THE ASHLEY BOOK OF
KNOTS

By

CLIFFORD W. ASHLEY

Author of THE YANKEE WHALER

"He'll allow his superiors on board to be tolerably good Navigators etc! But Alas! they want the Main Point; for shew me the Gentleman cries he, that can knot or splice?"—NED WARD in "The Wooden World"

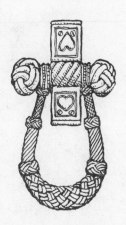

Doubleday & Company, Inc.

GARDEN CITY, NEW YORK

ISBN: 0-385-04025-3

COPYRIGHT, 1944
BY CLIFFORD W. ASHLEY
ALL RIGHTS RESERVED

PRINTED IN THE UNITED STATES

30 29

To my wife,
SARAH RODMAN ASHLEY,
who has lived with this book for eleven years
without losing her patience, her good humor,
or her faith in its culmination.

CONTENTS

CONTENTS

ILLUSTRATIONS

ACKNOWLEDGMENTS

They are too many, the sailors from whom I learned to tie knots, for me ever to accord them the credit that is their due. Many there were whose names I have forgotten, many more whose names I never even knew. For at the time our courses crossed nothing was further from my mind than writing a book of knots. My interest then was solely in tying, and it was a long while before I even started to keep a record.

Here and there in the pages to follow I shall have occasion to speak of someone in connection with a certain knot or splice, and if no name is mentioned, be assured that the ungrudging assistance that was given me is still fresh in my mind, and that the omission is due to a fault of memory and not of good will.

To the following friends I am indebted for assistance in the preparation of this book:

To Captain Daniel F. Mullins, who went to sea in the same year that I commenced the study of art. Coupled with a natural aptitude and curiosity for knots he has an amazingly retentive memory, and the assistance that he has given me, particularly with the splices, has been of incalculable service.

To Dr. Richard Knowles, who, while Headmaster of the William Penn Charter School, suggested that experience in teaching would aid me in writing a book of instruction. He arranged a series of lectures and classes in knots in several private schools near Philadelphia, and the experience that I acquired has been of great assistance to me in this work.

To Charles B. Rockwell, with whom I have often sailed and raced, and at whose instigation I made a WEAVER'S KNOT that is now used in mohair manufacture.

To Mr. Frederic A. Delano, who first became interested in my knot work at the time I was experimenting with SOLID SINNETS and who has followed the progress of this volume from its inception. He has read chapters from my manuscript and has made suggestions that have proved invaluable.

To Mrs. Frederick H. Brooke, onetime National President of the Girl Scouts, who, among other suggestions, proposed that the material should be arranged so that each chapter would be complete in itself and could be published separately in form suitable for the use of boy and girl scouts.

To Eugene E. du Pont, who for many years has patiently tolerated my preoccupation with knots and who, under protest, made the TWENTY-FOUR-STRAND, TWENTY-ONE-PART MATTHEW WALKER KNOT that is reproduced among the frontispieces. It was made, without previous experience, from my

ACKNOWLEDGMENTS

typed instructions and is probably the largest MATTHEW WALKER KNOT that has ever been tied.

To Rodman Swift, who sailed before the mast to China one June morning just after his graduation from Harvard University, thereby gaining an A.B. degree twice in the same year; a record not equaled even by Richard H. Dana, Jr., of *Two Years Before the Mast* fame. In recent years he and I have tied many knots together and the discussions that ensued have helped to settle many a debated point.

One institution I wish to thank in particular, The Mariners' Museum, of Newport News, Virginia, and also its President, Mr. Homer L. Ferguson, whose interest in the mariner and the sea has included knots, and whose encouragement of my research and writing has been one of the largest contributing factors to the completion of my task. While this work has been in preparation the museum has rendered material assistance by purchasing a number of my marine paintings.

Many of the illustrations have been drawn from old sailors' knot work that forms a part of the museum's permanent exhibit.

THE ASHLEY BOOK OF
KNOTS

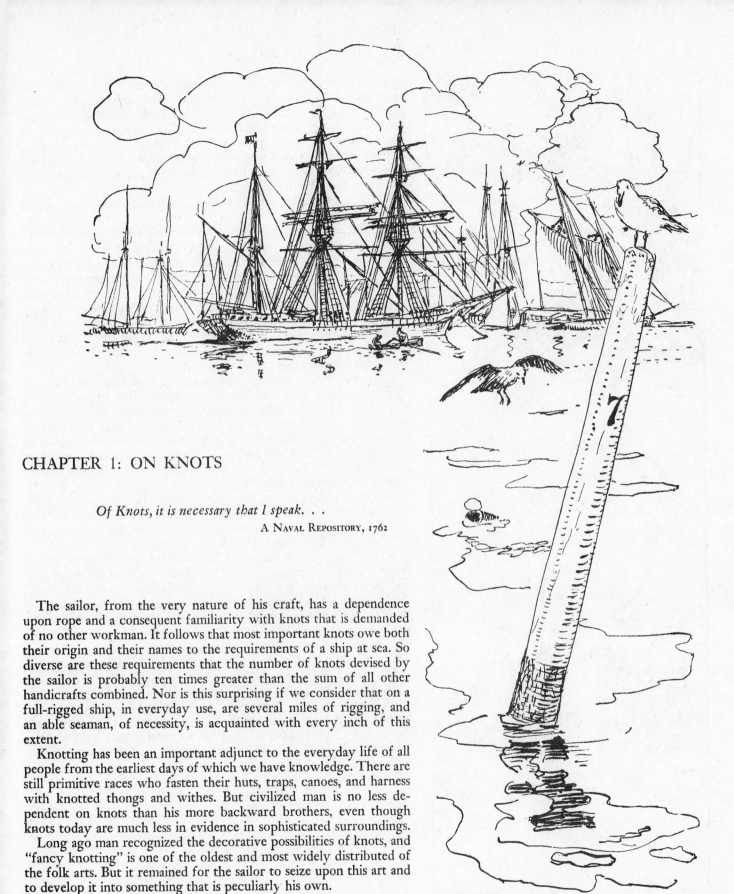

CHAPTER 1: ON KNOTS

Of Knots, it is necessary that I speak. . .
A NAVAL REPOSITORY, 1762

The sailor, from the very nature of his craft, has a dependence upon rope and a consequent familiarity with knots that is demanded of no other workman. It follows that most important knots owe both their origin and their names to the requirements of a ship at sea. So diverse are these requirements that the number of knots devised by the sailor is probably ten times greater than the sum of all other handicrafts combined. Nor is this surprising if we consider that on a full-rigged ship, in everyday use, are several miles of rigging, and an able seaman, of necessity, is acquainted with every inch of this extent.

Knotting has been an important adjunct to the everyday life of all people from the earliest days of which we have knowledge. There are still primitive races who fasten their huts, traps, canoes, and harness with knotted thongs and withes. But civilized man is no less dependent on knots than his more backward brothers, even though knots today are much less in evidence in sophisticated surroundings.

Long ago man recognized the decorative possibilities of knots, and "fancy knotting" is one of the oldest and most widely distributed of the folk arts. But it remained for the sailor to seize upon this art and to develop it into something that is peculiarly his own.

Aboard ship knotting had reached its flood early in the nineteenth century, and by mid-century, with the commencement of the Clipper Era, it had begun to ebb. Folk arts flourish best where there are leisure and contentment, and neither of these conditions obtained on clipper ships. After the American Civil War the economic situation in the merchant marine was such that all ships were undermanned; sailors had little or no time to spare from their labors, and knotting was pushed into the background.

At the beginning of the nineteenth century it was unusual to find in the forecastle of a sailing ship more than one or two sailors who could read and write. It was a common thing for boys to go to sea before they were ten years old, and cabin boys of seven and eight years' age were not unusual. Even ashore, at that time, education was considered unnecessary in the classes from which seamen were recruited. But the isolation of the sea was such that the sailor's inability to read and write was an almost intolerable hardship. In order to keep his mind occupied when off duty, it was necessary for him to busy his hands. Fortunately there was, aboard ship, one material that could be used for that purpose. There was generally plenty of condemned rope with which to tie knots.

A frugal owner would send his ship to sea with all the old running rigging in place that would pass inspection. But any shipmaster worthy of the name, once his ship was under way, began to reeve off new rigging wherever a long-jawed piece of gear met his eye.

There were two arts that belonged to the sailor: scrimshaw, which was the carving and engraving of whalebone and ivory and was peculiar to the whaling fleet, and knotting, which belonged to all deepwater ships, including whalers.

Jackknife industries also flourished aboard ship, and much of the tattooing of the old days was done in the forecastle. Sailors knitted, sewed, and crocheted; made baskets and straw hats. But the true shellback was more apt to specialize in knots.

Aboard coasters and fishermen knotting has never been so widely practiced. There is a fundamental difference between the deepwater and the coastwise sailor. The latter, in common with the fisherman, spends much of his time ashore, making harbor at short intervals. Usually he has a home and family ties of some sort. His excursions on the sea are too brief, and his hours at sea too busy, to encourage handicrafts. But the shellback, if he has a home, generally ignores it when ashore so long as his health and thirst last. Most of the days of his life are actually lived at sea.

The character of a sailor's knotting depends to a great extent on what branch of the service he is in. It would be impossible in the Navy to hand out rope in sufficient quantity for the large crews that are carried. Generally the men have to be content with log line, fishline, and such small stuff. This has resulted in the Navy's seamen specializing in "square knotting" or "macramé."

Merchant sailors have been better provided. Although they seldom obtain new material to work with, junk is generally issued, which they "work up" into foxes, nettles, and twice-laid rope.

It was the whaleman who fared best; his voyages were longer and less broken, and his ship was heavily overmanned. New whale line was frequently allowed, that had been broken in the whale hunt. This was the best quality rope that was manufactured, and could be worked up into any size material required. But to balance against these favorable conditions was the divided interest of the whaleman. Unless he possessed a special gift for knots he was apt to succumb to the lure of scrimshaw.

The interest of seamen in their knots was widespread and intense, and often decidedly competitive. Complicated knots were explained under pledge of secrecy; often a knowledge of one knot was bartered for another. I have heard of a sailor who carried an unfinished blackjack in his ditty bag for several voyages until at last he found a shipmate who could teach him the knot he wished to finish off with. A sailor was judged by his chest beckets and his bag lanyards. A superlative knot tier, in the middle of the nineteenth century, stood in the estimation of the forecastle about where the Artist of the Cavern Walls stood in the Cro-Magnon days.

Very little nationalism is evident among knots. One reason for this may be that the merchant sailor has never been too particular about what flag he sailed under, and in the general shifting about, knots soon became common property. Here and there we have a "Spanish," "Portuguese," "English," "French," or "American" Knot, but seldom is the application of such a name at all universal. The same knot may be attributed to several countries, just as Flat "Over-One-and-Under-One" Sinnet (#2976) is called by English-speaking sailors "French Sinnet" and by the ever-polite French "Tresse Anglaise."

It is impossible to make a distinction between the British and the American contribution to knots. There were English sailors in every Yankee forecastle. But it would seem that English-speaking people as a whole have made the largest single contribution to the subject. At the present time Scandinavian sailors are doing more toward preserving the traditions of marlingspike seamanship than any other seamen.

In the pages that are to follow, in order to save continual jumping between the past and present tenses, I shall speak in general as if square-rigged ships still sail the seas, as if Water Street and Front Street in every seaport town still teem with sailors. I for one wish that this were so, and it is no part of my task either to scrap the one or to bury the other. But it may well be that the assumption is not altogether too farfetched; for old customs die slowly; there are still a few square-riggers sailing out of Australia and South America. Rope standing rigging is still standard for small boats in the tropics, and on three quarters of the charted seas the internal-combustion engine is still a rarity.

A jagging wheel

In the middle 1800s the public of several nations became sailor-conscious. Organizations for "uplift" were formed, sailors' reading rooms and educational classes were established along the waterfronts. By this time the public- or common-school movement in America was well under way, so, unless a boy ran off to sea at a very immature age, the rudiments of the "three Rs" had begun to seep in.

"Sailors' Aid" societies in various ports placed compact little libraries aboard outbound ships. Voyages in the meanwhile had shortened. Ships were built more for speed and less for capacity; itinerant trading ventures had become infrequent. The best routes for making the long runs around the Horn and the Cape had been charted, and, except for the whaler, the day of the long voyage was past.

Usually the advent of steam is held accountable for putting a period to the art of knotting. But the fact that a sailor could not read and at the same time employ his hands may be accepted as in great part responsible. The higher education had taken its toll. To be sure, the books put aboard ship frequently had a Rollo-like flavor, more suited for juvenile Sunday-school classes than for the minds of adult men. But hungry minds will accept anything, and the average sailor was pretty young, and quite uncritical. Ship libraries were thumbed to shreds, the subject matter of books was discussed, and the comparative merits of heroes and the beauty of heroines argued aboard ship with a seriousness, even a partisanship, that would put to blush the efforts of many a Browning Society ashore.

But there were still men in the forecastle who preferred to work with their hands even when there was plenty of reading matter, which was not always the case.

A library of one hundred books was put aboard the bark *Sunbeam* in 1904 by the New Bedford Port Society. This library had been removed entire from the bark *Morning Star* on her return a few months earlier from a two years' whaling voyage. In theory the proceeding was sound, but in practice it presented flaws. Five of our crew were condemned to sail an additional two years, four years in all, with the selfsame one hundred books, all five men having just signed off from the *Morning Star*. Although at first there was grumbling, knotting and scrimshaw came to the rescue. Of the six men who started in at once to knot and scrimshaw, four were of the *Morning Star* group.

It was inevitable that when the sailor learned to read he would neglect the arts. Eventually good marlingspike sailors became scarce. Only the essential everyday knots were taught to the greenhorns in the forecastle, and work that formerly had been done at sea was turned out in the rigging loft.

Abruptly, however, in the second quarter of the twentieth century, knotting began to pick up again, and sailors the world over evinced a renewed interest. To the casual observer this might have seemed to be a fabricated or even a sentimental phenomenon. Yet on turbine and Diesel ships, on gasoline boats and piano-wired yachts, fancy knots were again in evidence.

Sailors once more compared and argued the relative beauties of the STAR, the ROSE, and the MANROPE KNOT; in the dogwatches knots were again a vital topic of conversation. The manifestation proved to be no mere transient fad. Nor was it the result of sentiment or of suasion. The answer was simple, and far deeper; the return to his first love was natural and wholly unpremeditated. The sailor's hand and eye, long slaves to magazine and book, were again free. The one no longer turned the leaf while the other scanned the printed page. Magazines and books were tossed aside unopened.

And now while the cheerful radio in the forecastle bleats out the latest baseball and cricket scores, or prize-fight gossip, from five hundred or two thousand miles away, the sailor's hands again deftly fashion a knotted belt or handbag for his lady, or for any one of his several ladies, in whatever port his ship is headed for; and if he is musically inclined he cheerfully whistles an obbligato to the radio soloist of the moment, while his fingers once more ply the knotted cords.

This I hold to be real progress; and the sailor today is a far happier mortal than ever he was before. Something of course is missing, for gone are the tall ships of yesterday, but somewhere in the offing may be something else quite as beautiful.

Also, just beyond the horizon is the threat of the cinema and television, which require only a little popularizing cheapness before they too will invade the forecastle; when they do the sailor's hands will again be idle.

My earliest schooling in knots was received from two uncles, who were whaling captains. One taught me the REEF KNOT when I was three years old, but a little sailboat model he promised to make me, when I had learned my lesson, was never completed, for he crossed the bar soon after. Years later my aunt gave me the model of a whaleboat that he had made for her, and which had traveled as far as the first Paris Exposition; and so the score was settled. My other uncle taught me to *sinnet*. He had agreed to make me a whiplash, but as he proved dilatory, or so it seemed to a boy of my age, I secured material and, with a little coaching, made the lash myself. When I was seven my father gave me a pony on condition that I master the HALTER HITCH.

Before I had reached the age of nine I was proprietor and chief canvasman of a two-ring circus that was widely, even if somewhat conventionally, advertised as the "Greatest Show on Earth." The tent was made of carriage covers that had been more or less honorably acquired, but the center poles had been pilfered from the clothesline. Besides being canvasman I was also trapeze performer, bearded lady, ticket seller, and ringmaster. It was in the first of my several capacities that I required a knowledge of splicing and the use of the sailor's palm and needle. My uncle at this time being away at sea, I found a teacher at the wharfside and cut out, seamed, and roped the tent with the assistance of Daniel Mullins (now Captain Mullins) and several other boys of the neighborhood. The circus presently took to the road, but it went into winter quarters abruptly and disbanded because of a misunderstanding over a piece of borrowed costume which the older generation deemed inappropriate for the street parade.

Eventually the tent was cut up into haycaps.

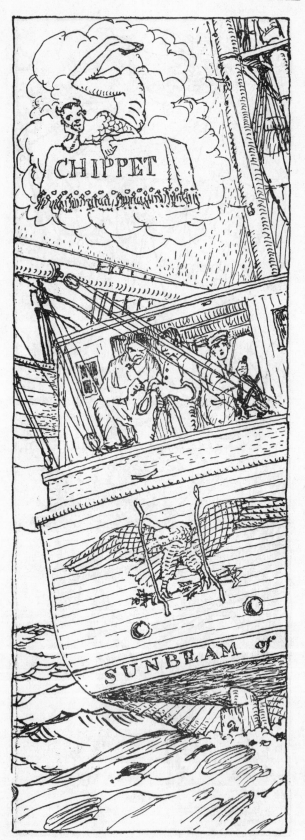

One day a dozen years later, in Wilmington, Delaware, the chief contortionist of Barnum and Bailey's Circus slapped me on the back and hailed me so boisterously that the embarrassed young lady who accompanied me made the error of attempting to continue her stroll as if nothing unusual were happening. But by the time she finally entered the big top, her circle of acquaintances had increased by three and she proudly held a handful of photographs, inscribed and autographed by the *Contortionist*, the *Tattooed Man*, and the *Expansionist*. "Chippet," the contortionist, was none other than the ex-"Bender" of my own defunct-but-never-absorbed-or-amalgamated circus, whom Barnum had succeeded in teaching to tie himself into a perfect FIGURE-OF-EIGHT KNOT. To this day I feel that P.T. had crowded me a bit.

When I arrived at a proper age I went to sea and served my apprenticeship in knots aboard the whaling bark *Sunbeam*. My chief instructor and the most quoted man in this volume was Captain Charles W. Smith, then acting mate, who afterward became master of the bark *Lagoda*, "the ship that never sailed" (the same being comfortably housed inside the New Bedford Whaling Museum). Under Captain Smith's tutorship I progressed rapidly in knots and marlingspike seamanship to a point where even my teacher admitted that if I persevered and retained my health I might someday hope to grasp the rudiments of the art.

When I had learned all that he offered I repaid him rather shabbily for all his kindness by slipping forward in the dogwatches and picking up, at the forecastle head, three knots with which he was unfamiliar.

From that day I have continued to collect knots wherever I could find them, and as unfamiliar sailors' knots became increasingly difficult to find I was attracted by the knots of other occupations. I hobnobbed with butchers and steeple jacks, cobblers and truck drivers, electric linesmen, Boy Scouts, and with elderly ladies who knit. Mr. Ringling himself, I cannot recall now which of the several brothers it was, took me about his circus and was pleased to be able to dazzle me with a score of knots with which I was quite unfamiliar. It was pleasant to talk to a brother showman again, and the meeting was not one bit too soon, for almost overnight the interior of the circus tent became a spiderweb of wire and turnbuckles instead of hemp and blocks.

Will James, "the Lone Cowboy," showed me the THEODORE KNOT one day while we were lunching with Joseph Chapin, then the Art Editor of *Scribner's Magazine*. In Boston I halted an operation to see how the surgeon made fast his stitches. I have watched oxen slung for the shoeing, I have helped throw pack lashings, I have followed tree surgeons through their acrobatics and examined poachers' traps and snares. But I never saw Houdini, never was present at a successful lynching, and never participated in a commercial second-story venture.

One spring soon after my whaling experience I spent several weeks on an oysterman in Delaware Bay, having been commissioned by *Harper's Magazine* to make a series of pictures of oyster culture. (Several of these now hang in the Mariners' Museum at Newport

News.) Over Sunday the fleet laid up at Bridgeton, New Jersey, and on Monday morning it got under way and sailed down the Cohansey Creek to dredge on the public beds off Ship John Light.

There was a fleet of perhaps two hundred sharpies, pungfys, bugeyes, canoes, schooners, and sloops, none with a motor, as the public beds are not open to power dredging. In the exodus down the narrow winding river the boats were crowded together as thick as a run of herring. At any time it appeared possible to walk ashore merely by stepping from rail to rail. But there was no fouling and no crowding; and what little chat there was consisted of friendly hails. It was just an average business day for the oystermen. Near the river's mouth a big bugeye overhauled us, and as she drew alongside my eye rested on a huge knot at the end of the foresail halyard; it was far bigger than the common FIGURE-EIGHT that is the universal stopper for the ends of running rigging. As we dropped astern I questioned the crew of the *Mattie Flavel* about the knot, which I assumed was one peculiar to the oyster fleet since I had not seen its like before. To my surprise no one aboard could identify it. So, as I carried a definite impression of its appearance, I hunted up a length of rope and in a little while evolved a duplicate, as I believed at the time.

That was the origin of the knot which I have since termed the "OYSTERMAN'S STOPPER" (#526). A few days later, in Bivalve, the same bugeye tied up near by. On going aboard I found that the glorified STOPPER KNOT was nothing after all but an ordinary FIGURE-EIGHT KNOT tied in the very gouty end of a long-jawed halyard.

That was my first original venture in knotwork, although at the time I had no idea the OYSTERMAN'S STOPPER was original, I supposed that everything of so simple a nature had already been discovered.

In the spring of 1916, George H. Taber mailed me a paper which he had received from a New Orleans correspondent, that purported to be an exposition of why a symmetrical sinnet of triangular cross section is impossible. The argument was unconvincing, and having conceived a mental image of how such a thing might appear, in a little while I held in hand a successful EQUILATERAL TRIANGULAR SINNET of nine strands (#3028).

Then, when my attention was called to the fact that Matthew Walker alone of all past knot tiers still holds the credit for his invention, I went to the trouble of patenting my sinnet.

From that day I have continued in my spare time, and also in time that perhaps I should not have spared, to search for new things in knots, in sinnets, and in splices. Occasionally I have set the subject aside for a while, but always to pick it up again sooner or later.

Some of my friends did not hesitate to take me to task for what they regarded as a flagrant waste of time. More than once I was tempted to explain my prodigality as an individual's protest against the materialism of his age. But even if that had been true, which it was not, it would hardly have been deemed a sufficient excuse.

Without doubt my critics would have been entirely satisfied if I had announced that I proposed to write a book on the subject, for the urge to write a book is nowadays accepted as ample excuse for almost any delinquency.

But I had given no thought at that time to writing a book of knots, a fact which I have had occasion to regret many times since, for my early notes were very fragmentary. However, I am not convinced that an excuse is called for. Throughout history, from the early peregrinations of Marco Polo and the first voyage of Christopher Columbus down to more recent explorations in Antarctica and the Himalayas, the thrill incident to the pursuit of untrodden ways and the joy that attends occasional discovery have ever been accounted sufficient reward in themselves for almost any human effort or sacrifice.

To me the simple act of tying a knot is an adventure in unlimited space. A bit of string affords a dimensional latitude that is unique among the entities. For an uncomplicated strand is a palpable object that, for all practical purposes, possesses one dimension only. If we move a single strand in a plane, interlacing it at will, actual objects of beauty and of utility can result in what is practically two dimensions; and if we choose to direct our strand out of this one plane, another dimension is added which provides opportunity for an excursion that is limited only by the scope of our own imagery and the length of the ropemaker's coil.

What can be more wonderful than that?

But there always seems to be another car ahead in every likely parking space. Here is a Mr. Klein who claims to have proved (*Mathematische Annalen*) that knots cannot exist in space of four dimensions. This in itself is bad enough, but if someone else should come forward to prove that heaven does not exist in three dimensions, what future is there left for the confirmed knot tier?

The basis of this work is the assembled notes of forty years' collection. My aim has been to write a comprehensive and orderly book on applied knots and to make whatever information it contains easily accessible.

Unless a knot serves a prescribed purpose, which may be either practical or decorative, it does not belong here. Knots that cannot hold their form when tied in tangible material are not shown, no matter how decorative they may be. Many such decorative knots appear in ancient architectural carvings, on early book covers, and in illuminated manuscripts. Old tombstones often bear them. The early Britons employed them in various heraldic devices. Many artists, including Leonardo da Vinci, have drawn elaborate knot forms in their decorations. These pictured and sculptured knots serve their purposes admirably, but they are not within the scope of the present work. A knot must have distinction of some sort to be included. Bad as the GRANNY KNOT is, it has borne a name, and been in use for many years. With such, I do not feel at liberty to be arbitrary, no matter how unimportant they may seem to be.

The purpose of a knot and the method of tying it are not less important than its name and aspect, the two features that are commonly stressed. The question of what knot is best for a particular need is perhaps the most important of all to be considered.

ON KNOTS

Often there is a certain way to make a knot that is either easy to remember, easy to tie, or so economical of effort that it deserves to be generally adopted. Usually this preferred way is the sailors', although in the case of *bends* for small material the weaver has been most prolific. Methods vary both with the vocation employing a knot and with the size and texture of the material used.

1, 2. The Sheet Bend (❋1) and the Weaver's Knot (❋2) are structurally identical but are tied by different methods and in different materials, the former being tied in rope, the latter in thread or yarn. A different way either of tying or of applying a form generally constitutes a second knot.

Methods of tying will be demonstrated with progressive diagrams in such manner that it is hoped they can be followed without recourse to the text.

This, however, may not suit all readers, for there are some people to whom diagrams are an annoyance. There are others to whom an arrow or the printed letters *A* and *B* savor of higher mathematics. On the other hand there are some who are irked by written or printed directions of any sort. Sometimes, with the latter, it is possible to have another person read aloud the directions. This alters the situation for them, since they can follow oral directions with ease. Apparently it is only the printed page that balks them.

But despite a few such individualists, no knot in my opinion is too complicated to be clearly illustrated and adequately described; and for any shortcoming in either direction an author should hold himself responsible. I do not mean by this that all knots are simple. There are some in the following pages that will tax the ingenuity and require the undivided attention of any adult expert, and there are practices for which the hand must be disciplined, the eye held steady, and the mind kept open and alert.

Several years ago, from my printed directions in the *Sportsman's Magazine*, and with no other assistance, my cousin, Hope Knowles, tied without error Knot ❋2217, which has forty-nine crossings, making therewith a covering for the knob of her father's automobile gear-shift lever. She was barely eleven years old at the time.

Previous to this demonstration I had considered writing two books, one of an elementary nature for boys and girls, and another, more advanced, for adults. But this decided me that one book was enough, and that there are few knots that an intelligent boy or girl of twelve or fourteen years, who is genuinely interested in the subject, cannot tie, provided the description is clear enough.

For several reasons drawings are used here for illustrations instead of photographs, the most important reason of course being that since I am an artist this is my usual method of expression. But drawings also have certain definite advantages over photographs. There need never be any doubt, in a drawing, as to which is the end of a rope and which is the standing part. In the photograph of an actual knot, the standing part appears cut off as well as the end, so that often the two cannot be told apart.

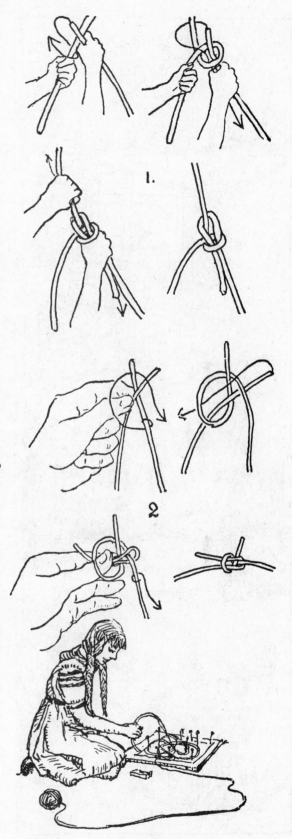

[9]

There need be no question in a drawing as to which strand is under and which is over at any point. In a photograph this is frequently obscured by shadow.

Anything may be omitted in a drawing that is not required, such as the individual strands and yarns of a rope. These are of importance in depicting MULTI-STRAND KNOTS but are superfluous and frequently confusing in the illustration of SINGLE-STRAND KNOTS.

In order to save the reader the annoyance of turning over leaves for reference, the text and the illustrations for each individual knot appear on the same page or, in a few instances, on the opposite or facing page. To make the two conform it has sometimes been necessary to condense either the text or the illustrations more than could be wished. It is hoped that this arbitrary pruning will not add appreciably to the reader's difficulties.

Knots that serve more than one purpose may be illustrated more than once. Many such knots are to be found among the *hitches*, where one that may be made fast to a rail may also be applied to a hook or ring. But even in such cases the methods of applying vary, the ends often are differently led, or the ways of tying are peculiar.

In Chapter 2, where the knots of each vocation or avocation are grouped together, regardless of their variety, many are shown that will reappear later in their regular classification. But here also the apparent duplication is usually within the spirit of the definition, that *either a different form, a different way of tying, or a different use constitutes a distinct knot.*

There are a number of practices closely allied to knotting—basketry, weaving, straw-hat making, rugmaking, bandaging, fly-tying, cat's cradles, embroidery, tatting, netting, macramé or square knotting, crochet, knitting; bead, quill, thong, sinew, cane, and hair work —which consist in the main of a multiplicity of simple forms built up into more or less elaborate patterns or designs. The basic knots of these are shown, but the subject of design itself is too large to be treated at length in any single volume.

A short list of books concerning these related subjects is given near the end of this volume.

Perhaps the most difficult task I have attempted is to sort out the terminology of knots and to ascribe to them their rightful names.

Preference has been given to the names that I have heard used, by sailors at sea, and by sailors, sailmakers, and riggers ashore. These have been compared with what could be gleaned from the best of the old works on seamanship and rigging. From these sources I have tried to sift the evidence and make a truthful record. I have refrained from advancing opinions of my own, except where the evidence was so slight, or the facts so obscured, that an opinion was all that could be offered. The date of a knot's first publication is also given when known.

It would seem that almost everybody has written about knots except the sailor himself. The many authors of excellent treatises on seamanship can hardly be regarded as exceptions to this statement, since most of them, save R. H. Dana, Jr., and W. B. Whall, were navy men, who presumably had no forecastle experience. They were officers, not sailors. Dana's discussion of knots is excellent but brief.

Whall is equally brief, and he expresses doubt of the success of his own effort. Unfortunately, a man is apt to forget in the cabin the things he learned at the forecastle.

The earliest, and still the outstanding marine authority on knots, is Darcy Lever, author of *Sheet Anchor* (London, 1808). Lever gave nearly forty knots and splices, and many of these had not appeared before in print. His plates and descriptions are clear and remarkably free from error; his terms are convincing. Many of the illustrations for his book have never been improved on, and most of them are still being copied.

Since the forecastle provided the best possible school for the professional seaman, no nautical authority ever considered it necessary to devote a whole volume to knots. Chapters on the subject were included in a number of early seamanship books, but these were hidden away in a mass of other technical material and were not open to the general reader. So it fell to the hands of a landsman first to bring the subject before the public in printed form.

This earliest English volume to deal exclusively with knots has been attributed to both Paul Rapsey Hodge and Frederick Chamier. It was entitled *The Book of Knots* and was published in London in 1866 under the pseudonym "Tom Bowling"—a name with a nautical smack well calculated to impress the sea-loving Britisher.

The original engravings, although clearly drawn, presented many errors, and owing to the engraver's process a number of the knots were reversed—that is to say, "mirrored." Being the first book in the field, it was given a prominence far beyond its merit, which was slight, and it is today by way of being considered a "source book." Much of the confusion that now exists in the terminology of knots may be traced to this one "source."

Presumably the material was abstracted from a French manuscript, since most of the knot titles are literal translations of the common French names. A total of *only eight English sailor names for knots is included*, which is an amazing discrepancy. Even such common titles as OVERHAND, FIGURE-EIGHT, HALF HITCH, CLOVE HITCH, SHEET BEND, WALL, and CROWN are lacking. The following parallel lists are given to illustrate Bowling's method of nomenclature.

COMMON ENGLISH NAMES	BOWLING'S NAMES	COMMON FRENCH NAMES
3. GRANNY KNOT	FALSE KNOT	NŒUD DE FAUX
4. OVERHAND KNOT	SIMPLE KNOT	NŒUD SIMPLE
5. BALE SLING HITCH AND RING HITCH	LARK'S HEAD	TÊTE D'ALOUETTE
6. SHEEPSHANK	DOGSHANK	JAMBE DE CHIEN
7. MARLINGSPIKE HITCH	BOAT KNOT	NŒUD DE GALÈRE
8. THE NOOSE	RUNNING KNOT	NŒUD COULANT
9. WALL KNOT	PIG-TAIL	CUL DE PORC
10. WALL AND CROWN	SKULL PIG-TAIL	CUL DE PORC AVEC TÊTE DE MORT

11. The CLOVE HITCH is called: (1) "WATERMANS KNOT," (2) "simple fastening in a rope," (3) "LARK'S HEAD, CROSSED," and (4) "BUILDERS' KNOT." The name CLOVE HITCH itself does not appear at all, and the old and reliable FISHERMAN'S BEND is called a SLIP KNOT!

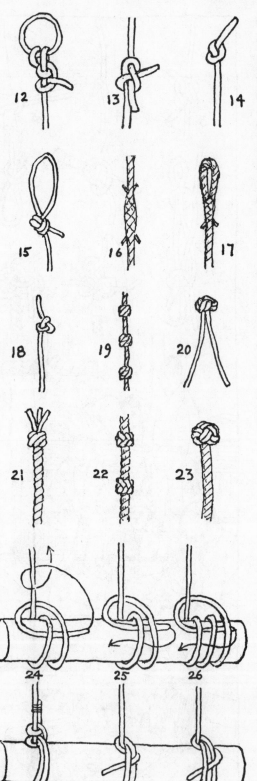

I have never found a sailor who used or even knew one of Bowling's titles, but I know of no current dictionary or encyclopedia that has not adopted some of them. With the exception perhaps of "SKULL PIG-TAIL," all of those I have listed are to be found in various commercial knot pamphlets, and in government, agricultural-school, and college knot bulletins.

Sailors have an idiomatic language of their own which provides about everything needed for a discussion of knots. A splice is *put in*, a hitch is *made fast* or *taken*, two ropes are *bent* together, a knot is *put in, made,* or *cast* in a rope. A sailor *takes a turn*, he belays; he *claps on* a stopper, he *slacks away*, and *casts off* a line. He *clears* a tangle, he *opens* a jammed knot, and he *works* a TURK'S-HEAD or a sinnet. But about the only time he actually *ties* is when, his voyage over, he *ties up to* a wharf. The word *tie* is used so seldom by the sailor only because it is too general a term for daily use, where something specific is almost always called for. But when a sailor refers to the subject as a whole he always speaks of "*tying knots*" or "*knot tying.*"

The word *knot* has three distinct meanings in common use. In its broadest sense it applies to all complications in cordage, except accidental ones, such as snarls and kinks, and complications adapted for storage, such as coils, hanks, skeins, balls, etc.

In its second sense it does not include *bends, hitches, splices,* and *sinnets*, and in its third and narrowest sense the term applies only to a *knob* tied in a rope to prevent unreeving, to provide a handhold, or (in small material only) to prevent fraying.

At sea, the whole subject of knots is commonly divided into four classifications: *hitches, bends, knots,* and *splices*.

12. A *hitch* makes a rope fast to another object.

13. A *bend* unites two rope ends.

14, 15. The term *knot* itself is applied particularly to *knobs* (14) and *loops* (15), and to *anything not included* in the other three classes, such as fancy and trick knots.

16. LONG and SHORT SPLICES are MULTI-STRAND BENDS.

17. EYE SPLICES are MULTI-STRAND LOOPS.

For the purposes of this discussion the word *knot* will be used in its broadest meaning, as an inclusive term for the whole subject, and the word *knob* will be used to designate a bunch tied in rope to prevent unreeving.

18, 21. There are two kinds of KNOB KNOTS: the STOPPER KNOT, in which the end of a rope, after forming a knob, passes out of the structure near the top; and

20, 23. The BUTTON KNOT, in which the end of a rope, after forming a knob, passes out of the structure at the stem, parallel with the standing part.

There are SINGLE-STRAND and MULTI-STRAND KNOTS of both these kinds.

Furthermore, the STOPPER KNOT is subdivided into two classes:

18, 21. The STOPPER KNOT proper, which is a TERMINAL KNOT; and

19, 22. The LANYARD KNOT, of similar construction, but tied in the bight or central part of a rope.

There are four exceptions, among sailors' knots, to the classification that has been given.

24. The FISHERMAN'S BEND is an ANCHOR HITCH.

25, 26. The STUDDING-SAIL HALYARD BEND (⋕25) and the TOPSAIL HALYARD BEND (⋕26) are YARD HITCHES.

The ROBAND HITCH is a BINDING KNOT (discussed in Chapter 12).

The verb *to bend* is used with considerable latitude: a sailor always *bends* a line to an anchor or to a spar, and he also *bends* a sail to a spar or stay. But with the exceptions here noted, all knots called bends are for lengthening rope, by tying two ends together.

Many *bends* and *hitches* are termed knots, but this agrees with the broadest definition of the term, *knot* being the generic term covering the whole subject.

For purposes of knotting, a rope is considered to consist of three parts:

27. The *end of a rope* is its extremity.

28. The *standing part* is the inactive part, as opposed to the bight and working end.

29. The *bight of a rope* is a term borrowed perhaps from topography, which has two meanings in knotting. First, it may be any central part of a rope, as distinct from the ends and standing part.

30. Second, it is a curve or arc in a rope no narrower than a semicircle. This corresponds to the topographical meaning of the word, a bight being an indentation in a coast so wide that it *may be sailed out of*, on one tack, in any wind.

31. An OPEN LOOP is a curve in a rope narrower than a bight but with separated ends.

32. A CLOSED LOOP is one in which the legs are brought together but not crossed.

When the legs of a loop are brought together *and crossed* the rope has "*taken a turn.*"

33. A LOOP KNOT is formed when the end of a rope is made fast to its own standing part, or when a loop in the bight of a rope is closed and knotted. Often a LOOP KNOT is called merely a "LOOP."

34. When a vessel, lying to two anchors, turns about, under the influence of wind and tide, she is said to have a *foul hawse*. If one cable merely lies over the other it is called a *cross* (of the cables).

35. If another cross is added the result is an *elbow* in the cables.

36. Another cross makes a *round turn*.

37. While still another cross constitutes a *round turn and an elbow* in the cable.

38. A *hitch* is a knot tied directly to or around an object; there are many hitches that will capsize if removed from the supporting object.

39. A LOOP KNOT, commonly called a LOOP, serves about the same purpose as a hitch, but it is *tied in hand*, which is the *chief distinction between the two*. After being tied it is placed around an object, such as a hook or a post. Its shape is not dependent on the object that it is fast to, and it may be removed at any time and will still retain its shape.

40, 41, 42. Alongside will be found illustrated (⋕40) a *single turn*, (⋕41) a *round turn*, and (⋕42) *two round turns*.

One of the few properties that would be desirable in every practical knot is that it should tie in an easily remembered way.

Decorative knots should be handsome and symmetrical.

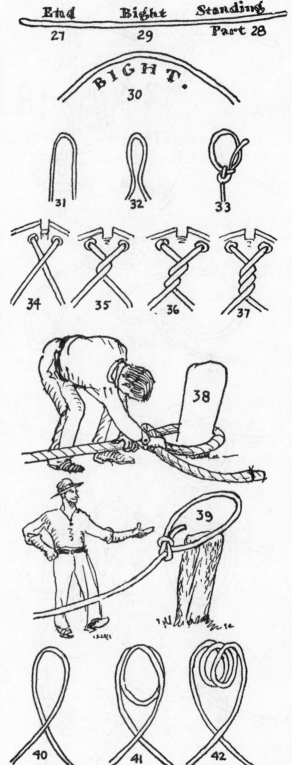

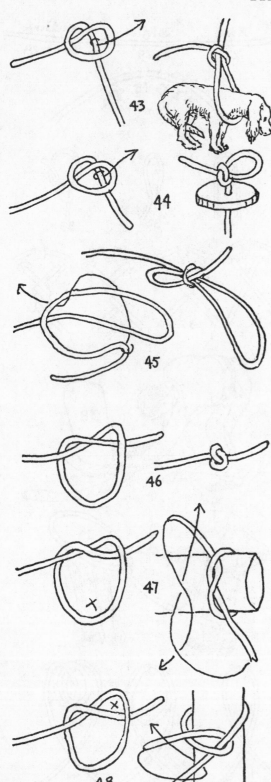

There are some knots that are commonly confused with each other because of some obvious similarity either of form or of name. Three outstanding examples are the Noose, the Slip Knot, and the Slip Noose.

43. The Noose is a sliding knot used in snaring birds and animals. It draws up and constricts when the standing part is pulled.

44. The Slip Knot is a Stopper Knot that may be spilled or slipped instantly by pulling on the end to withdraw a loop. There is but one knot entitled to the name; any others having a similar feature are merely "Slipped" Knots.

45. The Slip Noose starts as Noose ⌗43, but a bight is employed instead of an end for the final tuck. The knot may be spilled ("slipped") instantly, by pulling on the end, which withdraws the bight.

I have never seen an explanation of the differences between the Overhand Knot, the Half Knot, and the Half Hitch, three quite distinct knots of somewhat similar construction, but with clearly marked differences in their application. The three are often confused with each other.

46. The Overhand is the simplest of the Single-Strand Stopper Knots, and is *tied with one end* around its own standing part, its purpose being to prevent unreeving.

47. The Half Knot is a Binding Knot, being the first movement of the Reef or Square Knot. It is *tied with two ends around an object* and is used when reefing, furling, and tying up parcels, shoestrings, and the like.

48. The Half Hitch is *tied with one end* of a rope which is passed around an object and secured to its own standing part with a Single Hitch.

The difference between the Clove Hitch and Two Half Hitches is exceedingly vague in the minds of many, the reason being that the two have the same knot form; but one is tied around another object, the other around its own standing part. The illustrations of these and several other knots, given here in two parallel columns, may perhaps serve to make the differences clearer than a written description can.

In every instance opposite hitches in the two columns have the same knot form. But in the left column they are tied directly to another object, while in the right column they are tied around their own standing parts. The left column consists of snug hitches in which the ends are secured under the turns. The right column consists of loose hitches in which the ends, after passing around another object, are made fast to their own standing parts.

49. Single Hitch	50. Half Hitch
51. Slippery Hitch	52. Slipped Half Hitch
53. Clove Hitch	54. Two Half Hitches
	55. Buntline Hitch
56. Cow Hitch	57. Reversed Half Hitches
	58. Lobster Buoy Hitch
59. Bale Sling Hitch, Ring Hitch, or Tag Knot	60. Double Ring Hitch
61. Rolling Hitch, Magnus Hitch, or Magner's Hitch	62. Midshipman's Hitch

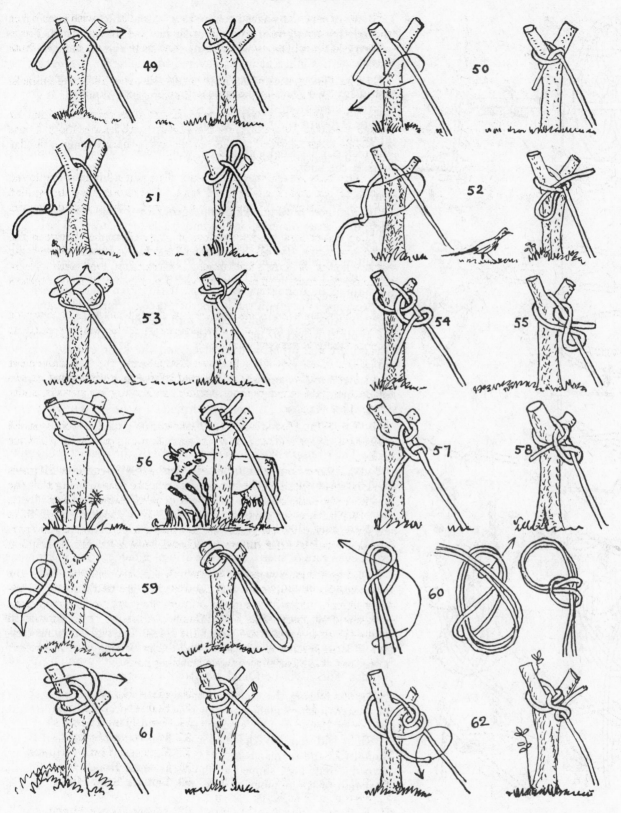

49   50

51   52

53   54   55

56   57   58

59   60

61   62

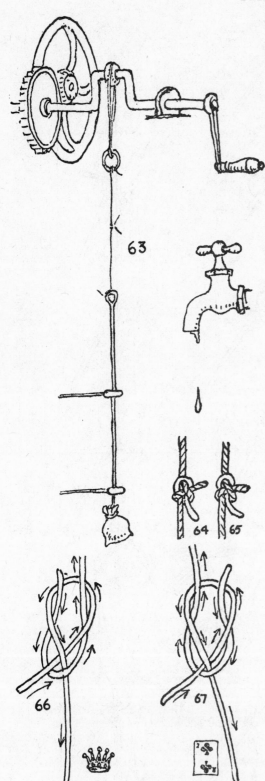

63

64 65

66

67

Many experiments have been made with the object of determining the relative *strength* of knots. But so far as I know the quality of *security* has not been considered, or else has been regarded as one of the properties inherent in, or covered by, the term *"strength."* Yet the two cannot be measured at the same time, and both are not present in any two knots in the same degree. A secure knot often breaks; a strong knot often slips.

The standard laboratory *test* of a knot has been to subject it to a gradually increasing load. Eventually either the knot has slipped or the material has tired and broken, which was usually at a point just outside the knot.

In everyday service, however, rope is seldom subjected to just that sort of wear.

In common use knots and rope generally break under a sudden jerk, or a series of jerks, or else under a sudden access of load.

63. Several years ago the Collins and Aikman Corporation, manufacturers of piled fabrics, asked me to find a knot for them that would not slip in the particularly coarse variety of mohair yarn required in automobile upholstery coverings. If this yarn once broke it was so "springy" that, with the knots then used, it untied over and over again before it was finally woven into the cloth. The great number of knots that had to be retied slowed down production seriously. Eventually the problem was solved and the knot evolved was put to use.

I started my experiments with the following premises for a point of departure.

A. The *security* of a knot is determined by the stress it will endure before it slips. To determine *security* a material is required that will slip before it breaks.

B. The *strength* of a knot is determined by the stress it will endure before it breaks. To determine *strength* a material is required that will break before it slips.

Some especially made mohair yarn, of large size and even quality, was provided, and I made myself some testing apparatus of material secured from a local junk yard.

My test of *security* consisted of a series of uniform jerks applied at an even rate of speed, using the drip of a faucet for a metronome. A bag of sand provided a weight, and the jerks were continued until they either amounted to one hundred in number or else the knot spilled.

Only bends were tested. Ten bends of each kind were tied with the ends trimmed to an even length. Only six knots failed to slip and only one of these was a well-known knot. One knot slipped at the first jerk each time it was tried, and other well-known knots gave unexpected results. These will be found tabulated on page 274.

64, 65. During the course of these experiments another question suggested itself, which was: what effect, if any, has the direction of the lay or twist of rope on the security of a knot?

Right-laid rope and left-laid rope have opposite torsion. It was found that the regular RIGHT-HAND SHEET BEND (#66), tied in the two different lays, slipped at about the same average rate, but the variation of the number of jerks required was about twice as great for the left-laid as for the right-laid rope, which suggests that the latter is more reliable.

The Right Overhand Bend (✻1410) showed a ratio of about two to three in favor of right-laid rope. An inferior material was used for these experiments, the excellent material of the earlier experiments being exhausted, so the actual figures of the experiments are not reliable.

To prevent slipping, a knot depends on friction, and to provide friction there must be pressure of some sort. This pressure and the place within the knot where it occurs is called the *nip*. The security of a knot appears to depend solely on its *nip*. The so-called and oft-quoted "principle of the knot," that "no two parts which would move in the same direction, if the rope were to slip, should lie alongside of and touching each other," plausible though it may appear, does not seem important. Even if it were possible to make a knot conform to any extent to these exacting conditions, it still would not hold any better than another, unless it were well nipped.

66, 67. An excellent example of this is the Sheet Bend. The Sheet Bend (✻66) violates the alleged "principle" at about every point where it can, but it has a good nip and does not slip easily. The Left-Hand Sheet Bend (✻67) conforms to the so-called "principle" to a remarkable extent, but has a poor nip and is unreliable.

It does not appear to make much difference just where the nip within a knot occurs, so far as *security* is concerned. But *the knot will be stronger* if the nip is well within the structure.

68. In the ordinary *strength* test, under a gradually increasing load, Dr. Cyrus Day found the Sheet Bend and the Left-Hand Sheet Bend about equal.

I tested strength with a series of single jerks of gradually increasing force.

A good quality of fish line was wound along a broadcloth-covered cylinder of two inches diameter. The lower end was secured to a weight, and the cylinder was placed horizontally near the ceiling of my studio. Only bends were tested. The knots were halfway between the cylinder and the weight, which were one foot apart at the beginning of each experiment.

The weight was dropped at regular intervals, and after each drop the cylinder was unwound one half turn, which lengthened the line approximately three inches. The number of drops required to break the line decided the knot's relative strength.

The break in material almost invariably occurred at a point just outside the entrance to the knot, which is usual in all tests.

A common statement that appears in many or most knot discussions is that "a knot is weaker than the rope in which it is tied." But since a rope practically never breaks within a knot, this can hardly be correct.

It appears to be true that a rope is weakest just outside the entrance to a knot, and this would seem to be due to the rigidity of the knot. These experiments were not carried far enough to give conclusive results, but some of the results indicated were quite different from what is generally accepted.

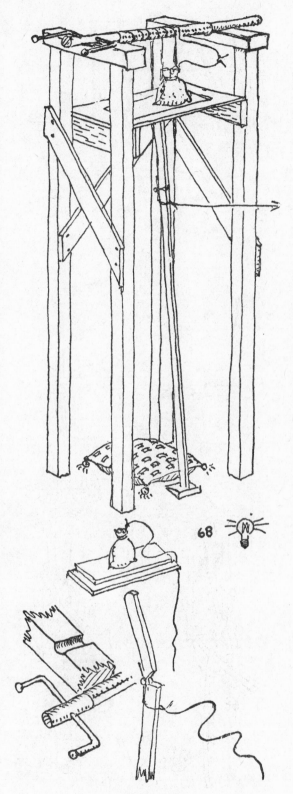

68

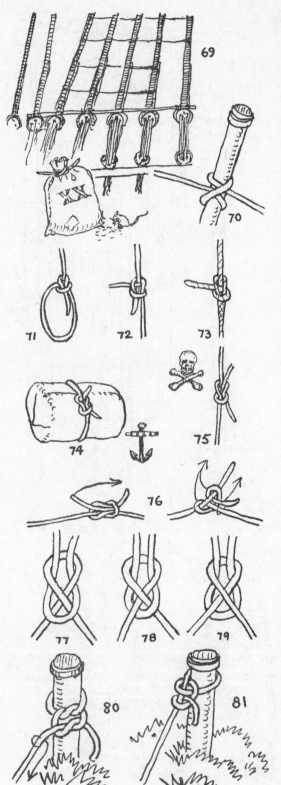

69. There is no such thing as a good general utility *knot*, although ashore the CLOVE HITCH (#1177) comes very near to filling the office of a general utility *hitch*. But at sea the CLOVE HITCH is employed almost solely as a CROSSING KNOT, for securing ratlines to shrouds, etc.

70. Although not a very secure hitch, it can be quickly tied in a great variety of easily remembered ways. It is the commonest of all POST HITCHES, and is often tied on a bag as a BINDING KNOT.

71, 72, 73. The purpose for which a knot is used and the way in which it is tied, rather than *its appearance*, decide its classification. This is clearly exemplified by three well-known knots of the same identical form: (#71) BOWLINE, (#72) SHEET BEND, (#73) BECKET HITCH. The end of a rope is made fast to its own standing part to form a BOWLINE (#71), which is a LOOP KNOT. The SHEET BEND (#72), of the same form, bends two rope ends together, and the BECKET HITCH (#73), also of the same form, secures the end of a rope to a becket, which is generally an eye or a hook.

74. One of the best but most misused of knots is the REEF or SQUARE KNOT (#1204). Employed as a BINDING KNOT, to reef and furl sails or to tie up parcels, it is invaluable.

75. But employed as a bend (to tie two rope ends together), the REEF KNOT is probably responsible for more deaths and injuries than have been caused by the *failure of all other knots combined*.

76. In fact the ease with which it is capsized by jerking at one end is its chief recommendation as a REEF KNOT. Tied in two ropes' ends of different size, texture, or stiffness, it is almost bound to capsize and spill.

77, 78, 79. A knot is never "nearly right"; it is either exactly right or it is hopelessly wrong, one or the other; there is nothing in between. This is not the impossibly high standard of the idealist, it is a mere fact for the realist to face. In a knot of eight crossings, which is about the average-size knot, there are 256 different "over-and-under" arrangements possible. (Wherever two strands cross each other, one must pass *over*, the other *under*.) Make only one change in this "*over-and-under*" sequence and either an entirely different knot is made or no knot at all may result. To illustrate this, let us consider #77, the REEF KNOT, and #78, the SHEET BEND, two totally different forms that do not resemble each other, that serve entirely different purposes, but that may be tied on the same diagram. One is a bend; the other is a BINDING KNOT. Yet there is precisely one point of difference in the "*over and under*" between the two. And if we make one additional change as indicated in #78, there will be no nip whatsoever and the two ropes will fall apart (#79).

80, 81. *There are very few knots, possibly less than a dozen, that may be drawn up properly merely by pulling or jerking at the two ends. There are few more important things to keep in mind than this* while knotting. Other knots must first be *tied* (formed) and then *worked* (drawn up into shape). The more elaborate the knot, the more deliberately must it be worked. Give one unconsidered pull, and a hopeless tangle is apt to follow. There are even cases where a totally different knot may result when carelessly pulled. Tie the GRANNY KNOT (# 80) around any object and pull one end, and it will capsize into TWO HALF HITCHES (#81). A REEF KNOT (#77) may be capsized into REVERSED HALF HITCHES (#1786) in the same manner.

Many or even most of the qualities that are considered desirable in a knot may on occasion be lacking and yet the knot be significant. A practical knot may either serve its particular purpose well or it may merely serve better than any other knot that offers. Here are shown three knots which have perhaps the smallest margin of safety among knots in everyday use. Yet each one appears to have been found the best for its purpose, and on one, at least, a man's life is daily balanced.

82. The SLIPPERY HITCH is often found in the sheets and halyards of small boats. It may be spilled instantly when required, yet it is a perfectly good hitch when properly applied and understood.

83. The AWNING KNOT is used as a stake hitch on marquees, and in lining off crowds on wharves and decks, at county fairs, parades, circuses, etc. It is instantly loosened by a jerk or blow, yet it is not a SLIPPED KNOT.

84. The BALANCING-POLE HITCH appears to have the smallest margin of all, but apparently it has proved adequate for the purpose it was designed for. When it is to be removed, the performer pauses, part way up his pole, then flirts the rope from the top of the pole and tosses it to the ground.

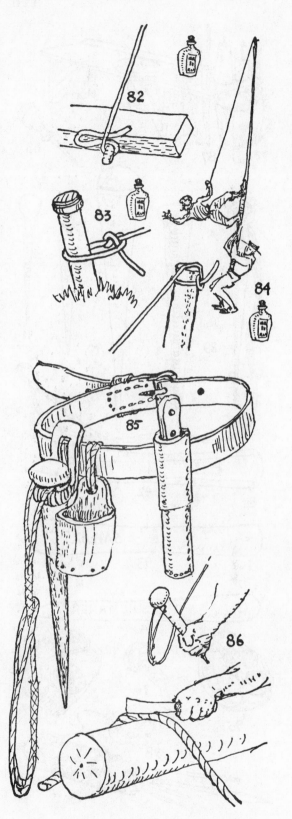

The tools of the sailor, the sailmaker, and the rigger, the three craftsmen whose work is primarily concerned with rope, are the result of years of selection and refinement. There can be nothing better for knot tying, although commercial tools are designed for heavy practical work. The confirmed knot tier aboard ship often has a few homemade miniature tools of similar design stowed away in his ditty bag.

85. The rigger commonly wears three articles on his belt: a *marlingspike*, a *horn* (called the *rigger's horn* or *grease horn*), and a *sheath knife* (#92). The horn contains tallow for greasing strands. A *marlingspike* (#89) is a long metal cone for opening strands in splicing and multi-strand knot tying. It has a protuberant head for pounding, and a hole for passing a lanyard. The bulging head distinguishes it from the *fid* (#90), which has none and is usually made of wood. For wire splicing the tapering point is usually somewhat flattened. The *rigger's knife* (#92) is "square-pointed" and is thicker-bladed than the characteristic *sailor's knife* (#93).

86. In cutting off lanyards and other rigging, the rope is held against a spar, and the back of the knife blade is tapped or pounded with the head of the *marlingspike*. A skilled rigger is one who can cut in this manner all but two fibers of a rope, without scoring the spar.

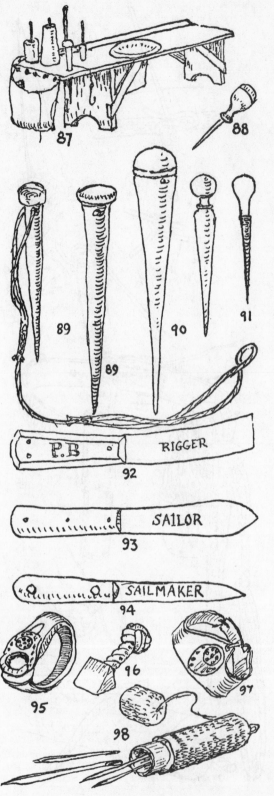

87. The sailmaker works in a loft while seated on a backless wooden bench with his tools stuck into various holes at one end, the right end if he is right-handed.

88. He has a small three-edged tool called a *stabber* for making eyelet holes.

89. Two different types of *marlingspike* are shown.

90. Several sizes of fids are required. Although commonly of wood, sometimes they are of whalebone, and often (in large sizes) of iron. A wooden *fid* may have a head, but it does not bulge, like the *marlingspike head*, beyond the line of the cone's taper.

91. A *pricker* is a smaller metal tool with a handle of other material (wood, leather, bone, etc.), or else it is an all-metal tool small enough to be held in the grasp of the hand (#99A). It is used by all three craftsmen but principally by the sailmaker. The *sailmaker's knife* (#94) is pointed and the back is often used in rubbing light seams; for heavy seams a *rubber* (also called *seam rubber*) (#96) is used. His *needles* (#98) are three-edged and of many sizes. A *marline needle* may be fully seven inches long with three flat sides three sixteenths of an inch wide. The shank and eye of a needle are smaller than the blade, so that needle and thread are easily pulled through after the *needle* point has once been entered. Instead of a thimble the sailmaker uses a *palm*, which is a checkered metal disk mounted in a sole leather or rawhide band. There are two sorts: a *roping palm* (#95), for sewing bolt rope to canvas, and a *seaming palm* (#97), for sewing cloths together. To hold his work in place he uses a *sail-hook* (#101D) which is made fast to his bench with a lanyard.

The sailor regularly employs any or all of the tools of the two other trades. His work at sea obliges him at times to be both rigger and sailmaker. A *sailor's knife* (#93) frequently has a blunt point and, in addition to its professional uses, is the sailor's only eating utensil, his fingers serving as boosters. On long voyages a cautious shipmaster will lead the whole crew aft to the carpenter's vise and have the point of each knife snapped off to resemble the *rigger's knife* (#92).

The best material I have found for practicing fancy and multi-strand knots is a round, flexible cotton braid called *banding* that is used for small "individual" drives in cotton mills. For general practical knot work, a good quality Manila rope is all that is required.

For making splices, bolt rope is excellent as it is soft-laid and of selected fiber. It is made with three strands only. Tarred ratline stuff (three-strand) and lanyard stuff (four-strand) hold the lay better than Manila and allow of more and easier correction.

For bag lanyards, leashes, etc., and for the standing rigging of ship models, there is a miniature rope in three and four strands of un-bleached linen, made in a number of sizes for Jacquard loom harness.

"Oriental" stores carry beautiful braided silk cord in various colors about five thirty-seconds of an inch in diameter. The P. C. Herwig Company, 121 Sands Street, Brooklyn, New York, has cotton cord for square knotting or "macramé" in almost every color and will send a catalogue if requested. They also sell an excellent pattern and instruction book on square knotting that is inexpensive and well illustrated.

Costly equipment is unnecessary. The fingers and a long round shoestring are all that is absolutely required for tying most of the

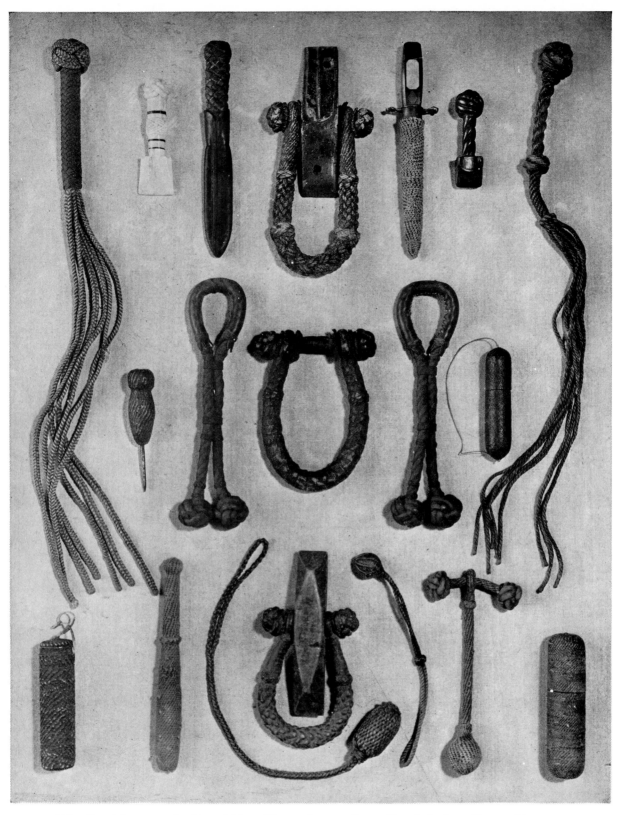

Old sailors' knot work. Cat-o'-Nine-Tails ⌗3719, ⌗509. Sheath knives ⌗3545. Two seam rubbers. Chest beckets, p. 573. Pegging awl ⌗3523. Needle cases ⌗3544. Policeman's night stick ⌗3717. Three blackjacks or life preservers, p. 580

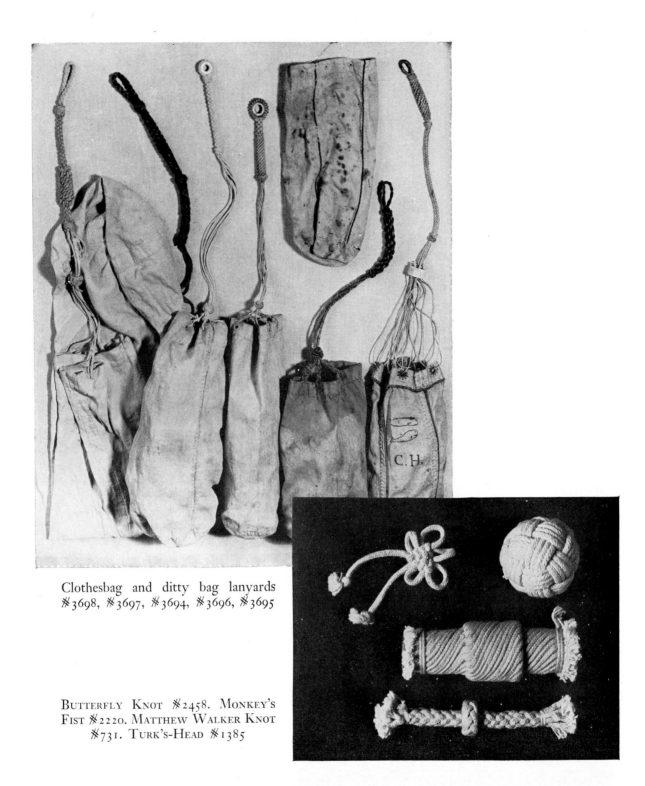

Clothesbag and ditty bag lanyards
#3698, #3697, #3694, #3696, #3695

Butterfly Knot #2458. Monkey's Fist #2220. Matthew Walker Knot #731. Turk's-Head #1385

Turk's-Head #1364

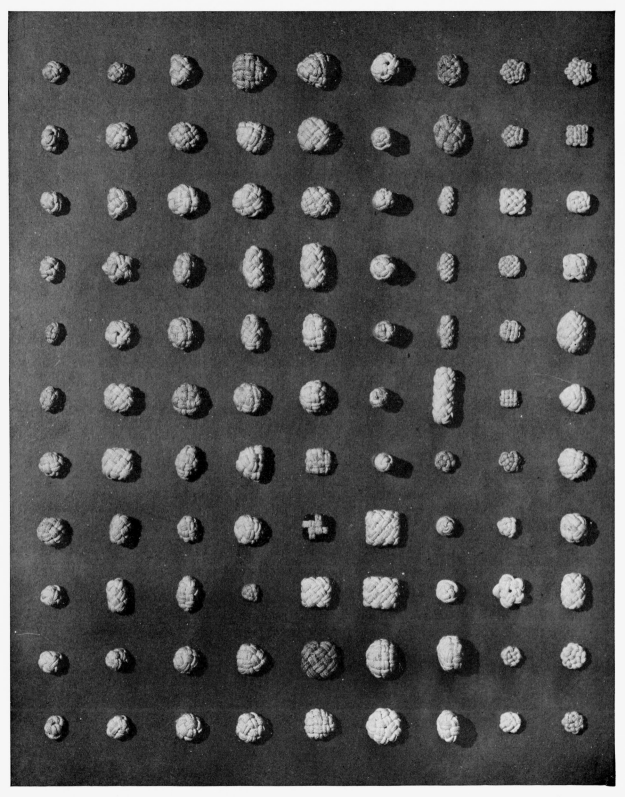

MULTI-STRAND BUTTONS of Chapter 10. Arranged in sequence from bottom to top and from left to right, Nos. 909–1008. #980 is missing

MULTI-STRAND BUTTONS, left to right, top to bottom, #898, #897, #896, #900, #899

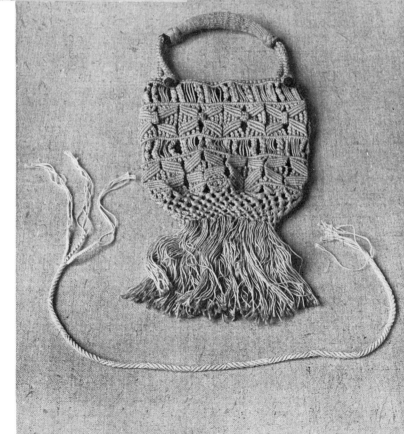

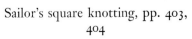

Sailor's square knotting, pp. 403, 404

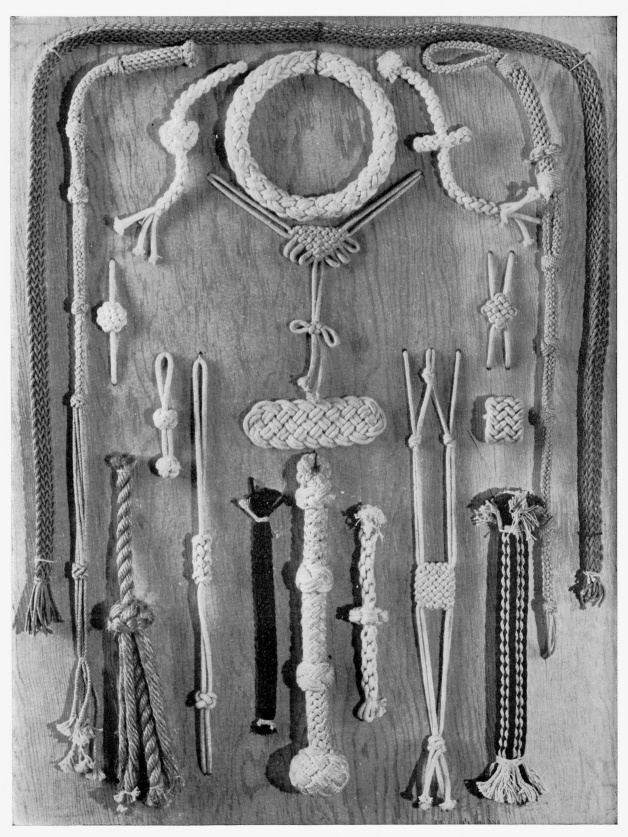

Knots and sinnets, mostly original. LANYARD KNOTS from Chapters 4, 7, 8. Sinnets from Chapter 39.
KNOTS #789, #980, #1381, #1382, #1590, #3590, #2217, #2275

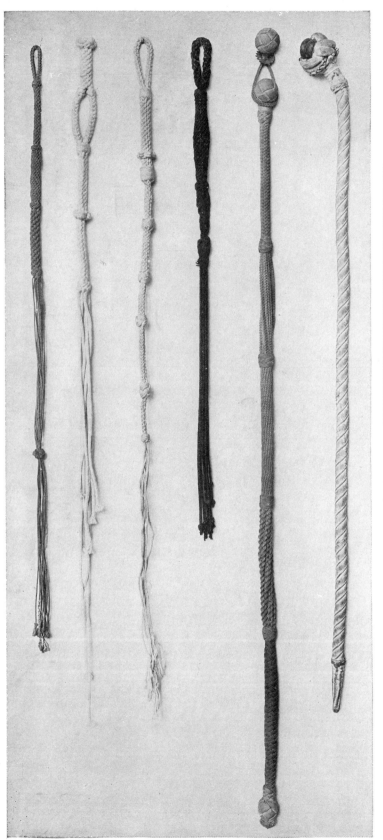

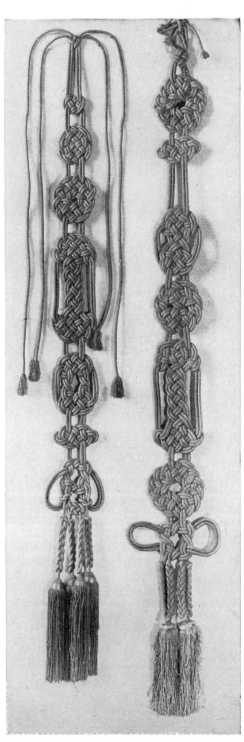

Bag lanyards #3691, #3689, #3692. Yoke rope #2523
Manrope #3758. Two Chinese priest cords, p. 381

Blocks, deadeyes, bull's-eyes, hearts, thimbles, etc., pp. 284–87, 521–25, 534, 544

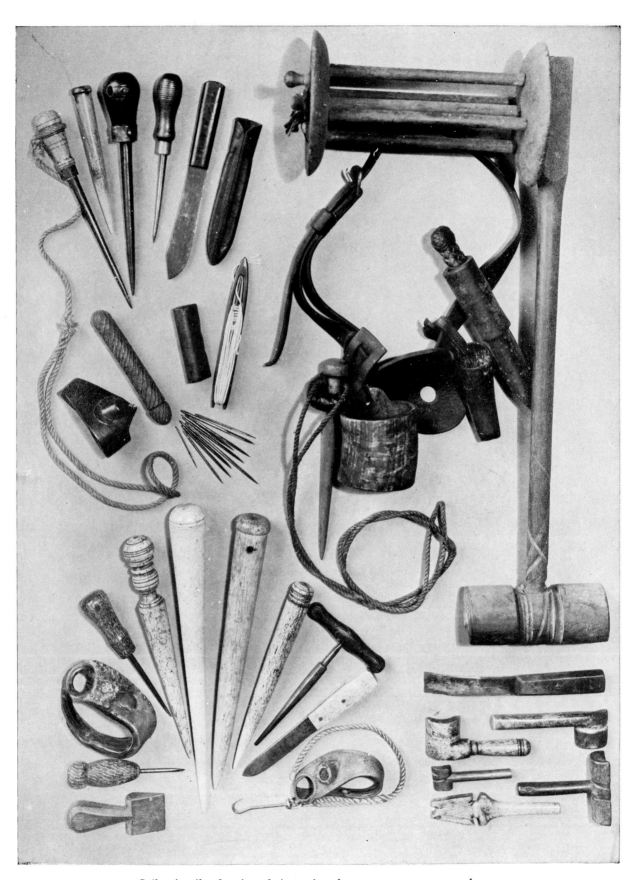

Sailors', sailmakers', and riggers' tools, pp. 19, 20, 21, 22, and 511

single-strand knots in this volume, and most homes will provide workable substitutes for the preferred tools that are described.

The Tools	Substitutes
Steel pricker or bodkin	Meat skewer, ice pick, or orange stick
Cork projection board	Breadboard or chair seat (and pins)
Loop buttoner	Hairpin
Wooden cylinders for Turk's-Head tying	Mailing tube
Knife	Scissors
Pliers	Fingers

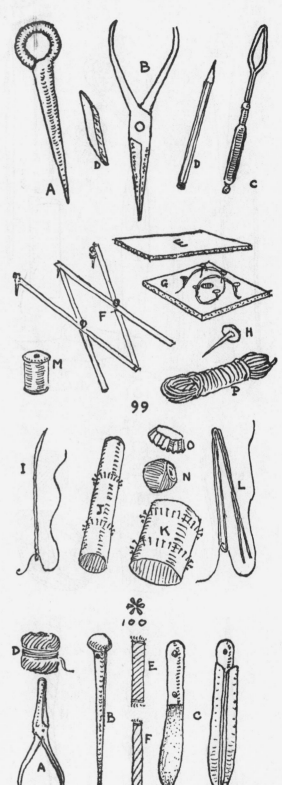

But, as in other handicrafts, the use of proper tools and materials will result in better workmanship and will save much inconvenience and consequent waste of time.

In the past I made many tools myself and had others made for me, before I learned where they could be procured. At least ten different kinds of shop would have to be visited by any would-be purchaser of the tools listed below, and the chance of finding everything in stock would be slight. To simplify this situation for any who might be interested I had arranged with a reputable ship chandlery to carry in stock the materials listed and to sell them either individually or in four numbered kits, ⚹99, ⚹100, ⚹101, ⚹102. Since this was arranged war has intervened and the arrangement has had to be canceled. However, if fifty cents is mailed to Warren Rope, Box 76, Westport Point, Massachusetts, a ball of cotton banding will be mailed to the reader.

List ⚹99 has everything needful for general knotting. Lists ⚹100 and ⚹101 are supplementary and are primarily for any who may be especially interested in splicing, in sailmaking, and in netting. List ⚹102 consists of occasional tools.

The illustrations, like the rest of the illustrations of the book, are not drawn to any especial scale.

KNOT-TYING TOOLS

General Kit ⚹99

A. Steel pricker, 4″
B. Long-billed pliers
C. Loop buttoner
D. Pencil and eraser
E. Block of tracing paper, 6″×8″
F. Pantograph
G. Cork projecting board, 12″ square
H. Long push tacks, for use with cork board
I. Packing needles
J. Wooden cylinders, 3″×6″, and 1½″×10″, for tying Turk's-Heads.
K. Pins for same
L. Flexible wire needle
M. Large black thread (used as a clue in making certain elaborate knots)
N. Twine for whippings and seizings
O. Beeswax
P. Ball of braided cotton "banding" for practicing knots

Supplementary Kit ⚹100 (including tools for splicing)

A. Duck-bill pliers
B. Marlingspike, 9″
C. Sheath knife, sailor's
D. Ball Italian yacht marline
E. Fifty feet four-strand rope (lanyard stuff)
F. Fifty feet three-strand rope (ratline stuff)

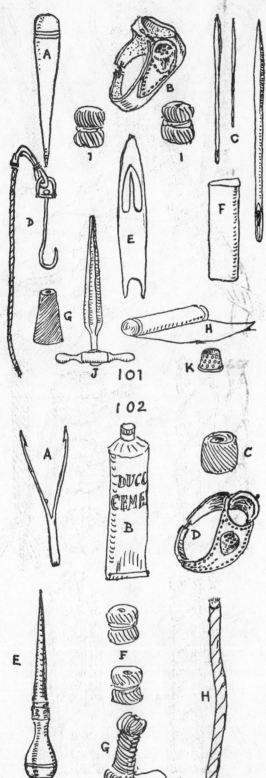

A. Hickory fid, 8½"
B. Sewing or seaming palm
C. Sail needles, three, assorted
D. Sail hook (for holding work)
E. Netting needle
F. Netting spool (1" practice spool)
G. Cord for netting
H. Five yards #10 duck (canvas)
I. Linen cord, three balls assorted (miniature rope)
J. Heaver
K. Thimble

Kit #102

Occasional Tools and Materials

A. Shouldered tweezers for "fancy knotting"
B. Duco cement
C. Sail twine
D. Roping palm
E. Pricker, 8"
F. Linen cord in various sizes
G. Larger-size banding for knot practice
H. Bolt rope, three-strand, for splicing

Perhaps the easiest way to tie many of the more elaborate knots is to place an outline of the knot desired on the cork projecting board, and to tie the knot directly over this diagram, pinning the cord at frequent intervals. A copy of the diagram is the first thing required. Tracing paper is the simplest thing to use, but carbon paper will serve equally well. Place the carbon paper between two sheets of white paper and make either a *direct* tracing or a *reversed* one, according to which side of the carbon paper is uppermost. To get a reversed tracing with ordinary tracing paper, merely turn the first tracing over and retrace on the back of it. If no tracing paper is handy, use ordinary typing paper against a well-lighted windowpane.

Some of the more elaborate diagrams will require enlarging. The pantograph provides an inexpensive and practical method of enlargement. One may be bought in any stationery shop for fifty cents and upward. There are also various reflecting and enlarging instruments of moderate cost, for sale in artists' materials shops, designed for the use of commercial artists. With these an enlarged tracing may be made in one operation.

A photostatic enlargement is perhaps the simplest means and is inexpensive, since a dozen diagrams may be traced on a single sheet of 8" × 10" paper and photostated directly onto a sheet of sensitized paper four times that size. If wished, one can be made directly from the book itself without any tracing.

Knots are tied in various kinds of flexible material: thongs, withes, roots, sinew, hair, and wire; but in this work, unless otherwise specified, rope and cord will be the materials considered. The term *rope* itself ordinarily applies to twisted vegetable fiber. The first operation in making rope of such material is to spin or twist a number of fibers into a yarn or thread. The ordinary twist is the same as that of a right-handed corkscrew, and is termed *right-handed*. If the yarns are twisted right-handed, the strands are left-handed and the rope itself is right-handed.

103. *Yarn:* Is a number of fibers twisted together, "right-handed." *Thread:* In ropemaking is the same as yarn.

104. *Sewing thread:* May be two, three, or more small yarns twisted together. *Sailmaker's sewing thread:* Consists of a number of cotton or linen yarns loose-twisted and is often called *sewing twine.*

105. *Strand:* Is two or more yarns or threads twisted together, generally *left-*handed.

106. *Rope:* Is three or more left-handed strands twisted together, right-handed, called plain-laid rope.

107. *Hawser:* Large plain-laid rope generally over 5″ in circumference is called hawser-laid.

108. *Cable* or *cable-laid rope:* Three plain- or hawser-laid ropes laid up together, left-handed; also called water-laid because it was presumed to be less pervious to moisture than plain-laid rope. Four-strand cable has been used for stays.

109. *Four-strand rope:* Right-handed, is used for lanyards, bucket bails, manropes, and sometimes for the running rigging of yachts.

110. *Shroud-laid rope:* Right-handed, four strands with a center core or *heart* (formerly termed a *goke*) was used for standing rigging before the days of wire rope. The heart is of plain-laid rope about half the size of one of the strands.

111. *Six-strand rope:* Right-handed with a heart, very hard-laid, was formerly used for tiller rope. The best was made of hide.

Six-strand "limber rope" was formerly laid along a keel and used to clear the limbers when they became clogged. It was made of horsehair, which resists moisture and decay better than vegetable fiber. Nowadays six-strand rope with wire cores in each strand is made for mooring cable and buoy ropes for small craft.

112. *Backhanded* or *reverse-laid rope:* In this material the yarns and the strands are *both* right-handed. It may be either three- or four-strand and is more pliant than plain-laid rope and less liable to kink when new, but it does not wear so well, is difficult to splice, and takes up moisture readily. Formerly it was used in the Navy for gun tackle and braces. Nowadays (in cotton) it is sometimes used for yacht running rigging. Lang-laid wire rope is somewhat similar in structure.

113. *Left-handed* or *left-laid rope:* The yarns are left-handed, the strands are right-handed, and the rope left-handed, the direct opposite of right-handed rope. Coupled with a right-handed or plain-laid rope of equal size, this is now used in roping seines and nets. The opposite twists compensate, so that wet seines have no tendency to twist and roll up at the edges.

In ropemaking, strictly speaking, yarns are "spun," strands are "formed," ropes are "laid," and cables are "closed," but these terms are often used indiscriminately.

Formerly plain-laid and hawser-laid meant the same thing. Now the term *hawser-laid* refers only to large plain-laid ropes suitable for towing, warping, and mooring.

It is a common mistake of recent years to use the terms *hawser-laid* and *cable-laid* interchangeably. This leaves two totally different products without distinguishing names, and it is no longer certain when either name is applied just what thing is referred to.

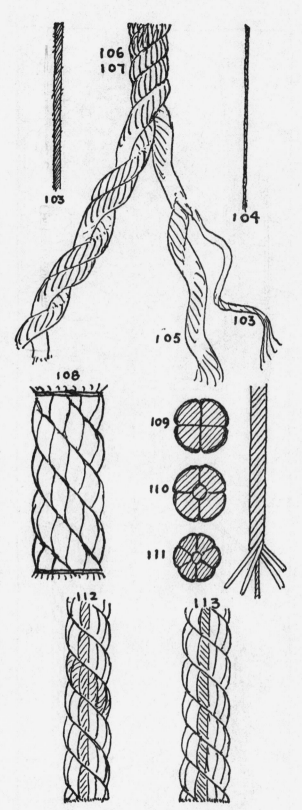

114

115

116

117

The fiber of *white rope* is moistened with water before laying, and for that reason it is also sometimes called *water-laid*. The fiber of ordinary rope is oiled, which makes a darker product.

114. *Soft-laid, slack-laid,* or *long-laid rope:* Handles easily, does not tend to kink, and is strongest. Whale line is soft-laid.

115. *Hard-laid* or *short-laid rope:* Gives better surface wear and is stiffer, but it is also weaker. Lariat rope is very hard-laid.

"Three-strand rope is approximately one fifth stronger than four-strand rope, and hawser-laid rope is said to be stronger than cable-laid in the proportion eight and seven tenths to six." This statement, which is frequently quoted, appears to have originated with Tinmouth, *Points of Seamanship* (London, 1845). Ninety-nine years is a long while for any statement to stand unchallenged. Although cable is harder laid than hawser, which tends to make it weaker, it is more elastic, which adds to its strength. I can see no reason why well-made cable in everyday service, where it is generally wet, should be inferior to hard-laid hawser.

Both wet rope and wet knots are stronger than dry ones, since water makes the fibers pliant and reduces the inside friction.

Corded is a general term applied to rope to indicate that it is twisted rather than braided, but more particularly it refers to *hard*-twisted stuff.

116. Rope that is stretched so that it has become attenuated and has lost much of its twist is termed "*long-jawed rope.*"

117. Swelled and weathered ends of rope are termed "*gouty ends.*"

Rope is anything in cordage above one inch in circumference; anything less is called "small stuff." Formerly the size of rope was always given in circumference, but now it is more commonly given in diameter, except "small stuff," in which the total number of the component threads (yarns) is mentioned to indicate the product. Ordinary clothesline is "nine-thread stuff," and "twenty-one-thread stuff" makes an adequate halyard for a small boat.

The word *rope* is seldom heard on shipboard, where it generally refers to new stuff in unbroken coils. But *rope* is also the inclusive term applied to all cordage, and a man is no sailor until he has "learned the ropes." There is an old saying that "there are seven ropes aboard a ship," but there are actually over sixty that have borne the name. Luce's *Seamanship* lists about forty which were presumably current when his book was first published.

Line is a common name for cordage aboard ship, but the word appears to be without specific meaning. Fishline, log line, ratline, clew line, buntline, whale line, heaving line, spring line, and towline indicate the indiscriminate range covered by the term.

There are several ways to break in new, stiff rope after it has been properly uncoiled. The best is to put it to use and to be very careful with it until it has adjusted itself. The worst way is to boil it in water, which removes the oil or tar and renders the fibers brittle.

118. A good practical way is to tow it overboard for one day, then turn it end for end and tow it for another day, having first made certain that both ends are well whipped. Afterward it should be carefully dried on a grating; wet rope should never be hauled taut and allowed to dry while made fast.

119. If a rope or splice is fuzzy, rub it with a clout of mail of the kind employed in kitchens for scouring pans. A piece of fine-mesh chicken wire will serve if the sharp wire ends are kept out of the way.

120. The neatest tool with which to cut rope is a sharp hatchet. The end of an ordinary fireplace log makes a good chopping block. A wide chisel will serve instead of a hatchet.

121. If the performer is not certain of his aim, or if the rope is large, lay it across the greased, upturned blade of a sharp ax, and pound it with a billet of firewood.

For smaller stuff the sailor's knife is the best all-around tool, and if kept sharp it will serve about every purpose.

Large cable may be whipped twice with wire and then sawed between the two whippings, with a fine-toothed saw, such as a hack saw, or a cabinet saw.

Before unlaying the strands of a rope to make a MULTI-STRAND KNOT it is best to put a stopping on at the length of strand required, and also to whip the ends of the individual strands. Use the CONSTRICTOR KNOT (#1249) for these purposes.

After splicing do not trim the ends of strands flush with the surface. Leave them longer until they have seen service and stretched and weathered a bit.

To fair the strands of an opened rope before tying a MULTI-STRAND KNOT, first whip them and then beat them well with a mallet; finally wax them.

122. A smoother knot, requiring more skill to tie, may be attained by first putting on a seizing, then dipping the strands for a few moments in hot water, without wetting the seizing. Twist up the strands tightly, attach ends to a board, and dry while under tension.

123. If the strands of a knot are to be canvas-covered, which is usual with MULTI-STRAND BUTTON KNOTS, first scrape the tips to a point and marl tightly with a fine, soft-twisted linen twine which has first been waxed.

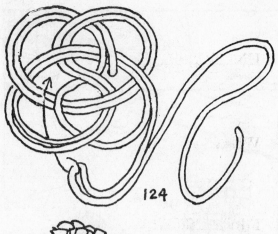

124. *When tucking a long cord, much twisting and kinking will be avoided if, instead of tucking the end directly, a loop is first stuck, and the long end pulled through after it.*

125. After tying, but before working, an elaborate MULTI-STRAND STOPPER or LANYARD KNOT, lay the ends up and stop them together. This will insure against unreeving, and will keep the ends of the completed knot well centered.

126. In tying any large knot, such as a TURK'S-HEAD or a MAT, in which the lead is to be followed twice or more, *middle your rope and tie the knot with one half.* Employ the other half later when doubling or trebling the knot.

127. To correct an error after a knot or sinnet is tied, employ a clue, preferably of a color and size different from the material of the knot. A shoestring is excellent for the purpose. Starting at a point *beyond the error* lay the *clue* in correctly, passing the error and continuing out to the end of the erring strand. Then remove the strand that was in error, and at once lay it in again correctly, parallel to and beside the *clue*. Finally remove the *clue*.

No amount of theoretical knowledge in any of the arts or handicrafts can compensate for the lack of practical experience.

A beginner should not be discouraged if he is not immediately successful with a complicated knot. Usually the first few examples that are given in each chapter are the simplest of their kind and are more fully described than the others which follow. For that reason they should be practiced first. A novice should avoid for a while anything in the nature of a short cut. He will find that the professional usually follows the charted course. If a failure is repeated, twist the diagram on the table and tie the knot again from a new angle.

From time to time, among the illustrations, a symbol has been placed to proclaim the merit or interest of a particular knot. It is hoped that the meaning of these symbols will be at once apparent—an anchor stands for security, a skull and crossbones implies the contrary, a star marks the best knot for a given purpose. These symbols will be found on the opposite page.

It is an integral part of the scheme of this book to give the sources of knots wherever possible. Various occupations are alphabetically arranged in Chapter 2, and their knots given. Among the practical knots, where nothing else is indicated a nautical origin is presumptive. Where the source is not made clear by the context, the practical knots, which I have evolved independently, are frequently labeled with the symbol of a spouting sperm whale. But this practice has not been consistently adhered to, and I have made no particular effort to mark my own contribution to decorative knots.

Certain chapters, such as those on the SINGLE-STRAND BUTTON (Chapter 5), MULTI-STRAND BUTTON, tied on the table (Chapter 10), the SHROUD KNOT (Chapter 19), the MONKEY'S FIST (Chapter 29), and the SOLID SINNETS (Chapter 39), are mostly or entirely original. Other chapters, such as those on the TURK'S-HEAD (Chapter 17), and the FLAT or Two-DIMENSIONAL KNOTS (Chapter 30), are the results of protracted research and experiment. They contain much original matter, but there is no way to determine what ground had previously been covered by others.

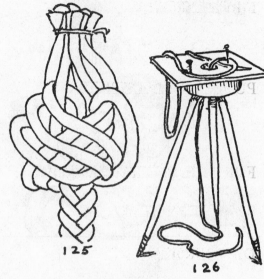

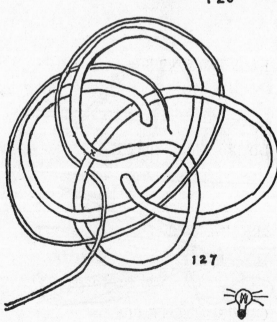

IMPORTANT

 UNIMPORTANT

 STRONG

 WEAK

 PRACTICAL

 IMPRACTICAL

 USEFUL AND ORNAMENTAL

 PURELY ORNAMENTAL

 BEST FOR THE PURPOSE

 FOR THE INITIATED ONLY

 RELIABLE

 DANGEROUS

 DIFFICULT TO UNTIE

 EASY TO UNTIE

 PROBABLY ORIGINAL

 LIABLE TO CAPSIZE

 OF THEORETICAL INTEREST

 DISTINCTIVE

 NEW LIGHT

 GENERAL UTILITY

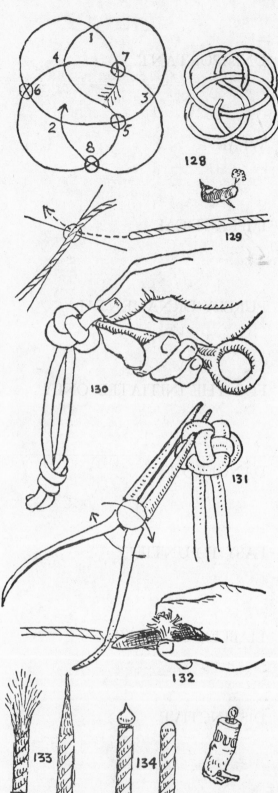

128. Diagrams are provided on which to tie the more intricate knots. On a diagram for an elaborate SINGLE-STRAND KNOT, the working end is indicated by an arrowhead, and the standing end with a feather. Each diagram is further marked with small circles around some of the points where two leads cross each other. At these encircled points the working end is always tucked under the other part. Knots which have a regular "over-one-and-under-one" sequence (basket weave) may have each alternate crossing numbered in regular sequence, 1, 2, 3, etc., and the end is tucked under each circle that is crossed in its regular numerical sequence.

To tie a knot upon such a diagram: Secure the cord, at the *feather end* of the line, by pinning it or else by dropping it down through a round hole in the center of the cork projecting board. Lay the cord along the line, pinning it at frequent intervals.

129. Wherever another lead is to be crossed, at a point that is marked with a circle, tuck the working end underneath.

Not more than two cords cross each other at any point in a diagram.

A knot having been tied or projected, the next thing in order is to "*work*" it, which means to draw it up snug while molding it into proper shape. The slack should be worked out very gradually. *This is a matter of no less importance than correct tying*, and often presents a more difficult problem, requiring both patience and practice. Carefully fair the knot, and, once having arranged the cord in symmetrical form, never allow it to become distorted, even momentarily.

130. A pricker, bodkin, or stiletto is the most practical tool for working a knot. Hold the point about even with the tip of the thumb and prick up the strand. Hold the strand firmly between thumb and the point of the pricker, and pull carefully.

For heavier pulling, use a marlingspike. The method is described in Chapter 27, "Occasional Knots" (⚹2029) and (⚹2030).

131. In finishing off a very tight knot employ a pair of pliers. Grip a part firmly and roll the pliers just enough to raise the required amount of material. Pull each part uniformly, and in regular turn.

Never try to complete an elaborate knot in one operation. Work a SINGLE-STRAND KNOT back and forth from end to end, tightening it gradually and prodding it constantly into its intended shape.

A MULTI-STRAND KNOT is always worked *toward* the strand ends. Each strand is tightened, one part only at a time, and the corresponding parts of the other strands are tightened before progressing to the next tier of parts.

132, 133. To assist in reeving: when tying an elaborate knot of small material, scrape the end to a point, saturate with Duco cement, add twist, and permit to dry.

134 To prevent fraying in braided material, cut the end square off and allow a round drop of Duco cement to dry on the very tip. This will scarcely be apparent when dry. A shoestring that has lost its metal tip may be repaired in this same way.

Round metal-tipped shoestrings are excellent for knot practice and are sometimes procurable in colors, but at the present time long shoestrings are difficult to obtain.

135. To wind cord into an ordinary ball, take a few turns around one hand, and make these turns into a wad by first twisting into a figure eight and then clapping the ends together. Wind as pictured, rotating the ball constantly and changing the axis from time to time.

136. To wind a kite string or a string that is wet, the following is perhaps the best method to employ. "S" turns, exactly the same as belaying-pin turns, are taken in the same manner, except that the hand which holds the stick is pivoted or twisted right and left, so the winding hand does not have to describe so large a figure "S."

To dry wet rope, coil loosely, and lay on a grating in a strong draft.

137. To uncoil large rope, or wire rope, place the coil on edge, make fast the end, and unroll. Wire rope must not be allowed to kink.

138. On shipboard new running rigging is rove off by leading it through a tail block that is bent to the rigging above the coil. The end of the rope is drawn from the center of the coil. Care must be taken that the proper end of the coil is uppermost; the rope should come out counterclockwise as shown in ⚓139, that is to say, in a direction opposite to the normal progress of a clock hand.

139. Kinks are removed from new whale line by making large successive left-hand coils and drawing up the lower end each time through the center of the coil. The rope is led through a tail block in the rigging. Whale line is finally coiled down right-handed in a tub, in a manner to be described later, as ⚓3105.

140. The common way of taking out kinks and excess twist from the end of a line is to twirl or spin it, beginning preferably at a distance from the end and working toward the end, but it is sometimes worked the other way. Repeat until the entire rope lies fair.

141. To untangle a snarl, loosen all jams or knots and open a hole through the mass at the point where the longest end leaves the snarl. Then proceed to roll or wind the end out through the center exactly as a stocking is rolled. Keep the snarl open and loose at all times and *do not pull on the end;* permit it to unfold itself. As the process is continued the end gradually emerges. No snarl is too complicated to be solved by this method; only patience is required.

142. To break twine or small cord, lay the right forefinger across the standing part and revolve the finger exactly as the marlingspike is revolved in making a MARLINGSPIKE HITCH, but pause when the cord is in the position shown in the first diagram. Hold the cord firmly in the palm with the thumb and fingers. Grasp the upper end with the free hand, and jerk either with the right hand, the left hand, or with both.

The method is used with varying technique; often the thumb is employed instead of the forefinger. *Do not allow the cord to slip while jerking, or a cut finger may result.*

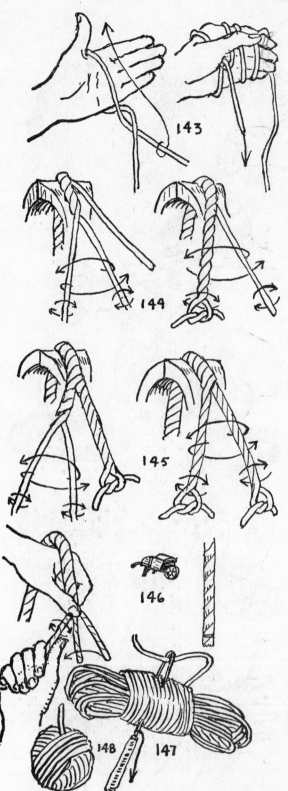

143. To break a heavy cord or string, take a turn of the cord around the left palm. Revolve the left hand so the cord is twisted in front of the palm, and wind the standing part several times around the fingers. Wrap the end (which is longer than illustrated) several times around the right hand; hold everything firm and jerk stoutly.

In each of the two methods given the string crosses itself at right angles, one part being held rigidly while the other part is strongly jerked.

My first impression was that the weakening effect of this harsh crossing was the important factor in causing the string to break invariably at this point. One of the "laws" quoted in dictionary and encyclopedia knot discussions is that "the strength of a knot depends on the ease of its curves," and of course a right-angle crossing provides the uneasiest curve that is possible within a knot.

But two BOWLINES tied into each other (the BOWLINE BEND, ⚓1145) have exactly the same right-angle crossing. And no less a naval authority than Admiral Stephen Luce, "father of our Naval Academy" and author of one of the best works on seamanship, says that it is "about the best." Richard Dana, Jr., says it is "the most usual" of HAWSER BENDS. On testing this bend I could find no tendency to break at the point of crossing. The material broke each time at a point just outside one of the BOWLINE KNOTS.

So it is evident that some factor other than a harsh curve is present when string is broken in the manner described. It seems probable that this is the shearing effect exerted by the taut cord where it is hacked across the section that is held rigid. At any rate the so-called "law" does not fit this particular case.

144. To lay up the opened end of a three-strand rope, grip the rope in a vise or clamp, or get someone to hold it. Take two strands, one in each hand, twist them simultaneously to the right, and at the same time lay the right strand over the left. Without rendering what has been gained, shift the hands and repeat. When the ends are reached half knot them together.

Then lay up these two strands with the single remaining strand in precisely the same way. The right twist will open the two strands already laid up, admitting the single or odd strand. Whip the end when completed.

145. To lay up the opened end of a four-strand rope, lay up each pair as already described, then lay the two pairs together in similar manner and whip.

146. If only a short piece of rope is opened, twist any strand a half turn to the right, then lay it to the left across the rope. Repeat with each strand one half turn at a time and continue until the rope is complete, then whip.

147. To secure the end after winding up a hank or ball, take a loop buttoner or a doubled piece of stiff wire and thrust it through the center of the ball. Thread the end of the cord through the wire loop and pull it back through the ball. To make up a hank, wind the cord around the palm of the hand and then add crossing turns.

148. A more common but less secure way to tuck the end is to stick it under the last few turns, and then work all snug.

In very slippery material a series of HALF HITCHES is often taken around the ball, but ⚓147 is probably preferable.

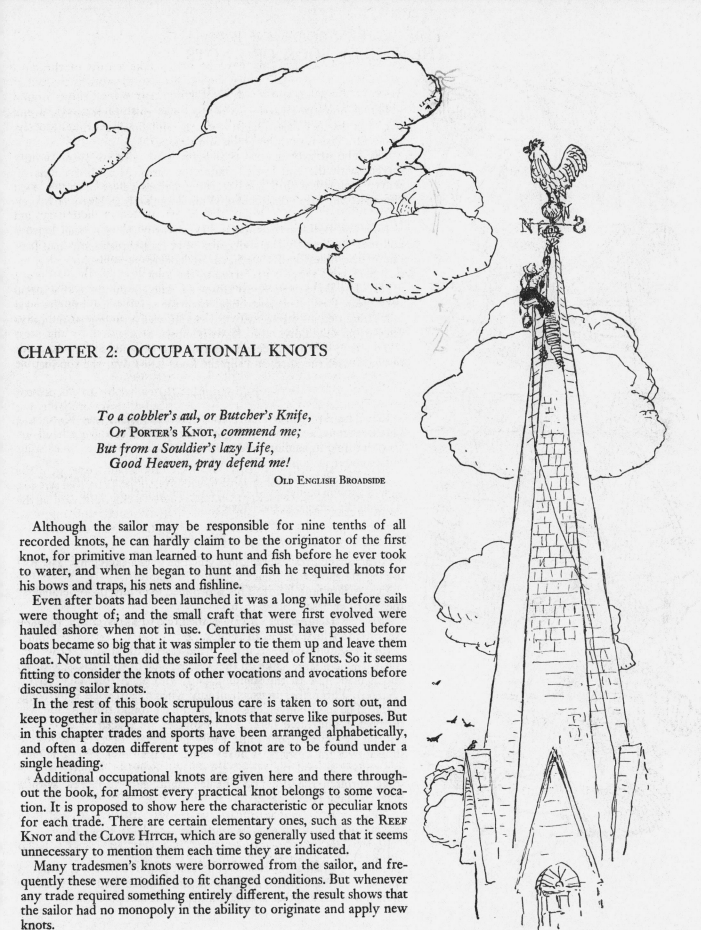

CHAPTER 2: OCCUPATIONAL KNOTS

To a cobbler's aul, or Butcher's Knife,
Or PORTER'S KNOT, commend me;
But from a Souldier's lazy Life,
Good Heaven, pray defend me!

OLD ENGLISH BROADSIDE

Although the sailor may be responsible for nine tenths of all recorded knots, he can hardly claim to be the originator of the first knot, for primitive man learned to hunt and fish before he ever took to water, and when he began to hunt and fish he required knots for his bows and traps, his nets and fishline.

Even after boats had been launched it was a long while before sails were thought of; and the small craft that were first evolved were hauled ashore when not in use. Centuries must have passed before boats became so big that it was simpler to tie them up and leave them afloat. Not until then did the sailor feel the need of knots. So it seems fitting to consider the knots of other vocations and avocations before discussing sailor knots.

In the rest of this book scrupulous care is taken to sort out, and keep together in separate chapters, knots that serve like purposes. But in this chapter trades and sports have been arranged alphabetically, and often a dozen different types of knot are to be found under a single heading.

Additional occupational knots are given here and there throughout the book, for almost every practical knot belongs to some vocation. It is proposed to show here the characteristic or peculiar knots for each trade. There are certain elementary ones, such as the REEF KNOT and the CLOVE HITCH, which are so generally used that it seems unnecessary to mention them each time they are indicated.

Many tradesmen's knots were borrowed from the sailor, and frequently these were modified to fit changed conditions. But whenever any trade required something entirely different, the result shows that the sailor had no monopoly in the ability to originate and apply new knots.

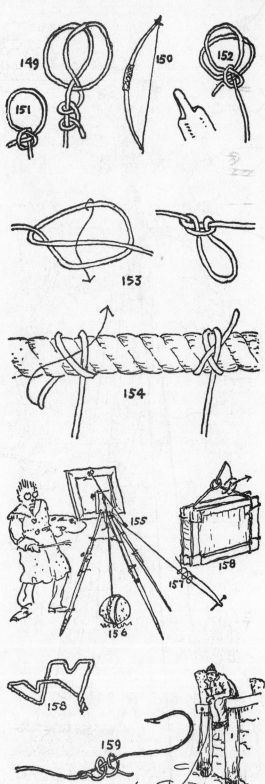

The Archer

149. A bowstring is secured to the lower end of a bow in a number of ways. A CLOVE HITCH with the end finished off with TWO HALF HITCHES is both common and practical.

150. The grip of a bow is sometimes of cord or yarn, tightly served, with the end buried under the turns. More often it is of woven material with a piled texture, such as velvet or plush. Occasionally the grip consists of a WIDE TURK'S-HEAD KNOT (Chapter 17).

151. The BOWSTRING KNOT is a LOOP KNOT that has been known and used for ages by the aborigines of at least three continents. It is one of the oldest knots we have. In modern archery, however, an EYE SPLICE (⚹2754) is preferred to the knot.

152. The BOWSTRING KNOT DOUBLED. The advantage of this is not very clear. Possibly it is stronger than the single knot, but the two loops might easily prove awkward in a hurried stringing of the bow. An ADJUSTABLE BOWSTRING KNOT is shown as ⚹1030.

To string a bow, place one end on the ground, spring the bow outward with the knee, and slip the LOOP KNOT over the top lug.

The Artilleryman

153. The ARTILLERY LOOP, also called MAN-HARNESS KNOT and HARNESS LOOP, is tied in the bight of a rope. It is used for a hand- or shoulder-hold in hauling field guns into position, and also in assisting horses either in uphill work or when mired.

154. The PICKET-LINE HITCH is used in tying up artillery horses. It was shown to me by J. Lawrence Houghteling, who learned it while in the service at the Mexican border.

The Artist

An artist requires several knots when he goes a-sketching. The following are those that I have found most helpful.

155. A BOWLINE KNOT. This is dropped over any protuberance at the top of an easel. (See ⚹1010.)

156. A KILLEG HITCH (⚹271) is then tied to a convenient stone or bag of sand which acts as an anchor.

157. A second cord, secured to the easel with another BOWLINE, is led around a large spike on the weather side of the canvas, and the end is made fast to the standing part with an ADJUSTABLE HITCH (⚹1800). This makes an excellent guy when a hard wind is blowing.

158. The most convenient way that I have found for carrying wet sketches is illustrated here. Two canvases are placed face to face, but not in contact; four clips, easily homemade of 3/32″ wire, slipped over the corners. A heavy cord, with a BOWLINE in one end, is wrapped around the clips between the canvases, and the end is stuck through the BOWLINE, hauled tight, and made fast with a SLIPPED HALF HITCH (⚹1476).

The Angler

159. A variety of ANGLER'S KNOTS will be found later in this chapter among FISHERMAN'S KNOTS. The knot pictured here is a common way of securing a line to a ring hook and is much used in the cruder branches of the art, that is to say, in hand-line and pole fishing.

The Automobilist

160. A method of affixing a towrope to an automobile or truck axle for very short hauls; this was devised by Captain Daniel F. Mullins, who needed something of the sort for dragging Diesel engines and other heavy equipment on rollers about the wharf. A most important practical feature of the knot is that it allows of instant and easy adjustment. Wharves are narrow, and a load frequently has to be hauled through narrow gaps in stacked merchandise. Often it is necessary to make a short pull and then back up to shorten the towrope. Almost any hitch in heavy rope is difficult to open, but this particular one slackens when the car stops, and the end is easily pulled through the hitches whenever it is necessary to adjust the length. Captain Mullins' hitch is the exact opposite of TWO HALF HITCHES, in which the hitches are in the end; in this the hitches are in the standing part.

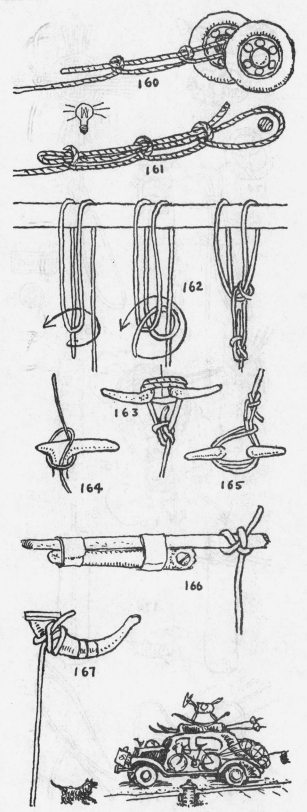

161. An amplification of the former knot: If the material is particularly large and stiff the end may be doubled and the knot will be found easier to make. It will also be more secure. Neither knot is suitable for hoisting.

162. The AXLE HITCH may be used for emergency towing. The knot is a variety of backhanded hitch, which requires but one passing of the line around the axle although the knot itself is double. Having rounded the axle, the loop is pulled out until all projecting parts of the car are cleared, where the hitch is completed and the BOWLINE (※1010) added. If a MIDSHIPMAN'S HITCH (※1027) is used to complete the knot instead of the BOWLINE, the knot will be less liable to jam.

163. There are many occasions for lashing suitcases and other luggage to the running board or other parts of a car, but the makers of cars so far have failed to co-operate by placing a few handy lugs here and there to lash to. Handles are about all we have for anchors, and the manufacturers' efforts have all been directed toward "streamlining" these to a degree where clothes cannot snag on them. If the handles of both doors approach each other with a long-horned effect nothing more is required than a round turn about both and TWO HALF HITCHES or else a BOWLINE to finish off with.

164. An application of the BUOY ROPE HITCH (※3323) is practicable if the handle of the door has a heel as well as a toe.

165. A BALE SLING HITCH (※1735) will never bind and may be applied in a variety of ways. Nothing else is required on a round knob save ※2018, which is the easiest thing there is to untie. If put in the bight as ※1816 *both ends* of the rope are available for lashing.

166. Where there is *danger of unlatching*, a small stick can be bound to the handle with electrician's tape and the knot secured to the stick close to the handle. The pull on the rope should be in the direction that will hold the latch secure.

167. If the knob or handle tapers, or if its shape is an obstacle, it can generally be taped in such way as to provide both a shoulder and a good surface to prevent a hitch from slipping. The ROLLING HITCH (※1734) is the safest knot to use in such a situation.

A method of roping a wheel when chains are lacking is given as ※2027.

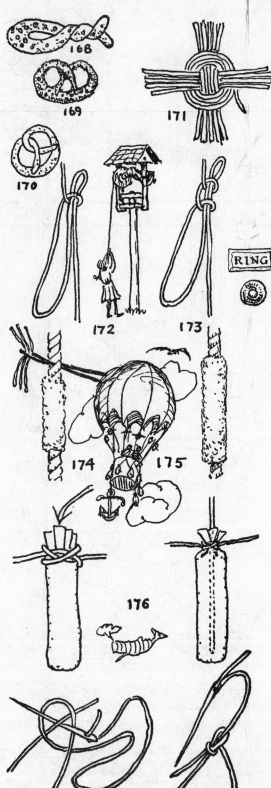

The Baker

168. The PRETZEL KNOT is too widely known to require much description, but there are several varieties, and often nowadays the pretzels are stamped out by machinery instead of being tied. The GIANT PRETZEL KNOT is from Lancaster County, Pennsylvania. It is about ten inches long.

169. The OVERHAND KNOT appears to be the oldest form of the *pretzel*.

170. A more sophisticated pretzel is a perversion of the FIGURE-EIGHT KNOT.

The Basketmaker

171. The SLATH or SLARTH KNOT appears at the bottom of splint baskets. The stakes are opened up fanwise and the basket woven in the regular "over-one-and-under-one" sequence that is known as the "basket weave." The JOSEPHINE KNOT (#1502) and the CROWN KNOT (#670) are also used in commencing baskets.

There is a great deal in basketmaking that approximates knot tying, but it constitutes a separate craft.

The Bell Ringer

172. The BELL RINGER'S KNOT is mentioned in Hutton's Dictionary of 1815. It is actually the first half of the ordinary SHEEPSHANK (#1153) and is probably a knot of considerable antiquity. Its purpose is to keep a long end of rope from lying on the belfry deck when not in use. The same knot is used in sail and rigging lofts and in ship chandleries to keep the ends of new rope off the floor.

173. If the rope is long and heavy two hitches are sometimes used instead of one, and, if necessary, several round turns may be taken instead of the single turn illustrated.

174. SALLIES, SALLY TUFTS, SALLIE TUFTING: A chafing gear of brightly colored yarns similar to "BAGGY WRINKLES" (#3485) is rove through the strands of a bell rope. These are packed hard and trimmed evenly. Different bells have different colors to identify them. The purpose of the tufting is to provide a proper handhold when ringing chimes. The SALLIES are usually several feet long, the length depending on the swing or scope of the bell.

The Balloonist and Parachutist

175. The basket or carriage of a balloon is generally *toggled* (#1922) to EYE SPLICES on the gas bag, so that the balloon may easily be disassembled, or cast adrift from the basket.

The Bicyclist

Among the occasional knots in Chapter 26 is shown a method of making an emergency, or jury, tire (#2028) out of a piece of old clothesline.

The Blaster

176. When a dynamite cartridge is to be exploded with a fuse, employ a CONSTRICTOR KNOT (#1249 and #1252). Pull the two ends tight and it will hold as if adjusted with a ratchet. The hole in the cartridge should be made with a *stick of soft wood and the* fuse inserted full length.

The Bookbinder

177. The BOOKBINDER'S KNOT is employed when sewing the leaves of a book. It is interesting, and quite unusual, because the knot, although tied with the working or needle end, is actually formed in the other end. It is identical in form with the LEFT-HAND SHEET BEND. Shown to me by Mrs. F. Gilbert Hinsdale.

The Bootmaker

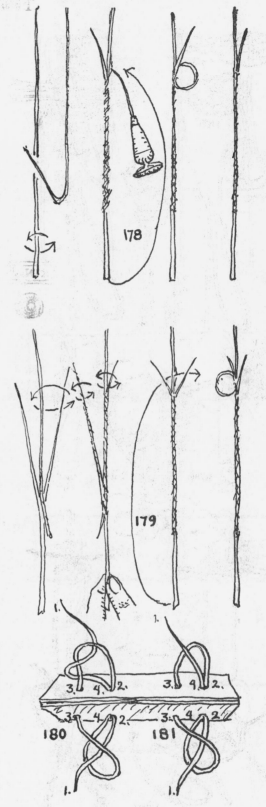

178. To secure thread to bristles: The preferred bristles are from the "ridges" of northern domestic boars. Wild-boar bristles, which make the best paintbrushes, are too large in diameter for sewing bristles and besides are frequently so covered with pitch that the expense of cleaning would make the cost prohibitive. Poland-China-hog bristles are the best, as a considerable length is required.

Several threads are laid together and at the required length are teased apart after rubbing out the twist on the knee. This divides the twine without breaking the fiber.

After the threads are well waxed the tip of the combined ends, which tapers to a microscopical point, is laid across the bristle near the hide end, which is the working end, at a 45-degree angle, the thread end pointing toward the tip. The thread is held in the right hand and rotated with the bristle when the butt or hide end of the latter is twisted between the thumb and forefinger. When the thread and bristle have been laid up together for about one fourth of an inch toward the hide end, the direction of the thread is changed so that it doubles back over the first laid section and to within an inch of the tip or small end.

With the bootmaker's awl a hole is then pricked through the thread at the point where it leaves the bristle. The hide or butt end of the bristle is then stuck through this hole and drawn taut. This locks the thread and bristle together. They are then rubbed smooth with the fingers.

Sometimes, for light work, the thread is left as in the second diagram, without sticking the bristle through the thread. By this latter method a bristle may be used over and over again.

179. The bristle is split in half at the tip end for about one third to two fifths of its length. The tapered end of the waxed thread is laid into the crotch so formed, overlapping about one quarter of an inch. The thread and one of the legs are twisted together to within an inch of the bristle tips. Holding this leg firmly, the second leg is twisted similarly by itself (same amount of twist, in the same direction). The two legs are then placed together and held at the tips, and the hide end is let go, whereupon the hide end twists reversely, of its own volition, and the two legs are laid up together exactly as rope is laid. A hole is next pricked where the thread leaves the bristle (three quarters of an inch to one inch from the tip), and the hide end is stuck through this opening and drawn snug. The whole is smoothed out with the fingers. This method is perhaps securer than the previous one.

180, 181. There are a number of simple ways of securing loose ends when sewing is completed; two of these are shown. In machine stitching, the untidy practice of back stitching is frequently resorted to.

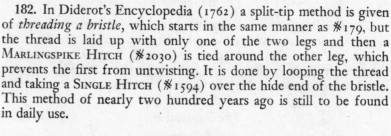

182. In Diderot's Encyclopedia (1762) a split-tip method is given of *threading a bristle*, which starts in the same manner as ✳179, but the thread is laid up with only one of the two legs and then a MARLINGSPIKE HITCH (✳2030) is tied around the other leg, which prevents the first from untwisting. It is done by looping the thread and taking a SINGLE HITCH (✳1594) over the hide end of the bristle. This method of nearly two hundred years ago is still to be found in daily use.

The Burglar

I would do nothing to encourage the activities of this archenemy of society, but I will urge him to consider the awful sequence of the following knots with all its direful implications: the BASKET HITCH (✳2155), the HANDCUFF KNOT (✳412), and the HANGMAN'S KNOT (✳366). If his interest is a morbid one he can find several more HANGMAN'S KNOTS in the chapter on nooses. And if he has any choice, I am told that the last wish of the hangee is always granted.

The Butcher

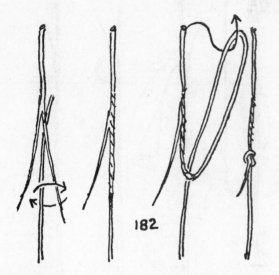

183. BUTCHER'S KNOTS are required in tying up "boned and rolled roasts" and in preparing corned beef and salt pork for pickling. After passing an end of twine around the meat a simple noose of some sort is made around the standing part of the twine. When this noose has been drawn up and held taut, the standing part is half hitched around the end. This is done by first taking a right round turn with the standing part around the tips of the left thumb and two or three adjoining fingers. The thumb and three fingers then grasp the end of the twine and the round turn is transferred to the knot, automatically forming a HALF HITCH, which renders all secure.

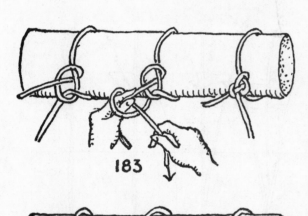

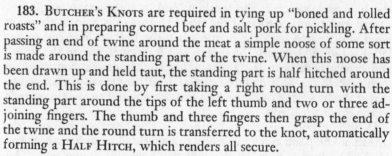

184. This final hitch is the salient feature of the BUTCHER'S KNOT, and it is so very efficient that any complication that will hold together while being drawn up around the meat will serve as the first part of a BUTCHER'S KNOT for a roast, which is hove taut, hitched, and shoved across the counter while you wait. The hitch is put around the end, not the end through the hitch.

For pickling and corning, however, something more is required. The noose must jam sufficiently to hold the meat firmly for several weeks until it is sufficiently pickled. During this process the meat shrinks constantly and the knot has to be tightened from time to time. The final hitch is not added until the pickling is concluded.

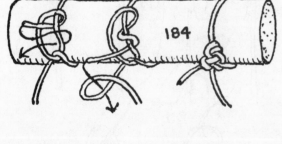

185. A SQUARE KNOT is tied and then capsized into a REVERSE HITCH, and the standing part is then *half hitched* around the end as already described. This is one of the commonest and also poorest of the series. It is apt to slip considerably in the drawing up, and occasionally spills and has to be retied.

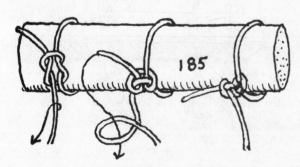

186. The GRANNY KNOT. If one end of a GRANNY KNOT is pulled, the knot will capsize into TWO HALF HITCHES, which makes a better knot than the REEF KNOT. The end is hitched as already described and as pictured in ⌗183.

187. The PACKER'S KNOT. This knot is sometimes used in baling and in parcel tying and is perhaps the most practical of BONED AND ROLLED ROAST KNOTS, for which purpose it is the one generally tied by the more skillful butchers. It is, however, hardly secure enough for a CORNED BEEF KNOT. The end has a nice lead and the completed knot is compact and neat.

188. I have found this knot in use in several widely separated places. But it is a clumsy one to tie, and I can see nothing in particular to recommend it. It is based on the PACKER'S KNOT, having one more turn, which does not help a bit and which was added by someone who could not leave well enough alone.

189. This knot is easier to tie than the foregoing and often appears on the table. KNOTS ⌗184, ⌗188, and ⌗189 are closely related although quite distinct. CORNED BEEF KNOT ⌗192, which is to follow, also has points of resemblance, but is vastly superior to the others.

190. This is perhaps the commonest of BUTCHER'S KNOTS and is the one generally used by those who have no particular affinity for knots. The OVERHAND KNOT in the end (⌗515) prevents it from spilling while being drawn up. The OVERHAND is tied first and then the noose is made around the roast.

BUTCHER'S KNOTS are a variety of BINDER KNOTS, and those just given were originally included in the BINDER KNOT chapter, (⌗16), where the reader may find several more knots of similar nature. When no final HALF HITCH is employed or required these knots are commonly called "JAM KNOTS."

The fact that the final hitch will make practically any BUTCHER'S KNOT secure undoubtedly explains why there are more BUTCHER'S KNOTS to be collected than any other kind of knot for a single purpose; more even than there are WEAVER'S KNOTS. I do not think I have ever failed to find at least one new knot in every butcher's shop that I have visited. In one market in Washington, D.C., I found butchers using five different knots. It would have been more remarkable, however, if I had found five butchers using the same knot. The few shown here are only a small part of the number collected. These have been selected because they are representative. They may be either the best, the most characteristic, the commonest, the simplest, or the most interesting.

In the illustrations the end of the twine is shown marked with an arrow which sticks through a turn in the standing part. This, of course, will tie the knot. But the technique of all BUTCHER'S KNOTS is the same, and all ends have the final hitch added over the end, as shown in KNOT ⌗183.

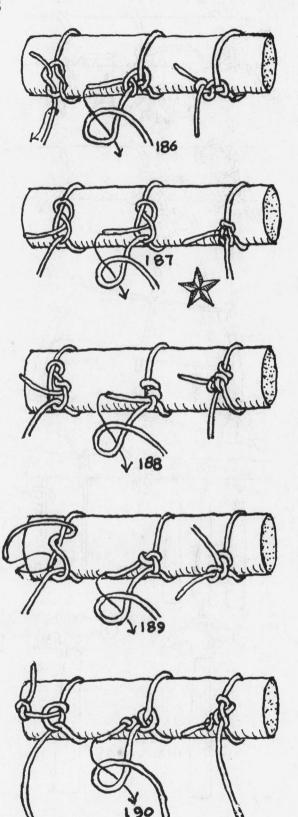

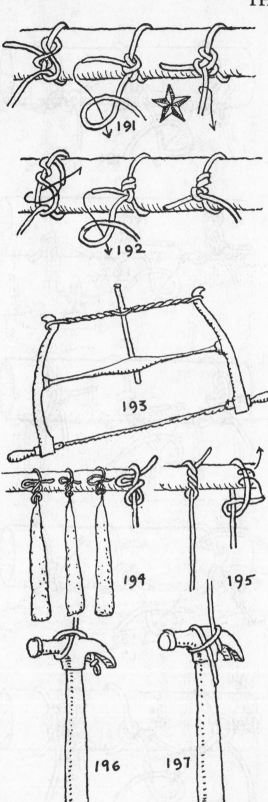

191. The Corned Beef and Salt Pork Knot. As already stated, meat shrinks appreciably while in the brine, and the knot has to be tightened from time to time before the final Half Hitch is added. This is Buntline Hitch ℀1711 tied around its own standing part. It is probably the best knot for the purpose.

192. This is another Corned Beef Knot, which appears to be more complicated than is necessary, but holds exceptionally well.

The Cabinetmaker

193. Cabinetmakers still tighten their scroll saws by twisting a cord with a short hardwood stick. This is inserted near the middle between the parts of a doubled cord. The stick is held nearly parallel with the cord and is twisted until the desired tension is reached. It is then turned at right angles to the cord and when let go fetches against the stretcher, which holds it in place. A thong is preferable for stringing a saw, but small hard-braided sash cord will do nicely. The same method is also employed when gluing up the legs of a Windsor or other chair to which clamps may not be easily affixed.

Wire used in fencing is tightened in the same way, but it requires more care, as it is apt to snap. A cordwood stick is inserted between two wires and twisted until the tension is sufficient. Then the end of the stick must be secured to a post or rail, or else driven into the ground.

The Camper and Canoeist

Knots of interest to these sportsmen will be found under "Mountain Climber," "Prospector," "Shooting," and "Cowboy" in this chapter, and under "Pack Lashing" in the chapter on lashing and slinging.

The Chandler

194. In candle dipping a dozen wicks may be tied to a stick, or to hooks on a stick or board, in the manner here shown. They are dipped into a kettle of simmering water on which an inch or so of melted wax is floating. A number of sticks are employed, and each stick is dipped quickly in turn. Between turns these are hung up on a rack to cool. A revolving rack is sometimes used.

The Carpenter

195. The Timber Hitch is very convenient for hoisting boards and timbers, as it cannot jam and may be instantly loosened. If timber is to be hoisted on end the Timber Hitch is made with the end of the rope below the center of the timber and then a Half Hitch is added in the standing part at the upper end of the timber (see Half Hitch and Timber Hitch, ℀1733).

196. This and the hitch which follows are practical ways to sling and hoist hammers. They are preferable to ℀198 because they cannot slip off while in mid-air. Here a Slip Knot (℀529) is placed between the claws and a Single Hitch is taken around the peen.

197. Two Single Hitches. This hitch raises an interesting point. Although in form the knot approximates the Clove Hitch, the intrusion of the handle divides the knot into "Two Single Hitches."

The carpenter is a very handy workman who is frequently called upon to meet new situations. The chapter on *lashing and slinging* should contain other matter of interest to him.

198. The commoner way to sling a hammer for lowering is by a CLOVE HITCH around the small of the handle. If not drawn tight, there is danger of the handle slipping out. In the dictionaries the CLOVE HITCH is sometimes called the BUILDER'S KNOT, a name apparently coined by Tom Bowling, who must have been unaware of the English name CLOVE HITCH, since he did not use it, although it had appeared as early as 1769 in Falconer's *Dictionary of the Marine*. In the trades, facts are generally passed along by word of mouth and very little is acquired from books, so the builder himself is probably unaware that he has a knot named for him.

199. The SASH WEIGHT KNOT is made as drawn. Before a sash is hung, the weights being already in position, the cord ends are tied into SLIP KNOTS (#529) so that the ends will not unreeve through the pulleys and disappear down the sash-weight wells.

200. The *method of slinging a plank* for use as a staging was shown to me by Arthur Carlsen. It is sometimes tied with three round turns instead of the two depicted, the left turns being worked the same way in both cases, and the final turn passing over all intervening parts to the end of the plank.

201. *To sling a plank, or joist, on edge*, make a CLOVE HITCH very loosely, and work into the form shown. It may be used with one less turn, if desired. The turns are taken loosely and must be extended, in order to pass over the end of the plank. A MARLINGSPIKE HITCH may also be made to serve a similar purpose.

202. When a carpenter *slings a ladder*, he generally uses a SHEEPSHANK KNOT over the ends of each side post. For the same purpose, a sailor would use a SPANISH BOWLINE, but he would have no ladder unless he were hauled out in drydock.

For the proper method of tying the SHEEPSHANK see #1153. Several feet above the DOUBLE LOOP the end should be bent to the standing part. The SPANISH BOWLINE is given as #1087. There are a number of knots among the DOUBLE LOOPS which will sling a ladder satisfactorily. Those that are rigid are to be preferred. The purpose of slinging a ladder is, of course, to make a staging for painting or incidental repairs. A board that in width is about equal to the length of the rungs of the ladder is required to complete the floor of the staging. Pothooks suspend the paint cans below the rungs.

203. The SASH CORD HITCH. The end of the sash cord is ordinarily hitched around a screw, which is recessed in an auger hole bored in the side of the window sash. Sometimes a SINGLE HITCH is employed, and sometimes a HALF HITCH. If there is no screw an OVERHAND KNOT suffices.

The Cartman

The cartman or carter generally gets along with very few knots; the LOOP KNOT (#1009), the OVERHAND (#515), and TWO HALF HITCHES (#1710) are his usual equipment. The more finished practitioners prefer the BOWLINE (#1010) and the FIGURE-EIGHT (#524). See under "Drayman" in this chapter for further information, and also "Crossing Knots," Chapter 15, and "Lashings and Slings," Chapter 28.

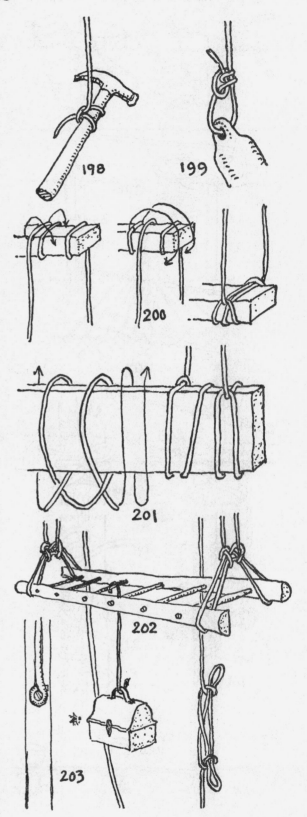

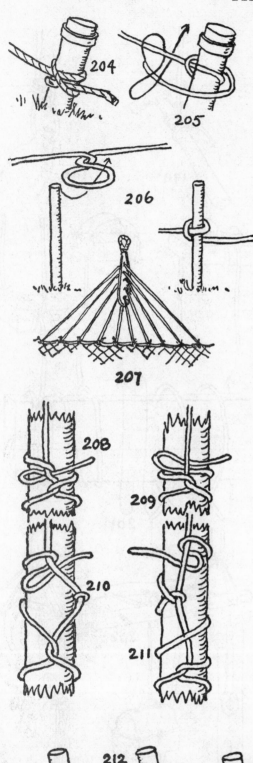

The Circus Man

The following series of knots is from Ringling Brothers' Circus. The knot tiers were "Mickey" Gray, "Frenchy" Haley, and William James O'Brien, who respectively represented the performers, the canvas, and the animals.

Latchings or latchets originally provided a method of adding temporarily to the area of a sail. They became obsolete for this purpose, but the circus today finds them invaluable. The top of a large tent consists of a number of separate rectangular mid-sections (one less than the number of center posts) and two semicircular ends. The several parts are laced together by a series of loops in one section called *latchings* which are rove through eyelet holes in the opposite section. They are illustrated in Chapter 27, "Occasional Knots," as #2064.

204. The DRY WEATHER HITCH. Here again appears that most universal general utility hitch, the CLOVE HITCH (#1178), which will be discussed at length in Chapters 23 and 33. It is quickly formed and easily adjusted, but tends to jam if wet.

205. The WET WEATHER or TAKE-UP HITCH. A SINGLE HITCH is dropped over the stake, the end is backed, and a SLIPPED HALF HITCH taken around the standing part. It is easily adjustable even when wet and never jams.

206. The CROSSING KNOT is used in staking out, one of its purposes being to define the straight and narrow pathway along which the circus patrons are herded. The circus way of making it is quite different from the way it is tied when making up bundles (#2077 and #2078). A bight is twisted a full turn and dropped over a stake.

207. The *euphroe block* and the CROW's-FOOT stretch the edges of a safety net for the aerialists. They are old sea practices now fallen into disuse on shipboard. Originally they stretched catharpins, awnings, and the standing ends of running rigging. Old practices are continually being revived for new purposes. For that reason many obsolete and obsolescent knots are shown with confidence in the belief that sometime, somewhere, they will be used again.

208. The ONE-LENGTH HITCH is used on a side-wall pole. A number of men haul down on the standing part, a SINGLE HITCH is taken around the base of the pole, and the end is brought around back of the pole and eventually is slip hitched to the standing part.

209. The WRAP HITCH is also for the side-wall pole, but is a more temporary fastening than the foregoing.

210. A QUARTER-POLE TWIST is a temporary hitch for the big top, but as there is more weight on the quarter pole than on the side-wall poles the rope passes around the pole a second time before being made fast.

211. A QUARTER-POLE HITCH that is more secure than the last one.

212. A HARNESS-CHAIN ANCHOR is to secure the end of a chain in the horse tent, over which harness is thrown. The stakes often are of iron; the chain passes shoulder-high down the center poles, secured to each with a CROSSING KNOT (#206) or a CLOVE HITCH (#204). A tackle between the anchor and the first pole makes all taut.

213. The JUMPER HITCH (for quarter poles). Circus poles can have no cleats or other projections, as they are unloaded in a heap on the ground and afterwards are dragged all over the lot. After the rope has been hauled hand taut, a SINGLE HITCH is taken around the pole waist-high, the line is backed one turn, or a round turn is put on (as in ✳212), and then a HALF HITCH is placed on the standing part above the first SINGLE HITCH. The rope is then staggered (zigzagged) up the back of the pole, and after each crossing it is strongly hauled and a HALF HITCH taken around the standing part. The mechanical principle involved is excellent, and it might serve well for reef pennants in small boats, as it is much neater than a tackle, quite as effective, and much less in the way.

214. The CENTER-POLE HITCH. A center pole has a shiv near the base. After the tent top is hoisted two turns are taken around the pole under the standing part just above the shiv and these are jammed down close to the shiv. The surplus rope is then wrapped around the pole until exhausted. In raising a tent the center poles are first erected and guyed, the guys being outside the tent, leading to the pole tops. The canvas is latched together and the top partially hoisted before the other poles are placed in position.

215. CAMEL HITCH. The camel is the most ruminative of animals, and he slobbers constantly while he ruminates, particularly on his PICKET-LINE HITCH, which he believes is provided for the purpose. His knot is always sopping, but it has been very nicely planned; and so, wet or dry, it is never difficult to untie and it does not slip in either direction.

216, 217. NET POLE KNOTS. These guy the short poles that stretch the safety net of the aerialists.

218. BALANCING-POLE HITCH: To support a man from the top of his balancing pole while he is climbing aloft. The knot is adjusted before the pole is elevated. Everything must be taut before the standing part is brought over the top of the pole. The rope is instantly removed by flirting the standing part. I know of no knot with a smaller margin of safety. Another and possibly better arrangement of the knot is given as ✳1812.

219. SLIP TACKLE KNOT. Practically all apparatus tackles in a circus are made fast in this manner, which at sea is merely a temporary expedient. House painters and carpenters also employ the knot.

220. Tent stakes are broken out by means of a lever on wheels. Several snug turns with a chain are taken close to the ground.

The Cook

221. *To spit and truss a fowl.* The spit is a long, flattened rod, sharpened at one end and with a wheel or crank at the other. Down its length are a number of slots through which to thrust skewers. After spitting the fowl, stick the first skewer through the meaty part of one leg, through a slot in the skewer, and then out through the other leg. According to the size of your fowl, stick either one or two additional skewers, which do not need to be so solidly imbedded. Middle a long cord and secure it with a RING HITCH (✳1859) to the eye of a skewer. Take several belaying-pin turns across the back of the fowl and around the two ends of the skewer; then do the same across the breastbone. Repeat with the other skewers. Splay the turns widely in order to support the tenderer parts of the fowl.

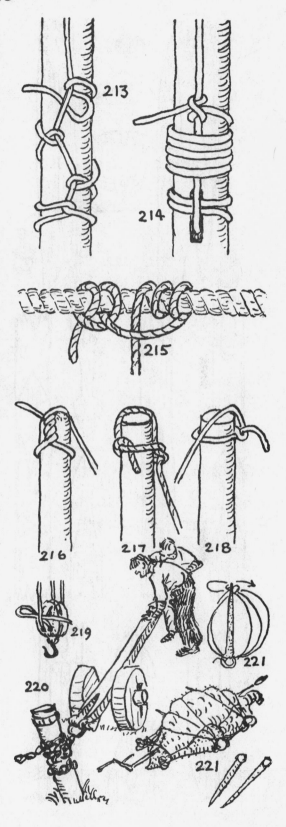

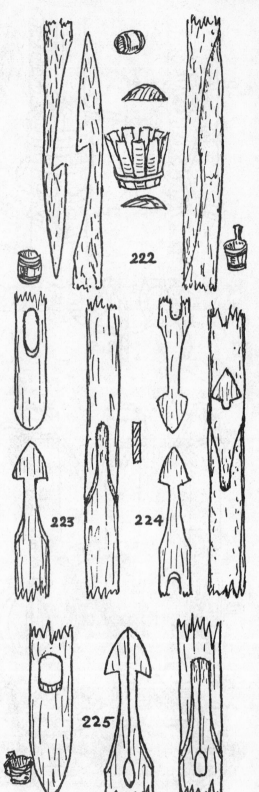

The Climber

(See pages 62, 63, and 77.) When climbing a tree without a ladder, wear rubber-soled shoes and pass a rope around the tree. Hold the ends in either hand or else bend them together around the body. Lean back against the rope and raise the feet, one at a time. Then swing the body toward the tree and jerk the rope a foot or so higher. Coconut trees are climbed in this way, a section of vine being used instead of a rope.

The Cobbler

See under "Bootmaker," near the beginning of this chapter

The Cooper

It may appear farfetched to include these split wood joints in a book devoted to knots, but they serve a purpose similar to the bend, and I know of no other place where they are to be found.

222. This is the ordinary hoop fastening for common commercial barrels, the average content of which is between thirty and thirty-three gallons. Hoops are of various kinds of wood. In New England wild cherry saplings are much used. They serve no other purpose, and farmers are anxious to be rid of them because of the caterpillars they shelter. Birch also is used and is better than cherry. Hoops are made up of green wood preferably, which is less apt to break in bending. The bark is left on, and great quantities are made up and stored in slack season. When making hoops by hand the cooper sits on a shaving horse, which has a clamp or vise on the forward end, operated by a wooden foot lever. The clamp grips one end of the sapling, and the cooper, sitting astride the bench with his feet on the treadle, pulls the drawknife toward him, riving the sapling into equal parts. After the hoop is shaped the joint is made, often with drawknife alone, sometimes with the assistance of a hatchet.

223, 224, 225. More elaborate joints are to be found on runlets, canteens, piggins, noggins, tankards, canopails, and other articles of domestic cooperage where the taste of the housewife has demanded more style and finish. These require better hoops, which in America are made of oak, hickory, ash, and maple.

Old wooden buckets are now seldom seen. Apparently they were worn out before the antiquarian arrived on the scene.

For many years a large proportion of the more substantial wooden hoops have been iron-fastened. According to the logbook of the Nantucket whaler *Beaver*, about one quarter of her casks in 1791 were iron-bound, but for small cooperage iron hoops had made little headway before the turn of the present century, and today wooden hoops are still used for many purposes.

Large hoops and hoops that were to be finished on both sides were riven from logs with a froe and then shaped up with the drawknife. Ash was the preferred wood, as it is the easiest to split.

The holes in evidence in the last three joints on this page were punched with a gouge and mallet, which is quicker than boring and if skillfully done requires no further shaping.

The Cowboy

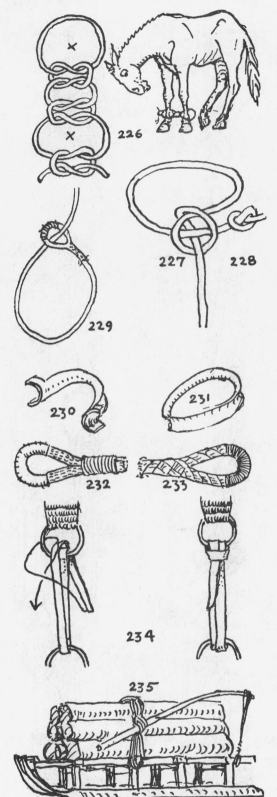

226. The HOBBLE KNOT was shown to me by Philip Ashton Rollins, who tells me that it is a common range knot and is also used by the prospector. It really consists of three REEF KNOTS and is preferably tied in a strip of hide. The first and second knots are several inches apart to give the horse's legs a little play.

227. The HONDA KNOT was first shown to me by Will James. It is based on the BOWSTRING KNOT (※151).

228. The OVERHAND KNOT (※515) is added for security. The two knots are drawn tight, then the standing part of the rope is rove through the hitch to form the noose required on a lariat.

229. An EYE SPLICE is preferable to the knot just given, but comparatively few cowboys know how to splice.

230. A *half thimble* is sometimes placed in a HONDA EYE SPLICE. Its four flanges are hammered tight around the rope.

231. An *oval thimble*, preferably of bronze, is also used.

232. A *braided rope* has some advantages over a laid rope. An eye (※2779) is formed by riveting the overlapping part with copper nails or tacks (two are sufficient); the overlap is then served snugly over, preferably with copper wire. A sole-leather or rawhide bushing sewed around the bosom of the eye is a common adjunct.

233. Sometimes a SPLICED EYE is served over with copper wire.

234. The CINCH, CINCHA, LATIGO, BELLYBAND, or GIRTH KNOT reached our Western cow country from South America via Mexico at the beginning of American ranching. It is a safer coupling than the buckle employed on sporting saddle girths, and is much stronger.

The THEODORE KNOT is sometimes used as a hackamore or emergency bridle by the cowboy. It was shown to me a number of years ago by Will James. James Drew, in *Rope and Cordage*, says that very few cowboys can tie it; that he knew of one who used to collect payment for each knot he made, and that this resulted in a considerable revenue. The method of tying is explained in Chapter 12, "Double and Multiple-Loop Knots," as ※1110. If seizings are used, while tying, the problem will not be found difficult. Philip Ashton Rollins writes me that the knot began life in the West under its correct Spanish name of "FIADOR" but that after the Spanish War, as a result of the publicity Theodore Roosevelt brought to the ranch and range, the name was corrupted to THEODORE.

Another knot, said to be employed as a hackamore, is the JUG or JAR SLING (※1142).

The Drayman

235. DRAYMAN'S KNOT. Logs are generally lashed to a cart or sled with loose turns which are twisted tight with a handspike or a pole (※2143). As they shift the lashings will slacken, but they are tightened by adding a further twist with the pole. Stone is slung under a high gear in about the same manner, chain being used instead of rope.

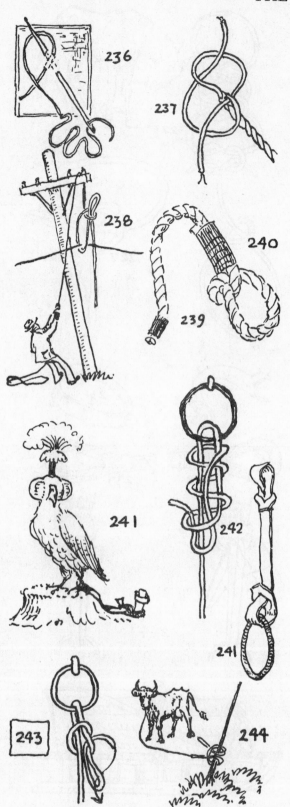

The Dressmaker

236. It is with some hesitation that I call the dressmaker's attention to the accompanying knot, which I have never seen anyone but a sailor use. The two stitches pictured here actually form an OVER-HAND KNOT in the fabric.

For other knots of interest to the dressmaker see the BUTTON KNOTS of Chapter 5 and the FLAT or TWO-DIMENSIONAL KNOTS of Chapter 30.

The Electrician

237. A Westport electrician tied this knot in a pull socket. It is a sailor's WALL KNOT (※671 and ※775) of two strands. I can recommend it unhesitatingly to electricians in general for employment where rough treatment is expected.

The Electric Lineman

238. To haul a wire to the arm of a pole, use this HALF SHEEPSHANK of the same knot formation as the BELL RINGER'S KNOT. It consists of a bight passed around the wire and half hitched to the standing part. See BIGHT KNOT ※1147.

A knot called the LINEMAN'S LOOP is described as ※1053.

239. The lineman whips the end of his rope with adhesive tape.

240. He makes a loop or eye with a SINGLE HALF HITCH and always seizes his ends with tape. These practices are exceedingly practical and expeditious.

It is characteristic of workmen that what the carpenter fashions of wood and nails the tinsmith makes of tin, the blacksmith of strap iron, and the pipe setter of pipe, the sailor gets his result with rope and spars.

The Falconer

241. The *jess* is a short strap which fits around the leg of a hawk; at the other end is a ring, which may be slipped around the forearm of the falconer. It is closely related to the *goose boot and hobble* (※434) shown later in this chapter.

The Farmer

242. The MANGER HITCH. The cow is an inveterate slobberer. Although not in a class with the camel, she should be made fast with a hitch that will not jam when wet.

243. HALTER HITCH. Horses are hitched with this knot the world over. The end is stuck loosely through the loop, which is not tightened. The knot is easily slipped after removing the end from the loop.

244. COW HITCH. Oddly enough, this name is generally used by the sailor, although the knot is also termed DEADEYE HITCH and LANYARD HITCH (※3317). It is the proper knot with which to secure a cow to a crowbar. The CLOVE HITCH, although more often used for the purpose, does not draw up snugly when the pull is all on one end, and it is apt to unwind under a steady rotating pull. I have seen a cow untie herself by walking around a crowbar to which she was

tied. This was undoubtedly without premeditation; the flies were bothering her at the time, and her initial step was in the right direction.

245. The BINDER KNOT is tied in a wisp of straw that is bound around a sheaf of grain. The two ends are brought together and laid up with a strong right-handed twist. The doubled end is then laid back on itself and the bight or loop so formed is thrust up to the right under the binding. The method of tying this knot is shown as ⚓1235 in several progressive drawings among the BINDER KNOTS, a chapter for which this knot is the prototype.

246. The knot tied by a mechanical binder is an OVERHAND BEND with bights tucked instead of the ends. Binder twine is a loose-twisted material similar to spun yarn, but wiry in texture. It is impractical to tie this knot for the purpose by hand.

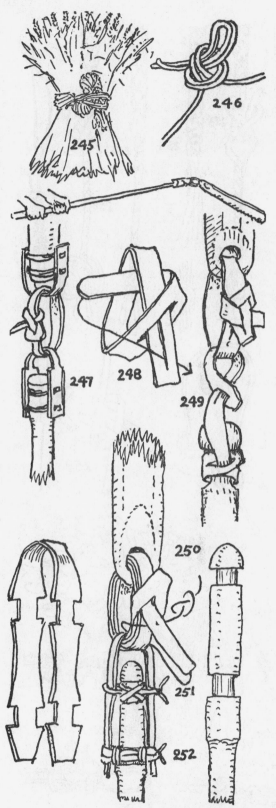

The remaining knots on this page apply to flails, which even in America are still used occasionally for threshing small crops of grain, although the mechanical threshing machine has superseded it where grain is grown in commercial quantities. Flails are also employed for threshing beans and peas.

The implement appears to have been fully perfected many centuries ago, and very few refinements have been added since Cain is alleged to have killed Abel with one. Some authorities state that it was invented in medieval times, but it would seem to be older, and the knowledge of it possibly reached Europe from Egypt or Asia at the time of the Crusades.

Practically all flails are jointed with rawhide, although I have seen them tied with cord, rope, tanned leather, rags, and shoestrings. It is necessary that the joint should pivot as well as hinge, which accounts for the elaborate nature of some of these fastenings.

247. This is a FLAIL KNOT from Diderot's Encyclopedia (1747). Small steamed and bent wooden yokes are lashed with rawhide thongs, let into circular grooves which are cut around the ends of the handle and the swingle, so forming two swivel joints. The rawhide connecting strap is tied in a BECKET HITCH.

248. A flail joint from Bristol County, Massachusetts. I have never seen this particular knot elsewhere.

249. This is a common fastening on flails. See STRAP HITCH ⚓1704.

250. A flail from Chester County, Pennsylvania. The strap is rove three times through the slit, and then the end is hitched around all three turns, forming something in the nature of a BECKET HITCH (⚓1900), although it is more a lashing than a hitch.

251. A turn having been taken around the yoke, X turns hold the thong securely in the groove of the handle. The two ends are reef knotted together (⚓1204).

252. In this, two round turns are taken about the yoke, and then frapping turns (⚓3120), at either side of the handle, hold the thong snugly in the groove. The average flail has a handle between four and four and a half feet long, and a swingle twenty-four to forty inches long. The length of the handle varies with the height of the thresher, and the weight and length of the swingle depend on the kind of grain to be threshed.

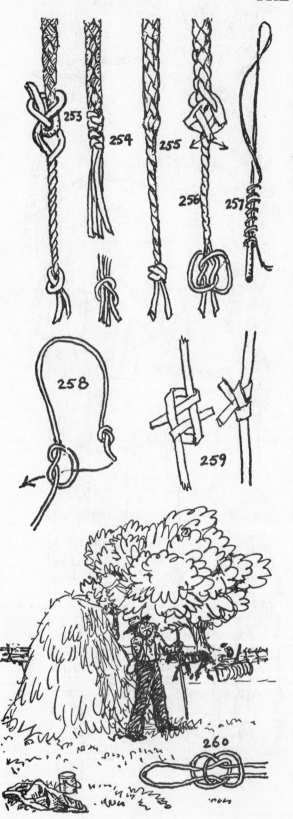

253. This is a method for making and attaching a *fly*, *snapper*, or *stinger* to an ox whip. The *whiplash* is made of two long rawhide thongs which are first middled and then doubled to form a loop at the thick or stock end. The four strands so formed are platted into a ROUND SINNET (⚹2999). Occasionally six strands (⚹3011) are used. From the loop end the width of the strands is widened for a foot or so and then is gradually narrowed again to the tip, so that when platted the lash has a snakelike form.

To add the fly to this braided lash, another short, narrow thong is required. This is doubled and tied at the center with a SHEET BEND to the end of the lash. The fly is then laid up (twisted as in ropemaking), and finally an OVERHAND KNOT is tied in the doubled end, which has been left long. The loop in the thick end of the lash is then made fast to the whipstock. Several different ways of securing whiplashes to whipstocks are shown on pages 544 and 545.

To make a neater job, take the tip ends of the sinnet and form an eye with two adjacent strands (⚹2800), and then lay in the other two strands, over and under, and contrariwise. Put on a whipping and then bend the fly to the lash as already pictured and described. Draw snug, wet with hot water, roll underfoot, and allow to dry.

254. Seize the thongs at the end of the sinnet and take a HALF KNOT (⚹1202) with each strand in turn around the other three. Each time take the strand next to the left of the one previously tied. Keep the strands fair and close together. Wet, roll underfoot, then dry. This will bulk very little larger than the platting.

255. Whip the sinnet and cut off both strands that rotate to the left. Make a slit in the end of each of these, and stick an opposing strand, which rotates to the right, through each slit. Be sure that everything is taut and fair. Lay up the two long ends and twist them together, being careful to arrange them so that they cover the ends of the short strands.

256. Lay up the fly for several inches and then tie a TWO-STRAND MATTHEW WALKER KNOT (⚹776) near the end. In New England a great many sailors were farm-bred, and they often returned to the soil, so hereabouts it is never surprising to find sailor's knots tied in farm gear.

257. The lash of an ox whip when out of use was generally tied in a MULTIPLE OVERHAND KNOT (⚹517) around the whipstock.

258. This is the universal farm method of tying a *neck halter* for either a horse or a cow. The part marked X surrounds the neck, and the halter cannot slip and choke the animal.

259. The GRASS KNOT is the best bend for broken straps or any other flat material such as shoestrings, straw, cane, etc. It is discussed more fully in the chapter on bends as ⚹1490.

260. Whenever you go afield, there is no better way to carry your water jug or bottle than suspended by a JAR or JUG SLING (⚹1142). The sailor's method of tying this is described in Chapter 14.

OCCUPATIONAL KNOTS

The Farrier

The farrier uses a NOSE TWITCH to steady a nervous horse while filing its teeth and sometimes when shoeing. This is tightened by twisting it around the horse's upper lip. On occasion it is applied to an ear. The instrument is illustrated (♯1261) in the chapter on BINDER KNOTS. Generally it is made of an old wagon spoke and a braided cord or else a thong.

The Fencer

These two practices I learned in Boston many years ago from Professor Rondelle, a fencing master.

261. A foil *handle* of twine closely half hitched in a helix along the full length of the hilt provides a grip not liable to turn in the fencer's hand. See ♯3450.

262. A *button* made of well-waxed twine. This is far superior to the commercial rubber button, as a raveled end will always give warning of its failure. The turns must be very snug and even. Start with a CLOVE HITCH. After the final surface turns have been taken toward the tip (tied as in WHIPPING ♯3443) the end is pulled taut and cut off short.

The Fireman

263. The SHEET KNOT: Sheets and blankets are torn into strips and bent together with BEND ♯1403, which consists of a REEF KNOT (♯1204) and two OVERHAND KNOTS (♯515) to serve as an emergency fire escape. One end is tied to a bed, which should be rolled close to a window. The window should be opened no farther than is necessary.

264. The FIRE-ESCAPE KNOT is for the same purpose, but it is generally a fixture found in country and seaside hotel bedrooms. The proper way of tying is most interesting and is described at the beginning of Chapter 4, "Single-Strand Lanyard Knots." In England this method of tying has long been a part of the regular drill in rural fire departments, and it is now being taught in America, where it is sometimes called the "PHILADELPHIA KNOT."

265. An injured or unconscious man is lowered by a SPANISH BOW-LINE KNOT (♯1087), each leg being stuck through one of the loops. After a hitch is passed close under the armpits, the man may be safely moved.

266. A ladder may be hoisted or slung by passing the loop end of a long BOWLINE KNOT (♯1010) under the upper rung and back over the side bar ends. This is similar to FORKED STICK HITCH ♯439.

267. Another common way to sling a ladder is to place a CLOVE HITCH (♯1177) around each side bar, immediately under the upper rung, before tying the BOWLINE.

268. A *fireman's ax* is slung by slipping an EYE SPLICE or a loop around the helve, leading the line over the head, and putting two hitches (♯3114) around the helve end.

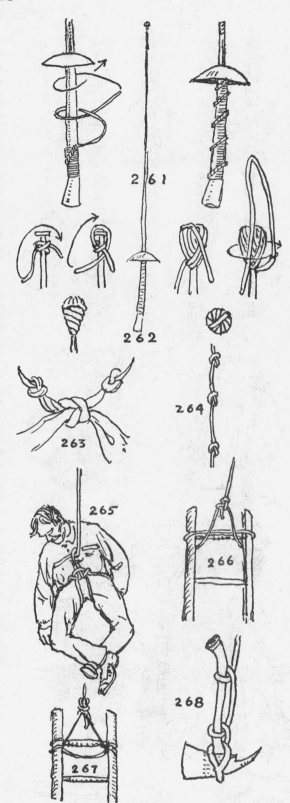

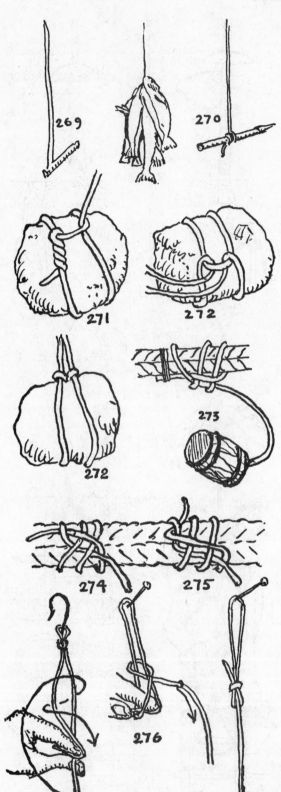

The Fisherman

The knots now to be shown apply to fishing as distinct from seamanship. The fisherman's knots, so far as his boat gear is concerned, do not differ much from other sailor's knots. But for his fishing he uses a number of original ones which, surprisingly enough, do not seem to have been recorded. For instance, the GROUND LINE HITCH (#277) and the GANGING KNOT (#276), which are the essence of cod fishing, do not appear even in the knot pages of the *Atlantic Fisherman's Almanac*, which is a trade journal that hangs in almost every fisherman's cabin.

The professed object of both the professional and the amateur fisherman's activities being to catch fish, and most of their practices being applicable or of interest to each other, their knots will be shown together. The use of the fly may be a little out of the professional's everyday requirements, but he occasionally uses spinners, eelskins, and other lures. On the other hand, there is no practice of the professional that will not provide sport for the amateur.

269, 270. These are the common ways of stringing fish, if you do not wish to hide your catch under a basket. In #269 the long end of the stick is shoved up through the gill and out of the mouth. In #270 a short, sharpened stick the size of a meat skewer is shoved into the mouth and out the gill, where it turns at right angles and acts as a toggle.

271. A KILLEG HITCH—also spelled and pronounced KELLIG, KELLAGH, Kellick, Killock, and Killick—consists of a TIMBER HITCH and HALF HITCH (#1733) that are drawn closely together around a stone. In its stricter application a killeg is a stone-weighted wooden anchor, while a stone used alone as an anchor is called a *slingstone*, and is used on rocky bottom where an anchor is apt to foul. It is employed in anchoring seines, lobster, crab, and eel pots, small boats, decoys, etc.

272. The SLINGSTONE HITCH comes from Sakonnet Point, where it is used in anchoring lobster pots. It may be tied either in the bight or in the end. Pull the ends strongly, and the turns in the standing part are spilled into the loops.

273. This is a BUOY ROPE HITCH from Polperro, England, used on seines.

274. NET LINE KNOT from Looe. A single headrope, when wet, will swell and consequently twist, thereby fouling and rolling up the edges of seines. To prevent this two headropes of equal size and opposite lay (twist) are led parallel with each other. This knot, which is of the type termed BINDER, seizes the two together. Except that it is used as a knot instead of a hitch, it is similar to #273.

275. A slightly different NET LINE KNOT from Clovelly.

276. The GANGING KNOT is used on codfish trawl. A soft line is cut into short, equal lengths, which are hung over a convenient nail or hook, and long loops of uniform length are tied in one of the ends of each, after which fishhooks are added to the loops as shown in #310 and #311. In the left drawing a hook is shown to indicate the

purpose of the knot, but in practice the hook is not added until after the loop has been tied.

Hold the end with the thumb and forefinger of the left hand, and with the standing part take a HALF HITCH around the two parts as pictured in the central diagram.

277. The GROUND LINE HITCH is the knot with which the gangings are secured to the trawl. A very short end is gripped under the left thumb, and the knot is tied with the loop end.

278. The same knot may be tied with the end while the loop hangs down at its fixed length. These are the two standard ways of securing the GANGING. It may be noted that this knot is closely related to ⚹273 from Polperro and that it is identical with the PICKET-LINE HITCH (⚹1676), although reversed.

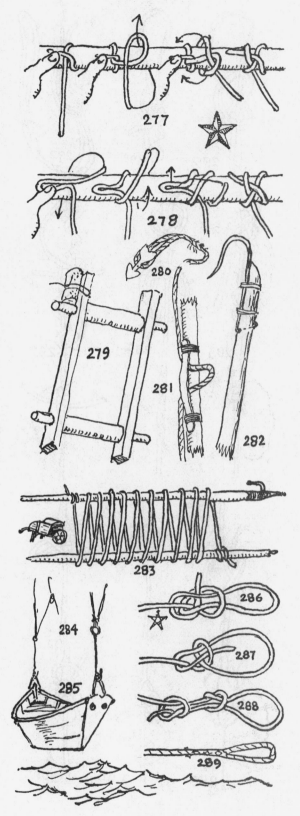

279. Split a cork lengthwise and secure it to a wooden reel with a CONSTRICTOR (⚹1249). This is to stick hooks into when they are not in use.

280, 281. A swordfisherman's iron has a long EYE SPLICE (⚹2733) made through the hole at the small of the head. The splice is stuck several feet from the head. On the underside of the head is a shoulder with a socket into which the iron end of the pole is fitted. The head is held in place by the tension of the line, which is hauled taut and jammed under a wooden cleat on the side of the pole. When a fish is struck the head pulls off the shaft, the line is snapped out from under the cleat, and the pole is recovered by means of a bib line attached to the end.

282. A *homemade gaff*. Nip the barb and ring from a halibut hook, and file smooth. Heat the ring end in a candle flame to take out the temper. Then bend it into proper shape. Bore a hole through the handle to take the end. Put the hook in place, rivet the end, and then serve over.

283. A *fisherman's litter*. This is quickly made by shoving two spare spars, oars, or poles through a coil of rope and making fast the ends of the rope.

284. A dory is always swung by two long hooks attached by RING or STRAP HITCHES (⚹1860) to tackles called Spanish Burtons.

285. The stern becket, to which the after tackle is hooked, is rove through two holes in the stern board, and each end bears a MATTHEW WALKER KNOT (⚹682). The forward tackle hooks to the EYE SPLICE in the painter.

286. The ANGLER'S LOOP has an excellent lead and is easily tied (see ⚹1017). This is unquestionably the most satisfactory LEADER LOOP.

287. The BOWLINE KNOT is often used for the same purpose, but it has a poor lead, is not quite secure in gut, and so is not recommended.

288. The FISHERMAN'S, WATERMAN'S, ENGLISHMAN'S, or TRUE-LOVER'S KNOT. This is much used and is interestingly tied by the method given as ⚹1038, but it is unnecessarily bulky and kicks up considerable fuss in the water.

289. A *made eye* is described as EYE SPLICE ⚹2792. For larger material EYE ⚹2794 is recommended.

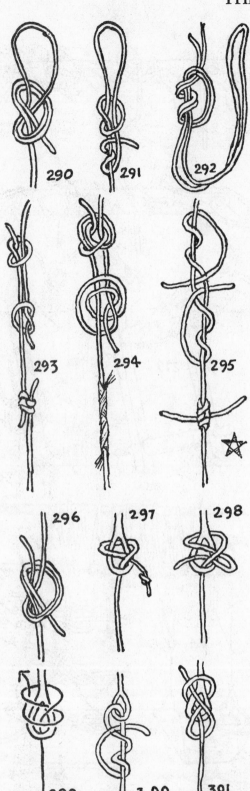

290. The LOOP KNOT is simple, secure, and strong, but without so good a lead as some of the others.

291. Another LEADER LOOP, which has a good lead.

292. The GUT KNOT is tied in the doubled end of a snell or snood. A doubled snell gives a stronger line with extra surface where wear is most severe. It also does away with a cumbersome knot at the eye of the hook, where it is apt to attract the attention of a fish. The loop is bent to a hook with a STRAP or RING HITCH as shown in ⌗310 and ⌗311. A snell is made of horsehair, gut, silk, or nylon for fresh water; for salt water, flax and hemp are also used. Hair and gut should be well soaked, for at least ten minutes, in lukewarm water before tying. Moisten in the mouth if no warm water is handy.

293. The ENGLISH, also called ENGLISHMAN'S, WATERMAN'S, FISHERMAN'S, and ANGLER'S KNOT, is much favored by anglers for bending two pieces of gut in a leader. Sometimes the ends are given an additional hitch, as in ⌗497, and one end is sometimes left long for affixing a dropper fly, the other being trimmed short.

294. GRAPEVINE KNOT, also called DOUBLE ENGLISH KNOT. For fishline, either braided or twisted, ravel the ends with a pin or the point of a hook. Draw the ends between the teeth to flatten them before tying. If well done, this will run easily through the guides of a rod.

295. The BARREL KNOT *for gut* is a compact knot that does not untie or slip. There is no better knot for making up a leader.

296. The WATER KNOT. The name is also applied to various other knots, but this is the one so termed in early editions of Izaak Walton, which should be sufficient authority for any angler. It is compact and reliable.

297. The BECKET HITCH is used to secure a reel line to the LEADER LOOP. For extra security an OVERHAND KNOT (⌗515) may be tied in the end.

298. This pictures the same knot "slipped," which is recommended for late afternoon fishing, when darkness is about to descend to make untying difficult.

299. The LORN KNOT was shown to me by Richard S. Whitney. It is an excellent LEADER LOOP KNOT, which makes very little commotion when whipped through the water. Hunter, in his *Fisherman's Wrinkles*, calls it the "FIGURE-EIGHT KNOT."

300, 301. Two well-known alternative methods for the same purpose as ⌗297, ⌗298, and ⌗299 are given here. All of these are more secure than the BECKET HITCH (⌗297), but they are also more prone to jam. Some anglers prefer bending a leader to the reel line with two loops, forming a STRAP BEND (⌗1493), in which case a permanent eye (⌗289) is made in the end of the reel line by first fraying and waxing the cord and then laying the frayed end against the standing part and whipping it.

302. A SWIVEL HITCH. The end of this may be cut fairly short. Often, in angling, two swivels are used in a single line, to diminish the possibility of jamming.

303. A SWIVEL HITCH. Another knot for the same purpose as the former. If the swivel ring permits, it is much better to pass the material through twice, as it will stand more wear and be stronger.

Swivels are necessary in lines bearing spinners and spoons or any other sort of tackle that tends to revolve and impart a twist that will eventually form a kink. A kink is almost certain to break a line, and of course a line never breaks except at an inopportune moment.

The BUNTLINE HITCH (#1847) is another excellent knot with which to make a line fast to a swivel.

304. A *cast*, also called a *whip*, includes leader, snell, dropper, and flies. It is more quickly attached and detached by a STRAP HITCH (#333) than by any other. This hitch, however, is objected to by some, because the commotion made in drawing it through the water tends to scare fish.

Several pieces of gut, termed leaders, are bent together into one line. In length a *cast* or *whip* may be as much as six or eight feet, depending upon the kind of fish sought. The largest gut is at the reel end, and each leader is smaller until the tail fly is reached. This tapers the line and puts the greater strength at the reel end. Dropper flies are generally attached at each joint in the cast, and the snells of the dropper flies should be of the same diameter gut as the section of the leader to which they are attached. A length of gut attached to a fly is variously termed a snell, snood, snooding, snead, sid, and tippet. They are closely related to the professional fisherman's ganging lines.

The final fly of a cast is termed the *end*, *tail*, or *drag* fly. When the cast is ready to be bent to the reel line it is said to be "made up," "fitted," or "rigged."

305. The TURTLE, MAJOR TURLE'S KNOT or TURL KNOT. For securing gut to an eye hook. This knot is much used and is dependable, but it has one bad feature: the fly is apt to become ruffled while being attached.

306. The JAM KNOT; **307**, the HALF HITCH; **308**, the FIGURE-EIGHT KNOT; and **309**, the DOUBLE OVERHAND KNOT, are all first stuck through the eye and then tied around the standing part before being pushed forward and capsized around the neck of the hook. They are then drawn taut. Knots tied in this manner are less apt to ruffle the fly than the TURTLE KNOT.

310. The TAG KNOT or RING HITCH. This shows the method by which loop #292 (the GUT KNOT) is secured to a hook by first reeving the loop through the eye and then passing it over the hook. If the eye in the hook is small and the light dim, the eye may first be stuck through a bit of white paper and then the knot tied with the paper for background. This makes the eye of the hook much more visible.

311. The end of a NOOSE may also be rove through the eye and looped over the end of the hook in the same manner.

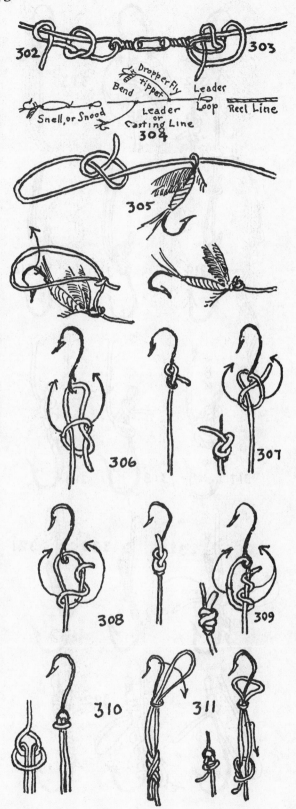

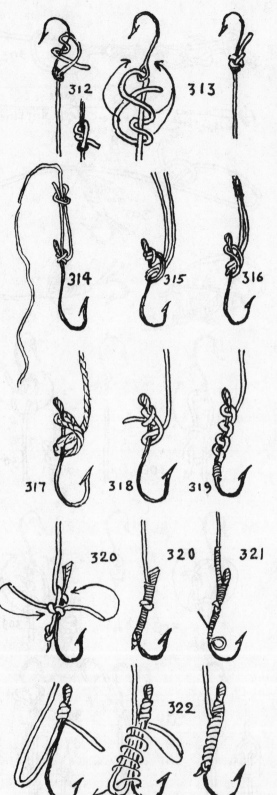

312. This knot is tied directly around the hook and requires no capsizing; it is Double Becket Hitch #1902.

313. The Salmon Knot, as shown to me by D. M. Beach, is both neat and compact. There are other knots which bear this name, or the name of some other fish, but there is too little uniformity in the terminology of anglers to admit of consistent labeling.

314. The hooks so far discussed have eyes. We now come to "flatted hooks" or "tad hooks," the flatted end being termed the *tad* by market fishermen. Commercially made fly hooks generally have neither tad nor eye, the gut being seized to a tapering shank. One of the commonest of market fishermen's ways of securing a flatted hook is with the Clove Hitch (#1775).

315. An old and established way of securing to both flatted and eye hooks.

316. This is neater and quite as satisfactory.

317. A refinement of the last two is shown here. To tie, wax and middle a piece of line, and lay up a snell or ganging by twisting the two ends together; add a Single Hitch.

318. An old favorite among hand-line fishermen.

319. A sound, practical method; can be tied by the unhandy. Longshore and wharfside fishermen use it without seizing the end. It consists of a series of hitches. Many very good anglers have five thumbs on each hand. They survive and actually catch fish by buying ready-to-wear tackle.

320. Diderot's Encyclopedia of 1747 contains this Hook Hitch. The hook differs from the modern one by having the end of the tad cut off square, or diagonally, instead of its being rounded. The line, with an Overhand Knot (#515) in the end, is single hitched below the tad and laid along the shank. A short piece of cord is half knotted (#1212) around the hook and line and is then served in either direction.

321. A Grand Banker's cod hook of 1840. The end of the line is scraped to a taper point, and an Overhand Knot (#515) is tied in it and placed about halfway down the shank. The standing part of the line is served down an inch or so before it is seized to the hook. At the lower end the line is stuck back under the service for four turns, is then whipped, and all is drawn snug. Small-sized angler's hooks are whipped with silk. This practice is termed *whipping* by anglers, but at sea it would be termed *seizing*. All whipping should be varnished if possible.

322. The method described here is found in an early edition of Izaak Walton. The end is first laid up the hook, and at the tad it is doubled back and about four turns made down the shank. Then the standing part is laid upward and the whipping continued down the hook around all parts. When the bight is reached the end is stuck through and hauled snug. Finally the standing part is pulled upon, which grips the end.

323. This modern way differs from Walton's only in lacking a collar of three or four turns at the tad end.

324. The usual way to mount a tapered hook that has neither tad nor ring is as follows: Wax a piece of fine silk about two feet long. Hold the barb end of the hook in the left hand; lay the end of silk against the shank at about half length, and wind it in several long turns up to the end of the shank. Now lay the end of the gut *over* these turns and along the shank, and whip neatly and firmly back to the bend of the hook. Finish off by sticking the end, as shown in ✳316. A neater job is made if the tip of the gut has been scraped to a taper. Large hooks may be whipped with fishline or sail twine.

325. If an eye is wanted on a flatted hook, it is made by doubling a short piece of line, tapering the two ends by scraping, and whipping them to the hook as shown.

326. Two hooks may be made up in this manner. The barbs may be turned in opposite directions if preferred.

327. The usual "whipping" employed on tackle may be made in a variety of ways. A convenient one is to make the last few turns around a hairpin; after threading the end withdraw the hairpin, pulling the end with it. A double string may be used instead of the hairpin. It is laid along the hook before the whipping is put on, and the whipping is served over it.

328. Fish that snap at the line require special tackle. Shark and barracuda hooks are usually mounted on chain. For smaller fish wire may be used. If chain or wire is not at hand, a hook may be attached to the line by one of the methods already given and the snell served with copper or flexible galvanized iron wire, or else it may be plaited over with rawhide thongs. Either shoestrings or belting laces will serve for the latter. Lacking these, use heavy fishline. If the fishline is tarred, dipped in fine *beach* sand, and allowed to dry, it will serve surprisingly well. Hold the hook in a vise and place the material around the shank. Start as in the left diagram and continue as in the right diagram. The top cord or thong is moved each time. Each cord, after being laid, returns to the side from where it started, but into the lower position. The cycle is always the same: move the top strand to the rear, across the back, forward between the two opposite strands, and back to its own side below its sister strand. This is Four-Strand Square Sinnet ✳2999. When the proper length has been made, tuck each end under a different strand of the fishline as in splicing. If the line is a braided one, cut the thongs off diagonally at different lengths and whip them over.

328½. An elastic span is sometimes added near the end of a line, in trap fishing and big-game fishing, to take up the shock of striking and playing the fish. A large band may be made from a cross section of a tire inner tube which is bale hitched at both ends. To tie the second end it will be necessary to reeve the end of the fishline through the knot. A Mouse (✳3498) is desirable for each knot.

A single strand of rubber is sometimes spliced into the line (✳2828), but it is better to employ a seizing. Take a silk thread or sail twine and lay a series of separated turns, place the end of the rubber over these, and then serve tightly over.

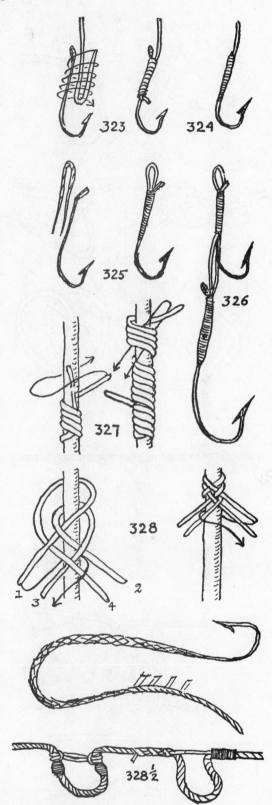

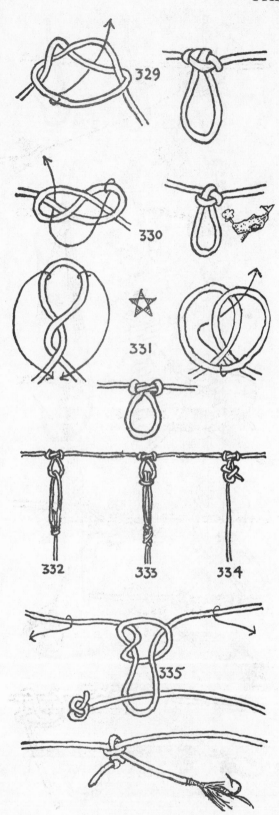

The SINGLE HARNESS LOOP (also called MAN-HARNESS KNOT and ARTILLERY LOOP) is shown in the chapter on SINGLE LOOPS in the bight (⚹1050). It is the LOOP KNOT generally recommended for attaching a dropper fly. This is undoubtedly because until very recent years only two SINGLE LOOPS in the bight appear to have been recorded, the other being *the* LOOP KNOT (⚹1046). In recent years, however, the agricultural college knot bulletins have published several others. THE SINGLE HARNESS LOOP (⚹1050) is not very secure under ordinary circumstances and is quite unfit for use in wet gut, where it is apt to slip. The LOOP KNOT (⚹1046) is secure, but is particularly weak, and also has a bad lead. All three knots to be given are slightly bulkier than the two mentioned, but they are stronger and more secure and have a better lead.

329. The DOUBLE HARNESS LOOP: For attaching a dropper fly. Form an ordinary noose in the line (⚹1052), and draw a bight through the noose as indicated by the arrow. When tying, one should allow much more material than seems necessary, as there is considerable slip while the knot is being drawn up; for that reason the two which follow will be found more practical, as they may be tied in a hurry and without taking any particular precautions.

330. This knot draws up easily into the desired shape and is simple to tie. It is both strong and secure, but it offers a little more water resistance than the other two.

331. The knot sometimes called the LINEMAN'S LOOP is secure and has an excellent lead. It is also compact and is the neatest of the lot. Of the three I should recommend whichever one is found easiest to tie.

332. A BOWLINE (⚹261) may be put in a dropper fly snell and attached to one of the three LEADER LOOPS that have just been shown.

333. SNELL LOOP ⚹265 may be secured to a leader by sticking one end of the snell through the LEADER LOOP and then reeving the hook through its own loop. This forms a RING HITCH (⚹1859), which is stronger than the previous hitch.

334. The BECKET HITCH (⚹1900) is easy to tie and untie. An OVERHAND KNOT is sometimes added to the end of the snell for greater security.

335. Tie a NOOSE in the leader bight, rather loosely. Insert the dropper gut as shown, and pull on the leader as indicated. This swallows a section of the dropper snell and gives KNOT ⚹2005 with the same formation as the SHEET BEND (⚹1431). But since the two ends of the leader are both actively in use and the snell is pulled at right angles, it can hardly be regarded as the same knot.

336. A DROPPER FLY or SNELL HITCH. This is the same formation as the SHEET BEND (#1431) but is differently tied. Make a round turn in the leader and reeve the snell as shown in the drawing. A large round turn is required, so that the hook will not foul in tying. Remember that the snell should be of the same size gut as the part of the leader to which it is bent.

337. A DROPPER FLY HITCH. This holds the snell at right angles to the leader and is particularly secure. Tie a HALF KNOT in the leader and reeve the snell as indicated by the arrow. If wished, both ends of the snell may be fitted to hooks. If only one hook is to be used, tie an OVERHAND KNOT in one end of the snell, draw it up close to the leader, and trim the end short.

338. A DROPPER FLY HITCH. This is a very popular method by which a dropper fly snell is attached to a leader. A BOWLINE (#1010) or ANGLER'S LOOP (#1017) is tied in the end of the snell, which is then secured to the leader with a LONG RUNNING HITCH (#1858). So that the hitch may be secure, it is tied around an OVERHAND KNOT (#515) which has been put in the leader for the purpose, or else it is put over one of the bends which join the several sections of the leader. Sometimes, instead of encompassing the knot, it is applied in front of it in the same way as the two knots that are to follow. This arrangement is strong and secure. It was shown to me by Ferris Greenslet, who has found it one of the quickest and most practical of knots to tie while fishing.

A knot attempted in the open, as the daylight is dimming and with hands that are thoroughly chilled, will present difficulties that are not apparent when the same knot is tied while sitting cozily before an open fire in the clubhouse.

339. The DOUBLE OVERHAND KNOT (#516) is frequently used as a STOPPER KNOT on a leader to prevent a DROPPER HITCH from slipping. It weakens the leader less than a SINGLE OVERHAND KNOT.

340. A well-known knot for attaching a snell to the leader, which seems bulkier than is necessary.

341. This is neater than the last knot and is probably adequate, but it would seem to me that the GROUND LINE HITCH (#252), which is equally firm and much smaller, would be preferable. So far as I know, however, it has not been tried out in gut.

342. This one is from W. Keith Rollo. The HALF KNOT in the leader holds the dropper at a most desirable angle, with the fly pointing toward the reel.

Another way of attaching droppers is to reeve the knotted end of a snell through one of the leader bends.

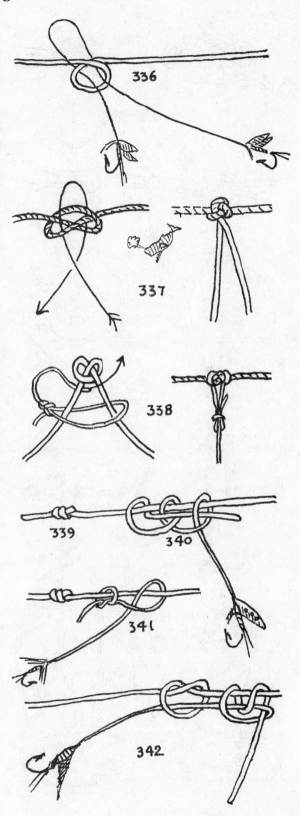

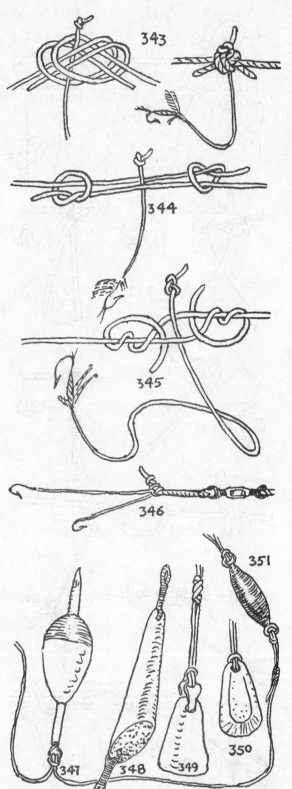

343. The WATER KNOT (⚹1412) utilized for this purpose is a bit bulkier than the two that follow, and the ends depart from the knot at such an angle that they are liable to snag on twigs or reeds, but the knot is both secure and strong.

344. The ENGLISHMAN'S KNOT (⚹1414) is the bend usually recommended for the purpose, but it is apt to loosen around the snell and is also liable to snag.

345. The BARREL KNOT (⚹1413) is the most secure of the three; the ends have a better lead, and they may be trimmed quite close. In the illustration a FIGURE-EIGHT KNOT (⚹524) is shown at the end of the dropper, instead of the OVERHAND (⚹515). But the OVERHAND is preferable, being smaller and, when used in this way, is sufficiently strong.

346. A double snell may be *clove hitched* (⚹1773) above an OVER-HAND KNOT (⚹515) in the end of the leader. This is a salt-water practice.

347. The familiar float or bob of the "pole" fisherman is secured to the line with a RING HITCH (⚹1859).

348. A codfish sinker or lead is fitted with beckets at either end to which the line is made fast.

Sinkers are made in an endless variety of shapes and are almost always attached with RING HITCHES (⚹1859). A narrow strip of thin sheet lead makes a good sinker. It is wrapped tightly around the line and pinched with pliers to hold it in place. An old favorite with anglers is a split bullet, which is tapped with a hammer to make it pinch the line. These bullets are procurable in different sizes, and if needed a number may be attached in a row.

349. A bottom sinker may have a leather bridle or strap to which the line is attached.

350. A line may be tied directly to a lead plummet. A heavy lead adds tremendously to the scope when casting.

351. A *swivel-shaped lead*. Excellent for both hand-line and rod fishing.

"Fishing tackle" is an angler's term not used by the professional fisherman, who calls the appurtenances of his fishing gear. The only tackle used at sea is an arrangement of blocks and rope required for hoisting. The name is always pronounced *taykle*.

Gear and tackle alike have to be suited to the fish, and the diversity of size and shape, appetite, and temperament of fish is amazing. There is no need for a fisherman or an angler ever to become bored.

A number of years ago R. R. M. Carpenter, author of *Game Trails, from Alaska to Africa* (Scribner's, 1939), said to me: "I hate to take a chance on sailfish and tarpon. I'm afraid they'll spoil me for trout and salmon." Fortunately, I was in a position to reassure him. "You don't need to worry about that. I find that I enjoy swordfishing now just as much as I did before I went whaling."

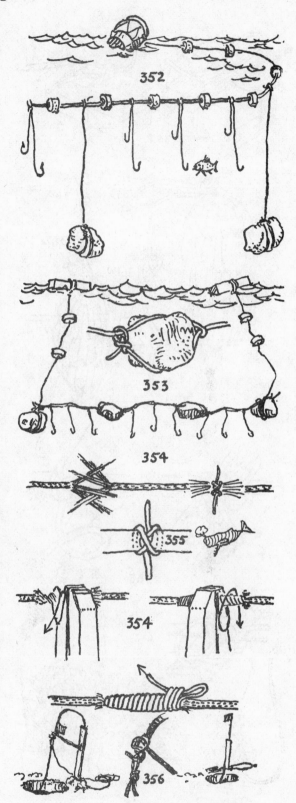

352. This illustrates a small *surface trawl*, which in principle does not differ from the large trawl of the professional fisherman. For an amateur a 150-foot length will provide plenty of interest and sport. The gangings (#276) should be about four feet apart, with ordinary disk-shaped cork floats in between. Tie OVERHAND KNOTS (#515) at each side of the floats. Every fourth line should be an anchor line about twenty feet long. Set the trawl in a tideway, bait with squid or any shiny fish, and visit it at each tide. If set from shore, only one marker buoy is required, and the apparatus is termed a "trot."

353. A *ground trawl* is similarly made, with *slingstones* (#271–273) between every three or four hooks. Markers are required at the ends. Set at low water and pull at the next tide.

354. Small FISHLINE SPLICE. Either ravel or unravel the ends of a braided line with a pin or fishhook one half inch to one and one quarter inches, depending on the size of the line. Divide the threads of each end into three equal parts. Scrape each group to a point and wax each point or strand thoroughly. Marry the two ends so that the tips overlap the unraveled parts of the lines slightly, as shown in the first illustration. Wax and middle a piece of fine silk thread. Tie a CONSTRICTOR KNOT (#1249) with the central section of it around the center of the splice and draw the knot taut. Grip the right half of the splice in a vise. Twist the left half of the splice strongly *away* from you, and serve tightly *toward* you with one end of the silk thread. Serve the whole end and then finish off as illustrated in the lower diagram. Next turn the splice end for end and repeat the first performance with the second end. The size of the thread is exaggerated in the illustrations. Some anglers consider it sufficient to lay the two waxed and tapered ends together and serve without either marrying or twisting. Finished splices should be varnished, but if made in the open, and to be used at once, grease with bacon fat, butter, or whatever else your lunch provides. A laid line may be spliced in the same way, or else with a SAILOR'S SPLICE, in which case the strands must be opened for several inches before marrying so that they can be threaded on needles, or else they can be tucked by pulling the ends through with a small hairpin.

355. If double gangings with two hooks are used as shown in #352 they may be secured with a CONSTRICTOR KNOT (#1249), which is more secure than a CLOVE HITCH (#1177) or a RING HITCH (#1859).

356. There are many different traps devised for *fishing through the ice*. The one given here is characteristic. It consists of a flat extensible spring at the top, with flag attached. When the flag flies high a fish is indicated. Formerly there was no limit to the number of traps allowed, and I have seen five hundred of them set at one time by three fishermen in a Massachusetts pond. But now in the same locality the limit is ten traps to the individual. The preferred baits are "shiner" and "mummychog," or "mumper." Pickerel and red perch will make up the bulk of the catch.

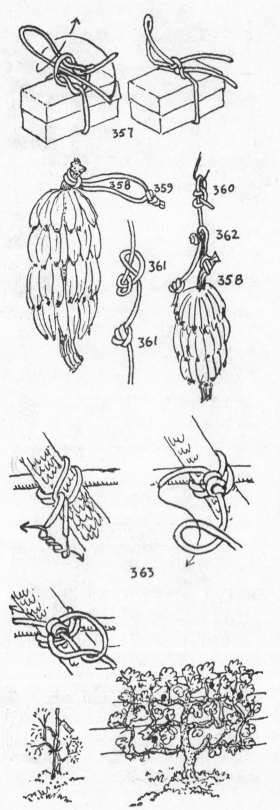

The Florist

357. A FLORIST'S KNOT: A parcel knot which does not slip, as the HALF BOWKNOT or DRAWKNOT (#1211) does, but nevertheless retains the loop for decorative purposes. This one is from Havana.

The Football Player

Laces his football as in #2036. He tightens the turns with a buttonhook.

The Fruiterer

358. In the banana trade stalks are equipped with a short length of rope yarn, secured to the stem with a strap or BALE SLING HITCH (#1759), so forming a loop at the top of the bunch, which is really the inverted bottom of the banana cluster.

359. The ends of the sling or strap are tied together with an OVERHAND BEND (#1410).

360. A lanyard of rope yarn, its length depending on the height of the storage-room ceiling, is secured to a hook with TWO HALF HITCHES (#1781). The end should hang about shoulder-high.

361. The BANANA KNOT. A series of three or four STOPPER KNOTS (Chapter 3) are tied in the lanyard from eight to twelve inches apart. The usual knot consists of a SINGLE OVERHAND with a HALF HITCH taken above it, as pictured. This is very much like the PEARL KNOT (#383). Sometimes FIGURE-EIGHT KNOTS (#520) are used instead.

362. The BANANA HITCH is an application of the BUTTON AND EYE (#1925). A porter enters the storage loft, a bunch of bananas on his right shoulder, with the knot end to the rear. He "eases" the bunch forward from his shoulder, and as he does so he reeves one of the lanyards through the loop at the end of the stalk. He allows the loop to close above one of the knots, #361, which suspends the stalk at a height above the reach of various pests. The porter holds the lanyard taut until the loop has settled snugly around the neck of the knot. These BANANA KNOTS were shown to me by Edward W. Sherman.

The Gardener

363. ESPALIER KNOT. This draws a plant and its support together and holds the adjustment without any bother while the knot is being completed. It is convenient to tie after once being mastered. A length of raffia is doubled, and a RING or BALE SLING HITCH (#1694) is placed around both the branch or stem, and the trellis or wire, and is then hove taut. A DOUBLE HALF KNOT (see the first diagram) is added and pulled up to give the proper tension. One of the ends is then hitched somewhat after the manner of a BUTCHER'S KNOT (#183), but the hitch is not superimposed on the knot already formed; instead, it is closed around the *neck* of the DOUBLE HALF KNOT. The knot may be tied in rope yarn or cord as well as raffia.

In bagging grapes, the CONSTRICTOR (#1249) works nicely, as the snugness may be accurately gauged. To tie: See #176 under "Blaster," this chapter.

364. To mend the garden hose when no wire couplings are handy, take a stout piece of fishline about one eighth inch in diameter, tie a CONSTRICTOR (⚹1249), place it around the hose, secure the ends of the cord to the centers of two sticks, and pull as illustrated. A ten-year-old boy can pull more effectively in this way than two strong men can, each pulling an end against the other.

There is only one satisfactory way to coil rubber hose, and that is with figure-eight turns, preferably flaked down as in ⚹3109 or ⚹3110.

365. The CROSSING KNOT should be employed in staking out newly seeded areas of grass. Number 206 gives the method of tying this knot.

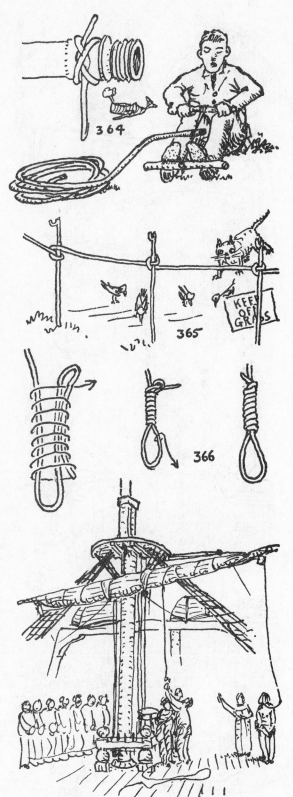

The Hammock Maker

The type of hammock recently termed "Cape Ann" has been used at sea for many years. I have an ancient one made of linen homespun sailcloth. There are two knots used by the commercial hammock makers in hitching to the eyelets, which are given elsewhere as RING HITCHES ⚹1832 and ⚹1833. Neither is particularly secure. At sea, hammock clews were made in several different ways, to be shown later in Chapter 41.

Very few net hammocks are now seen, and the old-fashioned barrel-stave hammock appears to have almost vanished.

The Hangman

366. The HANGMAN'S KNOT. There are several knots recommended for this purpose, and there are several variations of the one given here that may be found in the chapter on NOOSES. But this knot of eight turns appears to be the standard one, and it may be counted upon to draw up smoothly and snugly when it fulfills its office. The noose is always adjusted with the knot slightly below and immediately in back of the left ear. This is to provide the sidewise jerk, which is one of the refinements of a successful hanging.

Hangings at sea were infrequent. Such an occasion furnished a bit of extra-routine labor, in which the boatswain took especial pride, and in which no bungling was tolerated. A boatswain's reputation would be forever ruined if there were any hitch on such an occasion.

Although most of the details were left to him, there were certain well-established conventions which had to be observed. These are given in detail in an old work on seamanship. A fall was led through a single block at the fore yardarm and thence to a second single block under the fore cap. Between the two blocks was a SHEEPSHANK KNOT (⚹1154), the upper bight of which was not *half hitched*, as is customary, but was merely *stopped* with light twine. This stopping would carry away the instant the knot was hauled against the block, so spilling the SHEEPSHANK. The weight at the *noose* end at once dropped to take up the slack given by the spilled SHEEPSHANK, and it was brought up with a jerk by a toggle which fetched against the yardarm block. The toggle was *marlingspike hitched* (⚹2030) and seized to the rope at a point which allowed for an exact six-foot drop outside the rail.

In preparation for this the fall was laid at length along the deck "ready to be hurried aft" when "twenty stout fellows seized the rope."

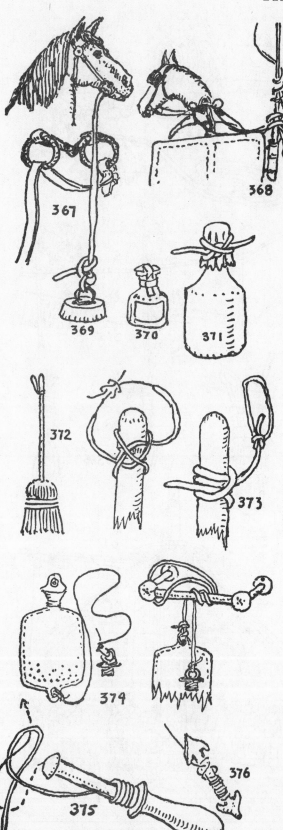

The Horseman

The horseman should consult Chapter 24 ("Ring Hitches") and also the last two pages of Chapter 26 ("Miscellaneous Holdfasts"), where a number of hitching posts are depicted. Other knots of interest to him may be found under "Cowboy," "Artilleryman," "Farmer," and "Prospector" in this chapter. Number 2057 shows how to tie up a horse's tail when the going is muddy.

367. When a horse was to be hitched by a rein, the left rein was left buckled to the bit ring and the other end was unbuckled and rove through the opposite bit ring on the right side. I use the past tense here, for I haven't seen a horse tied in this way in many years. Draft horses were sometimes hitched to a forward spoke, and a turn of the reins was taken around the hub, so that if the horses bolted the reins at once were pulled tight.

368. If a horse stood well, without hitching, the ends of the reins often were merely *clove hitched* around the handle of the whip as it stood upright in the whipsocket at the right side of the dasher, or dashboard. Everything was right-hand drive in the horse-and-carriage days.

369. A hitching weight was part of every doctor's buggy equipment. Generally it had a strap halter snapped to it, but if not, Two HALF HITCHES in rope or rein would make it fast.

The House Painter

See under "Carpenter" and "Steeplejack," this chapter. Also consult Chapter 27.

The Housewife

The housewife's needs are so multifarious that the following group of knots would seem inadequate but for the fact that most of her requirements are not peculiar and most of what she requires is to be found in the general classifications.

370. To hold the cork secure in a bottle, lay a piece of adhesive tape over the cork and down each side, then take two turns with another piece around the neck of the bottle.

371. The same result may be reached with cord and a CONSTRICTOR KNOT (#1249). Cover the top with a piece of heavy paper or cloth and tie a CONSTRICTOR close under the collar of the bottle.

372. To hang up a broom or mop, file a rough groove around the end of the stick and tie a CONSTRICTOR (#1249) in it, then knot the ends of the cord together.

373. A MAGNUS or ROLLING HITCH will suffice to tie a broom that has no groove, provided the surface is not too slick.

374. A hot-water bottle may be hung up and drained in the way illustrated. The same knot may be tied over a hook, in which case the left side, as here pictured, will be the top of the knot.

375. A knot at the end of a pillow-lace bobbin, which will prevent unwinding and at the same time allow easy removal.

376. A square knotting or macramé shuttle knot serves a similar purpose.

In Chapter 28 ("Lashings and Slings") parcel tying, a subject of importance to the housewife, is discussed.

377. The proper way to secure a wire to a screw eye: Small galvanized stovepipe wire is about the best picture wire; it is easier to work, easier to cut, cheaper to buy, and less in evidence than other wires.

378. The ordinary way of making a loop or securing the end of a wire to a screw eye.

379. If there is a vibration from the outside that tilts all your pictures askew, hang them from a single wire which passes through both screw eyes and makes fast to two picture hooks.

380. When walls are of brick and the plaster is powdery, take a half-inch board seven or eight inches wide and nearly as long as the width of your picture. Place a hook near the center, pepper the surface with small-wired brads, and drive them almost through the board. Put the board in place and drive the brads home with as little jar as possible. A "nail set" will help. This very practical method was shown me by a friend who had employed it to hang a six-foot canvas.

381. The common way of knotting a simple bandage. Anything more elaborate is generally fastened with adhesive tape.

382. A stubborn screw top on a jar may be started by winding a number of turns of string around the top to provide a better handhold. Elastic bands are even better, and adhesive tape will also serve the purpose well.

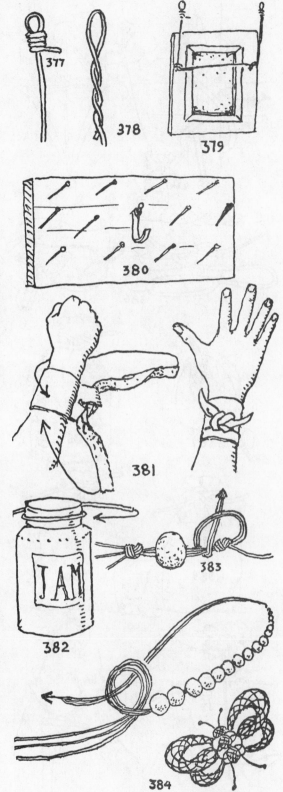

The Jeweler

"R. L.," of Tiffany and Company, very kindly supplied the method of stringing pearls. I do not feel that I can improve on the explicit instructions that were sent me, so I will quote them verbatim:

383. The PEARL KNOT. "The knot itself is only a simple single knot. There will be two, three, or four strands of silk, according to the size of the pearls and their holes. The knots will be as numerous as may be desired, sometimes one after each pearl, or after each five or more pearls.

"Each knot is tied by putting the pearls that have been strung through the loop [see second diagram], instead of the alternative of pulling the free end of the silk through the loop each time. The pearls on the string give weight in forming the loop, and thus make a better knot than the free silk would do.

"At both ends, where the clasp and click are, the silk is knotted back through the last pearl, so that the end of the silk is finally knotted between pearls and not tied simply to the clasp and click.

"Larger knots often have to be made if the hole in the pearl is too large for a single knot. These larger knots are made by knotting only two strands of the three." (See first diagram.)

384. This charming insect, made of knotted human hair, to serve as a breast pin, is abstracted from a commercial catalogue of the mid-nineteenth century, entitled *Jeweller's Book of Patterns in Hairwork*.

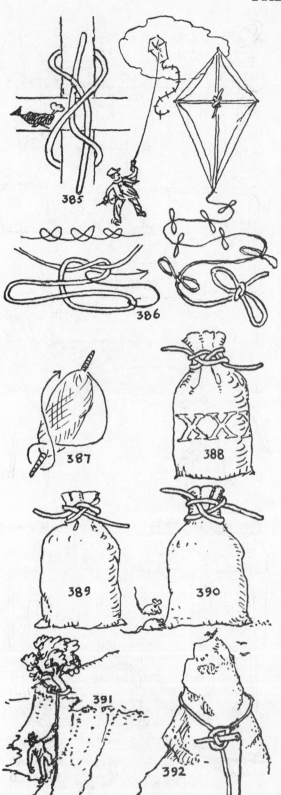

Kite Flying

385. To tie the ribs of a kite together, the TRANSOM KNOT (#1255), which is a modification of the CONSTRICTOR (#1249), will serve nicely.

386. Tails on old-fashioned kites almost always had crossbands called bobs designed to furnish aerial friction and so check the kite's tendency to dart here and there. For this purpose wads of paper are usually tied at intervals; sometimes, on large kites, short sticks are used instead. A cord or rope tail may have double loops added in the manner given here. First make a series of FIRE-ESCAPE KNOTS (#564) by the method that is given at the beginning of Chapter 4, then stick a loop in each knot as indicated in the diagram given here.

387. Kite strings were generally wound up on a stick in this manner, which is particularly adapted to wet or moist line. The turns are loose and open so that the cord will dry out readily if the reel is placed in a draft.

The Miller

388. The BAG KNOT.

389. The SACK KNOT.

390. The MILLER'S KNOT. The names of these three knots are interchangeable. Many millers use a round turn with the ends reef knotted or else secured with a DRAWKNOT or HALF BOWKNOT. Some employ a CLOVE HITCH, slipped, which is the least practical.

Additional BAG KNOTS are given in Chapters 16 and 27. The CONSTRICTOR KNOT (#1249) is the securest of all; but it is not easily untied unless a SLIP LOOP is added.

The Mountain Climber

These knots may also be of service to the bird nester and the tree scaler. Additional knots of interest to the climber may be found under "Steeplejack" and "Tree Surgeon" in this chapter.

I was once asked by an official of a mountain-climbing club to recommend a knot that could be used by a man while climbing alone. This necessitates a knot which can be spilled from below after the climber has lowered himself from a higher level. The following knots resulted.

391. The PRECIPICE KNOT is the SLIPPERY HITCH with an OVERHAND KNOT (#1606) added to the end.

The SLIPPERY HITCH is the answer to the sailor's favorite riddle for landsmen: "How would you lower yourself over a precipice with a rope that is just long enough to reach the ground, and then recover your rope before proceeding?" All that is necessary is to select a precipice with a convenient tree. When you have safely landed, flirt the rope to free the hitched end.

This knot should be studied carefully, since other knots require twice the length of rope; but it is no knot to trifle with. Unless the climber has an innate understanding or feeling for knots, he had better leave it alone.

392. Heavy weights are sometimes let go with an EYE SPLICE and a toggle. The method when applied to climbing requires an extra spill line. There is no danger of jamming.

393. If a rope is long enough, so that only half its length is required for the job, there are a number of SLIPPED HITCHES that may be used as climbing knots. This one is a modification of the TIMBER HITCH. It can be made fast around a small cylindrical object, such as a tree, a branch, or a post. The slipped loop should be nipped at the top of the branch.

394. A SLIPPED HALF HITCH. The nip should be at the top opposite the standing part.

395. The same knot may be slipped a second time. (To slip a knot is to reeve a bight for the final tuck instead of an end, so that the knot may be untied by pulling on the end.) This hitch may be tied around an object that is larger than №393 would be recommended for.

396. A knot that may be tied around a cylinder of fair size such as the branch of a tree. It is the most easily spilled of the knots that are given.

397. If the object to be tied to is large a SLIPPED BUNTLINE HITCH is a better knot than any of the foregoing. In tying any rope around a jagged stone arrange the turns carefully and draw up snugly, with the lead in exactly the direction in which the pull is to be exerted. If a rope shifts while supporting a heavy weight a sharp edge may easily cut a strand.

398. A knot that is closely related to №397, is amply secure, and spills smoothly.

399. Here is a knot that may be tied close to the ground around a clump of bushes and does not have to be drawn up snugly around the object. A clump of bushes or grass is a treacherous thing to tie to, for if either bends over enough to allow the rope to rise, a spill is inevitable.

In all these knots allow a good margin of safety by sticking a long slip loop. I do not like №392, although it is possibly the safest one for a person who does not know his ropes. Numbers 393, 394, 395, and 396 should be tied around comparatively small objects. Number 368 has less tendency to jam than the others, is the most easily slipped, and probably is the most satisfactory for tree climbing. Numbers 397 and 398 are perhaps the best all-around knots.

If you propose to trust your life to any knot, rehearse it a few times in the back yard before going afield, aloft, or afloat with it. Tie it carefully and deliberately, and add weight slowly. A knot is like an egg; it is either good, or it is rotten. A single difference in the "over-and-under" sequence will make a different knot out of any. If you are not accustomed to reading graphics and are tying from a diagram, have one or two friends with similar interests tie knots with you. Between you, the truth will out.

The Musician

A violin, guitar, or banjo string may be tied with a FIGURE-EIGHT KNOT (№520). If the hole is large, the end may be doubled before tying, as in №531. The OYSTERMAN'S KNOT (№526) is a neater one for the purpose, but is more complicated to tie.

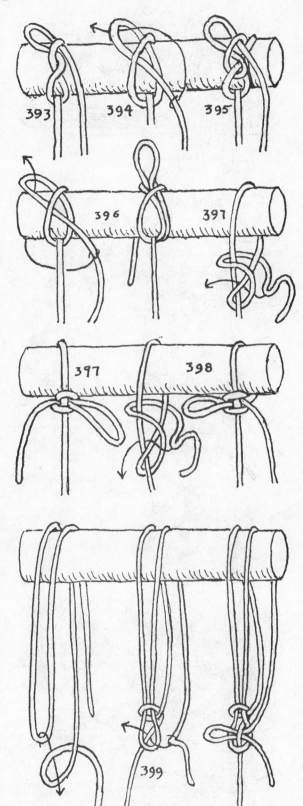

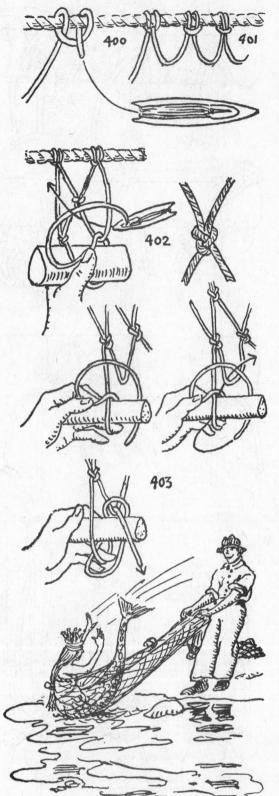

The Netmaker

400. The CLOVE HITCH (❋1177) is the customary knot with which to tie the first tier of meshes to the headline of a net.

401. Sometimes a COW HITCH (❋1802) is used for the purpose.

402. The MESH KNOT, sometimes called the FISHERMAN'S NETTING KNOT, is the ordinary way of tying the SHEET BEND when it is made with a netting needle.

403. The *Martha's Vineyard method* of tying the same knot, or rather the same knot mirrored (with the left and right sides reversed), was first shown to me by F. Gilbert Hinsdale, who had seen it tied by Captain James Look, of Chilmark. I afterwards learned it from the latter's brother, Captain Daniel C. Look, of Menemsha Bight. Although somewhat more difficult to learn than the usual MESH KNOT, it will prove much more rapid and exact when a little experience has been gained.

After reaching the position shown in the third diagram, continue to pull steadily on the needle while casting off the loop held by the thumb. While still pulling steadily on the needle, gradually let go the loop around the ring finger. When all material has been taken up, cast off the remaining loop around the little finger and draw the knot snugly against the spool. The spool regulates the size of the mesh. The spool is also called a "gauge," a "mesh," and sometimes a "mesh stick."

The same method of netting is given by Caulfield and Saward and also by De Dillmont, but with the fingers in somewhat different position, which is probably better for lightweight thread and smaller fingers.

Considerable has been written about netting from the needlework standpoint, where it is often difficult to differentiate clearly between netting and tatting, macramé and various other kinds of lacemaking.

Nets and seines are made in many different forms for different conditions and different fish, but although the nets of different continents, countries, and localities show a diversity of form, the MESH KNOT itself is universally the same. The various United States Government fishery and ethnological reports give a vast amount of information regarding all sorts of nets. These reports are always well illustrated and are to be found in most public and college libraries.

The only monograph that I know concerning fishermen's nets and seines is *Notes on Nets* by the Honorable and Reverend Charles Bathurst, LL.D., published in Cirencester about 1840. It contains a lot of practical information and also many quaint digressions, mainly on natural history. The author discusses such unrelated subjects as how to "clean the floor of a fishhouse," "Unusual Structure of Cervical Vertebre of a large Quadruped, found in a Boneyard," "A ball of Hair contained in a Horse's Stomach," and a "Tick that made a raft of its own detached stomach."

One interesting bit of information was: "Netting for fruit trees is made I believe by machinery, . . . I do not know that any other nets have as yet been [so] made for general purposes. . . ."

The subject of netting will be referred to again in Chapter 41.

404. In fringe making, and in nets made of material too heavy for the netting needle, *reef knotting* is sometimes resorted to.

405. This method is practiced with a needle. It results in a vertical REEF KNOT, where №404 is horizontal. A REVERSED or COW HITCH is first tied, which is capsized into a REEF KNOT by pulling, as shown by arrows in the diagram.

406. Dip nets and drawnwork fringes for canvas sea-chest covers may be tied with DOUBLE OVERHAND KNOTS.

The Nurse

407. Sometimes a delirious patient has to be spread-eagled to prevent exhaustion from constant tossing. Strips of sheeting are tied to the ankles and wrists. The other ends are made fast to the bedposts. Almost invariably the knots are tied so that they tend to shut off circulation and so add to the patient's discomfort. The proper way to tie is to make a smooth round turn about the wrist or ankle, and then finish off with a BOWLINE (№1010), close up, but not snug enough to cause any constriction. This will neither bind nor work loose, yet it is easily untied. For other knots of interest to the nurse see "Housewife" and "Surgeon," in this chapter, and "Tourniquets" in the binder chapter.

The Packer

408. The PACKER'S KNOT will hold a parcel snugly while the cord is being passed around a second dimension. It is also shown among the BUTCHER'S KNOTS, where it has a HALF HITCH added. Further knots of interest to the packer will be found under "Prospector," "Florist," and "Stationer" in this chapter, and also in Chapter 27, "Occasional Knots," and Chapter 28, "Lashings and Slings."

The Poacher

409. The POACHER'S KNOT is a noose used in snaring various game. A little stockade is built across a spot where woodcock or partridge are accustomed to pass. Usually it is disguised with a few leafed twigs. There are frequent arched openings, and in each of these is suspended a horsehair noose, lightly caught on the bark at the sides. Birds of this sort will walk along until they find an opening and will not fly unless startled.

410. "Springs" for larks are also fitted with horsehair nooses hitched to a staked-out anchor line. This trap is heavily baited; the former was not. Both Diderot (1762) and the *Sportsman's Dictionary* (1810) devote many pages to snaring, netting, and trapping birds and game; everything from larks to woodcock and from bears and wolves to mice is shown. Nooses were even suspended between trees for birds to fly into at dusk. See also under "Shooting" and "Trapper," this same chapter.

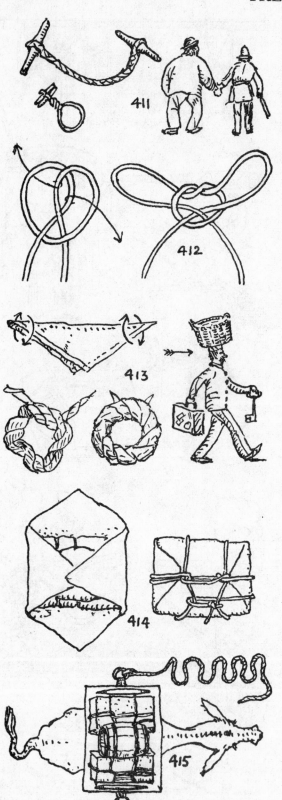

411. A *policeman's nippers*, sometimes called *twisters*, after encircling a wrist, are adjusted to a close fit by twisting; the two handles are brought together and held in the grip of one hand togglefashion, with the cord leading from between the second and third fingers. Formerly they were of rope, but nowadays they are more often of chain.

412. The HANDCUFF KNOT. After adjustment around the wrists of a culprit, the ends are half hitched around the neck of the loops (see ✳1140). The TOM FOOL'S KNOT (✳1141) has also been used for the same purpose and in the same manner.

The Porter

413. The PORTER'S KNOT consists of a loosely twisted grommet made of a large bandanna or other cloth. It dissipates the weight of a burden carried on the head so that even a novice can bear a difficult load with assurance and without the need of a steadying hand. First make a long left twist of the bandanna, and tie a large RIGHT-HANDED DOUBLE or THREEFOLD OVERHAND KNOT somewhat larger than the completed knot is to be. Continue to lay the material around the knot, parallel with the established strands and constantly imparting twist to the strand. Finally bury the ends between two leads, which secures them.

There is another apparatus that also bears the name PORTER'S KNOT which consists of either a rope or a long strip of cloth with the ends tied together in a REEF KNOT (✳1204), the whole apparatus being termed "PORTER'S KNOT." It is or was placed by the porters of London over their foreheads, and the loop which hung down the back helped to support whatever load was carried. It was mentioned in *Pills to Purge Melancholy*, by Thomas d'Urfey (1719). Much the same method of transport is employed by North American Indians and guides. A wide strap is used which is termed a tump or tote line or rope.

The Prospector

414. To make up a pack: The process of lashing a pack is described at some length in Chapter 28, "Lashings and Slings." The pack is made up in a square canvas cover called a *manta* and is lashed with a rope that is called a *lair rope*.

415. A pack animal may be a donkey, mule, horse, camel, llama, or elephant, but in our country a mule is preferred. The load is carried either on a packsaddle, which is a piece of furniture resembling a sawbuck, or on an aparejo, which is a heavy hay-stuffed pad, stiffened along its bottom edges with wooden battens.

All authorities are agreed that the first thing to be done in pack lashing is to blindfold the mule. This being attended to, the aparejo is secured in place and the load temporarily slung with a "sling rope" which holds the arrangement while the hitch is being "thrown" with the "lash rope."

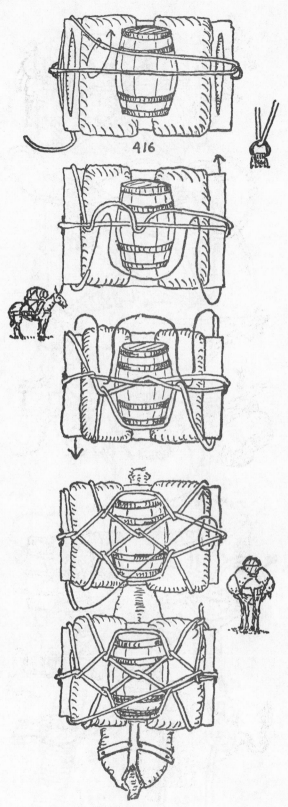

416. The Double Diamond Hitch, also called the Diamond Hitch, is a method of pack lashing used by the cowboy, the sheepherder, and the hunter, as well as by the prospector. It is widely known throughout the mountain country of both North and South America. The Double Diamond is a lashing for two *packs* with an additional *riding load*, the latter being a third object carried above the two packs. There is a ring in one end of the cinch to which the lash rope is either hitched or spliced. The lash rope is thrown over the mule's back by one packer, and the assistant passes it through the ring or hook at the other end of the cinch, which has been passed under the mule's belly to receive it. The packers proceed to "throw" the rope back and forth, each making his contribution to the hitch, as indicated in the drawings. There are various short cuts and refinements to the process, and some minor variations to the hitch itself are allowable. Different packers have different techniques. As each man throws, he calls out in appropriate words to announce progress and prepare his fellow packer for the next movement. The calls vary with different packers. After the hitch is made it is tightened and the end of the lash rope made fast with two or more Half Hitches. If there is an extra length of rope left it is led elsewhere and "hitched" again.

There is a great variety of hitches. Some are tied by one man, some by two. The Single and Double Diamond are shown here because the names are familiar to almost everybody.

The War Department has issued a comprehensive bulletin on packing, by H. W. Daly, of the Quartermasters Department (Document 360). Charles W. Post, in *Horse Packing*, has treated the subject very thoroughly for the general public, and his book contains many excellent illustrations.

Around animals in general, and on farms in particular, the word *hitch* is used as a verb, which is contrary to sea usage. A horse is hitched when he is tied up, and a rope is hitched when it is made fast. Moreover, when a horse is harnessed to a vehicle he is "hitched up."

I venture to say that before I started to write this book I never used the words *tie* and *hitch* as verbs except in reference to men's neck apparel and trousers, from one year's end to another, and the verb *hitch* passed entirely out of my vocabulary until a pony was added to the children's livestock a few years ago. But I now use both terms glibly, although I have been severely taken to task by several longshore purists for my lapses in these directions.

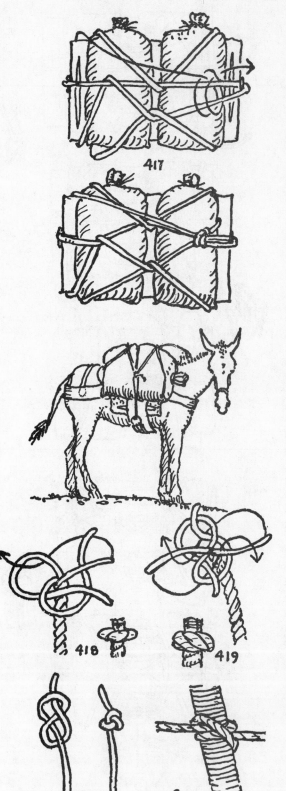

417. The SINGLE DIAMOND HITCH is for two packs with no riding load. It will be seen in consulting the sketches that the rope in this lashing forms a single diamond at the center top, and the previous hitch, a double diamond, which of course explains the names.

The Quilter

In quilting, the layers of material are often tacked together with strong twine, although much the nicer method is to stitch elaborate patterns which are first chalked out or stenciled on the quilt. In the more common method the needle, bearing several parallel cords, is first shoved down and then is stuck up again about three sixteenths of an inch to one side of and parallel to the first thrust. The ends are then square knotted together and "cut off long." A better practice, which is often followed, is to tuft with colored yarns, much as the upholsterer does (#483), but the knot used by the quilter is generally a SQUARE KNOT.

The Rigger

Nowadays a house painter or a steeplejack may be listed in the telephone directory as a rigger, but it is the ship rigger who is referred to here. Seizings, wormings, whipping, marling, parceling, serving, etc., are all to be found in Chapters 40 and 41, which deal with marlingspike seamanship and other rigging practices. Rigger's splices are to be found in three chapters devoted exclusively to splicing, and here and there throughout the chapters of practical knots are other rigger's knots. The several given here are peculiar to the rigger.

418. In *finishing off a seizing*, the rigger brings the end up between two turns, and if the material is small stuff he ties a WALL KNOT; if it is spun yarn he ties an OVERHAND KNOT (#515).

419. The LANYARD KNOT is tied in the ends of shroud and stay lanyards, and is employed in setting up and securing standing rigging.

420. A FIGURE-EIGHT KNOT (#520) is tied wherever a temporary stopper is needed and also near the ends of all running rigging, to prevent unreeving.

421. A CLOVE HITCH (#1177) is the CROSSING KNOT employed in *rattling down* rigging. Ratlines are the rope steps found on shrouds, by means of which the rigging is climbed.

In addition to the several knots that are illustrated here the rigger uses a BALE SLING HITCH (#1759) for a variety of purposes; a ROPE YARN KNOT (#1480) is called for in serving, and a HALF HITCH SEIZED (#1717) and Two HALF HITCHES SEIZED (#1719) are old rigger's stand-bys. The DIAMOND KNOT (#693) was formerly used in jib-boom footropes. Among the general sailor knots, which constitute the bulk of the material in this work, there are many knots for which the rigger has occasional use. The MARLINGSPIKE HITCH (#2030) is required constantly in tightening seizings and service.

The Rugmaker

422. The PERSIAN or SENNA KNOT. The second drawing shows the knot with the pile trimmed.

423. The GHIORDES or TURKISH KNOT. The second drawing shows the knot with the pile trimmed.

The hooked rug is made by shoving a series of loops through the coarse weave of heavy burlap with an instrument called a hook. Sometimes hooked rugs have been trimmed in the manner of "Orientals," but since they are made from long, narrow strips of woven fabric instead of yarn, the resemblance is not marked even when, as I have sometimes seen, an Oriental pattern is copied.

The Rush-Seat Maker

424. There is perhaps reason to include the rush-seat maker, since the course of his rush in rounding a chair leg approximates the course of a FIGURE-EIGHT KNOT, actually taking a series of BELAYING-PIN TURNS. Coarse marsh grass or rushes are twisted up by hand into long yarns, while either green or wet. A long overlap is required where rushes are joined, and the ends must be well hidden. When the two side rungs or stretchers do not lie parallel two FIGURE-EIGHTS are taken each time the front legs are passed, while only one is taken at the rear legs, until all parts are square. Extra rushes are laid along the side bars between the layers of seating to provide padding to save wear.

The Sailmaker

Curiously enough, the sailmaker does not use a great variety of knots, although he is an inveterate splicer. The needle and palm and a fid are his usual tools, and with them he does most of his work. The THUMB KNOT (#514) is employed constantly in the end of his sewing thread; it is tied with either hand, but generally with the left.

425. The CRINGLE is a knot required in most sails that is closely related to splicing and may be tied in a number of different ways. Several are shown in the chapter on odd splices. Formerly cringles were made *through* the boltrope; nowadays they are made *around* the boltrope, through eyelet holes in the sails.

Reef points were once knotted in, but nowadays they are sewed to a sail. In racing sails they are generally omitted, lace lines being substituted. Several methods of securing reef points are shown in Chapter 41.

There are a number of splices that are peculiar to the sailmaker: the TAPER SPLICE or SAILMAKER'S SPLICE, the ONE-STRAND or SAILMAKER'S SPLICE, the BACKHANDED or LEFT-HANDED EYE SPLICE, etc. These will be found in the chapters on splices, 34, 35, and 36.

Sailmaker's palm and needle whipping is described as #3446 in Chapter 40 on practical marlingspike seamanship. In Chapter 41, on applied knots, a number of sailmaker's stitches are given.

In making eyelets for cringles and reef points, a hole is stuck through the canvas with a stabber, and grommets are laid around the holes for reinforcement. These are closely stitched over and fidded out. The making of grommets is described as #2864 and #2865 in the chapter on odd splices, 36.

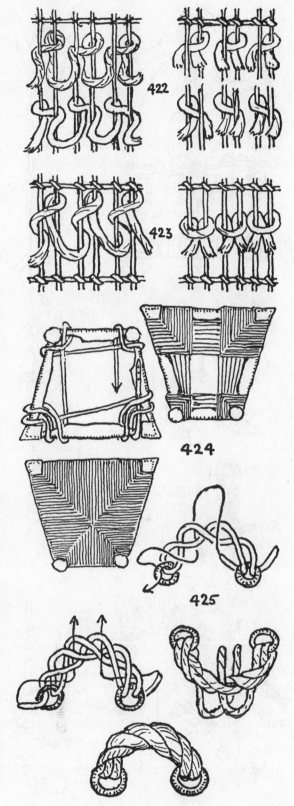

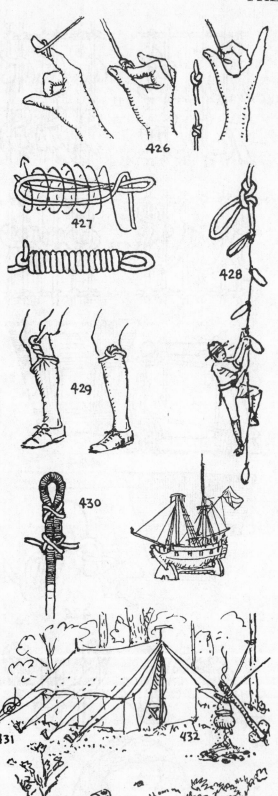

The Seamstress

426. The seamstress as well as the sailmaker constantly employs the THUMB KNOT (#514), which is generally either a SINGLE or a DOUBLE OVERHAND KNOT.

Girl and Boy Scouts

427. The SCOUT COIL is based on the HANGMAN'S KNOT (#366). After the end is stuck through the left loop, the right loop is pulled on until it is firm. A second tier of turns may be added and the other end be stuck instead. Whichever loop is left is hooked to the belt.

428. A long rope may have HARNESS LOOPS (#301) added to assist in climbing.

429. The GIRL SCOUT HITCH is in principle the same as the BINDER KNOT (#220). It is designed to hold up the stocking. There are a great many other knots throughout these pages that Scouts employ constantly. They will be found listed according to their uses.

The fisherman's litter (#283) is a bit of first-aid equipment that every Scout should know. It consists of two poles or oars, a coil of rope, and a bunch of seaweed.

The Ship-Model Maker

430. For *seizings* and whippings the CONSTRICTOR KNOT (#1249) is recommended. Wax a strong linen thread, tie the knot, draw snugly, and trim short (see #344). Instead of whipping small lines merely touch the tips with Duco cement.

To splice small lines: Thread the strands and thrust the needles without attempting to open the lay (see SPLICE #2685).

To make small wire rope: Take two or three fine wires. Fasten one set of ends in a vise and the other set in the chuck of a small hand drill. Twist hard and rub well with the round shank of a screw driver, while holding the rope taut.

To make small plain-laid rope: Take a large button having four holes, a hand drill, and a small fishline swivel. Secure three threads to one end of the swivel, hold the swivel in a vise so that it will not turn. Reeve each thread through one of the holes in the button, and hold the button close to the swivel. Secure *one* strand in the hand drill. Hold taut and turn the drill to add to the lay of the thread. Count the number of turns made with the crank and, when twisted sufficiently, keep it taut and make it fast. Repeat, giving the same number of turns to the other two threads. Place the ends together while holding them taut and secure them, or, better still, have someone else hold them. Hold the button in one hand, and adjust the vise so that the swivel can turn. Keep the strands taut, and move the button away from the vise steadily to the other end. If the strands have not been allowed to kink, the result should be a fair plain-laid rope. For four-strand rope use all four holes in the button.

Make cable-laid rope in the same way, but with opposite twist, using three of the ropes already made, or else three small twisted fishlines.

Shooting, Camping, Hunting, Etc.

431. An ADJUSTABLE HITCH (#1799) on a tent rope is about as easy to manipulate as a mechanical stake fastening and makes one thing less to carry on a camping trip. It is the same as a MIDSHIPMAN'S HITCH.

432. POT HITCH: Drive a stake at an angle into the ground. Middle a rope and tie a CLOVE HITCH near the top of the stake; lead the two ends to well-separated trees. The pot is hung from a stub that has been left near the top of the stake.

433. This is a leash for three brace of hounds from Diderot's Encyclopedia (1762). A is a STRAP or BALE SLING HITCH (#1694); B is a LOOP KNOT; C is an EYE SPLICE; and D is an OVERHAND KNOT. A number of leashes for house dogs may be found in Chapter 41 on applied knots.

434. A *goose boot and hobble,* shown to me by R. Eugene Ashley. It is used in staking out live wild goose decoys, a practice no longer legal in the United States. A goose picks continually at her fastenings, so rawhide is used exclusively, and nothing that can be untied will serve for a knot. The strap is first rove through the leather boot, then the end C is rove through the slit B. Next the end A is stuck through the slit C, which completes the boot end. The end A is then rove through the iron ring, after which the slit A is opened up and worked back over the ring, forming a RING HITCH (#1859). A stake is driven into the ground through the ring, and around the top of the stake is an iron hoop that is too large for the ring to pass. All this is so much bother that the goose will be fed where she stands for the whole shooting season unless there are spare decoys, in which case they may be relieved from time to time.

435. Generally a BALE SLING HITCH (#1694) in fishline or rope yarn is used on a short strap in hanging wild fowl by the neck or foot. In camp the same straps are used over and over again.

436. A live decoy duck has a leather foot strap or thong around her leg that is similar to the goose hobble but is not so elaborate. Frequently she is anchored with fishline only, which is tied with a STRAP HITCH precisely like #435. Nothing elaborate is needed, as a decoy duck is generally quite content to paddle around in shallow water for the few hours each day that are required of her. A short fishline is secured to the leather strap, the other end of which is fastened to an anchor, which may be a small stone, an old bolt or spike, a broken harrow tooth, or a lead sinker. In sand-dune country the anchor may even be a small bag of sand which is filled on the spot. There is no flesh, only sinew, in the legs of fowl and consequently no blood circulation, so contrivances of this sort cause little discomfort; they appear much worse than they really are.

437, 438. After a day's shooting, game often has to be carried by the gunner for considerable distances. Small birds fit into the pockets, but wild fowl are generally tied together, by the feet if few but by the necks if the day has been a lucky one. Two knots are commonly used for the purpose. The CLOVE HITCH (#1177) is easier to untie than the HALF KNOT (#1212).

439. A DEADEYE or LANYARD HITCH ties readily to a forked stake and as readily unties.

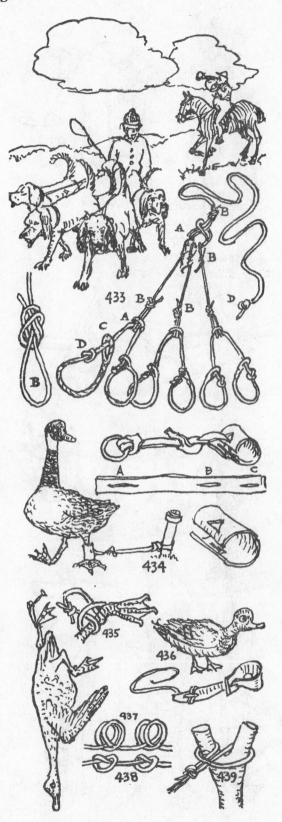

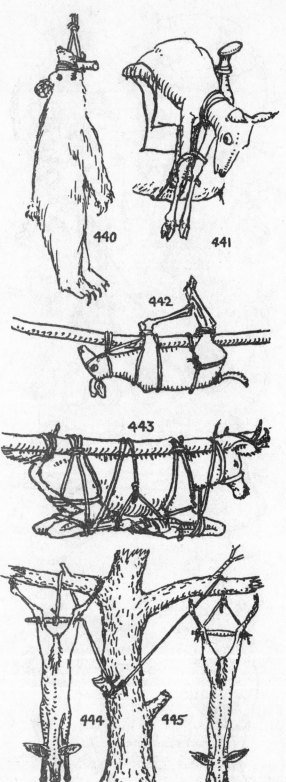

440. *To tump or tote a bear* without ruffling the fur: Place a small hardwood stick across the mouth, where the teeth will grip best, generally in back of the two fangs, and lash the mouth tightly around the snout and jaw with a Constrictor Knot (#1249). Lobster twine is excellent for the purpose. Then loop a rope over the nose and around the ends of the stick.

441. *To secure game across a saddle:* Middle a rope and make a Clove Hitch (#1177) around the pommel. Draw taut and make a Clove Hitch around the neck, and, if the animal is small, take a Marline Hitch (#2030) above the knees and make fast to the girth ring. Secure the other end of the animal in the same manner, taking a Clove Hitch around the small and a Marline Hitch above the hocks. If the animal is small the hitches around pommel, knees, and hocks may be omitted and the lashing secured to the rings of the girth only.

442. *To lash to a tote pole:* Lay the pole along the belly and clove hitch the legs together close above the knees and hocks. Lash the animal to the pole, and secure the end with a Clove Hitch to any convenient part.

443. *A buck lashed "right side up":* This will keep the antlers from snagging in the brush. Tote him "tail first." Tie all four feet together, clove hitch the dock to the pole, and lash each ham and shoulder singly. Next lash the antlers, then neck, knees, feet, and hocks. Last, pass stout turns around the lashings between the animal and the pole, and seize any turns that show a tendency to work loose. Marline or lobster cord makes a better lashing than rope, and is easier to pack on a trip.

444, 445. In *hanging large game*, the Clove Hitch and Two Half Hitches are commonly used. Sometimes a Clove Hitch is slipped over a hock or foot (or feet), the other end is tossed over a high limb, the animal is hauled aloft, and the end secured to a convenient branch. Dressed game is usually hung by sharpened crossbars impaled under the hamstrings.

The Skater

There is a club on the Wissahickon Creek named the "Philadelphia Skating Club and Humane Society." It has existed so long and so much water has passed down the stream since the club was founded that it may no longer be the duty of each member to wear, around his waist in skating season, a light knotted rope with which to rescue careless and unfortunate fellow skaters. Nevertheless, to this day the "Fire-Escape Knot" (#564), which appears to be the earlier name, is often termed by our firemen the "Philadelphia Knot," and it is, of course, quite possible that it was some eminent and skate-minded Philadelphian who first recognized the possibilities of this method of tying the Overhand Knot (#515). But as the knot was tied in jib-boom footropes at a much earlier date, the method probably belongs to the sailor. It is described at the beginning of Chapter 4 just as I learned it in Philadelphia thirty years ago, and the story that accompanies it was told to me by an octogenarian while sitting in the oriel window of the Philadelphia Art Club.

OCCUPATIONAL KNOTS

The Skier

446. A secure way to make fast a rawhide strap to a ski-pole handle. Cut a slit in each end of the strap. Reeve one end through the hole in the pole, and reeve the long right end through the slit in the left end. Thrust a bight from the right side up through the slit in the right end, and work the end down over the bight and continue down over the head of the pole to a point below the hole. Then straighten out all twists in the strap.

A comfortable way in which to adjust ski-boot lacings is shown as ⚓2039.

The Snowshoer

447. This shows a native Indian method of securing the moccasin to a snowshoe. It was found in *The Trapper's Guide* issued by the Oneida Colony of New York in the mid-1800s. The thong, after securing the toe, passes around the ankle, where it is reef knotted.

The Stationer

448. The STATIONER'S KNOT consists of a lashing that is finished off with a SLIPPED HALF HITCH.

The Steeplejack

The several knots to follow were provided by Laurie Young, a widely known steeplejack of eastern Massachusetts. His written description was illustrated with little sketches which are so graphic that I have copied them without change.

449, 450, 451. STEEPLE SLINGS. Two slings are required in climbing a steeple. They encircle the steeple, one above the other, and from each depends a boatswain's chair. The two slings are first put in place from windows at the base of the spire, and a chair similar to a boatswain's is hooked to each. The steeplejack climbs to the upper chair from the lower one. He unhooks the lower chair, draws it up, and temporarily hooks it to the upper sling. He stands on the upper chair, having taken the precaution to adjust his safety belt (⚓452) to the upper sling. He unties the lower sling and with his two hands swings it aloft to a level above the sling he is suspended from. He then ties its two ends together. Some steeplejacks use the REEF KNOT (⚓1204) for this purpose. Some have an EYE SPLICE in one end of the sling to which they bend the other end with TWO HALF HITCHES (⚓1710). The upper sling being in place, the extra chair is lifted and hooked to it, and then the steeplejack climbs again to the upper chair and repeats what has just been described. Chair ⚓450 is fitted with a hook, but the second chair, ⚓455 (on the following page), has an eye instead of a hook and is suspended from the tackle that will eventually be hooked to a strap and slung from the top of the steeple. From this chair the steeplejack performs his allotted task, which may be either a carpenter's, a tinsmith's, a slater's, or a painter's job.

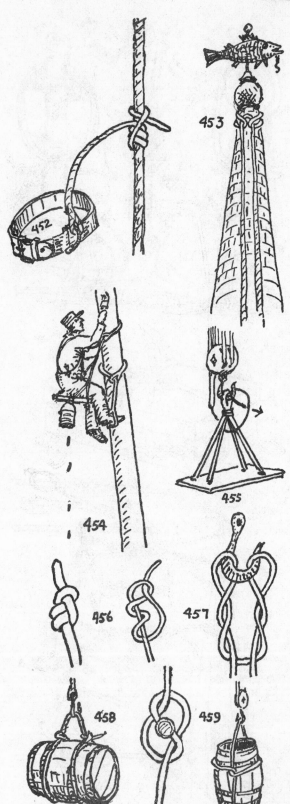

452. SAFETY-BELT HITCH. After a steeple has been climbed, the steeplejack's life belt is secured to a separate life line by a knot that is based on the MAGNUS or ROLLING HITCH, but the STEEPLEJACK'S KNOT has one more turn. It may easily be slid up and down the rope with the hand, but if the steeplejack should fall it will not slip when his weight falls on it.

453. The "ONE HITCH." His job complete, the steeplejack makes fast a double line to the steepletop in this manner and removes all other gear from the steeple, then lowers himself by means of the "ONE HITCH." This is easily shaken down, after he has reached the ground.

454. FLAGPOLE SLINGS. With these a man works himself aloft exactly as an inchworm progresses. First he stands on the foot sling and hitches his chair sling up, then he sits down and lifts the foot sling. Each sling has a NOOSE which passes around the pole.

455. A BOATSWAIN'S HITCH is used by all trades that go aloft: painters, ship riggers, steeplejacks, carpenters, and masons. A bight is pulled forward under the *eye seizing*, and a half turn of the wrist forms the SINGLE HITCH required on the bill of the hook.

The Stevedore

456. The STEVEDORE KNOT is a SINGLE-STRAND STOPPER KNOT tied in the end of a rope to prevent unreeving.

457. The DOUBLE CAT'S-PAW is the most satisfactory knot to secure slings to a cargo hook. Another twist may be added if desired.

458. HOGSHEAD SLINGS. The left end is rove through a thimble eye, forming a NOOSE; the right end is secured to the standing part with TWO HALF HITCHES. This is considered safer than *can hooks* for heavy casks.

459. To sling an open cask or barrel: Tie a large OVERHAND KNOT (#515) in the bight of the rope, lay the knot on the deck or ground, arrange it as in the illustration, and place the barrel over the center of it. Then bring up the ends and bend them together. This forms a MARLINE HITCH (#3115) at each side of the cask. Another method is to place the cask over the middle of the rope and tie a HALF KNOT (#1202) across the top. Open the knot at the center and slip it around the top of the cask. This forms HALF HITCHES at either side of the cask which are perhaps not so secure as the former. A third way is to place the cask over the center of the rope and then put an independent SINGLE HITCH (#1594) around the top with each end. This is the way usually recommended. The two hitches should be seized together.

The stevedore also uses the SHEEPSHANK (#1153) for shortening ropes, the BLACKWALL HITCH (#1875) for hoisting light goods, and the STRAP or BALE SLING HITCH (#1759) for slinging bales, crates, boxes, and sacks. Small articles are hoisted in cargo nets. Further stevedore's practices are included in Chapter 28, "Lashings and Slings."

OCCUPATIONAL KNOTS

The Surgeon

Surgeons, like artists, have always seemed to me to belong to two types. One, the nimble, intuitive mind, almost always is endowed with light hands and sensitive fingers, while the other, the methodical, reasoning mind, more often than not has heavy hands and clumsy fingers. The former will almost always tie excellent knots, while the latter, having no particular aptitude for them, is very apt to discount their importance, in which case the GRANNY KNOT is the best he produces.

But the GRANNY KNOT, although it has an initial tendency to slip, seldom spills entirely, so, although slipping in the early stages after an operation may aggravate bleeding, the common result of a poorly tied knot that has slipped unduly is nothing more than an unsightly and unnecessary scar. But too tight a knot, if there is inflammation, may cause a stitch to tear out.

For over twenty years, when opportunity has offered, I have asked surgeons to show me the knots they customarily tie. In this time I have questioned nearly two hundred individuals. A small proportion of these were physicians who also practiced surgery. Of all these over seventy per cent tied the GRANNY KNOT. Since every one of them was glad to learn how to tie the SQUARE KNOT, it would seem that there is an opportunity for the medical schools to hold more classes in knot tying.

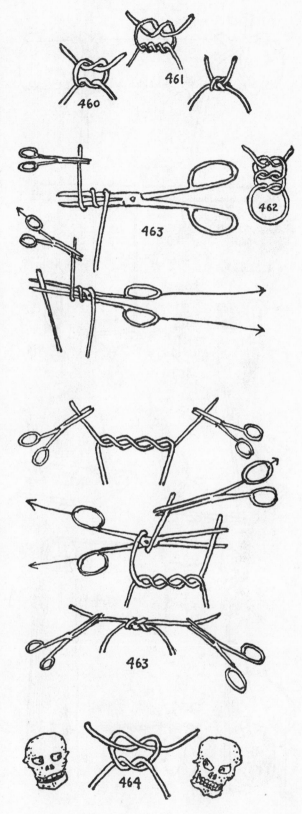

461

460

462

463

463

464

460. The REEF or SQUARE KNOT. This knot, used in tying a ligature, is preferred by many surgeons to the one which follows.

461. The LIGATURE KNOT is considered by some to use more gut than can be readily absorbed in the tissues, but the initial DOUBLE HALF KNOT is not apt to slip while the upper HALF KNOT is being added. For that reason it would seem to be better than the REEF KNOT.

462. Dr. C. W. Mayo, of the Mayo Clinic, Rochester, Minnesota, has written me that he uses the accompanying knot in tying a cystic duct, and also on all *large* blood vessels when ligature is necessary. Two identical HALF KNOTS are first tied, forming a GRANNY KNOT. This admits of a slight adjustment after the knot has been tied. When the tension has been adjusted, a third and opposite HALF KNOT is added, which locks the whole knot. The second and third HALF KNOTS, if considered as a unit, form a SQUARE KNOT.

463. The *aseptic method* of tying the SURGEON'S KNOT was shown to me by the late Dr. William C. Speakman, who learned it while serving in France with our Expeditionary Force of 1918. The REEF KNOT (#460) may be tied in the same way.

464. The GRANNY KNOT consists of two identical HALF KNOTS, the second being superimposed over the first.

Many surgeons tie *three identical* HALF KNOTS, one on top of another GRANNY-fashion, but even this is insufficient to fortify the GRANNY.

In making a suture, if the gut breaks, leaving only a short end, do not start over again but hold the end firmly and tie KNOT #2005 around it. Then, with the bight of the standing part that is held in one hand, add a HALF HITCH over the end in the manner employed for BUTCHER'S KNOTS (#183). This application of the hitch originated with Dr. Curtis C. Tripp.

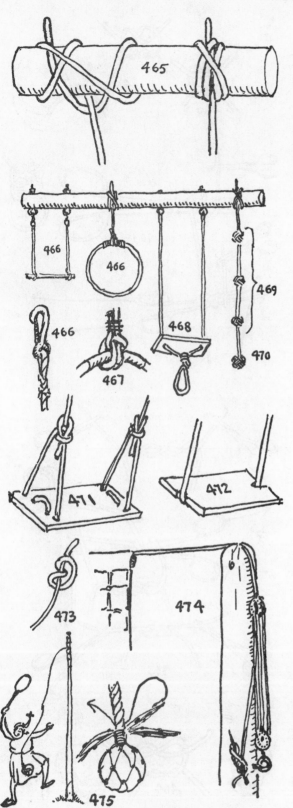

Swings and Swinging

465. To make fast a swing: The accompanying hitch is recommended, as it stays in place and does not chafe against the crossbar or limb.

466. A better method is to splice the ends of rope to snap hooks or sister hooks. These can be easily unhooked from the eye bolts and stored in winter. With this treatment ropes may be made to last several seasons.

467. A large ring such as an old mast hoop should be taped a short distance and the rope made fast with a ROUND TURN AND HALF HITCH (#1718), which should be stoutly seized close to the hitch. A CLOVE HITCH (#1670), well seized, will also serve.

468. Tie a LOOP KNOT (#1046), with the surplus material, under a swing seat. The height may be adjusted by this means, and the loop can be employed as a handgrip when swinging someone else.

An adjustable method of hanging a swing is pictured among the MULTI-STRAND STOPPER KNOTS as #726.

469. A series of STANDING TURK'S-HEADS (#1282) may be tied for handgrips on a climbing rope.

470. A MANROPE KNOT (#847) may be added to finish off the end.

471. A seat that will not teeter. The ends are secured with BOWLINE KNOTS.

472. This shows the ordinary notched swing seat. Other seats are illustrated near the end of Chapter 41.

The Tailor

473. The THUMB KNOT. "This is the simplest [knot] of all and it is used by Taylors [sic] at the end of their thread." (From Emerson's *Principles of Mechanics*, London, 1794.)

The Tennis Player

474. I have found that a tennis net is more easily and nicely adjusted with a small tackle, consisting of small two-shiv galvanized iron blocks and a small braided sash cord, than by any ratchet contrivance. No cleat is required for belaying. The end is hauled under the next running part and jammed against the block, as #1996 or #455. The method of making a tennis net is described as #3795.

The Tetherball Player

475. To make a tetherball, stretch a piece of small-meshed netting tightly over a tennis ball, and butt the rope against the ball. Split the skirts of the net into three ribbons of equal width and length, and splice these tightly into the whipped end of the rope, as in SHORT SPLICE #2635. Parcel with rubber tape and serve the splice tightly over with fishline.

The Theater

A great deal of rope and a trustworthy rigger are required in the theater. Clamps are used for holding sets together, but ropes secured to belaying pins hold them aloft.

Three-Legged Race

476. A HOBBLE KNOT is less complicated than it appears. Two round turns are taken with a strip of sheeting about a gentleman's leg, and then a SQUARE KNOT is added. Next, one round turn is taken with each of the ends around a lady's leg. One left leg and one right leg are tied together in order that the contestants may face in the same direction. Sometimes pads are added to prevent the knots from chafing.

The Trapper

477. There are fourteen folio plates of snares, nets, pitfalls, deadfalls, and traps in Diderot's Encyclopedia. The snare illustrated here is suitable for large game. A strong and resilient branch, longer than is represented in the illustrations, is bent down in a semicircular arch and its end placed against a smooth blazed spot on the trunk of an adjacent tree. The adjustment is very delicate. At the slightest disturbance of the rope the branch slips and straightens, jerking the noose aloft, with the quarry dangling.

A South American lizard trap is illustrated as ✳2061.

The Tree Surgeon

478. There is unsuspected virtue in a few turns of line. A single ROUND TURN on a branch will allow a man to lower several times his own weight. The device is much simpler to manipulate than a tackle but, of course, will not serve for hoisting.

479. The TIMBER HITCH unties readily and is one of the most practical of hitches for slinging cylindrical objects.

480, 481. These are tree surgeon's variations of the MAGNUS HITCH (✳1734). They work on the same principle as the CAMEL HITCH (✳215) and the steeplejack's SAFETY-BELT HITCH (✳452). All five knots may be slid up and down with the hand, but they remain firm under a pull on the standing part.

482. A loop in which the seat (✳472) is slung.

The Upholsterer

483. The TUFT KNOT. A length of strong twine is passed with a long needle first down and then up through a mattress, the two passages being about one eighth inch apart. A short piece of wicking is placed in the loop that is left at the bottom and another between the two ends at the top. Two HALF HITCHES are taken with one end around the other, which is held straight. The latter is then pulled taut and made fast with a HALF HITCH exactly as described for a BUTCHER'S KNOT (✳183). Soft round leather patches are sometimes used instead of tufts. These are notched at either edge.

484. Buttons are generally used on chairs and sofas instead of wicking. A button is threaded on a length of twine, and the two ends, being laid up, are put through the needle's eye together. The needle is next stuck up through the cushion, then one end of the twine only is put through the top button. The end holding the top button is held taut, and Two HALF HITCHES are taken with the free end, which is then hauled taut and locked with a HALF HITCH.

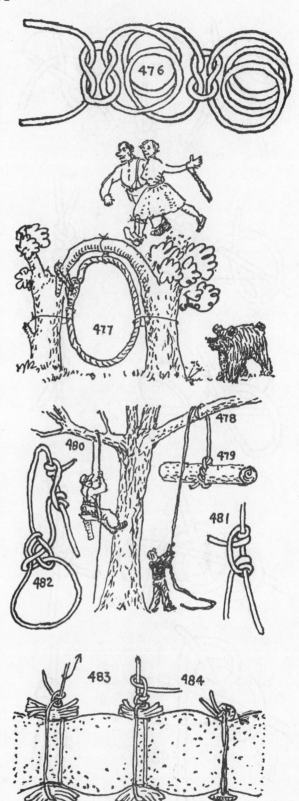

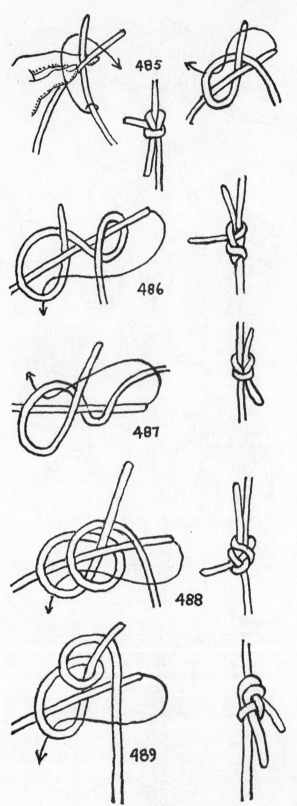

The Weaver

There are many WEAVER'S KNOTS. Some of them are the same in form as other well-known bends, but, being differently tied, they bear other names. The method of tying is the determining factor in the WEAVER'S KNOT, just as another method of tying characterizes the BUTCHER'S KNOT. Practically all WEAVER'S KNOTS are started by holding the crossed ends of two yarns between the thumb and forefinger of the left hand. All that are shown here conform to this rule until we come to ✂496, ✂497, and ✂500, which are used in springy mohair yarn, which requires a more secure knot than other yarns.

There is an astounding number of WEAVER'S KNOTS, a great many poor ones being used, but if a weaver can knot fast enough to turn out the cloth without stopping the loom this will usually escape notice unless his knots are so bulky as to affect the appearance of the finished cloth.

In Irish homespun even OVERHAND BEND ✂1410 is tied. But in this case the material is so rough in texture that the bunch formed by the knot is not sufficiently apparent to be objectionable.

485. The WEAVER'S KNOT shown here is the one usually tied in woolen cloth, and is the knot published in reference books as the "WEAVER'S KNOT." In form it is the same as the SHEET BEND, but it is tied in small material by weavers in a distinctive way that I have seldom seen tied for any other purpose. If a weaver himself tied the same formation in another way, the knot might bear another name.

Hold the ends in the left hand, as shown, and tie the knot with the right hand. Pass a bight around the left end. The right end is then stuck as indicated by the arrow in the right diagram and is held under the left thumb while the knot is pulled snug.

486. The DOUBLE POLISH KNOT was shown to me by Edward T. Pierce.

487. This knot is the same form as the REEF KNOT, but the method of tying is quite different. It was shown to me by Edward T. Pierce. It is hardly a good knot, since the end is apt to catch or snag and break the thread when passing through the reeds.

488. The DOUBLE WEAVER'S KNOT was also furnished by Edward T. Pierce. It is the same knot as the DOUBLE SHEET BEND (✂1434). Frequently it will pull up into the form here illustrated, which is equally secure. When tying these knots, leave the ends somewhat

longer than those shown in the diagrams, as there is generally an initial slip when a knot is drawn taut.

489. Another DOUBLE WEAVER'S KNOT from Edward T. Pierce. The two ends in this knot lead in the same direction, which is an excellent feature, as many threads are broken when the knots snag in passing through the reeds. The end that makes the final tuck should be held for a moment with the left thumb and finger while the knot is drawn up by pulling the two standing parts.

490. The BASTARD WEAVER'S KNOT was shown to me by Eugene Harrington. In form it is identical with the LEFT-HAND SHEET BEND (⌗1432), which probably accounts for its sinister name. As has been elsewhere stated in several different connections, either a different purpose or a different way of tying constitutes a different knot. This form is inferior to the regular RIGHT-HAND SHEET BEND (⌗1431), but the method of tying makes it one of the quickest of knots to form, which is a valuable feature.

491. The DOUBLE BASTARD WEAVER'S KNOT, also provided by Eugene Harrington, has the best lead of any WEAVER'S KNOT to be shown as both ends turn backward.

492. The LEFT-HAND SHEET BEND was supplied by F. Gilbert Hinsdale and is used in commercial lace manufacture. It can be very quickly tied. Although not so secure as the RIGHT-HAND SHEET BEND, unless the thread or yarn is very slippery it is quite adequate. About the two most important requirements of a WEAVER'S KNOT are these: it should pass through the reeds easily, and it should be inconspicuous in the finished cloth.

493. A WEAVER'S KNOT that is used in the manufacture of "banding," which is a small braided rope that is used in cotton manufacture for small drives. It was shown to me by Charles R. Gidley. The ends have an excellent lead.

It is seldom that a WEAVER'S KNOT is peculiar to a certain manufacture; it is more apt to be a characteristic of the individual weaver, and weavers drift from one mill to another. But on the other hand, an individual experienced in one branch of weaving is very apt to confine himself to that branch.

Generally a knot is woven into the cloth soon after it is tied, and in ordinary material a particularly firm knot is seldom required.

But mohair is a very slippery material, and special knots are needed for mohair manufacture.

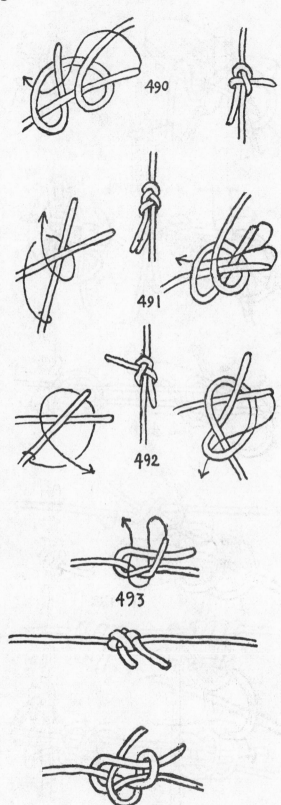

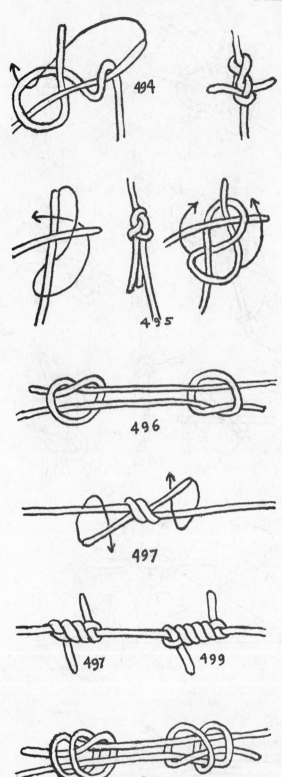

Mohair is the trade name for the wool or hair of the Angora goat, which may on occasion be fully seventeen inches long. The yarn is both slick and springy, in the same way that piano wire is. There is considerable variation in the material, depending on the variety of the goats and the country in which they have been raised. In automobile upholstery the coarsest wool or hair obtainable is required, and none of the customary WEAVER'S KNOTS will serve.

I was asked by the Collins and Aikman Corporation to find a mohair knot that would not untie in modern fast-running machinery. Manufacture had been speeded up to such an extent that several of the old knots which had been adequate in slow-running machinery could no longer be used. There is a jolt and jar to the modern mohair looms that cause the common knots to untie and reuntie, and when bulkier knots were used they snapped while being drawn through the reeds. Sometimes a single break had to be repaired a dozen times before the knot was finally woven into the fabric.

A satisfactory knot was found eventually, and a large proportion of the piled mohair fabric now used in automobile upholstery is tied with it. "One of the three commonest cars," I am told, has used it exclusively for five or more years.

Numbers 494, 495, and 501 are among the knots that were experimented with.

494. A compact knot that was based on the HARNESS BEND ($\#$1474) is shown here. It has a good lead and is more secure than the average bend, but in mohair it slips appreciably before it finally nips.

495. A FIGURE-EIGHT KNOT was tied in one end around the other, and was then spilled to engage the other end. The ends have a good lead, and the knot is tied in an interesting way.

496. The ENGLISH KNOT is an ANGLER'S BEND that is so bulky that it either untied or broke after a few jolts in the loom.

497. The ENGLISH KNOT with hitched ends is less liable to slip, but is more apt to break.

498. The DOUBLE ENGLISH KNOT is shown at the bottom of the page. The ends of both the ENGLISH KNOT and the DOUBLE ENGLISH KNOT have a bad lead, which resulted in many broken threads. Moreover, KNOTS #497–500 are all so bulky that, besides making weaving difficult, they are much too evident in the finished cloth.

499. The DOUBLE ENGLISH KNOT with the ends hitched. This knot is ungainly and was probably not used except experimentally.

500. For years the MOHAIR or QUEENSBURY KNOT has been the standard knot for mohair manufacture. It is tied in a most ingenious way. The two ends are brought together and joined in a HALF KNOT, then they are laid alongside each other and tied in an OVERHAND BEND (#1410) (also called THUMB KNOT). The HALF KNOT (#1212) spills into a HALF HITCH as shown in the right upper diagram and then slides up over the OVERHAND BEND.

It is a bulky knot that has to be woven into the cloth very slowly.

501. An attempt was made to embody the best features of the last knot in more compact form. The knot shown hardly seemed sufficiently secure for mohair and was bothersome to tie. But it draws together nicely in proper form when the two standing parts are pulled on.

502. A MOHAIR KNOT that is strong and symmetrical, besides being handsome and compact. It has too much initial slip and does not pull up inevitably into proper form, an important requirement in a WEAVER'S KNOT. This knot and also KNOTS #496–500 were shown to me by Charles B. Rockwell.

A characteristic WEAVER'S KNOT is started by holding two crossed ends between the thumb and forefinger of the left hand; it is then tied by adding one or two turns and tucking one or both of the ends. Few of the MOHAIR KNOTS, however, conform to these conventions.

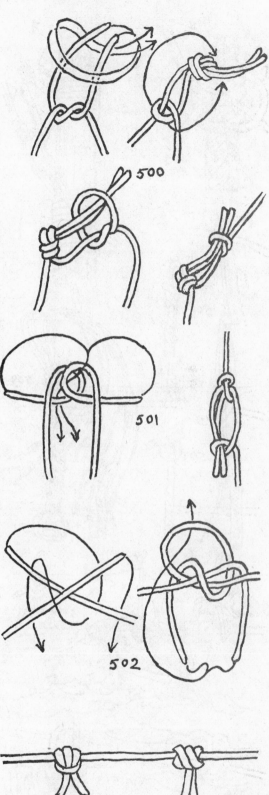

THE ASHLEY BOOK OF KNOTS

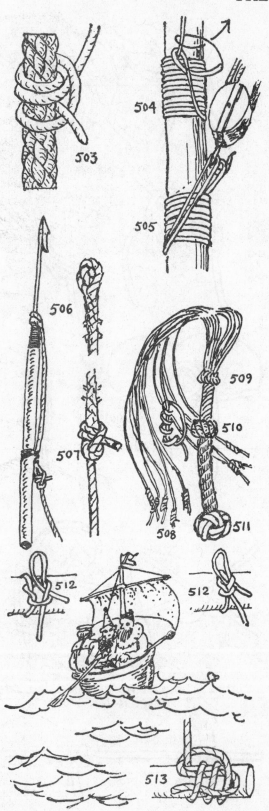

The Well Digger

503. The ROLLING HITCH (⌗1734) is made fast to a drilling cable to support the drill, whenever it is necessary to overhaul the drum end of the cable.

504. A WELL-PIPE HITCH is used to lower a pipe or hoist one.

505. A *sling* is wound around a well pipe in a way similar to the last, and the bights are clapped together and hooked to the block.
A MARINER'S SPLICE (see pages 441 and 442) is indicated when a Manila cable breaks.

The Whaleman

506. The *hitches*. Years ago, when hemp and flax whale line were used, a SEIZED CLOVE HITCH was made fast to a harpoon shank. The name *hitches* is a survival from that time, but in recent years the "*hitches*" consist of a ROUND TURN AND EYE SPLICE.

507. A DOUBLE BECKET HITCH is always employed in bending the line to the EYE SPLICE in the harpoon warp.

The Whipper

508. A DOUBLE OVERHAND KNOT (⌗515) tied in a cat-o'-nine-tails is termed a BLOOD KNOT; it may be double, treble, or even fourfold and is designed to add to the discomforts of whipping. I have never seen an actual BLOOD KNOT. Five old nautical cats, two of them in museums and the remainder in my own collection (see the frontispieces), bear no knots. I have examined a more modern cat that was used in the old jail at Newcastle, Delaware, and another in the Delaware workhouse, and both of these were devoid of knots. A number of museums have bag lanyards erroneously labeled "cats," and some of these have knotted ends. It is not difficult to tell the latter apart, as bag lanyards have an even number of legs and a becket to hang up by, while cats have an odd number of tails, generally nine, and the handles are finished off with KNOB KNOTS instead of eyes.
The *British Mariner's Vocabulary* (1801) says of cat-o'-nine-tails: "Nine cords about half a yard long fixed upon a piece of thick rope for a handle, having three knots on each at small intervals, nearest one end." According to the same authority a "Thieves' Cat" was heavier and the knots harder.

509. A NINE-STRAND SINNET KNOT is described (⌗757) in the chapter on MULTI-STRAND LANYARD KNOTS.

510. A THREE-STRAND MATTHEW WALKER KNOT is described among MULTI-STRAND STOPPER KNOTS as ⌗682.

511. A MANROPE KNOT (⌗847) is described among the MULTI-STRAND BUTTONS.

The Yachtsman

512. The HALF BOWKNOT or DRAWKNOT: Most sailor's knots have been adopted by the yachtsman. This particular knot, however, is peculiar to small pleasure craft; it is used in reefing, furling, and securing sail covers.

513. The TOPSAIL HALYARD BEND (⌗1679) is said to be a British yachtsman's knot. See also page 341.

CHAPTER 3: KNOB KNOTS. SINGLE-STRAND STOPPER OR TERMINAL KNOTS

One knot in a Thread will stay the Needle's Passage as well as five hundred.
R. BOLTON, 1633

The SINGLE-STRAND STOPPER KNOT is the first to be considered of the several varieties of KNOB KNOTS. Generally it is tied as a terminal knot in the end of a rope, where it forms a knob or bunch, the general purpose of which is to prevent unreeving. It is found in the ends of running rigging. It secures the end of a sewing thread; it provides a handhold or a foothold in bell ropes and footropes. It adds weight to the end of a heaving line, and it is often employed decoratively, but it *should not be used to prevent unlaying and fraying* except in small cord, twine, and the like, as a whipping is in every way preferable for large and valuable material. The distinction between the SINGLE-STRAND STOPPER KNOT and the SINGLE-STRAND LANYARD KNOT, which forms the next chapter, is an arbitrary one, and any decorative STOPPER KNOT with a good lead may also serve as a LANYARD KNOT, there being no fundamental structural difference between the two. The way the knot is used has determined its classification, and many of the knots belong equally in both classes. The purpose of the SINGLE-STRAND STOPPER KNOT is almost always a practical one, but the LANYARD KNOT is commonly tied in the central part or bight of a rope, and although it occasionally provides a hand- or foothold, it is more apt to serve a decorative purpose.

One interesting feature of this classification is that the LANYARD KNOT, per se, is pushed from its own nest and relegated to the chapter on MULTI-STRAND STOPPER KNOTS!

In working the following knots a small pricker will prove the most convenient tool.

[83]

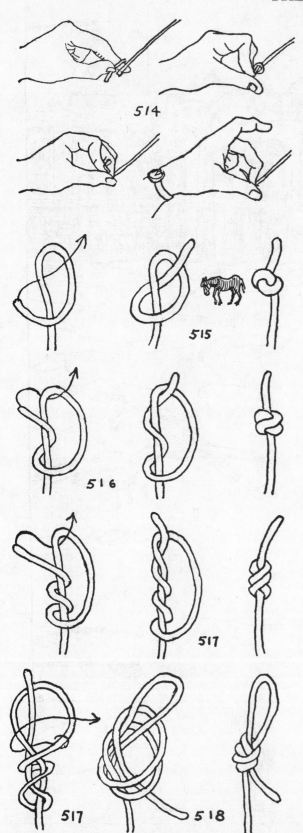

514. The OVERHAND KNOT, also called SIMPLE, SINGLE, THUMB, COMMON, and ORDINARY KNOT, is the simplest of all knot forms and is the point of departure for many of the more elaborate knots. It is quite secure but very weak, reducing the strength of the rope in which it is tied by perhaps as much as fifty per cent. It also jams and is difficult to untie, often injuring the fiber. For these reasons it should be tied only in small material that is not to be employed again, and where there is considerable margin of strength.

The name OVERHAND KNOT appears in Steel's *Elements & Practice of Rigging*, 1794. Formerly the knot was tied in square-sail reef points which, after reeving through eyelet holes in the sail, were knotted closely at either surface. It is the knot universally used in sewing thread and twine, and riggers put it in the ends of spun-yarn seizings.

On jib-boom footropes the OVERHAND KNOT is sometimes tied at regular intervals to prevent feet from slipping, but except for this single purpose it is seldom tied in rope at sea, as the FIGURE-EIGHT KNOT is both stronger and easier to untie.

Ashore the OVERHAND KNOT is frequently employed to prevent raveling and unreeving. Formerly carriage whips were hung up by OVERHAND KNOTS, which were tied in the ends of the fly or snapper.

Its chief merit is its compactness. It is the smallest of all knots, and expends the least material.

515. The name THUMB KNOT is applied particularly when the knot is tied by one hand, as it commonly is in sewing thread and twine. The name with this meaning is given in Emerson's *Mechanics* of 1794. So tied, it may be either a SINGLE or a DOUBLE OVERHAND KNOT. A loose round turn is made about the tip of the forefinger. When the thumb is extended the end rolls through the turn once or twice. The standing part of the thread is then pulled, and the knot is formed under the nail of the second finger. The technique varies, however, with the individual.

516. The DOUBLE OVERHAND KNOT is called a BLOOD KNOT when used on a cat-o'-nine-tails, or on the snapper of an ox whip.

517. A THREEFOLD OVERHAND KNOT, or even a larger one, may be tied, but beyond two turns the knot must be worked into shape, and for that reason it may be considered more decorative than practical. The FRENCH KNOT is a MULTIPLE OVERHAND tied over a needle in embroidery.

If a very large knot of this description is wanted it may be found easier first to tie in the usual way. Then add as many turns as desired by wrapping the loop around the end, as here illustrated.

518. An OVERHAND KNOT, tied in a doubled end, makes a bulky STOPPER KNOT that is sometimes put in the gut strings of a musical instrument. In construction this knot does not differ from LOOP KNOT #1009.

519. The OVERHAND KNOT is repeated here as the basic knot for another series of a different character, the second of this series being the FIGURE-EIGHT KNOT and the fourth the STEVEDORE KNOT.

To make the OVERHAND KNOT: First make a turn and then reeve the end through the turn as pictured.

520. The FIGURE-EIGHT or FIGURE-OF-EIGHT KNOT is also called (in books) the FLEMISH KNOT. The name FIGURE-OF-EIGHT KNOT appears in Lever's *Sheet Anchor; or, a Key to Rigging* (London, 1808). The word *of* nowadays is usually omitted. The knot is the sailor's common SINGLE-STRAND STOPPER KNOT and is tied in the ends of tackle falls and running rigging, unless the latter is fitted with MONKEY'S TAILS. It is used about ship wherever a temporary STOPPER KNOT is required. The FIGURE-EIGHT is much easier to untie than the OVERHAND, it does not have the same tendency to jam and so injure the fiber, and is larger, stronger, and equally secure.

To tie (for this series): Twist the bight pictured in the upper left diagram (#519) a half turn to the left, and stick the end as pictured here in the middle diagram.

521. An INTERMEDIATE KNOT between the FIGURE-EIGHT KNOT and the STEVEDORE KNOT (#522). Take the center diagram of the FIGURE-EIGHT KNOT and give it one additional half twist, then stick the end as pictured. This knot is seldom seen, and when it is tied it is generally by mistake, the intention having been to tie a STEVEDORE KNOT, which follows.

522. The STEVEDORE KNOT prevents the end of a cargo fall from unreeving; the cargo block, having larger shivs than the ordinary tackle aboard ship, requires a bulky knot. The bight is given one more half turn than in the former knot, before the end is finally stuck.

523. DOUBLE FIGURE-EIGHT KNOT. There are several ways of doubling the FIGURE-EIGHT KNOT, this one being perhaps the one most frequently seen. The number of racking turns may be increased as desired. A more symmetrical DOUBLE FIGURE-EIGHT, that is a little more complicated, will be found in the next chapter, on SINGLE-STRAND LANYARD KNOTS.

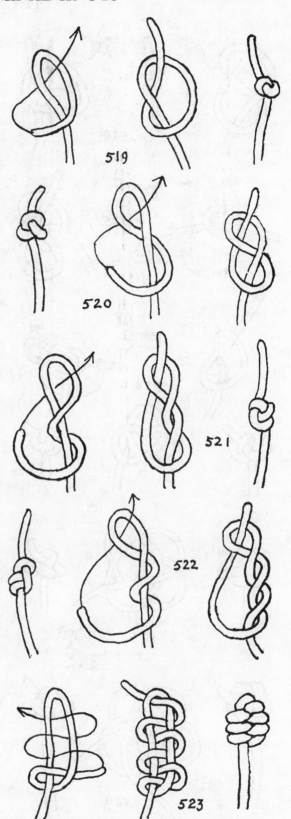

524. The FIGURE-EIGHT KNOT has a single rim part, which passes completely around the neck, and it has another single part at the top which nips the end. The OYSTERMAN'S STOPPER (#526) has three parts around the rim and one part at the top which nips the end. This suggests a knot, between the two, with two rim parts, and with the end nipped by a single top part.

525. The "TWEENIE" comes very near to filling these conditions, having one top part and two rim parts, but the end is nipped by one of the rim parts instead of the center part. It is nonetheless an excellent knot, although the stem is a bit off center. I have not as yet found a knot that precisely fills the gap between #524 and #526, but I do not question there is one to be found. In the search several other knots of interest have turned up, and several of them (#547, #548, and #549) are shown later in the chapter.

526. The OYSTERMAN'S STOPPER. The discovery of this knot is described in Chapter 1, page 7. It is a larger knot than the FIGURE-EIGHT, which has but one part around the stem. The OYSTERMAN'S STOPPER KNOT has three rim parts, and these are quite symmetrical when viewed from the underside. From this view it closely resembles a THREE-STRAND WALL KNOT. The end is nipped by a single top part. It is easy to tie and practical to use when the hole that is to be filled is too large for the FIGURE-EIGHT. Having reached the position of the upper right diagram and the end being rove as indicated by the arrow, the HALF KNOT shown near the end in the diagram must be pulled very snug; next the end is pulled and finally the standing part. Arrange the knot so that it is symmetrical as in the left and right bottom sketches. The center bottom diagram is given merely to show the over-and-under arrangement of the knot on a symmetrical diagram form.

527. The QUATREFOIL: This knot is one of the steps in the series beyond the OYSTERMAN'S STOPPER (#526). It has four rim parts and one center part, which nips the end. To tie: Pin the end along the diagram, tucking underneath where indicated, and work the knot taut with a pricker.

528. The CINQUEFOIL has five rim parts and a single center part and is symmetrical and handsome, but, unless tied very carefully and firmly, it tends to capsize and spill.

529. The SLIP KNOT is closely related to the OVERHAND KNOT, the difference between the two being in the treatment of the end. In the former the end is doubled before it is finally tucked. To untie, all that is required is a smart pull on the end of the rope, which withdraws the loop and causes the knot to spill instantly. A SLIP KNOT may be tied in the bight as readily as in the end, but the load must be on the standing part of the knot only. It is used wherever the necessity to cast off suddenly may arise.

Carpenters tie it in the end of a weighted sash cord before the sash is put in place. It is also used in adjusting a plumb bob.

In chandleries it is tied in the ends of wicks, and after the wax has hardened the knot is untied before removing the candle from the mold.

The SLIP KNOT is given in Moore's *British Mariner's Vocabulary*, 1801. The name has been loosely applied to a number of other unrelated knots.

530. A FIGURE-EIGHT KNOT may be slipped in the same manner as the above. This is about as easy to tie as a SLIP KNOT and is larger and much less prone to jam.

531. A FIGURE-EIGHT KNOT tied in the doubled end makes a strong, bulky knot for a violin string, which may be needed if the hole has been much worn. It is larger than ⌘518, which is also used for the purpose.

The same knot may be tied in the bight of a line, and either or both ends may be pulled, but the pull should not be on both ends unless the two parts have a parallel lead.

532. The HARNESS LOOP. If a stopper is required in the bight of a line where the pull may come from either direction, this knot will serve the purpose satisfactorily.

533. This LOOP KNOT, which is ⌘1055 of Chapter 11, may be used in the same way. It is more secure than the foregoing and is, in consequence, a little harder to untie.

In putting any of the knots in this chapter to work, if the hole is much larger than the rope, the use of a washer is advisable.

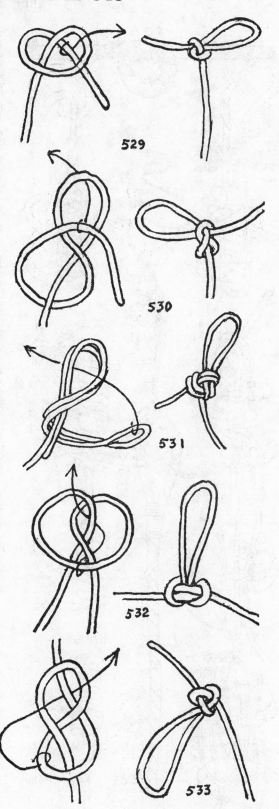

529

530

531

532

533

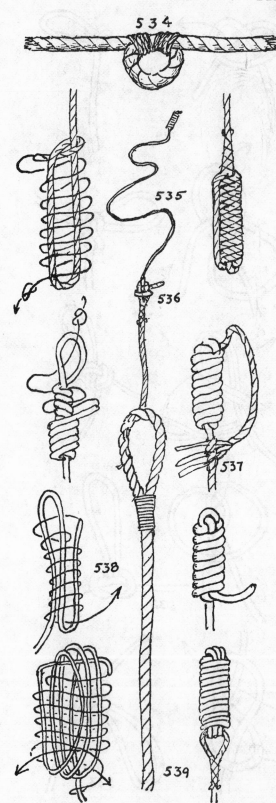

534. The MONKEY'S TAIL is a permanent or semipermanent stopper that is put in the bight as well as the end. It is also called SINGLE THROAT SEIZING, SEIZED ROUND TURN, CLINCH, and PIGTAIL. It is found, about ten feet from the ends, in running rigging. The purpose is to prevent unreeving at the racks or fair-leaders, which are seized in the shrouds seven or eight feet above deck. A small round turn is first taken, and a THROAT SEIZING (#3404), in length about a quarter of the round of the clinch, is put in.

The MONKEY'S TAIL is preferred for the purpose just described because it does less damage to rope than any knot. When the MONKEY'S TAIL fetches against the rack the seizing takes the burden.

535. The NORFOLK-TO-WASHINGTON BOAT HEAVING LINE KNOT. The HEAVING LINE KNOT is the least standardized of all knots. Every ferry boat and excursion steamer has its own version or interpretation. The purpose of the knot is to carry a light line ashore, by means of which hawsers are passed to the wharf. If the hawsers are very long and heavy, occasionally there is an intermediate line to be hauled first, which is larger than the heaving line, but smaller than the hawser.

The knot should be bulky enough to be plainly seen and heavy enough to carry the end of the heaving line well in advance of the coil when it is tossed, but it should not be heavy enough or hard enough to injure the wharf rat who catches it. Many knot tiers "load" their knots with sheet lead, lead foil, tinfoil "marbles," shot, or round stones. But there is a definite sporting limit to the weight that is considered good form.

The sample given here is about the simplest form of the knot. Two layers of sheet lead are wound around the standing part of the rope, and this is covered by the series of turns. The turns are hove taut and the end finished off with an OVERHAND KNOT (#515).

536. The HEAVING LINE LANYARD. The best way to rig a heaving line is with a lanyard. The lanyard should be larger than the heaving line and about four feet long. It is spliced into the bosom of the hawser eye, being tucked whole, three times, over and under (#2831). The other end of the lanyard has an EYE SPLICE to which the heaving line is bent with a BECKET HITCH. If the heaving line is bent directly to the hawser it is difficult to unbend it after the hawser eye is around a pile.

537. The HEAVING LINE KNOT is exposed to excessive wear, and the best practice is to side-splice the end into the neck of the knot (#2826) as the splice will hold the turns in place much better than a knot. The turns are put on as snugly as possible.

538. This particular HEAVING LINE KNOT is based on the well-known HANGMAN'S KNOT, and is perhaps the most common of all. The number of turns taken is optional, depending somewhat on the size of the ship.

539. MARTHA'S VINEYARD BOAT HEAVING LINE KNOT: Start with three round turns. Pass the end around the top turns and under its own part, and wind or round back snugly the full length of the knot. At the bottom, stick the end through the three original turns. Then, to make the knot symmetrical, stick the standing part through the same three turns in the reverse direction. Haul all taut, side-splice the end to the stem, and soak the knot in rigging tar.

540. There are numerous variations of this somewhat slovenly but very bulky HEAVING LINE KNOT which has a small coil for its base. Make the coil of three turns, and knot as shown in the first illustration. Round down snugly to the end of the coil, and stick the end as illustrated. Draw taut as possible with a marlingspike, and finally side-splice the end to the stem. Weight with sheet lead if desired.

541. An OVER-AND-UNDER HEAVING LINE KNOT. Make an S turn in the rope, and tuck the end of the rope through the bight at the bottom of the standing part. Lead the end to the right, alternately over and under the three parts of the S, until sufficient length has been made. When the number of "over" parts is a multiple of three, work the knot snug and splice the end to the standing part.

542. The MONKEY'S FIST. This has always been the standard HEAVING LINE KNOT of the square-rigger. Apparently it was first pictured by E. N. Little in *Log Book Notes* (1889). It was described by Dr. Cyrus L. Day in 1935. Take a piece of fifteen-thread stuff for the heaving line. Hold the working end with the thumb in the palm of the left hand, and with fingers separated a little, make two round turns about the hand and lay the working end back between the tips of the second and third fingers. Reeve the end to the front again, between the roots of the second and third fingers, and make two frapping turns around the original turns (the second one above the first). Remove the structure from the hand, and put on the final two turns as shown in the first and third diagrams. Tied in the way described, this knot may be worked into a compact ball, but it usually has a core, being tied around a ball of tea lead, a round beach pebble, or one of the cook's dumplings. If loaded in this way, three or even four turns are taken for each cycle, instead of the two turns described. In completing the knot the end is side-spliced to the standing part one foot from the knot, after which two seizings are put on, one at the end of the splice, the other at the neck of the knot. For additional discussion of the MONKEY'S FIST consult Chapter 29.

543. The DOUGHNUT, and KNOT #541, are my contribution to this series of knots. The DOUGHNUT was first published in *Sea Stories Magazine* in 1925. If desired, a narrow ribbon or tape of sheet lead may be served around the original coil of three or six turns before adding the service turns. In small material and without the sheet lead, the knot will serve a useful purpose about the house on the ends of jury shade cords and preventer electric-light pulls.

To tie, make a small coil of three or six round turns, which may be covered for convenience with adhesive tape. Then serve snugly as shown. Pack the turns tightly together, and haul them taut. Tuck the end as shown, and side-splice it to the stem.

544. The MAURETANIA KNOT is a loaded TURK'S-HEAD. A THREE-BIGHT, FOUR-PART TURK'S-HEAD is tied as in #1311. The knot should be doubled or tripled, and a large marble or small stone inserted, before working taut. Splice the end to the standing part one foot from the knot, and seize twice as already described for #542.

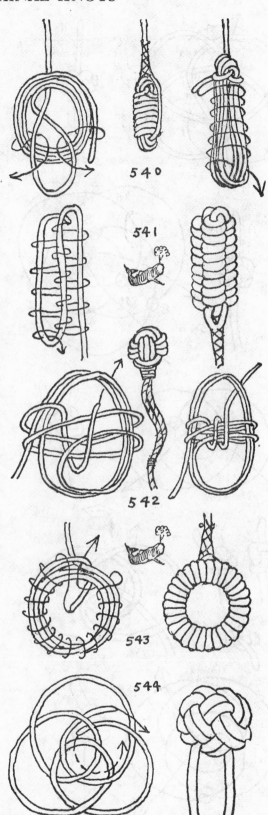

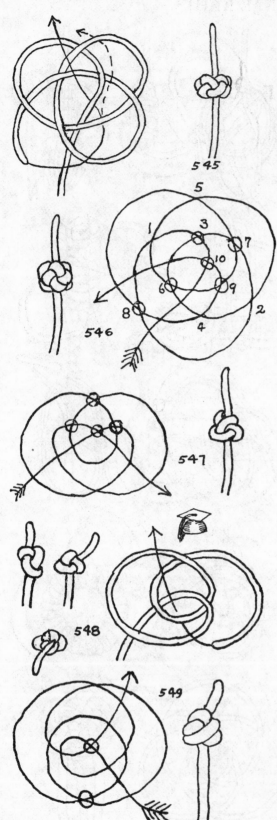

545. The smaller TURK'S-HEADS, with a little adaptation, may be converted into STOPPER KNOTS, and, since the lead is correct at both end and standing part, they also make handsome LANYARD KNOTS appropriate for the next chapter. TURK'S-HEADS are very decorative and, if well worked, are quite practical, when anything so large is needed. This one is based on the FOUR-BIGHT, THREE-LEAD TURK'S-HEAD described as ✳1305 in Chapter 17. The ends are arranged as pictured. These TURK'S-HEAD KNOTS are found on Chinese lantern cords, and they are sometimes used as TERMINAL KNOTS on dress and hat trimmings. They may be doubled if wished, in which case follow the lead of the dotted line for the second circuit, and finish off as the solid line.

546. The THREE-BIGHT, FOUR-LEAD TURK'S-HEAD (✳1311) may be utilized in the same way. The method of tying a knot over a diagram of this sort is described more fully as ✳128 in Chapter 1. Lay the diagram over a cork board, or else over an upholstered chair seat. Pin the cord at frequent intervals along the diagram, tucking the working end underneath a part encountered at any point that is *marked with a circle.* Use a pricker and work the knot tight, taking care not to distort it at any time.

547. The next few knots are the ones mentioned on page 86. They were by-products of the series given on that page, but are no less interesting than those already shown. Although made with only one cord, this knot resembles superficially a TWO-STRAND DIAMOND KNOT of two bights.

548. The stem of the accompanying knot is rimmed by two symmetrical parts, and the end is nipped by a single top part, but there are two top parts instead of one, which bars the knot from the previous series.

549. The knot alongside conforms to all the arbitrary conditions that were listed on page 86. But each of the two rim parts encircles the neck *a complete turn,* after the manner of the MATTHEW WALKER, so that its appearance denies relationship to the rest of the series. Although a good knot, it requires considerable working and is too elaborate to be considered a practical one.

550. All the conditions referred to are fulfilled in this example. There are two rim parts and only one top part; the end is nipped under the top part; and the knot is pleasing. But it easily distorts unless it is doubled. If, however, it is doubled, it is distinctive and handsome and not too difficult to tie. Half of the knot pictured in the diagram is merely the second parallel circuit.

551. Although the knot pictured here appears very simple after those that have just been considered, if it is not tied very carefully it tends to capsize into one of several forms; but once it is tied properly and drawn up carefully it will hold its shape. First make an OVERHAND KNOT, then lead the end as shown by the arrow, which will form another overhand through the first one. Draw up both ends at the same time, pulling slowly with both hands, and working the knot wherever it is necessary.

552. The DOUBLE OYSTERMAN'S KNOT. This is an outgrowth of the OYSTERMAN'S STOPPER KNOT (＃526) and it has a completely doubled rim of three leads while the top center part still remains single.

553. This knot is closely related to the last one. Superficially, the only difference is that the center part is double, where in the former it was single. For this reason perhaps it is more truly a DOUBLE OYSTERMAN'S KNOT than the last.

554. A decorative TERMINAL KNOT that is both individual and handsome.

The knots on this, and the preceding page, although they will serve nicely as practical knots after having once been made, are too elaborate to be tied unless they are to remain as fixtures.

Some of the illustrations on the next page might be called STOPPER KNOT substitutes, or perhaps they might better be called MECHANICAL STOPPERS.

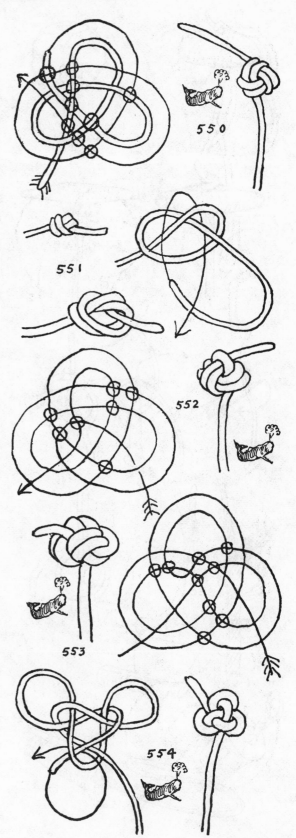

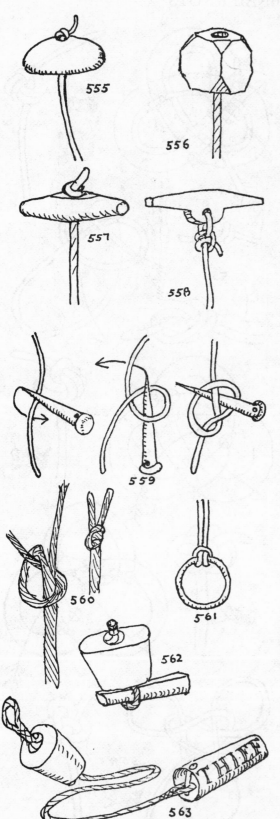

555. *Button molds* and *buttons* have for years been used by boys on their top strings. At sea in the time of Lever, 1808, a rope was rove through the pinhole of a block shiv and was used to haul on cables and hawsers, one or two HALF HITCHES being taken around the rope. This practice is illustrated among hitches for lengthwise pull (⚹1772).

556. Ashore, a *bead* or *button* is often found on the end of an electric-light pull. On catboats and other small open boats, the same thing, but larger, is to be found on the end of the centerboard pendant. In the latter case, a knot is countersunk into a wooden knob.

557. A *small hickory toggle*, inserted in the bunghole, is employed at sea when hoisting empty casks.

558. An *iron* one is used in hoisting water, gas, and oil tanks, where the large size of the manhole makes a wooden one impractical.

559. The MARLINGSPIKE HITCH is tied in the manner shown here, and makes an excellent temporary stopper.

560. The smallest practical STOPPER KNOT is made by taking one or more threads, yarns, or strands from the end of a piece of cordage and tying with it a SINGLE MARLINE HITCH around the rest of the end, just as one strand of a DOUBLE MATTHEW WALKER KNOT is led.

561. An *iron ring* makes a practical stopper. It will prevent unreeving and, if wished, it can be secured by dropping it over any projection such as a nail or peg. It is easily put in the bight of a rope by first reeving the bight through the ring and then reeving the ring through the bight, which forms a RING or BALE SLING HITCH (⚹1859). It is the common stopper for a window-shade cord.

562. *Hawse block* or *plug*. The hawse pipes or holes are usually stoppered at sea to prevent water coming inboard, particularly on a vessel that is not equipped with a "manger" with which to catch the water at the bows as it runs in and to hold it until the lift of the ship allows it to run out again. The block has a SPRITSAIL SHEET KNOT on the outside, and a short piece of rope is doubled to form an eye on the inside. The block having been driven into the pipe with a mallet from the outside, a wedge or fid is driven through the eye on the inside, which holds the contrivance secure. Similar plugs are used with scuppers that are not provided with flaps to keep the water out. These have lanyards attached to the outsides, by which the plugs are recovered when driven out.

563. No scuttle butt was to be found on a whaler. Water was bailed out of a large cask through the bunghole with an attenuated tin pail called a "thief," which held little over a cupful. The object of this was to husband water. The cask was lashed, bung up, to the ship's lash rail. The "thief" remained inside the cask and was attached to the bung by a lanyard and knot. There was also a cup to drink from. When water was scarce the cup was kept at the masthead, and any man who wanted water badly enough could go aloft and get it. When he was through, he had to take the cup aloft again. He was not allowed to pass it to another; each man had to make his own trip, or else go thirsty.

[92]

CHAPTER 4: KNOB KNOTS. SINGLE-STRAND LANYARD KNOTS

Jib Horses are knotted with an OVERHAND KNOT *at the distance of every Yard.*   DAVID STEEL: *Seamanship and Rigging*, 1794

There was, once upon a time, a sailor who had a sweetheart. The girl was beautiful, and the sailor was handsome—so the girl thought. But her father disliked all sailors, this one in particular, which may have been because he had another husband already picked out for her, a certain haberdasher's clerk, who had really very little to recommend him save that he managed to keep both feet on solid earth most of the time. That, as everybody knows, is too much to expect of a sailor.

But the girl found the haberdasher's clerk even less prepossessing than her father found our hero.

When the father saw which way the wind was blowing he pleaded with the girl, then he threatened and even stormed for a bit; but it was to no avail, and the ship of True Love was practically on the rocks.

But after a while the storm quieted down, as storms will. Although the father remained obdurate, which means stubborn, the girl too was stubborn, which means that she was her father's daughter.

But the haberdasher's clerk, although almost entirely devoid of charm, was endowed with a certain native cleverness, and it was not long before he thought of a plan which he communicated to the father. Thereupon the father appeared to relent, and soon after he suggested to his daughter that the selection of a husband should be decided in fair competition.

Amid general rejoicing it was agreed that the suitor who could tie the greater number of knots, while the father counted fifty, should marry the girl.

Now the father had argued to himself in somewhat this fashion: "Surely this haberdasher's clerk who does little from morning till night, save knot ribbons and tie up parcels, should have no trouble in besting this tarry-fingered son of a sea cook." But the girl needed no one to tell *her* that her Jack would win, by a long sea mile.

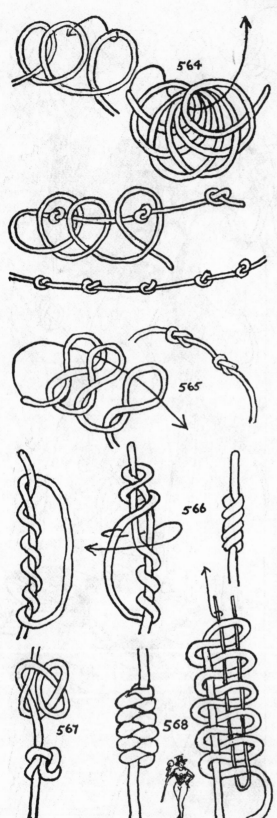

On the appointed day and hour the father commenced his count, and with nimble fingers the haberdasher's clerk tied OVERHAND KNOT after OVERHAND KNOT, with such celerity and precision that a doubt arose in the minds of the spectators whether his piece of string would be long enough to last the full count of fifty.

In the meantime our hero, with apparent unconcern, and so deliberately that it was maddening to watch, proceeded to cast one hitch after another over his left thumb. "Forty-two, forty-three, forty-four," counted the father; the race was practically over without a single knot having been chalked up to the credit of Neptune. The father was jubilant and had his blessing all ready. The poor girl was in tears, the haberdasher's clerk appeared even smugger than he had been before, but Jack remained calm as calm should be. "Forty-five, forty-six"—the hitches completely covered his thumb. "Forty-seven!" Our hero carefully tucked the lower end of his string up through the center of the tier of hitches (which he had by now shifted from his thumb). "Forty-eight! Forty-nine!" He pulled the end through *handsomely!* (See Glossary for definition of *handsomely.*) "FIFTY!" There on his string blossomed a hundred little flowerlike knots, all neatly spaced and exactly alike!

The race was won; the haberdasher's clerk was ignominiously defeated. There was nothing left for him to do but slink back to his shop and hide behind the counter; and there, so far as we know, he lurks to this day with his bit of string in one hand and his yardstick under his arm.

This bit of spun yarn, as you have guessed, is a fragment of the folklore of the sea. The FIRE-ESCAPE KNOT, on which it so happily hinges, belongs to the family of SINGLE-STRAND LANYARD KNOTS and is the first to be described in the present chapter. If there are any who would like to emulate our hero's feat they may quickly learn to do so (so far as the mere tying of knots is concerned) by carefully following directions to be found here and also later in Chapter 33.

A sailor has little opportunity at sea to replace an article that is lost overboard, so knotted lanyards are attached to everything movable that is carried aloft: marlingspikes and fids, paint cans and slush buckets, pencils, eyeglasses, hats, snuffboxes, jackknives, tobacco and money pouches, amulets, bosuns' whistles, watches, binoculars, pipes and keys, are all made fast around the neck, shoulder, or wrist, or else are attached to a buttonhole, belt, or suspender.

There is one physical characteristic required of a decorative LANYARD KNOT that is not required of a STOPPER KNOT. To be symmetrical the rope must enter and leave at opposite ends of the knot.

564. The FIRE-ESCAPE or PHILADELPHIA KNOT is tied at sea in jibboom footropes. A series of SINGLE HITCHES is first built up, one on top of another, each succeeding hitch being slightly larger than the previous one. Then the lower end of the rope is rove up through the center of all the hitches and is pulled out, one hitch at a time. This forms a series or chain of SINGLE OVERHAND KNOTS which is of assistance in lowering oneself hand over hand. Country and seaside hotel fire escapes are often so equipped.

565. A *chain* of FIGURE-EIGHT KNOTS is tied in a similar manner.

566. A MULTIPLE OVERHAND KNOT may be tied with any number of tucks. Small knots may be drawn up by pulling on the two ends, but larger ones must be worked.

Take the large bight at the right side of the left diagram and, beginning at the top, wind it downward to the left; this exhausts the original turns and replaces them with a series of left-hand turns that will all appear on the surface.

567. A BEAD KNOT. A while ago my daughter Phoebe, then aged seven, brought me this knot, which she had discovered for herself. It consists of a RIGHT HALF KNOT superimposed over the bight side of a RIGHT OVERHAND KNOT.

568. A MULTIPLE FIGURE-EIGHT KNOT is made by winding a series of turns around the standing part and then pulling the end up through these turns with a wire loop, after they have been arranged as shown in the right diagram.

569, 570. The basic knots for *twist braid* (or plat) are the OVERHAND KNOT (♯569) and the FIGURE-EIGHT KNOT (♯570). By giving the loop at the bottom an extra half twist and tucking the end once, the two plats may be lengthened. Each additional half twist and tuck adds a total of three bights to the two sides of the knot.

571. With an OVERHAND KNOT as a base, to tie a DOUBLE-TWIST BRAID KNOT: Plat alternately over and under, disentangling the working end from time to time until the lower end is again on the right side. To double this knot, withdraw the end from the last tuck and lead it to the right over one, as in the center diagram, then to the left under two and over one, and to the right under two and over one, which brings the end to the right top. Pass the end to the left under the upper end. Then tuck downward over two and under two alternately to the bottom.

572. With a FIGURE-EIGHT KNOT for a base, to tie a DOUBLE-TWIST BRAID KNOT, any section of which is the same as FIVE-STRAND FLAT SINNET: Make a SINGLE-TWIST BRAID KNOT with the lower end on the left side as in ♯569 and ♯570. Then tuck as shown by the single line in the diagram, upward under one and over two until the left top is reached. Cross underneath the whole structure to the right, then tuck downward as shown, over two and under two, to the bottom. The finished knot is the same as ♯573 (right diagram), except that it has nine bights on each side. The two knots just given may be lengthened further if wished.

573. A direct method of tying a FIVE-LEAD, FLAT-SINNET, TERMINAL KNOT in which the ends are diagonally opposite each other: Arrange the cord as in the left diagram and proceed to plat or braid. Bring the outside left strand over two strands to the center, then bring the outside right strand over two parts to the center. A knot is completed every time the end is brought over two strands, from the right to the left and tucked down at the center.

574. A direct method of tying a FIVE-LEAD, FLAT-SINNET, TERMINAL KNOT in which the two ends are on the same side of the knot: Arrange the cord as in the left diagram, and plat as directed for the last knot. A knot is completed every time the working end is brought over two strands, from the left to the right, and tucked down at the center.

575. It will be noted by consulting the five diagrams at the top of this page that the center one is an "impossible" one. The present knot tied by another method shows how that knot would appear if it were possible to tie it.

576. A FLAT LANYARD KNOT based on FIVE-STRAND FRENCH SINNET. Make a CLOVE HITCH, and arrange the strands as in the left diagram. Plat as FRENCH SINNET, employing the two loops and lower end only. A knot is completed each time the end strand has made a diagonal crossing to either side.

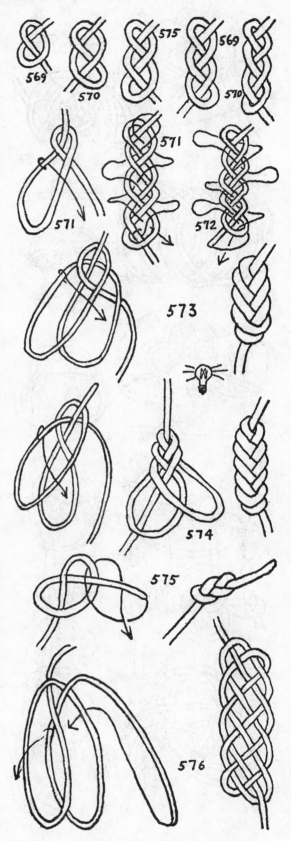

[95]

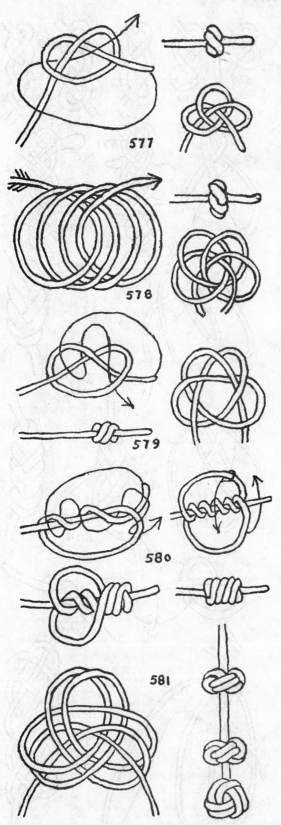

577

578

579

580

581

577. A THREE-PLY KNOT superficially resembles the MATTHEW WALKER KNOT after it has been drawn up evenly and tautly.

578. A FOUR-PLY KNOT superficially resembles the LANYARD KNOT. Tie with small right turns, and bring the working end at the conclusion of each turn up through all previous turns. Work out surplus material methodically.

579. A DOUBLE THREE-PLY KNOT superficially resembles a TWO-STRAND MATTHEW WALKER KNOT. Tie a RIGHT OVERHAND KNOT, and tuck as indicated by the arrow. The surplus cord from the inner turns must be worked out of the knot gradually and firmly before the ends are pulled on.

580. A LONG THREE-PLY KNOT is not so difficult to tie as might appear. Make a DOUBLE RIGHT OVERHAND KNOT, and tuck it as shown in the first diagram. Work it fairly snug so that it resembles the upper right diagram. Next wind the two bights from the right end to the left end as illustrated in the second and third diagrams. The surplus material must now be worked out from "end to end" until the knot resembles the final diagram.

581. A knot which superficially resembles a DOUBLE WALL KNOT requires considerable gentling before it takes its final shape, undistorted and perfectly symmetrical. The knot follows the general diagram of the THREE-PLY KNOT (#577). In one place the lead is deflected so that the ends may come out opposite each other to form a LANYARD KNOT. When the knot is completed, the ends are half knotted (as shown) before they are brought to the surface. When well drawn up the knot is both handsome and firm. It would make a practical STOPPER KNOT, but is somewhat overelaborate.

There are several knots among the MONKEY'S FISTS of Chapter 29 that will serve as SINGLE-CORD LANYARD KNOTS and are quite distinctive. It will be found possible to lead the two ends of a MONKEY'S FIST from the interior of the knot in such a way that they will be opposite each other when they appear on the surface.

In Peru, the ancient Incas used OVERHAND and MULTIPLE OVERHAND KNOTS in their account records, termed *quipus*. A series of lanyards depended from a ground line, and a chain or series of OVERHAND KNOTS was tied in each lanyard. It is presumed that each turn in a knot signified one digit and that the position of a knot on the cord decided its decimal value. The FIGURE-EIGHT KNOT also appears in these records.

582. A simple LANYARD KNOT based on the FIGURE-EIGHT makes a nice little knot for decorating a black silk eyeglass cord, and, besides acting as decoration, the series of knots will serve the purpose of preventing the cord's slipping through the fingers. The remaining knots on this page are original.

583. A symmetrical and somewhat larger knot, that will serve a similar purpose, draws up easily and inevitably. Knots of this description do not have to be crowded closely together, like beads on a lanyard, in order to present a decorative effect. A space between them equal to three or more times the length of the knot is not too great.

When tying, start with a NOOSE and after drawing that up quite snugly reeve the end through it as pictured. Keep in mind that there are two ways of tying the NOOSE, left and right, and whichever you start with continue to use unless you have a reason for alternating the knots, which does not appear necessary in this case. Tie the knot tightly, using a steel bodkin or stiletto for a tool.

584. The knots immediately to follow on this page resulted from an attempt to reproduce the appearance of the CHINESE CROWN KNOT (#808) while employing only one strand. This particular knot requires considerable prodding. But after working and tightening with the bodkin it will gradually assume the desired shape shown at the left and right. It tends to distort under pull. An interesting feature of the knot is that its basic construction is identical with #575 of this chapter. It is worked differently in the two cases, and must be completely loosened before it can be perverted into the other form.

585. A knot was finally produced that holds its shape under pull and has the crown on one of its faces, but the remaining faces are not particularly decorative.

586. A ONE-CORD KNOT, in form similar to the small TWO-STRAND BUTTERFLY, is easily produced. It has the crowned shape at the center with the addition of two close bights at the right and left. The bights may be extended if wished, but the knot will be insecure.

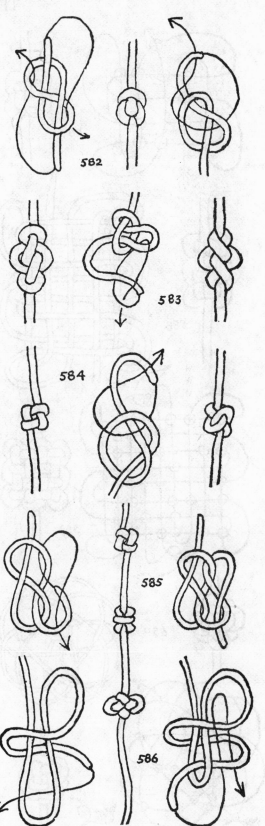

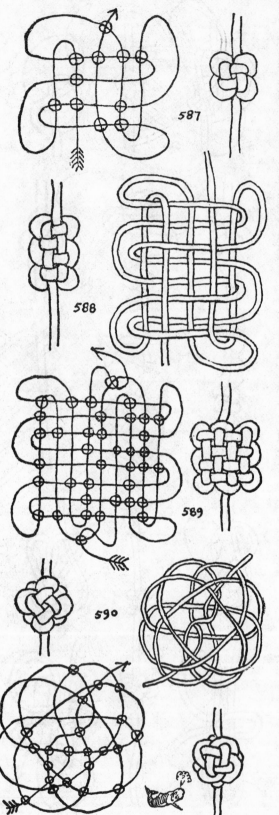

587. A Two-Plane Knot, with a crown center and four marginal loops tied in a single cord. The next three knots resemble the Chinese Butterfly Knot of Chapter 31, but the true Butterfly Knots require two cords. These are tied by a method already described in Chapter 1 (#128) and more fully discussed in the next chapter. The upper left diagram should be carefully copied about twice the present size, and the paper laid out on a cork board with pins or tacks placed where small crosses are marked. One end of the cord (preferably banding) should be attached to a pin at the feather end of the arrow and the cord led around the diagram line, rounding each pin in proper turn. Whenever another part of the cord is encountered at a point that is marked with a circle, the working end is *tucked underneath* the part encountered; at all other points the end is led *over*.

The knots of this and the following page must be drawn up very gradually. Tying the first three knots shown on this page may be facilitated if the two outer lines of the four sides of the diagram are tightened in pairs, the upper pair being worked to the left away from the looped end, the left pair next, and so on around the knot, in the same manner. It will be noted that the knot will resolve itself into two planes of similar aspect. When it has been drawn fairly snug there will be a large loop at each corner. These loops may be gradually worked out so the knot will resemble the final drawing at the right, or they may be left prominent as in the Chinese Knots of Chapter 31. Work the knot from end to end, each time in a direction the reverse of the last. Remove the surplus cord gradually, without distorting the knot at any time.

588. A Rectangular Knot is worked exactly as described for the last, except that there are four additional horizontal lines across the center. These should be tightened in pairs in regular order.

589. Except that this knot is larger, it presents no new problem. The final drawing at the right is the back side of the working diagram at the left. For the sake of a better lead the ends have been given an additional tuck, through one of the rim bights, which is not present in the previous two knots.

590. A circular diagram gives a knot of somewhat different aspect on the two faces. The forms are really the same, but on one side the crosslines are vertical and horizontal, while on the other side they are diagonal. Tie or project the knot as directed for the others, but draw up one part only at a time, as this knot does not lend itself to working two opposite parts together.

591. A PENTAGON IN TWO PLANES. The surface, instead of presenting a regular over-one-and-under-one texture, is tied over two and under two. The method by which this knot is formed is similar to CHAIN KNOT #34, which is tied in a straight line, but this is tied in a circle.

Beginning at the base, lay a loop in the end of your cord upward to the right, and thrust a similar loop at half length through the first one, from the right upward to the left. Thrust a similar loop horizontally from the right to the left through both of the others. Reeve the (single) end through the last two loops laid down, lead it round the neck of the first-laid loop (from bottom to top) and back parallel with its own part to the outside of the knot. Lead the single end through the two last-laid loops then over the two first-laid loops. Thrust the working end down, and lead back under the two first-laid loops and then through the two last-laid loops, parallel with its own part, to the outside again. Finally tuck the end through the knot as indicated by the arrow, and then work the knot taut.

592. A RECTANGULAR TWO-PLANE LANYARD KNOT of one strand. This is a practical knot which at first presented many difficulties. All elaborate knots of this and other sorts were first projected with pencil and paper, or else on a slate, before they could ever be committed to cord.

Tie the knot by the method given at the top of page 98 and draw up carefully and gradually.

593. This knot, tied by the same method, makes a CIRCLE IN TWO PLANES. In general, it may be said that the larger the knot the greater the care that must be taken in drawing it up. But this is not always so. Some knots have to be forced the whole way; others, apparently of their own volition, take their proper form almost inevitably.

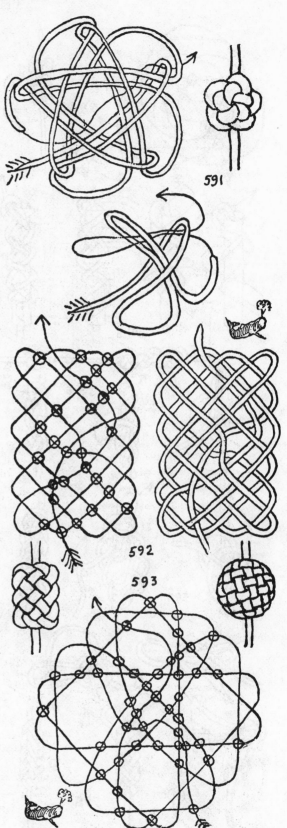

591

592

593

594. A THREE-BIGHT TURK'S-HEAD of any width may serve as a LANYARD KNOT. The cord ends emerge at opposite ends of the knot and cross each other as pictured. One end is led over the other and is then rove through the center to the bottom of the knot; the other end is brought out to the surface from under two parts.

The knot is shown here tied by the method elaborated upon in the two previous pages, but several ways of tying a THREE-BIGHT TURK'S-HEAD are given in Chapter 17, which may be found more expeditious.

595. A TWO-BIGHT TURK'S-HEAD LANYARD KNOT with an odd number of leads. Take a soda-fountain straw, or make yourself a small tube of a tight roll of paper by pasting the edges down. Stick one end of the cord through the tube. Take the long end that is left outside, and wind it in a helix downward at a 45-degree angle, to the right as pictured. When the desired length is reached wind it upward to the right at an equal and opposite angle, *all crossings being over*. Having crossed the first diagonal near the upper rim of the tube, lead the cord downward again in a third diagonal (being careful not to cross the parallel cord); all crossings up to this point are over. Now turn up at the bottom to make a fourth diagonal, but this time tuck *under* the first opposing diagonal, over the second, and so alternately to the top, where the last tuck will be under the part that was first turned down. A section of this is FOUR-STRAND ROUND (or SQUARE) SINNET (#2994), with one strand acting as a core.

596. MONKEY CHAIN LANYARD KNOT (#2868). This is the chain stitch of crochet and is often seen on window-shade pulls. Follow the diagrams, work the knot taut, and when long enough reeve the end as in the second diagram, instead of a loop, for the final tuck.

597. A TRUMPET CORD or DOUBLE MONKEY CHAIN LANYARD KNOT. Start this carefully by laying out the end as in the first diagram. Thereafter a series of loops are thrust each one through the *two* previous loops. When the knot is long enough the end is rove instead of a loop. TRUMPET CORD is also shown elsewhere as #2871.

598. A SQUARE LOOP SINNET LANYARD KNOT. Make a NOOSE KNOT as in the left upper diagram, and reeve a short bight through it as shown by the arrow in the first diagram. Reeve another short bight as shown in the second diagram, and then draw up the standing end snugly as in the third diagram. Lead the working end around in a right circle, tucking a short bight down through each loop in turn and tightening the loop as soon as a bight has been thrust through it by pulling the material into the opposite loop. Keep the sinnet snug as you progress. When the knot is long enough reeve an end instead of a loop twice in succession (through one loop from each side). Work the two ends fair, and they will be found identical.

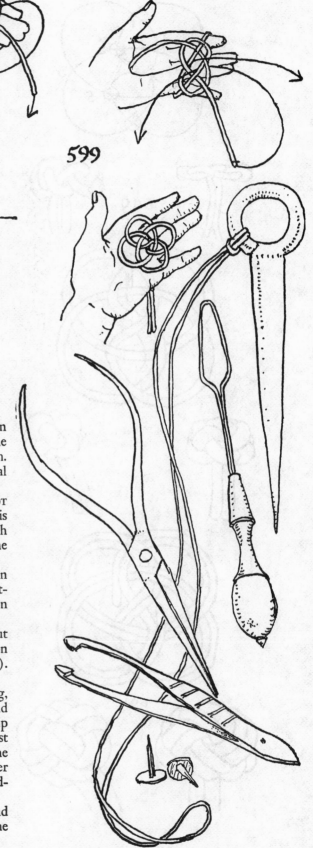

599

CHAPTER 5: KNOB KNOTS. SINGLE-STRAND BUTTON KNOTS

Pray you, undo this BUTTON . . .

WILLIAM SHAKESPEARE

The SINGLE-STRAND BUTTON is a third type of KNOB KNOT, in which the working end leaves the knot at the neck, parallel with the standing part, so that the two parts, or ends, together form a stem. The lay of the two ends is the same, and the knot is symmetrical throughout.

There is but one symmetrical CHINESE BUTTON or PAJAMA KNOT (₦599). There is another, larger CHINESE BUTTON (₦604), but it is not symmetrical, the two ends being off center and not parallel with each other. The first of these is the prototype for the knots of the present chapter.

599. The CHINESE BUTTON KNOT is worn throughout China on underwear and night clothes. Buttons of this sort are more comfortable to lie on and to rest against than common bone and composition buttons, and they cannot be broken even by the laundry.

A Chinese tailor ties the knot without guide, flat on his table. But one may be more quickly and easily tied in hand by a modification of the sailor's method of tying his KNIFE LANYARD KNOT (₦787). The two knots are tied alike, but they are worked differently.

To tie the button: Take a piece of banding about three feet long, middle it, and lay it across the left hand as pictured. Take the end from the back of the hand and make a right turn around the tip of the left thumb. Bend the left thumb and hold the turn against the standing part of the cord. Take the left end and tuck it to the right, under the first end and then to the left under the upper center part of the knot. The knot should now have a regular over-one-and-under-one sequence throughout.

Still keeping the knot in hand, tuck both ends under the rim and up through the center compartment of the knot as pictured in the third diagram.

[101]

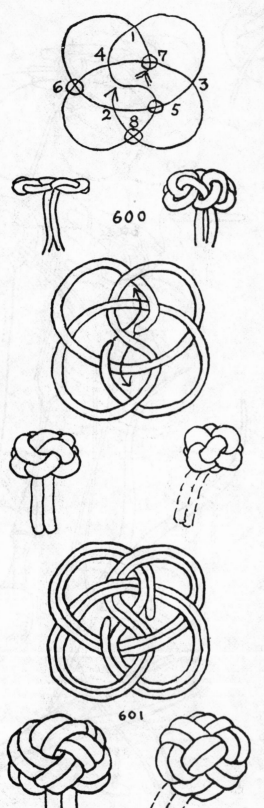

600

601

Remove the knot from the hand, turn it completely over, and allow the two ends to hang down between the two middle fingers of the left hand as drawn in the fifth diagram. Work out the surplus material of the loop without distorting the knot and arrange it to coincide with the large diagram of KNOT ⅍600.

In making KNOT ⅍602 by the KNIFE LANYARD method, the final tuck is rove differently, as shown in the diagram.

There is a certain knack to be acquired in working these knots, but with a little perseverance there should be no real difficulty. My daughter Phoebe, at the age of six, without assistance, made a set of four of these buttons for my painting coat, and after four years I am still wearing them.

There are several other well-known knots that are occasionally employed as buttons, among them the MONKEY'S FIST (⅍542) and the smaller TURK'S-HEADS of Chapter 17. The latter, tied in leather over molds, are commonly found on sport coats.

There is a close resemblance in diagram form between the THREE-LEAD, FOUR-BIGHT TURK'S-HEAD and the CHINESE BUTTON. This resemblance is particularly evident in ⅍601.

I found that by altering the lines of two opposite sides of the center or end compartment, so that they cross each other at the center, any FOUR-BIGHT TURK'S-HEAD diagram can be utilized for tying a BUTTON KNOT. With slight modification the THREE-BIGHT TURK'S-HEADS can also be adapted. But a FIVE-BIGHT TURK'S-HEAD is too large and a TWO-BIGHT TURK'S-HEAD too small at the center to be wholly practical.

TURK'S-HEADS of more than five leads are too wide to make satisfactory pellet-shaped knots, but they lend themselves to vertical "cattail" forms.

Some of the first BUTTON, as well as the first MONKEY'S FIST, diagrams to be experimented with were drawn with soft lead pencil on tennis balls, but the method was unhandy. I tried projecting them on a slate, with three- and four-sided planes, and the method proved more practical.

Eventually I found that any symmetrical design that was made with a single line that crossed itself but once at any point, forming planes of three and four sides only, and that had a crossing at the center, was a potential diagram for a BUTTON KNOT. Not all such diagrams, however, produced successful knots.

After a promising diagram had once been secured it often happened that it could be molded into two or even several different forms. That is, the final shapes, except in a few cases, were not necessarily inevitable. Certain forms that were searched for proved elusive, while other forms were easily found and frequently were duplicated, sometimes by quite different diagrams.

To assist in tying knots of a single strand that have a regular over-one-and-under-one weave, I have used a system that is not difficult to work and if followed methodically will tie the most complicated knot. This has already been referred to in Chapter 1. The single line of such a knot has an arrowhead at one end and a feather at the other to indicate the direction in which the cord is to be laid. After an enlarged working copy of the diagram has been made, the cord

602

603

is pinned at the feather end of the diagram or else it is tucked down through a hole in the diagram at that point. The working end is then led along the line of the arrow and pinned at frequent intervals. Every time another part of the cord is crossed at a point that is marked with a circle, the working end is *tucked under that part;* at all other crossings the cord is led *over.*

Many of the diagrams are numbered along the line of the arrow, every second crossing being numbered in regular numerical sequence. A knot so numbered is tied in the following manner: the cord is pinned at the feather end and then at 1, 2, 3, 4, 5, etc. Whenever any number that has a circle drawn around it is reached *in its proper sequence,* the working end is tucked *under* the part that lies across its path.

The point and feather of the arrow indicate where the ends drop down at the center of the knot to form the stem. In certain of these knots there will be found an irregularity at the centers in the over-and-under sequence, owing to the fact that the cord is led at this point out of one cycle into another, somewhat in the manner of the MONKEY'S FIST (∦2201).

600. A knot having been tied on the diagram by the method described, proceed to work out the surplus material. Keep the knot flat, as in the second diagram on the page, until it has been drawn fairly snug, then continue to tighten, allowing the rim to close downward in "mushroom" or "umbrella" form. Finally, using a pricker, work the rim tightly and evenly around the stem. At this point the top surface of the knot will probably resemble the right (finished) diagram for KNOT ∦602. The reason for this is that the top center part of the present knot has retreated from the surface. This should now be forcibly pricked to the surface and the surrounding parts tightened to hold it in place. This is the final form of the common CHINESE BUTTON KNOT. By counting, it will be found that the knot has nine surface parts.

601. The CHINESE BUTTON is often doubled, to make a larger knot. The lead for this is indicated by arrows in the lower center diagram of ∦600. Either one or both ends may be tucked parallel with the existing lead to make a TWO- or THREE-PLY (double or triple) KNOT. In a double knot it is unnecessary to prick up the top center part, as it is supported by parts that cross underneath.

In tying these knots, the Chinese employ either a silk cord or else a thin, compact roll of the material of the garment. This is strongly sewed and the seam carefully hidden on the underside when the knot is tied.

602. If the final tuck of the ends is the same as in the KNIFE LANYARD KNOT (∦787), a handsome EIGHT-PART BUTTON results, that, so far as I know, has not been utilized by the Chinese.

603. This EIGHT-PART KNOT may also be doubled. As the two ends have different cycles, both ends must be tucked each time a new ply is added to the knot. The illustration shows a DOUBLE or TWO-PLY KNOT, which may be doubled either as suggested by the solid arrow or by the dotted arrow in ∦602.

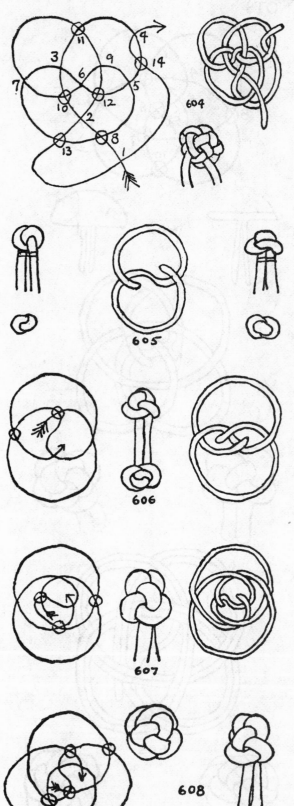

In working these knots the best tool is a pricker (#91). Lacking this, a dull ice pick or a meat skewer will serve. A cork board (see #99 and #126) is the best table top on which to pin a diagram, but a soft pine board or an upholstered chair seat is a practical substitute.

The word *part* is used in reference to each appearance of the cord on the surface of the knot.

The working diagrams represent the top elevation of a knot. Generally the finished aspect of a knot is also shown. Where the side of a knot is pictured, the stem or two ends are also shown.

"Working" a knot is apt to be more difficult than tying one, but once you have acquired the "feel" of the cord, working a knot, with its attendant prodding and molding, twisting and pulling, will have lost most of its difficulties.

In removing the slack cord from a knot, which is about all there is to working a knot, do not at any time distort the diagram form beyond recognition. Too strong a pull is apt to be fatal. One part at a time should be tightened, and then only by a slight amount. Use the fingers at first, but as the knot hardens employ the pricker. Work back and forth through the knot from one end of the cord to the other, drawing a little on each part until the desired firmness is achieved.

Many of these knots may be doubled or tripled, but the larger ones are generally big enough without addition and not only may lose some of their distinctive form but are apt to become flabby when enlarged too much.

A cord does not cross itself until it passes a point a second time, so a circle marked around a point is disregarded the first time it is passed.

604. There is a second CHINESE BUTTON, the sole merit of which is its larger size. Although it has a regular over-one-and-under-one texture, it is not symmetrical because the two ends leave the knot at right angles to each other and at a tangent with the surface of the knot.

605. A Two-Bight, One-Lead Turk's-Head is the smallest Turk's-Head form that can be adapted to tie a button. In its simplest form this makes an Overhand Knot, but if the center part is pricked to the surface, as in Knot #600, this makes a small but distinctive button.

606. A Two-Bight, Two-Lead Turk's-Head diagram makes a slightly larger knot, but one that is a little difficult to draw up into proper form.

The smaller examples of many kinds of knot are far from being the easiest to tie.

607. A THREE-LEAD, TWO-BIGHT TURK'S-HEAD makes a more practical knot for the basis of a button than the two previous ones, the two-bight series being on the whole unsatisfactory.

608. A BUTTON KNOT that is based on a triangular TURK'S-HEAD diagram of four leads and three bights. It is not possible with a three-bight circumference to make a button that is wholly symmetrical at the center. But by careful working the knot can be made to be approximately regular.

609. This knot with a six-bight rim and a three-bight center is not a TURK'S-HEAD form. It makes a satisfactory pellet-shaped knot. A six-part neck is about the practical limit in size for a SINGLE-STRAND BUTTON, as a larger one does not close snugly around the two-strand stem. This knot is shown doubled.

610. A four-by-four pellet-shaped knot does not have a regular over-one-and-under-one sequence. It is based on a FOUR-BIGHT by FIVE-LEAD TURK'S-HEAD, but at the center it has an over-two lead, which gives it the appearance of a ONE-STRAND, FOUR-LEAD by FOUR-BIGHT TURK'S-HEAD, which is an "impossible" knot.

611. A six-lead by four-bight diagram is about the limit in size for a pellet-shaped BUTTON KNOT. But it may either be molded into a flat or "cattail" form if preferred.

612. A FIVE-LEAD by THREE-BIGHT TURK'S-HEAD diagram tied in cat-tail form appears to be more practical than a THREE-BIGHT KNOT tied in pellet form.

613. A CATTAIL KNOT of any length, a section of which is FOUR-STRAND ROUND or SQUARE SINNET. After the desired length is reached the two strands are rove back through the center, the full length of the sinnet. To make: Start as in the first diagram. Having reached the position of the second diagram, take the outside right strand in hand, bring it around the back and up between the two opposing strands, and then down to the center and below its sister strand. Next take the outside left strand in hand, bring it around back and up between the opposing two strands, and then down to the center below its sister strand. Continue to alternate these two moves until the desired length is reached. Work the loop exactly as if it were two separate strands, and disentangle the two ends as often as necessary. At any time that the two ends are equal, a knot may be completed by reeving the ends up through the center of the sinnet. The material of the loop is then worked out and the knot worked snug.

The twist braids of page 485 will make excellent decorative buttons for the ends of shutters, lamps, and shade pulls.

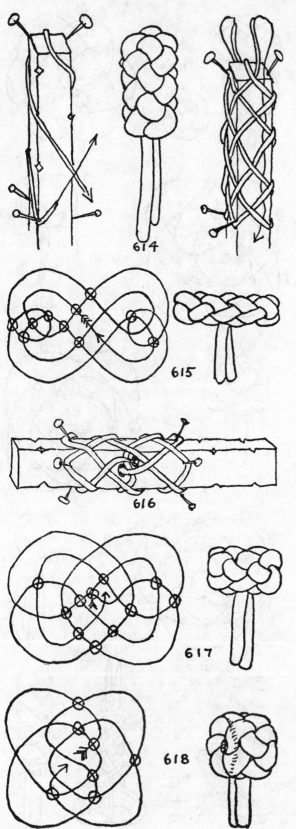

614. A cattail of any length, a cross section of which is Eight-Strand Round Sinnet. Take a stick of wood that is one inch square, and cut four notches in the centers of the edges at one end. Make a notch on each of the four edges, one half inch down from the end. Make four more notches *one inch* below the first four notches, and continue at one-inch intervals until the desired length is reached. Four notches to the row are illustrated here. Drive a tack into two opposite notches at the upper end and also four tacks into the four bottom notches. Middle a cord and lay it across the end in the un-tacked notches. Lead the two ends in a 45-degree right helix to the bottom, round the proper tacks, and lead the ends over all in a 45-degree right helix to the top. Round a top tack with each strand, lead the two ends over all down in a right 45-degree helix, and round the remaining two tacks. Now lead one end upward, *tucking underneath* the first strand encountered. Do likewise with the other end. Then tuck both ends alternately over and under to the top, when they will appear as in the right diagram. Finally, tuck both ends down through the center of the knot as indicated with the arrow, remove the stick, and draw up into cattail form.

615. A Toggle- or T-Shaped Knot. This is based on an Eight-Lead, Three-Bight Turk's-Head. The ends depart from the knot at the center length. Tie by the method described on page 102. When finishing this knot the center part must be pricked to the surface as in Knot ℵ600.

616. A Toggle-Shaped Knot may be tied with any even number of leads that is not divisible by four. The knot is marked out on a stick that is one inch square. Mark one of the central side compartments with the figure X instead of a square. Instead of marking out the knot with a pencil, it may be first laid out with a clue of black linen thread in which all the crossings are over, without considering the final over-and-under of the knot. Then pin one end of the banding as shown in the drawing and follow the clue, repeating to yourself over, under, etc., as you lead your cord, and take the crossings accordingly. Do not tuck through the clue; merely tuck under the final cord whenever you repeat "under." The ends depart from the knot downward through a hole in the compartment opposite the X at the center top.

617. This is exactly the same knot as the foregoing, except that the center lead happens to be reversed, and the knot is tied by the method described on page 102.

618. A short, cylindrical TOGGLE based on a TURK'S-HEAD having five bights. The center part between the two ends must be pricked to the surface to complete the knot.

619. A FLAT OBLONG TOGGLE. The final shape of this knot is almost inevitable, and the knot is one of the most practical of the SINGLE-STRAND BUTTONS. Its only drawback is that the center part has a slight tendency to sink from sight and must be pricked to the surface when completing the knot. This tendency can be corrected with a few stitches of a needle.

620. A FLATTENED CYLINDROID TOGGLE. Although the diagram appears much more complicated than those already shown, if the cord is pinned carefully as the knot progresses, it presents no additional problems, so far as tying is concerned. But the larger the knot, the more carefully must it be worked, and this of course takes more time. Work all knots deliberately and methodically.

621. An UPRIGHT CYLINDROID TOGGLE. This is the same knot as the above but projected from another angle, with the ends differently led.

622. An ELLIPTICAL KNOT that is compact and practical, but perhaps not so handsome as the one which follows.

623. An ELLIPTICAL KNOT of distinctive appearance. The top of this knot should be worked flat.

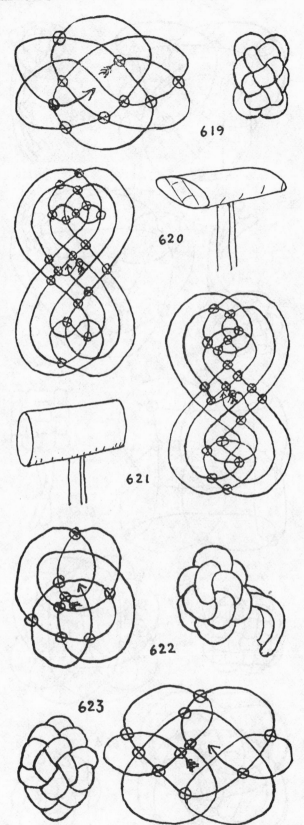

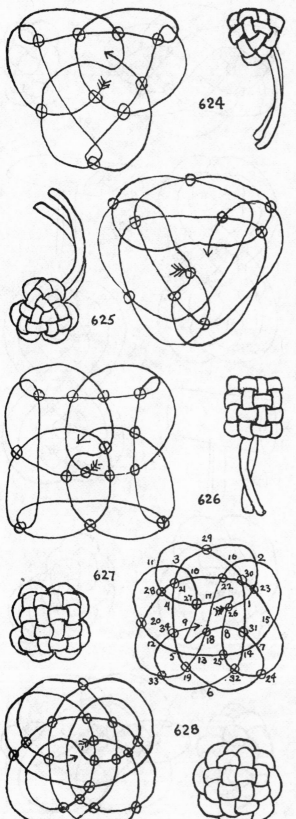

624. A Triangular Knot. To accent the corners of this, three two-sided compartments have been introduced. The knot is worked very flat, and the edges are kept very sharp.

625. A triangular shape with a series of snug bights around the edges. Although less distinctively triangular than the former knot, it is perhaps handsomer, and quite as practical.

626. A Square Knot with sharp edges similar to №624. All the knots shown on this page should be worked as flat as possible.

627. A Square Knot with the same characteristics as Triangular Knot №625.

628. A Circular Flat-Topped Knot tied and worked in the same manner.

629. The next few knots of this panel are based on the Chinese Butterfly Knot, which is more fully described in Chapter 31 ("Fancy Knots"). When tied as a fancy knot, the bights which are here tightly gathered around the crown of the knot are generally extended in long loops to form the fringes or wings that have given the name to the Butterfly Knots. Tied as a Button, there are four loops on this particular specimen, and the stem of the knot is at the center of the underside. Tied as a Butterfly Knot, the stem is at one corner, and there are three loops around the knot (№2451); while tied as a two-cord Lanyard Knot (№811), there are but two loops to the knot. These knots are tightened two parts at a time as described for Knot №587, in the last chapter.

630. An Oblong Knot which should be pinned out on the table for tying. Unless worked very firmly, it will distort.

631. One of the handsomest and most practical of all the Button Knots. Like the knots in the previous panel, this should be tied flat.

632. A larger Rectangular Knot.

633. A distinctive and individual *knot with a diagonal texture.*

634. An adaptation of the Butterfly Knot, in triangular form, may be tied as a Button Knot. Unless carefully worked, it is inclined to be too open at the edges to be practical.

635. A Pentagonal Butterfly Button. A five-bight center is inclined to distort. To obviate this the stem of the knot leads down from the lower instead of the upper plane of the knot.

636. A "Letter-Box" Shape, adapted from a Turk's-Head diagram.

637. A Truncated Pyramid.

638. A Rectangular Knot of individual form. It is not necessary in this one to prick up the top center part.

A practical way to copy diagrams that are not equipped with the circles which indicate the over-and-under sequence is to draw the diagram first with a single light pencil line. Then take a red pencil and draw a solid red line over each crossing in the direction to be taken by the upper lead or part.

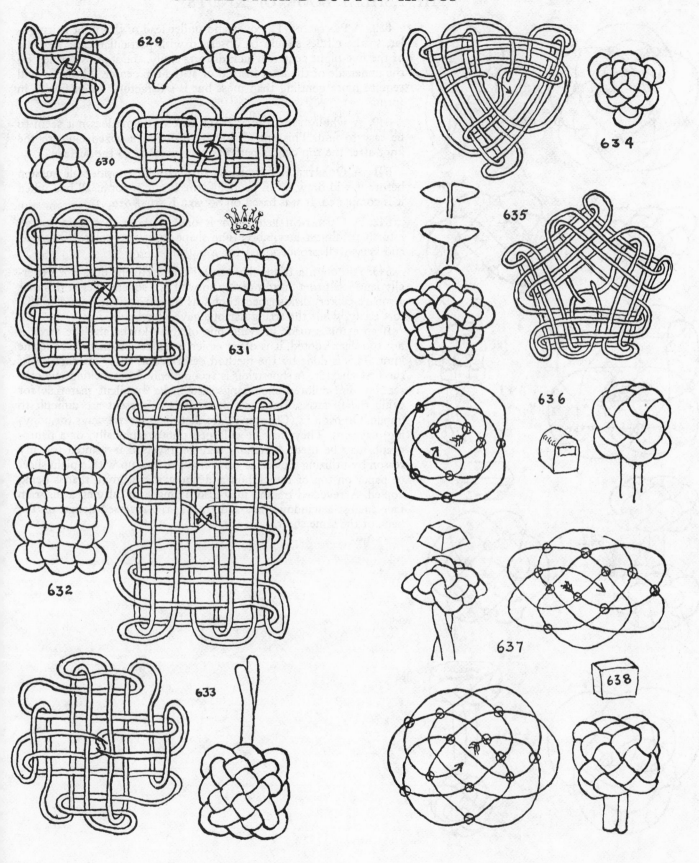

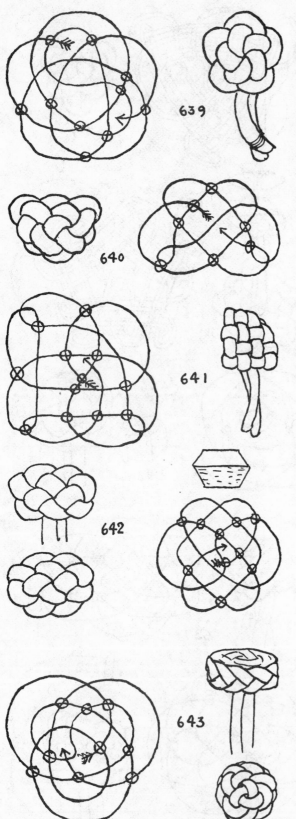

639. A PENTAGON. The over-and-under lead of this knot is irregular, so the circles should be observed with particular care. Because of the five-bight center, which distorts easily, the stem is formed on the underside of the knot instead of at the top center. The knot will require more gentling than most but is satisfactory when finally in form.

640. A wholly satisfactory HALF ROUND KNOT does not seem to be easy to find. This one should have the stem seized close to the knot after the top center part has been pricked to the surface.

641. A QUARTER ROUND KNOT may require considerable suasion before it will draw up in proper form, but it is not at all bad when it is completed. It was based on SQUARE KNOT #626.

642. A CASKET-SHAPED KNOT is one of those that seem to fall into shape almost inevitably. The shape itself is regular, handsome, and very well proportioned for a button.

643. Although a triangular central compartment does not generally lend itself to a button design so well as a square one, in this case a square-center, disk-shaped knot was striven for and found to distort easily, while the triangular one gave no trouble.

If an error is made in tying one of these knots, and the error is not too deep-rooted, it is often easier to correct it than to retie the knot. This is done by the method described as #127 on page 26 of the first chapter. A shoestring is recommended for making the correction, and colored shoestrings also make excellent materials for tying the BUTTONS. But such shoestrings at present are difficult to obtain. On page 22 (Chapter 1) are described several ways for copying diagrams. They may be enlarged photographically, or a pantograph may be used. A tracing may be reversed if wanted for any reason by utilizing a piece of carbon paper face up with a plain sheet of paper on top of the carbon and under the diagram that is being copied. A reversed tracing may also be made by placing a diagram face against a window glass and tracing the reversed design on the back of the same sheet.

In working knots of the BUTTERFLY variety, where, after they have been tied, there is always danger of distortion, secure a short piece of red twine temporarily through each one of the marginal bights to assist in identification.

On single-line diagrams I have found that it is not difficult to go astray at a crossing and lead the cord along the wrong line. A crossing may be considered either as two lines that intersect each other or as four lines that meet at a common point. A cord having been laid to such a point, there are three courses open, the cord itself already occupying one of the four lines. Number the three remaining radiating lines 1, 2, and 3, from left to right, and lay the cord along 2, which is always the center one. It makes no difference if the crossing is in the shape of a letter K, provided the lines are properly numbered.

644. An ELLIPSE with a regular over-one-and-under-one surface, and twenty-two parts.

The remaining knots on this page and the knots on page 112, with the exception of ⅋650, do not have the regular over-one-under-one surface that the knots already shown have had. KNOT ⅋656, although confused in the diagram by being tied in two planes, has a regular over-one-under-one surface texture in the finished knot.

645. This very small knot of four parts, the center two parts being parallel to each other, should be compared with KNOTS ⅋605 and ⅋606, to which it is closely related. Although small, the knot is wholly practical.

646. A knot resembling at the rim a MATTHEW WALKER and with a parallel two-part center at the top. After tying, this must be worked very carefully, keeping the turns well down around the stem until the knot is drawn up. Finally, the stem is pulled strongly to tighten the two center parts.

647. A knot similar to the foregoing, more individual perhaps but hardly as handsome.

648. A knot resembling a MATTHEW WALKER KNOT with a four-part crown at the top.

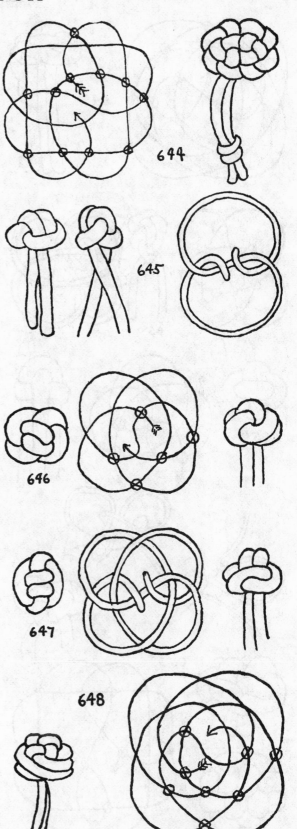

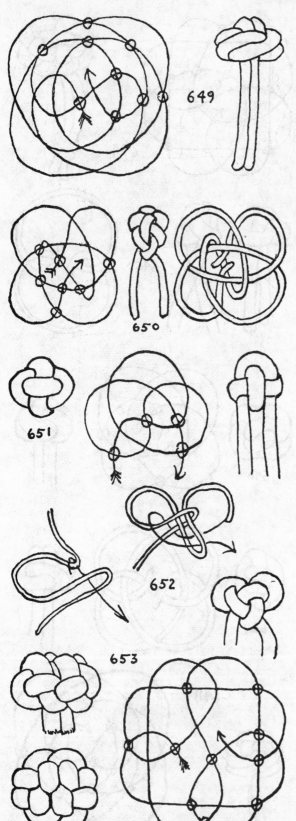

649. Here is a knot resembling a DOUBLE FOUR-STRAND MATTHEW WALKER, with two additional parallel center parts, similar to #646; but a much bulkier knot. When drawn up evenly this is quite handsome.

650. A sport that will serve better as a pendant on a window shade or light cord than as a practical knot, since it has champagne-bottle shoulders. The texture is regularly over-one-and-under-one.

651. Superficially this knot appears to be related to the MONKEY'S FIST, all parts being at right angles to each other.

652. A knot that has already been shown among the double loops. With the loops pulled up snugly, the knot makes a distinctive button.

653. The distinctive texture of this knot is due largely to the way in which it is drawn up. Although at first it may appear complicated, if a fairly stiff cord is employed, such as a braided curtain or sash cord, the knot will probably fall into proper shape of its own volition.

654. An ambitious knot that is not very successful. It was intended to be rectangular in form but is too large to be tied without a core. Take a piece of white pine about one inch square and three quarters of an inch thick. Bore a hole through this block from top to bottom large enough for the two ends to be tucked through, and countersink both ends of the hole.

Tie the knot, and when it is partly drawn up slip the wooden core inside. Reeve the ends through the hole and down through the bottom of the knot. Then work the knot snugly around the block.

655. A WAFER-SHAPED KNOT with the ends led out at the rim. This knot was first tied in two planes, as KNOT #656, by superimposing two identical single-plane diagrams, one on top of the other, one slued at a 45-degree angle to the other. This made the knot confusing to tie but easy to work.

The knot was later projected as given here and tied as SINGLE-PLANE KNOT #655. In this way it proved easier to tie but more difficult to work. As the knot does not have a regular over-one-and-under-one sequence throughout, the encircled points are not numbered, and the diagram must be followed very carefully. When the knot has been tied the outside rim or edge is lifted up and the rim closed together at the top center to form the upper plane of the knot, while the stem leads out of the knot at the right lower edge.

656. A little more care is necessary in tying the knot in two planes, but after it is once tied it is already in proper completed form and requires nothing further but a gradual working into the finished shape, shown in the illustration of the key guard. The cord moves from one plane to the other as it rounds the rim after each crossing. There is one peculiar feature to be noted, and that is where the second vertical from the left does not cross the diagram completely but turns downward and returns to the bottom in a right diagonal after going two thirds of the way to the top.

To tie a watch guard, middle a cord and tie the BUTTON KNOT, then at the proper distance tie KNIFE LANYARD KNOT #787. Finally form the key loop with one end, and tuck that end back into the knot, withdrawing the opposing end two full tucks. Draw all snug, and cut off the ends.

A similar diagram to #656 is utilized in Chapter 4 as SINGLE-CORD LANYARD KNOT #593.

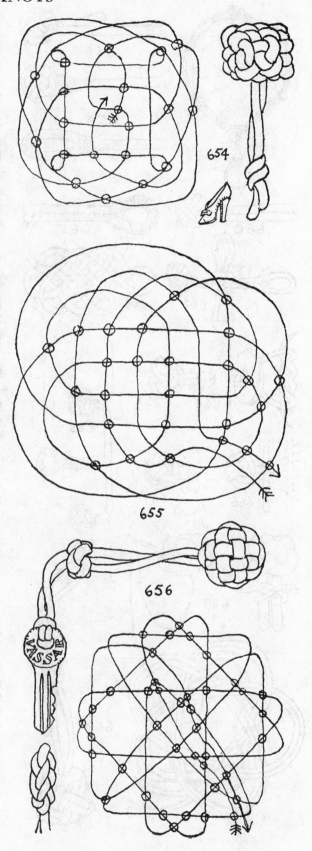

654

655

656

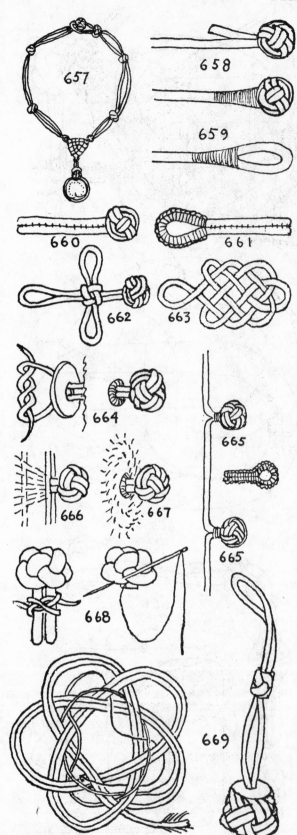

657. A decorative necklace is made by doubling a cord and making a small BUTTON (#600) which is to be worn at the nape of the neck. Two or three Two-Cord Lanyard Knots from Chapter 8 are then added. After that, PECTORAL KNOT #843 or #844 is tied, leaving either a small loop at the bottom with which to make fast a pectoral ornament, or else BUTTON #656 may be used for a pendant. If the latter, the PECTORAL KNOT is pinned out and half tied and not completed until the button has been made. The PECTORAL KNOT being tied, the remaining half of the necklace is completed to match the first half. Next, one end of the cord is doubled back to form the buttonhole, which may be done as in #659.

658. Having made a button on a single lanyard, cut and scrape the shorter end and serve it strongly and evenly, as in EYE SPLICE #2792, using thread of the same color. If it is sewed through a few stitches, as in #2793, it will be firmer.

659. To make a loop or eye for the button, scrape and taper the end and sew through several times before serving.

660, 661. The Chinese adjust pieces of the material of the garment into a firm, tight roll and sew the edge neatly down. The buttonhole is made in the same way, and when it shows wear it may be "buttonholed" over. The Chinese way of securing a button is to lay the ends parallel and sew them close together to the face of the garment.

662, 663. In silk cord the ends of the knot, and of the loop also, are often made into frogs of various sorts. See Chapter 30.

664. Where a strong attachment is needed the two ends are put through an eyelet and then rove through a leather washer or an ordinary button; they are then reef knotted together or else the ends are tacked down after passing through the leather washer.

665. Sometimes the buttons of a garment are all made in one cord and the cord is sewed along the edge of the garment to button into ordinary buttonholes, or else a set of loops is arranged in the same fashion as the buttons.

666. The seam of a heavy coat is sometimes opened and the ends of the knot frayed out and sewed flat between the two layers of material.

667. Button ends may be rove through eyelet holes and frayed and then sewed around on the back of the material.

668. The ends may be seized close and cut short, after which they are attached to the garment by sewing the knot itself "over and over," close to the stem.

669. The BASKET KNOT was described to me in a letter from Albert R. Wetjen, to whom I wrote for information after seeing it mentioned in *Fiddlers' Green*. I trust that it is correct as portrayed, but I am by no means certain. A THREE-LEAD, FIVE-BIGHT TURK'S-HEAD is made and doubled. After this has been faired, follow the arrow line which passes twice around the knot, and then double this. Seize the ends together and tuck them up through the knot; draw up, and employ the ends to conclude a lanyard.

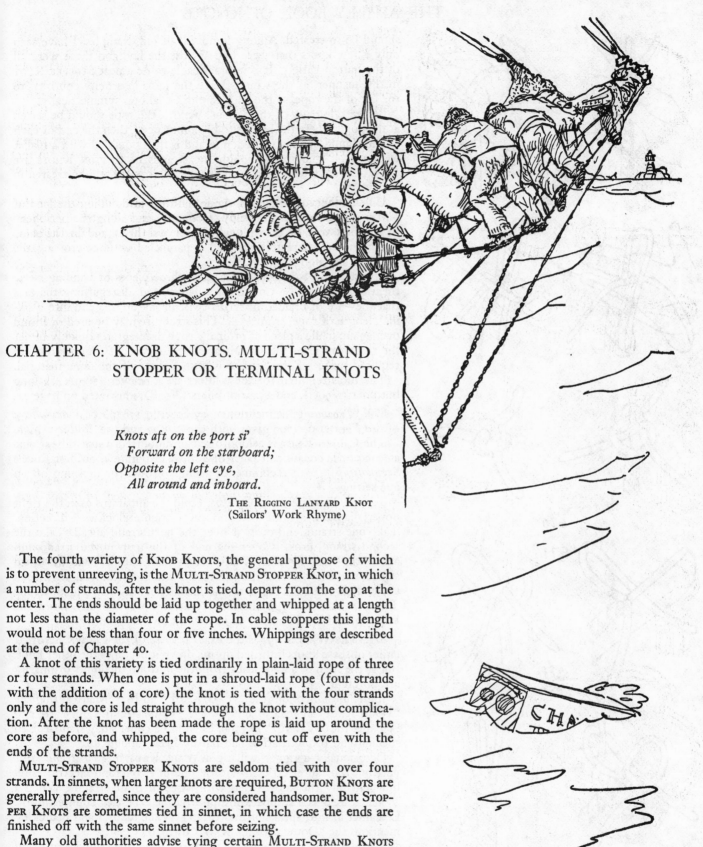

CHAPTER 6: KNOB KNOTS. MULTI-STRAND STOPPER OR TERMINAL KNOTS

Knots aft on the port si'
Forward on the starboard;
Opposite the left eye,
All around and inboard.

THE RIGGING LANYARD KNOT
(Sailors' Work Rhyme)

The fourth variety of KNOB KNOTS, the general purpose of which is to prevent unreeving, is the MULTI-STRAND STOPPER KNOT, in which a number of strands, after the knot is tied, depart from the top at the center. The ends should be laid up together and whipped at a length not less than the diameter of the rope. In cable stoppers this length would not be less than four or five inches. Whippings are described at the end of Chapter 40.

A knot of this variety is tied ordinarily in plain-laid rope of three or four strands. When one is put in a shroud-laid rope (four strands with the addition of a core) the knot is tied with the four strands only and the core is led straight through the knot without complication. After the knot has been made the rope is laid up around the core as before, and whipped, the core being cut off even with the ends of the strands.

MULTI-STRAND STOPPER KNOTS are seldom tied with over four strands. In sinnets, when larger knots are required, BUTTON KNOTS are generally preferred, since they are considered handsomer. But STOPPER KNOTS are sometimes tied in sinnet, in which case the ends are finished off with the same sinnet before seizing.

Many old authorities advise tying certain MULTI-STRAND KNOTS "against the lay," but there is little unanimity as to which knots

[115]

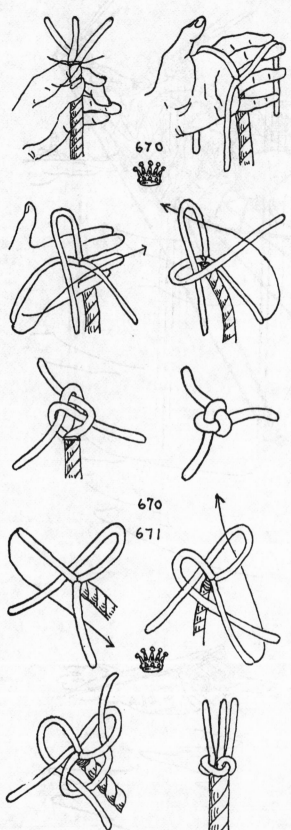

should be so treated. Among hundreds of old examples, I have seen only a few knots that were tied against the lay, and these were all of the button variety. It is impracticable to tie a neat STOPPER KNOT in this manner, as the strands leave the knot in a helix contrary to the lay of the rope, so the ends cannot be laid up symmetrically.

Before tying any of the STOPPER KNOTS, the rope should be seized at the point where the knot is to be commenced, then the end of each strand should be stopped. Each strand is then pounded with a mallet to render it smooth. Although the strands of BUTTON KNOTS are canvas-covered, MULTI-STRAND STOPPER KNOTS are seldom treated in that way.

Unless otherwise directed, the initial tuck in doubling the lead of a MULTI-STRAND KNOT is below or outside and along the periphery of the first wall or crown (whichever was first) and in the same direction, and thereafter the lead is paralleled without crossing the part that lies alongside.

In practicing STOPPER KNOTS, take three pieces of banding, seize them together with a CONSTRICTOR KNOT, and, disregarding the fact that they are of braided material, twist or lay up one end into a six-inch length of rope, as in ⁂144. This structure may be used over and over again, while a piece of ordinary rope disintegrates quickly under the treatment after the strands are once opened. If four strands are required make a FOUR-STRAND ROUND SINNET of the same material.

The tools required for these knots are a pricker (⁂99A), a loop buttoner (⁂99C), and a pair of pliers (⁂99B), illustrated on page 21.

670. "Crowning" is mentioned by Steel in 1794. *The Vocabulary of Sea Phrases* of 1799 gives both the *crown* and the *double crown*.

The CROWN KNOT is seldom used unsupported. Generally it acts as one of the constituent parts of a more elaborate knob. But Luce's *Seamanship* (1862) recommends a single crown for finishing off an eye seizing.

To tie a THREE-STRAND CROWN: Hold the apparatus as in the right upper diagram, and tie the knot in a counterclockwise direction. Take one strand, and cross it over the next strand ahead. Take the second strand, cross it over the end of the first-moved strand and across the standing part of the next strand ahead. Take the third strand, and cross it over the end of the strand last moved, then tuck the end through the bight of the next strand ahead (which, in the THREE-STRAND KNOT, is the first strand that was moved). Draw the knot up, and it will appear as in the last two diagrams.

671. The WALL KNOT is the exact reverse of the CROWN KNOT. If either of these knots is turned upside down it becomes the other knot. But as the stem of a knot leads from the bottom, the knots ordinarily are different.

John Smith mentions the "WALL KNOTT" in 1627, Manwayring the "WALE KNOT" in 1644, Blanckley the "WHALE KNOTT" in 1750, and Falconer the "WALNUT" in 1769. Even in Falconer's day standardized spelling and pronunciation had hardly been thought of.

Occasionally a rigger will tie a WALL KNOT in *two-strand stuff* (marline), or an electrician will tie one in two-strand electric wire, but generally the knot is tied with three or more strands. When a WALL is used as a stopper, unsupported, it is best to countersink it. Lescallier in 1783 speaks of the "SINGLE WALL KNOT," and Blanckley mentions the "DOUBLE WALL KNOT" in 1750.

To tie a THREE-STRAND WALL KNOT: Take one strand and bring it counterclockwise under the next strand. Take the next strand, and pass it under the end of the first-moved strand and under the standing part of the next. Take the third strand under the second end and up through the bight of the first-moved strand.

672. This is called the WALL AND CROWN KNOT, and was mentioned by Moore in 1801. The wall is tied first, and then a crown is superimposed.

The CROWN, the WALL, the DIAMOND KNOT (#693), and the FOOTROPE KNOT (#696) are the basis of the knots of this chapter. The four are tied in combination and with variations, and are doubled in a number of ways. This type of knot is spoken of as the "built-up" variety.

There are two ways of "following the lead" when doubling a knot. To follow *below*, lead the end below, or "outside" the initial wall, as indicated by the solid single line.

To follow *above*, proceed as indicated by the dotted line, and continue parallel with the same strand and without crossing it.

If a knot is tied flat on the cork board, with the stem dropped down through the hole, as in #674, #675, and #676, it may be pinned out symmetrically. So arranged, a knot is doubled "below the lead" when the second circuit of the strand is radially on the outer side of the first circuit, and the knot is doubled "above the lead" when the second circuit is inside the first circuit and radially nearer the center.

When the lead has been "followed" around the knot once, it is said to have been doubled and is a TWO-PLY KNOT; when followed twice it is tripled and is a THREE-PLY KNOT.

673. The DECK STOPPER provided the name for the whole class of STOPPER KNOTS. Its purpose was to secure the cables of a ship, which were too large to be belayed in the ordinary way, and to "stop" them from running out. A knot and a lanyard were in one end of the stopper, and the other end was hooked to the deck. The cable was secured with a lanyard lashing around the neck of the knot, the end being dogged and stopped along the cable.

674. The STOPPER KNOT, per se, is a SINGLE WALL with each strand given an additional tuck as shown by the arrow. The name is given by Steel in 1794. The *Manual of Seamanship* calls it the WALL and HALF WALL. In tying, draw up the strands firmly and evenly. When it is completed lay up the ends into a short section of rope, whip them, and trim. In speaking of the knot, the *Manual of Seamanship* further says: "Made in this way they will never capsize."

Lever, in 1808, stated that the ends of STOPPER KNOTS "if very short are whipped without being *stopped*." This statement is meaningless and is probably a printer's error, but it is still being copied. Brady, in 1841, straightened out the statement as follows: "The ends, if short, are *whipped* without being *layed up*; but if long, they are *layed up* and *stopped*."

675. The DOUBLE WALL (1) is given by Blanckley, 1750. Lever (1808) says the DOUBLE WALL is "tied in the ends of topgallant braces, to button into the clews of topgallant-sails." It was also used on stoppers instead of the STOPPER KNOT, and may be the earlier form of the two. In doubling this knot, it is preferable to follow *above* the first lead.

The *Manual of Seamanship* says: "a DOUBLE WALL KNOT will capsize when a great strain is brought on it."

676. DOUBLE WALL KNOT (2). This is a more compact and handsomer knot than the foregoing one and combines the best features of #674 and #675.

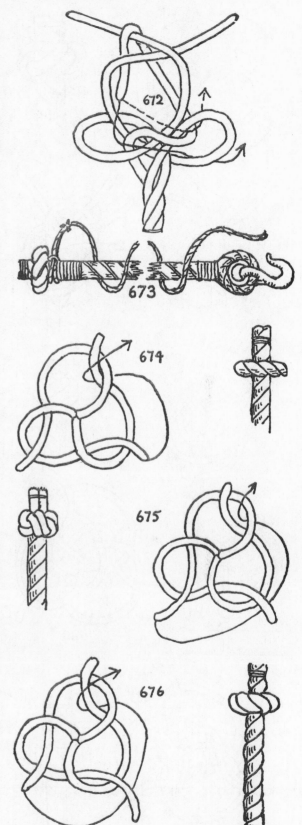

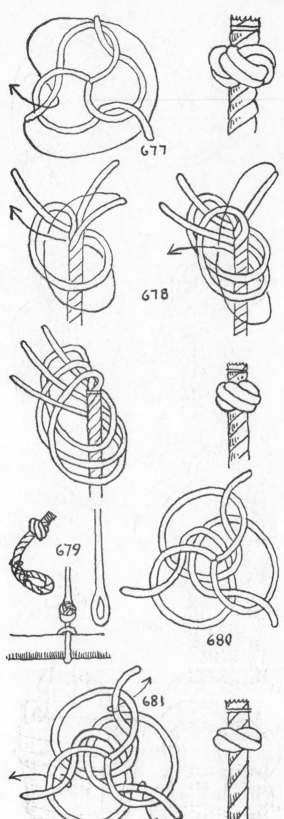

677. Double Wall Knot (3) is the most distinguished of the three given. After the basic Wall Knot has been tied each end is brought around the knot and thrust up beside the stem through its own bight.

678. The Full or Double Matthew Walker Knot. Lever in 1808 speaks of "Matthew Walker's Knot," and describes the knot which Alston in 1860 calls the "Double Matthew Walker Knot." A refinement of the original knot had in the meantime taken over the original name, which is now generally modified to "a Matthew Walker."

Lever's familiar expression, "Matthew Walker's Knot," suggests that he may have known the inventor, who was possibly a master rigger in one of the British naval dockyards. Many myths have grown up around Matthew Walker, "the only man ever to have a knot named for him." Dr. Frederic Lucas, of the American Museum of Natural History, once told me the following story of the origin of the knot, which he had heard off the Chincha Islands while loading guano in 1869.

A sailor, having been sentenced to death by a judge who in earlier life had been a sailor himself, was reprieved by the judge because of their common fellowship of the sea. The judge offered the sailor a full pardon if he could show him a knot that he, the judge, could neither tie nor untie.

The sailor called for ten fathoms of rope and, having retired to the privacy of his cell, unlaid the rope halfway, put in a Matthew Walker Knot, and then laid up the rope again to the end.

So Matthew Walker secured his pardon, and the world gained an excellent knot.

To tie the Double Matthew Walker: Hold the rope in the left hand. Arrange the strands as pictured. Take the backmost one, make a large left turn with it around the stem of the knot, and bring the end up through its own bight. Take the strand that is in front of the one just moved, make a left turn on top of the previous strand and bring the end up through both the bights. Take the third strand and lead it in the same way, bringing the end up through all three bights. The *Manual of Seamanship* says that the Double Matthew Walker is used on topmast rigging lanyards, bunt beckets, and the beckets of tubs and buckets.

679. Beckets are employed here and there about ships for suspending and securing objects. A common becket has either a stopper or a button at one end, and an eye at the other. It is sometimes called a "Strap and Button." Falconer describes this becket in 1769.

680. The Double or Full Matthew Walker may be tied on the cork board by pinning out on the diagram shown here.

681. The Matthew Walker proper is occasionally called Single Matthew Walker by the uninitiated. It is a much trimmer knot than №678 and it has almost entirely superseded the double knot on shipboard. It is the most important knot used aboard ship. Todd and Whall, in their *Seamanship*, go so far as to state: "Amongst knots proper the Matthew Walker is almost the only one which it is absolutely necessary for the seaman to know." The word *knot* is used here in its narrowest sense, meaning a Multi-Strand Knob, but even so this is high praise for the Matthew Walker Knot.

Alongside is shown the *lubber's* or *greenhorn's* way of tying the knot. First make a Double Matthew Walker (№678), and then withdraw each strand in turn, one tuck only.

682. The direct or *able seaman's* way of tying a MATTHEW WALKER KNOT was taught me by Captain Charles W. Smith, on board *Sunbeam* in 1904.

With any *two* strands, tie a WALL KNOT around the remaining strand. Lay the third (remaining) strand around the end that issues from the same compartment, lead it around the stem of the knot counterclockwise, and tuck it up through the only bight that does not already enclose an end.

683. The ordinary seaman's way of tying a MATTHEW WALKER KNOT is first to make a common WALL KNOT and then to tuck each end to the right through the next bight ahead.

Lever, in 1808, speaking of "MATTHEW WALKER'S KNOT," says: "This is a handsome knot for the end of a lannier." I do not recall any earlier direct evidence of the employment of a LANYARD KNOT.

Italian paintings of the period of the battle of Lepanto show the standing ends of lanyard lashings apparently secured with splices. (See Chapter 40.) The stone monument to Peter Martyr, erected in the fifteenth century in Milan, appears to show the same method. (See #3298).

Ship models made as early as the seventeenth century frequently carry LANYARD KNOTS, but ship models are untrustworthy. Under the best of conditions model rigging requires repair or replacement every fifty or sixty years.

Neither Manwayring, Smith, nor Boteler in discussing shrouds, deadeyes, and "lanniers" mentions either knots or splices. All mention the WALL or WALE KNOT, but always in connection with "Sheates, Tackes, and Stoppers."

But for many years, shroud lanyards have been secured at one end by a knot which passed through a hole in the upper deadeye. Fore and aft stay lanyards reeve through hearts. The latter are set up at both ends and have no knots, the ends being seized. One of the first knots to be used on the ends of lanyards was probably the STOPPER KNOT (#674).

684. The earliest LANYARD KNOT that I have found described is "Two SINGLE WALL KNOTS, one under the other, cast on the end." This is given by Lever (1808). Brady says in 1841, "Reeve the lanyards, *if* prepared with a knot on the end; a double wall is preferable"; which would seem to indicate that the use of a LANYARD KNOT was not universal even at that time. The MATTHEW WALKER KNOT, recommended by Lever in 1808, remained the standard LANYARD KNOT for topmast rigging as long as ships sailed the ocean.

685. It is probable that the LANYARD KNOT proper first appeared on clippers of the early 1850s, but it is not mentioned in naval treatises before 1860.

The LANYARD KNOT, per se, was tied in four-strand, tarred hemp, and was used for lower rigging only.

686. Deck bucket bails or beckets were of three-strand rope and had two MATTHEW WALKER KNOTS. Generally leather washers and collars were added. Fire-bucket handles were often four-strand rope and had either LANYARD KNOTS (#687) or else FOUR-STRAND SINGLE MATTHEW WALKERS (#692). Mess bucket bails ordinarily were of wood and pivoted on a wooden button.

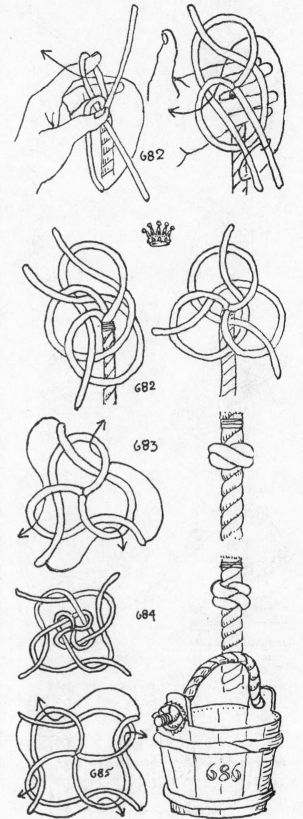

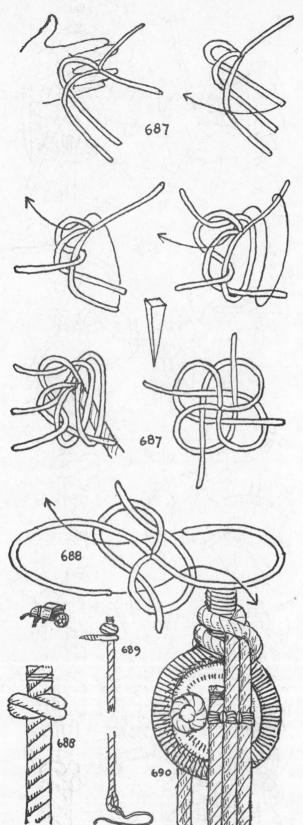

687

687

688

688

689

690

687. The orthodox way in which the *able seaman* ties the LANYARD KNOT is illustrated alongside. Very few have ever learned it except at the forecastle, and the way is easily forgotten. A bight is made with one strand, and the next strand is laid counterclockwise across this bight (figure 1). The third strand is then laid across the first two, and the end of the first-laid strand is led out to the periphery of the knot as in the second diagram. The third end is then led down under the second end and, continuing around the stem of the knot, is rove up through the first-laid bight. The fourth end is led down and around the second-laid strand end and, continuing around the stem of the knot, is rove up through the first and second bights. The knot is then worked close down on the seizing and drawn snug, after which the four strands are laid up for a distance equal to the width of the knot. It is finally given a palm-and-needle whipping (#3446).

688. The *ordinary seaman's* way of tying the LANYARD KNOT is perhaps the most practical of the lot. Two opposite strands are walled around the other two, which are held aloft without being involved. The second two strands are then walled, each being brought down around the stem and tucked up inside two bights as pictured.

The LANYARD KNOT may also be tied by first making a FOUR-STRAND DOUBLE MATTHEW WALKER, then withdrawing each end, one tuck at a time, exactly as in KNOT #681 and then withdrawing each end once more in the same manner. This is called the *lubber's* way.

Or the knot may be tied by making a FOUR-STRAND WALL, and tucking each strand under one more bight.

689. The knots of this series are very convenient for making rope handrails for the steps and ladders of cellars, attics, and barns. The lower end is finished off with an EYE SPLICE and lanyard for lashing.

Constant care must be taken to keep the lay of the strands fair. After each tuck, before drawing the knot taut, correct any unevenness, and when inserting the pricker or marlingspike be careful not to snag the yarns.

Captain Daniel F. Mullins tells me that he once sailed on a ship in which all the LANYARD KNOTS had square pegs driven into the hearts to keep the whippings snug. Undoubtedly it was a rigger's apprentice who made this mistake, since any sailor who could tie the knot at all would know that it had to be hove taut.

690. This pictures a LANYARD KNOT in position inboard at the left hole of an upper deadeye. On a few smart ships port lanyards were of left-laid rope and the port knots were at the forward hole, "opposite the *right* eye" and so were tied left-handed. But commonly the knots were "opposite the *left* eye," as described in the doggerel at the beginning of this chapter. Where cable shrouds were used—which was common on large naval ships in the last days of hemp standing rigging—all knots were opposite the right eye.

MULTI-STRAND STOPPER OR TERMINAL KNOTS

691. The FOUR-STRAND FULL or DOUBLE MATTHEW WALKER is tied as has already been described for the THREE-STRAND KNOT (₦678). Each strand is moved in turn, *counterclockwise*, once around the whole knot. Each strand ties a HALF KNOT to the left, the end being brought up through the structure as shown in the drawings for ₦678. The knot having been formed, place the ends together and arrange in the form of the upper left diagram of this page. Work the knot back against the seizing, and tighten each strand a little in turn, at all times keeping it symmetrical. But do not attempt to keep it in disk form. Get it promptly into cylindrical form as in the right upper drawing.

692. The FOUR-STRAND SINGLE MATTHEW WALKER is sometimes seen on fire buckets and is ordinarily tied by first making the FOUR-STRAND FULL MATTHEW WALKER as above, and then withdrawing each strand one tuck only, as illustrated for KNOT ₦681. The direct method, which is similar to KNOT ₦682, is as follows:

Make a bight with one strand, lead the next strand counterclockwise, making a wall with the first strand. Take the third strand and lead it down and around the stem and up through the second bight. Last, take the fourth strand, lead it down and around the stem and up through the third bight. Work the knot fair in disk form, then draw it taut in cylindrical form.

693. The DIAMOND KNOT, sometimes called the SINGLE DIAMOND, is an early knot. Falconer mentions it in 1769.

Seize three strands, turn down the ends for a good working length, and stop them. (A stop is less permanent, but it serves the same purpose as a seizing.) Hold the structure in the left hand, take any strand and pass it to the right over the adjacent strand and up under the second strand. Allow the end to hang down away from you over the back of the hand. Take the next strand to the right, and pass it to the right over the next adjacent strand and under the second strand. Repeat with the third strand. If there are more than three strands, continue until all have been passed in the same manner. Next, remove the stop and work the knot down hard against the seizing, at the same time working it taut by hauling up on each strand a little at a time and in regular order. The ends are finally laid up and whipped. This knot was first used on jib-boom footropes and later on side, yoke, and bell ropes.

When tied in a footrope, the strands were whipped and the rope was opened to *half length* and knots tied at the distance of a yard apart, to one end. Then the second end of the rope was opened and treated likewise. At first seize or stop the rope at the point where the knot is to be tied. But when the knot has become familiar, the strands need not be stopped before tying.

If a CONSTRICTOR KNOT (₦1249) is put around the ends of a DIAMOND KNOT after it is tied, close to the knot, and the ends pulled and tightened *through* the CONSTRICTOR, the ends of the knot will have a much better lead.

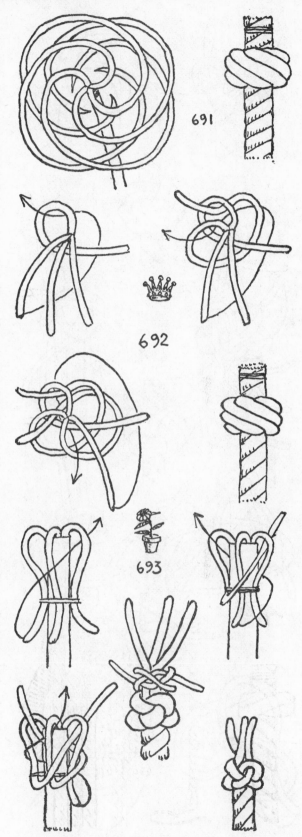

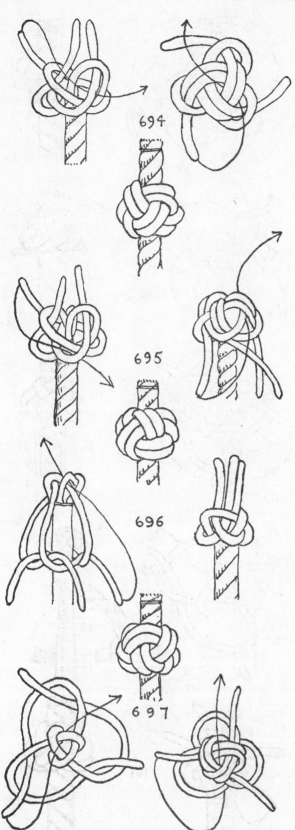

694. The DOUBLE DIAMOND (with the lead followed above) is given by Steel in 1794. The knot is doubled when a larger knot is desired, or if the knot is wanted for decorative purposes. If a doubled knot is tied in a footrope, the second lead is above the first as depicted here, as this brings the strands closer to the center of the knot and the rope lays up more snugly. The left diagram indicates how the lead is started, each strand being tucked once in turn. The second diagram indicates how the final tucks are taken to the center top. Draw up carefully. The knot was first tied in jib-boom footropes to prevent feet from slipping.

695. The DOUBLE DIAMOND (with the lead followed below) is illustrated here. When doubling most knots the lead is followed below, but DIAMOND KNOTS are tied in either way. The British Admiralty *Manual of the Sea* says that DOUBLE DIAMOND KNOTS are tied in "the lanyards of fire buckets."

The diagrams illustrate progressively how the strands are led. Once a lead has been started, an end must not be allowed to cross to the other side of the strand that is being followed.

696. The FOOTROPE KNOT. "First a crown, then a wall. Tuck up, and that's all." This is structurally the same as the DIAMOND KNOT, but it is tied "end for end"; that is to say, it is reversed. The lead being more compact at the end, the knot makes a far better appearing footrope than the DIAMOND KNOT, and, the lay being smoother, it is less subject to wear. It was first shown to me by Captain Charles W. Smith, who also supplied the work rhyme. After crowning and walling the rope, tuck the end to the top center as indicated in the drawings, and the single knot is complete.

697. The DOUBLE FOOTROPE KNOT is followed *above* the first lead. The left diagram shows how the ends are tucked at the center.

Tuck each strand once in turn, then tuck each strand in turn a second time up to the center as in the right bottom diagram. Each end passes under *four* parts.

698. The CAT STOPPER KNOT is used when the anchor has been catted (brought to the cathead). The stopper holds the anchor while the tackle is being shifted. One end of the stopper bears a knot, and the other end is pointed. The pointed end is rove downward through a hole in the cathead, passed through the anchor ring, led over a thumb cleat beside the hole on the after face of the cathead, and then is brought inboard and made fast to a timber head.

This knot was shown to me by Walter Thompson, head boat steerer on the *Sunbeam*, and afterwards mate. While boat steerer, he was called "Bosun" because of his proficiency with knots, there being no boatswain on a whaler. The rope is first crowned, next walled, and finally tucked to the top as illustrated. When tying the knot, if it is pinned out flat on the cork board with the stem tucked down through the center hole, there will be little chance of a mistake in tucking.

The end is stuck up immediately without following the previous wall; this is indicated by the arrows. If correctly tied the knot will resemble STOPPER KNOT #674, with a crown added.

699. A SINGLE CROWN AND DOUBLE WALL (1). Start as in the previous knot, but when the wall has been completed take one strand and follow *below* the strand ahead (counterclockwise) and tuck up to the center. Do likewise with the other two strands. The circuit of only one strand is illustrated here, but each strand in turn is moved counterclockwise.

The sequence of these three knots—#698, #699, and #700—should be compared with #674, #675, and #676.

700. A SINGLE CROWN AND DOUBLE WALL (2). The final tuck of this is made beyond one additional standing part. This gives a character quite different from the previous knot, which has a flat, even base.

701. SINGLE CROWN AND DOUBLE WALL (3). Having tied the crown and wall, tuck each end through the bight of the next crown to the right. Then bring each end around to the right, following under the adjacent parallel wall, and, passing by the next end to the right, tuck up to the center under three parts.

Unlike the BUTTON KNOTS, the *strands* of STOPPER KNOTS seldom are canvas-covered.

702. STOPPER KNOTS of different kinds are tied in life lines, etc., and are rove through stanchions at the ends of alleyways, companionways, and catwalks. The working end may have an EYE SPLICE (#2747), or it may be pointed and finished off with EYE #3550 or #3562.

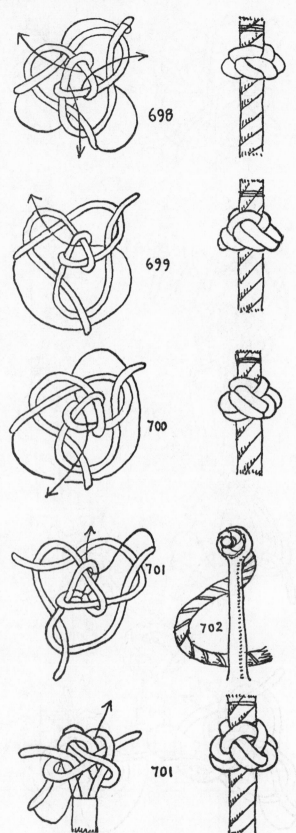

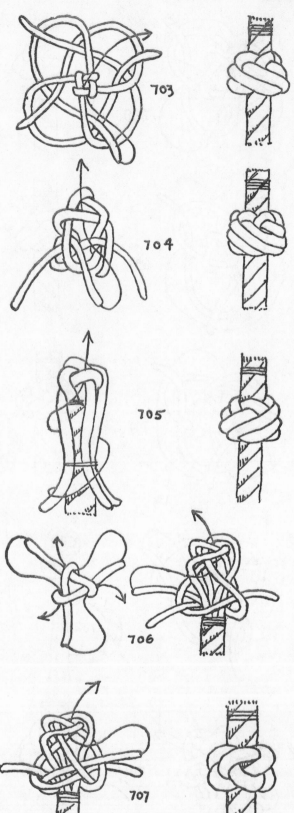

703. CROWN AND LANYARD KNOT (if tied with four strands) or CROWN AND MATTHEW WALKER KNOT (if tied with three strands). First make a crown in the usual way, then, below it, tie a LANYARD KNOT (#687) or a MATTHEW WALKER KNOT (#682), and tuck the ends up to the center, as indicated.

Most of the knots of this chapter should be fully and loosely tied before being worked taut. Then each strand in turn should be tightened a little, one part only at a time. Work as methodically as possible, and be careful at all times not to distort.

704. CROWN AND DOUBLE MATTHEW WALKER. A handsome knot which, if the ends are not laid up, is easily mistaken for SINNET KNOT #757 of the next chapter. Tie first a crown, then below it a FULL MATTHEW WALKER (#678), after which tuck the ends up through the center of the crown.

705. A FOOTROPE KNOT variation. Crown three strands *to the left*, stop the three strands to the stem, and take any end, leading it upward in a right diagonal completely around the stem and sticking it up through the center of the crown under its own part. Do likewise with the next strand to the right, and then with the remaining strand.

706. A DOUBLE CROWN AND SINGLE WALL. It may have been noted by the reader that the SINGLE DIAMOND KNOT (#693) is similar in appearance to a section of THREE-STRAND FLAT SINNET wrapped horizontally around the rope. The present knot is similar to FIVE-STRAND FLAT SINNET wrapped in similar manner. A DOUBLE CROWN and a SINGLE WALL having been tied with several strands, each end in turn is passed to the right over the first standing part and then is tucked up to center under three parts, as shown in the second illustration. The completed knot is shown as the final drawing of #707 (bottom right).

707. A DOUBLE CROWN AND MATTHEW WALKER. This being tied, the ends are tucked up under two parts to the center of the crown. This makes precisely the same knot as #706, but it is tied differently.

708. CROWN AND DIAMOND. First tie a crown, and, if wished, stop the strands to the stem as shown in #705. The ends below the stopping must be left long enough to tie the knot. Lead any strand to the right, passing over the first strand and under the second one.

Repeat with the other two strands in turn. Then tuck each strand up to the center top, passing under one part of the crown. This completes the SINGLE CROWN AND DIAMOND KNOT as pictured in the right top diagram.

709. A DOUBLE CROWN AND DIAMOND is started as the above knot, but the final tuck to the top center that was shown in #708 is not taken. Instead, when the diamond has been tucked "over one and under one" and the knot has progressed to the point shown in the left diagram, tuck any one end *down* through the crown, above and parallel with the adjacent strand of the original crown, as shown in the left diagram. Do likewise with the other two strands, and then follow the lead of the DIAMOND KNOT with all strands, one tuck at a time. Follow the original lead carefully and do not cross the strand you are following. Use the loop buttoner for tucking. When all parts have been doubled, the ends will issue from the tier shown in the left diagram. Sink the ends where they stand, and bring them out at the top. Fair the knot and work taut. In Sweden, according to Öhrvall, this is called ROSE KNOT (ROSENKNOP).

710. Twice crowned. Take four strands and tie two crowns, the second one outside (or below) the first. Draw the knot up loosely, and lead each end to the right over the next standing part and tuck up to the center under *two* parts as illustrated. The knot will have four flat faces.

711. WALL AND CROWN. Superficially this resembles #701, in which the crown comes first and the wall after. Often there are a number of ways in which to achieve a similar result. This fact makes the analysis of old paint-covered knots, that may not be opened, exceedingly difficult.

In this knot, after the wall and crown have been tied, the end parallels below the wall and is tucked up to the center inside four parts.

712. Another WALL AND CROWN. Start this like the last one, and then double the wall by following below the first lead. Do not stick up to the center, but take the ends and follow the lead of the wall a second time, making a THREE-PLY KNOT. Stick the ends up to the center under five parts.

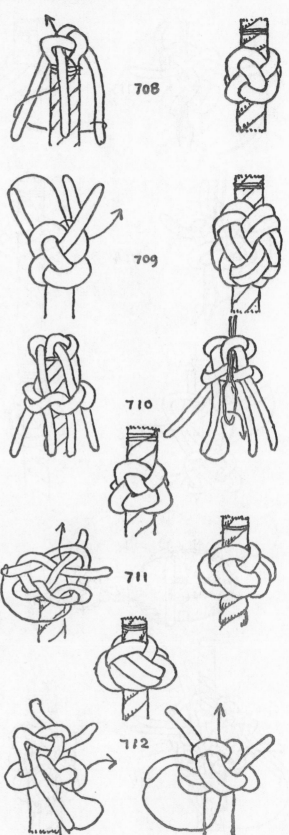

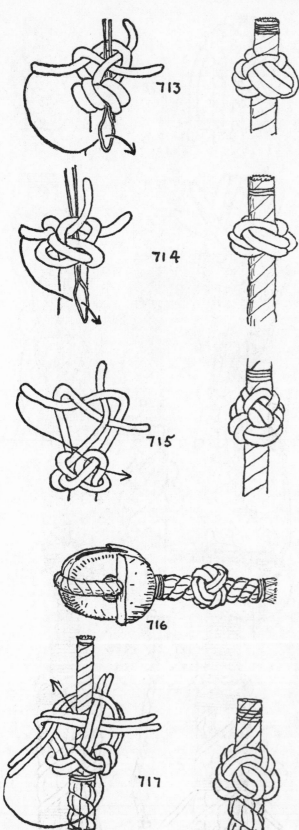

713. A number of old seamanship and rigging books, among them Bushell's (1854), recommend "*crowning* and *double walling*" the STOPPER KNOT when using it on a DECK STOPPER. The crown is designed to overcome a tendency to "roll" and capsize. I have found no description of the manner of disposing of the ends, but the ends could either be tucked to the stem, which would automatically make a BUTTON KNOT, eligible for the chapter to follow, or else they could be tucked up to the top center as shown here, making a true STOPPER KNOT.

714. A MATTHEW WALKER CROWNED, and tucked up in a manner similar to the last, makes a handsome knot resembling #701 and #710.

715. A DIAMOND KNOT CROWNED may be treated in the same way. After doubling the diamond by following *above* the original knot, tuck the ends where they lie up through the center of the crown to the top, without doubling the crown.

716. DIAMOND KNOT AND BLOCK STRAP. Seize a strap stoutly around the block, open the two ends, whip the six strands, and lay up the ends into three pairs—that is, into three two-strand ropes. Then close the three pairs into cable for the length required for the neck. Seize and tie a regular DIAMOND KNOT using the three two-strand ropes as strands. Lay up the ends for a further distance beyond the knot and whip. Directions for laying up ends will be found near the end of Chapter 1.

If difficulty is met in tying the knot with double strands, first tie it with single strands (employing every alternate one), and then double the knot with the three strands that were left out the first time. Lay up the ends as already directed.

717. Walter Thompson tied a CABLE STOPPER KNOT in the following way: Seize the cable stoutly, and open into nine strands. Take one inside strand from each rope, and lay the three up into a single rope for a core. Arrange the remaining six strands in pairs, and wall them around the structure, keeping the two strands of each pair parallel. Add a crown above the wall, and then tuck each pair of ends up to the top center as indicated by the arrow. Finally, lay the strands up right-handed into six-strand rope, around the single center core of three strands that was first made. Whip all ends, and trim them.

It is interesting to note that Walter Thompson, Captain Smith, and Captain Whitney all tied a number of knots, the knowledge of which they had acquired at sea many years after the practical needs for which the knots had originally been evolved no longer existed.

718. A CABLE STOPPER KNOT may be tied employing only six strands, using the remaining three strands as a core, in the follow-

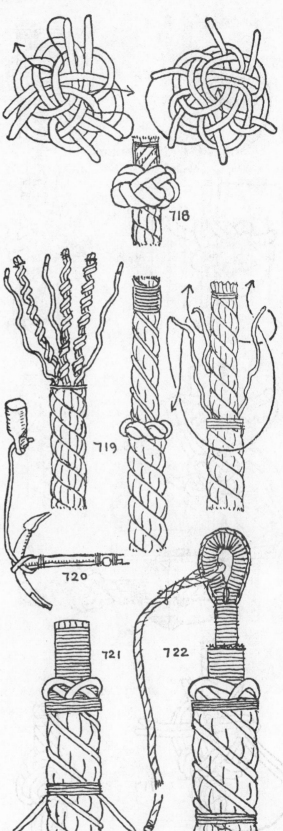

ing manner; or the knot may be tied in six-strand rope or sinnet, or else with the two ends of a three-strand strap or becket.

Single wall the six strands, then arrange the ends in three pairs of two strands each, and crown them as in the first diagram. Stick the left member of each pair under one additional part, as indicated by the arrow in the left diagram, and the knot will assume the appearance of the right diagram. Keeping the knot flat, follow below the original wall with each of the six ends and stick up to the center between two standing parts. Finally, lay up into SIX-STRAND ROUND SINNET or else six-strand right-hand rope.

719. The BUOY ROPE KNOT is described and named by Steel in 1794. It was put into the end of a cable-laid rope to provide a shoulder to assist in making the buoy rope fast to the anchor. First put on a heavy seizing, and open the cable into its three component ropes as far as the seizing. Next *lay out one strand from each rope end.* Stop all ends, and lay up the cable again with the three two-strand ropes that are left, having first beaten them well with a mallet. To do this, take two of the rope ends, twist them as hard as possible, and lay them up together. Then lay up the two with the remaining single rope end. Stop them, and beat them again to make them lie fair. Next, proceed to wall and double wall the three single strands where they were originally laid out. Draw the knot taut, and worm the three strands to the end of the cable. Finally, put on a strong spun-yarn whipping, which in width should equal the diameter of the cable.

720. In bending the buoy rope to an anchor the rope is first made fast to the crown of the anchor with BUOY ROPE HITCH ⚓3323, and then is seized next the crown. The knot is put halfway up the shank, and the rope is seized both above and below the BUOY ROPE KNOT.

721. To *crown a cable.* Put on a stout whipping some distance from the end, and open the cable into its nine separate strands. Take the three innermost strands (one from each of the three component ropes) and lay them up into a three-strand rope, to form a heart. Arrange the remaining six strands into pairs, take the right member of each pair, open it out and tease and fay it along the heart that was just made, and serve over all.

Crown the remaining three strands to the right, and worm them *back* along the cable their full length. Haul all taut and seize twice, once at the end of the worming and once close below the crown.

722. Luce in 1862 states that in crowning a cable "sometimes an artificial eye [⚓2796] is formed with the three inner strands." By means of this the cable is attached to a smaller rope and hauled out through the hawse pipe.

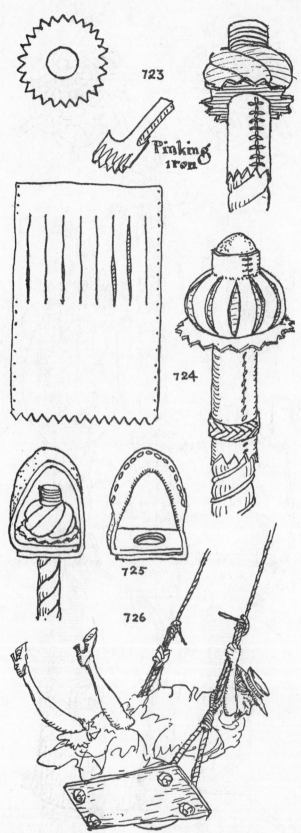

723. Wherever required, on both STOPPER and BUTTON KNOTS, *leather washers and often leather collars* are added to prevent excessive wear. The outer edges of the washers are always serrated, and the lower edge of the collar is treated in the same way. On smart ships "pinking irons" are provided the boatswain for the purpose, but a smart sailor can do quite as good a job with his jackknife—which, by the way, is a large, blunt clasp knife with a ring at the end, suspended from a neck lanyard and named after "Jack" himself. The stitches by which a collar is sewed are given as ⚓3538. There is always plenty of leather aboard ships, old boot tops, pump washers and rawhide chafing gear being the main sources.

724. A *slashed cap* was put over a MATTHEW WALKER KNOT whenever the knot was used on manrope and yoke ropes. This was done when a decorative knot smaller than the MANROPE KNOT was thought neater for the purpose. A piece of red leather was considered very smart, especially on a white-painted rope. A NARROW TURK'S-HEAD of small hard fishline added to the security of the collar.

After the MATTHEW WALKER KNOT had been tied, the piece of leather was slashed in the manner illustrated at the left. The length of the slashing and the spacing required careful planning. The width of the leather had to fit exactly the length of the rope and the circumference of the knot. The end fibers of the rope were trimmed to a dome shape. The holes for the stitches were punched with a bootmaker's awl. These things having been prepared, and the rope having been parceled and wormed, the sailor was ready to go to work. Is it any wonder that, with skilled labor at a dollar or more an hour, good knot work is pretty nearly a lost art?

725. A rope swivel requires an iron washer to provide a flat base on which the knot can revolve. A MATTHEW WALKER KNOT and a piece of sole leather are also required. The leather is cut as shown in the left diagram, and the center is piped around a short strand of rope and sewed to make a round member, through which an eye can be spliced. The washer and knot are greased with suet. If well made, no better swivel can be asked for.

726. STOPPER KNOTS, generally MATTHEW WALKER KNOTS, are used under the seats of swings and bosuns' chairs. For other seat arrangements, see the chairs on page 590. The height of the seat here shown is adjustable; see HITCH ⚓1800.

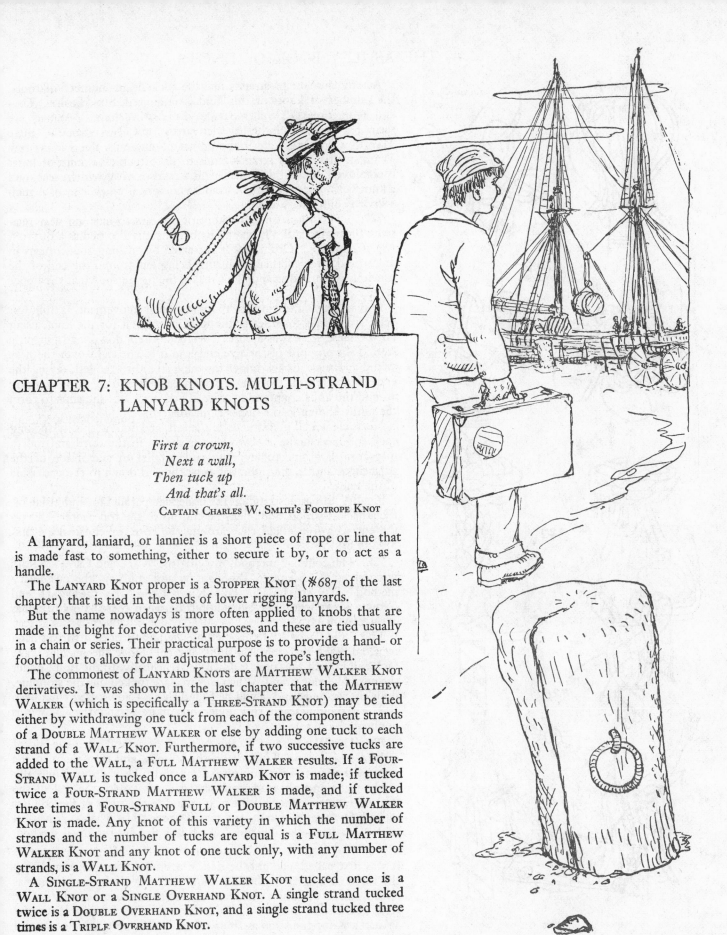

CHAPTER 7: KNOB KNOTS. MULTI-STRAND LANYARD KNOTS

First a crown,
Next a wall,
Then tuck up
And that's all.
CAPTAIN CHARLES W. SMITH'S FOOTROPE KNOT

A lanyard, laniard, or lannier is a short piece of rope or line that is made fast to something, either to secure it by, or to act as a handle.

The LANYARD KNOT proper is a STOPPER KNOT (#687 of the last chapter) that is tied in the ends of lower rigging lanyards.

But the name nowadays is more often applied to knobs that are made in the bight for decorative purposes, and these are tied usually in a chain or series. Their practical purpose is to provide a hand- or foothold or to allow for an adjustment of the rope's length.

The commonest of LANYARD KNOTS are MATTHEW WALKER KNOT derivatives. It was shown in the last chapter that the MATTHEW WALKER (which is specifically a THREE-STRAND KNOT) may be tied either by withdrawing one tuck from each of the component strands of a DOUBLE MATTHEW WALKER or else by adding one tuck to each strand of a WALL KNOT. Furthermore, if two successive tucks are added to the WALL, a FULL MATTHEW WALKER results. If a FOUR-STRAND WALL is tucked once a LANYARD KNOT is made; if tucked twice a FOUR-STRAND MATTHEW WALKER is made, and if tucked three times a FOUR-STRAND FULL or DOUBLE MATTHEW WALKER KNOT is made. Any knot of this variety in which the number of strands and the number of tucks are equal is a FULL MATTHEW WALKER KNOT and any knot of one tuck only, with any number of strands, is a WALL KNOT.

A SINGLE-STRAND MATTHEW WALKER KNOT tucked once is a WALL KNOT or a SINGLE OVERHAND KNOT. A single strand tucked twice is a DOUBLE OVERHAND KNOT, and a single strand tucked three times is a TRIPLE OVERHAND KNOT.

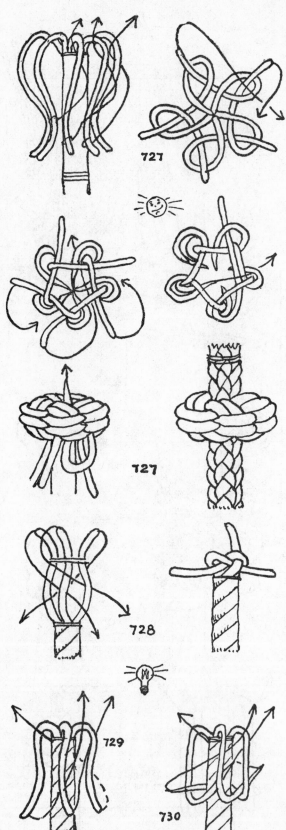

As any number of strands may be tucked any number of times, the number of knots of this kind is unlimited. Six-, Eight-, Ten- and (sometimes) Twelve-Strand Full Matthew Walkers are seen on sailors' clothesbag lanyards, and Nine-Strand Full Matthew Walkers are found on cat-o'-nine-tails. But a Matthew Walker of over six strands tends to distort unless a core or heart is employed, so anything over eight strands is very seldom seen, and a knot with more tucks than strands is practically never seen, as such a knot is difficult to work.

727. The Star is a unique knot; it appears to have no near relatives. Primarily, it is a Lanyard Knot, but it is also tied as a Button. (See Chapter 9.) Ordinarily it is started by making round turns in one strand after another, each turn being led around the end of the previously worked strand. This makes the figure shown at the upper right.

It may be found simpler to tie the first movement as follows: Seize six strands together at the length required for the knot, using one of these strands as a core. Turn the others down, and put on a stop. Take any one of the five and lead it to the right over the next strand and tuck it back under the same strand to the left, laying the end up at the top. Do likewise with each strand in turn, working around the knot counterclockwise. Then draw out the ends to form the figure shown in the upper right diagram.

Next, crown all five strands to the left, and follow this by tucking each end back under its own part as shown in the third and fourth diagrams. Continue to lay each end parallel to and inside of the adjacent strand to the right, and tuck the end down to the underside of the knot.

Finally, lead each strand on the underside parallel to, and inside of, the adjacent strand, and stick the end up to the top center. Lay up the end as a five-strand rope around the core, or else make a Six-Strand Sinnet.

728. The common methods of tying the Wall and Crown Knots were given in Chapter 6. By adapting and applying the customary method of tying the Diamond Knot (#693) to the Wall and Crown Knots the close relationship between these knots becomes at once evident.

To tie the Crown by this method: Seize and open a three-strand rope, and stop the strands a short distance above the seizing. Take each end in turn, and tuck it downward, helically, to the right, under the next adjacent strand. When all three are tucked cut the stopping, draw up the ends, and it will be found that a Crown Knot has been tied. By tucking each end under one more strand the Crown is doubled.

729. The Wall Knot by this method: Seize and open the end of a three-strand rope. Turn down the strands, and stop them to the stem of the knot. Take any one strand and tuck it upward helically to the right under the adjacent strand. Repeat with the rest of the strands, each time moving the next strand to the right of the one last moved. Draw up the knot, and it will prove to be a Wall, identical with #671 in the last chapter, which was tied by the usual method.

730. The Matthew Walker, or Matthew Walker's Knot as it was first called, can also be tied in a similar way: Seize and stop the three strands as in the last knot, and tuck each strand once as already directed. Then tuck each strand once more helically to the right in the same manner as before directed. This forms a Matthew Walker Knot the same as #682 in the last chapter, which was tied

by the usual sailor's method. If the ends are each tucked once more under the next intervening strand a FULL or DOUBLE MATTHEW WALKER is tied (#678), in which each strand has three tucks.

731. A MULTI-STRAND MATTHEW WALKER KNOT with *any number of strands and any number of tucks* may be tied by the method just given.

Take six (more or less) pieces of banding, eighteen or twenty inches long, seize, or stop, and "COACHWHIP" for a short length along a rope or other cylinder of about half-inch diameter. The seizings should be about two inches apart. Paste a piece of paper snugly around the cylinder. The paper should be large enough to cover the three seizings neatly, which hides the inert part of the knot. Turn down the top ends of banding, and stop them about three and one half inches down the paper sleeve that was just formed, and twist them to the right, countercorkscrew fashion, so that they form a 45-degree helix.

Take each strand in turn, and tuck it up under the adjacent strand to the right. Having completed one entire circuit or tier, tuck each strand again under one, and continue to add as many tiers as wished. The knot should now resemble the third or left diagram in the second row. Six or seven tiers will be sufficient, as it is difficult to work a knot if the number of tucks very much exceeds the number of strands. Arrange the knot neatly, and take a one-inch strip of wrapping or adhesive paper and wind it several times tightly around the waist of the knot, before pasting down the end (fourth diagram). Having added this sleeve, cut the stopping and remove the underneath paper sleeve. Working the knot constantly to keep it fair, pull each end gently in turn. The standing ends at the bottom may also be pulled, if they are not already made up into a rope or sinnet. As the knot is worked, the seizings may be removed, with the exception of the uppermost, which is permanent. Keep the edges of the knot parallel and regular. When the knot is taut remove the outside paper sleeve.

From these directions, Eugene E. du Pont, who had never made a MATTHEW WALKER KNOT before, tied in my studio, without other assistance, the TWENTY-FOUR-STRAND, TWENTY-ONE-TUCK MATTHEW WALKER KNOT that is reproduced among the frontispieces. This is probably the largest MATTHEW WALKER KNOT that has ever been tied. It would be impractical to tie a knot of this description by the sailor's method (#678) although it could be done by the method given as #683, of which method this is an elaboration.

732. A DOUBLE SINGLE MATTHEW WALKER KNOT is tied by following the lead below the next bight to the right. Tie an OVERHAND KNOT in each end *after* you have led it, to assist in identification.

733. A DOUBLE FULL MATTHEW WALKER KNOT of three strands: Tie a DOUBLE MATTHEW WALKER loosely. Take any strand and lay it parallel and below the next strand to its right. Tuck it up to the immediate *left* of the strand that is being followed, and draw it out at the top, immediately in advance of its own bight. *At once* tie an OVERHAND KNOT in the end so that the strand may be identified. Repeat with the other two strands, putting a knot in each end as soon as tied.

734. A CUBE-SHAPED DIAMOND KNOT. Take four strands, seize them to the stem, and tie a wall to the right. Having done this, tuck each strand in turn *over* one and *under* one. Work the knot into the form of a cube.

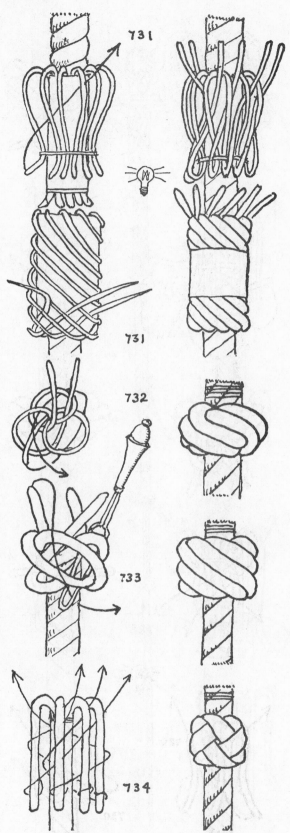

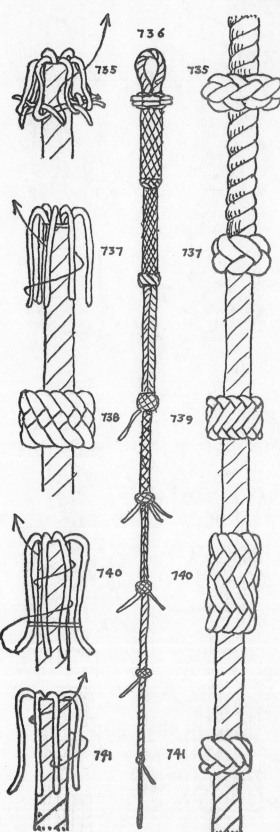

735. A HALF ROUND DIAMOND KNOT. With six strands tie in the same manner as the previous knot. Seize the strands and tie a WALL KNOT (#729), and then tuck each strand again, over one and under one. Draw up into half round form as depicted in the top right diagram. If the length of the knot is increased by additional tucks it will lose its shape and become cylindrical.

736. A *bag lanyard*, quirt, or leash is generally tapered. It is started at the larger end, and from time to time strands are "dropped out," one, two, or several at a time. While making, or when the sinnet of which the lanyard is composed has been completed, the ends that are laid out are tied into several kinds of knots: a single strand into a running TURK'S-HEAD, two strands into KNOT #792, three or more strands into FOOTROPE, DIAMOND, STAR, and other knots of this chapter. A variety of tapered lanyards are illustrated in Chapter 41, and others are shown in photographs among the frontispieces.

737. A DIAMOND KNOT which in texture superficially resembles a FIVE-STRAND FLAT SINNET (#2967) horizontally wrapped around a vertical section of rope.

Turn down a number of strands, and stop them to the stem. Four to eight strands are sufficient. Take any one strand and lead it in an upward helix to the right, over the first three strands, and under the next three, and lay the end out at the top. If preferred, tuck over two and under two instead. Take the next strand to the right and do likewise. Continue with each strand in turn until all strands have been passed. Work the knot taut.

738. A DIAMOND KNOT variation (1). Take six or eight strands (a knot with an even number is generally more practicable, since most sinnets have an even number of strands). Seize the strands to the stem, and tuck each strand to the right under the three adjacent parts. The knot having been carefully faired, each strand is tucked again in turn, *over one* and under three, then the knot is drawn up.

739. A DIAMOND KNOT variation (2). Take a number of strands (six or eight). Seize the strands, and then stop them to the stem below the seizing. Wall them to the right, and lead each strand in turn to the right, over four and under one.

740. A DIAMOND KNOT variation (3) with a twill weave. Take six or eight strands (the left illustration shows four, but a greater number is preferable). Seize them twice, leaving a considerable space between the seizings. Take any one strand and lead it to the right over the first two strands and under the next two strands. Move each of the remaining strands in turn to the right in exactly the same way as the first. Fair the strands, and then tuck each one again, in exactly the same manner as the first time, over two and under two, until all have been passed. Draw them up carefully, using a pricker at half length, as the knot will distort if the ends only are pulled. The knot may also be tied over three and under three.

741. A DIAMOND KNOT variation (4) that is an inversion of SINNET KNOT #704. Take four or any convenient number of strands and move each strand in turn to the right over one and under four.

742. The next two numbers are based on the FOOTROPE KNOT. With four strands make a crown and stop the ends down to the stem. Take any strand and tuck it to the right over one and under one. Repeat with the other three strands. Tuck all four strands to the right again, over one and under one, which forms a second tier. Repeat, tying as many tiers as desired below the original crown. When the wanted length has been tied, tuck each end up through the crown to the top center, *under two parts* as illustrated.

743. A second knot based on the FOOTROPE KNOT. This differs from the preceding knot in having a WALL KNOT at the base. Having been crowned and walled, the strands are tucked in tiers as before, over one and under one, as many times as wished.

To double this knot: When the point is reached where the final tuck under two parts was taken in the preceding knot, tuck *under one part only*, and proceed to follow (parallel) above the adjacent strand. When the knot is completely doubled, each of the four ends is tucked under four parts (two doubled parts) to the top.

744. A *knot tied in the end*, outside and above the seizing. Seize and open a three-strand rope, and put a stopping a short way above the seizing. Tuck each end in a downward helix to the right *under* the first obstructing strand. Then move all ends again, over the next strand and under the following one. Repeat as many times as wanted, then stick each strand up through the center to the top. Make certain that no two ends are tucked up between the same two strands; they should erupt at regular intervals.

745. The EMERALD KNOT. This knot is so named because it is closely related to the DIAMOND, but it appears distinctive enough to enjoy a name of its own. The distinguishing feature of the knot is that the strands at both ends enter or leave the knot at the surface instead of the interior, as the MATTHEW WALKER does, or from the center at one end and the surface at the other, as the DIAMOND and FOOTROPE KNOTS do.

The strands require careful preparation before tying, but the actual tying is quite as easy and much in the same manner as the DIAMOND KNOT. Take four strands and, having seized them, make a right hitch in each and stop the working half of the hitches together at the center. This is not quite so simple as it may appear, and it will be well to lay the four ends out flat on the table in the form of the second diagram. Having done this, work out some of the slack and arrange as in the fourth diagram. Tuck all strands to the right over one and under one, and then tuck them all a second time over one and under one. When making a lanyard employing these knots alone, tie them at close intervals, without laying up the strands between knots, and they will be most effective.

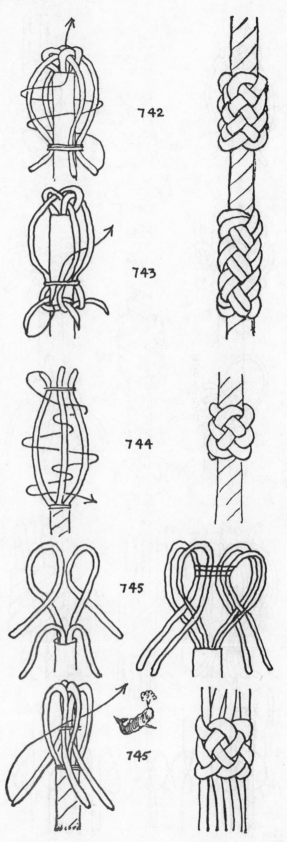

742

743

744

745

745

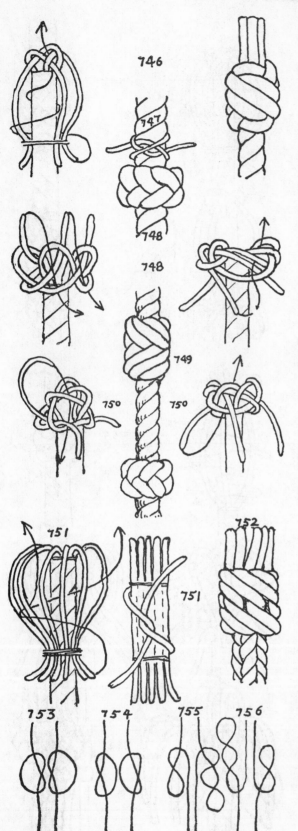

746. Another knot based on the FOOTROPE KNOT may be tied as follows: Crown three strands to the right, lay the ends down, and seize them to the stem. Tuck each end to the right in turn, over one and under three. After this, tuck each end up through the crown to the center top as in the illustration.

747. It has been recommended before that LANYARD KNOTS in which the strands at the end show a tendency to disperse should be tightened through a CONSTRICTOR KNOT, which is to be removed when the knot has been satisfactorily tied. This illustrates the process.

748. A DIAMOND KNOT may be doubled somewhat in the manner of the KNIFE LANYARD KNOT. It will resemble KNOT ⚓737, but it has twice as many parts as strands.

Having tied a DIAMOND KNOT of four (more or less) strands, tuck each end over the next strand and down through the next rim part to the right. After fairing the knot, take a loop buttoner (⚓99C) and draw each end up to the right, over the first two intervening parts, and under the next two parts. This should bring them out at the top center.

749. A knot of *herringbone texture*, that is twice the width of the former. Tie an over-two-and-under-two DIAMOND KNOT (⚓737). Then tuck each end down to the right under *two* rim parts. Finally, stick each end in turn up to the right over the first three parts and under the next three parts, which should bring it out at the top center. The whole cycle of the knot is now alternately over three and under three. The knot may require considerable gentling before it will lie fair.

750. A FOOTROPE KNOT can be doubled in somewhat the same way as DIAMOND KNOT ⚓748, the result being similar but reversed.

Crown and wall three strands in the usual way, then tuck each end down through the top and to the right of the next end as indicated by the arrow in the left diagram; finally, tuck up under four parts as indicated by the arrow in the right diagram.

751. A ZIGZAG LANYARD KNOT that is based on TURK's-HEAD ⚓1378. The strands in this knot do not encircle the stem. They are led in an upward diagonal to the left, and then returned an equal distance in an upward diagonal to the right.

Seize six or eight strands twice to the central part of a sinnet. Turn down the upper ends, and stop them below the lower seizing as shown. Take any one of the ends that were just turned down, lead it to the *left* over *four* strands, and tuck it up to the right under *one* strand. Do likewise with each of its sister strands. Then tuck each end in turn to the right under a second strand; repeat, tucking each end in turn under one strand only at a time, until all strands have been tucked four times to the right. Draw up the knot, and it will appear as depicted in the right diagram.

752. A *knot of similar aspect* but differently tied. Middle six or eight strands along the central part of a small core, and seize them twice, two or three inches apart. Twist the strands into a right (corkscrew) helix of about forty-five degrees. Lead the two ends of one strand around the structure as pictured, and tie them together with a LEFT HALF KNOT. Rotate the structure, doing the same in pairs with the other ends. Then tuck each upper end under the next strand to the right. Repeat until all strands of that end have been tucked four times. Turn the structure upside down, and tuck each of the opposing ends to the right three times in exactly the same way. All ends having been tucked four times, draw up the knot, removing the core, and lay the ends up into a sinnet.

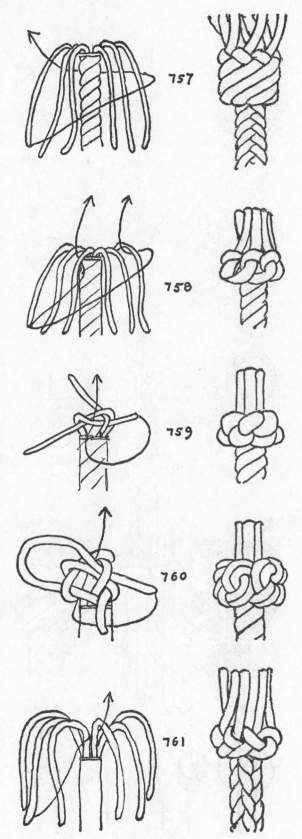

753. These diagrams illustrate the difference in cycles of the several knots that are under discussion. Number 753 is the MATTHEW WALKER KNOT. It is an imaginary profile of two strands that have made a complete circuit within the knot.

754. This shows the cycle of #745 and also of #752. In three dimensions the two strands interlock.

755. The DIAMOND KNOT of the last chapter and also #748 of this chapter conform to the profile at the left. The right side is #734 and #736 of this chapter.

756. The FOOTROPE KNOT, which has been discussed in both the last chapter and in the present one, is shown here.

The illustrations on this page represent SINNET KNOTS, which differ from LANYARD and STOPPER KNOTS in that the strand ends are left free, being neither whipped nor laid up. SINNET KNOTS are designed to grip the several strands so firmly that they may be separately employed, as in bag lanyards, cat-o'-nine-tails, and key guards.

757. The DIAMOND SINNET KNOT is the one most often seen. The SINNET KNOT was both named and pictured by E. N. Smith in *Log Book Notes* (1888). Generally the knot is tied in bag lanyards with either six or eight strands; occasionally they have ten and seldom twelve. Ditty-bag lanyards are sometimes tied with as few as four strands. Nine strands are required when the knot is tied in a "cat." Usually each strand makes a complete circuit of the knot, and the end is tucked under its own bight as illustrated.

758. Captain Charles W. Smith's SINNET KNOT is tied in the manner illustrated here. Each strand of his ditty-bag lanyard was passed around the second strand to the right. His clothesbag (which serves an officer as laundry bag) had eight legs in the lanyard. Each leg passed to the right over four strands and then rounded the fifth.

759. Captain Albert Whitney first crowned the legs and then tucked them up to the center reversely as pictured, to make his SINNET KNOT.

760. The LINK SINNET KNOT is crowned to the right and then walled to the left. Double the knot by tucking the ends above to the right and parallel with the crown. Continue to follow each lead outside its periphery, and finally tuck the ends up to the center as illustrated by the arrow in the first diagram.

761. Another SINNET KNOT. Seize a number of strands, and stop the ends to the stem. Pass any strand to the right, over the next strand and under or behind the standing part of the second strand, tucking it up to the left of the working end of the same strand (the second). Move each strand in turn in a like manner.

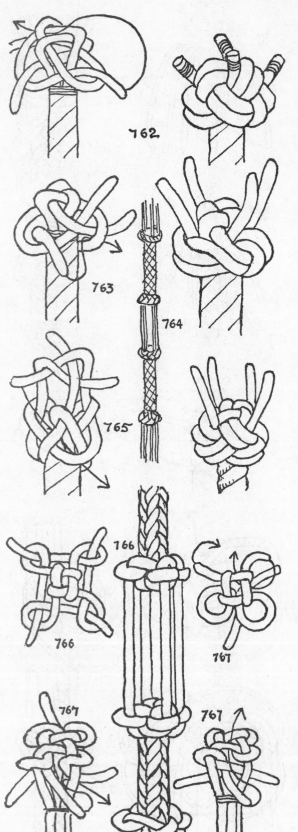

762. Admiral Luce's Deck Stopper Knot, from the 1884 edition of his *Seamanship*, is no longer used for its original purpose, and, as it has much in common with the Sinnet Knots of this chapter, it is introduced here.

With three or four strands make a crown and then a wall; double the crown by following the lead on the upper or inside. Continuing on the same side of the lead, double the wall. Whip the ends singly, if they are to be cut off, or else employ them for the legs of a lanyard.

763. A Single Crown and Double Wall. Crown and wall three or four strands. Double the wall only, by following below the next end to the right. Then stick the ends up to the right, under the two parts that lie immediately ahead, which brings the end outside of the original crown. If the knot has been correctly tied it will be found that in the last tuck each end passes under four strands.

764. The knots of this and the preceding page have this characteristic in common: the strands at one end enter the knot at the center and at the other end disperse at the outer edge. The Diamond Knot and the Footrope Knot of the last chapter also have this characteristic, but each is the reverse of the other. This is also true of Wall and Crown Knots. These two may be tied alternately to make a handsome lanyard. The strands between the two center leads may be made into two-strand rope or a Round Sinnet, and the strands between two outside leads may be left uncomplicated.

765. Manuel Perry's Sinnet Knot is larger than Admiral Luce's (#762) and it may be tied with any reasonable number of strands. With four or six strands the crown is closed at the rim, but with twelve it is wide open and the knot shaped like an umbrella or a mushroom. To make this, a Single Diamond Knot is first tied and then a Wall Knot is superimposed. After this the diamond is doubled or tripled by following below the initial lead, and the ends are laid out without doubling the crown.

I have seen a knot of sixteen strands, tied by Manuel Perry, that was commenced with an ordinary Diamond (#693), after which the present Sinnet Knot was added above that.

The remaining knots in this chapter are original.

766. A knot with very pronounced center and rim leads. Seize and crown four strands, draw the crown taut, and arrange the strands as in the left diagram, which is the same as the first movement of the Star Knot. Draw the knot taut.

767. Approximately the reverse of the preceding knot is tied in the following manner. Turn the first knot and structure upside down, and seize the strands at the length desired. Crown loosely, and then tuck all ends as indicated in the right upper diagram. Hold the knot vertically as in the left lower diagram, and tuck each end under the first standing part to the right as indicated by the arrow. Then stick each end in turn, as it lies, up under one part of the center crown. Draw up these two knots evenly, but not too tightly, so they are the same size.

The knots of this chapter have, so far, been of the sort known as the "built-up" variety. The Wall or Diamond, and the Crown

Knot have figured in each, and the final knot has been built up by a
series of more or less simple movements, in which each strand in turn
has progressed one tuck at a time, and the whole knot has grown
progressively in much the same way that a mechanical product is
added to, as it passes along an assembly bench. But the remaining two
pages consist of knots each of which is a unit in itself. To tie these
I know of no simpler way than to bring the strands up through a
hole in a board and then to pin the knots out over the clearly defined
lines of a diagram.

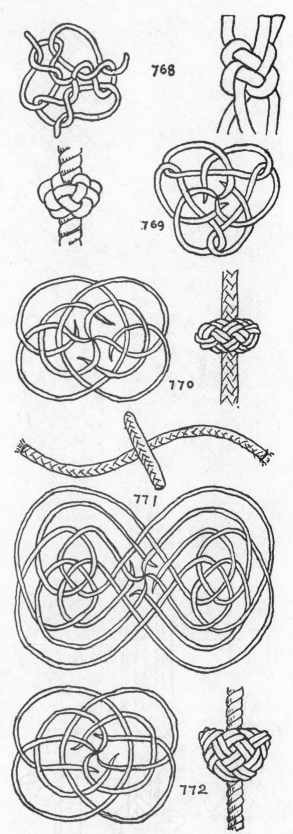

768. A knot with a triangular cross section and three square faces.
Seize three strands only, and bring the ends up through the hole in
the cork board. Place them over a diagram that is about three times
larger than the original shown here in the upper left corner. Pin one
cord carefully along the lines of the diagram for the complete circuit
of one strand, then add the other strands in turn and draw up the
knot with the rim part closed around the stem, mushroom-fashion.
If tied with four strands this knot will lose character.

769. The Lanyard Knot alongside is adapted from Multi-
Strand Button #624. To be suitable for such adaptation the outer
rim of a Button Knot should have preferably four bights or parts,
but this one has six. The standing part is led up through the hole in
the board, and, having formed the knot, the ends are led upward
and, after being drawn up, are made into a sinnet. The skirts of all
the knots on this page close downward around the stems, mushroom-
fashion.

770. A knot of four strands with an elliptical cross section based
on Button Knot #617. The stem is passed down through the hole
in the table or board, and the ends, *after the knot is made*, are stuck
to the top. This knot should be doubled. It will be found that two
of the strands that are required to tie the knot are much shorter than
the other two.

771. A Toggle-Shaped Knot of four strands. If it is required to
strengthen this knot a meat skewer of the proper length may be
thrust through it. Any knot of this size must be worked gradually
and methodically.

772. A Pocket-Shaped Knot of four strands. The diagrams of this
knot and of #770 have much in common. Nevertheless, their different shapes are both quite logical and require little prodding, provided
the knots are worked with precision.

It appears possible to adapt a section of almost any sinnet to form
a Multi-Strand Lanyard Knot diagram. A sinnet on end and projected into a circle automatically forms a Turk's-Head, and any
single Turk's-Head may be tied as a Multi-Strand Turk's-Head
if wished.

A Multi-Strand Turk's-Head with the several strands symmetrically arranged so that they pass out at opposite ends of a cylindrical-
shaped knot is potentially a Lanyard Knot. The ends may be laid
up into either a sinnet or a rope, or else merely laid out. The two
knots to be given here were first made as sinnets; later they were
made into Turk's-Heads. (See Chapter 17.)

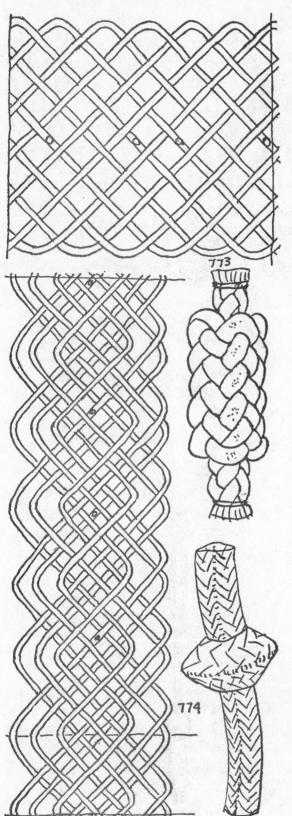

773. A Long Four-Strand Lanyard Knot with a square cross section is based on Sinnet #2998 and Turk's-Head #1390.

To make: Trace the diagram carefully on a piece of white paper (see directions, page 22). Take a strip of heavy Manila wrapping paper three inches wide and ten to fifteen inches long or longer according to the weight and stiffness of the paper. Cut off the ends of the white paper diagram flush with the two vertical lines, and paste the diagram to one end of the wrapping paper even with one edge. Roll the paper up with the diagram on the outside. When the two edges of the diagram coincide, paste the end down. Hold firmly with elastic bands, and set aside to dry.

Seize a Four-Strand Sinnet, leaving all strand ends about two feet long. Make holes where the four dots appear on the diagram, and, using a looped wire, reeve one of the strands from the left end of the cylinder out through a hole to the surface. Stick a pin at the center of each rim bight on the diagram, twelve in all. Lead the strand along its circuit, following the lead and the over-and-under of the diagram. When the working end reaches a convenient hole stick it down and out, to the right. Reeve the second strand through a hole, and continue in the same direction as the first. Do the same with the remaining strands, leading each, when it has completed its circuit, out of the cylinder and to the right.

Using scissors, cut away the paper cylinder without disturbing the knot, and draw all taut.

774. A Triangular Knot tied with four strands. Take a piece of paper eleven or more inches long. Start at the upper end of the tracing paper, and trace the full length of the diagram, then add another section to the bottom of the first tracing, beginning with the top of the diagram and stopping at the dotted line which lies about seven eighths of an inch from the bottom. The total tracing will be about ten and one half inches long. Take a large mailing tube, if one is available, and wind paper around it until it is the right size to fill the paper diagram, or else make a tube of stiff wrapping paper as directed for #773, but much stiffer, and tie in the same manner as above.

CHAPTER 8: KNOB KNOTS. TWO-STRAND LANYARD KNOTS

This is the knot sailors use to ornament the lanyards they hang their knives from, when they wear them round their necks.

CAULFIELD AND SAWARD: *Dictionary of Needlework*, 1882

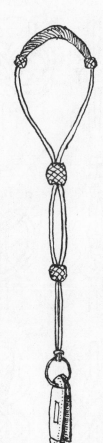

The knots of this chapter are tied with two cords which enter at the top or bottom of the knot and depart at the other end.

The quotation given above refers to the "FLAT LANYARD" or "BOSUN'S KNOT," as it is called by sailors, or the CHINESE KNOT, as it is called in needlework. The CHINESE KNOT is one of a large family, the smallest of which is the CARRICK BEND.

All the knots of this family have a regular over-one-and-under-one texture that is termed *basket weave*. They are tied in a plane, and their diagram forms consist of two sets of parallel lines, at right angles to each other and diagonal with the sides. the knots themselves being rectangular.

There is only one limitation to the size and proportions of the knots of this sort that can be made. The number of crossings in the two adjoining sides of a knot cannot have a common divisor. If this rule is violated more than two strands will be required to tie the knot.

The name BASKET WEAVE KNOT has been applied to all rectangular knots of this variety, of whatever proportions. The name BOSUN'S KNOT is limited to knots having one more or one less crossing in one side than in the adjoining side, and the name CHINESE KNOT is applied only to a BOSUN'S KNOT that has three by four side crossings. The CARRICK BEND has two by three side crossings.

[139]

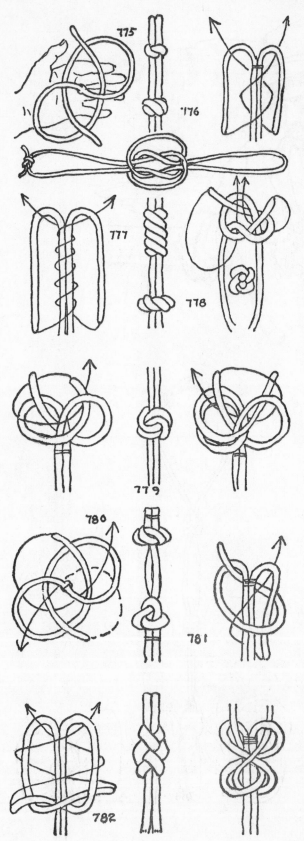

There are two general ways of "building up" or increasing the size of a BASKET WEAVE KNOT. The number of diagonals may be increased by reeving the ends, which enlarges the knot in both dimensions, or the cord ends and the intervening loops of one side may be extended and platted together, which lengthens the knot only.

Any BASKET WEAVE KNOT of two strands may be tied in a lanyard, but the BOSUN'S KNOTS have the ends of a single strand at two corners of the same side of the knot. So in order for the strand to progress from one knot to the next, that side must lie in the same direction as the lanyard itself. The number of crossings along the *side* will always be even. A corner crossing is counted in the census of both top and side.

Any (A ± 2 = B) KNOT (with two more or two less crossings on one side than on the adjoining side) can be tied, in which the number of crossings of each side is odd; and as the cord in such a knot progresses diagonally from corner to corner, a knot may be tied either vertically or horizontally to form either a lanyard, a net, or a fringe.

Although BASKET WEAVE KNOTS are distinctive and handsome, they have one characteristic that at times is a drawback. Being tied in one plane, they are as thin as potato chips and have the same tendency to curl and twist. To overcome this tendency I have experimented with similar knots in two planes, several of which will be given at the end of this chapter. Among these are included two knots of similar characteristics which require four cords.

But before proceeding with BASKET WEAVE KNOTS we will first discuss TWO-STRAND LANYARD KNOTS having other characteristics.

TWO-CORD LANYARD KNOTS are often tied decoratively in black silk cords. These are, or were, worn on spectacles, monocles, lorgnettes, watch chains, and guards, belts, necklaces, and hat cords.

Sailors use them tied in larger material, on knife, marlingspike, whistle, and pipe lanyards.

775. The TWO-STRAND WALL KNOT may be tied by the common sailor's method shown here, or by the method shown as ⚓729, in the preceding chapter.

776. A TWO-STRAND MATTHEW WALKER KNOT that was also tied as ⚓730 in the last chapter. This knot, besides making a decorative LANYARD KNOT, is a practical jug or jar sling. The neck of a jar or bottle is gripped in the center of the knot.

777. By tucking each strand in turn, a number of times, the TWO-STRAND MATTHEW WALKER KNOT can be lengthened, in the same manner that the MULTI-STRAND KNOT was lengthened in the preceding chapter.

778. A TWO-STRAND STOPPER KNOT is made by tucking the ends of a WALL KNOT beyond an additional standing part, and then sticking them up through the center. This gives four rim parts as against the two of the WALL KNOT.

779. A DOUBLE WALL KNOT of two strands, with the lead followed above, is quite different in character from the MULTI-STRAND KNOT. First tie the wall as in ⚓775, then hold the knot vertically and tuck the ends as shown by arrows in the two diagrams.

780. A DOUBLE WALL KNOT, with the lead followed below the first wall, closely resembles the MULTI-STRAND WALL KNOT.

781. The TWO-STRAND DIAMOND KNOT is tied the same way as the MULTI-STRAND KNOT. One working end is led to the right over

the next working end and up through its own bight. The second strand is moved in exactly the same way.

782. The Two-Strand Diamond may be lengthened by additional tucking. The drawing shows the knot first walled and then each strand tucked over the next standing part to the right and up through the following bight. Knot #781 may be lengthened in the same way.

783. The Two-Strand Footrope Knot is tied exactly as Three-Strand Knot #696: "First a crown, next a wall, then tuck up, and that's all." The tuck is through the center of the crown, and under one part only.

784. The Crown and Diamond. As the next four knots are a bit elusive, I suggest that the reader pin them out on the cork board and tie them flat as pictured.

After the Crown and Diamond Knot is tied, the ends are tucked up directly through the crown. The knot may be worked in flattened form as pictured, or else worked into a four-sided form.

785. The length of the Crown and Diamond Knot may be added to by further tucking. In this illustration each end is tucked over and under a second time only. It will be well to stop the strands to the stem before starting to tie the knot.

786. With two strands, crown the knot to the right, and then tie a single diamond, well below the crown. After that tuck each strand to the right under the next standing part and then repeat. This will give three consecutive underpasses for each strand. Finally, tuck the ends up through the crown to the center.

787. The Sailor's Knife Lanyard Knot, also called Marlingspike Lanyard Knot, Single-Strand Diamond Knot, Two-Strand Diamond Knot, and Bosun's Whistle Knot.

The several drawings alongside illustrate the common sailor's way of making the knot, which is also the most expeditious way of tying it. Middle a piece of banding three feet long, and hang it over the fingers of the left hand. With the right hand wind the back end around the left hand and take a turn over the tip of the left thumb. Transfer the turn that is around the thumb to the palm of the left hand directly over the other part of the cord. Continue to hold the turn in place with the thumb. Take the so far inactive front end and lead it to the right, tucking under the opposite end and continuing to the left, alternately tucking over and under as shown in the diagram. Fair the knot as it now stands, lead each end counterclockwise beyond the next part that passes around the back of the hand, and tuck it up through the center of the knot. Remove the knot from around the hand, and extend the loop that was originally around the back of the hand until it is long enough to form a necklace. Then draw the knot taut.

788. To double the Knife Lanyard Knot: Instead of tucking the ends as in the left diagram of the previous knot, tuck them as in the *right* diagram of the present one, then double by leading the two ends along the *inner* side of the initial lead. When all except the back loop and two rim parts have been doubled, tuck the ends as in the left diagram. The knot is then drawn up. In both knots the surface pictured in the diagram is the outside of the finished knot. The loop at the back of the hand is extended to form a necklace, and the rim is turned down to encircle the stem.

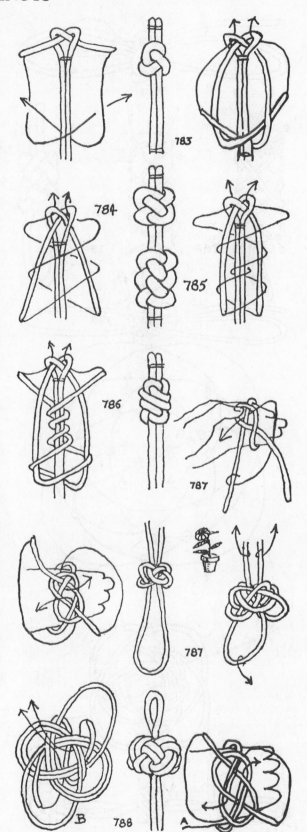

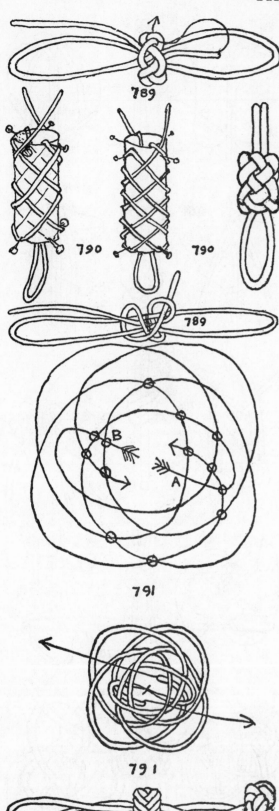

789

790   790

789

791

791

789. To conceal the ends of strands in a lanyard: This may be done by looping the right end back, seizing the two ends and the bight together strongly at the point where the knot is to be tied, and then making a Three-Lead, Four-Bight Turk's-Head around the structure with the right end. The start for this is shown just below diagrams of ⅍790. When this point has been reached, turn the structure end for end and with the same end *plat* as ⅍1316 until the end has been tucked *twice;* finally, stick the end as in the upper diagram, which completes a single knot. If an irregularity is met while tucking the second end, pass over the first end.

To double this knot, tuck the hitherto inactive end from underneath up through one of the center compartments and double the knot with it, laying it parallel with the first knot. The last tuck after the knot is completely doubled should be thrust underneath all to the rim. Draw up and cut the ends short.

An alternative treatment that will give practically the same effect is to seize the parts very firmly and cut them off. Then tie a Running Turk's-Head (⅍1305) over the juncture with a piece of the same sort of material. This may be doubled or trebled if wished.

790. To tie a Four-Lead Diamond Knot of any length with two strands only: Take a short section of mailing tube (the tube from a toilet-paper roll will do), and stick four pins equidistant around each end.

Double an eight- or nine-foot piece of banding, and tie an Over-hand Knot in it to make a loop at the center about six or seven inches long. Drop the loop down through the tube, leaving the two ends at the top. Lay the ends out opposite each other, and lead them around two pins in a right diagonal of forty-five degrees downward and parallel with each other. Round a pin with each end, and lead them upward in a right diagonal. When the top is reached, round the two empty pins that remain, and lead the cords downward in a right diagonal to the two empty pins at the bottom. Round these and tuck each strand up to the right, under the first opposite diagonal encountered. Then work one end at a time and stick it over, under, over, under, etc., to the top. The last tuck will be under the bight of the initial lead. Remove pins, draw the knot off at the top, guard against torsion, and work taut very gradually.

791. This knot, which superficially resembles ⅍737, is tied by bringing the two cords of the lanyard up through the hole in the cork board and laying first the end marked A and then B along the

[142]

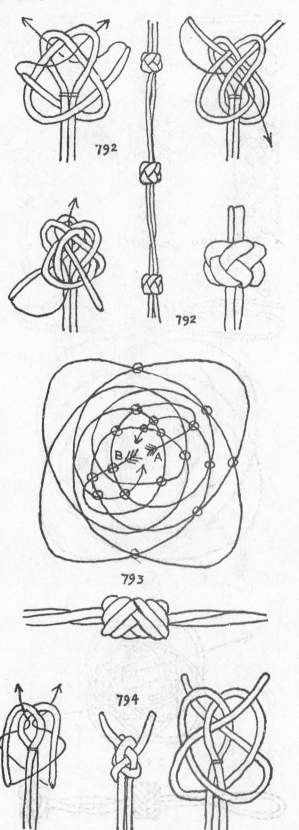

two arrow lines in the manner that has already been described. The working ends are finally lifted to the top.

Button Knot ⌗980 is tied at the end of a two-cord lanyard, if a button is required for the final knot. If the initial knot is to be a button, Chinese Button ⌗602 or any of the Single-Cord Buttons of Chapter 5 may be tied.

792. A Footrope Knot can be doubled so that the surface resembles a horizontal section of Five-Strand Flat Sinnet ⌗2967.

Crown and wall two strands, and tuck both ends up, over and under as illustrated. Tuck each end down to the right under the last bight that was made by the other end. Lead each end to the right beyond one standing part, and tuck up to the center. This knot is similar to ⌗791.

793. A Two-Strand Knot that is like ⌗791 and ⌗792, except that it is longer, is made on this diagram by the method first employed in the Single-Strand Button chapter, and that has also appeared several times in this chapter. Strand A is moved first along the line of the arrow, being pinned to the cork board at frequent intervals. Every time another part of the cord is crossed at a point marked with a circle the working end is tucked under. Having finished tucking the first cord, lead the second cord in the same manner.

In working this knot, constant care must be taken to work the bights away from the waist of the knot, as they have a tendency to pull up underneath and destroy the lay.

794. A knot similar to this, but unsymmetrical, was found in a Japanese book. The knot was altered as given here to make it symmetrical.

Many of the Single-Strand and Multi-Strand Button Knots can be tied as Two-Strand Lanyard Knots in the manner suggested by diagrams ⌗791 and ⌗793. Such knots should not have more than six parts around the rim, and four are better. It is not necessary that they should be round, although most of them are.

Additional Two-Strand Lanyard Knots flanked or fringed with loops will be found in the chapter on fancy knots. Chinese Priest Cord Knots are another variety of Two-Strand Lanyard Knots, but they are always tied with two sets of doubled parallel strands. These are to be found in the chapter on mats, or two-dimensional knots. Additional Multi-Strand Lanyards are discussed and illustrated in Chapter 32, "Square Knotting," and Chapter 41, on applied knots.

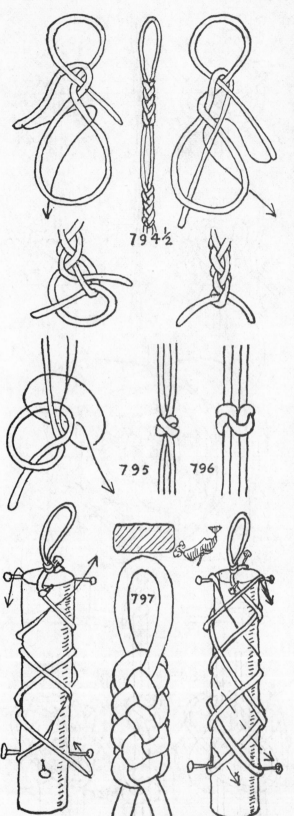

794½.

795   796

797

794½. ROUND SINNET in short sections may be tied in a two-cord lanyard by utilizing a loop to provide two additional strands for the length of the knot.

Arrange the cord as in the upper left diagram, and then plat as FOUR-STRAND ROUND or SQUARE SINNET, which is the same thing. The outer strands of either side are moved alternately. A strand is led around the back, then forward and down across the front of the lower of the two opposing strands, and finally down to the lower position of its own side. If the method is not familiar it will probably be easier to learn with four free strands (※2999). When the knot is of sufficient length, finish it off as in the two lower diagrams.

795. A LANYARD KNOT, made from two interlocked OVERHAND KNOTS. When completed, this turns out to be a TWO-STRAND MATTHEW WALKER KNOT.

796. A TURKISH LANYARD KNOT. Although the knot is tied with four strands, a section of the lanyard itself is made of the four ends of but two strands, which are doubled back on themselves at the knot.

The knot was tied in silk-wound silver wire and was found on a string of black amber beads that were shown to me by Mrs. George P. Gardner.

Öhrvall depicts the knot used architecturally in a Turkish stone column.

797. A knot of two strands with six diagonal leads. Take a round stick of wood about an inch or more in diameter and six or more inches long. Drive four equally spaced tacks around the top edge and a parallel row four or more inches below. Middle and knot or seize a loop six inches long into the doubled end of a piece of banding. Place the loop end across the end of the stick, to the left of two opposite tacks, and lead the two working ends in a right helix to the bottom of the stick, and there round two opposite tacks. Leave one end for a while, and tuck the other end in a right upward diagonal to the top *underneath* any *even* number of strands (in this case six) and round an empty tack at the top. Lead the other end *over all* to the top, parallel with the last laid end, and around the remaining tack. Tuck each end downward in a right diagonal, alternately over and under (or under and over), to the bottom.

Remove all tacks, and slip the knot from the stick, ready to draw up. Although there are six strands in the knot, four are in one diagonal and only two in the other. The number of crossings in the two sets of diagonals is, of course, the same. There will be a slight tendency to twist, but if the knot is worked gradually, this is easily overcome. A cross section of the knot is oblong, and it may be differently flattened, so that the center of the flat face may have the opposite diagonal from what is pictured. This will be equally firm and equally decorative.

798. The TRUE-LOVER'S KNOT. There are a number of knots bearing this name to be found in Chapter 31; this is one of the few that do not have loops at the edges. Like #796 and several knots that are to follow, it is made up of two interlocked knots, in this case two OVERHANDS.

799. Another LANYARD KNOT composed of two OVERHAND KNOTS. This is from a Japanese book.

800. A HORIZONTAL MATTHEW WALKER KNOT of two strands. Instead of being led through the knot from the same end, the two cords are introduced at opposite ends.

A LEFT HALF KNOT is tied with the two ends around a wire loop, the loop being to the left. Two round turns are next taken with the right end back around the wire and the HALF KNOT, which serve as a temporary core. Insert the end that was just moved, through the wire loop, and draw it through to the right, as shown in the first two diagrams. Then take the other end and make two and one half turns as pictured, paralleling the previous strand, but in the contrary direction.

Next, stick the wire loop through the knot from the left and parallel with the end that was previously drawn through. Reeve the second end through the loop, and draw it back through the knot to the left side.

Work this knot very carefully and methodically, as it can be easily distorted.

A knot of somewhat similar appearance that is easier to work is used in making a rope ladder. It is given in Chapter 41 as #3834.

801. The regular MATTHEW WALKER KNOT of two strands may be tied horizontally and in outward appearance is similar to the previous knot but is much shorter.

802. Captain Charles W. Smith's SINNET KNOT, #758 of the previous chapter, may be tied with two strands and has somewhat the character of a DIAMOND KNOT.

803. A FLAT SQUARE KNOT composed of two interlocked forms that are really OVERHAND KNOTS, although they are well disguised. Tie the left one first and arrange as pictured, then lead the right strand down, following the arrow line.

804. Another FLAT SQUARE KNOT in which the individual strands are not complicated. Although superficially alike, in this particular case they happen to be tied reversely. This knot is much flatter than the former, and the center part is less in evidence.

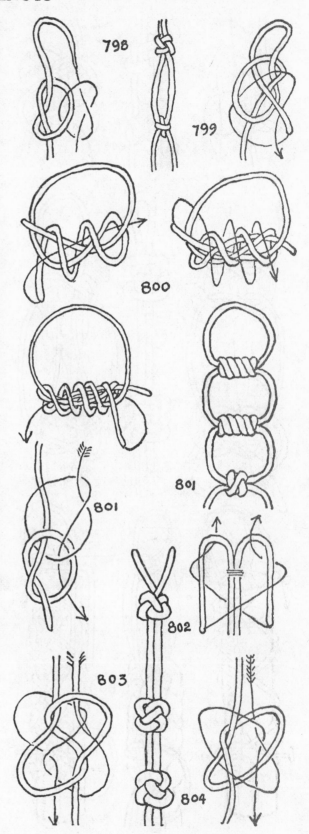

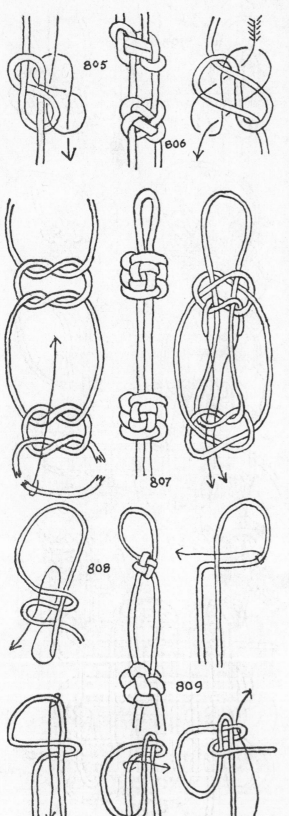

805. A FLAT LOZENGE-SHAPED KNOT of two strands composed of two interwoven FIGURE-EIGHT KNOTS. Each face has two flat parallel parts in the center. Although regular enough, this knot has an odd shape that makes it distinctive. It might prove effective tied in a cord fringe. A number of the knots in this chapter lend themselves to this purpose. (See page 284.)

806. A very symmetrical FLAT LANYARD KNOT composed of two OVERHAND KNOTS. Each face has two central parts.

807. A very handsome Two-Strand CHINESE LANYARD KNOT, from four identical HALF KNOTS. This is commonly tied in silk cord, but it is occasionally tied in colored cotton cord for cheaper lanterns.

Take a long cord with a loop at the bottom, and tie four identical HALF KNOTS in a row (two identical GRANNY KNOTS) in the ends of a cord, so that the cord corresponds with the left diagram, having a long loop at the bottom. Turn down the upper HALF KNOT as shown at the top of the right diagram. Reeve the bottom loop up through the upper GRANNY KNOT as shown in the right diagram. Then reeve the two ends of the cord separately. The right end passes under the right side of the original lower end loop, while the left end passes over the left side of the original lower end loop; the two ends are then brought together and are rove down through the center of the lower GRANNY KNOT.

In tying a number of these knots into a lanyard, leave each knot loose until the one ahead of it has been drawn taut. This is necessary, as the knots must be evenly spaced in order to carry the proper decorative effect.

808. The CHINESE CROWN KNOT is perhaps the most common of CHINESE LANYARD KNOTS. The cord is laid flat on a board, with the two ends downward. The left leg is brought over the right leg and a bight tucked back under the right leg. The right leg is then tucked up underneath three horizontal parts to the center of the loop that has been formed, and is tucked down through the bight that was formed in the left leg.

809. The sailor ties the knot as a FOUR-STRAND CROWN. But as the two sides of a loop must be worked instead of two uncomplicated strands, the technique is slightly different from that of the ordinary CROWN KNOT. Lay out the cord as in the upper right diagram, and start the crown with the right half of the loop, which is led to the left; the other leg of the loop is then led down (second diagram). The left end of the cord is drawn up through the loop and led to the right (third diagram), and the other leg is then led upward and tucked under the first-laid part of the crown (fourth diagram). This makes exactly the same knot as the CHINESE one (#808). If the knot is turned over, a similar one may be tied on the back, which makes a thick, practically cubical knot with two identical faces; this opposite face cannot be added by the Chinese method. The Chinese method is quicker and for that reason preferable when tying a lanyard of several single knots.

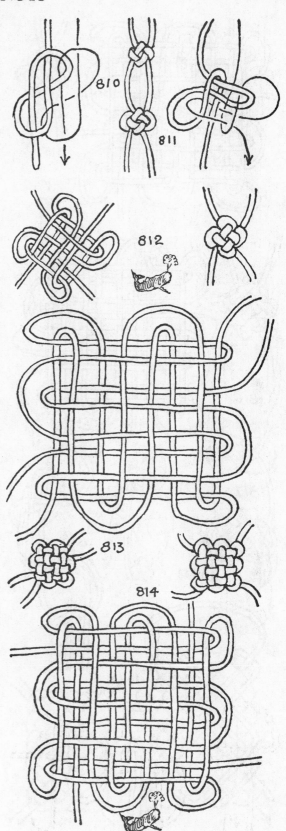

810. It required a long search to find a practical knot with two faces precisely alike, both resembling the CHINESE CROWN KNOT. But when it was found it proved very simple indeed. Two OVERHAND KNOTS are interwoven, and the outer edges of the diagram are brought forward and closed together.

811. The CHINESE BUTTERFLY KNOT is tied in several sizes and is arranged in a number of ways. It will be found further elaborated upon in the chapter on fancy knots (31). This is the smallest knot of the set and is here tied in lanyard form. It is of the same form as the CHINESE CROWN but with the addition of two bights at the rim.

812. By adding two lines to the diagram to form an X across the center of the knot above it was possible to arrange it so that there would be a bight at each of the four corners of the rim.

813. The commoner and best-known CHINESE BUTTERFLY KNOT is the one given here. It is generally tied either as a TERMINAL PENDANT KNOT or as a component part of an elaborate design. In both cases the loops at the sides and corners are extended to act as a decorative fringe or else to interweave with the loops of other knots.

814. By introducing one extra lead across the knot in either direction in the manner of KNOT #812, making nine leads in all, it was found possible to supply two corner bights that are missing in #813. By closing the two ends at each corner of #813, these rim parts will be present, but there is left no cord with which to form a lanyard. In the present knot both are there.

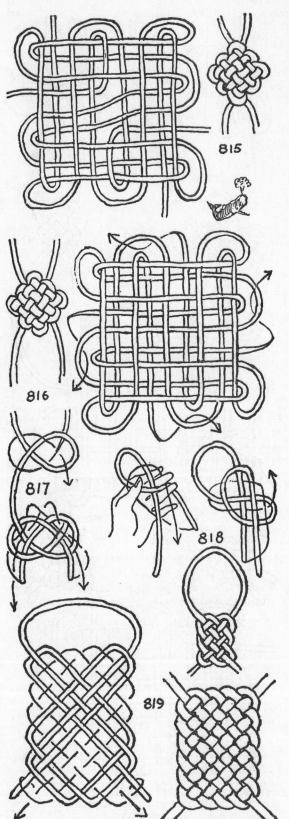

815. With the strands leading in the same tangent from the four corners as in ⌘814, the knot did not lend itself to tying in lanyard form. After considerable experiment the knot alongside was evolved, in which the strands entered near one corner and departed at the diagonally opposite corner, but on the adjacent side. A little gentling is necessary to make the center surface lie fair.

816. There was another possibility, and that was to have strands enter or emerge from the sides at half length. This knot gave more trouble than the others, since it is impossible to have more than one end lead to a single line. An approximately central lead was finally gotten by tucking each end through one of the side loops. This method, of course, cannot be applied to knots in which the loops are to remain extended in "butterfly" form.

817. The series of FLAT LANYARD KNOTS to follow have been termed BOSUN'S KNOTS and are already mentioned at the beginning of this chapter.

The CARRICK BEND is the smallest of the series. There are several ways of increasing the dimensions of this knot, to be given here, and several others are given later in Chapter 30.

Hold the CARRICK BEND horizontally. Turn back the lower right end, and lay it parallel and above its own part to the top rim of the knot. Turn it downward to the left, and lay it to the lower corner of the knot with over-and-under contrary to the other end.

Take the lower left end, cross it up over the end that was just laid, and lead it parallel and to the top with contrary over-and-under. At the top turn down to the right, and lead to the lower right corner with contrary over-and-under. This makes a knot the diagram form of which is given as ⌘830. To raise to a larger size, repeat the directions just given. Each performance adds one bight to each end and two bights to the top and bottom. The number of bights at the top and bottom is always twice the number at the ends.

818. The FLAT LANYARD KNOT, also called the BOATSWAIN'S LANYARD, the WHISTLE LANYARD, and the CHINESE KNOT, is the next enlarged size possible for the BOSUN'S KNOT. In needlework this has also been referred to as the NAPOLEON KNOT, undoubtedly because it is larger than, and has features in common with, the JOSEPHINE KNOT. The knot is customarily tied in hand, the cord being held as illustrated. The course of the cord after reaching the second diagram is along the arrow line with the over-and-under contrary to that of the parallel strand.

819. The FLAT LANYARD KNOT just given may be raised to yet larger dimensions in the same manner described. Take either end and turn it downward and back into the structure of the knot. Follow the circuit and the over-and-under pictured in the accompanying diagram. Do likewise with the second end. The size of the knot may be increased by continuing to repeat in the same manner.

820. The PROLONG KNOT is so called because the knot may be lengthened without changing its width. It is first mentioned by name in Boyd's *Manual for Naval Cadets* in 1857. C. H. Smith, in the *Artificer's Guide* (1876), calls it the "PROLONGED" KNOT. Admiral Luce, to whom the knot was apparently unfamiliar, added a letter *e* to the name and gave a drawing, but he ascribed no purpose and gave no description. Since a prolonge is a rope used in the field artillery, most subsequent authors have attributed the knot to the artillery and frequently have called it GUNNER'S or ARTILLERY KNOT.

821. To prolong the knot shown in the upper left diagram extend the two bottom loops to the desired length and plat them with the two ends into a FRENCH SINNET. A knot is completed each time the ends are brought to the sides (lower corners). The smallest is the knot shown here, with four bights to a side.

822. To increase the length of the knot, plat again as before, which will bring the two ends out on the original sides. Each time that the knot is lengthened by crossing the ends, three bights are added to each side.

823. OCEAN PLAT is the name given to the second start for this knot, in the South Kensington Museum collection. A HALF KNOT is its point of departure. With these two starts, every possible BASKET WEAVE KNOT of this width may be tied. With this particular start, the first prolongation is the CHINESE KNOT, which has four crossings (three bights) to each side. Each time the knot is further platted three bights and three crossings are added to each side.

824. When tying any of the BASKET WEAVE KNOTS, if flat material is used instead of round, such as flat shoestrings, thongs, tape, etc., it may be turned over as each edge or rim is rounded, instead of merely deflecting it, which is all that is necessary with round material. The result will be a straight edge at the rim instead of a series of bights or scallops.

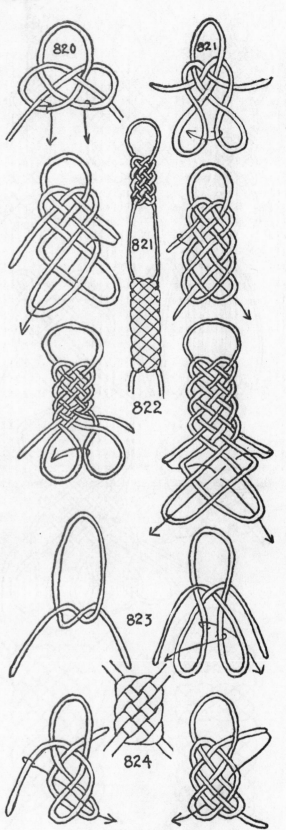

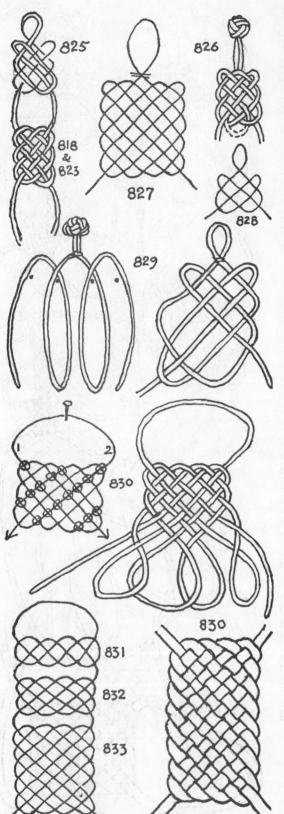

825. A belt in wearing apparel is often knotted, and the flat knot shown here may be tied to furnish a means of buckling. The loop at the end of the knot is seized in with silk or other thread (#2792).

826. A similar knot, terminating in a button, is tied reversely at the other end. The illustration also shows the knot tied as a frog, but in a belt the knot is merely the final one of the series, and the loop shown here at the bottom of the knot is really the continuation of the two cords of the lanyard. The TERMINAL KNOT shown at the top right is TWO-STRAND BUTTON #980.

827. A wider knot for the end of a belt is depicted here. The belt is started with this knot and is finished off with a similar one bearing BUTTON #980 on its end. The first knot and the final knot are each the reverse of the other. Knots of this width are made and lengthened as described for #830.

828. This knot is similar to KNOTS #825 and #826 but is shorter, having one less crossing on each side. It may be lengthened by extending the loops and platting as illustrated below.

829. Knots similar to #825 and #826, and any prolongation of the same form, may be platted directly without first tying a knot. Make a right-hand coil of three turns and arrange as in the left diagram, then plat as in FRENCH SINNET #2977, bringing strands alternately from either side and tucking them alternately over one and under one. A knot is completed every time the two ends have been brought down to the lower corners. Similar knots of greater width may be tied in this way with the two ends and a larger number of turns (or loops).

To tie all possible knots of this particular width it is necessary to utilize another start, which has been shown as #828.

830. Wider knots similar to the PROLONG KNOT and OCEAN PLAT may be made with ten, fourteen, or more leads if wished.

Four starts are required to exhaust the possibilities of this particular width knot. Each has five crossings along the top edge. The four starts have respectively two, three, four, and six crossings at the side edges.

The knot shown here has four side crossings and may be made by tucking as explained at the bottom of page 102, or it may be tied by method #2248.

To tie by the method given alongside for two ends: Middle the cord, and pin to the cork board over the diagram. Pin the left end at (1) and lay along the line of the diagram, tucking under any section of cord encountered at a point that is marked with a circle. When that cord has completed its circuit, lay in the right end at (2) and tuck in the same manner. The basic knot (left diagram) having been tied, extend the bottom bights and proceed to plat as FRENCH SINNET (over one and under one). This knot raises first to nine and then to fourteen crossings at each side.

831. With two side crosses, the knot raises first to seven and then to twelve crossings to the side.

832. With three side crosses, the knot raises first to eight and then to thirteen crossings to the side.

830. With four side crosses, the knot raises first to nine and then to fourteen crossings to the side.

833. With six side crosses, the knot raises first to eleven and then to sixteen crossings to the side.

While platting these knots keep the top edge pinned securely on the board.

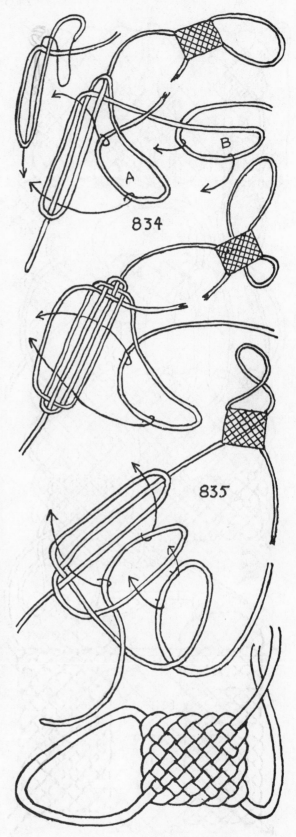

834

835

834. A series of BOSUN'S KNOTS (A ± 1 = B) may be tied in a lanyard by platting with loops as well as ends. This method is quite the most expeditious way of making the knot.

The first to be discussed is the narrow knot in which the number of crossings along the side exceeds the number of crossings in the top by one, the number at the top being always odd. Arrange the cord as pictured in the upper left diagram. The *right* or bight cord between the knot that is being worked and any previous knot should be long enough to tie *half* of one knot, plus the distance between two knots. This is actually a bight between the two knots and will be spoken of as "the bight." The unused length of the left or end cord should equal merely the projected distance between two knots.

Take the left or end cord and make a SINGLE HITCH, as in the upper left diagram. Then take a part of the right or bight cord, allowing extra material for half the knot, and arrange as in the second diagram (top right). After arranging the knot as in the second diagram, make a hitch in the bight cord close to it and weave the left side of the hitch from *right to left*, over, under, over. Then arrange the cord in a rectangular form as in the third diagram.

Take a hitch in the end cord close to the knot and weave it as before, over, under, over, and continue under, over. Repeat with the bight cord. Each hitch in turn is tucked under and over once more than the previous one. When the knot is large enough, tuck the end cord singly to the left; do not tuck a hitch. This completes the knot. The CHINESE KNOT is the smallest to be made by this method.

835. A wide BOSUN'S KNOT in which the number of crossings at the top exceeds the number of crossings on a side by one and the number of crossings at the top is always odd.

Take the right cord and make a SINGLE HITCH at some distance from the previous knot, leaving the end at the bottom. Lay the left cord under this hitch, and lead it to the right over the first-laid end. The knot should now coincide with the first diagram. Proceed to tuck alternate hitches over, under, etc., as in the previous knot; but these hitches are tucked upward to the left instead of downward to the left, as in the other knot. When the knot is of sufficient size, tuck the working end instead of tucking a hitch. Each knot should be worked snug and placed at the proper length in the lanyard before the next knot is commenced.

These knots are easily raveled by retracting the end and pulling at the cords alternately.

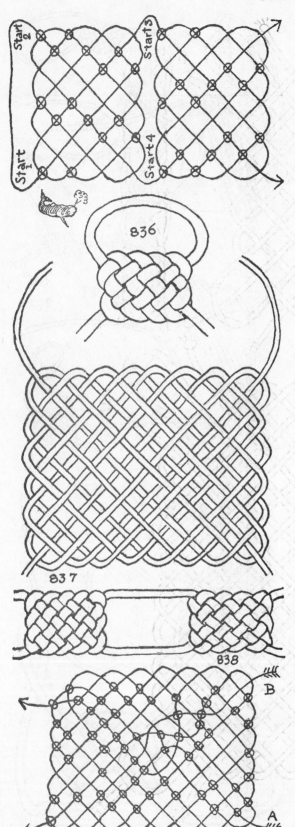

836. In tying a lanyard composed of flat knots arrange the lead so that between two knots at one side the lead is over-over, and at the other side under-under. This does away with the tendency of the lanyard to twist.

To tie any knot reversely, lay the diagram face outward against a windowpane and trace the form on the back, then tie knots alternately first over the front diagram and then over the back diagram.

The two accompanying knots are the first successful ones in an attempt to make thicker knots of this description. They have a twill weave and are less apt to curl and twist than knots with a basket weave.

The diagrams for this knot are marked with encircled points and are to be tied by the method described as №830.

837. The first Two-Plane Basket Weave Knot that worked out satisfactorily was the accompanying one. The two faces are not replicas, one being flat while the other is beveled or chamfered at the edges.

838. A Pillow-Shaped Rectangular Knot in two planes. The knot is tied by leading one cord at a time in the order marked on the diagram. There are two surfaces between which the ends may be led to any desired point.

839. A Two-Plane Knot of 136 crossings, which is tied with four cords. This knot is large and regular and has a machine-made appearance that is, ordinarily, foreign to knots. Two of the cords are much shorter than the other two, but this can be allowed for by turning the lanyard over each time before tying the next knot. No general rule for the length of strands can be given, since the length required is dependent on the size and firmness of the cord used. Tie the knot directly over a traced diagram, carefully following the over-and-under sequence depicted in the illustration.

To make an encircled diagram by which to tie the knot proceed as follows: Letter the four ends; make a light, single-line tracing across the top, with a hard pencil, from left to right, A, B, C, and D. Take a soft pencil (3B or 4B) and, starting at A, accent the light line already made. Wherever the dark line is about to cross *itself* note whether the section of line you are following should pass over or under at this point to accord with the printed diagram; if *under*, draw a neat circle around the point. Disregard the light lines. When line A is completed, continue with line B in the same manner, and then with lines C and D. When the points have all been marked tie the knot as already directed.

840. A Two-Plane Bosun's Knot of 304 crossings. A photograph of the completed knot is given among the frontispieces. The knot is neither difficult to tie nor hard to draw up. Having formed the knot and removed the pins from the projection board, pull the two planes apart. Any irregularity in the weave will at once be apparent. Examine the surface carefully, and if an error is found take a shoestring in hand and correct the error as directed on page 20 in Chapter 1.

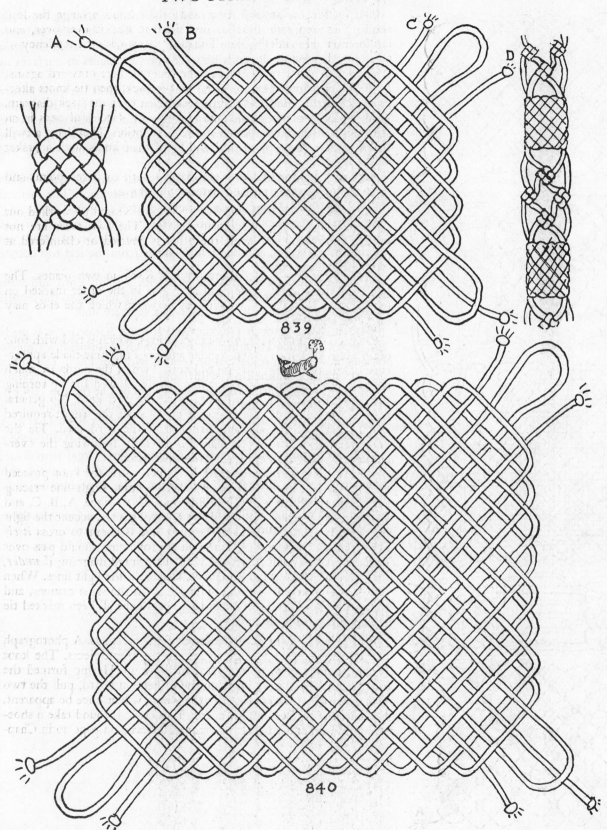

839

840

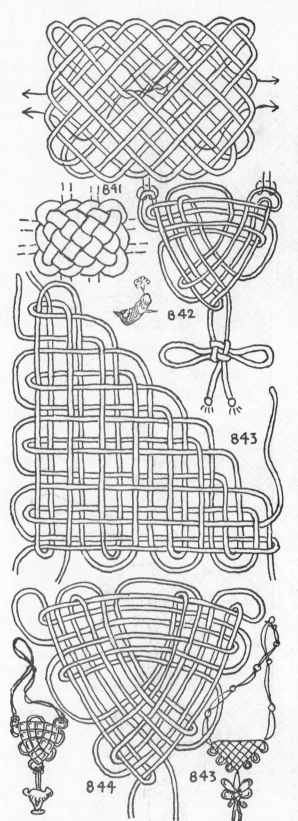

841. A PILLOW-SHAPED KNOT, with the cords emanating from the ends. This is practically the same knot as ⌗836, but the ends are differently treated. The two ends are half knotted inside the knot and are then led to the ends between the two planes or surfaces of the knot.

If the two LEFT HALF KNOTS, which are tied in the ends before they leave the knot, are reversed and two RIGHT HALF KNOTS are tied instead, the cords that now emanate from the left side may be led between the two plane surfaces to the top of the knot, and the two cords from the right side may be led to the bottom, which will make a horizontal instead of a vertical knot.

842. A TRIANGULAR KNOT of the BUTTERFLY variety, which makes a handsome pectoral ornament for a knotted necklace. The method of making this lanyard is also described as ⌗3708 in Chapter 41. The ends of the necklace button together at the nape of the neck. There are three different sections of cord in the knot, two that pass from top to bottom, and one which passes from the left top corner to the right top corner.

If preferred, the knot may be tied with a single cord and with loops at the upper corners. In this case it is ring hitched to the looped ends of the necklace, which is made as a separate unit.

843. A RIGHT-ANGLED TRIANGULAR PECTORAL KNOT that was made for Mrs. Lawrence Houghteling from which to suspend a Chinese ornament. A short necklace is preferable with this knot. The upper corners may be finished off with loops described for the previous knot, to which the necklace can be ring hitched at the top corners. The lower corner should have a small LANYARD KNOT ending in a loop to which the ornament is secured with another RING HITCH. A photograph of the finished knot is included among the frontispieces.

844. An EQUILATERAL TRIANGULAR KNOT a little larger than ⌗842, to be used when the necklace is a long one. If tied too tightly, this knot may tend to distort; for that reason ⌗842 is preferable, since it is fully as handsome and is simpler and firmer.

The form of ⌗842 is also shown in the chapter on fancy knots as a TERMINAL KNOT and in Chapter 5 as a BUTTON KNOT.

CHAPTER 9: KNOB KNOTS. MULTI-STRAND BUTTONS, TIED IN HAND

First a wall,
And then a crown,
Next tuck up,
And then tuck down.

THE MANROPE KNOT (Sailors' Work Rhyme)

Steel (1794) and Lever (1808) both speak of BUTTONS being put through beckets and clews, to secure the standing ends of running rigging. Steel describes the knot that was then customarily used as a "WALNUT KNOT, crowned," and Lever as a "DOUBLE WALLED KNOT, double crowned."

MULTI-STRAND BUTTON KNOTS are the last variety of KNOB KNOT to be discussed. Like the knots of preceding chapters, their purpose is to prevent unreeving, but unlike SINGLE-STRAND KNOTS, MULTI-STRAND KNOTS are never untied. Wherever they are put, they remain fixtures. The strands of MULTI-STRAND BUTTONS are almost always canvas-covered before the knots are tied. After they are tied the canvas covering is generally filled (hardwood filler) and painted, often in several colors; for although their purpose is essentially practical, the knots are usually tied where they will also serve decoratively.

The knots which form this chapter are, with the exception of the STAR, of the built-up variety, being generally a combination of two elementary knots. The CROWN KNOT is almost invariably one of the two component knots, and the WALL KNOT, in a majority of cases, is the other. But the DIAMOND KNOT is also common, and there are several other knots that are occasionally used in combination with the CROWN. With these few basic forms, many different combinations are possible. The "lay" of these knots is usually doubled or tripled, and there is considerable latitude in the ways in which this may be done.

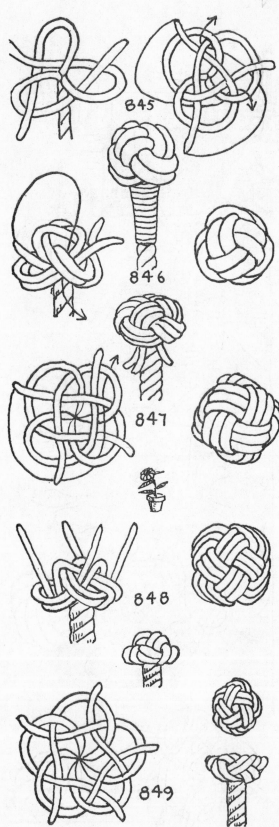

There are, moreover, two different ways of tying most knots that are a combination of two. The commoner way is to have both the CROWN and the second component knot (WALL, DIAMOND, FOOT-ROPE, etc.) lead or rotate in the same direction, which is generally counterclockwise. But another way, which makes a different knot, is to have the two lead or rotate in opposite directions.

845. A WHALE OR WALE KNOT, according to the *Naval Expositor* of 1750, "is a round Knot or Knob made with three Strands of Rope at one End of the TACKS, Topsail Sheats and Stoppers, so they cannot slip."

Manwayring, Captain John Smith, Boteler, and the Anderson-edited manuscript of 1625 (circa) speak of the WHALE, WALE, and WALNUT KNOT, names which at that date appear to have been applied indiscriminately to any of the WALL AND CROWN derivatives, or to the WALL alone.

The SINGLE WALL AND CROWN was the first knot of this sort to be described.

846. The *tack* is a large, tapered *three-strand* rope which hauls forward and trims the weather clew of a course or lower square sail. This is to prevent the sail from being taken aback. The knot is buttoned to the clew (#2837 and #3397) and seized in.

The TACK KNOT, as given by Steel in 1794, was a DOUBLED WALL AND CROWN. To tie the knot: Take a *three-strand* rope, seize, and open the end. Make a WALL AND CROWN as shown in the first two diagrams, allowing the stem to drop down between the two middle fingers and holding the knot in the palm of the left hand.

To *double* the knot, follow with each strand in turn *below* the first wall and tuck as illustrated in the right upper diagram. Then follow outside the crown with each strand in turn, and finally stick all the ends down to the stem. I have found no evidence that the knot was ever tripled, but there is no reason why this should not have been done.

The strands of the TACK KNOT were *not covered* with canvas as most MULTI-STRAND BUTTONS are nowadays, and the ends of the strands were left long and scraped. A part of each strand was wormed, and the remaining yarns were fayed (combed out), marled, and served over.

The practice of putting buttons in the ends of tacks ceased when the tack itself was doubled and rove through a block at the clew. The TACK KNOT was later modified, and, having been differently applied, its name was changed to MANROPE KNOT.

847. MANROPE KNOTS were first mentioned by Brady in 1841. They were tied in manropes, which are ropes leading to either side of the gangway. The knots provide a handhold for anyone climbing the side ladder. At an early date manropes were called entering ropes, a name mentioned by Captain John Smith in 1627; for a while in the nineteenth century they were called sideropes. The MANROPE KNOT proper is four-strand, the strands being invariably canvas-covered and trimmed flush at the stem. When doubled, the lead is commonly followed on the lower or outer side. Generally the knot is tripled, and often it is four-ply, but I have seen the knot tied with as many as six ply on a pair of naval chest beckets. The earliest name for the knot was "DOUBLE WALL AND DOUBLE CROWN." Occasionally it has been called "TOPSAIL SHEET KNOT," and Norie, in 1804, called it "KOP KNOT." Wetjen, in *Fiddlers' Green*, says: "A man who can make a MANROPE KNOT, STAR KNOT, or ROSE KNOT is an object of respect"—and at sea this statement still holds true.

847½. Left-handed specimens of the MANROPE KNOT are often found. This knot is shown at the right of 847.

848. A MANROPE KNOT with the lead followed above is less common than one with the lead followed below. The result is a flatter knot. Generally this knot is merely doubled, for if tripled it crowds the center.

849. The FIVE-STRAND MANROPE KNOT is also tied, and generally it is doubled only. But with more than five strands the center of the knot is too open to be altogether pleasing, and the knot tends to be flabby unless it is made over a core.

850. On old chest beckets the MANROPE KNOT is sometimes found tied with a reversed crown. I have one chest with double beckets in which one only of the four knots is tied in this manner. In this case it must have been by mistake. The knot, however, is pronouncedly square and distinctive in character and is not at all an unusual knot. A flatter knot will result if the lead is followed above when doubling.

851. A DIAMOND AND CROWN is an uncommon knot, and few sailors tie it. It makes a larger knot than the WALL AND CROWN or MANROPE KNOT and is usually doubled; for if tripled it may require a core. There is an example of this knot on exhibit at the U.S. Naval Academy in Annapolis.

852. The same knot tied with five strands may be worked into a flat form to give a starlike knot quite dissimilar in character to the last. A TWO-PLY or DOUBLED KNOT is quite sufficient; a larger knot unless very carefully worked will not be firm.

853. The *Vocabulary of Sea Phrases* of 1799 mentions the "DOUBLE CROWN KNOT." A CROWN, either doubled or tripled, forms a BUTTON KNOT. The lead may be followed either above or below. Although distinctive in appearance, it is hardly a practical knot.

854. Steel (1794) gives two different descriptions of a TACK KNOT (Vol. I, pp. 180, 182), one of which may be a CROWN AND WALL with the ends tucked down at the center.

MULTI-STRAND BUTTON KNOTS are used as terminal knobs for a great variety of purposes, both practical and decorative. They are found on yoke lines, bell lanyards, watch guards, manropes, chest beckets, etc. Many of these applications are illustrated in Chapter 41.

For tying the knots of this chapter I recommend banding, the material that is described on page 20 in the first chapter. After being filled and painted, the strands are scarcely distinguishable from canvas-covered ones. Either a hardwood filler, shellac, or a coating of casein glue may be first applied, and when dry this is followed by a coat of paint. Whiting may be added to the casein.

Brady (1841), in describing how knots are doubled, says: "Follow the lead until it shows three parts all round, and it is completed."

Many nautical authorities recommend tying BUTTON KNOTS against the lay. This is contrary to the common practice, as exemplified by the sailor's knots that have survived. Presumably the recommendation has been abstracted from Steel, who first published it.

A left-handed man will naturally tie a MULTI-STRAND KNOT in right-handed rope *against the lay*, and a right-handed man will tie a knot in a left-handed rope against the lay, because it is easier for them to do it that way. I do not doubt but what this was the occasion for the recommendation. A knot tied against the lay, in theory, is a little firmer and a little weaker, but not enough of either to be of much moment.

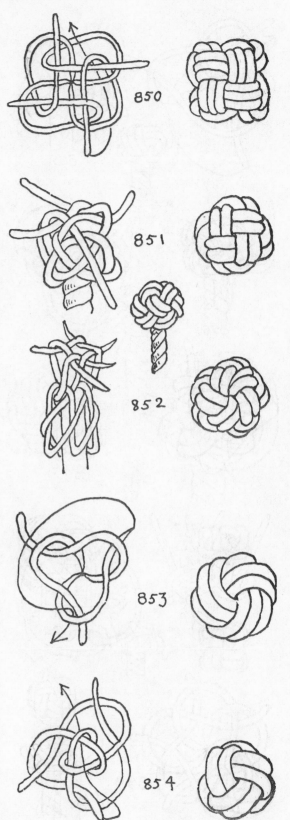

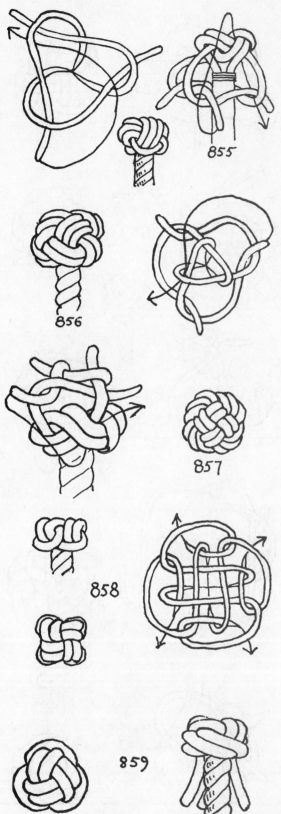

855. Make a double crown with the lead followed above. Next, tie a wall below the double crown, and finally lead the ends above the double crown and tuck them down at the center. The top of this knot is pronouncedly triangular. Like #854, this is decorative but not very practical.

856. Another interpretation is given here of Steel's TACK KNOT (Vol. 1, p. 180, *Seamanship and Rigging*, 1794). It consists of a triple crown and a double wall.

Crown three strands, and wall below them. Follow both the crown and wall once around on the outside. Then lead the ends parallel again to the outside of the crown, and tuck down to the stem. This knot is very frequently tied but is usually unrecognized, being taken for the MANROPE KNOT. Taper, fay, and serve the ends as in #846.

857. Bushell, in speaking of the DOUBLE WALL KNOT, says: "Some people will crown them, but there is no need of it." This shows the DOUBLE WALL crowned and then the whole knot doubled as a unit. The DOUBLE WALL is first tied as #675, and the crown is superimposed. If the CROWN KNOT is undoubled, the result is a ROSE KNOT. Doubled, this knot has a triple wall and a double crown. Compare it with the preceding knot (#856). In the former the crown is triple and the wall is double.

858. A distinctive RECTANGULAR KNOT of four strands. Crown the four strands to the right, and then wall them to the left. After this tuck each end to the right, through the bight of the original crown, and finally down to the stem. Like many another good knot, this one must be gentled into shape. Work slowly, and tighten each part a little only at a time.

859. First crown three or four strands, and then tie a SINGLE MATTHEW WALKER KNOT. Follow the lead above the initial crown and tuck the ends down at the center.

Ends of MULTI-STRAND BUTTONS are generally tucked out at the stem and cut off flush; but on occasion, if a large lanyard is wished with a small knot, three or four loose strands may be seized together and the knot tied, after which the ends and standing part are laid up together, making six or eight strands (or any even number), and a SIX- or EIGHT-STRAND SINNET is formed of the aggregate, leaving no ends to be trimmed.

860. A "THRICE-CROWNED KNOT" is mighty like a ROSE in appearance, but in construction it differs essentially.

Make a snug crown, which forms the top center of the finished knot. Crown *below* this, and then double this last crown by following below the lead of the second one. Draw up snugly. The result makes a handsome and distinctive knob.

861. We are now approaching the ROSE KNOT, an early form of BUTTON that was sometimes tied in the ends of deck stoppers instead of STOPPER KNOT #117. So far as I know, this knot has never been described, although it is referred to from time to time in the literature of the sea and was mentioned as early as 1769 in Falconer's *Dictionary of the Marine*. The ROSE consists of a DOUBLE KNOT surmounted by a single crown. This much at least is known. But the knot is the least standardized of all, and there are so many different ways in which a similar result can be obtained that there can be no certainty as to which was the earliest form. A number of the forms given here I have seen tied; others are the results of my attempt to identify the logical pretender to the title.

The knot alongside is the simplest form that I have seen. A DOUBLE WALL (#140) is tied, and each strand in turn is stuck to the stem as indicated by the arrow.

862. The DOUBLE WALL, crowned, may be the original and true ROSE KNOT. Moore (1801) speaks of the "DOUBLE WALL, crowned," but pictures a STOPPER KNOT, crowned (#864).

The Portuguese apply the name "PINHA DE ROSA" to the DOUBLE DIAMOND KNOT. The Swedes apply the name "ROSENKNOP" to a DOUBLE DIAMOND AND CROWN. But both of these are STOPPER KNOTS instead of BUTTONS, and we know the English ROSE KNOT is the latter.

863. The STOPPER KNOT tucked to the right without crowning makes a very handsome flat-topped knot, that belongs in this series.

864. The STOPPER KNOT, crowned, is pictured by Vial Du Clairbois (1783) and by Moore (1801). Brady in 1841, speaking of the STOPPER KNOT, says, "Some persons will crown them but there is no need of it." Bushell also speaks of this knot being used as a stopper. Its claim to the name *rose* is at least as good as that of the DOUBLE WALL AND CROWN (#862).

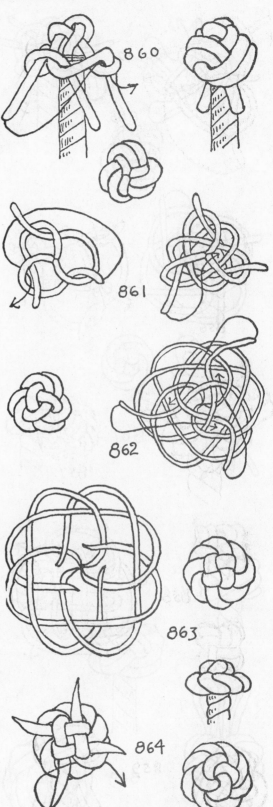

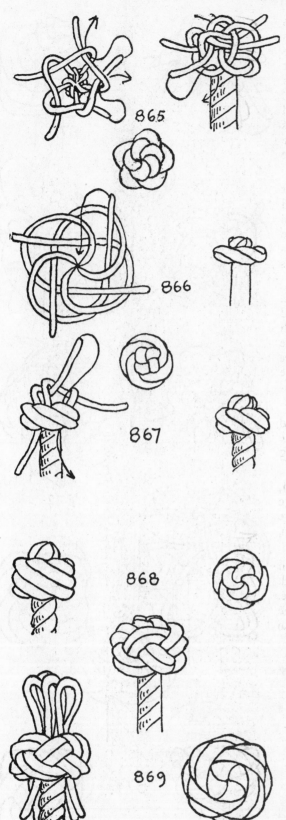

865. A FIVE-STRAND MANROPE KNOT with a double crown and a single wall. This crown is doubled in a way that has not been shown before in this chapter. After a WALL AND CROWN has been tied, each strand is tucked through the next bight of the crown to the right, as shown in the left diagram. The ends are then tucked down to the stem through the initial wall as shown in the second diagram. When completed as directed, the knot can be doubled in the ordinary way.

866. A LANYARD KNOT, crowned, makes a handsome ROSE KNOT. After crowning, the strands are tucked to the stem in the usual way.

867. A FOUR-STRAND SINGLE MATTHEW WALKER may have a crown of the sort described and illustrated in №865 and, so tied, is a very effective knot.

868. A FOUR-STRAND DOUBLE or FULL MATTHEW WALKER may be crowned in the same way as №865, or the crown may be tucked one additional part, which will make a fuller center.

869. A DOUBLE FOOTROPE KNOT (№697), with the lead followed above, may be crowned in one of the ways that have been described to make a bulkier knot than has yet been shown. The crown should be doubled, and the ends led to the stem, before the FOOTROPE KNOT is finally drawn snug. Having worked the FOOTROPE KNOT, each end of the crown is in turn tightened a little until the top of the knot has sunk to the desired level. The ends may then be trimmed.

The *Naval Repository* of 1762 described a manrope of the period in the following terms: "The entering Rope is suspended from the Top of the Ladder by which you enter the Ship; and for the most Part [is] covered with Scarlet Cloth curiously fringed and tasseled." It would seem that the rope described must have had an eye for lashing purposes, instead of a knob, since a tassel could scarcely be rove through the small hole of a stanchion. Later descriptions of the *entering rope* describe a knot, however.

MANROPE KNOTS are often mistakenly called TURK's-HEADS. This is probably because certain sciolists have made the error in their magazine articles, which have had a wide circulation. There is no excuse for the mistake, as one is a solid MULTI-STRAND KNOT in the end of a rope, and the other is a SINGLE-STRAND CYLINDRICAL BINDING KNOT around the bight of a rope. All they have in common is a basket-weave surface.

In tying MULTI-STRAND KNOTS, do not allow yourself to become confused. Tie methodically, one move after another. Do not become impatient, for there is a lot to be learned. Not more than six ordinary seamen out of a hundred could tie even a MANROPE KNOT, and the MANROPE KNOT is about the easiest knot of the present chapter.

A plumber's apprentice labors for several years before he becomes a full-fledged plumber. At the expiration of that time, if he has worked conscientiously and has talent, he is permitted to screw up pipes and apply solder and may even have advanced to the point where he rates a helper to carry his tools for him. Knotting is no simple craft, and there is a great variety.

Most MULTI-STRAND BUTTONS are tied with canvas-covered strands. The ends are sometimes tapered slightly, and the canvas seams are turned, rubbed down, and sewed (♯123). In working the knots constant care must be observed to keep the seams on the underside.

870. This illustrates a FOUR-STRAND DOUBLE DIAMOND KNOT that has been crowned to form a ROSE KNOT. The lead of the diamond is followed above, before the crown is added and the strands tucked to the stem. If tied as described, a slightly convex top results. If the lead of the diamond is followed below, the knot will have a somewhat different character, being possibly rounder. But the form is largely the result of the way the knot is worked.

871. A knot with a double crown and collar and a single girdle. First tie a single diamond (♯693). Above this tie a single crown and stick the ends to the stem under three parts. Tuck up with each end following below the lead at the rim. Then follow outside the lead at the crown, and tuck down to the stem. This last tuck passes under five parts. The parts forming the collar are double, and the crown is double, but the upper rim is left single. In the left illustration the single parts are shown at the four corners.

872. A *rosebud* shape is secured by tying a single diamond and adding a single crown above the diamond. Then follow above the lead of the diamond, tucking down to the stem without doubling the crown.

873. A bulkier knot is obtained by first tying a diamond (♯734), tucking each strand to the right in turn, under, over, under. Arrange the knot symmetrically, and add a crown at the top. Follow above the lead, doubling only the diamond, and stick the ends to the stem, leaving the crown single.

874. Another knot is tied exactly like ♯873, and the difference in appearance is due entirely to the difference in the way it is worked. The third tier of parts is pulled tight to withdraw it from the surface. The top of the knot then automatically assumes a flat surface. The side elevation of the knot is similar in appearance to a THREE-LEAD TURK'S-HEAD.

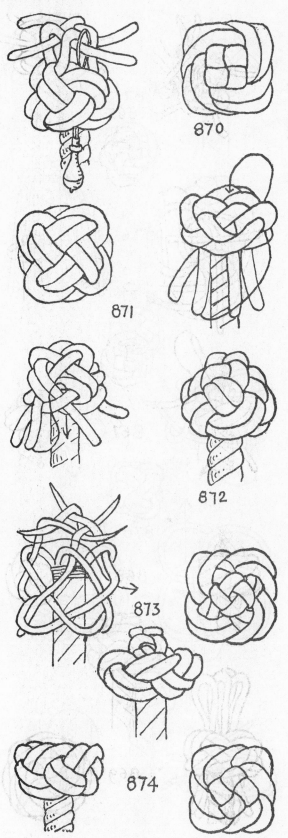

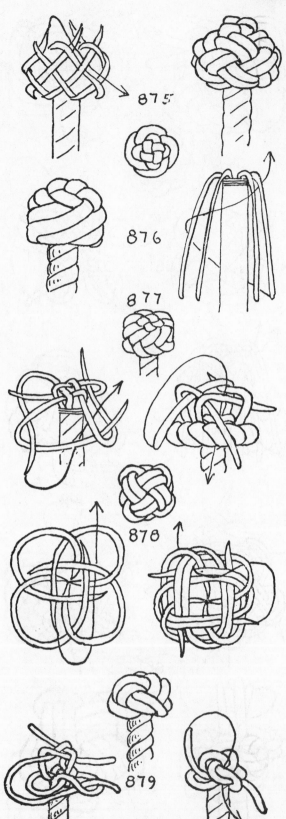

875. With four strands tie a DIAMOND KNOT, *under, over, and under,* as pictured. Turn the ends down, and double the knot in tiers; that is to say, tuck each strand in turn under one part at a time, until the whole diamond has been doubled and the ends are again at the top. Then crown the four strands to the right, stick the four ends down to the stem, and trim them.

876. With four strands tie SINNET KNOT #757. First stop all four strands to the stem, lead each one in turn to the right over the first three strands and under the fourth (which is the bight of the same strand that is being led). Crown the four ends, and stick them to the stem.

877. A very flat and handsome knot, the side elevation of which resembles FIVE-STRAND FLAT SINNET.

Seize and crown four strands to the *left,* and draw them up snug. Next wall them to the right. Then tuck each end up as in the left illustration. Ignore the first crown, and superimpose another right crown outside the first one. Stick the ends down *outside* the *first crown* and *inside* the *last crown* as illustrated. The first crown appears on the surface when the knot has been worked, making a perfectly flat top.

878. Captain Charles Smith's TACK KNOT was shown to me aboard ship in 1904. At this time the original TACK KNOT (#846) had been out of use for its original purpose for at least fifty years. This furnishes a good illustration of the tenacity with which old customs and names persist at sea. Captain Smith knew what the TACK KNOT was for, although he had never seen one used practically. He had learned the present knot about 1870 on his first whaling voyage.

I have seen examples of this twice, on old chest beckets and there is an old sample of the knot in a hemp rope's end in the New Bedford Whaling Museum.

The knot is begun with a WALL AND CROWN. Each end in turn is then tucked regularly over and under as indicated by the single arrow line in the left illustration. Note that at the third crossing (which is over) the lead appears to be over two parts, where the two parts of the same cycle overlap to form the end and standing part. When the knot is drawn up it will be quite regular. The ends are tucked down at the center as shown by the arrow in the right illustration, after the crown has been doubled or tripled.

879. A MANROPE KNOT with the wall doubled somewhat after the manner of the DOUBLE WALL KNOT has a character of its own. First wall and crown in the usual manner. Then tuck the ends *up* through the wall as pictured. After this follow the crown on the outside with each strand and tuck down to the stem.

880. A knot of different character, but tied in somewhat the same way, is made as follows: Wall and crown three or four strands.

Tuck up each end in turn through the next bight to the right and in advance of the next end. Then tuck each end down to the center in advance of the second standing part to the right. The working drawings show a THREE-STRAND KNOT, and the final drawing shows a completed knot with four strands.

881. Perhaps the most distinguished of sailor's BUTTON KNOTS, and certainly the most individual, is the STAR KNOT. It is occasionally mentioned in nautical fiction of the nineteenth century, but the first illustration of it is, I believe, in *Log Book Notes* by E. N. Little (1888).

The knot is tied preferably with five strands, but four and six strands are common, and I have a pair of early nineteenth-century chest beckets (#3639) bearing THREE-STRAND STAR KNOTS.

To tie with five strands, splice an extra strand to the core of a shroud-laid rope (#2660), or else seize stoutly and cut out one strand from a piece of tiller rope or SIX-STRAND ROUND SINNET. To tie a SIX-STRAND STAR use six-strand rope or sinnet or else tie it in the doubled ends of three-strand rope. A SIX-STRAND STAR may also be tied in cable-laid (nine-strand) rope by cutting out the three central strands. This leaves six surface strands with which to tie the knot.

To tie a FIVE-STRAND KNOT: Take any strand and, with the next strand to its right, make a SINGLE HITCH around the end of the left strand. Take the next strand to the right and with it make a SINGLE HITCH around the second strand. Take the fourth strand and make a SINGLE HITCH around the third. With the fifth strand place a hitch around the fourth, and finally with the bight of the first strand (the end being already engaged) make a hitch around the fifth end. This is shown in the first two diagrams. A less confusing way is to turn down the five strands to the neck as in the third diagram, lead any strand to the right, and tuck the end upward and back to the left under the next strand. Repeat with each strand in turn, progressing to the right. The form will be identical with the second diagram after a little rearrangement. Next, crown the five strands to the left (fourth diagram) and tuck each strand around to the right toward the center and under its own part. Continue to follow the lead to the right on the inside of the parallel strand (fifth diagram) and tuck down through the two superimposed parts at the corner. Turn the knot upside down, continue to lay the strand parallel as shown by the sixth diagram (which represents the essential parts of the bottom of the knot at this juncture), and stick the ends up to the top center as indicated by the arrow. Turn the knot right side up again, parallel the lead on the inside to the right with each strand in turn and finally tuck the ends down to the stem under four parts. This is the simplest of the several forms of the knot, but none of them is so difficult as the diagrams suggest, since the knots are tied in easy progressive steps.

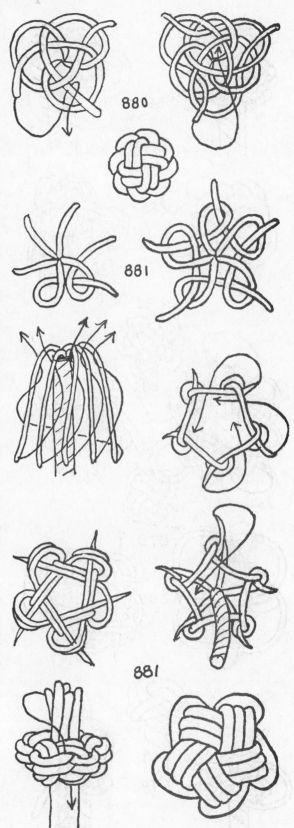

880

881

881

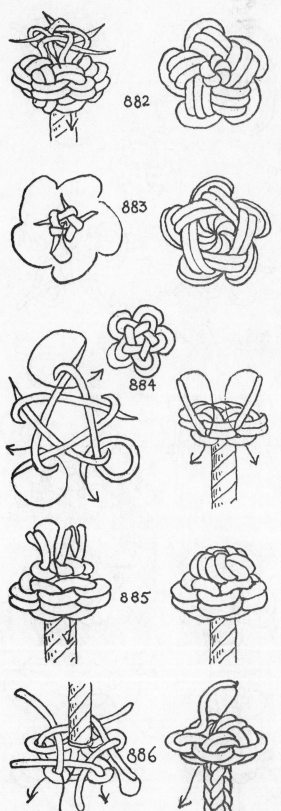

882. Proceed as in the previous knot until the seventh diagram. At this point a crown is added to the present knot. The crown is then doubled by sticking each end to the right through the next bight as shown in ⚹865. After this the whole STAR with the exception of the crown is drawn up snugly in final form, and not till then is the crown tightened, one strand at a time and only a little of each strand at a time lest it disappear from sight. When completed the crown should protrude slightly. Trim the ends with scissors.

883. The STAR KNOT is tied as before, and a single crown is superimposed. The ends are stuck down at the center to the stem, as illustrated, which doubles the crown. The crown is not tightened in the least until the STAR itself has been worked snug.

884. A STAR variation. Having reached the position of the second diagram in ⚹881, proceed to crown the ends as in the left diagram alongside. Then continue to stick each of the five ends as shown in the two bottom points of the same diagram. Having reached this juncture, stick each end down under one bight to the stem as pictured.

885. A DOUBLE WALL KNOT superimposed on a STAR KNOT. When the initial STAR KNOT is completed tie a SINGLE WALL KNOT at the top, lead the ends somewhat to the right, and stick them down to the stem outside the first WALL KNOT. Work the STAR KNOT snug. Draw up the first wall so that the strands are well centered, and then pull down the ends carefully so as not to spill the double wall.

886. A STAR KNOT with a single rim. Seize five strands and, holding the structure with the stem aloft, tie the first movement of the STAR, as shown in the second diagram of ⚹881. Continue to hold the knot in the same position, and crown the strands to the left as shown in the first diagram alongside. Stick each end down through the next bight to the left as shown by arrows in the same diagram, and then turn the knot right side up and lead each end to the right, parallel to the proper strand, and tuck down at the center.

When under considerable strain, this knot tends to distort, becoming somewhat concave.

CHAPTER 10: KNOB KNOTS. MULTI-STRAND BUTTONS, TIED ON THE TABLE

*In the way of knots, especially for sea use, there can be nothing more,
I think, to invent.* SIR EDWIN ARNOLD, 1900

With the exception of the STAR KNOT, the knots of the preceding chapter were built up of two basic knots, one superimposed on the other. Generally these were doubled, and almost invariably one of the two knots was a regular CROWN. Occasionally the CROWN was tied first, but usually it followed a WALL KNOT or, less frequently, a DIAMOND or a FOOTROPE KNOT. Upon examination it will be found that each strand of a CROWN regularly passes over another strand and under a second one, so that a diagram of any of these CROWNS consists of several symmetrical lines, each of which has two crossings only.

The first knot to be considered in the present chapter is the SPRITSAIL SHEET KNOT, which originally was tied in a block strap. The two ends of the strap were brought together, and the six strands, after being rove through holes in the block, were walled and topped off with an irregular crown, two of the strands of this crown having four crossings each, and the four remaining strands having two crossings each.

Although the crown of the SPRITSAIL SHEET KNOT is irregular, each strand has an even number of crossings, all crossings are taken alternately over one and under one, and all the compartments are either three- or four-sided.

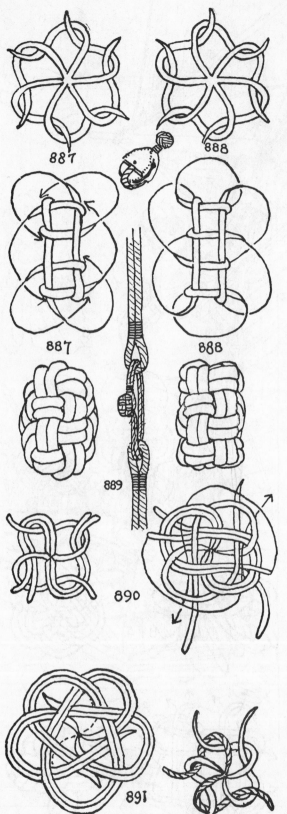

887

888

887

888

889

890

891

So far knots that commenced with a wall have had the same number of rim parts as strands. But knots that are started with a crown have the same number of sides to the center compartment as there are strands, while the number of rim parts may vary.

It is unnecessary, however, that either the number of center parts or the number of rim parts should coincide with the number of strands. Number 980 has a center compartment of four sides and four rim parts and is tied with two strands only, while ⌗1000 is tied with *two* strands only, but has six rim parts and no center compartment at all, having a cross at the center instead of a compartment.

887. The SPRITSAIL SHEET KNOT was first given by Steel in 1794. To tie: Seize two parallel rope ends together, open and wall all six strands regularly to the right, and then crown them as illustrated. The knot may now be doubled by following outside the original wall and continuing on the same side of the strand without crossing it. If any difficulty is encountered a study of the method of tying described as ⌗907 and ⌗908 may be of assistance.

Work the knot into the shape of the lower left diagram.

888. Knots that are crowned in a direction opposite to the wall are marked by a difference in appearance as well as structure. If it is desired to tie a knot in this way it may be found simpler to reverse the original wall instead of reversing the crown, the crowns being always tied as in the diagram that is given. The top right diagram illustrates a left wall, and below this is the diagram form of the SPRITSAIL SHEET KNOT tied with a *left wall* and a *right crown*. Below this is a picture of the completed knot which shows how rectangular it becomes when the wall and crown are tied reversely.

In ordinary sea practice the SPRITSAIL SHEET KNOT was generally tied as nearly round as possible. In this form it was put in messenger straps (⌗889) and in the straps of tack, clew line, and spritsail sheet blocks.

Sometimes the knot was tied in deck stoppers when they were of cable-laid rope. In this case the three central strands were cut out, and the knot was tied with the six remaining surface strands.

889. The two ends of a messenger strap were buttoned together with a SPRITSAIL SHEET KNOT after being rove through the eyes of the messenger.

890. If there are *too many strands* in a sinnet with which to tie a desired knot, lay up the strands symmetrically in pairs until there are the right number of *units* with which to tie, and make the knot with these units. Then double the parts that are still single, and triple the knot, finally tucking all ends to the stem as they lie.

891. When there are *too few strands* for a knot that is planned, stop a sufficient number of extra strands along the stem of the knot, having them evenly distributed. These extra strands should be of different color or texture from the permanent strands. Tie the knot, and double or triple it *without* sticking the ends to the stem. Double the lead of one of the extra strands with a convenient permanent strand, after which remove the extra strand so that the knot is the same size as before. Then remove and replace another strand. In some cases, such as the STAR KNOT and the FOUR-STRAND DIAMOND

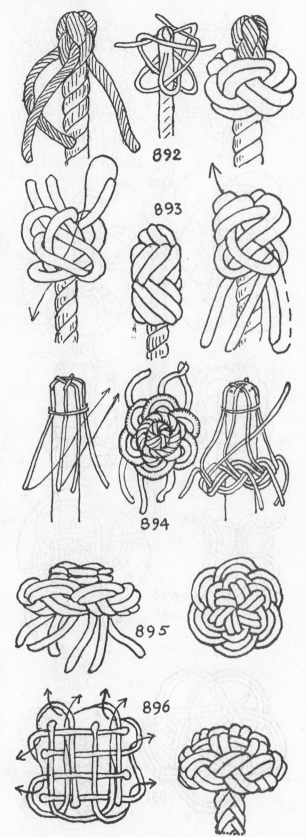

AND CROWN, where each strand has an individual circuit, the method does not work as it stands. In such cases employ one long working end and reintroduce it after the knot has been tied, as a substitute for one of the extra strands.

892. A BACK-SPLICED WALL AND CROWN. Seize and open a three- or four-strand rope, and back splice (#2813), tucking each strand once only. Then tie a DOUBLE WALL AND CROWN, following below the lead.

This knot is sometimes seen on bucket ropes and does away with the whipping that is required when a MATTHEW WALKER KNOT is used.

A somewhat similar knot may be made by first back splicing one tuck and then tying (upside down) LANYARD KNOT #119.

893. A TERMINAL KNOT with a twilled texture. Take three strands and tie a diamond *to the left*, leading each strand in turn over two and under two.

Take any one strand, turn it down to the left, and tuck it over two parts and under two parts, as pictured in the left diagram. Repeat with the other two strands.

Take any end and lead it upward to the left, over four and under four, as pictured in the right diagram. Do not draw the knot taut as yet.

Crown the ends to the right, and tuck each end a second time to the right and then through the bight of the next strand. Finally tuck them down to the stem. Work the diamond very carefully into cylindrical form, and at the last moment, with very great care, haul the ends taut.

894. Captain Albert Whitney's ROSE KNOT. Three long strands are stopped at the centers and seized over the end of a small stick. With the six ends a DIAMOND KNOT is tied and doubled by following below the lead. An additional upward tuck is given to each end (over one and under one), as shown in the third diagram.

The stick is removed and the knot flattened out. The six ends are walled above the knot just tied, and this wall is doubled. Each strand is then tucked up to the center of the knot. Finally, the ends are crowned again over all and stuck down to the stem.

The knot is then removed from the stick, and, after careful fairing, the ends are laid up into a ROUND SINNET.

895. A knot may be started as Captain Whitney's ROSE KNOT (#894), but instead of the final crown a STAR KNOT (#881) is added, after the directions for the extra tucks in the right diagram of #894 have been followed.

896. Esparteiro gives a ROSE KNOT with a crown of larger dimensions than the SPRITSAIL SHEET CROWN. This crown was first given by Alston in 1860 for the purpose of finishing off the ends of fenders. Seize an EIGHT-STRAND SINNET, and make "first a crown and then a wall" as here depicted. Then double the crown only. Outside the double crown add a *wall and crown*, and double these by following above the lead. This acts as a frame for the first *crown and wall*. Stick all ends down to the stem, to the right of two of the parts that bridge the space between the inner and outer knots.

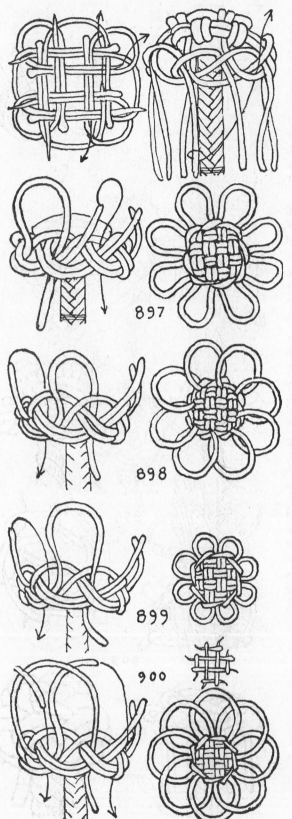

897

898

899

900

The remaining knots of this chapter are original. The series given on the present page, and shown among the frontispieces, were designed as hats for my wife and three daughters. One hat only was delivered, as it appeared that they were a bit sophisticated for the children.

897. The DAISY. Crown and wall, and double the crown only. Draw up snugly.

Below this a wall and crown is tied, the lead of which is doubled *below* and the ends tucked down to the stem as illustrated in the third diagram. After this has been drawn up very tightly, the bight of the last parts to be tucked (shown elevated in the third diagram) is pulled out to the desired length to form the petals of the flower. The strands are seized to the stem with a CONSTRICTOR, close to the knot.

898. The "PROPELLER" is started the same as the foregoing knot, but when doubling the final wall and crown, the lead is followed *above*. The ends are tucked differently down to the stem immediately after crossing a single part as shown in the diagram. The knot is next worked taut, seized, and the propeller blades drawn out.

899. The "NOSEGAY" is started in the same manner as the others on this page. When doubling the final wall and crown the lead is above the first-laid strand. After the ends are stuck to the stem and the knot has been worked taut, the loops which form the leaves are extended.

900. The "SUNFLOWER" has a smaller crown, somewhat rounder in form than the others. Follow the crown with a wall and then double the crown only. Draw up taut, and add another wall and crown below. Double this latter knot above the established lead, and finally tuck to the stem, as in the "NOSEGAY," *but one compartment farther to the right.* That is to say, skip the first compartment and tuck down through the second.

Draw up taut, and extend the loops to the desired length. When converting this knot into a hat my wife frayed out the ends of the sash cord, of which the knot was composed, and sewed them flat to the underside of a wide pleated fillet or snood of unbleached linen duck.

The more elaborate knots of this chapter are scarcely practicable in the strands of ordinary rope. At sea "fancy knots" are apt to be tied with log, lead, or codfish line. I have found banding (see page 20) a very satisfactory material for practicing knots, and for many purposes it is an excellent material for finished knot work. After it is painted it has a texture very much like canvas-covered strands.

Many of the completed Stopper Knots of Chapter 6 and the Lanyard Knots of Chapters 7 and 8 may be satisfactorily converted into Multi-Strand Button Knots by crowning them and then tucking the ends of the strands to the stem, or, in some cases, by tucking the ends to the stem without first crowning them.

901. The Cauliflower Knot. Crown and wall six strands, and then double the crown only, as in the knots on the two previous pages. Draw up the knot, then turn the structure upside down, and, in this position, tie a diamond with all six strands as shown in the second diagram. This is to be doubled similarly to Lanyard Knot ⌗120.

To do this, tuck down over one and under one, as shown in the second diagram, and tuck each strand up over two and under two, as indicated by the arrow in the third diagram. Finally, turn back this second knot around the neck of the first knot, and draw all taut.

902. With five strands make a crown like the diagram given here at the left. Add a wall, and then double the crown only, following the lead on the inside. Stick the ends to the stem, add a Star Knot (⌗881) below the knot already described, and finally tuck the ends out at the stem.

903. Crown upon Crown. Seize six strands and tie two crowns, one outside the other (see second diagram), and draw all taut. Turn the structure upside down, and stop the strands to the stem as in the third diagram. In this position make a crown and wall to the right, and double this, following above the lead, the stem still being held aloft. Finally, stick the ends to the stem as they lie.

Knots of the Wall and Crown variety generally require doubling if they are to be firm. But if the centers are tied before the rims, knots can be made that do not require doubling. The Single-Strand Buttons of Chapter 5 are tied in this way; that is to say, the strands are introduced at the center. Most of the Single-Strand Buttons that have a square compartment at the center, or that can be adapted to that arrangement, may be tied as Multi-Strand Buttons. But Single-Strand Button diagrams in which the *parts around the center* do not rotate in one direction do not easily permit the introduction of strands at the center. Moreover Single-Strand Buttons in which the *parts around the rim* do not all rotate in the same direction may not be started with a Wall Knot.

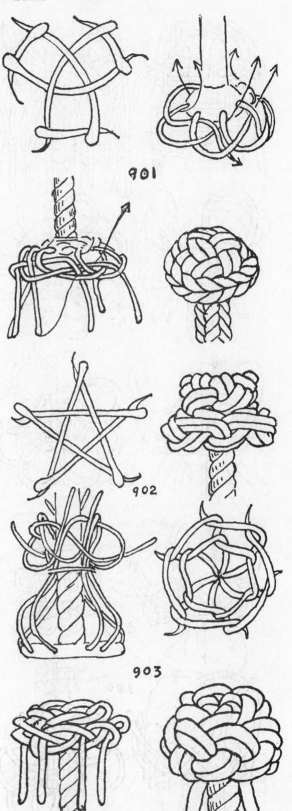

901

902

903

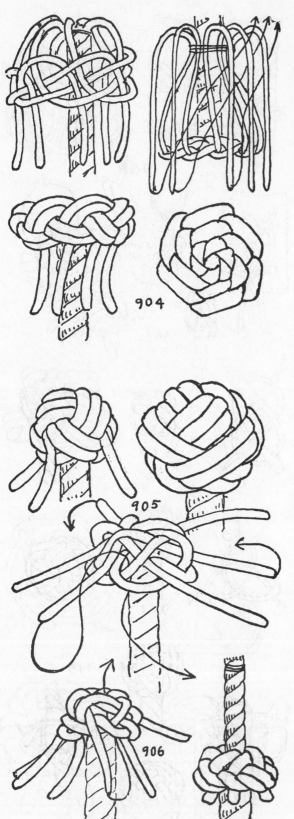

904

905

906

904. Seize six strands. Lay the ends down, and tie a RIGHT-HAND DIAMOND KNOT. Above the diamond superimpose a crown (also to the right), and tuck each end down under a rim part, as shown in the first diagram, following the parallel lead on the near side. This is shown completed in the first diagram.

At this point work the knot taut and flat, as it is to be completed before proceeding with the next move. Having worked it carefully and progressively, proceed to pull the ends so that only right diagonals show, and the doubled parts which lead to the ends, and the standing parts, are hidden. When complete, the top must be flat, and in appearance like the center of the fourth diagram.

Turn the structure upside down, and stop the strands to the neck, as in the second diagram. Allow the strands to hang downward, and in this position tie a diamond to the right, as shown in the same diagram.

Double this, as shown in the third diagram, in which the structure has returned to an erect position, and finally draw up the knot.

Work methodically until the knot is regular and conforms to diagrams 3 and 4.

While working, continually force the final double diamond downward, so that its outer rim closes tightly around the neck and the inner rim is flush with the first-made knot. Finally, pull on the stem and make certain that the top of the knot is flat.

905. ACORN KNOT. Make "first a crown and then a wall," with either three or four strands. Follow below the lead on the outer periphery, until the crown is tripled and the wall is doubled. Turn the knot upside down, and tie a diamond (⚹693) *to the right, outside* the first knot. Double this, and work the knot carefully, making certain that only the crown of the original knot is still apparent.

906. A HYBRID KNOT that has some of the characteristics of the BUTTON and some of the LANYARD KNOT, half the strands being tucked to the stem and the other half being laid up at the top. Take six or eight strands, and single wall and single crown them. Tuck each end of the crown through one additional bight, then stick each alternate end down to the stem under *two* parts. Stick the remaining ends up to the center top after the manner of the STOPPER KNOT, as shown in the third diagram. Each interstice between two standing parts should be filled with an end.

If six strands were used, the three top strands might be laid up into rope. If eight strands were used, the four left at the top might be either laid up or platted as SQUARE SINNET. The strands of the neck are trimmed short, whatever their number.

907. So far the knots of this chapter have been tied in hand. The knots which immediately follow, through KNOT ⚹967, are tied on a cork board or table, having a hole in the center through which the stem departs out of the plane of the knot. The knots are first walled, generally to the right, and then are crowned. The considerable variety in the shape and character of these knots is caused by the difference in the design of the crowns, since they all start with a single wall unless otherwise stated.

MULTI-STRAND BUTTONS, TIED ON THE TABLE

An enlarged copy of a crown is made on a sheet of paper, and a hole is pierced (with a pencil point) where each strand is to be introduced. A single right wall having been tied, the strands are rove upward through these holes in the paper diagram in their proper order, after which the stem and WALL KNOT are lowered down through the hole in the cork board or table. The diagram is flattened out on top of the board, and the crown is tied over the diagram, one strand at a time being pinned at frequent intervals. After this the knot is removed and drawn taut.

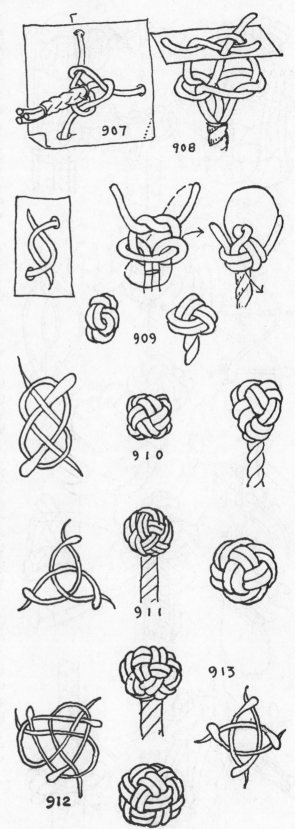

908. The knot illustrated here is TACK KNOT #846, now called MANROPE KNOT. Sometimes it is easier to double a knot before removing it from the board. Often it is simpler to work it into smaller compass before doubling, particularly if the strands are short. In doubling, the lead may be followed either below or above as described in #672.

909. A very simple TWO-STRAND CROWN is given here, and the knot is doubled by following below the lead, which is the common way. The ends of the strands are tucked to the stem after the knot has been doubled or tripled. The larger knots of this series, however, are often left single, the pictured form being of ample size. Many of the SINGLE-STRAND BUTTONS of Chapter 4 may be tied as TWO-STRAND BUTTONS. (See #980 and #1000.)

The following knots are at first limited to a few strands, but the number of strands increases as the chapter progresses, a TWELVE-STRAND KNOT appearing on page 180. If sinnets of more strands are tied the strands may be seized and the superfluous ones trimmed out. Beyond twelve strands the knots become hollow and require a core.

910. A TWO-STRAND BUTTON that is based on a CARRICK BEND CROWN. After a TWO-STRAND KNOT is completed the ends and standing parts may be laid up together into a neck of FOUR-STRAND SQUARE SINNET or else four-strand plain-laid rope.

911. A THREE-STRAND BUTTON KNOT. The crown that is pictured here, if added to a single *wall*, makes the same knot as a DIAMOND KNOT with a superimposed *single crown*. The crossings in all these crowns are taken alternately over and under. It does not appear necessary to elaborate the drawings of each one. Sufficient is drawn to indicate the order of the over-and-under. After the initial wall, the first tuck of the crown is always over and then under.

Any diagram composed entirely of lines with an even number of crossings is a potential crown for a BUTTON KNOT.

912. A larger knot than the foregoing, also of three strands, the top aspect of which is somewhat similar.

913. A FOUR-STRAND KNOT that gives the same result as a DIAMOND AND CROWN of four strands.

The forms of many of these knots are more or less inevitable, provided they are evenly worked. But some have to be prodded and molded before they take shape. Knots, like children, should be gently urged in the direction it is hoped they will follow.

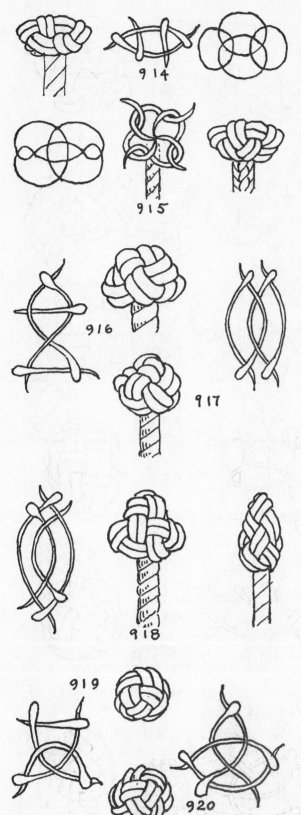

914. This is a compact, FOUR-STRAND KNOT a little smaller than the SPRITSAIL SHEET KNOT. These knots hold their distinctive forms better when they are either single or double; tripling tends to "round them out" too much.

915. It has been mentioned elsewhere, in connection with the SPRITSAIL SHEET KNOT, that the character of a knot is often altered if the crown is tied reversely. It was also suggested that the same effect, but mirrored, may be gained by reversing the original wall. This makes it unnecessary to illustrate the crown tied in both ways. The center diagram is a left wall, and the left diagram here gives the complete diagram form of the knot tied with the left-handed wall. The crown of both ⚓914 and ⚓915 is at the top center of the page, and the single-line diagram at the top right is the complete cycle of the knot with a right wall.

916. Knots of irregular shape are possible with an even number of strands.

917. To exhaust the possibilities even of a four-strand diagram would appear to be a considerable task.

918. This knot is both distinctive and practical.

919. Compare this with regular TURK'S-HEAD diagram ⚓911.

920. A FOUR-STRAND KNOT built on an irregular diagram with a three-sided center compartment. The effect, however, is quite regular.

921. A somewhat conical knot of four strands with a three-sided center compartment. Except occasionally at the center, the surface of these knots is limited to three- and four-sided compartments, and the texture appears quite regular, even though in the diagrams it may appear uneven at times.

922. A TOGGLE-SHAPED KNOT.

923. A SADDLECLOTH-SHAPED BUTTON.

924. A SQUARE KNOT with a diagonal weave.

925. An inverted truncated PYRAMID.

926. The FIVE-STRAND KNOTS commence with a FIVE-POINTED STAR. This may be tied in four-strand rope by splicing an extra strand to the core. It consists of a wall and a *star-shaped crown*. An identical knot may be made by tying a diamond and a single crown. This is shown as ⚓852.

927. A different knot with the wall tied to the right, but with the crown reversed. This makes a more pronounced STAR than the last, quite different in character and very flat on top.

928. A HALF-ROUND KNOT.

929. A FIVE-STRAND KNOT with a four-part center that is approximately round.

930. A FIVE-STRAND KNOT with a four-part center. Somewhat elliptical in form.

931. A neat FIVE-STRAND KNOB with a three-part center.

932. A taller and larger knot than the last, somewhat egg-shaped. Tie these knots tightly, and, if necessary, beat them into compact and regular form with a wooden mallet.

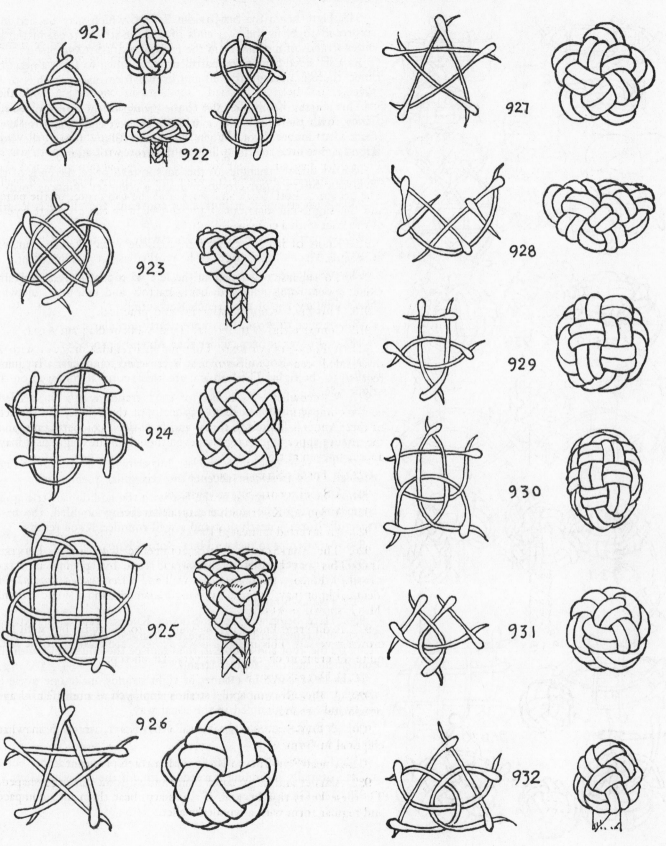

921

922

923

924

925

926

927

928

929

930

931

932

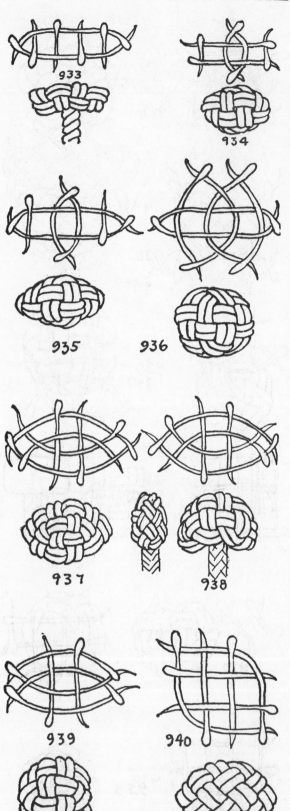

933. Here begin the SIX-STRAND KNOTS, which may be tied in a six-strand rope, in the two ends of a three-strand rope, in the six outer strands of a cable, or in the ends of a SIX-STRAND SINNET.

As a six-sided center compartment is too open to form a practical knot, there is no regular wall and crown form in six strands to be given.

This diagram form is similar to the crown of the SPRITSAIL SHEET KNOT, with the addition of a triangle at each end, which makes a somewhat longer knot. When doubling, follow below the lead. Don't tighten the two long lines of the crown too hastily.

934. By adding triangles to the sides instead of to the ends of the SPRITSAIL SHEET KNOT crown diagram, a compact ellipse is formed.

935. With triangles, at both sides and ends, the ellipse is lengthened.

936. A particularly handsome knot with a flat top.

937. A MELON SEED shape: to be worked as flat as convenient.

938. With the crown tied to the left on top of a right wall, the knot is completely changed, being narrow and tall, and somewhat like a military hat of the French Revolution.

939. Similar to #936, but more nearly circular.

940. A PUMPKIN SEED, wider than MELON SEED #937.

941. A HALF-ROUND KNOT that is crowned to the left after being walled to the right. The lead is more satisfactory if followed on the right side.

942. A neat CIRCULAR KNOT.

943. A TRIANGULAR KNOT that was doubled, and the lead followed on the outside.

944. The same diagram as the last, but crowned to the left and not doubled. This treatment accents the triangular form.

945. The same diagram as the last with the addition of triangular compartments at the side centers. After being doubled, the basic triangular form is nearly lost and a well-rounded KNOB results.

946. An attempt to make a HALF-ROUND KNOT.

947. A very regular KNOB shape.

948. A KIDNEY BEAN shape.

949. TOGGLE-SHAPED.

950. Here begin the SEVEN-STRAND KNOTS. Take a SIX-STRAND SINNET and temporarily seize an extra strand of other material to the stem, tie the knot and double it, then replace the odd strand with the convenient end of a regular strand.

If the knot is tied in a sinnet of eight strands, make one cycle of the diagram with two parallel strands employed as a unit. This leaves six strands to be doubled in the usual way.

951. A SEVEN-STRAND QUARTER-ROUND KNOT, which in shape resembles a wedge of pie.

952. The HEART. It is hardly necessary to name a knot, but it assists materially in finding it a second time if the occasion arises.

953. The GRASSHOPPER.

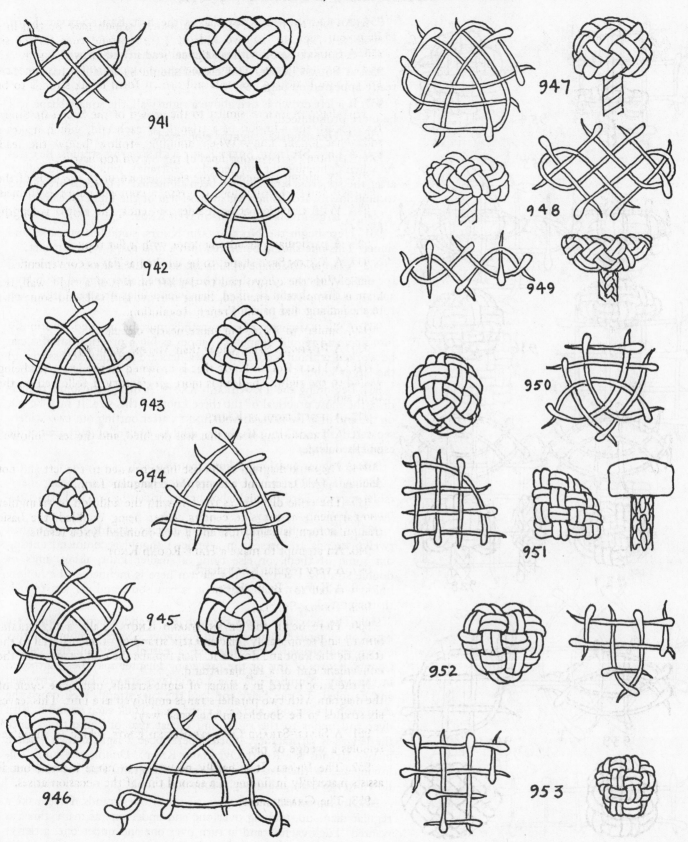

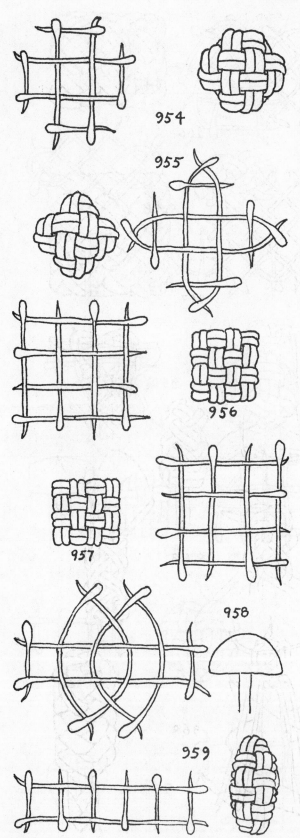

954

955

956

957

958

959

954. An OCTAGONAL KNOT that is the first EIGHT-STRAND KNOT to be given.

955. A SQUARE KNOT with a diagonal lead in the crown.

956. A SQUARE KNOT. This crown should be familiar, having already appeared on page 167.

957. If a left crown is tied above a right wall, the square shape will be more pronounced.

958. A HEMISPHERE, slightly elongated.

959. A LONG SPRITSAIL SHEET KNOT with six cross strands. Be careful when tightening the two lengthwise strands, which should follow after the six cross strands have been tightened. The ends are bound to pull downward, somewhat in the form of the kidney bean.

960. A large inverted BASKET-SHAPED KNOT.

961. Here begin the NINE-STRAND KNOTS, suitable for cables and sinnet. This one should be beaten into a *disk shape* with a mallet.

962. A larger disk shape of nine strands. If these knots are intended for out-of-door use, they should be tightened after a good pounding, and then they should be filled (hardwood filler or casein glue) before shellacking and painting.

963. A TETRAHEDRON of nine strands must be worked laboriously into firm and regular shape. It is about as big a practical knot as can be worked without a core. Metal washers are practical accessories to the larger knots.

964. Beginning the TEN-STRAND KNOTS. A firm, handsome, regular disk, the most practical of the three knots of this size. It may be put on the end of a TWELVE-STRAND SINNET after cutting out two widely separated strands. In this knot, double by following *above* the established lead.

965. A bigger and longer knot than #958.

966. A large OBLONG of ten strands. The shape, not being inevitable, requires hard manual labor before it can be worked into satisfactory form.

967. A somewhat similar knot of twelve strands. If more than twelve strands are present in a sinnet I should recommend cutting out some of them, or else tying a smaller knot, using units of double strands. Even the knot shown here is inclined to be hollow unless worked to the limit. But it is handsome and no less regular than pictured.

968. The next few knots through #978 and excepting #972 are based on elongated DIAMOND and FOOTROPE KNOTS combined with a crown and shaped somewhat like a cattail. Any of the smaller CROWN KNOTS of this or the preceding chapter may be lengthened in this way. Number 968 is a LONG TWO-STRAND KNOT, crowned and doubled. To tie: Seize and lead the two strands well down the stem, stop the strands, and tie a right wall. Tuck each strand in turn over and under to the right, and repeat two or three times until the length is satisfactory. Then superimpose a right crown (which in two strands is a RIGHT OVERHAND KNOT). Double the knot, following below the lead as in the fourth diagram. Pull the two ends down to the stem, using a wire loop for a tool.

969. In somewhat similar way, tie with four strands. First make a regular diamond, tucking over one and under one as many times as wanted. Tuck each strand in turn over one and under one, a tier at a time. Finally, crown and tuck the ends to the stem without doubling.

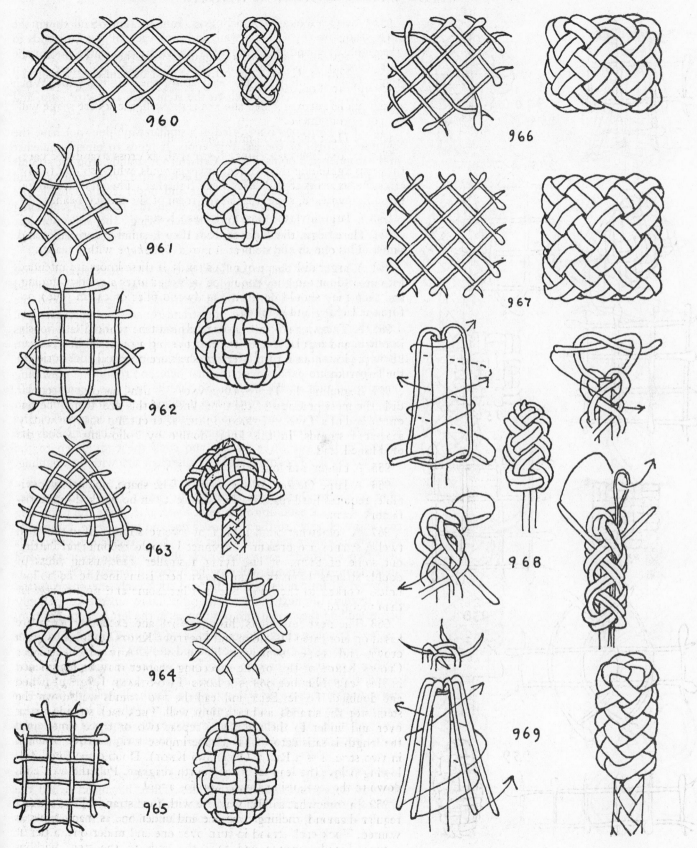

960

966

961

967

962

963

968

964

969

965

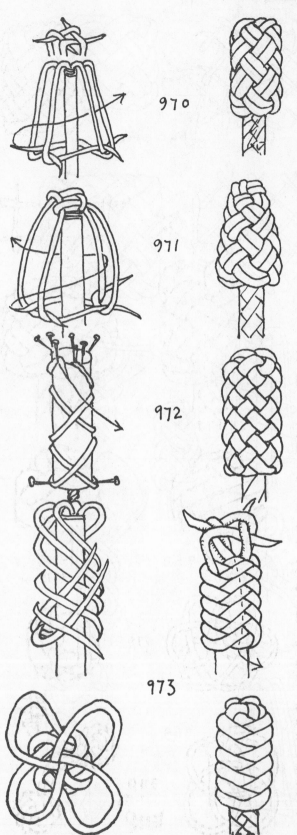

970. Seize a FOUR-STRAND SINNET, lead the ends well down the stem, and stop them. Tie a wall, and tuck each of the four ends to the right, over and under once, as shown by the single line in the left diagram. Repeat this with all four strands, and then crown them. Double, following the lead above the original knot. When complete, pull the ends down to the stem with the wire loop, and work the knot taut.

971. The FOOTROPE KNOT, tied in a similar way, does not have the cylindrical form of the last few knots. It tends to taper somewhat in the manner of a pointed rope. Crown four strands, stop the strands well down the stem, and wall them. Tuck in turn to the right over and under. Then tuck each strand over and under again. Double the original crown by following the lead on the *outside*. Continuing parallel, double the whole knot, which brings the ends out just *below* the crown. Tuck the ends as they lie, into the center of the knot and down to the stem.

972. This LONG TERMINAL KNOT is tied with three strands. Seize the strands and tuck up through a short mailing tube. There should be six evenly spaced pins around each end of the tube. Lead the strands out at the top, so that one strand rounds each alternate pin. Lead them downward in a 45-degree helix and round alternate pins at the base. Lead all strands upward over all in a 45-degree helix to the top, passing each of the ends around an unoccupied pin. Lay the ends down again parallel with the first helix and round the remaining unoccupied pins at the bottom. So far the lead has been over all. Lay each strand in turn to the top, tucking it *first under* one, then *over* one, and *under* one and so on, alternately, to the top. The last tuck will be under one of the first rim bights. When all ends are tucked, crown the three strands and stick the ends down to the stem, as they lie. The knot will be of sufficient size without doubling.

973. A knot with a twilled surface. Lay down four strands in a right 45-degree helix, and seize to the stem. Take two *opposite* strands and tuck each up to the right *under one*. Take the remaining two and tuck them to the right *over one* and *under two*. Now tuck the first pair over *two* and under *two*. Next tuck all four strands over two and under two, then tuck all four again, over two and under two. The strands will now be in two different tiers.

Crown all four ends as they lie, and stick each one down to the stem beyond the next bight to the right. Draw up the knot snugly before pulling the crown into position, as in the left bottom diagram.

974. The next three knots consist of LONG DOUBLE DIAMOND KNOTS, in combination with compound crowns.

Seize five strands, or take a SIX-STRAND SINNET and cut out one strand. Stop the five ends at some distance down the stem below the seizing, and there tie a WALL KNOT. Tuck all strands upward in a right diagonal, over one and under one, and then over and under a second time. Add a star-shaped crown to the top, and double the whole knot, sticking all ends down at the center, parallel with the stem.

975. With four strands tie a diamond, tucking each strand over one and under one and repeating this. Then, having crowned the knot as in the diagram, follow the lead with the two *end* strands of the crown *below* the first lead (imperative). Then with the two remaining cross strands of the crown follow the lead *above* until the whole knot has been doubled, when the ends are tucked down to the stem in the usual manner.

No trouble should be occasioned by the fact that some strands follow above and some below the earlier parallel strands. All that is necessary is to remember that if you *cross a strand* that is alongside, you are not paralleling it. When the knot is completed the crown should be flat.

976. With six strands make a wall, and then tuck each end over and under once only. Superimpose the crown that is pictured here and double the knot, following below the lead and finally sticking the strands down to the stem in the usual manner. The crown of the completed top takes the form of a lengthwise arch.

977. The two knots to follow are LANYARD KNOTS that are crowned and have the ends stuck down to the stem. Begin with a FOUR-STRAND DIAMOND KNOT (⋕693). Each strand having been tucked in turn over one and under one, all four strands are tucked again *under* one, and this is repeated twice more, so that each strand of the knot lies over one and under four. Crown this knot, and tuck the ends down to the stem.

978. With four strands, tie a DIAMOND KNOT in which each strand, when the knot is complete, has been tucked over two and under three. Crown this knot, and stick each end of the crown through one additional bight to the right. Tuck the ends down to the stem, and draw the knot up carefully.

979. The diagram given here depicts the *wall*, not the crown, of the knot. Heretofore the walls have been regular, so that it was not necessary to show them. In this case an irregular wall is called for. Copy the diagram, and stick the strands up through the paper. Then tie the knot shown, and add a single crown. Finally, stick the ends to the stem without doubling the knot. The result is a very regular disk.

980. I found myself away from home one evening without any cuff links, on an occasion when a black tie was to be worn. I was able to find a pair of round black shoestrings and evolved the following.

I first tied, in the center of one shoestring, a CHINESE BUTTON KNOT (⋕601) which I doubled. I then drew a diagram of the TWO-STRAND BUTTON KNOT pictured here. After tying it, I proceeded to double it, following the lead indicated by the dotted lines. A hairpin served to draw it taut.

In most of the knots so far shown in this chapter the number of rim parts has coincided with the number of strands employed. In this knot the number of bights at the rim is twice the number of the strands.

Most of the knots in this chapter have had the standing parts introduced at the rim, by tying either a WALL KNOT, a DIAMOND KNOT, or a FOOTROPE KNOT. The knots on pages 179–180 have the strands introduced at the center, which requires a different method of tying. Some knots may be tied by both methods, but when tied in different ways they will differ somewhat in character. Generally a knot in which the strands are introduced at the center does not require doubling, being sufficiently firm, while a knot that is started at the rim is less firm and should be doubled.

981

982

983

984

985

981. A LONG TOGGLE-SHAPED KNOT may be tied by first walling and then crowning four strands, over the accompanying diagram. This knot should be *doubled*.

982. But the same knot, tied with four strands introduced at the center, does not need to be doubled. The diagram should be placed on the cork board or table, the stem dropped through the hole, and one cord at a time pinned along the lines of the diagram. At the crossings repeat to yourself, "Over," or "Under," as the case may be, and continue repeating, alternately at each crossing, and tucking the cord accordingly. When one strand has finished its circuit, continue with the next one.

983, 984. Two somewhat similar knots that can be tied only with strands that are introduced at the centers. These diagrams are not suitable for the rim method, as different parts of the rim rotate in contrary directions.

985. A small, exceedingly practical ELLIPSE that cannot be tied by the wall and crown method.

986. A large, flat, and very compact ELLIPSE.

987. An ARCHED DISK which can also be tied by the rim method but, so tied, will not hold its distinctive shape so well.

988. A knot that may be tied by either method, but changes character. The rim (wall) method is shown as ✵940. If the ends are tucked beyond the second standing part the center will be fuller and the knot firmer.

989. Here is another way in which to tie a PENTALPHA, which should be compared with ✵926 and ✵927.

990. A TRIANGULAR KNOT of three strands and six rim parts. When the ends are led to the stem, the knot will be improved if they are tucked beyond the second standing part, as indicated by the arrows.

991. A handsome and distinctive TRIANGULAR BUTTON of three strands. This may be tied either as a SINGLE or as a DOUBLE KNOT.

992. A SQUARE BUTTON with crisp, angular edges. This should not be doubled, as, when doubled, ✵956 and ✵957 have much the same appearance and are simpler to tie.

993. The same knot as the last with the addition of bights to the rim.

994. A ROUND FLAT KNOT.

995. A SQUARE KNOT with a diagonal weave.

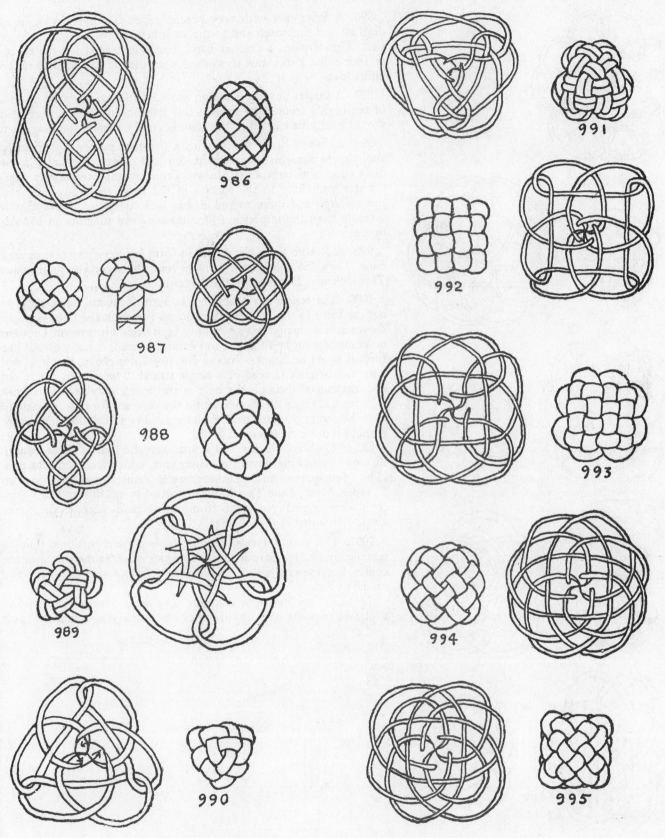

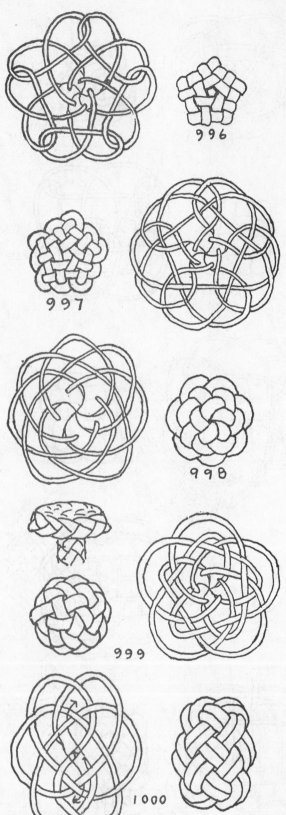

996. A PENTAGON with very precise edges. Tie over an enlarged diagram and tuck each end to the stem beyond the second standing part. This requires a craftier hand than was needed for the three- or four-sided knots, but if worked with care it should present no difficulties.

997. A similar but larger design provides a PENTAGON with a series of ten bights around the rim. In this knot, as in the last, each end should finally be tucked to the stem beyond a second standing part.

998. A SEVEN-BIGHT KNOT with a five-part center. Surprisingly enough, despite this disparity of rim and center, the knot is the most successful large DISK shown. Probably this irregularity contributes something to the success of the knot, for №994, which is just as large and quite as round, has such a regular weave that it detracts from the impression of roundness and suggests an angular figure.

999. A ROUND FLAT KNOT that in form is a very short, truncated cone. Tuck the ends of the knot beyond the second standing part. This is clearly illustrated in the diagram.

1000. The remaining knots may be termed SPORTS, since they do not conform to the arbitrary limitations to which the knots already shown in this chapter have generally been held. The present knot has no compartment at all in the top center; instead, it has a cross. The form is based on SINGLE-STRAND BUTTON KNOT №619, but it is tied with two strands instead of a single strand. The strands are seized and introduced through the hole in the board or table. If the knot is to remain single after completing the diagram form, lead one end over the center diagonal before sticking it down. If doubled, the knot perhaps is more satisfactory.

Other ONE-STRAND BUTTON KNOTS may be tied as TWO-STRAND BUTTONS by pulling down the center part, which automatically provides a four-part stem. Still others may be easily tied as FOUR-STRAND BUTTONS. Most of the TRIANGULAR SINGLE-STRAND BUTTONS of Chapter 5 were originally adapted from multi-strand diagrams that were already included in this chapter.

1001. This shows a very regular knob pattern that may not be completely tied by introducing the strands either at the rim or at the center, because one line of the diagram fails to touch either the rim or the center.

To tie: Copy the right diagram, take a SIX-STRAND SINNET, and stick two opposite ends up through holes on the diagram at the spots marked X. Wall the four remaining strands beneath the diagram and around the two inactive strands, and stick them up through the remaining holes on the diagram, in the order indicated. Crown as shown in the lower right diagram. Then remove the diagram, and double the parts not already doubled, finally sticking the ends down at the stem. This is a very neat design, which presented a nice problem in tying.

The more elaborate knots of this volume were drawn on slate or paper before they were committed to cord or rope. Some of the knots have several hundred crossings and could hardly be tied off-hand.

1002. A knot without any wall. Double the crown as shown. Six strands are required. The knot is regular and of good appearance.

1003. None of the conventional methods appear to be absolutely necessary for there is generally another way to tie any knot. If strands are diverted, after completing their regular cycles, into other cycles after the manner of the MONKEY'S FIST (see Chapter 29) almost any regular design appears to be a possible knot. The present diagram may be tied by the rim method with six strands. But by the center method alone, only half the knot will be tied. To make with three strands, by an adaptation of the MONKEY'S FIST method: Make an enlarged copy of the diagram, introduce the strands at the center, and pin out according to the diagram. After each cord has been led and doubled one cycle, it is diverted into another cycle. This makes a successful knot that is superficially the same as #943, but it is much more trouble to tie.

1004. The accompanying knot is the result of an attempt to vary the texture of these knots, which has so far been regularly over one and under one. The sequence in this knot, after a basic wall has been tied, is over two and under one, or else over one and under two. It is not a bad knot, but it was a difficult one to plot and draw up. It must be worked skillfully and unhurriedly.

1005. A distinctive knot that has four six-sided compartments, which are not, however, very apparent when the knot is completed. Take four strands, wall and then crown them, as in the left diagram. Tuck the ends as indicated by the arrow in the left diagram, pull them and arrange the crown to take the form of the right diagram. Follow the lead below the wall to the right, and after doubling the entire knot stick the ends down to the stem beyond the first bight to the right.

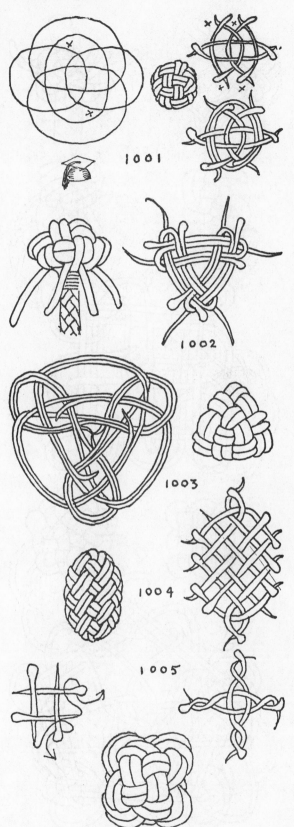

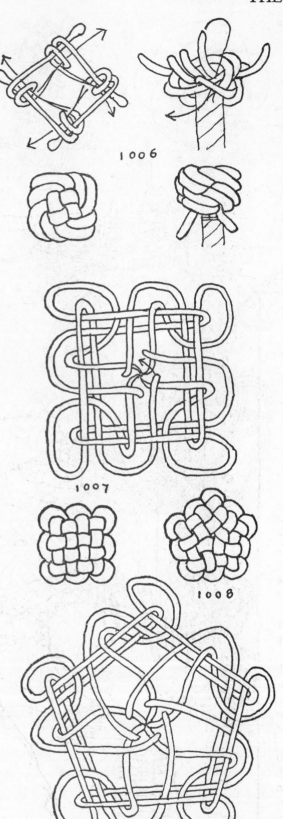

1006

1007

1008

1006. A SPORT that has a character of its own. Seize four strands and tie a wall to the right. Stick each strand up through a hole in the paper. The holes should be about one and one half inches apart, at the four corners of a square. It is not necessary to copy the diagram as in this particular knot a diagram does not seem to help much.

Tie a right wall *above* the paper, and lead each strand an additional right tuck around the strand ahead of it to the right. Lead each end back to the left, tucking it parallel to its own part and through the round turn, that is, to its left. The visible knot should now exactly resemble the first diagram.

Tuck each end down through the original wall to the stem, under two parts, as shown in the second diagram.

Double the original wall, following *below* the lead and *to the left*, and stick the end directly down to the stem, as shown in the right lower diagram.

1007. The two remaining knots are depicted in two planes, one over the other, so that, although the completed knots have a regular over-one-and-under-one surface texture, the drawings do not show it.

This SQUARE KNOT is based on the CHINESE BUTTERFLY KNOT (#2460). The same form is also used as SINGLE-STRAND BUTTON KNOT #631. A knot of somewhat similar appearance, but tied in a totally different way, is given as #993; in the latter knot there are two bights at each side of the square, while in the present knot there is a bight at each corner and also one at the center of each side.

In working the knot, the central part may be gradually tightened, drawing the material out into the bights around the rim. After the knot has taken form, the superfluous material in these bights is worked out.

The center of the knot will be strengthened by sticking the ends down to the stem beyond the second standing part. This is indicated by an arrow on one of the ends.

After the knot is completed, if the four strands were not originally made into FOUR-STRAND SINNET, the ends and standing parts may be worked together either as EIGHT-STRAND SQUARE SINNET #3001 or as EIGHT-STRAND ROUND SINNET #3021.

A TRIANGULAR KNOT (#991) is tied by the same method as #993, but a TRIANGULAR KNOT tied by the present method is less successful, since it does not close compactly at the center edges.

1008. The PENTAGON is tied in a similar way, but as it has a five-part center it requires five strands. The HELICAL CROWN SINNET (#2931) will provide the necessary strands, or the FOUR-STRAND ROUND or SQUARE SINNET (#2999) with a core added may be used. An extra strand may be spliced to the core of a shroud-laid rope (#2828) or a single strand may be cut out of a SIX-STRAND ROUND SINNET. The knot is tied in any of these materials in the manner of #1007.

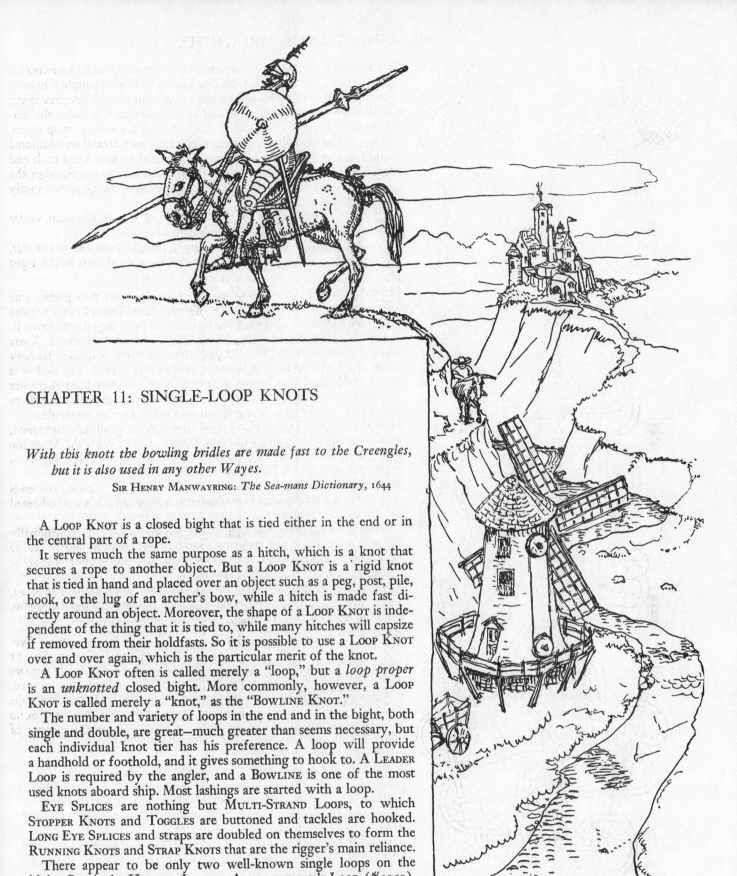

CHAPTER 11: SINGLE-LOOP KNOTS

With this knott the bowling bridles are made fast to the Creengles, but it is also used in any other Wayes.

SIR HENRY MANWAYRING: *The Sea-mans Dictionary*, 1644

A LOOP KNOT is a closed bight that is tied either in the end or in the central part of a rope.

It serves much the same purpose as a hitch, which is a knot that secures a rope to another object. But a LOOP KNOT is a rigid knot that is tied in hand and placed over an object such as a peg, post, pile, hook, or the lug of an archer's bow, while a hitch is made fast directly around an object. Moreover, the shape of a LOOP KNOT is independent of the thing that it is tied to, while many hitches will capsize if removed from their holdfasts. So it is possible to use a LOOP KNOT over and over again, which is the particular merit of the knot.

A LOOP KNOT often is called merely a "loop," but a *loop proper* is an *unknotted* closed bight. More commonly, however, a LOOP KNOT is called merely a "knot," as the "BOWLINE KNOT."

The number and variety of loops in the end and in the bight, both single and double, are great—much greater than seems necessary, but each individual knot tier has his preference. A loop will provide a handhold or foothold, and it gives something to hook to. A LEADER LOOP is required by the angler, and a BOWLINE is one of the most used knots aboard ship. Most lashings are started with a loop.

EYE SPLICES are nothing but MULTI-STRAND LOOPS, to which STOPPER KNOTS and TOGGLES are buttoned and tackles are hooked. LONG EYE SPLICES and straps are doubled on themselves to form the RUNNING KNOTS and STRAP KNOTS that are the rigger's main reliance.

There appear to be only two well-known single loops on the bight. One is the HARNESS LOOP or ARTILLERYMAN'S LOOP (#1050), a knot that is used to provide a hand- or shoulder-hold in manhandling guns. The second is the ENGLISH, ENGLISHMAN'S, WATER,

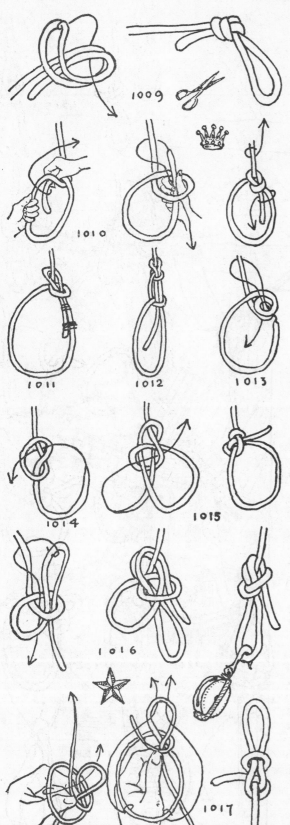

WATERMAN'S, FISHER'S, FISHERMAN'S, FISHERMAN'S EYE, FISHER-MAN'S LOOP, LOVE, TRUE-LOVE, or TRUE-LOVER'S KNOT (#1038), which is an angler's loop and rather a cumbrous one; but it is a very well-known knot, mainly, I think, because of the manner in which it is tied.

1009. The LOOP KNOT, also called OVERHAND LOOP, is the simplest as well as the commonest of loops. It is used in the home and the shop when tying up parcels and on the farm and in general carting for hooking the ends of lashings. It is not suitable, however, for rope, being difficult to untie.

1010. The BOWLINE, BOWLING, or BOLIN KNOT, sometimes called BOWLING'S KNOT. The name is derived from *bow line*, a rope that holds the weather leech of a square sail forward and prevents the sail from being taken aback. As the line or rope that provided the knot is no longer in use, the BOWLINE KNOT is nowadays very apt to be termed merely the "BOWLINE," the word *knot* being dropped.

It is sometimes called STANDING BOWLINE in contradistinction to RUNNING BOWLINE (NOOSE #1117).

Captain John Smith says of the knot: "The Boling Knot is so firmly made and fastened by the bridles into the creengles of the sailes, they will breake, or the saile split before it will slip." But no knot is safe that is not properly drawn up, which will explain probably the following contradictory statement from Alston's *Seamanship* of 1871: "With a heavy strain a bowline knot often capsizes." However, it is a fact that no knot is safe except under reasonable conditions. Properly tied in ordinary rope, there is little or no danger of a BOWLINE KNOT's capsizing before the breaking point of the rope itself is reached. It is so good a knot that the sailor seldom uses any other LOOP KNOT aboard ship.

A BOWLINE is frequently used as a hitch when tying a boat painter to a ring. On a whaler it is tied around a man's waist to make a "monkey rope," which is required if he is to be lowered overside for any purpose. When mooring, BOWLINES are tied in hawsers and tossed over bollards. Two interlocked BOWLINES are a common form of HAWSER BEND. It is often said at sea that "the divil would make a good sailor, if he could only tie a bowline and look aloft."

To tie the knot: Grasp the end of a rope in the right hand and the standing part in the left hand. Cross the end of the rope over the standing part, and with a turn of the right wrist put a single hitch around the rope end. Without shifting the grip of the right hand, pass the end of the rope to the left under the standing part, then down through the hitch that was first formed.

1011. The STANDING BOWLINE. This name properly belongs to a BOWLINE KNOT that has been seized, as on a boatswain's chair.

1012. If a BOWLINE is to be towed through the water a second HALF HITCH may be added. Wet knots are apt to jam, and the extra hitch lessens this tendency.

1013. The DOUBLE or ROUND TURN BOWLINE is put into stiff or slippery rope and is the same knot formation as the DOUBLE BECKET HITCH. It holds the BOWLINE together in such a way as to lessen the danger of its capsizing, which is liable to occur when a SINGLE BOWLINE is carelessly drawn up.

1014. The HAWSER BOWLINE is a "trick" way of forming the knot. A turn is formed in the standing part of the rope, and the end is brought around a post and tucked as shown. The swing of a boat will haul the knot taut.

1015. Alston, who complained of the unreliability of the BOWLINE

Knot as quoted under ⚓1010, gives this method of tucking the end of the knot to render it more secure.

1016. Luce and Ward, and also Nares, give this knot, based on the Bowline, as the proper loop for the hook of a light tackle.

1017. The Angler's Loop has the best lead of any loop and is one of the best of single loops for the ends of small lines such as fishline, twine, etc. But as it jams, it is not suitable for rope.

Take a long end (a little practice will show how long) and form a bight. Hold as shown in the first diagram. Make two turns around the finger tips, the first equaling the size of the proposed loop, the second being snugly taken around the small of the knot. Lead the large turn over the second turn and through the first bight, and pull taut.

1018. Department-Store Loop. One of the commonest of Loop Knots for tying bundles, but not a particularly strong one.

1019. Eskimo Bowstring Loop Knot from an ethnological report (Washington, 1892). The same knot is given in Diderot's Encyclopedia of 1762 as a Weaver's Knot for a loom adjustment. The knot is also employed by anglers. Its merit is that the length of the loop is easily altered, when necessary, after the knot has been tied.

1020. A Slipped Loop is used by anglers so that a leader does not jam and is easily removed.

1021. An Adjustable Loop is another Leader Loop with features similar to ⚓1019 and ⚓1020.

1022. An improved Englishman's Loop (see ⚓1039). It is strong and handsome but cumbersome. It may be untied by separating the two knots of which it is composed and then capsizing them one at a time.

1023. The Farmer's Halter Loop does not slip and choke an animal that is being led. A Single Hitch may be added around the nose to allow easier leading. It is similar to ⚓1018, but the loop is rounder. In teaming, it is applied to hooks and stakes when lashing a load.

1024. The Bowstring Knot or Honda Knot appears to have been used by the aborigines of several continents. It is the most compact and open of all loops. Mexican and American cowboys have adopted it for their lariats and call it the Honda Knot. The end may be either seized or knotted.

"Tom Bowling" confused the Bowstring Knot with the Bowline Knot, so that, amusingly enough, the Bowling or Bowline Knot, proper, does not appear in "Bowling's" book!

1025. There are always people who believe that if a single thing is good two are bound to be better. So they overburden their knots with extra turns and flourishes. The accompanying knot, which is often shown, is a good example of this, the previous knot being quite adequate, and the latter no improvement over it.

1026. A Stopped or Seized Half Hitch is compact, strong, and secure in large rope, and is much used by both sailors and riggers.

1027. The Midshipman's Hitch, seized or stopped, is another semipermanent loop, one of the strongest.

1028. An Eskimo Loop or Strap Loop, tied in rawhide. Make a long slit near the end of a strap and a shorter slit in the bight at the length desired for the loop.

Reeve the end through the bight slip for a short distance, next reeve the loop that has been formed completely through the end slit, and then carefully remove all superfluous turns and kinks from the material.

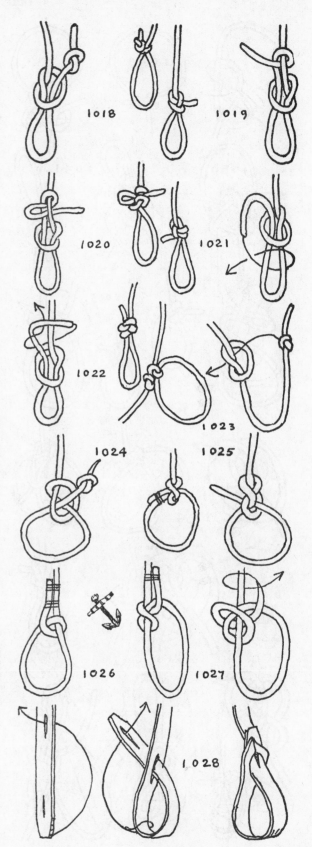

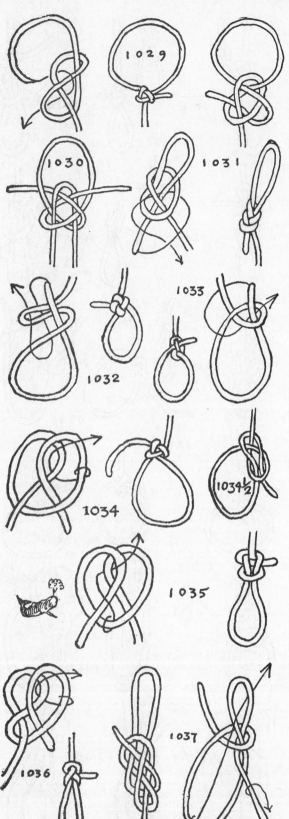

1029. A decorative loop that starts with an OVERHAND KNOT. Arrange the OVERHAND as in the left diagram, then tuck as shown by the arrow. Draw up evenly. The eye that is formed is compact and symmetrical.

1030. This ADJUSTABLE BOWSTRING LOOP from the Orient was shown to me by George L. Aspinwall. The ADJUSTABLE LOOP is made of a short cord that is added to the upper loop of the BOWSTRING proper. The ends are regulated to suit and may be seized to the sides of the loop. One leg of the BOWSTRING proper is inert and is made fast to the bow just above the grip.

1031. A decorative loop, that is given in both French and Japanese books, may be tied in the bight (see #1048) as well as in the end.

1032. A decorative CHINESE LOOP. This is commonly employed as a LANYARD KNOT. It is handsome and secure.

1033. The CARRICK LOOP has the same formation as one of the so-called single CARRICK BENDS. It is easy to untie, but it has no advantages over others that are simpler.

1034. The following knots (through page 189) are tied *in the end, with a bight.* Many of them are suitable for pull exerted at either or both ends. Start with a CLOVE HITCH (#1177), and reeve a bight as indicated by the arrow in the first diagram.

1034½. In formation the LEFT-HAND BOWLINE KNOT is similar to the LEFT-HAND SHEET BEND (#67). It is often tied directly around a post, in mooring (probably by mistake), instead of tying a RIGHT-HAND BOWLINE (#1010), to which it is distinctly inferior.

1035. The ANGLER'S LOOP (the same as #1017) may be tied in the bight. It is started with a round turn as here pictured, or it may be tied exactly as it was in #1017. There is no better loop for small stuff than this; it is unsuitable for rope only because it jams. Only the method of tying is original, but the emblem was added to fill a vacant space on the page.

1036. Another excellent loop with a good lead: Start with a CLOVE HITCH (#1177), and add half a turn to the left hitch as shown in the left diagram.

1037. A good loop that starts with a BELL RINGER'S KNOT (#172). Twist the upper loop of the BELL RINGER'S KNOT one full turn to the right, and then reeve the lower loop up through the upper one and pull on the standing part. Work the knot tight.

1038. The ENGLISHMAN'S, FISHERMAN'S, and ANGLER'S LOOP, or the TRUE-LOVER'S KNOT. There is a story that goes along with this knot that is given with KNOT #387. Middle a cord, and turn down a bight. Twist the two center parts one half turn, and draw the bottom part of the original bight up through the two legs, as indicated by the arrow at the right. Pull the knot that is formed in the right leg down below the knot in the other leg, and draw all snug. Although tied by anglers for leader loops, the knot is so bulky that it makes considerable commotion in the water. Number 1017 will be found better for the purpose.

1039. An IMPROVED ENGLISHMAN'S KNOT. You will have noticed that the last knot consisted of two OVERHAND KNOTS, one tied in each leg around the bight of the other leg (see ⌗1022), and that the knot as a whole was unsymmetrical. Tie it as shown here by the arrows, and the irregularity disappears. The knot form will be the same as BEND ⌗1414.

1040. A second way to make the knot that has just been shown is to form a round turn, with the upper single turn at the left of the lower one. Draw a bight through the two as indicated by the arrow, and then pull the right knot down below the left one.

1041. A third way to tie the knot is to first reproduce diagram ⌗1040, then turn the right turn over to the left so that the two faces come together to form the present diagram. Thrust the looped end down through the center of the turns, and pull the larger hitch down below the smaller.

1042. The "FIGURE-EIGHT" ENGLISHMAN'S LOOP. A knot may be made that will give a similar knotted aspect on both faces. Turn down a loop over the legs as in ⌗1038. Give each of the two loops that are now formed an outward turn or twist, as shown here in the first diagram. Then tuck the lower bight as indicated by the arrow. Pull the upper loop down outside the lower one to the bottom, and draw up the knot. Sometimes this knot will give a little trouble. You may either retie it or else attempt to arrange the two component knots into the form of the third diagram.

1043. A strong, secure loop that is tied with a bight and may be put either in the end or in the bight of the rope.

1044. A very compact loop tied with a bight, for use in the end only. It is made by tucking a doubled end very carefully to conform with each of the three diagrams in turn. In these drawings or diagrams I have frequently shown the finished aspect of the knot in the central position. Except for this occasional departure, the diagrams are intended to progress from left to right and from top to bottom throughout the book.

1045. Another compact loop, which may appear to be insecure up to the very moment that it is hove taut. Hold it in shape until snug, and it will be found both trustworthy and easy to remember.

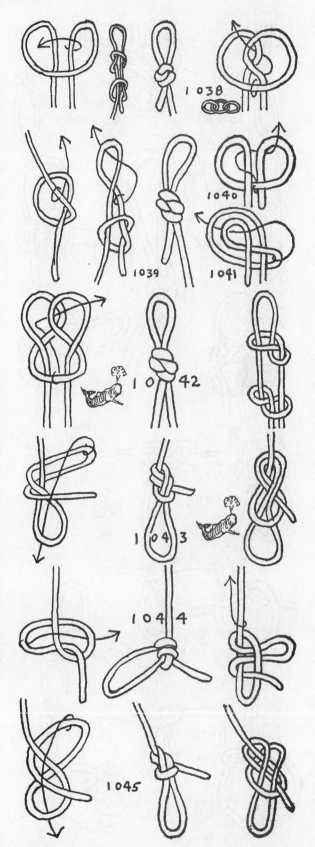

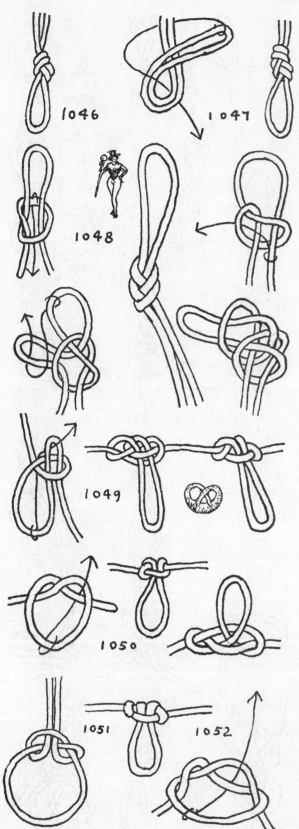

1046

1047

1048

1049

1050

1051   1052

The next two pages are given to single loops tied *with a bight, in the bight*. Such knots are employed to supply a hand- or foothold, or else to provide a becket to which another line may be bent or, in the case of a lashing, through which another or the same line may be rove and tightened. Loops in the bight may be tied in bell or climbing ropes. On a picket line they will provide beckets that will keep halters separated, and on a clothesline they will keep coat hangers from sliding to a common center.

Generally the pull on the two ends of a bight loop is opposite, but in the first three knots to be shown the pull is parallel.

1046. The LOOP KNOT or OVERHAND LOOP is often used in the lashing of a wagon load where both ends are to be further employed

1047. The FLEMISH LOOP or FIGURE-EIGHT LOOP is perhaps stronger than the LOOP KNOT. Neither of these knots is used at sea, as they are hard to untie. In hooking a tackle to any of the loops, if the loop is long enough it is better to arrange the rope as a CAT's-PAW (#1891).

1048. A decorative loop in the bight, suitable for a handbag handle. This is shown by Bocher; although made in the bight it is tied with an end.

1049. The SPAN LOOP. Start as if about to tie a SHEEPSHANK (#1153), make a BELL RINGER's KNOT (#1147), tuck it as shown, and draw the knot taut. This is exceptionally easy to untie and is, moreover, one of the strongest and most secure of the series.

A span is made fast at the ends and is hauled at the center. It is used in slinging and in rigging. The knot described is for hooking a tackle block. Do not stretch the rope too taut, as a direct sidewise pull is too much for any tight-stretched rope.

1050. The HARNESS LOOP was shown in 1862 by Admiral Luce, who called it the HARNESS HITCH. It is an ARTILLERYMAN's KNOT, to be used in manhandling guns on boggy and hilly ground. The loops should be made large enough to pass around a man's shoulder so that he may keep both hands free. The knot may be tied in any tow or climbing rope. It has been used by anglers for attaching dropper flies.

1051. Loosen the HARNESS LOOP, pull at either end, and the knot will capsize into a loop that is almost round and which has a structure identical with the previous knot before it was capsized, but with ends and loop transposed. Both this and #1050 should be tied with a much longer loop than is finally wanted, as considerable length may be lost by slipping before the knot is nipped.

1052. DOUBLE HARNESS LOOP. The HARNESS LOOP is not secure under all circumstances, and for that reason doubling the knot is sometimes recommended. This makes a safer knot, but one that does not tie so readily. There are a number of loops to be given here that will be found more practical.

1053. LINEMAN'S LOOP. J. M. Drew was the first to publish this knot, and he is probably responsible for the name. It has an excellent lead and is strong, secure, and easily tied; a better knot in every way than the HARNESS LOOP.

1054. The FARMER'S LOOP is shown by Professor Howard W. Riley in a Cornell reading course pamphlet of 1912, which is devoted to knots employed on the farm. The knot is a good one on all three counts—lead, security, and strength. Moreover, the method of tying it is both ingenious and distinctive, and, once mastered, it is not apt to be forgotten.

To tie: Take three turns around the left arm or hand, according to the size of the material being used. Move the center turn to the outside three times, as indicated by the arrows, first right, then left, and finally right again. Finally, pull out (extend) the center turn, and the knot is ready for use.

1055. A BIGHT LOOP. Another LOOP KNOT in the bight that is somewhat similar in aspect is made by laying out the cord on a figure-eight diagram, but without tucking the lower end. Tuck the upper bight as indicated by the arrow in the first diagram, and extend it to form the loop that is shown.

1056. A LOOP KNOT in the bight, which is started in the same way as the last knot, but with the bight, although tucked under the same part, tucked in the opposite direction. The result is a knot of the same form as Professor Riley's FARMER'S LOOP (※1054).

1057. The SINGLE BOWLINE *on the bight.* There are a number of knots that have been given this title, including the HARNESS LOOP (※1050), but none of them have parallel ends, as the real (DOUBLE) BOWLINE *on the bight* has. The present knot is from Esparteiro. Although it is a good knot, it tends to distort when the pull is on opposite ends.

1058. The SINGLE BOWLINE *on the bight.* This knot, in appearance at least, appears to have a better claim to the title than the others. It should be drawn up snugly and evenly and is not difficult to untie.

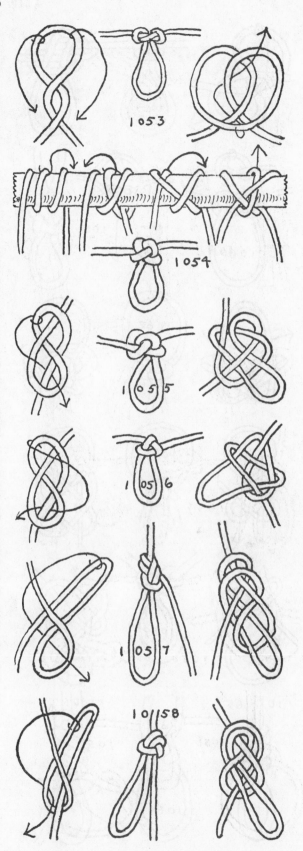

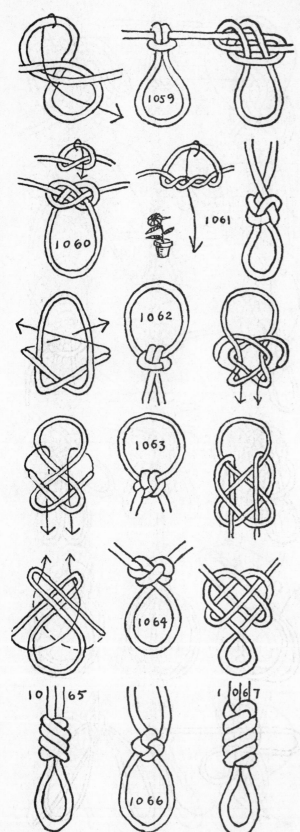

1059. A single loop in the bight that is made from a CONSTRICTOR KNOT. First tie a CONSTRICTOR KNOT, and then reeve either of the loops down through the other. The left diagram shows the CONSTRICTOR KNOT opened out flat, with the upper loop about to be passed through the lower one.

The merit of this particular knot is its almost absolute symmetry. The loop is at right angles to the rope or cord, and there is no irregularity apparent. It must be worked carefully by drawing on all four parts: that is, the two ends of the loop and the two ends of the rope.

This same knot tied as an end loop is given as ⚓1045, but tied in the bight a SINGLE HITCH remains visible at the upper part, so that the relationship is scarcely noticeable.

1060. The remainder of the knots of this chapter are tied into the bight by employing the ends, so they are not proper "BIGHT KNOTS." Since this also entails an additional amount of labor, the knots may be considered decorative rather than practical. These may be used on necklaces, and ring hitched to lockets, crosses, etc. The present one starts with an OVERHAND KNOT. The bight is rove through the crown to form a loop and is then given a strong right-hand twist and the ends hauled taut. If the loop is given a left twist the knot will tend to slip.

1061. A similar knot is started with a DOUBLE OVERHAND KNOT. This may have either parallel or opposite ends. In either case, the loop should be given a right twist.

1062. A round, rigid loop with parallel ends. Tie a LEFT HALF KNOT, and tuck the ends progressively as indicated by arrows in the diagrams.

1063. Tie a LEFT HALF KNOT, lay it flat on the table, and give the loop a half twist to the right as shown in the left diagram. Reeve the ends first through the loop and then downward, as pictured.

1064. The knot given here has much in common with the DIAMOND KNOT, but if tied with more than two strands it is difficult to draw up. The two ends are splayed.

1065. A Two-Strand MATTHEW WALKER KNOT that is tucked several times. It is tied as described in Chapter 8 as ⚓777. In a similar way a loop may be started with any of the Two-Strand LANYARD KNOTS of that chapter, and any small ornament or implement may be ring hitched to the loop.

1066. The CHINESE CROWN LOOP is distinctive and decorative. The method of tying it is described as ⚓808 in Chapter 8.

1067. The SINNET KNOT described as ⚓757 is another LANYARD KNOT that, tied with two strands only, may be recommended for decorative use. The loop may be of any practical length. Another very handsome loop from the same chapter is KNIFE LANYARD KNOT ⚓787.

CHAPTER 12: DOUBLE- AND MULTIPLE-LOOP KNOTS

Nor aine skild in Loupes of fingring fine,
Might in their divers cunning ever dare
With this so curious Networke to compare.

EDMUND SPENSER

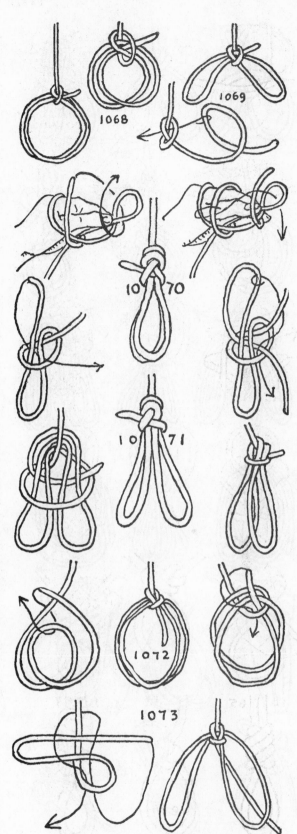

There are only two well-known DOUBLE LOOPS, and both of these are tied in the bight. They are the BOWLINE on the bight and the SPANISH BOWLINE.

1068. The DOUBLE BOWSTRING KNOT is a DOUBLE LOOP tied in the end of a bowstring. Start with KNOT ✳1024, and tuck the end through the knot a second time as shown. It does not appear to be any improvement over the single knot.

1069. A FORKED LOOP. A SINGLE HITCH is made and thrust half-way through the initial OVERHAND KNOT.

1070. The DOUBLE ANGLER'S LOOP is the same knot form as the SINGLE ANGLER'S LOOP (✳1017), except that two turns instead of one are taken around the fingers, and both of these are thrust through the initial end loop.

1071. A FORKED LOOP similar to the foregoing is started with NOOSE KNOT ✳1114, and a long working end. Two drawings of the finished aspect of this knot are given.

1072. The PORTUGUESE BOWLINE is tied in the end of a rope. Although a sailor's knot, it appears to be little known among English-speaking seamen. I first saw it used as an ANCHOR BEND by the quahog boats of the "Portuguese Navy Yard" in New Bedford. Felix Riesenberg mentions it in *Under Sail* (1915) and describes it in *Standard Seamanship* (1922) under the name "FRENCH BOWLINE." He points out that the knot makes an excellent emergency boat-swain's chair. A man may sit in one loop, while the other loop provides a back to his chair. Bandeira gives a drawing of the knot in *Tratado de Apparelho do Navio* (Lisbon, 1896). After making a round turn with the left hand, the knot is tied in much the same way as the ordinary BOWLINE.

1073. This has the same knot formation as the foregoing, but the loops are splayed, instead of being parallel to each other.

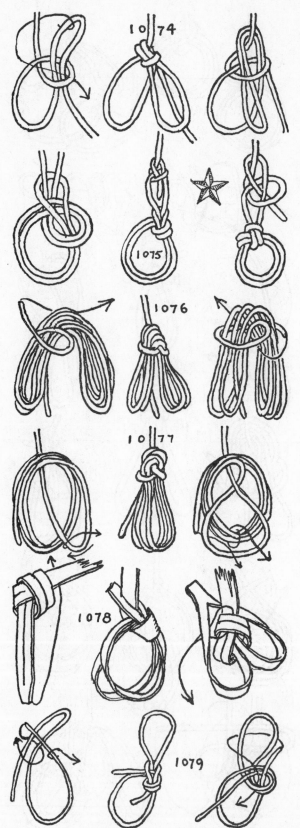

1074. The BOWLINE *with a bight* is tied in the end of a pendant to which to hook a tackle. Whenever possible a hook should have a double bearing when it is to be hitched to a rope. The loops should be of equal length for otherwise the wear on them will be uneven.

1075. BOWLINE *on the bight* and BOWLINE. Tie KNOT ⚹1080 near the end of a rope. Then take the end, and with it tie BOWLINE ⚹1010 to the standing part of the rope.

1076. A MULTIPLE LOOP starting from a small coil. Make a coil of several turns that are twice the length and half the number of the final loops. Middle and fold the coil and with the standing part make a small right turn at the top of the doubled coil (as in the first diagram), then bring the standing part of the rope around the back and stick it through the small right turn and the top of the coil. This makes a practical and reasonably firm knot if the number of loops is not too large.

1077. MULTIPLE PARALLEL LOOPS, from a coil. Make a number of turns, of the size and number required. Stick the standing part down through the coil. Take the bottom of the last turn and give it a half turn to the right as in the left diagram. Spread open the loop that was just formed and bring all the lower end of the coil up through it as shown in the third diagram. Draw the knot taut. Either this or the previous knot will be sufficiently firm for ordinary usage but if objects of different weights are to be suspended from the different loops the present one is the more dependable of the two. It may be made fast to a rafter and any number of blocks or tackles suspended from it.

1078. A DOUBLE LOOP in the end of a strap. Split the end of a strap or thong for a distance a little greater than the circumference of one of the loops that are to be made. Tie a RIGHT OVERHAND KNOT in the end of the strap near the upper end of the slit. Arrange as in the left diagram and lay the end back, underneath. Open the slit end as in right diagram. Loosen the OVERHAND KNOT and extend the bight as indicated by the arrow down through the slit end, gathering the material for this from the slit end itself and from the standing part. Take out all unwanted twists and turns before drawing the knot taut. This is tied exactly as the BOWLINE in the bight (⚹1082). So if difficulty is encountered a study of that knot, which is tied in rope, may serve to make this one clearer.

1079. SISTER LOOPS. Double back one end of a short rope. Treat the doubled end as if it were the standing part of the rope and tie a BOWLINE to it with the other end. Then adjust the length of the loops before drawing taut.

This brings us to DOUBLE and MULTIPLE LOOPS tied in the bight, a much more prolific family than DOUBLE and MULTIPLE LOOPS tied in the end. In fact there seems to be no end to the number of knots of this nature that are possible. Of those to be given here the BOWLINE in the bight ✳1080, ✳1081, ✳1083 and the SPANISH BOWLINE (✳1087) are well known. Number 1088, the SHEEPSHANK, was published in *Sea Stories* in 1925 and ✳1097, ✳1102, ✳1105, and ✳1113 are well-known "fancy knots." Number 1110 is the rather rare "THEODORE KNOT," of the cowboys. The remainder are mostly the result of my own investigation.

1080. The BOWLINE, *on, in*, or *upon, the bight*, or *a* bight, was mentioned by Lever in 1808, who called it "BOWLINE upon the bight." Roding gives a picture of it in 1795. It consists of two parallel rigid loops which may be used individually if desired. The pull on the two ends should be approximately parallel. It is the knot generally used at sea for lowering an injured man from aloft. One leg is put through each loop and if conscious the man holds the double standing part in hand, but, if unconscious, a SINGLE HITCH from the standing part is placed around his chest and under his armpits.

To tie: Double a line, and with the loop end, tie a BELL RINGER'S KNOT (✳1147), as in the second diagram. Then open the single end loop and pass it around the whole knot and close it about the neck of the knot, as pictured. Draw out the two loops and the knot will be complete.

1081. A second method of tying the BOWLINE on the bight: Double a rope and tie an OVERHAND KNOT with the looped end. Following the diagram, fold the loop up over the front of the knot, placing the bight across the neck. Holding the loop in place, pull forward the double part that is indicated by the arrow in the second diagram and work the knot taut.

1082. A third way to tie the BOWLINE on the bight: Tie an OVERHAND KNOT with a looped end, exactly as in the foregoing knot. Double the loop back, but this time double it *underneath* instead of on top. The doubled bight that is marked with an arrow in the right lower diagram forms the two loops. The material from the single loop is worked out and the knot drawn taut.

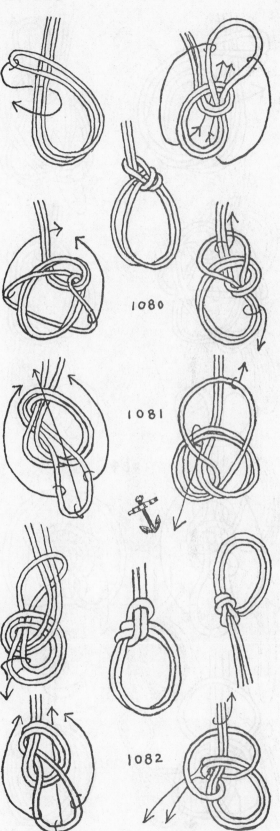

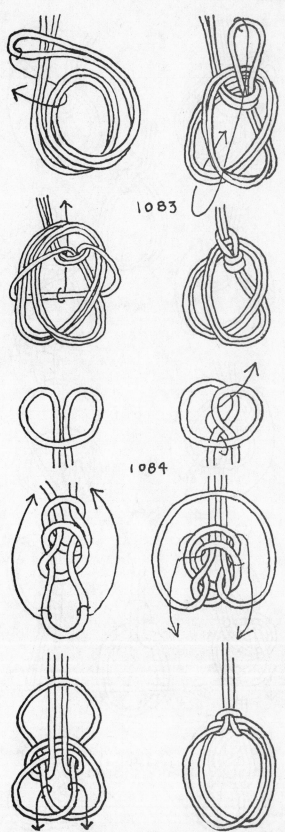

1083

1084

1083. A DOUBLE BOWLINE on the bight is tied with two turns of a doubled rope which gives four loops, or if wanted, an additional turn will add two more loops. But as the number increases the knot becomes less secure, so that if more pull is put on one loop than upon its sister loops, that loop is apt to lengthen.

To tie: Turn back a rope upon itself so that a loop is formed at the place where the knot is to be. Take the doubled rope in hand and make a round left turn. Lay the loop end across the standing part as in the left diagram and, following the direction of the arrow in the first diagram, capsize a double turn around the neck of the single loop. Extend the single loop to a size large enough to pass around the whole knot (upper right diagram). Then, after you have arranged the lower loops so that they are of equal length, bring the opened single loop down and completely around the rest of the knot and to the top again, closing it about the neck or standing part. Draw all snug. This knot is an adaptation of the PORTUGUESE BOWLINE, shown as ⚹1072.

1084. Two PARALLEL ROUND LOOPS with a knot formation that suggests the SPANISH BOWLINE, yet is not the same since the SPANISH BOWLINE has forked or splayed loops.

The knot begins with an ENGLISHMAN's or TRUE-LOVER's KNOT. To tie this, turn down a loop over two parallel legs. Above the loop lift the right bight over the edge of the left bight, to form a narrow compartment. Then *tuck down* the bottom loop between the two legs and draw it up through the center compartment. This forms the ENGLISHMAN's KNOT (⚹1143).

Arrange the ENGLISHMAN's KNOT so that it conforms exactly with the third diagram. Keep the knot open and loose. Next turn up the bottom loop of the ENGLISHMAN's KNOT, so that the bight of it lies across the doubled standing part of the knot.

Grasp the upper bights of the two component OVERHAND KNOTS which form the ENGLISHMAN's KNOT and draw them downward, holding the large single loop in place at the top. The knot should now appear as shown in the fifth diagram. Proceed to draw all extra material from the single loop down into the two lower loops, being careful that they remain of equal size. Finally draw the knot up snug.

If any difficulty is experienced, retie the knot from the start, keeping all the turns loose and open.

1085. A rigid DOUBLE FIGURE-EIGHT LOOP. The loops are narrow and parallel. Double your rope and tie the looped end in the form of a figure eight but without making a final tuck. It should coincide with the left diagram. The loop that was formed should be laid back *underneath* against the doubled standing part which is to form the neck of the knot. See the right diagram. Two bights from the neck of the single loop are then grasped (third diagram) and pulled down through the DOUBLE LOOP. Draw up evenly to form the knot pictured in the center.

1086. MULTIPLE PARALLEL LOOPS in the bight. Double your rope and with the looped end make a right round turn, then lay the loop on top of the upper end of the coil with the standing part underneath. Pull the bight of the standing part up through the structure, and give it one complete *left-hand twist* or turn; after which draw all four loops down through the doubled bight from the standing part, and work the knot taut. Another turn will add two more loops to the knot.

If, instead of placing the single end loop on the top of the coil (left diagram) and drawing the twisted standing part up through it, the single loop is merely coiled down to the right side as suggested by the dotted line, five instead of four loops will then be made and the knot will be quite as symmetrical and as satisfactory in every way.

1087. The SPANISH BOWLINE is a well-known DOUBLE FORKED LOOP. It is presumably a sailor's knot and possibly an old one, but I have not succeeded in finding any early reference to it. It is generally tied in hand, but may perhaps be more easily tied on a table while learning.

Middle a rope and hold aloft with both hands, dropping a single loop down and away from you. Holding the tops of the two upstanding loops that are formed, twist each one of these a half turn toward the center as in the second diagram. Without further twisting pass the left loop through the upper compartment of the right loop to assume the form of the fourth diagram (the third or center diagram being the finished knot).

Raise and reeve each of the two lower bights back through the bight that is immediately above it and draw all snug.

The knot is employed in sending or lowering a man from aloft. One leg is thrust through each loop, and, if an unconscious man is to be lowered, a hitch is added around the chest and under the armpits. It may also be used in slinging a ladder for a staging. But as the material from one loop may be drawn into the other loop, the knot must be firmly drawn up.

1088. A SHEEPSHANK KNOT with HALF HITCHES drawn together will serve the purpose of slinging a flat ladder as well as the last knot. But it has the same fault—that the material from one loop may be drawn into the other loop, so that if tied loosely the ladder might tilt sidewise.

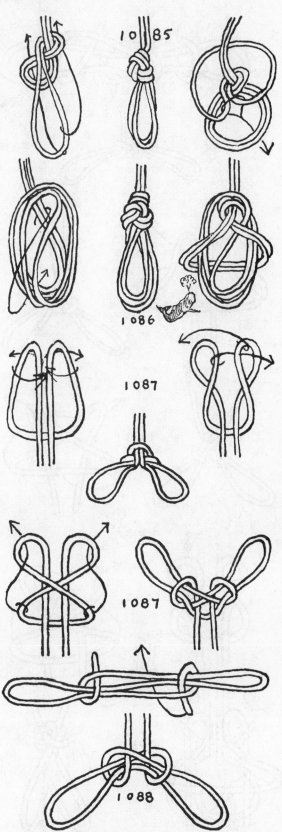

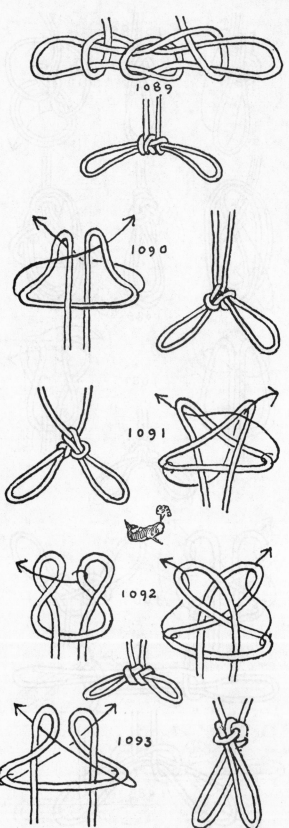

1089. The HITCHED TOM FOOL'S KNOT will be more secure than the two former knots for slinging a ladder, since the material from one loop may not be directly drawn to the other loop.

1090. A DOUBLE FORKED LOOP on the bight. The method of making the remaining knots on this page was suggested by MULTI-STRAND DIAMOND KNOT ✳693 and SINNET KNOT ✳757, although the application is somewhat remote. They are all trustworthy knots provided they are well tied.

This knot is commenced with two round turns. These are distorted a bit to provide bights for tucking, and for tucking through. The two lower bights are carried around the stem and tucked to the right through the next upper bight.

1091. A DOUBLE FORKED LOOP in the bight. This knot also starts with two round turns which are arranged in the shape of a pentagon. In this case a lower bight passes to the left over the adjacent bight and through the opposite upper bight. It more closely resembles the method of tying a DIAMOND KNOT than the last knot did, but in these knots, bights instead of ends are tucked.

1092. This knot, which is perhaps the most secure of the series, is tied somewhat in the manner of the SPANISH BOWLINE (✳1087), but the finished knots have little in common. This one is the more secure of the two since the material of the two loops is not readily drawn from one to the other. The knot is started with a CLOVE HITCH; each of the two SINGLE HITCHES which compose the CLOVE HITCH is given an added half twist to the right. The right-hand hitch is then crossed over the left so that the knot assumes the form of the second diagram. After this the two lower bights are rove through the two upper bights as indicated by the arrows. The knot is then drawn taut.

1093. A DOUBLE LOOP KNOT in the bight that is not so pronouncedly forked as the others of the series. It is started with two round turns and the top of each of these is given an additional half twist to the right, before the lower bights are tucked, as shown in the lower left diagram. The resulting knot is firm and strong.

1094. The knots on this page are more easily tied on a table than in hand. This knot starts with a CONSTRICTOR (※1249) that has been flattened out on the table. The center part is arranged in a reversed curve, and the two central bights that are formed are led over and under as indicated by the two arrows. The ends of the rope in this case are opposite each other, instead of parallel, as most of the previous ends in this chapter have been.

1095. Another knot, which starts with a CONSTRICTOR, has PARALLEL LOOPS and a strong family resemblance to KNOTS ※1090 and ※1091. The ends may be pulled and led either opposite or parallel to each other.

1096. Here is a knot that, in drawing up, will distort into several different forms, a number of which are symmetrical DOUBLE LOOPS. Except for its variety the knot appears to have no particular interest, since others that are more inevitable in form are more practical.

1097. A THREE-PART CROWN in the bight. As this knot is easily remembered and is exceedingly secure, it would probably be the most practical of all SPLAYED LOOPS were it not for the fact that it is harder to untie than some others.

The back may be crowned a second time if a decorative knot is wished.

1098. A decorative JAPANESE LOOP in the bight. The ends must be rove in order to complete the knot. A HALF KNOT is first tied in the two ends of a cord. The ends are passed around the loop that is formed, one end in front and one in back, and after being crossed as shown in the left diagram they are tucked through the HALF KNOT that was first formed (as shown by the two arrows in the same diagram). This is not very secure as the material from one loop is easily drawn into the other loop.

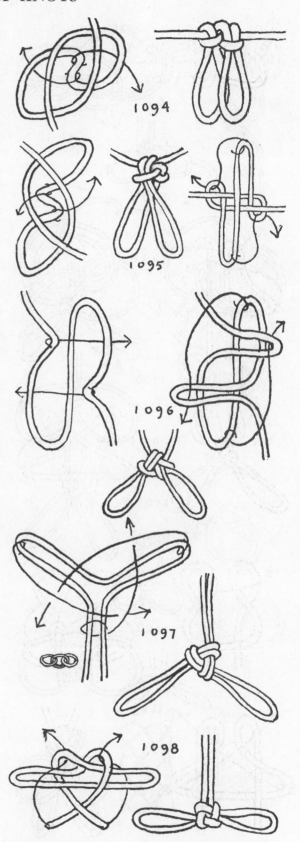

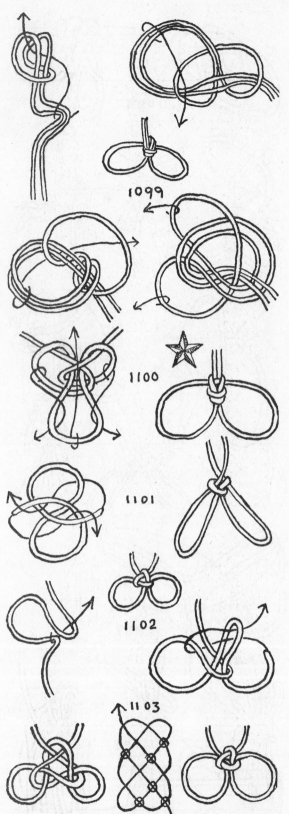

1099. A DOUBLE FORKED or SPLAYED LOOP in the bight that commences with a STRAP HITCH (⚹1694). The rope is doubled to form a loop. The loop is turned down over the doubled standing part, so forming two loops, and the two loops are brought together to form a STRAP HITCH. A bight is then taken from the double stem and tucked through the STRAP HITCH as in the first diagram. The turns are then carefully arranged to conform with the leads of the second diagram. The DOUBLE LOOP of the second diagram is laid down as indicated by the arrow and arranged to conform with the lower left diagram. The left DOUBLE LOOP is moved underneath to the right to conform with the lower right diagram. The stem is next drawn taut; at the same time the two single loops are extended. The resulting knot is strong, compact and handsome, but it is not rigid since the two loops may be withdrawn into each other.

1100. A rigid DOUBLE SPLAYED LOOP in the bight. This is one of the firmest of the DOUBLE LOOPS since the two loops do not directly communicate with each other.

Make SINGLE BIGHT LOOP KNOT ⚹1053, extend the two bights that encompass the legs and reeve them through the single loop in the direction shown in the left diagram; at the same time turn back the single loop so that it surrounds the neck of the knot. Arrange the length of the two loops carefully before drawing the knot snug. There is no stronger or more secure DOUBLE LOOP than this one.

This completes the loops that are tied in the bight, with bights. The remainder of the knots to be shown are tied in the bight with the *ends* and are mainly for decorative purposes.

1101. A FORKED LOOP tied with the ends. Tie a CONSTRICTOR (⚹1249) and lay it flat on the table. Tuck the two ends as indicated by the arrows in the left diagram. Draw the two ends upward and hold the two loops down. This is one of the most compact of all DOUBLE LOOPS, but it is not a rigid one.

1102. A loop based on the CHINESE CROWN KNOT. The latter is described in Chapter 31, "Fancy Knots."

One bight is thrust through another bight as shown in the left diagram. The end is then rove, as indicated in the right diagram, to complete the knot.

1103. A knot of similar appearance to the last but differently constructed. This may be tied on the table directly by following the lead shown in the left diagram. Or it may be made by the method described as ⚹128. To do this, make an enlargement of the center diagram shown here, and pin a cord along the line of the diagram beginning at the feather end. Wherever another cord is to be crossed at a point that is marked with a circle, tuck the working end underneath. At all other points disregard the circles and lay the working end over.

1104. This decorative DOUBLE LOOP was the result of an attempt to make a DOUBLE CROWN with single loops. To tie: Make an enlarged diagram and pin the cord along the line, observing carefully the correct over-and-under sequence.

1105. A FOUR-LOOPED KNOT with a DOUBLE SQUARE CROWN at the center. A cord is arranged with five loops, one of which consists of the two ends knotted together. The two ends are disregarded and the four loops are crowned to the right. The knot is carefully faired and crowned a second time, this time to the left.

1106. If the three snug loops or bights present at the three outer corners of ✻1105 are extended the knot will have seven loops.

1107. A decorative DOUBLE LOOP KNOT is based on SINGLE-STRAND BUTTON ✻600. A cord is laid out as pictured in the center, and when it has been tied the loops are pulled down as shown by the upper left and lower right arrows, while the ends are extended as shown by the upper right and lower left *arrows*. Draw up methodically and mold the knot into the flat form pictured.

1108. If KNOT ✻1107 is worked into a round shape it will resemble closely the KNIFE LANYARD KNOT (✻787), except that it will have two loops instead of one.

1109. A somewhat larger knot is worked in the same way. The knot is pinned out and tied, the two bights are pulled downward to form the loops and the two ends are lifted.

1110. The THEODORE KNOT is a single-strand adaptation of the SAILOR'S DIAMOND KNOT (✻693) which is tied with four strands. Cowboys have employed the knot as a hackamore or emergency bridle. According to Philip Ashton Rollins, the method originated in the South American pampas and worked its way, via Mexico, to our Southwestern cow country, arriving there soon after the conclusion of the Spanish-American War. When Theodore Roosevelt, "the hero of San Juan Hill," visited the Southwest, shortly after the war, it was a foregone conclusion that the Spanish name "Fiador" would be corrupted to "Theodore" in his honor.

To tie: Double a rope, then redouble it. Hold it in hand with the two ends and the single bight uppermost and stop it a little below half length. Then turn down the ends and single bight from the top. Put a second stop above the first around the structure as it stands.

Turn up the last-laid loop in a right diagonal and tuck the two single ends downward through them as pictured. Next, reeve the two single ends upward and to the right, moving the left one first and tucking it through the top bight of the left leg of the loop that was first tucked. Then tuck the remaining end through the next bight to the right. Cut the second stop and tighten the knot, then remove the first stop.

The knot may be very simply and easily tied by using a clue. Take two long cords of different color, middle them and seize them with the four ends uppermost and the colors alternating. Tie a SAILOR'S DIAMOND KNOT (✻693). Leaving it quite loose, bend any two adjacent ends of different color together. Take a long cord of the permanent material and with it follow the lead of the first knot. Finally remove the first knot, and there will remain a THEODORE KNOT.

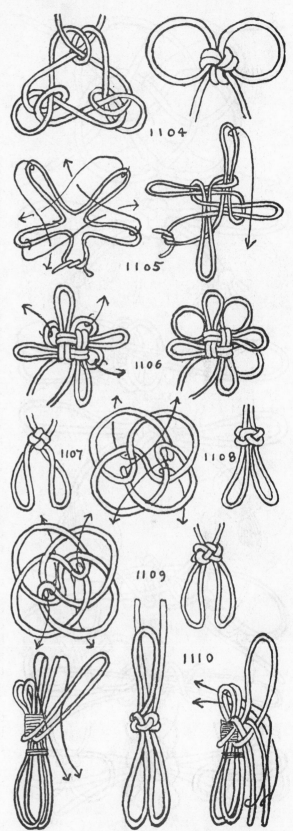

1104

1105

1106

1107

1108

1109

1110

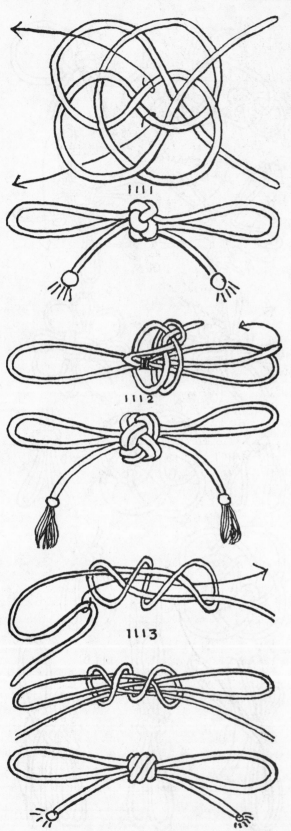

1111. The knots on this page are designed primarily for curtain holdbacks. The first is a knot with two rigid loops which suggests the Boatswain's Lanyard Knot, but which structurally is quite different. It is best tied on a cork board, pinning the cord at frequent intervals. Make an enlarged copy of the diagram and follow over this with the cord. Do not begin to draw the knot taut until certain that the over-and-under sequence of the cord corresponds at every point with the diagram. One of the ends and one of the two central parts are pulled downward out of the plane of the knot and the other two are lifted upward to form a loop with a tassel at either side of the knot. Various tassels are shown in Chapter 41.

1112. A Curtain Holdback with a Turk's-Head Knot. Take a cord of the required length and lay it up into three parallel parts, the end parts being somewhat longer than the bight part. Seize the three parts together at the middle. Take the end which leads to the left and tie a Three-Lead, Four-Bight, Two-Ply Turk's-Head around the place where the seizing occurs. Then with the other end follow the lead a third time. Introduce this strand at the right side and follow around the circuit of the knot in the same direction as the first end. Draw the knot even and snug and add tassels to the ends as described in Chapter 41.

About the same effect may be achieved by seizing the three parallel parts of the cord permanently and then tying a snug Turk's-Head around it with a second cord.

1113. The common Commercial Cord Curtain Holdback. Unlike the two knots just given, the loops in this are not rigid, but the knot is fully as practical and is distinctive in appearance. Superficially it resembles the Matthew Walker Knot.

At about one third of the length of the cord tie a Three- or Four-Part Strangle Knot (❊1240). While it is still loose reeve a loop from the left end through the knot, leaving enough material at the left side to form a loop. This makes a loop at either end. Draw the knot snug and arrange so that the lengths of the two loops and the ends are equal. Add or make tassels as described in Chapter 41.

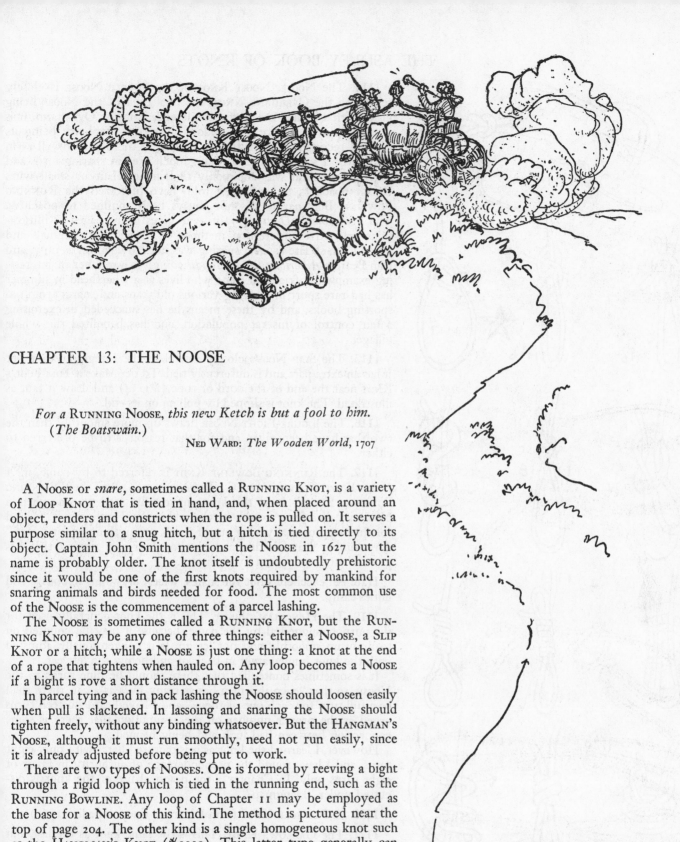

CHAPTER 13: THE NOOSE

For a RUNNING NOOSE, *this new Ketch is but a fool to him.*
(*The Boatswain.*)

NED WARD: *The Wooden World*, 1707

A NOOSE or *snare*, sometimes called a RUNNING KNOT, is a variety of LOOP KNOT that is tied in hand, and, when placed around an object, renders and constricts when the rope is pulled on. It serves a purpose similar to a snug hitch, but a hitch is tied directly to its object. Captain John Smith mentions the NOOSE in 1627 but the name is probably older. The knot itself is undoubtedly prehistoric since it would be one of the first knots required by mankind for snaring animals and birds needed for food. The most common use of the NOOSE is the commencement of a parcel lashing.

The NOOSE is sometimes called a RUNNING KNOT, but the RUNNING KNOT may be any one of three things: either a NOOSE, a SLIP KNOT or a hitch; while a NOOSE is just one thing: a knot at the end of a rope that tightens when hauled on. Any loop becomes a NOOSE if a bight is rove a short distance through it.

In parcel tying and in pack lashing the NOOSE should loosen easily when pull is slackened. In lassoing and snaring the NOOSE should tighten freely, without any binding whatsoever. But the HANGMAN'S NOOSE, although it must run smoothly, need not run easily, since it is already adjusted before being put to work.

There are two types of NOOSES. One is formed by reeving a bight through a rigid loop which is tied in the running end, such as the RUNNING BOWLINE. Any loop of Chapter 11 may be employed as the base for a NOOSE of this kind. The method is pictured near the top of page 204. The other kind is a single homogeneous knot such as the HANGMAN'S KNOT (❋1119). This latter type generally can be spilled without untying after it has been removed from its object.

To make a NOOSE of the first type: Put a loop in one end of the rope. Then reeve a bight from the standing part of the same end through the loop and place it around the object to be secured, or else, if the rope is short, reeve the end its full length through the knot.

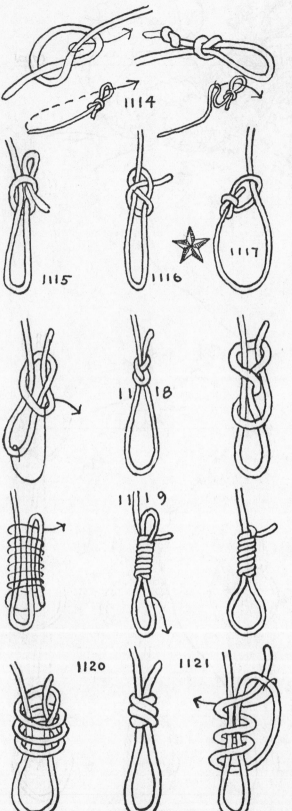

1114. The NOOSE, NOOSE KNOT or the SIMPLE NOOSE is closely related to the OVERHAND KNOT, the final tuck of the NOOSE being made with a bight instead of a single end, as in the OVERHAND. It is often employed ashore, but seldom at sea, its simplicity being its greatest recommendation. It may be tied in the bight as well as in the end of a rope. Formerly it was much used in snaring birds and small animals and was commonly tied in horsehair or small wire. British poachers, I have been told, have preferred the RUNNING BOWLINE. But snaring has not always been confined to poachers. The *Sportsman's Dictionary* of 1778 gives many pages of illustrations devoted to interesting methods of snaring both animals and birds. Even so late as 1893 snaring was not frowned on as now, and Dan Beard's *American Boy's Handibook* gives a number of interesting examples. A friend of mine who lives at a wharfhead in summer has had rare sport in copying various old traps and snares from old sporting books, and by these means he has succeeded in exercising a fair control of his rat population, and has benefited the whole village.

1115. The SLIP NOOSE closely resembles the foregoing knot but it has an extra part and is differently tied. To tie: Make a TOM FOOL'S KNOT near the end of the cord or rope (※1134) and draw it taut as illustrated. The knot is slipped by pulling on its end.

1116. The FIGURE-EIGHT NOOSE draws up more smoothly than the two that have been given and for that reason is to be preferred to either.

1117. The RUNNING BOWLINE KNOT is referred to by name, in *A Four Years' Voyage* by G. Roberts (1726), as the "RUNNING BOWLING KNOT." It is the knot universally used at sea when a NOOSE is called for. According to an old nautical authority it "is used for throwing over anything out of reach, or anything under water." Any lumber that has dropped overboard or any rigging that has gone adrift is recovered by its means.

1118. An excellent knot for snares, which draws up smoothly and unties easily.

1119. The HANGMAN'S KNOT. This is the knot generally used for the purpose suggested by the name, because it may be counted on to draw up smoothly and not let go. It is conventionally adjusted with the knot immediately in back of and below the left ear.

It is sometimes contended that there should be nine turns to the NOOSE, so that "even if a man has as many lives as a cat, there shall be a full turn for each one of them," and I have heard thirteen turns urged as the proper number on the assumption that there is some connection between bad luck and being hanged.

However, I learned the knot as it is pictured here, with only eight turns, and I have found the preponderance of authority in favor of eight turns only. In Chapter 2 the practical use of the knot is discussed under "Hangman."

1120. A SCAFFOLD KNOT from Diderot's Encyclopedia (1762).

1121. The GALLOWS KNOT. This is the same knot as the last, but differently tied.

1122. The NEWGATE KNOT is given by Gibson. It is differently tied from #1121, but it is exactly the same knot when drawn up in final form. Both are THREE-FOLD OVERHAND KNOTS with the standing end rove back through the knot.

1123. The ICHABOD KNOT was shown to me by the attendant at the old Newcastle jail in Delaware. It appears to be an adequate knot for its purpose. A very similar knot was shown to me in near-by Wilmington, Delaware, for tying up a cow (#1828).

1124. The GIBBET KNOT was first shown to me by Captain George H. Grant, of Nantucket, and later the same knot was shown to me by Ole Jackson.

1125. A decorative NOOSE which superficially resembles a MATTHEW WALKER KNOT.

1126. A DOUBLE RING or TAG KNOT, also called DOUBLE RUNNING KNOT, is used by lobster- and crabmen around their pots. As it has no ends, its security is never in question. It is an exceedingly practical knot that is commonly tied in hand.

1127. The LARIAT or LASSO NOOSE is made by reeving the end of the lariat through a HONDA KNOT. The latter knot is based on the BOWSTRING KNOT and is described in the chapter on single loops (#1024). The HONDA differs from the BOWSTRING KNOT in having a single OVERHAND KNOT in the end of the rope. To tie, first make an OVERHAND KNOT in the bight and then reeve the end through it, after which the knot in the end is added.

1128. A four-strand lariat often has a HONDA that is formed by reeving the end of the rope between the strands of the standing part. An OVERHAND (#515), WALL (#671), or (less frequently) a MATTHEW WALKER KNOT (#682) is put in the end. The opened strands are seized close to the knot. The end of the rope is also whipped. The MATTHEW WALKER KNOT is said to be common in Mexico.

1129. One of the most common HONDAS consists of a copper riveted eye with the bosom served over with heavy copper wire. A description is given in Chapter 35, which deals with EYE SPLICES.

1130. The INSIDE CLINCH consists of one or two seized round turns in the end of a rope. The rope is rove through the turns. The turns are held together with either two or three *round seizings*. The clinch is tied in hawsers and cables that are too large for easy knotting, but it is also tied in buntlines and leech lines, and is used for the latter purpose in preference to hitches, since the seizings are less liable to be loosened by continual slatting of the sail. The buntline is first rove through the cringle in the boltrope and then through the turns of the clinch.

1131. The OUTSIDE CLINCH is not so secure and is employed wherever it is necessary to cast off smartly, which is done by cutting the seizing. The size of a clinch must always be less than the size of the ring or cringle to which it is secured.

1132. The THIMBLE AND EYE is the neatest of NOOSES. Nowadays it is often tied in wire, sometimes with a bull's-eye instead of a thimble, as in cargo slings.

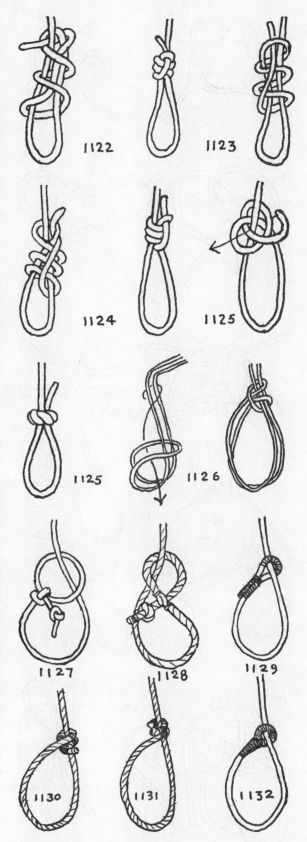

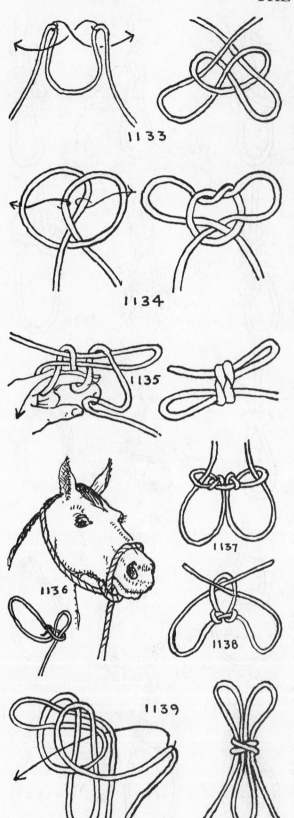

1133. This page consists of DOUBLE NOOSES, that are used for such purposes as handcuffing and binding prisoners, and hobbling, slinging, and throwing animals.

The TOM FOOL'S KNOT has long been used and recommended for handcuffing.

1134. The HANDCUFF KNOT, per se, is, however, a firmer knot, less apt to spill while being put to work, and consequently to be preferred to the TOM FOOL'S KNOT. A loop having been adjusted around each wrist, both ends are pulled on to tighten the knot; finally a hitch is added to each end around the neck of the loop, close up to the wrist.

1135. A decorative loop that will prove quite practical in any place where a DOUBLE LOOP is called for.

1136. A DOUBLE NOOSE may serve as a halter with which to lead a refractory horse. A loop (#1009) or a spliced eye is put in the end of a halter-length rope. The NECK LOOP is held at the horse's throat, and a SINGLE HITCH is passed around the snout. Although this holds everything taut it does not choke the animal.

1137. The SPANISH BOWLINE may be employed as the base for a DOUBLE NOOSE to be placed around the pasterns of a horse or cow. This knot will be useful either as a preventive of kicking or an adjunct to throwing or slinging. The center of the rope is made fast to a surcingle or sling.

1138. A DOUBLE NOOSE may be evolved from a single bight loop, starting with the HARNESS LOOP. It probably is not so strong as the knot made with a SPANISH BOWLINE.

1139. A DOUBLE NOOSE based on the MATTHEW WALKER KNOT. This knot will draw together from three points.

Middle a short line and, holding it in hand with the two ends uppermost, tie a TWO-STRAND MATTHEW WALKER KNOT, but with this difference: in the last movement, instead of sticking the ends up singly, turn them back along themselves and stick up a bight from each instead.

There are many knots included here for which there appears to be little present use. But the practicality or impracticality of a knot can be too much stressed. History teaches us that sooner or later a purpose is discovered for everything that exists. Old knots long out of use have a way of coming back into this workaday world with renewed vigor and usefulness.

CHAPTER 14: KNOTS TIED IN THE BIGHT

Here I have made the True Lovers Knott,
To try it in Marriage was never my Lott.

STEPHEN BLAKE: *The compleat Gardener's Practice*, 1664

BIGHT KNOTS are tied without the employment of ends and so are very apt to mystify the layman. For that reason, in addition to their practical purposes they are frequently tied as tricks or puzzles. (Chapter 33).

A number of the loops in Chapters 12 and 13 are tied in the bight, and in almost every chapter will be found one or several knots so tied. Of the knots that are commonly grouped under the heading, "BIGHT KNOTS," the SHEEPSHANK and the MASTHEAD KNOTS are most typical.

Captain John Smith, in his *Sea Grammar* (1627), while enumerating the knots required by the sailor, which he limits to three in number, says as follows: "The last is the *Shepshanke* [sic] which is a knot they caste upon a Runner, or a Tackle, when it is too long to take in the Goods, and by this Knot they can shorten a Roape without cutting it, as much as they list, and presently undoe it againe, and yet never the worse." And in another place: "*Sheeps Feet* is a stay in setting up a topmast and a guie [guy] in staying the tackles when they are charged with goods." Also: "Strike your topmasts to the cap, make them sure with your *sheeps feete*."

Previous to the days of the clipper ship, it was the usual practice of merchant ships, when approaching Cape Horn, to send down their topgallant masts before an expected blow. It was also a part of the regular drill aboard the square-rigged ships of the Navy. The eyes of the topgallant backstays were lowered and lashed at the topmast caps and the slack material of the stays was made up into SHEEPSHANK KNOTS.

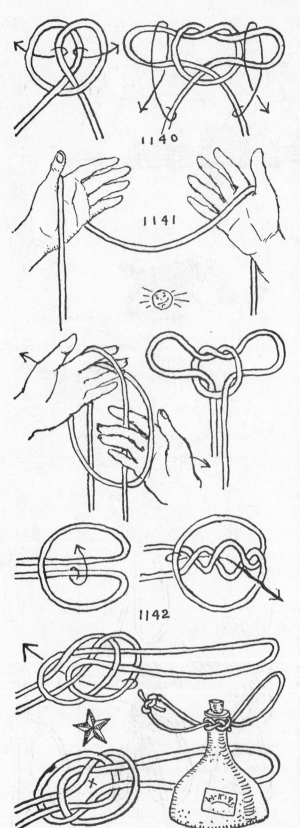

Another temporary use for the knot was to ease the strain around a weak or wounded section of rope. Nowadays the knot comes in handy to shorten an automobile towrope or a hay tackle fall.

The MASTHEAD or JURY MAST KNOT provides a strap to which the several stays are bent when jury rigging is required after a storm or a battle. It also comes in handy on the stays of a derrick. A pair of cleats, nailed to the head of the mast or pole, should be added if possible, to make the knot doubly secure.

1140. The HANDCUFF KNOT is often confused with the TOM FOOL's KNOT. But it is commenced with a CLOVE HITCH while the latter knot is evolved from a round turn. After the HANDCUFF KNOT has been drawn up snugly, each end may be half hitched around one of the loops to render the knot secure.

1141. The TOM FOOL or TOM FOOL's KNOT may be used for the same purpose as the former but is not so satisfactory a HANDCUFF KNOT, as it is more difficult to draw snug and make fast, if the prisoner proves fractious. Generally it is employed as a trick knot and as such will be found more fully described at the beginning of Chapter 33.

1142. The JUG SLING or JAR SLING KNOT is invaluable on picnics or wherever heavy bottles, vacuum jars, or jugs have to be lugged considerable distances. Sailors find it useful on "wooding" and "watering" parties ashore. On sketching expeditions I have found it invaluable for carrying fluid with which to wash brushes. The JUG SLING is pictured by Roding in 1795. E. N. Little, in 1889, pictures and labels it JAR SLING KNOT, the two terms being interchangeable.

Cowboys are said to have employed it as a hackamore or emergency bridle. The two center bights of the knot proper form the bit, the outer bights surround the muzzle, the long loop forms the headstall and the ends are used for reins.

To tie the knot: Middle a stout cord and turn back the center to form a loop or bight (first diagram). Holding the center of the bight with the left thumb and finger so that it will not shift, twist the two parallel center parts one full turn, as pictured in diagram 2.

Insert the right thumb and forefinger *down* into the center compartment of the twisted section and with the *forefingernail uppermost* grasp the center of the original bight (see arrow in the second diagram).

Holding the two legs of the knot with the left hand, lift the knot with both hands, and, without changing the grip of the right hand, hold the knot out before you, allowing the right hand to turn away from you so that the thumb is toward you. Then separate the two hands slowly, drawing out the knot into position 3.

If you haven't succeeded in achieving position 3, repeat from the beginning and it will probably fall into correct form.

Slip the left hand under the knot and withdraw the bight that is indicated by the arrow in the third diagram. Finally place the center of the knot marked X in the bottom of the left diagram around the collared neck of a bottle (a milk bottle will do nicely) and draw up the knot.

Tie the legs together (BEND #1474), making a second loop the size of the first, fill the bottle, take the two loops in hand and proceed according to plan.

1143. The name TRUE-LOVER'S KNOT is mentioned by Stephen Blake in 1664. The knot is also called ENGLISH, ENGLISHMAN'S, WATER, WATERMAN'S, FISHER'S and FISHERMAN'S KNOT or LOOP. A bit of folklore goes with this that may be found in Chapter 31 (#2420). The knot commences in much the same way as the previous knot, but only a single half twist or turn is taken in the two parallel parts at the center. The bight is then pulled up through the center. Occasionally one of the two component OVERHAND KNOTS slips over the other and has to be righted, but generally it ties correctly without any bother. A strong but clumsy loop is formed that is much favored by anglers.

1144. A MONKEY CHAIN or CHAIN SHORTENING is generally given as a BIGHT KNOT, but hardly belongs in the class as the end has to be rove through the final loop of the chain, in order to make it secure. Or the end may be seized, stopped or toggled instead. It is the most common shortening for domestic purposes, being nothing more than the crochet chain stitch, which is familiar to all good housewives. It is used on window-shade cords and electric-light pulls. Roding gives a picture of it in 1795.

1145. If a MONKEY CHAIN is toggled at either end it is not liable to jam. Sometimes a MONKEY CHAIN is used to shorten a hay tackle fall but this is severe treatment for rope.

1146. KNOT SHORTENING. Turn back two bights as if starting a SHEEPSHANK KNOT (#1152). Twist both ends and lead around the standing part in opposite directions to half knot the two bights together. The practice is not suitable for rope but it may be used in packing cord when tightening a slack lashing. It is difficult to untie.

1147. The BELL RINGER'S KNOT is mentioned in Hutton's *Mechanics* (1815). A single bight is lifted and the standing part above is half hitched around it. The purpose is to keep the rope from the belfry deck when the bell is not in use.

1148. Sometimes two hitches are made, which is more secure. This may be required when the rope is so long that several turns are hitched.

1149. The YARDARM KNOT is described in an old book on seamanship. The upper part of the knot is lightly stopped with twine and the lower end only is hitched. It is the same form as #1147 with the addition of a stopping, but it is the other side up. The knot was employed in a hanging at sea (see #366). Precisely six feet of rope was expended in the knot and when the seizing fetched against a block it broke and the load was dropped six full feet.

1150. When a rope is only a little too long for its purpose a BOWLINE SHORTENING will be found reliable, expeditious and not liable to jam.

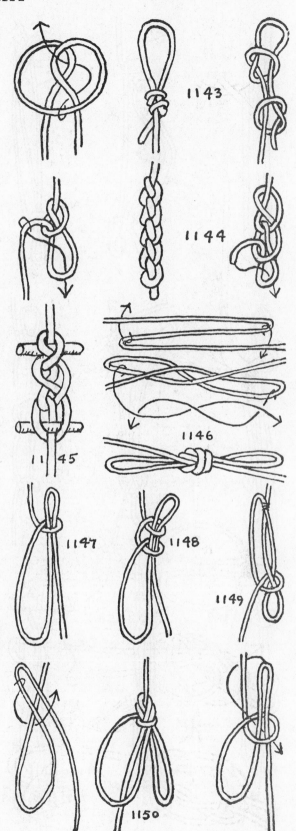

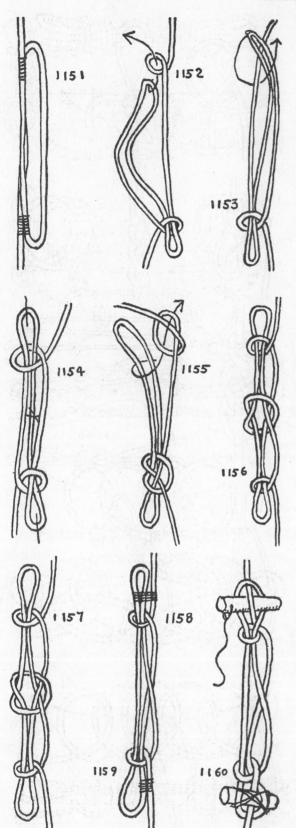

1151. A SEIZED SHORTENING is sometimes put on a new rope that has not yet been weathered. It is neat and dependable. The seizings may be made as ⚓3385.

1152. There are two practical ways of tying the SHEEPSHANK KNOT. The slack in the rope may be laid out on deck in three parallel parts, forming two bights as in the first diagram of ⚓1146. A HALF HITCH is formed in the standing part and placed over the end of one of the bights. Then the other bight is treated likewise. This is the preferred way for large rope.

1153. In light rope the three parallel parts of the SHEEPSHANK KNOT are laid out as before, the upper bight is grasped in the right hand, laid across the standing part of the rope and then given a turn which picks up a hitch exactly in the same way that is employed in tying a BOWLINE KNOT. This is repeated with the lower end.

1154. If a SHEEPSHANK KNOT is to be tied around a wounded or chafed part of a rope it should be arranged so that the weak point will be where X is marked on the accompanying drawing. Sometimes this knot is employed as a "trick" and the rope is cut at X. Under steady pull, even when cut, the knot is reasonably secure.

1155. The SHEEPSHANK WITH MARLINGSPIKE HITCHES is the safest of the SHEEPSHANK KNOTS. All other varieties should be seized or otherwise secured to make them safe, unless the need is very temporary.

1156. A SHEEPSHANK based on the TOM FOOL'S KNOT. Sailors tie a number of more or less decorative SHEEPSHANKS for the edification of landsmen. A TOM FOOL'S KNOT having been tied, a HALF HITCH is added to the end of each loop.

1157. A SHEEPSHANK from a HANDCUFF KNOT may be made by adding two hitches in similar manner to the last knot, or it may be tied directly with four hitches as ⚓1164.

1158. The common SHEEPSHANK, if carefully tied and drawn up and kept at even tension, is fairly dependable, but it should be examined after each haul or lift, and if it is to remain in place any considerable length of time it should be stopped. This is usually done as shown alongside.

1159. Perhaps a better way to secure the SHEEPSHANK is to include only two parts and to add crossing turns to the seizings. Arranged in this way, the knot will be safe.

1160. In heavy material a SHEEPSHANK may be toggled. Slightly tapering fids should be driven in and these in turn should be secured by taking belaying turns of marline around the two ends. If the fids are notched at the center the knot will be safer.

1161. If there is a considerable length of material to be expended in the SHEEPSHANK, a number of turns may be taken. To make this coil doubly secure, place a CLOVE HITCH at each end. I have seen this knot used in color halyards that are to be hung well above deck.

1162. The "parlor method" of tying the SHEEPSHANK is one of the sailor's standard tricks. The knot is tied almost instantaneously from three hitches which are arranged one on top of another as shown here. Each side bight of the center hitch is grasped *through* an outer hitch, and extended for a short distance. Then the bights are cast off in mid-air, the grasp being shifted to the two ends of the rope.

If small stuff is used, this knot is tied, inchworm-fashion, by pulling out the loops with thumbs and forefingers, and as the loops are extended the ends of the cord are grasped at either side, with the ring and little fingers. The trick is practiced until only one continuous movement is evident. The finished knot is shown as ⚹1154.

1163. The SHEEPSHANK WITH A SWORD KNOT has also been called NAVY SHEEPSHANK, and occasionally MAN-O'-WAR SHEEPSHANK. Four hitches are made which should overlap each other in pairs. The bights from each pair are pulled through the center of the opposite pair and are tightly drawn together. It is well to jerk them a few times to make them tighter. In this form the knot is quite irregular and unprepossessing. Now take the ends in hand and jerk them apart. The knot should now appear as in the lower drawing of ⚹1164 but it may require a little prodding to make it quite regular.

1164. The same knot may be made in a less spectacular way. Note that two adjoining bights are crossed and that each of the single bights at the center is rove through the two opposite hitches. This is HANDCUFF KNOT ⚹1157 with the two loops half hitched.

The whole series of SHEEPSHANKS are practical knots; I once tried them all when hauling a heavy skiff across a wide beach. On account of the sand there was only about fifty feet in which to work the car to advantage, so the boat had to be hauled in short hitches. I put a different SHEEPSHANK in the rope each time the car was backed up and had no trouble with any of them; they neither jammed nor slipped.

1165. Make four hitches and overlap the two center hitches. Then tuck each of the center bights in alternate over-and-under sequence, to the side. If the two outer hitches are made a little smaller than the two inner ones, the knot will require little or no adjustment.

1166. "TWO HEARTS THAT BEAT AS ONE." Sailors ring all the changes on this knot, using any number of hitches. But beyond five the SHEEPSHANK soon loses distinction.

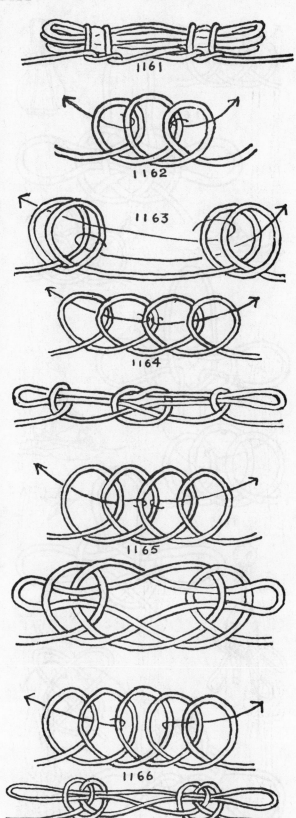

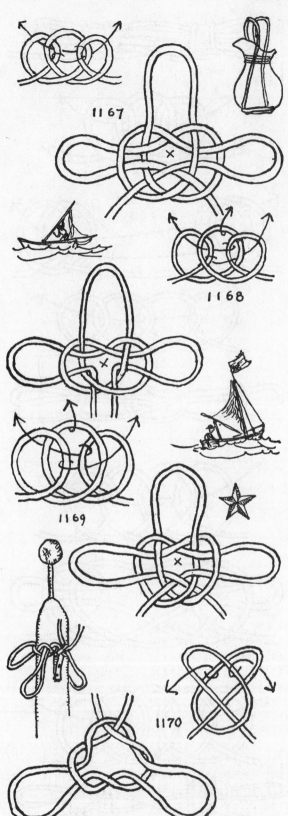

1167

1168

1169

1170

1167. The MASTHEAD or JURY MAST KNOT is generally to be found among the "fancy knots." This is because it is decorative, and it may also be because the occasion for its practical use is fortunately seldom encountered.

The original purpose of the knot is to place a strap around a temporary masthead to which stays can be made fast. The knot binds well and provides several loops to which the stays are secured with BECKET HITCHES. If possible cleats should be nailed below the knot. It has also been called a "PITCHER KNOT."

Ashore it is employed practically at the head of a derrick pole. It has frequently been recommended as a means of lugging shot about ship, but I have never seen this purpose mentioned by a nautical authority and the usual means for transporting shot was a heavy "CABBAGE NET" (#3792).

The common MASTHEAD KNOT, which is the one pictured here, is commenced with three overlapping hitches. The inner bights of the two outer hitches are led in regular sequence over and under to the opposite sides of the knot, while the upper bight of the center hitch is merely extended. The teeth are sometimes used for the latter purpose.

When the knot is put to use the ends may be employed for additional staying or they may be seized to the side loops after the knot is drawn taut.

1168. A second method is commenced by laying down a SINGLE HITCH, followed by a round turn, and then a second hitch, the first hitch being at the left of the knot.

It is possible, of course, to tie any knot reversely (except one that is dependent on the lay of the strands or rope) but for purposes of practice it is simpler for the reader to disregard that possibility and to tie the knots as they are described.

This particular knot is less complicated than #1167, at the point where the ends depart from the knot. Here they may be reef knotted together, to which treatment the former knot does not lend itself readily.

1169. A third method of tying the JURY MAST KNOT is started with three round turns. The bights are woven in regular over-and-under sequence as already described, and as indicated by the arrows in this diagram. After this the center loop or turn is extended. The ends may be seized to the stays after the knot is in place, or they may be used for additional staying.

The sketch at the left shows the knot in place at the masthead ready for the addition of stays. Notice that wooden cheeks have been nailed to the mast to prevent slipping. There may be some protuberance already on the jury mast that will serve the purpose. If nothing is found an attempt to provide something should be made, or else a slight groove can be whittled, rasped or chopped around the spar. Only if it is absolutely necessary should the knot be used unsupported, in which case KNOT #1167 may have the firmer grip. If nothing else offers, parcel the mast with rubber or canvas.

1170. A FRENCH MASTHEAD KNOT which has but two loops is shown by Challamel (Paris, 1891). By using the legs of the knot to secure the headstay, with the two loops for the backstays, there will be three leads, which is the number usually required. All stays should be secured to the loops with BECKET HITCHES (#1900).

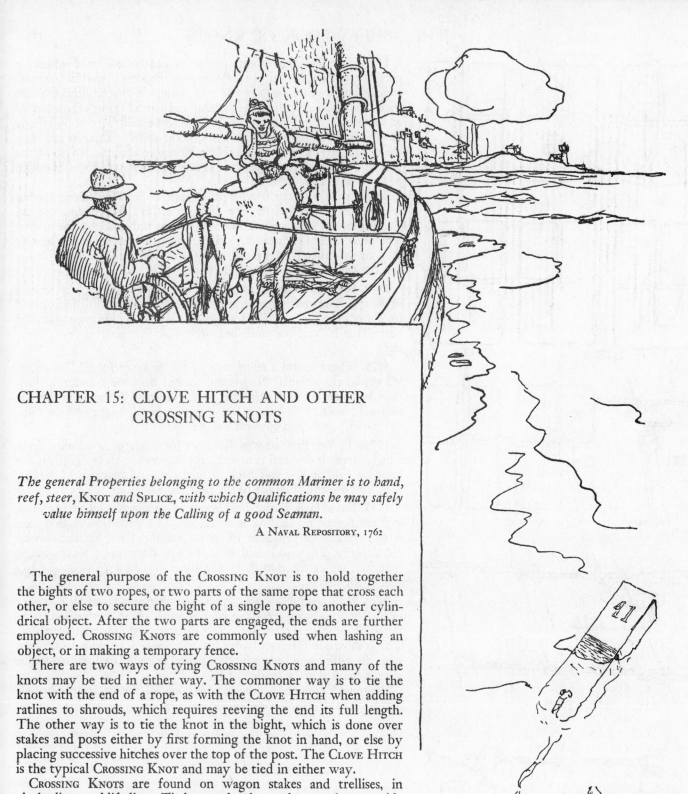

CHAPTER 15: CLOVE HITCH AND OTHER CROSSING KNOTS

The general Properties belonging to the common Mariner is to hand, reef, steer, KNOT and SPLICE, with which Qualifications he may safely value himself upon the Calling of a good Seaman.

A NAVAL REPOSITORY, 1762

The general purpose of the CROSSING KNOT is to hold together the bights of two ropes, or two parts of the same rope that cross each other, or else to secure the bight of a single rope to another cylindrical object. After the two parts are engaged, the ends are further employed. CROSSING KNOTS are commonly used when lashing an object, or in making a temporary fence.

There are two ways of tying CROSSING KNOTS and many of the knots may be tied in either way. The commoner way is to tie the knot with the end of a rope, as with the CLOVE HITCH when adding ratlines to shrouds, which requires reeving the end its full length. The other way is to tie the knot in the bight, which is done over stakes and posts either by first forming the knot in hand, or else by placing successive hitches over the top of the post. The CLOVE HITCH is the typical CROSSING KNOT and may be tied in either way.

CROSSING KNOTS are found on wagon stakes and trellises, in clotheslines and life lines. Tied around stakes and posts, they provide a barrier for "roping off" crowds at fires, circuses, parades, weddings, country auctions, lawn parties and inaugurations. They serve to make temporary fences around clambakes, broken shopwindows, street trenches and shell holes.

They are required in lashings on chests, trunks, bales, bundles and parcels, and in standing rigging, scaffoldings, stanchions and rope ladders.

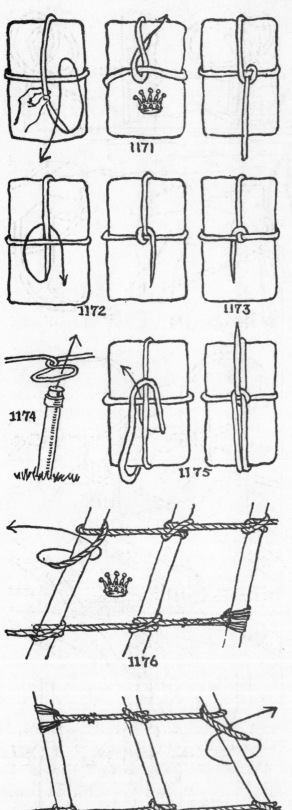

1171. The CROSSING KNOT, per se, is known and used wherever parcels are made up, but it is seldom that the knot is tied in the most expeditious way. Generally the end is tucked twice, although one tuck is all that is needed. As lashing and parcel tying are discussed at some length in Chapter 28, little need be said here about them. Ordinarily a NOOSE is tightened around the girth of a parcel and then the cord is led at right angles to the NOOSE around the length of the parcel. Wherever the cord crosses itself a CROSSING KNOT is added to hold the lashing firm.

To tie the preferred way, with a single tuck: The lashing having reached the position of the first diagram and the cord having crossed the original NOOSE, make a HALF HITCH as indicated by the arrow. The cord is then tightened by first pulling it back as in the second diagram and then forward as in the third. The end is secured on the reverse side with Two HALF HITCHES.

1172. The *usual shopkeeper's way* of tying the knot is the reverse of #1171. The end is rove under the NOOSE and is hauled back and tightened. It then is tucked a second time under its own standing part. This is "end-for-end" but otherwise the same as the former knot.

1173. There is still a *third way* to tie the same form. The end is led across the original NOOSE and tucked backward under it. It is then led over its own standing part and stuck forward under the original NOOSE. This knot is the upside down of #1172 and the "upside-down" *and* "end-for-end" of #1171.

1174. To tie the CROSSING KNOT *in the bight* over a stake: Seize a bight, twist it one full turn and drop it over the stake. Tighten the knot by hauling the end back as in the second diagram of #1171, then lead the end forward to the next stake.

1175. Sometimes, if the cord is not so strong as might be wished, it is reinforced by leading it twice around a parcel. In such a case it will usually be sufficient to tie a CROSSING KNOT on the second circuit only. The end is laid as in the first diagram of #1171 but it is tucked under the two parts that have formed a cross on the top side of the parcel.

1176, 1177. Although the name CLOVE HITCH is given by Falconer in his Dictionary of 1769, the knot is much older, having been tied in ratlines at least as early as the first quarter of the sixteenth century. This is shown in early sculpture and paintings. A round turn is taken with the ratline and then a hitch is added below. The forward end is always the first to be made fast.

Diagram #1176 shows the outside view of the starboard shrouds and #1177 the outside view of the port shrouds.

In tying up heavy bundles and bales the CLOVE HITCH is the CROSS-ING KNOT favored by manufacturers, since the whole lashing is not apt to give way if any part of the cord or rope chafes through.

1178. When placing a CLOVE HITCH over a post or stake it may be tied in hand by first making two turns and then bringing the lower turn atop the first one. (See first diagram.) Or a SINGLE HITCH may be tied around the post and the rope tightened and held while the second hitch is added.

Additional ways of tying the CLOVE HITCH are given in POST HITCHES, Chapter 23. "Trick" ways are shown in Chapter 33.

1179. Frequently it is a great convenience to be able to tie the knot with one hand. The rope, as shown here, comes from the left and is led beyond the post. With the palm of the right hand held away from you, grasp the rope on the right side of the post. Cross the hand to your left, and turn the palm toward you. This imparts a twist to the rope which is then dropped back (away from you) over the post. Take the end again in your right hand, pull it to the left to tighten the rope, then make and place a second turn, over the top of the post, exactly as described for the first one.

1180. If it is desired to haul the line between posts very tight, the following is the way to do it. Pull with both hands and when the rope is taut, hold what you have gained with the left hand. Twist the rope to the right with the right hand, which will cause a turn to be formed, and allow this turn to drop over the end of the post. Pull this turn tight around the post with the right hand, without rendering any that is held in the left hand. Hold all taut with the left hand while adding a second hitch to complete the CLOVE HITCH.

1181. An AFRICAN RAFTER LASHING from the 38th Annual Report of the National Smithsonian Museum. The framework of the hut is of bamboo and the roof is thatched with grass. The rope is brought from the left parallel with the purline. It passes a rafter on the under-side and takes a turn around it; it then takes a turn around the pur-line and is tucked forward again under the first turn that is around the rafter. The knot is repeated at each rafter crossing.

1182. The TRANSOM KNOT is closely related to the CONSTRICTOR. It was first made to hold together the crossed ribs of a kite. If un-supported it is more secure than the previous knot, and has little or no initial slip. It may be used for a series of knots in a single rope or it may be tied singly. If pickets, pales, or transoms are spaced widely apart much material will be saved without any loss of security by closely clipping each knot.

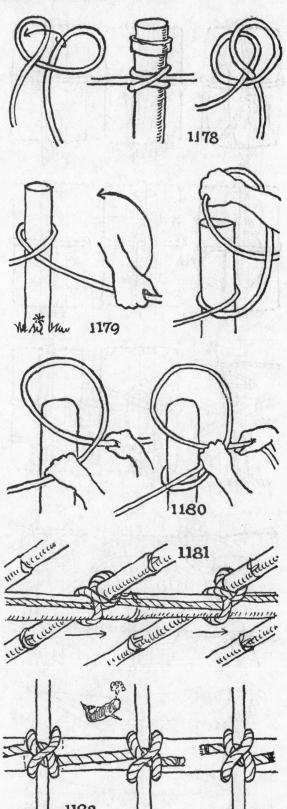

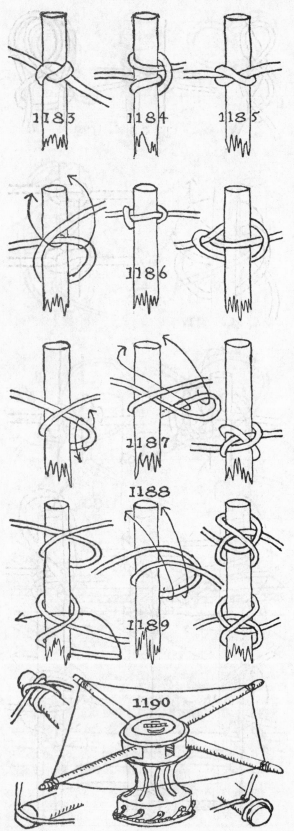

1183. The HALF KNOT is the commonest of the CROSSING KNOTS and the least efficient. Sometimes it is tucked a second time to make a DOUBLE HALF KNOT, which is more secure but still is hardly to be recommended. I have seen the HALF KNOT used for the sides of a rope ladder to the trapezes, in Lowney Brothers' Circus. As the knots of each rope were tied on opposite sides of the rungs there was no tendency for the rungs to turn and the knot served its purpose. The chief objection would be that when not in use they would be liable to loosen and get out of adjustment.

1184. The COW HITCH is used as a CROSSING KNOT on the farm. It is not particularly firm, but it does not become untied, since both ends are engaged; moreover it cannot jam. It has the further advantage that it is easily tied, either in the end or bight of a rope.

1185. The HALF HITCH is often used in roping off street construction activities. It is perhaps the least satisfactory of CROSSING KNOTS in common use since it is very apt to slip down the iron stake to which it is ordinarily tied. The rope may first be tied in a series of OVERHAND KNOTS (⚹564); then each knot is opened as ⚹48 and dropped over a stake.

1186. The MARLINGSPIKE HITCH is tied in the bight and is often seen on iron stakes. It may slip if the rope is slack but it is easily untied, and the pull on the ends is at opposite sides of the stake.

1187. SPAR HITCH ⚹1244 makes a good CROSSING KNOT. It is firm, has an excellent lead and may be tied in the bight.

1188. The CONSTRICTOR KNOT is the firmest of the CROSSING KNOTS and may be tied either in the end or bight but it is one of the most difficult of knots to untie and is not suitable for *rope* unless the purpose is a permanent one (such as on a rope ladder). For this purpose the two ropes are led down opposite sides and ends of the rungs.

The three CROSSING KNOTS (⚹1186, ⚹1187 and ⚹1188) are each started with a similar turn around the stake. The same bight is lifted in each case from under the same part and then passed over the top of the post. But in ⚹1186 the bight is lifted over without twisting to form a MARLINGSPIKE HITCH; in ⚹1187 it is given a half twist or turn to the left to form HITCH ⚹1674, and in ⚹1188 it is given a half twist to the right to form the CONSTRICTOR KNOT—three very different hitches which make excellent CROSSING KNOTS.

1189. When the CONSTRICTOR KNOT is tied around a stanchion or a tall pole, where there is no access to the top, a round turn must be made and the end rove as pictured here.

1190. If there is to be considerable sidewise pull, as in swifting the bars of a capstan, the ROLLING HITCH, originally the MAGNUS or MAGNERS HITCH, is the best CROSSING KNOT to employ. It is easily tied in the bight by winding the standing part for two backward turns and then adding a hitch over the end of the bar with a bight from the working end. A deep slot is often put across the ends of capstan bars, or else a hole is bored through the end, to hold the swifter in place. When there are holes POST HITCH #1199 should be tied to save the trouble of reeving. The two ends of the swifter are bent together.

With the possible exception of the MARLINGSPIKE HITCH (#1186), the knots so far shown in this chapter have had the pull of the two ends from the same side or rather surface of the knot. In the MARLINGSPIKE HITCH the pull is from opposite faces, which is a desirable feature for some purposes as there is less tendency to disturb the stake. But the MARLINGSPIKE HITCH does not always stay in place, if the rope slackens. KNOTS #1191, #1192, #1193 and #1196 are the results of an attempt to find a satisfactory knot for this purpose.

1191. Of the next four knots the first and #1194 can be tied in the bight. For that reason they are the most practical of the lot. In #1191 the bight of the rope is twisted one full turn, the two legs where they cross each other farthest from the bight are pulled up through the bight to assume the shape of the right diagram, the post is inserted at the spot marked X and both legs are pulled on while they are still parallel. When the slack has been taken up sufficiently the knot is further tightened by pulling the ends in opposite directions.

1192. A knot of more regular appearance which has to be rove twice in the making. It is commenced with a HALF HITCH around a post and is completed with a second one, around the post and through the first HALF HITCH.

1193. A knot, also of regular appearance, which requires but one reeving and the passing of a single bight over the top of the post.

1194. The MOORING HITCH (#1815) adapts itself very nicely to the purpose of a CROSSING HITCH; it is easily tied and untied and is both strong and secure.

1195. The ZIGZAG KNOT is a common STAKE HITCH employed in lashing wagon, sled and truck loads. The end of the rope in making the lashing is passed in a coil, when possible, which saves much reeving.

Pass the rope around a stake and haul it taut. Stick the end down behind the standing part. At this point it is a replica of KNOT #1173. Pass the end behind the stake again and around the standing part and then behind the stake again. Haul on it strongly and any slack will be taken up. After this bring the end to the next stake and repeat the operation that has just been described.

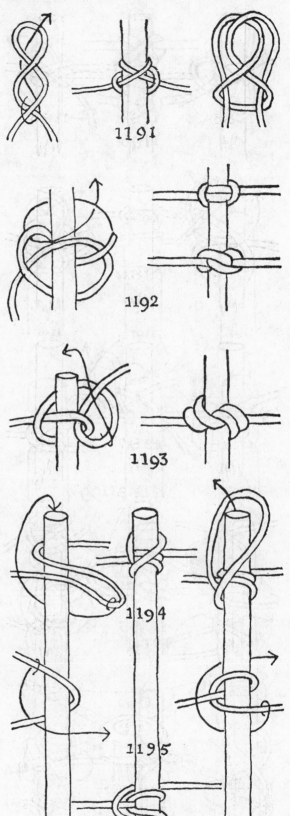

1191

1192

1193

1194

1195

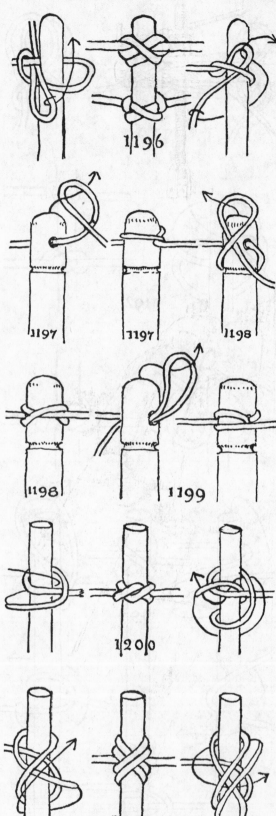

1196. A fairly symmetrical knot, that is pulled from opposite sides. This builds up with a few simple moves and requires but a single reeving. Pass the rope around the post and make a SLIPPED HALF HITCH. Pass the end of the rope around the back of the post and reeve it through the SLIP LOOP. The knot will require a little adjustment before it will lie fair, and is probably the least satisfactory of the four knots with opposite pull that are given.

1197. If a post has a hole through it, as is sometimes the case with fence posts and clothes poles, the end of the line may be rove through the hole, hauled taut and then a hitch dropped over the end of the post to make a very secure hitch. In this case the ends will be about opposite each other.

1198. If, after reeving the line through the hole, the end is carried around the back of the pole and under the standing part before adding the hitch over the top, the pull may not be so symmetrical but the knot will be strong and secure.

1199. If the hole is large enough, the common way of making a CROSSING KNOT is to reeve a bight through the hole. The bight is next dropped back over the top of the pole or post and the working end is led forward.

1200. The next two knots are symmetrical and decorative. They may be used practically for any purpose for which the other knots, that have been described, are used. But the extra work required to tie them will be justified only if they are used for staking off on very special occasions, such as a lawn party or a wedding.

Tie by following the course indicated by the successive arrows in the right and left drawings. By inadvertence, the rope which forms this knot has been illustrated as leading from right to left instead of left to right as the others have been drawn. There is no especial reason for this.

Moreover, in the final crossing of the arrow line, from right to left, the second of the four crossings should be *over* instead of *under* as it is drawn. The knot is correctly shown as ⚹1253 among the BINDING KNOTS.

1201. Although handsome, this knot is somewhat ponderous and I would hesitate to recommend it for anything less than a meeting of the Garden Club itself. The purpose of the knot under the circumstances would be to provide roped-off areas so that guests might be spared the embarrassment of trampling on the flower beds.

First tie a CLOVE HITCH and arrange the turns as in the left diagram, continue as in the right diagram and complete as shown in the center.

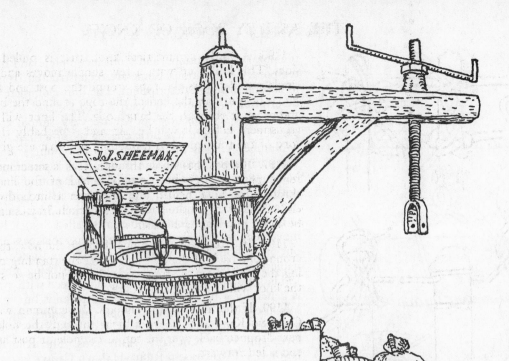

CHAPTER 16: BINDING KNOTS

Dry sun, and dry winde;
Time to reap, and time to BIND.

OLD WEATHER ADAGE

BINDING KNOTS are of two sorts. The first sort passes around an object or objects one or more times and the two ends are snugly tied together; the second passes around an object or objects two or more times and the ends are stuck under the turns.

The knots serve two purposes. Either they confine and constrict a single object, or else they hold two or more objects snugly together. The *whippings* and *seizings*, shown in Chapter 40, serve much the same purpose as BINDING KNOTS, but they contain too many turns to be considered as knots, being more akin to lashings.

On the other hand, the TURK'S-HEAD is a legitimate BINDER KNOT of the second variety, but the family is so large, and has so many ramifications, that it is given a whole chapter to itself.

The last page of the present chapter deals with the ROBAND HITCH, the knot that bends a square sail to its yard or to a backstay. It is a subject of considerable historical interest, particularly for ship-model builders; many of its forms are applicable to present-day needs.

At a time when all sail was bent directly to the yards, the ROBAND HITCH was seldom a recognizable knot; it was more apt to be a seizing or a lashing of small stuff. But by 1840 a knot was the common means of bending sail. With the advent of the clipper ship, however, in the 1850s, seizings of marline became the standard, perhaps due to lighter cotton canvas, and after 1860 the ROBAND HITCH was seldom seen except in the Navy and on school ships, where bending and unbending sail was a part of the regular drill.

I have never seen a complete contemporary illustration of any ROBAND HITCH. The knots shown here are reconstructed from con-

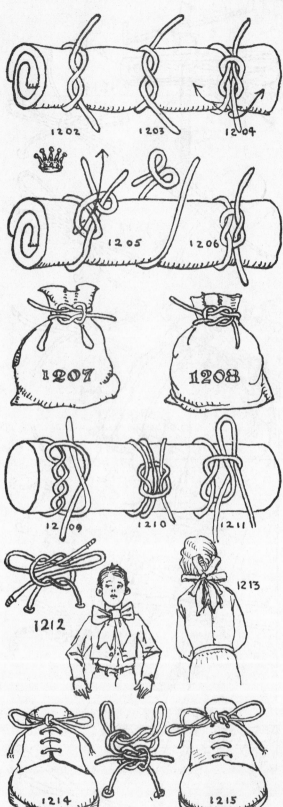

temporary descriptions, and from incomplete and often faulty contemporary illustrations. Some are reconstructed from a combination of several different descriptions. The only complete and satisfactory description is by Lever of KNOT ⚓ 1267.

The first six ROBANDS shown are very simple and probably are correct, since there was little chance to go wrong.

Number 1270 is the ROBAND HITCH of our sailing Navy, which was adequately recorded, in most of the contemporary seamanship books, except for the one detail of finishing off at the top of the yard with a final REEF KNOT. This was omitted in both description and illustration by all authorities until mentioned by Taunt in 1883.

1202. The HALF KNOT, sometimes called SINGLE KNOT, is the first movement for the class of BINDER KNOTS that pass around an object but once. Both Brady and Dana in 1841, and Luce, in 1862, use the name HALF KNOT, the name SINGLE KNOT being a needlework term.

The HALF KNOT is tied around an object with two rope ends. It is generally a part of a more elaborate knot but it also has several solo uses. It is tied singly in rope yarn knots, and in finishing off grommets, cringles, LONG and BACKHANDED SPLICES, ARTIFICIAL EYES and WEST COUNTRY WHIPPINGS. The RIGHT-HANDED HALF KNOT is a TWO-STRAND RIGHT-HANDED CROWN.

1203. The LEFT-HANDED HALF KNOT is a TWO-STRAND LEFT-HANDED CROWN.

1204. The REEF KNOT or SQUARE KNOT consists of two HALF KNOTS, one left and one right, one being tied on top of the other, and either being tied first.

Captain John Smith gives the name REEF KNOT in 1627. Dana gives the name SQUARE KNOT in 1841. Few sailors speak of SQUARE KNOT except in contradistinction to GRANNY KNOT but it is the common shore name for the knot and is in good repute among sailors. Other names for it are TRUE, HARD, FLAT, COMMON, REGULAR, ORDINARY.

When adding the second HALF KNOT to the first, the latter is often held in place by a thumb, a finger or by another person, until the second HALF KNOT has been drawn up.

The REEF KNOT is unique in that it may be tied and tightened with both ends. It is universally used for parcels, rolls and bundles. At sea it is always employed in reefing and furling sails and stopping clothes for drying. But *under no circumstances should it ever be tied as a bend*, for if tied with two ends of unequal size, or if one end is stiffer or smoother than the other, the knot is almost bound to spill. Except for its true purpose of binding it is a knot to be shunned.

1205. One of the distinguishing features of the SQUARE KNOT and the one which gives it its chief value as a REEF KNOT is the ease with which it may be untied. Jerk one end in a direction away from its own standing part (that is, toward the other end) and the knot capsizes; all the turns are left in one end and these are easily stripped from the other end with a sweep of the hand.

1206. The GRANNY KNOT is also called the FALSE, LUBBER'S, CALF and BOOBY KNOT. Patterson's *Nautical Encyclopedia* calls it "OLD GRANNY KNOT" and Sir Edwin Arnold calls it the "COMMON or GARDEN KNOT." The name GRANNY is given in *Vocabulary of Sea Phrases* (Anonymous, 1799) and Roding pictures the knot in 1795.

The GRANNY consists of two identical HALF KNOTS, one tied on top of the other. It has but one practical purpose that I know of and that is to serve as a SURGEON'S KNOT (see Chapter 2). Formerly it was employed for tying up parcels in five-and-ten-cent stores, but the practice was given up and paper bags substituted as they were found to be simpler.

1207. The THIEF or BAG KNOT is also called BREAD BAG KNOT. It appears very like the REEF KNOT, but there is one real and scarcely evident difference. It does not consist of two HALF KNOTS. There is a legend that sailors tie clothesbags, and bread bags with this knot and that thieves always retie them with REEF KNOTS and so are inevitably detected. It is a pleasing story that should encourage honesty. However, if I have ever met this knot in practical use, I have neither recognized it nor paid penalty for my failure to do so.

1208. The WHATNOT. This is the same knot formation as the GRANNY KNOT, but the ends are diagonally opposite each other. It is hardly a practical knot. But with the ends seized it is called the REEVING LINE BEND (♯1459), and it also serves as an interesting trick (♯2579).

1209. The LIGATURE KNOT is commonly called by laymen the SURGEON'S KNOT. But surgeons do not speak of the "SURGEON'S KNOT" any more than a sailor would speak of a "SAILOR'S KNOT."

1210. A knot that is used by shoemakers, harness makers and sailmakers for tying up parcels. The thread is led twice around the parcel. A HALF KNOT is tied in which one end is led under both parts before the final HALF KNOT is added.

1211. The HALF or SINGLE BOWKNOT, called, in Emerson's Dictionary of 1794, DRAWKNOT. It is called the SLIPPED REEF KNOT by yachtsmen and small boatmen. It is much used in parcel tying.

1212. The BOWKNOT or DOUBLE BOWKNOT is closely related to the REEF KNOT, the difference being in the second HALF KNOT, which is tied with two bights instead of two ends. It is often tied in ribbons and tape. Its practical importance lies in the ease with which it may be untied, by pulling at one or both of the ends.

1213. With additional bows worked into circular form the BOWKNOT is sometimes termed a ROSETTE or a ROSETTE KNOT.

1214. The BOWKNOT is the universal means of fastening shoestrings together.

1215. The SHOE CLERK'S KNOT is the BOWKNOT with the addition of an opposing HALF KNOT tied in the two loops.

1216. This pictures the DOUBLE SHOESTRING KNOT as tied by Mrs. Charles S. Knowles. After a BOWKNOT has been loosely tied, the right forefinger, or the right middle finger, pushes the left loop through the knot a second time, from the back forward as shown by the arrow in the left drawing.

1217. A SQUARE SHOESTRING KNOT is tied with two bights. This holds well and is untied by spilling in the manner described for the REEF KNOT (♯1206).

1218. A SQUARE KNOT for shoestrings is tied with one end and one bight.

1219. The DOUBLE SLIP KNOT is also applied to shoestrings. Each of the two loops in the second knot is tucked once after they have been crossed, as in the left diagram.

1220. A SHOESTRING or PARCEL KNOT was shown to me by George H. Taber. Tie a regular BOWKNOT and stick the right loop through the left loop, then pull the left loop tight around the right loop.

1221. A SHOESTRING or PARCEL KNOT. Tie a SINGLE BOWKNOT, tuck a bight from the secure end, through the single loop, and draw up the loop tightly around it. Spill the knot by pulling the two ends one after the other.

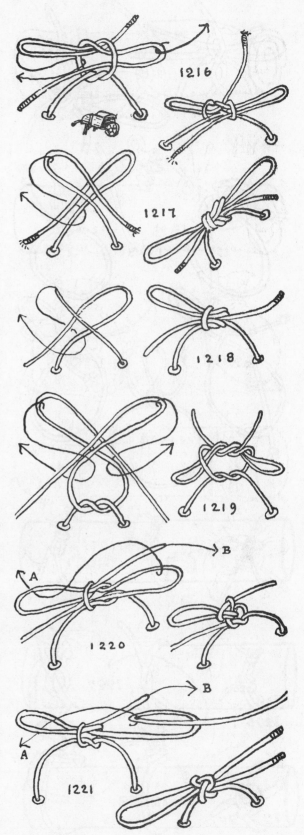

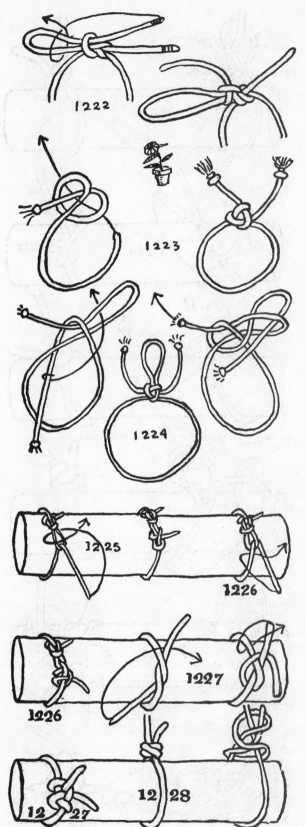

1222. The STATIONER'S KNOT came from Havana. A HALF HITCH is tied with the "slippery end" around the loop of a SINGLE BOWKNOT. Hold the loop while drawing up the hitch. This is not a SLIP KNOT, as the hitch must be removed before the knot can be spilled.

1223. A decorative BATHROBE CORD KNOT. Like the SHOESTRING KNOTS on the previous page, these two knots are pictured from the viewpoint of the wearer. The loop at the bottom presumably encircles a waist. Arrange the knot as in the left diagram, tighten as much as desired by pulling the uncomplicated end (indicated by the arrow). Then, before slacking off, pull the other end smartly, which "sets" the knot. Finally arrange the turns so that they are symmetrical.

1224. A somewhat similar-appearing knot for the same purpose but with the addition of a loop. Half knot the single right cord and the looped left cord together. Thrust a bight from the right cord through the loop of the left cord and draw up the end of the left cord. Arrange the knot so that the parts are symmetrical.

1225. The HITCHED LOOP is a secure knot sometimes seen in a chest lashing. A LOOP KNOT or an EYE SPLICE is tied in one end, the other end is rove through the eye, and after it has been drawn up to the requisite tautness, a SINGLE HITCH is made with the end around the eye in the manner shown in the illustration. The form is the same as the BECKET HITCH.

1226. A HITCHED LOOP. This is a more practical DRAWKNOT for heavy parcel tying. Make LOOP KNOT ⚭1009 or BOWLINE ⚭1010 in one end. Reeve the free end through the eye or loop and after pulling to the desired tautness add TWO HALF HITCHES. This is not so neat in appearance as the previous knot, but it is easier to draw up and make fast.

1227. A PARCEL KNOT based on the HARNESS BEND (⚭1474). With one end tie a CROSSING KNOT around the other. Hold snug and pull the uncomplicated end through to the required tautness. Without slacking or rendering anything that has been gained, add a HALF HITCH with the free end. This is a particularly secure knot and, once the technique is mastered, a most practical one.

1228. A "JAM" KNOT. There are several of these to be given. They are akin to NOOSES but, once drawn up, they are not intended to render, or else they are supposed to hold temporarily while the end is being made fast. They may be tied in the initial girth of a lashing and do not have to be held in hand while the lashing is completed as the ordinary NOOSE does. This well-known knot was shown in Diderot's Encyclopedia (1762).

1229. The BUNTLINE HITCH serves well as a JAM KNOT. It consists of a CLOVE HITCH tied around its own standing part in the opposite way to which Two HALF HITCHES are taken.

1230. The MAGNUS or ROLLING HITCH may be tied in the way pictured with the round turn outside and the HALF HITCH within the encompassing circuit of the knot. This is the reverse of the MIDSHIPMAN'S HITCH. Cotton brokers used to carry their samples in a large roll of paper tied about with either this or a worse knot, this being the best for the purpose.

The knot, having been placed around the roll, was pulled snug and there it stayed until it was time to open, when all that was required to slacken it was to grasp the knot and slide it down the cord. When the package was rewrapped the knot was once more slid into position to tighten it.

1231. An original knot which answers the same purpose as the former. It is simple to tie and easy to untie.

1232. Another which belongs in the class with ⚹1228 and ⚹1229 but is not so secure as ⚹1230 and ⚹1231.

BUTCHER'S KNOTS belong among the knots given here. They have the general characteristics of KNOTS ⚹1228–⚹1232. They do not, however, hold fast until the standing part has been half hitched around the end. The method of doing this, and a number of the knots, are to be found among the vocational knots of Chapter 2.

1233. We have now come to the second variety of BINDER KNOTS in which the rope passes twice or more around an object or objects and the ends are tucked under the turns.

The "DIPLOMA KNOT" is tied around an object of cylindrical form, mainly for decorative purposes.

Take three turns around the cylinder, the second and third turns crossing the first in left diagonals.

Lead the working end across the standing end. Tuck to the right under the second and third turns and then to the left under the first turn. The cord is further tucked as shown in the doubled line of the second drawing. As it stands now it is an excellent BINDER KNOT.

1234. Continue from ⚹1233 and tuck the ends as indicated by the single line arrows in the second drawing to form the double lines of the third drawing. Then tuck both ends again across the knot as shown by the arrows in the third drawing.

Draw up the knot carefully and tautly. The ends may be left long and knotted or else tasseled, or they may be trimmed flush. If tied in soft wire of gold or platinum a handsome ring is formed.

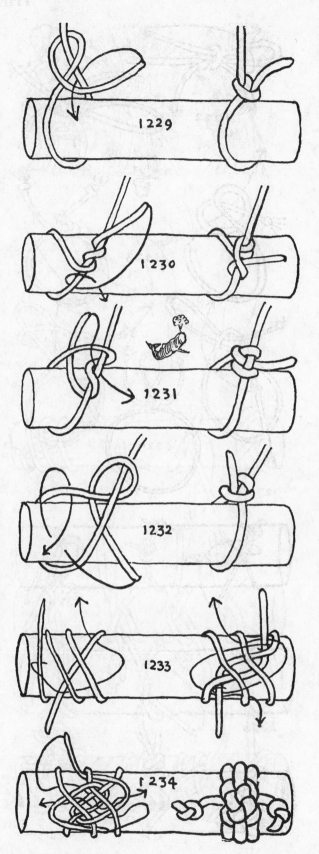

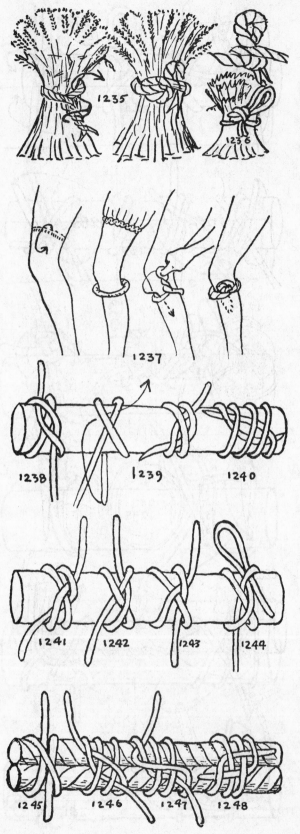

1235. The early BINDER KNOT, that has supplied the name for the knots of this chapter, was made from wisps of the straw that was being bound. A handful was teased out to the required length and rough-twisted to form a strand sufficient for the purpose. The two ends were brought together around the sheaf and were laid up together with a hard twist that was opposite the twist of the strand itself. A bight from the end was tucked back under the binding, in the direction shown.

1236. The knot tied by a mechanical binder is the OVERHAND BEND, sometimes called the THUMB KNOT. It is quite impractical to tie this by hand for this purpose.

1237. The GIRL SCOUT HITCH is closely related to the BINDER KNOT (❋1235). The stocking is rolled down, a finger is inserted below the roll and the roll twisted several turns, after which the end is tucked down inside the stocking. It should be tucked "against the twist."

1238. The knot shown here has a good grip and is the easiest ligature there is to tighten. If out of position, however, it spills easily. So a HALF KNOT should be added to make it secure.

A round turn is first taken and a HALF KNOT is made over this with the two ends.

1239. The STRANGLE KNOT starts with a round turn and the end is stuck under two parts. It may be used to tie up a roll. If required, a loop may be stuck instead of the end, which makes a SLIPPED KNOT that is one of the best for tying up sacks and meal bags.

1240. With one or two additional turns the STRANGLE KNOT makes an excellent temporary whipping for the end of a rope. The drawing shows the knot tied with turns the reverse of ❋1239.

1241. The MILLER'S KNOT (1) is a fairly good BINDING KNOT that is often given in farm bulletins. Any of the MILLER'S KNOTS may employ a bight or loop for the final tuck instead of an end. This makes SLIP KNOTS of them and saves the bag from being injured when the cord is being cut.

1242. MILLER'S KNOT (2). This is the first move for a THREE-LEAD, TWO-BIGHT TURK'S-HEAD. It is a fairly good knot for a bag, being simple to tie, but it sometimes capsizes.

1243. The SACK KNOT is of the same formation as the FISHERMAN'S GROUND LINE HITCH, and also the ARTILLERYMAN'S PICKET-LINE HITCH. Moreover it is the start of the THREE-LEAD, FOUR-BIGHT TURK'S-HEAD. Added to these uses, it serves very well around the neck of a sack.

1244. The BAG KNOT constricts better than most of the knots so far given and makes a very practical MILLER'S KNOT.

1245. The CLOVE HITCH, although an excellent CROSSING KNOT, is not a good binder, although often used for the purpose.

1246. A NET LINE HITCH from Looe. This holds together two lines of opposite lay at the head of a seine.

1247. A NET LINE HITCH from Clovelly which serves the same purpose as the last.

1248. The ESKIMO SPEAR LASHING is a strong and decorative binder that is closely related to the STRANGLE KNOT (❋1239).

1249. The CONSTRICTOR KNOT. At the time when the sinnets of Chapter 39 were being made there was no knot that would hold secure the large number of strands that were required for some of them. For a while seizings were employed, which served the purpose well but took too much time to tie. Then the knot shown here was evolved, which proved in every way adequate. So long as the CONSTRICTOR is tied over a convex surface it will not slip. It draws up easily, has a ratchetlike grip and is the most secure of all BINDING KNOTS.

In the twenty-five years and more that have elapsed since I first tied the knot, I have shown it to many people, and a number of fishermen sailing out of New Bedford now use it for whippings and stoppings. It is also used for the same purpose in several chandleries.

I have found it convenient for tying any kind of a roll, for hanging Christmas stockings to a crane, and for seizing garden hose and atomizer bulbs.

1250. The CONSTRICTOR may be slipped, which greatly simplifies untying, and, so made, it is one of the best of MILLER'S KNOTS.

1251. To tie the CONSTRICTOR in the bight, over the end of a mailing tube or other roll, or over a stake: Make a round turn, pull out a bight and bring it over the end as pictured.

1252. An extra turn may be taken in the CONSTRICTOR to provide a wide permanent whipping.

1253. Another knot that will serve well as a whipping. To tie, follow the right-hand diagram.

1254. A BINDING KNOT of three turns that was made to hold a lanyard in place in the eye of a pricker.

1255. The TRANSOM KNOT was originally made to hold together the two cross sticks of my daughter's kite. It will also serve well in rope but does not untie easily. If more strength is required another knot of the same kind may be tied on the back at right angles to the first.

1256. A *rubber band* is an excellent binder for small objects. It may be wound until it is tight.

1257. Two rubber bands may be doubled together as shown.

1258. A *tourniquet* is ordinarily made of a piece of cloth; a pad should be added where the twist pinches. Its purpose is to stop bleeding, so it should be placed either above an artery or below a vein. An OVERHAND KNOT may be placed where the pressure is wanted.

1259. Another way of tying a *tourniquet* is shown. This same method is applied to tightening rope lashings for heavy logs.

1260. *Nippers* or *twisters* are twisted around a prisoner's wrist, and the handles are held in the grasp of the policeman's hand.

1261. A *nose twitch*, used by farriers and veterinaries, is generally made of a wagon spoke and a piece of small sash cord. It is passed around a horse's upper lip below the nostrils and is twisted sufficiently to hold the horse steady. Sometimes it is put around the ear but this is not good practice. It is required when teeth are to be filed, or eye drops are to be given.

To tie: Hang the rope loop around the left wrist, seize the upper lip with the left hand, hold tightly and with the right hand slip the loop over the left hand and into place. Still holding the lip with the left hand, twist the spoke with the right hand.

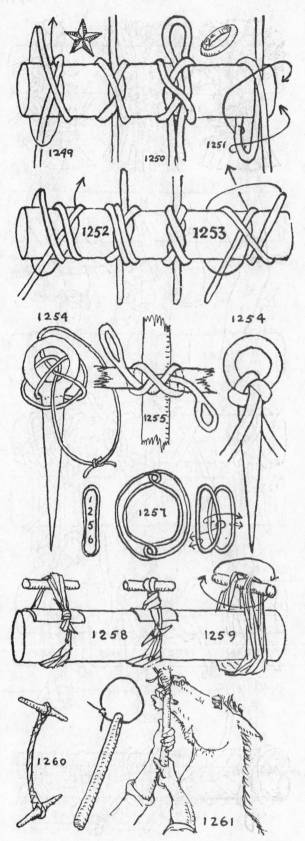

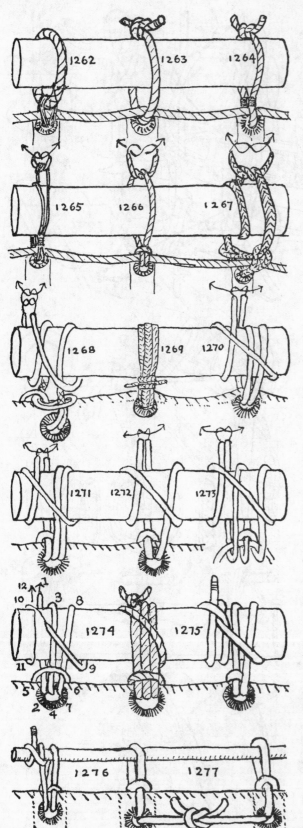

1262. (Circa 1600.) The earliest hanks and mast hoops were *grommets*, and from the evidence of early prints it seems probable that grommets were used on yards for bending square sails. The early grommet was a short rope with the ends short spliced together.

1263. (Circa 1625.) The earliest authorities agree that "*robins* are small lines rove through the eyelet holes of the sayles and made fast on the top of the yeards."

1264. (Circa 1650.) A print of this period appears to show robins with a seizing above the head rope.

1265. (Circa 1750.) Falconer says of robins: "Small rope or braided cordage—of sufficient length to pass two or three times around the yard."

1266. (Circa 1775.) Du Clairbois says that "*robands* may have either one or two legs."

1267. (Circa 1800.) Steel (1794) and Lever (1808) describe robins of two legs, which are put through the eyelet hole as shown. A round turn is taken with the long end, the short end is brought up abaft and the two ends are reef knotted on top of the yard. Steel gives sinnet robands and Lever illustrates rope ones.

1268. (Circa 1805.) The first intimation of the evolution of the ROBAND HITCH from a lashing into a knot was given by Mason (1806). A turn was made with each of two legs and together these formed a CLOVE HITCH.

1269. (Circa 1845.) Young (1847) says: "Rope-bands are small pieces of 2 yarn foxes plaited, or of sinnet or spun yarn, they are not used with jackstays, a number of turns of a single rope yarn being sufficient."

Biddlecomb (1848) says: "Knittles are to bend the squaresails to the jackstays in lieu of ropebands."

1270. (Anno 1860.) The remaining knots on this page were bent to jackstays. This is the standard ROBAND HITCH of both the American and the British Navies. Admiral Nares asks the following question: "How are *all* sails bent to the *jackstays?*" Answer: "With a ROBAND HITCH." To tie the knot: Make two round turns around the jackstay and through the eyelet hole, and clove hitch the long end around the jackstay over the turns already made.

1271. (Anno 1866.) Make a BACK-HANDED HITCH to the eyelet hole with a short end and with the long end make two turns around the jackstay and through the eyelet hole. Put a CLOVE HITCH around the jackstay over the first two turns.

1272. (Circa 1880.) Similar to ⌘1271 but has one less turn around the stay and through the eye.

1273. (Circa 1880.) Middle a roband and tie a BACK-HANDED HITCH. Make a round turn with one end and with the second end tie a CLOVE HITCH over the first end.

1274. (Circa 1880.) This is the handsomest and most shipshape of all the ROBAND HITCHES. Follow the numbers in regular sequence.

1275. (Circa 1880.) Make fast a SHORT RUNNING EYE to the eyelet hole, take a round turn around the jackstay and through the eyelet. Tie a CLOVE HITCH over the turns and add a SINGLE HITCH.

1276. (Anno 1891.) A roband with a *single* leg is secured with a running eye to the eyelet hole of the sail and finished off with a CLOVE HITCH to the jackstay.

1277. (Anno 1860.) Alston gives this method for topgallant and Royal sails. The robands are bent to the sail with running eyes "the two nearest robands being knotted together."

CHAPTER 17: THE TURK'S-HEAD

Made on the footropes of jibbooms in place of an overhanded knot, the Turk's-Head is much neater—and considered by some an ornament.
William Brady: *The Kedge Anchor*, 1841

The Turk's-Head is a tubular knot that is usually made around a cylindrical object, such as a rope, a stanchion, or a rail. It is one of the varieties of the Binding Knot and serves a great diversity of practical purposes but it is perhaps even more often used for decoration only; for which reason, it is usually classed with "fancy knots." Representations of the Turk's-Head are often carved in wood, ivory, bone and stone.

Lever's *Sheet Anchor* (1808) states that a Turk's-Head, "worked with a logline, will form a kind of Crown or Turban." This resemblance to a turban presumably is responsible for the name "Turk's-Head."

There is no knot with a wider field of usefulness. A Turk's-Head is generally found on the "up-and-down" spoke of a ship's steering wheel, so that a glance will tell if the helm is amidship. It provides a foothold on footropes and a handhold on manropes, yoke ropes, gymnasium climbing ropes, guardrails, and life lines. It serves instead of whippings and seizings. It is employed as a gathering hoop on ditty bags, neckerchiefs and bridle reins. Tied in rattan, black whalebone or stiff fishline, it makes a useful napkin ring, and it is often worn by racing crews in "one-design classes" as a bracelet or anklet. It will cover loose ends in sinnets and splices. It furnishes a handgrip on fishing rods, archery bows and vaulting poles. It will stiffen sprung vaulting poles, fishing rods, spars, oars and paddles. On a pole or rope it will raise a bole big enough to prevent a hitch

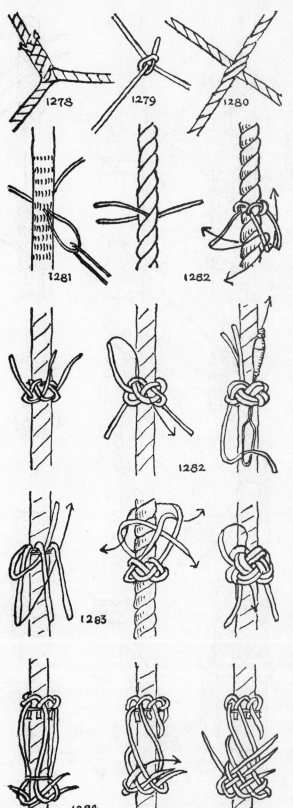

in another rope from slipping. On edged tools it makes an excellent hand guard, and on oars and canoe paddles, a drip guard. It is found employed decoratively on whips, lanyards, telescopes, hatbands, leashes, quirts, and harness; on wicker chairs and basketry; on bell ropes and tassels. Old chest beckets, bell ropes and yoke ropes are resplendent with them.

There are three distinct kinds of TURK's-HEADS that are much the same in appearance, but are differently constructed. They are: (1) the STANDING TURK's-HEAD, which is tied with *any number* of strands; (2) COACHWHIPPING, which is tied with any *even* number of strands; and (3) the common TURK's-HEAD, sometimes called the RUNNING TURK's-HEAD, which is tied with a single strand.

The name, "STANDING TURK's-HEAD," appears in Nares' *Seamanship* of 1860. The knot is employed where any slipping would be disastrous. It is found particularly on footropes, and also on Jacob's ladders, where it serves to hold the rungs in place.

1278. If a STANDING TURK's-HEAD is to be made around a three-strand rope, take two pieces of small stuff, one piece being half the length of the other, and side splice the shorter piece to the middle of the longer piece.

1279. If small braided material is used for the TURK's-HEAD, half hitch the end of the short piece around the center of the longer piece.

1280. If the STANDING TURK's-HEAD is to be tied around a four-strand rope, two pieces of the same length are required. Open one piece at the center and reeve the other piece halfway through it, or else merely cross the two pieces at half length.

1281. If a TURK's-HEAD is to be made around a *large braided rope*, double the small stuff and reeve the bight through the larger rope to half length. Then cut the bight to provide four ends.

1282. To tie a STANDING TURK's-HEAD: Insert the three-legged structure (※1278) into the heart of a three-strand rope, so that a leg projects from between each two strands. Hold the rope vertically and crown the three legs to the right. Then, holding the rope as before, wall below the crown, and in the same direction (to the right), in the manner already described for FOOTROPE KNOT ※696. After that, double the lay of the knot by following below each established lead a second circuit, as described for FOOTROPE KNOT ※696. The ends are finally stuck out, under the crown, lengthwise of the rope. It should now be worked snug and each leg hauled on strongly. Finally the ends are trimmed as close as is practicable. The knot may be followed again, which triples it, making a THREE-PLY KNOT. A FOUR- or even a FIVE-PLY KNOT can be made, but the latter is not always satisfactory.

1283. To make the above around a four-strand rope: Arrange the strands as in ※1280 or ※1281, and tie in exactly the way described for three strands.

If a sailor wishes to tie a wider STANDING TURK's-HEAD, he first ties a DIAMOND KNOT and then crowns it, making a FOUR-LEAD KNOT. This is doubled, tripled or quadrupled, if desired.

1284. To tie a WIDE STANDING TURK's-HEAD of any width and any number of strands: Seize a number of cords securely to a rope with CONSTRICTOR ※1249. Hold the rope vertically and crown the

legs to the right. Lead the legs down the rope in a right helix and
stop them. Wall the legs to the right. Disregard the stopping and
take each leg in turn, passing it over the next leg to its right, and
tucking it under the second. This process may be repeated as many
times as desired. The legs are tucked in tiers; that is, each leg is
tucked only *once* in turn, and at no time is any leg advanced more
than one tuck beyond the others. When the knot is wide enough,
double or triple it, as already described.

Each leg of the knot that was just described may be tucked down
to the neck as it lies, or else it may be tucked independently somewhat further, the opposing leg being withdrawn at each tuck so
that the joints are well scattered to prevent unsightly bulges. The
two opposing ends should emerge from under the same part.

1285. The foregoing knot may be doubled or trebled by paralleling one end with the other. Work the knot snug, pull the ends tight
and trim them close. The number of bights is always equal to the
number of strands and the number of leads is always odd.

The foregoing describes the usual sailor's variety of WIDE STAND-
ING TURK'S-HEAD. There are really four varieties of the knot, #1284
and the three which follow.

Condensed directions for #1284 and #1285 are as follows: Seize
several strands and crown to the right and then helix downward.
Seize again and wall to the right, then tuck upward over and under,
any number of times. The number of leads is always odd. (This
is the common STANDING TURK'S-HEAD.)

1286. Seize, *crown* to the right and helix downward, seize again
and tuck upward, over and under any number of times. The number of leads is always *even*.

1287. Seize, turn down strands in a right helix (without crowning), seize again and *wall*, then tuck upward over and under any
number of times. This is the reverse of #1286. The number of leads
is always even.

1288. Seize, turn down strands in a right helix (without crowning), seize again and tuck upward over and under any number of
times. This is the reverse of #1284 and #1285. The number of leads
is always odd. The cycle of this is the same as that of the DIAMOND
KNOT.

By the above four methods a STANDING TURK'S-HEAD of any size
may be made.

1289. The following method, however, gives the same result, and
is the one I have found most convenient. Take a number of legs
equal to the number of bights desired. Middle the legs and seize
them at the center to a rope or other cylinder. Twist the lower set
of legs in a 45-degree helix downward to the right and seize again.
The two seizings should mark the position and length of the projected knot. Crown the upper set to the left and (1) wall the lower
set to right, or else (2) tuck the lower set upward over and under
without walling. Proceed to tuck both upper and lower sets of legs
over and under until they meet. Opposite ends are then laid in
parallel with each other and the knot is doubled or tripled. The ends
should be scattered so that they do not all project at the same circumference, which would cause bulging. Draw the knot snug and
trim all ends. With these two starts knots of any size may be made.

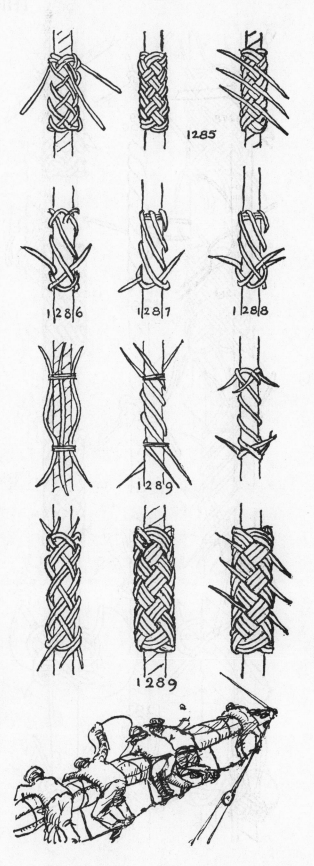

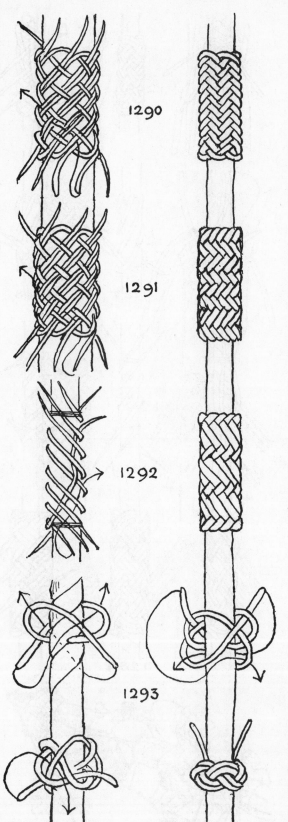

1290

1291

1292

1293

1290. *Herringbone weave.* Take six or eight rather long strands. Lay them along a cylinder, and seize them twice as before. Make a helix between the two seizings as directed for the last knot.

Tuck the lower legs up and to the right over one and under one to the rim.

Turn the structure end for end and do the same with the other set of legs. The right diagonals will now be double and the left diagonals single, and will appear as in the first diagram.

Stick the lower set of legs to the left *over* two and under two as illustrated (study the diagram carefully).

Turn the structure end for end and do the same with the other set of legs.

Continue to stick all legs over *two* and under *two* until they meet. Scatter the ends well and, finally, stick opposing legs under the same two parts, cut the seizings, draw up the knot evenly, scatter the ends and trim them. This makes herringboning that runs with the width of the knot.

1291. *Herringboning, parallel with the length of the knot,* is started in the same way as the last. After one helix has been doubled stick the lower set of legs to the left *under* two as illustrated. Then turn the structure end for end and do the same with the second set of legs. Continue to stick all the legs over *two* and under *two* and repeat until they meet. Finally scatter the ends, stick the opposing legs under the same two parts, cut the seizings, draw up the knot and trim the ends.

1292. Herringbone weave by another method: Middle and seize a group of legs sufficient in number to fit closely together around the cylinder that is to be covered. After the legs have been helixed and seized a second time at the bottom, take the set of lower legs and stick each one to the right over one strand and under three strands, then over one and under three again. Turn the structure end for end and tuck each strand over one and under three, and continue to tuck over one and under three until the two sets meet, where care must be taken that the over-one-under-three sequence is unbroken. The ends are to be well scattered and trimmed as already described.

Other textures may be made by this method such as over-two-and-under-two, or over-two-and-under-three, etc.

1293. *Cutting out strands.* The STANDING TURK'S-HEADS are often used for "cutting out" strands on sinnet lanyards which it is desired to *taper.* Two, three, four, or even five strands may be laid out of the sinnet at one time and STANDING TURK'S-HEADS are tied with them after the lanyard is completed. If one strand only is to be cut out, TURK'S-HEAD ⌗1304 may be tied. If, however, *two* strands are to be cut out of a sinnet, the accompanying knot, which has four bights and is handsomer than the straight crown and wall of two bights, may be used. This knot may also be made in an untapered sinnet with the two legs of a single cord which has been *thrust through* the sinnet.

To tie: Lead the two ends as shown in the diagram, then double as many times as desired and draw up snugly. Finally trim the ends.

1294. Structurally *cross grafting* or *cross pointing* is the same thing as ROUND SINNET except that the former is employed as a *covering* around a rope or core. More strands (always an even number) may be used and the ends are "finished off" decoratively, instead of being seized as in the ROUND SINNET. This is the preferred method for covering long rails and stanchions aboard ship.

Take any number of strands (in this case an even number is not required), seize them at the middle around a rope or rail and twist slightly so that the upper ends all rotate to the right, as in a right corkscrew, and the lower ends to the left. Now turn the upper set downward, and using both sets, one leading to the right, one to the left, lay up a section of ROUND SINNET of the length wanted for the knot. Make as directed for SINNETS ✻3021 and ✻3022. But use the rope or rail as a core. Seize at the end and fair all strands. If it is desired to double this, work the ends back into the structure parallel with the legs of the opposing set, using a sail needle if convenient. Do likewise with the other legs until the whole surface is closely doubled or tripled. Scatter the ends well and trim the knot closely.

1295. The term COACHWHIPPING is also commonly applied when a covering is made by the SQUARE SINNET method (✻3001). Several parallel strands are worked as a unit, around a rope or rail, the whole surface being covered in one operation and the ends tucked back at the rim and scattered.

The name COACHWHIPPING is given in Alston's *Seamanship* of 1860 and the name "WHIP STICH" [sic] was applied to it by Ned Ward in 1707.

A COACHWHIPPING of four leads is the usual thing. It is made with doubled or tripled strands as described for SINNET ✻3015. In covering a long rail the boatswain should have the assistance of a "mate." The parallel cords are wound in balls or on bobbins.

1296. With six leads (SINNET ✻3016) a boatswain's mate is indispensable, if the bobbins are to remain disentangled.

1297. In making the knots of this chapter the direction of the strands around the cylinder can be deflected so that the same material will cover a very varied circumference.

1298. Instead of sticking the ends back into the structure they may be tied at the rim in a DIAMOND KNOT, each set of parallel ends being worked in a unit, after which the ends are sometimes "trimmed long" and left to form a fringe. This is quite common on stanchions. The top edge of the knot may be straight, not scalloped, if arranged as shown in ✻1895. Ordinarily the knots of the TURK'S-HEAD family have scalloped rims as detailed in ✻1896.

1299. A commoner method of finishing off COACHWHIPPING on long rails is to trim all ends close to the seizings and then to cover them with narrow independent TURK'S-HEADS made of the same or smaller material. For such purposes tarred fishline is often used.

TURK'S-HEADS may be made of cord, thongs, tape, shoestrings, straw, cellophane, wrapping paper and other flattened materials, and the rims turned as illustrated in ✻1895. The ends of flat materials are laid above and underneath each other before trimming. (Round material is laid alongside.) Flat ends can be pasted, cemented, glued, riveted, seized, sewed or spliced together. Pull them forcibly to the surface, distorting the knot no more than is necessary, fasten them and when fast, work them back out of sight again before cutting them off. It is commonly unnecessary to fasten the ends of ordinary TURK'S-HEADS if they have been properly drawn up.

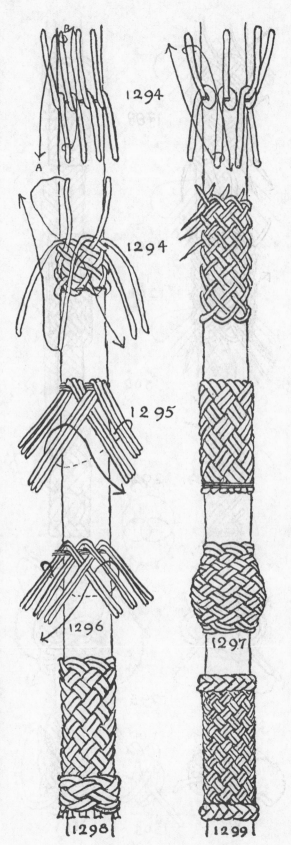

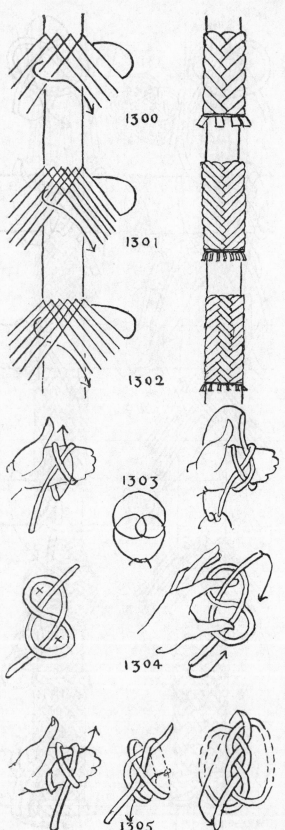

1300

1301

1302

1303

1304

1305

1300. COACHWHIPPING, based on SQUARE SINNET, makes a herringbone weave. The directions for SQUARE SINNET are given on page 493. This may be made with eight strands around a rope or rail, and gives four lengthwise rows of "herringboning." The legs may be left long enough for sticking back at both ends, which is done in the manner shown as ⅜1290.

1301. SQUARE SINNET of twelve and sixteen strands can be employed in the same way, using three or four strands to each unit, as the case may be.

1302. Six rows of herringboning will result if the strands are led as shown here. Care must be exercised in these last two to arrange the seizings so that the rims will be symmetrical. The ends should be stuck back with a needle before removing the seizings. Some of the ends are stuck once and trimmed, others are led back two and three tucks in order to scatter them. COACHWHIPPING ordinarily is not doubled; it is completed in one operation. But if the surface has not been completely covered, double the knot, using a needle.

The common TURK'S-HEAD is made of a single continuous line and is an older knot than the multi-strand one. Sometimes it is called the RUNNING TURK'S-HEAD, a term which may have been applied in contradistinction to STANDING TURK'S-HEAD, or it may be descriptive of the sailor's use of the knot as a gathering hoop or puckering ring to slide up and down on bag lanyards, neckerchiefs, etc. It should be understood that whenever the name "TURK'S-HEAD" is applied by sailors without qualification, the single-line knot is always the one that is referred to.

The name "TURK'S-HEAD" first appears in Darcy Lever's *The Sheet Anchor* (1808), but the knot is much older. I have a powder horn dated 1676 which has several TURK'S-HEADS carved around it, and Leonardo da Vinci (1452–1519) shows a number in disk form, in a drawing that is reproduced by Öhrvall in *Om Knutar* (1916).

In discussing the SINGLE-STRAND TURK'S-HEAD the use of the word *strand* will be avoided as it is ambiguous. *Cord* or *line* will designate the material of the knot and the word *lead* will designate a single circuit of the cord around the cylinder or barrel. The size of a knot is designated by the number of its leads and bights. Bights are the scallops or coves formed by the cord where it changes direction at the rims. The total number of leads denotes the width of a knot along the cylinder, and the total number of bights denotes the length of a knot *around* the barrel or cylinder.

Each reappearance of the *cord* or *lead* on the surface will be termed a *part*. Only one part, the upper one, is in evidence at each crossing in the finished knot. To *follow* a cord or lead is to parallel it with identical over-and-under sequence, which alternates in the common TURK'S-HEAD. When a lead has been followed throughout a whole knot, the knot is said to have been *doubled*.

The sailor interprets the word *double* in his own way. When a finished knot consists of two parallel cords the sailor describes it as having been *doubled twice*; when it exhibits three parallel cords throughout, it has been *doubled three times*.

A knot that is doubled three times is said by sailors to have three lays. It is also called a THREE-PLY KNOT.

Tucking over a cord is the same as *passing* or *crossing over*. A sailor may *tuck* either under and over, or over and under.

1303, 1305. Ordinarily the sailor ties a TURK'S-HEAD directly around his fingers. When it has been formed it is placed around the object that is to be its permanent support.

THE TURK'S-HEAD

There are two sizes that the sailor commonly ties in this direct manual way: ⚹1303, which has three leads and two bights; and ⚹1305, which has three leads and four bights.

1304. An unusual but simple method of tying the THREE-LEAD, TWO-BIGHT TURK'S-HEAD is to first make the FIGURE-EIGHT KNOT, then insert thumb and finger into two compartments as shown, and pinch them together. When the two ends meet the knot is complete.

1306. The sailor also ties the THREE-LEAD BY FIVE-BIGHT KNOT, either directly or more often by lengthening ⚹1305, a process that is later described as ⚹1316.

1307. Occasionally he ties directly the FIVE-LEAD BY THREE-BIGHT KNOT as shown here. After reaching the position of the left diagram, the left turn of the two center leads is shifted to the right over the next one to assume the position of the right diagram. To complete the knot, follow the line indicated by the arrow. Any of the TURK'S-HEADS may be doubled or tripled by paralleling one end with the other.

1308, 1309, 1310, 1311. There are several manual methods of tying the FOUR-LEAD by THREE-BIGHT KNOT. No particular technique is required. After reaching the position shown in any final diagram the knot is placed around its permanent support and "faired," but not drawn up. The lay is then paralleled as many times as wished by "following the lead" that has been established. To do this tuck in one end beside its opposing end, and continue to tuck contrariwise and parallel with the other end, following the lead with identical over-and-under sequence. The second lead must be kept always on the same side of the first lead, either right or left according to how it was started. When the knot has as many plies as desired it is worked snug with a pricker. This is done by progressing from one end of the cord to the other through the whole knot, back and forth, gradually pricking up and hauling out the slack. The knot must not at any time be distorted by pulling too strongly on any one part. When completed it should be so snug around its support that it will not slip. To tie ⚹1311: Start as if you were making KNIFE LANYARD KNOT ⚹781.

I have known several sailors who could tie directly in hand 4L × 5B and 5L × 4B TURK'S-HEADS but in each case their methods were individual and often too cumbersome to be generally practical. They were also perhaps unnecessary, as it is easier to tie large knots by *raising* smaller ones to larger dimensions. For this purpose there are several different methods to follow.

There is but one actual limitation to the size and proportions of SINGLE-LINE TURK'S-HEADS: *A knot of one line is impossible in which the number of leads and the number of bights have a common divisor.* All others are possible if the knot tier has sufficient time and cord at his disposal.

This "Law of the Common Divisor" was discovered at the same time by George H. Taber and the author.

The operation of the Law of the Common Divisor is quite simple. For example, within the limits of twenty-four leads and twenty-four bights there are 576 combinations. Of these combinations, 240 have a common divisor and cannot be tied as a TURK'S-HEAD, and 336 have no common divisor and can be tied. If a knot is attempted in one cord with dimensions that possess a common divisor, the working end and the standing end will meet before the desired knot is complete. Such a knot, being composed of more than one line, can be tied only as a MULTI-STRAND KNOT.

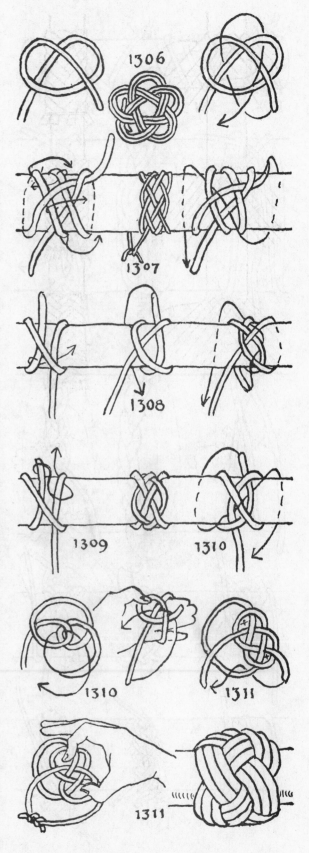

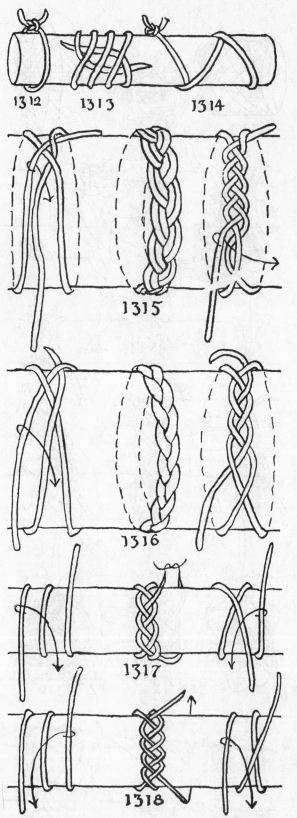

1312   1313   1314

1315

1316

1317

1318

1312. There is one exception to this "law": knots of *one bight* may be tied with one strand and with *any number* of leads.

This provides, among other anomalies, the only TURK'S-HEAD in which the number of leads and the number of bights is equal (1L × 1B).

1313. The same knot may be doubled if wished; the illustration gives a FOUR-PLY KNOT of one lead and one bight.

1314. A knot of three leads and one bight only is here illustrated.

A CENSUS OF ALL SINGLE-LINE TURK'S-HEADS CONTAINING NOT MORE THAN 24 BIGHTS AND 40 LEADS

X stands for an impossible knot; all others may be tied.

```
                         NO. OF LEADS
          (10)      (20)      (30)      (40)
    1234567890123456789012345678901234567890
 1
 2   X X X X X X X X X X X X X X X X X X X X
 3    X  X  X  X  X  X X  X  X X  X  X  X
 4   X X X X X X X X X X X X X X X X X X X X
 5      X    X    X    X    X    X    X    X
 6    XXX X XXX X XXX X XXX XX X XXX X XXX X XXX
 7        X    X   X      X    X
 8   X X X X X X X X X X X X X X X X X X X X
 9    X  X  X  X  X  X  X  X  X  X  X  X  X
10    X XXX X X X XXX X X X XXX X X X XXX X X
11   X          X          X
12    XXX X XXX X XXX X XXX XX X XXX X XXX X XXX
13   X          X          X
14    X X XXX X  X X X X X XX X X X X  X XXX X X
15    X XX  XX X  X  X X X  XX X  X  X XX  XX
16   X X X X X X X X X X X X X X X X X X X X
17   X            X            X
18    XXX X XXX X XXX X XXX XX X XXX X XXX X XXX
19   X                X
20    X XXX X X X XXX X X X XXX X X X XXX X X
21    X  XX X  X XX  X  X  X  XX X  X XX  X
22    X X X X X XX X X X X X  X X X X  XXX X X X
23   X                    X
24    XXX X XXX X XXX X XXX XX X XXX X XXX X XXX
```

All TURK'S-HEADS of two leads are OVERHAND and MULTIPLE OVERHAND KNOTS.

A good practical way to plan TURK'S-HEADS is to take a prime number for the larger dimensions (5, 7, 11, 13, 17, 19, 23, 29, 37, 41, etc.) and to use any smaller number, either odd or even, for the other dimension.

1315. The simplest method of enlarging or raising TURK'S-HEADS to larger dimensions is based on KNOTS ※1303 and ※1305.

After first tying a 3L × 4B TURK'S-HEAD KNOT (※1305) very loosely, bring the left bight under the next and down to the center position and continue to plat, leading alternate sides under to the center, exactly as in ordinary THREE-STRAND SINNET. One end and both bights are platted and the working end has to be disentangled from time to time from the bights. A new knot is completed each time the working end is brought to the same rim with the standing end; and each time this occurs three new bights have been added to the knot.

1316. After tying KNOT ※1303 (3L × 2B) or KNOT ※1305 (3L × 4B), start with the left end, bring it *over* to the center, and continue to plat as THREE-STRAND SINNET.

With these two starts, all possible TURK'S-HEADS of three leads are made. These may be doubled, tripled or quadrupled if wished. Numbers 1315 and 1316 are the common methods that have "always been used" for lengthening THREE-LEAD TURK'S-HEADS.

1317. Recently I have found what appears to be a simpler method.

Take two right round turns about an object (the left hand) and start at once to plat, leading with the left end. Hold the upper end and bights firmly in position until the plat is well started. A TURK'S-HEAD is completed each time both ends are brought to the same rim. The start shown makes a 3L × 4B TURK'S-HEAD which, by continuing to plat, will build up into 3 × 7, 10, 13, etc.

1318. Arrange two round turns in the same way as ※1317 but commence to plat with the right end instead of the left. Numbers 1317 and 1318 will give all possible THREE-LEAD TURK'S-HEADS.

1319, 1320, 1321. In the methods just given the TURK'S-HEAD was increased in only one of its two dimensions, its *length;* the number of bights was added to, but the number of leads remained the same, and its width was unchanged. The TURK'S-HEADS immediately to follow are increased in both dimensions at each operation. There are three different groups to consider:

1319. In "SQUARE TURK'S-HEADS," as sailors call them, the number of leads is always one greater, or one less, than the number of bights.

1320. In WIDE TURK'S-HEADS the number of leads exceeds the number of bights by two or more (with one exception only).

1321. In NARROW TURK'S-HEADS the number of bights exceeds the number of leads by two or more (with one exception, of theoretical interest only).

Several authors have discussed the way of "raising" SQUARE TURK'S-HEADS to larger dimensions: Taber, Öhrvall, Saito, Bocher, Spencer, and Griswold. But Taber alone has noted that it takes four different starts to make all possible SQUARE TURK'S-HEADS. (*Method of Making C ~ L = 1 Turksheads* by George H. Taber, Pittsburgh, 1919, privately published.) His paper covers SQUARE TURK'S-HEADS exhaustively in mathematical terms. Öhrvall gives three of the starts, Saito and Griswold give two each, the other authors give but one. Griswold's illustrations are excellent. He describes SQUARE TURK'S-HEADS made of thongs over leather collars.

In addition to the SQUARE TURK'S-HEAD discussions, Taber, Griswold and Spencer give methods of raising WIDE TURK'S-HEADS, in which the number of leads exceeds the number of bights by two or more.

So far as I know, there has been no description published of a method of raising NARROW TURK'S-HEADS, in which the number of bights exceeds the number of leads by two or more (except methods ⚓1315 and ⚓1316 in which the number of leads is always three). But NARROW TURK'S-HEADS may be made by methods similar to those given for WIDE TURK'S-HEADS and they have a greater variety than the wide ones.

1322. The sailor commonly employs two ways of raising SQUARE TURK'S-HEADS to larger dimensions: He may start with either a 4L × 3B TURK'S-HEAD or a 3L × 2B TURK'S-HEAD tied in hand and, each time two circuits around the hand are added, a larger TURK'S-HEAD results. The 4L × 3B TURK'S-HEAD is commenced with an OVERHAND KNOT, and the end is led as shown here.

1323. The 3L × 2B KNOT is first tied as ⚓1303 and is then raised as shown here in the left and right diagrams. In both these knots (⚓1322 and ⚓1323) the working end is constantly laid parallel and ahead of the last previously laid circuit and with the contrary over-and-under. The method is described in detail on the page to follow.

To make all possible SQUARE TURK'S-HEADS two more starts are required; the 3L × 4B and the 4L × 5B (or 2L × 3B). I have never seen a sailor employ either of these.

1324. TURK'S-HEADS may be more easily tied around a wooden cylinder than around the hand, using pins to hold the bights in place.

To tie a SQUARE TURK'S-HEAD on a cylinder: Take a wooden stick approximately round and about four inches in diameter and twelve inches long, a more convenient apparatus is shown at the end of this chapter. Draw two parallel lines around the circumference four inches apart and equidistant from the ends of the log. Two elastic bands will serve to establish and fair the lines. Mark thirty-one evenly spaced points around these lines, employing a pair of dividers, or else follow the directions for spacing given on the last page of this chapter. Drive small brads at these established points and leave about a quarter of an inch projecting.

Place the cylinder or barrel across the knees and number the pins, away from you, 1 to 31; opposite pins in the two lines are to be numbered alike. Take a piece of small braided cord and tie an end to left pin 1.

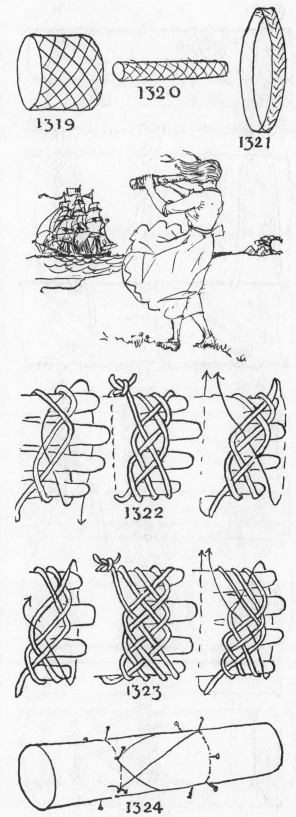

1319

1320

1321

1322

1323

1324

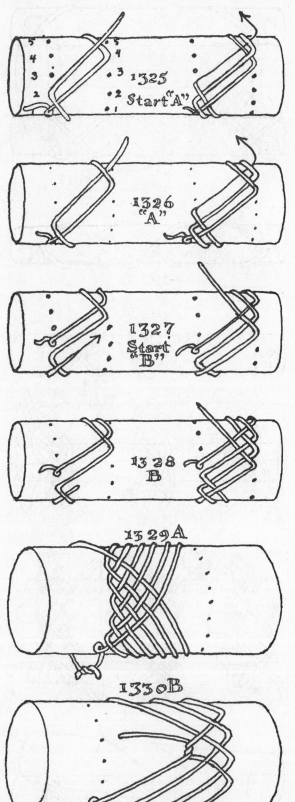

1325. Start "A." Knots having an odd number of leads and an even number of bights. (3L × 2B raises to 5L × 4B, 7L × 6B, etc.)

Lay cord diagonally away from you to the right and around pin 17. Lay cord diagonally away from you to the left and around pin 2. Lay cord diagonally away from you to the right and around pin 18. Continue to lay the cord parallel to and in advance of the established lead. Turn so that the work is constantly on top. All crossings are *over* until two adjacent parallel leads are to be crossed at the end of the fourth diagonal. Cross these with under-and-over that is contrary to the parallel lead, forming a regular "basket weave." The working end crosses a standing part each time it is led to the left rim. With this start a knot is completed each time the ends are brought together around the barrel outside the left rim, as in illustration ⌗1329. The number of bights is even.

1326. Start "A." Knots having an even number of leads and an odd number of bights (starts with 2L × 1B and raises to 4L × 3B, 6L × 5B, etc.).

Lay cord 1, 17, 2, 18 as before, and continue to lay parallel with established lead. The first crossing is *over* (17 to 2), the second crossing is *under* (2 to 18). All crossings thereafter are contrary to the parallel lead. A knot is completed each time both ends are at the left rim and the number of bights is odd.

1327. Start "B." Knots having an odd number of leads and an even number of bights (starts with 3L × 4B which raises to 5L × 6B, 7L × 8B, etc.).

Lay cord diagonally away from you to the right and around pin 16. Lay cord diagonally away from you to the left and around pin 31. Lay cord diagonally away from you to the right and around pin 15. Continue to lay cord parallel to other diagonals. All crossings are *over* until two parallels are to be crossed. Cross these with over-and-under, which is contrary to adjacent parallel lead, and continue contrary to parallel lead. A knot is completed each time the ends cross on the barrel to the left of all other leads and the number of bights is even.

1328. Start "B." Knots having an even number of leads and an odd number of bights (starts with 2L × 3B which raises to 4L × 5B, 6L × 7B, etc.).

Lay cord 1, 16, 31, 15, 30, 14 as before and continue to lay cord parallel with the established lead. The first crossing is *over* (15 to 30) and the second crossing is *under* (30 to 14). Thereafter crossings are contrary to the parallel lead. A knot is completed each time the ends cross on the cylinder to the left of all other leads and the number of bights is odd. Whenever, in tying the four knots just given, the required number of leads and bights have been attained, the knot may be doubled or tripled as already described. All possible SQUARE TURK'S-HEADS may be tied with one of these four starts.

1329. The illustration shows how to complete a knot commenced with Start "A" as either ⌗1325 or ⌗1326.

1330. The illustration shows how to complete a knot commenced with Start "B" as either ⌗1327 or ⌗1328.

WIDE TURK'S-HEADS WITH AN EVEN NUMBER OF BIGHTS, IN WHICH THE NUMBER OF LEADS EXCEEDS THE NUMBER OF BIGHTS BY TWO OR MORE (WITH ONE EXCEPTION)

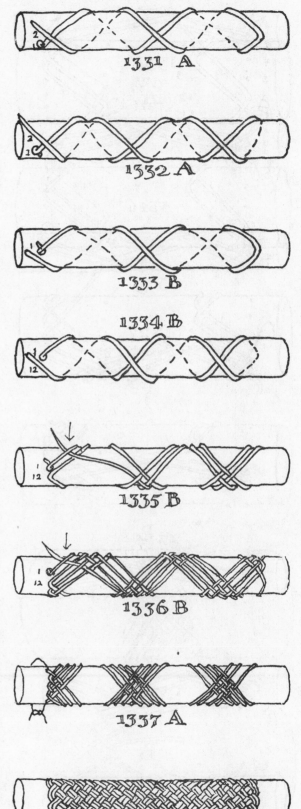

This group also has four different starts. In Start "A" (⚹1331) and Start "B" (⚹1333) the cord encircles the cylinder any even number of times beginning with two before returning to the left rim and in Start "A" (⚹1332) and Start "B" (⚹1334) the cord encircles the cylinder any odd number of times beginning with three before returning to the left rim.

Take a wooden cylinder about twenty inches long and one and a half inches in diameter. Make two parallel rows of pins around it twelve inches apart, with twelve pins in each row. Place the cylinder or barrel across the knees and number the pins 1 to 12 *away* from you, and with the same numbers opposite each other in the two rows. Secure a cord to left pin 1.

1331. Start "A."
Lead the cord away from you in a right diagonal to pin R. 1. Lead the cord away from you in a left diagonal to pin L. 2. (Take care that the two diagonals progress the same distance, which will be either once, twice, etc., around the cylinder.) This makes an even number of turns. Note that in Start "A" ⚹1331 and ⚹1332 the working end is always led on the far side of the previous diagonal.

1332. Start "A."
Lead the cord away from you in a right diagonal to pin R. 7. Lead the cord away from you in a left diagonal to pin L. 2. This makes an odd number of turns. Be certain that both diagonals progress the same distance.

1333. Start "B."
Lead the cord away from you in a right diagonal to pin R. 1. Lead the cord away from you in a left diagonal to pin L. 12. This makes an even number of turns. Be certain that both diagonals progress the same distance. Note that in Start "B" the working end is always led on the near side of the previous diagonal.

1334. Start "B."
Lead the cord away from you in a right diagonal to pin R. 7. Lead the cord away from you in a left diagonal to pin L. 12. This makes an odd number of turns. Be certain that both diagonals progress the same distance.

1335. To complete a TWO-BIGHT KNOT from Start "B" ⚹1334.
All crossings are over until the fourth (left) diagonal. The first crossing after the fourth diagonal is under. Thereafter continue to tuck contrary to the established lead of the adjacent parallel diagonal. The knot is completed where the arrow indicates in the illustration.

1336. To increase KNOT ⚹1335 or any other Start "B" knot, to a larger knot of four or any other number of bights, proceed as follows:

All crossings are over until the fourth diagonal. The first crossing of the fourth diagonal is under. The first crossing of the fifth (right) diagonal is *under* and the lead thereafter is contrary to the lead of the adjacent parallel diagonal. Continue until the knot has four, six, eight, or any even number of bights and complete by bringing the ends together as in the diagram.

It will be found that every TWO-BIGHT KNOT may be made with either Start "A" or Start "B" (except 3L × 2B) but that in enlarging a knot by different starts they will increase at different rates.

1337. In Start "B" all crossings are *over* until the fourth diagonal; and in the fourth diagonal, and thereafter, the lead is contrary to the established lead of the adjacent parallel diagonal. A knot is completed whenever there is an even number of bights at both rims: 2, 4, 6, 8, etc., and the ends have been brought together.

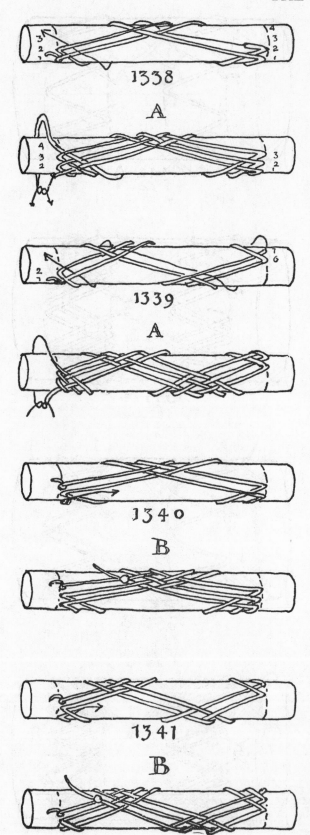

1338

A

1339

A

1340

B

1341

B

WIDE TURK'S-HEADS WITH AN ODD NUMBER OF BIGHTS

Starting with knots of three bights, which may be raised to any odd number of bights, the number of leads may be either odd or even but the number of bights and the number of leads may have no common divisor.

1338. Start "A." The cord is secured at L. 1 and encircles the cylinder an *even* number of times (two or more) before returning to the left rim. The second diagonal crosses the first diagonal an even number of times. (The smallest knot is 7L × 3B.)
1. Make a right diagonal and round pin 1. 2. Make a left diagonal and round pin 2. Lead is over and under. 3. Make a right diagonal and round pin 2. Lead is over and under. 4. Make a left diagonal and round pin 3. Over and under is contrary to adjacent parallel lead. 5. Make a right diagonal and round pin 3. Over and under is contrary to adjacent parallel lead. 6. Make a left diagonal and round pin 4, then bring ends together as in second diagram.

1339. Start "A." The cord encircles the cylinder an *odd* number of times (three or more) before returning to the left rim. The two diagonals are equal.
The second diagonal crosses the first diagonal an odd number of times. (The smallest knot is 10L × 3B.) 1. Make a right diagonal and round pin 6. 2. Make a left diagonal and round pin 2. Lead is over and under. 3. Make a right diagonal and round pin 7. Lead is contrary to parallel lead and alternately over and under. 4. Make a left diagonal and round pin 3. Over and under contrary to the parallel lead. 5. Make a right diagonal and round pin 8. Over and under contrary to parallel lead. 6. Make a left diagonal and round pin 4. Bring the ends together around the barrel.

1340. Start "B." The cord encircles the cylinder an *even* number of times (two or more) before returning to the left rim. The two diagonals are equal.
The second diagonal crosses the first diagonal an odd number of times. (The smallest knot is 5L × 3B.) 1. Make a right diagonal and round pin 1. 2. Make a left diagonal and round pin 12. Lead is over and under. 3. Make a right diagonal and round pin 12. Over and under contrary to parallel lead. 4. Make a left diagonal and round pin 11. Lead is first over, then contrary to the parallel lead. 5. Make a right diagonal and round pin 11. Lead is first over, then contrary to the parallel lead. 6. Make a left diagonal and round pin 10. Lead is over and under. Knot is complete at last crossing.

1341. Start "B." The cord encircles the cylinder an *odd* number of times before returning to left rim. The two diagonals are equal.
The second diagonal crosses the first diagonal an even number of times. (The smallest knot is 8L × 3B.) 1. Make a right diagonal and round pin 6. 2. Make a left diagonal and round pin 12. Lead is over and under, etc. 3. Make a right diagonal and round pin 5. Lead is under and over, etc. 4. Make a left diagonal and round pin 11. First over, then contrary to parallel lead. 5. Make a right diagonal and round pin 4. First under, then contrary to the parallel lead. 6. Make a left diagonal and round pin 10. Lead is over and under. Knot is complete at last crossing. To raise any of these THREE-BIGHT KNOTS to larger size: Continue to lay cord with over-and-under contrary to adjacent parallel lead. A new knot results each time the number of bights is odd. If the number of pins on the cylinder is equal to the number of bights desired for the completed knot, there will be less distortion than when there is a surplus of pins, and the knot will require less working. This is true of any TURK'S-HEAD. But a slight initial distortion is unimportant if it does not confuse the tier, as it disappears quickly when the knot is worked. The knots are doubled exactly as other regular OVER-AND-UNDER TURK'S-HEADS.

THE TURK'S-HEAD

TO RAISE NARROW TURK'S-HEADS IN WHICH THE NUMBER OF BIGHTS EXCEEDS THE NUMBER OF LEADS BY TWO OR MORE (WITH ONE EXCEPTION, 2L × 3B)

"Staggered" Pattern

Take a wooden cylinder four inches in diameter and twelve inches long, encircled with two rows of pins, the circles four inches apart, with 31 pins in each circle. Hold the cylinder across the knees with the cord secured at pin L. 1.

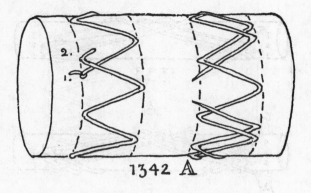

1342 A

General Directions for All Sizes

Lay the cord diagonally away from you and around a pin at the right rim. Continue to stagger your cord left and right any even number of diagonals (not less than four, and, for this apparatus, not more than sixteen). Round a pin at each rim, selecting pins that are equidistant from each other. When one circuit of the barrel has been made, the cord is led around either left pin 2 (Start "A") or left pin 31 (Start "B"). Thereafter continue to parallel the lead established until the TURK'S-HEAD is formed.

With four diagonals (Start "A"), start at left 1–9–17–25–2. The cord is led alternately from left side to right side but starts at left (1).
With four diagonals (Start "B"), left 1–9–16–24–31.
With six diagonals, left 1–6–11–16–21–26 (to 2 or 31).
With eight diagonals, left 1–5–9–13–17–21–25–28 (to 2 or 31).
With ten diagonals, left 1–4–7–10–13–16–19–22–25–28 (to 2 or 31).
With twelve diagonals, left 1–4–6–9–11–14–16–19–21–24–26–29 (to 2 or 31).
With fourteen diagonals, left 1–3–6–8–11–13–15–17–19–21–23–25–27–29 (to 2 or 31).
With sixteen diagonals, left 1–3–5–7–9–11–13–15–17–19–21–23–25–27–29 (to 2 or 31).

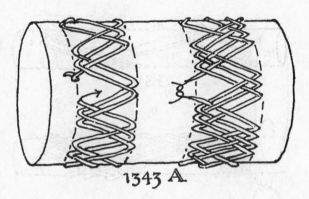

1343 A

If a barrel with a greater number of pins is used, more initial diagonals may be employed or the knots may be raised to larger sizes. There is no theoretical limit to the size. To arrange a larger knot: Divide the number of pins in one circle by the number of diagonals to be laid and advance between *two* diagonals (on one side) a number of pins equal to the whole number resulting from the division, disregarding all fractions.

Specific Directions for Tying Narrow Turk's-Heads

Start "A." With an even number of leads the smallest knot is 2L × 3B. Fasten cord to pin 1.

1342. Having reached left pin 2 by passing *over the first* lead beside left pin 1, continue with alternating under-and-over, etc., until a TWO-LEAD KNOT is complete.

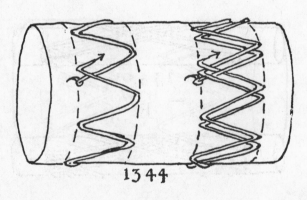

1344

A

1343. To raise KNOT #1342 continue with a lead contrary to the adjacent parallel lead.
With an odd number of leads the smallest knot is 3L × 5B.

1344. Having reached left pin 2 by passing over the first lead beside pin 1, the lead is *over* in the second circuit until, when approaching pin 3, the lead is already found established. Thereafter take all crossings contrary to the lead of the parallel cord. And if larger knots are required continue as already directed.
Start "B." With an even number of leads, the smallest knot is 2L × 5B.

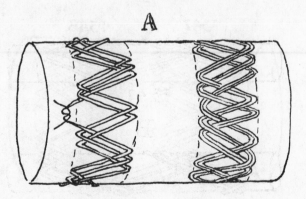

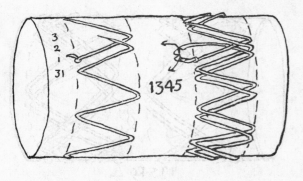

1345

B

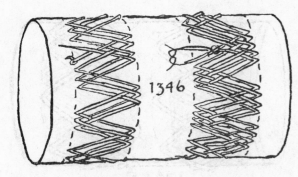

1346

B

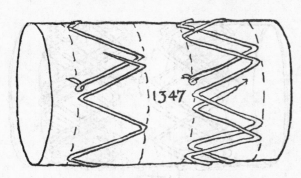

1347

B

1347   **1348**

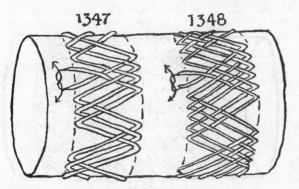

1345. Start at pin 1 and round pins in the same order as Knot ⌗1342 until the last, when pin 31 is rounded instead of 2.

Having completed the first circuit, tuck over and under until a Two-Lead Knot is completed.

1346. To raise ⌗1345 to a larger size continue with over-and-under contrary to the parallel lead.

With an odd number of leads, the smallest knot is 3L × 7B.

1347. Having rounded pin 31, continue *over* at all crossings until the second circuit is completed at pin 30. The following tuck is *over* and thereafter all crossings are contrary to the adjacent parallel lead.

1348. Raise to larger size by continuing with over-and-under contrary to the parallel lead.

All knots termed *even* are completed each time the number of leads is even; all knots termed *odd* are completed each time the number of leads is odd.

Condensed Directions for the Knots on This Page and the Preceding One

To make a Narrow Turk's-Head on a diagram consisting of a single staggered line:

If the number of leads is to be even, with either Start "A" or "B," the second circuit is alternately over and under. To raise such a knot to larger size, the over-and-under is contrary to the established parallel lead.

If the number of leads is to be odd, with either Start "A" or "B," all is over until two parallel leads are to be crossed. Cross these with over-and-under contrary to the established parallel lead. To raise such a knot to larger size, continue with alternate over-and-under.

A knot starting with an odd number of leads always raises to an odd number of leads. A knot starting with an even number of leads always raises to an even number of leads.

The three varieties of enlargement that have been given, Square, Wide and Narrow, are convenient and comparatively simple to work. There are, however, considerable gaps between these three in which lie knots of other proportions. The several methods that will now be given fit into these gaps, although they by no means fill them. They serve, however, to show that while it is possible to carry the method farther, it is scarcely practical. The method tends to become elaborate and involved, so that beyond these it will probably be found easier to tie absent knots by one of the several direct methods that are to be given.

A "DIAMOND PATTERN"

Between Square and Narrow Turk's-Heads

(Directions for knots with only three diagonals in each circuit)

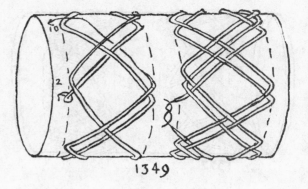
1349

1349. Start "A."
5L × 7B
9L × 13B
13L × 19B

With cord fastened to left pin 1, lead to R. 10, L. 20, R. 1, L. 10, R. 20, and then to L. 2.
The lead is *over* except where a parallel lead is established; there the over-and-under is contrary to the parallel lead.
The first knot is 5L × 7B, which raises to 9L × 13B, 13L × 19B, etc.

1350. Start "A."
3L × 4B
7L × 10B
11L × 16B

This is the same sequence of pins as ⚹1349 but at the end of the second circuit stick *under* the opposing lead when passing pin 1 before rounding pin L. 2. Thereafter the lead is alternately over and under until a 3L × 4B Turk's-Head is complete.
To raise this knot: Where the lead is not established, the first tuck is *under* at each rim; elsewhere tuck contrary to the parallel lead.

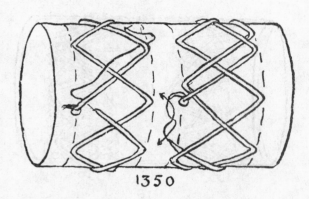
1350

1351. Start "B."
5L × 8B
9L × 14B
13L × 20B

Follow the same sequence of pins as above until, at the end of the second circuit, left pin 31 is rounded. Thereafter the lead is parallel and opposite to the established lead. The lead is over-all the first *three* circuits. Continue to cross *over* the first lead encountered after rounding each pin. All other crossings are contrary to the over-and-under established by the parallel lead.

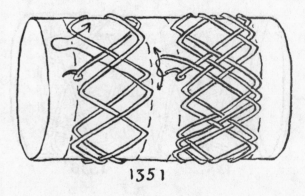
1351

1352. Start "B."
3L × 5B
7L × 11B
11L × 17B

Follow the same sequence of pins as above until the third circuit, which starts at 31 and continues *over* at center and *under* at rim and thereafter alternates over and under until a 3L × 5B knot is completed.
To raise this knot to larger dimensions stick *under* at the first crossing after rounding each pin. Elsewhere the over-and-under is contrary to the established parallel lead.

Following the same directions, with any of these four "starts" knots with any odd number of diagonals in the first circuit may be tied. At the end of the second circuit pass around either left pin 2 (which is Start "A") or around left pin 31 (which is Start "B"). In the first circuit take care that occupied pins are evenly spaced.

A STAGGERED "THREE-LINE PATTERN"

Between Square and Narrow Turk's-Heads

(Somewhat wider than the last)

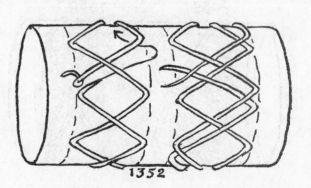
1352

In the next four knots, ⚹1353–56, the course of the cord for the three circuits that are required to establish the lead is as follows:

1–13–24–5–16–28–8–20–(2 for Start "A") (31 for Start "B")

Thereafter the cord is led parallel with the established lead. With Start "A" a knot is completed as ⚹1329; with Start "B" a knot is completed as ⚹1330.

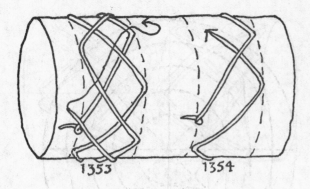

1353. Start "A." 3L × 4B. 7L × 9B. 13L × 17B. 19L × 25B.

The number of leads is odd. With the cord fast to left pin 1: The lead is over-all around the pins in the order given above (which is for three circuits) and continues over-all for one more circuit parallel to the established lead. After reaching pin 6 the lead is *over* at each crossing that is next to the rim and elsewhere the over-and-under lead is contrary to the adjacent parallel lead. To enlarge this knot continue to lay the cord parallel with the lead and with over-and-under contrary to the adjacent diagonal.

1354. Start "A." 4L × 5B. 10L × 13B. 16L × 21B. 22L × 29B.

The number of leads is even. The lead is over-all until, in second circuit, pin 5 is reached. Pass under between pins 5 and 16. Pass over between pins 16 and 28. Pass under, over between pins 28 and 8. Pass over, under between pins 8 and 20. Pass under, over, under between pins 20 and 2. Thereafter the lead is under at *left* rim and over at *right* rim. Elsewhere the lead is over and under, contrary to the adjacent parallel lead.

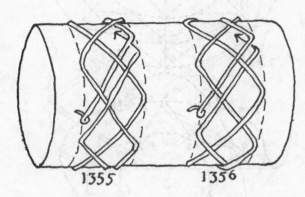

1355. Start "B." 5L × 7B. 11L × 15B. 17L × 23B. 23L × 31B.

The number of leads is odd. The lead is over-all until pin 31 is rounded. Thereafter the lead is under at each rim crossing and elsewhere the over-and-under is contrary to the parallel lead.

1356. Start "B." 2L × 3B. 8L × 11B. 14L × 19B. 20L × 27B.

The number of leads is even. The lead is over-all until pin 5 is reached. Pass under between pins 5 and 16. Pass over between pins 16 and 28. Pass under, over between pins 28 and 8. Pass over, under between pins 8 and 20. Pass under, over between pins 20 and 31. Thereafter the lead is under at the right rim and over at the left rim. Elsewhere the over-and-under is contrary to the parallel lead.

A STAGGERED "THREE-LINE PATTERN"

Between Square and Wide Turk's-Heads

In the next four knots the course of the cord, for the three circuits that are required to establish the lead, is as follows:
Secure the cord to left pin 1, and lead first to the right.

1–27–17–10–(2 for Start "A") (31 for Start "B")

Thereafter continue to lay the cord parallel to the adjacent lead and with the opposite over and under.

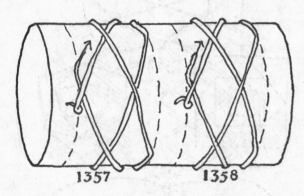

1357. Start "A." 8L × 5B. 14L × 9B. 20L × 13B. 26L × 17B.

With the lead as above. Between pins 1 and 27 over-all. Between pins 27 and 17 pass over. Between pins 17 and 10 pass under. Between pins 10 and 2 pass under, over, over. Continue with over-and-under contrary to parallel lead. At right rim tuck *under*, at left rim pass *over*.

1358. Start "A." 5L × 3B. 11L × 7B. 17L × 11B. 23L × 15B.

Between pins 1 and 27 over-all. Between pins 27 and 17 over. Between pins 17 and 10 over. Between pins 10 and 2 pass over, over, under. Continue with over-and-under contrary to established parallel lead. At right rim tuck *under*, at left rim tuck *under*.

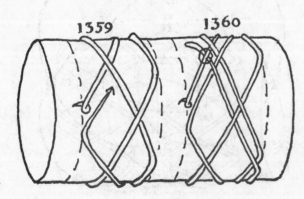

1359. Start "B." 7L × 5B. 13L × 9B. 19L × 13B. 25L × 17B. Between pins 1 and 27 over-all. Between pins 27 and 17 over-all. Between pins 17 and 10 pass over. Between pins 10 and 31 pass over, over. Continue with over-and-under contrary to the established parallel lead. The first crossing at both rims is *over*.

1360. Start "B." 4L × 3B. 10L × 7B. 16L × 11B. 22L × 15B. Between pins 1 and 27 over. Between pins 27 and 17 over. Between pins 17 and 10 under. Between pins 10 and 31 under, over. Continue with over-and-under contrary to established parallel lead. Crossings at the right rim are *over*. Crossings at the left rim are *under*. The illustration shows a completed 4L × 3B. TURK'S-HEAD. Continue as directed to complete a TURK'S-HEAD of 22L × 15B.

VARIOUS DIRECT METHODS FOR TYING TURK'S-HEADS

The Disk Method

1361. There are a number of direct ways by which TURK'S-HEADS that do not lend themselves readily to one of the "enlargement" methods that have been given, may be tied.

The projection of a TURK'S-HEAD on a plane has certain advantages. It is easy to plan, easy to form, and the whole knot is visible at all times. But it is not so easy to work as a TURK'S-HEAD that has been tied around a cylinder, as the knot is distorted by having one rim much larger than the other. This is not always important and there are certain complicated knots that can hardly be projected by another method. (See ✷1394 and ✷1395.) For regular knots, a large disk may be used with radiating lines and equispaced circles about the center and with pins at all crossings, around which different-sized TURK'S-HEADS may be tied. But the method is unwieldy. When a knot is to be tied on a plane surface, it will probably be found easier to make a diagram that agrees with the knot, such as the two which follow.

1362. Take a twenty-five-cent piece, place it in the center of a sheet of paper, and pencil a line around it. Divide the circumference with a pair of dividers into a number of parts equal to the intended number of bights.

Make a series of regular triangles around the outside of the circumference just made, using the ends of each arc to limit one side of each triangle. From each apex of these triangles, draw two divergent legs, each foot of which meets the foot of its neighbor. This completes a diagram for a THREE-LEAD TURK'S-HEAD. To make a wider TURK'S-HEAD, continue to add other legs in the same manner. When certain that the diagram consists of only one line (the number of bights and leads have no common divisor), you are ready to tie the knot. But if the diagram is found to consist of more than one line, add another tier of legs. Then, starting at the center, pin a cord along the line, repeating alternately at the crossings, "Over, under," etc., and tucking the end accordingly. Use a cork board and pin with large flat-headed tacks.

At every point on a diagram four lines meet, or else two lines cross, which is the same thing. To make a crossing with a cord at such a point, leave one line to the right, one line to the left, and follow along the line that remains, which is opposite the standing end.

When a knot has been tied it may be placed around a cylinder, doubled, and worked as already described. There will be considerable surplus material to be worked out of the rim before the knot takes a proper cylindrical form.

1363. Another and perhaps easier way to tie a knot on a disk is to use the system of notation that has been described in Chapter 1, as ✷128.

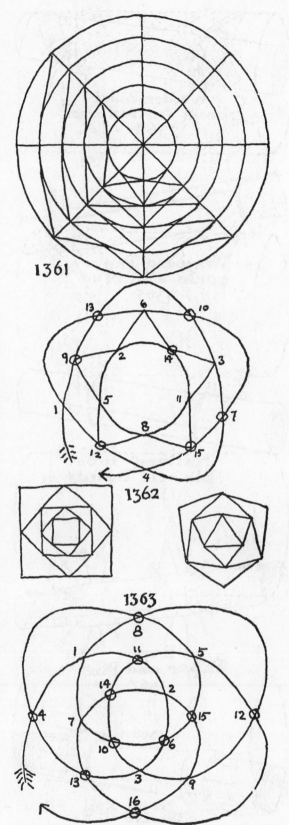

1361

1362

1363

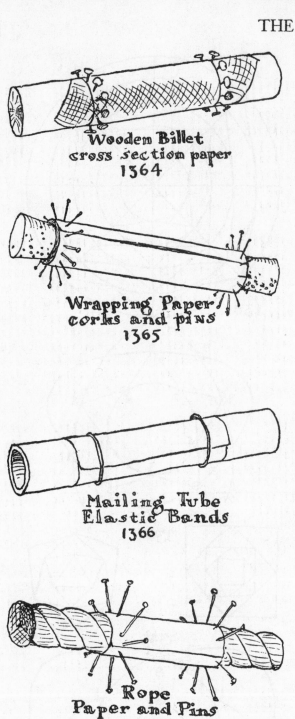

Wooden Billet
cross section paper
1364

Wrapping Paper
corks and pins
1365

Mailing Tube
Elastic Bands
1366

Rope
Paper and Pins
1367

1368

Metal Rail
adhesive Tape

"Cross-Section" Paper Method

1364. In tying large knots by any direct method, lines of some sort are wanted for guidance.

One effective way in which to tie a regular TURK'S-HEAD is to follow the guidelines on a sheet of cross-section paper which has been wrapped diagonally around a cylinder. If the scale is small, use only every second or every third line. The sole drawback to this method is the difficulty of making the two edges of the diagram coincide when brought together around the cylinder. It is rarely that a wooden cylinder or a mailing tube of precisely the right size is at hand.

1365. If the cylinder is a little too small, bind heavy paper tightly around it to bring it to the right size. If a wooden cylinder is too large, it may be planed down. If nothing is at hand approximating the required size, I have found it very convenient to begin by pasting the edges of the cross-section paper accurately together without support. After this make a tight roll of a number of thicknesses of heavy wrapping paper, slip the roll inside the cross-section paper cylinder and twist the inner roll open until it fits the cross-section paper snugly. Stick two cork stoppers tightly into the ends of the roll (which should be the width of the diagram). Finally stick tacks through the paper into the corks at every dotted bight of the diagram or, if preferred, at every crossing.

1366. If no cross-section paper is handy, wrap a blank sheet of paper around a mailing tube of any size and snap two elastic bands around it. Using the elastic bands as guides, draw two circles about the barrel to represent the rims of the knot and make an even row of dots around each line to indicate where the pins are to be. (An easy way to space these dots equally is given on page 256 of this chapter.) Remove the paper and draw a diagonal line in a 45-degree angle, away from you, from a left dot to a right one. In the same manner draw the other diagonals parallel with this one. Then start at any right point and make a left diagonal away from you to a left point, *crossing a number of lines that is one less than* the required number of leads. Draw other diagonals parallel with this one until the knot is complete. Replace the diagram, drive tacks and tie the knot.

1367. To make a large knot around a *rope*, wind several thicknesses of heavy paper around the rope with a diagram on the outside. Stick heavy pins through the paper, well into the rope. Stretch the rope between two belaying pins or other supports several feet apart. This will allow the rope to be twisted sufficiently so that every side of the knot may be worked with ease.

To tie a knot by this method: Secure an end of cord by thrusting it through the lay of the rope, to one side of the knot, and, starting at a left pin, lay it along the line of the diagram, rounding each pin as it is reached and tucking as already directed.

1368. If a knot is to be tied around a metal stanchion or rail, build up a shallow collar at either rim with a dozen or so turns of adhesive tape, and insert pins or brads between the layers of tape, as illustrated. After the knot is made and the pins are pulled out, the knot may be slipped to one side, the tape removed and the knot doubled or tripled. If the tape is put over a paper sleeve, the TURK'S-HEAD can be turned around the cylinder while being made, which is very helpful if the cylinder is fixed.

THE TURK'S-HEAD

FOUNDATION METHODS

1369. A *guide cord* or PILOT KNOT.

The proper number of pins for the knot should be placed in two rows around a wooden cylinder and a temporary structure of black linen thread laid around the pins, following the line of the projected TURK'S-HEAD, all crossings being *over*.

Tie an end of black linen thread to a left pin, lead it away in a right diagonal of 45 degrees and around a right pin. Next lead the thread in a left diagonal to a left pin. If the knot is to have eight leads, this should be the eighth left pin beyond the initial one. If the knot is to have eleven leads, it is the eleventh left pin, etc. Continue to lead the black thread parallel with the initial leads and, if the Law of the Common Divisor has not been violated, the two ends will meet when all the pins have been rounded.

Tie the final knot over the PILOT KNOT with other material, taking the crossings over one and under one.

1370. The "PERRY BASKET" was originated by Manuel Perry.

A FOOTROPE KNOT (#743) is tied with tarred codfish line, making a stiff basketlike structure. This knot is doubled and tripled with a single piece of other material, after which the initial basket is removed. The method is ingenious but the stiff basket is difficult to remove without capsizing the knot. The inventor found that his knots sometimes could not be made with a single cord, and he finally adopted the WIDE STANDING TURK'S-HEAD method (#1284) when he required a large knot. I was told that he always had started his BASKET with a CROWN AND WALL KNOT. If he had also employed a CROWN AND DIAMOND (#708), his difficulties would have been lessened. For with these two starts all possible ONE-STRAND TURK'S-HEADS can be formed.

1371. The *clue method* provides an accurate way to make a large knot.

Although it requires considerable preparation it is one of the easiest to tie. The pins having been arranged as usual, fasten a black linen thread to a left pin, and lead it away from you in a 45-degree angle to the right. Secure it with a SINGLE HITCH to a convenient right pin and cut off the end at two and a half times the length of the diagonal. Tie another end to the next left pin and lay a second cord parallel with the first, securing the end and cutting it off in the same manner as before. Repeat until all pins are occupied with a series of right diagonals.

Take any one of the long ends, round the right pin, and *tuck* it, *once only*, away from you and to the left. If the number of *leads* is to be odd, this tuck is *over* the first contrary strand, and *under* the second; but if the number of leads is to be even, the first tuck is *under* the *first* contrary strand. Having tucked an end once only, proceed to tuck each of the other ends in the same manner, until all have been tucked, thereby forming a tier of single tucks; then tuck each strand again, over and under, and continue to repeat, one tier at a time, until the number of strands *crossed* by one thread is one less than the number of leads that is planned. Then tie each end to its proper left pin.

To tie the permanent knot on this foundation: Take a single cord of different material, middle it and tie the *center* temporarily to a left pin. Follow the lead established by the clue until the cord has been doubled or tripled, using both ends of the cord as needed. Then remove the pins and the original thread, cutting the clue with scissors wherever necessary. Work the knot taut.

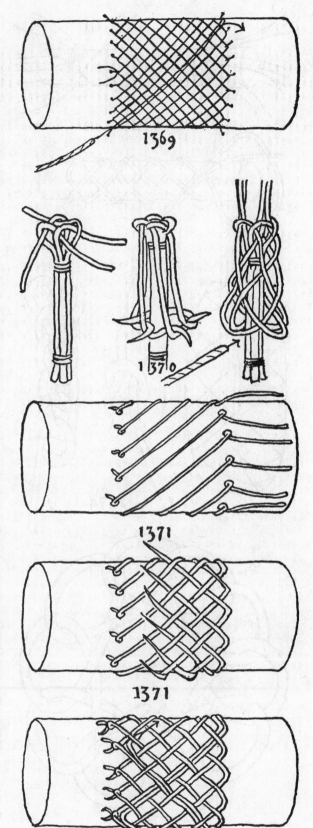

1369

1370

1371

1371

[245]

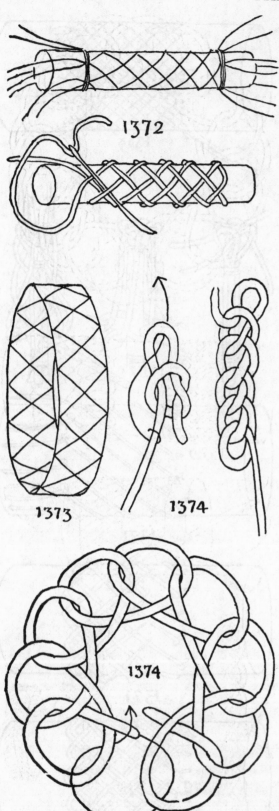

1372

1373

1374

1374

TO TIE A WIDE KNOT

1372. If an exceptionally wide TURK's-HEAD with a small number of bights is to be tied, a *foundation* of cross grafting (ROUND SINNET) will provide an even knot requiring little adjustment before working.

To tie: Middle and seize an even number of strands around the cylinder (not too many, if the knot is to be doubled). Form a MULTI-STRAND KNOT of the projected size exactly as described under cross grafting (#2677). When this FOUNDATION KNOT is complete, tuck all ends back into the structure, count the leads carefully and compare with the number of bights (each strand makes one bight) in deference to the Law of the Common Divisor. When satisfied, introduce a long single cord and double the knot before removing the grafting foundation. Continue to follow the lay until the cylinder is covered.

Each of the methods that has been given has its individual merit and the reader may find one among them more to his liking than another.

Except in a few cases under COACHWHIPPING and grafting, the discussion so far has been limited to a straight alternating over-one-and-under-one lead, which results in a woven surface that is ordinarily termed "basket weave." This has been doubled or tripled to make a weave resembling the textile fabric called monk's cloth.

Any section of an ordinary TURK's-HEAD, before doubling, is identical with FRENCH SINNET. There appeared to be no reason why other sinnets, made in circular or wreath form, should not fall under the definition of TURK's-HEAD, and there is probably no sinnet that cannot be made in such a form. A sinnet in which the various strands helix independently in different cycles will, of course, require more than one cord. But most sinnets of practicable size can be arranged to require not more than two cords.

1373. Paper, straw and other flat material may be turned over at each rim where a round cord is always *slued*. This results in a TURK's-HEAD with a straight edge, while round cord gives a scalloped edge.

CHAIN SINNET TURK's-HEADS

1374. Any of the CHAIN SINNETS may easily be made into TURK's-HEADS by making a section in hand in the usual way (see Chapter 37), and then relaying one end back into the other end. The cords may be joined on the underside by bringing them together and putting a CONSTRICTOR KNOT (#1249) of waxed sail twine around them, but sewing the ends together will be better. The example given on this page is common MONKEY CHAIN, which is a crochet stitch that is sometimes called SINGLE TRUMPET CORD.

1375. The illustration shows a DOUBLE TRUMPET CORD TURK's-HEAD and the way in which the two ends are joined. The sinnet on which it is based is #2870.

1376. The FIGURE-EIGHT CHAIN is joined in the same manner, using a needle. The knot may be doubled if wished.

1377. A DOUBLE FIGURE-EIGHT CHAIN TURK's-HEAD offers no difficulties. The crossings are taken with alternate over-and-under.

1378. NETTING-NEEDLE SINNET (#2943, #2944, and #2945) is the basis for this TURK's-HEAD, but there is little resemblance between them, for there is so much torsion in the sinnet that it is perfectly round in cross section while in the TURK's-HEAD the sinnet is held flat. The knot is very handsome when made with a "patent-leather" thong, the grain of the leather being always outermost.

FLAT SINNET TURK'S-HEADS

An ordinary THREE-LEAD TURK'S-HEAD may have its width raised to five or seven leads, and the over-and-under sequence tucked, so that it resembles FLAT SINNET #2967. The final sequence of the lead is over two and under two for a FIVE-LEAD KNOT and over three and under three for a SEVEN-LEAD KNOT. If made very carefully, even nine leads, which is over four and under four, may be successfully worked, but beyond this the TURK'S-HEAD is flimsy.

These knots are made in hand without the use of a cylinder. To tie: Take a piece of cord about five feet long, middle the cord and tie a TURK'S-HEAD in one end. Make either #1305, a 3L × 4B, or #1306, a 3L × 5B TURK'S-HEAD.

After the single TURK'S-HEAD is made, at each tuck either to left or right, stick the end down at the center beside the first lead which is being paralleled, until the end is about to cross a doubled strand at the center; there the end is stuck down between the two lays.

When the standing end is passed a second time it should be passed with either Start "A" or "B," in whichever way it was passed the first time.

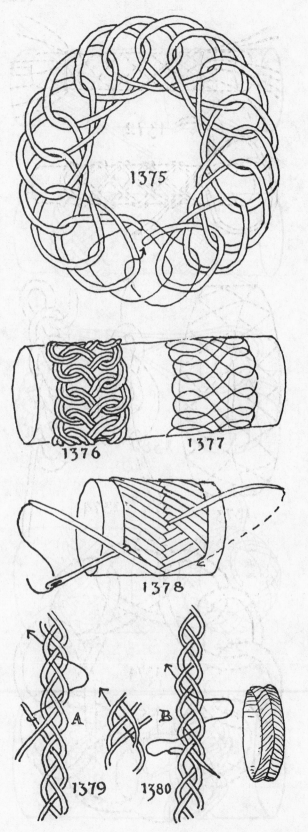

TO MAKE A FLAT SINNET TURK'S-HEAD
Starting with a Regular 3L × 4B Turk's-Head

1379. Start "A."
Cross the working end under the standing end as shown.
1. Tuck to right over one and under two and continue over one and under two until four leads are met at the end of the circuit.
2. Then tuck over two and under two until five leads are met (second diagram). To enlarge this:
3. Then tuck over three and under two until six leads are met.
4. Then tuck over three and under three until the end, which makes a 7L × 9B FLAT SINNET TURK'S-HEAD.

With a 3L × 5B Turk's-Head for a Base
Start "A."
1. Tuck right over one and under two until four leads are met.
2. Tuck over two and under two until five leads are met, which makes a 5L × 8B FLAT SINNET TURK'S-HEAD. To enlarge this:
3. Continue over two and under three until six leads are met.
4. Then over three and under three until seven leads are met, which makes a 7L × 11B FLAT SINNET TURK'S-HEAD.

With a 3L × 4B Turk's-Head for a Base
1380. Start "B."
1. Tuck over two and under one until four leads are met.
2. Tuck over two and under two until five leads are met, which makes a 5L × 7B FLAT SINNET TURK'S-HEAD. To enlarge this:
Continue to right.
3. Tuck over three and under two until six leads are met.
4. Tuck over three and under three until seven leads are met, which makes a 7L × 10B FLAT SINNET TURK'S-HEAD.

With a 3L × 5B Turk's-Head for a Base
Start "B."
1. Tuck right over two and under one until four leads are met.
2. Tuck over two and under two until five leads are met.
3. Tuck over two and under three until six leads are met.
4. Tuck over three and under three until seven leads are met, which makes a 7L × 12B FLAT SINNET TURK'S-HEAD.

HERRINGBONE WEAVE

1381. The four SQUARE TURK'S-HEADS of page 236 lend themselves readily to different weaves, of which over-two-and-under-two and over-three-and-under-three are the simplest. The knots are tied on the barrel in much the same manner that has been described already for KNOTS ✻1325–28. With an over-two-under-two lead, a knot is completed each time four bights are added to each rim, and with over-three-under-three, a knot is completed each time six bights are added to each rim.

To tie an "OVER-TWO-UNDER-TWO" KNOT: Start as in first diagram in KNOT ✻1325. Take all crossings *over* until three *parallel* leads are encountered. Tuck *under* the first one in each group of three, until a group of four parallel leads is met. Thereafter tuck over two and under two. A knot is completed at any time when the lead runs over-two-under-two throughout. Then tie the two ends together.

To tie an "OVER-THREE-UNDER-THREE" KNOT: When the knot has progressed as far as the first diagram, make one more circuit *over-all*. When four parallel leads are encountered, tuck under the first one of them; when five parallel leads are encountered, tuck under the first two of them; and when six parallel leads are encountered, tuck under the first three of them and over the second three. When completing the knot, butt the ends together as in ✻1329 and ✻1330, and withdraw them into the middle of the knot without "doubling."

A ROUND SINNET TURK'S-HEAD

1382. TURK'S-HEADS of FRENCH SINNET, CHAIN SINNET and FLAT SINNET have been shown, and only SOLID SINNETS have been left unconsidered. The first attempted was the ROUND SINNET of six strands, which makes a TURK'S-HEAD of two cords. A working drawing was made in circular form, with strands widely separated so that all crossings were clearly depicted. This proved feasible, but a more practical method suggested itself. A very loose grommet (✻2864) was made. Into this the ends of three shoestrings were tucked over and under, exactly as in short splicing, until they encircled the grommet, after making the same number of turns but in the opposite direction as the banding. Opposite ends were then knotted together, taking care that two ends of the same string were not bent together. The shoestrings serve merely as a clue. Next untie one of the three knots and replace the shoestrings with a long cord of the same material as the grommet. Double the knot that has been made, using a wire needle. Half knot, and "bury" opposing ends as in LONG SPLICING ✻2697.

A core consisting of an ordinary grommet (✻2864) is advisable, if the knot is to be doubled or tripled.

1383. To make a TURK'S-HEAD employing a *continuous length* of THREE-STRAND FLAT SINNET for the basic material: First form an ordinary THREE-LEAD TURK'S-HEAD (✻1306) and double it, leaving one long end. With this end and the two parallel leads already established proceed to plat a THREE-STRAND FLAT SINNET in the ordinary way (✻1315 and ✻1316) but following the line of the TURK'S-HEAD that has been formed.

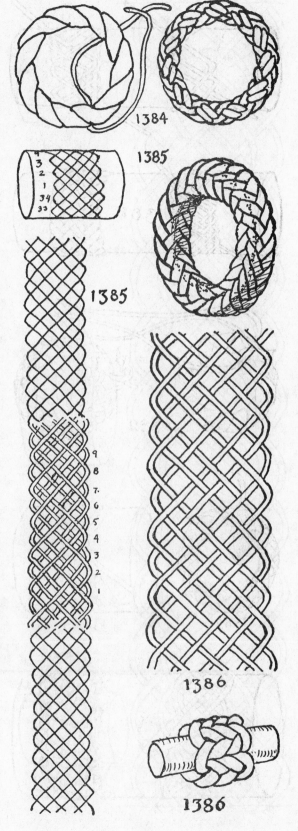

As it stands this knot has no particular charm or use and is generally regarded as a "trick knot" but it may now be redoubled by following its nine leads, in the ordinary manner of doubling Turk's-Heads (#1311), or it may be made into a Five-Lead Flat Sinnet, as pictured in the last diagram, by following the directions given for #1379 and #1380.

1384. A *grommet of four strands* is tied in much the same way as #1382 and may be doubled in the ordinary way. If tripled, this will need a core, for which purpose a small ordinary grommet (#2864) will serve. This makes an excellent *deck tennis ring*, preferable to the commercial rubber variety since it is much kinder to the fingernails, and it also has a better grip than the ordinary rope grommet.

The Four-Strand Round Sinnet Turk's-Head, tied with rawhide thongs, shoestrings or belt laces, makes an excellent *slipover dog collar*.

A TURK'S-HEAD OF SQUARE SINNET

1385. Square Sinnet can also be made into Turk's-Head form by the grommet method, but I will give a "cross-section" or "plotting-paper" diagram for tying it, the projection of which provides an interesting problem and also serves to familiarize the method by which several knots that are to follow are projected. There are two cycles in this knot, requiring two cords.

Drive two evenly spaced rows of pins four inches apart around a wooden barrel, with thirty-four numbered pins in each row. Make a Guide Knot of eight leads. To do this: Secure a black linen thread to left pin 1 and progress in the following order from rim to rim: 1, 4, 9, 12, 17, 20, 25, 28, 33 and thereafter parallel to the established lead until half the pins are occupied and the cord has returned to left pin 1. All the crossings are *over*.

Then tie another piece of thread to left pin 2 and complete the other half of the Guide Knot in the same manner, all crossings having been over.

Secure the permanent cord to left pin 1 and follow the lead of the pilot thread.

All right diagonals are *over*-all.

All left diagonals are *under*-all.

Finally knot the two ends together, which completes the first cycle.

Secure another permanent cord to left pin 2 and follow the pilot thread.

All right diagonals are under four, over one, under one, over one. (Count the leads of the pilot thread but do not tuck under them.)

All left diagonals are over four, under one, over one, under one. (Count the leads of the pilot threads but do not tuck under them.)

Each pair of ends is half knotted under opposing parts.

A FLAT KNOT WITH A DOUBLED EDGE

1386. Make a Guide Knot (#1369) of eight leads and ten bights. This being done, follow carefully with one cord the sequence shown in the diagram. Draw up snugly around a cylinder.

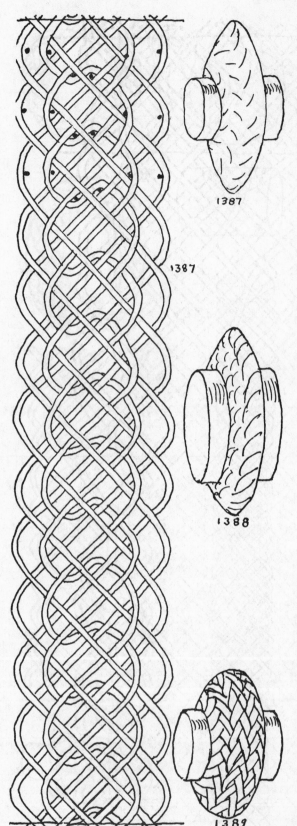

1387

'1387

1388

1389

SOLID TRIANGULAR TURK'S-HEADS

The next three knots, based on original SOLID SINNETS, have a complexity not to be found in the other TURK'S-HEAD diagrams. All the lines in the three diagrams do not progress at the same rate around the cylinder or barrel; in places they cross and recross each other. This makes it necessary to place pins in the central part of the diagrams, between the rims.

A Triangular Turk's-Head of Nine Leads and Two Strands Based on Sinnet #3028

1387. Make a single-line copy of the diagram by tracing, photostating, or otherwise.

Take a barrel of the right size (build up by wrapping with adhesive paper if necessary).

Drive pins at the rims and at other places indicated by dots.

Tie the knot by following the over-and-under of the diagram. There are two circuits and two cords required. When tied, half knot opposite ends and bury them carefully before working the knot, which may either be removed to a smaller cylinder or else drawn up in hand.

A Triangular Turk's-Head of Thirteen Leads

1388. The diagram given here represents one half the actual length of the knot. Two tracings of it must be made, each exactly abutting the other, so that all lines lie fair. A fireplace log slightly under five and a half inches in diameter will do for a barrel and 180 pins are required. No one is advised to attempt this who does not take his knots seriously.

A HALF ROUND TURK'S-HEAD OF SEVENTEEN LEADS BASED ON SINNET #3054

1389. If you have successfully made the previous TURK'S-HEAD this one holds no new problem, but it will take longer to tie and to work. Both concentration and patience will be required. Tie with banding, not with a twisted cord, as the torsion of the latter is bound to prove bothersome.

Do not allow yourself to become distracted; mere size is nothing to be afraid of. If you can tie one knot, you can tie another. Do one thing at a time and take plenty of time. Stop now and then to search for errors. It is better to work deliberately than to make false starts and have to undo and repeat. If you find an error after finishing, consider KNOT #127 before deciding to start afresh.

If a knot becomes too tight for inserting the flexible wire needle (#99), open with a pricker and pull the cord through with a loop buttoner (#99C). A hairpin will serve. An upholsterer's needle is also an excellent tool for small cords, if the point has first been dulled and smoothed with a file and emery cloth.

With small cord a knot is sometimes worked snug before adding the final doubling. This is then put in with a sail needle.

If a particularly tight knot is wanted use a pair of long-jawed pliers for the final pulling. Grip the cord close to the knot and with a rolling motion tighten each part in turn, being careful to exert an even pull throughout the knot.

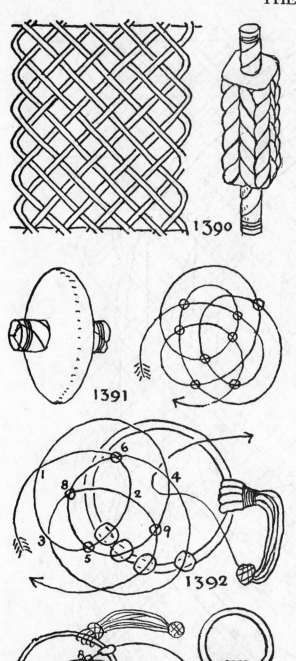

A TURK'S-HEAD OF ELEVEN LEADS WITH SQUARE CROSS SECTION TIED WITH ONE CORD

1390. This TURK'S-HEAD is based on a sinnet similar to the one from which ⚹1386 was evolved. Make a GUIDE KNOT of eleven leads and six bights (six tacks or pins around the barrel). The sequence in the right diagonals is over one, under two, and in the left diagonals, under one, over two. But the diagram is required to guide the start of each diagonal.

The knot should be worked around a rope or other cylinder of about twice the diameter of the cord that is used for the TURK'S-HEAD. Mold the knot into a square shape and pound it, if necessary, with a mallet. Draw up, sink the ends, and trim them off.

A HALF ROUND TURK'S-HEAD

1391. The objection to many of the SOLID SINNETS that are applied to TURK'S-HEAD forms is that they bulk too large around the inner circumference, which causes a crowding there, and there is also a stretching around the outer circumference. The sample given here makes a very nice HALF ROUND TURK'S-HEAD, which does not have this tendency. It is based on SINGLE-STRAND BUTTON diagram ⚹643. The lay may be doubled, in which case a small STANDING TURK'S-HEAD or a small MOUSE may be used as a core. Besides rendering the knot firmer, this will make it more secure. Although much simpler than ⚹1389, this makes quite as effective a HALF ROUND KNOT.

A TENNIS BAG LANYARD KNOT

1392. This was made to secure a lanyard to the iron ring of a netted tennis-ball bag (⚹3811). The knot is formed through the ring, after which the lanyard and net are rove through one of the compartments. It is here tied by the disk method as a comparatively simple introduction to several more elaborate knots which follow.

Pin the cord at 1 and tuck the end *underneath* wherever the cord crosses itself at a point that is marked with a *circle*. In this case the metal ring is also marked with circles and the end is tucked under the ring wherever it is so marked. When the knot is complete, reeve the lanyard and net through the compartment indicated by the arrow and draw it snug.

1393. It seemed probable that a knot which formed a collar around the neck of the lanyard might be more practical for the purpose than the last.

An ordinary 5L × 4B TURK'S-HEAD was selected, but this was tied *on end*, and the ring passed through opposite side compartments instead of through the end compartments of the knot. Another knot, somewhat in the shape of the letter T, was the next TURK'S-HEAD to be tied.

1394. To tie the letter T: Pin the cord at 1, then follow the line, pinning at 2, 3, 4, 5, etc., and tucking underneath wherever a circle is passed *in regular numerical sequence*.

The first T that was made proved unnecessarily large and the crossbar of the T was of greater diameter than the standard.

A later trial resulted in the present knot, which corrected these faults, but is much too large for the purpose for which ⚹1392 and ⚹1393 were used.

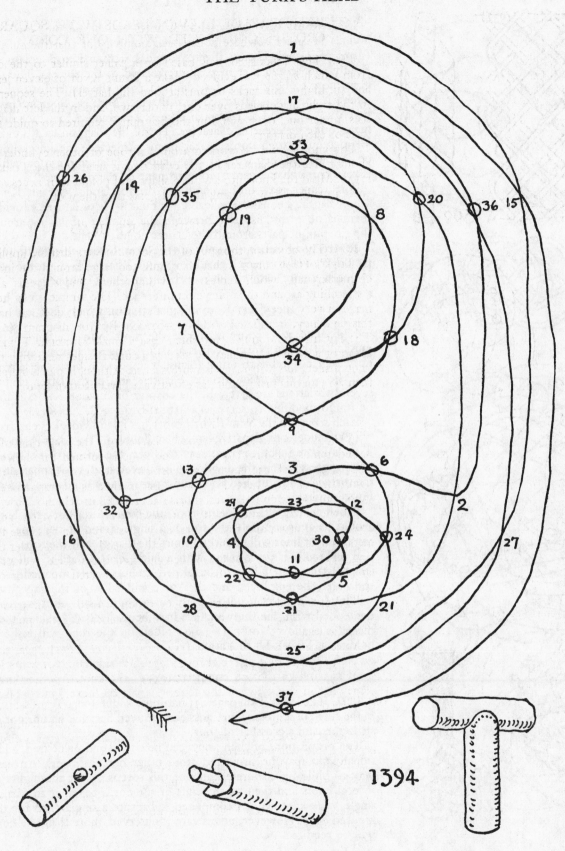

1394

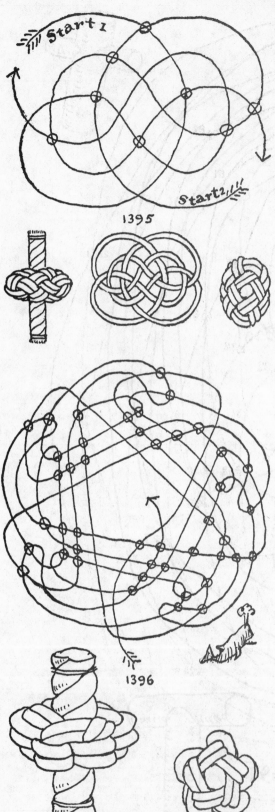

1395

1396

1395. It has been shown how sinnets can be adapted to form Turk's-Heads. Elsewhere it has been pointed out that the simpler forms of Turk's-Heads, Buttons, and Lanyard Knots are superficially similar and that they all are related to the sinnets. The diagram now to be given is far removed from the sinnet form. Elsewhere it appears as Multi-Strand Button ⚹922, as Single-Strand Button ⚹617, and as Lanyard Knots ⚹770 and ⚹772, each form being quite different in character. To tie the diagram as a Turk's-Head requires two cords. After being projected, the knot should be doubled and then worked very deliberately around a rope, which is rove through the center compartment of the diagram.

The reader may find among the Button and Lanyard Knots other diagrams equally applicable to Turk's-Head Knots, provided there is no great disparity between the number of bights around the rim and of parts around the center compartment.

Before tying either this knot, or the Star Knot which follows, it would be well to place a small Standing Turk's-Head on the rope to act as a core with which to prevent the knot's slipping.

THE STAR KNOT TURK'S-HEAD

1396. The Star Knot is one of the most individual and distinguished of knots. Normally it is a Multi-Strand Stopper, and it is not easily adaptable to other forms. It appears in both the lanyard and the Multi-Strand Button chapters and in the latter chapter several variations are given. In the chapter on Shroud Knots it may be found modified to serve as a Multi-Strand Bend (⚹1582).

Each strand in the Star Knot proper has its individual cycle, from which it does not depart even when doubled. To adapt it to the Turk's-Head form it is necessary to divert the line so that the cord will progress around the diagram. The altered lead is not apparent on the surface of the finished knot, and a particularly handsome Turk's-Head results.

If tied around a three-strand rope, the material for the Star Knot should be approximately the size of a single strand of the rope, and the resultant knot will be several times the diameter of the rope.

If a Turk's-Head is made with a fairly elastic cord it will constrict better. But if it is to be placed around a soft rope, stiff material may be employed and the "give and take" of the rope itself will hold it in place. If both a shiny surface and a stiff cord are to be contended with, the shiny surface may be shellacked. Lacking these means, a shallow Mouse (⚹3499) raised on the rope will assist in holding a Turk's-Head stationary.

THE CROSS

1397. The letter T on page 253 naturally suggested a Turk's-Head in the form of a cross. The Cross that is given here has an upright of six bights and a crossbar of four.

The proportions of such knots can be varied and, if desired, additional arms may be projected from other compartments. An easy way to build up elaborate knots of this sort is to cut the bights of several knots and then tie the ends of the cords together to form a single large knot. When completed, substitute a single cord for the knotted cord. However, unless care is observed, more than one cord will be required.

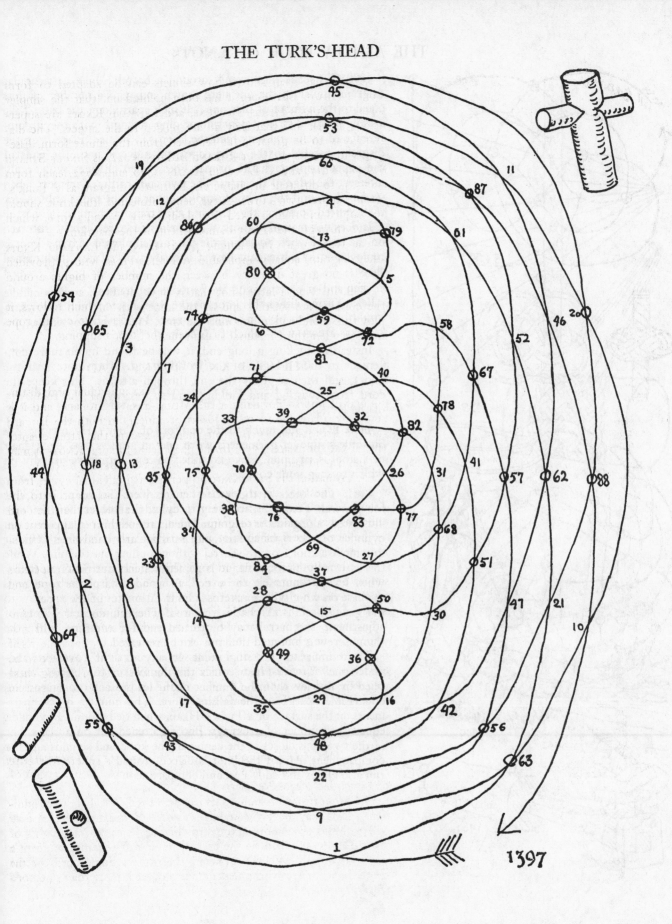

1397

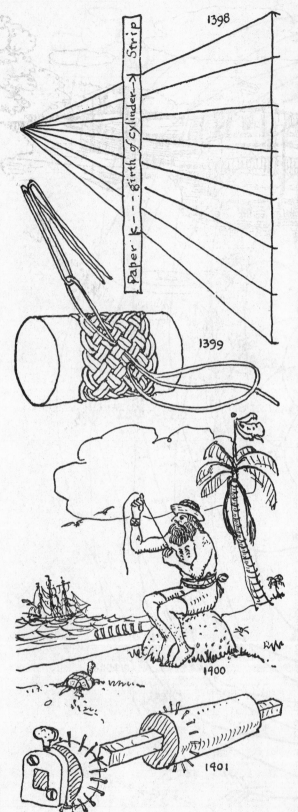

1398. To space pins evenly around a barrel: Make a triangular diagram similar to the one here shown and with a number of dots equal to the number of pins one half inch apart along the base. Take a straight-edged strip of paper coinciding in length with the circumference of the barrel on which the knot is to be tied. Place it on the diagram, parallel to the right edge, and move it until the ends of the paper strip touch the proper lines, when all lines will evenly intersect the edge of the strip. The two ends of the strip meet when wrapped around the cylinder and so count as one point only. Mark the required points on the strip and then transfer them to the barrel.

It does not matter if knots, while being tied, are slightly distorted on the barrel when not all of the pins are employed. After a knot is removed to its permanent base it is easily worked into its intended shape.

1399. In tying a large knot that is to be doubled, always middle the cord before starting and tie the knot with one end only. Employ the second end in doubling the knot. This saves dragging an unnecessary length of material at each tuck.

Instead of tucking a long end, it will be found much more convenient to tuck a bight of the working end (from quite near the knot), and then to draw the end through after it. This keeps the cord from twisting and kinking, and so destroying the regularity of the lay.

1400. It will add much to the comfort of Turk's-Head tying if a buttonless slipover garment is worn and an armless bow-back chair or a stool is sat upon. Have no other piece of furniture near by on which to snag your cord.

1401. The knots of the last few pages were tied on a board, but for general Turk's-Head tying a cylindrical object of the sort illustrated alongside is recommended, although a plain wooden cylinder of the right size is quite satisfactory. It is often difficult to remove a knot from the barrel without pulling out the pins. While this is usually practicable, it is sometimes inconvenient, especially when several knots are to be tied. A wooden carpenter's gauge is the base on which the apparatus is built. A long cylinder to screw to the gauge head is all that is required. The thumbscrew allows of adjustment, the barrel may be turned end for end, and when the thumbscrew is loosened the knot can be removed.

The number of crossing points in any straight "over-one-and-under-one" Turk's-Head equals the number of the bights, multiplied by one less than the number of the leads. Each crossing makes one visible "part" on the finished knot. The number of compartments on the surface of a Turk's-Head, when tied around a cylinder, equals the number of crossings. But if flattened out on a plane, one of the two rims closes at the center of the knot, and so adds another compartment. And if the knot is placed around a sphere, the outer rim also closes and adds a second compartment.

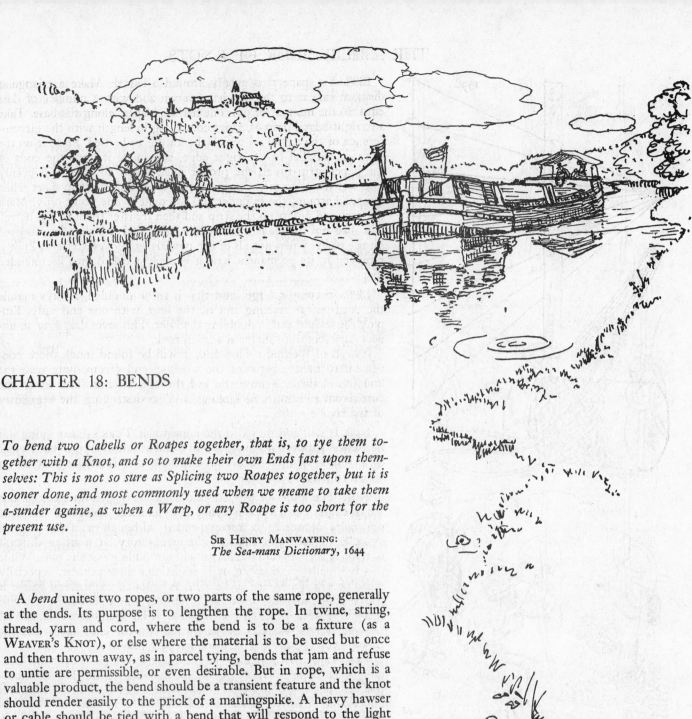

CHAPTER 18: BENDS

*To bend two Cabells or Roapes together, that is, to tye them to-
gether with a Knot, and so to make their own Ends fast upon themselves: This is not so sure as Splicing two Roapes together, but it is
sooner done, and most commonly used when we meane to take them
a-sunder againe, as when a Warp, or any Roape is too short for the
present use.*

SIR HENRY MANWAYRING:
The Sea-mans Dictionary, 1644

A *bend* unites two ropes, or two parts of the same rope, generally
at the ends. Its purpose is to lengthen the rope. In twine, string,
thread, yarn and cord, where the bend is to be a fixture (as a
WEAVER'S KNOT), or else where the material is to be used but once
and then thrown away, as in parcel tying, bends that jam and refuse
to untie are permissible, or even desirable. But in rope, which is a
valuable product, the bend should be a transient feature and the knot
should render easily to the prick of a marlingspike. A heavy hawser
or cable should be tied with a bend that will respond to the light
tapping of a mallet or fid. In such material a marlingspike should be
employed only as a last resort for, once abraded, the life of a rope
is short. The larger the rope, the easier the bend should open.

Unless particularly advised, no bend is recommended for use
except with two ends of identical material. Bends in which one rope
is larger, stiffer or smoother than the other are not to be trusted
unless they have been selected to meet these particular conditions.

Bends for tying two ends of different characteristics may partake
somewhat of the nature of a hitch, since one rope is more active than
the other. In the chapter on hitches for lengthwise pull will be
found additional knots for bending small ropes to large ones, which
can be considered as either bends or hitches.

A wet rope is both stronger and more slippery than a dry one.
This is a point to be considered when tying hawsers and cable.

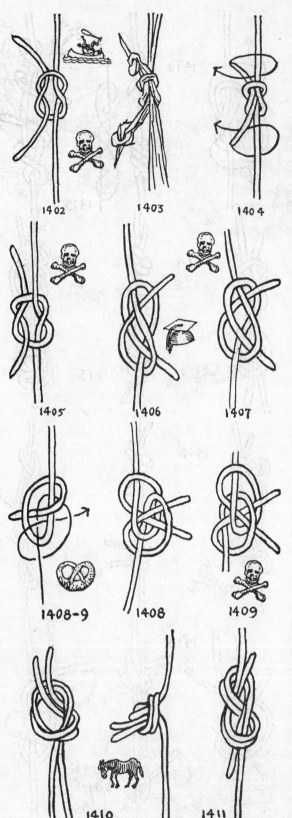

1402   1403   1404

1405   1406   1407

1408-9   1408   1409

1410   1411

Bends in general should be regarded as temporary expedients. Where something permanent is required, SHROUD KNOTS and LONG and SHORT SPLICES are used. These are MULTI-STRAND BENDS, which are dealt with in separate chapters.

1402. The REEF or SQUARE KNOT is a true BINDER KNOT (Chapter 16), for which purpose it is admirable, but under no circumstance should it be used as a bend. If tied with two ends of unequal size, or if one end is stiffer or more slippery than the other, it is bound to spill. Unfortunately it is about the most easily remembered knot there is, and the uninitiated commonly employ it as a bend. *There have probably been more lives lost as a result of using a SQUARE KNOT as a bend (to tie two ropes together) than from the failure of any other half dozen knots combined.* This was stated in the first chapter and may be repeated again. In fact it is the ease with which the knot may be spilled that gives it its value as a REEF KNOT.

1403. The SHEET KNOT is a means of knotting strips of sheeting and blanketing if a quick exit from a second-story window is imperative. With OVERHAND KNOTS added in this way, the REEF KNOT becomes secure.

1404. Another bend from a REEF KNOT. This method of half hitching the ends has been used on WEAVER'S KNOTS but is unnecessarily cumbersome.

1405. The GRANNY is another questionable knot that is often tied as a bend. Its use is inexcusable but it is hardly so bad for the purpose as the REEF KNOT, for although it will slip, it does not have the same tendency to capsize and spill.

1406. The WHATNOT (1). There is little danger of anyone ever tying this knot by mistake: the method is too unhandy. It really belongs among the "trick knots" of Chapter 33. With the ends arranged as shown, it is a more secure bend than many far more trustworthy knots.

1407. The WHATNOT (2). With the ends twisted as given here, the WHATNOT is the most insecure bend there is. At all times it is quite unpredictable.

1408. Here is another bend with the same untrustworthy features as the "WHATNOT," yet in the form shown here it ranks among the securest bends known.

1409. But in this second form it is one of the least secure knots known, its only rival being the WHATNOT. The change from one of its forms to the other may occur accidentally or intentionally. So the knot is quite untrustworthy.

1410. The OVERHAND BEND, also called THUMB KNOT and (by Bowling) OPENHAND KNOT, ranks higher than the SHEET BEND in security but is among the weakest of the bends. It is used in joining the ends of rope yarns by which hams, bacon, and bananas are hung, and it is also the knot tied by a mechanical binder.

1411. The FLEMISH BEND, also called FIGURE-EIGHT BEND, is often given in knot monographs but is seldom used. It is bulky and bothersome to tie, and not to be preferred to the following knot, which is made in a similar manner.

1412. This bend is called the RING KNOT in Hutton's Dictionary of 1815. At an earlier date Izaak Walton calls it the WATER KNOT, and Dr. Holden, in *Streamcraft* (1919), follows the latter authority. But as there are several other WATER KNOTS the name RING KNOT is perhaps preferable.

It is also known as the GUT KNOT.

The RING KNOT is an excellent bend for wet gut. It may be tied in the way illustrated here or a SINGLE OVERHAND KNOT may be put in one of the two ends and then the other end "backed" for the length of the first knot.

1413. The BARREL KNOT, called BLOOD KNOT by Keith Rollo, is the best bend there is for small, stiff or slippery line. The ends may be trimmed short and the knot offers the least resistance possible when drawn through water. It is sometimes tied with additional turns, which are unnecessary unless the material is piano wire. Sometimes it is tied with opposite twists, or with ends leading from opposite sides, none of which is an improvement. Before tying piano wires, shellac and dry them. Even then the chances of success are relatively small.

1414. WATER KNOT, also called WATERMAN'S, ENGLISH, ENGLISHMAN'S, FISHERMAN'S, TRUE-LOVER'S and ANGLER'S KNOT. Hutton (1815) calls it WATER KNOT. It is very strong and one of the commonest of bends employed by anglers, but it is needlessly bulky.

1415. GRAPEVINE KNOT, also called DOUBLE ENGLISH KNOT. This is used by anglers in knotting horsehair and gut. If the latter is well frayed the DOUBLE KNOT does not bulk objectionably.

1416. This DOUBLE FIGURE-EIGHT BEND is of interest because both faces present the same appearance, which is identical with one of the faces of the WATER KNOT (#1414).

1417. This bend, based on the TIMBER HITCH, is strong and secure. Moreover it may be tied successfully in galvanized iron and copper wire.

1418. The WEAVER'S KNOT is the simplest way in which the SHEET BEND may be tied in yarn and twine. It is employed for joining threads that have parted in the loom, and it has been known and used for this purpose the world over for as long as there is record. It is not recommended for stiff material that is to be in constant use, as it may spill on occasion. For ordinary purposes where a safe knot is required, #1474, which does not spill, is preferable.

1419. A WEAVER'S KNOT that is closely related to the REEF KNOT was shown to me by Charles R. Gidley. Both ends tend to lie in the same direction, which allows the knot to pass through the reeds easily.

WEAVER'S KNOTS are bends that are designed to be permanently tied in small material. There are four pages of WEAVER'S KNOTS near the end of Chapter 2, and in the same chapter among FISHERMAN'S KNOTS are a number of methods for attaching a line to a LEADER LOOP which are closely akin to bends. Among the BECKET HITCHES of Chapter 25 will be found others that serve a similar purpose.

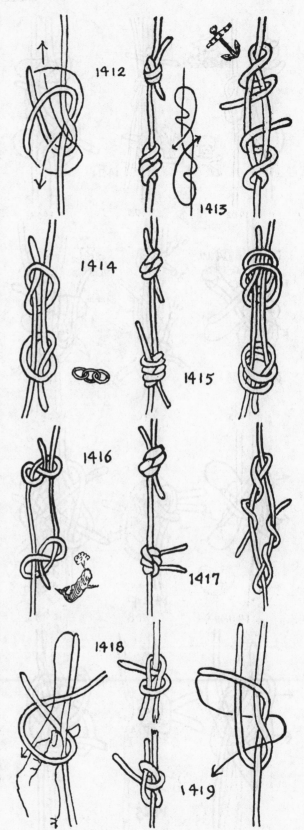

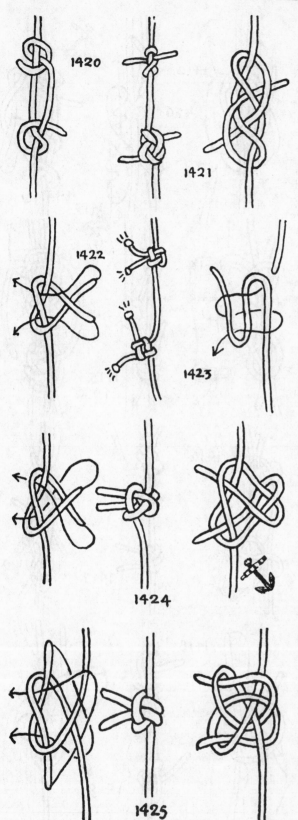

1420. The DOUBLE HARNESS BEND is tied with two CROSSING KNOTS, one in each of the two ends, around the standing part of the other end. The two knots draw together. It is strong and secure, but the SINGLE HARNESS BEND (※1474) is simpler to tie. Both of them are exceedingly hard to untie, after they are once drawn up.

1421. The DOUBLE HARNESS BEND with parallel ends appears to be preferable to the former. It is distinctive in appearance and the ends may be cut short after the bend is tightened.

The bends that have so far been shown in this chapter are for use in small stuff such as twine, cord and fishline. For that reason none of them, except ※1418, unties readily.

The bends to follow on this page and the next, although practical enough for many purposes, are designed particularly for decorative use.

1422. A decorative bend. If carefully drawn up this is one of the most secure of all bends, but it is bulky and apt to snag. It may be tied in flat material as well as round, and has the distinction of being one of the most difficult bends there is to untie.

1423. The JAPANESE BEND may be used decoratively on girdles and curtain holdbacks, but it tends to distort if subjected to any considerable strain.

1424. Another decorative bend that is very secure and may be used for the same purposes as the last. Both faces of this particular knot are similar in appearance to one of the faces of the SHEET BEND. (See ※1431.)

1425. A knot that is equally decorative and suitable for the same purposes as the last. Unless a bend, requiring as many crossings as this one, possesses some particularly desirable feature beyond other bends, it is of interest only if it is decorative. A practical bend, lacking other outstanding qualities, must tie in a very simple manner.

1425A. HUNTER'S BEND (Also see facing page 261) consists of two interlocked overhand knots, and is a comparatively new arrival on the knotting scene. Its cruciform layout (ends at right angles), however, is where it differs from 1408, 1409, 1425 and the two-strand Matthew Walker knot

The bend's first appearance in print seems to have been in 'Knots for Mountaineering' by Phil D. Smith, published in the U.S.A. in the 1950s; but about the same time Dr. Edward Hunter, a British physician, had discovered the same bend for himself.

By 1978, the bend was receiving publicity worldwide, linked to the doctor's name, but the first designation probably belongs to Smith who labelled it 'Rigger's bend'.

Tested to breaking point by the Royal Aircraft Establishment (Materials Department), in parachute cordage, it was found to be "... not as strong as the blood knot, similar to the reverse figure of eight and stronger than the fisherman's bend, sheet bend or reef knot".

Dr. Hunter's method of tying the bend is to hold both strands together and parallel, throw a bight as shown (taking care to keep the strands parallel without any accidental crossovers), then simply tuck each working end through the bight from opposite sides as indicated.

A new knot added 1979

BENDS

1426. Twofold Overhand Bend. In actual formation this is the same as a Two-Strand·Full Matthew Walker Knot but one of the two ends leads reversely. It is decorative and symmetrical.

1427. The Double Twofold Overhand Bend in formation is the same as a Two-Strand Four-Part Matthew Walker. (See Chapter 7, "Multi-Strand Lanyard Knots.") A Double Overhand Knot is tied in one end and a similar knot is tied reversely through the first knot with the other end. In the true Matthew Walker Knot the two Overhands are tied in the same direction.

1428. The Carrick Bend or Full Carrick Bend may be tied flat for decorative purposes. If tied in needlework, so that all four ends are to be employed, it is called the Josephine Knot. The drawing illustrates the Carrick Bend with both ends on the same side of the knot, which is less secure than the same knot formation with the ends diagonally opposite each other.

1429. If the lower bight is extended, the Carrick Bend may be platted a further length (as long as desired). This is often seen in trumpet cords and in military braids. A knot is completed each time the two ends are tucked down to the bottom. (See Knots ⚹2254 and ⚹2255.)

1430. Similarly the form of Four-Strand Square or Round Sinnet may be adapted to form a decorative bend. The outer members are moved alternately from either side, across the back, forward between the two opposing parts and down the front to a position parallel to, and below, the other sister strand.

The bends that have been shown so far are tied in small material such as twine, cord and fishline, where they are seldom untied. Either these knots are permanent or the material is cut and thrown away when they have served their purposes. When we come to rope, a knot that may be untied is called for, as the material is valuable and not to be squandered.

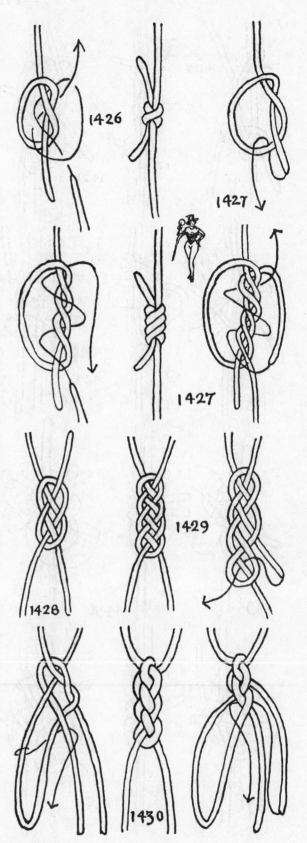

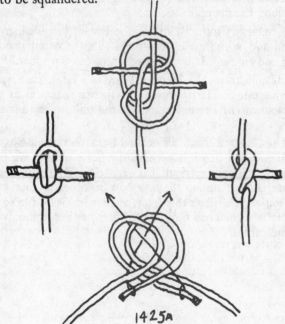

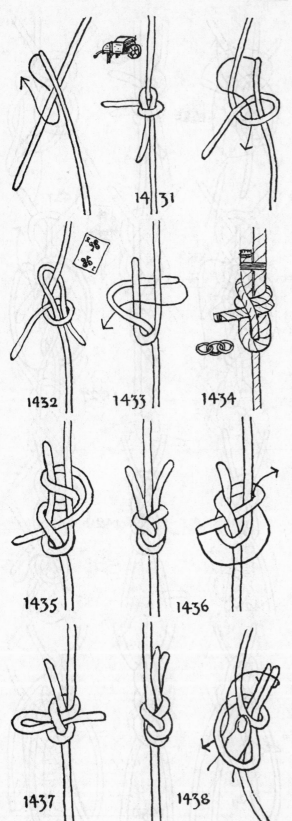

1431. The SHEET BEND is the common general utility bend aboard ship. It was formerly tied in a sheet, which is a piece of running rigging that trims a sail, and this accounts for the origin of the name. It serves almost every purpose well, and unties readily without damaging the rope. It is always tied in the manner that has been described for the BOWLINE KNOT (※1010), which is a LOOP KNOT of similar formation. But instead of tying an end to its own bight, one end is tied to a bight in another end.

The SHEET BEND bears a number of other titles including THE BEND, SIMPLE BEND, ORDINARY BEND, COMMON BEND, SINGLE BEND. It is also sometimes called, in error, BECKET BEND. But a becket in this case is an EYE SPLICE and the knot resulting is a hitch, which at sea is called the BECKET HITCH. The SHEET BEND should always be tied with two ends of similar material, as otherwise it may spill, unless it has been seized. Steel gives the name SHEET BEND in 1794.

1432. The LEFT-HAND SHEET BEND is often tied by landsmen and is not so reliable a knot as ※1431. It will be noted in the diagram that the pull on the bottom rope is the reverse of the SHEET BEND. Consult the table on page 274 to gain an idea of what degree of security this knot possesses.

1433. When tying the SHEET BEND in large or stiff material, turn up one end as pictured and hold the loop that has been formed with one hand and reeve the other end as indicated by the arrow.

1434. The DOUBLE SHEET BEND is mentioned by Luce in 1862. If the material is very stiff and large, seize an eye in one end and reeve the working end two turns instead of one. The DOUBLE BEND is no stronger but it is more secure.

1435. The DOUBLE SHEET BEND is sometimes tied by another method. It may be more quickly made in this way, since it has one less tuck.

1436. The SHEET BEND may have the end tucked as illustrated. This is recommended either for towing or for a rope that is to be dragged along the ground.

1437. A SLIPPED SHEET BEND may be instantly spilled, by pulling on the end and withdrawing the bight. This is often handy when launching and rigging. It is also used on circus tent gear.

1438. This illustrates the DOUBLE WEAVER'S KNOT that was shown to me by Eugene S. Harrington and which is identical in structure with TUCKED SHEET BEND ※1436, but the pull on the upper end is reversed.

1439. The CARRICK BEND, also called FULL CARRICK BEND, SAILOR'S KNOT, and ANCHOR BEND, is perhaps the nearest thing we have to a perfect bend. It is symmetrical, it is easy to tie, it does not slip easily in wet material, it is among the strongest of knots, it cannot jam and is readily untied. To offset this array of excellencies is the sole objection that it is somewhat bulky. It is the bend commonly tied in hawsers and cables.

When we come to consider hawsers and cables we are confronted with a new factor. The material is heavy and inflexible and the bend must take its form correctly and inevitably while under strain, as it cannot be worked into shape by hand alone. It also must untie easily, as the force that a man can bring to bear is relatively small and a marlingspike is apt to break the fiber of a wet rope.

The CARRICK BEND, when under stress, pulls up into easy loops, which may be readily opened with a few light taps from a belaying pin, fid, or other implement. It may be watersoaked indefinitely, and even then it will not jam.

Sometimes the CARRICK BEND is illustrated with the ends both on one side (❊1428) instead of diagonally opposite, but this is not so secure. At sea it is tied as shown here.

Lescallier gives the knot by name in 1783.

1440. The SINGLE CARRICK BEND. Almost every knot that can be conformed to the CARRICK BEND diagram, and that has a different over-and-under from the regular CARRICK BEND, has at one time or another been termed the SINGLE CARRICK BEND. Not one of these, however, has the desirable features of the TRUE CARRICK BEND (❊1439). (See table, page 274.) Riesenberg's *Standard Seamanship* gives the CARRICK BEND correctly.

1441. As these so-called SINGLE CARRICK BENDS are always seized, their true character is generally obscured. Several nautical authorities have even given the REEF KNOT labeled CARRICK BEND.

1442. Du Clairbois has gone so far as to give the GRANNY KNOT. With such a bend there is little between the sailor and eternity save the seizings. But the three that have just been shown and commented on are superior to what is to follow.

1443. This SINGLE CARRICK BEND, as shown by Brady, Luce, Alston, and others, slipped and spilled in mohair yarn with an average of 4.5 jerks. It is among the poorest of all the bends tested. (See page 274.)

1444. Another SINGLE CARRICK BEND, that is frequently published, slipped with an average of 4.6 jerks, very slightly better than ❊1443.

1445. But here is the worst SINGLE CARRICK BEND, shown by Knight, Nares, Todd and Whall, Henderson, etc. It slipped with an average of 2.6 jerks. Only one of all the other knots tested was worse than this. Yet it is recommended for towing and is said not to jam. Of course it was always seized.

All the so-called SINGLE CARRICK BENDS without seizings proved to be worthless, or worse. The fact that they ever appeared in print in the first place may be due to a blind faith in the CARRICK BEND diagram, and the fact that they have survived must be due to the fact that anything at all, even the WHATNOT, will hold if well seized. But the danger is always imminent that some poor unfortunate may tie one without adding seizings.

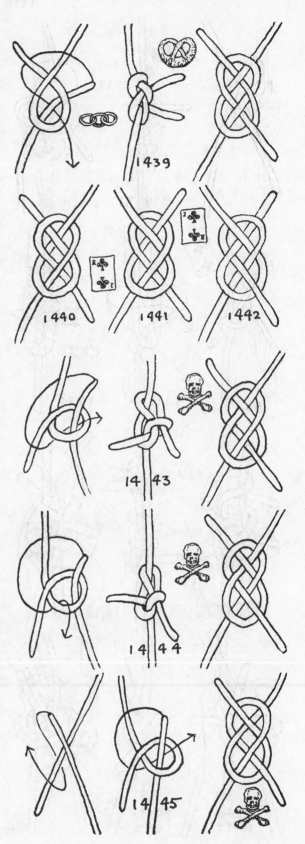

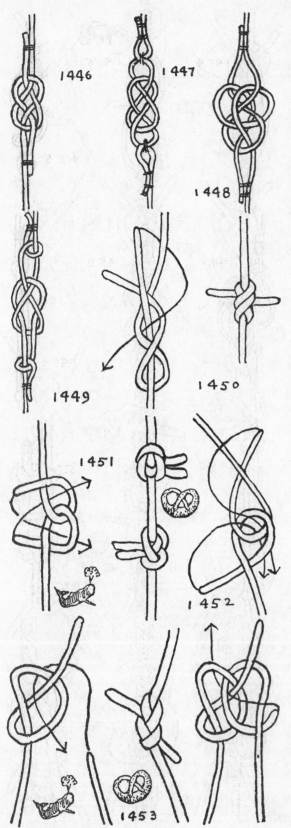

1446 1447

1448

1449

1450

1451

1452

1453

1446. HAWSER BENDS are always seized and frequently are parceled to save wear. Two round seizings are sufficient for the FULL CARRICK BEND.

1447. The SPANISH HAWSER BEND is made secure with two throat seizings and two round seizings. It is an old method in good standing.

1448. The OPEN CARRICK BEND will not jam and is strong and easily tied. But it is a clumsy affair. In bending cables, always leave long ends.

1449. Diderot's SINGLE CARRICK BEND is really the SHEET BEND. It is finished off with Two HALF HITCHES and if well seized should prove amply secure. The sketch here is copied from his Encyclopedia of 1762.

1450. (4/10/29.) There are no other well-known and easily untied bends suitable for large material. The present original bend is compact, has an excellent lead, and is not difficult to untie. By raising the upper loop the knot is easily loosened.

1451. (3/16/37.) This has less initial slip than the CARRICK BEND, opens almost as easily, is possibly not so strong, but would seem to be about as secure.

1452. (2/3/34.) Another original bend that is as easily untied as #1451. It appears to be strong, secure and compact. As it stands, the method of tying is more complicated than could be wished but this can probably be remedied.

1453. (5/27/24.) This bend appears to be the most easily untied of all.

1454. Two BENDS is a good method of securing two light hawsers together, but the two legs require careful adjustment so that they will have an equal pull. If it is to be used for towing, the ends should be seized.

1455. Two BOWLINES, or the BOWLINE BEND, given by Dana (1841), is more quickly tied than the preceding and is about the most common of all HAWSER BENDS.

1456. Lever, in 1808, says, "Hawsers are sometimes bent together thus. The hawser has a half hitch cast in it, a throat seizing clapped on the standing part and a round one at the end. Another hawser is

BENDS

rove through the bight of this, hitched in the same manner and seized to the standing part." Most of the "Seamanships" still continue to copy this description verbatim.

1457. Roding (Hamburg, 1798) gives a bend similar to the last except that round turns are taken by each hawser through the other.

1458. The TEMPORARY BEND given by Steel in 1794 consists of three throat seizings and two round seizings (for seizings see Chapter 40). The seizings bear the whole burden and if they fret away, the bend will part. When in use, seizings should be examined frequently.

1459. The REEVING-LINE BEND, which is pictured by Roding in 1795, is so named because it passes easily through hawse pipes and fair-leaders. The Two HALF HITCHES relieve the load on the seizings. Admiral Alston (*Seamanship*, London, 1860) says this "is about the best." Mechanically the knot is the exact duplicate of the WHATNOT (⚓1406) and the GRASS KNOT (⚓1490).

1460. Esparteiro, in his *Dicionario de Marinharia* (Lisboa, 1936), gives the same bend as the last but with two additional hitches.

1461. DOUBLE and TRIPLE SHEET BENDS are often employed when shifting hawsers and cables, in getting them through hawse pipes, and in passing them to shore. The knot will be more secure if the loop in the end of the hawser is seized in, or better still, eye spliced. Its purpose is to secure a small rope to a much larger one.

1462. The RACKING BEND does not require seizing as each turn of racking is hove on as it is laid, and the hawser parts draw snugly together. The end may be half hitched or stopped.

1463. The HEAVING-LINE BEND, given by Öhrvall, is used to attach a heaving line to the eye of a hawser.

1464. A SINGLE STOPPER is passed as illustrated. Two turns are taken, the standing part is passed and the tail dogged with the lay of the larger rope, which may be either hawser, cable or standing rigging. In this way a tail block is secured to a shroud or stay.

1465. The ROLLING HITCH was formerly called MAGNUS HITCH and MAGNER'S HITCH. If the latter is correct, Mr. Magner is the only rival that Matthew Walker has. Of the latter, it has been said that he is "the only man to have a knot named for him." The ROLLING HITCH is the best-known knot for bending a small rope to a larger taut one, and it is one of the most frequently used knots on shipboard.

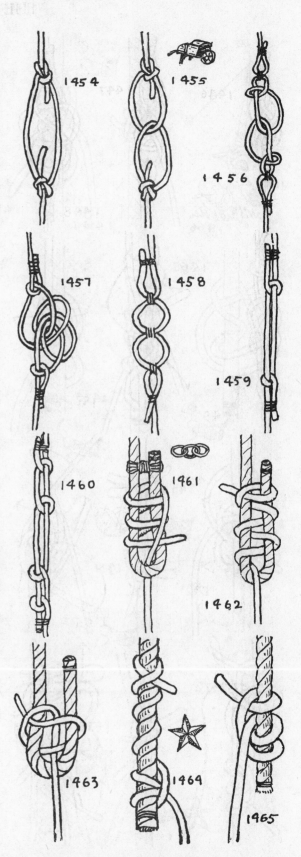

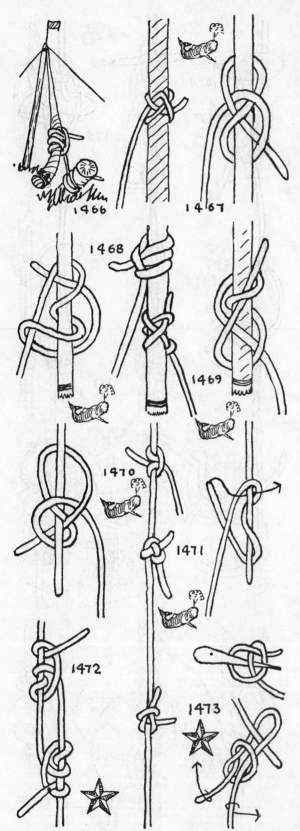

1466. If the ROLLING HITCH is tied to an inert end and the final hitch, which terminates the knot, is taken reversely, there will be less tendency to twist than in ⚹1465.

1467. (3/1/34.) The bend pictured here appears to be particularly secure for bending a *very small* line to a much *larger* one. This series of knots (⚹1464-71) could as well be considered hitches as bends, since only the smaller rope is active. But as they serve the purpose of uniting two ropes, they also belong here.

1468. A SLACK-LINE BEND to a larger line. Draw up carefully and pull both ends of the small line strongly in order to "set" the knot. Watch the knot and add weight gradually.

1469. For the same purpose as the last, this knot appears to serve equally well.

1470. (4/7/30.) For two ropes of the same material but tied with one end only. When this end is pulled carefully the other end is gripped.

1471. (2/5/39.) A JAMMING BEND is tied with one line to the bight, or end, of another of the same size. Both ends of the active line are pulled, which engages the other end, and the bend is formed in the parts of both.

1472. An ADJUSTABLE BEND is formed by tying a ROLLING HITCH in each end around the standing part of the other. The knots may be easily slid, even when the rope is under tension, and will hold when the hand is removed. Excellent for guy ropes of any sort where adjustment is required, and for lashing a load that may require tightening after it has shaken down.

1473. A SHORT END BEND was shown to me by Mrs. Thomas Knowles, who used it constantly in her knitting. I have often used it as a temporary expedient when a shoe lacing has parted. Any end that is long enough to drop a loop over may be bent to, if sufficient care is exercised. Form a NOOSE or a MARLINGSPIKE HITCH as illustrated. Place the NOOSE around the short end, in the direction shown, or else substitute an end of rope for the marlingspike and pull both the end and standing part of the NOOSE as illustrated; the short end will be "swallowed" and a SHEET BEND formed. The method is quite practical and requires half the material needed for other methods. So little length is required for the tying that the knot may be tied successfully as a "trick." (See Chapter 33.)

1474. The DRAWING BEND, HARNESS BEND or PARCEL BEND is about the most practical bend for twine. There is no danger of capsizing as there is with the WEAVER'S KNOT, and it is very secure. It has an added feature which makes it invaluable in parcel tying: it may be tied tightly while under tension. To tie: Form a CROSSING KNOT with one end around the other end. Hold this knot with the left hand and pull the upper end until taut. When taut enough, hold with the left hand and half hitch the upper end snugly around the upper standing part.

1475. The BECKET HITCH makes an effective DRAWING BEND. Put a BOWLINE KNOT in a rope's end. Reeve the other end through it, draw taut and hitch as shown by the arrow.

1476. A BOWLINE AND TWO HALF HITCHES. This one is easier to draw taut and hold under stress and is the most common of DRAWING BENDS. Commonly used in parcel tying and lashing wagon loads.

1477. The MARLINE HITCH AND HALF HITCH is also a good DRAWING BEND. If tied as illustrated it is secure, but with the final HALF HITCH reversed it is not so wholly dependable. Diderot (1762) gives it as a WEAVER'S KNOT.

1478. A TURK'S-HEAD BEND may be used in forming a handle for an umbrella, cane, sea chest, etc. Reeve the rope through the cleat and strongly seize at the desired size of the ring. Tie a 3L × 4B TURK'S-HEAD (#1305) with the end that leads to the right and double it. Then enter the heretofore inactive end, and with it triple the knot.

1479. A 4L × 3B TURK'S-HEAD KNOT may be made on the diagram given. Starting at the feather end, form the knot by tucking underneath an opposing strand, when passing an encircled point, for the second time. Reeve the end through the center compartment when it has been reached. Draw up the knot loosely into shape before doubling it, and in doubling it avoid doubling the loop which passes through the hole.

Another way to arrive at a similar result is to first tie the WHISTLE or KNIFE LANYARD KNOT (#787). Then reeve one of the ends of the knot through the hole in the cane or cleat. Cut the loop at the other end of the knot and lead the working end into the loop end parallel with the correct loop part, withdrawing the loop part at each tuck. When the working end has been substituted for the original half, draw up the knot.

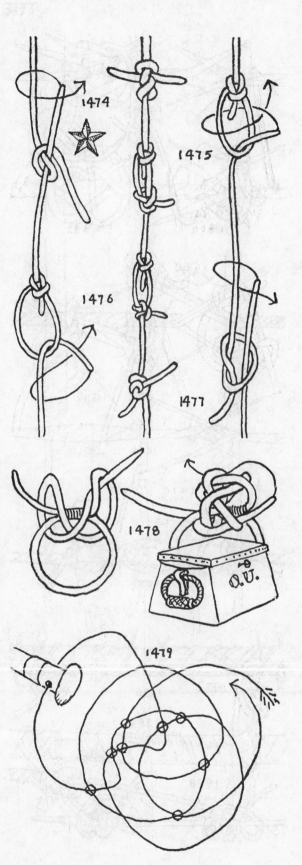

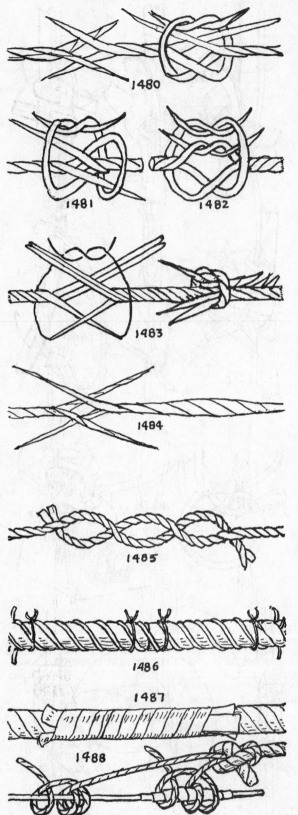

1480. The Rope Yarn Knot is used when serving standing rigging. It bulks three times the size of the rope yarn, while a Reef Knot bulks four times the size. To tie, split each rope yarn into two equal parts and tease all parts to a point, then crotch or marry the two ends. Cross two opposing parts and tie a Half Knot in them on the opposite side of the structure. Sometimes the knot is tied contrary to the lay of the rope yarn. Either way will serve, but the former makes a smoother knot. Rope yarn generally has a right lay.

The ends are buried underneath the service as it progresses and the knot is hardly evident. This is neither strong enough nor secure enough to be used as a general-purpose bend.

1481. Sometimes the knot is pictured with an extra turn. This might prove to be a little stronger, but it also may not be quite so secure.

1482. A Marline Bend. Marline has a left lay generally, being composed of two right-laid yarns. It may be tied with any of the Rope Yarn Knots. The underlying Half Knot shown here is optional.

1483. A Rope Yarn Bend in three-strand small stuff is sometimes pictured, but generally in serving with *small stuff* a Short Splice tucked either once or else once and a half is used.

1484. A Yarn Splice was shown to me by S. R. Ashley, who employs it in her knitting. The yarn is teased, split, and married, then is twisted with the lay and knitted in, while holding the twist intact with the fingers. Worked in this way, the knot or splice cannot be detected. As the splice is made at the exact point where the yarn is about to enter the fabric, the knitting presents no manual difficulties.

1485. The Tucked Bend is now very generally used when serving with either marline or small stuff, having to a large extent superseded the Rope Yarn Knot and the Marline Bend. Each end is tucked twice through the other end.

1486. Reeving-Off Bend, also called *marrying a rope*. When reeving off new running rigging, butt the ends of the new and old ropes together. Worm three short pieces of marline into the cuntlines, bridging the joint. Seize the wormings twice in each end. Then tuck the three ends "as they lie"; that is to say, tuck *under*, not *over and under*.

1487. Nowadays this may be more quickly but less safely done with "electric tape." Butt the ends as before and lay a number of lengthwise strips of rubber tape across the joint until it is covered. Then bind or serve helically with tape. Cover completely with tallow or talc powder; otherwise the tape may pull off in passing through the block. The best method is to serve with marline over several lengthwise strips of tape.

1488. To bend to a telephone or other wire. This will hold better if the wire is first shellacked. Take a short flexible cord or small rope that is slightly larger than the wire and, using this as a bridle, secure both ends to the wire with ROLLING HITCHES, then bend the hauling rope to the slack of the bridle between the hitches. The wire may be taped, but sometimes sticky tape will crawl.

1489. The STRAP KNOT is the common method of repairing a broken strap in·harness. In form this is similar to the BECKET HITCH. Although more used on the farm than at sea, I have seen the lanyard of a binocular case repaired with it.

1490. The GRASS BEND provides the best method of joining any flat, semiflexible material, such as straps, chair cane, thongs, grass, and straw. It has an excellent lead and is quite secure. Although in formation it is the same as the WHATNOT (※1407), when the ends have been arranged as shown, due to the flatness of the material they cannot shift into an insecure position.

1491. STRAP KNOT. A bend that cannot untie may be formed by cutting a slit in each strap end and reeving as illustrated in the right-hand diagram. One of the ends may be fast to another object.

1492. A STRAP BEND of another sort. The circular piece of rope which passes around a block and provides the eye from which it is suspended is called a strap. Also a rope wreath, or a single rope with an eye in one or both ends, which is to be made fast in the rigging and to which a tackle is hooked, is termed a strap.

When the two ends of a cargo sling or a strap are to be bent together, reeve one doubled end through the other in the way a BECKET HITCH is tied.

1493. A bend for rubber bands. Two or more slings or straps may be bent together as illustrated. In formation this is the same knot depicted as ※1491. It is the best way to bend elastic bands together. Drop the end of one band over the end of the other. Then reeve the outer one through the other.

1494. A SLING or STRAP TOGGLE. If a third end is not available for tying ※1493, or if it is desired to cast off quickly, arrange the ends as pictured and insert a toggle. Hold the toggle secure until the load has been added.

1495. EYE TO EYE. This may be tied with a somewhat different technique than is given for ※1491. Reeve the upper end of the lower strap through the eye of the upper strap. Then reeve the lower eye of the lower strap through its *own* upper eye. This forms a SLING HITCH in one of the eyes which, with a little assistance, will capsize into a STRAP BEND.

1496. Two clinches may be used to form a HAWSER or CABLE BEND. The illustration shows two OUTSIDE CLINCHES. The turns should be as small as possible. The INSIDE CLINCH is more secure than the OUTSIDE CLINCH but is not so easily cast off.

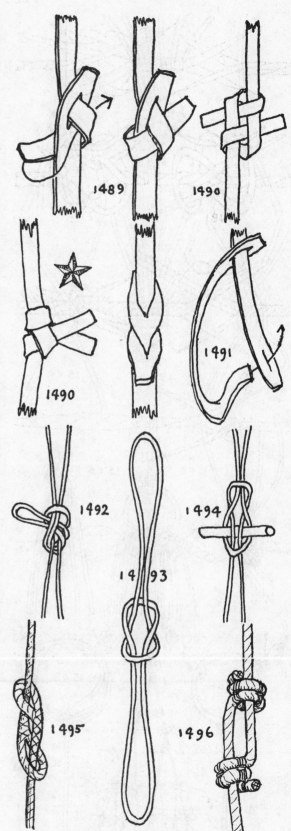

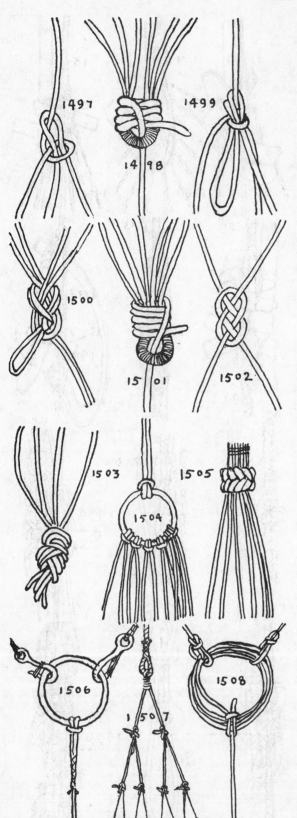

1497. MULTIPLE BENDS of more than two ends are occasionally called for on nets, tents, awnings, hammock clews, etc. The common SHEET BEND will provide either three or four ends and the pull may be either two against two or one against three.

1498. A MULTIPLE RACKING BEND can be formed by seizing a number of small lines together at the center and bending a larger line to them with racking turns.

1499. The BOWLINE may be tied with a bight so that, when the bight is cut, five ends are available.

1500. If bights are to be bent together to furnish a number of ends, the knot pictured here will be found firmer than similar KNOT #1492.

1501. A MULTIPLE SHEET BEND. If a considerable number of straddled lines are needed, it is well to serve or ringbolt hitch them at the center and then to seize in an eye before bending to it with a MULTIPLE SHEET BEND.

1502. The JOSEPHINE KNOT. When used in decorative needlework with four working ends, the CARRICK BEND bears this name. A loop is made in the center of one thread and the end of the other thread is sewed through the first one with a needle.

1503. A MULTIPLE FIGURE-EIGHT KNOT appears to be a practical and compact means for bending several ends together.

1504. For hammock clews a number of small lines are often secured to a metal ring with a series of RING HITCHES.

1505. If lines are to be pulled not too widely apart the DIAMOND KNOT, elsewhere described as #693, will be found quite practical.

1506. Snap hooks to clews and metal rings are often employed at sea.

1507. The device pictured here is given in Diderot's Encyclopedia. It is the hoist rope of a pile driver which was worked wholly by man power. An individual line is provided for each man.

At sea, BOWLINE BRIDLES are similarly constructed, having three or four legs.

1508. An expeditious way of bending several lines at a common point is to first form a MULTIPLE PORTUGUESE BOWLINE in one rope's end, and then secure the others to the bights of this with ordinary BOWLINE KNOTS.

1509. Several ends interlocked with either BOWLINE KNOTS or EYE SPLICES may be rove together as pictured and will be as secure as it is possible for rope to be.

1510. CROW'S-FEET. The edges of awnings on shipboard were stretched with euphroe blocks and so also were catharpins. The web so formed was termed a CROW'S-FOOT. The standing ends of running rigging in the seventeenth century were secured in similar manner to the top ends of fore and aft stays.

1511. A multiplicity of small lines are sometimes toggled or fidded to a spliced eye in a larger rope.

1512. The FIGURE-EIGHT LASHING was used in bending the two ends of a messenger together. A lanyard was spliced to one of the eyes, the two eyes were lashed together "figure-eight"-fashion and the end secured with HALF HITCHES.

1513. The WEDDING KNOT was a somewhat similar method of lashing two eyes together. Both ends of the lashing were passed in round turns through the two eyes. When sufficient lashing turns had been taken the two ends were crossed in the center of the lashing and frapping turns taken, the ground turns were led away from the center, and the riding turns back to the center where the ends were reef knotted. The two halves of a rope jackstay were bent together by this method.

A RIGGING STOPPER (#3302) is closely related to the bends. It serves to repair a break in a stay or shroud.

1514. A LOOP LASHING also partakes somewhat of the nature of a bend. This is used about deck, and ashore it is used on wagon-load lashings. A BOWLINE KNOT (#1010) is put in one rope's end and a single loop in the bight is added to the standing part of the other rope. Either a HARNESS LOOP (#1050) or a SINGLE BOWLINE on the bight (#1058) may be used. Teamsters generally employ LOOP KNOT #1046, which is weak but secure. The working end is rove through the BOWLINE in the other end, then led back through the BIGHT LOOP. One or several turns are made through the two loops, and these are tightened at every turn. The end is finally made fast with HALF HITCHES near the loop last rove through.

1515. This illustrates a rope with selvagee tails stopped to a chain. The end of the rope is opened and divided into two equal groups of yarn. These are marline hitched to form two tails. Formerly this was used on the end of chain gammoning.

1516. Rope stopped to chain. The rope is half hitched around the third link, the standing part is seized to the first link and the end is seized to the fifth.

1517. Three selvagee tails are made fast to a chain. Each strand is opened up into its separate yarns and then the three strands are marled down separately to make three equal tails. These are hitched to the chain and then are platted to the end and stopped, the chain having first been parceled.

1518. A FISHERMAN'S BEND made fast to a chain cable. The Yankee bank fisherman's cable is half chain, half rope. The chain is for the stony bottom and the rope for its easier riding qualities. The end link is parceled, and the bend is seized.

1519. The *Shiver and Eye* provides a handy method of quick bending and unbending. One rope's end is rove through an old shiv and a STOPPER KNOT holds it in place. It is buttoned into an EYE SPLICE in the other rope's end.

1520. A SPRITSAIL SHEET KNOT was tied in the ends of a messenger strap. The strap being rove through the eyes of the messenger, the ends were buttoned together.

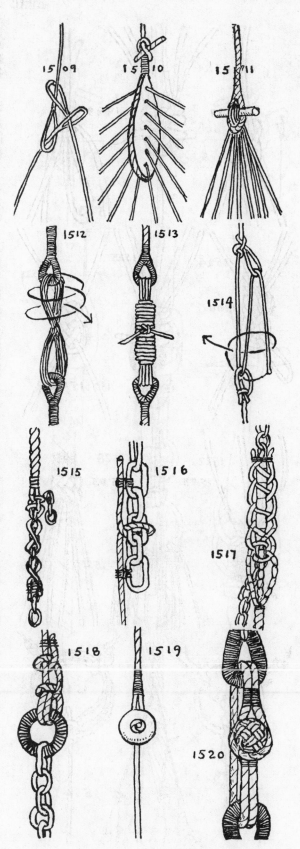

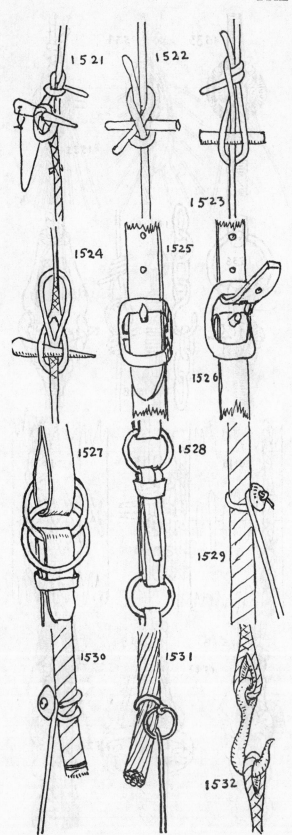

1521. *Toggle and eye* or *two eyes toggled*. A toggle is easily freed even when under strain, which is sometimes a great advantage. It is used to support a heavy weight that is designed to be dropped rather than lowered, such as a mooring or anchor.

1522. In heavy lifting a SHEET BEND is often toggled. Adjusted in this way, it never jams and is less liable to spill.

1523. The DOUBLE SHEET BEND can be toggled in this fashion and instantly spills when the toggle is removed. All toggles must be held in place until the load has been added.

1524. Two eyes may be toggled together in much the same way and will spill at once when the toggle is withdrawn.

1525. The common *buckle* and *strap* serves the purpose of a bend although it is of a mechanical nature.

1526. A less common buckle bears a stud instead of a tongue.

1527. A buckle that consists of two rings. This is an old form that has been revived in recent years.

1528. The CINCH or CINCHA KNOT, which started out in life either in Mexico or in South America. It is now universally used on pack saddles and on most riding saddles except the English type.

1529. The SHIVER HITCH is made of an old block shiv and a MATTHEW WALKER KNOT. It was formerly used in the merchant service to hold on to the cable at a time when a tackle was used for heaving. A SINGLE HITCH was taken around the cable and the shiv jammed when hauled taut.

1530. The DOUBLE SHIVER HITCH may be used for the same purpose and also for hauling unfinished spars about in a spar yard. It would be excellent for hauling circus poles around the lot.

1531. A *chain* and *ring* are used in the rigging loft when putting wire rigging on the stretch. The method is also used on the rigger's bench when tightening wire rope strands.

1532. The HOOK AND EYE is one of the simplest means by which rope may be lengthened and shortened, and if the hook is moused it cannot spill.

1533. *Bull's-eyes* are among the earliest surviving bits of apparatus that are still used on shipboard. They are to be found on Egyptian models from the Pyramids. In our Merchant Marine they are used to secure the ends of fore and aft stays. One end of the stay is seized into the groove around a bull's-eye. The other end is rove through the bull's-eye. After the stay has been set up with tackles the second end is made fast with round seizings.

1534. A *single shell* has two grooves but no holes.

1535. A *double shell* has two holes. Nowadays it is made of pottery ("stoneware") or glass, and is to be seen on telephone-pole guy ropes, where it provides electrical insulation as well as a means of tightening.

1536. Large hemp cables usually had a thimble eye in either end, and when it was necessary to lengthen the cable, two eyes were shackled together, or one was shackled to a chain cable. Often the eye was put in when the cable was made. Swivels were often added.

1537. An S hook provides the simplest method of coupling two pieces of chain. The hook is put through the two links and closed with a hammer.

1538. The most secure way to bend two wires together is with two loops. The ground turns in the wire should be close together and riding turns should be added.

1539. This is a coupling from an Eskimo seal harpoon line, made of reindeer marrowbone. One end of sinew rope is rove through a hole across the knucklebone. The other end has a loop which is thrust into the end of the bone and buttoned to a carved stud inside the base of the coupling. The drawing was taken from the Smithsonian Museum *Report* of 1900.

1540. There are many different ways of lacing a belt drive. The way given here is characteristic and simple. The left illustration represents the grain side of the leather, which comes in contact with the drive wheel. With the skived side uppermost, lace up through 1, down through 2, etc. The two ends are left out at 1 and 16 respectively and are cut off "long."

1541. A direct way of joining two wire ends. The ends are led past each other and each end is twisted in two layers (with both ground and riding turns) around the standing part of the other end. Three or four *ground turns* are led away from the center, then the *riding turns* are led back toward the center. The two ends should be twisted in opposite ways so that they cannot "corkscrew" and come apart.

1542. The *skater's chain grip* illustrates how two hands should be bent together in rescuing someone who has fallen through the ice. Fingernails should first be close-pared.

1543. The POLICE-LINE KNOT is recommended for holding back a crowd or for use when kissing the Blarney Stone.

The following table gives the results obtained in the *security* tests that were described on page 18. The knots are listed in the order of their security, the most insecure being mentioned first. The left column gives the average number of jerks necessary to make a knot of each kind spill.

1.0	WHATNOT (#1407)
2.6	SINGLE CARRICK BEND A (#1445)
3.	GRANNY KNOT (#1442)
4.5	SINGLE CARRICK BEND B (#1443)
4.6	SINGLE CARRICK BEND C (#1444)
12.2	THIEF KNOT (#1207)
14.6	LEFT-HAND SHEET BEND (#1432)
19.	REEF KNOT (#1441)
19.6	CARRICK BEND, both ends on same side of knot (#1428)
22.3	SHEET BEND (#1431)
22.8	OVERHAND BEND in left-twisted yarn (#1548)
25.8	WHATNOT, jammed (#1406)
30.9	HARNESS BEND, single (#1474)
33.1	OVERHAND BEND, left-handed in left-twist yarn (#1547)
36.2	DOUBLE SHEET BEND (#1434)
42.9	ENGLISHMAN'S or WATERMAN'S KNOT (#1414)
70.8	CARRICK BEND, with diagonal pull (#1439)
100.	RING KNOT (#1412) Slight slip but did not spill.
100.	BARREL KNOT (#1413) No slip.
100.	(2/3/34) (#1452) No slip.

Some readers may be surprised to find the SHEET BEND with so low a rating, but these tests were made in exceptionally slippery material. The SHEET BEND is the most practical of bends and quite secure enough for ordinary purposes. The SINGLE CARRICK BENDS (#1443, #1444, #1445) are among the least secure of all bends, and depend almost entirely on their seizings for whatever security they possess.

1544. A swivel may be added to a rope by utilizing two small boards nailed together at right angles. Three holes are to be bored and a MATTHEW WALKER KNOT with a collar and a leather washer is needed. The swivel is improved if three rim holes are bored. A BOWLINE is made through two of the holes and the end is led to the third hole and knotted.

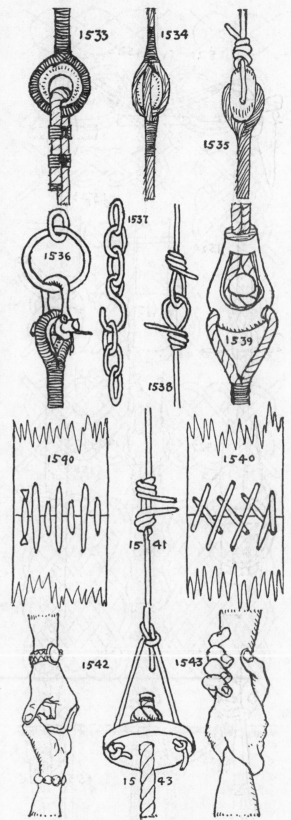

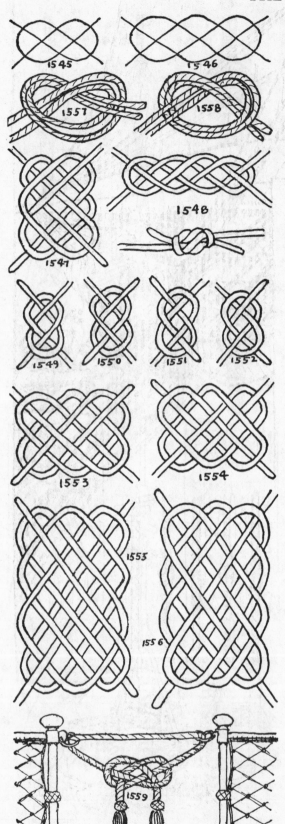

1545. Many bends in common use may be tied on the CARRICK BEND diagram. By using a larger diagram of similar characteristics it seemed probable that other bends could be projected.

1546. A bend diagram one part longer than the CARRICK diagram is impossible, as it consists of more than two lines, and so cannot be tied in two ends.

1547. The CHINESE KNOT diagram not only was productive of more elaborate knots, such as the HARNESS BEND (⚹1474) and the ENGLISHMAN'S KNOT (⚹1414), but also could be used to depict all the knots of the smaller CARRICK diagram. The REEF KNOT is illustrated here tied in the larger diagram. See also KNOTS ⚹1553 and ⚹1554.

1548. A one-bight-by-four-bight diagram was not very productive although the DOUBLE HARNESS BEND (⚹1420) can be tied on it. The knot depicted here was one of its results; although symmetrical and secure, it is unwieldy.

The following knots are projected on the CARRICK BEND diagram:

1549. The REEF KNOT.

1550. The SHEET BEND.

1551. The CARRICK BEND.

1552. The GRANNY.

The following knots are projected on the CHINESE KNOT diagram:

1553. The DOUBLE HARNESS BEND.

1554. The ENGLISHMAN'S KNOT.

1555. A diagram the next size larger than the CHINESE KNOT contains all the knots of both the CARRICK BEND and the CHINESE KNOT diagrams, as well as an assortment of still more elaborate knots. Shown here is the DOUBLE WEAVER'S KNOT (⚹1438).

1556. If the pull is on diagonally opposite ends this diagram will give the OVERHAND BEND, but if the pull is on two ends of the same side it will give the RING KNOT.

1557. (At the top of the page.) The OVERHAND BEND is shown tied left-handed, in left-laid yarn.

1558. The OVERHAND BEND, tied right-handed, in left-laid yarn. The left-hand knot is almost fifty per cent more secure. If right-handed yarns were used the right-handed knot would be equally secure.

1559. The CHECK or DELAY KNOT is employed semidecoratively on passenger ships to block off alleyways, companionways and doorways from inquisitive passengers, when painting or other business is in order. It is also tied in idle manropes when they are left hanging at the sides.

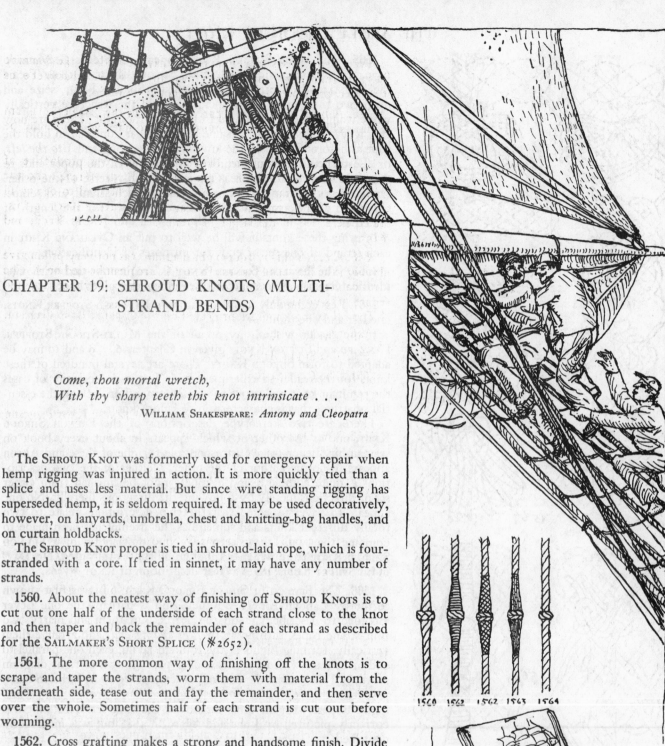

CHAPTER 19: SHROUD KNOTS (MULTI-STRAND BENDS)

Come, thou mortal wretch,
With thy sharp teeth this knot intrinsicate . . .

WILLIAM SHAKESPEARE: *Antony and Cleopatra*

The SHROUD KNOT was formerly used for emergency repair when hemp rigging was injured in action. It is more quickly tied than a splice and uses less material. But since wire standing rigging has superseded hemp, it is seldom required. It may be used decoratively, however, on lanyards, umbrella, chest and knitting-bag handles, and on curtain holdbacks.

The SHROUD KNOT proper is tied in shroud-laid rope, which is four-stranded with a core. If tied in sinnet, it may have any number of strands.

1560. About the neatest way of finishing off SHROUD KNOTS is to cut out one half of the underside of each strand close to the knot and then taper and back the remainder of each strand as described for the SAILMAKER'S SHORT SPLICE (#2652).

1561. The more common way of finishing off the knots is to scrape and taper the strands, worm them with material from the underneath side, tease out and fay the remainder, and then serve over the whole. Sometimes half of each strand is cut out before worming.

1562. Cross grafting makes a strong and handsome finish. Divide the yarns of each strand into four parts, cut out the lower quarter, worm the second quarter, use the third quarter in faying and re-serve the outside quarter for cross grafting (#2677). The length of the knot should be about four times the diameter of the rope. Both ends should be covered with a snaked whipping. (See #3453.)

1563. A grafted SHROUD KNOT is prepared in the same way as the last. The individual yarns should be tapered slightly. (See #2678.)

1564. Provided they have been snugly worked, most of the more elaborate knots given in this chapter are sufficiently secure to allow trimming the strands close to the knots.

[275]

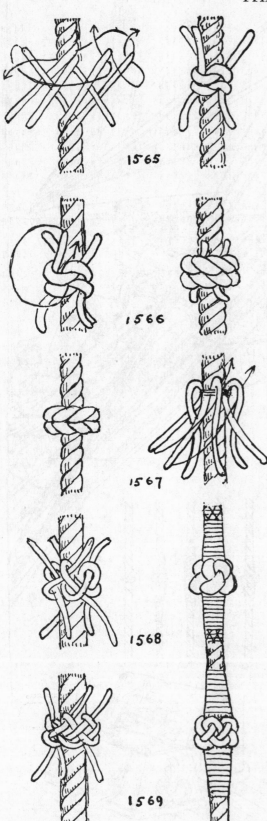

1565

1566

1567

1568

1569

1565. The name SHROUD KNOT appears in Steel's *Seamanship* (1794). Lever speaks of the FRENCH SHROUD KNOT in 1808. To tie the "COMMON," "DOUBLE" or "ENGLISH" SHROUD KNOT, seize and open two rope ends, marry them and hold the structure vertically while walling the upstanding set of ends to the right. There are now two ways of describing the same thing. Either continue to hold the rope as before and crown the lower (downhanging ends) *to the left*, or else turn the structure, end for end, and wall the upper ends to the right as directed before. One knot is the reverse of the other. Draw all snug, scrape and worm a part of each strand, and scrape, taper and fay the remainder. Serve over snugly for the length of the taper.

In tying these knots it will be well to put an OVERHAND KNOT in each strand of one set of ends for purposes of identification.

1566. The ENGLISH SHROUD KNOT is frequently tied with two identical STOPPER KNOTS (#676) which makes a fuller knot.

1567. Less commonly it is tied with two REVERSED STOPPER KNOTS, one left and one right.

If the reader wishes, any or all of the MULTI-STRAND STOPPER, LANYARD and BUTTON KNOTS given in Chapters 6, 7, 9 and 10 may be adapted to form SHROUD KNOTS. There are several hundred of these knots for the reader to experiment with. But in the majority of cases the resultant knot will prove to be a clumsy affair, lacking the essential smartness that is characteristic of sailor's knots.

There are two stereotype descriptions of the FRENCH SHROUD KNOT, one or the other of which appears in about every book on seamanship. Lever (1808) is responsible for one of these and Alston appears to be the author of the other. Neither of the two descriptions is quite complete, and a knot cannot be finished from either set of directions merely by following the directions literally. No one appears to have suspected that the two descriptions relate to two totally different knots and sometimes the attempt has been made to combine the two. I have seen only one description of a FRENCH SHROUD KNOT from which a knot can be successfully tied. Dr. Day, in his *Sailor's Knots*, gives a clear description of KNOT #1568.

1568. The FRENCH or SINGLE SHROUD KNOT (1) was first shown to me by Captain Albert Whitney, and is perhaps the one Lever intended to describe. Cut off the hearts, butt them and marry two four-strand ropes, turn down the *upstanding ends* and arrange them vertically, forming bights at the top and laying each one parallel to and in contact with its own standing part (shown as right diagram #1567). Take one of the original *downhanging ends*, hitherto inert, pass it to the right, past the first bight and up through the second bight. Repeat with the other strands of the same set. This knot was correctly pictured by Luce and Ward in 1884 but was incorrectly described.

1569. The FRENCH or SINGLE SHROUD KNOT (2). Lever directs tying as follows: "Single wall the ends round the bights of the other three and their own standing parts." This leaves the knot incomplete. But if we pass the first bight and stick each end up through the second bight to the right, the result is a practical and symmetrical knot.

1570. Alston's (1860) description of the FRENCH or SINGLE SHROUD KNOT (3). "Crown backwards, lefthanded, the strands of each end; then dip the ends that lie *from* you to the left of those that fall down *towards* you: haul them into their places . . ." He then directs: ". . . tuck the ends as in splicing, or tease the strands out and marl down." But the strands are not in position for doing either.

If, after having followed Alston's directions literally, up to the point where he mentions tucking "as in splicing," the ends are tucked instead as shown here, a satisfactory knot results which may well be the knot Alston had in mind. This knot under tension will distort somewhat. I have never seen any of the foregoing "FRENCH SHROUD KNOTS" tied by a sailor except ✳1568.

1571. The FRENCH SHROUD KNOT (4), that I have always seen tied by sailors, I first learned from Captain Charles W. Smith on board the *Sunbeam* in 1904, and I have seen many other sailors tie it. Olsen, in *Fisherman's Seamanship* (Grimsby, 1885), describes it correctly but uses for illustration Alston's drawing for a quite different knot.

The four foregoing knots (✳1568–71) include all the FRENCH SHROUD KNOTS either published or unpublished that I have been able to trace.

1572. To double SHROUD KNOT ✳1571: Tie the knot and then tuck each end directly through the next bight to the right, which doubles or enlarges the knot. Superficially it will now closely resemble FIVE-STRAND FLAT SINNET ✳2967, tied horizontally around the rope, and if each strand is tucked through an additional bight the surface will resemble SEVEN-STRAND FLAT or ENGLISH SINNET, also tied horizontally.

1573. A firm knot, superficially resembling some of the FRENCH SHROUD KNOTS already given, is crowned to the right (upper ends only). Then the lower strands are tucked up to the left, over one and under one to the top center.

1574. A wider knot than has been given, which superficially resembles FOUR-STRAND FLAT SINNET or a FOUR-LEAD TURK'S-HEAD, is tied as follows: Without changing the grip on the structure, crown the upper strands to the right and wall the lower strands to the left. Then tuck the ends as shown, first the lower ends upward, then the upper ends, which are not tucked immediately down under the bight below, but are tucked *under the next bight to the right*, as shown in the right diagram.

The tools required for these knots are pricker, scissors and loop buttoner. For practicing the knots double two pieces of banding and lay up into about five inches of FOUR-STRAND SQUARE SINNET ✳2999. Seize and leave the ends about two feet long. Two of these sinnets are required for one SHROUD KNOT. Boil or soak one of the two sinnets in tea or coffee and the other in plain water for the same length of time. When dry, they will be of different color but of the same texture.

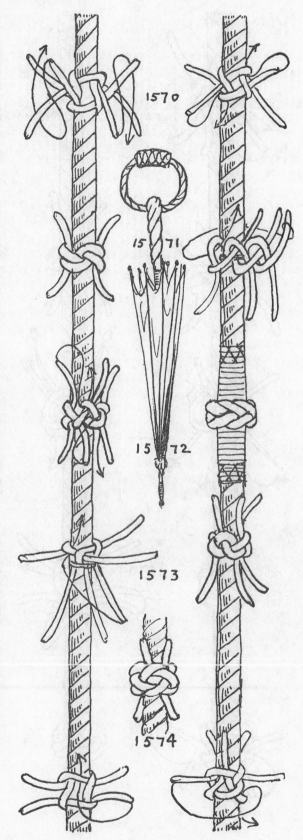

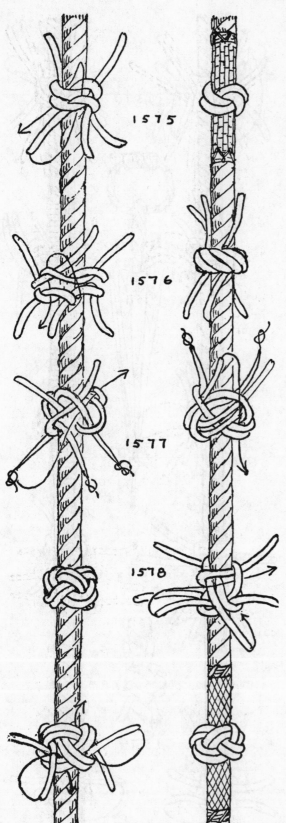

1575. A SHROUD KNOT superficially resembling the DOUBLE WALL KNOT is built up from an ENGLISH SHROUD KNOT base. First tie KNOT ⌘1565. Withdraw each lower strand in turn and stick it, as indicated by the arrow, under two parallel bights. This knot is less apt to distort than ⌘1570, which it resembles in appearance.

1576. A SHROUD KNOT superficially resembling the STOPPER KNOT is also based on the ENGLISH SHROUD KNOT. Each lower strand is carried beyond one upper end to the left, before sticking down under the same part from which it was earlier removed, passing under three parts in all.

1577. A DOUBLE SHROUD KNOT. Bushell (1854) recommends that "strands be tucked without doubling," which indicates that a DOUBLE SHROUD KNOT of some sort was used in his period. This is not to be confused with the ENGLISH SHROUD KNOT (⌘1565), for that consists of two separate knots, instead of a single knot that is doubled. First tie ⌘1571. Then pass each lower *end* to the right, parallel with and under the next adjacent lower *bight*, then up under *two upper* bights. At this point there will be two ends issuing from under each upper bight. Lead the lower one of each of these pairs downward, following the established lead, and tuck out at the stem under two parallel bights.

1578. Another DOUBLE FRENCH SHROUD KNOT is based on ⌘1574. Marry two rope ends and, holding the structure vertically and without shifting the grip, crown the upper strands to the right and wall the lower strands in the same direction. Tuck each lower end once to the right, following below the upper crown; next tuck each end of the original crown *once* parallel with and below the bight which issues from the same compartment. This brings all ends out at the middle cross section of the knot. Stick all up-pointing ends to the top stem under four bights (right arrow) and stick all down-pointing ends to the lower stem under two bights (left arrow).

Directions are often given in old seamanship books to tie SHROUD KNOTS *left-handed*. This, I think, may have reference to cable-laid shrouds, which are, of course, left-handed. SHROUD KNOTS are commonly wormed and served, and if tied against the lay the strands would lie in the wrong direction for worming. In general it may be said that all MULTI-STRAND KNOTS should be tied with the lay, unless for a good and specific reason. Sailors, like other people, are apt to do things the easiest way, which for a left-handed sailor would be "against the lay" of plain-laid rope.

1579. To shroud knot two ends that have an unequal number of strands: With three- and four-strand rope the most practical way is to seize the four-strand end carefully and cut off one strand close to the seizing. Then knot as two three-strand ropes by one of the methods that has been given.

In shroud knotting four-strand rope or sinnet to six-strand material proceed as follows: Crotch the two ends in the manner pictured, the double strands and the single strands in the larger end alternating. Work the double strands as units and tie exactly as ⌗1578. From this point follow the lead wherever it is required to make all parts double. Finally stick all ends out at the rim. Work snug and trim the ends.

1580. A SHROUD KNOT based on Captain Whitney's SINNET KNOT ⌗759. Marry the ends, crown the upper strands to the right and wall the lower strands to right as in ⌗1578. Lead an end from the upper crown down and *to the left* around a lower end and up through its own bight in the original crown. Repeat with the rest of the strands of the crown. Then take an end from the lower wall, lead it to the *left*, which brings it below the original crown, and stick it down to the stem as pictured. Draw taut and finish off in any of the five ways shown on page 275.

1581. The NAPKIN RING. With two pieces of three-strand rope, crown and wall as ⌗1574. With the strands of the upper crown tie a SINGLE MATTHEW WALKER KNOT and stick each end in turn up through the crown to the top. Then lay an end from the lower wall up between the strands of the MATTHEW WALKER and parallel to it and stick it down under four parts to the stem. Repeat with the rest of the strands of the lower wall; the last strand is stuck down under five parts.

1582. The STAR SHROUD KNOT. Marry two ends with four, five or six strands each. With the lower strands tie the first movement of the STAR KNOT with strands leading to the right. Having done this, turn the structure end for end and tie another first movement of the STAR KNOT but with *ends leading to the left*. The second sketch shows the knot at this point with *all ends* leading to the left, as the structure was turned end for end after the first operation, which reversed the lead of the first part of the knot. Bring the two knots close together with bights opposite each other and reeve the opposite ends of each knot through the bights of the other knot, parallel to each other, so that all ends emerge close to the stem. Next lead all ends parallel to the established lay and stick all to the stem, half of them up and half of them down.

To make a FIVE-POINTED STAR with shroud-laid rope: splice an extra strand (one tuck each way) to the small rope heart. (See SPLICE ⌗2828.)

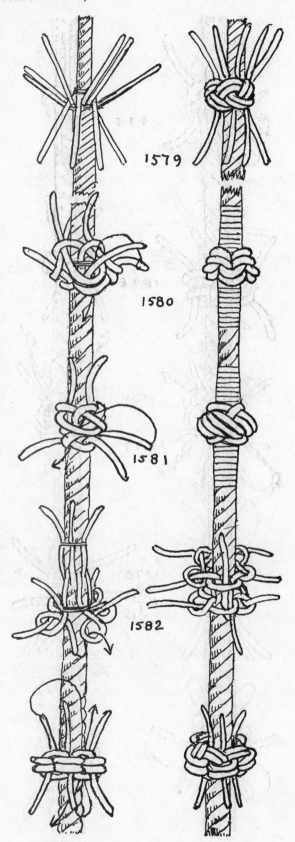

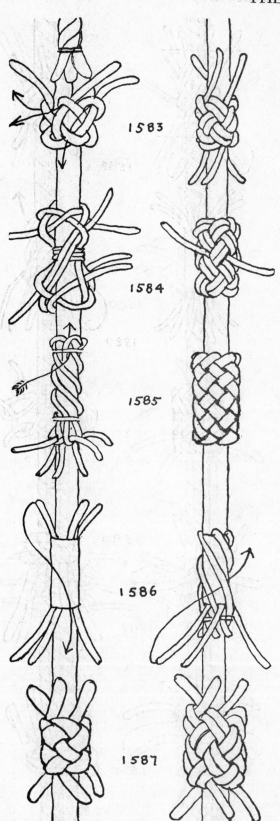

1583. A Shroud Knot based on the Diamond Knot. Take two ends, but do not crotch them. Turn down the ends of one rope and wall them, then tuck them in turn over one and under one as illustrated. Open the other rope and stick the ends reversely, parallel with the knot already tied. With these ends double the first knot and as each end reaches the upper rim tuck it under all to the lower rim.

1584. To make a Double Diamond Shroud Knot. Open, marry and seize two ends together. Tie a right-handed Diamond Knot (❋693) in the lower strands, then turn the structure end for end and tie a similar knot with the other strands. Cross and tuck two adjacent strands from opposite ends as illustrated and arrange the other opposing pairs in the same way. Tuck all ends parallel with the established lead until they have returned to the center length of the knot again, as the pair illustrated in the right diagram. Then, using the loop buttoner, draw all strands underneath and out to the rims.

The size of this knot may be increased by making additional tucks before doubling, or it may be made smaller by tying an initial wall instead of a diamond at one of the ends.

1585. To make a Single Diamond Shroud Knot. Marry two sinnets of six strands each (or any number of strands). Crown the upper ends to the right and seize them just below the crown. Lay them downward to the right in a 45-degree helix for the length desired for the knot and seize again, having first arranged the strands of the two ends so that they alternate in proper order around the rope or sinnet. Bring the lower strands (hitherto inactive) forward, each between two of the opposite strands, and tie them in a right wall around the other set. Next tuck each of these ends to the right and over the first diagonal and under the second diagonal of the opposing set. Tuck each end again in turn until as many tiers have been tucked as are required. Then stick the ends up under two parts as shown by the arrow in the left diagram. Work snug with the pricker and trim all ends. Remove the end seizings as soon as they are not required.

1586. A single knot. This provides a method that may be tied either single or double, and will make as large a knot as may be desired. Marry two ropes and seize twice at the length where the rims are to be. Paste a piece of paper to form a sleeve around this central section, which will hide all parts that are not being worked. Helix each upper strand downward over the sleeve to the right and lay it between two lower strands. Bring the lower strands forward and seize the upper strands below the edge of the paper sleeve. Tuck the lower strands upward and to the right, each in turn, *over one and under one*. Repeat again with each strand in turn until the knot is the desired width. The knot may now be worked taut, and as the work progresses remove the sleeve and seizings.

1587. *To double the last knot:* Bring each strand to the right above and parallel with the bights of the strands that were first turned down. Tucking each strand once in turn, repeat until the knot is completely doubled.

1588. A knot that superficially resembles the MATTHEW WALKER KNOT. Marry two ends of three strands each and put on two seizings at twice the diameter of the rope apart. Bring the upper strands down in a right helix and lay the lower strands upward between them in a left helix. Seize all strands outside the previous seizings as indicated by the dotted lines. Take a lower end and tuck it upward and to the right *under* one strand; repeat with the other two lower strands. Turn the structure end for end and repeat with the opposing ends. Tuck all strands *under* in tiers until each has been tucked under six. Draw taut and trim the ends.

If a larger knot is wanted, employ more strands and tuck under additional parts as wished.

1589. A HERRINGBONE SHROUD KNOT. Take two sinnets of six strands each (or some other number), marry the ends and seize in two places, about twice the diameter of the sinnet apart. Lead the upper set in a right downward helix and seize at the bottom, leaving the lower set free. Take any one of the free strands of the lower set and tuck it upward to the right over *two* and under *two*, then repeat with each lower end in turn. Continue to tuck over two and under two until the knot is the desired width. Work taut and trim all ends.

1590. A "TASSEL" SHROUD KNOT. This is best made with three-strand Manila rope. Crotch two ends and put on a *very strong and narrow seizing* (the CONSTRICTOR KNOT in five- or six-ply sail twine will serve). *Single wall all six strands* together to the right. Be certain that the strands of the two sets are led alternately into the knot, first an upper, then a lower one. Next *crown* the six strands to the right above the wall and finally tuck all ends down to the stem as shown by the arrow. Work the knot very snug.

If, instead of employing this as a SHROUD KNOT, it is desired to make a TASSEL of it, cut off the lower rope at the length of the other strands. This gives nine strands in all to be opened into yarns. Put a drop of Duco cement on the end of each yarn if it is desired that they should not ravel.

1591. Another SHROUD KNOT with all ends pointing in one direction. Marry two ends and seize them strongly at the crossing, hold them vertically and, without shifting the grip, wall the upper strands; then wall the lower strands (both sets to the right). Stick the lower ends up to the stem, through the upper wall, as pictured in the left diagram. Draw all snug, working the two walls together while pulling at the ends. This may also be used as a TASSEL by cutting the rope off at the length of the strand ends. But it will not prove so secure as the previous TASSEL.

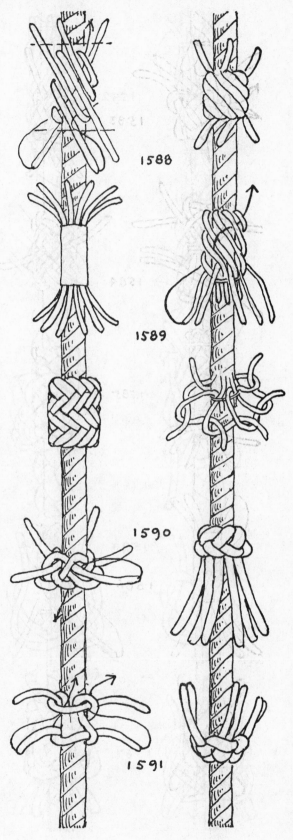

1592

1593

1592. A CUBE-SHAPED SHROUD KNOT. Marry two ends of four strands each, seize stoutly at the point of crossing with a CONSTRICTOR KNOT (#1249). Lay each set of strands a short distance along the opposite structure and seize again (four or five times the diameter of the rope apart). Roll a strip of white paper tightly around the section between the seizings and paste down the end to form a sleeve. This is merely to save confusion.

Helix the upper strands downward to the right, passing with each end *all the strands of the other set*. Seize the four ends below the paper sleeve and bring each of the lower strands forward between two of the strands that have been seized together. Lead the lower set in a left helix to the top, laying each strand between two strands of the opposing set and parallel with them. Seize these strands at the top just beyond the edge of the paper cylinder. The structure should now resemble the second diagram.

Tuck each bottom end to the right under the first bight of the opposing strands. Turn the structure upside down and tuck each of the lower ends to the right under the first bight of the opposing strands. Then tuck the second set only, once more over one and under one.

Note that at this point with sister strands the over-and-under is parallel, not contrary.

Next, without further tucking, arrange the opposing ends in the center to lie alternately, exactly as in the fourth diagram. If it seems impossible to arrange any two opposing strands in this way, try the next strand of the opposing set instead, either the one to the right or the one to the left of the one that proved bothersome.

Having arranged the strands as directed, tuck all ends one set at a time over one and under one. One of the two sets will have to be tucked a second time over one and under one, to bring all ends out at the rim. This makes a regular basket-weave surface. The knot must now be worked methodically and deliberately and prodded constantly to make it assume its proper cubical shape. The end seizings and the paper sleeve are removed as the knot is drawn up. (Scissors will be of assistance.) Only the original basic seizing is left.

A similar knot of triangular cross section may be made with three-strand rope, but it is not so satisfactory.

1593. A TWO-STRAND SHROUD KNOT. Wall the strands of the lower end and insert the strands of the upper end as indicated by the arrows in the second diagram. Work the knot a little more snugly into shape and then tuck the ends as in the third diagram. This knot, in common with many of the smaller knots of other series, is very easily spilled until well drawn up. In knot tying, simple forms frequently are more difficult to work than the more intricate ones.

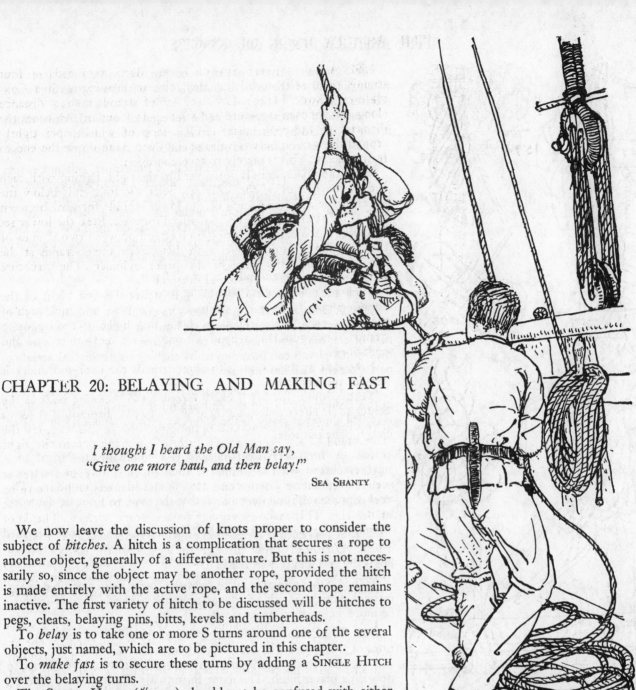

CHAPTER 20: BELAYING AND MAKING FAST

I thought I heard the Old Man say,
"Give one more haul, and then belay!"

SEA SHANTY

We now leave the discussion of knots proper to consider the subject of *hitches*. A hitch is a complication that secures a rope to another object, generally of a different nature. But this is not necessarily so, since the object may be another rope, provided the hitch is made entirely with the active rope, and the second rope remains inactive. The first variety of hitch to be discussed will be hitches to pegs, cleats, belaying pins, bitts, kevels and timberheads.

To *belay* is to take one or more S turns around one of the several objects, just named, which are to be pictured in this chapter.

To *make fast* is to secure these turns by adding a SINGLE HITCH over the belaying turns.

The SINGLE HITCH (⚓1594) should not be confused with either the SLIPPERY HITCH (⚓1620) or the HALF HITCH (⚓1662). It consists of a single turn around an object with the end laid *under* its own standing part.

This holds the end *against* the object.

The SLIPPERY HITCH is similar, but a bight instead of the end is tucked under the standing part.

The HALF HITCH (⚓1662) consists of a SINGLE HITCH made with an end *around its own standing part*. The SINGLE HITCH (⚓1594) is one half of a CLOVE HITCH (⚓1178), while the HALF HITCH (⚓1662) is one half of Two HALF HITCHES (⚓1710). The SINGLE HITCH spills when removed from its object, while the HALF HITCH, upon removal, pulls up into an OVERHAND KNOT (⚓515). The CLOVE HITCH spills upon removal, while Two HALF HITCHES capsizes into a GRANNY KNOT (⚓1216).

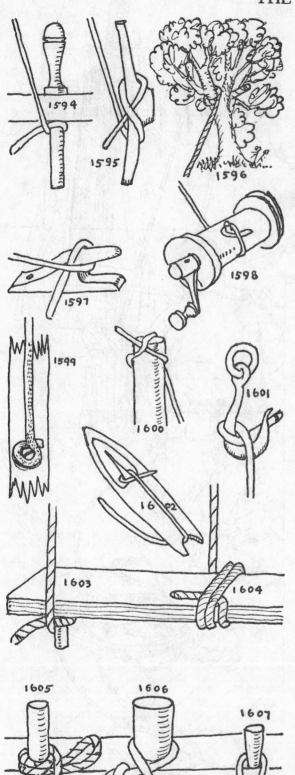

The SLIPPERY HITCH, having been put to work, spills instantly when the end of the rope is pulled. This withdraws the bight and releases the rope.

The SINGLE HITCH must first be relieved of its load, after which it can be untied by flirting or jerking the standing part.

The HALF HITCH must be opened and the end withdrawn by hand.

1594. A HITCH, or a SINGLE HITCH, is sometimes, but not often, termed a SIMPLE HITCH; the name SINGLE HITCH was applied by Lieutenant (subsequently Admiral) Luce in his *Seamanship* of 1862. The end of the rope is nipped under the standing part against an edge or shoulder, and if the adjustment is good the knot is secure.

Unless the end of the rope is very short, and the need temporary, a SLIPPERY HITCH will be found preferable, as it is easier to untie.

1595. A *single turn* and a SINGLE HITCH is often used for temporary purposes on either a belaying pin or a cleat.

1596. A SINGLE HITCH, applied to the crotch or branch of a tree, is quite secure but is apt to pinch or bind on account of the roughness of the bark and may have to be removed by hand. Generally the SINGLE HITCH can be removed by shaking or flirting the standing part after the load has been removed.

1597. Jib sheets on a small boat are often belayed to *thumb cleats* in this fashion. By lifting the end behind the standing part the hitch is spilled almost as easily as the SLIPPERY HITCH, which is more often used for the purpose.

1598. A SINGLE HITCH to a stud is a common attachment to a small ratcheted windlass which is used for a variety of purposes, such as tightening lawn-tennis-net ropes and awning hoists. The stud is preferably countersunk so that the rope will not be damaged by it.

1599. A sash cord is recessed in a groove and socket in the side of a sash. A flathead screw through the center of the SINGLE HITCH holds the end securely in place.

1600. A SINGLE HITCH taken over the top of a post or pole in the manner pictured, with a groove across the post end, would seem to be more secure than KNOT #218.

1601. The BLACKWALL HITCH is one of the most common applications of the SINGLE HITCH, but it is not to be trusted too far. At sea it is used in setting up rigging lanyards when they are too short to tie with a better hitch. The name BLACKWALL HITCH was applied by Steel in 1794.

1602. The SINGLE HITCH is always used when starting to wind material on a netting needle. It is also used when starting to wind a kite string on a stick, or a line on a reel.

1603. Whaleboat and other small-boat halyards are made fast to a peg on the underside of a coaming or thwart with either a SINGLE HITCH or a SLIPPERY HITCH.

1604. When no peg is at hand, a number of turns of rope may be taken around a thwart and the end jammed as pictured. This hitch may be slipped if desired.

1605. If the rope is too small for the peg, lay back the end and twist the two parts together to increase its bulk, then make a SINGLE HITCH with the doubled part.

1606. If you are at all nervous when lowering yourself from aloft with a SINGLE HITCH, tie an OVERHAND KNOT in the end before forming the hitch. When you have returned to deck the hitch is removed by shaking or flirting the rope.

1607. The knot pictured here is in formation a HALF HITCH. But the principle by which it is nipped is the principle of the SINGLE HITCH (⚹1603).

1608. *Pin racks* are seized in the rigging well above deck and are belayed to in bad weather, or when there is a deck load, or if the deck is cluttered.

1609. A *right-hand turn* on a pin is the one that is naturally taken by a right-handed sailor. When running rigging has been hauled taut the mate usually shouts, "So!" "Enough!" "Hold!" "Hold it!" "There!" or any other individual expression that he fancies, and to which the crew must become accustomed. The next order is, *"Belay,"* which may be followed by "Make fast," after sufficient turns have been taken. The preferred way is shown in which to take the initial turn when the standing part leads from the left.

1610. A left-hand turn is the one naturally taken by a left-handed sailor. Right-hand turns are sometimes insisted on, as uniformity is desirable, particularly at night, when a sailor has to "see with his fingers." But the direction of the initial turn is usually determined by the lead of the rope, except when a rope leads up and down.

The length of a belaying pin depends on the thickness of the rail. Generally a pin projects six or seven inches below the rail, but the handle of the pin may be anything up to twelve or fourteen inches above the rail, depending on the size of the coil that is hung from it. Sometimes coils are divided and hang from two neighboring pins.

1611. Right-hand belaying-pin turns are taken in this way, but there is no tendency for a rope to twist, whichever way the turns are taken, as the turn at the top is always the reverse of the turn at the bottom, so that the two compensate each other.

1612. An initial *round turn* on a pin is common, in fact preferable, but after the first turn a round turn is lubberly and not to be countenanced.

1613. When possible, a cleat should be fixed so that the lead of the standing part is at an angle with it, be it either from the left or from the right.

1614. *"Make fast"* (*contra,* "Cast off"). This is the order to add a SINGLE HITCH to the top of the coil on a pin, or on the forward or upper horn of a cleat.

1615. ANTI-GALLIGAN HITCH. The name is derived from "anti-Gallican" and is a survival from the Napoleonic Wars. Incidentally it is the most polite name I know for a "left-hand" BELAYING-PIN HITCH, which is at times very difficult to untie.

1616. *Belay and stop.* A method of relieving the strain on a belaying pin by means of a stopper. This is also known as "backing" a sheet, brace, etc.

1617. A *deck lead* allows of stronger hauling than a straight lead.

1618. A "permanent lead" is generally rove through an eye or a block that is fast to a staple or ring on deck.

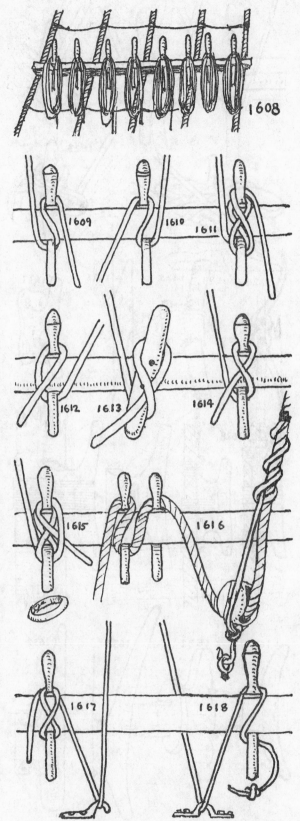

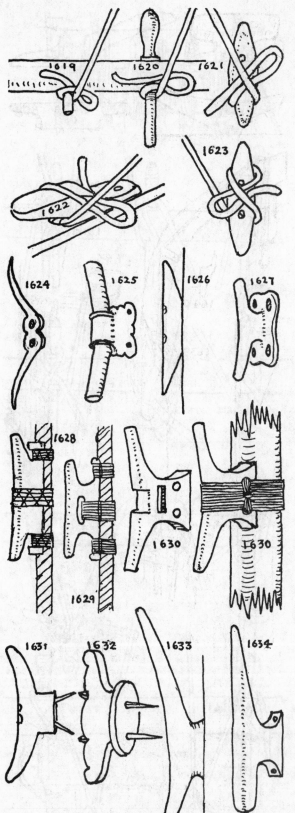

1619. The name Slippery Hitch is given in the anonymous *Vocabulary of Sea Phrases* (1799), and Norie (1802) speaks of the "Slippering Hitch." On shipboard the knot is seldom called for, but in small boats, especially open boats that are easily capsizable, the necessity frequently arises for instant casting off, and the Slippery Hitch is found indispensable. A whaleboat's halyards as well as sheets are always secured with them, since a Slipped Knot admits of casting off without first removing the load.

1620. The former knot is *the* Slippery Hitch. This one is called a Slippery Pin Hitch, and is for the same purpose.

1621. A Slippery Hitch may be *applied to a cleat* as illustrated. On small boats the cleat takes the place of the belaying pin.

1622. A Slippery Hitch to a *thumb cleat*. In this manner the jib sheets of small boats are often secured.

1623. A *slipped turn on a cleat* is often confused with the Slippery Hitch.

1624. A clothesline cleat of galvanized iron. The acute angle of the horn pinches the line enough to hold it taut while the turns are being added.

1625. A composite cleat with iron standard and wooden horns; the date is around 1875.

1626. A pinch cleat is designed to grip a rope instantly and hold it without rendering until turns can be added. In various patterns they are found on small racing boats, in stage scenery, etc., wherever quick handling is required.

1627. A common commercial galvanized iron cleat for awnings, clotheslines, etc.

1628. A shroud or rigging cleat is shown by Lever in 1808. It is scored for three seizings, which are to be snaked.

1629. The modern shroud or rigging cleat is similar in shape but is made of galvanized iron or bronze.

1630. A *mast cleat*, that is shown by Lever, has a score for the seizing and a long hole through which the under turns are laid. When these have been tightly applied, crossing turns are added through two round holes, which tightens or fraps the seizing and holds the cleat snugly to the mast. The crossing turns may be snaked.

1631. The horns of an old-fashioned cleat were more curved than those in common use today.

Screws are a nineteenth-century invention and cleats of an early date were nailed or, occasionally, bolted. Nails should be shellacked, dried and well toed when driven.

1632. This cleat is copied from Roding (1795). The nails are exceedingly long and were not toed.

1633. A *horn cleat* from the davit tackles of the bark *Sunbeam*. The specimen was eighteen inches in length. The upper horn is made long in order to hold the turns of a large coil.

1634. An *anvil cleat* for the halyards of a small yacht.

1635. On small craft, where decks are always crowded, deck cleats, if they are used at all, should have wide flat tops. These are much easier on the feet than upturned horns. Moreover the horns should

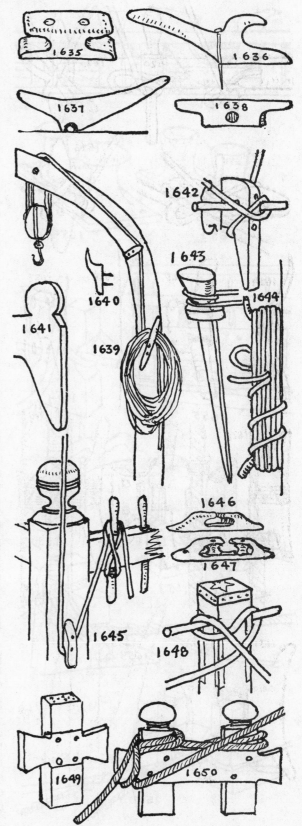

either be very close to deck or else so open that bare toes will not be pinched under them. It is preferable to have cleats fixed to houses and masts and at an angle with the lead.

The cleat pictured was made about 1800. More recent deck cleats are tapered instead of being square-horned. On coastwise vessels, both sail and steam, and on scows, barges and canal boats, large iron deck cleats are common. They are also much used on modern cement wharfs, which have little piling to make fast to. But on deep-sea sailing craft they are not often seen. Clear decks are needed for the day's work and deck cleats are very apt to foul running rigging.

1636. A combined *thumb* and *pinch cleat* of bronze has been used for jib sheets.

1637. A bronze *rocker cleat* is made for a similar purpose. It requires very few turns and no hitch, as the pull of the sail clamps the forward horn hard down on the turn of the sheet.

1638. For small craft a *mainsheet cleat* is sometimes fitted with a hole. A FIGURE-EIGHT KNOT is put in the end of the sheet to prevent unreeving. The illustration shows an early example.

1639. This illustrates horn cleat ⌗1633, in use on the davit of a whaler.

1640. A thumb cleat on the side of the davit serves as a fair-leader to keep the fall from fouling the whaleboat.

1641. The shoe cleat is somewhat similar in form to ⌗1642, but it does not have the "norman," as the iron crossbar is termed. The one given here is copied from Roding (1795).

1642. The ram's-head cleat is an old form that is now being revived. It is used to make fast a schooner's halyards.

1643. A loggerhead in the stern of a whaleboat is the means of snubbing and also holding fast the whale line with a series of round turns.

1644. As an iceboat has no deck, it is important that all coils should be fixed. This method of belaying exhausts the halyard and serves the double purpose of coiling and belaying. It was pictured and described by Öhrvall in *Om Knutar* in 1916, and is found on lake scows and other light racing craft.

1645. A thumb cleat is sometimes used as a fair-leader at the fife rail.

1646. A chock is commonly used to provide a proper lead for various heavy warps.

1647. A fair-leader with "*rollers*" serves the same purpose with less friction.

1648. A single bitt with a norman (an iron crossbar) is often used for the mainsheet bitts of a small schooner. S turns are taken on bitts exactly as on cleats and pins, only, of course, horizontally. A similar bitt forward is often placed on small motor craft for the "anchor warp."

1649. A *mainsheet bitt* may have a mortised oak cleat which takes the place of the norman. This is commonly found on fishermen.

1650. Double bitts were formerly mortised with a similar cleat. On schooners main- and foresheets were made fast to them, and, on square-riggers, sheets and braces.

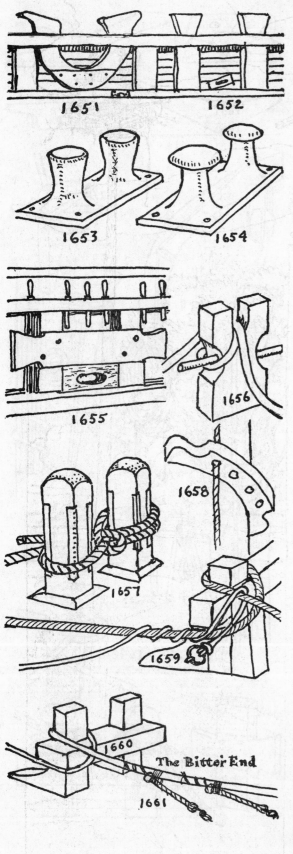

1651. *Kevels* or *cavils* are a seemingly obsolete variety of cleats or bitts that were let into the bulwarks of a ship and to which braces and sheets were belayed. The present drawing is abstracted from Du Clairbois, *Encyclopédie Méthodique Marine* (1783).

1652. Timberheads are ribs that are carried well above deck and mortised through the rail to serve as bitts.

1653. A *bollard* was originally a knighthead and, later, a large post at either side of a dock. Nowadays the name generally refers to round bitts of cast iron which may be either single or in pairs and are to be found either on the dockside or on shipboard, in the latter case generally on steamships.

1654. On wharfs and on steamships *iron bollards* are apt to have mushroom tops to prevent the hawsers from riding. It is generally easier to seize the ends (of hawsers) than it is to make them fast with hitches. But a large spliced eye placed over the bollard is preferable to either.

1655. A long *quarter cleat* bolted to the starboard stanchions was employed on a whale ship either in tying up or when getting a whale alongside. A similar cleat was generally to be found forward. It was not an uncommon fixture in other kind of craft.

1656. A *single bitt*, from *Histoire de la Marine* by De Joinville, is illustrated here. There is a similar one at the main fife rail of the British school ship *Implacable,* but without the norman, and with the addition of several shivs close to deck.

1657. A hawser belayed to double bitts, and made fast with a Single Hitch, is shown by Steel in 1794. Generally a round turn is first taken about one bitt with which to snub the line, before the S turns are added.

In large stuff it is good practice to put on sufficient turns to make it unnecessary to make fast at all, although, if desired, stops can be added. Hitches are difficult to put in heavy stuff and turns are more easily cast off.

1658. A mainmast fair-leader from an old square-rigger. A fair-leader serves several purposes. It lessens the slatting of the rigging, it also prevents loose ends from going adrift, since the Figure-Eight Knots in the rope's ends cannot pass through the holes. When several lines are slacked off at a time the positions of the holes serve to identify them. Fair-leaders, similar to pin racks, are seized in the shrouds about ten feet above deck, where they fill much the same purpose as the one given here for the mast.

1659. *Bitts and bitt stopper* from Gower (1808). The stopper is secured to a ring on the bitts with a Long Running Eye. After passing once around the cable, the end is dogged forward around the cable and "attended" by a sailor. Any running out of the cable nips it more firmly to the bitts.

1660. A cable is always "turned" around the bitts as pictured here, a turn in the starboard bitt being the reverse of the turn in the port bitt. The end of the cable abaft the bitts is the "bitter end." The common expression, "reached the bitter end," refers to a situation of extremity and has nothing at all to do with lees and dregs and other unpalatable things. It means literally that someone has "got to the end of his rope."

1661. Deck stoppers are passed and secured to the eyebolts down both sides of the deck on the way to the chain locker, which used to be just forward of and below the main hatch.

CHAPTER 21: HITCHES TO SPAR AND RAIL
(RIGHT-ANGLE PULL)

To Hitch, Is to catch-hold of Anything with a roape, to hold it fast.

SIR HENRY MANWAYRING:
The Sea-mans Dictionary, 1644

The verb *hitch* is seldom heard at sea. The expression *make fast* is used instead, and *hitch* as a verb is applied only to various marling-spike seamanship practices, such as *half hitching, marling, palm and needle,* and *ringbolt hitching.*

But there is also an exception in the use of the expression *make fast.* Although the knots employed are really hitches, the sailor *bends* instead of making fast to an anchor or a spar. There are three hitches so used that are always termed *bends.* They are the STUDDING-SAIL BEND, the TOPSAIL HALYARD BEND and the FISHERMAN'S BEND. These three knots are basically alike and the differences between them consist either in the number of the turns or the method of tucking the end.

This chapter is composed of hitches to objects of more or less cylindrical form, the pull being at an angle with the object. These are of two general sorts, the first treated being SNUG HITCHES of *two* or more turns, in which the ends are secured under one or more of the turns. The second variety consists of LOOSE HITCHES of *one* or more turns in which the ends are secured to the standing part, generally with one or two HALF HITCHES.

The TIMBER HITCH is an exception to this classification, for, although it has but one turn around the spar, the end is secured under the one turn.

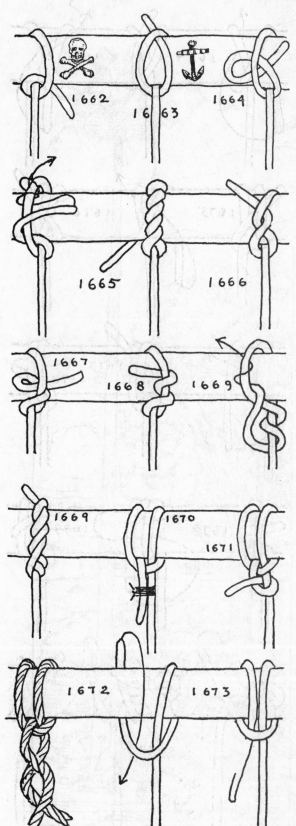

1662. The HALF HITCH as shown here is generally the first step in tying some more elaborate hitch. It should not be used unsupported, as it is by no means dependable. But, if seized, it becomes secure. The name HALF HITCH is given by Falconer (1769).

1663. The HALF HITCH, with the nip adjusted to bear at the top of the spar, is quite a different thing. So long as the pull is constant, and the adjustment is not altered by loosening or shaking, the hitch is adequate for almost any temporary purpose.

1664. A SLIPPED HALF HITCH, with the nip near the top of the spar, may also be used with discretion.

1665. The TIMBER HITCH, sometimes called LUMBERMAN'S KNOT and COUNTRYMAN'S KNOT, was used at sea for securing the standing ends of topsail clewlines and fore and main clew garnets, according to the *Manual of Seamanship* (1891). In the *Manuscript on Rigging* (circa 1625), edited by R. C. Anderson, and published by the Society for Nautical Research, is the statement: "The tymber Hitch is to fasten the truss to the middle of ye Mayne yearde." Diderot illustrates the knot in 1762 and Steel illustrates and names it in 1794.

The hitch is much used in handling cargo, for which it is very convenient, as it practically falls apart when pull ceases. It is used for spars, timber, small crates and bales. The turns should always be "dogged" *with the lay* of the rope. Three tucks or turns are ample.

1666. A FIGURE-EIGHT HITCH is more secure than the HALF HITCH (#1662), particularly if the encompassed object is small.

1667. The above knot, slipped, was formerly tied in wicks and used in candle dipping.

1668. The FIGURE-EIGHT TIMBER HITCH is approximately as secure as #1665 and requires one less tuck.

1669. The FIGURE-EIGHT HITCH and round turn. If the rope is weak and the hoist is heavy, a round turn on the standing part adds materially to the strength of the knot.

1670, 1671. The CLOVE HITCH is a common POST HITCH. When made fast to a spar, the end should either be stopped (#1670) or half hitched (#1671) to its own standing part, as the knot has a tendency to slip. The name CLOVE HITCH appears in Falconer's Dictionary (1769).

1672. The CLOVE HITCH with the end tucked through the standing part is a semipermanent hitch that is used in boat lashing.

1673. The Cow HITCH or LANYARD HITCH is the knot that is employed in securing a lanyard to a shroud. It is the same knot formation as the BALE SLING HITCH, or RING HITCH (#1859), and the RUNNING EYE (#1699), but the Cow HITCH is tied in the end of the rigging lanyard while the Bale Sling Hitch is tied in the bight of a continuous strap or wreath and a Running Eye is tied in an Eye Splice.

1674. This brings us to Snug Hitches, in which the end is secured under a turn. This one is both strong and secure. It is well to draw up all knots carefully before putting them to work.

1675. Another hitch that is equally secure and, moreover, does not bind or jam. In big material particularly a knot that does not jam is most desirable.

1676. The Picket-Line Hitch is a practical Snug Hitch that does not slip when properly drawn up. It was shown to me by J. Lawrence Houghteling, who learned it while in service with the artillery. It does not appear to be a regulation army knot. It should be noted that this knot is the start for a 3L × 4B Turk's-Head. The same formation, reversed, is used by fishermen on their trawl and is shown, at the bottom of this page, as the Ground Line Hitch.

1677. Gaff Topsail Halyard Bend. This is a neat and snug hitch that is very easily untied. The tucked end should be nipped well up on the top of the spar.

1678. The Studding-Sail Bend is used for bending topgallant and royal studding-sail halyards. Except for the manner of securing the end, it is the same knot as the Fisherman's Bend (#1722). Having tied the previous hitch (#1677), lead the end back over the first turn and tuck under the second. It is not necessary to lead the end toward the top of the spar as the additional tuck makes it sufficiently secure. Brady names and describes the knot in 1841, saying, "The advantage is this, that it lies close to the yard and consequently permits of little or no drift between the yard and the block."

1679. The Topsail Halyard Bend is said to be a yachting hitch, but it is possible that it has never appeared outside the covers of a book. It has one more turn than the Studding-Sail Bend and this, like the second tablespoonful of castor oil, savors of redundancy.

1680. The Ground Line Hitch is the standard knot of the cod fishermen. It is used in affixing ganging lines to the ground line of Codfish Trawl #277. A short bight near the end is held with the left thumb against the heavier ground line, and two tight turns are taken to the right with the end, and the end is then stuck through the bight that has been held by the left thumb. The standing part is then pulled snug. Tied in this way, very little end is wasted. The gangings are fixed to the ground line at frequent intervals and the loose ends of the gangings, before they are secured to the ground line, are fitted with loops to which, at the proper time, hooks are attached by means of Ring Hitches (#311).

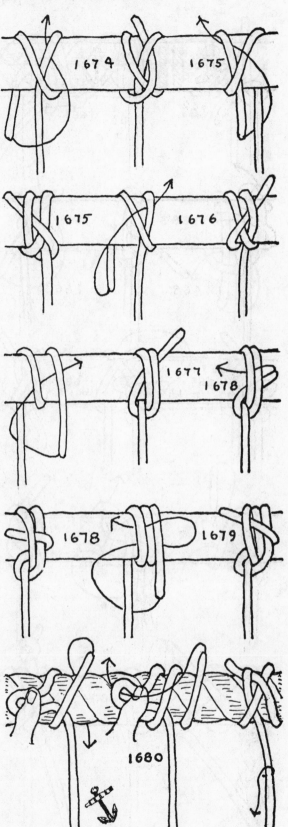

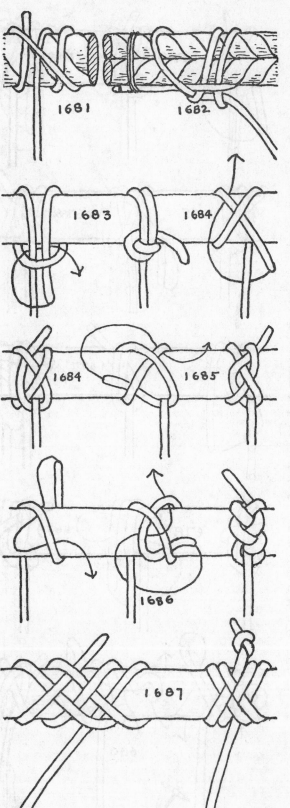

1681. The ROLLING HITCH was named by Dana in 1841 and the title is nowadays universally applied to the knot. But earlier authors, Lever, Biddlecomb and others, including Steel (1794), called it MAGNUS HITCH and sometimes MAGNER'S HITCH. KNOT #1721 was the original ROLLING HITCH (Falconer, 1769), but Dana and subsequent authors have renamed it "TWO ROUND TURNS AND TWO HALF HITCHES."

The feature of the present-day ROLLING HITCH (formerly MAGNUS HITCH) is its non-liability to slip under a lengthwise pull in the direction of the round turn. To tie: First make a round turn to the right, pass the end to the left in front of the standing part and add a HALF HITCH to the left. Sometimes an additional HALF HITCH is added to the neck of this knot, with the idea that this checks the tendency to slip if the pull is reversed.

1682. A BUOY ROPE HITCH, collected at Looe, in Cornwall. The headrope of a seine is generally double, with two ropes of opposing lays, which prevents twisting and rolling up the head. The hitch may be used with either a single or a double headrope.

1683. The next four knots are the results of an attempt to make a compact SNUG HITCH for semipermanent use. This one is compact but requires considerable arrangement.

1684. This knot is neater, requires less tucking and is every bit as satisfactory in other respects. The appearance is augmented by the resemblance to THREE-STRAND SINNET.

1685. The sinnet effect is also in evidence in this one, and the end, being tucked twice after passing the standing part, is more secure.

1686. In this knot the sinnet effect is carried still farther, and a very regular SNUG HITCH is the result. These are all handsome knots that would serve well on a boat boom and are fairly easy to untie.

1687. A decorative hitch for a boat boom that needs but one tuck. For the first three turns the lead is taken over all. After the required single tuck has been made, the knot must be worked taut.

1688. The knots on this page resulted from a search for a hitch that will draw snug without any working. The last four or five knots of the previous page must all be worked.

The present hitch appears to be the simplest and most secure of the lot. It draws up inevitably and has an excellent nip under all circumstances. Moreover it is exceptionally easy to untie.

1689. Make a round turn about the spar, pass the end behind the standing part and tuck under the first turn. This requires but one tuck and is as easy to untie as the former knot.

1690. A BACKHANDED HITCH. The next two knots, although they have a double bearing, require but a single pass around the spar. To tie this: Pass a bight up the back and down the front of the spar with the loose end at the right. With the end reach through the bight and half hitch around the standing part and its parallel part, as indicated with the arrow. Tie with a long end.

1691. In this case the bight is led over the spar from front to back and a single tuck of the end is all that is required. It may be somewhat simpler than the foregoing. The knot is hardly so snug as the rest of the series, but it draws up inevitably and is eminently practical. Tie with a long end.

1692. This is an interesting knot that, if worked tight as in the second diagram, will make a very satisfactory SNUG HITCH. It is easily untied and has but two turns around the spar. If tied slackly with a long end, the standing part may be pulled on until a third turn appears around the spar. This forms a very secure hitch that is quite as symmetrical on the back as on the front and does not jam. Moreover it is one of the easiest of all to untie.

1693. The left diagram shows a CLOVE HITCH. Pass the end to the left in back of the standing part and under the crossed turns. The result is a hitch that is firm, strong, secure and easily untied once the load has been removed.

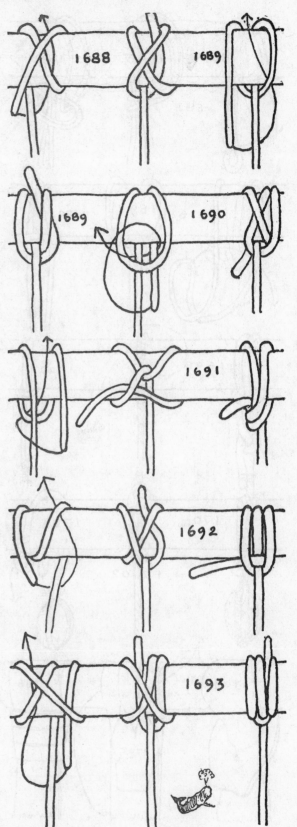

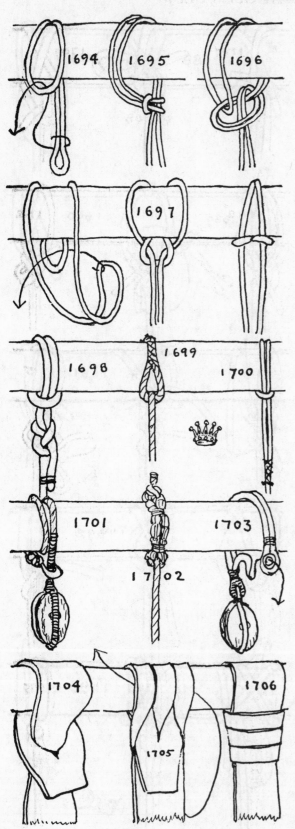

1694. The STRAP HITCH or BALE SLING HITCH is the most secure of all hitches, since it has no ends to untie. Moreover it cannot jam, being one of the easiest of hitches to loosen. It is used in rigging straps, in cargo slings and in elastic bands.

1695. The DOUBLE STRAP HITCH is tied in hand by drawing a bight from the standing part through the DOUBLE LOOP already formed. Used in longshore fishing gear.

1696. A KNOTTED STRAP HITCH which cannot untie. Add a HALF HITCH close outside the bight. It is found on lobster, eel and crab pots.

1697. The KELLIG HITCH, also called SLINGSTONE HITCH, is found on lobster- and crab-pot gear, where it is secured to the stones by which the pots are anchored.

1698. STRAP AND BECKET HITCH is one of the commonest methods of fastening slings, halyards and other gear, both standing and running. In standing rigging most hitches are seized.

1699. A RUNNING EYE is a neat hitch of the same basic sort as the last by which tyes, studding-sail halyards, stays, and other gear are made fast to different spars. The EYE SPLICE, which is generally served over, is held in place while the whole length of the line is rove through it. But if a LOOP KNOT should be used for a similar purpose (temporary) it may be tied in the standing end directly around the standing part so that no reeving is required.

1700. A LONG RUNNING EYE serves a similar purpose and is easier to adjust. The great length of the eye allows a whole coil of line to be passed through it at one time, dispensing with the tedious reeving required for the previous knot. It is used on yards in bending and furling sail, and is tied to the lead on a sounding line.

1701. A PENDANT HITCH consists of a hooked round turn and is "hitched" to a yard. Here the verb *hitch* is nautically correct as a hook is always "hitched," although a rope may not be. A *quarter tackle* is made fast in this manner and is used for getting aboard provisions.

1702. A STUDDING-SAIL HALYARD STRAP consists of a short selvagee made about the standing end of a studding-sail halyard. A button-and-eye fastening is made which is quickly and easily put in or cast off.

1703. A *permanent strap* is a convenient arrangement for hooking a block to a yard.

1704. A LEATHER STRAP HITCH, used for various purposes ashore. The end is rove through the slit as ⚹ 1699.

1705. Another STRAP HITCH. This must be slipped over the end of the object to which it is fastened. Take a strap, soften the leather in warm water, and cut two parallel slits dividing the strap into three equal parts. Double the strap back across the two slits and twist or slue each of the three bights that are formed one half a turn. Reeve the cylinder through them and pound smooth.

1706. Continuing from ⚹ 1705, remove the cylinder, take the free end of the strap and stick it through the three loops from right to left, keeping the *hide or grain side to the front*. Draw up firmly and carefully until it fits the cylinder snugly in the form pictured and then pound the knot smooth. This is given by Lester Griswold in *Handicraft*, which is a very informative book that is very well illustrated.

1707. The remaining knots of this chapter are Loose Hitches in which one or more turns are taken about the spar and the end is secured around the standing part.

The Half Hitch is the basic knot in this series as well as in the last. But with the end drawn close around the standing part, it is quite undependable. In order to hold well, it should be arranged as ⚓1663.

1708. The loop of the Slipped Half Hitch bulks larger than the single end of ⚓1707; for that reason it is perhaps a better hitch. It is a very common knot, but it is improved when arranged as the following knot.

1709. The "Half Hitched Half Hitch" is a good knot that cannot jam, will not slip, and unties easily.

1710. Two Half Hitches is the commonest of all hitches for mooring in particular and also for general utility. Steel gives the name in 1794. The difference between Two Half Hitches and the Clove Hitch is that the former, after a single turn around a spar, is made fast around its own standing part, while the latter is tied directly around the spar.

1711. The Buntline Hitch, when bent to a yard, makes a more secure knot than Two Half Hitches, but is more liable to jam. It differs from Two Half Hitches in that the second Half Hitch is inside instead of outside the first one.

1712. The Slipped Buntline Hitch has been recommended in agricultural college bulletins as a means of "tying up" horses.

1713. Reverse Hitches has less tendency to jam than Two Half Hitches (which has practically none) and is not a bad hitch for many purposes. It hardly seems to deserve the opprobrium that has been heaped upon it. Captain Benjamin A. Higgins, in answer to a question of mine, said: "I don't know what *you* call it; but if I catch the Greenie that tied it, I know what *I'll* call *him!*"

1714. The Lobster Buoy Hitch was shown to me years ago by John B. Cornell, of Cuttyhunk, who used it for about every purpose and claimed it was particularly good to tie to timber. As the chief industry of Cuttyhunk was wrecking, I value his opinion highly on such a point. The knot is tied tightly around the standing part and then is slipped along the rope snugly into place. Compare with ⚓1711.

1715. The Slip Noose Hitch is a common farm knot, and is used the world over for "tying up" or hitching horses to fence rails.

1716. The Bowline Hitch: A *sailor* will often, having passed his rope around an object, face about and tie a Bowline in the regular fashion. A landsman who is acquainted with the knot will usually form the round turn (shown in second diagram) with his left hand and reeve the end as shown by the arrow. The preferred sailor way is to make a Half Hitch, as in the first diagram, and then capsize it by pulling the end. The knot is then completed as shown by the arrow.

1717. A Half Hitch in standing rigging is always seized.

1718. A Round Turn and Half Hitch is also seized.

1719. Two Half Hitches, on deck, is not seized; but aloft or in ground tackle it is seized once and (rarely) twice. The greater the permanency of any gear, the greater is the care exercised in its tying. Riggers never seem to tire of adding seizings.

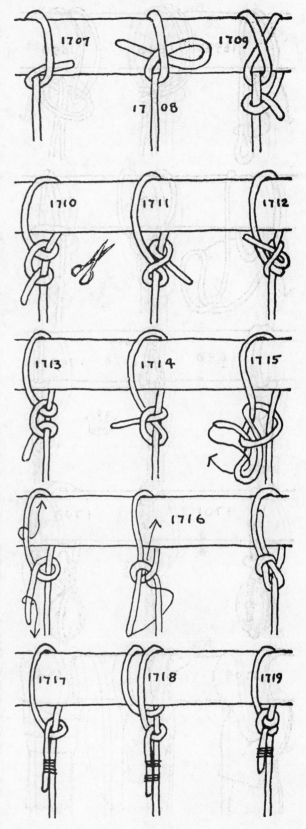

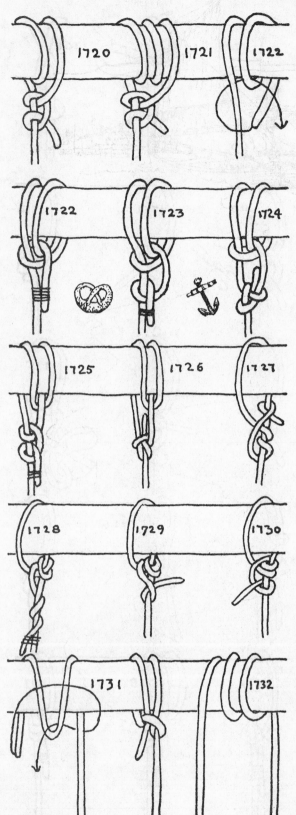

1720. The ROUND TURN AND TWO HALF HITCHES is named by Steel in 1794. If a spar is small a round turn is preferable to a single turn. It makes a stronger knot and dissipates the wear.

1721. TWO ROUND TURNS AND TWO HALF HITCHES, so called by Dana in 1841, and by subsequent authors, was originally called ROLLING HITCH (Falconer, 1769). It is a strong, old-fashioned knot that is excellent to tie to the limb of a tree.

1722. The FISHERMAN'S BEND is occasionally tied in this manner with one hitch only, which is always stopped or seized.

1723. The FISHERMAN'S BEND: The common way of tying this knot (1808) is with two hitches, which, Lever says, "is used for bending the studding-sail halyards to the yards."

1724. The FISHERMAN'S BEND AND BOWLINE: A quick and convenient way in which to finish off this hitch is with a BOWLINE KNOT when no seizing stuff is handy.

1725. The BACKHANDED HITCH is used in tying up to the stringpiece of a wharf, where it is usually difficult to reeve the warp underneath the timber. Only a single pass is required. A bight is pushed through the gap under the stringpiece and the end is then rove through the bight to be half hitched twice, and then stopped or seized.

1726. The BACKHANDED HITCH AND BOWLINE makes a good TOW-ROPE HITCH to an automobile axle. An axle is difficult of access, and the single pass required of this knot is a great convenience. The BOWLINE is quicker to tie than a seizing; moreover it can be applied where the knot will clear the car.

1727. The JAM HITCH. In structure this is closely related to the three knots to follow. It belongs equally with the BUTCHER'S KNOTS of Chapter 2 and with the BINDER KNOTS of Chapter 16. The peculiarity of the knot is that it closes easily but does not tend to open, which is the opposite of the hitch which follows. The latter is similar in construction but reversed. It opens easily but does not tend to close.

1728, 1729. The MIDSHIPMAN'S HITCH bears the same relation to the ROLLING HITCH (※1735) that TWO HALF HITCHES (※1710) bears to the CLOVE HITCH (※1178). That is to say, the knot is made fast around its own standing part, while in the ROLLING HITCH it is made fast around another object.

1730. If you have fallen overboard the MIDSHIPMAN'S HITCH (※1728) is the knot to tie in the end of the rope that is tossed to you. Dog the end and hold it in your hand while you are hoisted aboard. But in big stuff the knot is tied as shown here. In ※1728 and ※1729 the second turn is jammed under the first taken turn. In big stuff the end is generally seized. In small stuff it is more convenient to hitch as in ※1729. If the second turn is not jammed down over the first one, the knot will be adjustable and may be slid with ease to any place on the standing part where it will hold its position under tension.

1731. A SINGLE PASS HITCH that must be tied with a very long loose end. The bight, which, in the first diagram, is at the front, must be pushed to the back as the knot is drawn up.

1732. Three round turns are excellent for lowering heavy weights from aloft or from the branch of a tree, and four or five will serve temporarily as a hitch. Be certain that the turns are snug before lowering away. "There's a lot of virtue in a round turn."

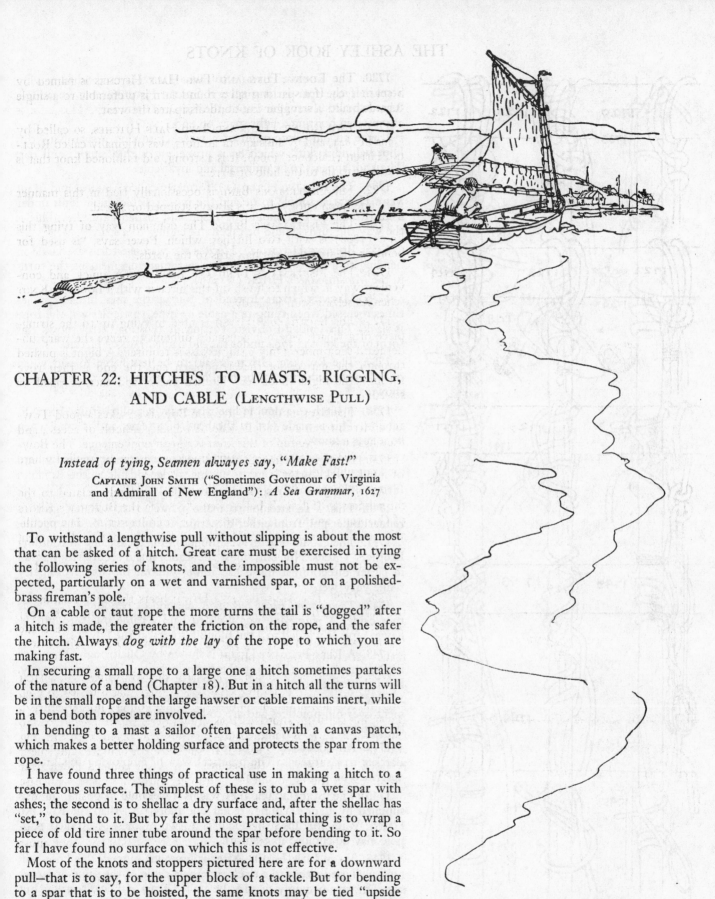

CHAPTER 22: HITCHES TO MASTS, RIGGING, AND CABLE (LENGTHWISE PULL)

Instead of tying, Seamen alwayes say, "Make Fast!"

CAPTAINE JOHN SMITH ("Sometimes Governour of Virginia
and Admirall of New England"): *A Sea Grammar*, 1627

To withstand a lengthwise pull without slipping is about the most that can be asked of a hitch. Great care must be exercised in tying the following series of knots, and the impossible must not be expected, particularly on a wet and varnished spar, or on a polished-brass fireman's pole.

On a cable or taut rope the more turns the tail is "dogged" after a hitch is made, the greater the friction on the rope, and the safer the hitch. Always *dog with the lay* of the rope to which you are making fast.

In securing a small rope to a large one a hitch sometimes partakes of the nature of a bend (Chapter 18). But in a hitch all the turns will be in the small rope and the large hawser or cable remains inert, while in a bend both ropes are involved.

In bending to a mast a sailor often parcels with a canvas patch, which makes a better holding surface and protects the spar from the rope.

I have found three things of practical use in making a hitch to a treacherous surface. The simplest of these is to rub a wet spar with ashes; the second is to shellac a dry surface and, after the shellac has "set," to bend to it. But by far the most practical thing is to wrap a piece of old tire inner tube around the spar before bending to it. So far I have found no surface on which this is not effective.

Most of the knots and stoppers pictured here are for a downward pull—that is to say, for the upper block of a tackle. But for bending to a spar that is to be hoisted, the same knots may be tied "upside down."

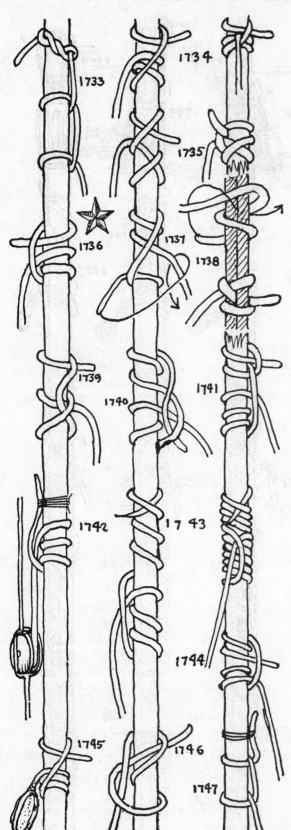

1733. The Timber Hitch and Half Hitch is used when towing a spar. If the spar is long several Single Hitches may be added. There should always be one at the forward extremity. This knot is also used in hoisting a light spar "on end."

I have an old photograph of a wrecker towing a spar with this knot behind a skiff, which he is propelling with a single scull oar. The knot appears to be universal and invariable.

1734. The Rolling Hitch (1), formerly called Magnus and Magner's Hitch, is simple to tie and the most reliable single knot under a lengthwise pull. It should be made and loaded carefully. This is the way the turns should be taken in bending to a spar.

1735. Rolling Hitch (2). Here is the way the turns are taken in bending to a rope, which is similar to the arrangement of the turns in the Midshipman's Hitch (#1729).

1736. Magnus Hitch. Instead of #1734, the final hitch is sometimes reversed when tying to a cable or rope, particularly if the rope is slack. This tends to obviate torsion or twisting. Steel shows this form of the knot in 1794 under the old name Magnus Hitch.

1737. The Rolling Hitch is said to be less liable to slip when pulled in the direction of the final hitch if a Half Hitch is added as shown.

1738. A hitch to a double line that may be pulled from either direction. This is made fast to the head of a seine, and is used when attaching a buoy.

1739. A single-hitched Clove Hitch is sometimes put in the end of a tail block, but it is by no means so dependable as the Rolling Hitch and presumably is tied by the inexpert.

1740. This is an attempt to make a hitch that will not give or render under pull from either direction. It appears to be dependable.

1741. The Camel Hitch was found on the picket line in Ringling Brothers' Circus. Not only must the knot remain secure from a pull in either direction; it must also untie without too much difficulty while very wet.

1742. *Two round turns seized.* A method of bending a *ring rope* to a cable. A *ring rope* was used to haul a cable out through the hawse pipe. It was led to a tail block fastened at the bowsprit.

1743. A Reef Pendant Hitch is shown by Qualtrough. This is an improvement over a cleat on the boom, which is always in the way. But I think that some of the Circus Pole Hitches shown in Chapter 2, which also properly belong in the present chapter, are an improvement over old practices and are to be recommended for purposes of this nature.

1744. An Arboreal Hitch or Tree Surgeon's Knot from the Bartlett tree surgeons. The practical way of employing this knot is described on page 77.

1745. The Steeplejack's Hitch is found on page 74. It was supplied by Laurie Young. It has one more turn than the Rolling Hitch. With stirrups suspended from two of these, the tallest flag-pole may be climbed in comfort.

1746. Slack Line Hitch. After it has once nipped, this knot will hold well, tied either to a slack rope or a cable of the same or larger size. Drawn up snugly, it may be pulled from either direction. But it is not wholly satisfactory if tied to stiff braided rope.

1747. The coastwise steamship sailor of today is apt to secure a tail block with a series of HALF HITCHES and a stopped end.

Stoppers and *straps* are always "passed." In using the term in this way, the implication is that, on account of the intricacy of the hitch, the size of the material, or the heaviness of the task, it is necessary to *pass* the rope from one hand to another, or else from one sailor to another.

1748. A tail block stopped in the rigging. This consists of a SINGLE HITCH only, but it is dogged half a turn, and it is this dogging which makes it better practice than ✳1747. The hitch is also taken so that any tendency to slip is *with the lay* of the rope.

Strictly speaking, a hitch in a small rope around a bigger one is a SINGLE HITCH, but custom dictates that so long as the hitch is around a rope of sorts, the formation may be called a HALF HITCH. It is more liable to be called a SINGLE HITCH when it is taken around a spar. But here again it is impossible to make a rule, for the terms nowadays are very loosely applied, even by the sailor himself.

1749. This is similar to the last, but the end is turned back and "stopped." It was given by Roding in 1788. The dogging is left-handed since this is stopped to cable-laid rope.

1750. Knight shows this method of lashing the eye of a tackle block to a cargo boom with racking turns. Cheeks should be nailed to the spar if possible.

1751. A tail block hitched, dogged and hitched. This is similar to ✳1748, but it is dogged several turns, and the end is hitched instead of being stopped. Although not so good practice, it is quicker in an emergency.

1752. A tail block with the tail round turned, then dogged, and finally secured with a hitch.

1753. A tail block with turns arranged as in a MIDSHIPMAN'S HITCH (✳1735), and with the end dogged and stopped.

1754. A tail block showing a MIDSHIPMAN'S HITCH, hitched, dogged, and hitched.

1755. A cross-lashed strap made fast in the rigging, to hook a block to. Shakespeare terms this method of lashing (differently applied) "cross-gartering."

1756. A cross-lashed strap, for hooking a block or hoisting a spar. For the latter purpose the drawing should be turned end for end.

1757. A double tail block. The tails are half hitched, dogged and seized in the same direction, but with opposite twist. They should be longer than pictured. If the tails are long, they may be dogged several turns and the ends reef knotted.

1758. A sling to which a tackle is to be hooked. Selvagee slings and straps are easier on spars and rigging than corded rope, besides being less liable to slip.

1759. A STRAP or BALE SLING HITCH to mast and rigging. This is much used at sea. Nares states, "If steadied until under proper strain any weight may be lifted." Number 1757 would, on the whole, seem preferable.

1760. A single strap for a well pipe.

1761. A single strap to a telephone pole.

1762. A double strap for hoisting a spar or hooking a tackle.

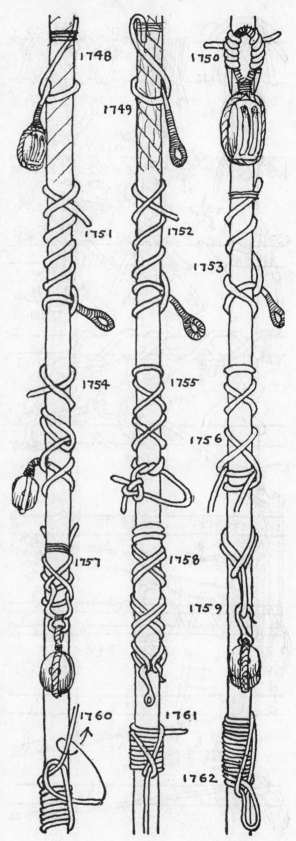

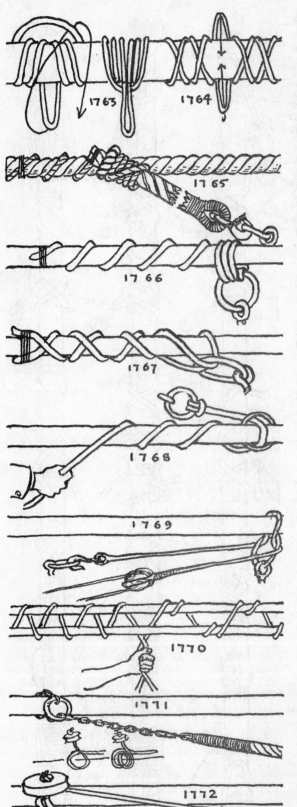

1763. A double strap or sling for hoisting a spar at middle length. One bight is rove through the other and a tackle is hooked to the single bight.

1764. A CROSS-LASHED SLING is also to be used in the middle of a spar; the two bights are clapped together and hooked to a tackle block.

1765. A *stopper*, in the eighteenth and nineteenth centuries, provided the means of making fast a hemp cable, when a ship rode at anchor, since a cable was too large for belaying in the ordinary way. At an earlier period, when ships were smaller, cables were made fast to the foremast, with seized turns and hitches.

The *deck stopper* is a piece of deck furniture that apparently has not changed since it first appeared. On large naval vessels cable-laid rope has at times been used with a SPRITSAIL SHEET KNOT in the end. But as a rule deck stoppers were of hawser-laid rope and either a STOPPER KNOT or else a DOUBLE WALL KNOT was tied in the end. A lanyard half the circumference of the stopper was spliced around the neck, and the lower end was hooked or shackled to a ring on the deck. The average deck stopper was five or six feet long, but on naval vessels they sometimes reached a length of twelve feet. The length of the lanyard depended on the size of the cable. Four or five turns were taken around both stopper and cable close to the knot, and after that four rounds of "dogging," with an ample length left over for stopping, were allowed.

1766. The ordinary SINGLE RING STOPPER. These automatically became DECK, WING, HATCHWAY, or BITT STOPPERS, according to where they were made fast.

1767. The DOUBLE RING STOPPER.

1768. A RING STOPPER that was shown by Gower.

1769. A RING STOPPER given by Knight for use with a wire hawser.

1770. A nipper secures the cable to the *messenger*, which is a continuous belt of smaller cable half the circumference of the cable itself, passing around two capstans, one forward, the other near the mainmast. The capstans and messenger provide the means of heaving in the cable.

The cable was lashed to the messenger with nippers, which were attended by "nipper boys," while the cable was being hove in. The nipper boys walked aft, holding the ends in place, and after they were untied brought them forward again for another nip. The illustration shows two ways of passing the nippers.

1771. A small chain with a ring attached to a tackle is used on a rigging table for heaving on the strands of large wire rigging while splicing.

1772. The SHIVER HITCH is shown by Lever in 1808. It was used in the Merchant Marine for fastening a jig tackle to a cable when getting up anchor. Either a SINGLE HITCH or a round turn and hitch were used. The Navy did not employ tackles for the purpose, having plenty of hands for manning the capstans and nippers.

CHAPTER 23: HITCHES TO STAKE AND POST, PILE AND BOLLARD

The work was hard an' the wages low,
   (Leave 'er, Johnny, leave 'er!)
The grub was bad, an' the voy'ge was slow,
   (Leave 'er, Johnny, leave 'er.)

Oh Make 'er fast, an' Stow yer gear,
   (Leave 'er, Johnny, leave 'er!)
An' tie 'er up to the bloomin' pier,
   It's time for us to leave 'er!

OLD SHANTY

About the only time a sailor "ties" is when, his voyage over, he "ties up" to the wharf, but, once arrived there, he may even go so far as to "tie up for the winter." A sailor speaks of "tying a knot in the devil's tail" when he has completed a difficult job to his own satisfaction. In fact the expression *to tie* always seems to carry with it a note of conclusion or finality.

Piles and bollards are the usual furniture of the wharf. Stakes are commonly associated with tents, fences and guy ropes.

The word *post* does not at first appear to have much nautical flavor, but Falconer, in his *Dictionary of the Marine* (1769), under *Hitches*, speaks of posts and does not mention either piles or bollards. Bollards may be either double or single and so may bitts. Bitts and stanchions are generally rectangular in cross section. They are discussed further in Chapters 20 and 27.

The commonest of all POST HITCHES is undoubtedly the CLOVE HITCH. It is the one almost universally used on tent stakes. But the sailor himself seldom employs it as a hitch.

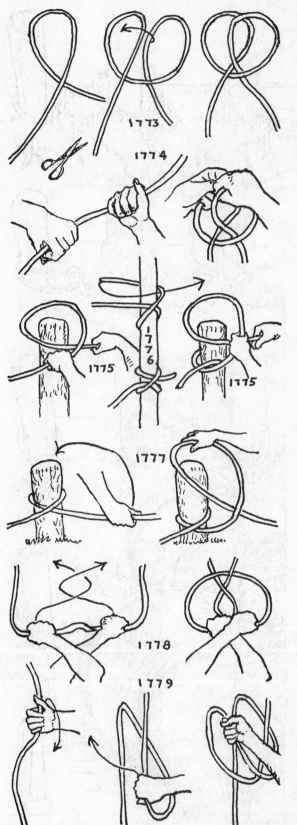

The importance of the CLOVE HITCH as a STAKE HITCH rests largely upon the ease, celerity and variety of the ways in which it may be formed. It can be tied with either one hand or two, picked with one hand off the deck or out of the air, as easily by night as by day; but, except as a CROSSING KNOT, there is a better holding knot for about every purpose to which the CLOVE HITCH can be put. Nevertheless the CLOVE HITCH is a very important knot and the most used of all POST HITCHES. At sea it is sometimes tied as a hitch in the ends of seizings, and ashore it is the nearest thing there is to a general utility hitch. It is by no means secure, but it is the quickest hitch there is to tie, and one of the easiest to remember.

Besides the several methods of tying given on the following page, there are a number of additional ways shown among the tricks and puzzles on page 485.

1773. The CLOVE HITCH was mentioned by Falconer in 1769. "Tom Bowling," in 1866, called it the BUILDER'S KNOT. It consists of two SINGLE HITCHES, the second one superimposed over the first. It is commonly tied in hand and then dropped over a post.

1774. A *quick way of tying* the CLOVE HITCH in medium-weight rope is here shown. With the back of the left hand and the palm of the right hand uppermost, grasp the rope with the two hands several feet apart. Rotate each hand one half turn as indicated by the arrows and clap the knuckles of the right hand into the palm of the left hand. Transfer the upper hitch into the grasp of the left hand and drop the knot over a post.

1775. To *make the hitch directly over a post* while pulling on the rope: Pull with the left hand and impart a right twist with the right hand, which will cause the bight between the two hands to form a SINGLE HITCH. This is dropped over the post while the left hand still holds the standing part of the rope taut. A second hitch is then added in the same way.

1776. To *tie around a tall post:* Where the post or pole is too tall for dropping hitches over the top, there is but one way to tie the knot. Make a turn with the end below the standing part, then put a hitch above by reeving the end without reversing the direction of the turns.

1777. A *one-hand method of casting* a CLOVE HITCH directly over the post. It is accomplished with a half turn of the right arm, which is repeated in adding the second hitch.

1778. The STEAMBOAT HITCH is the quickest and most convenient way that I know of tying the CLOVE HITCH in medium- or heavy-weight rope. It was first shown to me by E. E. du Pont, who had seen it tied on a Chesapeake Bay steamer. H. W. Riley, in a Cornell Agricultural School knot bulletin, calls this the *"Circus method."*

The CLOVE HITCH does not draw up snugly when pull is exerted on one end only and there is almost always an initial slip that cannot be gauged with certainty. The hitch may be unwound with a rotating pull in one direction, particularly if it is tied to a square post and the rope is stiff.

1779. This shows the *sailor's trick of picking up a* CLOVE HITCH *from deck*, employing one hand only. Between the second and third diagrams the loop is laid to the left across the lower part of the rope and the hand grasps the two parts pictured. With a little practice this may be done with a bale hook instead of the hand (⚹2544). Other ways of tying the CLOVE HITCH are given in Chapter 33,

"Tricks and Puzzles." The knot is also discussed in Chapter 15, "Crossing Knots," which is its most distinctive use, and also among the BINDING KNOTS of Chapter 16.

1780. The SEIZED HALF HITCH is mentioned by Falconer in 1769. Formerly the knot was used much more than at present; in fact the use of seizings and stoppings, except by riggers, has become infrequent. But if an eye is needed in very large rope, there is nothing better than this. A hitch is made around the standing part of the rope with its own end and then is drawn up snug and either stopped or seized.

1781. Two HALF HITCHES is mentioned by Steel in 1794. An expeditious way in which to tie the knot to a post is to first form a loose GRANNY KNOT, leaving a long end. As the ship swings she will take up the slack and the GRANNY will capsize into Two HALF HITCHES. Warps on coastwise ships, however, are generally fitted with spliced eyes to drop over piles and bollards, but deep-sea sailing craft usually keep the ends of their hawsers clear.

"Two half hitches will never slip"—Admiral Luce.

"Two half hitches saved a Queen's Ship"—Anonymous.

"Three half hitches are more than a King's Yacht wants"—Admiral Smyth.

1782. If a ship is to remain tied up for several days, Two HALF HITCHES, seized, is preferable to ⚓1780.

1783. In making small craft fast to a wharf the BOWLINE is sometimes tied as a hitch. Two loose HALF HITCHES are made and well separated. The one closest to the post is then capsized by pulling sufficiently to straighten out the turns, as shown by the arrows in ⚓1781. The end is then tucked, as shown by the arrows in the center diagram, to form a LEFT-HAND BOWLINE (⚓1034½).

1784. The ROUND TURN AND TWO HALF HITCHES is mentioned by Steel in 1794. It should be used when the object to be tied to is of small diameter, since the second turn dissipates the wear. The hitch is seized often but not invariably.

1785. The ROUND TURN AND SLIPPED HALF HITCH is an excellent temporary STAKE HITCH.

1786. REVERSED HALF HITCHES bears the same relation to a COW HITCH that TWO HALF HITCHES bears to a CLOVE HITCH. The same knot formation is either tied around its own standing part, which forms REVERSED HALF HITCHES, or around another object, which makes the COW HITCH. The knot is often seen on tent stakes and is more easily untied than TWO HALF HITCHES.

1787. A RIGHT-HAND BOWLINE is formed when REVERSED HALF HITCHES are put around a stake and then are capsized and further tucked in a manner similar to ⚓1782.

1788. A BOWLINE may be tied quickly in still another way. Form the standing part into a MARLINGSPIKE HITCH and reeve the end as indicated by the arrow. Adjust the loop to the desired size, then pull the hitch taut. The end of the rope is at once swallowed, and a BOWLINE KNOT is formed.

1789. The MARLINGSPIKE HITCH, given by Dana in 1841, has sometimes been called, in magazine articles, "the BOAT KNOT" and is said to be used over a stake for tying up. If this spills, it becomes the ordinary NOOSE HITCH shown as ⚓1803, a knot which is seldom allowed to approach salt water.

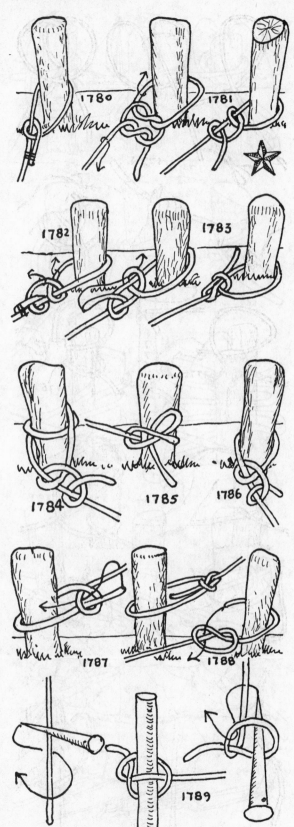

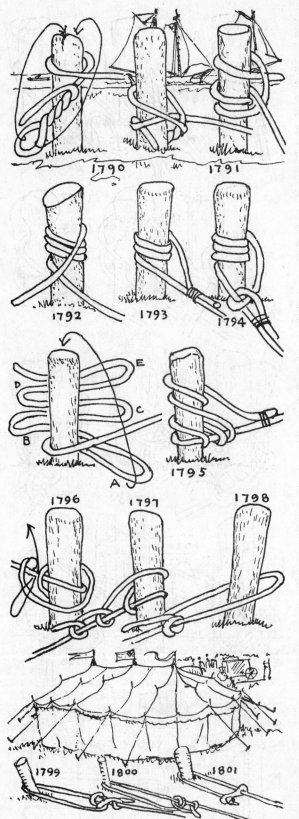

1790. A safe STAKE HITCH of simple construction that is distantly related to the TIMBER HITCH (※1665), consists of a SINGLE HITCH around the stake and a twisted loop in the end, which is dropped over the top of the stake.

1791. "MOORING HITCH" appears to be a fairly old name for the MAGNUS or ROLLING HITCH when made fast to a post. The merit of the hitch is that, when snugly applied, it will not slip *down* the post. Anyone who has found himself at full tide, after a hard day's fishing, with his painter fast to a stake four or five feet below high-water mark, will be inspired to learn this knot. First make a round turn below the standing part of the rope and then add a SINGLE HITCH above it.

1792. Several *snubbing turns* are taken with a warp around a pile and the headway of a ship is gradually checked before the warp is made fast.

1793. *Seized round turns.* When the ship has been brought to a standstill, if the hawser is a large one, the end may be merely seized or stopped to the standing part.

1794. *Round turns hitched.* A medium-sized hawser, or one that is pliant, is generally half hitched before seizing.

1795. The BACKHANDED MOORING HITCH. A single turn is first made around the post. When all headway is checked, a flake from the right is dragged forward *under* the standing part and turned over the top of the post without twisting it. The first left-hand bight is next lifted directly over the post without turning it. Then the next right-hand bight is dragged under the standing part and turned over the post as before. Alternate with left- and right-hand bights until the cable is exhausted, then stop the end to the standing part. It may take several hands to do this in very heavy stuff.

1796. The WET WEATHER HITCH is a circus-tent STAKE HITCH that has already been described in Chapter 2. A SINGLE HITCH is first taken around the post, several hands haul in the slack while one man, at the end, holds what is given. The end is backed around the stake and a SLIPPED HALF HITCH is added. If the rope shrinks in the rain one man can slack away and make fast alone.

1797. The BACKHANDED HITCH is a sailor's knot very similar to the circus hitch just shown. Instead of the SLIPPED HALF HITCH, TWO HALF HITCHES completes the knot. This is easily held and made fast at the exact point where the hawser is checked.

1798. The AWNING KNOT is an uncompleted MIDSHIPMAN'S HITCH (※1799). The second turn is carefully jammed so that the knot will hold until jerked or jarred, when it will spill instantly. It is used in roping off sections of decks and as a temporary tent STAKE HITCH on marquees, etc.

1799. The MIDSHIPMAN'S HITCH is the same as the foregoing with the addition of a HALF HITCH. It is a fixed knot that holds well and has a variety of uses.

1800. The ADJUSTABLE HITCH is based on the MAGNUS or ROLLING HITCH and is closely related to the MIDSHIPMAN'S KNOT, the difference being in the arrangement of the second turn. If the concluding hitch is reversed there will be less tendency to twist. Slide the knot either way and it should remain without rendering.

1801. The ordinary commercial stake adjustment serves the purpose no better than the ADJUSTABLE HITCH and is much more trouble to pack on a camping trip.

1802. The COW HITCH differs from the STRAP or BALE SLING HITCH in that the pull is on one part only and the knot is tied in the end instead of in the bight. The form, however, is the same; it is the hitch by which farmers stake out their cows to nibble favored grass in restricted places. It is also the knot by which the ends of rigging lanyards are secured. Other names for it are LANYARD HITCH, DEADEYE HITCH and STAKE HITCH. But the sailor himself is more apt to call it COW HITCH.

1803. The NOOSE HITCH or FARMER'S HITCH. A much-used but poor fastening unsuited to a post since it jams and is difficult to untie.

1804. The HALTER HITCH is based on the preceding knot but the tuck is made with a bight instead of the end. After the hitch has been carefully drawn up the end is dropped loosely through the final bight so that the knot cannot spill accidentally.

1805. A HALF HITCHED CLOVE HITCH. Although seldom mentioned, this hitch is not infrequently seen even on shipboard and is by no means a bad one. It is much used by cartmen. The HALF HITCH makes the basic CLOVE HITCH secure.

1806. A FARM HITCH for a halter: An OPEN OVERHAND KNOT is tied some distance from the end. The end is passed around the small of a post or a rail and is rove through the knot and drawn snug. The OVERHAND KNOT is pulled tight and a SLIP KNOT (#529) is added close to the original knot.

1807. The SLIPPED BUNTLINE HITCH is used both for hitching horses and for tying up small boats.

1808. Many of the SNUG HITCHES shown in Chapter 21 are suitable POST HITCHES. This illustrates the PICKET-LINE HITCH with the end slipped.

1809. A HIGH POST HITCH. Sometimes it is necessary to tie a boat to a pile or post where the drop of the tide is considerable. It will be found convenient to make fast with a SLIP KNOT and to lead a long end back to the boat. After you have returned to your boat and got all your gear stowed, have your oars or outboard motor in readiness and then cast off by hauling on the end of your painter, which slips the hitch. The rope is hauled back into the boat by pulling on the standing part after it has been untwisted.

1810. A HIGH POST HITCH *tied in the bight*. This is a great convenience on occasion. Middle the rope, pass the bight around the post and lay it around the two standing parts, then tuck a bight from the end part as indicated by the arrow. When the end is pulled the rope is drawn back into the boat.

1811. For temporary tying to a tall wharf, nothing can be more convenient than the SLIPPERY HITCH.

1812. A SINGLE HITCH to a post top. If tied in rope of proper size, texture, pliability and stretch, this is surprisingly secure until the rope is slacked off. A groove across the post top will render it doubly secure. It is probably a safer knot than #218 of Chapter 2.

1813. A CLOTHESLINE HITCH to a post that has a hole bored through the top.

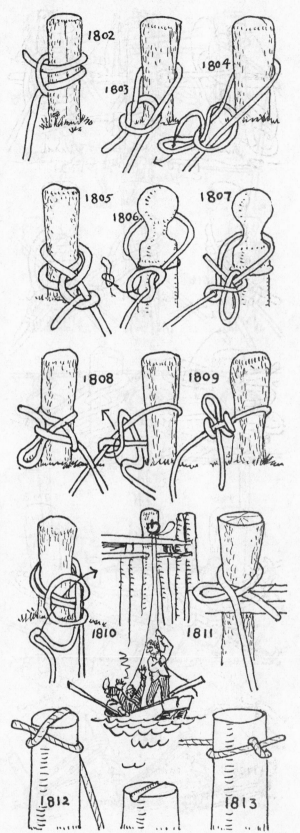

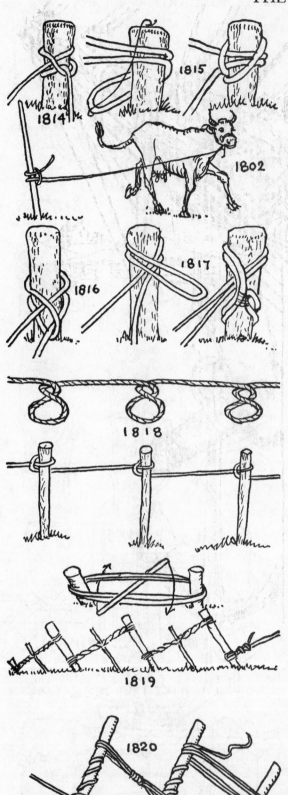

1814. A CLOVE HITCH is used in tying the bight of a line to a pile. Sometimes it jams, but not often.

1815. A PILE HITCH may be easily and quickly tied either in the end or bight of a heavy line. It is remarkably secure and is easy to cast off when the left bight has been loosened by a single well-aimed kick. Recommended for medium and heavy lines.

To tie: Lead a loop from either the end or center of a line once around the post from either direction and *under* the standing part, then drop the loop over the post.

To remove: When tied in the bight, slack off the line and force the left bight to the left and then lift the loop from the pile, or, if tied in the end, withdraw the end from under the bight, after which the knot may be unwound.

1816. A BIGHT HITCH is often required when tying up to a wharf with a single long line. This knot, the form of which is the same as a Cow HITCH, is made by dropping two opposite SINGLE HITCHES over the post. It will never bind or jam and requires little length of rope but, like all the other BIGHT HITCHES so far given, it must be slackened before it can be removed.

1817. If a BIGHT HITCH is wanted that may be untied without slacking off the line, which is sometimes difficult to do, particularly in the swift-flowing water of a river or canal, start as if to tie a Cow HITCH but, instead of tucking under at the final turn, merely seize the loop as pictured. To untie, cut the seizing.

1818. A CROSSING HITCH is required on posts in staking out lines with which to guide the populace at circuses, inaugurations and similar occasions. Proceed along a line of stakes, twisting one bight at a time and dropping it over the head of a stake. Draw the hitch taut by first pulling the end backward and then forward; it will assume the form shown in the lower drawing.

1819. In hauling out a boat or in moving a building it is often necessary to anchor the standing end of a rope or tackle with a series of stakes. Large drills or crowbars may be used for the purpose. The stakes are driven at such an angle that a line connecting the top of the forward stake with the base of the next stake will be approximately at right angles to both. A number of turns of a short rope are hauled hand-taut between the two stakes and stout sticks are introduced in the center of these straps. The sticks are twisted until the straps are taut and then the lower end of each stick is driven into the ground.

1820. If large wooden stakes are used, the straps can generally be tightened sufficiently with a few frapping turns, requiring no twisting. Sometimes a long rope made fast to the base of the forward stake is wound to the top and then led to the base of the next stake with a few turns, in which case no individual straps are needed. The bottom turns may have frapping turns added or they may be twisted as ✳1819.

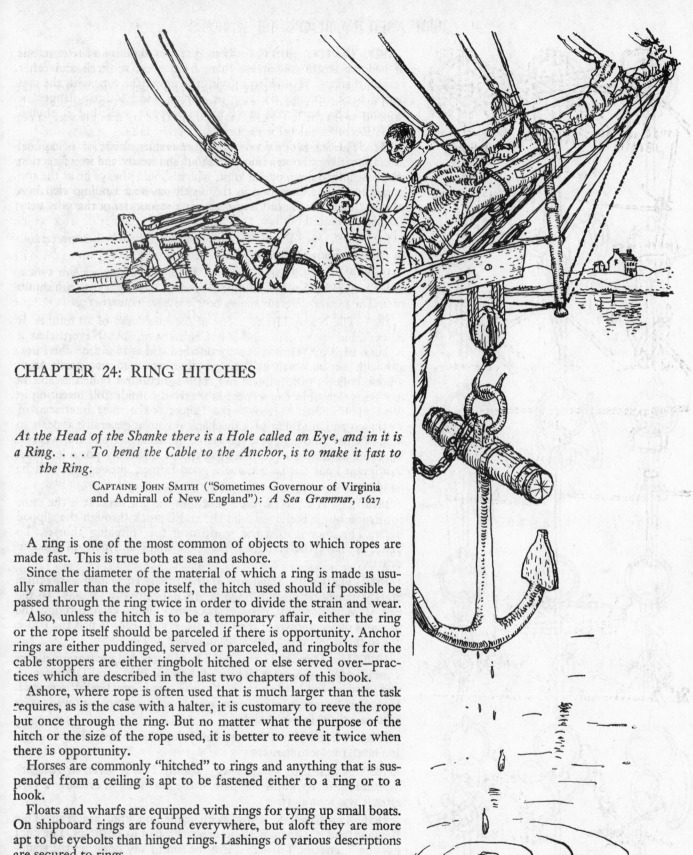

CHAPTER 24: RING HITCHES

At the Head of the Shanke there is a Hole called an Eye, and in it is a Ring. . . . To bend the Cable to the Anchor, is to make it fast to the Ring.

CAPTAINE JOHN SMITH ("Sometimes Governour of Virginia and Admirall of New England"): *A Sea Grammar*, 1627

A ring is one of the most common of objects to which ropes are made fast. This is true both at sea and ashore.

Since the diameter of the material of which a ring is made is usually smaller than the rope itself, the hitch used should if possible be passed through the ring twice in order to divide the strain and wear.

Also, unless the hitch is to be a temporary affair, either the ring or the rope itself should be parceled if there is opportunity. Anchor rings are either puddinged, served or parceled, and ringbolts for the cable stoppers are either ringbolt hitched or else served over—practices which are described in the last two chapters of this book.

Ashore, where rope is often used that is much larger than the task requires, as is the case with a halter, it is customary to reeve the rope but once through the ring. But no matter what the purpose of the hitch or the size of the rope used, it is better to reeve it twice when there is opportunity.

Horses are commonly "hitched" to rings and anything that is suspended from a ceiling is apt to be fastened either to a ring or to a hook.

Floats and wharfs are equipped with rings for tying up small boats. On shipboard rings are found everywhere, but aloft they are more apt to be eyebolts than hinged rings. Lashings of various descriptions are secured to rings.

Lashings are discussed in Chapter 28, and ring stoppers are to be found on page 300.

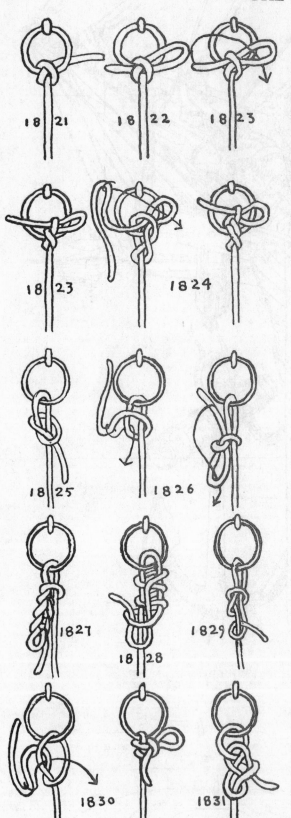

1821. The HALF HITCH. In a storage room there is no better means of hanging stores to remove them from mice, squirrels and other vermin than the HALF HITCH; with the nip at the top, with the end passed back through the ring as shown, there is little danger of slipping. This knot will serve many purposes well, but it should never be disturbed while at work.

1822. The SLIPPED HALF HITCH. A convenient knot for occasional use. The pull on the standing part should be steady and in a direction that is against the nip of the knot, which should always be at the top as pictured. The knot is seen frequently on boat landings tied in a painter, but this is hardly legitimate use unless the occasion is very temporary indeed.

1823. A SLIPPED HALF HITCH, with the end tucked, is preferable to the last knot.

1824. A FIGURE-EIGHT KNOT may be slipped either once or twice; the left diagram shows one bight slipped and the right diagram shows two. The center diagram shows how they are constructed.

1825. The NOOSE HITCH is one of the most used of all hitches. It is weak and apt to jam, and is not entirely reliable. Nevertheless it is much used by teamsters and truckmen and is found on the farm, although not so much as formerly. Farmers read and profit from school, college, government and state agricultural bulletins, and in late years the subject of knots has received considerable attention in these publications. Moreover the farmer is the most interested of workmen and anything of a mechanical nature generally appeals to him. But unlike the rigger, the sailor, the sailmaker and the weaver, knots are incidental to his labor, so that it is entirely possible for an indifferent knot tier to become a good farmer, although he will be handicapped.

1826. The HALTER HITCH is based on the last knot. It is the same formation but it is slipped, and the end is stuck through the slipped bight. The knot is used the world over for "hitching" horses. To untie: Remove the end from the loose bight and pull on the end smartly.

1827. The CHAIN SLIPKNOT. If the end is very long a practical SLIPKNOT may be made by adding a CHAIN SINNET (#2868) to the end. This is done by passing successive bights each through the previous one as shown in the right diagram #1826. When the end is pulled the whole chain ravels, or unravels.

1828. The MANGER HITCH must have been designed originally as a pacifier for a cow that slobbered. I found it in rural Delaware. A wet knot is very hard to untie, but this one is practically jamproof. However, halters in cow barns are about as common nowadays as buttoned shoes in night clubs.

1829. A knot from Diderot's Encyclopedia of 1762. It was given as a hitch for loom harness.

1830. A SLIPKNOT for passing a *lizard*. This is given in Knight's *Seamanship* of 1901 and was part of the gear used in crossing a yard after it was sent aloft.

1831. The CAPSTAN KNOT. Both name and knot are from Tom Bowling, and it is given without explanation of its purposes. The knot has one interesting feature: it may be slid to any point on the standing part and there "locked" by pulling smartly on the end.

1832, 1833. These two Hammock Hitches were found on "Cape Ann hammocks," one from Portland and one from New Bedford. The Cape Ann hammock is much older than the present trade name suggests. I have seen a number of them that were made of homespun. The knots shown are employed in tying the nettles to the eyelet holes.

1834. The Round Turn and Half Hitch is given by Steel as the proper knot for bending to a stream anchor.

1835. A Round Turn and Two Half Hitches is given by both Biddlecomb and Luce as an Anchor Bend. Although often used without stopping, it is better to add one as it prevents jamming.

1836. Two Round Turns and Two Half Hitches is a very old and strong hitch that will never jam. Under the name Rolling Hitch it is described by Falconer in 1769.

1837. The Round Turn and Reversed Hitches holds about as well as the Round Turn and Two Half Hitches and is easier to untie.

1838. The Round Turn and Buntline Hitch is snugger than either Two Half Hitches or Reversed Hitches; for that reason it is preferred for buntlines and clew lines where the slatting of the sails tends to loosen the knot.

1839. The Lobster Buoy Hitch holds about as well as #1838 and is more easily opened.

1840. The Fisherman's Bend consists of a round turn with a hitch through the turns and customarily a second hitch that is added around the standing part. The knot is often illustrated without the second hitch but is seldom tied in that way. Some find it handier to tie the knot with overhand turns instead of underhand turns as shown here.

1841. The Fisherman's Bend, also called the Anchor Bend, is one of the strongest of hitches. Steel gives it as the proper bend for a kedge anchor. There is no better Anchor Bend but in stiff, heavy cable it is not so easily applied as the Round Turn and Two Half Hitches.

1842. The Fisherman's Bend and Bowline Knot is probably the *most practical* Anchor Bend for small craft with anchor warps under three inches in circumference. Beyond this point the cables are generally of chain.

1843. An Anchor Bend from a *Handbook of Boat Sailing* (Anonymous, London, 1904). A compact knot that is interestingly related to the Fisherman's Bend.

1844. The Outside Clinch is bent to the *bower anchor*, according to Biddlecombe. The British Admiralty *Manual of Seamanship* states that it is used on "any rope you wish to let go smartly." The name *Clinch* is given by Boteler in 1685 and the Outside Clinch is first mentioned by Steel in 1794.

1845. The Inside Clinch is also mentioned by Steel (1794) and is pictured by Roding in 1795. Steel gives the Inside Clinch for bending to a bower anchor. The knot is further used to secure buntlines to the foot of a sail, and to attach bowline bridles to the cringles. It is not so easily cast off as the Outside Clinch, but is safer.

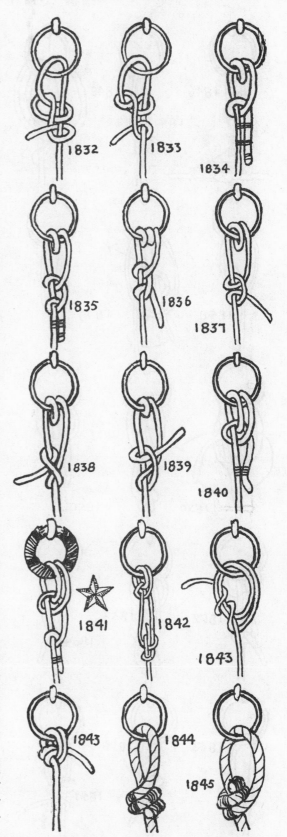

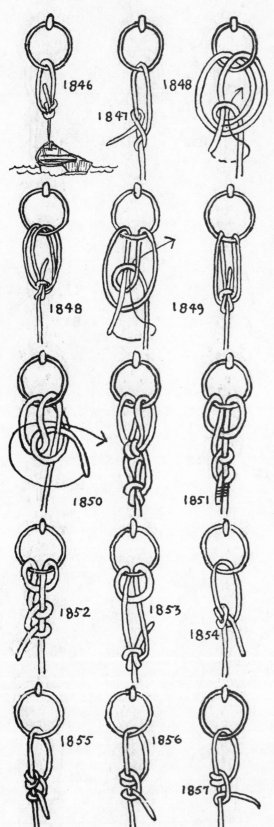

1846. The BOWLINE KNOT is often tied in a painter to the ring of a float. Sometimes where there is considerable tide the painter is rove through a ring on a wharf, led back to the boat and tied in a BOWLINE close to deck. In this way it is not necessary to cast off until ready to pull away.

The ROUND TURN AND BOWLINE is a very handy ANCHOR BEND for a small boat.

1847. The BUNTLINE HITCH is ordinarily tied with one turn only through a cringle or eyelet. It is used to bend a buntline to the foot of a square sail.

1848. The PORTUGUESE BOWLINE. I first saw this knot used as an ANCHOR BEND in the quahog fleet at the "Portagee Navy Yard" in New Bedford. It is shown by Bandeira (*Tratado de Apparelho do Navio*, Lisboa, 1896). Felix Riesenberg, in his *Standard Seamanship*, calls it "FRENCH BOWLINE" and points out that it makes an excellent boatswain's chair, with one loop serving as seat, the other as back. It must be drawn up very carefully and snugly. The way of tying the knot *in hand* is given among the DOUBLE LOOP KNOTS (#1072).

1849. This ANCHOR HITCH, based on the PORTUGUESE BOWLINE, is tied with a single pass.

1850. Another hitch with a double bearing that requires only a single pass.

1851. The BACKHANDED HITCH. There are several hitches bearing this name. This one requires only a single pass through the ring but it must be seized or stopped, otherwise it tends to capsize.

1852. A BACKHANDED HITCH that does not require stopping.

1853. A BACKHANDED HITCH AND BOWLINE. A good single-pass hitch, with a double bearing. Tuck a bight up through the ring and then draw the end through the bight and add the BOWLINE.

1854. The AWNING KNOT is an incomplete MIDSHIPMAN'S HITCH. Make a loop through the ring. Pull the rope taut and take a round turn inside the loop and jam the second turn hard inside the first. I have seen this used on shipboard in roping off the passengers who had surrendered their tickets before the ship was docked. It is also used on awnings, as its name indicates, and as a temporary tent STAKE HITCH. The hitch is spilled by jerking or jarring the rope.

1855. The MIDSHIPMAN'S HITCH is the same as the last knot with the end half hitched or else dogged and seized. This is an exceptionally practical knot much used about ship. Properly tied, it does not slip or jam.

1856. The ROLLING HITCH may be used on a ring by reeving the end of the rope through the ring and then bending the hitch to its own standing part. The advantage of this over the last knot is that it is easily adjustable. It may be slid by hand either to lengthen or shorten the rope but, left alone, it stays where it is.

1857. If the HALF HITCH is reversed most of the torsion is eliminated and there is little tendency for the knot to twist.

1858. The LONG RUNNING EYE or HITCH is the common rigger's method of making fast to eyebolts on spars aloft. A LONG EYE, spliced in the end of the line, admits the passing of a whole coil at one thrust. SHORT EYE SPLICES are not so good for this purpose as they require reeving the full length of the line through the eye.

1859. The RING HITCH and TAG KNOT are of the same formation as the BALE SLING HITCH (#1694) but are not necessarily tied in a wreath. This knot is found on rings and tags, as well as on key and curtain rings.

1860. The LEAD LINE or STRAP HITCH. Either a LONG EYE (as in a lead line) or a long bight as in the fall of a Spanish burton, is passed through the eye or ring; then the lead, hook or other object is passed through the bight and the line is drawn up. Note that the knots already described on this page, although similar in form, are tied in individual ways.

1861. A more transient fastening to a ring is made as described for the LONG RUNNING HITCH (#1858) by employing a BOWLINE KNOT instead of an EYE SPLICE.

1862. A RING HITCH may be doubled without removal from the ring by drawing and twisting a bight to the right, as shown in the left drawing, then reeving the ring through the bight in the direction indicated. This may be tied to a key or watch.

1863. The next two drawings on this page show two ways in which the number of parts having a bearing on a ring may be increased without removing the ring. I became interested in the problem when I found that a watch guard, which I prized, was showing signs of wear. To tie: Reeve the guard through the ring from the back and pass the end behind the standing part as indicated by the arrow.

1864. Arrange the loop that passes through the ring in the form shown and then reeve the end of the guard once as indicated by the arrow.

1865. If the loop of the guard is too long for the purpose, a decorative LANYARD KNOT may be added while the loop is still on the ring. Extend the loop as shown and twist the end one half turn to the right. Stick the end of the guard in the direction of the arrow downward through the loop that was just formed. Arrange the knot so that the loop is kept long. *Turn the apparatus over* and repeat a second time exactly as before, except of course on the other side. Arrange the knot at the proper length and work snug. This is the same knot as BEND #1414.

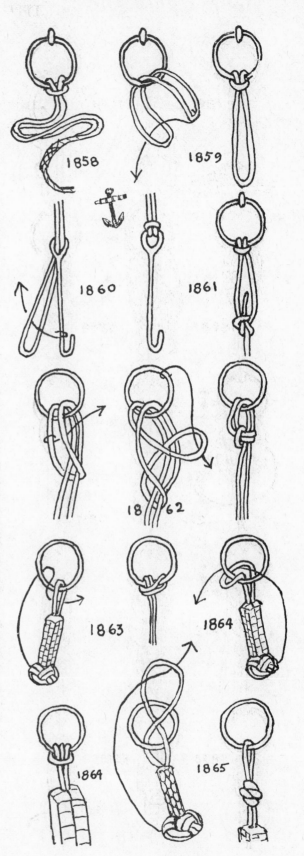

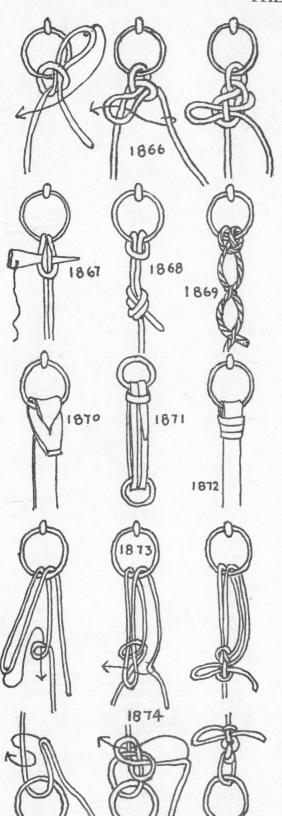

1866. The SAMPAN HITCH is used very generally throughout the East for tying up river boats, according to Captain E. H. Pentecost, who first showed me the knot.

The end of the painter, after passing through the ring, is led back to deck. The hitch is completed by sticking successive loops. It is instantly spilled from deck by a smart pull on the end of the line.

1867. A TOGGLED BIGHT is sometimes labeled a BOAT KNOT by unnautical authorities but it does not appear suitable for a BOAT HITCH. For hurried casting off, however, nothing is quicker than a toggle.

1868. The TEAMSTER'S HITCH is used when lashing a load to a truck or wagon. A LONG OVERHAND LOOP is tied, long enough so that after sticking the bight through a ring the whole coil may be rove through the bight. If the truck is fitted with hooks, the RING HITCH is tied in hand without any necessity for reeving. The end of the loop is folded back against the standing part and the hook stuck through the knot that is formed.

1869. A semipermanent loop sometimes used on the standing part of a boat lashing consists of a CLOVE HITCH with the end tucked twice through the lay. The end is sometimes stopped.

1870. The common way of securing a leather strap to a ring is to make a lengthwise slit in the strap near the end and to pass the unslit end through the ring and then through the slit.

1871. The LATIGO, CINCH or GIRTH KNOT which secures an American saddle to a horse's back is added to the cinch strap or latigo after it has been passed several times through the two rings of the saddle and girth. The cinch strap is tightened and then a COW HITCH tied to the upper or saddle ring. The grain side of the strap is at all times on the outside of the turns.

The same knot is sometimes made on a man's "sport" belt, and I have seen it tied in the rattlesnake-skin band on a ten-gallon hat.

1872. This STRAP HITCH to a ring has already been shown in detail as #1705. The knot is started as in the first two figures and attached to the ring as in the last.

1873. To *tie up to a ringbolt* on a wharf when the tide is dropping. It is sometimes difficult to free the whole length of a painter from a ring. If the painter is long this knot will be found most convenient. Reeve a bight through the ring and bring it down to the boat just above deck. Put a SINGLE HITCH with the standing part around the downhanging loop or bight, just as you would start a SHEEP-SHANK KNOT. Then reeve a bight from the loose end of the painter as shown in the second drawing. By pulling on the end the whole knot is easily spilled and withdrawn.

1874. Another knot for the same purpose may be tied either close to the ring or near the deck, and is also spilled by pulling on the end. Start as a BOWLINE WITH A BIGHT. Arrange the bight as in the middle diagram and add a SLIP LOOP.

CHAPTER 25: HOOKS, BECKETS, AND TOGGLES

A Blackwall hitch is used with a lanyard in setting up rigging, where the end of your lanyard is not long enough to form a catspaw; but a strap and toggle is preferable to both.

WILLIAM N. BRADY: The Kedge Anchor, 1841

A good HOOK HITCH should tie simply and spill the instant it is removed from the hook, without requiring any loosening.

For the bight of a slings, a DOUBLE CAT'S-PAW leaves nothing to be desired. But none of the well-known SINGLE HITCHES are wholly trustworthy. The BLACKWALL HITCH fills some of the requirements but is prone to slip. The BILL HITCH is recommended by the British Admiralty *Manual of Seamanship* but is not safe in small rope if tied to a large hook. The MARLINGSPIKE HITCH appears to be about the best of the lot.

In an attempt to find a satisfactory SINGLE HOOK HITCH, ⚓1886 was evolved. This appears to have certain advantages over the others. It ties and casts off easily and holds well when fast to a large hook. It should not be tied, however, in a large rope that overflows the hook.

A *becket* may be any one of a number of small objects to which ropes are secured. The thimble on a block to which the standing end of the fall is spliced, the hook of the block itself, or the eye in a pendant to which the block is hooked are, all three of them, *beckets.* Any EYE SPLICE is a becket, and a BECKET HITCH is the knot that commonly is made fast to an EYE SPLICE. The rope handle of a sea chest is also called a becket.

Any short rope that is employed for securing objects on shipboard is termed a becket, provided it has an eye in one end. Generally it has a KNOB KNOT or toggle in the other end, to button into the eye. (See ⚓679.)

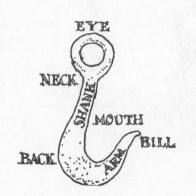

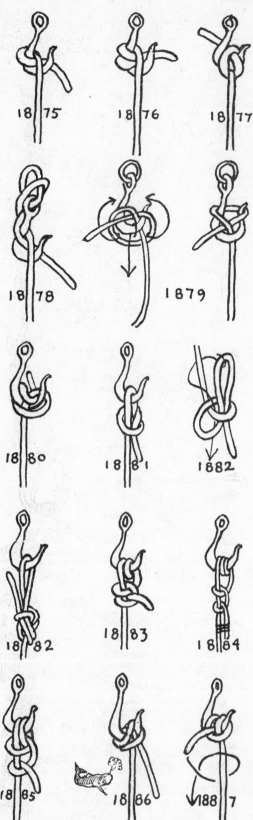

1875. The BLACKWALL HITCH is given by Steel in 1794. It is used in setting up rigging when the lanyard is short, but is never quite safe unless the rope is large enough to nearly fill the mouth of the hook. It should never be tied to a cargo block.

1876. The DOUBLE BLACKWALL HITCH has one more turn and is often recommended as preferable to the former knot. It appears, however, to be even less reliable. The second turn is sometimes jammed below the first in the manner of the AWNING KNOT, but this appears to be no improvement.

1877. The HALF HITCH, tied with the nip at the top with the end leading back through the hook, is secure if it is carefully adjusted before each fresh hoist.

1878. The STUNNER HITCH is somewhat similar to the common DOUBLE BLACKWALL HITCH but the second turn is taken above the eye of the hook. Bushell, Knight and other nautical authorities ascribe this name, but it is also called DOUBLE BLACKWALL HITCH, the true DOUBLE BLACKWALL HITCH being seldom used. This one appears to be no better than ✕1876.

1879. The BILL HITCH is the same form as the BECKET HITCH and is sometimes called by that name. It is secure if the rope fills the hook snugly. It may be made by tying a MARLINGSPIKE HITCH and then lifting the bight at the back so that it encompasses both the bill and neck of the hook.

1880. The MARLINGSPIKE HITCH "is used for the hook of a tackle, to any rope where a smart pull is required," according to the *Manual of the Sea* (1891).

If tied loosely, the MARLINGSPIKE HITCH will generally draw up to have a double bearing. In this form it is secure and easy to loosen.

1881. The MARLINGSPIKE HITCH will also on occasion take the form of the FARMER'S NOOSE HITCH (✕1825). In this form it is given in the French *Encyclopédie Méthodique Marine*, of 1783 by Vial du Clairbois. It may be formed by extending the loop of the MARLINGSPIKE HITCH, or it may be tied directly as pictured. Nares says, "This is used to hook an up and down tackle to a luff tackle fall."

1882. The BOWLINE WITH A BIGHT is employed "for heavy pulls on the ends of rigging Luffs," according to Luce and Ward (*Seamanship*, 1884). The second diagram shows the knot turned "end for end" and suspended from a hook.

1883. A ROUND TURN AND TWO HALF HITCHES. Any Hook Hitch with a double bearing is stronger than one that passes through the hook but once.

1884. A ROLLING HITCH is less apt to jam than the former knot and is exceptionally strong.

1885. The FISHERMAN'S BEND is strong and will not jam. These last three hitches are found on hooks in running rigging when it is not necessary for them to spill on removal, and where they are always moused.

1886. This is the hitch mentioned on page 313. To tie: Double back the end and twist it with the lay. Lay the doubled rope through the hook from front to back, bring it around the back of the hook and drop the loop over the bill of the hook. Pull taut and crowd all parts well down into the mouth of the hook.

1887. The CLOVE HITCH is sometimes used for a HOOK HITCH. Although it is apt to have an initial slip it is convenient.

1888. The SINGLE CAT'S-PAW. After winding, as pictured, the two ends of the coil should be twisted in opposite directions and hooked to the cargo block.

1889. The COW HITCH is sometimes found on a hook. If used at all, the end should be left long.

1890. The RING HITCH is similar in form to the COW HITCH. It may be tied in slings and straps, where it will serve well, as both parts are pulled on equally.

1891. The CAT'S-PAW is the common HOOK HITCH for slings. It is the same basic form as the BALE SLING HITCH but has additional twists. Brady says "two or three altogether," and Steel, who mentioned the name in 1794, says "three twists." It is the best of all SLING HITCHES and is often recommended for a slippery rope. But no hitch can slip when tied in a slings since it has no ends. All that is needed is a hitch that cannot jam, and this requirement the CAT'S-PAW fills admirably. The knot spills instantly when removed from the hook. It is the hitch always used for heavy lifts. Occasionally it has been called the RACKING HITCH, being confused with the knot that follows (\#1892), which nowadays is seldom seen.

To tie the CAT'S-PAW in cargo slings: Grasp two bights and hold them well apart. Twist three full turns with both hands (away from you), then clap the bights together and place them over the hook.

1892. The RACKING HITCH is similar to the CAT'S-PAW, the difference being that the two bights are twisted in opposite directions. Steel (1794) says that the RACKING HITCH is used for shortening slings, a purpose which the CAT'S-PAW also serves.

1893. Wherever any HOOK HITCH is to be used for a series of lifts, or the same load is to be slacked away and relifted, the hook should be moused. Middle a short piece of marline, take a number of turns around the shank and bill of the hook. Cross the two ends of marline at the center and serve each end a short distance away from each other, then add riding turns back again to the center and square knot the two ends together.

1894. To *shorten slings*. A method shown to me by Captain Daniel F. Mullins. After a BALE HITCH has been put around the object to be lifted, extend the slack in two long equal bights. Half knot the two bights and clap them together over the hook.

1895. The CROW'S-FOOT serves a similar purpose. After the knot is formed the two loops may be pulled out to any required length to take up the superfluous material.

1896. A *selvagee strap and toggle* is considered the best way of hooking to a lanyard in setting up rigging. The method does not injure the lanyard, which, if old, has lost much of its pliancy.

1897. A *hook and eye*. A common way of hooking a block to a pendant. The hook should be moused.

1898. HOOK AND STOPPER KNOT. I have seen the traces or tug ropes in horse harness so fitted, and also a hammock slung by similar means.

1899. This method of lashing a hook block to a shroud is given by Admiral Nares. The standing end of a single strap takes a round turn down the lay of the shroud. Then the shank of the hook is seized with five or six ground turns and three or four riders, and the end is laid up the rope and square knotted to the standing end.

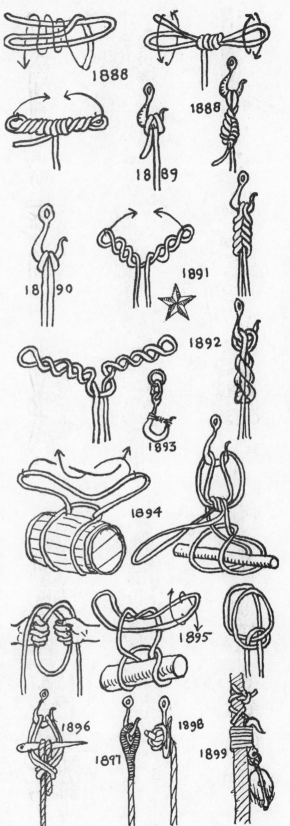

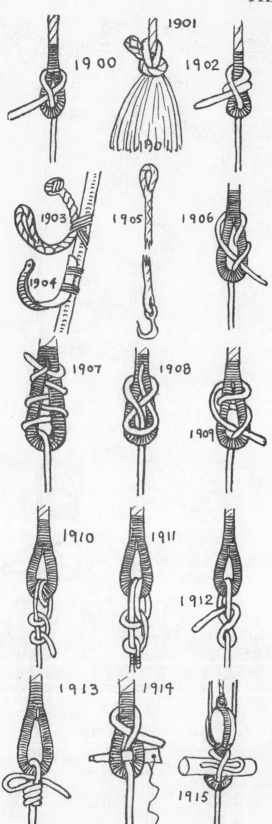

1900. Any hitch that is attached to an EYE SPLICE becomes a BECKET HITCH, but this is *the* BECKET HITCH, proper. In form it is similar to the SHEET BEND. But the end is bent to an eye instead of a loop. The name BECKET HITCH was applied by Nares in 1860.

1901. The SWAB HITCH is of similar construction. Customarily a *dog's point* is spliced in the end of a swab lanyard so that the end of the SWAB HITCH may be short. This adds greatly to the security of the hitch. When not in use, lanyards are removed and swabs are often suspended to dry along the end of the mainstay at the fore-castle head. New swabs are frequently four to six feet long. On small craft the lanyards may be long enough to admit dipping overboard. But on large craft they are dipped in a tub at the waist, which is kept filled by one or more draw buckets.

1902. The DOUBLE BECKET HITCH is more secure than the SINGLE BECKET HITCH and is the method by which a whale line is always made fast to the harpoon becket.

If a very small line is bent to a large eye the BECKET HITCH may be tripled or even quadrupled by adding further turns.

1903. This is *a becket* (not a BECKET HITCH). It is seized in the rigging and used as a fair-leader for running rigging or else for confining and storing coils, oars, spars, etc.

1904. An iron hook, used in the same way and for the same purpose, is also termed a *becket*. This is moused when in use (※3267).

1905. *Steering-wheel beckets* are used in pairs. They hook to the deck, and an EYE SPLICE slips over a spoke at either side of the wheel to hold it steady when the ship is not under weigh. The wheel is then said to be "in beckets"; hands are "in beckets" when in the trousers pockets.

1906. Another DOUBLE BECKET HITCH is formed as shown here; if desired, the end may be stuck through both the turns instead of through the lower one only.

1907. A BECKET HITCH is given by Öhrvall, for bending to a large eye with a small line, employing racking turns. This is given among the bends as ※1462.

1908. The FIGURE-EIGHT HITCH is an angler's method of attaching a fishline to a LEADER LOOP. There are a number of LEADER LOOP HITCHES shown in Chapter 2, which are potential BECKET HITCHES provided the LEADER LOOP is a spliced eye.

1909. A DOUBLE BECKET HITCH that is often shown. It is inferior to ※1902 but requires one less tuck.

1910. A ROUND TURN AND TWO HALF HITCHES is a strong hitch that is to be recommended where there is a considerable discrepancy between the size of the line and the becket.

1911. If a mooring line is to remain long under water the FISHERMAN'S BEND, parceled and seized, cannot be bettered.

1912. A temporary hitch that is found in lifeboat lashings. It is insecure and must be used with discrimination. The knot should be pushed hard up to the becket.

1913. The same knot with additional turns is frequently slipped. The turns serve to expend the surplus line.

1914. A TOGGLED BIGHT is used where it is necessary to cast off quickly. It cannot jam and is spilled by removing the toggle.

1915. A SLIPPED AND TOGGLED BECKET HITCH is used in setting up topmast rigging. It is slipped by pulling on the end. It is popular because it "favors" the stiffened ends of old lanyards.

1916. *Bowline bridles* are attached to the bowline cringles either with toggles or (an earlier practice) with BOWLINE KNOTS.

1917. In the mid-nineteenth century bowline bridles were also *inside clinched* to the cringles. The BOWLINE holds the luff of a square sail to windward when a ship is sailing "full and by." Buntlines on large craft were also secured with INSIDE CLINCHES.

1918. The BUNTLINE HITCH, according to Kipping (1840), was tied through eyelet holes in the foot of a sail, *not* to a cringle, which was the earlier practice. Buntlines are employed to lift the square sails preparatory to furling. The BUNTLINE HITCH is a very secure knot and is not easily loosened by the slatting of the sail. Toggles also have been employed for securing buntlines, Luce showing them in 1862.

1919. The TOGGLED BIGHT is employed in hoisting sail preparatory to bending. A spill line or trip line is attached to the toggle.

1920. The TOGGLED BIGHT is more secure if extra turns are added.

1921. A BIGHT AND EYE, toggled: This provides a way to secure slings to an eye strap.

1922. TOGGLE AND EYE: Lever, in 1808, gives this as the Merchant Marine way of bending the tack to a clew.

1923. EYE TO EYE (about 1800). In this case the clew is rove through the eye and then the sheet is rove through the clew. The toggle is to prevent the two eyes from jamming.

1924. EYE TO EYE (1808). The clew is rove through the eye and the toggle is stuck under a bight of the sheet. When the toggle is removed the knot spills.

1925. Sheet block and TACK KNOT made fast to a clew. Lower and topsail sheet blocks were fastened in this manner a hundred and fifty years ago with TACK KNOTS, and topgallant and royal sheets with STOPPER KNOTS or DOUBLE WALL KNOTS.

1926. Nares, in 1860, gives this method of attaching the BOWLINES. When tacking ship, the lower toggle is slipped and the BOWLINE is instantly cleared from the sail. The upper toggle is spliced to the bowline bridle.

1927. An eye toggled to a bight is given in several seamanship books as a means of securing the standing part of a topgallant halyard purchase. A hitch is first made around the neck of the block strap and then a bight is shoved through the becket. The toggle is inserted as shown.

1928. When rafting water, the cask hoops are driven up and beckets inserted. Before driving the hoops home, moist sand is rubbed on the staves to prevent riding. The towlines are either toggled to the beckets or else made fast with BECKET HITCHES.

1929. Signal flags are fitted with toggles at one end of the hoist and eyes at the other, so that a number can be buttoned together without loss of time.

1930. A topgallant, studding-sail tack block, toggled to an eye in the end of a studding-sail boom (1860).

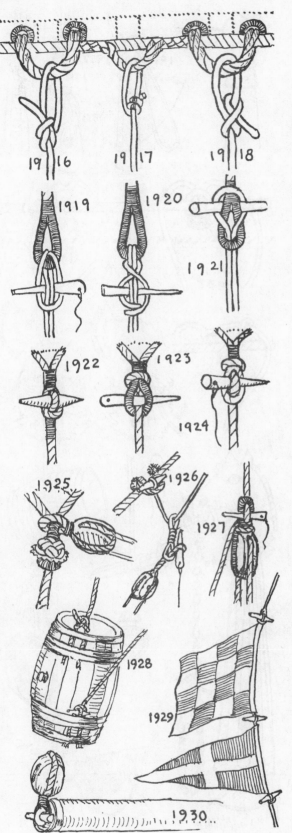

1931. An *anchor post*. A bight or loop, passed through a hole in a post, is held fast with a toggle.

1932. A *hand lead* (for sounding the depth of water) was formerly fitted with a short leather strap or becket with a slit or hole at either end of it. A LONG RUNNING EYE in the end of the lead line was rove through the two slits in the strap.

1933. A *grommet* is made through the eye of a deep-sea lead and the lead line is attached with a LONG RUNNING EYE to the grommet or becket.

1934. A wire grommet is best for a heavy lead. The sides of the grommet are seized together so as not to disturb the passage of the lead through the water.

1935. Robands, robbins or ropebands were required in bending square sail. A single roband is made fast with a TAG HITCH through the eyelet holes in the head of the sail.

1936. Storm trysails are often secured to the mast with toggles and beckets.

1937. Double robands were generally of FLAT SINNET ⌗2968. One end of each had an eye and the other end was pointed. The shorter tail was rove through the eyelet hole, from aft forward, then through the eye or becket of its mate. The second ropeband was then rove through the eye of the first one.

1938. Single reef points of small stuff were knotted at half length through the sails. Nowadays they are sewed in.

They are called points because the early ones, which were of sinnet, were always tapered or pointed. Reef points of small stuff are always whipped twice, sinnet ones once. The name *whipping* comes from the whipping or lashing received by reef points from the wind.

1939. Double reef points of sinnet with an eye or becket in each leg were common before the clipper days. The eye was made long and a round turn was taken in it to serve as a stopper. The end of each point passed through a grommet eyelet in the sail and through the doubled eye of its mate. Then they were hove taut.

1940. A T chain hitching post was, in the horse-and-carriage days, one of the commonest means of temporarily "hitching" a horse. The chain passed around the horse's neck before it was toggled. As I recall it, the toggle was always spoken of as "the bar."

If it was necessary to "hitch" a *pair* of horses—a very poor practice indeed, for people who can't afford a coachman really should limit themselves to one horse—the toggle was rove through all the rings of both bits and toggled to the nigh bit ring of the nigh horse.

1941. For hoisting empty casks, a railroad spike makes an excellent toggle that is inserted at the bunghole. A lanyard of fishline should be made fast around the head of the spike with which it is to be recovered when the lift is over, as otherwise it is likely to foul in the bunghole.

1942. A watch chain ordinarily toggles to a waistcoat buttonhole with a gold bar.

1943. A whaler's blubber toggle and eye strap will hold under a strain where a 100-pound iron hook will straighten. The toggle is worked out by hand from a section of six-inch white oak or hickory.

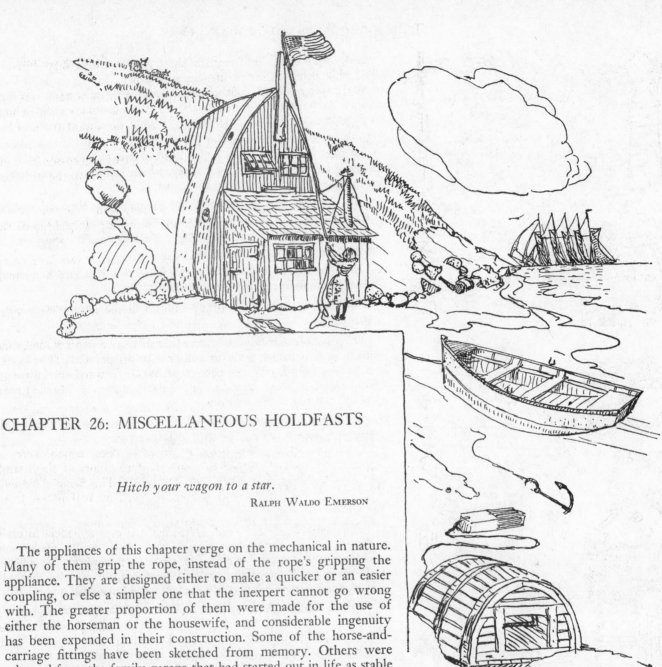

CHAPTER 26: MISCELLANEOUS HOLDFASTS

Hitch your wagon to a star.

Ralph Waldo Emerson

The appliances of this chapter verge on the mechanical in nature. Many of them grip the rope, instead of the rope's gripping the appliance. They are designed either to make a quicker or an easier coupling, or else a simpler one that the inexpert cannot go wrong with. The greater proportion of them were made for the use of either the horseman or the housewife, and considerable ingenuity has been expended in their construction. Some of the horse-and-carriage fittings have been sketched from memory. Others were salvaged from the family garage that had started out in life as stable and carriage house.

It may seem unprofitable to resurrect such material, much of which is obsolete today. But knotting is merely the application of certain mechanical principles, and a principle itself can hardly become obsolete. As conditions change, new applications are bound to appear. The fact that something is not required today is no reason for believing that it will not be needed tomorrow.

Latchings and euphroes, that one time were used at sea, of late years cannot be found serving their original purposes on shipboard. But they have now become circus stand-bys. Toggles, at one time common aboard ship, are now to be found on balloons and parachutes.

Different ways of making a rope fast to blocks and hooks were given in the last chapter. Here are illustrated a number of smaller snap hooks that snap into beckets and eyes of various sorts.

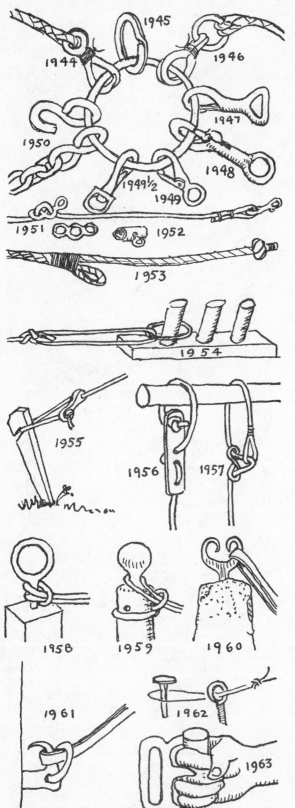

1944. *Sister hooks* are found on sheet blocks, where they are usually a semipermanent or permanent attachment. They consist of two parallel reversed hooks, with flat sides adjoining each other. When stopped or seized at the neck or small, they cannot loosen. These hinge around a thimble.

1945. A *key ring* consists of a close helix of two turns made of spring steel. It is often fitted with a cord or small chain lanyard. The spring opens sideways to admit a key which has to pass completely around the ring before it drops into place.

1946. Another variety of sister hooks, sometimes called clip hooks, hinges on a ring. In this one the eyes are at right angles to the hook.

1947. The ordinary *snap hook* has a flat sheet-metal spring which bends to admit a ring or other object.

1948. The common *halter snap hook* has a bolt which is opened with the thumb and is closed by a coil spring.

1949. A *tongue hook* is a more modern type of snap hook.

1949½. A *swivel hook* saves a rope from twisting.

1950. An *S* or *Ess hook* is used to permanently join two links of a chain, or to fasten a chain to a bucket or other object. The hook is closed by hammering the parts together.

1951. The law still requires the seller of a horse to furnish a *halter* to the buyer. The halter pictured here was of jute and once retailed for fifteen cents.

1952. The ordinary eye for the *snap hook of a neck halter* has a galvanized iron cylinder into which it screws.

1953. An old New Bedford neck halter which consisted of a MATTHEW WALKER KNOT that buttoned to an EYE SPLICE. It was made and used by Captain William I. Shockley.

1954. A *tension adjustment* from an old hand loom consisted of a series of pegs over one of which an iron ring was dropped.

1955. Another *tension adjustment*, that can be used for many purposes, is the commercial tent-rope fastening.

1956, 1957. Here are two *rope-end adjustments* found in children's gymnasium apparatus of today. But #1956 was illustrated in Emerson's *Principles of Mechanics* (London, 1794), while #1957 is fashioned from an ordinary S hook.

1958. To secure the bight of a rope to an eyebolt, screw eye or knob, tie a RING HITCH around the neck.

1959. To "hitch" a bridle rein directly to the ring of a common hitching post was always considered bad form, since a horse would be apt to pull back and break the rein. Often hitching posts were installed quite as much to protect trees from horses as to accommodate the drivers.

1960. An early *bridle-rein catch* from five stone posts that were bought in Middleboro, Massachusetts.

1961. An early *bridle-rein catch*, set in masonry.

1962. A *screw eye and a nail* makes a good fastening on the same principle as #1959, #1961 and #1963.

1963. The *"Black Boy" hitching post*. This was taken from the familiar cast-iron hitching post representing a Negro jockey whose business it was to hold your horse.

1964. An iron *gondola-mooring hook* from Venice, which operates on the same principle as ⌗1959, ⌗1961, ⌗1963.

1965. A *hitch to the eye of a hook*, that was found in modern hay hoisting gear.

1966. A Single Hitch *to a stud* on a tennis-net winch. Sometimes the stud is countersunk so that the rope will not be bruised in the winding.

1967. *Peg and hole*. A method employed in caning chairs and stringing racquets. For temporarily holding a string or gut in a hole, thrust in either an awl or a pricker in the direction shown here for the wedges. Shellac or glue may be added to hold the gut secure.

1968. A *window-shade pulley* for raising and lowering large shades. The window-shade cord leads through this pulley, which is screwed to the wall. Raise the shade to the required height, hold the cord off center, either to the right or left, and continue to lower. The cord will switch to the side track and jam. To lower: Pull down to loosen the cord, then hold the cord straight up and down and lower away.

1969. This buttonlike fitting is almost always found on *Venetian blinds* and *jalousies*. A few turns of the cord around the disk-shaped head hold the cord secure. Several cords may be wrapped parallel with each other to the same anchor.

Ansted, in his *Dictionary of Sea Terms* (Glasgow, 1917), shows what he calls *sheet clips*, that are the same as the Venetian-blind catch except that the disk or button is at right angles to the screw plate. He recommends them for use with jib sheets in single-handed sailing. I have not heard of their being employed in America.

1970. There have been many attempts to produce a perfect *clothesline fastening*. But it would seem that the average laundress is not mechanically minded. Number 1972, patented many years ago, is still the favorite, although the ordinary wire nail runs a close second.

The appliance shown is a variety of *pinch cleat* and the rope is made fast with one or two round turns. I am not certain just how old this is, but as it is better made than ⌗1972 it is probably older.

1971. A cheaper, newer and perhaps as efficient a pinch fastening is made of heavy bent wire. A couple of turns around the horn should hold the clothesline adequately.

1972. This *patented cleat* of fifty years or more ago will hold, no matter how the turns in the clothesline are taken, provided they are sufficient in number. The maker's name and the patent number both indicate that the hook or cleat should be fastened in the position in which it is here drawn. The hook at the top, to which the line is first led, appears to belong logically in this position. But I have never seen one so placed. Evidently laundresses are unwilling to jeopardize their luck, as the horseshoe is always secured with the other side up.

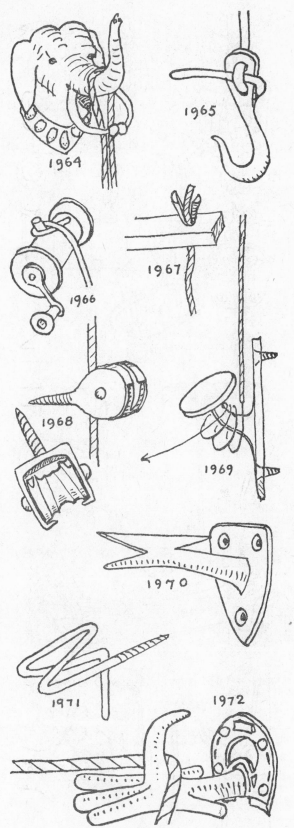

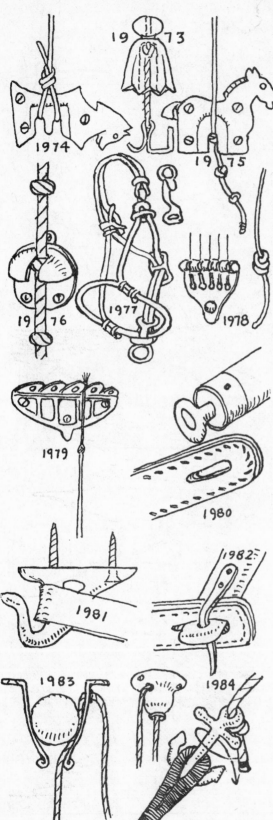

1973. This *counterweight, of gilded cast iron* in the form of a tassel, was suspended by a rope from the ceiling of the harness room.

1974. The *cast-iron horse* was attached to the wall and a rope led up the wall and across the ceiling to the middle of the room, where it terminated in the counterweight pictured above; to the bottom of the iron tassel was attached a leather-covered hook. Harness was hooked to this and cleaned. When not in use the counterweight was hauled to the ceiling and the height was adjusted on the iron horse with a series of loops.

1975. A more realistic animal was found in a friend's stable. An OVERHAND KNOT instead of a loop was used in making fast, and there was a second OVERHAND KNOT higher up, with which to hold the hook to the ceiling.

1976. A *reversed cup* held open the carriage-room skylight. Several OVERHAND KNOTS were tied in the rope at different lengths to allow of adjustment. Almost the same thing, but upturned, is found in gymnasiums for holding dumbbells.

1977. This shows a *modern head halter* of sash cord with a great variety of cast-iron and bent wire couplings.

1978. Strings are secured to the tailpieces of musical instruments with STOPPER KNOTS. These are generally DOUBLE OVERHAND KNOTS. The knots are dropped through large holes and then slipped forward into narrow slots which pinch the string.

1979. The "fly" or "snapper" of a carriage whip is held in a similar way. Generally a half dozen or more whips are hung against the carriage- or harness-room wall from a cast-iron rack, the edges of which are slotted. Each slot tapers to pinch the fly below a TERMINAL OVERHAND KNOT. Whips were very personal things and each member of a family often had his individual whip and place in the rack.

1980. The *clip* on the end of a whiffletree, if of iron, was tilted forward at a 45-degree angle. The trace or tug had to be lifted to admit of buttoning to the clip. When traces were slack they sagged forward at right angles to the clip, when taut at about 45 degrees, so they could not become unbuttoned without assistance.

1981. The holdback was often a leather loop nailed to the underside of the shaft; the strap took a round turn through the loop and around the shaft. But in the final quarter of the last century an iron casting was screwed to the shaft. The bight of the holdback strap was bent forward and the edge farthest from the shaft was slipped into place first. Once adjusted, there was no tendency to slip out.

1982. On light carts a wooden clip, which was a continuation of the whiffletree, held the trace, and a leather tongue was thrust through a hole, which prevented its slipping. On farm wagons and heavy carts the whiffletree was fitted with curved iron hooks to which chain tugs were hooked.

1983. A ball-and-socket adjustable fastening for a punching bag. The first illustration gives a vertical cross section. To shorten the rope, pull on the standing part; to lengthen, insert a nail to lift the ball and pull down the end.

1984. A hammock anchor was a common contrivance for hooking a rope to a hammock clew. The hook on the post or tree was generally out of reach. The knotted end could be extended and a BECKET HITCH made, as shown by the arrow.

CHAPTER 27: OCCASIONAL KNOTS

With old sailors it was, and is, a matter of pride to be able to make knots, the more difficult and obscure the better.

ALBERT R. WETJEN: *Fiddlers' Green*, 1941

This chapter is devoted to knots that serve a special or individual purpose. Either they serve the purpose especially well, or else merely better than other knots that offer.

Quite a number of the knots that are given here for special purposes will also be found elsewhere serving general purposes.

The chapter also includes a number of odd knots that do not fall easily under the listings of other chapters, or that here fulfill other needs that do not appear under their regular listing. Here also will be found knots that belong to classes so small that they were deemed insufficient to command a chapter for themselves. There are some knots here that might have been included among the vocational knots of Chapter 2, or that are eligible for one of the chapters on hitches. The present chapter really serves as a catchall for anything that does not definitely belong somewhere else.

I was once asked to tie a rope to the tapering end of a spar. The spar tapered only slightly and it was not a difficult thing to do, but there is a definite limit in that direction to what may fairly be asked of a knot. If a hitch is made on a cone with a taper that is not too pronounced, a fairly good knot can be made, provided the very tip of the rope can be held stationary under a slight pull.

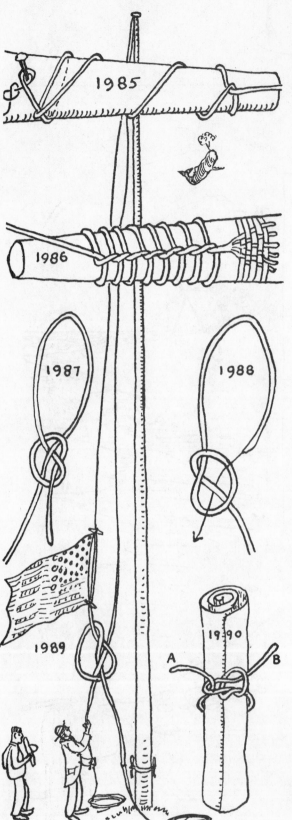

1985. If permissible, drive a tack or small nail into a spar and make a SINGLE HITCH with the line below it. Marl a piece of old inner tube lengthwise, not bandage-wise, down the cone. Put a hitch snugly around the tube close to the nail. Wrap the rope tightly in a long helix toward the end of the cone and, when near the end, put on a final hitch. Add the load gradually.

1986. Another way is to open the end of the rope, tease it out and with a narrow strip of adhesive tape graft it to the cone. A third way is to cover the cone with an old inner tube and add a series of SNUG HALF HITCHES toward the end, being careful that the knots lie in a straight line. Add the load slowly.

1987. The CRABBER'S EYE KNOT, also called the CROSSED RUNNING KNOT, is similar in form to the BOWLINE, but the pull is different and it is more apt to distort. Its salient feature is that the standing part may be hauled on and the knot slid to a desired position. When the desired position is reached the knot may be "locked" by hauling stoutly on the end.

1988. The LEFT-HAND SHEET BEND is a more secure knot than the foregoing and may be utilized in the same way. Haul on the standing part until in the correct position, then hold it steady and haul or jerk on the end.

1989. FLAGSTAFF KNOT. But if you have decided to hoist the flag and have it remain where it is hoisted, it is no longer necessary to nail your colors to the mast. Merely use the knot shown here and a steeplejack or a tree scaler will be required to haul it down.

The lead is better than in the two previous knots and it draws up more smoothly. If there is much at stake, seize the knot open with worsted yarn before hauling it aloft. A jerk on the end will break the yarn and lock the knot.

1990. A LOCK KNOT around a parcel or roll can be tied on somewhat the same principle. An ordinary NOOSE is made in the end around its own standing part. Draw the standing part snug, and then, while holding it snug, pull stoutly on the end. Pull until a bight of the standing part is swallowed by the NOOSE. The knot capsizes into a SHEET BEND and, after once being adjusted, will hold its position.

OCCASIONAL KNOTS

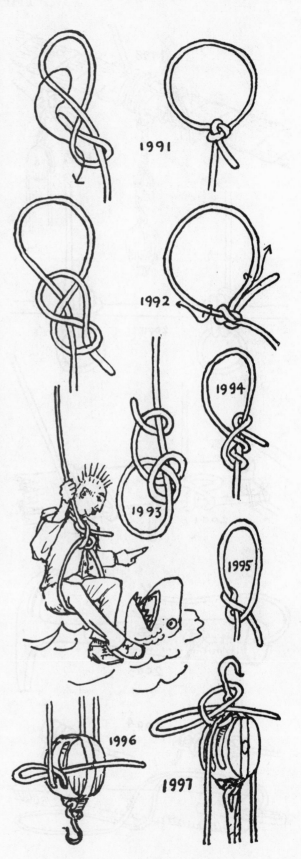

1991. A JAM HITCH may be slid up and down the standing part until the proper adjustment is reached; then, by pulling smartly on the end, the knot is jammed and thereafter will not slip.

1992. A JAMMING HITCH that closes easily, but does not render easily. This may be tied around a bale or roll and after being drawn taut may be slid to any position and will stay in place after the hand has been removed.

1993. The MIDSHIPMAN'S HITCH. When you have fallen overboard, which happens to us all, sooner or later, grab the end of the line that is tossed you, pass it quickly either through your legs or under your seat, make a HALF HITCH around the standing part with the end, then jam a second turn on top of the HALF HITCH. If no more time is available, hold the end tightly grasped to the standing part. If you still have opportunity make a HALF HITCH above the structure that is already tied. Either way, you are now quite ready to be rescued.

1994. An ADJUSTABLE JAM HITCH. This knot is based on the ROLLING HITCH, and is also closely akin to the MIDSHIPMAN'S HITCH that has just been shown. The round turn is on the outer side of the knot and the HALF HITCH is inside. The knot may be slipped close to hold a bale or roll as described for ⌗1992. It will hold stoutly wherever it is left but it is nevertheless easily adjusted to any other position.

1995. The AWNING KNOT is often used as a temporary POST HITCH in "staking off" to hold a crowd in check, or else as a STAKE HITCH for an awning. It is immediately loosened by a jar or jerk, the former generally being administered by the foot and the latter by hand.

1996. When no belaying pin or cleat is handy, a tackle fall is often temporarily made fast by jamming the end against the block under an adjacent lead. Generally a bight is jammed, but if the end is short it is led singly. This is more apt to be used ashore than at sea because at sea, particularly on deck, a belaying pin is generally handy. The circus man calls it the "SLIP TACKLE KNOT."

1997. Painters and carpenters, when securing their stagings, sometimes jam the end as just directed and then add a hitch around the neck of the hook. They do this on the assumption that a knot need fail but once to be fatal. The preferred way is to make fast to the *lower block* as KNOT ⌗455.

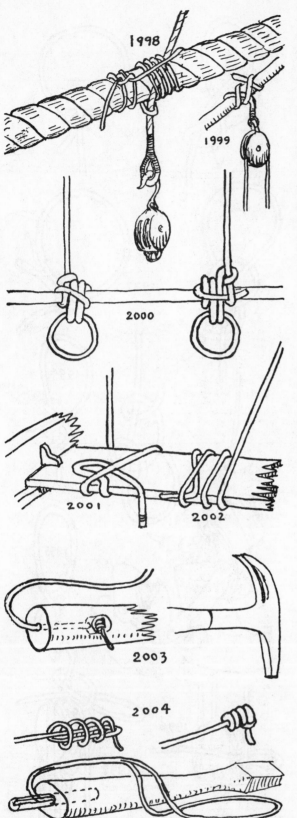

1998. For a *heavy lift from a stay*, a pendant is secured to the top-mast head, having first been led through a thimble or bull's-eye in the end of a lashing. The lashing is passed four or five times around the stay and pendant. The end, having been brought forward from behind the pendant, is clove hitched around the stay.

1999. For a light lift, a *tail block* is made fast to the stay with a ROLLING HITCH.

2000. The ROBAND HITCH (⌗1270) is given by Lieutenant Emery H. Taunt, in *The Young Sailor's Assistant* (Washington, 1883), as a means of boating an anchor, which is far from its original purpose of bending sail. The end of the rope is tucked similarly to the TOP-SAIL HALYARD BEND. I have found the knot useful in securing a lantern to the end of a boat boom. It might also serve to support the arm of a makeshift derrick. To tie: Lead the end downward and put a CLOVE HITCH around the spar, then reeve two turns around both spar and ring (or becket) within the CLOVE HITCH. Tie a SINGLE HITCH around the standing part and tuck under the turns as pictured.

2001. A SLIPPED HITCH to a boat thwart is a good method for securing the halyards in a sailing skiff or dinghy when the craft is not fitted with cleats.

2002. Öhrvall shows a somewhat similar knot for the same purpose.

2003. To secure a lanyard to a tool handle: Bore a hole slightly larger than the size of the lanyard for two or three inches into the end of the handle and countersink the hole slightly to save chafe on the lanyard. Then bore a larger intercepting hole from the side. Reeve the lanyard in at the end and out at the side hole, tie a FIGURE-EIGHT KNOT or OYSTERMAN'S STOPPER in the end and with-draw it into the handle. Fill the hole with plastic wood and, when dry, sandpaper and varnish it.

2004. Another method is to bore a somewhat larger hole three or four inches into the end of the handle. Tie a large knot in the end of the cord. Make a peg that fills the hole tightly, groove one side of the peg to receive the cord. Insert the knot, lay the cord into the groove, swab the peg with glue and drive it home. When dry, trim the end of the peg.

2005. The SHORT END BEND. Although this knot has already been shown among the bends, its specialty differentiates it from all other bends. It can be tied to a fixed end that is far shorter than can be tied to by any other method that I know.

Its final form is identical with the SHEET BEND. A NOOSE KNOT is made in the long end and drawn up a little less than snug. The NOOSE is dropped over the short end, which remains inert, and the two ends of the NOOSE are pulled apart until the NOOSE capsizes and swallows the short end. If the NOOSE is wrongside up when placed over the short end, a LEFT-HAND SHEET BEND will result, which is not so secure as the RIGHT-HAND SHEET BEND shown here.

2006. A TWO-STRAND MATTHEW WALKER KNOT makes a good jug, jar or bottle sling if the available cord is too short for BIGHT KNOT ✷1142. To tie: Follow the diagrams given and insert the neck of the bottle at X.

2007. I have seen the JUG SLING (✷1142) recommended for carrying a heavy bag. Tie the cord ends together with HARNESS BEND ✷1420 so that the loops are of equal length.

2008. If no cord is handy and the neck of the bag is long, grip well down on the neck and tuck the end as in the illustration. This is a form of the BECKET HITCH.

2009. Another way is to take a turn around the wrist with the neck of the bag and grip the end in the hand. If the neck is twisted a little it will be easier to handle. Although these knots tighten about the wrist, they cause very little discomfort.

2010. A third way to hold a bag is shown here. As a heavy bag is a tiresome thing to carry under any circumstances, all three of these grips will be welcome if the carry is a long one. It is useful when either loading a boat or making a portage.

2011. The next three knots are employed in finishing off seizings. They are rigger's ways of securing the working ends, and are not shown elsewhere among knots proper, although they are given under marlingspike seamanship in Chapter 40, where their applications are shown.

This one is sometimes spoken of as "finishing off with a CLOVE HITCH," but it is not quite a CLOVE HITCH. In construction it is similar to the GROUND LINE HITCH (✷277) except that it is tied end for end.

2012. The FLAT KNOT. The crossing turns start downward at the top back when there are three crossing parts at the back and two at the front. The knot is formed as shown. Sometimes it is mistakenly called the "SQUARE KNOT," but "FLAT KNOT" is the rigger's name.

2013. Öhrvall shows a slightly different FLAT KNOT that is used for the same purpose.

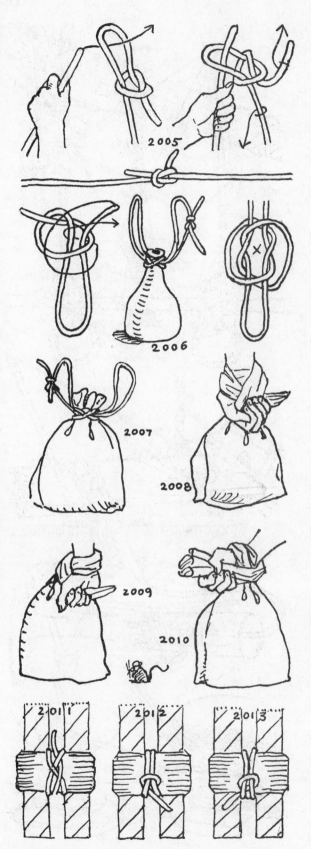

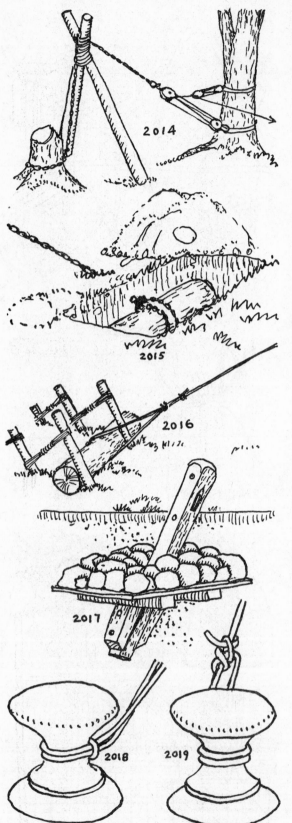

2014. In pulling posts and stumps when heavy tackle is lacking, gear can be compounded by utilizing the principle of the lever and adding a "tail jigger" to the end of the lifting tackle. In the illustration the lever is a pair of shears. In stump pulling I have used an old door, leading the chain over the center top, and holding it in place by driving a spike down through one of the chain links at the top into the door top. To hold what has been gained, lead a rope from the anchor (post, crowbar, or tree) and put a ROLLING HITCH on the chain.

2015. A *dead man* is an anchor made by burying some bulky object, such as a log. It is used for various guys and as an anchor for a tackle in heavy hauling.

2016. A log similar to the one just shown may be used above ground by compounding several rows of stakes. It is more quickly arranged and will serve well where the pull does not depart too much from the level, or where the ground is not too soft.

2017. A *heaving-down post.* This post was found on an old wharf. It may at some time have been called a "heaving-down pile" but in late years it has been called "post." The British speak of *careening* instead of *heaving down* and without doubt there are still piles or posts for careening preserved in British naval dockyards. This one was the last to remain on Merrill's Wharf in New Bedford. The post was sunk and a heavy floor built around it at a depth of several feet. The floor was buried under stone with earth on top. The remainder of the heaving-down gear, including winch and tackles, is pictured as ⅜3250 in Chapter 40.

2018. A BIGHT HITCH to a knob. If a door sticks, tie a BALE SLING HITCH around the knob with as large material as practicable. The ends of the rope should be knotted together, forming a wreath or grommet fifteen or eighteen inches long. Having attached it to the knob, slip the hand into the loop, hold the loop firmly and, using your hand as a hammer, drive open the door. If necessary, use a section of iron pipe instead of the fist but, as this may break the knob, examine the hinges of the door first to make sure that the pins cannot be driven out, allowing the door to open at the hinge edge.

2019. A SINGLE HITCH to a knob. If a knob must be secured with an end of rope, make two round turns about the neck, then fasten the end of the rope to the standing part with a ROLLING HITCH. With this arrangement the rope may be tightened or slacked off by sliding the knot up the standing part.

2020. A *parbuckle and skids* furnishes a convenient means of loading or unloading cylindrical objects, such as casks and spars. The two encircling ropes serve to steady the rolling object along its path. The skids are not required but make the task easier.

A long rope may be middled and secured at the center, to a post, ring or other fixture on shipboard, preferably with a BALE SLING

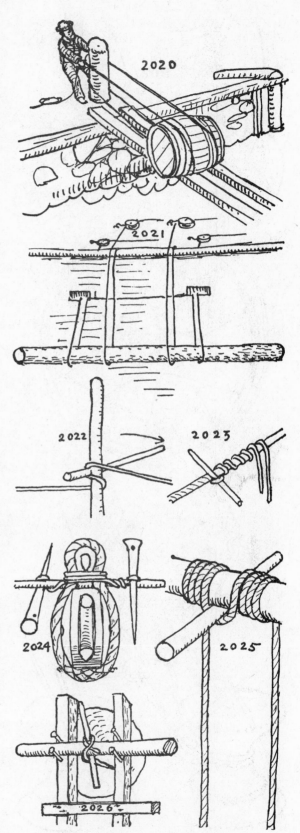

HITCH. The two parts of the rope are laid under the object and the ends are led back in the direction of the post or ring. Care must be taken to haul equally on the two ends. The power exerted is doubled.

2021. If an object, such as a spar, is too long or wide to pass through the gangway, *return parbuckles* must be added and the object lifted over the rail. The regular parbuckle is rigged with the two parts leading over the rail of the ship.

The return parbuckle must be led at the level of the deck, so the bights are passed out at two scuppers.

When the spar has been hauled to the top of the rail, the two return parbuckles take over the load. They are first made taut and then slacked off at an even rate to lower the spar to deck.

2022. The *Spanish windlass* imparts power to a rope by means of a lever, which is pried around a spar, stake or other object. There are several forms of the Spanish windlass.

To haul out a boat, or to move an automobile from a ditch: Make fast the standing end of the rope to a fixed object and have a second person hold a stake erect. Slush the stake well and also the part of the lever around which the rope is to pass. Arrange the rope as in the drawing and pull the lever around the stake. It may be necessary to overhaul your windlass frequently. This may be done by applying a STOPPER which by-passes the windlass stake and makes fast to the rope at either side with a ROLLING HITCH.

2023. A *heaver* works on much the same principle and, when used in this way, it may be termed a Spanish windlass. It is used in setting up on a *rounding*, on a *hawser* or *cable* (#3350).

2024. A Spanish windlass is generally used when strapping a large block at sea. A piece of well-slushed ratline stuff is passed one round turn about the neck of the strap. The most convenient fulcrum is a sheer pole which is already fast in the rigging at the correct height. The power is applied with two marlingspikes or belaying pins which are secured with MARLINGSPIKE HITCHES. When the two sides of the strap have been hove together a seizing is put on.

2025. To twist a pipe, spar or post: Middle a rope and take a number of turns as pictured. *Do not slush*, as in this case it is not intended that the rope should slip. If, when the lever is turned, the rope should slip, add more turns with each end of the rope or sprinkle the surface with ashes.

2026. To lift a heavy load where no tackle is handy: Drive two spikes into two heavy beams. Take a heavy round hardwood stick for a fulcrum and, having arranged the rope, twist the bar around the stick to lift the load. Slip another stick under the bar to hold the load when the right level is reached. For light lifts a ladder may be used. To lift a stone from a hole, lay beams horizontally and elevate them above the opening, so that cribbing can be placed under the stone after it is high enough.

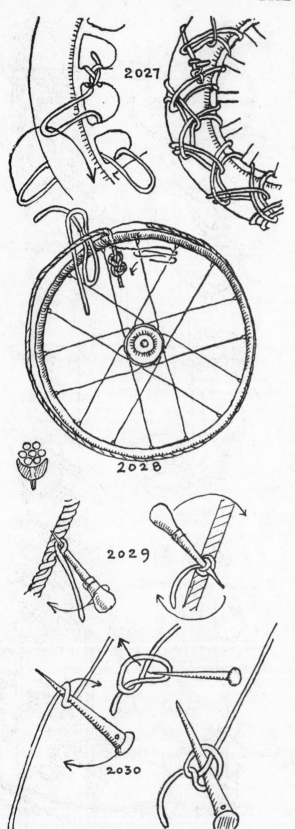

2027

2028

2029

2030

2027. A rope "mud chain" for an automobile wheel, that does away with the necessity of reeving the whole rope at each spoke. Make fast to any spoke and reeve a short bight forward through the adjacent opening. Bring a short bight from the rear around the tread and through the first bight. Bring a bight from the rear out through the second opening in the spokes and through the second bight. Continue reeving alternate right and left bights in this same manner. To finish off, reeve the end of the rope through the last bight and make fast.

If any considerable length of rope is left, exhaust it in tightening the structure already made, by making frapping turns.

2028. A jury bicycle tire. This is a rough-riding substitute but it will get a person home without damage to rim or tire. Remove the tire and take fifty-two feet of old clothesline (for a 28-inch tire). Stick an end down through the valve hole in the rim. Tie a FIGURE-EIGHT KNOT in the end. Then, facing the right side of the wheel, lay another short piece of rope across the rim in a round turn, as pictured at the left. Lead the long rope counterclockwise two turns (in one layer) and draw as taut as possible. Add three more turns in a second layer and heave all taut. Then add two more turns in a third layer and stick the end of the rope through the near side of the loop that was laid across the rim and draw the end through to the opposite side of the wheel. Heave the rope taut and put on several S turns around the two nearest spokes. The success of this "tire" depends entirely on how tautly it has been passed. If the rope stretches, it will have to be readjusted. So don't wait for it to come off. Ride a short distance and then examine the tire, and adjust it if necessary.

If the rope is small, three turns may be required for the ground tier, four for the middle tier and three for the upper tier.

2029. To heave on a strand when splicing: Take a hitch with a strand around the tip of the pricker point as pictured and draw it up close to the rope. Hold the end of the strand tightly with the left hand and twist the pricker clockwise. Change the grip as often as is necessary.

2030. The MARLINGSPIKE HITCH is always used for heavy heaving on splices, seizings and service. To tie the knot: With the marlingspike in the right hand, lay the point across the marline and with the left hand add a turn of marline around the tip. Lift the spike and place the tip to the right of the standing part and slip it under the bight.

2031. A practical girdle or belt, that is easily adjustable, may be made of a short piece of rope by tying two ROLLING HITCHES (#1734), which form the ADJUSTABLE BEND shown elsewhere as #1472.

2032. Beads ordinarily are strung with OVERHAND KNOTS of various sizes. The Chinese are said to employ a worm to carry a thread through a crooked hole. Where a thread is large for the hole, it is possible to splice a smaller one to the end of the larger one (⁂2681) by scraping both ends; then the smaller one is rove first and the larger one is dragged through after it. The splice should be waxed before stringing the beads.

If the hole is large, as is often the case with wooden beads, a single cord may still be used by increasing the size of the knot. A large knot of the kind shown here adds very much to the decorative effect of the beads. The knot is formed loosely by interlocking two OVERHAND KNOTS. The first OVERHAND is drawn up snugly, close to the bead, and the second OVERHAND KNOT, shown by the single line arrow, is next pulled tight. The result outwardly resembles a Two-Strand MATTHEW WALKER KNOT.

2033. An ordinary way of lacing a shoe is pictured here. On the surface, the parts lead horizontally, and on the underside diagonally, similar to ⁂2036.

2034. Perhaps the more common way is this, in which the parts are diagonal on the surface and horizontal on the underside, and are led similarly to ⁂2035.

S. R. Ashley laces her skating and ski boots with two short strings on each boot. The method saves much loosening and tightening and allows of a much nicer adjustment at different parts of the lacing (shown as ⁂2033 and ⁂2034).

2035. The method shown here is designed to do away with the tying of lacings. The fact that there is very little pull on the bottom parts of a lacing makes the method practicable. The strings are led from *top to bottom*, the reverse of ⁂2034. The lace is led in regular over-and-under tucks in the order marked on the drawing. The ends may be led under the loop at top between 6 and 7. After the lacings are tightened (from top to bottom) the ends are tucked out of sight under the shoe tops. It is particularly neat, but will prove uncomfortable unless the metal tips are cut off. A buttonhook will be of assistance in tightening.

2036. The concealed-end "horizontal lace" is preferred by many. It was shown to me by Bruce McRae. The string is rove in the order marked on the illustration. A football is laced in much the same manner, a buttonhook being used for tightening.

2037. A method of lacing the cuffs of riding breeches was shown to me by my brother, Burton M. Ashley. The long diagonals allow considerable elasticity. All the parts on the underside are led vertically.

2038. A lacing with a cross-gartered effect.

2039. Ski and skating boots may be laced so that no cord crosses in contact with the instep.

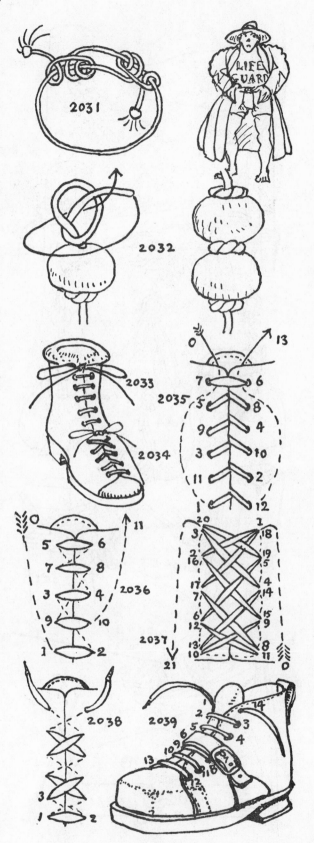

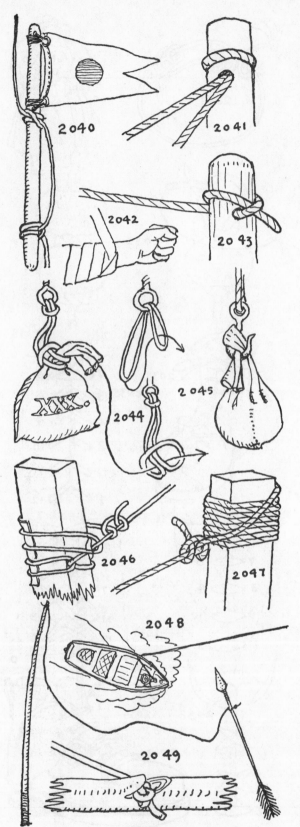

2040. Signal flags on yachts are commonly sent aloft on a small staff. The flag is seized twice to its staff and the halyard is clove hitched just below the lower seizing, and single hitched or clove hitched near the bottom of the staff. The two ends of the halyard are generally bent together.

2041. To secure the *bight* of a rope *to a perforated post:* Reeve a bight through the hole and turn it back over the top of the post. This is used in *staking off* and on clothes posts.

2042. In *parceling*, in *bandaging* and in *passing gaskets* or other flat material, if the lead requires deflection, fold the material half over, crease and smooth down the fold, and lead in the direction wanted.

2043. To secure the end of a line to a perforated post: Reeve the line through the hole in the post, then make a SINGLE HITCH over the top of the post with the end.

2044. To *hang a loaded* sack from an eyebolt or a hook. Make fast a strap, of marline or heavier material, to the eye with a RING HITCH (#1859). Then make a BALE SLING HITCH (#1694) in hand and slip it over the neck of the sack.

2045. To *hang a partially loaded sack* to a hook without employing a rope, tie a BLACKWALL HITCH with the neck of the bag. First lay the end in the mouth of the hook, then lead the neck around the back of the hook and through the mouth.

2046. To *hitch to a stanchion:* Haul the rope taut. Bring the end around the post and take a turn around the standing part. Bring the rope back around the post in the contrary way and take a turn around the standing part and lead back again. Take as many of these turns alternately left and right as desired, hauling each taut, and finally half hitch the end to the standing part. If possible wrap the stanchion first with old canvas, gunny sacking, or a piece of newspaper. This hitch must be made tightly so that it cannot "work."

2047. Another method of *tying to a rectangular timber.* Take five or six close turns around a timber and with the end take Two HALF HITCHES around the standing part.

2048. To tow a boat alongside in such a way that she will sheer off and be in no danger of colliding: Bring the painter aft, passing it under a thwart, then lead it forward through a rowlock to the side of the ship.

2049. A notched arrow for a throwing stick. An OVERHAND KNOT is tied in the end of a cord that is fast to a whiplike stick. The knot is adjusted in a shallow slot or notch near the fore end of the arrow which has been whittled from a shingle. The arrow is thrown with a lash of the whip. I learned this, when a boy, from Dan Beard's *American Boy's Handibook.* In this book was the first discussion of knots that I had ever read.

2050, 2051. In fishing, off a beach, a bag of sand is about the best anchor that can be found. On a wide beach the distance that the boat must be dragged or rolled, to reach the water's edge, or to be above the reach of the tide, is often so great that the extra weight of an iron anchor is no small thing, and as it is no longer safe in this country to leave anything smaller than a large boat around loose, an iron anchor would have to be taken home after each trip, along with the oars and fish. A strong and close-woven canvas bag is required. Two bucketfuls will be enough sand for an ordinary skiff in any weather that is fit for fishing.

2050. Lay your anchor warp across the neck of the sack and turn the neck back. Take a number of turns around the neck (seven or eight), lead the end of the rope between the neck and the bag and make the end of the rope fast to the standing part. This is a method I have often seen employed on Horseneck Beach.

2051. The method that I have used myself is to tie with a MULTI-FOLD BECKET HITCH. (See #1902).

2052. A well-rounded stone from a shingle beach or an old cannon ball makes an excellent *counterweight for a gate* or a cellar door. Place the stone in the center of a square of canvas. Gather the canvas at the top and tie closely with a CONSTRICTOR KNOT (#1189). Bend the end to the standing part with a BOWLINE KNOT.

2053. To carry or hang up an irregular or globular object, such as a watermelon or a roast of beef, take a piece of old hammock or seine. Cut it to a size a little bigger than appears necessary and reeve the end of a rope in and out in a rough circle through the outer meshes. Place the object in the center and draw up the rope, which acts as a puckering string. Secure with Two HALF HITCHES. If the net fits too loosely, add a seizing close to the object that is to be suspended. Carry over your shoulder, or on a tote pole between two men.

2054. A *Spanish reef* is an emergency method of shortening sail in a small boat. Sometimes the mainsail of a sloop, when close reefed, is too small for the jib as a whole, yet the boat will not steer without some headsail. Unsnap the upper stay hooks of the jib and tie an OVERHAND KNOT in the head of the sail.

2055. *Bracing a drum.* A drumhead is tautened by hauling down on the leathers, one at a time. This tightens the cord which holds the two ends of the drum together. When not in use the leathers are slackened, so as not to stretch the head.

2056. To hitch to the side of a ladder at the end of a rung, employ the BUOY ROPE HITCH (#720).

2057. A *horse's tail is tied up,* when sleighing in slushy snow, or whenever the going is muddy. There are a number of ways of doing this. Often the hair is twisted and laid up in the manner of rope; sometimes it is platted. A good practical way is to divide the tail and *half knot* the two parts, then wind the two ends tightly upward in opposite directions. As the dock tapers toward the end the whole tendency is for the hair to slip downward. It is prevented by the bulk of the first HALF KNOT. When the tail has been wound sufficiently, half knot the two ends together, and tuck the ends of hair under the outside turns.

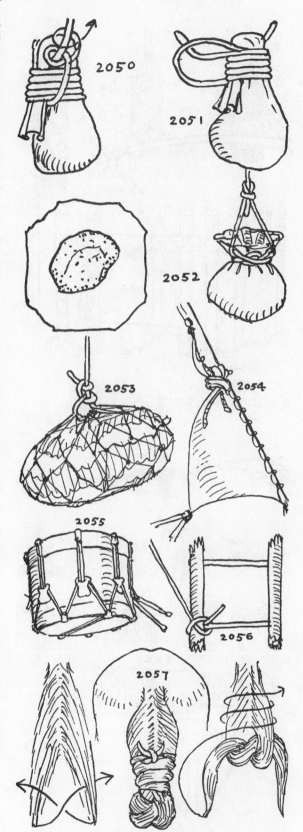

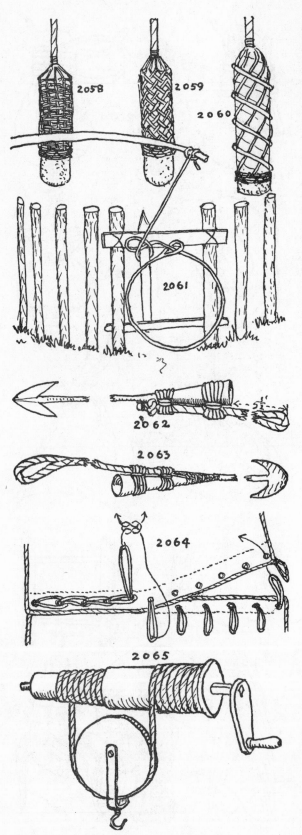

2058. A *hitch to a cylinder*. If a window weight is too large it may be broken with a hammer and both halves used. One end, having no hole, requires a special attachment. First seize the rope and open it to the seizing, then open the strands into their individual yarns. With the standing part upward and the yarns hanging downward, arrange them evenly around the end of the weight and seize with a Constrictor Knot (#1249). Next proceed with marline to graft the yarns to the cylinder as described in #3557. Finally seize all ends.

2059. Cross Grafting is more secure than regular grafting for this purpose. The method is described as #3563.

2060. A practical and expeditious way is to tape the window weight in a right helix, then to twist the yarns evenly over the taped section in an opposite helix to the left. Finally *round* over the yarns with *marline* in a tight right helix. Whip and snake the ends.

2061. A *lizard trap* from Guinea, taken from a *Smithsonian Ethnological Report*. A gap is left in the wall of a light stockade and a crossbar is lashed across the top. The rope is secured to a strong springy sapling, the end of which is to be hauled down above the gap. A Noose is put in the end of the rope. Two loose sticks are arranged as in the picture, and a Slippery Hitch holds the Noose and the otherwise loose sticks in position, until one or the other is disturbed by an animal attempting to pass through the gap. The knots are a Slippery Hitch and a Noose arranged as shown. Other traps are shown under "Shooting," "The Trapper," and "The Poacher" in Chapter 2.

2062. An old mounting on a Provincetown Arctic "iron" or harpoon. A Wall Knot (#671) is tied in the end of the mounting, which is made fast to the harpoon socket with two round seizings (#541). The rope is five and a half feet long. The whale line is bent with a Double Becket Hitch (#1902).

2063. The mounting for a sperm-whale iron, which is about twelve inches shorter than the former, due to the thinner blubber of the Temperate Zone whale. It is seized in the same way as the former, but the two seizings are nearer together to allow of grafting (#3557), which starts well up on the socket of the iron.

2064. *Latching* is an old method of attaching a drabbler to a jib, or a bonnet to a fore and aft sail. Nowadays it is the method employed by circuses in assembling the canvas sections of the tents. A series of eyelets in the upper section of the sail are opposite a series of loops, termed "keys," in the headrope of the bonnet. Starting at one side, a key is rove through the opposite eyelet and hauled to the next eye. The next key is rove through its opposite eye and through the key that was first led. This process is continued until the center is reached. The process is then repeated, beginning at the other edge of the sail. The two center loops, being twice as long as the rest, are reef knotted together. Captain John Smith described them in 1627, calling them "latchets."

2065. The *Chinese windlass* is the grandfather of the present-day differential chain hoist. One end winds, while the other unwinds, and the right end of the barrel, being larger than the left, winds or unwinds a greater length of rope than the left end, with each revolution of the crank.

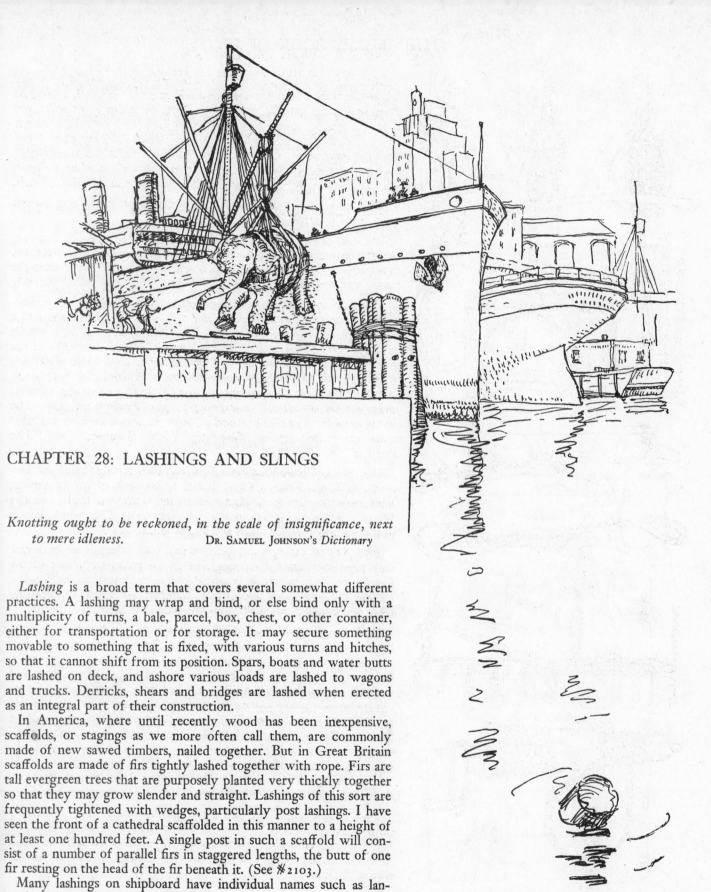

CHAPTER 28: LASHINGS AND SLINGS

Knotting ought to be reckoned, in the scale of insignificance, next to mere idleness.   Dr. Samuel Johnson's *Dictionary*

Lashing is a broad term that covers several somewhat different practices. A lashing may wrap and bind, or else bind only with a multiplicity of turns, a bale, parcel, box, chest, or other container, either for transportation or for storage. It may secure something movable to something that is fixed, with various turns and hitches, so that it cannot shift from its position. Spars, boats and water butts are lashed on deck, and ashore various loads are lashed to wagons and trucks. Derricks, shears and bridges are lashed when erected as an integral part of their construction.

In America, where until recently wood has been inexpensive, scaffolds, or stagings as we more often call them, are commonly made of new sawed timbers, nailed together. But in Great Britain scaffolds are made of firs tightly lashed together with rope. Firs are tall evergreen trees that are purposely planted very thickly together so that they may grow slender and straight. Lashings of this sort are frequently tightened with wedges, particularly post lashings. I have seen the front of a cathedral scaffolded in this manner to a height of at least one hundred feet. A single post in such a scaffold will consist of a number of parallel firs in staggered lengths, the butt of one fir resting on the head of the fir beneath it. (See ⚓2103.)

Many lashings on shipboard have individual names such as lanyards, gripes, gammoning, fishing, etc.

[335]

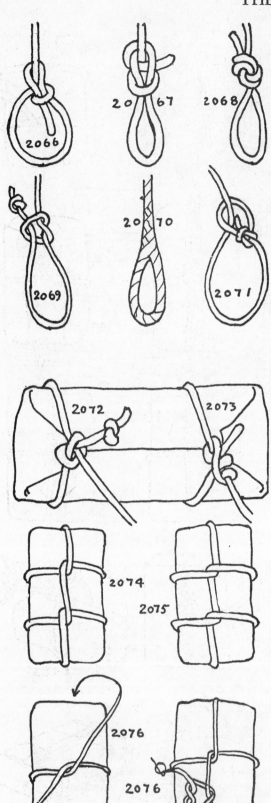

2066 2067 2068

2069 2070 2071

2072 2073

2074

2075

2076

2076

Lashings that are in constant use are apt to be fitted at one end with a ring, an EYE SPLICE or a hook, and with a lanyard at the other end.

Frapping turns are round turns which heave the several parts of a lashing together to tighten them, and *racking turns* are taken S-wise around two parts for the same purpose and also to hold them securely in position.

Service, seizings and whippings are closely related to lashings but are made of smaller material.

2066. In making up a parcel, bale, bundle, or roll (the commonest form of lashing), the lashing is generally started by tying a loop in the end of the rope. At sea the BOWLINE KNOT (※1010) is used for the purpose.

2067. For tying in twine the ANGLER'S LOOP is to be recommended; it is as easily tied as the BOWLINE, is neater, has a better lead and is quite as strong; but it is not so easily untied.

2068. The LOOP KNOT (※1009), sometimes called "THUMB KNOT," is commonly used in shops when tying up heavy parcels.

2069. The LOOP KNOT (2) is more often tied in the manufacturing and wholesale districts, where heavier cord is required.

2070. If a lashing is permanent, such as that on a boat or on a sea chest, where it is replaced after each opening, an EYE SPLICE is put in the end.

2071. The RUNNING BOWLINE is the Noose that is customarily put around any parcel or bale that is made up at sea. Ashore a LOOP KNOT (※1009) is more apt to be used in forming the Noose.

A NOOSE is formed by reeving the end through any of the five loops that have just been shown. But a much quicker way to form a NOOSE is to lay a bight from the standing part across the loop and pull the bight through until it is the size required.

2072. When a loop is not made in hand the common shopkeeper's way is to tie it directly around the parcel in the manner pictured here. An OVERHAND KNOT is added to the end of the cord to prevent spilling. This is not quite the same as NOOSE ※2069 but the OVERHAND KNOT makes it about as secure.

2073. In the days when the cotton brokers of New Bedford used to carry their samples from mill to mill, the bundles or rolls were sometimes tied with the knot shown here, which is the opposite of the MIDSHIPMAN'S HITCH (※1856). The advantage of this knot was that the NOOSE could be drawn as tightly as wished, and would not render, so no further lashing or knotting was necessary. All that was required when the samples were to be displayed was to slide the knot open. It was closed in the same way.

2074. Where a long object is to be lashed, a series of SINGLE HITCHES, or MARLINE HITCHES, is required along its full length.

2075. MARLINE HITCHES are preferable, since they are firmer. In the Navy seven such hitches were formerly required when a hammock was to be lashed, but nowadays five appears to be the standard.

2076. The most elementary method of making up a bundle is to middle a cord and pass a single turn around the waist. Cross the ends, making an elbow, and bring them around at right angles until they meet again, and there tie them snugly with a REEF KNOT. This is a proper way to use the REEF KNOT and it is as good a way as any to "tie" bundles that are to be stowed away. It is not, however, sufficiently secure for post and express parcels; but a close OVERHAND KNOT in each end will make the REEF KNOT safe for the purpose.

Bundles in the home are always "tied," and in some quarters a tightly lashed bundle is said to be "corded."

2077. The CROSSING KNOT. In a proper lashing two parts do not cross each other without being engaged. The common CROSSING KNOT is often used at sea because a sailor abhors anything in rope that jams. Lay a bight of the working end across the transverse part, then tuck the end as pictured.

2078. The common shore way of tying this knot requires two tucks. The knots are identical, or they may be left and right perversions, as the drawings here show them.

2079. The CLOVE HITCH is ordinarily tied in heavy cord by manufacturers' shipping departments, whenever a CROSSING HITCH is required. However, if the cord is worth saving, the CLOVE HITCH is an annoyance, as it is difficult to untie. The hitch in the illustration is tied in the horizontal cord.

2080. This shows the top of a parcel with a RUNNING BOWLINE secured about its waist. On the bottom is CROSSING KNOT ℀2077. To draw taut and make fast, pass the end upward across the waist; stick from right to left under the upper vertical part and form a HALF HITCH in what is practically one motion. Haul taut and add another HALF HITCH above the first, then draw up and add an OVERHAND KNOT to the end. This is about the simplest way to make up a parcel.

2081. The commoner but by no means better way of securing the end is to pass it around the upper part of the lashing and to add the two HALF HITCHES below.

2082. The first HALF HITCH may be taken after the end has been rove under the knot at the waist. Tied in this way, no finger is required to hold the first HALF HITCH while the second one is being added. What is gained, however, scarcely pays for the extra trouble of reeving.

2083. The PACKING KNOT consists of a FIGURE-EIGHT KNOT tied around the standing part. It may be drawn up snugly and ordinarily will not render while the cross turn is being added. If a hitch is put around the end, with a bight from the standing part, the waist is permanently locked after the manner of a BUTCHER'S KNOT.

2084. To *wrap up bottles:* Take an oversize piece of heavy Manila paper, much wider than for an ordinary parcel, open and place several thicknesses of old newspapers on top. Close the side edges together and roll them up tightly two or more turns. Turn up the edges of one end and fold or roll up that end so that it forms a heavy pad. Treat the other end likewise and lash with a heavy cord, as already described for ℀2080.

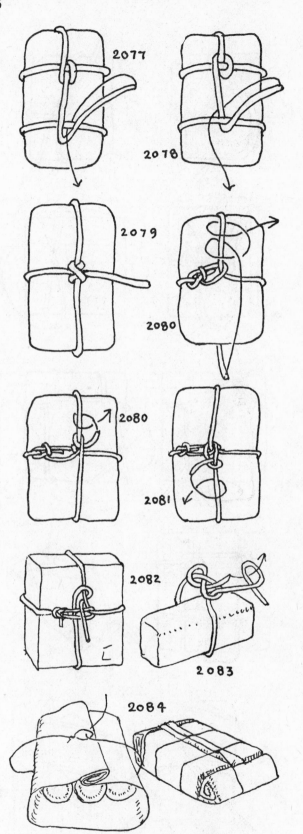

2085. These drawings represent a *parcel lashing* that is much affected by "shoppes of the better sorte," but it is to be found in the cash-and-carry zones as well. Middle a cord or ribbon and loop it over one corner of the box or parcel. Cross the ends on the underside and bring them to the top. Here the end from the left is led through the loop as pictured, and the end leading from the bottom is tucked to the left under the upper vertical part. The two ends are then tied in a Bowknot which may be as elaborate as desired.

2086. A *square parcel lashing*. Hold one quarter of the length of a long cord in the left hand and take a full turn with the right hand, around the right end of a flat and approximately square-topped box, passing the long end to the left of the short end. Still with the right hand lead the long end to the right end around the upper end of the box, passing below the short end. Turn the long end upward, crossing the short end, and lead the long end around the left end of the box, bringing it up to the right of the short end. Cross the long end to the left over the short end and lead it around the lower end of the box and finally tie the two ends together with either a Reef Knot or Parcel Knot #2095. A Bowknot from Chapter 31 should be added. If desired, the lashing may be further complicated while being made by adding Crossing Knots to the reverse side.

2087. This depicts a *method of parcel tying* that is common in dress shops, haberdasheries, laundries, "dry cleaning" and pressing establishments. Besides being decorative it is essentially practical. It may be tied in cord or ribbon but colored cotton tape is customarily used. The girl who ties the parcel generally drops a large loose turn of the cord over the counter or over the box and then arranges it in two loops around opposite corners. The cords are next crossed at one end of the box and the long end is passed again around the box with an alternating over-and-under that is the opposite of the first course. When the cord has returned to the front, both the top and bottom lashings will be found to bear a neat diamond pattern. The ends are crossed as shown in the fourth diagram and after being drawn taut are finished off with a Bowknot.

2088. The transportation of goods by pack animals is still important in mountainous country. But lately we have heard less of the army mule and more of the automobile truck. Mountain highways are rapidly paralleling the old pack trails.

A characteristic *pack* is shown here, but every packer adds his individual refinements to the task, and these he varies to suit the char-

acter of the load. The various articles that are to be carried are assembled and wrapped in a canvas *manta*. The turns of the lashing
are arranged so that they can be progressively tightened by heaving
sideways on the various parts. A rope called a *lair*, having an EYE
SPLICE AND THIMBLE at one end, is needed for the lashing. A NOOSE is
formed by means of the EYE SPLICE and is placed lengthwise around
the pack. A hitch is led around the pack at one-third length, as shown
in the first diagram. Another SINGLE HITCH is added around the pack
below the first, so that the length of the pack is divided approximately into equal thirds by the two hitches. The lair rope is next led
up the back of the pack, forming two CROSSING KNOTS (※2089) on
the way. It is brought down the front on the right side where it
rounds the lower of the two encircling hitches, and is then made fast
to the upper one, generally with a CLOVE HITCH. While being made
up, the pack is not hove on—it is merely adjusted "hand taut." But
when all the turns are in place it is set up, or hove taut. It is then
tightened gradually from beginning to end, and the end of the lair
rope is expended with further turns if necessary.

2089. The CROSSING KNOTS, on the back of the pack lashing, differ
somewhat from the ordinary one, shown as ※2077 and ※2078, because it encompasses a parallel section of rope. Only one tuck is
required, however, but this is taken under two parts simultaneously,
as shown in the illustration.

2090. The ordinary method of lashing a chest or trunk is shown
here. A piece of rope about clothesline size is employed. The lashing
is started with a NOOSE (※1114) or a RUNNING BOWLINE (※1117),
and a series of hitches follows, which may be two to five in number.
These are taken along the length of the chest. The end is then rove
through the becket on the chest end, and passed the length of the
bottom with a series of CROSSING KNOTS (※2077). After the rope has
been rove through the becket on the other end, it is half hitched to
the original RUNNING BOWLINE. The whole lashing is now set up before a second HALF HITCH is added.

If there is a long end, the lashing is continued as follows: The end
is led around the nearest hitch and hove taut. It is next led back to
the farthest unsecured hitch, and hove taut and hitched. In this way,
it is led back and forth until the rope is expended or all the original
hitches around the chest are secured. An OVERHAND KNOT may be
added close up to the final HALF HITCH.

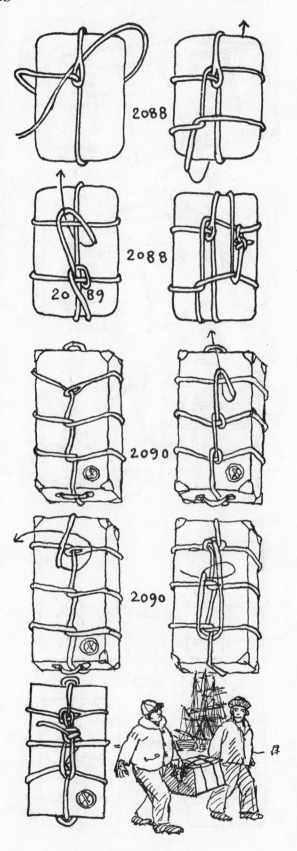

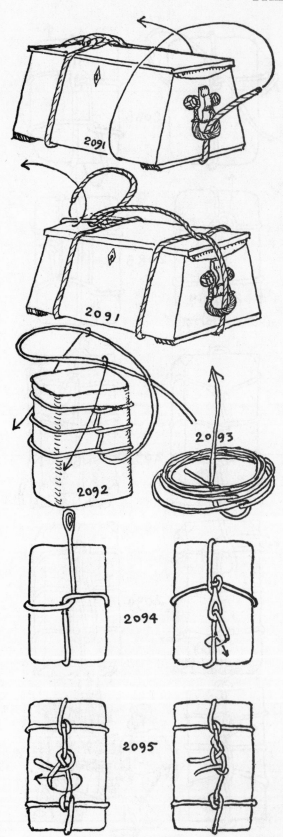

2091. Many sailors keep their sea chests lashed at all times to discourage prying, particularly when a lock is untrustworthy. The method of lashing shown here admits of opening the lid without casting off the turns of the lashing, which is a great convenience.

A NOOSE, preferably an eye spliced one, is passed around one end of the chest and the rope end is rove downward through the becket of the same end. A CROSSING KNOT is added at the bottom and the end is rove up through the opposite becket. A hitch is passed around the second end, with a CROSSING KNOT at the bottom, and the end is then secured to the EYE SPLICE as in ⚓2080.

To open this lashing: Cast off the final knot and slip the original NOOSE and the hitch at the other end down over their respective ends. This allows the lid to be opened.

2092. To lash a chest with MARLINE HITCHES: Stand it on end and put a NOOSE around the top, then, beginning near the top, put on a series of snug SINGLE HITCHES. Each of these, after being formed, is hove snug below the preceding one, which capsizes it into a MARLINE HITCH.

2093. To remove MARLINE HITCHES quickly and easily, remove all other complications in the rope and then drop the hitches to the floor. Remove the chest and haul the lower end of the lashing up through the center of the turns. This unties the series in the manner described for TRICK KNOT ⚓2582.

2094. Instead of starting a lashing with a NOOSE, it is sometimes started with a hitch around the girth. A CROSSING KNOT (⚓2077) is added to the working end on the reverse side and the working end is half hitched to the ring, eye or loop with which the standing end is fitted.

2095. A most expeditious way to tie small parcels and rolls is with KNOT ⚓1227. The lashing having been put on, tie a HALF KNOT with the two ends. Lead the upper end to a position below the lower end of the HALF KNOT, as pictured in the left diagram. Then draw the knot taut and add a HALF HITCH around the lower part with the working end.

2096. A lashing that passes around the girth only of an object, without having any frapping turns, is termed at sea a *stop* or a *stopping*. Furled sails are "stopped" and sails that are to be "set flying" are first "put up in stops."

The common knot for finishing off a stopping is the REEF or SQUARE KNOT.

2097. For stopping rolls of moderate circumference—rugs, papers, and such—nothing can be snugger than the CONSTRICTOR KNOT (⚓1249). But as the CONSTRICTOR KNOT binds so tightly that it must be cut or broken to release an object, it is not suitable for rope unless it is slipped as ⚓1250.

2098. In racing craft, light sails are "sent up in stops," that is, they are tied in a long roll with a series of light stops before hoisting. At the proper moment they are "broken out" by hauling on the sheet. To set or make up a jib or staysail in stops: Fold the sail lengthwise so that the clew projects beyond the luff, and the luff and bunt are parallel. Then roll up the bunt tightly to the luff and stop at the width of every cloth or seam, with a single piece of sail twine tied in a Reef Knot. Omit the head stop. At either side of the projecting clew put on a double stop.

2099. To make up a spinnaker: Bring the two clews, or the clew and tack, together and, holding the head at a loose stretch, put long zigzag folds in the sail as pictured. Be careful that the clew and tack are both accessible. Stop the sail at even intervals with a single yarn if adequate. Leave an appreciable length at the head without any stop, as there is little pull there and in a light wind the sail may fail to break out. At the foot put on a double stop.

The spinnaker is a very light sail and too heavy a stop may damage it. On small boats white woolen knitting yarn makes a good stop and may be used single or double as required. On a very small open boat I have seen candle wicking used on a sail that scarcely rated any stops. Every man has his own technique for making up sails in stops, but the principle does not vary.

2100. When a heavy swell is running and there is practically no wind, there is always danger of the sail breaking out before it is wanted. Under these circumstances a sail may be made up with a "chain stitch." The rope required is very long, so that, when breaking it out, one man should "run away" with it aft, while another stands by at the clew, to run away with a second length when the time arrives. This was tried, when twine was lacking, on a Genoa jib and worked satisfactorily. But under some circumstances it seems possible that it might foul and perhaps injure the sail.

2101. Colors are sent aloft in stops to prevent their fouling in the rigging. The upper end of the lashing shown is the downhaul end of the halyard which is bent to the lower end of the hoist. Double the flag by laying head and foot together, then roll it up tightly.

Studding sails were once sent up in the manner last described or else they were stopped with rope yarns. In both cases they were stopped to their yards. They were sent aloft abaft the square sails on the weather side, and forward on the leeward side. The stops were cut by a sailor, who stood on the yardarm to which the studding sail was *clewed*.

In a light wind, a spinnaker sometimes has a rope with a Stopper Knot in the end. The rope is laid up outside the sail. The upper stop, which is double, is made fast to the knot, and about every fourth stop is fast to the rope.

Sometimes a sheet is laid up to the peak and stopped in, the end being brought to deck outside all. This insures instant breaking out.

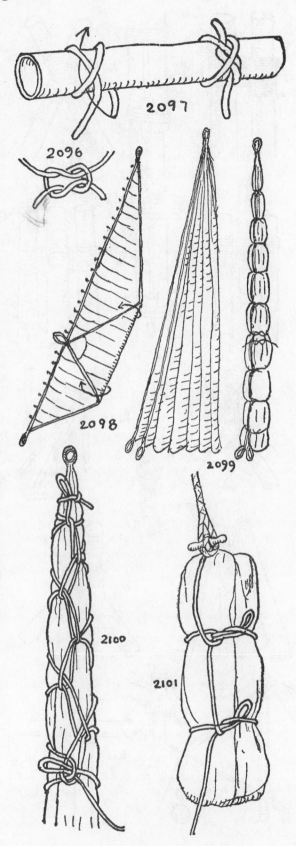

THE ASHLEY BOOK OF KNOTS

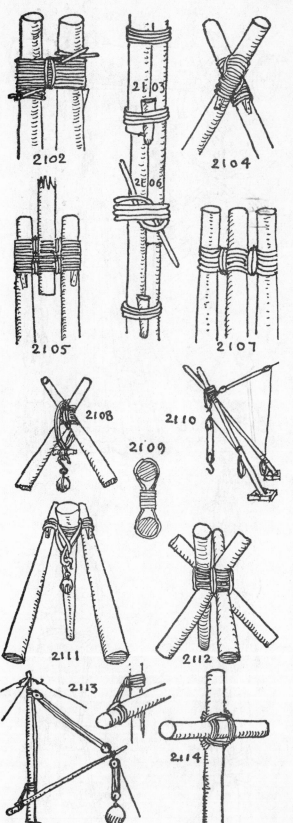

2102. *Shear leg lashing* is much like seizing, but is on a much larger scale. Start with a CLOVE HITCH around one leg, then pass a series of round turns, eight or nine, rather loosely. Put them on just tightly enough so that the several frapping turns which are to be added will heave the round turns closely together between the two legs. The lashing is finished off with a CLOVE HITCH around the second leg. Nail cheeks to the posts when practicable.

2103. A *pole* or *post* for a *scaffolding*. A tall pole is built up with a series of parallel poles. The joints are evenly staggered. The bigger firs are at the bottom of the pole and the butt of an upper fir rests on the head of a lower one. There is a lashing above and below each joint, consisting of four to eight turns. These are first made hand taut and then are hove taut with a marlingspike. After this they are wedged, the wedge always being driven downward from above.

2104. A *shear leg lashing* is more secure if taken with racking turns. Several frapping turns are added with the two ends, which are then reef knotted together. When the shears are opened the lashing is further tightened by the process.

2105. *Tripod lashings* are made with seven or eight loose turns Frapping turns are taken in the two intervals between the three legs, one of the rope ends being expended in each interval. These crossing turns may be finished off with any of the three knots shown in the previous chapter at the bottom of page 327. In the tripod shown here the center leg is lashed in a direction opposite the two side legs. When the tripod is erected the feet may have to be made fast to each other to prevent spreading.

2106. A good way to pass *pole lashings* (⚹2103) is to tie as pictured here, and then tighten one turn at a time with a marlingspike. This is discussed as KNOT ⚹1240.

2107. A lashing that is passed the same as ⚹2105 but the odd leg is laid parallel with the other two instead of opposite. If the lashing is made too taut it will be necessary to stake out the feet.

2108. To support the *tackle of a shears* take a round turn with a heavy strap as pictured, and hook the tackle to this.

2109. *Frapping turns* in a lashing are similar to the crossing turns in a seizing. Around large spars frapping turns give great leverage and often provide all the power that is necessary to tighten the lashing.

2110. A shears requires the support of a single guy which may be led to a mast, a tree, or a distant stake. If led to a stake, the guy is sometimes braced with a pole in the manner that a clothes pole is elevated. If erected on deck, the feet of the shears will require nailed cleats to prevent shifting.

2111. To suspend a *tackle block* under a tripod, put a BALE SLING HITCH over the top of the pole of the center leg and work it well down on the pole.

2112. Esparteiro gives this method of *lashing four legs;* it is similar to Seizing ⚹3398.

2113. A *derrick* consists of a mast and boom. Three or four guys are made fast to a Masthead Knot at the top, and the lower ends are fast to stakes. The boom is secured to the mast as pictured.

2114. A *square* or *transom lashing* is used in scaffolding, temporary bridge building, trellises, grape arbors, etc. The ends of the frapping turns are reef knotted together.

2115. A *crossed lashing* is used when one spar is vertical, the other horizontal. It is also used when battens are lashed or seized to shrouds instead of ratlines. Frapping turns will add to the security.

2116. A *square* or *right-angle lashing* from the outrigger of a South Sea Island boat, shown to me by Alexander Brown of the Mariners' Museum. A similar practice in basketry is found on the common market baskets of the British West Indies. It fastens the handle of the basket to the rim.

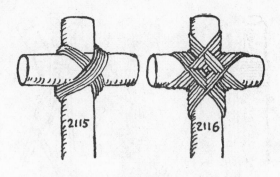

2117. *Fishing* strengthens and arrests further damage to spars when they are sprung, cracked or split. Several small spars serve as splints for a larger one, and the interstices are strengthened with old oars, handspikes, etc., for a distance much longer than the actual injury. Seizings of rope with riding turns are applied at intervals; these should be wide enough to cover approximately one third of the total surface of the repaired area. The lashings are tightened with marlingspikes and handspikes, and are made doubly secure with wooden wedges.

2118. The *wedges for fishing* are wide and flat with the outer edges rounded so they will not injure the lashing.

2119, 2120, 2121. *Boat lashings* are hove taut with lanyards that are secured either to an eye, a ring, or a deck bolt. As boat lashings should be ready at all times for instant removal they are applied with that purpose in mind. A series of loops are passed and the end is made fast to the last loop, often with a Slipped Half Hitch (⚹1664).

2122. *Boat gripes* are made of several thicknesses of canvas. Formerly they were of Sinnet ⚹2976 and ⚹3477, or (the best practice) of sword matting (⚹2964 and ⚹3817). The lanyard may be spliced to the ring or it may be secured with a Long Running Eye.

2123. If a boat is to be lashed while on the davits, the *gripe lanyards* may be coiled and the coil rove halfway through the gripe rings. One end of the coil is then passed around the davit and the two ends are toggled together with a fid. The gripes are made taut at the upper end.

If a boat is to remain long uncovered, particularly in the tropics, a narrow strip of wood termed a *stretcher* is placed between the gunnels to prevent warping. The gripes shrink when wet and slacken when dry, which puts a constant strain on the boat.

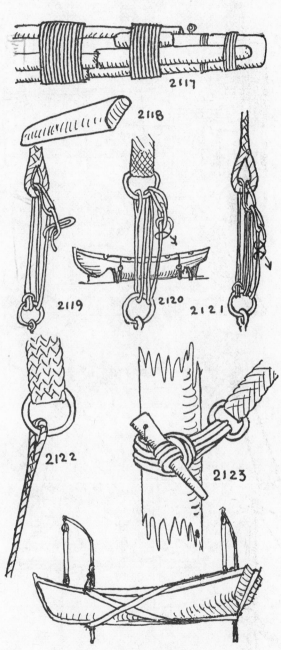

2124. In lashing a wagon or truck load, the length of a lashing is variable. A LOOP KNOT on the bight (HARNESS LOOP ⚓1050 or FARMER'S LOOP ⚓1054) can be put in at the proper length and a lashing made as shown here.

2125. To finish off such a lashing, bring the end up through a lower ring or hook and expend it with a series of tight turns or hitches. Reeve the end below the final turn and between two of the lashing turns. Work all taut and tie an OVERHAND KNOT close to the turns.

2126. A quicker but less dependable lashing is based on BELL RINGER'S KNOT ⚓1148. It is made fast in the way already described.

2127. Trucks and wagons are generally fitted along the sides with a series of rings, hooks, stake holes or else with a superstructure having lengthwise boards to lash to. With a smooth and even load, which is to be tarpaulin-covered, pass a series of crosswise lashings over the top of the load and then add two lengthwise ones with CROSSING KNOTS at the top wherever they pass the vertical ropes. Secure one end partway up one side and well forward and put a CROSSING KNOT loosely around the first and second upright. Do the same with the third and fourth and then the fifth and sixth until all the uprights around the load are taken care of in pairs. Then tighten from the beginning. Add another staggered row of knots above this, draw taut and the lashing will resemble the second drawing if the load is a soft one; but if it is a rigid one, the up-and-down ropes will merely stagger and will not meet. The lashing is completed with a lengthwise member along the top.

2128. In starting wagonload lashings a half hitched CLOVE HITCH is frequently used by teamsters.

2129. In finishing off a wagon lashing TWO HALF HITCHES is generally used.

2130. In passing a CROSSING KNOT around two upright parts of a wagon lashing, lead the working end underneath the two parts and back under its own standing part. Heave the two upright parts halfway together before leading the end forward to the next pair. In heaving on the next pair the first pair will receive additional tightening and may close together.

2131. Everything movable on the deck of a ship should be lashed when not in use. Boats, scuttle butts, spare spars, harness cask, sail bench, hen coops, blacksmith's forge, chopping block, workbenches, etc., are all secured. Many of these articles have permanent lanyards attached to them by which they are made fast.

The essence of good lashing is to first place the turns so that the object is held against shifting in any direction and, secondly, to tighten these turns by heaving on them with a sidewise pull at half length, which compounds the tension of the whole fabric.

2132. Movable objects about deck are generally lashed with a lanyard having a LONG RUNNING EYE in the end, and this is usually made fast to a ringbolt.

2133. A whale ship is fitted with a *lash rail* to secure things to, but this is very seldom found in other craft. An oil or water cask is lashed as pictured. Round turns are hove together with frapping turns.

2134. This illustrates a single turn around the middle part of a lashing. It is one of the best of devices for tightening a rope.

2135. A *scuttle butt* lies on its bilge and requires chocks to make a firm cradle for it to rest on. Sometimes small tackles are used to set up lashings of this sort, but usually rings and eyes are sufficient.

2136. The turns around a *horizontal cask or scuttle butt* often are set up with nothing save frapping turns.

2137. The *end of a lanyard* may be finished off around two parts in such a manner as to heave them together and so add to the effectiveness of the lashing.

2138. One of the most common ways of securing the end of a lashing is with TWO HALF HITCHES made fast to an eye.

2139. *Scuttle butts* sometimes have hinged metal straps fitted with rings in the ends and these are lashed to ringbolts on the deck.

Catharpins were sometimes frapped together in the manner of a lashing, although they were more often led through a euphroe or centipede block. *Catharpins* were of small stuff and their purpose was to take up the slack in the stays, to prevent jerking and slatting. They are pictured on page 533.

Besides tightening a lashing, frapping turns are employed to draw together the falls of a tackle, in order to tighten them, to strengthen them, or to hold them secure. The halyards of a sailing yacht at anchor are often frapped at night, to prevent slatting against the mast and keeping guests awake. Frappings of this nature are added with rope yarn. In a lashing, when the length is sufficient, the end of the rope itself is employed in frapping.

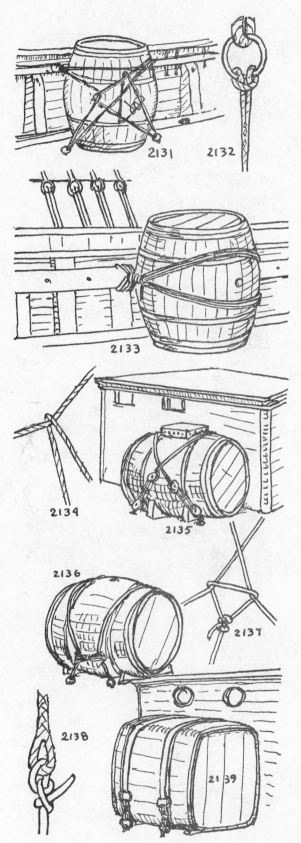

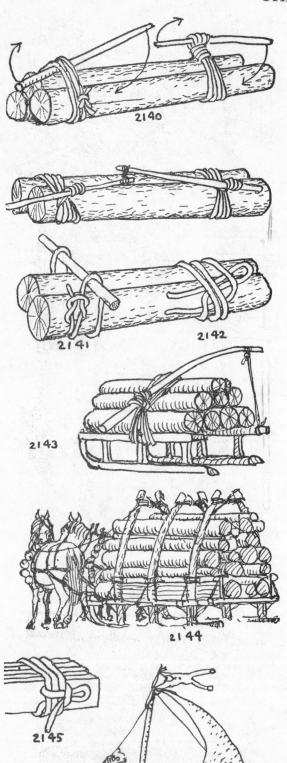

2140. In the timber industry, rope is used in making log rafts and in lashing loads. On the west coast huge rafts several hundred feet in length have been lashed with chain cable and towed many hundreds of miles. Log booms are found in spar yards and along rivers. Long spars are either lashed or chained together to form an enclosure around the floating logs.

Army engineers have in all past wars used a great deal of *rope lashing* in bridge building, field fortification, etc. This is gone into exhaustively in the United States Government *Engineers' Field Manual.*

In *raft making*, after several turns of rope have been passed loosely around two floating logs, a rack bar or pole is inserted under the turns and the lashing tightened by twisting with the bar horizontally. Two of these lashings are made near enough together so that the ends of two bars can be tied to each other. The lashings of the two must be twisted in the same direction, preferably "with the lay" of the rope. A hard-laid rope will not stand as much twisting as a soft-laid one.

2141. If rope is very large it will be found simpler to make up the lashing as pictured here. It is twisted horizontally as before described. In principle this does not differ from the surgeon's tourniquet given as ⌗1259.

2142. Ropes may be knotted as here shown and tightened with a bar. Put a MARLINGSPIKE HITCH in one end of a rope and pry, using the side or end of the log for a fulcrum. With large material a rack bar will be necessary.

2143. A load of logs may be secured to a sled with a lashing similar to ⌗2140. A much longer bar is used and the end is made fast to the sled.

2144. Stakes are required if a considerable number of logs are to be lashed. Tough green saplings are cut for stakes and the tops of these are notched and lashed together across the load. The lashings are tightened by twisting in a vertical plane and tying the ends of the rack bars together the same as in ⌗2040.

2145. The knot shown here is used in lashing timbers. The edge of the timber provides a shoulder for the end of the rope so that little strain comes on the SLIP LOOP. A bight is tucked under all three turns, then another bight through the first one.

Stones are slung under a high gear, using one or more straps of chain, which are twisted tight with rack bars.

Slinging is the arranging of ropes or straps around an object by means of which the object is to be hoisted and lowered, or else suspended. Tools are slung when sent aloft on the end of a rope, cargo is slung when taken aboard, a sunken vessel is slung before it is "raised," and a sick horse is slung in its stall when it is unable to stand without assistance.

2146. A *marlingspike* is slung ready for sending aloft by taking a SINGLE HITCH with its own lanyard around the pointed end.

2147. A simple way to *sling a hammer* is with a BUOY ROPE HITCH.

2148. Ashore a *hammer* is often slung with a CLOVE HITCH around the neck of the handle but a MARLINGSPIKE HITCH is often used at sea and is preferable.

2149. To *sling a pitchfork* for conveyance to the mow: Lead the end of a rope between the tines and make fast to the shank with a CLOVE HITCH.

2150. A CLOVE HITCH placed around the peen and a SINGLE HITCH near the end of the handle is good sound practice for hoisting a hammer.

2151. A *crowbar* may be sent to the upper floors of a building, which is being wrecked or is under construction, or it may be lowered into a cellar or well. Tie a ROLLING HITCH (※1734) to the handle end and add a SINGLE HITCH near the working end.

2152. To *sling a shovel* for lowering down a well, make a BECKET HITCH fast to the handle.

2153. A *maul, sledge hammer, grub hoe, pickax, mattock* or other heavy-headed tool should have the rope led under the head. Pass the end of a rope around the neck of the handle and twist the end and standing parts together a number of turns. Bring the standing part under the head and put two SINGLE HITCHES on the handle, spaced as pictured, one at the shank and the other at the grip.

2154. To *lower a bucket* by the handle and then to recover the rope from aloft: The handle is held firmly while lowering and is released instantly when the long end, which has been retained, is pulled and the knot is spilled. Objects may be lowered in this way from a window or down a stair well, saving many steps.

Middle the rope and pass two bights, one after the other, as pictured. Both ends are retained at the higher level, but the *working end* is merely to spill the knot after the object has reached bottom. Lower away with the standing end, at the same time paying out the spill line. When the object brings up, jerk the spill line or *working end*, which slips the knot, so that the rope may be retrieved.

2155. If the rope is too short for the knot just described, a basket with a flat bail may be lowered by means of a SINGLE HITCH. The end of the rope should have an OVERHAND KNOT. Adjust very carefully and test to make certain that it has nipped before lowering the basket. When the basket touches the ground, shake the rope to release the knot. This knot may be used on any flat-handled container such as a bucket, can-o-pail, or suitcase.

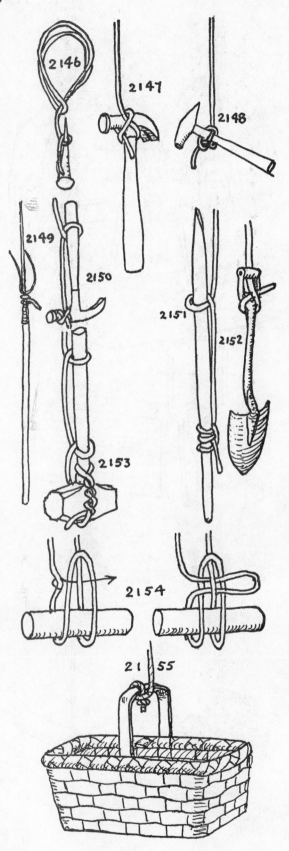

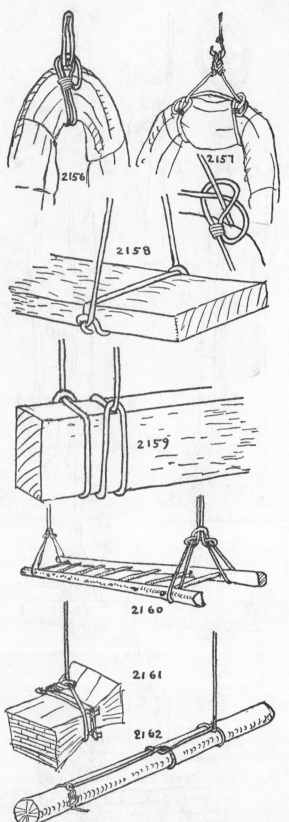

2156. Knight's *Seamanship* gives this strap for sending sails aloft. A selvagee should be employed as it is less liable than rope to pinch and bruise the canvas. The large DOUBLED EYE does not have to be unbent in order to remove the strap. It is merely necessary to cut the stopping.

2157. A better way perhaps is to hook to the block with a CAT's-PAW (#1891) and then to lead the sling down the back of the sail with the two parts well separated. Pass the sling under the sail and lead it back through the legs that were formed. From each side twist and seize in a turn around each of the two legs. When the two seizings are cut the sling spills instantly.

2158. To *sling a plank staging overside:* Tie a MARLINGSPIKE HITCH and insert one end of the plank. Do likewise with the other end.

2159. To *sling a plank on edge:* This is sometimes required as a fender when tying up to a stone pier that has neither stringpiece nor piling. Make a CLOVE HITCH much larger than the girth of the plank, and work the ends around until the knot is in the form shown.

2160. There are several knots that may be employed in *slinging a ladder* horizontally for use as a staging, the best known of these being the SPANISH BOWLINE (#1087). Others are given on pages 198 and 199. A loop is placed over the ends of each side post or rail and a wide board is laid over the rungs to complete the staging. In Chapter 12 several other DOUBLE LOOPS are given that will serve the same purpose and the subject of stagings is also discussed further in Chapter 2, under "Carpenter."

2161. For *slinging a bundle of shingles,* a carpenter generally employs the TIMBER HITCH.

2162. At sea if a small spar or some other lengthy object is to be hoisted on end through the tops, a TIMBER HITCH is made at the lower end and a series of SINGLE HITCHES added, finished off generally with a CLOVE HITCH at the upper end.
For towing, a spar is slung in the same way.

2163. The BALE or BARREL SLING is the most generally useful method of slinging. Sacks of sugar and flour, barrels, and bales are all slung with it. The sling is passed under the object to be hoisted and the longer bight is then rove through the upper one. The two turns which are formed around the bale should be well separated.

2164. If sufficient length is left, after the BALE SLING is in place, the longer bight is made fast to the cargo hook with a CAT's-PAW, which is the most practical of HOOK HITCHES. It is easily formed by grasping two bights and twisting the sling three or four turns away from you. The bights are then clapped together and put over the hook.

A stone is slung as the foregoing except that a chain is used and the loop of the chain is hooked directly without having any hitch put into it.

2165. The illustration shows the common way of turning over a stone while pulling it out of a hole; this doubles the power of the pull.

2166. The chain strap may be secured with a BLACKWALL HITCH to the tackle hook. It is one of the few knots that can be tied in chain without fear of jamming.

2167. A CASK SLING for use when the slings are short. The ends of slings, unless they are made selvagee fashion, are short spliced together and the strand ends are "cross seized." (See SPLICE ✳2639.)

2168. If a cask is to be hoisted with the end of a line, a Cow HITCH is tied around it and a BOWLINE KNOT tied with the end to the standing part. This is the same knot formation as the BALE SLING HITCH but it is tied in the end instead of the bight.

2169. A BUTT or HOGSHEAD SLING is made of heavy hawser-laid rope with a thimble eye cast in one end. The end is rove through the thimble and the NOOSE that is formed is put around one end of the hogshead and the other end hitches around the other end of the hogshead and is made fast to the standing part with TWO HALF HITCHES. In such heavy rope the cargo block is hooked directly to the bight or span of the slings.

2170. The *cargo block* pictured here is from Diderot's Encyclopedia of 1762. No knotting is required and the cask or pipe has little tendency to twist or turn in mid-air.

2171. *Can hooks* are used to lift a barrel by the chines.

2172. A four-strand rope has a ROUND EYE formed in the center by reeving one end through the strands of the other. A round thimble is seized in and chine hooks are spliced in at either end of the span. Nowadays this is usually made of chain.

2173. An older way of rigging can hooks or chine hooks that serves the same purpose. A grommet is made through the chine hooks and the eye is seized in with a round seizing.

2174. A *crate sling*. The slings are passed lengthwise and crossed in the mouth of the hook. The two parts are strapped across the ends to prevent their closing together and spilling the load.

2175. If a single sling is too short, two slings may be bent together with a STRAP BEND (✳1493).

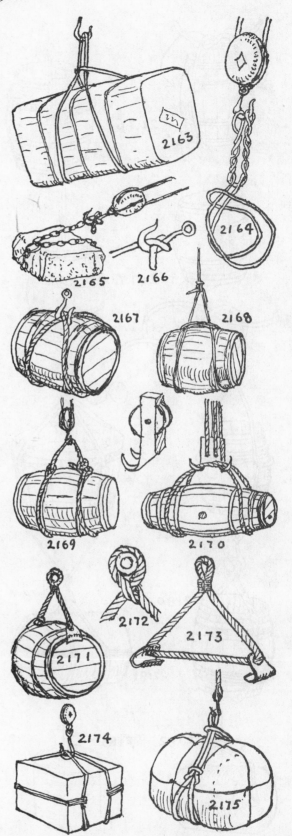

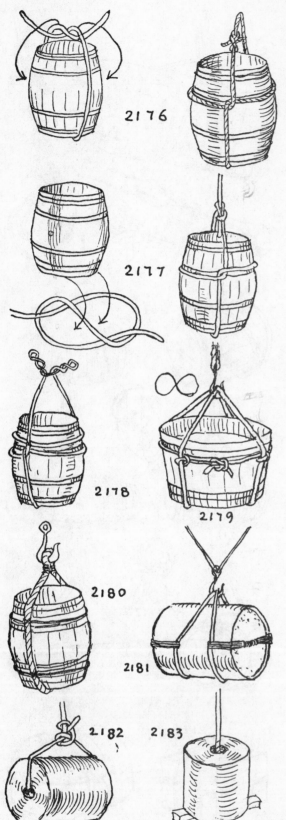

2176. There are a number of ways in which to *hoist or lower an open barrel or cask* that is partly full. The simplest is to take the bight of a rope fifteen to twenty feet long, stand the cask over the center of it and half knot the ends loosely across the top. Open the HALF KNOT and slip one half around either side of the bilge. This makes a SINGLE HITCH on either side of the cask. The ends are bent together.

2177. Another way is to first tie a large OVERHAND KNOT, open it wide and arrange it flat on the ground as pictured. Stand the cask over the center part and lift the knot until the cask is surrounded. This makes a MARLINE HITCH at either side of the cask, which is more secure than the SINGLE HITCH. Bend the ends together or bend one end to the bight of the other.

2178. To *hoist an open cask with a slings:* Stand the cask over the center part of the slings. Then put a SINGLE HITCH with either side of the slings a little way below the head. Make a CAT'S-PAW at the top of the slings and hook to the cargo block. Put on stops where the hitches cross the lengthwise parts of the slings.

If the slings is very long, double it and tie as before but with a doubled line. Hook the two loops to the tackle block.

2179. To *hoist an open and loaded tub:* First lash a sack over the head of the tub with several round turns of marline to keep the contents from slopping. Make a figure-eight turn in your slings and set the tub over the X crossing at the center. Bring the two bights together and put them over the hook. Lead a smaller rope around the bilge of the tub, adding knots wherever there is a crossing. It is well to stop the CROSSING KNOTS with a few turns of marline as there is a chance of their slipping down.

2180. If *an open cask is to be slung* with a short slings, seize in an eye and arrange as pictured. Put on a cross lashing with small stuff around each end of the cask. Use the CLOVE HITCH where the small stuff crosses the slings. There was a time when practically all ship's stores were kept in casks, and these methods were of vital importance. Nowadays fishermen occasionally use them.

2181. To *hoist or lower a boiler* or other heavy cylindrical object, use doubled slings and mouse the cargo hook stoutly. Keep the slings well separated by lashings across the two ends of the boiler.

2182. To *sling a coil of rope horizontally:* Reeve the end of a rope through the center of the coil and make fast the end to the standing part with Two HALF HITCHES.

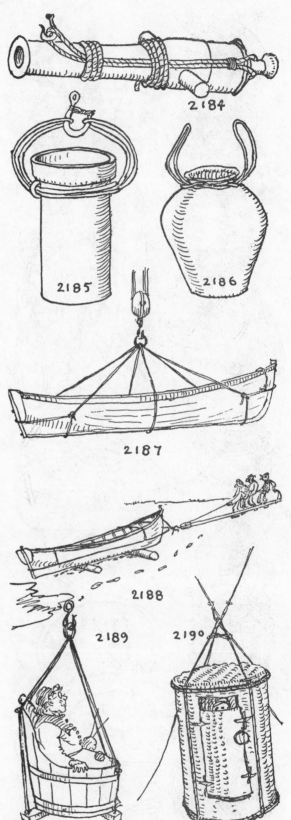

2183. To *sling a coil of rope on end:* Reeve the end of a rope through a coil and make it fast to the middle of a stout billet of wood, which will act as a toggle.

2184. An old method by which to *sling a gun or cannon:* Arrange the slings as pictured. The trunnions must be kept free so that the gun can be lowered directly into the carriage. If a gun is to be merely moved about deck the slings may be seized around the cascabel and a stout oak plug driven into the muzzle. Sometimes this plug was furnished with shivs for direct hoisting, in which case a block was made fast to the cascabel.

2185. To *sling an earthenware pipe* or other heavy cylindrical object that has a shoulder: Double two short slings and reeve one end of each through the bight of the other. Insert the pipe as shown.

2186. If the shoulder is slight a JUG OR JAR SLING (※1142) is safer as it does not give when the load is eased away.

2187. When a *boat is hoisted on a crane* she has to be slung but, when hoisted on davits, eyebolts are provided for the tackles. The crane slings have to be arranged to dissipate the strain on the structure of the boat and, as there is little or nothing to fasten to, the lashing may sometimes be quite elaborate. The method given here is from Luce and Ward. A wooden *spreader* should be inserted amidship to strengthen the gunnels.

2188. If a *heavy boat* is to be *hauled ashore* on rollers and the boat is not sufficiently strong to make use of such rings and eyebolts as are provided, more rope is called for. Sometimes there is a mast to tie to, but generally it is best to pass a rope horizontally around the boat and suspend it at intervals. If the painter is secured well down on the stem, which is the proper place to tow from, the strap around the boat may be stopped to it merely to hold the slings at the proper level, but it should not bear any part of the pull.

2189. A *"lady's chair"* from a whale ship. This was made from an oil cask and was provided so that the captain's wife, who often accompanied her husband on voyages of three or four years' length, could be hoisted and lowered to the whaleboat whenever boats went ashore or gammed with other ships at sea.

2190. A *passenger basket* used in offshore work in the Orient, from a photograph taken in Natal. Passengers are landed in small boats and rowed ashore. Many important harbors in the East are not provided with wharves, and many are so unhealthy that ships do not care to tie up even where there are facilities.

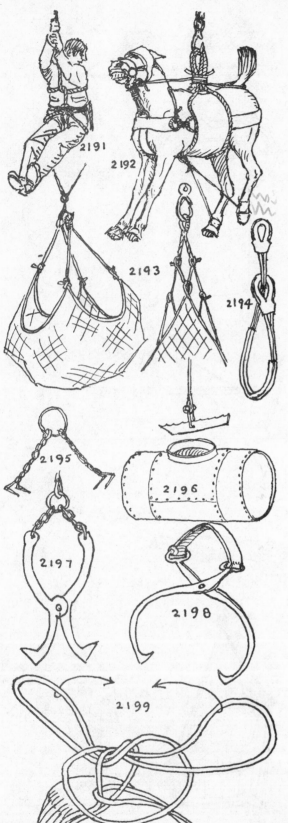

2191. To *sling a man* who is incapacitated. Tie either a PORTUGUESE BOWLINE, a BOWLINE in the bight or else a SPANISH BOWLINE. Put each leg through one loop of the BOWLINE and make a SINGLE HITCH in the standing part around the man's chest, close under his armpits.

2192. To *sling a horse*, for hoisting from a lighter: Take a length of heavy canvas, one and a half times the girth of the horse and one cloth wide. Double this lengthwise, then middle and sew a three-inch (circumference) boltrope to the selvage edge down each side of the sling, leaving loops at both ends two feet long and splicing the ends together. A breastplate, a breeching and a martingale of doubled canvas six inches wide are also to be made. One end of each of these is sewed to the sling and the other end has a strong eyelet hole worked into it. The boltrope of the sling proper has two cringles (⚹2843) worked into it for lashing the lanyards of the breastplate and breeching. The martingale eyelet is lashed to the halter ring and the head of the horse should be hove well down. A strong lanyard is lashed to one of the large loops in the ends of the sling proper. When the sling is in place this lanyard is employed to seize the two supporting loops and hold them together as snugly as possible. The other lanyards are spliced to the martingale, the breastplate and the breeching eyelets. If the horse is a heavy or a fractious one, kicking straps may be added. Be certain that the animal is well blindfolded.

2193. Odd-shaped merchandise will have various projections which may be utilized in lashing. This usually simplifies the task instead of complicating it. Such objects may be put into a *cargo net* if not too heavy. All small packages are handled in this way including the passengers' luggage.

The construction of a cargo net is described in Chapter 41.

2194. STEEL WIRE CARGO SLINGS are fitted with oversize thimbles as pictured, and the doubled wire itself is racked with marline and then served over. Often it is covered with hose pipe.

2195. *Sling "dogs"* are closely related to can and span hooks (page 349). Logs are hoisted with *single "dogs"* which are driven into the log with a maul; bales of wool, cotton, jute and Manila fiber are hoisted with *forked or double dogs*, which are also hammered into place and later removed with a crowbar.

2196. A *tank* is *slung* with an *iron toggle* inserted in the manhole.

2197. *Inside tongs* are employed in hoisting iron pipes and small tanks.

2198. *Outside tongs* are employed in hoisting ice, baled hay and other merchandise that will not be injured by the treatment.

2199. To *shorten an ordinary slings* after a BALE HITCH has been applied. Arrange the slack into two equal loops, half knot the two loops together, and clap them over the hook.

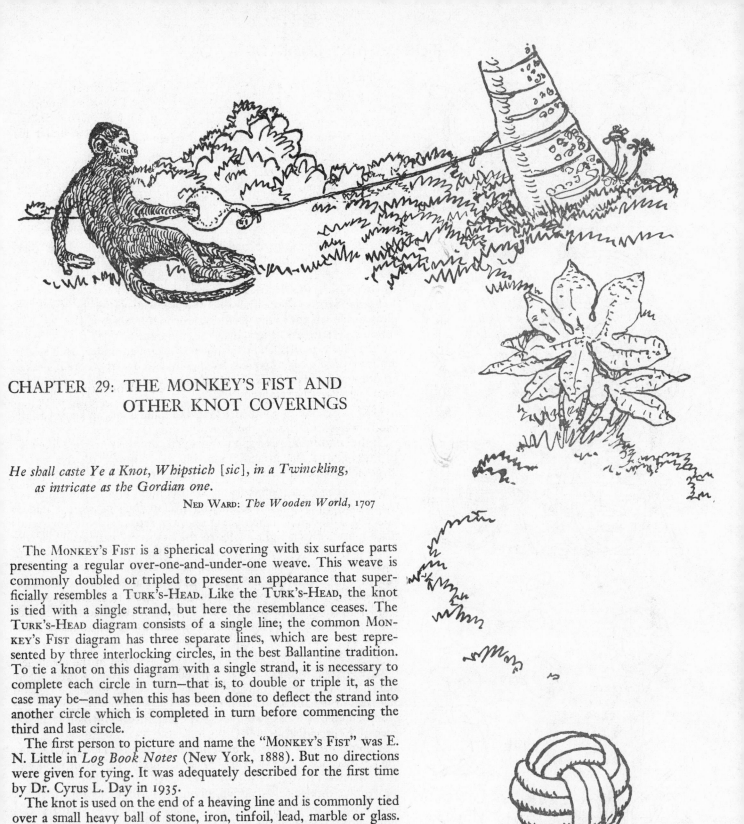

CHAPTER 29: THE MONKEY'S FIST AND OTHER KNOT COVERINGS

He shall caste Ye a Knot, Whipstich [sic], in a Twinckling,
   as intricate as the Gordian one.

NED WARD: *The Wooden World*, 1707

The MONKEY'S FIST is a spherical covering with six surface parts presenting a regular over-one-and-under-one weave. This weave is commonly doubled or tripled to present an appearance that superficially resembles a TURK'S-HEAD. Like the TURK'S-HEAD, the knot is tied with a single strand, but here the resemblance ceases. The TURK'S-HEAD diagram consists of a single line; the common MONKEY'S FIST diagram has three separate lines, which are best represented by three interlocking circles, in the best Ballantine tradition. To tie a knot on this diagram with a single strand, it is necessary to complete each circle in turn—that is, to double or triple it, as the case may be—and when this has been done to deflect the strand into another circle which is completed in turn before commencing the third and last circle.

The first person to picture and name the "MONKEY'S FIST" was E. N. Little in *Log Book Notes* (New York, 1888). But no directions were given for tying. It was adequately described for the first time by Dr. Cyrus L. Day in 1935.

The knot is used on the end of a heaving line and is commonly tied over a small heavy ball of stone, iron, tinfoil, lead, marble or glass. This heavy core is required to carry the weight of the heaving line when it is cast in a coil from ship to wharf, or from ship to towboat or lighter.

At sea the knot has been tied in three ways as shown in ⌗2200 and ⌗2202. These three knots, and some of the smaller TURK'S-HEADS, appear to be the only knots of record that have been used for coverings.

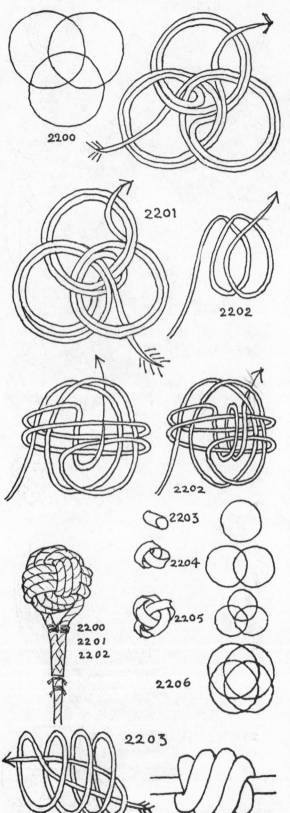

Some of the coverings that are to be shown may be used to cover balls, knobs and cane heads; the rectangular ones can be used to cover doorstops, book stops and paperweights. In general the drawings indicate the logical shapes of the knots but the proportions are capable of considerable molding and stretching.

2200. The MONKEY'S FIST. The first illustration shows the diagram form of the regular MONKEY'S FIST. It may be noted that this is also the diagram of the THREE-STRAND MANROPE KNOT, the THREE-STRAND DIAMOND KNOT, and the THREE-STRAND FOOTROPE KNOT.

All four of these have a regular alternate over-one-and-under-one lead.

Ordinarily the knot is tied three-ply—that is, the lead has three parallel parts; less often it has two and four ply. To simplify the drawings the TWO-PLY KNOT is the one that is often illustrated even when a THREE-PLY KNOT is described.

To tie: Start at the feather end of the arrow and make three complete circles to the right. Deflect the rope or cord and make three complete circles to the left, over the first circles. Tuck the end back, under the first circles, and continue to tuck, over, under, over, under, until the third set of three circles is complete. Insert a core if desired or draw up without one. With three-ply the core is optional but with four-ply it is required.

2201. A second method for tying the same knot. Make three left-hand circles each inside the previous one. The second cycle starts with the inside circle and spirals outward, and the third one likewise. In both KNOTS #2200 and #2201 the ends appear on the surface diagonally opposite each other, at either end of one of the parts.

2202. The sailor commonly makes the knot around the fingers of his left hand. He takes three turns around the fingers, the middle finger and the ring finger being slightly separated. He then adds three more turns at right angles to the first three turns and *through* the two fingers that were separated. The final three turns are wound outside the second three turns and inside the first three turns. The knot is worked taut around a large marble, rubber ball or whatever is handy. It should be pounded smooth with a mallet. The sailor's way of finishing off is to side splice the end of the rope to the standing part about a foot from the knot, and to put on a seizing close up to the knot. The splice is also whipped near the end. This does not differ from KNOT #2201.

2203. As the MONKEY'S FIST is based on a diagram of three interlocked circles it seemed probable that other knots could be tied on diagrams of one, two, and four circles. A five-circle diagram did not promise much as it has two five-sided compartments which seem too open to be practical.

A single circle was tried which produced SINGLE, DOUBLE, TRIPLE, and QUADRUPLE OVERHAND KNOTS in a napkin-ring form. Number 2204, of two circles, gives two interlocked rings. Number 2205 is the regular three-circle diagram, giving the MONKEY'S FIST that has been already described; and #2206 makes a very satisfactory and much larger knot on four interlocking circles.

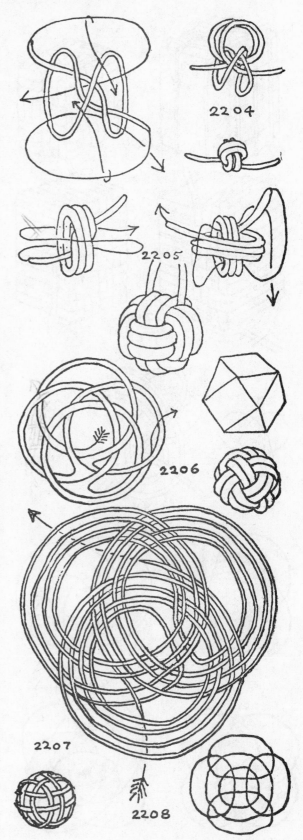

2204

2205

2206

2207

2208

2204. A MONKEY'S FIST on a *two-circle diagram* may be tied in several ways, of which the following seemed to be the most practical.

Tie a DOUBLE or TRIPLE OVERHAND KNOT, then tuck one end once as pictured and the other end either once or twice according to whether a double or triple knot is wished. The illustrations show a doubled one. Draw up the OVERHAND KNOT first and then the second cycle.

2205. This shows a fourth way to tie the regular MONKEY'S FIST of six parts that has already been discussed as ✳2200, ✳2201, and ✳2202. The method was suggested by the foregoing way of tying a two-circle knot. Begin by tying a TRIPLE OVERHAND KNOT. With the lower left end take three turns around the OVERHAND KNOT, as diagram 1. Then with the remaining upper end make three turns outside the last turns that were taken, and inside the initial TRIPLE OVERHAND KNOT. Draw the knot taut and side splice the end to the standing part. Tie around a ball if desired. The two ends of this knot are laterally opposite each other instead of diagonally opposite as in ✳2201, ✳2202, ✳2203.

2206. A *four-circle diagram* coincides with the edges of a cubocta-hedron. Each square is bounded by four triangles and each triangle by three squares. The single line of the diagram represents the knot doubled. It is quite a handful and it will be found easier to project it by pinning out on the cork board than to try to tie it directly in hand. The knot is handsome and regular and so large that even the two-ply specimen requires a core.

This form provides the normal limit for a regular MONKEY'S FIST diagram based on interlocking circles, as beyond this point com-partments of large size appear which make irregular knots.

2207. We will now go back to the original *three-cycle diagram* (✳2200) and will tie each *cycle* with two different sets of leads (inner and outer), six sets in all, and each of these six will be fol-lowed twice, making a Two-PLY KNOT. The first *cycle*, consisting of four clockwise *circles*, is pinned out flat, each *circle* inside the previous one. The rope is then diverted to the second *cycle*, and the cord is tucked counterclockwise over two and under two. Hav-ing finished laying out the first two of the second set of four *circles*, the sequence is altered and becomes under two and over two, for the remaining two *circles* before entering the third and last *cycle*. The end is now led counterclockwise and continues two more full *circles* in unbroken *over*-two-and-*under*-two sequence. It then alters to *under*-two-*over*-two sequence to finish the last two *circles*. This will require a core (a ball) even for a Two-PLY KNOT. A THREE-PLY or FOUR-PLY KNOT may be tied if a large enough core is pro-vided. The knot tied is four times the size of ✳2200.

2208. This knot gives an interesting example in projection. If ✳2207 is tied with single instead of parallel lines it will be exactly the same knot as this. It is very difficult at times to detect the differ-ences and similarities of two knots even when they are logically drawn.

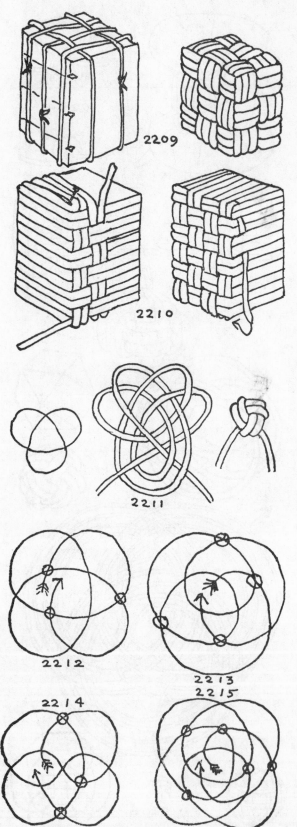

2209

2210

2211

2212

2213

2214

2215

2209. A *rectangular block* may be covered with any number of strands parallel with the edges, in regular over-one-and-under-one sequence, provided the strands are evenly spaced to accord with the proportions of the block. A MULTI-STRAND KNOT is more easily tied than a single-cord one, as the length of strand to be reeved is much shorter.

Take a block and measure its proportions. Notch the edges so that all spaces are even or very nearly so. Except at the corners the spaces should be half length. Lead parallel cords singly around the block lengthwise, sufficient to fill all notches, and square knot the two ends. Next tie a cord around the block in a sidewise direction, crossing the first-laid cords at each side at right angles. If there is an even number of notches in the *length* of the block the first and the last tuck on the side will have contrary over-and-under. But if the number of notches is odd the first and the last tuck will be the *same*. An adjacent parallel strand will be tucked with opposite lay until all strands of the set are in place. Then lay the strands of the third and final set so that the lay for the whole block is alternately over and under. Proceed to double, triple or quadruple the lay of the knot, and scatter the ends well. Pull them taut and cut them off close.

2210. Any block knot may be tied as a true MONKEY'S FIST—that is, with a single cord. This may be done either directly or else by paralleling the knot last described, which in such a case serves merely as a clue.

To tie the single-cord knot directly: Wind the cord around the block, end for end, neither too tightly nor too closely. When a side is covered turn a corner as in the third diagram and add the second circuit (fourth diagram), turn into the third circuit as in the fourth diagram and complete the knot. Use a packing needle with blunted point for a tool.

KNOT #2208 is actually a CUBE KNOT of the present series, 2 × 2 × 2 in proportion, and the original MONKEY'S FIST (#2201) may also be tied as a cube covering, 1 × 1 × 1.

2211. This is the "TWEENIE" (KNOT #525) of Chapter 3, doubled. It has some of the characteristics of the MONKEY'S FIST and, having three parts, it will fit in between the two-part #2204 and the six-part #2202.

2212, 2213. The smaller TURK'S-HEADS are often used for knob coverings and are followed or doubled, sometimes as many as six times.

2214. The CHINESE BUTTON diagram (#600) makes a good covering of nine parts.

2215. Larger TURK'S-HEADS than this have been used for spherical coverings. Five leads and four bights appears to be about the practical limit, as the proportions soon become ungainly and the end compartments overlarge.

The first spherical covering that I attempted was at the suggestion of Eugene E. du Pont, who thought that such a knot would be effective on the knob of an automobile gearshift lever.

Spherical covering may also be utilized over smaller knots on the ends of manropes, bell lanyards, etc. On a small boat they make handsome coverings for knobs on the ends of centerboard pendants, where they save marking and wear on the top of the centerboard box. Made of small material, they serve well as buttons on garments.

2216. This knot is normally an oblate spheroid, an excellent shape for the end of a centerboard pendant or a gearshift lever knob. The slight flattening at the poles will not be noticed if a spherical core is used.

Make a copy of the diagram twice the size of the original and place the paper on the center of the cork board. Take about thirty feet of fishline or other material and reeve half the length through the center hole. Lay the top section of cord along the line of the diagram, pinning it at frequent intervals. Whenever the cord crosses itself in regular numerical sequence *at a point that is marked by a circle,* tuck the working end under the bight that is to be crossed. At all other points the cord is overlaid and the circles disregarded.

Follow the lead around a second time, laying the second length parallel with the first. Then place the knot over the core that is to be covered and work it into loose spherical shape. Follow the lead a third or fourth time if desired, using the other end of the cord when it is needed. Gradually work the cord taut. Both ends are brought to the surface under the same part, pulled tight and cut off short. They will generally shrink from sight. The knot may then be shellacked and painted.

2217. This is perhaps the most practical knot of the series. It was originally described and illustrated for the *Sportsman Magazine* and I have since met several individuals who had tied knots from the original description. My cousin, Hope Knowles, at the age of eleven tied one without assistance by following the printed directions. A photograph of the knot is shown on the end of a bell rope among the frontispieces.

If to be used on the end of a centerboard pendant, bore a hole through the wooden knob and countersink an OVERHAND KNOT into the hole. Fill the gap in the hole with plastic wood, place the knot over the core and work it snug.

2218. This knot is quite symmetrical and spherical and is possibly the handsomest of the lot. Tie as already directed for #2216.

2219. A *prolate spheroid.* The bulk of any knot, as well as its shape, is of course dependent on the number and disposition of its parts. This particular knot has sixteen parts around the central girth and twenty-four parts around its lengthwise circuit, which account for its elongated shape. But the shape of these knots, as with the TURK'S-HEADS, is capable of much distortion without detracting from their appearance, and so they may easily be tied in spherical form if desired.

KNOTS #2216 and #2217 may be doubled, with one end only, but #2218 and #2219 require both ends for doubling as the two ends have separate circuits or cycles.

If the neck of a knob is small, three or four bights around the rim will be a sufficient number, but if the neck is large in proportion to the knot, as in a cane-head covering, six or even eight bights may on occasion be required.

If a knob or other covering is to be tied regularly with one cord, it is limited to a one-cycle diagram. If it has two or more cycles it must either be tied as a MULTI-STRAND KNOT or else it can be tied irregularly with one cord, no matter how many cycles it has, providing one cycle is completed at a time and the cord thereafter is deflected to another cycle as in the MONKEY'S FIST, per se.

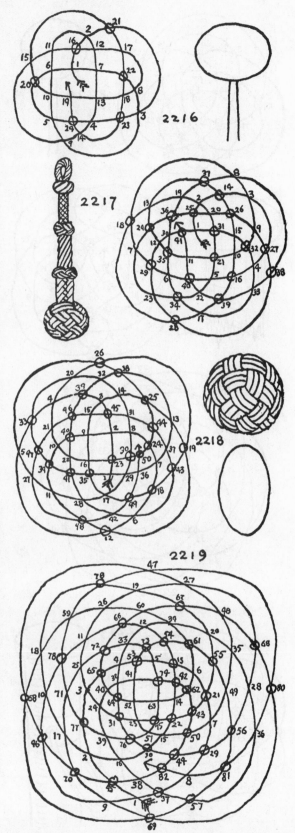

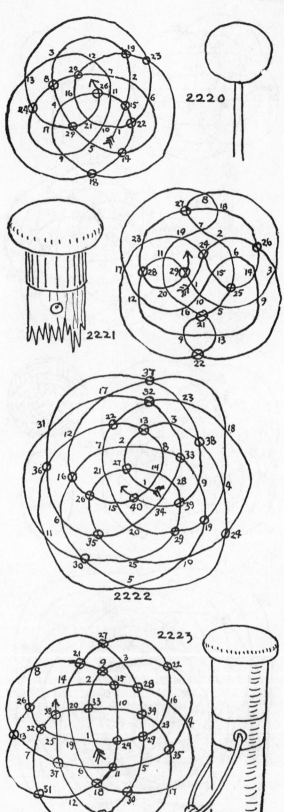

2220

2221

2222

2223

It may be well to repeat that the success of any elaborate knot depends largely on gradual and unhurried working. Do not at any time pull one part enough to distort the knot materially. Work from end to end, and finally pull the ends very tight and cut them off flush with the surface. They should shrink enough so that they will not be in evidence.

2220. The four knots last shown were based on two square figures at opposite sides of the sphere.

When tied and drawn together, the rims of these knots close and the bottom half of each knot will be found to be exactly a duplicate of the top half but slued to a different angle.

The present knot is similarly based on two triangular figures, one at the top and one at the bottom. Except for ⚹2216, this is the smallest spherical covering to be given.

2221. The knot alongside is the result of an attempt to follow the general pattern of a tennis-ball cover. It is somewhat flattened at the poles and is perhaps the least satisfactory of the series, as it tends to bulk considerably at the four places on the diagram where two triangular compartments have a common side.

2222. This knot was made to cover a cane head for Robert Cushman Murphy. The stick was of considerable diameter so that a four-part rim was insufficient to close evenly at the edges. So six rim parts were tried and found to serve well.

2223. A heavy stick, with a shallow knob having very little overhang, will require even more rim parts.

2224. By adapting the method of the MULTI-STRAND BUTTON KNOT, knobs of a variety of shapes may be covered.

To tie: Select a crown from the diagrams given below (⚹2224–31) of approximately the shape of the cross section wanted. Middle the strands and stop them twice to the end of your stick as illustrated in left top diagram. Arrange them evenly around the stick in a right diagonal of forty-five degrees, and crown the upper ends in the form of the diagram selected.

Take one of the lower ends, cross it over the next strand to the left, and under the second strand. Take each one of the remaining lower strands in turn, and tuck it to the left over one and under one. Take one of the upper strands and tuck it downward to the right, over one and under one. Take each strand in turn and do likewise. Tuck as many tiers as wished. When the length is sufficient take any end and stick it in parallel with the opposite end. If the over-and-under arrangement is not correct, stick it in beside the *next strand* to the left or right, whichever one of the two appears most convenient. Tuck all strands in regular order until the whole knot has been doubled or tripled. Scatter the ends so that the final tucks are not all in the same neighborhood. Work the knot taut and cut the ends off short.

An ovate object—an egg, for instance—can be covered in this way, working both ways from the center and crowning both ends in exactly the same way.

2225–31. Seven additional diagrams are given here from which to choose; others may be found in Chapter 10.

2232. A disk-shaped covering makes a particularly smart knot. The underlying block in thickness should be about one third the width. I have used this one on a centerboard pendant. Bore a hole halfway through the wooden core, large enough to take a STOPPER KNOT; then bore a smaller hole the rest of the way to take the rope. Tie the knot as already directed on page 357.

2233. To cover a wooden *cylindrical toggle* with a THREE-BIGHT TURK'S-HEAD. This may be done with any number of leads. If the number of leads is divisible by four the toggle rope will enter the cylinder at *a center compartment in line with a rim crossing*. If the number of leads is divisible by two but not by four (six, ten, etc.) the toggle rope must enter the cylinder at a center compartment that is *in line with the center of a rim bight*. To tie, see the chapter on TURK'S-HEADS. The illustration gives an EIGHT-LEAD, THREE-BIGHT TURK'S-HEAD.

2234. A *toggle* with a square cross section is a little more complicated. If the rope is to enter at the center of a side, either a four-cycle diagram is needed (a MULTI-STRAND KNOT) or the bights at either end must run parallel with the rim as shown here. The illustration gives a TEN-LEAD, FOUR-BIGHT TURK'S-HEAD.

2235. A cylinder may be covered with any width FOUR-BIGHT TURK'S-HEAD if the toggle rope is to enter the core at the end. (See TURK'S-HEAD chapter.)

2236. If the rope is to enter at the end of a stick that has a square cross section, a FOUR-BIGHT KNOT may be tied with a single cord, so that the bights cross the corners of the ends diagonally. To do this a TURK'S-HEAD must be tied in which the number of leads is a *multiple of two, but not of four*. The cord must be deflected once as pictured, as a TURK'S-HEAD in which the number of leads and the number of bights have a common divisor may not be tied regularly with one cord. The stick pictured is covered with a SIX-LEAD, FOUR-BIGHT TURK'S-HEAD.

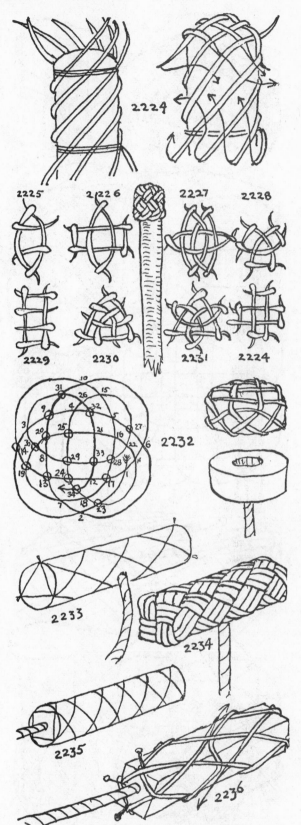

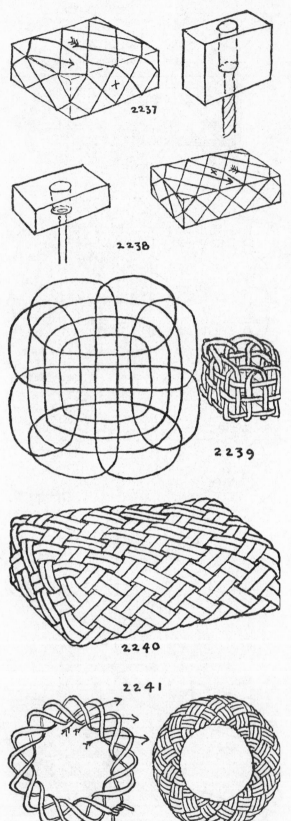

2237

2238

2239

2240

2241

The *block or brick coverings* of page 356 have a lead that is parallel with the sides of the block. The blocks of this page have a diagonal lead and the lead of each knot has two cycles, so they must be tied with two cords, or else it will be necessary at some place on the surface to deflect the line from one cycle to the other in the same way that the strand of a MONKEY'S FIST (#2201) is deflected.

Evenly spaced notches are placed along the edges of the block used as a core, and at each of these notches two cords cross each other at right angles, making a 45-degree angle with the edge. The knot about to be shown has 1 × 2 × 3 notches.

2237. A block of 1 × 2 × 3 notches. It has a central compartment on the 1 × 3 side so that it will make a symmetrical toggle if one is wanted, or it will make a book or doorstop, or a paperweight. The cord is deflected from one cycle to the other near the center of the largest side. Around this compartment the cord should be pinned with four tacks. Take a spool of black linen thread and, ignoring the over-and-under arrangement, lead the thread once around the complete diagram. To tie the knot: Follow above the black clue and tuck a piece of banding alternately under and over at the crossings except at the diagonal between the head and feather of the arrow, where both ends of the diagonal are under.

2238. A block with 1 × 2 × 4 notches. This is tied in the same way as the foregoing. If it is required to be made as a toggle, the only central compartment will be found on the 2 × 4 side.

2239. To *cover five sides only of a rectangular block:* This makes a basket of stiff fishline. Tie as a MULTI-STRAND KNOT with five cords and take the crossings alternately over and under. Turn the edges as illustrated along the open side and make a Two-, THREE-, FOUR- or FIVE-PLY KNOT. Shellac before removing from the block.

2240. A 2 × 3 × 5 block is made as already described for #2237 and #2238. If desired, 1 × 3 × 4, 2 × 3 × 6 and 3 × 4 × 7 may be tied in the same way, but beyond this I have not carried the knot, and so far I have discovered none of the sort that can be tied without adaptation in a single cycle diagram.

2241. A *covering for a ring or grommet.* Make a loose *three-strand grommet* by winding a cord in a widely and evenly spaced helix three times around the circuit of the ring that is to be covered. Tie the two ends together, leaving them long enough for doubling. Count the turns and take another cord of another color or size material and wind it the *same number of turns* in the opposite direction three times around the ring. This is to act merely as a clue. Take a longer cord of the first material and with it follow parallel with the *second* cord but tucking alternately over and under at the crossings. Next remove the clue and double both strands throughout or triple and quadruple them if necessary to cover the ring. Use a wire needle (#99L) to tie the knot and work it taut with a pricker (#99A).

CHAPTER 30: FLAT OR TWO-DIMENSIONAL KNOTS

. . . are those which by a peculiar Name to a Ship are called Mats.
Boteler's Dialogues, circa 1634

Mats are used aboard ship for chafing gear. They are nailed to the deck at gangways, thresholds and companionways, and, where needed, to rails and spars. They are employed to take up the thump of jib sheet and traveler blocks and they appear alow and aloft wherever wear or galling is to be expected.

Platted, woven and thrummed mats are also used in chafing gear but these will be dealt with in Chapter 41. In this chapter only mats that are tied as knots will be shown.

Many of the FLAT TWO-CORD LANYARD KNOTS of Chapter 8 will serve well as mats, and the PRIEST CORD KNOTS, which are given in this chapter, are also a variety of LANYARD KNOT, tied in double parallel cords.

Mats make most satisfactory hot pads for the dining table, stove lifters for the kitchen, and cushion covers for hard-seated chairs.

Frogs are two-dimensional knots that are appliquéd on overcoats, pajamas and uniforms. These are commonly tied in gold braid or in colors and attain their full splendor on the uniforms of the band-master, the ringmaster and the college drum majorette.

A flexible wire needle (#99L) is an excellent tool for matmaking, but a packing needle with a dulled point is better if the material is small, and with anything so large as *priest cords*, fingers will be found the best tools of all.

The first mats to be discussed are a variety termed "BASKET WEAVE KNOTS" in which the weave throughout is alternately over one and

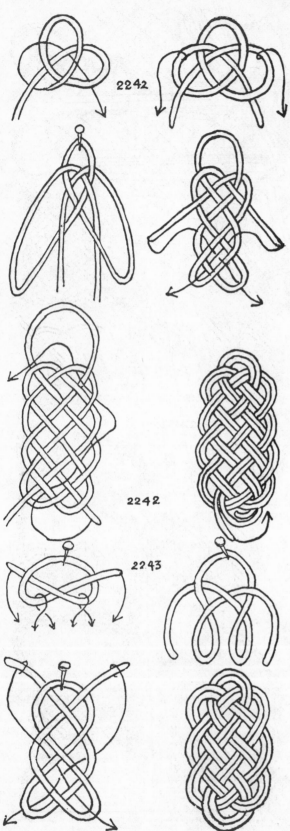

under one or, if doubled, over two and under two. A small knot is first tied and thereafter, either by adding further diagonals or else by platting the loops and ends of one side, the size of the knot is increased. In the former the proportions are unchanged, and in the latter the knot is lengthened. When the knot that was decided on has been made, its size may be further increased by doubling or tripling the established lay or ply in the manner that was described for the TURK'S-HEADS of Chapter 18.

2242. The PROLONG KNOT was so named because its length may be added to—that is, it may be prolonged. Boyd (*A Manual for Naval Cadets*, 1857) first called attention to it by name. But Luce, a few years later, pictured only the simplest form of the completed knot, which is the first diagram given on this page, and failed to mention either the method of tying and enlarging or the purpose of the knot. Furthermore he misspelled the name, calling it PROLONGE, which is the name of a rope used by the field artillery. C. H. Smith called it "PROLONGED KNOT" in 1876, which appears to be a common name for it.

In the braid trade the form of the upper right diagram has been termed the "PRETZEL" KNOT, and under the name "AUSTRIAN" KNOT the same form has been employed as an officer's insignia in the United States Marine Corps.

The PROLONG is a common mat for stair treads on shipboard. It is loosely formed, as in the first diagram, in regular over-one-and-under-one sequence, then the ends and two lower bights are loosened and extended, after which the six strands are platted as FRENCH SINNET, each of the loops or bights serving as two strands. Each time the two *ends* have been led to the corners a knot is completed. The first completed knot has four side bights and the second time the ends are crossed the knot is increased to seven bights on each side. The smallest number of side bights in a completed PROLONG is four and each enlargement adds three more.

To double or triple the ply of this knot: Lead either leg back into the knot parallel with and in contrary direction to the lead of the other leg. The method is shown in the fifth and sixth diagrams on the page. The ends should not be left permanently near the rim but should be withdrawn into the central structure, sewed down or seized on the underside.

2243. The OCEAN PLAT is a companion knot that is commenced with an OVERHAND KNOT. The central bight should be hung over a convenient nail or hook and the two ends and two bights extended as in the previous knot. When this has been done the knot is platted as before. The smallest number of side bights in this knot is three and each enlargement adds three more bights. With these two starts (#2242 and #2243) every possible number of bights for knots of this width is tied. Five, eight, eleven bights, etc., are impossible knots to tie with a single strand, two or more cords being required for them.

In construction the present knot, which is the smallest knot of all, is identical with the CHINESE or FLAT KNIFE LANYARD KNOT, although the ends are differently disposed. The name OCEAN PLAT was found on the specimen in the South Kensington Museum collection.

2244. The accompanying diagram represents the first enlargement of the PROLONG KNOT (#2242). This, when tripled, makes an excellent tread for a companionway step.

2245. The OCEAN PLAT first enlarges to a six-bight length, and then to a nine-bight length.

2246. To enlarge the CARRICK BEND, which is the smallest of the series, by tucking two diagonally opposite ends: Tuck one end back into the knot parallel with its own standing part and with the same over-and-under. Tuck it completely across the knot, alternately over and under, as shown by the arrow.

Take the opposing end and cross the end that was just tucked and which now lies alongside, and, tucking alternately over and under, cross the knot diagonally between the opposing two parallel leads with opposite over-and-under.

This enlarges the CARRICK BEND to the size of the CHINESE KNOT. The two knots that have been given are alike in form except that this is tied with two cords; the other was tied with the two ends of one cord. The CARRICK BEND design may be increased to any size but may not be tied in a two-cord lanyard by this method. To make a rug or mat of this knot tuck the ends back underneath the rim and sew them flat, or else bring them out at the corners and add four tassels.

2247. To enlarge a CARRICK BEND by reeving alternate loops instead of ends. A knot is completed any time a single end is rove instead of a loop.

2248. A WIDE BASKET WEAVE KNOT. To tie and enlarge a horizontal CARRICK BEND in which the two corners of a longer side are already united, so that the knot is tied in a single cord suitable for a lanyard (in this the number of top bights is always even and exceeds the number of side bights by one): Start by tying the second diagram of the PROLONG (#2242), arranging a long upper loop, and tuck the lower right end to the upper left, as in A, parallel with its own part. A knot is completed each time the number of top bights is even. This differs from #2247 in which the number of bights at the top may be either odd or even. Having reached the position of the upper left diagram B, make a right round turn in the left upper end of the long loop, pass it over the single upper left end and tuck it downward in a right diagonal between the two parallel parts. Repeat this, alternating with loops from the two upper left parts, until the knot is the size wanted, then tuck the end cord singly down to the lower right corner.

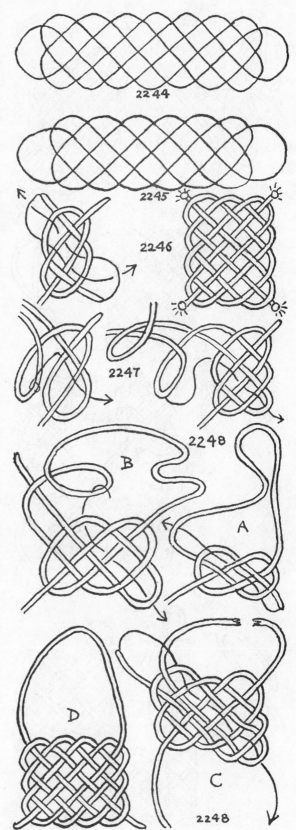

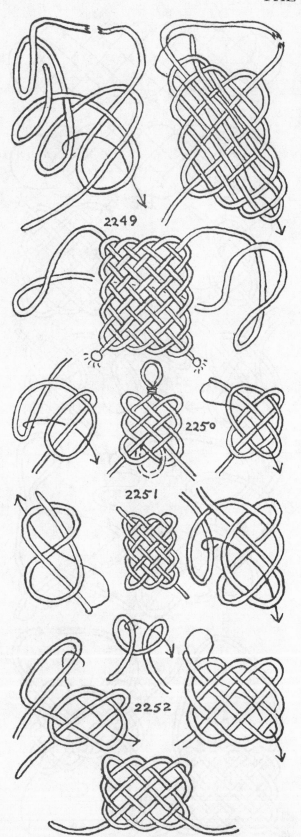

2249

2250

2251

2252

2249. A Long Basket Weave Knot. Arrange the knot as pictured in the upper left diagram, with a long neckband and a short lower left end. The two corners of a short side are united with a loop at the top, and by the method a series of knots can be tied into a lanyard. Loops from the two different parts at the upper left corner are tucked alternately until the knot is completed by tucking the single end. A bight is added to both sides each time a loop is brought to the lower corner. The number of side bights is one greater than the number of top bights and the number of top bights is always even.

Knot ⚹2246 on the previous page ties every possible knot of the Basket Weave variety in which there is a strand at each of the four corners and in which there is one more bight at the side than at the end.

Methods ⚹2248 and ⚹2249 tie all possible Basket Weave Knots of a single cord in which the length equals the width plus, or minus, one. The loop in these lanyards is always on the side with the even number of bights.

2250. A knot of one cord in which both ends depart at the bottom corners and the number of the top and side parts is equal. The knot is increased by one bight on each side, per operation. Successive bights are tucked from the upper left corner only, while the lower left end and the right upper end are held inert. Start as in the left diagram and tuck successive bights or turns. When the size wanted is reached, tuck the end instead of a bight as shown in the right diagram. The eye, shown at the top of this knot, is seized in after the knot is finished, if required.

2251. A knot of the Basket Weave variety in which a single cord enters at one corner and departs at the diagonally opposite corner. Tie a Figure-Eight Knot, then tuck the lower end diagonally upward, above and parallel to its own part. In regular over-and-under sequence tuck a turn from the second end under the first end and downward diagonally to the right across the knot in regular and contrary over-and-under sequence between the two parallel parts leading from the other end. Repeat this with loops from alternating ends as many times as may be desired. When the size wanted is reached, tuck either end across the knot singly, which completes the knot.

2252. To tie a knot in which the cord enters and leaves the knot at the two lower corners and in which the number of top bights is one greater than the number of side bights: First tie a Clove Hitch and stick the left bight through the right bight and arrange as pictured in the left diagram, with both ends at the left. Form a loop with the upper left end and tuck it diagonally down to the lower right as pictured. Tuck another loop from the same upper left end cord in the same way. When the size wanted is reached, tuck the end singly as pictured in the right diagram, which completes the knot.

2253. A knot of the BASKET WEAVE variety in which the proportions are so wide that two diagonals are required to enlarge the knot. Tie the basic knot, illustrated with doubled lines, by pinning it out on the cork board. Lead each end parallel with its own standing part for one diagonal (to the top), then cross the two ends and tuck each end down to the corner between two parallel parts and with the opposite over-and-under. This adds two parts to the width of the knot but only one part to the length. Repeat until the size wanted is attained.

2254. A *platted mat of four lengthwise leads* may be started with an OVERHAND KNOT. As in ⁂2242 a knot is completed every time the two ends are brought down to the corners. Two side parts are added at each operation.

2255. In order to make all possible knots of this width, a second start is necessary. Make a single round turn and plat as before. Two side parts are added at each operation. With these two starts any length is possible.

2256. To make a *six-strand platted mat:* First tie a knot as in the left diagram, which may be started as ⁂2252. Extend the two lower bights and proceed to plat all six as in FRENCH SINNET. A section of this knot is similar to ⁂2242 and ⁂2243, but the rectangular top is peculiar to the present series. Each time the two ends are brought down to the corners three bights have been added to each side and a knot is completed. Like KNOTS ⁂2242 and ⁂2243, a second start is necessary to make all possible sizes of this knot.

2257. The second start is similar to KNOT ⁂2255 but requires two loops instead of one. Arrange the cord in two round turns over three nails or hooks and have the ends slightly longer than the loops. Counting each loop as two strands, these altogether make a total of six strands. All six are platted to form the knot. But it may be found easier to first cross the two loops in the manner illustrated in the lower part of the right diagram of ⁂2256, and then to tuck the two ends as illustrated by the arrows. This has already been illustrated for KNOTS ⁂2242 and ⁂2243. The smallest knot by this method has three side parts, which may be raised to six, nine, etc. The previous knot starts with a completed knot of two side bights, which raises to five, eight, etc. The two starts will make all possible knots of this width and sort.

2258. While considering the possibilities of these knots it should be noted that two strands only, platted alternately over one and under one, is two-strand rope and is the basic form for all the plats utilized on this page. This may also be considered the basic form for the knot series, since knots similar to ⁂2254 and ⁂2255 can be tied by adding upward diagonals with the two ends as suggested by the arrows that are shown in the center diagram.

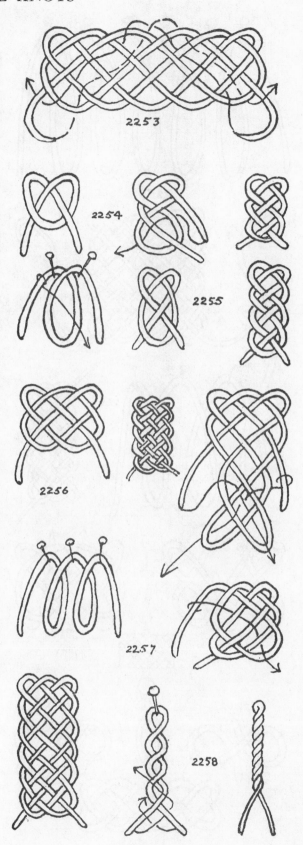

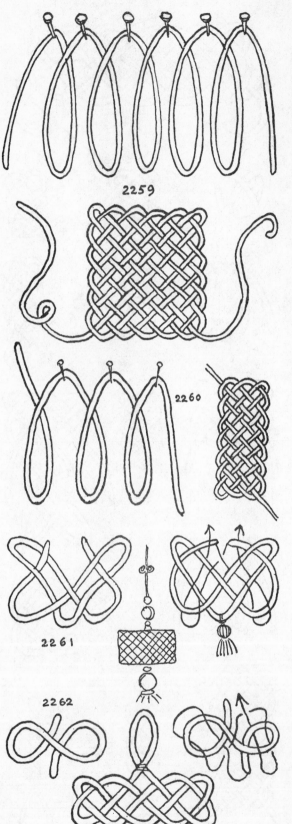

2259

2260

2261

2262

2259. The knot given here is of the same sort as KNOTS ⚹2255 and ⚹2257, which are the simplest forms of the kind. It may be started with *any* number of very long round turns, which are laid out with tacks on a board, and are platted as FRENCH SINNET (page 490). Each loop is worked as two strands, the upper half being led to the left and the lower half to the right exactly as single strands are worked in the sinnet. The loops and ends should be much longer than needed for the finished knot and the knot is first tied very loosely and then worked taut. It will be better to start with a knot of three or four loops and make one or two practice knots before attempting a large one. A knot is completed each time the ends reach opposite sides.

To tie the TWELVE-STRAND KNOT illustrated: The overlaid strands which lead to the left are moved in turn. Lead the second (left) strand in a left diagonal under the left end strand. Lead the third (left) strand to the left (parallel with the first one that was led), under one strand, over the next and under the outside one. Lead the fourth (left) strand to the left parallel with the others and alternately under, over, under, over, under to the left side. Lead the fifth (left) strand likewise. Disentangle the loops after each strand is crossed. Take the *right end strand* and lead it to the left, under, over, etc., to the left edge, where *it is laid out.*

Bring the next right upper strand, which is part of a loop, to the left in correct (alternate) over-and-under sequence to the bottom. *Lay this out.* Lay the next upper right strand to the left in similar way and lay out. Do the same with the next, and so on until only a single end strand remains at the right corner. This is tucked out as pictured for ⚹2257, after which the knot must be faired.

If the right end had not been laid out when it reached the lower left corner, and if, instead, each strand had been platted one more diagonal in the manner already described, the knot would be twice the length.

2260. To prolong a knot of a single strand in which only one end of the strand is worked. This may be done with any desired number of loops, and is worked the same as the last knot except that, as the upper left end is not active, the number of the strands is always odd instead of even. The knot is completed when the working end reaches either the left or the right side. Compare with ⚹2251, center diagram, which has a different number of bights, and which, if desired, may be platted farther by the present method.

2261. A RECTANGULAR KNOT without ends at the corners. It may be enlarged as shown, to any size. After the knot is completely formed, one end is withdrawn two or three tucks, while the other end is tucked in to take its place. The ends are cut and sewed one over the other. To tie: Make an OVERHAND KNOT and tuck the two ends upward to coincide with the left diagram. Cross the ends at the top center and tuck them to the lower corner and then back to the top with both ends and with alternate over-and-under. Repeat until the knot is the proper size.

2262. A narrower RECTANGULAR KNOT is formed as shown by these diagrams, beginning with an S turn. This is enlarged by tucking one end as shown.

FLAT OR TWO-DIMENSIONAL KNOTS

Any of the BASKET WEAVE KNOTS, when tied in flat material, may be turned at the edges instead of being slued, as is usual in round material. This makes a knot with an even or flush edge.

2263. A knot with the strands introduced at the side, suitable for frogs carrying loops and buttons. To tie: Draw a diagram two bights wide and seven bights long, place it on the cork board and stick a pin at each rim crossing. Start at the center bottom and lead the cord around the pins. After tucking under at the first crossing, repeat aloud, "Over, under, over," etc., and take the crossings accordingly. When the knot has been removed from the board and faired, it may be enlarged by following the lead indicated by the arrows in the upper diagram. The knot is increased by four side bights and one end bight at each enlargement.

2264. This is another way to increase the size of KNOT ⌗2262. The operation may be repeated as many times as desired. But after a certain size has been reached, it will be found that often a knot of larger material and fewer crossings will prove handsomer than an elaborate knot.

The second diagram shows a TWO-STRAND BUTTON KNOT (⌗601) added to the knot just described. It should be paired with a similar frog bearing a loop instead of the button. When making the loop withdraw one end of the cord into the knot several tucks. Form the loop with the other end and tuck it back into the knot to fill the space that was vacated. Sew the joint on the underside.

2265. The method of raising these knots appears to have endless ramifications and I have made no effort to exhaust the possibilities. This shows the same basic knot as the last, raised to a knot of 3 × 8 bights; the last one was 3 × 7. If it is to be used as a frog the strands, to be symmetrical, must lead from the center end.

2266. A RECTANGULAR KNOT with the cords entering at the center of the end. First lay out a 3 × 4 KNOT on the board, then raise it to a 5 × 7 (or larger) KNOT by following the leads indicated by the arrows. The sides increase by three and the ends by two at each operation.

2267. The CHINESE FROG KNOT is found on Chinese pajamas. Each knot is tied entirely with one end of a cord or tape. The two knots are tied with different pieces of tape and the stem of each is concealed under the corner loop of the other.

A long left loop is pinned out on the board. A similar loop is taken close to the first one and is slipped downward under the standing part and over the lower bight of the first one. A third one follows, and is tucked under the first part encountered, over the next, then under and over. A fourth loop follows and is tucked under, over, under, over, under, over. This is continued until the knot is the right size, then the single working end is tucked, instead of the turn or loop, and is sewed flat at the bottom. When the knot is worked taut it should be perfectly rectangular and, the larger it is, the nearer square will the rectangle be.

When the two knots are arranged on the garment the two standing ends are laid parallel and each is sewed down under the rim of the opposite knot.

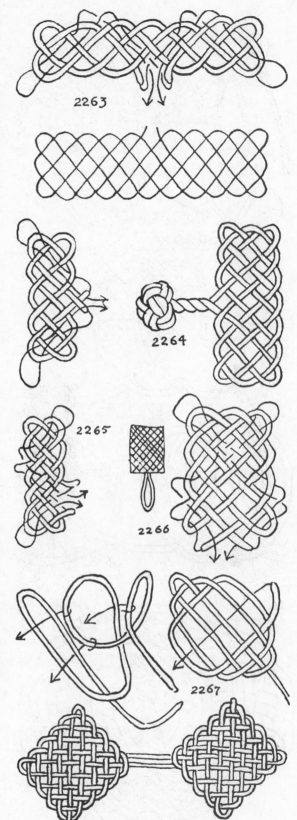

2268. A nearly *square mat* is tied with a single cord and with both ends at one corner. Tie the knot shown in the left diagram. Take the upper end of the cord and cross it over the lower end and tuck a bight parallel with the other end, over, under to the upper left corner. Reverse the direction and continue to tuck it over and under downward in a right diagonal between the two leads that are parallel, which brings it to the right lower corner. Repeat this operation with alternate ends until the knot is the required size. A netting needle may be used to advantage in tying this and other knots of the sort in which an end and not a bight is tucked. When completed, if it is to be a mat or doily, lay one of the ends out for several tucks and inlay the opposite end so that the joint is hidden on the underside, well away from the corner.

2269. A *hitched mat* is made with one or any number of hitches for a base.

Middle a cord, make a SINGLE HITCH and then lead the left end in a right upward diagonal across the hitch. Continue the lead along the line indicated by the arrows until the two ends have met. Fair the knot and then double and triple it, using both ends.

2270. A knot from two hitches. Middle a line as before and, after the two hitches are arranged as shown, take the left end, lead it in a right upward diagonal, over and under, to the center, then under and over to the side. Continue to tuck as indicated by the arrows, then double and triple the knot, using the surplus material of both ends.

2271. A larger knot of the same sort is made with any number of hitches. After the first hitch each succeeding hitch is tucked to the left, over the first bight (in every case) and under the second, and so alternately to the center. The desired number of hitches being in place (in the knot pictured there are five), the left end is led in a right upward diagonal over the first hitch, under the second and so alternately until the center part of the knot is reached. When the center has been reached, note whether the last tuck was over or under. Whichever it was, the next tuck away from the center toward the right side will be the same, and the rest are taken alternately.

The centers of all knots that start with an odd number of hitches will be like ⅜2269; the centers of all knots that start with an even number of hitches will be like ⅜2270. Three diagonals cross the hitches of each knot and in every case the first (outside) crossing of each diagonal is *over*.

These mats may be used for companionway treads, hot pads for dining tables, and chair-seat covers. There is no limit theoretically to their size, although practice is required to tie almost any large knot successfully, and difficulties multiply with each slight increase in size.

2272. The remainder of these *single-strand mats* do not "enlarge." They are tied directly, after which they may be doubled or tripled in the usual way. A rectangular mat with well-rounded corners may be tied over a diagram by the method described at some length at the bottom of page 102. These make particularly handsome stair treads. First make an enlarged copy of the diagram, which is very easily done by utilizing the lines or the alternate lines on a piece of cross-section paper. Pin the cord along the line in the direction indicated by the arrow. Wherever a cord lies across the path, at a point that is *marked with a circle*, tuck the working end under the cord at that point. Disregard the circles if no other part is already there. This knot has three bights at the ends and five at the sides. Its finished aspect is shown in the second row below. A THREE-LEAD BY SIX-BIGHT and a THREE-LEAD BY TEN-BIGHT KNOT may also be tied and undoubtedly many others that have not been checked.

While tying, repeat to yourself, "Over, under," etc., in alternation, and take the crossings accordingly.

2273. The FIVE-BIGHT BY SEVEN-BIGHT KNOT, illustrated here, may be tied by the method described for the previous knot, and a FIVE-LEAD BY TEN-BIGHT and a SEVEN BY NINE KNOT may be tied by the same method.

2274. In diagram form this knot resembles the PROLONG (#2242) "widened out," but it does not appear to be suited to any enlargement method.

The present knot has three side bights and makes a symmetrical elliptical mat. It may be tied on the cork board over a diagram by pinning the cord at frequent intervals and tucking the working end underneath another part at every encircled point that is passed in regular numerical sequence.

2275. The finished aspect of a similar knot with seven side bights is shown here. To tie: Outline the knot on cross-section paper and pin a cord along the line, repeating as you do so, "Over, under," etc., and tucking the end accordingly. This knot may be tied with 2, 3, 7, 8, 12, 13, 17, 18, etc., side bights, 7 bights being illustrated on this page.

2276. A square mat of the same nature as #2272 and #2273 in any size is tied as a MULTI-STRAND KNOT. It is to be formed over a diagram and requires a separate cord for each cycle within the knot, if tied regularly, or, if the reader wishes, he may tie the knot after the manner of the MONKEY'S FIST (Chapter 29), deflecting the cord from one cycle to another after it has been doubled or tripled.

A most practical way to tie this particular knot by such a method would seem to be with two cords. Take one of the two central horizontal cycles; begin at the middle and follow it three times around, then lead the cord into the adjacent central horizontal cycle after the manner of the MONKEY'S FIST KNOTS, and follow that three times around.

Take another and longer cord. Start at the center of the extreme left vertical line, follow around the rectangle three times to the right, then deflect the line to the second vertical, follow three times and move to the next. Continue with the same method until the knot is completed.

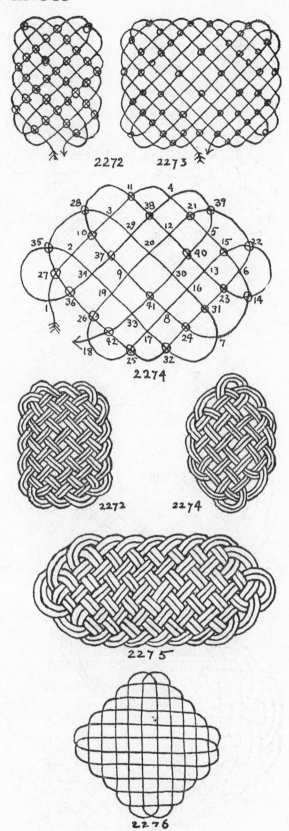

2272   2273

2274

2272   2274

2275

2276

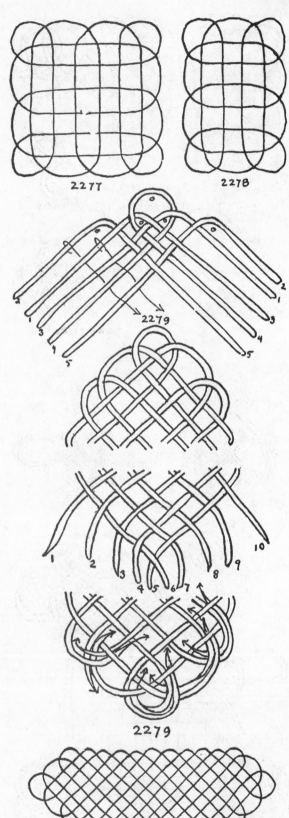

2277

2278

2279

2279

2277, 2278. Multi-strand mats of rectangular form in which the corners of the diagram are borrowed from the ends of diagrams #2274 and #2275. The well-rounded corners of these and of diagrams #2272 and #2273 lend themselves particularly well to doubling and tripling. Corners similar to #2268, on the other hand, are more successful when the knots are left single.

A mat of the sort given here may be made in any size or proportion and tied either multi-strand, or two-strand by the MONKEY'S FIST method which was described for KNOT #2276 on the preceding page. Make a large cross-section paper diagram of the knot wanted and lay it out on the cork board.

2279. A platted MULTI-STRAND KNOT of any length that is based on SINGLE-STRAND KNOTS #2274 and #2275.

Take five long cords and middle them, making ten strands of equal length. Drive five pins at the top of the board and arrange the strands as pictured in the upper diagram. Make certain that the weave is in regular over-and-under sequence throughout.

Take the second strand at the left top (numbered 1) and tuck it to the right and center, under, over, under (passing *three* strands).

Take the opposite cord on the right side, also numbered 1, and tuck it to the left and center over, under, over, under (passing *four* strands).

Take the left top strand 2 and bring it to the right and center over, under, over, under.

Take the right top strand 2 and tuck it to the left and center under, over, under, over.

Continue to work the two outer top strands alternately as FRENCH SINNET, according to these last two directions, until sufficient length is made for the knot wanted.

Do not draw the ends too tightly together. They should be left longer than pictured. long enough to allow doubling or tripling the knot.

When the length is satisfactory, see that the strands are arranged as in the third diagram, which represents the way they should appear each time a right upper strand has been tucked to the left and center.

All ends are now led back into the knot, each one to the *right* of an opposing end, and parallel with it, in the contrary direction.

To do this:

Transpose ends 1 and 3 (tucking each end to the *right* of the other) and passing *over* strand 2.

Transpose ends 8 and 10, tucking under strand 9.

Transpose ends 4 and 7, passing under 5 and over 6.

Transpose ends 2 and 5.

Transpose ends 6 and 9.

After doubling or tripling the knot, and working it taut, dissipate the ends away from the edges and sew them down on the underside. Most of the foregoing knots of this chapter may be doubled or tripled if desired.

FLAT OR TWO-DIMENSIONAL KNOTS

The next knots to be considered are often tied as frogs. They are flat knots that are appliquéd to cloaks, dressing gowns, dresses, men's bathrobes and pajamas, band and yacht uniforms. Formerly they were worn on fur overcoats, fur-lined evening overcoats and servants' livery. In the Army such knots are nowadays confined to dress uniforms.

In most MAT KNOTS the crossings are taken alternately over and under but this is not strictly adhered to in military frogs where the gold braid is often so dazzling as to obscure the lead.

2280. The OVERHAND KNOT is the simplest form of all. If the ends are brought together ⚹2285 results, which is the form of a Two-Lead, Three-Bight Turk's-Head.

2281. A TREFOIL KNOT which does not hold form when removed from the sleeve.

2282. The BAKER'S and the COWBOY'S PRETZEL KNOT; the cowboy employs it as a "trick" LARIAT KNOT, which spills into the FIGURE-EIGHT KNOT (⚹2284).

2283. The PRETZEL KNOT of the braid trade, which is also the start of PROLONG KNOT ⚹2242. If the ends are closed together KNOT ⚹2287 results, which is a THREE-LEAD, FOUR-BIGHT TURK'S-HEAD.

2284. The common FIGURE-EIGHT KNOT is often used as a "repeat" motif in conventional design.

2285. A TREFOIL KNOT that is also a TWO-LEAD, THREE-BIGHT TURK'S-HEAD KNOT.

2286. A TREFOIL KNOT. A FOUR-LEAD, THREE-BIGHT TURK'S-HEAD KNOT.

2287. A THREE-LEAD, FOUR-BIGHT TURK'S-HEAD KNOT, in disk form.

2288. A THREE-LEAD, FIVE-BIGHT TURK'S-HEAD KNOT with bights extended to make a flowerlike form.

2289. A THREE-LEAD, EIGHT-BIGHT TURK'S-HEAD KNOT. A comparison of the last three knots will indicate the way in which the character of a knot may be modified by rearranging its curves. Four of the bights of this knot are retracted and the diagram form is exactly the same as the TRUE-LOVER'S KNOT (⚹2419), although the over-and-under sequence differs.

2290. The TOM FOOL'S KNOT. This is also shown in Chapters 14 and 33.

2291. The TOM FOOL'S KNOT with the loops rearranged.

2292. The HANDCUFF KNOT cannot be arranged to coincide with the diagram of ⚹2290 but easily conforms to ⚹2291.

2293. Two THREE-LEAD, SEVEN-BIGHT TURK'S-HEADS, arranged as practical frogs. One part bears a loop which serves as a buttonhole, the other part has a BUTTON KNOT from Chapter 5. The ends of the cord are hidden. They are brought together and sewed on the underside of the knot.

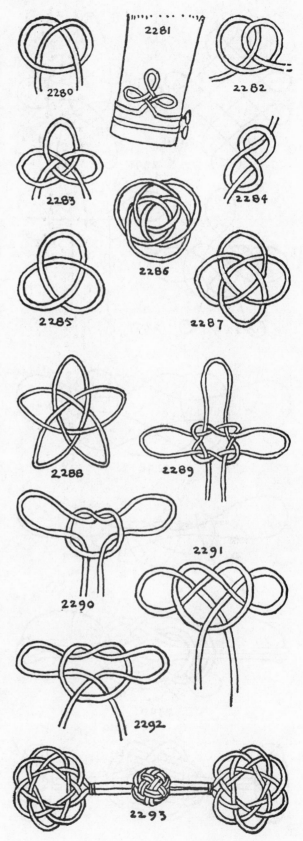

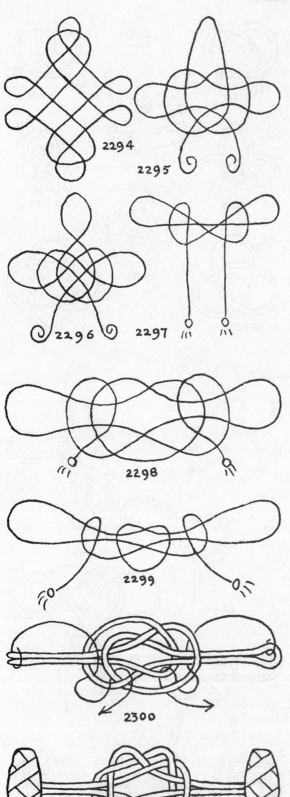

2294. An arbitrary knot form which may be lengthened by repeating the central motif.

2295. The MASTHEAD KNOT (#1167).

2296. The MASTHEAD KNOT with a single twist added to each of the three loops. It will be noted that these rearranged sailor's knots, although they are symmetrical, do not rigidly conform to a regular over-and-under sequence, unless they are retied with that in view.

2297. A SHEEPSHANK KNOT is formed from three hitches (#1162).

2298. A SHEEPSHANK formed from four hitches. The method is given as KNOT #1165.

2299. This shows a somewhat similar knot of four hitches differently arranged. It is described as KNOT #1164.

2300. The JUG SLING (#1143), arranged as a frog or FROG KNOT. Sometimes the distinction is made that the button and buttonhole is the frog but in the braid trade the appliquéd knots themselves are the frogs. This knot is used on a double-breasted coat, one button being a dummy that is sewed directly to the frog itself, while the other is not attached to the frog but buttons through the buttonhole from the underside. After the JUG SLING has been tied the ends are rearranged as shown by the arrows.

2301. The TRUE-LOVER'S KNOT. In form this does not differ from the diagram of TURK'S-HEAD #2289, but the over-and-under arrangement differs.

2302. The "FALSE-LOVER'S" KNOT is closely related to the above, but the two OVERHAND KNOTS are differently interlocked.

2303. A dissimilar knot, tied with two OVERHAND KNOTS, which do not interlock.

2304. A knot of two loops. There are other knots given in the chapter on DOUBLE LOOPS that may be employed as frogs.

2305. Another forked loop, which can be decoratively arranged.

2306, 2307, 2308. Three arbitrary forms. The center one is from Bocher, who devotes considerable space to decorative TWO-DIMENSIONAL KNOTS. The knots are to be pinned over a diagram. Repeat to yourself, "Over and under," as you pin the cord and take the crossings alternately.

2309. A knot closely related to #2303 which does not have a regular over-one-and-under-one sequence.

2310, 2311. These two are from Japan. Knots of this kind are superimposed on parcel lashings and are often made of several parallel copper wires that are silk-covered and parti-colored. The loops are bent into decorative forms.

2312. Another knot from Bocher.

2313. This knot, also shown by Bocher, is found tied on almost every Chinese priest cord. It will appear again in this chapter #2362.

2314. The BUMBLEBEE. It is hard to resist the temptation to name a knot when the title seems as appropriate as this is.

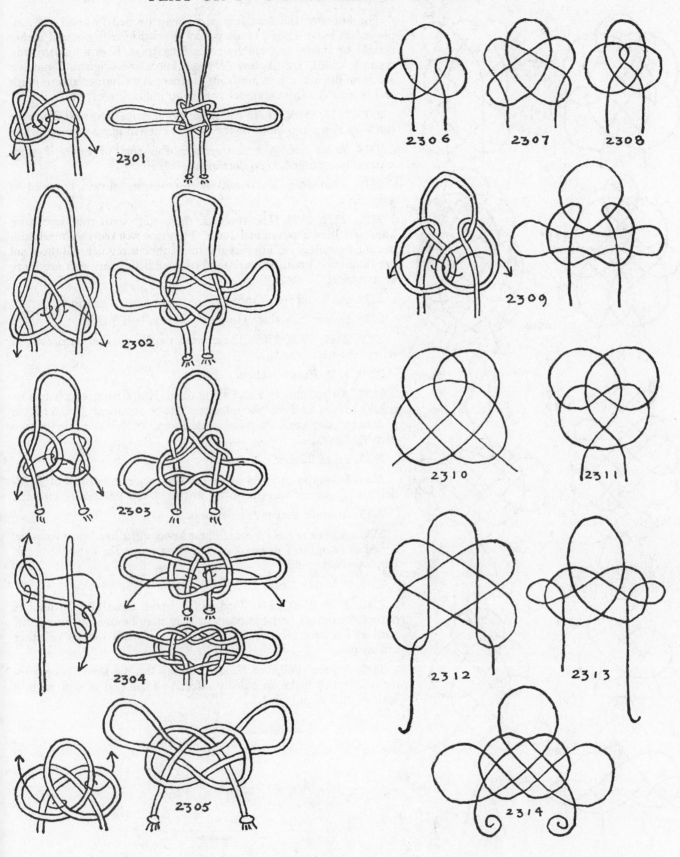

2301

2302

2303

2304

2305

2306

2307

2308

2309

2310

2311

2312

2313

2314

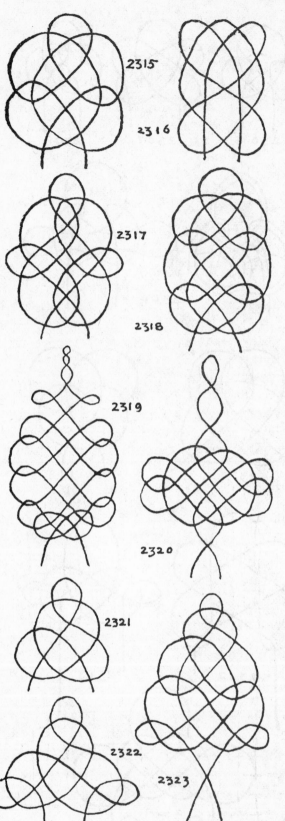

The knots of the next few pages may be tied in braid and employed as FROG KNOTS, or they may be tied in stiff material, either double or single, and employed as TERMINAL KNOTS on lanyards, trumpet cords, etc. A few of these knots are original, a number are from Bocher, others are from Japanese and Chinese lantern cords and several are from trumpet cords and military uniforms.

2315, 2317, 2318. These will make symmetrical LANYARD KNOTS if the loop at the top bight of the knot is cut (to make two cords).

2316. A six-sided compartment in this sort of knot, if symmetrically arranged, is no detriment.

2319, 2320. *Ring* and *bandmaster frogs* are always required in pairs.

2321, 2322, 2323. The three of these start with the same basic knot and have a pyramidal form. They are not truly symmetrical, but the irregularity is internal and the outline is regular. All three are very common knots, and are used oftener than many that are more symmetrical.

2324. An elementary knot.

2325. Bocher calls this "MORS DU CHEVAL."

2326, 2327, 2328, 2329. These were tied in parallel parti-colored wires on lantern cords.

2330, 2331. From Bocher.

2332. An attempt to make a PECTORAL KNOT from which to suspend a carved Chinese "semiprecious" stone ornament. It was tied in a doubled silk cord. A more satisfactory knot was made in two planes (#843).

2333. From Bocher.

2334. From the end of a bugle cord by Seiderman Bros. of Philadelphia. The knot was drawn up so that it was practically circular.

2335. Another nearly circular knot.

2336. A SQUARE LEAF FORM. These knots make handsome frogs or, if tied in round stiff material, excellent terminals for light-cords and window-shade pulls.

2337. A MAPLE LEAF.

2338, 2339, 2340, 2341. Tied in flat braid, these may be used as corner ornaments on band coats or they may be used in round stiff cord as PECTORAL KNOTS from which to suspend lockets or other ornaments.

2342. A knot similar to #2340, but this has the lower corner removed. It will make an equally effective knot tied in stiff narrow braid or stiff round cord.

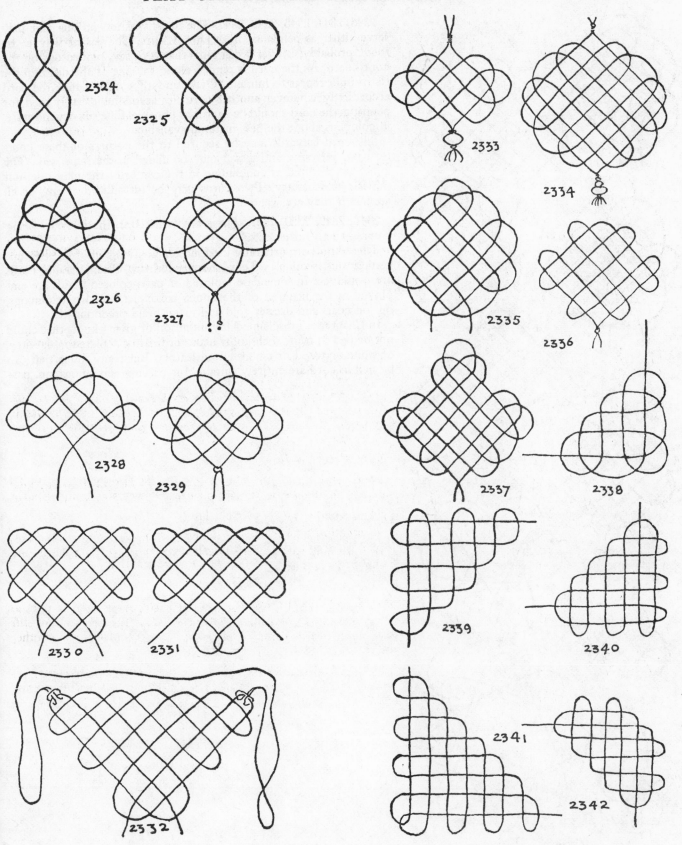

2324
2325
2333
2334
2326
2327
2335
2336
2328
2329
2337
2338
2330
2331
2339
2340
2332
2341
2342

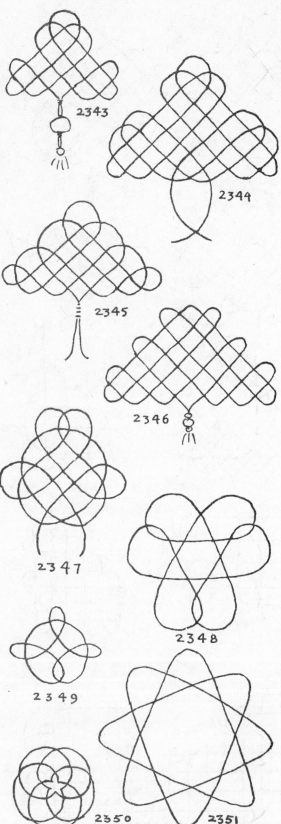

2343, 2344, 2345, 2346, 2347. The first five knots on this page may serve either as pendants or as FROG KNOTS. The easiest way to tie them, probably, is over a diagram—that is to say, pinned out on the cork board. As the cord is pinned along the line of the diagram the tier should repeat to himself "Over, under," etc., and tuck the cord accordingly wherever another cord lies across his path. If used for pendants the cord should be as stiff as possible. Fine silk-wound wire, in colors, is about the best material available.

Silk cord lanyards may be secured to the corners of these knots by RING HITCHES, and tassels may be added in the same way. The knots are pictured as concluding in the center of the long side, but this is not necessary. Two cords may be introduced at any or all corners if they are wanted.

2348, 2349, 2350, 2351. These are *medallions*, the last two being TURK'S-HEAD forms.

These knots are generally used in combination and often with uncomplicated sections of cord between them. Often parallel cords are employed. In some cases colored or parti-colored braids are employed as the material of the knots, particularly in hat trimmings, but on coats and dresses gold and metal braid predominate.

In Chapter 1, I disclaimed any intention of giving knots that could not be tied in rope, such knots being ordinarily depicted in carvings of stone or wood or embossed on leather. But many knots that can be tied in cord are entirely suitable for carving and embossing, particularly those of the present chapter. I do not scorn intangible knots, but they form another subject that is not under consideration, and the size of the present volume is already large enough.

Many of the knots of the last few pages would make appropriate and decorative escutcheons, medallions and corners for the covers of books. To save myself unnecessary labor, many of these knots have been drawn in single line only and the over-and-under sequence has not been indicated. It is alternate throughout, unless something else has been indicated, as in the knots of pages 371, 372, and 373.

2352. The two knots at the top of this page together form a very simple escutcheon. Other, and in some cases more elaborate, knots will lend themselves to similar treatment.

2355, 2356. These medallions are carved on the sides of a flattened powder horn in my possession. The strands of the rope in the Turk's-Head are carved in detail. The horn has been mentioned already in the chapter on Turk's-Heads, and is dated 1675.

2360. The knot pictured here would make a good thump mat for a sheet or traveler block, if tied in heavy rope and followed two or three times, in the manner of a Turk's-Head.

Many of the One-Strand Button diagrams, if sufficiently decorative, may be made to serve as medallions and also many of the Monkey's Fist diagrams. The Multi-Strand Button diagrams of Chapter 9 can be tied as mats provided the large number of strands used is no objection.

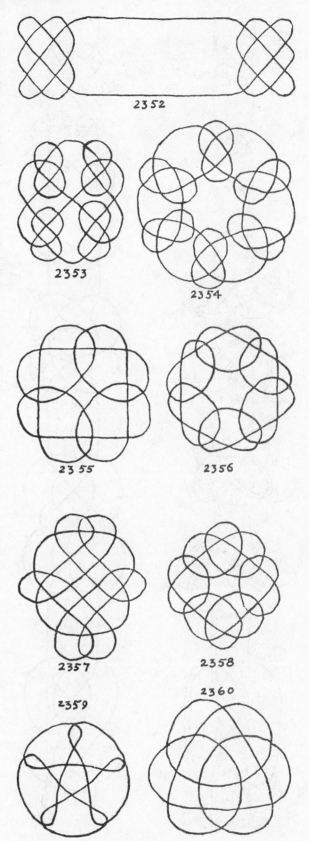

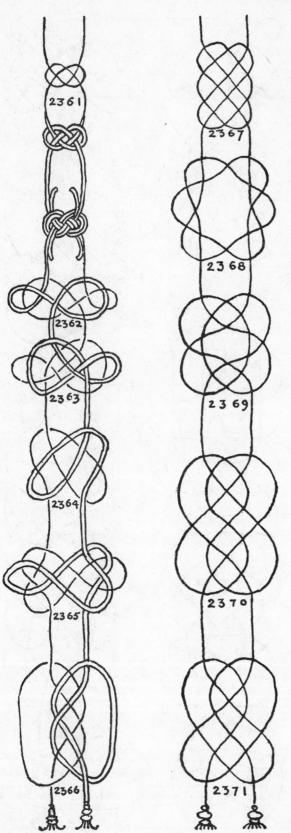

Chinese *priest cords* are very uniform in character, although there is a great diversity in the knots that compose them. The material is invariably heavy silk-covered cord about a quarter of an inch in diameter. There are always two pairs of strands and each pair is parallel throughout the cord, except generally in the initial and final knots, and occasionally in the large knot, which is second from the end, in which the strands are led independently.

All the cords I have examined have each contained eight or nine knots. The length of a cord varies from about four and one half to five feet from the top of the upper knot to the bottom of the tassels. They are presumably either part of a Buddhist priest's costume or else they are temple ornaments on curtains or banner staffs.

To tie: Pin the cords out on a board, using four cords, two in each set. Work two parallel strands as a unit. The order of tying is alternately over and under throughout, with one important exception. In order to prevent torsion, the order between two knots is either under, under or else over, over. That is to say, if the cord leaves one knot "under," it enters the next knot "under" in the same way. Otherwise the priest cord would tend to "corkscrew" or twist. The end of each cord is finished off with twist braid, and each of these braids terminates in a tassel.

2361. The first knot shown here is the JOSEPHINE KNOT, which in form does not differ from the CARRICK BEND. It appears on every priest cord that I have seen, as both the second and the final knot before the twist braids and the tassel.

2362. This is another knot that is on almost every priest cord. The reason for the almost universal use of the last two knots is probably that they are the smallest to be found that fulfill all requirements of a priest cord.

2363, 2364, 2365, 2366. These are small knots that often appear near the ends of the cords.

2367. The CHINESE KNOT or FLAT KNIFE LANYARD KNOT I have never seen on a priest cord, but I have seen it tied in association with PRIEST CORD KNOTS in other kinds of lanyards. Tied in a uniform series, the CHINESE KNOT makes an excellent belt or bell pull.

2368. The THREE-LEAD, EIGHT-BIGHT TURK'S-HEAD.

2369, 2370, 2371. These knots are progressively larger, but are still small. The biggest knot in a cord is always just below the center.

2369. A knot with four outside parts and a six-sided center.

2370, 2371. Knots which do not have the characteristic CARRICK BEND motif which appears as a component part at the top and bottom of the majority of PRIEST CORD KNOTS. They have other of the characteristics however. They were tied in Chinese lanyards of four strands in the manner of priest cords, but not in priest cords. It is quite possible that the knots of the priest cord are held sacred and are deemed inappropriate for other purposes.

2375. This was tied in heavy sash cord on the lanyard of a boat fender that was owned by the Boston Antique Co.

2372, 2373, 2374, 2376, 2377. These knots and a number on the subsequent pages were shown to me by Louise Delano Cheney, who lived in China a number of years, and who first introduced me to this variety of knot. She made several priest cords herself and devised a number of original knots suitable for them.

Priest cords can serve one very practical domestic purpose: they make very attractive and decorative bell pulls. Usually they are of a single solid color except when there is a splash of gold or bright color which shows through the simple knotting or network covers of the tassel molds.

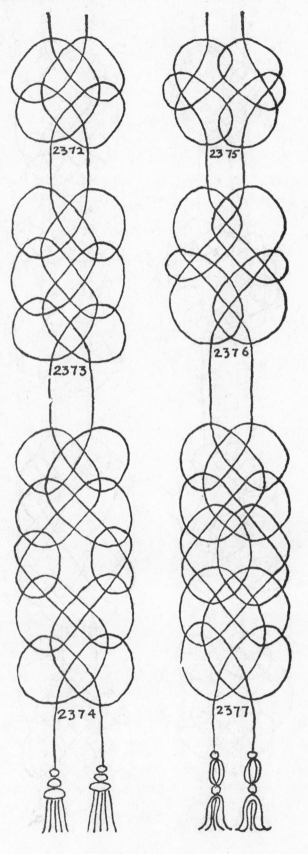

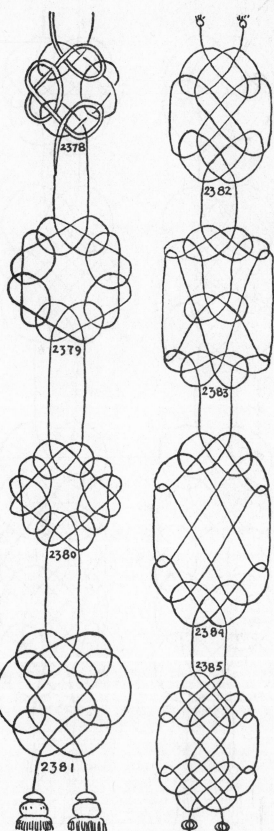

The three complete priest cords detailed in the left, center and right areas of page 381 belonged respectively to Louise Delano Cheney, to the author, and to Mrs. Frederic Stone. The left is gray lilac in color with a gold-leaf tassel mold. The center cord is dark golden ochre, and the right cord is a rich orange. The tassels of the latter are of gold cord formed over an emerald-green mold. The other tassels are the same color as the cords.

2378, 2379. These should be compared with Knots #2355 and #2356, which are from the powder horn of 1675. Knot #2378 appears in both the lilac and the orange priest cords; #2379 appears in the ochre cord.

The diagrams in general will indicate the finished form of the knots but a better idea may be formed from the photographs of two cords among the frontispieces. These also will indicate how the knots should be spaced.

Having tied a cord in regular over-and-under sequence, except that between two knots the sequence does *not* alternate, proceed to draw up the knots evenly, beginning at the top and completing each knot before progressing to the next.

2380. An original knot supplied by Mrs. Cheney.

2381. Appears on both lilac (left) and orange (right) cords.

2382. Found on both the ochre and the orange cords.

2383. Found on a priest cord in the stock of a New York Chinese "notions" shop.

A knot similar to either #2386 or #2391 appears as the initial knot of every priest cord that I have seen except one on which the first two knots were missing.

The semifinal knots for the cords that I have seen are almost invariably derived from the True-Lover's Knot or else follow it closely in diagram form, as does Knot #2387, (which is an Eight-Bight, Three-Lead Turk's-Head); so also does semifinal Knot #2392. (See Knot #2289, this chapter.) When the semifinal knot is not a True-Lover's Knot, it still has the two flanking loops that are characteristic of that knot. Generally below this the two center strands are held together with Knot #2361, which serves to secure two of the four ends, while #2387, #2393 or some similar knot holds the other two ends.

2388. When the four ends are ready they are each made up into twist braid of seven to nine bights each. The method of making this is shown at the top of page 95.

It seems probable that the center (ochre) cord originally had a Carrick Bend (#2361) at the top in place of Knot #2379. This would explain the shortness of the lanyards and would make the three cords, right, left and center, quite uniform in their proportions.

2393. Two Overhand Knots hold the loops of the True-Lover's Knot in place.

2394. To tie a True-Lover's Knot: First make two *interlocking* Overhand Knots and then pull the bights out as indicated by the arrows in the fourth-column diagram. (See Knot # 2418.)

2395. A knot supplied by Mrs. Cheney.

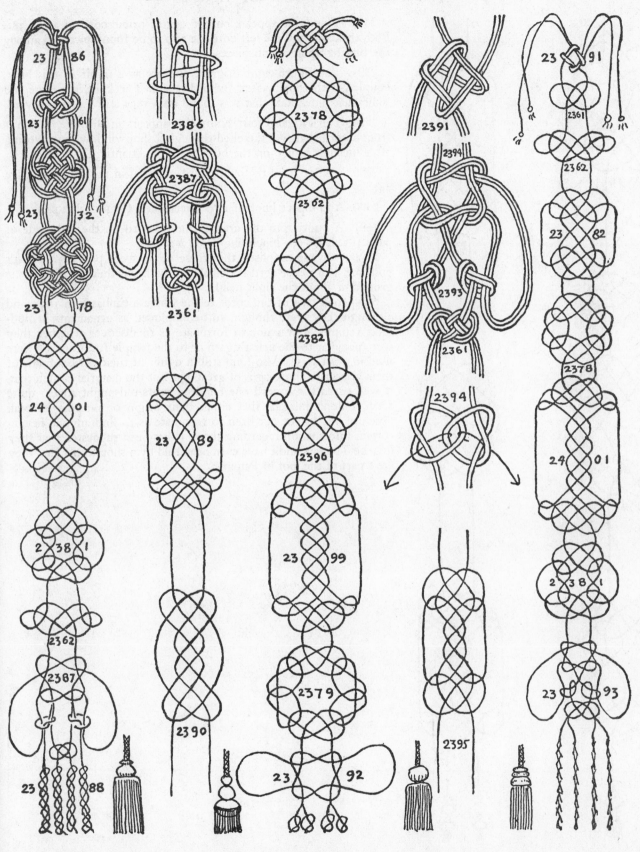

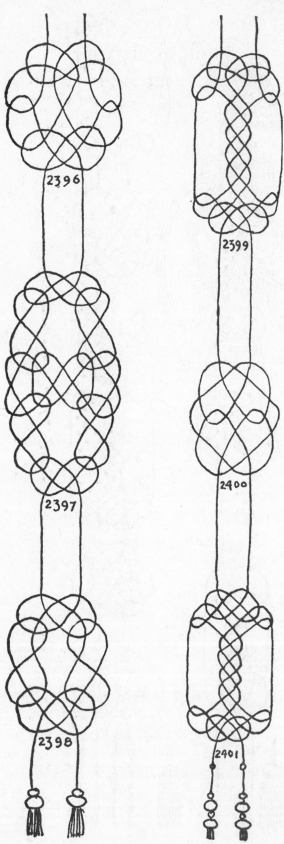

2396. This knot appears on the center priest cord of page 381. Both this cord and the left cord are also to be found pictured among the photographic frontispieces.

2397. The figure-eight diagram appears as a motif in this knot, coupled with the CARRICK BEND diagram. The knot is a large and somewhat flimsy one that was found on a very stiff lantern lanyard.

2398. The FIGURE-EIGHT KNOT also appears in this one, which is from a cord that was sketched through a shopwindow, one evening after business hours, on the boardwalk of Atlantic City.

2399. A knot from the ochre cord pictured in the center of page 381.

2400. A compact knot of two interlocked CARRICK BENDS.

2401. A knot from the orange-colored cord on the right side of page 381. It is very much like KNOT #2399.

I have always supposed that these cords were part of a priest's costume. If a priest cord is tied about the neck, the tassels clear the ground at about the right height.

But I took two of the cords to the Chinese Embassy in 1935, and although they were thought to be employed as ornaments in Buddhist temples, I was not so fortunate as to discover whether they were peculiar to the priest's garb or to the temple furniture, or were used in both ways. Also I am still in doubt of their period. Some of them appear to show signs of great age, but the material is such that, if well cared for, a cord one hundred years old might appear quite fresh. I don't imagine that either their origin or purpose is at all obscure, but I have not been so fortunate as to find anyone having certain information regarding them. It has been suggested that they may be Tibetan, and I have even been told by a shopkeeper that they are a part of the loot of Peiping.

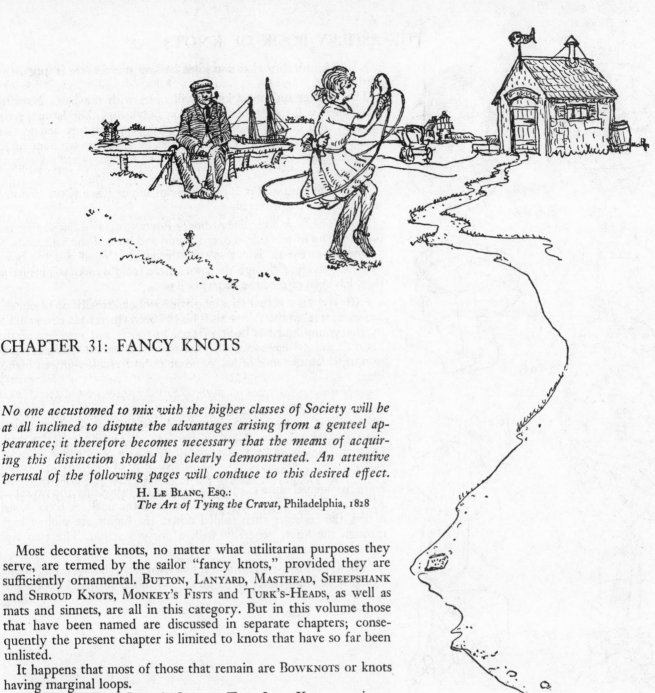

CHAPTER 31: FANCY KNOTS

*No one accustomed to mix with the higher classes of Society will be
at all inclined to dispute the advantages arising from a genteel appearance; it therefore becomes necessary that the means of acquir-
ing this distinction should be clearly demonstrated. An attentive
perusal of the following pages will conduce to this desired effect.*

H. Le Blanc, Esq.:
The Art of Tying the Cravat, Philadelphia, 1828

Most decorative knots, no matter what utilitarian purposes they
serve, are termed by the sailor "fancy knots," provided they are
sufficiently ornamental. Button, Lanyard, Masthead, Sheepshank
and Shroud Knots, Monkey's Fists and Turk's-Heads, as well as
mats and sinnets, are all in this category. But in this volume those
that have been named are discussed in separate chapters; consequently the present chapter is limited to knots that have so far been
unlisted.

It happens that most of those that remain are Bowknots or knots
having marginal loops.

Of these the True-Lover's, Love or True Love Knot constitutes
the largest single group. The name being a very popular one, there
are many knots that bear it. The oldest description that I find of the
True-Lover's Knot says: "A sort of double knot with two bows."
This is so broad that almost any of the knots bearing the name can
be made to fit it. Webster labels both the ordinary Bowknot and
the Carrick Bend, "True Love Knots." There is just one point on
which most authorities agree. This is that the True-Lover's Knot
consists of two intertwined Overhand Knots that are brought together in such a manner as to form a charming and symmetrical
unit.

The conscious romanticism that has fixed this name upon two
quite commonplace forms which, when drawn together, make a
single beautiful and harmonious knot, should leave no doubt in the

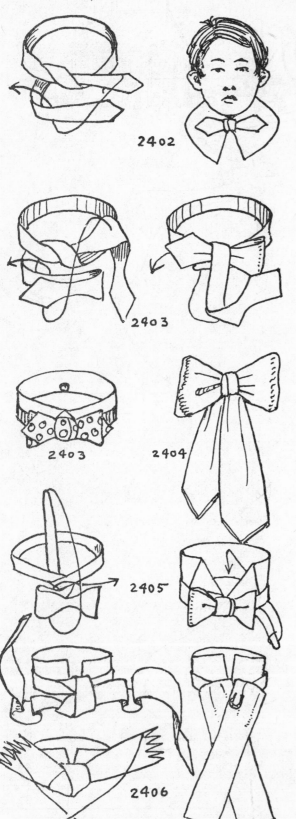

minds of all idealists that any knot lacking this feature is unworthy of the name.

The chapter on fancy knots will open with the basic NECKTIE KNOTS and will then touch briefly on BOWKNOTS. The latter part is devoted to a certain variety of CHINESE KNOT that is tied in two planes and is commonly called BUTTERFLY KNOT on account of its marginal loops or bows, which are fancied to resemble the wings of the insect.

2402. The STRING TIE is merely a SQUARE or REEF KNOT tied in a well-stiffened flat material.

2403. The BOW TIE. The ordinary BOWKNOT is tied flat so that the bow and end of one side is over the end and bow of the other side.

Sometimes the tie is cut so that the waist is small and the bows flare excessively, although the knot is free from wrinkles. This latter form has been termed the BATWING TIE.

2404. If a bow is tied in a long wide ribbon, usually of black, the necktie is termed the WINDSOR. This has been worn with Eton collars by the young and has been affected by poets and students of the Latin Quarter. I have seen a photograph of Edmund Clarence Stedman in which the ends of his Windsor tie were fully eighteen inches long.

2405. The COVENTRY DRESS TIE is based on the DRAWKNOT or single bow. It is the easiest dress tie for the non-adept to master. One half of the tie tapers to an end that is stiffened at the very tip with a small metal disk which is to be stuck in between the collar and neckband, and then pushed downward from sight.

2406. The ASCOT. This tie is still associated with horses and is today worn by women quite as much as by men. It is possibly the easiest of all to tie. The ends are drawn even around the neck. A REEF KNOT is tied, the ends are then folded down, the bights are pinned high through the knot, generally with a horsy scarfpin. The two legs cross each other at a moderate angle.

2407. The FOUR-IN-HAND. This tie also has a horsy background, which it has long since lived down. So much so that I found one person who thought that the name was in some way descriptive of the manner of tying, and that two people with four hands were required for the job.

The simplest way to knot the FOUR-IN-HAND is to form an OVER-HAND KNOT with the wider end and to reeve the more attenuated end through the knot.

2408. A fuller and handsomer knot is formed, however, by bringing the wider end twice around the narrower end, then reeving it up beside the neck, finally sticking it down under the outer one of the first two turns. This is the common FOUR-IN-HAND KNOT, called by M. Le Blanc "the CRAVAT KNOT." It must be worked and prodded before perfection is attained.

Every few years scarfpins are worn with this tie. But when the pins have grown so conspicuous that they transcend good taste the scarfpin is relegated for another period to the tack room or the jewel box, to stay in quod until another generation comes along.

The knot has the same form as the BUNTLINE HITCH.

2409. If the material of a FOUR-IN-HAND tie lacks substance it may be passed three times instead of twice when starting the knot. The end, however, in the final tucking down is passed only under the last or upper turn. This knot bulks much larger than the one last described.

2410. The STOCK. M. Le Blanc terms this tie and method "En Cascade." The stock is middled at the throat and then one end goes around the neck, one part passing above the other, at the nape. At the front a GRANNY KNOT is tied, care being taken that all parts are flat and fair. The upper end is turned directly down over the lower or smaller end and the scarfpin holds everything firm after the folds have been carefully arranged.

If the knot is to be tied around a collar the tie is merely passed around the back of the neck and either a HALF KNOT or a GRANNY KNOT tied at the front before adjusting the pin.

M. Le Blanc credits Lord Byron with being the first to cross a tie at the nape of the neck instead of (stockwise) at the front.

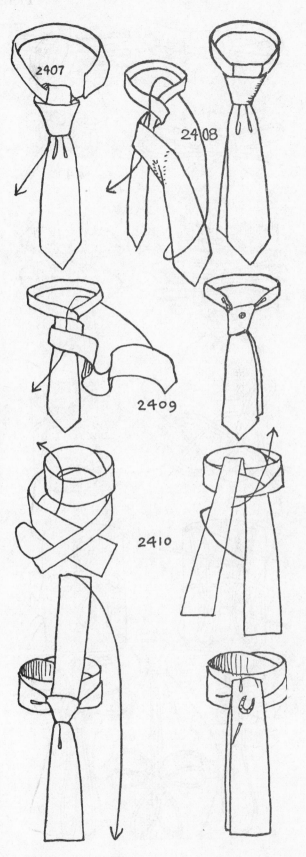

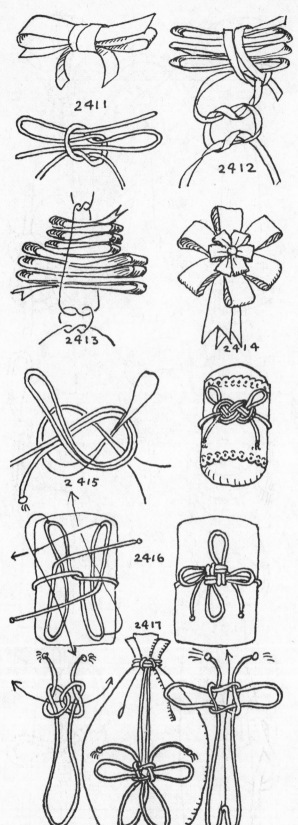

2411. The ordinary BOWKNOT of the shops, as used by dressmakers, florists, confectioners, hatters, etc., does not differ essentially from the necktie bow except that usually a ribbon has one right side, so that it is necessary, by twisting the ribbon, to keep that side uppermost at all times.

2412. If a considerable number of loops are to be added, for decorative effect, they may all be made with one end and then *clove hitched* with the other end, the ribbon being first secured firmly in place with a SQUARE KNOT. The loops are smoothed out and disposed of as the tier wishes, after which they may all have one or both sets of ends trimmed with either a swallowtail or a diagonal cut. The trimmed ends are always left longer than the loops.

2413. For a particularly full knot an extra piece of ribbon is often superimposed over the original knot and, after the folds are arranged, is square knotted firmly in place.

2414. If a BOWKNOT is worked into circular form it is termed a "ROSETTE" or "ROSETTE KNOT." In any of these knots the several loops may be of equal length or of graduated lengths.

2415. The "GIFT KNOT" is a JAPANESE PARCEL KNOT consisting of a CARRICK BEND, tied in doubled ends. If of cord, little tassels on the ends add much to the decorative effect.

2416. A parcel is sometimes tied with a crown of four loops. Arrange the cord as in the first diagram and, disregarding the two ends, crown the four loops or bights to the right. Lay the left upper loop down to the right of the next or second loop, then cross the second loop to the right, over the first and above the third. Take the third loop, cross it up over the second loop and to the left of the fourth loop. Take the fourth loop and cross it over the third loop and tuck it under the double bight that was formed when the first loop was moved. Arrange all parts so they are smooth and fair and draw up taut. By crowning all four loops again in the opposite direction, the knot is made more secure.

2417. This brings us to the TRUE-LOVER'S KNOT that was mentioned at the beginning of the chapter. One of these knots may be added, for decorative effect, to any bag or parcel lashing. In a short length of cord tie two interlocked OVERHAND KNOTS. Pull two bights through the OVERHAND KNOTS as shown in the left diagram. Then pull the bottom loop up through the knot as shown in the right diagram. The upper bight that has just been pulled through the knot is secured to the parcel lashing with a RING HITCH (#1859). The two ends may be tasseled or finished off with OVERHAND KNOTS; if of cord, or if of ribbon, the ends may be trimmed either with a diagonal or swallow-tailed cut.

2418. The TRUE-LOVER'S or TRUE LOVE KNOT is sometimes pulled up snugly without adding loops and bights. So tied, it makes a handsome TWO-CORD LANYARD KNOT and in small black silk cord is quite effective on a monocle cord where a series of small knots assists materially in preventing slipping when any twirling is resorted to.

2419. With the two side loops arranged conventionally as pictured, this has been called the "SAILOR'S CROSS" and also the "SOUTHERN CROSS." Tied in two cords and pulled up snugly, this also makes an attractive TWO-CORD LANYARD KNOT.

2420. This ENGLISH, ENGLISHMAN'S, WATER, WATERMAN'S, FISHER'S, FISHERMAN'S or TRUE-LOVER'S KNOT is perhaps the least pleasing to the eye of all TRUE-LOVER'S KNOTS, but it has a legend attached to it that more than makes up for any lack of symmetry in the knot itself. The story was first told to me by Mrs. E. E. du Pont, who had heard it from a boatman in Sidney, N.S. It concerned a certain bashful sailor who could not screw up his courage to the point of inviting his girl to marry him. After some delay he sent her a TRUE-LOVER'S KNOT tied in a piece of fishline and with the two knots wide apart as in the left illustration. It transpires that, if the knot is returned as it was sent, the sailor will be welcomed when next he comes ashore, at which time he will still be on probation. If, however, the knot is returned snugly drawn together as in the right illustration, it means that, if he can't borrow a boat with which to row ashore, he'd better swim, for it's high time for the banns to be published. But if his knot should be capsized and nothing remain of it, it means: "You'd better ship around Cape Horn, and you can't do it too soon to suit me."

But the story has it that our sailor had shilly-shallied so long that his boat sailed codfishing before his girl had time to return his gift, so we don't know what happened when he got back, or even whether he caught his boat.

2421. The TRUE-LOVER'S KNOT. This again consists of two interlocked OVERHAND KNOTS which form what is actually a TWO-STRAND MATTHEW WALKER, and makes a very nice LANYARD KNOT.

2422. The FALSE-LOVER'S KNOT. The two knots are interlocked reversely; otherwise it is tied as ⌗2419. The knot has a character of its own and, appliquéd in flat braid, will make a good frog.

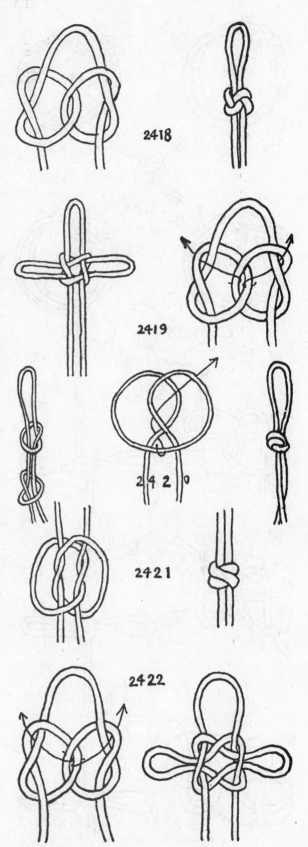

2418

2419

2420

2421

2422

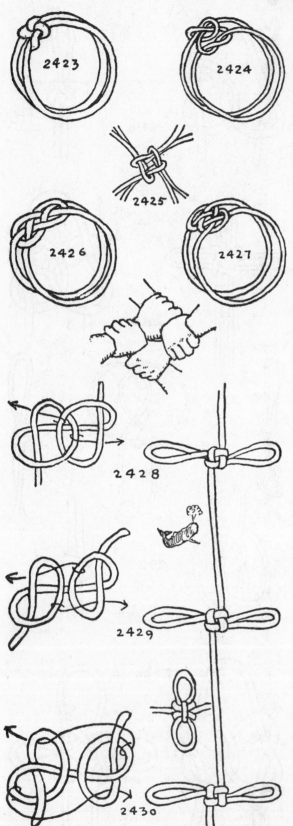

2423. This is Knot #2418 tied with gold wires. Formerly this was a very characteristic gift from a sailor to his sweetheart. The two rings could move independently but could not be separated, which undoubtedly carried a meaning to the young couple that made the long separation entailed by a sea voyage more tolerable.

2424. Jewelers not conversant with the symbolism of the previous knot were apt to make the True-Lover's Knot in this form, which, while it superficially seemed about the same, consisted of but one wire and held the two rings rigidly together.

2425. A True-Lover's Knot tied in the bights of four short strands symbolizes the four clasped hands of two lovers arranged in the manner called a "hand chair." The knot was shown to me by Mrs. Osborn W. Bright.

2426. A True-Lover's Knot in ring form, based on the Carrick Bend. This, like #2424, is made of a single wire, and I cannot but feel that it was less popular than the one to follow, which does not submerge all individuality. One reason that I believe that this knot is held in lower esteem by the sailor is that the only two specimens I have ever seen were both of silver. Certainly the baser metal must bear some significance. Moreover one of them was exposed for sale in a pawnshop window.

2427. A Carrick Bend in two separate rings which interlock harmoniously, perhaps the handsomest of the four rings shown.

There are probably other knots that are called by the name True-Lover's, but these are all I have found that fill the specifications that were somewhat arbitrarily adopted. These are outlined on page 383.

2428. The following knots, through page 389, are Single-Cord Lanyard Knots with a loop at either side and a four-part crown at the center. Two-Strand Knot #2451 is the well-known Chinese Crown Knot. I set out to find a knot of similar appearance for a *single-cord lanyard* and this series resulted before I was through. The first five are of similar aspect. The simplest is #2432, which is the common Sheepshank Knot with the parts pulled together. This knot will serve on a lanyard, and I have also used it for kite tails to the entire satisfaction of my children.

2429. This knot and the previous one are easily formed. They should be drawn up firmly, for if the pull is excessive they tend to distort.

2430. A knot that is firmer and will stand a considerable pull. Moreover the back of the knot is more regular than the others.

2431. Having found №2430 satisfactory on the front side, I next attempted to find a ONE-CORD LANYARD KNOT with a loop at either side and a crown at both front and back. This occasioned a longer search, but the knot alongside was finally evolved, which, if carefully worked and pulled taut, fills all requirements. It needs some "gentling" before it is quite satisfactory.

2432. The common SHEEPSHANK KNOT, when pulled compactly together, presents a crown on one side only and distorts easily. Nevertheless it had the desired aspect and was the point of departure for the series.

2433. The loops of this knot run parallel with the cord.

2434. The crown of the knot alongside is not square with the cord, but the loops are; and if drawn up well, the knot is quite firm. The simpler the formation is, the harder some kinds of knots are to keep in hand. This knot is quite handsome when tied with a doubled cord. Some of the others might be doubled as satisfactorily. All must be worked methodically, and as complete success never comes until the very last moment, the tier must not allow himself to be easily discouraged.

2435. A DOUBLE CROWN with single loops. This knot is more successful perhaps than the drawings indicate. It is very firm and does not easily distort. It is, however, quite a handful to tie, and it will be well to make a large-size diagram and pin the cord at frequent intervals. Although about as much trouble to work as to tie, once it has been drawn together compactly the form is both symmetrical and inevitable.

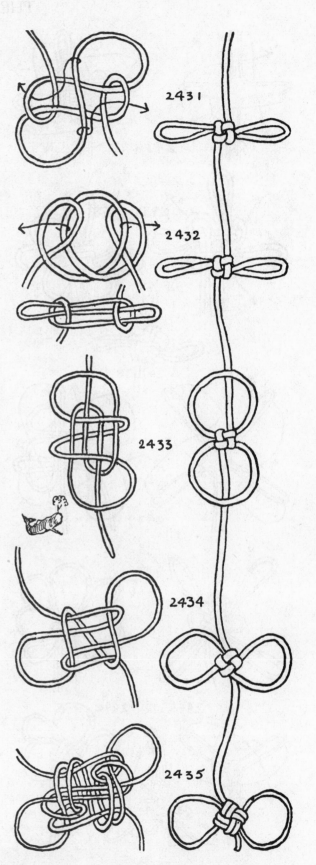

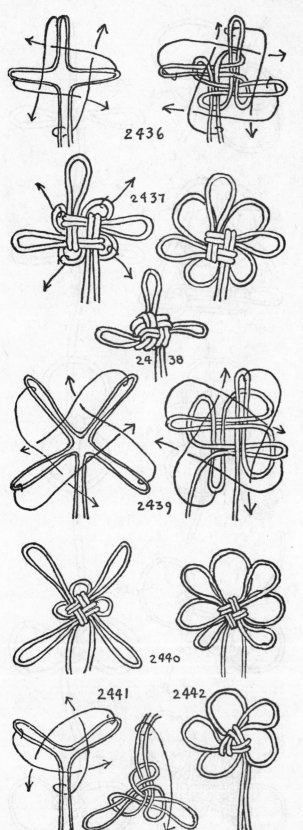

2436

2437

24 38

2439

2440

2441   2442

2436. The SHAMROCK KNOT. With a single cord arrange three loops and the two standing parts into the form of a cross. Arrange symmetrically and crown the loops and ends to the right, the two ends being worked as a unit. *Without turning the structure over,* reverse the direction of the ends and loops and crown them back to the left. This completes the SHAMROCK KNOT as shown in the third diagram.

2437. To make a *knot of seven loops* from the same start, extend each of the four close bights indicated by the arrows in the third diagram of ⚹2436. Arrange them symmetrically, in the form of the fourth diagram.

2438. A THREE-PETAL KNOT with a cuboid center is made from the same start. Crown as in the first diagram of ⚹2436. Having drawn this up snugly as in the third diagram, *turn the structure over* and crown again reversely. The second crown will cover the bights that are evident in the third diagram of ⚹2436, giving the knot an entirely different character.

2439. A *knot of four loops:* Arrange a cord with four equal loops and with the two legs parallel. Crown the loops only, to the right. Then, keeping the structure the same side up, arrange the cord as shown in the second diagram and crown a second time, this time to the left. The completed knot is shown in the third diagram.

2440. The three bights that are closely drawn around the center of KNOT ⚹2439 may be extended to make a SEVEN-PETAL KNOT that is somewhat different from ⚹2437. If the legs of the present knot were included in the original crown, an arrangement is made, similar to KNOT ⚹2437, which will have nine petals.

2441. If a *knot of two loops only* is to be crowned, employ the ends as well as the loops. The resultant knot will have three close bights and two forked loops extending from a double triangular crown.

2442. If the three close bights are extended, a LEAF-SHAPED KNOT of five loops is formed, which is shown as the final drawing on this page.

The knots of this series make decorative terminals that are effective on the ends of window-shade pulls, electric-light pulls, curtain and bell cords, and dress and hat trimmings.

2443. A knot somewhat similar to the last may be made by crowning three loops without engaging the ends, and then reversing and crowning the loops a second time on the same side of the structure. If the two close bights are extended the knot will have five petals.

2444. A knot of five loops crowned without engaging the ends. The loops are crowned a second time in the reverse direction. The four bights may be extended if desired so that the knot will appear as in the right diagram with nine loops. If the legs are crowned as well as the loops a larger knot with a center crown of six parts will result.

2445. An interesting knot with three well-rounded marginal loops and a double four-part crown center. This knot does not promise much until it is nearly finished. Then it suddenly becomes compact and regular. Except that it has a double center and single loops, it is similar in character to ⅍2451. Its structure may be compared with ⅍2435, which was evolved first and upon which this knot was based.

2446. A JAPANESE KNOT with a single four-part crown center and two opposite loops.

2447. The VIOLET. This is from a French book, and was ascribed to Japan. After the knot has been formed, as in the left diagram, the parts marked with arrows are extended to form petals and the other parts are contracted.

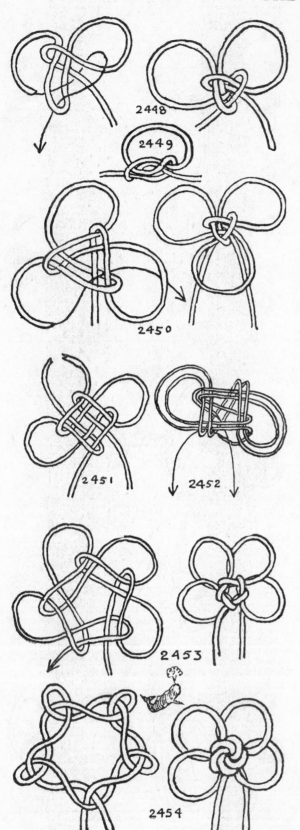

"BUTTERFLY KNOT" is the name commonly applied to a variety of CHINESE KNOT that is tied in two planes. It consists of a central part or body in two layers, both having a straight over-one-and-under-one weave, and a series of marginal loops, which protrude from between the two central planes or layers. Since the knots are tied directly in two layers, but are illustrated or projected with one layer over the other, the over-and-under weave is not evident in the diagrams. By observing closely it will be seen that a loop passes through or between the two parts of another loop in each case and then passes *around* the two parts of the next loop that lies at right angles to it; and in the larger knots, this continues through another loop and *around* the next and continues to pass any other loops that lie ahead of it in the same manner—that is, alternately "through" and "around."

Although in practice it is often necessary to reeve the working end of the cord forward and then back in order to make a loop pass around other loops, it is simple, once the knack is acquired, to repeat as you pass another loop (either a pictured one on the diagram or a tangible one in the knot), "Through," and "Around," in alternation, and to tuck the cord accordingly.

The BUTTERFLY may be tied either as a LANYARD KNOT or as a TERMINAL KNOT. By studying ⚹2448, ⚹2451, ⚹2453, and ⚹2455, it will be seen that the simplest forms of these knots may be tied in a circle with a "CHAIN SINNET" or crochet chain stitch and that the knots are concluded by interweaving the two ends. This is shown clearly in the first diagram on the page.

2448. A three-part crown center is the simplest practical form of the knot.

2449. The simplest and basic knot of the series is nothing other than a SQUARE KNOT.

2450. If, when one of these knots has been tied, the working end is tucked ahead through its own bight and through the legs of the first bight that was tucked, the knot will have one additional loop. Any of the regular BUTTERFLY KNOTS may be so treated. The present diagram shows KNOT ⚹2448 completed in this way.

2451. The commonest and best known of the BUTTERFLIES. Instead of having a top center loop and being employed as a TERMINAL KNOT, it is here tied as a LANYARD KNOT, two ends being substituted for the top loop that is shown in ⚹811. In tying knots ⚹2448, ⚹2451, ⚹2453, and ⚹2455 by the CHAIN SINNET method, take a flat board or table and, keeping the knot continually in exact diagrammatic form, thrust one bight at a time through the previous loop and pin the knot at intervals to avoid capsizing.

2452. Compare this knot with ⚹2435 and ⚹2445. The centers are the same but in this case the loops too are double. Moreover it is not suitable for use as a LANYARD KNOT without modification.

2453. The five-part center crown is tied as already described on page 392. It may have five loops if the working end is stuck as described for ⌗2450.

2454. This is a surprising knot, as it is quite flimsy until almost completely drawn up, when it falls into shape nicely. Superficially it cannot be told from Knot ⌗2457, if the latter is tied with five loops instead of six.

2455. A Five-Bight Knot with a six-part crown in the center is the practical limit in size for this type of Butterfly. The method of tying a smaller knot of the sort has already been shown as ⌗2448, ⌗2451, and ⌗2453. The present knot makes a handsome Two-Cord Lanyard Knot which is shown as ⌗2484. If another rim bight is desired one may be added as in ⌗2450.

2456. A Five-Bight Knot with a more elaborate over-and-under arrangement. The first bight is laid out and pinned as in the former knot. The second bight is laid around, instead of through, the first one. The third and fourth bights are tucked through one bight and around the second one. The fifth bight is tucked through the first bight and around the next two and the final one is passed through the first, around the second, through the third and around the fourth to complete the knot. To do this the end has to be rove both forward and back. In this knot the two planes in which the series is tied become very evident.

2457. A knot may be based on a hexagonal diagram and the sequence of the crown will be over two and under two. The first bight is pinned out flat on the board. The second bight is tucked through the first. The third and fourth bights tuck through both the previous bights, the fifth bight tucks through two bights and around the third bight and the final bight tucks through two and around two. The working end in this knot may, if desired, be tucked as indicated by the arrow to add another rim bight, which makes a flowerlike knot of six petals, with a six-part center.

2458. A Triangular Butterfly Knot may be tied either with the rim bights extended or else drawn up, which will make two knots of quite different character. The diagram should be enlarged and the knot pinned out on the board when tying. Before working the knot, check the over-and-under sequence. Then work it snug, very carefully and methodically, with a pricker.

2459. If desired, the stem of the last knot may be introduced at the side instead of at the corner. This also may be tied either with or without the marginal loops. The two ends may be seized together or sewed to make a compact stem.

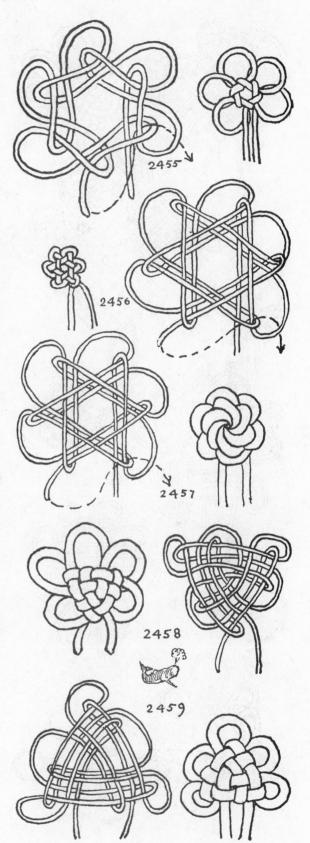

2455

2456

2457

2458

2459

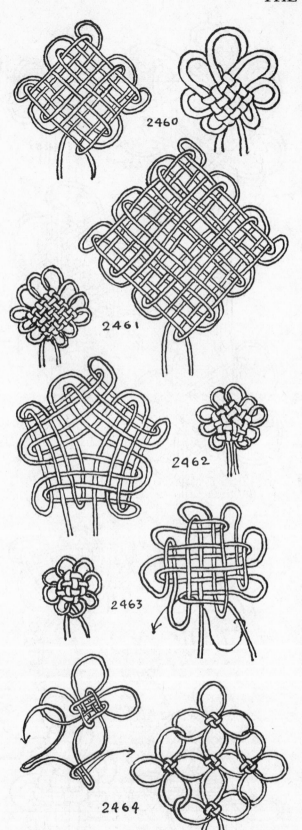

2460. The CHINESE BUTTERFLY KNOT is the prototype of this whole series. The knot, being tied in two planes, is more difficult to visualize than the SINGLE-PLANE KNOTS of the last chapter. It can be diagrammed without too much difficulty and the crossings marked with circles for each underpass. But I have found it simpler to repeat to myself as I tie a knot of this sort, "Around, through; around, through," and to take the crossings accordingly.

Copy the diagram about two or three times the size of the original on the page, and with the drawing alongside to check with. The knot will not be found difficult, once the method has become familiar. Insert pins along the outer edge, two for each rim bight and one for each inside bight, making six pins to the side. In drawing up, prod the knot constantly, and do not allow it to become distorted by uneven pulling.

The loops around the edges may be drawn up snug or they may be extended. On the next two pages the Chinese method of intertwining the loops is indicated. Wherever this intertwining occurs the crossings are taken alternately over and under.

2461. A larger knot of the same description presents no new problem.

If the top loop is cut to make separate ends at the top, the two knots that have just been given will serve as TWO-CORD LANYARD KNOTS.

2462. A PENTAGON is tied in the same way, but is perhaps more difficult to tie regularly.

2463. This diagram, if tied and worked carefully and then prodded into shape, will make either a SQUARE or a CIRCULAR KNOT.

2464. An assembled knot may be tied directly over a diagram. Another way to tie knots consisting of a number of units, which are to be combined into a single elaborate knot, is to tie each with a separate cord. Assemble these units and pin them out on the board, cut the loops and tie the ends together, so that the pattern ultimately consists of a single connected, but knotted, cord.

This having been done, take a single cord long enough for the whole pattern, and, using the knot already formed as a clue, double it with the new cord. When complete remove the CLUE KNOT and work the SINGLE-CORD KNOT snug. Very intricate patterns can be formed in this way, but it is best to try assembling a few simple knots first in order to become familiar with the method. On occasion it will happen, in projecting such knots, that they cannot be tied with a single cord.

2465. The CHINESE BUTTON KNOT was discussed at length in the beginning of Chapter 5; here it forms the head of an interesting insect. It may be found easier to tie the knot by the diagrams and directions that were given on page 103.

2466. The TRUE-LOVER'S KNOT has already been dealt with in detail on page 387 of this chapter. It seems to be universally known, which can be explained by the fact that sailors, the world over, tie it. But so far as I know the sailor ties it only as a trick knot (#2420). It would seem that the Chinese people have found uses for knots in home decoration beyond all other people.

2467. The DRAGON FLY is a quaint little insect made up very simply from the two knots that were just shown.

2468. I found the CATERPILLAR KNOT in a Japanese knot book; it is made of "square knotting," which is an Occidental form of knotting to be discussed in the chapter to follow. In the next chapter also are two Japanese lanyards which combine square knotting with CHINESE PRIEST CORD KNOTS and also a SAILOR'S STOPPER KNOT, a knot which I have never known to be tied, save on this lanyard, by anyone except a sailor. The lanyard is shown on page 403.

The CATERPILLAR KNOT consists of a series of alternating RIGHT and LEFT HALF KNOTS, tied with the ends over a short foundation loop. In *square knotting* these are called SOLOMON BARS. They are explained more fully in the next chapter.

2469. A BUTTERFLY KNOT. This is based on KNOT #2460. It is seldom in Chinese knotting that one of these knots is tied alone and unsupported; usually they are tied in combination with other knots and with additional flourishes of the marginal loops. All crossings outside the central structure of the knot are in a single plane and with regular over-one-and-under-one sequence. The diagram may be reversed.

2470. The Japanese specialize in parcel tying, and to this they bring a great deal of ingenuity. Most of the basic knots, which are quite simple, are borrowed from the Chinese. The Japanese contribution is principally in the nature of arrangement. Many of these knot forms are tied in cord consisting of a minute silk-covered copper wire. Several parti-colored wires are led in parallel strands, and once the knots are tied they are bent into leaf, flower and geometric forms. The charm of these designs depends largely on the bent wire forms, the knots being on the whole subordinate. There are several Japanese books devoted solely to the subject. The knots that are included in the design given here are #2311 and #2391.

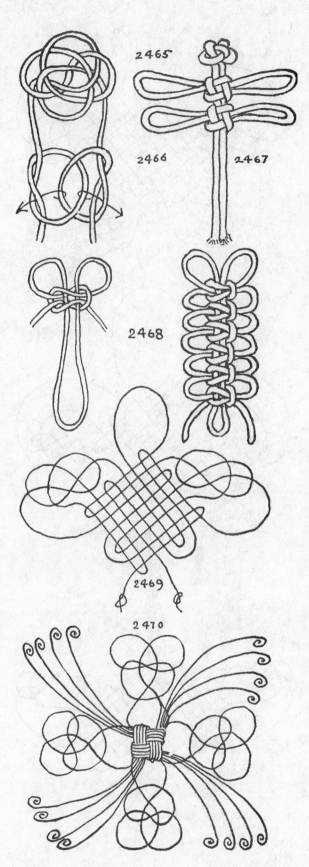

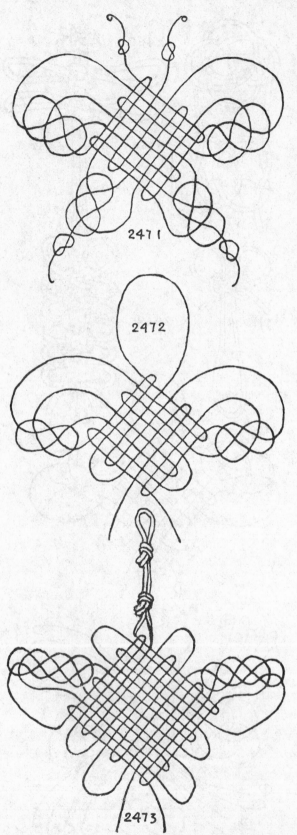

2471

2472

2473

2471. The Moth. The knots on this page are further amplifications of Butterfly Knots ⚹2460 and ⚹2461, the centers of which are here copied, but the marginal loops are further complicated in flat over-one-and-under-one sequence. In this knot the Carrick Bend motif is repeated four times in the loops and the Overhand Knot four times, one in each end of the two cords.

2472. The Owl Knot, like the last, is based on Butterfly Knot ⚹2460. Two Carrick Bends are tied in the wings. To add a knot in the marginal loops, pin out the first strand of the knot carefully. No tucking is required until the second strand is introduced, but the loop receives a single twist, which may be in either direction, provided the knot on the opposite wing is twisted contrariwise. When the strand is led for a second time to one of these knots, make certain while laying in the strand that the over-and-under is alternate throughout.

2473. The Wild Goose Knot is based on Butterfly ⚹2461.

Two Loop Knots (⚹1046) are tied in the neck of the bird and the knot tied in the wings is ⚹1429, which is similar to but longer than the Carrick Bend. Great care must be taken in drawing up this knot, for if it is once distorted by drawing any one part too tight it is difficult to make it lie fair again. The effort should be made to tie it just a little slacker than desired, and this should be done by working entirely through the knot, from end to end of the cord, each time taking out a very little of the slack. If preferred, work the knot from the center toward both ends. Often it will be found that a knot that has been tied a little slacker than was at first thought desirable has really about the tension that is wanted. But often when it seems that all reasonable restraint has been exercised it will be found that the knot is still tied tighter than the Chinese prototype.

The Chinese, in addition to the priest cords of the last chapter, have given us lanyards of surpassing beauty which are best exemplified by their lantern lanyards. Undoubtedly inside their homes are many other examples of this variety of knotting other than the lantern cords. But the lantern hangs in full view for all to see. Beside the lacery of these cords, in which many different kinds of knots are intertwined in a variety not equaled even in their priest cords, the Chinese have added color and texture. Tied in both silk and cotton, they are studded with semiprecious stones, glass and metal ornaments in the form of beads, disks and pendants.

FANCY KNOTS

I have never missed an opportunity to study Chinese lanyards wherever I have met them, but the Chinese have carried the art of knotting so far that there seems to be no end to their variety, and whenever I have found a good collection of Chinese knot work I have never failed to see something with which I was unfamiliar. When there isn't an entirely new knot, there is either a new twist to an old knot or a different way of combining two.

2474. Alongside is a Chinese lantern cord that was tied in a small, round, blue-silk braided cord.

To tie: Take a long cord and double it, leaving a loop four inches long. Proceed to complete one knot at a time, taking care to keep the length of the two strands, as well as the knots themselves, symmetrical.

Hold the structure with the loop down, and tie a SAILOR'S ROUND KNIFE LANYARD KNOT, sometimes called TWO-CORD DIAMOND KNOT. The method of tying this is given as ✳787.

2475, 2476. The KNIFE LANYARD KNOT is followed by two opposite (left and right) CARRICK BENDS a short distance apart. The drawing will give an idea of the spacing and proportions of the cord.

2477. The assembled knot which comes next consists of two small FOUR-PART CROWN BUTTERFLY KNOTS and two CARRICK BENDS, which should be worked until the combined knot is nearly round.

2478. Two WALL KNOTS follow, separating two colored and gilded beads.

2479. Another assembled knot is in the center of the cord and is made up of two FOUR-PART CROWN BUTTERFLIES and two THREE-PART CROWN BUTTERFLIES.

2480. Around the two cords in the center is a THREE-LEAD, FOUR-BIGHT, THREE-PLY TURK'S-HEAD in silver-wound wire cord.

2481. Then follow two WALLS (✳2478) separating two beads, and below that a soapstone disk in imitation of mutton-fat jade. Additional silk threads lead across the disk and these are seized to the cords with silver thread at the top and bottom of the disk. In the center of the disk is a silver TURK'S-HEAD.

There are three more beads below the disk and after a considerable uncomplicated length of two parallel cords a tassel is added.

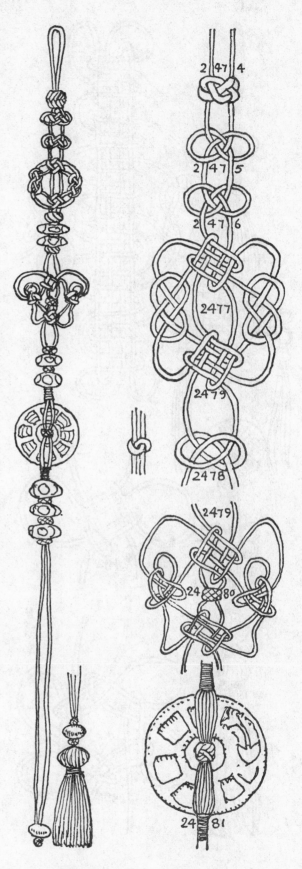

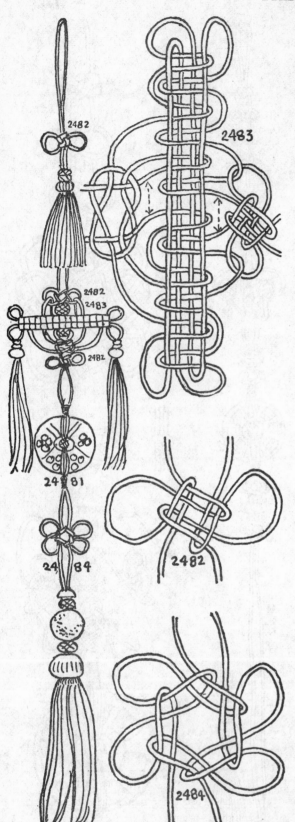

2482. A more elaborate Chinese lantern cord is made of narrow sage-green cotton sinnet, platted as ⌗2967, twenty-seven inches in length. The tassels are of red silk thread and the TURK'S-HEADS are of parti-colored wire-wound silk and silver-covered wire. To tie: Double a long cord. As the take-up differs with the size of the cord, it is difficult to specify the length. Leaving a five-inch loop, tie a FOUR-CROWN BUTTERFLY KNOT (⌗811).

Below this are two THREE-LEAD, FOUR-BIGHT, TWO-PLY WIRE TURK'S-HEADS, the upper one silver-covered, the lower blue-silk-covered. Close to this is a tassel of red silk thread, three and one half inches long.

2483. A second FOUR-CROWN BUTTERFLY (⌗2482) is added below the tassel and then the elaborate KNOT ⌗2483 (detailed at the left) is carefully pinned out on the board. The horizontal bar of the original knot was stiffened with a piece of bone, two and one half inches long, in shape exactly like the mahjong counters we used to play with. There are two THREE-LEAD, FOUR-BIGHT, TWO-PLY TURK'S-HEADS which encircle the center cords. The positions of the TURK'S-HEADS are indicated by double-headed arrows in the right upper diagram. The upper of these two TURK'S-HEADS is of silver, the lower red.

Suspended from the ends of the crossbar are tassels made over round buttons one half inch in diameter. The tassels are four and a half inches long and of red silk. Above each of these are two TURK'S-HEADS, the upper one silver, the lower one blue. Tasselmaking is described in Chapter 41.

Close to KNOT ⌗2483, but not interlocking with it, is another knot (⌗2482).

An inch and a quarter below the last-mentioned knot is the top of a glass disk, one and five eighths inches in diameter, of imitation jade. The disk is perforated at the center and a red silk TURK'S-HEAD (⌗2481) holds the strands together through this. A smooth seizing, a quarter of an inch wide, of dark linen thread, holds the disk in place at both top and bottom. The seizing has been wound with silk thread to make a blue stripe around the center at either side of the TURK'S-HEAD. The outer edges of the seizing are of dark blue, the center light blue and the whole stripe is not more than one sixteenth of an inch wide.

2484. An inch and a quarter below the disk is tied a BUTTERFLY KNOT of the same form as ⌗2455, already shown in this chapter.

An inch below this knot are two TURK'S-HEADS, the upper one silver, the lower one red. These are of larger wire (about one thirty-second of an inch) than those previously described, which so far have been of uniform size.

Below these two TURK'S-HEADS is a round silver-lined glass bead five eighths of an inch in diameter and below this is a bright green wire TURK'S-HEAD, about a quarter larger than those last described. Close to this is a ten-inch tassel of red silk made over a wooden mold seven eighths of an inch in diameter.

Methods of making tassels are shown in Chapter 41.

CHAPTER 32: SQUARE KNOTTING

But here's a Queen, when she rides abroad,
Is always knotting threads.

SIR CHARLES SEDLEY (1639–1701): From a Poem
Dedicated to Mary, Queen of William of Orange

Mary is held responsible for having introduced square knotting
into England, having herself become adept in the art while living
in Holland.

Square knotting is supposed to have originated in Arabia, where
it was called macramé which means in Arabic *fringe*. Apparently
the practice was first applied and limited to coarse cord fringes,
until it became known in Italy, at the time of the Crusades. Here
nuns, using a much finer material, developed it into a lacelike textile
of great beauty and strength. For a long time it was employed almost exclusively for altar cloths, church vestments and the like.
There was (at least until recently) in the Louvre a painting by Paul
Veronese (1528–88) of "The Supper of Simon the Canaanite." A
square knotted table cover formed an important part of the painted
design.

Exactly when the sailor first took up square knotting is not known.
But in the middle of the nineteenth century crews in both the American and British Navies specialized in square knotting, perhaps because their narrow quarters gave little or no opportunity for stowing larger work.

Much of the square knot work aboard ship took the form of
fringes for sea-chest covers, tablecloths, shelf covers, binnacle, sky-

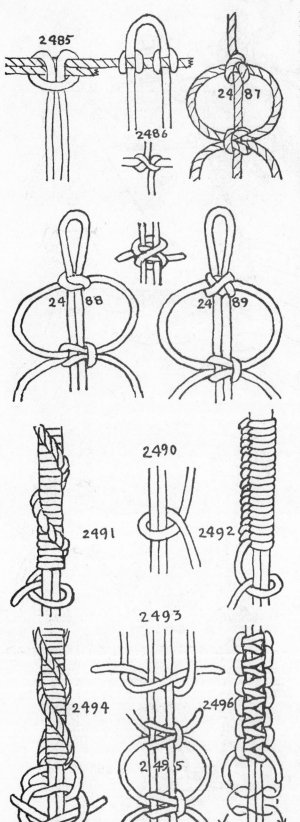

light, capstan, wheel and bell covers and, on whalers, line tub covers. Bell and yoke ropes and occasionally even manropes were square knotted. Spray screens for launches, and also "eye screens," for accommodation ladders, were required at a time when women were less frankly bifurcated than at present. Knotted belts, handbags, watch guards, leashes, lanyards, light, shade and bell pulls are made at the present time, and no longer ago than last summer I saw, in a magazine advertisement, the photograph of what was unquestionably a knotted bathing suit.

Square knotting is essentially a variety of lacemaking that is closely related to tatting and pillow lacemaking. Like tatting, the component knots are simple and few and the beauty of the product depends on both the design and the uniformity of the workmanship.

Only two elementary knots are essential. These are the HALF KNOT (called the "MACRAMÉ KNOT") and the HALF HITCH (called the "TATTING KNOT"). Various combinations of these two, in varying numbers, are termed *bars*. About a dozen of these bars are important enough to bear distinguishing names.

Merchant seamen are apt to introduce sailor's knots into their square knotting, but the great majority of examples of square knotting that I have seen contain no knots beyond the two that have been named.

Square knot design is too large a subject to be considered here, even if design were not outside the scope of the present work. The basic knots and bars of square knotting are given and several examples of the work will be described, including the sailor-made handbag that is reproduced among the frontispieces.

Those who are interested in square knot design will find the following current books of assistance. They are replete with practicable designs and suggestions and moreover are inexpensive. Herwig, *Square Knot Book* (elementary instruction); and De Dillmont, *Macramé*, which is very handsomely illustrated.

2485. Square knotting is started with a series of cords made fast to a foundation cord, which may be either single or double. For close spacing, the cords are middled and secured to the heading or foundation with COW HITCHES (#56). The length of the cords required is generally about seven or eight times the length of the finished product. Each cord is middled and made fast to the foundation.

2486. If wider spacing is required, secure the cords to the foundation with CLOVE HITCHES (#53) which may be either single or double. Long cords may be either wound on bobbins or they may be wound over the fingers and held with elastic bands (#3085).

2487. To add two strands to one, in a lanyard or other pattern: Tie a HALF HITCH in the shorter cord around the center of the long or leader cord.

2488. The HALF KNOT is ordinarily used in adding two cords to a double warp, but the ends are not quite at the same level.

2489. The CONSTRICTOR KNOT will be found firmer and more symmetrical for the purpose, although it bulks somewhat larger.

2490. The HALF HITCH, also called the TATTING KNOT, is one of the two basic knots of square knotting, the HALF KNOT being the other one. One or the other or both of these appear in every square knotted bar.

2491. The CORKSCREW BAR shows the HALF HITCH tied in a uniform series which causes it to helix down the leader cord.

2492. The BUTTONHOLE BAR is exactly the same as the foregoing, except that it is not allowed to twist. It is tied a little slacker and forced to lie straight until the end is secured.

2493. The HALF KNOT, also called the MACRAMÉ KNOT, is the second of the basic knots of square knotting. Both of these are tied around a *leader cord or warp* which hangs from the foundation cord.

2494. If a series of identical HALF KNOTS is made the bar will helix, forming what is called a TWISTED or BANNISTER BAR. Two identical HALF KNOTS constitute a GRANNY KNOT.

2495. The SQUARE KNOT consists of two HALF KNOTS, one left and one right, one superimposed over the other. This is called a SOLOMON KNOT when tied around a leader cord.

2496. A series of alternating LEFT and RIGHT HALF KNOTS forms a SOLOMON BAR, which has no tendency to twist. This is the typical knot that is responsible for the name *square knotting*.

2497. The SINGLE TATTED BAR may have either a single or double warp and is tied with a single cord in alternating LEFT and RIGHT HALF HITCHES. There is no tendency to twist and the effect is somewhat similar to buttonholing.

2498. The DOUBLE TATTED BAR is tied with two cords over either a single or double warp, a COW HITCH being tied alternately with first one and then the other cord.

2499. If a cord proves too short, splice it while it is being used as the core for a BEADED BAR (#2508). Tease the two ends and scrape them to a taper. Divide each end in three parts and crotch the two ends. Twist them to the right, and, with a piece of thread the same color as the cord, serve them against the twist or lay. This splice is described more fully as #2686.

2500. The SINGLE GENOESE BAR consists of LEFT and RIGHT HALF HITCHES tied alternately with two cords around a double warp.

2501. The DOUBLE GENOESE BAR consists of CLOVE HITCHES tied alternately with two cords around a double warp.

2502. The WAVED or SHELL BAR is tied with two warps and two cords. Put on five identical LEFT HALF HITCHES or TATTING KNOTS with the left cord while the right cord remains inert. Then lay out the left cord and tie five identical RIGHT HALF HITCHES with the right cord. Continue to do this, alternating with the right and left cord. Don't allow the cord to twist.

2503. The WAVED or SHELL BAR may be tied with seven identical HALF HITCHES. Seven and five appear to be the conventional number of hitches to employ for this particular bar.

2504. SINGLE TATTED CHAIN is also called the "SEESAW KNOT." Although much used in square knotting, this is not termed a bar. The distinction is made because this knot is not tied over a warp. It consists of alternate HALF HITCHES tied in two cords alternately around each other.

2505. The DOUBLE TATTED CHAIN is similar but is tied with two double cords. Care must be exercised to keep the knots uniform.

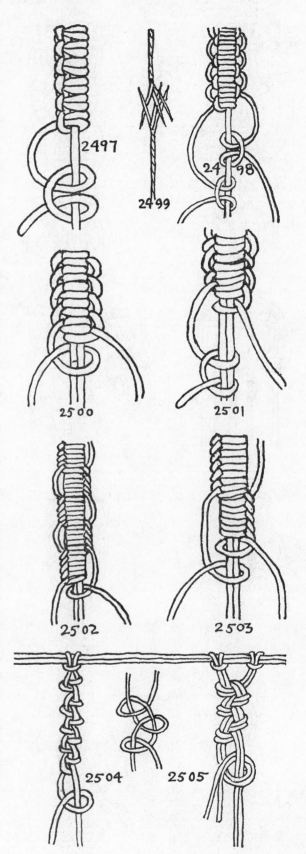

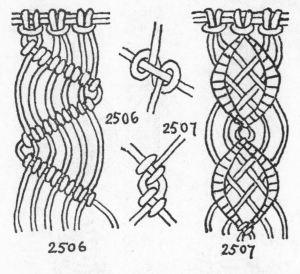

2506. ZIGZAG BARS. Three working cords are doubled and secured to the foundation cord. The *leader* or *warp* zigzags the whole length of the structure and the *working* or *knotting* threads are tied to it with CLOVE HITCHES. A line of knots staggers right and left down the length of the structure.

2507. INTERTWINED BARS. Three strands are doubled and secured to the foundation. The two center ones are employed as leaders. The outside ones are turned inward and each is clove hitched to the nearest leader. The four working strands are then crowned as illustrated and, continuing in the same diagonal in which they were started, are clove hitched again, but to the opposite leaders, which have been turned inward. The leaders are now at the center, where they are clove hitched to each other as shown in the lower drawing. After this the same figure is repeated until the structure has the desired length.

2508. A BEADED BAR starts the same as the ZIGZAG BAR (#2506), but several bars are made parallel and close to each other, and one cord serves as a leader for only one diagonal, after which the next cord becomes the leader.

2509. OPPOSED BARS. The illustration shows two parallel BEADED BARS tied in close contact. Six doubled strands are employed and are divided into two units, the right unit being tied the reverse of the left.

When two BEADED BARS have been tied in both halves, the right leader is clove hitched around the left and the two leaders cross to opposite sides. The BEADED BARS are made as before, but in such way that a DOUBLE BAR zigzags down each half of the pattern.

2510. A JAPANESE KNOT that was tied with several SOLOMON KNOTS (#2496).

Two cords are doubled and laid parallel. At the center they are doubled, forming two bights and four parallel strands. The outer ends of the two bights are square knotted around the two center strands. After this knot is tied the two working strands are formed into the large circle and remain inactive while the other two ends that served as leaders for the first SQUARE KNOT are each half hitched to one side of the circle and then tied together in a SQUARE KNOT at the center. They then are each half hitched again to the side of the circle. Having completed this, they are brought to the center as leaders and the ends which form the large circle are square knotted around them.

2511. This tassel from a gangway fender was one of a pair. It was made of white painted sash cord, and is the only thing of the sort that I have ever seen. It is sailor work and was found in the Boston Antique Shop. The end bears a TURK'S-HEAD tassel.

2512. A knot shown by Bocher. It is built up of several TRUE-LOVER'S KNOTS, and only the two wings suggest square knotting. First tie the top and center TRUE-LOVER'S KNOTS without any interlacement. Then cross the loop tips at either side and pin out on a board. After this tie the lower HALF KNOT of the lower TRUE-LOVER'S KNOT, reeve the ends as pictured, tie the upper half of the TRUE-LOVER'S KNOT and stick the ends down through the lower half.

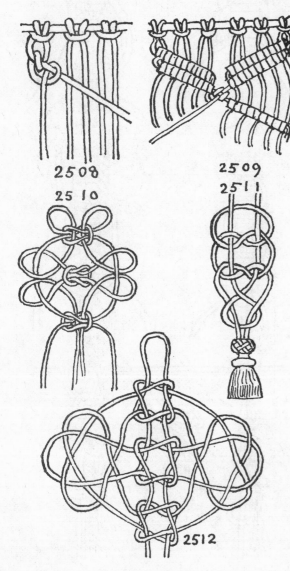

2513. The Japanese lanyards shown on this page are interesting because they combine sailor's knots, fancy knots, PRIEST CORD KNOTS and macramé. No one except a Japanese or a sailor would attempt such a salmagundi.

In the left lanyard one cord is half hitched to the bight of another, as №2487, and, using the single cord as a warp or leader, a SOLOMON BAR of six HALF KNOTS is made with the other two strands, as №2496. This is followed by an uncomplicated section of two and one half inches, then a SOLOMON KNOT (№2496), followed by another uncomplicated two and one half inches. It is then finished off with six HALF KNOTS.

2514. A FOUR-BIGHT, THREE-LEAD, THREE-PLY TURK'S-HEAD.

2515. A knot similar to PRIEST CORD KNOT №2379 except that it has one less OVERHAND KNOT to a side and is made with a single strand instead of a doubled one.

The lower half of the lanyard is a replica of the upper half in the reverse except that the final knot is a THREE-STRAND DIAMOND KNOT (№693) instead of a TURK'S-HEAD.

2516. This diagram portrays one of the eight vertical panels that are repeated around the old sailor's handbag which is shown as one of the frontispieces. The handle (see frontispiece) has no square knotting on it. The grip is needle hitched (№3544) and finished off with a FOUR-LEAD, THREE-BIGHT, FOUR-PLY TURK'S-HEAD, edged and tipped with turkey-red cotton cloth. The legs are FOUR-STRAND ROUND SINNET, four cords to each strand, and the knots in the ends are the ACORNS described on page 565.

Each of these vertical sections consists of twenty cords. They are secured to a double foundation cord with COW or BALE SLING HITCHES, and a second (single) foundation below the first is secured with CLOVE HITCHES. There are four horizontal sections in the bag, divided horizontally with single foundation cords, and the first and third of these consist of a series of "bars," each bar of four cords, and every fourth bar around the bag consists of four uncomplicated parallel cords. The remaining three spaces are filled up with four different bars in no regular order, except that two alike are not found in the same panel. The four are DOUBLE TATTED BAR №2505, TWISTED BAR №2493, SOLOMON BAR №2496, and GENOA BAR №2500.

The second and fourth horizontal sections are made of BEADED BARS (№2508), the strands between them being made up into SINGLE TATTED CHAINS (№2504). Vertically around the center in the second horizontal section a SOLOMON BAR is arranged TURK'S-HEAD fashion.

2517. Below the fourth horizontal section SINGLE BEADED BARS are made (№2508 and №2509) and then a knotted fringe is added (see page 584).

2518. The second Japanese lanyard is started as the other and made into a long BANNISTER BAR with a single cord warp (№2493).

2519. When close to the center, a DOUBLE WALL KNOT is tied, as detailed at the bottom of the page.

2520. The center knot consists of two TRUE-LOVER'S KNOTS with the loops interlaced so that they form a CARRICK BEND. A THREE-LEAD, FOUR-BIGHT, THREE-PLY TURK'S-HEAD is added at the center.

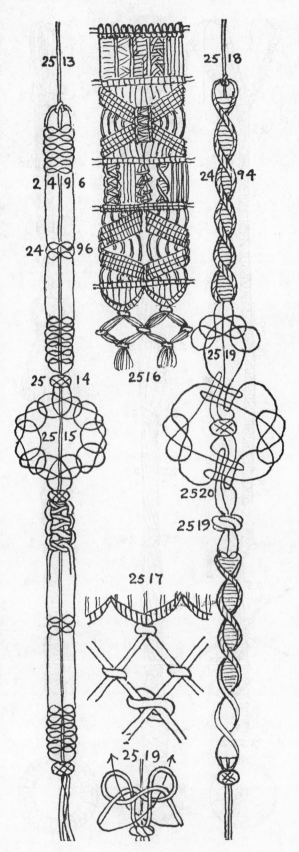

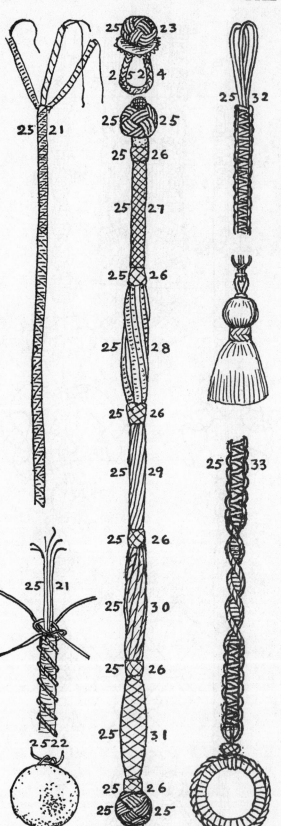

2521. Captain Albert Whitney, of Staten Island, made the accompanying lanyard of twelve small cords.

The ball was probably made first, and the six cords were middled and seized around it. Eight of these strands form a core for the lanyard.

The four remaining strands are spaced evenly around the core and two opposite ones are knotted together. Then the other pair is knotted in the same direction with identical HALF KNOTS. They must be tied tightly and care exercised that the corkscrewing pairs are evenly spaced ninety degrees apart. Each pair is knotted forty times (the two pairs make eighty times) to form a section. Then the knots are reversed and another section of eighty knots is made, which helix in the opposite direction. The cord has twelve sections of this helix, after which the end is finished off by dividing the twelve strands into three parts. Two parts of four strands each are made up into TWISTED BARS (#2493) and one into SOLOMON BAR #2496. Presumably this cord was intended for a bell lanyard.

2522. Directions are given for making the ball on page 568.

2523. A square knotted yoke rope is in the collection of the New Bedford Whaling Museum, made over a two-inch cotton rope.

The top section is seized into the rudder yoke of a yawl boat or gig. The round knob consists of a FIVE-LEAD, FOUR-BIGHT, EIGHT-PLY TURK'S-HEAD that is tied over a MANROPE KNOT.

2524. A section of EIGHT-STRAND SQUARE SINNET (#3001) into which the yoke rope is buttoned.

2525. The end of the yoke rope, which is tied into a MATTHEW WALKER KNOT, is tufted. Below this knot thirty-two strands of fishline are evenly seized around the rope. The joint is covered with TURK'S-HEAD #2523.

2526. A FIVE-LEAD, FOUR-BIGHT, FOUR-PLY TURK'S-HEAD divides the several sections.

2527. COACHWHIPPING or CROSS-POINTING (#3022) of sixteen leads, two-ply (thirty-two strands of fishline in all).

2528. Ten SOLOMON BARS. Two of them have a double warp, the rest have single warps. There are thirty-two strands in all and seventy HALF KNOTS in each of the SOLOMON BARS.

2529. Needlework (#3547) which resembles a ribbed stocking.

2530. TWISTED or BANNISTER BARS of the same length, number and size as #2528.

2531. EIGHT-LEAD, FOUR-PLY COACHWHIPPING. This section of rope is moused (#3499) to make a good handle with which to steer. Numbers 2527, 2529, and 2531 should be a little shorter than #2528 and #2530. The end is the same as #2525.

2532. A window-shade or electric-light pull may be tied with any of the bars shown on pages 400 and 401 using two doubled cords for a loop, and finishing off with one of the tassels shown in Chapter 41.

2533. This is similar to the last except that a loop is formed in the end, under the TURK'S-HEAD.

The lanyard is made of alternate sections of SOLOMON and BANNISTER BARS. A metal ring is ringbolt hitched (#3605) and secured to the lanyard with a RING HITCH.

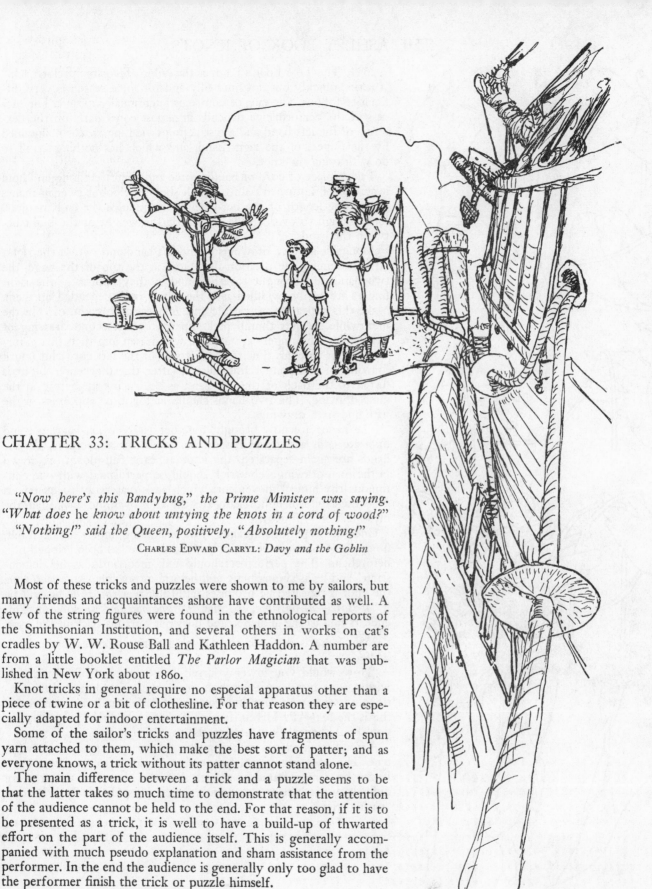

CHAPTER 33: TRICKS AND PUZZLES

"Now here's this Bandybug," the Prime Minister was saying.
"What does he know about untying the knots in a cord of wood?"
"Nothing!" said the Queen, positively. "Absolutely nothing!"
CHARLES EDWARD CARRYL: *Davy and the Goblin*

Most of these tricks and puzzles were shown to me by sailors, but many friends and acquaintances ashore have contributed as well. A few of the string figures were found in the ethnological reports of the Smithsonian Institution, and several others in works on cat's cradles by W. W. Rouse Ball and Kathleen Haddon. A number are from a little booklet entitled *The Parlor Magician* that was published in New York about 1860.

Knot tricks in general require no especial apparatus other than a piece of twine or a bit of clothesline. For that reason they are especially adapted for indoor entertainment.

Some of the sailor's tricks and puzzles have fragments of spun yarn attached to them, which make the best sort of patter; and as everyone knows, a trick without its patter cannot stand alone.

The main difference between a trick and a puzzle seems to be that the latter takes so much time to demonstrate that the attention of the audience cannot be held to the end. For that reason, if it is to be presented as a trick, it is well to have a build-up of thwarted effort on the part of the audience itself. This is generally accompanied with much pseudo explanation and sham assistance from the performer. In the end the audience is generally only too glad to have the performer finish the trick or puzzle himself.

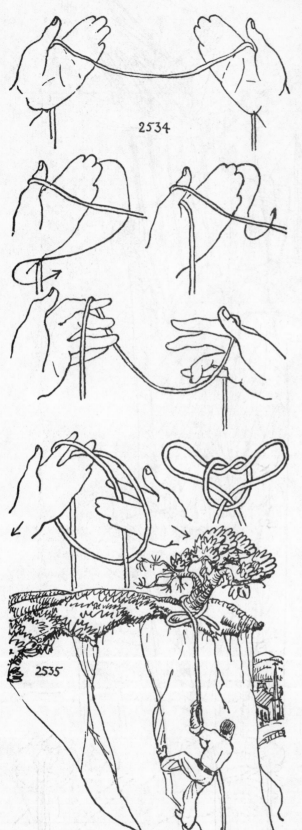

2534

2535

2534. The TOM FOOL'S KNOT is the sailor's favorite "parlor trick." It is tied quickly but not hurriedly and for some reason is very difficult to follow. The eye, of course, is intentionally misled. The success of the performance depends in almost equal parts on the dexterity of the left hand and a distracting twiddling that is maintained by the fingers of the right hand, and which has nothing at all to do with tying the knot.

Take a piece of cord or banding five and a half feet long and hold it across the upturned palms, which should be about twenty inches apart. The length of the cord is important since the ends must be long enough to overbalance by a little the weight of the bight between the hands.

Alongside are five drawings of the left hand and two of the right. After assuming the position illustrated at the top of the page, the two hands are brought together, and as they approach, the right fingers are busily twiddled as if the whole trick depended on them. Make this appear as reasonable and as necessary as you can. In the meanwhile the left thumb picks up the cord (second drawing of left hand). The fingers are at once withdrawn and then thrust forward again, but this time to the left side of the left cord end (third drawing of left hand). Immediately after this the center bight is flirted to the back of the left hand as shown by the arrow in the same drawing. The two hands should at this time appear as in the fifth and sixth drawings.

The hands are now brought together (left lower diagram), and opposite ends are grasped with the finger tips as pictured. As the hands are again separated, the knot appears, full-blown, as drawn in the final drawing. The trick should be performed with one continuous rhythmical movement, which adds materially to its effect.

As the exhibitor unhurriedly ties the knot over and over again the mystification will grow.

Once the hypnotic influence of the twiddling fingers has been felt, no one is going to solve the problem unless he has been "tipped off" beforehand. The performer should talk incessantly as he demonstrates and be as sympathetic and helpful as possible. And each time the knot is repeated he promises faithfully that *this time* he will tie it "*as slowly as possible,*" so that "*no one can fail*" to solve it. This endears him to the audience and does not hurt his trick in the least.

2535. Here is depicted the sailor's favorite puzzle for the landlubber.

"How would you lower yourself from the edge of a precipice, with a rope just long enough to reach the ground, and then continue on your way carrying your rope with you?" The answer to this is the SLIPPERY HITCH. It is a safe knot when tied properly, but you should never allow anyone else to tie it for you.

A good trick should always puzzle, but the reverse is not always true. The knot just given, I should say, belongs to the latter class. It can be demonstrated as a trick, but the place and the tree are difficult to produce at a moment's notice. Most decidedly it is not a "parlor trick."

TRICKS AND PUZZLES

The problems that are based on well-known practical knots generally prove the most interesting, since the spectator finds himself on familiar ground. The next few examples depict one-hand methods of tying practical knots that ordinarily require two hands.

2536. The OVERHAND KNOT. To tie with one hand: Pick up the string, and allow a short end to fall to the back of the hand; engage the little finger in the bight that crosses the palm, turn the hand palm downward, and grasp the short end with the fore and second fingers. Incline the hand downward; shake the loop from around the hand and an OVERHAND KNOT will be found in the string.

2537. To tie a NOOSE with one hand is almost a repetition of the last knot. But the end at the back of the hand must be longer, and the fore and second fingers grasp a bight instead of the end. When the loop around the back of the hand is shaken off it will form a NOOSE. Do not hesitate to show this knot immediately after the other, as the spectators will assume that the difference is fundamental although it really is superficial.

2538, 2539. The next two knots are cowboy tricks to be tied with a lariat; they were shown to me by a trouper who used to spin a rope in the Pantages circuit. A stiff rope, either hard plain-laid, or of the sash-cord type, is employed with a heavy honda in the end. This may be an EYE SPLICE around a thimble, or an eye that is wrapped or served with copper wire.

The standing end of the rope hangs over the back of the wrist and a loop is formed in the hand which is held in two places as illustrated, the little finger and the thumb and forefinger being engaged. The loop should be about six inches in diameter. The honda end is now dropped over the back of the hand. Hold the forearm horizontal with the honda hanging just clear of the ground.

A smooth upward jerk is made, strong enough to bring the honda to hand. As it pauses at the top of its trajectory the loop in hand is gently swayed either left or right, around the honda, as indicated in the diagram. Number 2538 forms an OVERHAND KNOT.

Number 2539 forms either a FIGURE-EIGHT KNOT or its perversion, which is called by the cowboy a PRETZEL KNOT. The latter is the knot shown at the left of the FIGURE-EIGHT. The aim is to swing the loop so smoothly and slightly that it appears as if the jerk were the whole trick. This is easier than one might think.

2540. To tie a RING or BALE SLING HITCH with one hand: Hang a loop over the thumb, with both ends crossing the palm. Engage the little finger with the end that hangs from the back of the thumb and bring it forward *underneath* the other end. Then transfer it from the little finger to the tip of the forefinger. The knot is completed when the thumb and forefinger are brought together and the two bights are slipped to the thumb.

The following series of knots consists of "trick" ways of tying the familiar and practical CLOVE HITCH. Most of these will, on occasion, prove to be practical methods. Number 2543 is perhaps the best and certainly the quickest way there is to tie the CLOVE HITCH in large rope.

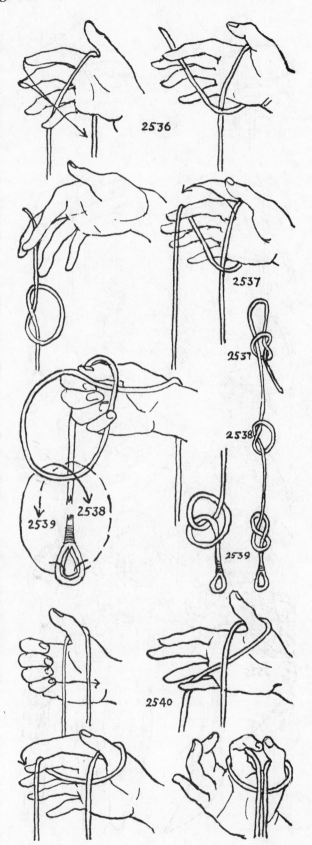

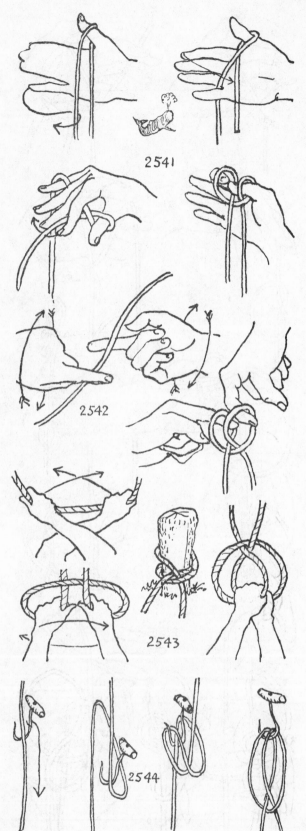

2541

2542

2543

2544

2541. A method of tying this familiar knot with one hand. If the technique given is followed carefully, after a little practice it will be found that the knot can be tied almost instantaneously. After the position of the third diagram is reached and the cord grasped with the two fingers, the hand should be held erect (fingers up) and at once the loops will fall into the position of the fourth diagram; which completes the knot as the thumb and forefinger are brought together.

2542. To tie a CLOVE HITCH with two fingers is far simpler than it appears. It is based on a common practical method which follows this, in which two hands are employed. Hold the right hand palm up. Place the forefinger under the string, which is laid flat on the table. Hold the left hand palm down, forefinger on top of the string. Grip the string with the forefingers and rotate each hand a half turn. Then without turning them further place the hitch from the right finger against the tip of the left forefinger, which completes the knot.

2543. The last two knots, #2541 and #2542, should be tied in small material but this one is ordinarily tied in heavy rope or hawser. It was shown to me by E. E. du Pont under the title "STEAMBOAT HITCH." It is employed on coastwise and river steamers. In a large hawser the bight, which in the first diagram is pictured as a straight piece of rope held between two hands, should be gathered into a loop or bight containing sufficient material to pass around whatever object the hitch is designed for. If this is a pile on a wharf, as much as six or ten feet of rope may be required between the two hands. The hitch formed will be in diameter about one third the length of this bight, but sufficient allowance must be made so that it will drop easily over a post, bollard or pile.

The arms are crossed as far as possible, backs of hands are held uppermost and with right forearm on top. The rope is grasped firmly, and, with the backs of the hands kept constantly uppermost, the arms are rotated until the left hand is on top in the position of the last diagram. Examination will show that a CLOVE HITCH of large size has been tied. Although often tied as a trick, this is one of the most practical ways to form the knot.

2544. The *bale hook method* of tying the CLOVE HITCH was shown to me by a North River stevedore. It is the same thing as the common sailor's way of picking one from the deck with one hand while his other hand is occupied. In the latter case use a hand instead of a hook. A little practice may be required to learn the ways of the bale hook, unless you were born a stevedore.

2545. This knot was mislaid.

2546. To convert an ordinary NOOSE into a CLOVE HITCH. This may be used successfully either as a puzzle or a trick. Arrange the NOOSE carefully as pictured before going ahead with the trick. It must be tied very loosely so that the bight may be pulled out sufficiently to pass around the post. As it is pulled out it is given a half twist to the left before being dropped over the post. To make it lie fair this bight should be dropped below the turn that is already around the post.

2547. A CLOVE HITCH from two round turns. Nothing could be simpler than this, but it is rather surprising when the hitch appears. The turns are not twisted sidewise in the same plane; the right one comes forward and up, the left one goes backward and up. When the two meet the knot is formed.

2548. A series of hitches formed over the left hand. Flexible clothesline is recommended for this trick. Loops are twirled with the right hand and caught on the left hand, which is darted forward to intercept them. With a little practice the process can be exceedingly rapid. If two hitches only are made the result is a CLOVE HITCH.

2549. To convert Two HALF HITCHES into a BOWLINE. Captain Charles W. Smith always told a story while tying this knot. The story is employed as patter and with the last word the knot is completed. I have heard the same story told by other sailors without any considerable variation, and it is apparently old and a part of the folklore of the sea. This is Captain Smith's story as nearly in his own words as I can recall them:

"A bum caught a line that was tossed to shore *from a ship*, and made fast with two half hitches. 'Not that way, you damn ninny!'" (Ninny was Captain Smith's ultimate cuss word.) "'Put a bowline in that there blankety-blank line and be damn quick about it,' bawls the mate from deck.

"'Bowline it is, sir!' says the bum, and he puts the end down through and hauls her taut, and damned if it *wa'n't* a bowline!" Of course this procedure makes a LEFT-HAND BOWLINE which is not so secure as the BOWLINE proper. After the TWO HALF HITCHES have been loosely tied the end is laid up parallel with its own part and the two are together hauled down through the loop of the original TWO HALF HITCHES. In this way a new loop is formed and the first one is removed by pulling on the standing part.

2550. The following is a somewhat more cumbersome method that sometimes goes with the same story. But this one retains the original loop made by the first TWO HALF HITCHES. Like the former, it makes a LEFT-HAND BOWLINE when the rather elaborate conglomerate of the second diagram is capsized into its final form. It was first shown to me by John B. Cornell, of Cuttyhunk.

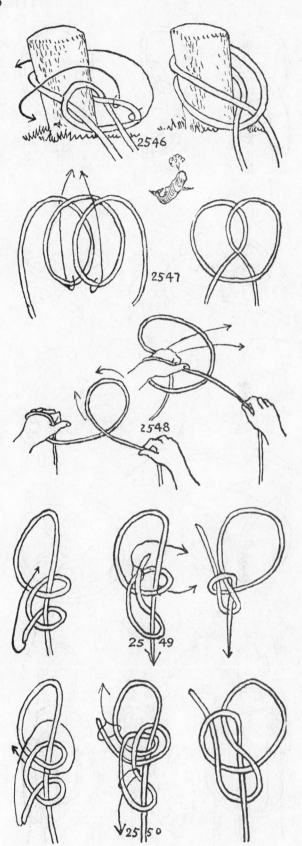

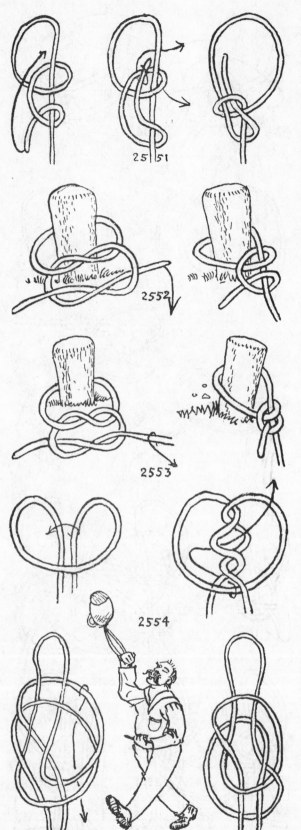

2551

2552

2553

2554

2551. As a trick the foregoing seems preferable to this which follows, for the reason that Two Half Hitches is the commonest of all hitches; but the fact remains that they capsize into a Left-Hand Bowline, which is scorned by the sailor. The Right-Hand Bowline, which is a real sailor's knot, may be made in a manner similar to ⚓2549 but is commenced with Reversed Half Hitches. The latter is a knot that is occasionally used ashore but is seldom seen aboard ship. In performing the knot as a trick the same "business" and "patter" are used and the knot tied in the same way as ⚓2549.

2552. A Square Knot may be capsized into Reversed Half Hitches, and under some circumstances this is a very practical way to make the knot. When tied as a trick, the audience should be requested to name the knot that is being tied. After they have announced that it *is* a Square Knot, the performer examines it with some surprise and is forced to announce that it is something quite different, in fact Reversed Half Hitches.

2553. A Granny Knot capsizes into Two Half Hitches. As Two Half Hitches is more common, and the name much better known to the layman than the last, this perhaps provides the better trick. Most of the audience will be able to recognize and name the Granny, which is first tied. When the performer produces the Two Half Hitches, the finished knot proves equally familiar. If the single jerk, which is all that is required to effect the change, is somewhat obscured, the mystification is complete and the fact that most everyone knows both these knots adds greatly to the interest.

2554. The Jug or Jar Sling is a highly specialized knot that serves one exceedingly practical purpose. But it is little known to the general public. Years ago I carried an alcohol cookstove in my boat, and one day I cruised into a small Cape Cod harbor where I replenished my supply of fuel at the local drugstore. Someone became interested in the Jug Sling Knot that I had on my one-gallon bottle, and to demonstrate its security I swung the bottle around and over my head, and of course up over the glass counters, much as one would whirl an Indian club. I was intent on my demonstration and the barks and screams of the druggist at first failed to distract me. It seemed that he resented the performance but dared not physically interfere for fear of precipitating a catastrophe. I have always attributed my safe exit from the shop to the presence of mind which prompted me to continue to oscillate the bottle until I was well outside the door.

I believe that a knowledge of this particular knot would have been of great value to that druggist. It would have helped him to market larger and fuller bottles. Moreover a demonstration now and then, of the sort that I had afforded, would undoubtedly have brought trade to his door.

2555. The Magnus or Rolling Hitch is an exceedingly practical knot that is easily converted into a trick. Its success depends on the glibness of the performer.

After the knot is tied, ask a spectator to pull on it strongly. Put your hand on the rope, ostensibly to find if it is working satisfactorily, and with an easy sweeping gesture slide the knot toward the puller, who will at once seat himself on the floor.

All humor, according to Mark Twain, is based on the enjoyment of a little suffering that is experienced by someone else.

2556. A puzzle. If you ever find yourself up a pole, with a rope just long enough to reach the ground, how do you lower yourself by means of the rope and then continue on your way, taking the rope along with you? Tie the knot shown and shake it from the pole when you've reached the bottom. It is, however, a dangerous knot to be careless with.

2557. The AWNING KNOT. Tie the knot and jam the second turn down, inside the first, and place a cushion on the floor. Announce that you will pull against the knot and that at "the word of command" the knot will spill and that you will then seat yourself on the cushion. Make your own choice of a magic word. Pronounce it, and in all probability nothing will happen. If anything does happen the trick is at once successful and you pass on to something else. But if nothing happens "command" the knot several times with rising anger, pulling steadily against it, then, losing your temper completely, you kick the knot, and at once you find yourself seated.

2558. The "TUG-OF-WAR KNOT." This provides a variation of the trick already given as ⌗2555. Secure two ardent young investigators.

Put one hand on each knot and tell the contestants to "start pulling gradually." When they are well off balance and have pulled to their hearts' content, slide the two parts quickly together and the knot will decide the winner. Select boys from twelve to fifteen, because at that age they do not bruise easily and will enjoy the fun as much as anyone else.

2559. The MONKEY CHAIN. A CHAIN SINNET is often used in vaudeville and circus to give the audience a mild thrill. The performer, suspended aloft and swinging over the heads of the audience, lets go the ends of the chain and apparently is flung at the heads of the audience, but the drop is at most only two or three feet.

2560. To tie up a "Houdini." Take a soft cord and put a CONSTRICTOR KNOT about the two wrists of the victim. Draw up snugly but not enough to cut off circulation. Have a sharp knife ready to cut the cord.

2561. The BAG KNOT, also called the BREAD BAG KNOT. At sea a certain amount of hard bread or sea biscuit was allowed each watch and was kept in a heavy canvas bag. The story is that a thief was suspected and that a knot was fashioned, as here shown, which at first sight is hardly distinguishable from a REEF KNOT. The unwitting culprit, of course, always retied the bag with a REEF KNOT and so was invariably detected.

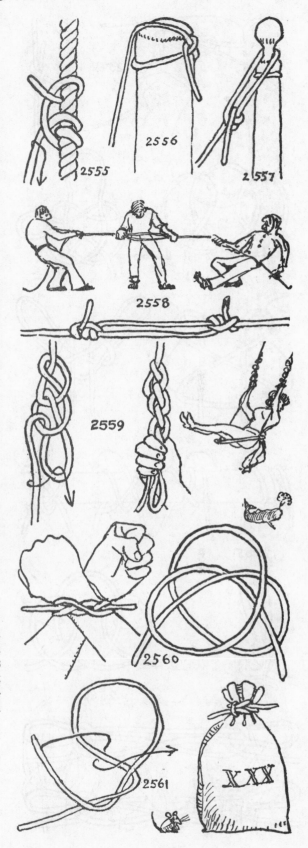

2556

2555

2557

2558

2559

2560

2561

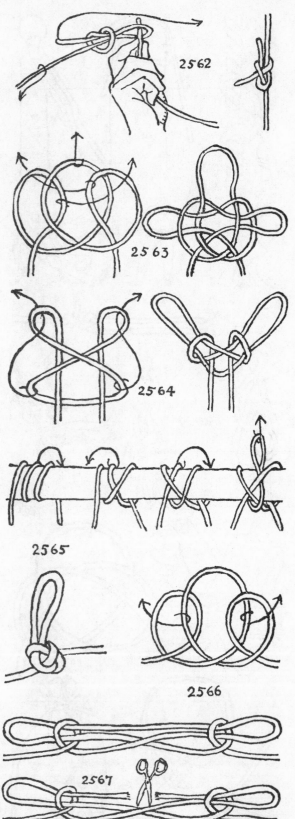

2562. The method of tying a SHEET BEND *to a short end* was taught me many years ago by Mrs. Thomas Knowles, who used it in her yarn while knitting. It is a knot with which to astound even the initiated. Few sailors know it, probably because it is unsuitable for large material.

A little practice will be required to find just how short an end may be tied, which varies with the material used, and also just how snug the NOOSE is to be drawn before it is slipped over the short end.

A spectator is asked to hold up a short end and a slack NOOSE is slipped around the upheld end. The two ends of the NOOSE are then pulled apart, until the short end that is held by the spectator is "swallowed," when it will be found that a SHEET BEND has been tied.

2563. In the next few tricks, certain well-known symmetrical knots are produced unexpectedly from a few simple turns or hitches. Their interest depends entirely on the ease and celerity with which they are tied. The first to be shown is the sailor's MASTHEAD or JURY MAST KNOT, which is employed practically as a temporary strap to which stays are led when erecting a jury mast or derrick. Three hitches are made, fairly large, and the three are extended as indicated by the arrows. Sometimes the top loop is pulled out with the teeth in lieu of a third hand, but a skillful sailor uses only his two hands. The side loops should be completely interlaced and then all three loops are extended in the same instant.

2564. The SPANISH BOWLINE, when put in heavy rope, provides an excellent means for slinging a ladder as a staging. When tying the knot as a "parlor trick" the two extended loops of the final diagram are drawn simultaneously through the upper loops shown in the first diagram. Start the knot as in the first diagram of ⅜2554, twist the two top loops a half turn each, turn the knot around and arrange as shown in the first drawing here.

2565. The FARMER'S LOOP. I found this knot in a farm bulletin, published at Cornell University and written by Professor H. W. Riley. Three loops may be taken with a soft cord around the left forefinger. Then with the right hand these loops are jumped, right, left, right, with dazzling rapidity, to form the finished loop, which is shown partly drawn out in the fourth diagram and completed in the fifth.

2566. The trick method of tying a SHEEPSHANK KNOT. Three hitches are made exactly as in ⅜2563 for the MASTHEAD KNOT but only the center hitch or loop is extended. For this reason the center hitch may be larger than the end ones. The two sides of the center hitch, shown in the first diagram, are held with the thumbs and forefingers and the ends of the cord are encircled with the little fingers and pulled upon. The end hitches close around the two end loops. The knot is produced with what appears to be a single jerk. This will require a little rehearsal.

2567. Cut the knot that was last tied, as shown in this diagram, and two spectators may be allowed to pull *steadily* on the two ends, but if jerked upon, the knot is apt to upset.

2568. The SHEEPSHANK WITH AN OVERHAND KNOT, also called "SWORD KNOT." So far as the sailor is concerned, this is purely a trick knot. Four hitches are made and then the four bights are pulled or jerked through opposite sides of the knot. Do not be concerned if at this point the knot appears bunchy and unattractive, as this merely adds to the effectiveness of the trick. Grasp the ends of the cord, count three and, at the count of three, give a strong jerk. If the rope straightens (as it sometimes will) and nothing results, do not allow your audience to think the failure wholly unexpected. The next time make the hitches or loops a little larger. When the knot finally appears, a quick prod may be needed to make it absolutely symmetrical.

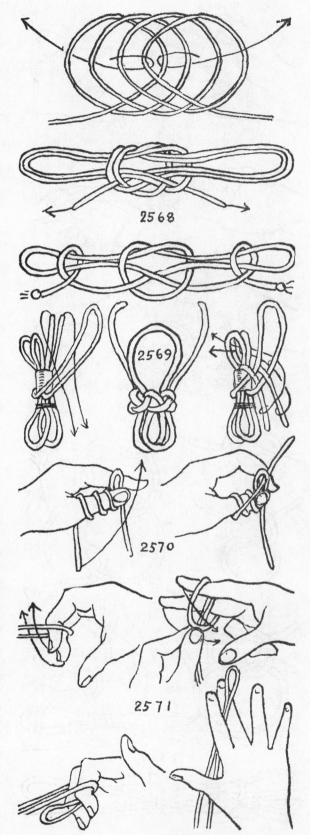

2569. The THEODORE KNOT. This is the cowboy's most elaborate *hackamore*, a name applied to any temporary or emergency bridle or halter. The knot was shown to me by Will James. It is based on the sailor's MULTI-STRAND DIAMOND KNOT and the trick is to succeed in tying it.

To tie: Double a long piece of cord and turn the ends up even with the center loop. Stop all four parts together at half length. Allow the ends and center loop to hang downward and stop the loop only above the first stop.

Turn the original center loop upward in a right diagonal, and reeve the ends down through it as in the first diagram. Next reeve the two ends upward and to the right, moving the left one first and tucking it through the top bight of the leg of the loop that was first tucked. Tuck the remaining end through the next bight to the right, cut the second stop and tighten the knot partially. Finally cut the first stop and draw the knot snug. After practice the knot should be tied in hand without employing any stops.

Philip Ashton Rollins tells me that this knot was originally called "FIADOR." It came from South America by way of Mexico. When Theodore Roosevelt visited our Southwest after the Spanish-American War, the name was changed to "THEODORE" quite spontaneously.

2570. Threading a loop: Leave an end about ten inches long and take several turns around the left thumb (four is about the right number) in the direction shown in the diagram, finishing with a *very small loop*, at the thumb end. The smallness of the loop makes the trick more effective. Announce that you will *drive* the end through the loop with one dart of the right hand. Take the left end in the right hand, aim the tip at the loop and approach the loop several times, then quickly dart the end directly *by the tip of the thumb* until it fetches, when it will be found that the loop is threaded. If the end is held taut it will not be noticed that the loop has been threaded in the wrong direction, but to make the matter doubly sure, the forefinger of the left hand may be retracted a bit, which will turn the loop in the right direction. The end that was darted has passed under the thumb, and one turn has disappeared from the thumb.

2571. "Rabbit in the Hole." Shown to me by Dr. John H. Cunningham, Waldo Howland and Melbourne Christopher, the professional knot magician. The latter is the most finished performer of knot tricks that I have ever had the pleasure of seeing at work.

This one belongs to that annoying "Just-see-if-you-can-do-it" class of tricks. The string is held for a moment as in the first diagram, then the remainder is done in a flash, and the little loop which represents the rabbit is held aloft.

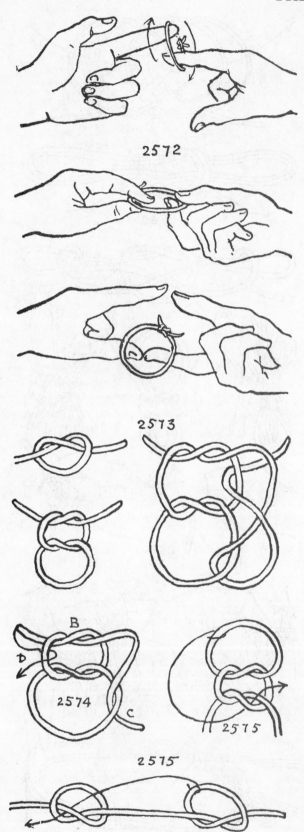

2572

2573

B
D
2574
C

2575

2575

2572. The Whirling Ring. Another "See-if-you-can-do-it" trick, equally easy, and just as annoying as the last. To perform the trick spin the hands around with the two finger tips inside the loop or ring. First one way, then reverse. Close the thumbs and forefingers of both hands when in the position of the second diagram, then move the hands together until the thumbs touch the tips of the opposite forefingers. Open both hands without separating opposite thumbs and forefingers. Although the ring appears to be still involved, it falls to the floor quite free. The trick is ridiculously simple and somewhat pointless, yet there are over one hundred million people in these United States alone who won't have the least idea of how to do it even after they have been shown. Dr. John H. Cunningham first showed it to me.

2573. An elusive knot. The effectiveness of this trick depends almost entirely on the patter. The feebler the patter, the more suitable it seems to be. This is the way I got it from Arthur Carlsen, who showed it to me.

"This is one of the queerest knots. Some days I can tie it, some days I can't. First I will tie a half knot, then I will add another half knot, which makes a good solid square knot. Anyone may examine this who wishes to. I am going to add a hitch *here* and then I will stick the end *there*. Now when I pull the two ends be prepared to see something remarkable." The knot disappears. "H-mm, I think I shall drop this knot from my act; this is the third day in a row that it hasn't worked."

2574. A similar trick was shown to me by its originator, Melbourne Christopher; I do not believe I am betraying a trust in showing it and I wouldn't know how to gain his permission as his last address was somewhere in central Europe.

A, B and C are tied slowly for the audience to observe, but D is stuck without the knowledge of the audience at the same time C is being stuck. The knot is tied for the ostensible purpose of selecting a suitable rope for something else that is to follow. So, after the knot has spilled completely two or three times, the rope is discarded as unsuitable, and another rope is substituted, with which the act passes on to something else.

2575. To change a REEF or SQUARE KNOT into two OVERHAND KNOTS, and to change these back again. Given as a puzzle, this is not apt to be solved in a hurry but it may also be treated as a trick. The REEF KNOT (diagram 1) falls very simply into the form of two OVERHANDS (diagram 2), but the reverse may not be so inevitable, as often the second HALF KNOT takes the form of a HALF HITCH, in which all the turns are in one end. But it is only necessary to move the left end to the right, the right to the left and the REEF KNOT will materialize. In both cases a knot is pulled as indicated by the arrow but the end of the rope must not be allowed to follow through.

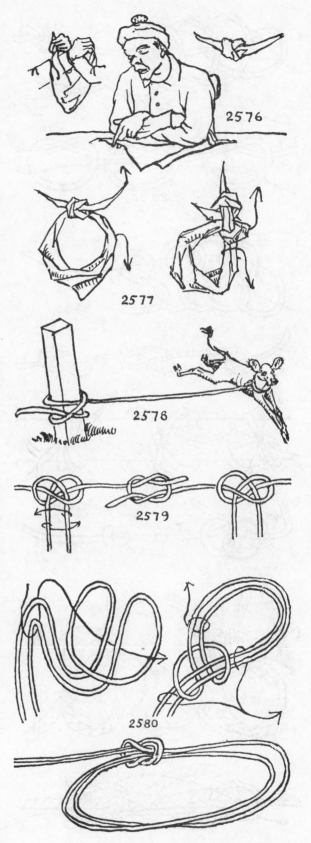

2576. Puzzle: To hold in hand the opposite corners of an un-knotted handkerchief and, without once letting go, to tie a knot in the handkerchief. This has also been called the "FOURTH-DIMEN-SIONAL KNOT" because it appears from nowhere in particular. The spectators having failed to solve the puzzle, the performer seats himself at a table with a handkerchief stretched before him. He folds his arms and dallies negligently, first with one end of the hand-kerchief, then the other; suddenly, as he unfolds his arms, the knot appears.

It is necessary to get hold of both ends of the handkerchief with the finger tips while the arms are folded. When the arms are un-folded the knot is transferred from the arms to the handkerchief.

2577. To spill a REEF or SQUARE KNOT that has been tied by one of the audience. While talking you ostensibly tighten the knot by pull-ing at first one end and then the other, and at the right moment, un-seen by the audience, you pull and straighten out the knot as shown by the diagrams. Cover the knot with your hand. When you open your hand there is no knot, it having slipped off the end as shown by the arrows in the second diagram. This is the way sailors untie reef points.

2578. To untie a CLOVE HITCH. Take a stiff piece of rope about four yards long; new sash cord three eighths of an inch in diameter is recommended. Have a member of the audience tie a CLOVE HITCH with a long end tightly around a *square* upturned table or chair leg.

Then in an unhurried way stroll around and around the table leg, and the audience, to their amazement, will see the much-respected knot unwind itself without offering any resistance what-ever.

2579. The WHATNOT provides one of the prettiest of rope tricks. Take two pieces of *sash cord* or banding each five feet long. Tie the knot loosely as in the center diagram and grasp the two untied ends in the hands. Pull on the two ends and the knot will take the form of the left diagram and *roll* before the spectators' eyes from one end of the rope to the other. Watch the rope carefully and as it twists (which it will) *untwist* the ends just enough to relieve it. Shift your grip as frequently as is necessary. When the knot has traveled the full length of the ropes, let go the two ends you have in hand, and roll the knot back again by pulling on the other two ends. If the knot tends to tighten shift back to the opposite ends and *keep the knot moving*. Finally, as you watch closely, you will see the two ends shift position and take the form shown in the right diagram. (The difference is in the upper center crossing.) At once stop pulling and invite two spectators to assist you. Give each one an end to pull. They will be utterly unable to move the knot the fractional part of an inch.

2580. To tie a SQUARE KNOT in the bight. A puzzle, shown to me by Arthur Carlsen. Get your cord into the form of each diagram in turn, before proceeding to the next.

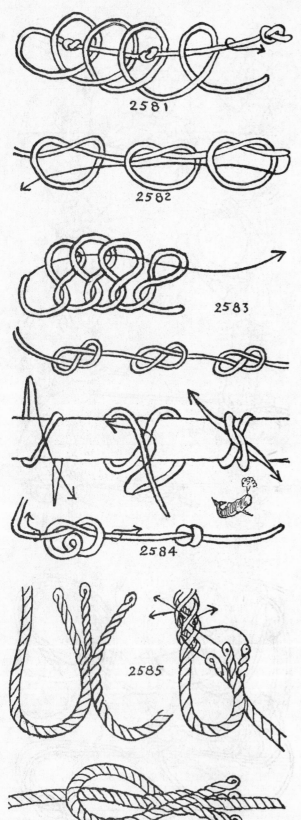

2581. The "MAGICAL KNOT," also known as the "FIREMAN'S KNOT" and the "PHILADELPHIA KNOT."

To tie: Take a long piece of banding and build up a series of hitches over the left thumb. Remove from thumb and stick the lower end of the cord up through these hitches. Cover all with the hand except the upstuck end. Lean over your hand and whisper some magical word that you may think of, then pull steadily on the protruding end and a long series of knots will march out from under your fingers. In the meanwhile the twiddling left fingers hold everything back except the one knot whose turn it is to come forth. Pull gently so that the knots will remain *loosely* tied. A series of at least a dozen are easily made.

2582. Continue to talk animatedly to your audience while you unostentatiously rearrange the knots as in the diagram, merely tucking one end through each knot in turn. Let two of the audience step forward, give each an end (the knots being well bunched and hidden in your hand). Ask them to pull the knots as tight as possible so that they will be hard to untie, keep your hands over the knots and, when they have finished pulling, remove your hand; and the knots will have entirely disappeared. Six or eight knots are enough for the trick, but there is no limit to the number that is possible.

2583. Both the FIGURE-EIGHT and the STEVEDORE KNOT may be tied in similar manner. The FIGURE-EIGHT is illustrated, but if one more half turn is added to each upstanding loop in the first diagram the result will be a series of STEVEDORE KNOTS.

2584. An unrecognizable knot. This is a puzzle rather than a trick. Make one, two or three round turns around a pencil, and add a HALF KNOT. Remove and work the knot taut, pulling as little as possible on the ends and retaining all possible twist within the knot.

The knot should already be in pocket when you announce to your audience, preferably a small one and of the sporting gentry, that you have in your possession a knot that no one present has ever seen before. There are always people present who have seen everything there is to be seen, so in the ensuing argument produce the knot and place a few judicious bets. State that you will pay all bets if anyone present can produce a duplicate.

Allow no one to touch the knot, for there is always someone who will innocently attempt to untie it. Put it on the table in full view and allow anyone to turn it over with a match or pencil. Finally someone will tie a FIGURE-EIGHT KNOT in another cord, which will appear to be the same thing. You must have both knots opened without permitting an end from either to be withdrawn. It will at once be evident to all that your trick knot is merely an OVERHAND KNOT.

2585. A puzzle. How to put an EYE SPLICE in the bight of a rope. Twist the rope and crowd a central section together, which will cause the three strands to protrude separately in three bights. This is called *crowfooting a rope*. Make an ordinary EYE SPLICE tucked twice, sticking bights instead of ends. This splice is valueless except as a trick, being ruinous to rope.

2585½. *False braid.* Take four strands, secure them to a hook or other holdfast and arrange with three strands in the left hand and one in the right. Take the outermost left strand and cross it over its two sister strands, laying it snugly parallel and below the single right strand. Now take the *next* (outermost) *left* strand and lay it snugly across its one remaining sister strand and parallel to and below the preceding one. This completes one cycle.

There will now be three strands in the *right* and only one in the *left* hand. Take the outermost right strand and lay it across its two sister strands and place it parallel to and below the single left strand. Take the next (outermost) strand of the right side, lay it across its single sister strand and place it parallel to and below the two left strands. This completes the second cycle. Repeat alternately left and right until the desired amount of braid is completed. Lay the strands snugly and the product will resemble ordinary FLAT SINNET. If well made, it will stand ordinary usage, but give it several smart jerks and perhaps a little assistance with a finger if necessary, and it will at once resolve itself into two two-strand ropes, one right-laid, the other left-laid. To make an effective trick for a large audience use material that is large and soft.

2586. Having tied a BOWLINE into a BOWLINE *on the bight*, the trick is to remove the latter without disturbing the former. This interesting puzzle was propounded to me by a sailor of the Eastern Shore of Maryland. He had heard the problem but did not know the answer. After experiment it was solved in two ways.

A piece of banding may be used, the loops should be large and the rope between long. The standing part of the rope should be held by a spectator or else be secured to another object, and is not to be tampered with.

The BOWLINE on the bight can be very quickly and easily removed by first loosening it and then rolling it back away from the standing part, exactly as a stocking is rolled inside out but without disturbing the single BOWLINE. This is a method used at sea for disentangling small lines. All that is necessary is to keep in mind that at no time must the standing part be pulled or tightened. This is so simple that after a little practice the knot may be easily untied behind the performer's back, while held in full view of the audience. Moreover if the fingers are kept "busy" the audience may require a number of demonstrations before they will understand how it is done.

2587. The BOWLINE on the bight can be tied back into the BOWLINE without employing either end of the rope. The method is illustrated step by step in the accompanying diagrams. Having mastered these, the reader will not find it difficult to answer the original proposition by reversing the order of these diagrams.

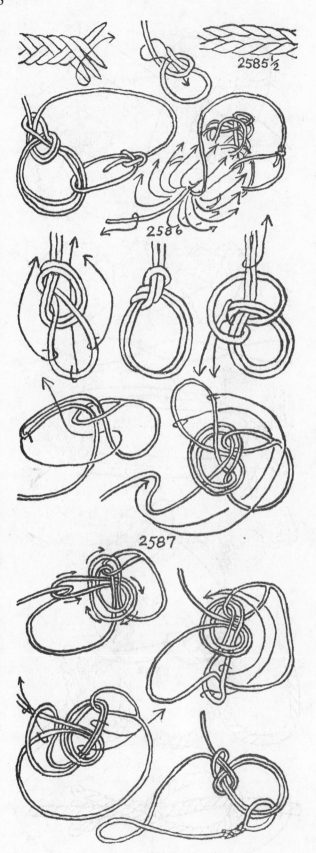

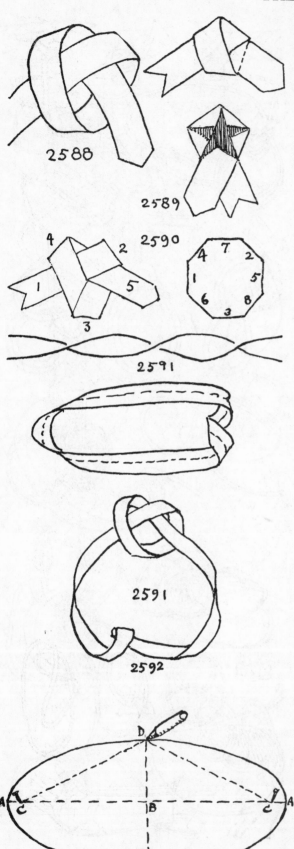

2588

2589

2590

2591

2591

2592

2588. Puzzle: To make a regular PENTAGON with an OVERHAND KNOT. The answer: Take a ribbon of paper and tie an OVERHAND KNOT in it. Draw up gradually and closely, keeping it flat at all times. When snug, fold back the ends and as perfect a PENTAGON will result as can be secured with drawing instruments.

2589. Puzzle: To make a regular PENTALPHA with the same material and a pencil. Hold the knot against a lighted windowpane and a PENTALPHA or five-pointed star is silhouetted. Outline this with your pencil.

2590. To make a regular OCTAGON. This is from Admiral Luce's *Seamanship* (1862). The knot is given as a method of making the straw button required in the top center of a sailor's hat.

Take a paper ribbon and tie an OVERHAND KNOT in it, tying from left to right. *Every time* the ribbon is folded, the end is turned downward. Be certain that the OVERHAND KNOT takes the open form of the first diagram. Now turn down the end at point 5 and reeve it through at 3 and lead it to 6. Stick the end down at 6, lead it *over* 1 and *through* 4 to 7. Turn it *down* at 7 and stick it through 2 *and* 5. Turn it down at 8 and stick it through 3 and 6.

Cut the standing end (1) off even with the edge of the OCTAGON and leave the working end just long enough to turn down and sink out of sight on the underside, in the direction of 2.

2591. To tie an OVERHAND KNOT with a pair of scissors: Take a paper ribbon one inch wide and about two feet long. A piece of paper from a narrow adhesive-paper roll is excellent, as the ends are to be pasted together and the adhesive on such rolls dries quickly. Twist this ribbon three half turns and stick the ends together.

When the ends are secured, take a pair of scissors and divide the ribbon lengthwise in two. It will be found to be still a single ribbon, but of twice its original length, half its original width, and with an OVERHAND KNOT tied in it.

2592. To make an ELLIPSE by means of a piece of cord, three brads and a pencil.

Draw two lines at right angles to and crossing each other in the middle. They should equal the length and width of the proposed ellipse. The distance C–D is equal to A–B. Take the distance A–B on a pair of compasses or a ruler and, using D as a center, establish C–C. Now drive three brads (at C, C, and D). Tie an *inelastic* cord snugly around the three brads. Remove the brad at D and insert the point of a sharp pencil on the inside of this continuous cord. Keeping the cord at an even tension around both remaining brads, draw an ellipse along the periphery that is allowed by the cord.

Aside from being an amusing puzzle, this is an exceedingly practical way to draw any wanted ellipse.

2593. Snare (1). Bend together the two ends of a string five or six feet long and hold the knotted part in your hand. Without turning the hand lay the cord on a table from east to west, to south, to north. From south to north the doubled string crosses itself at right angles. Ask someone to place his finger within the string, so that the string may not be removed. The chances are that he will put it on the spot marked X, in which case the string easily slides off the table without engaging the finger. Now lay the cord down again, but this time, in passing from south to north, twist the cord one half a right turn as in the second diagram. Then ask the owner of the finger to try again, but this time to allow the string to be removed. But this time the string will engage the finger if he places it at X.

2594. Snare (2). This trick differs from the previous one, in that a turn of the wrist is made each time the direction of the cord is changed. The trick is started at N.W. and moved S.E., then S.W., then N.W., to N.E. The only difference between the left and right diagrams is in the over-and-under at the last turn (at W.). Here the wrist was turned left for the left diagram and right for the other. In the left diagram the finger will not be snared at X and in the right diagram it will be.

When a finger is placed at X on either diagram, any of the six bights at the rim may be pulled on and the result is the same for all six. The knotted ends are generally pulled.

2595. "Nailed to the mast": In addition to a piece of string, a knife, nail or ice pick is required, and one's hostess should be consulted before sticking the knife into any of her woodwork. A tree or a fence post provides a satisfactory prop. Wind the string or rope as pictured. Hold the two ends in hand. (It is not necessary to tie them together.) Remove the knife and jerk the string, which will then apparently pass through the tree. It may be tied with a spectator's forefinger serving instead of a knife or nail.

2596. "La Garrotte": Take a right round turn about the victim's neck, cross the cord in front, and, with the part leading from below the right ear on top, move the doubled portion over the victim's head to the nape of the neck. Pull snappily on the front bight and, although the neck is apparently severed, the head will not fall off.

2597. "Fingering the Nose" is claimed by *The Parlor Magician* to be "irresistibly funny": Tie the ends of a thirty-inch cord together. Take a left round turn and grasp the center between the teeth. Hold the *upper* and *longer* loop with the left hand and move the *lower* and *shorter* loop from underneath around and up to the right, turning it *over* the longer loop (right upper diagram). Stick the left thumb up through the longer loop, the right forefinger through the shorter loop. Place the right forefinger against the tip of the nose, face your audience, laugh loudly and draw the string away with the left hand while the right hand remains in position, devoid of string.

If the whole right hand is passed through the shorter loop instead of a mere forefinger and the thumb is brought in juxtaposition with the nose the joke becomes even more irresistible and more up to date, particularly when the fingers are distended.

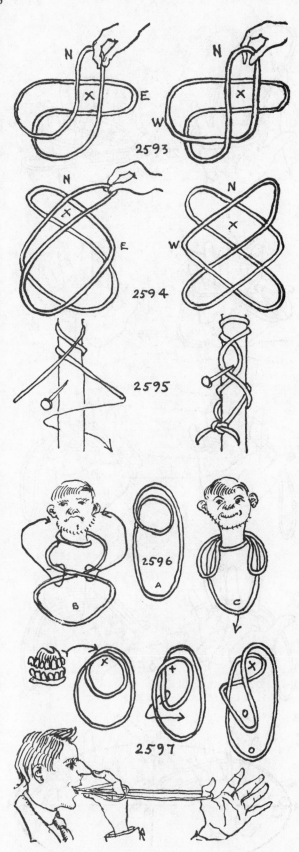

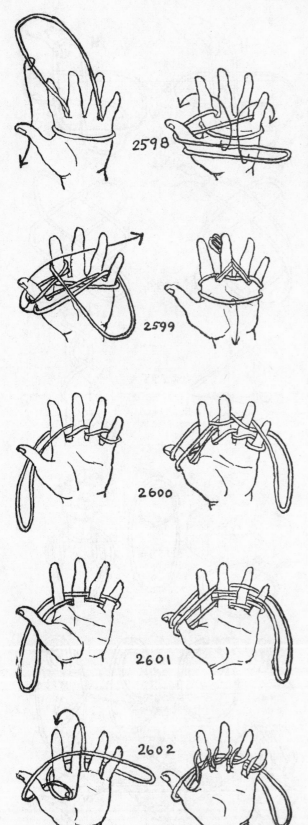

The next five numbers are of the type ordinarily termed "Cutting the Fingers." These tricks are common with most primitive people and are recorded in ethnological reports from almost every quarter of the globe.

2598. "Cutting the Fingers" (1) was first shown to me by Waldo Howland. It is given in the Smithsonian *38th Annual Report* (Washington, 1916–17) and also is described by W. W. Rouse Ball, Kathleen Haddon, and C. F. Jayne in their works on string figures. When diagram ✻2599 has been reached, *ignore the arrow that is drawn*, and cast off the two loops from the thumb, pull forward on the loop shown at the heel of the hand, and all the fingers will be neatly severed and the cord removed.

2599. "Cutting the Fingers" (2). If, however, the arrow in the final diagram of ✻2598 is followed and the two loops around the thumb are led to the back of the hand and pulled back taut between the second and ring fingers, it will be found that the loop which was pulled in ✻2598 will no longer be in evidence. An entirely different and solitary loop or bight now crosses the palm as in ✻2599. This is seized and pulled to cut the fingers and spill the knot.

2600. "Cutting the Fingers" (3). Shown to me by Waldo Howland, given also in the Smithsonian *38th Annual Report*. When placing the cord around the fingers it is given a half turn in the same direction at each finger. But when the thumb is reached the direction is changed and the twist also is reversed.

Finally the two bights in the second drawing are removed from the thumb, the long loop at the little finger is pulled, and again the fingers are cut.

2601. "Cutting the Fingers" (4). Shown to me by my mother when I was a child. I have never forgotten it or found it elsewhere and I still recall how the dispatch with which my fingers were severed filled me with horror. How children ever survive having their noses alternately removed and replaced, their fingers lopped off, their ears snipped, their thumbs twisted off and other like acts of mayhem is a mystery to me; and yet we live and joyfully pass the ghastly practices along to the next generation.

2602. "Cutting the Fingers" (5). This one I also learned when a child, from my uncle, Captain Albert Robbins. I would very much like to know in just what quarter of the globe he found it. A loop encircles the thumb and fingers of the left hand. The forefinger of the right hand is passed between the thumb and forefinger of the left hand, which leads across the left palm, to hook the back cord. A bight is pulled forward and twisted half a right turn and then is dropped over to the back of the finger. Each finger is hitched in proper turn. When all are arranged, the single loop over the thumb is cast off, and only the forward half of the cord across the palm is pulled on to cut the fingers.

In each of the tricks now to be considered the string or cord at

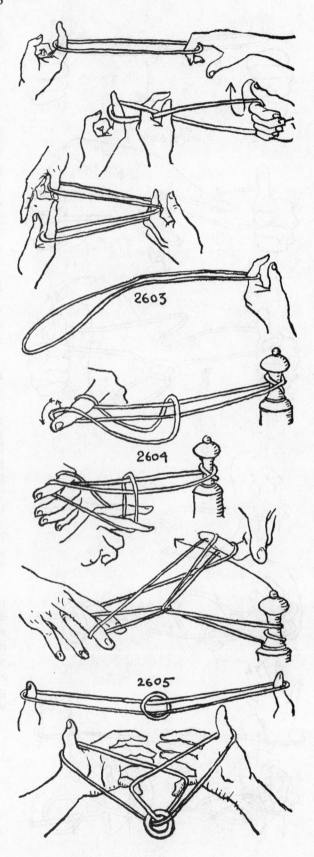

2603

2604

2605

some point reverses and "backtracks." At some central point the performer's hand or thumb holds the cord until the performer wishes to spill it. In a number of the knots a spectator's finger or a chair knob is substituted, which allows the performer's hands to be free.

2603. Have a spectator hold his forefinger upright. (See left drawing.) Over this you pass one of the two looped ends of a continuous string. The other looped end is held in your right hand. Twist the right hand to give the cord a right half twist and insert the left forefinger downward to the left of the crossing and grasp the crossing with the thumb and finger. Turn the left finger and thumb upward. The cord is now arranged as in the second drawing, the spectator's hand being the one farthest to the left. Announce that you are going to remove the cord *without* passing *any part* of it *over* the spectator's finger. In the meanwhile the cord in the right hand should be shifted to the thumb as shown by the arrow in the second drawing. Holding the center of the cord taut with the left hand, the right end is passed toward the spectator's hand and the tip of the right thumb is placed on the tip of the spectator's finger. The performer's left hand now casts off either of the two loops it holds and smartly pulls on the one that remains. Nothing has passed over the tip of the spectator's finger, yet the cord is free!

For this reason, perhaps, the trick is more mystifying than others in which extra loops are added around the spectator's finger.

2604. "Cutting off the Chair Knob." A spectator's finger will make quite as satisfactory an anchor as a chair knob.

A right round turn is placed over the knob. The cord is held taut with the performer's right hand while he places his left forefinger across the two parallel parts at about mid-length and drops the looped end over the two taut parts of his cord. The right hand is then brought up underneath, two fingers are splayed, right and left, and stuck up through the two loosely hanging loops; after which remove the single twist from the outer loop around the left forefinger tip so that it appears as in the second drawing. This can be done with the thumb and forefinger without the assistance of the right hand. Next, with the left forefinger crooked toward you, transfer both loops to the knob. Hold all taut and cast off the loop from the right forefinger and at once pull out the loop that remains on the second finger. All complications will at once vanish.

2605. To *remove a string from the buttonhole* without letting go the string. Use either your own or a spectator's buttonhole. If desired, a ring, key or the thumbhole of a pair of scissors may be substituted. Reeve the string through the buttonhole and be certain that the string is not crossed between the thumbs. Hold the string taut, reach out the little finger of the right hand and hook the nearest bight from the left hand, then hook the other bight with the other little finger. Then cast off the loops from the *left little finger* and the *right thumb* simultaneously and pull the hands apart. The string will apparently snap directly through the material of the coat.

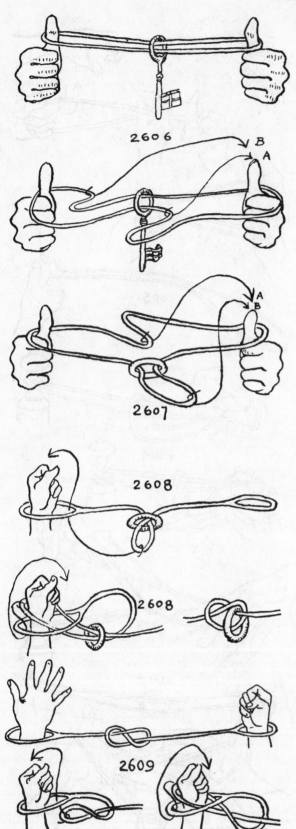

2606. To *remove a ring* (or key) *from a doubled string* which is passed around the two thumbs of a spectator, without disturbing the spectator. Neither of the loops is to be lifted from the spectator's thumbs.

Two bights are made, one in the back part of the string at the left of the ring and one in the front part at the right of the ring (from the performer's viewpoint). These bights may be treated in two ways; they may be moved one at a time and placed over the left thumb of the spectator in the order A, B or bight B may be placed over bight A and then the two together may be placed over the spectator's left thumb (which is, of course, the thumb at the right side of the diagram). In either case do not let go until the spectator starts to spread his arms. The spectator's hands have been at first held loosely in order to allow bights to be formed and placed over the thumbs, but when the performer casts off, the spectator's hands are stretched apart and the ring or key drops off the cord.

2607. To *replace the ring*. First stick a bight from the near side of the string through the ring and hold in place with the right hand. Next, with the left hand place a bight from the rear part of the string over the spectator's thumb and then place the bight from the ring also over the thumb. When the spectator's hands are spread apart the ring is found neatly restored to the string.

2608. To *knot a ring to a single string*, the two ends of which are tied around your wrists. (If preferred, this may be done around the wrists of a spectator.)

A loop (a BOWLINE KNOT) is tied around each wrist. They should not be tight enough to cause discomfort. Pull forward a bight from the center and stick it through the ring, give it half a left turn and, keeping the pictured side uppermost, reeve it up through the loop that is around the left wrist, then over the left hand and down the left wrist until it has passed under and below the loop that was first tied around the wrist. Now lift it off over the hand. The ring will be found securely knotted to the string.

To *remove the same knot:* Take the left bight of the knot which is shown in the right final diagram and place it *over* the left hand and over and below the loop that was first tied around the wrist. Then reeve it up *under* the original loop and cast off over the hand.

2609. To tie a FIGURE-EIGHT KNOT in the bight without removing the loops from the wrists: The first diagram shows the finished aspect of the trick. In the second diagram is shown a full left turn made in the bight, which is to be pushed up under the loop around the left wrist, and then brought down over the hand and under the wrist loop and finally is cast off over the hand and wrist loop. To remove this knot proceed exactly in the way described for the previous knot (⚹2608), the left bight of the FIGURE-EIGHT being well opened and pulled out before proceeding to untie.

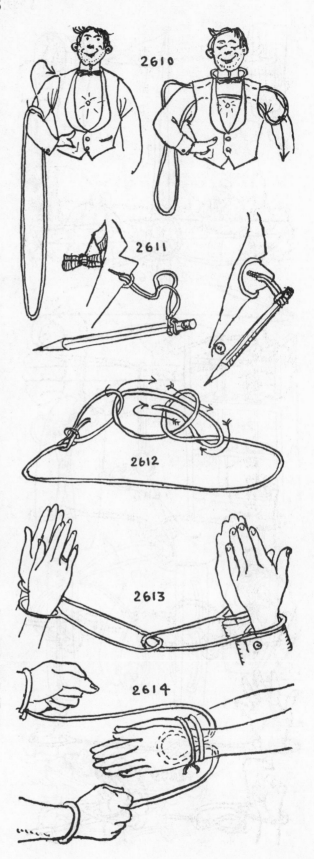

2610. To *remove a circular cord from around the arm*, while the hand is held in a waistcoat pocket: Take a piece of cord eight feet long and tie the ends together. Remove the coat, put the right hand through the looped cord and into the waistcoat pocket. The problem is to remove the cord without untying it and without removing the right hand from the pocket or passing the cord through the pocket.

With the left hand pull the cord to the top of the shoulder. Stick the left hand under the lapel and out through the waistcoat armhole and pull the cord to the collar and over the head, leading one part around the back of the neck, the other under the chin. Thrust the bight out through the left armhole and stick the left arm through the bight. As the waistcoat is buttoned, a few moments may be required to work the cord down inside the waistcoat until it has reached the waist; from there it will drop to the ground.

2611. To *remove a pencil that is fast to a coat:* Tie a RING HITCH into the buttonhole of a spectator's coat with a short piece of cord that has been doubled. Secure the ends to a *long* new lead pencil. The length of cord between the buttonhole and the pencil should be about two thirds the length of the pencil. The problem is to remove the cord from the coat without untying the pencil end. This was shown to me by J. M. Drew. The solution is to remove the coat from the back, then open the RING HITCH and work the whole coat gradually out through the bight of the RING HITCH in the manner indicated by the arrows in the second diagram. Select for a victim someone who, you feel certain, can well afford to have his coat pressed.

2612. To separate two interlocked BOWLINES without untying either: The loop end of one BOWLINE must be backtracked into the other knot until it has capped the other end of the rope and is withdrawn. The second knot must be well opened before it is entered.

2613. *Insecure shackles.* Two persons are tied together in the manner pictured. The problem is for them to rid themselves of each other without untying the knots. The cords should be just long enough to encourage the couple to attempt various absurdities, but not so long that they will lose all sense of intimacy. To divorce the couple: Take a bight from near the center of one cord and, without twisting it, stick it up under and through one of the end loops in the other cord, then over the hand, under the loop at the back, and cast off over the hand.

2614. The "Russian Escape." A prisoner is supposed to be secured to his guard in the manner pictured. In his efforts to escape he rubs his hands together until the heels of his hands pinch a bight of the rope. It is then an easy matter to roll the bight down as far as the roots of the fingers, where it can be grasped with the finger tips of one hand and slipped over the backs of the fingers of the other hand. The prisoner then pulls away and the cord or rope slips over the back of his hand and under the handcuff lashing. The latter may be tied fairly tight without endangering the trick.

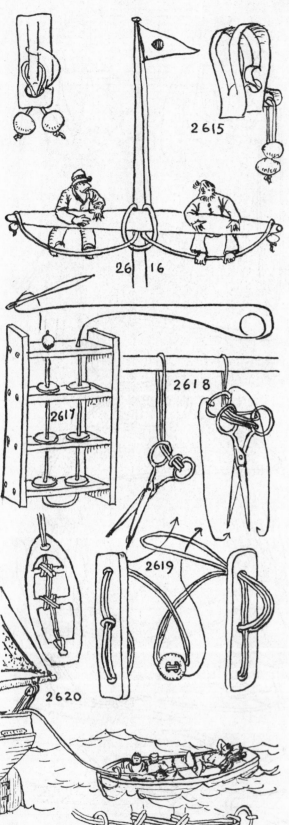

2615. A puzzle: To *remove the cord* from a card without untying the beads. A flexible card or strip having two slits and a hole, and two buttons larger than the hole, are required.

The solution is to bend the flexible strip at the middle and pull it, by means of the cord, down through the hole. Then withdraw one of the beads through the loop that has been formed by the strip.

2616. "Two Sailors Out on the Yardarms." To get them both on the same yardarm without passing the knot. This was shown to me by Lovell Thompson, who learned it in Nova Scotia.

Pull out a bight from the center knot and stick it down through the near side of an end hole. Drop the knot at the end of the foot-rope down through the bight and withdraw the bight over the knot to bring it back to where it started from. Treat the other end similarly and the knot at the center will disappear. One sailor then crosses to the opposite yardarm. The knot is replaced by reversing the process described.

2617. The *oriental ladder trick:* To remove the string from the ladder without disengaging the string from the buttons.

Take a turn about the upper right post of the ladder and then reeve the needle reversely the full length of the cord so that two parallel cords pass through the whole structure. Reverse the needle and this time reeve *only through the buttons*, passing *outside* each rung of the ladder. Take the turn off the ladder post, pull out the doubled cord and nothing will remain on the cord except the buttons.

2618. To *disentangle scissors:* The Ring Hitch is pulled out and led through the upper thumbhole of the scissors, and then passed entirely around the scissors, which frees them.

2619. To *remove the button:* Two sticks, with three holes in each, and a button with large holes are required. These are arranged as pictured.

Extend the loop at the center hole of one of the sticks, reeve it through the upper hole, then pass both the opposite stick and the button through the loop. The loop can now be withdrawn from its own stick and the button removed. After this the stick may be replaced by reversing the process.

2620. "The Pirate and the Jolly Boat."

A pirate, having more prisoners than he has room for, tows one boatload astern.

All knives are taken away, and the boat made fast with the bight of a doubled line. The after end of the line is ring hitched to a stern ringbolt. Clove Hitches are put around each thwart, and the line is rove through the bow ringbolt and brought to deck. They are told to escape if they can.

How do they escape?

The reader should make a rough cardboard replica of the top elevation of the boat to work with.

The solution: The boat is hauled close to ship, and the loose rope, so gained, is led aft through all the Clove Hitches until the Ring Hitch in the after ringbolt can be loosened. The bight of this knot is extended to its limit, after which it is led forward, paralleling the rope through its successive hitches, and after leading it out through the forward ring it is dropped into the water and the boat itself is hauled through it.

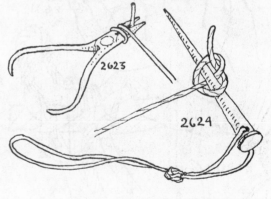

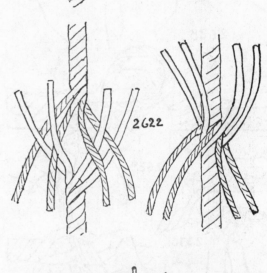

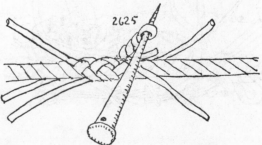

CHAPTER 34: LONG AND SHORT SPLICES
(MULTI-STRAND BENDS)

Splicing—is fastening two Ends of a Rope together, with uncommon Slight—to execute which requires no ordinary Skill; as I can venture to say not one Seaman in twenty can perform it.

A NAVAL REPOSITORY, 1762

2621. This pictures the proper way to crotch or marry two three-strand ropes preparatory to short splicing.

2622. The proper way to crotch or marry two four-strand ropes is shown here.

2623. Small strands may be hove with round-jawed pliers.

2624. Larger strands are hove taut with a marlingspike and a MARLINGSPIKE HITCH.

2625. Medium-size strands may be tightened with the point of the marlingspike by imparting a strong twist.

There are three angles of approach to splices—the sailmaker's, the rigger's and the sailor's.

Sailmaker's splices are put into the boltrope of sails, which is three-strand. They are supported by being strongly sewed to the sailcloth. The strands of a sailmaker's splice are always "backed"—that is, each end is tucked around and around a single opposing strand, forming a long helix, instead of being tucked over one strand and under the next as in other splices. The ends are cut off on the underside of the splice, a few yarns at each tuck, and are covered up at the next tuck.

The sailmaker works while sitting on a bench in the sail loft. He opens his strands with a wooden fid. When his splice is complete he pounds it with his fid and often spits on the handle and burnishes the splice to make it lie fair for the stitching.

The final splice on a sail is always called the "CONFINE SPLICE," whatever its variety, since it is the splice that closes the end of the boltrope around the sail.

Rigger's splices belong principally in standing rigging and its appurtenances. Many of them are tied in shroud-laid rope, which is four-strand and has a core. But block straps, pendants, slings, lifts, etc., are three-strand.

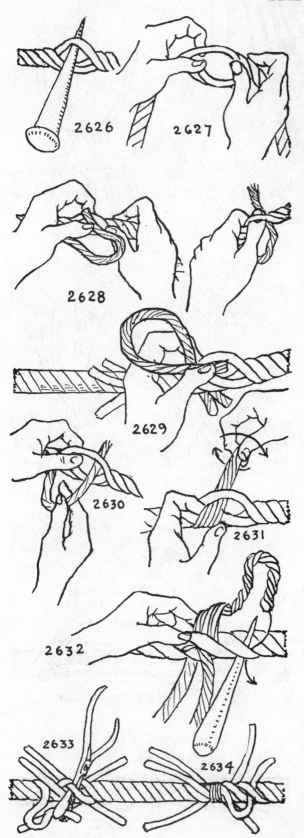

The rigger splices while standing at a workbench in the rigging loft. He opens a rope with an iron marlingspike. His strands are greased with tallow before they are tucked. The ends are cut shorter than sailmaker's and sailor's splices, and they are teased out and served over.

Sailor's splices are found principally in running rigging, cargo and deck gear, and in ground tackle. They are unsupported by either stitches or service. If the rope allows, he prefers to splice with his fingers alone. When completed, his splice may be rolled underfoot or else pounded with a fid or marlingspike. Unlike sailmaker's and rigger's splices, the ends are left long and in full view.

2626. For opening strands a sailor employs his fingers wherever practicable, but if the rope is large or new, a marlingspike or pricker is required. The rope is twisted strongly to the right and the point is entered carefully so that none of the fibers are disturbed.

2627. When opening a strand with his fingers, the sailor grasps the rope as pictured, and, with the right thumb against the strand that is to be lifted, he imparts a strong twist.

2628. To *stick or tuck the strands*, the first step in making a SHORT or LONG SPLICE. After opening the rope, hold it firmly and turn back an end from the left rope (counterclockwise). Shove it through the opening with the left thumb, the hands and strand assuming the positions pictured.

2629. The second tuck is taken differently. A left twist is given to the strand, sufficient to make it form the small left turn that is illustrated, with a gesture that is similar to adding a turn to a left-hand coil. The end is directed to the right, instead of to the left as in ✥2628. The left thumb pushes the strand through as before. The reason for the different technique is that the latter way skillfully removes just sufficient twist from the working strand to make it lie fair over the next strand. Both ✥2628 and ✥2629 are employed by the sailor in the OVER-AND-UNDER SPLICE, which is the first to be described. But ✥2628 is employed only for the initial sticking or tuck, the reason being that it is less liable to disturb the lay of the two crotched ropes.

2630. The rigger, having opened his rope with a marlingspike (✥2626), holds it open with the left thumb and forefinger just long enough to thrust a strand directly through as shown. Much of a rigger's work is with tarred hemp, which is quite the handiest material there is to splice with. I would recommend the beginner buying a few yards of small three-strand "ratline stuff" and four-strand "lanyard stuff" to practice with.

2631. This shows how the rigger, and sometimes the sailor too, will make a strand lie fair by twisting after it has been thrust.

2632. Sailmaker's splices, being backhanded, require a different technique for arranging the lay, so that the yarns in the overlaid section of strand will coincide with the lay of the strand underneath. Having reached the position shown in this sketch, the yarns are closely held and flattened with the thumb at the same time directing the lay with the forefinger.

2633. I have found that splicing moderately stiff material of medium size is much speeded by entering with a pair of duck-billed pliers and pulling the end through without the use of a fid.

2634. This diagram shows the first strand of a SAILOR'S SHORT SPLICE in process of being tucked. The end is led over the first opposing strand and under the next. Then the rope is turned toward you into position for the next strand, which is shown above the first one. After the three ends are each tucked once the splice is turned end for end and the other set is tucked the same. When splicing, be seated if possible, with the splice laid across the lap.

2635. The "OVER AND UNDER," or "SAILOR'S SHORT SPLICE," also called "SHORT SPLICE" and "REGULAR SHORT SPLICE." All early nautical authorities, beginning with Captain John Smith, called this the ROUND SPLICE. Falconer, in 1769, was the first to call it the SHORT SPLICE. The earliest SHORT SPLICE was tucked twice full size.

The rope is crotched, stopped, and held across the splicer's lap. The first tuck is taken as shown in ⁂2634, after which the rope is turned one third of a revolution toward the splicer and the next sister strand is tucked in exactly the same manner. After the rope is turned end for end, the other three strands are tucked the same as the first end. The way of taking the first tuck has been described as ⁂2628.

Having removed the stop and drawn all the strands snug, proceed to tuck all six ends a second time, as described in ⁂2629. The ends are trimmed at a length equal to the diameter of the rope. The second diagram shows the appearance of the completed splice.

2636. The diagram alongside shows the SHORT SPLICE opened and flattened with every strand in evidence. The drawing was made in answer to the suggestion of several knot enthusiasts, who felt that it was inadequate to show one face of the splice only; that all strands should be shown to make the construction clear. The diagram is interesting mainly because, although it shows everything regularly and as simply as may be, it fails to make the splice clearer.

2637. Illustrative of the sailor's common way of *cutting a strand*. The knife is drawn toward the splicer to the right, and the strand is cut diagonally. But the best way to cut strands is probably with a pair of shears; the quickest way is with a hatchet.

2638. Captain Charles W. Smith's GENERAL UTILITY SPLICE was tucked full twice, both ways. Then the yarns of each strand were divided and the lower half of all six was stuck once more. As it is ordinarily expressed, each strand was "tucked two and a half times." The splice was then either rolled on deck underfoot, or else was pounded with a marlingspike, after which it was given two palm-and-needle whippings at each end. The whippings were put over the well-rounded section, where the strands cross each other. The ends were trimmed to a length equal to the diameter of the rope.

2639. A CARGO SLINGS SPLICE is also put into large hawsers. One full turn must be taken out of the twist before crotching for a slings. The ends are tucked twice full, and then one half a strand from each of two adjacent ends is securely whipped or seized together. This is called CROSS WHIPPING. This scheme is followed until all ends have been given a strong whipping. The ends are trimmed to a length of four to six inches according to the size of the rope. Sometimes they are whipped twice.

2640. The ordinary FARM SPLICE ashore is tucked three times full. Ends should always be cut long (preferably one and one half times the diameter of the rope), and then be allowed to wear off in use.

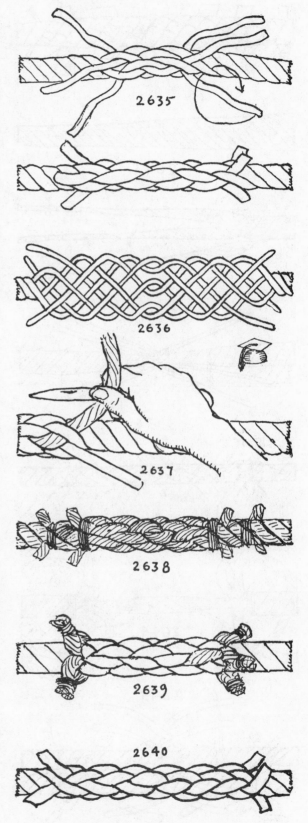

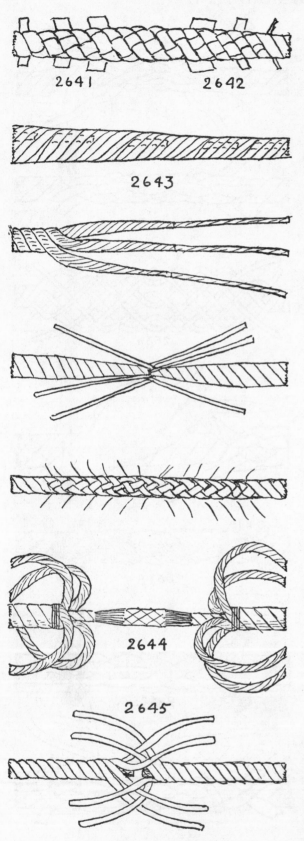

2641. It is often stated that a SHORT SPLICE is stronger than a LONG SPLICE. This is probably taken from the testimony of the testing machine. But in practical use the rather abrupt shoulders of the SHORT SPLICE continually fetch against various obstructions and eventually the rope is weakened at the entrance to the splice. If a SHORT SPLICE is carefully tapered it will give better service, and if a number of yarns are wormed, its strength is increased. There is a great variety in the ways that splices are tapered. It has often been stated: "Every ship has its own long splice and every sailor has his own short one." A splice tucked "once full, once two thirds and once one third" has a nice taper. This is mentioned in Steel's *Elements and Practice of Rigging and Seamanship* (1794).

2642. The more usual way is to tuck each strand "once full, once one half, and once one quarter." Some splicers will tuck the strands twice full before starting to taper, or one end once and the other end twice. The material itself should decide the splice. A hard-laid rope requires fewer tucks than a soft-laid rope, and a soft, well-stretched and well-worn old rope should have additional tucks.

2643. A "LONG SHORT SPLICE": I have made a very satisfactory SHORT SPLICE having a diameter no greater than a LONG SPLICE, when the material was of insufficient length for the latter. The splice should be about three times the length of the ordinary SHORT SPLICE and careful workmanship is necessary. Open and seize each end at a length equal to about six times its circumference, and whip all strands.

Count the yarns in one strand, and taper each strand evenly for one third of its length, beginning at the *seizing*, so that in that length exactly one half of the yarns are cut out.

The tapering is done in this manner. Without disturbing the outside lay of the strand, lift out one of the *interior* yarns and cut it off at an inch and a half from the seizing. Carefully unwind the yarn to the end of the strand and cut it off close to the whipping. With the left thumb, siip the short remaining end back into the interior of the strand. This is called *sinking* or *burying* a yarn. At short regular intervals, cut out other inside yarns one at a time, sinking the upper end and cutting off the lower end. When the inside yarns are exhausted, remove outside yarns but *do not remove adjacent yarns consecutively.* Scatter and bury the ends. When all three strands have been tapered regularly to half size at one-third length, lay them up again as described in ✳144. Lay them up *as tightly as you can*, and whip them strongly. Marry the two ends and short splice as already described, cutting out yarns at the same rate as in tapering. When three yarns are left in each strand, back the yarns twice *through* the proper opposing strand and cut them off short. After rolling, the splice should be about the size of the rest of the rope.

2644. A SHROUD SPLICE. Short splice the hearts of two shroud-laid ropes (✳110). One tuck each way is sufficient, after which the ends are scraped down and marled with twine. Next, short splice the shrouds, tucking them once and a half, scrape all strands and serve over. Snake the ends of the service (✳3453). This was the early SHROUD SPLICE.

2645. As the heart of a four-strand rope is not intended to add to the strength of the rope, but is merely to give it firmness, a neater splice, that is about as strong, is made by cutting off the ends of the hearts and butting them, after which the outside strands are spliced as in ✳2644.

2646. A FOUR-STRAND OVER-AND-UNDER SPLICE. In the illustration, for the sake of compactness, the splice is shown tucked only once at the left and twice at the right. The technique is the same as already described. But as four-strand rope is not so firm as three-strand rope, each strand should be tucked at least twice full, then once one half, and once one quarter. The last tuck in any FOUR-STRAND SPLICE should always be under two strands whether the splice is long, short, backhanded, or over-and-under.

2647. An alternative way of sticking a SHORT SPLICE. This makes a splice that is scarcely distinguishable from the ordinary SHORT SPLICE. It is tucked as in the diagram alongside, which illustrates two opposing strands. The others are tucked the same way, and after all are tucked once they are spliced regularly over one and under one as in ✻2635 or ✻2638.

The ordinary OVER-AND-UNDER SHORT SPLICE, tucked once only, each way, is often used in the straps of single blocks. Thicker blocks will require more tucks, so that the length of the splice equals the thickness of the block. The sharp angle of the shell, at the bosom, adds to the security of the splice and often the ends are trimmed short. But on smart ships the straps are wormed and the splices teased, parceled and served or grafted over.

2648. The RIGGER'S SHORT SPLICE. Opposite strands are half knotted together and then are tucked over and under once in each direction, as shown by the arrow in the diagram. The splice belongs on the strap of a single block. For a double block it would be tucked twice each way and the ends cut off short.

2649. This is the SAILOR'S BACKHANDED SHORT SPLICE, which is often confused with the SAILMAKER'S SHORT SPLICE. It is, however, made with a different technique and has several structural differences.

After crotching the ropes, the ends are half knotted as in the RIGGER'S SHORT SPLICE (✻2648), and then each of the six strands is backed once in turn. They are not backed, however, as the sailmaker backs them (✻2632). The sailor backs them in his own way. Each strand is tucked *forward over one and under two, instead of over one and under one*, which is the usual sailor's splice. In three-strand rope this is structurally the same as a sailmaker's backhanded tuck, and in four-strand rope the splice is not attempted. All six strands are tucked in turn four times, the three strands of each end being kept "a-tier," not "run down" one at a time as the sailmaker does it. The tucks are taken twice full, once three quarters, once one half and once one quarter. The splice is put into boltrope and is appreciably longer than an ordinary SHORT SPLICE.

2650. The sailor enters his fid for the BACKHANDED SPLICE either at right angles to the rope or else pointed a little to the left. The strand end, which should be whipped, is thrust through end first as shown by the arrow.

2651. The first mention of SAILMAKER'S SPLICES is by Kipping (1847), who says "Left-handed splices are best for roping straight." He does not describe the "LEFT-HANDED" SPLICE, and earlier works on sailmaking give only the OVER-AND-UNDER SPLICE. This illustration is given here to show the structural difference between the SAILMAKER'S SPLICE and the RIGGER'S SPLICE (✻2648). The former is backed once either way, which gives four bights as shown here, while the latter is half knotted, which gives two bights only. Each time all the ends are tucked a total of four bights is added.

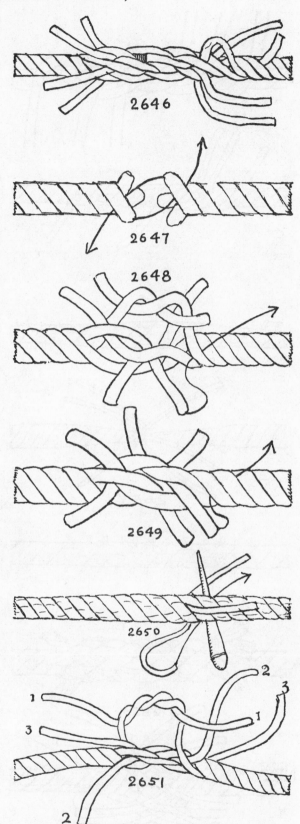

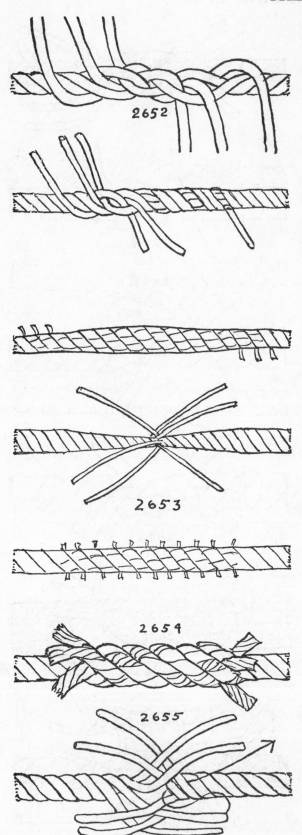

2652

2653

2654

2655

2652. The value of the LEFT-HANDED or SAILMAKER'S SHORT SPLICE is that it preserves the lay of the rope so that the sail may be sewed more evenly to the boltrope. Although when unsupported the BACKHANDED SPLICE is less secure than the OVER-AND-UNDER SPLICE, the sailmaker's stitches render it secure. Splices are always cross stitched to the canvas. Kipping, in 1847, speaking of square sails, says: "The SHORT SPLICE is used upon the foot of sails, under the service, or where the splice is not required to be made very long."

Crotch two three-strand ropes together, open the rope with a fid and stick a strand left-handed as pictured in ⚹2632.

All strands having been stuck once, as in ⚹2651, it will be found that they will "set" more snugly if permitted to stagger as illustrated at the top of this page, instead of being held a-tier. After all strands have been stuck once the sailmaker takes the forward strand at the right end and leads it to the right around and around the same strand, cutting out a few yarns on the underside after each tuck so that the tuck completely hides all ends. This is called "running down" a strand. When the yarns are reduced to three or four, the next strand is taken and "run down" in the same way and then the third. The final tucks of the three strands are carefully arranged so that they are not in the same cross section of the rope.

2653. By tapering the strands, as described for SPLICE ⚹2643, a particularly smooth SAILMAKER'S SPLICE may be made, backing the strands as described in the last splice and cutting out the yarns as described in ⚹2643. The two final tucks of each end should be *through* the strand that is being followed. The ends are trimmed off short. The splice must be much longer than the OVER-AND-UNDER SPLICE (⚹2543) and its security depends almost entirely on the tightness with which the ends are laid up after tapering. Unless the workmanship is really excellent the splice is not dependable.

2654. "The divil himself, with all hell to help him, couldn't make a FOUR-STRAND, BACKHANDED SHORT SPLICE that was worth a damn." This is an old sea adage which I first heard from Captain Daniel F. Mullins. It is as true as it is terse.

2655. The course of a strand in an ordinary SAILOR'S SPLICE is over one and under one. In the THREE-STRAND BACKHANDED SPLICE the course is over one and under two (see ⚹2649).

But in the FOUR-STRAND BACKHANDED SPLICE (⚹2654) that has just been commented upon, the course would be over one and under three.

This leaves a splice that is over one and under two in four-strand rope and that so far has not been considered. A splice made in this manner is more compact than ⚹2654 and perhaps more secure. But even ⚹2654 will be secure if served over. This method of tucking has been used with six strands in wire splicing.

2656. The SAILMAKER'S SPLICE, per se, also called the TAPER SPLICE, the SAILMAKER'S TAPER SPLICE and the SWEET POTATO SPLICE.

LONG AND SHORT SPLICES (MULTI-STRAND BENDS)

This was formerly much used on square sails where the diameter of the boltrope was changed for each side of the sail.

In general there is no clear line of division between the splices of the different crafts. Many sailors have served an apprenticeship in rigging or sailmaking and many sailmakers and riggers have made at least one voyage to sea. Generally it is in the details and refinements that the practices overlap, for the requirements of the three trades are different and basically the splices must differ. There should seldom be any doubt in identifying the source of a splice.

To make the TAPER SPLICE: Open the smaller rope a short distance and open the larger rope several times that distance, possibly eighteen inches, but be governed by the size and the degree of disproportion between the two ropes. Marry and stop at the crotch.

Cut away one fourth of the yarns on the underside of one of the larger strands *before* backing it into the smaller rope. Follow down the same strand of the smaller rope with backhanded tucks, cutting out a few yarns of the larger strand at each tuck until the strand is reduced to a very few yarns. Repeat with the second strand. When the third strand is tucked the cutting-out may have to be varied somewhat to make the strand fill the space evenly. The ends are carefully arranged a-tandem, not a-tier. The small rope strands are now spliced *over one and under one* into the larger rope, three or four times, tapering as you go and *backing* the final tuck.

2657. To short splice two left-laid ropes together: Proceed exactly as with right-laid rope but the tucks are taken in the contrary direction.

2658. When a left- and a right-laid rope are short spliced together the strands of both ends already point away from the splicer in the direction they are to be tucked. Structurally the whole length of this splice is identical with SIX-STRAND ROUND SINNET.

By short splicing together twenty- or thirty-foot shots of alternating left-laid and right-laid rope, of the same size, an anchor warp may be made that will have no tendency whatever to kink, that will lie fair at all times and that may be coiled in either direction. Such a rope will ride easier than any other kind of cable, and if the splices are well tapered there is little loss of strength and little trouble will be had at the winch. The same splice, used on a seine or net, will do away with the tendency to roll up at the edge.

LONG SPLICES are impractical in left- and right-laid rope, but if one should be put in, for any reason, it should be served over.

2659. In the same way as #2658 a cable may be spliced to a hawser as if both were three-strand ropes. Seize both rope and cable before opening and stop the six working ends. Tuck twice full in each direction, then divide the ends and cross whip as in a SLINGS SPLICE.

2660. A strand may be spliced to a heart in a similar way. This is required when tying a FIVE-STRAND STAR KNOT in a shroud-laid rope. One tuck is sufficient.

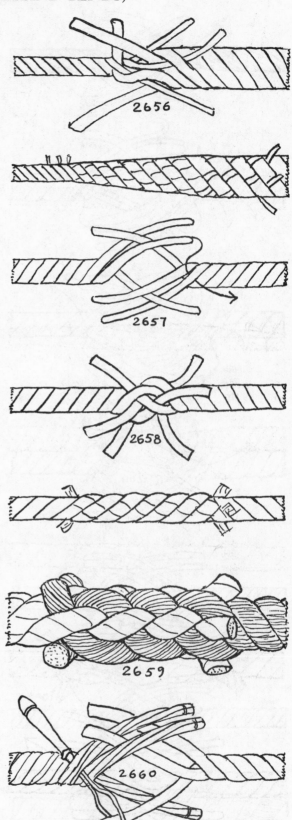

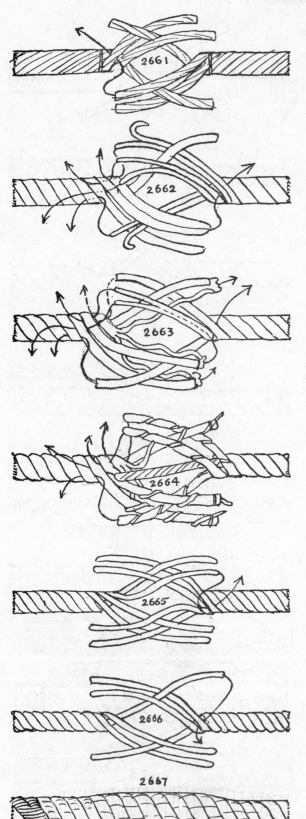

2661. To *splice two strands together:* Stop them at the length of the splice and cut out the heart yarns, leaving all outside yarns undisturbed. Divide the remaining yarns of each end into equal thirds and crotch them. Then, using a loop of stiff wire, short splice as ⚹2365, but reversely since the lay is left. Care must be taken to tuck under an equal number of yarns at each operation. The ends of the splice should be whipped with sail twine. If the strands are to be worked up into sinnet this will not be necessary.

2662. A SHORT SPLICE of four-strand material to three-strand material. At times considerable four-strand rope has been used in the running rigging of yachts. It is more pliant than three-strand rope and is smoother and softer to handle, but many chandleries do not carry it and replacements while cruising are sometimes difficult. Consequently the occasion will arise for a THREE-STRAND TO FOUR-STRAND SPLICE. This splice is often required by lobstermen and other longshore fishermen who collect and use secondhand gear.

The common way to make the SHORT SPLICE is to crotch two strands of the four-strand rope end for use as a unit and to divide a single strand of the three-strand rope. Tuck all ends once as in the illustration. After the first tuck of the two-strand unit, half of each of the two strands are laid together to make a single strand and the three strands are then tucked full once more, and then once one half and once one quarter.

Turn the structure around, divide the three full strands in half and lay out half from two of them. Tuck the remaining *four half strands* as a four-strand rope, twice full and once one half.

2663. A THREE- BY FOUR-STRAND SHORT SPLICE, from Alston's *Seamanship.* Seize both ends. Divide one strand of the four-strand rope into thirds and lay up one of these thirds with each of the remaining three full strands. Crotch the ends as in three-strand rope, stick twice full, once one half and once one quarter. Turn the splice around and divide one strand of the three-strand rope into two parts and tuck as described in the previous splice.

2664. In this splice the four-strand end is treated as in the previous splice and the THREE-STRAND SPLICE has one fourth of the yarns from each strand laid out and then laid up into a fourth strand. The ends are then married and are short spliced in the usual way, four strands into the four-strand rope and three strands into the three-strand rope.

2665. Lay up the three-strand rope into a four-strand rope by robbing one fourth of the yarns from each strand to make a fourth that is long enough for a regular FOUR-STRAND SHORT SPLICE. But if the three-strand rope is the smaller one an extra strand may be side spliced into it for a length as long as the whole splice.

2666. Lay up the four-strand rope into three strands by dividing the extra strand among the three that remain, for a distance long enough to allow of a regular THREE-STRAND BACKHANDED SPLICE.

2667. If a single strand of the four-strand rope equals in size a strand from the other rope, one of the strands of the four-strand rope may be sunk or buried before it would enter the splice, and a THREE-STRAND SHORT SPLICE made. The method of sinking a strand is shown as ✕2707.

2668. A REVERSED SHORT SPLICE. Crotch the ropes as usual, and tuck one set of strands back into their own rope end, as pictured. Do likewise with the other end. Make all fair and tuck all strands full a second time and then half strands for the third tuck. The splice is perhaps more flexible than the usual SHORT SPLICE. It was shown to me as a "trick" and so far as I know it has no practical purpose.

2669. The "LONG ROLLING SPLICE" or LOG LINE SPLICE was used in lead and log lines before machine-braided "sinnet rope" made its appearance. It is actually a LONG CUT SPLICE with the two component SIDE SPLICES more widely separated than is usual. After one of the SIDE SPLICES has been made, the two parallel parts are twisted and laid up tightly together before the strands of the second splice are stuck. The legs must be of equal length. Four palm-and-needle whippings are added. The avowed purpose of this splice is to prevent unbending while in the water. For this purpose it was deemed more secure than the SHORT SPLICE. The method of making the SIDE SPLICE required is shown as ✕2826.

2670. A HAWSER SHORT SPLICE. Crotch and stick one end only. Next halve all six strands and tuck both ends once, then halve them again and tuck all six once more, and if the hawser is to be towed through the water, *back all ends once*. Give the splice six strong seizings, or else serve over for the full length.

2671. The CABLE SHORT SPLICE. Seize very strongly before opening the ends. Stick each rope, of the three which form the cable, twice in each direction, then cut out one strand from each of the six ropes and stick the ropes again. Cut out another strand from each of the six ropes and tuck the remaining six strands once more. Trim the ends and serve over with spun yarn a distance somewhat more than the full length of the splice. The illustration shows only the right end of the splice.

2672. A CABLE SHORT SPLICE. In this splice, given by Steel (1794), Gower (1808) and Blount (1811), each end of the ropes is stuck full twice. Then one strand from each rope is wormed along the cable and the rest are teased, scraped, tapered, marled and given a round and two end seizings. Gower says this is "the snuggest cable splice."

2673. The TAPERED CABLE SHORT SPLICE is described by Steel in 1794. The splice is tucked full twice each way and then the ends are opened, teased, scraped and served over with spun yarn; the ends of the service are "snaked."

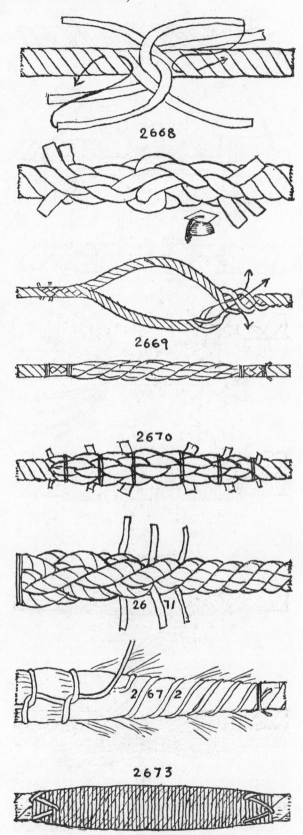

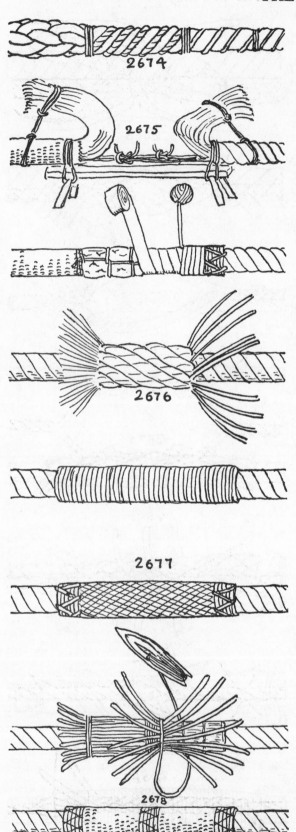

2674. The (CABLE) DRAWING SPLICE "is esteemed the best for cables as it may be readily undone." The cable is seized and opened about ten feet. The three ropes of each end are tapered the full length. A SHORT SPLICE is put in and tucked twice full, each way. At each end of the splice a "quarter seizing" is added. The tapered tails are next tightly wormed along the cable, and middle and end seizings put on.

2675. A SINNET ROPE SPLICE. This method was also used for sinnets, plain-laid hawsers, for cables, and for splicing any one of the three to any one of the others. The rope should be opened for a distance equal to twelve or fifteen times its diameter. The two ends should be held rigidly with vises, clamps or lashings at two points about ten times the diameter of the rope apart. The opened ends should be turned and held back with a RING KNOT (#1859) in the manner pictured. Take two of the bottom yarns and bend them together either with ROPE YARN KNOT #1480 or with a SQUARE KNOT. The tension of the yarns *must be kept uniform* throughout but not too taut. Tie opposite *bottom* yarns together first. Scatter the knots evenly throughout the length of the splice. If the yarns prove troublesome, wax them. Cut the ends fairly short. When through knotting, stop the splice securely in several places, or else bind tightly with adhesive tape. Serve over and snake the ends of the service.

If the yarns of the two ropes are of unequal size, knot two of one side to three of the other, employing a REEF KNOT.

2676. The GRECIAN SHROUD SPLICE (1). Short splice the hearts of two shroud-laid ropes two full tucks each way, and cut off the ends short (see #2644). Serve the heart over hard with marline. Divide each of the four surface strands into three parts, making twelve in all. Twist up each part in turn tightly, wax and rub well with a rag. Marry the twenty-four parts. Put a stop around them at the center, and proceed exactly as in the ordinary SHORT SPLICE, tucking over one and under one. Each end is tucked twice full. Scrape ends, tease, taper, parcel and serve.

2677. The GRECIAN SHROUD SPLICE (2). This is the same as the above but the center of the splice is cross-pointed (#3023) and the ends are whipped and snaked.

2678. GRAFTING is an old splice employed on block straps and standing rigging. The two ends are crotched and seized and, if the ropes are shroud-laid, the hearts are cut out. The underside of each strand is also cut out. The ropes are then wormed with yarns from the undersides of the already reduced strands. More yarns from the undersides of the strands are teased out and marled down with waxed sail twine.

The remaining surface yarns from both ropes are crotched so that they lead alternately left and right.

The center of the splice having been whipped with Italian marline, fishline, lobster cord or other material, employ one end of the whipping as a warp and revolve the rope away from you, laying the yarns of the right end alternately to the left and right of the warp (which leads toward you). The warp passes over only the yarns that are laid down to the right. The total number of yarns must be odd, so that at each new circuit the lead will alternate. If the number is even, cut out a single yarn.

Proceed until sufficient grafting has been made to cover the end you are working. Finish off the end with a whipping the same width as the middle one and snake it. Make the other end of the splice to correspond, and then snake the middle whipping in the same way as the ends.

2679. *Splicing a chain cable to a hemp one.* This splice was described by Nicholas Tinmouth in 1845. No stronger method of bending chain to hemp has since been discovered. Three chain tails of sixty-five links each, made tapering, were shackled to the large end link of a large chain cable. A further tapered ten-foot hemp tail was spliced to the end link of each chain tail (%2858). One or two strands from a large hemp hawser were laid along each of the chain tails, the yarns completely covering it, and these were served over first with spun yarn and after that, were parceled and served a second time with marline.

The chain tails were next laid up tightly into three-strand rope and the hemp cable and chain cable were short spliced to each other in the usual way—three full tucks. Five seizings were put over the splice, the center seizing two inches wide, and the end and quarter seizings one and a half inches wide. The tails of the chain cable were next wormed along the hemp cable and secured with two flat seizings, which were snaked.

The first chain cable for ship use is said to have been made in England about 1812. Previous to that hemp cables were used exclusively. For ships of the line they were sometimes as large as thirty inches in circumference.

The first flexible wire hawser appeared on shipboard about 1875.

Specimens of wire rope have been found in the ruins of Pompeii. Wire rope was rediscovered about 1831 by a man named Clausthal, and at first was used only in mining operations. Wire standing rigging came into use with the advent of the clipper ships in the 1850s.

2680. A TWO-STRAND SHORT SPLICE (marline). Tuck three times full and roll underfoot. If very soft-laid, tuck each strand four times. Structurally a section of this splice is the same as a FOUR-STRAND ROUND SINNET.

Marline is left-handed so it is spliced the opposite of right-laid rope.

2681. A TWO-STRAND BACKHANDED SPLICE. Open and tie a TRIPLE OVERHAND KNOT in each pair of strands. Tighten strongly by pulling alternately at the two pairs of ends. The direction of the knots *must be contrary to the lay of the marline*. Roll underfoot *when tight*.

2682. An INVISIBLE SPLICE for knitting yarn was shown to me by S. R. Ashley. Make the splice when the end is about to disappear into the knitted or crocheted object. Divide and crotch the two ends of yarn and twist the legs around outside the yarn in the same direction as the lay at both ends. Do not twist the body of the yarn itself. Hold with the fingers while knitting it into the material and straighten with a needle if necessary. The splice will not be evident in the finished garment and does not tend to loosen. Do not cut off the ends, if in evidence, but tease them out.

2683. A SINGLE-TUCK SPLICE for twine, cord, yarn, marline, etc. Split one end into two parts and leave the other end unopened. Lay the tip of the large single end into the crotch of the split end and, beginning at that end, plat a very tight three-strand braid for a considerable distance (twice as long as for an ordinary splice). Unless the platting is very firm the splice will not hold. When the two ends are about exhausted stick *one* of them through the center of the unopened yarn. Wax and rub well with the fingers or else roll underfoot.

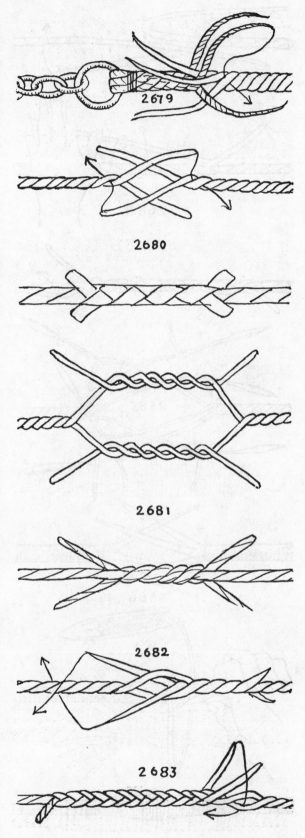

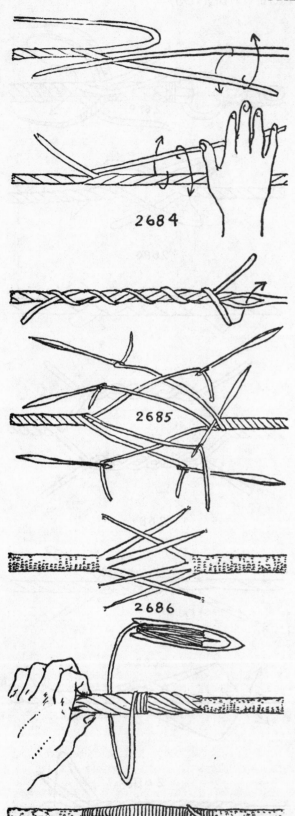

2684

2685

2686

2684. This splice is based on the shoemaker's way of securing a bristle to his thread, but it works very nicely tied in small loose-twisted twine or thread. Open one end into a long fork. If there is any difference in size between them, open the larger end of the two. Wax all three ends and lay out one end of the pair. Overlap the tip of the single end into the crotch of the forked end. Rub the right hand on the knee, away from you if the lay is right, twisting and laying up the two opposite ends. Next, rub the hand reversely on the knee (toward you), twisting both remaining parts but keeping them separated as pictured. When the left end is let go the second leg will overlay the rest. Finally tuck the last-laid tip through the standing part of the single end as pictured. Wax the whole splice and rub well with the fingers.

Sometimes, in stringing beads, a thread is too tight for the hole, making reeving difficult. A piece of smaller thread may be spliced to the end in the manner just described, but before splicing scrape the larger end to a tapered point. Wax the finished splice, reeve the small end and haul the large end through after it.

The same method makes an excellent MARLINE SPLICE but is tied with a different technique. Open one end into a long fork and place the other tip overlapping the crotch as before. Then, twisting with the fingers of both hands, lay up the single tip with the lower leg of the fork. Then, with a reverse twist and two hands, lay up the part that was first made, with the remaining leg. Finally tuck the tip of this leg through the lay of the single marline, and roll underfoot.

2685. A SHIP MODELMAKER'S SPLICE. In splicing very small material, the splice, except for one minor difference, is the same as the ordinary SHORT SPLICE (⚹2635). The ends are opened for a considerable length and a sail needle, the smallest that will serve, is threaded to each strand. A sailmaker's palm is worn and the splice is made by thrusting the needle instead of tucking with the fingers. No effort should be made to tuck *under* the opposing strand; the splice will be firmer if the needle is thrust directly through a strand from one cuntline to the next. Ordinarily two full tucks are taken and only in ship models of exceptional size is any effort made to taper the strands. Another good way to splice in very small stuff is to draw the ends through with a hairpin.

2686. An ANGLER'S SPLICE for small braided fishline. With the point of a pin, needle or fishhook ravel the ends for an inch, more or less, depending on the size of the line. Divide each end into three equal parts, wax well and scrape each part to a taper point. Marry the ends, allowing tips to overlap the solid part of the line very slightly, as in the first drawing. Seize with a CONSTRICTOR KNOT (⚹1249) at the center of the splice, and hold in a vise at the middle. Twist one half strongly one way and with a fine waxed silk thread serve it *tightly* the other way to a point beyond the frayed ends. Secure the end under several turns as in a whipping and repeat with the other end of the splice. Roll between two boards and cover with thin spar varnish.

2687. A "Snakehead" or "Telescope" Splice for *banding* or *tubing*. There is a special tool called a *banding splicer* made for this particular splice which is a variety of wire loop, but a sail needle will serve as well or better. All round commercially braided cord is tubular and this splice is used with most sorts except sash cord. Take a sail needle and work it carefully along the interior of the banding. Start about six inches from the end and, pointing the *eye end* of the needle toward the end, bring it to the surface four inches from the end. To do this, work the material back over the eye end of the needle and, when the proper spot is reached, work or force the eye end out through the side to the surface at a spot about four inches distant from the end. Next reeve the tip of the other piece of banding through the end of the needle, scraping it to a point if necessary, and draw the second piece of banding lengthwise through the first and out at the spot where the needle was first entered. Smooth the banding carefully where it is doubled and leave six inches of the second end protruding. Stick the eye of the needle into the second end two inches behind the spot where the second end enters the first end, and bring it out beside the spot where the first end protrudes. Reeve the first end through the eye and withdraw the needle through the banding. Draw the two doubled parts together and smooth out the splice, stretch it and cut the ends off flush. If the banding is hard and has a core or heart, the hearts or cores must be pulled out at the end and cut off for a length of six inches before starting the splice.

2688. The Rope Yarn Knot or Marline Bend (1) is crotched as a splice but is tied as a knot. Split the ends of two rope yarns, crotch them and leave two of the halves inert while the other two opposite halves are knotted as pictured. This knot bulks three times the size of the rope yarn where a Reef Knot bulks four times the size. It may be tied in any one- or two-strand material.

2689. Rope Yarn Knot or Marline Bend (2). This bulks the same size as the previous knot and is perhaps more secure. Neither of the knots is particularly strong, but they are usually employed in serving and for such purposes have been found adequate.

2690. Occasionally three-thread marline is found and it may be bent together in this manner, two yarns from each end being knotted. But, if there is time, a splice is preferable in every way, as it will bulk only twice the size of the material and is stronger.

2691. A Tucked Marline Bend. This is a recent way of joining marline for serving and it bulks less than a Rope Yarn Knot. The ends are overlapped for several inches and each end is stuck twice through the standing part of the other end. The strands are generally opened with a pricker and the splice must be well rubbed down with the fingers or rolled under the foot before being put to use. The ends of the marline should be carefully buried under the turns of the service. The splice will lie flat and be almost indistinguishable. Nowadays this knot is more popular than the Rope Yarn Knots, being neater and of smaller diameter.

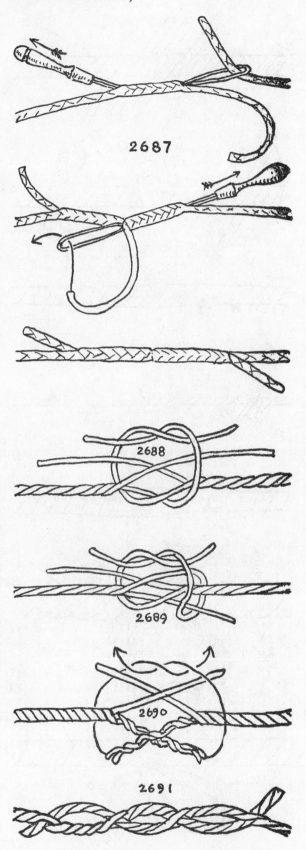

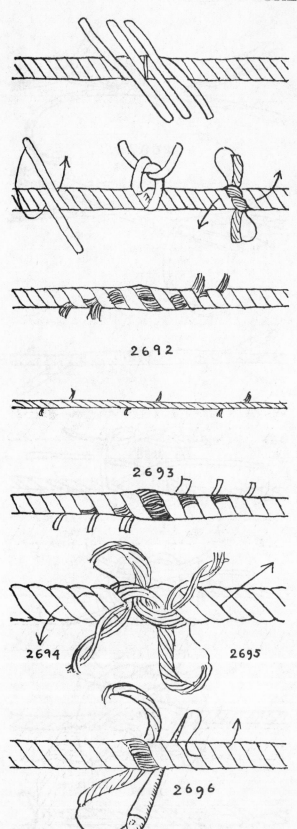

2692

2693

2694   2695

2696

2692. LONG SPLICES are mentioned by Falconer in 1769. They are used wherever it is necessary for a splice to pass through a block, since they are smaller in diameter than SHORT SPLICES. But they are practical only if the two ropes to be joined are of the same size.

Some of the ropemaking concerns state that a LONG SPLICE weakens a rope as much as fifty per cent. But unless a splice is very badly made indeed this can hardly be true, since there are at every length in a LONG SPLICE two untouched strands. This leaves sixty-six and two thirds per cent of the rope at all times intact. So even if the third strand has no strength at all, which can hardly be imagined, fifty per cent is still too low an estimate.

To tie a long splice: Marry the rope as in a SHORT SPLICE, but make the legs much longer (about fifteen inches for each inch of circumference in the rope). The strands may be arranged as depicted in the upper diagram, and stopped at the point in the center where a vertical line is drawn. Proceed with the two opposing strands at the right end, laying one out to the right and laying the other one into its score, "one turn out and one turn in," at one time. When the length of one strand is reduced to nine inches, arrange the two ends as the left ends in the second diagram and, pulling them snugly together, leave them for the moment. Proceed to lay out and lay in the two left strands in the same manner described for the right-hand ones, but, having made about two circuits of the rope, stop and examine the center of your splice carefully. If the two continuous sections at the center are not even and smooth you must rearrange the tension with the left end with which you are now working. Failing to do this, your splice will be worthless. *This is the danger point for a beginner.* When the left strands are correctly laid, half knot all ends as pictured in the second diagram, removing enough of the lay or twist so that the yarns will lie fair. Having knotted the ends, work the center pair first, tuck each end over and under twice full and then a half. Treat the other ends in the same fashion.

2693. This differs from the last only in being tucked once full, once one half and once one quarter. It is also good practice to tuck once full, once two thirds and once one third.

2694. The present splice and the other LONG SPLICES to follow are all arranged as in the previous description until three sets of opposing strands face each other along the rope. A more uniform splice than those already shown is made by laying out one half of each strand *before* knotting. The two opposing half strands are then knotted together. Tuck the ends over and under twice, divide the remainder and stick once more.

2695. The sailmaker, having laid out one half the strand as above, knots the two ends and "backs" the remaining part once, then halves it and backs it a second time.

2696. The Sailor's Backhanded Long Splice. Knot full, then *back* (over one, under two) twice, then divide and tuck once more, over one and under two.

2697. A Sailmaker's Long Splice. Lay out half of each strand before half knotting the ends and tuck the parts that were laid out as shown by the center arrow. A few yarns, the same number each time, are then cut out *on the underside* at each tuck. Each end is run down singly until only two or three yarns are left. These are cut off short.

2698. If there is plenty of time, and the material is good, a neat Sailmaker's Splice may be made by tapering each strand to half size at the point of knotting. For the method of tapering see #2643 in this chapter. Lay the ends side by side and knot as shown by the arrows. Then back the full distance of the taper, cutting out yarns on the underside at a rate corresponding to the taper that was previously made. Arrange the lay of the strand after each tuck so that it corresponds throughout the rope.

2699. A Long Splice for larger material. In hawsers, the strands are not half knotted for the reason that a Half Knot in large material is exceedingly difficult to draw up. Opposite strand ends are placed alongside in the same way as heretofore and then each is tucked full *over* the opposing end and under the next strand as indicated by the arrows. It is then halved and tucked over and under once more.

2700. This splice, which is also recommended for hawsers, is tucked once full, and then is backed (tucked backhanded) once one half. It is always better for towing to have the final tuck of any splice a backhanded one.

2701. A Hawser Splice. The strands are first halved and tucked, as shown by the arrows, over one and under two. They are then tucked over one and under two a second time.

All the methods given are in good standing: some of the differences are slight but others are greater than they may seem at first glance. The first essential in any of them is good workmanship. In fact, good workmanship is of more importance than the method.

2702. The Sailmaker's "Quick" or "Chain Lightning" Splice (the latter being the common name). One end only is stuck full, just once. This splice has been widely used on quick jobs for the merchant service. The knot is on the forward side of the boltrope, next to the canvas. The ends are seized and cut short. When cross stitched to the canvas, the splice has been found secure enough for practical commercial use.

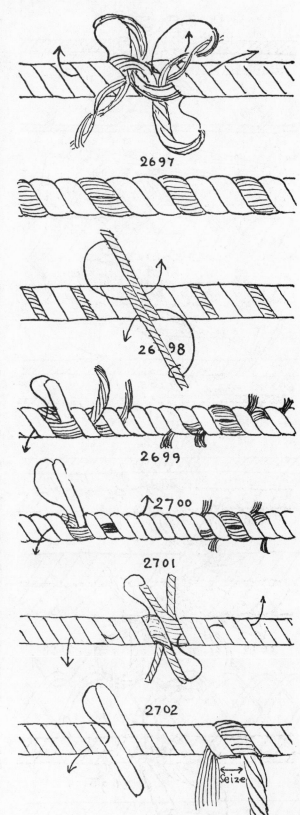

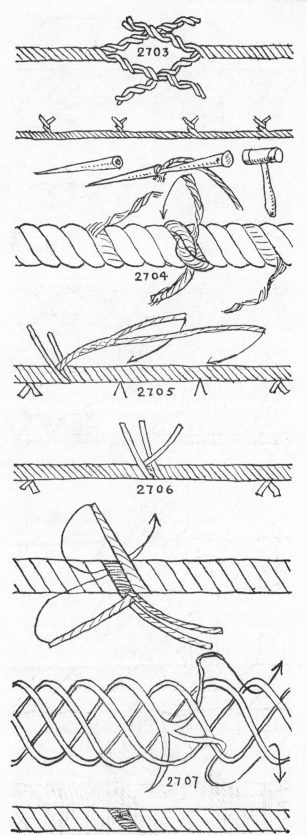

2703. To *long splice two four-strand ropes:* Open each rope end into one fork of two legs, each leg containing two undisturbed strands. Crotch these two forks, cutting out the cores if there are any so that they do not quite butt. In length the legs of each fork should equal about one foot for each inch of the rope's circumference. Lay out one leg and lay in the opposing leg one quarter of its length. Separate the two pairs of legs into their two component single strands. Lay up and half knot one opposing pair where it lies and proceed to lay out and lay in the remaining opposing pair for two thirds of the remaining length. Half knot this pair.

Treat the other end of the splice in like manner. The four pairs of strands should now be evenly spaced along the rope. The ends may now be spliced as in ⚓2696 or ⚓2697.

2704. A TRANSMISSION ROPE SPLICE. Open the two ends of a four-strand rope into a fork one third longer than in the last splice. Take out the twist of the rope one full turn and crotch the two ends. Proceed to arrange as in the second diagram of ⚓2703.

When the eight strand ends are laid up in four equidistant pairs the procedure changes. Unlay the two strands of the left pair two full turns each, and, without disturbing the lay of the yarns, divide the ends carefully into two even parts. Lay out one half and then lay back the remaining one half from each end back to the center (not too tightly) and half knot them together as in the diagram.

Use a wire loop and with it *back* the proper center half strand to the left, preserving the lay carefully, until it butts the left half strand that was laid out. The lay should be kept so even that it will not be evident that it has been disturbed. Do likewise with the other pair of half strands, after which the other three pairs of strands are to be treated in the same manner.

There should now be eight joints laid up together, each consisting of two half strands. The rope should be smooth and even throughout, but if it is not that should now be corrected.

Take the left pair of half strands that have been laid up, and knot them as ⚓2698, then back each end three times full, or else back and taper them by cutting out a few yarns on the underside at each tuck. Pound well with a mallet and trim the ends. In making such splices two marlingspikes with cupped ends are often used. The point of the second spike grips the strand in the socket of the first marlingspike and the end is driven through the rope with a mallet.

2705. To long splice a three-strand rope to a four-strand rope. Open and crotch the ropes as for a THREE-STRAND LONG SPLICE but with two strands of the four-strand rope opposite a single strand at the center. Side splice an extra strand to the single strand. After the yarns are stuck, taper and back them several turns, so that the lay is kept fair. Lay out the opposing two strands to the right and lay in the single and the side spliced strands to the points marked below the rope. When properly spaced, splice them exactly as the other strands.

2706. Lay out as described for the previous splice. Divide the single strand and back the halves to the right around the opposing full strands as if they were two full strands. Taper the two strands from the four-strand rope, lay them up into a single strand and back them around the single opposing strand to the left.

2707. To *sink a strand:* Instead of laying up two strands into one, as in ⚓2706, many splicers prefer merely sinking the extra end where it lies before it enters the splice. Split the end into three equal parts, stick the three parts as in the diagram and tuck as in SIDE SPLICE ⚓2826.

2708. Cables consist of three plain- or hawser-laid ropes twisted together left-handed. Each component rope having three strands, the cable itself has nine strands. In the following descriptions, when *a rope* is spoken of it will refer to *one third of the cable*, and when a strand is spoken of it will mean one third of a rope, or one ninth of the cable.

An old nineteenth-century custom was to call the ropes strands, and the strands "readies," but the different rope works today have each their own names for the different parts of a cable.

A cable is hard-laid and the work of splicing one is, at times, exacting. But these mechanical difficulties are discussed under ⚓2714. Until that is reached we will merely describe the mechanics of the splices.

The splice pictured is perhaps the simplest of the LONG CABLE SPLICES; it bulks four ropes at the center, or thirty-three per cent larger than the cable itself, but it requires less material than the other LONG SPLICES and is one of the most practical for towing, warping, etc.

The ends are opened up each into its three ropes for a length equal to about ten times the circumference of the cable. The two ends are married and "laid out and laid in" to the right and left just as *strands* were treated in the ROPE SPLICES last described. These two drawings depict the splicing of two *rope* ends—that is, one third only of a whole CABLE LONG SPLICE. The two rope ends are married as shown at the top. After having been crotched, if the ropes prove too loose, the upper strand end should be carefully unlaid (withdrawn) one full turn and will then occupy the lowest position of the three strands. It may be necessary to repeat this operation until the right tension is achieved. This having been done, the strands that point to the right are all three tucked *under the adjacent rope* to the right and the left-hand strands under the adjacent rope to the left. The bottom strand at the right is now left out and the remaining two are tucked once, over and under the *ropes* to the right. Again the bottom strand is left out and the remaining strand is tucked over and under the next rope to the right. The splice is now turned end for end and the other end is spliced as the first. If the cable is to be used for towing the last strand should be backed one tuck.

2709. The MARINER'S SPLICE. Alston, Luce and other nautical authorities say this "can only be done with old soft cables which are not worth the trouble and for these a shroud knot is the best treatment." However, the drilling cable of today is smaller than the ship cables that the naval gentlemen referred to, and a LONG CABLE SPLICE is required nowadays. The MARINER'S SPLICE is always described as "a long spliced cable with long spliced strands" (ropes).

A cable is opened and the ropes laid out and in as pictured in the second diagram. The ropes in turn are opened and the strands laid out and laid in so that there are nine pairs of strands to be spliced as shown in the third diagram. Each strand is divided and one half is tucked over one and under one as shown in the upper diagram, all the tucks being kept on the surface of the rope. For these tasks a marlingspike and considerable force are required.

2710. Bushell's MARINER'S SPLICE. The illustrations show the method of tucking two opposing strands. There are nine such joints in the splice.

2711. The British Admiralty MARINER'S SPLICE from *The Manual of the Sea* (1891). The method of tucking two opposite strands is shown.

2712. Admiral Luce's MARINER'S SPLICE. The HALF KNOT is difficult to draw up and it cannot fail to be objectionably prominent in the finished splice.

2713. A CABLE SPLICE given by Murphy and Jeffers (1849). Two opposite rope ends in the cable are treated as described in ⚓2675.

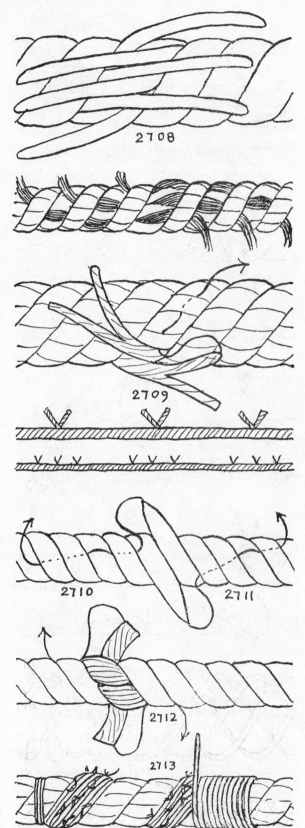

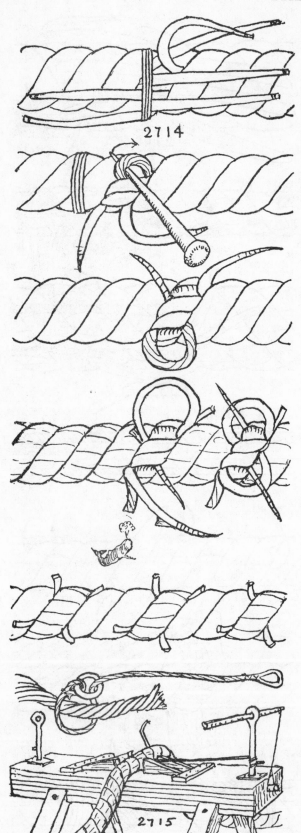

2714

2715

2714. All the descriptions that I have found of the MARINER'S SPLICE are perfunctory and inexplicit.

A rope manufacturer once asked me to describe the MARINER'S SPLICE for use in drilling cable. It seemed probable that the technique of tying could be simplified, even if the splice itself could not. The splice that follows was finally evolved. It has several new features and is not too difficult for one man to tie. Without a helper, I put the splice into a new nine-inch cable. The nine-inch specimen that was made is now shown in the Mariners' Museum at Newport News.

Even large cable is quite simple to marry. The first difficulty is encountered when the strands are to be tucked. This difficulty was met by rough-tapering the strands with a pair of shears and pointing with rubber tape for about fifteen inches (#3570). The cable ends were arranged as already described (#2708). The following description is for one joint of two ropes—that is, one third of the whole splice.

Each pair of *ropes* was married as pictured at the top of the page. One strand at the top having been left out of the seizing, the two upper strands were "laid in and out" to the right. Both strands were greased with tallow, and with a marlingspike the turn *from* the right was pricked up and, using a heavy pair of blacksmith's tongs, was *twisted* out. The greased point of the opposite strand was inserted in the vacated score far enough to be seized with the blacksmith tongs. In this way the strands were laid out and in, *three* full tucks, the trailing end being hove taut after each tuck. The way in which they were tightened is described below as #2715. The bottom pair of strands was then treated in the same way as the top ones.

The next thing to be done was to knot the center pair of strands. This is shown in the fourth diagram. It is this knot and the pointed ends that make the splice practicable. Both points being well tallowed, the upper one was withdrawn *nearly to the tip* and the lower one was rove, as pictured at the right of the fourth diagram. Half of each strand was then cut out, after which the two ends were pulled through simultaneously with the winch that is pictured below. Even with well-tallowed strands it will help to pound with a mallet while heaving on the strands. When all is faired, the other two pairs of strands are knotted in the same way and the splice is one third complete.

When all nine points have been tucked, beat the splice thoroughly with a mallet from end to end several times, and trim all ends to a four- or five-inch length.

In small-sized cable, the knotted strands may be pulled taut with two marlingspikes and MARLINGSPIKE HITCHES. Place one spike under the insteps, the opposite one across the knees, as in #364.

2715. In making large CABLE SPLICES, I employed the winch that is pictured alongside. Four one-inch boards were nailed together, with an inch hole bored in each end. Then a whole board was added below to stop the holes. The threaded ends of two long one-inch eyebolts were sawed off with a hack saw. Two pairs of cleats were nailed down the center of the bench, forming a four-inch groove. The gap between the ends of the two pairs of cleats was five inches. A lug was put on each bolt. Two small flexible wire ropes were spliced to two rings and the other ends each had an eye to go over a lug on the eyebolts. With this apparatus strands could be pulled on as strongly as needed.

There are no new principles involved in wire splicing, but a different technique is required on account of the stiffness of the material. A SHORT SPLICE in wire is seldom seen.

2716. A SHORT BACKHANDED WIRE SPLICE. Seize the ropes at the length of the splice. Tape the end of each strand and open the ropes, cutting out the cores. Spread the strands fan-shape, and bring them together just as two hands are clasped with interlocked fingers. Force the ends closely together so that the two cores butt and seize strongly at the point of crossing. The cores of the separate strands are usually cut out before a splice is tucked. Hold in a vise at half length, and *back* each of the six ends of one side under one strand as shown in ⚓2632, except that in wire splicing the marlingspike points to the left when entering a rope, and the rope is entered and tucked on the near side of the spike. Reverse the splice in the vise end and tuck the other six ends once. Work them all snugly back toward the center. Then tuck until all twelve ends have been tucked four times full. Now *back each alternate strand* once more. Pound well with a mallet, cut all ends flush and parcel and serve over the whole splice.

2717. An earlier SHORT SPLICE is given by Admiral Knight in his *Seamanship*. Each strand was tucked *over one and under two*, twice full, once one half and once one quarter. The British Admiralty (1932) specifies an ordinary OVER-ONE-AND-UNDER-ONE SPLICE, tucked four times full, once two thirds and once one third.

2718. A LONG WIRE SPLICE. Take two small wire ropes (five eighths of an inch in diameter will do), and seize each at a point ten feet from the end. Tape the strands of each end *in pairs*, and open each rope end into a three-legged fork. Crotch the two forked ends and lay out and lay in the pairs to the right and left so that they are evenly spaced five feet apart. Stop the right pair and the center pair and open the ends of the left pair. Tape each strand and lay out and lay in one opposite pair to the left for three feet. Then put stops on both pairs. Open the center two pairs and lay in and lay out one pair to the left two feet and the other to the right the same amount and stop both pairs. Turn the splice end for end and treat the second end the way the first was treated. The ends are now in six pairs.

Cross a pair of ends as in the fourth diagram and cut them all to a one-foot length, first taping five or six inches of each end. Drive a marlingspike between two ends and through the center of the rope. Cut the core and lay out the core ends a short distance. Hold one end of the splice in a vise, put a heaver (first diagram) on the other end and have a helper twist the latter sufficiently to open the rope so that the strand end can be thrust into the center, replacing the core, as the spike is revolved. At the same time remove the core and cut it off flush with the strand end. The remaining ends are worked in the same manner.

2719. In lang-laid rope the strands and the rope have the same lay or twist. The splice is made the same as ⚓2718, except that the ends are crossed differently for the final laying in.

2720. A *wire rope spliced to a Manila tail*. When wire halyards were first introduced this splice was used. The wire end was opened into three legs of two strands each and each leg was served or taped the full length, and laid up again. The two ropes were then short spliced together, the Manila legs being tucked six times, the wire three. The splice is served over.

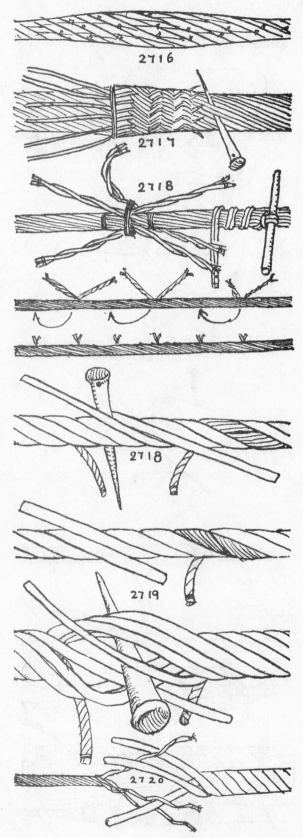

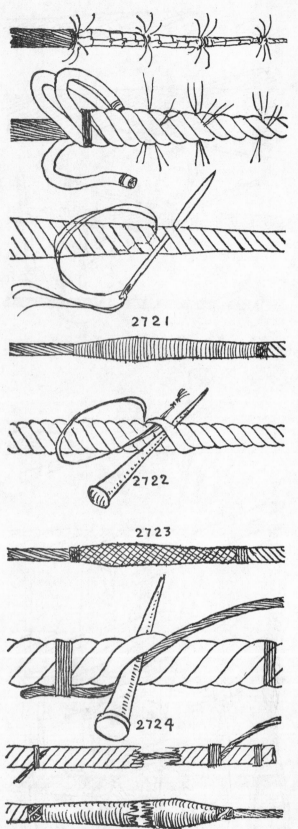

2721. A Tail Splice, that is said to have originated in Bristol, Rhode Island, was shown to me by Arthur Carlsen.

Seize a one-half-inch (diameter) wire rope at three feet from the end. Lay back three alternate strands to the seizing and lay out one half of each. Lay in the three remaining halves for nine inches, seize the rope a second time and lay out the three remaining half strands.

Seize the three full strands that remain at nine inches from the last (second) seizing and lay out one half of each strand. Lay up the three half strands that are left for nine inches, put on a fourth (and last) seizing and lay out the ends. Parcel and serve each section. There should now remain only a nine-inch core. Taper this to a point.

Open a Manila rope end two and a quarter inches in circumference for about five feet and lay it up tightly over the tapered end of the wire rope. Each set of wire ends should be divided evenly in thirds and led to the surface between two Manila strands. Stop the rope frequently, wherever needed. Seize the ends of the Manila strands several inches to the left of the protruding wires (second diagram).

Thread several or one of the right-hand wires on a large sail needle and stick them over and under into the Manila rope, but in a peculiar way. In passing over (which comes first) the wire is pulled down completely out of sight between two surface yarns. In tucking under (which follows) the needle is thrust through the middle of the next strand at right angles to it. In this way no wires appear on the surface. Each group is differently led and is sewed from six to ten tucks, so that the ends are well scattered. The last tuck should be *backed* through the strand, and the end trimmed short. Pound with a mallet. Tease and scrape the ends of the Manila rope and lay it up around the wire. Parcel it and marl and serve the whole length of the splice with Italian marline or fishline.

2722. Before the technique just described was generally adopted, much the same splice was made by crotching the two ropes. A number of wires were taped together and tucked in the regular short splice manner except that the "over" wires were sunk between two yarns as in the last splice. The wires were cut out at regular intervals.

2723. A *somewhat earlier* Tail Splice was made as follows: The wire end was rough pointed by cutting out one strand at a time. The Manila rope was opened for several feet and the strands were also opened. The lower half of the yarns were marled down over the end of the wire, the ends being scraped down. The remaining yarns were then cross-pointed for a distance somewhat longer than the wire point, and the ends were then seized.

2724. *Drilling cable to Manila cable.* Point the end of the wire cable for about fifteen feet by first cutting out the core and then reducing the strands, one at a time, until only one is left. If the Manila cable has a heart it should be cut out for the full length of the splice. Whip the end of the Manila cable. Seize the tip of the wire cable to the Manila cable at the point where the Manila heart was cut out and, with a marlingspike, lay the wire into the heart of the Manila cable until within a foot of the whipping. Seize it there. Next with a marlingspike lay the tip of the wire cable into the Manila rope and remove the seizing. Taper the end of the Manila cable for a foot and marl it down around the wire rope. Serve over the whole length of the splice and snake the ends.

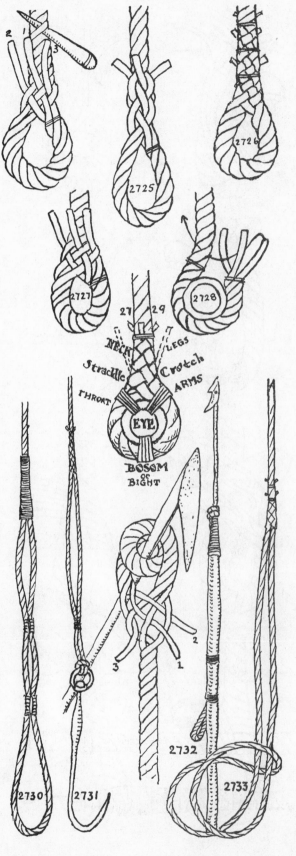

CHAPTER 35: EYE SPLICES (Multi-Strand Loops)

Every finger a marlingspike,
Every hair a rope yarn.

Sailors' Adage

2725. The Sailor's Eye Splice. Form the eye and spread the strands away from you fanwise, placing them against the rope where it is to be entered. Untwist the rope one half turn, open the top or center bight with a small fid, and stick the center strand under the center bight from right to left, then stick the left strand under the next bight to the left in the same direction and lastly stick the right strand, from right to left, under the remaining bight. After this, tuck all strands once more, over one and under one. Trim the ends at a length equal to one diameter of the rope.

Ship-model builders should make this splice with three sail needles, or else by drawing the ends through with a hairpin.

2726. The *same splice tucked twice full,* and *once one half* (called two and a half tucks). If the rope is "long-jawed," the splice may be tucked four times full. The ends are often whipped twice, over the last two tucks.

2727. Darcy Lever's Sailor's Eye Splice, from the *Sheet Anchor* (1808). Tuck the left strand a second time as shown, to bring all the ends into the same tier, and then tuck all strands two and one half times further.

2728. A Thimble Eye. Put on a stop or else chalk-mark the rope at the point where the strands are to be opened, and also the point where the ends are to be stuck. This length is equal to once the round of the thimble, plus once the round of the rope. One half a turn is taken out of the eye before the strands are stuck. After the eye is completed, it is opened out with a fid and greased with tallow, before driving in the thimble.

2729. In heavy rope the eye is made directly around the thimble. In Rigging Splices the part that rounds the thimble is served over, but hawsers are not served, as they do not dry out readily. After looping the rope around the thimble, seize it at the bosom and then again at either leg, close to where the strands are to be stuck. It may be held vertically in a vise and a Spanish windlass used to heave the legs together, or else use a marlingspike and heave with racking turns.

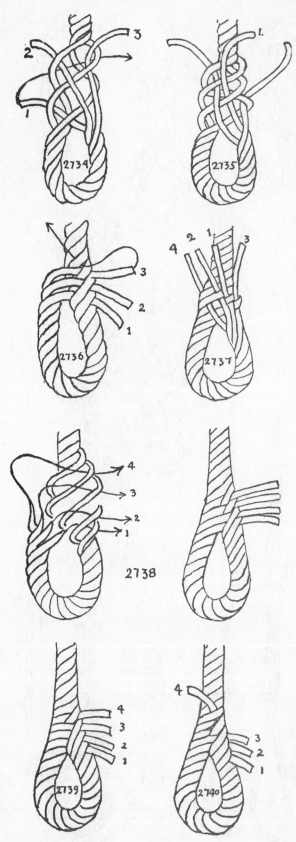

2730. A LEAD LINE EYE SPLICE. The eye is made very long, the splice is tapered and seized, or else served over.

2731. A RUNNING EYE for a sail hook. The eye is made long and seized over the final tuck. After it is in place, it is seized again, close up to the hook.

2732. The WHALEMAN'S EYE is called "THE HITCHES." A round turn is taken about the shank of a whale iron and the rope in the eye is untwisted *one full turn*. It is spliced as ⚓2726.

2733. A LONG EYE or LONG RUNNING EYE is used in making fast to a spar aloft. This saves the need of long reeving. The eye can be tossed over a yard and lowered to deck, where a whole coil can be passed through it before hauling it back to the yard.

Manwayring speaks of the "EYE SPLICE" in 1644. Of all splices, it is the most important. Twenty or thirty of them may be required aboard ship before a SHORT SPLICE is needed.

Anatomically, the EYE SPLICE is one of the queerest things that exists. Its neck is between its legs, its crotch is between its arms, its throat and bosom are in its eye, and it has but one eye.

In long and short splicing, the first direction given is to marry or crotch the strands, but in eye splicing the first direction is to "stick" the strands. Thereafter the strands are "tucked," although the terms are often used interchangeably. The technique of tucking was discussed at the beginning of the preceding chapter.

A seizing should be put around the rope before it is opened, which should be at a distance from the end equal to about four and one half rounds of a strand. Another seizing sometimes is added where the strands are to be entered or stuck; it is sufficient to mark this with chalk. Before sticking, one half a twist must be removed from the lay of the part that forms the eye. Hold the bosom of the eye toward you and the standing part away from you as you work. A WIRE EYE SPLICE is held vertically in a vise with the standing part aloft, and is worked with a marlingspike. Manila is spliced with a fid. pricker or marlingspike, whichever is easiest.

The beginner should whip the ends of all strands before commencing work.

2734. The next two are experimental eyes. They are interesting mainly because they indicate that with only three strands there are still many different ways of starting a splice. Tuck strand 1 over and under once, which brings all the strands in a tier. Then continue to tuck as directed for ⚓2726.

2735. This is another experimental eye that appears to have a good lead. Stick the center strand, which in this case is the bottom one, first. Tuck all strands two and one half times.

2736. The RIGGER'S EYE. The greater number of the eyes which follow belong to the rigger, but this particular one is the eye that is called "RIGGER'S EYE" by both the sailmaker and the sailor. The strands are stuck as the sailmaker sticks them and are then tucked over and under as the sailor tucks them, once full, once one half, and once one quarter.

2737. The SAILOR'S FOUR-STRAND EYE SPLICE. Tuck over and under twice full, then divide each strand and tuck again. This splice is strong, but not so neat as could be wished. The heart, if there is one, is cut out in all FOUR-STRAND SPLICES, unless otherwise directed, and the *final* tucks are improved if they are made over one and *under two* strands.

2738. The RIGGER'S FOUR-STRAND EYE. Stick backhanded as shown and then tuck over and under once full and once one half. This is to be served over. All the tucks may be taken backhanded, in shroud-laid rope, with fair success.

2739. Captain Daniel F. Mullins' FOUR-STRAND EYE SPLICE. Stick as shown and tuck over and under as in #2738. This makes a good THIMBLE EYE.

2740. An experimental FOUR-STRAND EYE. Stick as illustrated, then tuck strands 1, 2, and 3 over and under once more, which brings all four strands into the same tier. After this, tuck all four once full, once one half and finally one quarter. The splice is improved by serving over.

2741. Another experimental FOUR-STRAND OVER-AND-UNDER EYE that is compact and strong.

2742. An experimental FOUR-STRAND OVER-AND-UNDER EYE that is firm and neat.

2743. A FIVE-STRAND OVER-AND-UNDER EYE SPLICE is given in Nares' *Seamanship* (1874). Five-strand rope is unknown to me.

2744. Six-strand rope was once made of hide as well as of very hard-laid hemp and was used primarily for tiller rope, which established the connection between the wheel and the helm. It was used for a few other purposes where there was excessive surface wear. The EYE SPLICE was stuck as shown, and tucked over and under three or four times full, after which it was tapered and served over.

2745. The FLEMISH EYE (1) is a RIGGER'S EYE that was mentioned by Lever in 1808. Nowadays it is frequently miscalled "ARTIFICIAL EYE." One strand is laid out, and the eye is formed with the two remaining strands. The strand that was laid out is now laid around the eye in the contrary direction. No strands are tucked. After everything is fair, seize the strands at the straddle; scrape, worm, tease, taper and fay all ends before serving them over.

2746. The FLEMISH EYE (2). This is started in the same way as the foregoing, but after forming, it is seized at the straddle to hold the strands in place. The innermost of the two strands that lead together is cut off short in the straddle. The two remaining ends are tapered and scraped, wormed and teased along the neck. The eye and splice are both served over.

Some splices as well as knots bear several names; but if the exclusive use of one name for a certain splice or knot would leave another equally worthy without a distinguishing title, I favor the arrangement that allots at least one name to each, provided it is not contrary to the best usage.

When Dana's *Seaman's Friend* was published (1841), the names FLEMISH EYE and ARTIFICIAL EYE had become confused. Speaking of the latter, Dana said, "This is now usually called a FLEMISH EYE."

But Admiral Luce in 1862, speaking of the ARTIFICIAL EYE, says: "Sometimes, though improperly, called a FLEMISH EYE."

If EYE SPLICES are unfamiliar to the reader, banding will be found an excellent material to practice with. Take three equal pieces (or four for a FOUR-STRAND SPLICE), seize them, and *lay them up* into a rope for a length of about ten inches, as described in #144 or #145. This structure will be found easy to tuck and easy to follow and correct. It will hold its shape indefinitely, and will not fray out.

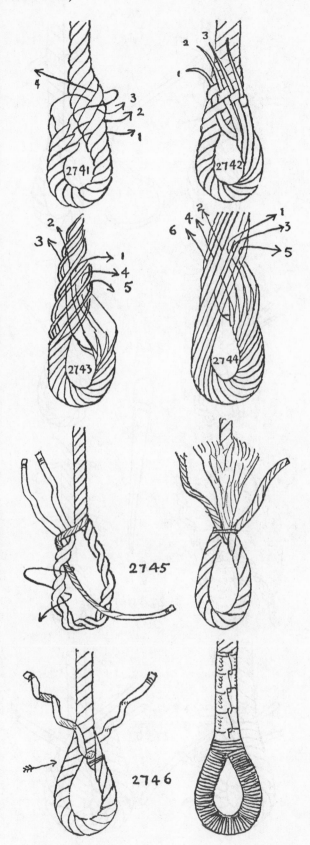

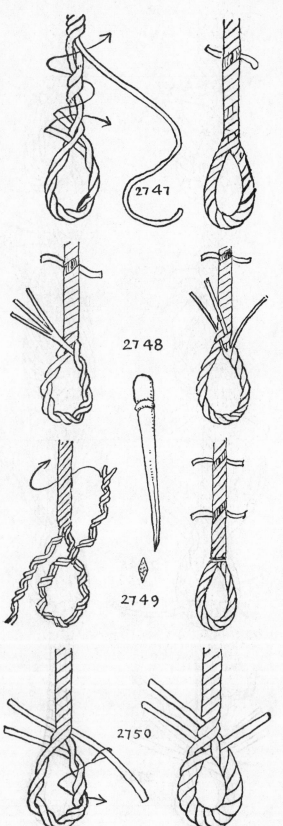

2747. The REEVING EYE was first shown me by Captain Charles W. Smith. As the eye bulks only four strands it can easily be rove through a block if the block is of a proper size for the tackle. One strand is laid out for a considerable length and the eye is formed with the other two strands. When the eye has been turned, one end is stuck as pictured and the other end is laid along the standing part of the rope into the score of the long single strand that was previously laid out. After laying the first end out and the second end in for four or five rounds, half knot the two ends together and finish them off by tucking as in a LONG SPLICE, once one half, and once one quarter. The end that was tucked at the straddle is now *backed* into the neck of the eye as pictured and is tapered and trimmed.

2748. A THREE-STRAND JIB-STAY EYE is similar to the foregoing except that the second end is not backed at the straddle. When the position of the first illustration is reached the end of the strand is divided equally into three parts and opened fanwise. The left part is tucked over one and under one, the center part is tucked under one, and the third part stands as it lies until the second tuck, when all three are tucked over one and under one. Each of the parts is then divided, the lower parts are wormed and the upper parts are teased and scraped and fayed. The whole eye and standing part are served over.

2749. A FOUR-STRAND JIB-STAY EYE. This is very similar to the REEVING EYE (⚓2747). Two strands are laid out and the eye is formed with the other two. The two strands that formed the eye are laid up the standing part into the score vacated by the pair that was laid out. After several turns two of the opposing ends are knotted and the remaining pair of strands are further laid out and in for several turns, where they too are knotted. All ends are spliced as in a LONG SPLICE, once one half and once one quarter, the whole eye and splice are served over, and a strong racking seizing is added at the straddle.

2750. The MAIDEN'S EYE is one of the neatest of the THREE-STRAND OVER-AND-UNDER EYE SPLICES. It was shown to me by Captain Daniel F. Mullins. The strands have an excellent lay and the splice is firm, strong and neat. The eye is formed as the FLEMISH EYE SPLICE and is stuck as illustrated. The single strand (in the right diagram) is stuck under the bight of the uppermost strand of the pair that first formed the eye. All three strands are tucked over and under, twice full, then two thirds, and finally one third.

2751. An eye somewhat similar to the foregoing is also started as the FLEMISH EYE, and is stuck as shown by the arrow. Then it is tucked over and under twice full, once two thirds and once one third.

2752. A FOUR-STRAND EYE. Open the end into two long forks of two strands each. Knot the two forks at the bosom, taking out a little of the twist, and lay up both legs as far as the straddle. Stick them as in the third diagram, both sides being the same, and tuck the splice over and under. Taper as desired.

2753. A FOUR-STRAND BACKHANDED EYE. Tie in shroud-laid rope. Cut out the core for the length of the splice. Form the eye as in the foregoing and stick as depicted in the first of these two illustrations. The front and back faces are identical. Back and taper each strand in turn.

A FOUR-STRAND BACKHANDED SPLICE is generally considered impractical, but if well served over this will prove satisfactory.

The sailor allows for his EYE SPLICE to weaken the rope by about one eighth. Some of the rope manufacturers say that the loss of strength is as much as one half. It would seem to me that, if an EYE SPLICE is well made and the yarns are afterwards *wormed, teased,* and *served over* for a distance greater than the length of the splice, such an allowance is excessive. In fact I think such a splice should not prove weaker than the rope.

The sailmaker waxes his strands, the rigger greases his with tallow but the sailor does neither.

The sailmaker taps his finished splice with a fid, spits on it and burnishes it with the handle of the fid. The rigger pounds his with a marlingspike or a mallet, while the sailor rolls his underfoot on the deck.

The point of a fid, pricker or marlingspike should not be too sharp or it will snag the yarns. A small fid of greenheart, with a diamond-shaped cross section at the tip, and no sharp edges, is the handiest tool I know. It is illustrated on the opposite page. Greenheart is recommended because it is slippery without being greasy.

A good working fid may be made from a hickory hammer handle. It should be sandpapered with the grain, and soaked in linseed oil or even boiled in oil to make it hard and smooth.

In tucking splices, the overlaid part of a strand should be flattened somewhat by the removal of a certain amount of the twist or lay; the method was described near the beginning of Chapter 34. Rigger's splices have the fewest tucks and sailmaker's the most.

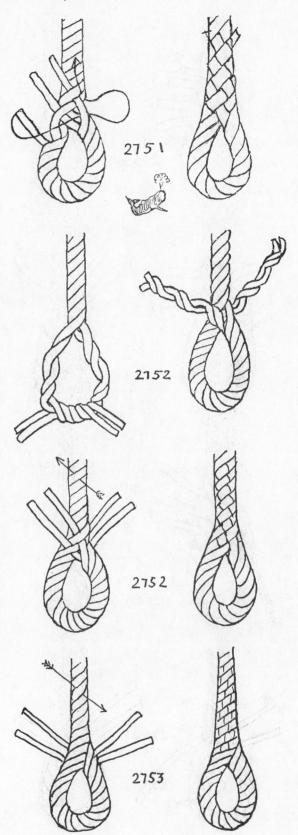

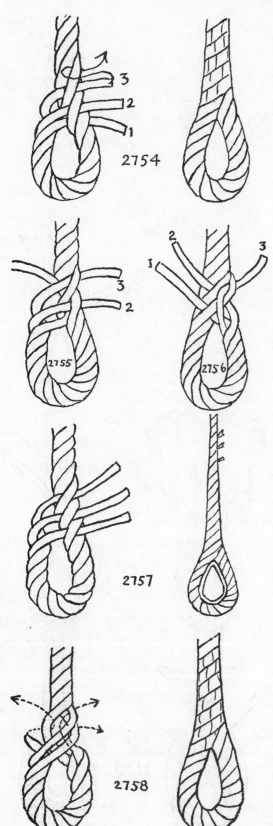

2754. SAILMAKER'S EYE SPLICES are shown on this page. Boltrope being three-strand, the sailmaker is not concerned with FOUR-STRAND EYES. The first three shown are actually identical in structure, although this may not at first be apparent. They are different methods that sailmakers have of sticking the same splice. The strand ends are numbered in the order in which they are stuck.

The SAILMAKER'S SPLICE is not intended to be used unsupported by stitches. Recently in a sail loft I noted that twelve sail bench hooks out of fifteen bore ordinary OVER-AND-UNDER SAILOR'S EYE SPLICES. This may be taken as an expression of opinion from the sailmaker himself.

The common way of sticking the SAILMAKER'S EYE SPLICE (1) is the one given first. The splice being arranged as in the first diagram, each strand is run down in turn—that is to say, it is backed—the full length of the splice, then the next strand is run down. At each tuck a few yarns are cut off short on the underside. The number of yarns removed should be the same for each tuck. The three ends should terminate in a row, along the rope, when reduced to three or four yarns. This is illustrated as ⚹2757.

2755. SAILMAKER'S EYE SPLICE (2). Although differently stuck, this is identical with ⚹2754. At the beginning of Chapter 34, the method of backing a sailmaker's strand is described.

2756. SAILMAKER'S EYE SPLICE (3). This is also the same as ⚹2754.

2757. SAILMAKER'S EYE SPLICE (4). The sticking of this splice is structurally different. It is frequently seen, but is not often used without a thimble. It is more regular, but a little less compact than the common SAILMAKER'S SPLICE. When sewed to a sail, this last is unimportant. It is tucked as directed for ⚹2754. SAILMAKER'S EYE SPLICES average about fifty per cent longer than the SAILOR'S EYE SPLICE. All splices in a sail are cross stitched for their full length.

A modification of this splice is used in archery to form the loop of a modern bowstring. The "string" is a single yarn consisting of a multiplicity of small linen threads. These are laid up by hand for about fifteen inches into three firm strands (⚹144), having the *same lay* as the bowstring itself. After being laid up about nine inches, the strands should be tapered gradually to the ends and, having been beeswaxed, they are stuck at the nine-inch point and backed for their full length. The right-hand illustration represents the finished aspect of a SAILMAKER'S EYE SPLICE. The eye of a bowstring is proportionately longer and has no thimble.

2758. A BACKHANDED EYE SPLICE that is stuck in the manner of the FLEMISH EYE (⚹2745). Open a rope and lay out a single strand, for a length equal to the round of the eye. Form the eye with the two ends which are still laid up together. The odd strand is then laid back around the eye into its own score but in the direction contrary to its original lay. Stick the three ends, as indicated by the arrows in the diagram, and back the strands as previously directed.

2759. The RIGGER'S LASHING EYE is stuck as the SAILOR'S EYE SPLICE (#2725). It is employed on footropes, bobstay collars, top-gallant sheet blocks, etc. Eleven lays of the rope are allowed for the eye, which is stuck once and one half only, the ends are tapered and scraped and the whole is served over with spun yarn. A lanyard, half the size of the rope, is eye spliced into it.

2760. A HAWSER EYE is often very large, suitable for throwing over posts and piles. Stick as EYE SPLICE #2725, and tuck twice full. Leave the strands long, divide the ends and cross whip them. Sometimes they are whipped twice at intervals of a few inches apart.

2761. A CABLE EYE for a mooring is made in exactly the same way but the cable has a reverse lay. The three ropes of the cable are tucked exactly as if they were the three strands of an ordinary rope.

2762. A HAWSER THIMBLE EYE. Stick the strands once full, divide them and tuck them once, one half. Divide the remaining halves, worm a part, tease the remainder, parcel, marl and serve over all.

2763. A CABLE EYE. Open the cable and form an eye similar to #2745, but employing the three ropes of the cable for strands. Take the rope end indicated in the first illustration, open it into its three strands (a cable consists of three three-strand ropes), stick one of these strands (which is one ninth of the whole cable) under the *rope* indicated in the first diagram. From each of the other two rope ends lay out one strand. Worm these three strands up the cable. This leaves six strands which are now opened, combed out, scraped, teased, parceled, marled, tarred and served over.

2764. The ROPEMAKER'S EYE. In the ropewalk an eye is formed in a cable, while it is being made, by doubling a long rope in the middle and laying it up with a single rope of half its length. A long end is left in the single rope end, and an eye is formed in this end, which is laid parallel with the eye that is formed in the bight of the long rope.

The eye in the single rope is made in this manner: The rope is opened and the strands stuck as illustrated. Half of each strand is wormed and the remainder is scraped, teased and marled over. The whole eye is then served with small stuff. A thimble is seized in and a shackle is put through the thimble. The eye is used in the inboard end of a cable.

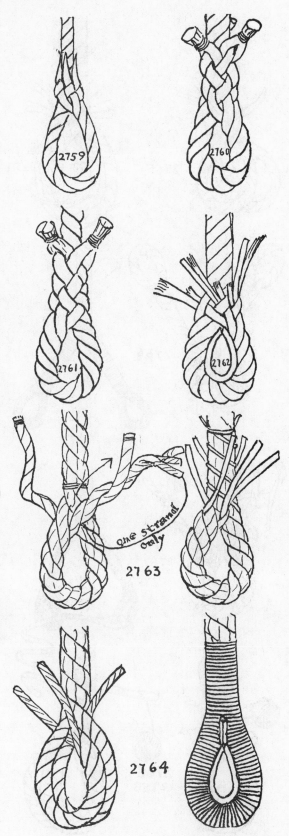

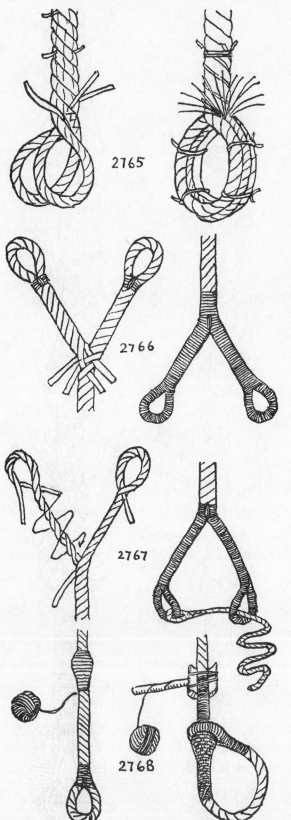

2765

2766

2767

2768

2765. "ADMIRAL THE HON. SIR GEORGE ELLIOT'S EYE," as it was called by Biddlecomb (1848), was later called "ELLIOT'S EYE." The cable is opened for a considerable length and stopped. Two of the rope ends are "short long spliced" together; the ends, after half knotting, are tucked but once. The single rope end is carefully chalk-marked to show where it is to be spliced, in order to exactly parallel the eye already made. The eye is formed and tucked twice only. The two eyes are clapped together and stopped. A smaller rope is laid into the score between the two eyes. The ends of this are cut and butted and the eye is ringbolt hitched (#3605) with small rope. The eye is made a little larger than the oval thimble used and is seized in. It is used on the outboard end of a cable and is the eye that is shackled to the anchor.

2766. A FORK SPLICE WITH LASHING EYES. Open a four-strand rope into a fork of two legs. At a short distance from the crotch form eyes in each of the two forks at the same length and seize them in with a racking seizing. Lay the ends back again to the fork, which makes two legs of four strands each. Stick the ends at the crotch as in SPLICE #2752. Tuck over and under, once full, once one half and once one quarter. Taper and scrape the ends and serve over the whole structure with spun yarn. The back and front are alike.

2767. The following is similar but neater. After forming one of the eyes lead only one strand back to the fork. The other end is tucked and backed as in REEVING EYE SPLICE #2747. At the fork each end is stuck under one strand and is then backed and tapered. The whole structure is served over with spun yarn or marline or, if very large, with small stuff. By means of this splice a stay is secured by lashing the two eyes together around the mast with a small lanyard, which is first spliced through one of the eyes.

2768. COLLAR AND EYE or FORESTAY EYE, also called MOUSE AND COLLAR. At an early date the "MOUSE" was raised with spun yarn. But Admiral Luce, in 1866, says that parceling has been "found sufficient for the purpose." So raise your MOUSE firmly and symmetrically by either method and graft the whole structure over carefully. This having been done, form Eye #2745 in the end of the rope, of a size to fit around the stay. The whole length of the stay has to be rove through the eye when the ship is being rigged.

2769. To put an eye in the single strand of a rope: Seize the strand and cut out the heart yarns below the seizing, leaving only the surface yarns. Divide these into three equal parts, and stick each of these parts, after the ends have been whipped, exactly as in Splice #2726, under one third of the surface yarns of the standing part. Use for a tool a wire loop, tuck full four to six times according to the slackness of the strand. Whip the splice once or twice with sail twine or serve over the whole splice.

2770. A Marline or Two-Strand Eye Splice (1). Stick the strands as shown and then tuck, over and under, four or five times as needed.

2771. A Marline Eye Splice (2). Open into two long legs, half knot at the bosom and make a Multiple Overhand Knot. Tighten by pulling on the ends. Pass over two or three lays, sticking each end through the same aperture, and then tuck both ends over and under once.

2772. The Marline Eye Splice (3) or Tucked Eye is much used in the ends of seizings and service. If several turns of service are led over the loose end of the eye it will make it secure and it is exceptionally neat. Tuck twice as shown. Leave the end rather long and bury it under the turns.

2773. Somewhat the same method is employed in lashings of small stuff, a Clove Hitch being made before the two tucks are put in.

The splices in most of these drawings are shown "opened" so that the reader may easily discover the lead of the various strands. But the actual splices must be made as snug as practicable.

The ends of strands are often drawn in the illustrations much shorter than is required for the tying. This is so that the scale of the drawings need not be reduced to make room for the extra length of the ends. For an average Eye Splice the opened ends should not be less in length than ten times the diameter of the rope.

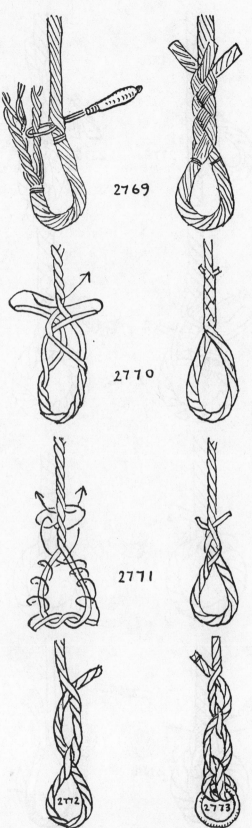

2769

2770

2771

2772

2773

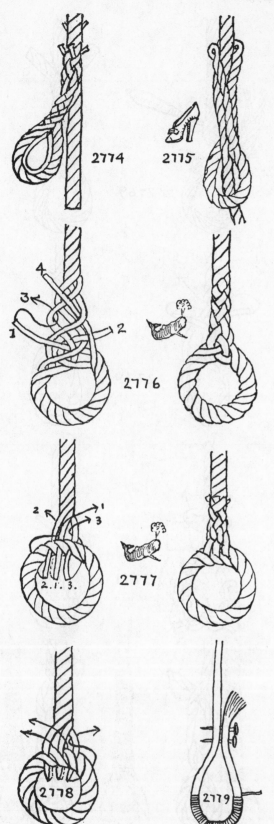

2774. A Bight Eye Splice. This is used in boat lashings, in securing whaleboat stays, etc. Eye ⚭2725 is put in a short rope's end, the other end of which is then side spliced to the stay or lashing. The lower end of the stay is rove through a ring or eye at the gunnel, and is then led up through the Bight Eye Splice. One or two round turns are taken through the opposing eyes and are hauled taut. Frapping turns are added and the end is made fast around the turns.

2775. An Eye Splice in the bight. This knot or splice is to be found described in the chapter on tricks and puzzles (⚭2585). It is slovenly in appearance and will injure the rope if used practically.

2776. A Round Eye. This is the result of an attempt to make a Round Eye for the honda of a lariat. The inside of the eye presents an even lay.

2777. A Grommet Eye. This was made for a fair-leader. The grommet itself is described in the following chapter on odd splices as ⚭2864. It does not have to be of the same weight as the rope to which it is spliced. Each end after tucking under one strand as pictured is led around the back of the grommet and is there tucked into its own standing part as indicated by the arrows in the first diagram. After this the ends are tucked regularly over and under, once full, once one half and once one quarter. The Right-Angle Splice which attaches the rope to the grommet is also given as ⚭2851 in the next chapter.

2778. This is a similar eye based on William A. Larson's Backhanded Ring Splice (⚭2859).

2779. A honda on a braided rope lariat is commonly made by raveling and tapering the tip and then forming the eye and riveting the end above the tip to the standing part with copper tacks. The whole eye and neck is then served over with copper wire, or only the bosom with copper and the rest with strong fishline.

2780. A Honda Knot with a *side spliced end*. Make a round turn in the end of a rope and side splice the end to the inside of the turn. Tuck the strands once, cut the ends off at a length equal to twice the diameter of the rope and scrape to a taper. Serve the length of the splice snugly with small fishline and add a Half Hitch with the standing part.

2781. A Mainsheet Eye for a small boat is shown by Qualtrough. When on the wind, the eye is fast to a hook, aft. When before the wind, the hook is cast off and the knot above the eye fetches against a metal eye or ring on the boom. This allows of a much shorter mainsheet than is customary. Cut the ends of the splice short.

The eye is stuck as in a SAILMAKER'S EYE and the ends are tucked (backed) once only. After this a FOOTROPE KNOT (#697) is tied and doubled, close to the splice.

2782. A RIGGING STOPPER EYE. Stick once only as in the foregoing splice and then tie a MATTHEW WALKER KNOT with the ends. Two of these were made in the ends of a long lanyard that was rove through two deadeyes and used in repairing standing rigging that was shot away in action. The RIGGING STOPPER or FIGHTING STOPPER is shown as #3302.

The same knot has been used on a cargo fall to support a heavy counterweight with which to overhaul the tackle.

2783. A JIB SHEET EYE is designed to absorb a portion of the slatting of the sheet. Stick as in the foregoing, and tie a STOPPER KNOT (#676). Scrape, tease and serve the ends.

2784. A "fancy" eye found on an old whale harpoon now in the Mariners' Museum collection. Open a rope for a considerable length, make a very careful SAILMAKER'S EYE, having first laid out two yarns from each strand. Lay up the yarns into three tight two-yarn foxes and worm them the length of the splice. Put a wide whipping of Italian marline at the throat and another over the final tuck and snake the whippings.

2785. A GRAFTED EYE. Open the rope for a considerable distance, lay out half of each strand and with the remainder make a smooth SAILMAKER'S SPLICE, well tapered. Worm and parcel this (adhesive tape will be found convenient for the purpose). Lay out six yarns and graft over the splice with the remainder (see #2678). Tie a THREE-PLY STANDING TURK'S-HEAD with the six yarns that were laid out. Seize the end of the splice and add another TURK'S-HEAD. Cut all ends short.

2786. A COACHWHIPPED EYE is tied similarly to the last but the surface is cross-pointed (#3026) instead of being grafted. First lay out twelve yarns at the straddle, to be made up into two-yarn nettles. With these a SIX-STRAND MATTHEW WALKER is made at the throat and another is made at the end of the splice with the ends of the COACHWHIPPING, the superfluous ends being cut off close to the seizing. Both #2785 and #2786 are often made of fishline instead of the yarns of the rope itself.

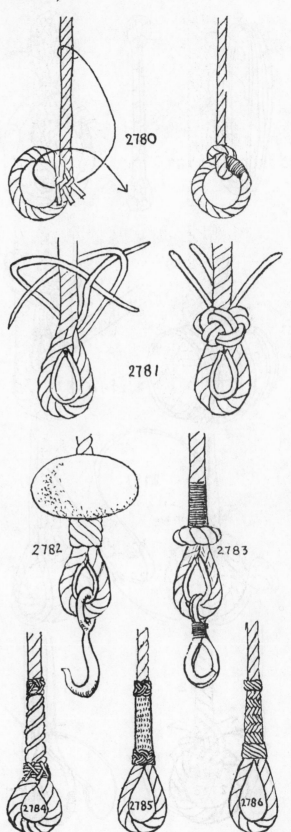

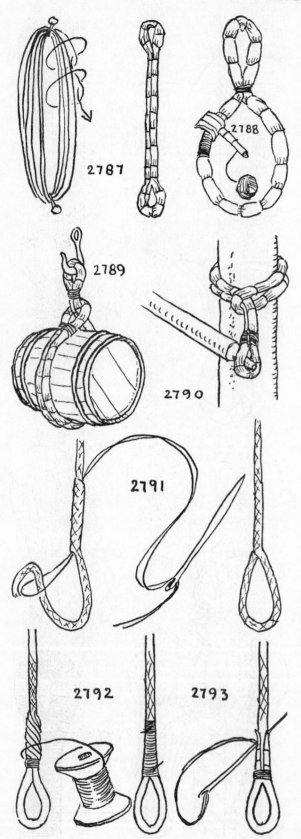

2787. SALVAGEE or SELVAGEE STRAP EYES. Marline or rope yarn is wound around two pegs or nails which are spaced according to the length required. The strap is marled over and may be served as well. The cores for chest beckets are often made in this way. The center between the eyes is generally raised with spun yarn in order to increase the size of the grip. The details of this are given in Chapter 41 (#3622). The eyes of chest beckets are commonly covered with ringbolt hitching.

2788. Block straps were formerly made selvagee-fashion and were either grafted or served over, after which the block was seized in. Nowadays *grommet straps* are more commonly used.

2789. Slings or cargo straps are sometimes made with eyes tightly seized into the doubled ends. These are seldom served over as the selvagee has an excellent "cling" that is most desirable in slinging cargo.

2790. A snotter for a spritsail rig has a large eye at one end and a small one at the other. Generally these are regular SAILOR'S EYE SPLICES, but, when made selvagee-fashion, they are seized in and served over.

2791. An EYE SPLICE for banding or other tubular braided material. Pull out the heart and cut off about nine inches of its length. Skin back the surface yarns in order to reach the heart. Then stretch the cord and work the remaining heart back into place. Insert a large sail needle six inches from the end and reeve it eye end first through the tube for four inches, sticking it out to the surface. Thread the needle with twine or copper wire, leaving a loop. Loop the bight end of the sail twine or copper wire over the end of the banding and pull the banding end through the tube until the eye is of the desired size. Then smooth out the neck and stretch well before trimming the end. If the material is soft, sew through with a few stitches of twine near the cut-off end.

2792. An *eye for a braided fishline*, or a silk cord. Ravel for an inch and a half. Twist strongly to the left and serve tightly to the right with silk thread, holding one end of the splice in a vise or clamp. This makes an excellent buttonhole in a cord for the knots of Chapters 5, 9 and 10 when they are required in the end of a lanyard.

2793. An *eye for a braided silk cord*. Scrape to a taper, wax the end and form the eye. Take a long thread of the same color and material, thread it through the needle, seize with a CONSTRICTOR and serve. Every two or three turns shove the needle through the material instead of passing around it. Finish off as a whipping or sew with the needle. See that all frayed ends are covered and that the finish is smooth and even.

2794. A SASH CORD EYE. Open the cord and comb out the threads for twice the length of the eye. Divide the threads into two equal legs and form the eye by double half knotting the ends at half length with a CONSTRICTOR KNOT at the bosom and serve both ways toward the throat with sail twine or fishline.

2795. An EYE SPLICE in sash cord or other hard braided rope. Open the end for a length equal to four or five diameters of the rope. Drive a sharp marlingspike through the rope where the throat of the eye is to be, and stick one quarter, one third, or one half, if possible, of the end through the hole. Scrape and tease both parts of the end and serve over tightly or, for a neater job, graft over. This splice is often made without sticking any part, but the method described is more secure.

2796. SPINDLE, ARTIFICIAL or MADE EYE, often inaccurately called a FLEMISH EYE. Steel gives "MADE EYE" in 1794, Lever "ARTIFICIAL or SPINDLE EYE" in 1808. Dana, in 1841, says, "This is now usually called a FLEMISH EYE," but Luce in 1862 prefers "ARTIFICIAL EYE." Formerly, this eye was put in the ends of stays but it is well adapted to braided rope. Seize a rope at a distance from the end that is a little longer than twice the length of the proposed eye. Take a billet of wood, the size of the eye, to serve as a spindle. With strips of canvas, spun yarn or adhesive tape raise two ridges around the spindle, about the diameter of the rope apart. Lay five or six pieces of marline lengthwise across these ridges and stop them in place with rope yarns.

Open the rope to the seizing, and proceed to half knot opposite yarns around the spindle. Scatter these HALF KNOTS well around the spindle. When all have been half knotted, seize the ends to the throat. Remove the stops and reef knot the short lengths of marline firmly around the knotted yarns. Remove the structure from the spindle, scrape the ends to a nice taper and serve over both neck and eye.

2797. A SPINDLE EYE for a jib stay is made of shroud-laid rope. The heart is cut out. One fourth of each of the four strands is laid out for a worming. Each worming is brought over the spindle and half knotted to an opposite one. Bring the ends down and seize them at the neck; worm them into the rope and seize them again. Open the remainder of the strands and *reef knot* the yarns at widely scattered points around the spindle. Cut off the ends, parcel, tar and serve over the eye. Put in the thimble and serve over to the end of the worming.

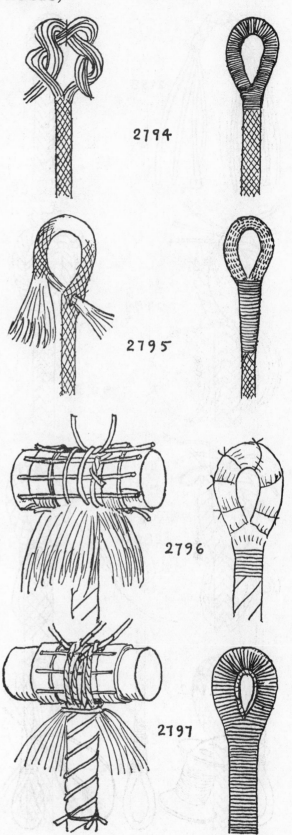

2794

2795

2796

2797

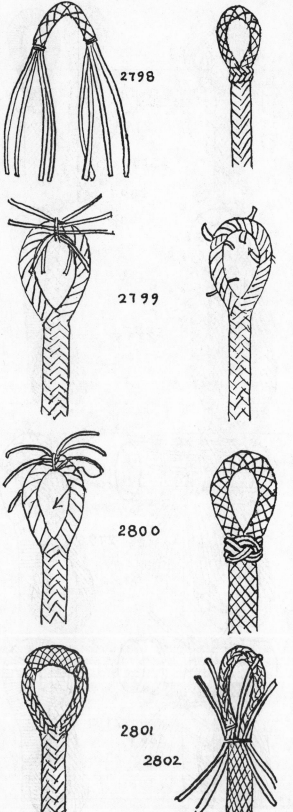

2798. This page consists of eyes in sinnet or braided rope. THREE-STRAND FLAT SINNET EYES are found in gaskets and reef points. FOUR-STRAND and SIX-STRAND ROUND SINNET EYES, tied in the manner here depicted, are to be found on sailors' clothesbag and ditty-bag lanyards. Generally the eye is made first, then all ends are brought together and the sinnet is continued with double the number of strands. Two, three or four of the strands may be laid out at the crotch and after the larger sinnet has been well started a STANDING TURK'S-HEAD (※1284) is made with the strands that were laid out. This covers the joint completely.

2799. If the eye is to be tied in the end instead of the bight of the sinnet, the sinnet is stoutly whipped, the strands are divided and laid up into equal lengths of three- or four-strand rope. The two ends are next crotched or married and then the strands are scattered as in a LONG SPLICE.

2800. In this the two arms are laid up into ropes in a manner somewhat similar to the foregoing. But one arm is *right-laid* rope, the other *left-laid* rope. The lay is loosely twisted. Having been crotched, the two legs are next tucked into the opposite leg in an OVER-AND-UNDER SPLICE to the straddle. Then seize or else add a SIX- or EIGHT-STRAND STANDING TURK'S-HEAD, or some other desired MULTI-STRAND LANYARD KNOT.

2801. Instead of splicing the ends as in the previous eye, lay up both arms with the same lay or else make a FOUR-STRAND SINNET of each. Marry and seize the two ends at the bosom and there tie any desired SHROUD KNOT from Chapter 19. Place a TURK'S-HEAD at the straddle or if the joint between the standing part and the legs is neatly arranged no knot need be added.

2802. Seize an eight-strand lanyard strongly and, employing each alternate strand, make a FOUR-STRAND SINNET and form the eye with it. *Crotch* the two groups of four strands at the straddle of the eye so that they are alternately spaced around the neck. Seize well and tie a SHROUD KNOT, such as ※1585. Rigging lofts employ a "turning-in machine" or a rigging screw when putting a WIRE EYE SPLICE around a thimble or a deadeye.

2803. Often a Spanish windlass was used at sea for the purpose. Two thimbles were seized as in the illustration, the lower one being merely for temporary use in closing the eye. A well-greased strand from a large rope was led around the shear pole as shown in the illustration and was set up by twisting with two marlingspikes. When the rope was brought together at the throat, two seizings were added, as at the top of ※2804, and a round seizing was put on at the throat, after which the temporary thimble was removed.

2804. The same operation may be more easily done with a vise, but the jaws of the vise must be grooved or else have a grooved bushing, preferably of lead; for otherwise there is danger of the rope snapping out and injuring someone. Rope that is temporarily served with marline is of course much less apt to slip than uncovered wire rope.

2805. The British Board of Trade specifications (1932) call for an OVER-ONE-AND-UNDER-ONE WIRE EYE SPLICE. The technique of handling wire strands has already been discussed somewhat at the end of the previous chapter. The ends of all working strands should be kept taped, or whipped. The rope itself should be strongly stopped just above the point where the strands are to be stuck. It is well to serve the rope over for the round of the thimble before the thimble is seized in. After the heart has been cut out the strands are stuck in the order marked on the diagram and pounded with a mallet *until all lie fair*. After sticking as pictured, each strand is tucked three times more over one and under one, then each alternate strand *only* is tucked once, *over one and under two*, which serves to taper the splice. After a thorough pounding with a mallet all ends are cut short with nippers. Sometimes strands are split and tapered as described for Manila splices, in which case the cores are first removed. Finished wire splices should always be covered, as otherwise hands are bound to be torn on the sharp ends. Sometimes, instead of being served over, an EYE SPLICE is covered with canvas or else rawhide. The seam goes around the outer edge of the eye and the wire beneath should be painted with thick white lead. The thimble is driven in with a hammer or a mallet.

2806. This is perhaps the most satisfactory way of sticking an OVER-ONE-AND-UNDER-ONE WIRE EYE SPLICE. Stick the strands in the order numbered on the diagram, but after strand 3 is stuck do not remove the marlingspike until 4 has also been stuck; this should be under the same strand but in the opposite direction—that is, to the left. Moreover be careful to observe that, after the end has been opened fan-fashion and strands 1 and 2 have been stuck, strand 3, which is actually the right-hand strand of the group, is passed to the left under strands 1 and 2 and is tucked beyond them and to the right. Strands 4, 5 and 6 are next tucked to the left. Work wire strands firmly back into the splice but *do not force them* sufficiently to kink or bend them out of shape. Half the success of a wire splice is in a thorough and proper pounding after all tucks have been made.

Stick the splice four times full. Then stick *alternate strands* once more over one and under two. Pound, cut off ends and serve over.

2807. An early form of OVER-AND-UNDER WIRE EYE SPLICE, now seldom seen, was tucked *over one and under two*. The strands were tucked full twice, then tapered three quarters, one half, and one quarter; or else two thirds and one third.

2808. This splice was lost in the shuffle.

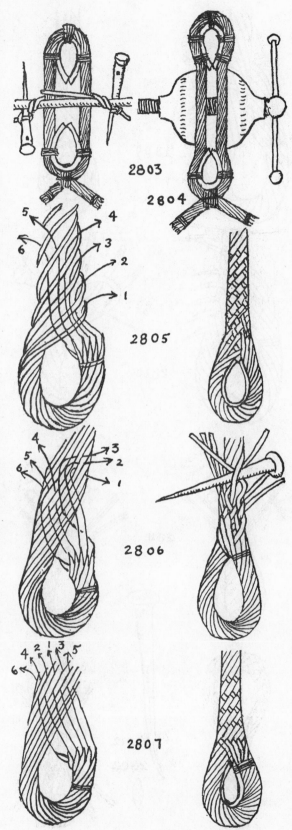

2803

2804

2805

2806

2807

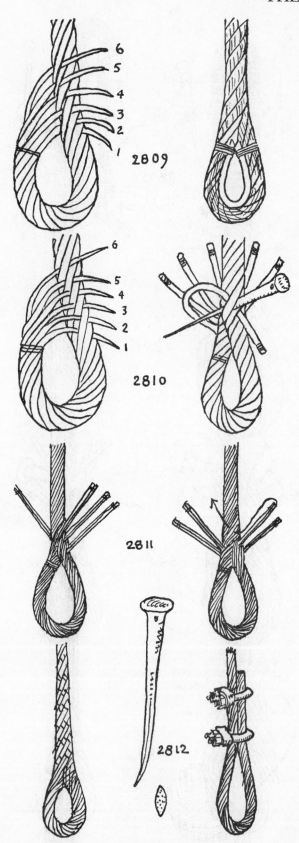

2809. The BACKHANDED WIRE EYE SPLICE (1). In America today most WIRE EYE SPLICES are made backhanded. And if an occasional OVER-AND-UNDER SPLICE does appear, the initial sticking is generally the same as for a BACKHANDED SPLICE. In wire the splice is almost always made directly around a thimble.

After sticking the strands as shown alongside, pound them lightly to make them lie fair and then back them four times. Sometimes each strand is backed twice in succession instead of once only at a time; this saves time but the strands are not run down as in a SAILMAKER'S SPLICE. Start with the most backward strand and progress regularly from one to the next. In a BACKHANDED SPLICE it is not necessary to make the strands lie all in one tier. Work them well back toward the throat but, without bending the wires, let them choose their own beds. After having tucked the strands four times full, some riggers will taper by cutting out one third at each subsequent tuck. But it seems sufficient merely to back each alternate strand once more, but under two strands, and then to trim them all as they lie.

2810. BACKHANDED EYE SPLICE (2). This way of tucking is seen about as frequently as the former and is the one preferred by Captain Daniel F. Mullins. After the initial tucking the splice is put in exactly in the same manner as the last.

2811. An OVER-AND-UNDER SPLICE, for single-strand ropes, or for ropes of more than six strands. Seize the rope at the point where it is to be opened and cut out not only the heart but all other wires or strands except those on the surface. For the purpose of this description we will assume that there are twelve surface wires. Divide the surface wires into four groups of three wires each, taping each group of three together at the ends and spreading the four fanwise. Tuck the right group of three to the right under six wires. Stick the next group in the same place but under only three wires, then the third group to the right under the next three wires, and finally tuck the last set of three under the remaining three wires. Then stick all groups of three to the left as in any OVER-AND-UNDER SPLICE. Tuck each time in regular rotation under one of the original groups of three strands. A single-strand rope is generally left-laid, so it will be spliced in the opposite direction from this description. A six-wire *strand* (left-laid) should be spliced exactly as ⚓2810 (but reversely). If there are eighteen surface wires (or strands) divide into six groups and stick as in ⚓2810 (or reversely) and thereafter tuck over and under as described for ⚓2805 and ⚓2806.

2812. In making eyes for wire guy ropes on telegraph poles and derricks ashore, U-bolt shackles are ordinarily used. The nuts should *always be beside the standing part of the rope* and never beside the end.

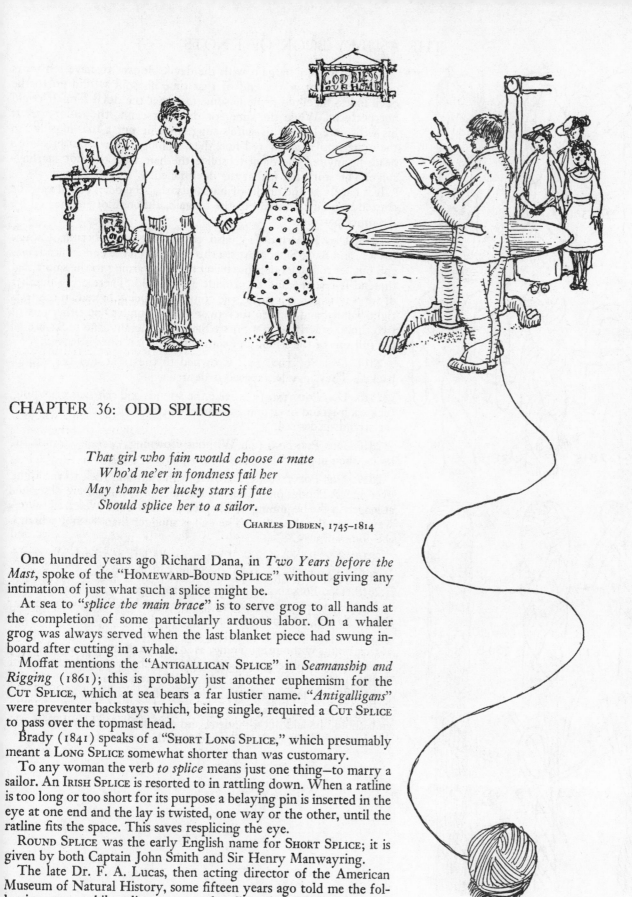

CHAPTER 36: ODD SPLICES

That girl who fain would choose a mate
Who'd ne'er in fondness fail her
May thank her lucky stars if fate
Should splice her to a sailor.

CHARLES DIBDEN, 1745–1814

One hundred years ago Richard Dana, in *Two Years before the Mast*, spoke of the "HOMEWARD-BOUND SPLICE" without giving any intimation of just what such a splice might be.

At sea to *"splice the main brace"* is to serve grog to all hands at the completion of some particularly arduous labor. On a whaler grog was always served when the last blanket piece had swung inboard after cutting in a whale.

Moffat mentions the "ANTIGALLICAN SPLICE" in *Seamanship and Rigging* (1861); this is probably just another euphemism for the CUT SPLICE, which at sea bears a far lustier name. *"Antigalligans"* were preventer backstays which, being single, required a CUT SPLICE to pass over the topmast head.

Brady (1841) speaks of a "SHORT LONG SPLICE," which presumably meant a LONG SPLICE somewhat shorter than was customary.

To any woman the verb *to splice* means just one thing—to marry a sailor. An IRISH SPLICE is resorted to in rattling down. When a ratline is too long or too short for its purpose a belaying pin is inserted in the eye at one end and the lay is twisted, one way or the other, until the ratline fits the space. This saves resplicing the eye.

ROUND SPLICE was the early English name for SHORT SPLICE; it is given by both Captain John Smith and Sir Henry Manwayring.

The late Dr. F. A. Lucas, then acting director of the American Museum of Natural History, some fifteen years ago told me the following story while splices were under discussion. He had heard it aboard ship on his first voyage to the Chincha Islands in 1861.

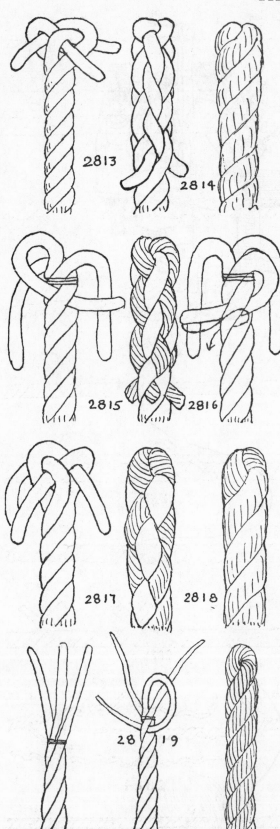

A sailor made a bargain with the devil. He was to have ten years of affluence, but at the end of that time his soul would go to the devil unless he could provide some task that the devil himself could not perform. When the time for payment came, the sailor was at his wit's end, but at his wife's suggestion he put a marlingspike in the grate until it grew red hot, then, pulling a hair from his wife's head, he invited the devil to splice the hair with the hot marlingspike. The story has it that the devil failed.

It is hardly to the credit of humanity that the devil can always be trusted to hold to his end of the bargain, although often cheated by the other party.

2813. DOG POINTING (1), also called SPANISH POINTING, CROWN SPLICE, and BACK SPLICE. At sea this is found on the ends of lead lines and bucket ropes, its purpose being to give warning to the sailor that the end is reached and to provide a handhold. There are a number of ways in which it is made, the commonest being to crown the ends right-handed and then to tuck over one and under one either one or two times, exactly as in a SHORT SPLICE. Generally, the tucks are all the full size of the strand but sometimes the last tuck is halved.

2814. DOG POINTING (2). Crowned to the right and the strands backed. They may be tapered if desired.

2815. DOG POINTING (3). Seize the strands and *without* crowning, tuck each strand over one and under one two or three times. Taper the strands if desired.

2816. DOG POINTING (4). Without crowning, *back* all strands full twice, then one half and finally one quarter.

2817. DOG POINTING (5). Crown to the left and tuck to the right, over one and under one. The two methods of tucking were described at length in the beginning of Chapter 34. This is the preferred sailor's way of making the splice. The end is snugger than #2813, which is the common way.

2818. DOG POINTING (6). Crown to the left and back all strands (the first two tucks are full), then taper if desired.

2819. DOG POINTING (7). Open the rope for a considerable length and make an *exceedingly tight* taper or rattail, as described in SHORT SPLICE #2643, until one half of each strand has been cut out. At this point put on a temporary whipping and then begin to back splice at that point, without crowning, as in #2816. Remove the whipping as soon as the splice is well started. Cut out yarns at the same rate that they were cut out while making the rattail. Back splice the full length of the taper and stick the last few yarns of each strand *through* the strand that is being followed instead of under it. The ends should be laid out a-tandem, and cut off flush. If well done, the pointing should be uniform in size with the rest of the rope.

2820. To *repair a stranded rope* (1). Remove the chafed or galled strand. Lay in a new strand of the same size but longer. Half knot opposite ends where they meet and tuck once one half and once one quarter, or else back and taper.

2821. To *repair a stranded rope* (2). *If the chafed section is long,* the splice to follow may be found more practical. Remove the chafed section of strand. Divide the two-strand section that is left into three equal parts and mark with chalk. Cut through one of the two strands at one mark and the other strand at the remaining mark. Telescope the two rope ends until the three pairs of strands overlap. Lay the strands of the two ropes into each other as in any LONG SPLICE. Half knot all ends, see that the rope is fair, then tuck all ends once full, once one half and once one quarter. If a four-strand rope is to be mended, care must be taken that the joints of the cut strands rotate around the rope in regular progression.

2822. To *repair a stranded rope* (3). *If the galled section is short,* remove it and, with a chalk, mark off on the rope at either side of the two-strand section a length equal to or greater than the removed part. Carefully cut one of the two remaining strands at each of these marks and *be certain not to cut the same strand twice.* Lay the ends together and splice as directed for the last splice. The outer ends will require considerable overlap before the middle ends will be long enough for splicing.

2823. To *shorten a rope in the center.* This splice is often required by sailmakers when cutting down the size of a sail. Mark the rope in three evenly spaced places a foot or more apart and cut one strand at each mark. Then the rope is laid up again at the correct length and the splice is made exactly as directed for #2821. In the present splice, however, the original strands are rejoined.

2824. The ONE-STRAND SPLICE, often called SAILMAKER'S ONE-STRAND SPLICE. The purpose of this is to lengthen a rope; it is often required by sailmakers when the width of a sail is to be increased by the addition of one or several cloths. Cut the rope strands at three evenly separated points. The distance between two adjoining points must equal the required extra width of the sail plus an amount sufficient to tuck the two strands. A single long strand of the same size material is laid in for the full length, beginning at the extreme left and allowing sufficient material for tucking. Splice as already directed for #2821. It will be noted that there are four joints in this THREE-STRAND SPLICE while there are only three joints in the others.

These splices are required in boltrope. For all other purposes ropes are added to, or shortened, at the ends. Similar splices, of course, could be put into four-strand or six-strand rope. But the sailmaker uses only three-strand rope, so ordinarily the occasion does not arise.

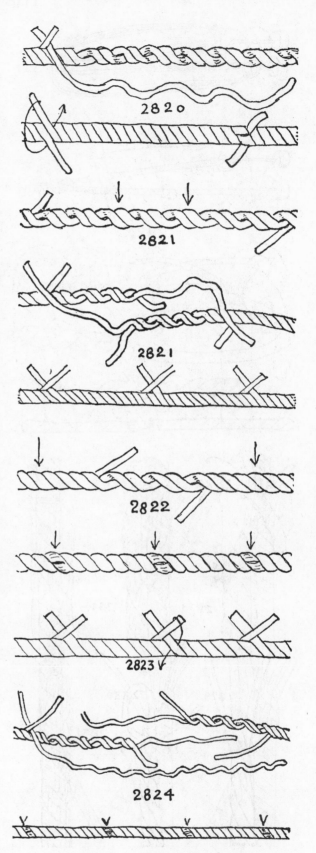

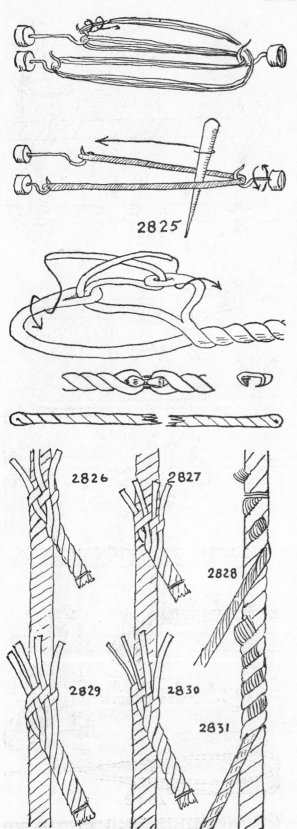

2825. A DOUBLE LOOP SPLICE for small rope drives (belts) is of hard-twisted cotton. The rope and splice are made together on a "coning machine," so called because the rope, being of only two strands, does not require a "top" to guide the strands, and instead is closed with a metal cone which is held at right angles to the rope.

Four or five cotton yarns are middled and placed around the upper left hook. They are led parallel, first around the single hook at the right, next to the lower hook at the left, and back to the single hook at the right. Finally they are made fast with a CLOVE HITCH to the upper and longer hook at the left. The two hooks at the left are revolved at equal rate until the strands are tightly twisted. The cone is then inserted between the two strands close to the hooks at the right; the single hook at the right is disengaged so that it may turn freely, and as the cone is moved to the left, the twist in the strands causes the single hook at the right to spin, and as the cone moves from right to left a two-strand rope is formed.

The CLOVE HITCH on the upper left hook is now removed and the two single ends from the lower hook are rove through the eye (see the bottom illustration). One of the two single ends from the upper hook is next rove through the smaller eye. The two ends, being led beyond each other, are laid into the strand and buried or sunk, as shown in the drawing.

The single large loop that has just been formed is now put over a left hook. The left hook is revolved until the rope is entirely untwisted again and reduced to two tightly twisted strands. The cone is introduced between the two strands at the extreme right, the right hook is disengaged so that it may revolve freely, and the cone is moved at a steady rate to the left, which lays the rope up again and completes the belt. When the belt is to be put to use, the two eyes are joined together with a little metal clip.

2826. SIDE SPLICE (1). A *three-strand end* to a *three-strand bight*. The strands are stuck as pictured and tucked over and under twice full, then they are split and one half the strand tucked again. This is structurally the same as EYE SPLICE #2726. To side splice two strands of a rope, proceed as in EYE SPLICE #2769.

2827. SIDE SPLICE (2). A *four-strand end* to a *four-strand bight*. Stick the strands as pictured and splice over and under exactly as in the SAILOR'S FOUR-STRAND EYE SPLICE #2737.

2828. SIDE SPLICE (3). A single strand is spliced to a rope with three full tucks and then is split and stuck one half and a whipping is added. The end should not helix around the rope but should progress as pictured.

2829. SIDE SPLICE (4). A *four-strand end* to a *three-strand bight*. Stick the strands as pictured. Lay together one half of each of the two left strands and tuck them as a single strand. Then tuck all three strands, full twice, and once one half.

2830. SIDE SPLICE (5). A *three-strand end* spliced to a *four-strand bight*. Divide the left strand into two equal halves and stick all four ends as in a regular FOUR-STRAND EYE SPLICE (#2737); then divide and lay out half of each of the two full-sized strands and tuck the four half strands that are left twice more.

2831. SIDE SPLICE (6). A small rope is side spliced to a larger one in much the same way as #2828, except that the small rope is opened out fanlike and the three strands are combined and tucked as a unit, four or five times full. If the splice is seized, three tucks are enough. The tucks should be parallel with the length of the rope, not at right angles to the lay, as the latter method tends to twist when pull is exerted.

Buoy ropes and heaving lines are often spliced to larger rope in this manner.

2832. The name CUT SPLICE is mentioned in Phillips' Dictionary of 1658. Other book names for the splice are CONT, BIGHT and ANTIGALLIGAN. The splice is put in standing rigging for pendants, jib guys, breast backstays and odd shrouds. The slit passes around a spar or block and the ends are side spliced each to the standing part of the opposite end, and the ends are secured with racking seizings or else the splice is served over.

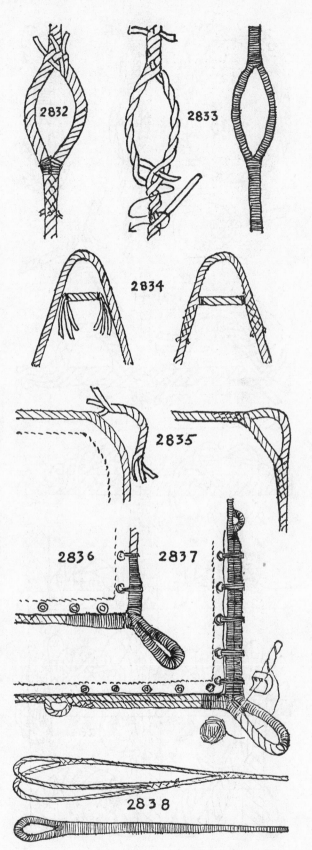

2833. This CUT SPLICE bulks only one strand larger than the rope itself. One strand at each end is laid back for a distance greater than the splice. One of the two remaining strands at each end is then laid into the opposite rope for some distance and spliced to the opposite end that was laid out. The two ends that were left, one at each straddle, are tucked where they lie over and under, three and a half times. Seize each end of the splice with racking turns (※3403). Compare with the REEVING EYE SPLICE (※2747) in the last chapter.

2834. The HORSESHOE or SPAN SPLICE is used in standing rigging when the lead of either shrouds or stays diverges too much for a seizing. The two ends of a short piece of rope are side spliced as ※2827.

2835. The early EARING CRINGLE was side spliced to the head and leech ropes of a square sail. Later EARING CRINGLES are given on page 468.

2836. Square-sail clews of 1847. The clew rope of courses and topsails on ships of over five hundred tons was the same size as the boltrope. On other square sails it was one inch larger in circumference. Staysail clews were half an inch larger than the boltrope. The clew itself was fourteen lays of the rope in length. It was stoutly seized and then the legs were side spliced to the boltrope. The whole splice and the eye itself were parceled and served. Eyelet holes were worked into the tablings of the sails, and the clew was marled to the boltrope for the length of the service.

2837. In 1794 the clew rope of the topsails and courses was *spliced into the leech at the lower* BOWLINE CRINGLE and to the footrope at the first BUNTLINE CRINGLE. It was necessary to marl the sail to the boltrope because the service was too hard to thrust a roping needle through. But in all small sails of this period the clews were seized directly into the boltrope itself, requiring no splices.

2838. A *bull earing*, also called a *head earing*, is the rope which lashes the upper corner of a square sail to its yard or jackstay. It is interestingly tapered by means of a series of SIDE SPLICES. The end of a long rope is first laid back and side spliced (※2826) to the standing part at the desired length of the taper. The doubled length is next divided into thirds and marked with chalk. A short piece of the same size rope is laid parallel with the eye already formed and is side spliced at the marked points. An eye is seized in and the whole splice parceled, marled and served over.

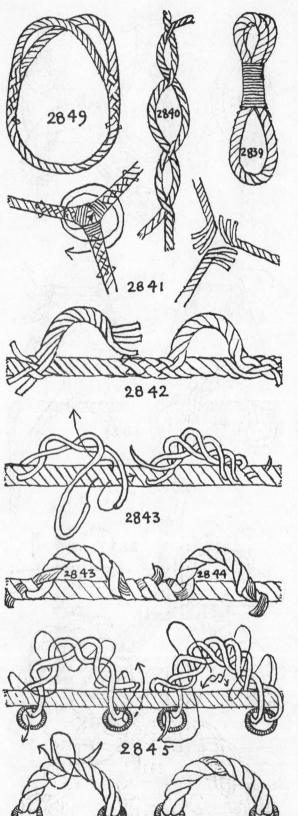

2839. "Hitches" found on an old *grommet iron*. This was an experimental toggle iron or whale harpoon, circa 1830–34. Two ends of a short 1¾-inch hemp rope were spliced together with a CUT SPLICE. The doubled part was closely seized around the shoulder of the harpoon socket. The eye formed was about eight inches long.

Another similar "hitches" of the same period consisted of eyes in the two ends of a short span that were spliced directly around the harpoon shank and then seized together.

2840. A TUCKED CUT SPLICE is tied in marline and is used as a bend in service.

2841. *Three ropes side spliced together* (see ⚹2826). The splice is snugly seized by passing the seizing stuff alternately over and under, around the juncture.

2842. *Cringles* are tied in the boltrope of sails, and bowlines, earings, reef tackles, buntlines and leech lines are secured to them. They are also used in tacks and clews, being easier to replace than seized-in eyes. The earliest cringles were merely short pieces of rope somewhat smaller than the boltrope, which were side spliced at each end as ⚹2835. REEF TACKLE CRINGLES were tucked three and one half times at the lower end and only two and one half times at the upper end, the lower end being more apt to draw. Bowline and buntline cringles span only four lays of the boltrope.

2843. "MADE" CRINGLES, tied directly into the boltrope, are made with a single long strand of new rope a half inch smaller in circumference than the rope in which they are stuck. According to Lever (1808), "All these cringles are now generally worked around thimbles." But Alston, in 1860, states that REEF CRINGLES have thimbles but BOWLINE CRINGLES do not require them. Cringles without thimbles are by no means rare even at the present day. The three turns, shown in the first diagram here, are enough for an ordinary cringle but as many odd turns as seven may be required on occasion.

With the back of the sail toward you, stick a long strand under two lays of the boltrope, draw through until one third of the strand is toward you and two thirds of it is away from you. Lay the two ends up loosely together to the right, finishing with the long end toward you. Stick the long end away from you at the right end under two lays, leaving the short strand in the position pictured. Lay the long end back again to the left. When the position of the second diagram is reached, stick the two ends over and under twice.

2844. This is the same cringle as the last except that the two ends are backed instead of being tucked over and under. The date of this is much later than the former; in fact it can hardly be much earlier than 1850.

2845. The seamanship books, as late as 1860, show cringles tucked through the boltrope, but as early as 1794, Steel states that "beckets for reefing are made through eyelet holes in the tabling."

This cringle is made with any odd number of turns (as described above) and the strand is stuck through eyelet holes instead of through the boltrope. Instead of splicing-in the ends they are passed a second time through the eyelet and knotted together on the underside of the cringle. Divide the strands and then tuck once more.

2846. The ENGLISH CRINGLE, as tied by William A. Larson, foreman of the C. E. Beckman sail loft.

In all these cringles an even lay must be maintained. This is not hard if the twist of the strand is not forced in any way and is tied loosely and later worked snug. Sailmakers frequently wax the strands.

Cringles may be tied around thimbles and worked snug or they may be completed first and the thimbles pounded in after. In the latter case the thimbles must be *entered on the canvas side*. If entered on the boltrope side they are apt to foul the edge of the canvas.

If you are employing a tarred hemp strand, rub the strand well with a piece of canvas to smooth out the lay. A handsome cringle can be made with hemp small stuff, the full size. The lay, of course, is right-handed, so the cringle is tied the reverse of the directions given here for a single-strand cringle. If you are tying with Manila, employ if possible a single strand from a *four-strand rope* of the same size as the boltrope, and disturb the lay as little as possible.

Stick the strand through the left eyelet with the long end at the back. Take any desired number of turns and tuck the long end through the right eyelet (from front to back) and continue to lay in the long end to the left eyelet and this time tuck from back to front. Tuck the short end through the right eyelet front to back and to the right of the part already there. Each end is now backed, as illustrated in the second diagram, until the two ends are tucked down past each other as shown in the third diagram. Open the cringle well with a fid before pounding in the thimble.

A cringle will make an excellent emergency handle for a suitcase.

2847. A *cringle finished off on the crown*. William A. Larson calls this the DUTCH CRINGLE. It is the one tied when the thimble is to be put in place before the cringle is worked snug. It was first shown to me by Rodman Swift. It is started exactly as the last but, after passing through the eyelet a second time, is tucked as shown in the upper left diagram, continued as in the lower left diagram and finished off as in the upper right diagram.

2848. AMERICAN CRINGLE, also called FRENCH CRINGLE. This is similar in appearance to the last, but the ends are tucked instead of being knotted. It may be made around a thimble without additional tucking.

2849. A SINNET CRINGLE can be made of signal line. Reeve the cord through the outer side of the left eyelet, leaving the upper end very short. Pin out the cringle over a copy of the lower diagram.

Tighten and sew or seize the two ends together on the inside.

If a shorter cringle is desired, leave out the section between the two dotted lines of the lower diagram. If a longer cringle is desired, add one or two of these sections.

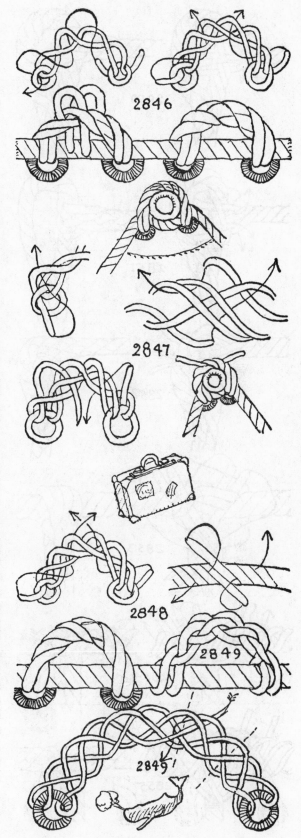

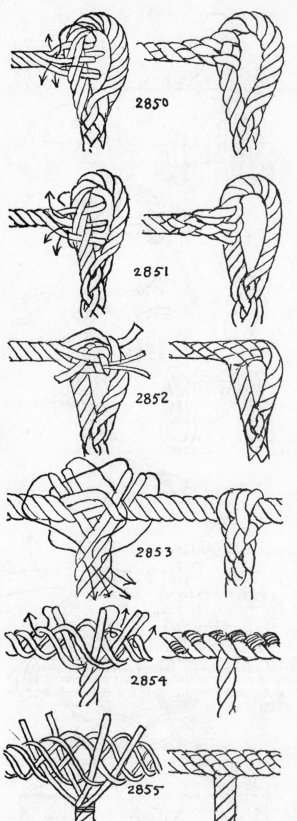

2850

2851

2852

2853

2854

2855

2850, 2851. The HEAD or EARING CRINGLE consists of an EYE SPLICE in the head of the leech rope, and a RIGHT-ANGLE SPLICE in the headrope stuck into the crown of the leech rope EYE SPLICE. This forms an eye by which the upper corner of a square sail is bent to its yard. The descriptions of the EARING CRINGLE are very meager. All the definite information that I have found is the statement that it has fourteen turns in the eye. The eye was an ordinary OVER-AND-UNDER SPLICE, since the BACKHANDED SPLICE had not been invented. The earliest HEAD EARING CRINGLE is shown as ⁘2835. The one we are discussing was first described (as above) in 1794. The two that are given here are attempts at reconstruction. Stick as in the diagrams and tuck all ends over and under twice full, once one half, and once one quarter. This will make an excellent splice to the bolt-rope in a cargo net.

2852. Kipping (1847) describes a somewhat different splice in which one strand is turned back into the headrope, the other two strands being spliced into the eye. In all three splices the eye in the leech rope should be made as ⁘2726. Kipping allows only eight turns for the eye, which appears rather small. The splice given here conforms to Kipping's description quite well. The center strand is stuck and turned back, the lower strand is split and stuck as shown. All three ends that point to the right are tucked over and under twice, then the full strand has one half laid out and all three (half strands) are tucked once more and then are redivided and given a final tuck.

The single strand to be spliced back into the headrope is divided into thirds, one third is left where it stands, the two remaining thirds are tucked under the adjacent strand to the left and the left one of these two is tucked under one additional strand—that is, under two in all. All three are now spliced as they lie, over one and under one, twice full.

2853. A RIGHT-ANGLE SIDE SPLICE of four strands. Use two ropes of the same size, stick as shown and then tuck three times full and taper if desired. This splice makes a considerable bunch around the rope.

2854. THREE-STRAND SIDE SPLICE. Stick as shown and then tuck the single left strand once over and under to the left and the two right strands over and under once to the right. Stick each of the two right ends once more over *one* and under *two*. Now either back the single end several times or else split the strand and stick one half over one, under one, and the other half over one and under two. Lastly stick both halves over one and under one.

2855. A FOUR-STRAND SIDE SPLICE that is more symmetrical and handsomer than the three-strand one just shown. Open your rope and whip it at the straddle and stick as pictured, each strand under one bight. Now tuck the strands over and under full twice, once one half and once one quarter. Work the parts back snugly toward the center.

The HEAD CRINGLE SPLICES described as ⁘2850 and ⁘2851 may be stuck into a straight piece of rope to form RIGHT-ANGLE SPLICES,

nd any of the splices might serve as RIGHT-ANGLE SPLICES on cargo
nd boarding nets.

2856. The FOOT STOPPER or BOOM STOPPER KNOT, by which the
oot of a fore-and-aft sail is bent to the boom. It appears to be a
British or European product not often seen on this side of the At-
antic. A short piece of rope is middled and stuck through an eyelet
n the foot of the sail. Each end is stuck through the strands of the
opposite end at the proper point to form a small eye around the
ootrope. This is drawn up snugly and then the two ends are reef
knotted around the boom. By means of this contrivance a sail may
be foot loosed or bent as quickly as a reef can be put in or shaken
out, and exactly in the same way. They are cast off when sailing
free and tied in when on the wind. Used on small craft.

2857. A REEF BECKET EYE. Reef beckets for a while in the 1880s
superseded gaskets for securing furled sails. Often they were of sinnet and the rope was seized at a distance from the toggle equal to
one round of the yard to which it was to be attached. Some of them
were seized to the jackstay at the neck of the toggle, others were
passed around the yard.

A toggle was spliced into the end of a short piece of four-strand
rope. The rope was divided into two-strand legs, which were laid
parallel for four inches and then laid up four-strand again for four
inches more. Then once more they were laid up into two parallel
two-strand ropes for eight inches; two eyes having thus been formed,
the rope was laid up four-strand for nine inches to the end, and
whipped.

A single strand of the same material, about two feet long, was next
middled and laid into the lower crotch of the four-inch eye; one
end was laid up into each leg of the eye to the top where it was
spliced in, over and under two and a half or three tucks. The ends
should be stuck so that they tuck over and under alternate strands.

2858. The LINK or CHAIN SPLICE has long been used in securing
hemp tails to chain running rigging. Reeve two strands through a
chain link or a ring, and lay one of these strands back into the rope,
at the same time laying out the strand that did not pass through the
chain. Join the ends as in a LONG SPLICE. The remaining strand is
backed and tapered as described in SPLICE ⌗2747.

2859. William A. Larson's RING SPLICE, made on a ring clew in
yacht sails. It is stuck as illustrated, then each strand in turn is tapered
and back spliced seven or eight tucks. The last two or three yarns
are stuck and backed through the strand, instead of under it.

2860. A splice that is very similar to the foregoing except that it
is stuck reversely and then tucked over and under while being tapered. SPLICE ⌗2851 is based upon this one.

Grommets (pronounced *grummits*) are used for block straps,
quoits, deck-tennis rings and eyelet hole reinforcements. They are
sewed to the bottoms of draw buckets. Loosely tied in dish towels,
they are used on cabin tables to prop dishes in a seaway. Tied in a
neckerchief, they form the PORTER'S KNOT.

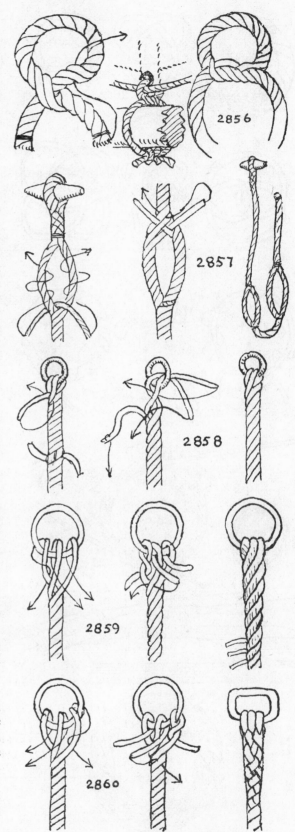

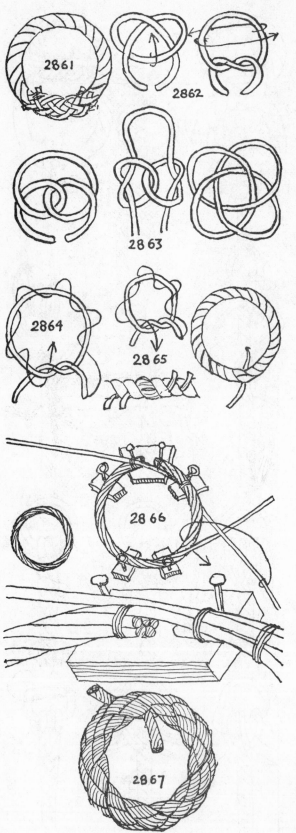

2861. The earliest form of grommet is a short piece of rope in the shape of a circle with the two ends short spliced together. One half a turn from the lay of the rope is removed before crotching. These were the first mast hoops and also the first jib hanks. Block straps are sometimes still made in this way.

2862. A grommet of *two leads* and *three bights* may be capsized into a grommet of *three leads* and *two bights*.

2863. A TRUE-LOVER'S KNOT, consisting of two interlocked OVER-HAND KNOTS, when drawn together and a single tuck added, becomes a THREE-LEAD, FOUR-BIGHT GROMMET.

2864, 2865. The COMMON GROMMET is made with a single strand in two ways. After completing two circles with any wanted number of loose turns, start the third circuit either as ✳2864 or as ✳2865, and continue to lay the strands parallel. The ends are finished off as in a LONG SPLICE. These two starts make all possible grommets of three leads. A grommet in Manila is tied preferably with a single strand of four-strand rope. In tarred hemp, grommets are made of small stuff, the full size. EYELET HOLE GROMMETS in sails are of marline or small wire. The length of strand required for a grommet is three times the circumference of the grommet plus six times the round of the rope.

Grommets of ROUND SINNET are shown as TURK'S-HEADS ✳1382 and ✳1384.

2866. To make a WIRE ROPE GROMMET: Nail five small blocks of wood to the top of a workbench, with two projecting nails in the upper and wider block, and a screw eye in each of the others. Bend a full-size piece of wire rope into your frame for a clue so that each nail holds one of the two ends, which are separated several inches. Turn the screw eyes to hold the rope in place.

Take a single strand of wire rope twenty-two times the diameter of the proposed grommet. Lift a strand from the end of the clue rope in the frame and seize in its stead *the center* of the single long strand. Continue to lay out the end that was lifted and lay in the long strand in its place. Keep the screw eyes turned so that the strands will not spring out. Keep all ends stopped with marline. When the working strand is to be led across the gap between the two ends, *it must be laid in beside* its own first-laid section, *on whichever side is the easier.* If the ends are not exactly opposite they can be *untwisted* a little with a pair of pliers, but they *cannot be twisted tighter.* If necessary, change the size of the grommet slightly.

When one end of the single strand is exhausted, use the other end. When the six full rounds of the grommet are completed, hammer lightly with a mallet, then lay the ends into the core as described for LONG SPLICE ✳2718.

2867. A CABLE GROMMET: Take a piece of tarred halibut line fourteen times the circumference wanted for the grommet. Middle the cord and make one complete turn at the center, imparting no extra twist. Then half knot the ends *with the lay* and proceed to make a very *loose* ordinary grommet of three circuits (✳2864). When, after three rounds, the two ends meet, half knot them in a *direction opposite to the lay* and with one end continue to helix around the other end of the *single cord.* Follow the single cord three full times around the circuit and then place one end beside the other and follow three more circuits between the two strands that are already in place. Knot the ends and bury them well.

CHAPTER 37: CHAIN AND CROWN SINNETS

Sinnet is a Line—made of Roape Yarnes—which are divided and platted One over Another, as they plat Horses Maines.

SIR HENRY MANWAYRING, 1644

There are several forms of the word *sinnet*, among them *synet*, *sennet*, *sennett*, *sennit* and *sinnit*. But the older sailors that I have known invariably pronounced the word *sinnet*; and the early and best nautical authorities—Captain John Smith (1627), Sir Henry Manwayring (1644), Thomas Blanckley (1750), and R. H. Dana (1841)—agree on the spelling as I give it.

Falconer (1769) appears to be responsible for the present dictionary form of the word, *sennit*, which he attempts to derive from *seven* plus *knit*. But the sailor is perhaps more familiar with netting than he is with knitting, and I hazard that *sin*(gle) plus *net* is a more plausible derivation, and that most derivations are mere guesswork anyway.

The word *braid* appears to have been applied almost exclusively to FLAT SINNETS.

The word *plat* or *plait*, besides meaning braid, also means a fold in cloth. It is often spelled *pleat*, but is always pronounced *plăt* at sea. Sailors use the word when platting a mat.

Sinnet appears to be the only comprehensive term for the present subject that carries no other meaning.

On shipboard sinnet is employed for chafing gear; it was formerly used for service and for reef points, gaskets, robands, earings and lashings.

CHAIN SINNETS are made of one or more strands that are formed into successive loops, which are tucked through each other. They savor of crochet and knitting, and as such are often termed "chains" or "chain stitch."

[471]

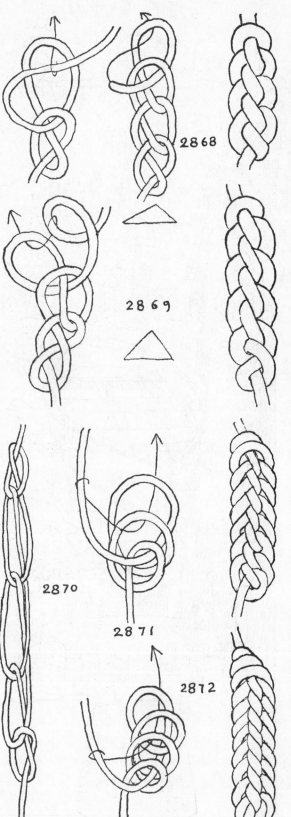

We are all of us familiar with the "spool" reins that are made by children in parti-colored worsted. But fewer will know that this is the way that purses were commonly made so late as 1840, and that crocheting was at that date just being introduced into England. Most of the sinnets to be shown here, although they may be made with a crochet needle, were first made either with fingers alone or else on one of these spools, of which there are several sorts.

2868. CHAIN SINNET, also called *monkey chain, monkey braid, single trumpet cord, single bugle cord, chain stitch, crochet stitch,* and *chain braid*. This is one of the most universal of sinnets and is employed for a variety of domestic purposes. It is often found in gold on dress uniforms. It is used as a shortening on window-shade and electric-light pulls and on aerial circus apparatus, where the end is freed and pulled to ravel the sinnet when it is time to put the rope to use. It is built up on a uniform series of single loops and is completed by drawing the working end through the final loop, which prevents raveling.

2869. Made with a series of hitches instead of loops, the chain is handsomer, thicker, possibly stronger, and certainly more shipshape.

2870. The method is sometimes used when larger and stronger cordage is needed than is quickly available. One end of a long cord or string is held and wound by a second person while the maker with alternate hands sticks a finger through the loops in turn and hooks a bight each time, and with a constant swinging of the arms makes a chain of long loops as rapidly as the other person can wind. This threefold chain is then tripled in the same manner that the single cord was, after which the operation may be repeated. Finally an ordinary THREE-STRAND PLAT may be made, or three sections of the resulting chain may even be loosely twisted into a rope of sorts. The method provides about the quickest way there is to make a strong rope without tools, and with only small material to work with.

2871. CHAIN SINNET, doubled, is called "*trumpet cord*"; sometimes it is called "*double trumpet cord*." To double, with the standing end take two full turns around the working part. Successive bights from the working end are then tucked through *two bights*, the surplus material of the earliest tuck being worked out after each new tuck is made. If built up with a series of hitches instead of turns (illustrated in ⚹2869), the product is more compact, being pronouncedly triangular, and the bottom side in particular is much improved in appearance.

2872. Trumpet cord may be tucked through triple loops if desired, which produces a larger but no handsomer cord. This also may be made with hitches instead of turns in a manner similar to ⚹2869. To finish off the sinnet, stick the end through the three final hitches in precisely the way illustrated for tucking the loops. In ⚹2871 the end is tucked through two loops or hitches as shown in the illustration.

Any of the sinnets on this page may be made with a crochet needle. They may also be made on a spool of *one peg* by the methods described on pages 474 and 476. Number 2869 is made by placing successive hitches over the pin; the rest by merely making a turn. Either method may be doubled by passing a turn of the strand a third time around the pin, then casting off the lower turn only at each operation.

2873. The chains that were just shown resemble closely, on the reverse side, the ordinary FLAT SINNET, of the next chapter. By tucking each loop alternately over, under and over, instead of under all three parts, a sinnet will be made that closely approximates FRENCH SINNET and that will make a very handsome trumpet cord. The final illustration shows the reverse side.

2874. This illustrates a chain carried one step farther than the last and tucked over, under, over and under. The method rapidly becomes cumbersome and it would seem that these two are sufficient for all practical purposes. But there is no limit to the number of loops and sizes that are theoretically possible.

We have now finished with the FLAT CHAIN SINNETS of one strand and most of the remainder of the LOOP SINNETS may be characterized as TUBULAR SINNETS, since they have a roundabout circuit. Many of them can be made by hand alone, and most of them may be made on a spool, but if large cord is used the hand method is recommended.

2875. The chain "fork" is an old apparatus for making square chains of small thread, generally of silk. This was the common cord for hanging lockets, eyeglasses, etc.

Sometimes the forks are of ivory, often they are of ebony or holly. The one pictured, which is my own, is made of boxwood. Sailors make this sinnet in larger material by hand and it can scarcely be told from ordinary EIGHT-STRAND SQUARE SINNET. Miss Lambert in her *Hand Book of Needlework* (1842), illustrates a chain fork which does not have the shoulders that are pictured here.

2876. The braiding spool pictured is a familiar contrivance that is generally considered a child's toy. It commonly has three or four pegs, which makes a SIX- or EIGHT-SIDED SINNET that is practically round. With one peg only a SINGLE CHAIN SINNET (#2868) can be made. Spools are commercially made in different forms, sometimes with a sliding wire carrier to lead the yarn around the pegs. One can be made with a large base, and with a hole entering at one side so that the finished sinnet may be led from the side or front while the spool rests solidly on the table. By this means both hands are left free.

2877. Miss Lambert gives a "purse mould" of many pegs. She minutely describes the old method of making purses, of the sort that Cyrano de Bergerac, in the persons of Mansfield, Coquelin and Hampden, used to toss about the stage so carelessly, but states that "since the introduction of crochet, these moulds have not been much used." A large CYLINDRICAL SINNET of sail twine, made on a mold of this sort, after being moistened, stretched and dried, makes a strong bag or pocket for holding odds and ends.

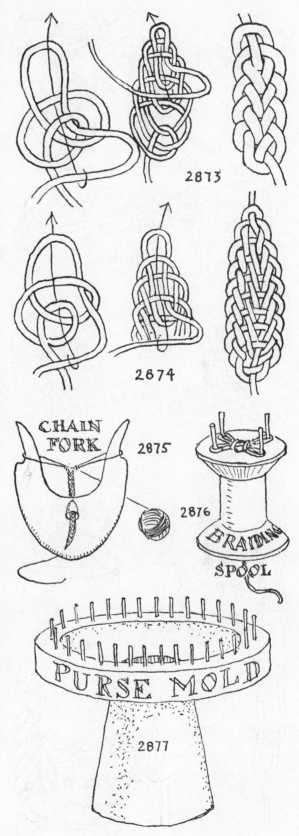

2873

2874

CHAIN FORK 2875

2876 BRAIDING SPOOL

PURSE MOLD 2877

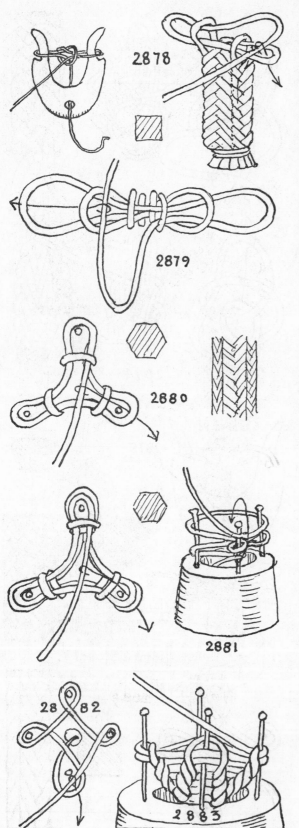

2878. SQUARE LOOP SINNET. To work on a fork (or on a two-pegged spool): Tie a TOM FOOL'S KNOT in the end of a cord. Put one loop over each arm or peg and drop the short end of the cord down through the hole in the bottom of the fork. Lead the working end of the cord around the fork to the left, laying it outside the fork and above the first loop. Lift the first-laid loop over the peg and cast it off over the top of the last-laid part to the inside of the fork. Lead the cord around the next peg, laying it just above the previous loop, and lift the first-laid loop over the last-laid part and cast it off on the inside. Continue in the same way, always working to the left or, if more convenient, to the right. From time to time pull the completed end down through the hole in the fork or spool.

To make the same sinnet in hand of larger material. Tie a TOM FOOL'S KNOT in the end of a fishline. Revolve the structure counterclockwise. Pass the line *over* the first loop of the TOM FOOL'S KNOT and pull a short bight of the working part down through the loop of the knot. Continue to revolve the structure counterclockwise and pull down another short bight through the other loop of the knot. Then work the knot snug. There are now two new loops in the structure. Revolve it counterclockwise a half turn at a time and pull down another loop through the next lower loop. From time to time draw out the surplus material from the lower loops. Continue tucking new loops and tightening lower loops, keeping the sinnet even at all times. Each time a loop is tucked down through the earlier loop, the earlier loop is at once drawn snug.

2879. A DOUBLE SQUARE LOOP SINNET. Work as before until two loops have been stuck through each end of the original TOM FOOL'S KNOT. *But do not draw up the knot.* Continue around once more and then draw up the material from the original knot. Continue in this way, each time reeving bights through two loops and always having two loops ready to stick through at the next operation.

To *make the same on a spool* having two pegs or pins. Start with a TOM FOOL'S KNOT, then wrap the yarn two turns around the pegs above the TOM FOOL'S KNOT. This gives three bights at each peg. Lift the bottom loop over the top of the peg and cast off on the inside. This leaves not less than two bights at any time around each peg.

2880. THREE-LOOP (SIX-SIDED) SINNET. Make exactly as described for LOOP SINNET %2878, but, when tied on a spool, three pegs are employed. Start by making two turns about the pegs, then proceed to work each peg in regular rotation as before. To tie in hand, use three loops and tie in the manner described for %2878.

2881. THREE-LOOP (SIX-SIDED) SINNET, doubled. This is doubled the same as %2879.

2882. FOUR-LOOP (EIGHT-SIDED) SINNET is the largest that I have seen tied in hand without employing a spool. Even larger sizes of the same sort present no manual difficulties but they tend to become hollow. To start this on a spool, make two complete turns around the four pins. Then work as already described.

2883. This illustrates the FOUR-PEG or LOOP KNOT doubled. Start as ⁂2882, but with three turns around the pegs, and work in the manner described for ⁂2879.

2884. A SPOOL SINNET that is made with one cord less than the number of pegs and is worked counterclockwise. Tie the ends together and arrange as pictured. Note that the bottom cord has turned two pegs. Lift the right bottom loop over the top of the peg and cast off to the center; next work the upper right peg, leading the cord from peg 3, above the bight that is already at 2. Lift this bight and cast it off over the top of the peg. Rotate the apparatus *clockwise* ninety degrees and lead the next cord likewise and cast off the bottom loop over the top of the peg. Continue to rotate the apparatus clockwise, working each cord in rotation. In appearance, this is about the same as a sinnet of one strand, around four pins (⁂2882), but it is a little fuller and it has the advantage of allowing several colors to be used if they are wanted.

2885. This shows the same method doubled, employing three pegs and two cords only.

2886. A SPOOL SINNET employing *one more cord* than the number of pegs. The strands are led clockwise and the sinnet also is *worked clockwise*, the apparatus being *rotated counterclockwise*. With three pins this will admit of the employment of four different colors. It may be made double if wished. The cord marked 1 is the first to be worked.

2887. The same method may be worked with two pegs and three strands. This may be made on a fork and will give three colors, the cross section being square.

The cross-sectional shapes of the LOOP SINNETS are quite as well defined as the cross sections of the PLATTED SINNETS which are to follow.

2888. An EIGHT-SIDED LOOP SINNET of two strands is more compact than the SINGLE-STRAND EIGHT-SIDED SINNET (⁂2882) of similar aspect. Each peg is worked in turn counterclockwise, the cord each time being led from the opposite peg.

2889. A SQUARE SINNET of four pegs made with round *turns* instead of loops. Note that there are the same number of sides in the completed sinnet as there are pegs; the previous SPOOL SINNETS have had twice as many sides as pegs. This sinnet was first shown me by Dean Longfellow: it is described in Volume III of Emmanuel Bocher's book on needlework. A considerable number of sinnets are to be found in this work, but most of them are limited to the transposition of two strands at each move. In general, they savor somewhat of crochet and interior decoration, lacking the crispness and severity that is characteristic of sailors' work. This is to be expected, considering the purpose of the book, but it does not apply to all of the sinnets that are included.

To make: Proceed as in ⁂2878, except that a round turn is taken in passing each pin. The cord is led rather loosely to the left, and the spool is rotated counterclockwise.

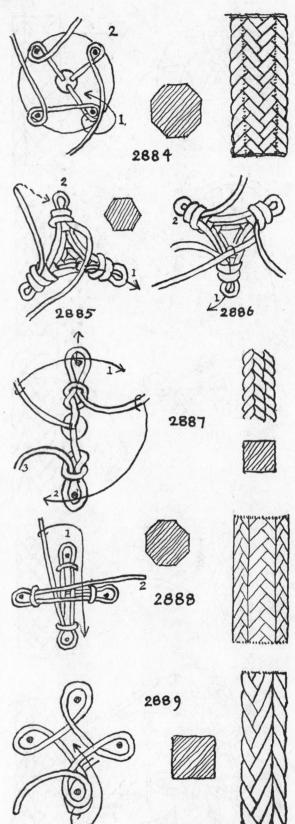

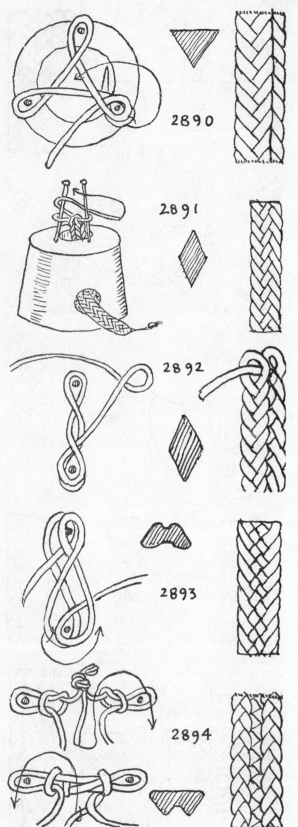

2890. This sinnet, which was suggested by the foregoing, is a most successful EQUILATERAL TRIANGULAR SINNET of one strand. The drawing illustrates it made with SINGLE HITCHES, but this has no advantages over making it with round turns, as shown in ⚓2889. If doubled, the sinnet loses some of its distinction. The illustration portrays one side only.

2891. A DIAMOND CROSS-SECTION SPOOL SINNET. Start with a TOM FOOL'S KNOT, thereafter pass each peg with a belaying-pin turn (figure-eight or S turn). Hold the apparatus, without shifting, in the position depicted (do not rotate), lift the cord over and cast off inside the pins alternately. The spool pictured here is the wooden plug from one end of a roll of paper; one may be secured in almost any shop that uses wrapping paper.

2892. A sinnet somewhat similar to the one just shown may be made by employing a series of identical hitches. The apparatus may be rotated in the direction found more convenient, when only two pins or pegs are employed. Generally I have found a counterclockwise direction the easier, but the reverse will probably suit the left-handed person better.

2893. If alternating left and right hitches are taken with the single strand a sinnet somewhat similar in appearance to ⚓2894 results, but the latter has three strands.

2894. A sinnet of two loops and three cords, taken from the *38th Annual Report* of the Bureau of American Ethnology. There are several examples of LOOP SINNETS given in an article on the arts and crafts of the Guiana Indians. For the most part they are not symmetrical. In the description of this particular sinnet the loops are held on the thumb and forefinger of the left hand. But it may easily be made on a spool. Three cords of equal length are tied together. NOOSES are made in two of them close to the knotted end and these are put over the pegs on the spool. The third cord is placed between the two knotted ones at the front. Lead the unengaged end to the back and then to the right around the right pin; then lift the loop (NOOSE) and cast off over the pin. The cord that has just been cast off is next led to the back and counterclockwise around the left pin, and the loop on that pin is lifted and cast off over the newly arrived cord and the pin. There is always one unengaged cord at the front center ready to be used and this is always the strand to be worked. It is carried to the back across the center of the structure, and then around one of the two pins which are worked alternately.

2895. The remaining LOOP SINNETS are made in hand. The present one is the only sinnet of distinctive equilateral triangular cross section that I have ever seen, except those that I have made myself. This is of a loose texture which suggests crochet, and I imagine that it is made with a hook.

I have made it upside down on a spool of two pins. The loops are stuck toward the center instead of outward. To make: Start with a TOM FOOL'S KNOT. The working end of cord is led to the right, and the structure is turned clockwise. Successive hitches are stuck as shown. Exercise great care in tightening the loops and employ a soft cord.

2896. IDIOT'S DELIGHT is tied with a single loop and two cords. Arrange as in the left drawing with the center of the material over a hook or nail. Stick the left forefinger through the single loop and withdraw a short loop, pulling it tightly. Through this loop insert the right forefinger and withdraw a short loop from the left cord in similar manner. Pull this tight and continue to alternate until sufficient sinnet is made. Note that each time the forefinger is inserted through the loop it is put *under* the part that leads to the working end. Made in this way, the sinnet will be almost round when pulled up carefully. If made in large cord, the surplus material will have to be worked out. But in small, smooth material it will be sufficient to pull it tight after each move.

2897. This is almost the same sinnet structurally but it has a different character. On one side (the left side in this case) the left finger is inserted *over* instead of under the part of the loop leading to the working end of the cord. The other side is entered as in the previous sinnet. Worked in this way, the resulting cord is very much flattened.

2898. IDIOT'S DELIGHT may be doubled successfully. Instead of sticking a loop through a single bight it is stuck through one bight and around the next and left well extended. Pin it out on the projection board when you first attempt it and work the sinnet upward or away from you.

2899. An easier way to double the sinnet, presenting quite a different appearance, is to stick each loop through two bights, leaving the end of the loop well projected. This sinnet builds rapidly and is not hard to work.

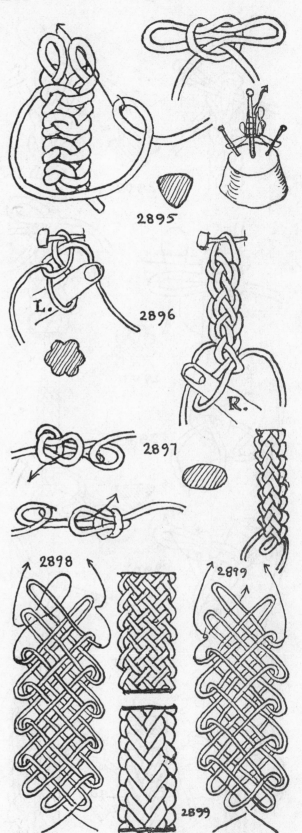

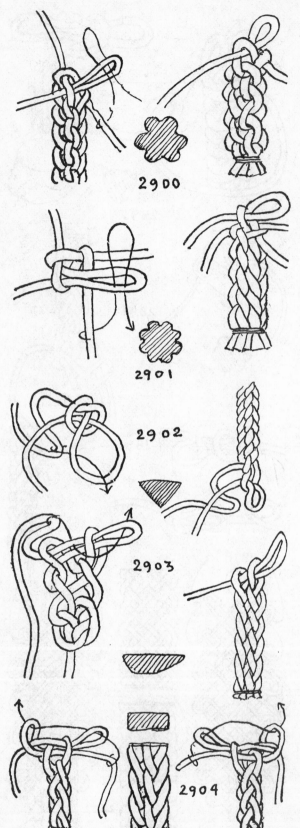

2900. A sinnet of three strands and one loop. Revolve the sinnet clockwise, stick a bight from each strand in turn. After the bight is stuck the previous bight is tightened around it, and then a bight from the next strand ahead is shoved through the new bight.

2901. With four strands the sinnet is made in the same manner. The four strands are tied together and a hitch or Noose formed in one. After the bight of the next strand to the right is stuck through this the first loop is drawn up and tightened and the sinnet continued.

2902. An irregular Triangular Spool Sinnet from Bocher. It is effective and pleasing. Two of the sides are alike. There are two strands and but one loop in evidence at one time. Middle the cord and make a Noose at the center, arrange as in the illustration and lead a bight from each cord in alternation up through the other loop. The two strands are worked in the same manner, the loop has the same face up and both ends are always on the left side.

2903. This is a crocheting stitch from Caulfield and Saward's *Dictionary of Needlework*, where it is termed "double foundation." Commence with a Tom Fool's Knot and stick a loop of the working end from the left through both loops of the knot. Then take another loop from the working end and lead it to the right, tuck it forward through the bight that lies between the two loops of the original Tom Fool's Knot and through the last-laid loop at the right. It should be led exactly as pictured, after which the previous bight or loop should be tightened, and another one added in exactly the same way.

2904. This sinnet was accidentally discovered while working for something quite different, an unusual event. The method is so obvious that it would be strange if it has not been made before. The cross section is a neat oblong and is the only Loop Sinnet I know of that shape. Single bights from the left and right sides are stuck alternately through both loops, and the second loop that was stuck through is tightened before the bight is stuck from the other side.

The narrow dimension of the oblong is lengthwise of the two loops, which is rather unexpected.

This completes the Chain or Loop Sinnets and brings us to the Crown Sinnets. A Crown is a knot of a number of strands in which each strand in regular turn passes over an adjacent strand and under the bight of another. A Half Knot of two strands is the smallest Crown possible.

In the upper left corner of this page is illustrated a Right Half Knot and in the upper right corner of the page is illustrated a Left Half Knot. This is in agreement with the Crowns shown in #2911, #2912 and #2913.

2905. A Crown of two strands, made of alternating Left and Right Half Knots. This is often used on a decorative cord and it illustrates the way HALF KNOTS or TWO-STRAND CROWNS are made, two of them forming a SQUARE or REEF KNOT which separates each two links of the sinnet.

2906. Sinnet of square knotting. This is the same as the previous sinnet but with all the parts drawn together. It bears a close relationship to the SOLOMON BARS in macramé but it lacks the inert foundation cords which pass lengthwise through the latter (see #2496).

2907. A series of identical HALF KNOTS of two strands makes a CROWN SINNET of two strands, the surface of which helixes to resemble quite strongly a plain-laid rope.

2908. With four strands worked alternately in pairs, and LEFT and RIGHT HALF KNOTS tied alternately, the resulting sinnet is square. The same face is kept constantly toward you, as you work.

2909. Four strands worked alternately in pairs and tied in identical HALF KNOTS make a bulkier ROUND SINNET than #2907.

2910. An EIGHT-STRAND HALF KNOTTED SINNET. Seize the strands and right half knot the opposite strands of two parallel pairs. Then left half knot the other two parallel pairs and continue to alternate. Keep the same side of the sinnet constantly toward you while you work.

2911. A CROWN SINNET of three strands. Crown in one direction, in this case right-handed. Lay one strand to the right in front of the next strand to the right. Lay that strand tightly over the end of the first-laid strand and in front of the next strand. Lay the third strand over the end of the second strand and stick it through the bight left by the first-laid strand. Draw all strands tight. This forms what is termed a SINGLE CROWN. The sinnet is built up of successive CROWNS exactly like the one just described. The success of these sinnets depends on drawing up the CROWNS evenly.

2912. FOUR-STRAND CROWN SINNET is made in the same way as the foregoing.

2913. FIVE- and SIX-STRAND CROWN SINNETS are made in the same way.
    The sinnet may be made with even more strands if a core is used, six being about the limit when there is no core.

2914. With three strands make alternate RIGHT and LEFT CROWNS. The result is roughly triangular.

2915, 2916. Sinnets of four and five strands, made with alternate RIGHT and LEFT CROWNS.
    The above sinnets from #2908 to #2916 are round, with the exception of #2914.

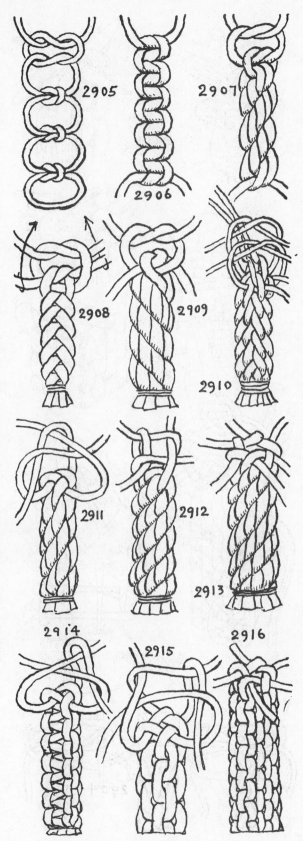

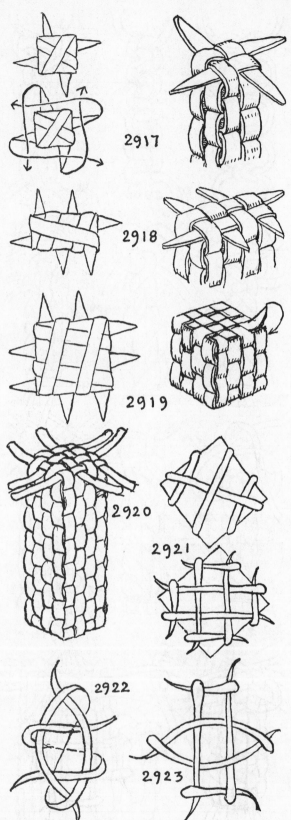

2917

2918

2919

2920

2921

2922

2923

2917. CROWN SINNETS are often made of flat thongs (leather and woven shoelaces). Sinnet watch guards and bracelets appear periodically, and are generally made by the amateur, while umbrella guards, leashes and dog collars are commercial products shown in Chapter 41. When made of flat material, these are almost invariably of *reverse crowning* (the first CROWN being to the right, the second to the left). The simplest employed is the regular four-strand (⚓2915), three strands not being very satisfactory. Flat fabric shoestrings may be used when no thongs are handy. The first diagram shows the bottom of the initial CROWN. Middle the strands, cross them as shown in this diagram, and crown them. Now, holding the first knot bottom up, as pictured, cover the initial crossing with a second CROWN as indicated by the arrows. Continue, with the same side up, to build the sinnet with alternate LEFT and RIGHT CROWNS.

2918. An OBLONG CROSS-SECTION, CROWN-AND-REVERSE SINNET is made in the same manner. The single thong which goes lengthwise must be about forty per cent longer than the other two. If all the thongs are drawn up with equal tension this will be very handsome. If desired, two more crossing cords may be added, which will double the width of the sinnet.

2919. This CROWN diagram, shown in Alston's *Seamanship*, for finishing off a fender, makes a very large and handsome cube if, after tying alternately, left and right, at the proper length, the ends of the strands are pointed and tucked back into the structure.

2920. This shows Alston's CROWN worked into a sinnet by crowning first to the left and then to the right. If crowned continuously in one direction, a large ROUND SINNET would result.

The remaining sinnets on this page are best made in cord; either banding or fishline will serve.

2921. The diagram shown here will make a sinnet that is more or less octagonal. It is worked in the same manner as the others but it may also be tied continuously with a RIGHT CROWN if desired, in which case it will be round. Compare with ⚓2930.

2922. A decided ELLIPSE, but to hold this shape it must be made with REVERSE CROWN. If tied with a continuous crowning to the right, it will be round.

2923. A rather full ELLIPSE with six strands, the diagram to be worked with CROWN and REVERSE CROWN.

Except for page 486, most of the remaining sinnets of this chapter are original. Captain Charles W. Smith is responsible for ⚓2931. There are several well-known ones on pages 484 and 485.

2924. A roughly triangular REVERSE CROWN SINNET. If rolled underfoot, the cross section will be practically round. It is not particularly distinguished, but, as it requires only six strands to work, it is quite practical. The advantage of this series of CROWN SINNETS is that large sinnets of differing forms, that do not distort, may be made with very few strands. Moreover, while being worked, they may be laid aside to be picked up later without danger of raveling or untying. The PLATTED SINNETS of the next chapter, when put down before completion, often prove confusing to pick up again.

2925. An EQUILATERAL TRIANGULAR REVERSE CROWN SINNET. This is very handsome. It should be worked snug, but not hove on, as this will destroy its regularity. If tied with right crowning only, it gives a ROUND SINNET with a handsome helixed surface.

2926. A REVERSED PARALLEL CROWN TRIANGLE. This was one of the earliest successful EQUILATERAL TRIANGULAR SINNETS to be made. It is not at all bad-looking and, if pulled up very carefully, the sides will have no bulge.

2927, 2928. A SQUARE PARALLEL-STRAND REVERSE CROWN SINNET and a FIVE-SIDED SINNET of the same sort as the last. These are both exceedingly practical and the latter is one of the most clear-cut of all FIVE-SIDED SINNETS.

2929. This is made on the same diagram as ⚓2924 but the strands that form the center triangle of the diagram pass over two and under two and the illustration shows the sinnet crowned constantly to the right. This makes a good ROUND SINNET that draws up more easily than ⚓2924.

2930. This shows a similar diagram form tied with reverse crowning. Most of these may be tied satisfactorily with the CROWN constantly revolving in the same direction, in which case, however, they all become approximately round. But by reverse crowning they maintain very closely their diagram shape. This diagram is the same as ⚓2921 but the strands that pass the center pass over two and under two. For that reason the sinnet is easier to make and easier to draw up than the other. In none of the sinnets of this series that have so far been given are cores required.

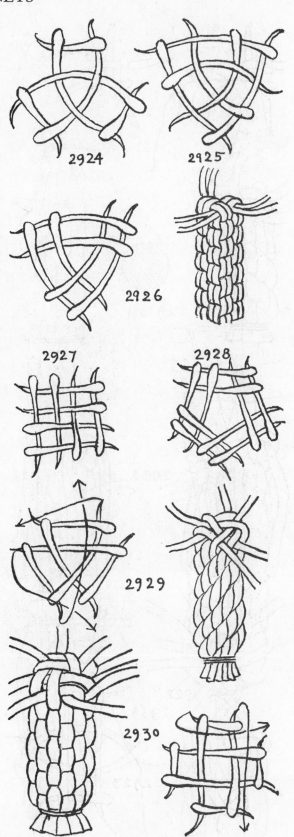

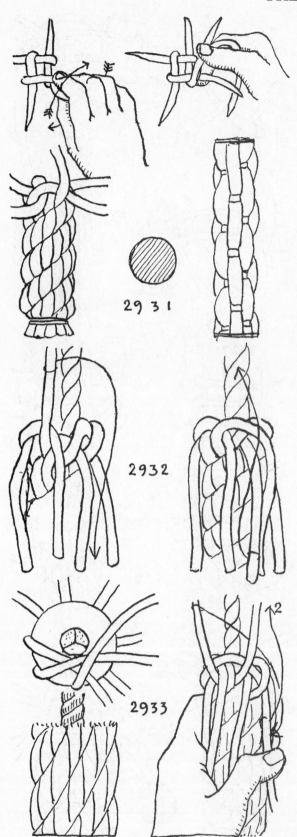

2931

2932

2933

2931. The method of continuous (helical) crowning was shown to me by Captain Charles W. Smith. It does not appear to be recorded in seamanship books although the mechanical sash cord braider employs it.

The method requires not less than five strands. Three strands worked in this way will give ordinary plain-laid rope; four strands will make a two-strand left-hand rope, with two yarns to each strand. With five strands a sinnet outwardly resembling FOUR-STRAND CROWN SINNET #2912 is made. The sinnet builds very much faster than the knotted variety, but it must be made very snugly indeed as it stretches considerably. The third sketch illustrates the sinnet of five strands, completed, and the fourth sketch shows the same sinnet after being stretched. With more than seven strands the use of a core is indicated. Six strands requires no core and is a practical size.

The method is similar to the sailor's way of making a punch mat (#2963) which will be shown in the next chapter.

To make: Secure five strands with a CONSTRICTOR KNOT (#1249) with the ends uppermost. Grip any two adjacent strands and impart a hard right-hand twist, or half turn, to the right. Drop the first strand and engage the next one to the right in exactly the same manner. Continue dropping the earlier strand and picking up the next to the right before each twist, and at each operation twist the two strands clockwise until the next one is in position. The motion in twisting strands is much the same as that employed in driving a wood screw with a common screw driver and, if continued long enough, is liable to cause sore fingers.

2932. The same, by another technique. Seize six or seven strands. Upend one strand only and hold the rest in the grasp of the left hand. Bring the upright end down into the grasp of the hand, crossing over the next strand to the right as you do so. Then extend the strand that was crossed. Pull on the new strand strongly, then cross that one over the next strand to the right, grasp it in hand and extend the strand just crossed. Continue until sufficient sinnet is made.

If a core is employed, this is about the quickest way of making a covering.

2933. A method of making a similar DOUBLE SINNET. Take eight or nine strands and seize them. Upend *two* strands and hold the rest in the grasp of the hand. Take the left upstanding strand, bring it to the right in back of its sister strand and cross it over the next downhanging strand to the right. Extend the strand that was just crossed. Take the left upstanding strand and repeat. Exercise care not to extend by mistake the end that was last laid down. Except for this, there is little opportunity to go wrong. If a core is used the core may be secured aloft.

2934. To make a PARALLEL CROWN SINNET by the helical method. The upper drawing shows an outside circuit of the strands at the upper edge of the sinnet. Take eight strands, extend two alternate strands and hold the rest in the grasp of the hand. Move the right member of the pair to the right, crossing *one* downhanging strand, and extend the strand that was just crossed. Take the strand that was the left-hand one of the original pair, pass it behind the strand that was last extended and cross the next downhanging strand. Extend the strand that was just crossed. Continue to work the new pair just as the first pair was worked. The right member of the pair is moved first and crosses the first adjacent downhanging strand, the left strand is then passed in back of the newly extended strand and continues until it has crossed over the next adjacent downhanging strand. Take care not to extend a strand that has just been turned down.

2935. This sinnet is made with ten strands; in cross section it is similar to ⚹2930, of eight strands, which does not helix. It is made in exactly the same way as ⚹2934. The method may be used with twelve strands, no core being required, but with fourteen strands a core is indicated.

2936. A ROUND CROWN SINNET with two sets of strands. Make with a total of either six or eight strands. Arrange the strands in two equal sets and crown the sets alternately to the right. This makes a firm and handsome sinnet. Tie knots in the ends of one set of strands, for purposes of identification, extend one set and drop the other set into the grasp of the hand. Crown the four uppermost strands. Then lift the lower set of strands and crown them above the first knot. Next arrange the lead of the *first-made* CROWN so that each end passes inside two strands of the upper knot.

2937. With six or eight strands tie this knot the same as the foregoing, except that the lead of the lower knot passes inside *one strand* of the upper knot instead of two strands.

2938. A ROUND CROWN-AND-REVERSE SINNET with two sets of opposed strands. One set is crowned to the right and the other set to the left. The lead in the lower CROWN is from one side to an adjoining side, not across the structure.

2939. A TWELVE-STRAND SINNET made with three sets of crowns, which are crowned alternately right and left. As the number of sets is odd, each set of strands is itself crowned alternately left and right. Knot the ends of the strands of two of the sets differently to assist in identification, an OVERHAND in one set, a FIGURE-EIGHT in the other. Lift four bottom strands up to the left of the next opposing strands and crown them to the right, then lift the next four bottom strands up to the *right* of the opposing strands and crown them to the left. Continue alternating in the same manner. This bulks larger than ⚹2938 but has about the same characteristics. It is large, firm and handsome.

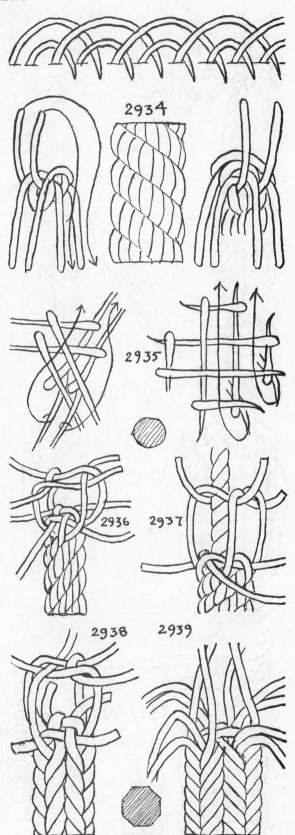

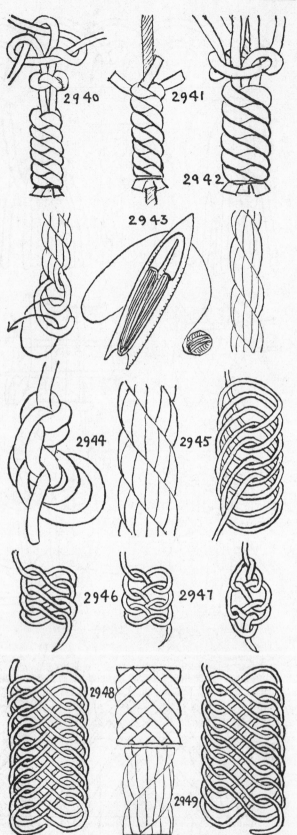

2940. Wall Sinnet. This is sometimes seen, but stretches so easily that it is scarcely practical unless it has a core. An old sample of this with a core is shown on the becket of the second bag lanyard among the frontispieces.

2941. This shows the sinnet with a single strand serving as core. This will take care of the stretch, but all the strain is on the core.

2942. With two groups of strands alternately walled the sinnet is larger, handsomer, stronger and has little tendency to stretch.

2943. A *netting needle* is a practical tool for making a sinnet that builds very rapidly. But it may be tied either with the netting needle or with the fingers alone. The needle is preferable if any considerable length is to be made, or if the material is small. Sew over and over, or under and under, through the last loop made, and draw up carefully and evenly. The result is a nicely rounded helix.

2944. The same sinnet, with the needle thrust through two loops each time instead of one, bulks larger and has a better appearance.

2945. The same sinnet with the needle thrust through three loops at each operation. This would seem to be about the practical limit of the sinnet, which, in this size, resembles left-laid rope. Draw up the next to the last stitch after each passage.

2946. A Figure-Eight Chain. This does not seem to have much merit, but it is always given in books on the subject. A netting needle is the best tool for the purpose. Start with the top of the design and tuck through the bottom bights of the figure eights alternately down through the left bight and up through the right bight.

2947. The same diagram is perhaps more often worked down through the right and down through the left, which makes a regular over-one-and-under-one design.

2948. An elaboration of the Figure-Eight design makes an effective Flat Sinnet. This should be done with a netting needle and drawn up after each stitch. The cycle of this is down through two bights and down through two other bights.

2949. A Round Sinnet may be made on the same diagram. The cord is led down through two bights on the right and up through two bights on the left. The resulting sinnet superficially resembles ⁂2944.

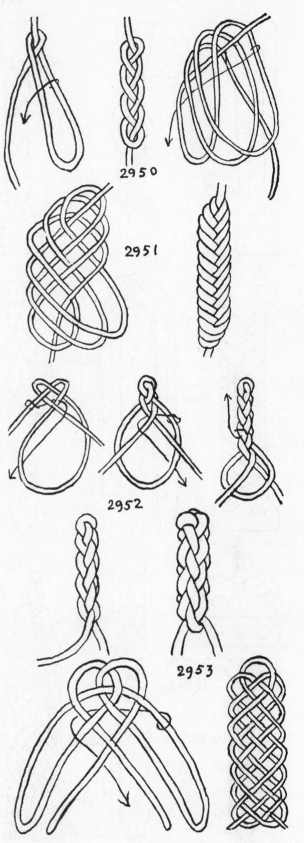

2950. Twist braid, sometimes called trumpet cord and bugle cord. This is frequently seen in trimmings of one sort and another and often is used as a shortening on window-shade pulls. There are two different starts for this sinnet. Make either an OVERHAND KNOT (illustrated) or a FIGURE-EIGHT KNOT. With these two all possible lengths may be made. A sinnet is completed each time the end of the strand is stuck through the bottom bight.

The ordinary THREE-STRAND PLAT is the basic form of both FRENCH and FLAT SINNET and either of these sinnets may be worked in a single cord in this manner with any desired odd number of leads. For further sinnets of both sorts see page 95 in the chapter on single-strand lanyards and also see mats in Chapter 30.

2951. A twist braid based on a FLAT SINNET of seven leads. The strands are arranged as shown, and are platted as described for FLAT SINNET in the next chapter. The sinnet may also be made with five strands. A sinnet is completed each time the end of the strand is led to the left lower corner.

2952. A ROUND TWIST SINNET based on FOUR-STRAND SQUARE or ROUND SINNET. Follow the diagrams in rotation to make this one. A sinnet is completed each time both ends are brought through the same bight in opposite directions. When the sinnet has been faired the bight at the bottom is withdrawn and the surplus material worked out to the end of the strand.

2953. ROUND TWIST SINNET based on SIX-STRAND ROUND SINNET. Arrange the strand as in the lower left diagram, then plat as indicated by the arrow, alternately from each side, withdrawing the two ends from time to time. The method is further described as ✳3011. When the two ends in the left diagram have each made one more diagonal and the two loops are disentangled, proceed to complete the arrangement of the strands that is shown in the bottom right diagram and work up into a snug braid as shown in the upper drawing of the knot. This is by no means a simple accomplishment, and it may prove easier for a beginner to pin the knot out on a board directly as in the right lower diagram. But in this case it becomes a knot and automatically ceases to be a sinnet. Aside from being a handsome TWIST SINNET, this makes a distinctive BUTTON KNOT.

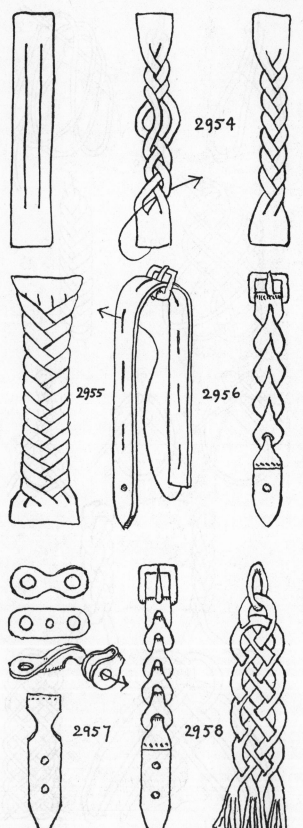

2954

2954

2955

2956

2957

2958

2954. Twist braid may be made in a single piece of leather and is quite similar to ✳2950. A leather strap is slit twice so that it has three equal lengthwise parts in the center length, while the ends remain uncut. Soak the leather in warm water before proceeding with the braid.

Make a very tight THREE-STRAND PLAT in the upper end, starting with the left strand and moving left and right strands alternately. It will be found that a similar but reversed plat forms in the lower end, and if the two ends are jerked sufficiently the two compensating plats will ravel and disappear.

The upper plat should be held firmly in one hand while the lower plat is worked out in the manner indicated in the second sketch. The plat may be made in any length that is a multiple of six moves. The strands are generally kept the same side up at the edges so that the grain of the leather will remain uppermost.

2955. Theoretically FLAT SINNET, with any odd number of strands, may be worked into twist braid in the way first described, but the practical limit is perhaps five, or at most seven, leads. A section of sinnet is completed each time a number of moves to the center has been made that is twice the number of the strands employed; this will bring all strands back to their original positions. Each time that this is done the opposing plat at the bottom should be raveled out before adding further to the length. To ravel, always pass the lower end through the *lower part* of the plat as illustrated in ✳2954. The illustration for this plat (✳2955) shows five strands, turned over each time they pass an edge. This, of course, will not give a pleasing appearance unless the split side of the leather is well finished.

2956. A slit leather plat is made by reeving the two ends of a strap alternately through slits in the opposing end. This is often seen in the leather shops but may easily be made at home.

2957. LINK SINNET. As links are best cut out with a stamp, the sinnet generally is commercially made. This and ✳2956 are found on luggage tags, wrist straps, dog collars, leashes and such commodities.

2958. This shows a Western bridle tassel which closely resembles a plat. But it is made by reeving the ends of two middled rawhide thongs through a series of evenly spaced slots. The ends are fringed.

A number of knotted cords that suggest sinnets will be found in the chapters on macramé (32), mats (30), and fancy knots (31). A LONG DIAMOND of two or more strands may be considered platting, and of course a LONG TURK'S-HEAD is of a very similar nature.

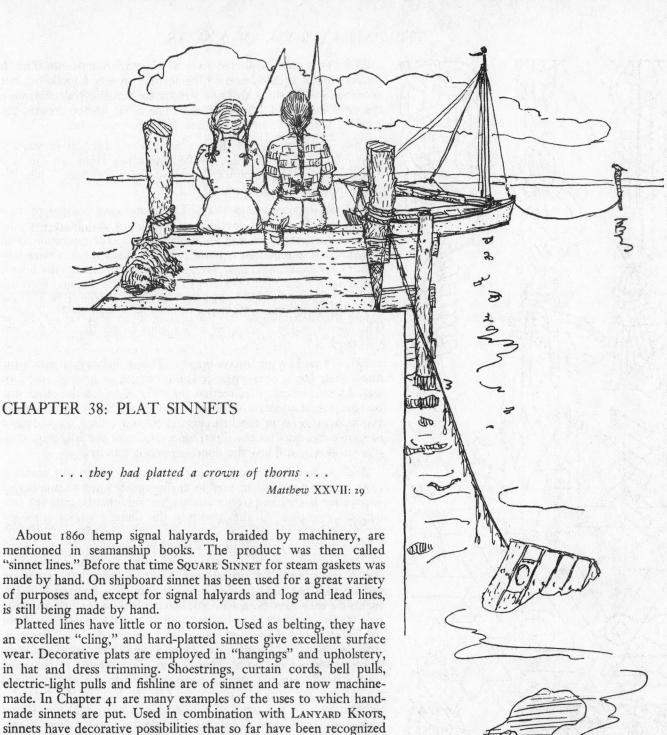

CHAPTER 38: PLAT SINNETS

. . . they had platted a crown of thorns . . .
Matthew XXVII: 29

About 1860 hemp signal halyards, braided by machinery, are mentioned in seamanship books. The product was then called "sinnet lines." Before that time SQUARE SINNET for steam gaskets was made by hand. On shipboard sinnet has been used for a great variety of purposes and, except for signal halyards and log and lead lines, is still being made by hand.

Platted lines have little or no torsion. Used as belting, they have an excellent "cling," and hard-platted sinnets give excellent surface wear. Decorative plats are employed in "hangings" and upholstery, in hat and dress trimming. Shoestrings, curtain cords, bell pulls, electric-light pulls and fishline are of sinnet and are now machine-made. In Chapter 41 are many examples of the uses to which hand-made sinnets are put. Used in combination with LANYARD KNOTS, sinnets have decorative possibilities that so far have been recognized only by the sailor. By dropping out strands at intervals, with which knots are to be tied, a lanyard is given a nice taper.

The usual way of starting a sinnet is to bind the required number of strands together and to begin at once to plat. Later the uneven beginning is either straightened out or cut off.

In most sinnets allow a length of strand about forty per cent greater than the length of the projected sinnet.

If strands are very long, wind them around the hand as ✳3085 and then snap elastic bands around them. If carefully wound in this way, when additional length is required, it may be pulled out without disturbing the elastic band.

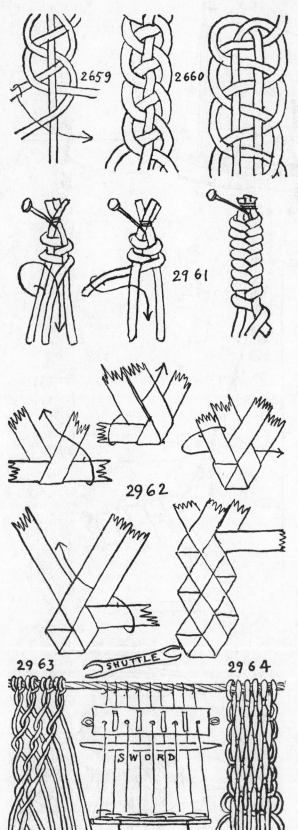

2659   2660

2961

2962

2963   SHUTTLE   2964

SWORD

2959. Two strands platted over a one-cord foundation. This is reminiscent of square knotting, being built over a foundation, but examination will show that the strands are actually platted around the cord instead of being knotted. The outer or top strands are worked alternately, first from one side, then the other.

2960. This is similar to the last but has two foundation strands. The outer or top strands are worked alternately from first one side and then the other in regular over-and-under sequence, while the foundation strands are inactive.

2961. A THREE-STRAND PLAT. The foundation consists of two strands and there is but one filler or working strand. Start with the filler in the center and lead all strands to the center position as in ⅋2965, but the sequence is quite different. Lead the left strand to center (a foundation strand); next lead the left to center (the filler); follow with the right to center (a foundation strand); and then the right to center (the filler). Plat very firmly and from time to time crowd back the filler so that the foundation is completely covered. The filler strand is at least five or six times longer than the foundation cords.

2962. PLAT, HAT or STRAW SINNET. This is the way in which the first "sailor hats" were made at sea, of straw, or of split palmetto leaf. At each change of direction the straw is folded the other side up. Be careful to draw up snugly and neatly before creasing the edges. Arrange as in the first illustration and follow the sequence of moves indicated in the illustration. To make the hat, start with BUTTON ⅋2590 and sew the sinnet around it spirally.

2963. A *punch* or *wrought mat*. A narrow punch mat makes a FLAT SINNET that is often used in chafing gear. An even number of single strands are hung over a foundation rope that is stretched taut between two pins. All the strands in this sinnet continue throughout to hold their original positions. Since the strands are "laid up" with each other—that is to say, a slight individual twist is imparted *to each*, which is contrary to the way they are twisted *together*—they have little tendency to untwist. The two upper left strands are laid up together right-handed, one turn, and are knotted together each time they have been worked. Having laid up the first pair, the second pair (3 and 4) are laid up together in the same way. Then the left strand of the second group (3) is laid up one complete turn with the right strand of the first group (2) and then 1 and 2 are again laid up together one turn. Then 5 and 6 are treated in the same way. After laying two strands together the left one of the pair is always engaged with the next strand to the left. In this way the sinnet is built up in a series of long diagonals from right to left, the back and front being identical. The finished appearance is also shown as ⅋3492.

2964. A *woven* or *sword mat*. Ashore this is used for girths in horse harness. At sea this is made on a rough loom as illustrated. Originally the sword was a flat, pointed, swordlike stick used to open the warp for each strand of filler, after which the sword hammered the filler into place. The shuttle was generally a ball or hank, or else a large homemade netting needle consisting of a flat stick deeply notched at each end. A sword is still used in beating back the filler.

2965. FLAT, ENGLISH, ORDINARY or COMMON SINNET is the plat or braid seen in schoolgirl pigtails. It is made of three strands and is the simplest possible plat.

To make: Secure three strands together and make the end fast to a hook or nail. Hold two strands in the right hand and one in the left. Bring the outer right strand down across its sister strand and lay it parallel to and below the single left strand. Now bring the upper left strand down across its sister strand and lay it parallel to and below the single right strand. Repeat alternately.

2966. Possibly a quicker but less usual way to make this plat is to pass the strands at the back, employing only the first and second fingers and the thumbs.

2967. With more than three strands it is well to secure the strands in a straight line. Two pencils and two elastic bands are sufficient apparatus. FLAT SINNET may be made with any odd number of strands in the way already described. The outer strands are moved alternately, and the tension is correctly and evenly arranged as each strand is passed.

2968. Seven strands is about the practical limit of the method. Beyond that there is difficulty in keeping it even. Even if a degree of success is achieved, a very little rough treatment will cause it to distort.

2969. Unless for some special purpose, this method is usually limited to an odd number of strands, as with an even number of strands the sinnet is unsymmetrical. But I have seen the braid, made as if with three strands in the left hand and one in the right hand, as here pictured, used as edging on theater-seat upholstery. Of course it was machine-made.

2970. If made of flat thongs, straw or shoestrings, the strands may be turned over at each edge. This will result in a sinnet with straight even edges.

2971. If the same method of turning edges is applied where units of two or three parallel round cords are used, instead of single strands, a distinctive sinnet results.

2972. In this sinnet the strands are double and parallel. The effect is very different from the last, in which the edges were turned.

2973. The number of sinnets that are possible with three strands only seem very limited. Three are given on these two facing pages.

2974. With four strands the horizon is somewhat widened.

2975. This sinnet is of interest as it has the same diagram form as ⌗2972, but the strands, instead of being parallel in pairs, are all laid alternately over one and under one.

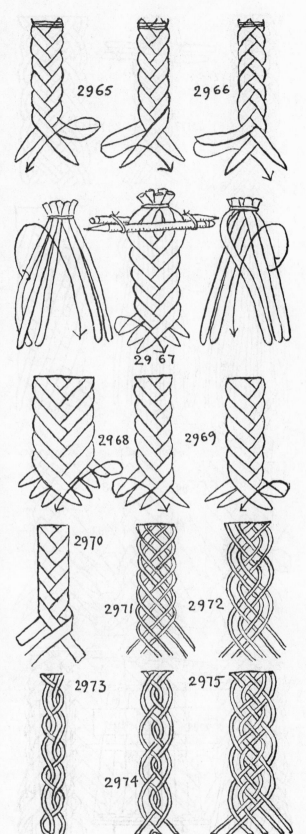

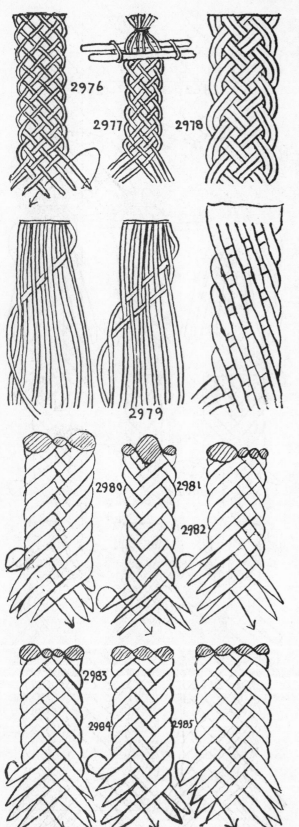

2976. FRENCH SINNET is a flat plat in which the strands have a regular over-one-and-under-one weave. The French call it "TRESSE ANGLAISE." As this has occasionally been translated literally in English books, it has caused some confusion. FRENCH SINNET is generally tied with an odd number of strands but may be tied quite as satisfactorily with an even number. In working it the strands are customarily divided so that if there is an odd one it is placed with the group that is held in the left hand.

FRENCH SINNET (1). The example given here is of seven strands. With four strands in the left hand, take the upper left strand and lead it diagonally down to the center, crossing its three sister strands alternately under, over and under. It has now become the lowest member of the right-hand group. Next take the upper member of the right-hand group (which now has four strands) and lead it to the left in the same order as before, under one, over one, under one. Repeat these two operations until sufficient sinnet is made.

2977. SIX-STRAND FRENCH SINNET with three strands in the left hand and three in the right. Lead the top left strand to the center over one and under one. Follow with the top right strand under one, over one and under one, and repeat from the start.

2978. DOUBLE FRENCH SINNET. This drawing illustrates a FRENCH SINNET of five leads platted with doubled strands, ten in all.

2979. FRENCH SINNET (2). In the braid and trimming trades ashore a different technique from ✂2976 is used, which gives a different character to the product, although it is structurally the same. All the strands are held in the left hand and only the top right strand is worked. This strand is led almost horizontally across *all the other* strands, in alternate over-and-under sequence. Then the next top right strand is treated likewise, and the process continued. The much shorter diagonal of the right strands is responsible for the changed appearance.

2980. The texture of sinnets based on FLAT and FRENCH SINNETS has a range of possibilities analogous to weaving and the range widens rapidly as the number of the strands is increased. But the comparative narrowness of the sinnet limits the size of the patterns employed.

With eight strands (five in the left hand) lead the top left strand under three, and over one to the center. Then lead the top right strand over three to the center. Repeat the two movements.

2981. Six strands (three in the left hand). Lead the left strand over one and under one. Lead the right strand under one and over two. Repeat.

2982. Seven strands (five in the left hand). Move the left under three, over one. Move the right under one, over one. Repeat.

2983. Seven strands (four in left hand). Move left outer strand under two, over one, move right strand under two, over one. Repeat.

2984. Seven strands (five in left hand). Move left strand under two, over two to center. Move right strand over two. Repeat the two movements.

2985. Nine strands (five strands in left hand). Move left strand under two, over two; move right strand the same.

2986. An ELEVEN-STRAND SINNET (six held in the left hand). Move left strand under two, over three to center. Move right strand the same.

2987. ELEVEN-STRAND SINNET (six held in left hand). Move left strand under two, over two, under one. Move right strand the same.

2988. A FIVE-STRAND FRENCH SINNET suggested by Captain Charles Smith's SQUARE SINNET (#3017, #3018). Hold three strands in the left hand. Lead left strand *over* two to center. (1). Lead right strand *over* two to center. (2). Lead left strand *under* two to center. Lead right strand *under* two to center. Repeat the four moves from the start. As this requires no tucking under and over, it builds very rapidly. But as it is folded in the center lengthwise, it must be folded back and creased reversely in order to flatten it out.

2989. SIX-STRAND DUPLEX SINNET. Two superimposed THREE-STRAND PLATS can be made simultaneously. Four strands are held in the left hand. Lead the left strand *over* three to center. Lead right strand *over* two to center. Lead left strand *under* three to center. Lead right strand *under* two to center. Repeat from the beginning.

This method may be carried farther with different numbers of strands differently divided. Six strands equally divided and worked in the same way gives a sinnet the same as #3003.

2990. The sinnets that have just been described have all had a single cycle for each set of diagonals. The remaining FLAT SINNETS of this chapter have two cycles for each set of diagonals, with the exception of #2998, which has three for each set of diagonals. That is, each of these sinnets is made with either four or six distinct movements.

A NINE-STRAND TWILL SINNET (five strands in the left hand). Lead first the left and then the right upper strand under one, over three. Follow this, first left and then right, under two, over two. Then repeat from the start. Work carefully and very firmly.

2991. A TEN-STRAND TWILL SINNET (five strands in the left hand). Although less individual, perhaps, than the last, this holds its shape better. Lead the left strand over two and under two. Lead the right strand over two, under two, and over one. Next lead the left strand over two and under two, and lead the right strand over two and under *three*.

Although banding has been recommended for general practice work in these sinnets, when making them for practical use something else will often be required. In small material nothing is superior to fishline. For decorative purposes the colored cords mentioned on page 20 will serve nicely. If a nicer material is needed it may be found either in "notion" or "Oriental" shops. Small silk fishline is also obtainable.

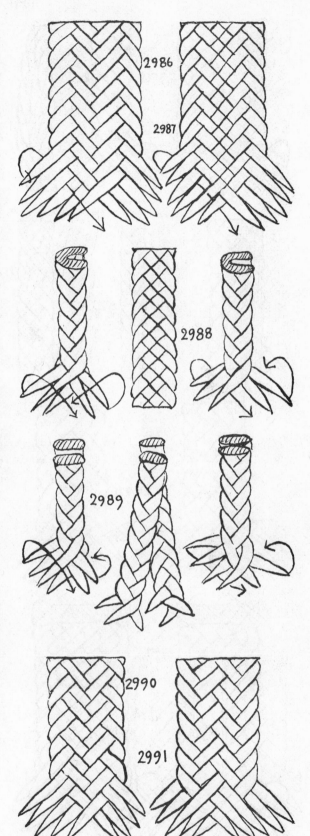

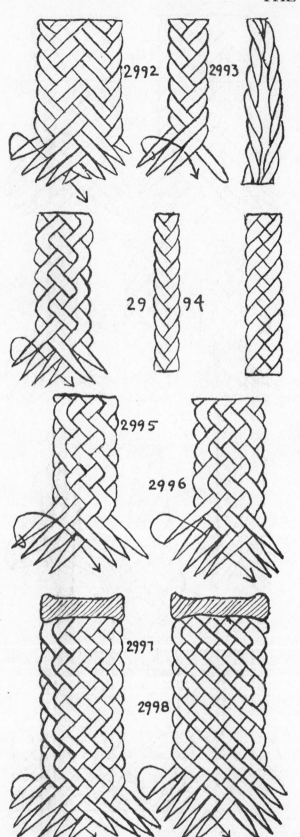

2992. A TEN-STRAND TWILL SINNET (hold five strands in the left hand). Move the left upper strand over one, under three to center. Move the right upper strand over one, under three, over one to center. Move the left upper strand over one, under three, to center. Move the right upper strand over one, under four, to center.

2993. A FOUR-STRAND "TRICK" SINNET. Superficially this appears to belong with the TWILL SINNETS, and if it is made firmly and not roughly used, its shortcomings will not be at once apparent. But actually it does not "jell." To expose its weakness, grasp the two ends and give a series of sharp jerks and somewhere in its length will appear a separation of strands. Grasp the two halves at this point and pull them strongly apart and the sinnet at once resolves itself into two separate two-strand ropes with opposite lays.

To make: With three strands in the left hand, lead the *left* upper strand to the center, then at once lead the next *left* upper strand to the center parallel with the first. Lead the right upper strand to the center, and then at once lead the next right upper strand to the center. Continue laying first two left strands and then two right strands one after the other.

Before this has been separated into two parts it is easily mistaken for SIX-STRAND SINNET (※2971).

2994. The remainder of the sinnets on this page are flat and have a doubled edge. The present one of the series is so narrow, however, that its cross section is oblong. It must be platted very firmly. Having made certain that you have followed directions correctly, do not feel concern about its success. Having made the desired length, beat it well with a mallet first along its edge, then along the flat. Finally its surfaces will appear as depicted in the center and right diagrams.

To make: Take six strands (four in the left hand). First lead the left strand over one, under two. Second, lead the right strand over two. Third, lead the left strand under one, over two. Fourth, lead the right strand under two. Repeat from the beginning.

2995. A SEVEN-STRAND DOUBLED-EDGE FLAT SINNET (hold four strands in the left hand). Lead the upper left strand over two, under one. Lead the right upper strand under one, over two. Lead the left upper strand under two, over one. Lead the right upper strand over one, under two. Repeat.

2996. An EIGHT-STRAND DOUBLED-EDGE FLAT SINNET (hold five strands in the left hand). Lead the left strand under one, over two, under one to center. Lead the right strand under one, over two to center. Lead the left strand over one, under two, over one to center. Lead the right strand over one, under two to center.

2997. A TEN-STRAND DOUBLED-EDGE FLAT SINNET (hold six strands in the left hand). Lead the left under two, over two, under one to center. Lead the right under two, over two to center. Lead the left over two, under two, over one to center. Lead the right over two, under two to center.

2998. An ELEVEN-STRAND DOUBLED-EDGE FLAT SINNET (hold six strands in the left hand). Lead the left upper strand under one, over two, under one, over one. Lead the right upper strand under two, over one, under two. Lead the left upper strand over one, under one, over two, under one. Lead the right upper strand over one, under two, over one, under one. Lead the left upper strand over two, under one, over two. Lead the right upper strand under one, over one, under two, over one. The visible parts on the face of this sinnet pass regularly from the left, in a downward diagonal over two and under one and from the right in a downward diagonal over one and under two.

2999. SQUARE SINNET of four strands. Used for lanyards, whips, whiplashes, quirts and leashes.

With strands of two colors, arranged as pictured, the two colors helix around the sinnet, giving a barber-pole or candy-twist effect. The sinnet is made in two movements.

First, take the top left strand, bring it around to the back of the other strands and then from back to front between the opposing strands. Finally lay it beside its sister strand into the lower position at the left.

Second, take the right upper strand, bring it around to the back of the other strands and then from back to front between the opposing strands. Finally lay it beside its sister strand into the lower position at the right. In this size, this sinnet, although made by the SQUARE SINNET method, is identical with ROUND SINNET of four strands.

3000. The same sinnet as the above with the colored strands differently arranged. Two strands of the same color are held in each hand. The colors in the sinnet alternate and a scaly effect is secured.

Roll this sinnet underfoot and it will be round; pound it thoroughly with a mallet, first one side, then the next adjacent side, and it will be square. It is generally made by the SQUARE method as the ROUND SINNET method (※3021) is much slower.

3001. EIGHT-STRAND SQUARE SINNET. One of the best known and most used of the sinnets. Often a core is added and is rolled, under pressure, to form a ROUND SINNET. Arrange with four strands in either hand. Like the FOUR-STRAND SINNET, this is made in two movements. First, lead the upper left strand, bring it around in back of its sister strands, and from back to front between the center of the opposing strands, and then down parallel with its sister strands, into the lowest position in its own group. Second, lead the right upper strand around back of its sister strands and from back to front between the center of the opposing strands and down parallel with its sister strands into the lowest position in the group.

If two colors are employed (white and green) and one color is held in the left hand, the other color in the right, the resulting sinnet will have four alternate-colored vertical stripes, one at each edge.

If the colors are arranged so that the four top strands are alike the sinnet will have belts of alternating color.

The strands may be arranged with the two top left strands green, the bottom white, the two top right strands white, the bottom green. Or the strands may be alternated on the left side and arranged either the same or opposite on the right side. The results are all distinctive.

This is the sinnet that has always been used for steam gaskets, and until comparatively recent years it was made by hand.

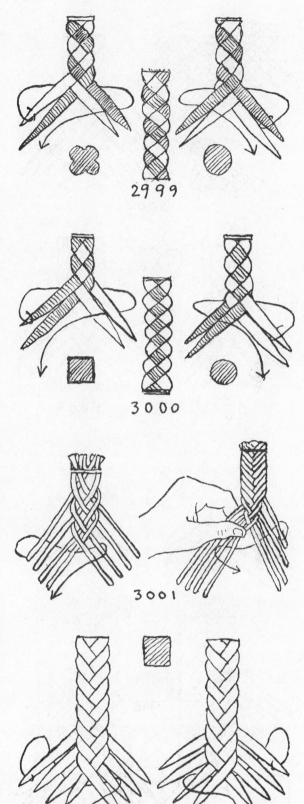

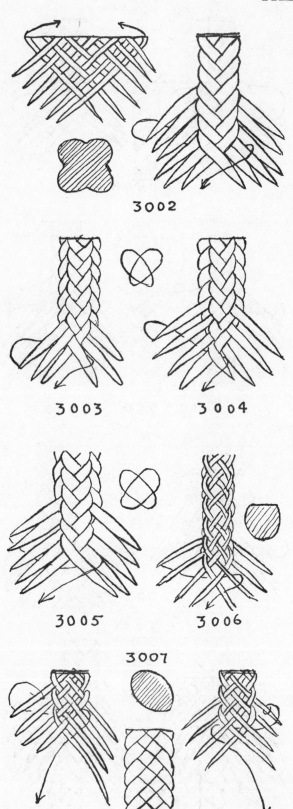

3002

3003   3004

3005   3006

3007

3002. Twelve-Strand Square Sinnet is sometimes seen. It bulks larger than the Eight-Strand Square Sinnet, but it is neither so firm nor so handsome. Sixteen-Strand or even Twenty-Strand Square Sinnet can be made if desired, but they have little distinction. All of these can be made around a core and rolled into a round form.

To make Twelve-Strand Sinnet, bring the upper strand of the right set around back, up between the third and fourth opposing strands and back into the lower position beside its sister strands. Do likewise (reversely) with the upper strand of the left set, and repeat these two operations alternately until the sinnet is the required length.

3003. The following sinnets through #3014 are variations of the Square method. The first four to be given are ordinarily termed "Half Round." Unless otherwise noted, the strands are equally divided, and the directions for the two sides are the same but reversed. With six strands lead the upper left strand around back, forward between the opposite bottom and second strand and then back, beside and below its sister strands. Do likewise with the right upper strand and then repeat from the beginning until sufficient sinnet is made.

3004. A Half Round Sinnet of eight strands. Lead the upper left strand around the back, then forward between opposite first and second strands (counting from the bottom) and place it below its sister strands. Do similarly with the right upper strand and then repeat from the beginning.

3005. A Half Round Sinnet of ten strands. Lead the upper left strand around the back, then forward between opposite second and third strands (from the bottom) and place it below its sister strands. Do similarly with the right strand and repeat from the beginning.

3006. A Half Round Sinnet of eight strands. Lead the upper left strand around back, forward between the two center right strands, then down again between the first and second strands (from the bottom) and lay it beside and below its sister strands in the left-hand group. Do likewise (reversely) with the upper right strand, and repeat from the beginning.

3007. An Ellipse of eight strands. First, lead the upper left strand around back, forward between the third and fourth strands (from the bottom), then down between the second and third strands (from the bottom) and lay beside and below its sister strands. Second, lead

[494]

the upper right strand around the back, forward between center strands, down between the first and second strands (from the bottom) and lay beside and below its sister strands in the right-hand group. Repeat from the beginning.

3008. A SIX-STRAND ELLIPSE. Lead the upper left strand around back, and bring it forward between the second and third strands (from the bottom), laying it beside and below its sister strands. Next lead the right upper strand around back and bring it forward between the first and second strands from the bottom and lay beside and below its sister strands. Repeat from the beginning.

3009. An EIGHT-STRAND ELLIPSE. First, lead the left upper strand around the back and bring it forward between the third and fourth strands (from the bottom), laying it beside and below its sister strands. Second, take the right upper strand around the back and bring it forward between the first and second strands (from the bottom), laying it beside and below its sister strands. Repeat these two directions in alternation.

3010. A TEN-STRAND ELLIPSE. First, lead the left upper strand around the back and bring it forward between the third and fourth strands (from the bottom), laying it beside and below its sister strands. Second, take the right upper strand around the back and bring it forward between the second and third strands (from the bottom), laying it beside and below its sister strands. Repeat these two directions alternately until sufficient sinnet has been made.

3011. SIX-STRAND ROUND SINNET, by the SQUARE SINNET method. Lead the left upper strand around the back, and forward between the third and second strands (from the bottom), then down between the first and second strands (from the bottom) and lay beside and below its sister strands. Lead the right upper strand around the back and forward between the first and second strands (from the bottom) and lay beside and below its sister strands. Repeat from the beginning.

3012. EIGHT-STRAND ROUND SINNET may be made by the same method but requires a core. It is impractical unless worked by two men. Lead the left upper strand back, forward between three and four, back between two and three, forward between one and two and down beside and below its sister strands. Lead the upper right strand similarly but reversely. Method #3022 will be found more satisfactory.

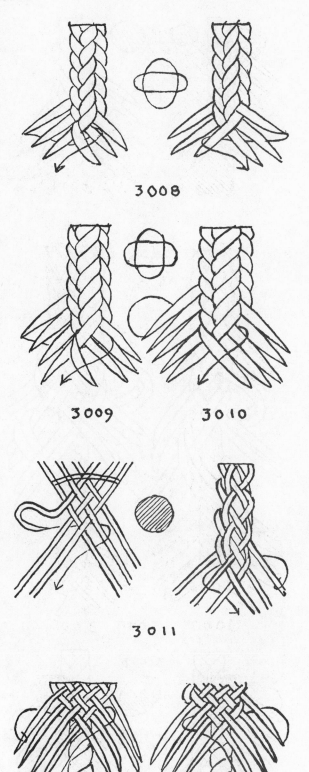

3008

3009   3010

3011

3012

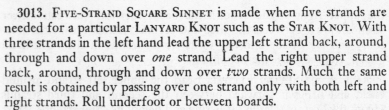

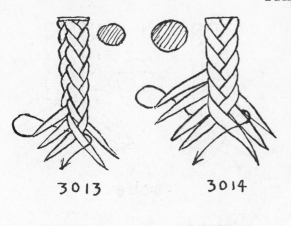

3013   3014

3015   3016

3017

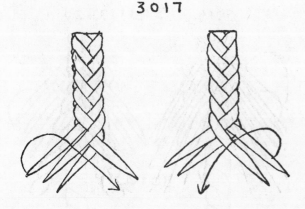

3013. FIVE-STRAND SQUARE SINNET is made when five strands are needed for a particular LANYARD KNOT such as the STAR KNOT. With three strands in the left hand lead the upper left strand back, around, through and down over *one* strand. Lead the right upper strand back, around, through and down over *two* strands. Much the same result is obtained by passing over one strand only with both left and right strands. Roll underfoot or between boards.

3014. SEVEN-STRAND SQUARE SINNET is for the same purpose as the above. Four strands are held in the left hand and three strands in the right hand. The sinnet is made in two movements like the rest of the sinnets given here. First, lead the upper left strand around in back and then forward between the second and third strands from the bottom and finally back parallel with its sister strands into the lowest position of the group. Second, lead the right upper strand around in back and forward between the center opposing strands and then back parallel with its sister strands into the lowest position of the group. Repeat these directions from the beginning, and roll the sinnet thoroughly.

3015. COACHWHIPPING is made over stanchions and rails with two or several parallel strands. Generally fishline is used. It is worked as SQUARE SINNET ⚹2999 but with two, sometimes three or even four, strands as a unit, instead of one. Under some circumstances, when the strands fail to cover the core or foundation, extra strands are added with a sail needle.

3016. SIX-STRAND COACHWHIPPING. This is made as ⚹3011 but with doubled, tripled or quadrupled strands. This sinnet is almost invariably made with the aid of a "mate" or helper. "Mate" is the preferred name; it comes from "boatswain's mate." Sometimes the sinnet is made as ⚹3011 and the strands are doubled or tripled with a needle as in a TURK'S-HEAD. COACHWHIPPING is also made as EIGHT-STRAND SQUARE SINNET ⚹3001 with either doubled or tripled strands moved as units.

3017. This was, so far as I know, Captain Charles W. Smith's individual method of making SQUARE SINNET. With four strands, hold three in the left hand and one in the right hand. First, lay the upper left strand across the *front* to the center below its sister strand. Second, lay the upper right strand across the *front* to the center below its sister strand. Third, lay the upper left strand across the *back* to the center below its sister strand. Fourth, lay the upper right strand across the *back* to the center below its sister strand, and repeat the directions from the beginning.

3018. EIGHT-STRAND SQUARE SINNET by Captain Charles W. Smith's method. Hold five strands in the left hand and three strands in the right. First, bring the upper left strand down the *front* to the center into the lower position on the right side. Second, bring the upper right strand down the *front* to the center into the lower position on the left side. Third, bring the upper left strand down the *back* to the center into the lower position on the right side. Fourth, bring the upper right strand down the *back* to the center into the lower position on the left side. Repeat from the beginning until sufficient sinnet has been made.

This builds much faster than the usual method (#3001) but it requires more skill to plat it snugly. I have experienced some difficulty, after putting this sinnet aside, in picking it up again just where I left off. Structurally it is identical with #3001. Either sinnet may be interrupted and then continued by the other method.

3019. TWELVE-STRAND SQUARE SINNET by Captain Charles W. Smith's method. Hold seven strands in the left hand and five in the right and follow the directions already given for #3018.

3020. If it is desired to get the effect of a CROWN SINNET in a hurry, take some fishline or marline and lay up into a SIX-STRAND CABLE by hand. Fasten one end of a fishline to a hook or nail on the side of a building, fasten the other end in a hand drill in the place of a bitt. Holding the line taut, turn the hand drill until the lay is as tight as practicable. Keep the line tight and have your "mate" rub it well with a piece of waxed canvas. Then have him grasp the strand at half length and hold it taut while you place the two ends together and make the second end fast. Grasp the bight in the drill. Keeping the doubled line taut, loosen the ratchet of the drill, and the two parts will lay up together. Make three of these doubled lines. With the brace impart extra twist to the lay of each of the three and then, using the ratchet of the drill as before, lay the three doubled lines up together. Your mate should rub the line well with the waxed canvas patch before slackening the tension that is held with the drill. The six strands, which really form a cable of sorts, can hardly be told from CROWN SINNET.

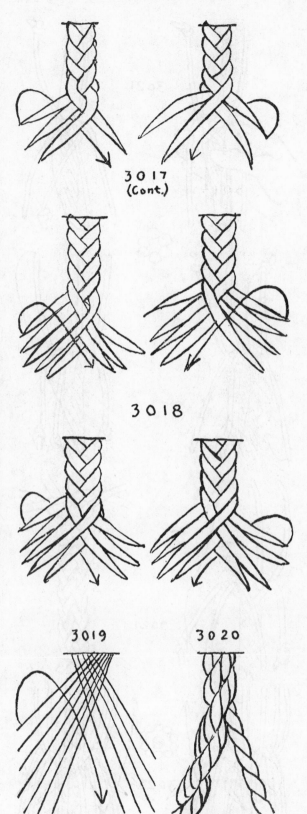

3017 (Cont.)

3018

3019   3020

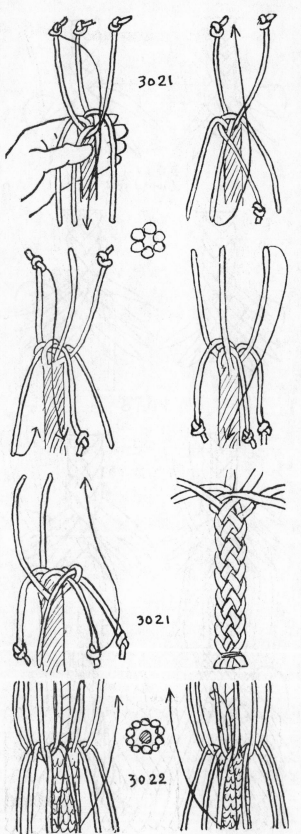

3021. ROUND SINNET requires an even number of strands. With four strands it is identical with ✳2999, which is made by a quicker and simpler method. Six is the preferred number of strands for ROUND SINNET but it may also be made satisfactorily with eight strands if worked carefully. With more than eight strands, being tubular, it is prone to distort and should have a core. Made with a core, it is often termed COACHWHIPPING, although COACHWHIPPING proper is made with doubled or tripled strands (✳3015) and, if made on the tapering end of a rope, is called CROSS-POINTING.

To make a SIX-STRAND ROUND SINNET: Tie six strands together and hold them in the left hand with three alternate strands extended over the back of the hand and the three lower strands held in the grasp of the hand. Tie an OVERHAND KNOT in the end of each upper strand to identify it. Take any upper knotted strand, lay it diagonally down to the right, crossing the first lower strand, and place it in the grasp of the hand. Extend the lower strand that has just been crossed, pull on it firmly and lay it over the back of the hand. Turn the whole sinnet in the hand, counterclockwise, a hundred and twenty degrees (one third of the circuit), which brings the next pair of strands to the front. Treat these in the same manner as the first pair. Turn the structure again counterclockwise a hundred and twenty degrees farther and do likewise with the third and remaining pair. This completes one of the two cycles that are required to make the sinnet.

Without changing the grip of the left hand, grasp with the right hand the upper strand to the right. (The upper strands at this time are the unknotted strands that originally were in the lower position.) Lead this strand down in a left diagonal, crossing the next lower strand, and extend the strand just crossed. Count aloud as you cross strands, one number for each crossing, "1, 2, 3," and at 3 it is time to reverse the direction again. At the completion of one cycle the three knots are aloft; at the completion of the next cycle the knots are down. Continue to alternate the two sets of directions that have been given.

The first two diagrams show the first two strands being exchanged. The third diagram shows the beginning of the second interchange. Diagram 4 shows the completed cycle, after all strands have been interchanged, and also the beginning of the first reverse interchange. Figure 5 shows the continuation of this interchange, and figure 6 shows the completed sinnet.

3022. Unless very firmly made, EIGHT-STRAND ROUND SINNET will require a core. With more than eight strands a core is imperative and the resultant sinnet is called CROSS-POINTING. CROSS-POINTING is worked as ROUND SINNET, with any even number of strands.

If worked around a core with units of two or three strands instead of single strands, this is generally called COACHWHIPPING. But almost any sinnet worked around a core may be called COACHWHIPPING.

3023. In MULTI-STRAND CROSS-POINTING one end of the core should be secured to some object aloft. For small sinnets a hook is convenient as the length must be changed frequently. Have the hook at not less than eye level. But the best way is to lead the core aloft through a single block and to make the end fast to a pin or cleat so that it may be adjusted at frequent intervals as the sinnet grows.

3024. Cyrus L. Day, in his book *Sailors' Knots*, gives the method of making ROUND SINNET in a position the reverse of what I have described, with the strands hanging downward. I have never seen this method described elsewhere. If a core is used (CROSS-POINTING) there seems to be little to choose between the two methods, but I prefer the old way for a regular ROUND SINNET, without a core, as it gives a firmer mass to grasp in the hand.

The directions for making this are identical with what has already been given, the sole difference in working being that the strands are pulled downward when tightening instead of upward.

3025. ROUND SINNET. A "skip-strand" method for ROUND SINNET and CROSS-POINTING, with eight strands. The strands are divided and arranged as in the ROUND SINNET just described but the upper strand in its downward diagonal crosses two lower strands instead of one, and it is the second one to be crossed that is raised or extended each time. It will assist greatly when first making this sinnet if the strands of the two sets are marked (one set moves to the right, the other to the left). If two colors are not available, dip one set in strong tea or coffee, the other in water, and dry them. But if time is lacking, tie an OVERHAND KNOT in the ends of one set. It will also assist materially if the strands are started as SINNET #3021, until they are in regular formation.

To make: With *eight* strands in hand, raise each alternate one and lay it back over the forefinger and hold the remainder in the grasp of the left hand. Do two movements of #3021, one set to the left and then one set to the right; the sinnet is now ready to start. Take any upper strand and lead it downward in a right diagonal, crossing two lower strands. Grasp the strand that was moved in the left hand and extend the last or second strand that was crossed. Rotate the structure counterclockwise one quarter turn, so that the next upper strand to the left is in position. Repeat with this and then with the remaining two strands. When the fourth upper strand has been moved, do not shift the grip but grasp the second upstanding strand to the *right* of it, lead it in a left diagonal downward over the two lower strands and extend the last or second one that was passed. Rotate the structure one quarter turn clockwise and repeat with the next upstanding strand to the right. Do likewise with the remaining two. The two complete cycles of the sinnet have now been made.

This sinnet may be made without a core up to ten, or possibly twelve, strands. But a core of about twice the diameter of a strand can be employed to advantage with twelve and fourteen strands.

3026. A "SKIP-STRAND" SINNET (three strands are skipped). This is made in the same manner as the foregoing except that three lower strands are crossed instead of two by each upper strand when it is worked.

3027. A "SKIP-STRAND" SINNET with alternating short and long diagonals. In the left diagonals the upper strands are each led over three lower strands at each move and in the right diagonals the upper strands are each led over only one lower strand.

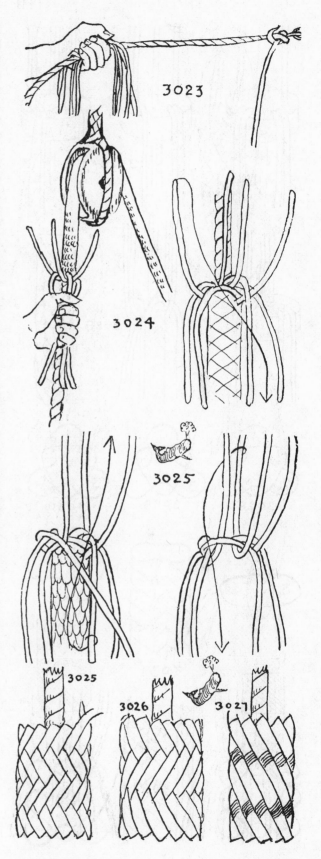

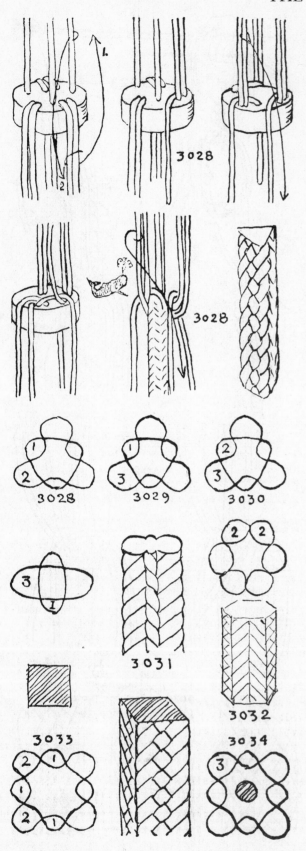

3028

3028

3028   3029   3030

3031

3033

3032

3034

3028. A TRIANGULAR SINNET of nine strands. This was the first EQUILATERAL TRIANGULAR SINNET to be made. It is easy to make and "builds" rapidly. Tie nine strands together, three white and six colored strands. Hold in the left hand and extend the three white strands over the back of the hand, arranging the six colored strands regularly in the grasp of the hand. Take one of the single white strands and lead it to the *left* down over the next pair of lower strands and extend the *pair* that was just crossed. Rotate the structure a hundred and twenty degrees clockwise, which brings the next single white strand into position. Move this strand the same as the previous one and extend two colored strands as before. Then move the remaining single strand exactly as the first strand was worked, extending the remaining colored strands. There are now three pairs of upper strands and three single lower strands.

Take the bottom or left strand from a convenient upper (colored) pair and lead it to the right across the next single lower white strand (see fifth illustration) and extend the single white strand. Now *drop* the remaining member of that colored pair down into the grasp of the hand. Move the structure a hundred and twenty degrees counter-clockwise and repeat with the next set of strands. Repeat with the remaining set.

Start from the beginning and repeat. It will be found, when it is time to work the pairs, that the two strands are arranged one above the other. Each time, it is the *lower* strand of the pair that is led and the remaining or upper strand of the pair is dropped inert, into the hand, without making any crossing.

Although at first the method may prove a little confusing (probably due to the inert member of each of the pairs), it will be found to work very quickly and smoothly when once learned. The colored pairs form the edges of the finished sinnet and the white strands the sides.

3029. A TRIANGULAR SINNET of twelve strands is worked similarly. At the edges the colored strands are arranged in groups of three instead of pairs. The sole difference in working is that after the bottom strand of a group of three has been crossed to the right and the single white strand that was crossed has been extended, two remaining strands are dropped into the grasp of the hand, instead of one.

3030. A TRIANGULAR SINNET of fifteen strands introduces a new feature. The edge strands are worked as before, to the right, and the white or side strands to the left. But in this sinnet there are two white strands to each side group and they are worked similarly to the edge strands. The white strand in the *lower* tier is crossed over the opposing group of three colored strands, while the remaining white *one* is dropped into the grasp of the hand.

3031. A SQUARE SINNET with four groups instead of three, worked in the same way. If four equal groups are used, the result is ordinary SQUARE SINNET (#3001). The number of strands at each point is indicated on the diagrams. If there is a difference in the number of the two sets, the white strands are always the smaller in number.

3032. A ROUND or SIX-SIDED SINNET. This sinnet has six groups of strands but the groups are even, having two strands each. If a core is used, this may be made with three strands to the group.

3033. A handsome SQUARE SINNET may be made with eight groups, four being singular and pairs being introduced at the corners.

3034. A SQUARE SINNET. With three strands in each corner group, a small core is indicated.

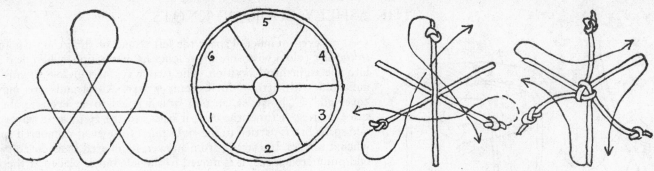

CHAPTER 39: SOLID SINNETS

It can be done in another way, but it requires a good and neat MAR-
LINGSPIKE SAILOR to do it.

WILLIAM BRADY: *The Kedge Anchor*, 1841

The PLAT SINNETS of the previous chapter are either flat or tubular. Larger and different-shaped sinnets have always required cores.

My first experiments in sinnets began with a search for a sinnet
of equilateral triangular cross section and the first successful sinnet
of this shape was a tubular one (※3028) of the last chapter.

In a later attempt to find a larger sinnet of the same shape, a CROWN
SINNET was produced on diagram ※3047. Still later it was found
that a smaller CROWN SINNET of the same sort could be made on a
smaller diagram. This was ※3035, which follows:

3035. The method of making is illustrated in the series of diagrams
at the top of this page. Six strands are seized together with a CON-
STRICTOR KNOT and an OVERHAND KNOT is cast in three alternate ends
to assist in identification. The knotted ends are first crowned as
shown in the third diagram. The unknotted ends are next led without crowning as in the fourth diagram, which completes one operation. The sinnet is continued by crowning the knotted strands again,
as shown in the fifth diagram of the series, and then the unknotted
set is led again, as in the fourth diagram. The two movements are
repeated in alternation until sufficient sinnet has been made.

The sinnet produced is triangular, but due to the bulkiness of the
CROWN KNOT, it is somewhat irregular, and this irregularity is very
much accented in larger sinnets, in which both sets of strands are
crowned.

3036. I found that, by introducing extra or duplicate strands at
various places in the circumference, the sinnet could be made to build
in a helix instead of in tiers, so eliminating the necessity of crowning
the strands. The extra strands were so introduced that no space in
the circumference was left vacant, when the strands were moved.

The spaces are regularly numbered around the diagrams counterclockwise. All *odd* strands, when they are moved, are led to the
right, counterclockwise; all *even* strands are led to the left, clockwise. The earliest strand to occupy any space is always the next one
to be moved from that space. The earliest odd-numbered strand is
always the right-hand strand of its group; when it is moved it is led
to the right, counterclockwise, until it reaches its destination, where
it is put into the near or left-hand position of an odd-numbered
space.

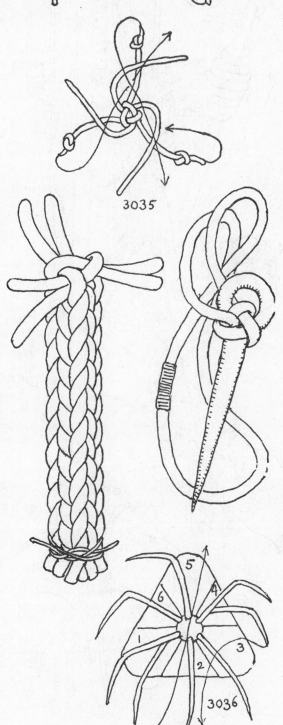

3035

3036

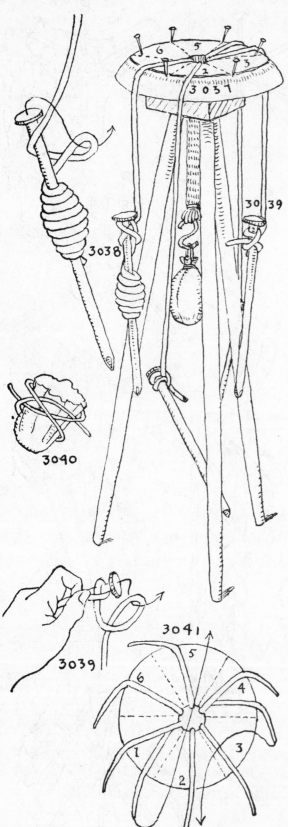

At an even-numbered space the left strand of the group is moved *to the left* (clockwise) until it reaches its destination, where it is put into the right-hand position. The two ways of moving strands are indicated with arrows in diagram ✳3041. All strands are moved "over all." If, however, an odd strand is led to an even-numbered space, as is sometimes the case, it passes to the *right* as it leaves the odd space but is carried to the *right side* of the even-numbered space when it arrives. If a strand from an even-numbered space is led to an odd-numbered space, it is moved to the left but is placed at the *left* side of the odd-numbered space.

3037. To hold the strands in place, while working these sinnets, a table, similar to the one shown, will be found a great convenience. Take the round bottom of a peach basket with an inch-and-a-half hole in the center and peg in three broomsticks for legs, about forty inches long. Chamfer the top edge. At the top the legs should be close together and at the floor about eighteen inches or more apart.

3038, 3039. As many bobbins are required as there are strands, and these should be weighted. Seven-inch wire spikes will be found satisfactory and inexpensive. Two ways of securing them with Clove Hitches are illustrated.

3040. Use a small bag of BB shot for a counterweight, as this is easily adjustable and will not mar anything if it falls. But a weighted stocking foot or a beanbag will serve as well. The counterweight should be a little heavier than the combined weight of the bobbins.

3041. The cross-sectional shapes of the completed sinnets are closely approximated by the outline of the diagrams, which show the cycles of the various strands. But it is unnecessary to make the sinnets directly over the diagrams. It will be sufficient, and less confusing, to take a paper disk the size of the table top, with a hole in the center of the proper size, and to draw on it a number of evenly spaced radial lines equal to the number of spaces that are called for. Number the spaces between the lines in rotation, counterclockwise, with large heavy figures. After putting the paper disk on the table, preparatory to making a sinnet, drive an inch brad near the outer end of each line. These will serve to keep the strands apart.

The least number of strands with which a sinnet may be made by the helical method, to conform to the first triangular diagram of this chapter, which is at the top of page 501, is eight. There are three different sequences of moves by which the sinnet may be made with eight strands. There are six sequences by which it may be made with nine strands and three by which it may be made with ten strands. One of the Eight-Strand Sinnets is round, two are barely triangular, all six of the Nine-Strand Sinnets are triangular, but irregular. The remaining three Ten-Strand Sinnets are all triangular and symmetrical. By introducing one additional strand, at each corner or edge, the non-triangular Eight-Strand Sinnet becomes triangular. By introducing extra strands where required, the six irregular Nine-Strand Sinnets will become regular.

3042. Five of the sinnets that may be made on six-space diagram ✳3035 are to be given on the next page. Except for the present sinnet, the outward appearances of the five are much alike, all being triangular.

Seize together the ends of eight strands of banding; arrange them on worktable (✳3037) over a paper disk (✳3041) that is divided by radial lines into six equal sectors. Number these sectors, one to six, counterclockwise, and mark in each space the number of strands that are indicated in the second column of table ✳3042 (next page).

SOLID SINNETS

Attach a bobbin (⚹3038–39) to the end of each strand, and counterbalance as ⚹3040.

Move the strands as described in ⚹3036 and in the sequence directed in the two right columns of table ⚹3042 (see below), and continue to repeat these directions in the same order.

Odd numbers are always moved to the right, and even numbers to the left. The *right*-hand strand from space 1 is moved *to the right* and put into the *left*-hand or near position in space 5. The *left*-hand strand in space 4 is moved *to the left* to take the *right*-hand or near position in space 2. Work the strands firmly, but not forcefully, and continue to move strands as directed in the two right-hand columns until sufficient sinnet is made.

3043. By the addition of one extra strand at each edge or corner, ⚹3042 is transformed from a ROUND SINNET into a satisfactory TRIANGULAR SINNET of eleven strands. A corner in a diagram represents an edge of the completed sinnet. The directions for this sinnet are tabulated below. It is worked the same as ⚹3042.

3044. An EIGHT-STRAND SINNET that is triangular. Observe that whenever a side strand is moved to the left in this sinnet it crosses *two* adjacent corner strands, while in ⚹3042 a side strand crosses only *one* adjacent corner strand. This is responsible for the differing bulk, at the edges of the two sinnets. Directions for making this are given in the table below (⚹3044).

3045. The handsomest TRIANGULAR SINNET made on the six-bight diagram has ten strands. Its triangular shape is regular and practically inevitable if the bobbins and counterweight are correct and the edge of the table is well rounded. See table ⚹3045 below.

3046. A fuller-appearing SINNET OF THIRTEEN STRANDS which bulks very little more than the others. With one more strand added to each corner a handsome SIXTEEN-STRAND SINNET is made. See table ⚹3046 below.

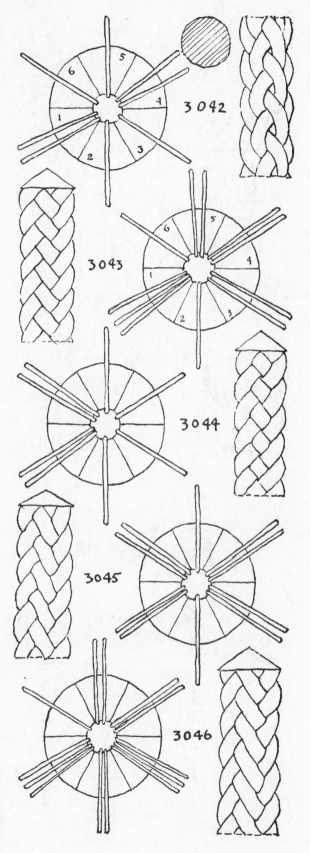

⚹3042 (8-STRAND ROUND)

Space	Strands	Move
1	2	1–5
2	1	4–2
3	1	5–3
4	2	2–6
5	1	3–1
6	1	6–4

⚹3043 (11-STRAND TRIANGLE)

Space	Strands	Move
1	3	
2	1	Directions
3	2	the same
4	2	as ⚹3042
5	2	
6	1	

⚹3044 (8-STRAND TRIANGLE)

Space	Strands	Move
1	2	1–5
2	1	6–4
3	1	5–3
4	1	4–2
5	1	3–1
6	2	2–6

⚹3045 (10-STRAND TRIANGLE)

Space	Strands	Move
1	2	1–5
2	1	4–2
3	2	3–1
4	2	6–4
5	1	5–3
6	2	2–6

⚹3046 (13-STRAND TRIANGLE)

Space	Strands	Move
1	3	1–5
2	2	2–6
3	3	3–1
4	2	4–2
5	2	5–3
6	1	6–4

Any *sinnet with an uneven number of edges* (or sides), in order to be symmetrical, must have all the strands at the edges rotate in the same direction.

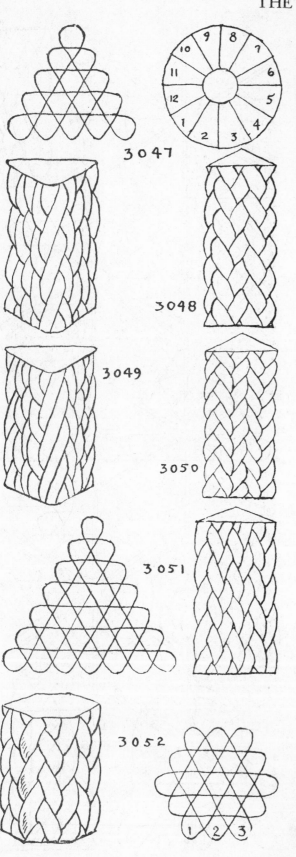

3047

3048

3049

3050

3051

3052

3047. This is the first HELICAL SINNET that was made. It is a triangle of twelve bights.

To tie: Make a paper disk with a hole in the middle, divide the circumference into twelve equal parts and draw radial lines to the center. Number the spaces in numerical order, counterclockwise. Place the disk on the table and drive in brads near the ends of the lines. Having arranged the strands, spindles and counterweight, introduce the strands of banding at the different spaces as shown in the two left columns of the table below and move the strands as directed in the table.

3048. The edges of this sinnet are not prominent.

⚹3047 (19-Strand Triangle)			⚹3048 (17-Strand Triangle)		
Space	Strands	Move	Space	Strands	Move
1	2	1– 9	1	2	1– 9
2	1	8– 2	2	1	8– 2
3	2	3– 7	3	2	3– 7
4	1	6– 4	4	1	6– 4
5	2	5– 1	5	1	9– 5
6	2	12– 6	6	2	4–10
7	1	7–11	7	1	11– 3
8	2	10– 8	8	2	2–12
9	1	9– 5	9	1	5– 1
10	2	4–10	10	1	12– 6
11	1	11– 3	11	2	7–11
12	2	2–12	12	1	10– 8

⚹3049 (22-Strand Triangle)			⚹3050 (29-Strand Triangle)		
Space	Strands	Move	Space	Strands	Move
1	3	1– 9	1	3	
2	1	8– 2	2	2	
3	2	3– 7	3	3	
4	1	6– 4	4	2	Directions
5	3	5– 1	5	2	same as
6	2	12– 6	6	3	⚹3048
7	1	7–11	7	2	
8	2	10– 8	8	3	
9	2	9– 5	9	2	
10	2	4–10	10	2	
11	1	11– 3	11	3	
12	2	2–12	12	2	

⚹3051 (28-Strand Triangle)			⚹3052 (20-Strand Hexagon)		
Space	Strands	Move	Space	Strands	Move
1	2	11–13	1	2	12– 8
2	1	12– 2	2	1	7– 1
3	2	3–11	3	2	1– 7
4	1	10– 4	4	1	6– 2
5	2	5– 9	5	2	2–10
6	1	8– 6	6	2	9– 3
7	2	7– 1	7	2	3– 9
8	2	18– 8	8	1	8– 4
9	1	9–17	9	2	4–12
10	2	16–10	10	1	11– 5
11	1	11–15	11	2	5–11
12	2	14–12	12	2	10– 6
13	1	13– 7			
14	2	6–14			
15	1	15– 5			
16	2	4–16			
17	1	17– 3			
18	2	2–18			

Corners "take up" faster than sides.

3049. The edges of this one are more prominent.

3050. The texture here has been doubled by the introduction of additional strands. Any of the other diagrams may have their texture doubled in a similar manner. Moreover any may have their edges accented by adding an extra strand at each corner as in ⚜3049.

3051, 3052. These are worked as the others.

If a sinnet is not sufficiently compact when first tied, which is very likely to happen, particularly when making the larger ones, they may be easily worked over, along their length, with a pricker, first tightening all the even strands in sequence and then tightening the odd ones. This is not so arduous a task as might appear, although it may take a little while before the knack is acquired.

3053, 3054. In these diagrams, for the first time a strand from an odd-numbered space is led to an even-numbered space, and a strand from an even-numbered space is led to an odd-numbered space.

But having once departed from a space, that space should be forgotten and the new space approached in the manner that is peculiar to it, and which has already been described. The tension of SINNET ⚜3057 should be handled carefully. The texture differs from anything that has heretofore been shown.

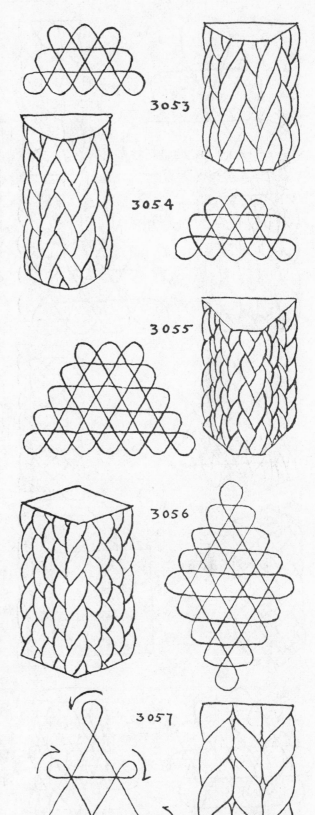

⚜3053 (19-STRAND HALF HEXAGON)

Space	Strands	Move
1	3	6– 4
2	1	3– 7
3	2	7– 2
4	1	1– 8
5	2	8– 5
6	2	4– 9
7	3	9– 3
8	1	2–10
9	3	10– 6
10	1	5– 1

⚜3054 (17-STRAND HALF ROUND)

Space	Strands	Move
1	3	
2	1	
3	2	
4	1	
5	2	Move
6	2	as ⚜3053
7	2	
8	1	
9	2	
10	1	

⚜3055 (26-STRAND FANBELT SHAPE)

Space	Strands	Move
1	2	12– 7
2	2	6–13
3	1	13– 5
4	2	4–14
5	1	15– 3
6	2	2–16
7	1	1–12
8	2	11– 2
9	1	3–11
10	2	10– 4
11	2	5– 9
12	2	8– 6
13	2	7– 1
14	1	16– 8
15	2	9–15
16	1	14–10

⚜3056 (26-STRAND DIAMOND)

Space	Strands	Move
1	2	1–12
2	1	11– 2
3	2	3–10
4	1	9– 4
5	2	6– 1
6	2	16– 7
7	1	8–15
8	2	14– 9
9	2	2–16
10	1	15– 3
11	2	4–14
12	1	13– 5
13	2	5–13
14	2	12– 6
15	1	7–11
16	2	10– 8

⚜3057 (9-STRAND TRIANGLE)

Space	Strands	Move
1	2	1–5
2	2	2–4
3	2	3–1
4	1	4–6
5	1	5–3
6	1	6–2

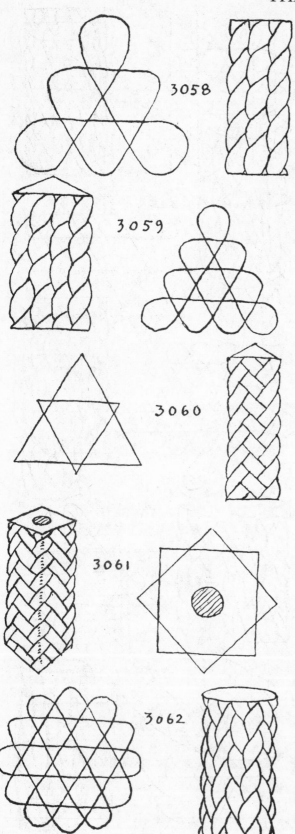

3058. The same diagram is employed here as for the sinnets of pages 501–03, but all the strands here rotate in one direction only.

3059. With the strands all rotating in one direction it is possible in a sinnet with an uneven number of edges (and sides) to have an even number of spaces on each side (or face). Heretofore, with an odd number of faces, an odd number of spaces to the side was required.

3060. The present diagram is the exact cycle of SINNET ⌗3028 of the last chapter, and the same number of strands is employed, but they are differently disposed. In SINNET ⌗3028 six strands rotate to the right and three to the left. In the sinnet given here five rotate to the right and four to the left. But the present sinnet is made by the helical method while ⌗3028 does not helix, although three strands from each set are moved simultaneously without being knotted. The completed sinnets can hardly be told apart.

3061. A SQUARE SINNET of twelve strands made on a diagram of eight spaces. This is tubular and a small core is indicated. But if one strand is added to each even space a ROUND SINNET will result.

3062. The ROUND SINNET given here is made on the same diagram as HEXAGONAL SINNET ⌗3052, but with the addition of extra strands to the sides the form becomes round. Being solid, the final round shape is practically inevitable, which is true of most of the sinnets of this chapter. This is, of course, dependent upon a proper tension for each strand.

⌗3058 (9-STRAND TRIANGLE)
(All strands move to the right.)

Space	Strands	Move
1	2	1–5
2	2	2–4
3	2	3–1
4	1	4–6
5	1	5–3
6	1	6–2

⌗3059 (13-STRAND TRIANGLE)
(All strands move to the right.)

Space	Strands	Move
1	2	1–7
2	2	2–6
3	2	3–5
4	2	4–1
5	1	5–9
6	1	6–8
7	1	7–4
8	1	8–3
9	1	9–2

⌗3060 (9-STRAND TRIANGLE)
(Strands move right and left.)

Space	Strands	Move
1	2	1–3
2	1	6–4
3	1	5–1
4	1	4–2
5	2	3–5
6	2	2–6

⌗3061 (12-STRAND SQUARE [CORE])

Space	Strands	Move
1	2	2–8
2	2	1–3
3	1	8–6
4	1	7–1
5	2	6–4
6	1	5–7
7	2	4–2
8	1	3–5

⌗3062 (26-STRAND ROUND)

Space	Strands	Move
1	2	12– 8
2	2	7– 1
3	2	1– 7
4	2	6– 2
5	2	2–10
6	3	9– 3
7	2	3– 9
8	2	8– 4
9	2	4–12
10	2	11– 5
11	2	5–11
12	3	10– 6

3063. A large, compact ROUND SINNET of forty-five strands with a doubled texture resembling a ribbed stocking.

3064. A ROUND SINNET with a distinctive texture, that is quite handsome but is not so simple to draw up as some of the others.

3065. A ROUND SINNET with three different cycles each in the shape of an S turn.

3066. The strands in the next four sinnets rotate in one direction only—to the right. They are related to the CROWN SINNETS, but helix so that they require no knotting. This one has two extra strands introduced at 1 and 5. But it may be attempted with one extra strand, at 1, or it may be made with four extra strands introduced at 1, 3, 5, and 7.

3067. A ROUND SINNET made on the table but without the employment of pins or numbers.

Take seven or eight strands (with six strands the result is merely a plain-laid rope), lead any strand to the right over the next four strands. Take the third strand to the left of the one that was just deposited, and cross the next four to the right. Draw up firmly after each strand is passed and continue to repeat the *last direction* that was given until sufficient sinnet is made.

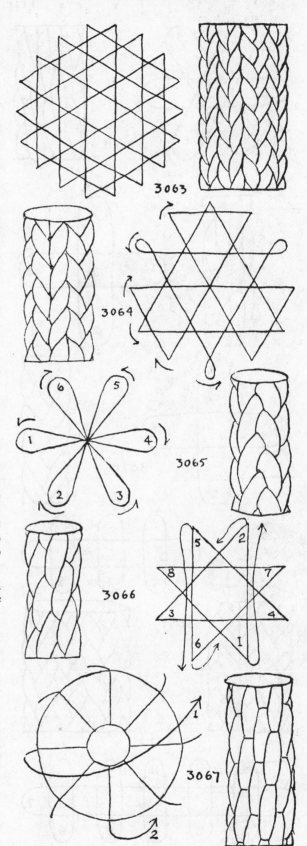

3063

3064

3065

3066

3067

#3063 (45-Strand Round)

Space	Strands	Move
1	3	16–12
2	2	11–17
3	3	18–10
4	3	1– 9
5	2	8– 2
6	3	3– 7
7	2	4–18
8	3	17– 5
9	2	6–16
10	2	7–15
11	3	14– 8
12	2	9–13
13	2	10– 6
14	3	5–11
15	2	12– 4
16	3	13– 3
17	2	2–14
18	3	15– 1

#3065 (9-Strand Round)

Space	Strands	Move
1	2	5–2
2	1	1–4
3	2	3–6
4	1	2–5
5	2	4–1
6	1	6–3

#3064 (19-Strand Round)

Space	Strands	Move
1	1	7–11
2	1	6–12
3	1	5– 1
4	2	4– 2
5	2	11– 3
6	2	10– 4
7	2	9– 5
8	2	8– 6
9	2	3– 7
10	2	2– 8
11	2	1– 9
12	2	12–10

#3066 (10-Strand Round)

Space	Strands	Move
1	2	1–2
2	1	5–6
3	1	2–3
4	1	6–7
5	2	3–4
6	1	7–8
7	1	4–5
8	1	8–1

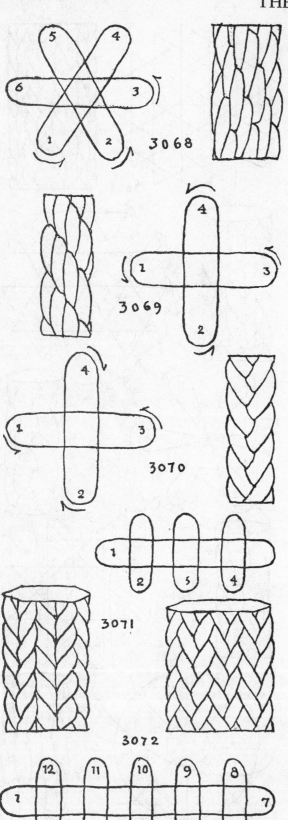

3068. All strands are moved to the right in accordance with the tabulated directions.

3069. All strands are moved to the right on a four-space diagram. The result resembles a cable-laid rope.

3070. This is ordinary SQUARE SINNET ✳3001 made on the table. This seems to be a quicker method than the ordinary way and with practice might prove even faster than the Captain Charles W. Smith method (✳3018). After a little experience the operator will be able to move opposite strands simultaneously; two strands (1–3, 3–1) are moved together, then 2–4, 4–2. Even-numbered strands, as usual, go to the left and odd strands to right.

3071, 3072. FLAT CHISEL-EDGED SINNETS. These are quite handsome and may be made wider if desired. Many of the sinnets that are shown here lend themselves to amplification.

✳3068 (12-STRAND ROUND)
(All strands move to *right*.)

Space	Strands	Move
1	2	1–4
2	2	4–1
3	2	2–5
4	2	5–2
5	2	3–6
6	2	6–3

✳3069 (6-STRAND ROUND)
(All strands move to *right*.)

Space	Strands	Move
1	2	1–3
2	2	2–4
3	1	3–1
4	1	4–2

✳3070 (8-STRAND SQUARE)
(Odd strands move right, even strands left.)

Space	Strands	Move
1	2	1–3
2	2	3–1
3	2	2–4
4	2	4–2

✳3071 (14-STRAND CHISEL-EDGE)
(Odd strands move to right, even to the left.)

Space	Strands	Move
1	2	5–1
2	1	8–2
3	2	3–7
4	1	6–4
5	3	1–5
6	2	4–6
7	1	7–3
8	2	2–8

✳3072 (20-STRAND CHISEL-EDGE)
(Odd strands move to the right, even strands move to the left.)

Space	Strands	Move
1	2	7– 1
2	1	12– 2
3	2	3–11
4	1	10– 4
5	2	5– 9
6	1	8– 6
7	3	1– 7
8	2	6– 8
9	1	9– 5
10	2	4–10
11	1	11– 3
12	2	2–12

The sinnets on the next page, being four-sided, are not limited to edges rotating in the same direction, or to sides with an odd number of parts. Odd numbers move to the right and even numbers to the left as usual.

SOLID SINNETS

Always place an arriving strand, if *odd*, at the left of its group, and if *even*, at the right of its group, and always move a departing strand, if odd, from the right of a group and, if even, from the left of a group.

✳3073 (20-Strand Square)

Space	Strands	Move	
1	2	2–12	
2	2	11– 3	
3	1	4–10	Left
4	2	10– 4	"
5	2	5– 9	
6	1	8– 6	
7	2	3– 5	
8	2	6– 2	
9	1	1– 7	
10	2	7– 1	
11	2	12– 8	
12	1	9–11	

✳3076 (20-Strand Oblong)

Space	Strands	Move
1	2	4– 2
2	1	1– 5
3	2	6– 1
4	2	12– 7
5	1	7–11
6	2	10– 8
7	2	2–12
8	1	11– 3
9	2	3–10
10	2	9– 4
11	1	5– 9
12	2	8– 6

✳3074 (26-Strand Square)

Space	Strands	Move
1	2	2–16
2	2	15– 3
3	1	4–14
4	2	13– 5
5	2	5–13
6	1	12– 6
7	2	7–11
8	1	10– 8
9	2	6– 4
10	2	3– 7
11	1	8– 2
12	2	1– 9
13	2	9– 1
14	1	16–10
15	2	11–15
16	1	14–12

✳3077 (32-Strand Oblong)

Space	Strands	Move
1	2	2–20
2	2	19– 3
3	1	4–19
4	2	18– 5
5	1	6–17
6	2	16– 7
7	1	8–15
8	2	14– 9
9	2	9–13
10	1	12–10
11	2	10– 8
12	2	7–11
13	1	11– 6
14	2	5–12
15	1	13– 4
16	2	3–14
17	1	15– 2
18	2	1–16
19	2	17– 1
20	1	20–18

✳3075 (20-Strand Oblong)

Space	Strands	Move
1	2	2–12
2	2	12– 3
3	1	4–11
4	2	10– 5
5	1	6– 9
6	2	8– 6
7	2	5– 7
8	2	7– 4
9	1	3– 8
10	2	9– 2
11	1	1–10
12	2	11– 1

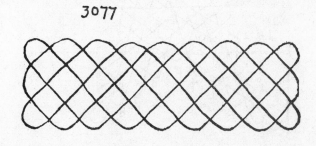

3073

3074

3075

3077

3076

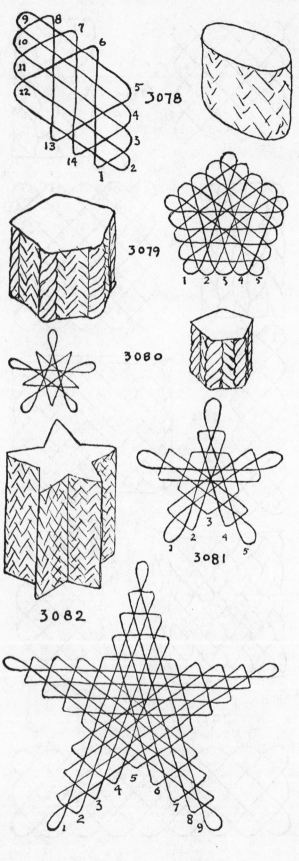

3078

3079

3080

3081

3082

3078. An ELLIPSE of twenty strands. Although this design appears to be a bit irregular, it works out into a very handsome ELLIPSE with an even surface. The tension of the strands must be carefully handled, and the sinnet will require fairing with a pricker after removal from the table.

3079. A PENTAGON of thirty-six strands. Although the lines in this diagram lead in five directions it is no more complicated to work than the others. The specimen was made with red corners, green center strands and the remainder white, the result being a series of lengthwise stripes.

3080. A smaller PENTAGON.

3081, 3082. Two PENTALPHAS. The latter was the first made, the shape is inevitable if worked methodically.

✳3078 (20-Strand Ellipse)

Space	Strands	Move
1	2	1– 3
2	1	4–14
3	1	13– 5
4	2	12– 6
5	1	7–11
6	1	10– 8
7	2	8–13
8	1	14– 7
9	1	6– 1
10	2	5– 9
11	1	9– 4
12	2	3–10
13	2	11– 2
14	1	2–12

✳3079 (36-Strand Pentagon)

Space	Strands	Move
1	3	1–13
2	1	12– 2
3	2	3–11
4	1	10– 4
5	3	5–17
6	1	16– 6
7	2	7–15
8	1	14– 8
9	3	9– 1
10	2	20–10
11	1	11–19
12	2	18–12
13	2	13– 5
14	2	4–14
15	1	15– 3
16	2	2–16
17	2	17– 9
18	2	8–18
19	1	19– 7
20	2	6–20

✳3080 (16-Strand Pentagon)

Space	Strands	Move
1	2	1– 7
2	1	6– 2
3	2	3– 9
4	1	8– 4
5	2	5– 1
6	2	10– 6
7	1	7– 3
8	2	2– 8
9	1	9– 5
10	2	4–10

✳3081 (31-Strand Pentalpha)

Space	Strands	Move
1	3	18–16
2	3	15–19
3	1	1–13
4	1	12– 2
5	3	2–20
6		19– 3
7	1	5–17
8	1	16– 6
9	3	6– 4
10	1	3– 7
11	1	9– 1
12	2	20–10
13	1	10– 8
14	1	7–11
15	2	13– 5
16	1	4–14
17	2	14–12
18	1	11–15
19	1	17– 9
20	1	8–18

✳3082 (61-Strand Pentalpha)

Space	Strands	Move
1	3	34–32
2	1	31–35
3	2	36–30
4	1	29–37
5	1	1–25
6	1	24– 2
7	2	3–23
8	1	22– 4
9	3	2–40
10	1	39– 3
11	2	4–38
12	1	37– 5
13	1	9–33
14	1	32–10
15	2	11–31
16	1	30–12
17	3	10– 8
18	1	7–11
19	2	12– 6
20	1	5–13
21	1	17– 1
22	2	40–18
23	1	19–39
24	2	38–20
25	2	18–16
26	1	15–19
27	2	20–14
28	1	13–21
29	2	25– 9
30	1	8–26
31	2	27– 7
32	1	6–28
33	2	26–24
34	2	23–27
35	1	28–22
36	2	21–29
37	1	33–17
38	1	16–34
39	2	35–15
40	1	14–36

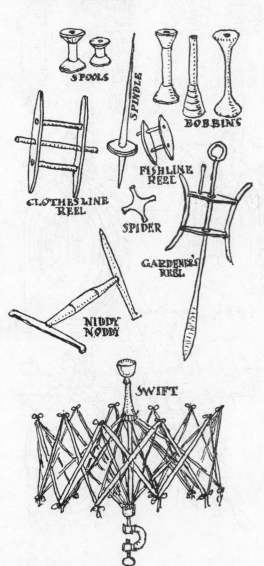

CHAPTER 40: PRACTICAL MARLINGSPIKE SEAMANSHIP

Worm and parcel with the lay,
Turn about and serve away.

SAILORS' WORK RHYME

The subject of marlingspike seamanship is to be divided into two chapters. The first of these is concerned primarily with what is elementary and practical, while the one to follow is devoted mostly to knots in combination. More often than not these combinations are deliberately decorative, although they are scarcely less practical than the contents of the present chapter.

Much of the matter of both chapters consists of details of the rigger's craft. There has never been a handicraft in which innovations have been more critically examined or more grudgingly accepted. But this, perhaps, is well, since many lives must have been spared as a consequence.

This conservatism is evidenced by the fact that many of the smaller riggers' practices of today are exactly what they were in the days of Lever and Du Clairbois. There was quite as much difference to be found in the detail work of two contemporary rigging lofts at any one time in this period as there was between the characteristic work of any two dates that are a century apart.

The bark *Sunbeam*, on which I sailed in 1904, was probably the last merchant square-rigger to put to sea with hemp standing rigging. The whalers that remained at that time reflected the practices of a day fifty or seventy-five years earlier. So I can fairly claim, with a few reservations, a first-hand acquaintance with the rigging prac-

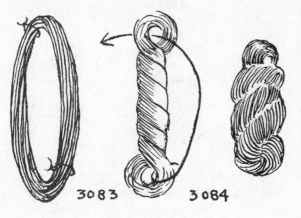

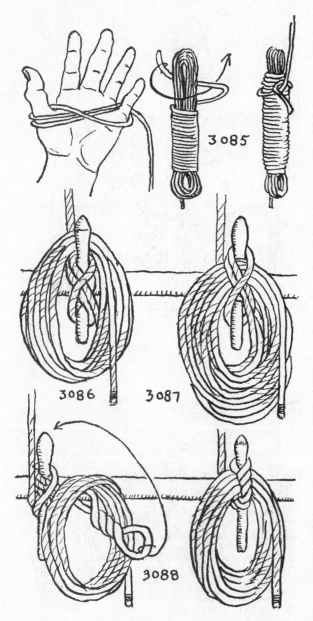

tices of a full century. Wire rigging began to appear with the advent of the clipper ships and rigging at that time became loftier and lighter. But the day of the clipper was a short one. It has been only within the last twenty-five or thirty years, when the relative importance of commercial and pleasure sailing craft has been shifting, that the clamor for lighter gear aloft has again been heard.

Ropes and line for convenience in handling, or else for purposes of storage, are coiled or wound on reels of various sorts, which vary all the way from a flat stick to elaborate ball-bearing anglers' reels. Gardeners have their edging and hose reels and laundresses their clothesline reels. There are table swifts for yarn, and spools for thread. Spindles, bobbins, cops and shuttles are employed in spinning and weaving. There are tatting needles and netting needles. Reels may vary in size all the way from a ten-foot seine wheel, on a river bank, to the quarter-inch bobbin of a sewing machine.

Right-hand or plain-laid rope properly is coiled clockwise but it is sometimes simpler to coil new rope left-handed. The right way to coil a cable, of course, is counterclockwise, its lay being opposite to plain- or right-laid rope.

Many of the illustrations in the next two chapters have been drawn from objects from my own collection and from the collection of the Mariners' Museum in Newport News. Others are from sketches that I have made on ships that I have visited, since the days when I first began to draw.

Ship models as a source of contemporary information are usually untrustworthy. Models are delicate things that require frequent repair, and they offer too much temptation for the amateur rigger, who sometimes has more zeal than knowledge. Most ship models at one time or another have fallen into the hands of at least one of these.

3083. Coils in fishline and twine are called hanks. The two ends are stopped at opposite sides of the coil. Broken coils of rope in chandleries are stopped in the same way, but in several places.

3084. After woolen yarn is wound into a long skein it is twisted hard with the hands, the two ends are brought together and one end is tucked a short way through the other. When the ends are released the material lays itself up as pictured. A hank may be several skeins tied up together, or it may be a series of connected and uniform short lengths of a single line, wound as in ⚓3085. When so made, the purchaser may buy the length required without the necessity of rewinding or measuring.

3085. When making punch mats or long sinnets a sailor makes up his foxes or nettles into small hanks that are first wound in S turns around the thumb and finger of one hand and then have frapping turns added. These are more easily disposed of, while working, than long loose ends. The third drawing shows a way of holding a hank, while working, with an easily adjustable hitch.

3086. The ordinary method of disposing of a coil at sea. A right-hand coil is hung directly over a pin and jammed down firmly. The end is left a little longer than the coil. The turns of a coil should be started next the pin and concluded at the end of the rope. If the end is coiled first the rope will kink.

When working ship, coils are dropped to deck face down, in front of their pins, from which position they will generally run clear.

In making fast, if a coil is very large, it may be divided and hung over two neighboring pins.

3087. After turns have been put on a pin, the upper part of the coil may be flattened against the pin rail, the standing part of the rope pulled forward through the coil and several turns and (possibly) a hitch added. The end of the line is not disturbed.

3088. This is the preferred way of securing coils that bulk too large for hanging directly on the pins or cleats. A bight is pulled forward through the coil from the standing part and is twisted to the left until it will just slip over the handle of the pin.

3089. To coil *sea gaskets* or *furling lines*. Furling lines were used in the Merchant Marine after about 1850 and in the Navy probably not earlier than 1875. Previous to these dates sea gaskets had been made of FLAT SINNETS and *harbor gaskets* of FRENCH SINNET. When in use they were seized or bent to the yard or jackstay with a RUNNING EYE. They were used, when furling, to lash the sail to the yard. When not in use they were coiled as pictured and brought over the top of the yard to hang down in front of the sail.

After a coil had been made, four or five frapping turns were taken near the head of the coil with the *standing* part of the line and then a bight of the standing part was thrust through the head of the coil above the turns and looped back over the head of the coil, where it was jammed down close to the frapping turns and was worked snug.

3090. Ropes are often coiled and hung up in lofts for storage. They are also hung over stakes in farm wagons and on hooks in moving vans, fire apparatus and linesmen's repair trucks. For such active storage coils must be well made.

The coil given here is a particularly neat one. The working end is brought to the head of the coil where, after a short round turn has been made on the face of the coil, it is passed to the left, around the back, and then at the front, is tucked back through all the turns at the head of the coil. If the coil is to be stowed down, a single end is passed, but if it is to be hung up, the end is doubled. In either case this is one of the easiest coils of the sort to remember and for that reason it is essentially practical. Instead of a single crossing turn, two or three may be taken.

3091. A coil that is based on the ANGLER'S LOOP. Take a round turn in the working end at the head of the coil. Make a bight in the standing end at the back, and shove this bight up through the head of the coil, and around all parts, then back through the head of the coil and *under* the doubled part that was first rove through the head of the coil. The coils illustrated as #3089–95 are for active storage, while #3096, #3097 and #3098 are for dead storage.

3092. Make a coil as pictured in the left sketch. Arrange the end and hold at the head with the left hand, then add one or two frapping turns and stick the loop down as indicated by the arrow.

Lashing ropes on trucks and vans are very apt to have EYE SPLICES in one or both ends, in which case they are hung up by these and it is not necessary to double the ends when coiling.

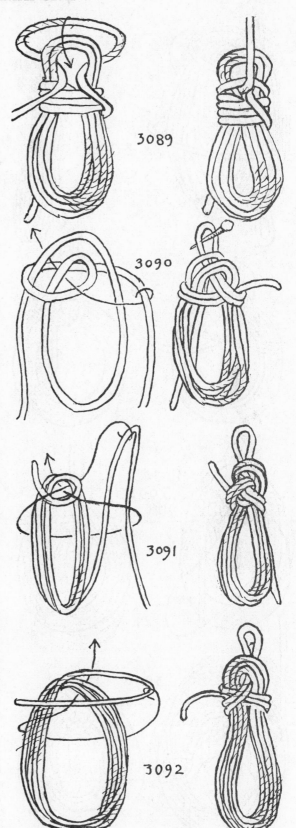

3089

3090

3091

3092

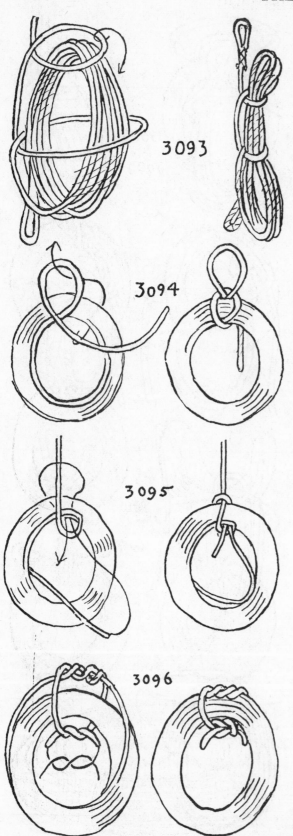

3093. This coil resembles the SHEEPSHANK KNOT (#1153), and is a purely temporary expedient, generally to be seen in lofts, fishing shacks, outbuildings and junk yards. A loose end is gathered up into several turns and the standing part is half hitched twice at whatever height the coil is to hang. If there are only one or two turns, one hitch is quite sufficient, in which case a BELL RINGER'S KNOT (#1147) has been tied.

3094. The fireman's coil was shown to me by George Paselle. It is very neat, and is quickly cleared when needed. A hitch is made near the end and laid against the top of the coil. A bight in the end is passed from front to back through the head of the coil and up through the hitch. The hitch must be drawn up snugly.

3095. A coil may be made in the manner of the PORTUGUESE BOWLINE. A round turn is put in the standing part of the line. Then the lower end of the rope is drawn up through the *coil* and knotted as shown in the diagrams. Draw all taut and hang over a peg or nail with a COW HITCH, which is less liable to jam than a CLOVE HITCH. In this coil neither end can work loose.

3096. A short-line coil for storage. Bring both ends together at the head of the coil and form a DOUBLE HALF KNOT. Bring both ends together around the coil, one under and one above, and reef knot the two together.

3097. A fisherman's coil, for stowing down short lengths, is usually secured with a CLOVE HITCH. It is tied by making first a round turn and then a HALF HITCH, both to the left. This is the coil often seen in fishermen's shacks. It must be drawn up snugly and carefully and adjusted as illustrated in the second diagram. The method is inferior to the one which follows and it is possible that it is mistakenly tied instead of ⚹3098.

3098. The sailor's coil, as customarily used at sea for stowing down, is more secure. The construction of the knot is similar to the GROUND LINE HITCH, shown as ⚹278, but is reversed. A SINGLE HITCH is first taken with the end to the right tightly around a section of the coil, then a second hitch is taken to the left. This is a very satisfactory knot and, when used for coils of average size, will stand considerable handling. If desired, the end may be left long for the purpose of hanging up. It is often mistakenly called a CLOVE HITCH, although the two knots have little in common.

3099. This is an excellent coil that is rarely seen, the previous coil being easier to remember and, on the whole, better. But there is never a knot without a friend, and many people swear by it. It is tied by first making a round turn to the right, then a turn to the left and finally the end is tucked as shown.

3100. The STRANGLE KNOT (⚹1239) will hold a coil well and is easily remembered. But, if drawn up too tightly, it will jam; for that reason it had better be slipped. Tied in this way, it is both neat and practical.

3101. Large coils are generally stowed down with three or four rope-yarn stops. This is also the way rope is commonly delivered to customers in chandleries, two stops being sufficient for small stuff, and four or five for large stuff.

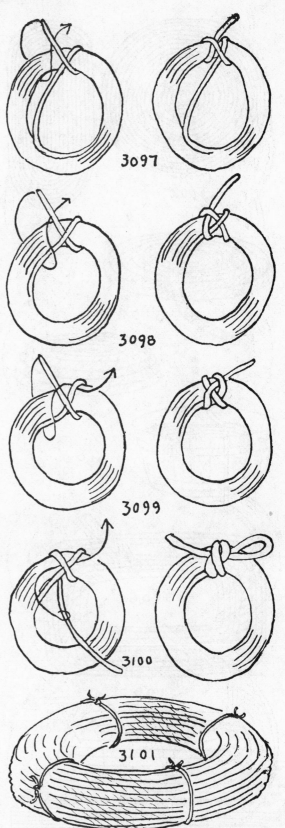

3097

3098

3099

3100

3101

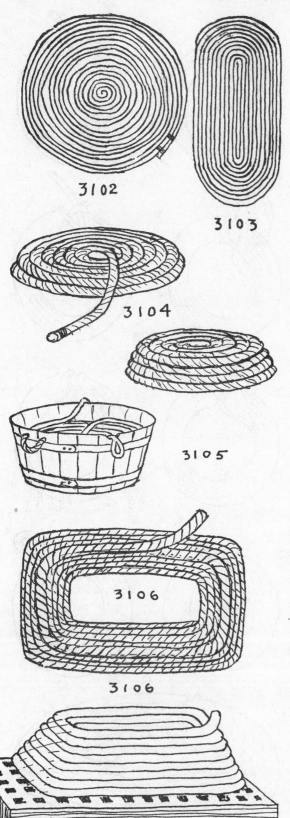

3102

3103

3104

3105

3106

3106

3106

3102. Admiral: What mean you by flakes?
Captain: They are only those several circles or rounds of the roapes or cables, that are quoiled up round.

Boteler's Dialogues, circa 1634

A flake is the sailor's term for a turn in an ordinary coil, or for a complete tier in a flat coil, as a French or *Flemish flake*. The current dictionary form of the word is *fake*, a word that I have never heard used with this meaning.

A Flemish flake is a spiral coil of one layer only. It is made on deck, in this manner, so that it may be walked on if necessary. Sometimes the outer turn is stopped to the end with sail twine, which keeps the flake from being accidentally uncoiled. Commonly it is circular. Often in yachts and training ships Flemish flakes are sewed together on the back and placed about deck for ornament. (See #3491.)

3103. Sometimes a Flemish flake is made in elliptical form, when this shape better suits the space that is to be filled.

3104. A French coil is made of several (usually three or four) Flemish flakes, one on top of the other. The first one is laid from the center outward, the next from the outside, inward. Each flake is made one turn smaller than the preceding one.

3105. The whaleman's coil is somewhat similar to the last but is made inside a line tub, which it completely fills, and each spiral flake is begun at the outer edge. The initial end, which bears an EYE SPLICE, is left hanging out through a notch in the rim of the tub. When the center of each flake is reached, the line is led to the outer edge and a second and succeeding flakes are added until the tub is full. Each time the line is led from the center to the side, it is advanced clockwise several inches beyond the previous radius. If we consider the top plane of the coil as a clock face, the lines radiate clockwise at five- or six-minute intervals.

3106. An anchor cable is coiled on a grating close to the hatch, between decks. The grating allows for the circulation of air, which assists in drying and prevents mildew. Being left-laid, a cable is coiled left-handed—that is, counterclockwise or "against the sun," usually in a somewhat angular ellipse which is made as large as the space will admit. The first flake is from the outside inward, and the second from the inside outward, each flake being one turn smaller than the previous one. The center of the coil is left well open and is reserved for stowing smaller hawsers, rope and warps. The space is called the "cable tier."

3107. A *rocket coil* is arranged for shooting a light line to a wreck, by means of which a life line is hauled to ship. It is also used at sea for passing a line to a disabled vessel from another.

The cover of the "flaking box" has a series of pins over which the line (a braided one) is coiled in the manner pictured, alternate flakes being coiled from front to back and from side to side. The box is then placed over the coiled lines and pins and is *turned over*. When the coil is put to use the cover with the pins is *lifted*, which leaves the line loosely coiled in the box. The box is placed with a corner facing the line of trajectory, so that the flakes are diagonal. The back corner of the box is lifted to allow the rope to run out easily when the rocket is fired.

3108. A *British method of coiling* a line for the rocket gun is described by Todd and Whall and pictured in the Admiralty *Manual of Seamanship* for 1932. The turns are taken diagonally instead of square, alternate flakes having opposite diagonals. The rocket end of the line leads from the side of the box, which is placed all square, and with the back side lifted.

3109. *Racked turns.* If a new sheet is inclined to kink, coil it flat on deck in this manner with figure-eight or belaying-pin turns, which will neither add to nor detract from the amount of twist. Make the turns as large as space will admit. After a few days the sheet will adjust itself. Coil garden hose in this manner around two large stones which will hold the turns in place while coiling. Coiled in this way, hose may be hung up on two pegs or beckets against the side of a building and may be hauled directly from the coil without danger of kinking.

3110. *Figure-eight flakes.* A series of overlapping figure-eight turns, advancing, in the direction illustrated, about one or two diameters of the rope at each turn, is an excellent way to range a new stiff cable. It is also a very satisfactory way of coiling down large hose.

3111. A *long flake* in a chain buoy cable is ranged thwartship the full width of the deck opposite the companionway and, when the anchor is dropped, whips out, end for end, with a fearful commotion, raising a cloud of dust. After it has once started to run, no human agency can stop it. It does not require so wide a companionway as the French flake which follows.

3112. The *French flake* is made exactly as the *long flake*, but it leads from the side instead of the end when planting buoys. It is also used in hawsers and warps for towing, when it is ranged thwartship and the lead is aft.

3113. To "*Flemish down*" is a little different. Although it is very closely related to the French flake, it bears no resemblance to the Flemish coil. It is employed with a stiff line, not necessarily a large one, although usually so. The ends of each succeeding flake are pushed slightly under the preceding one, which holds it in place. One man coils down, while another arranges the turns.

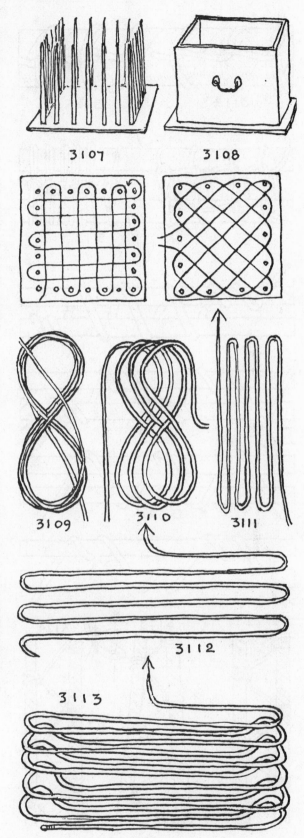

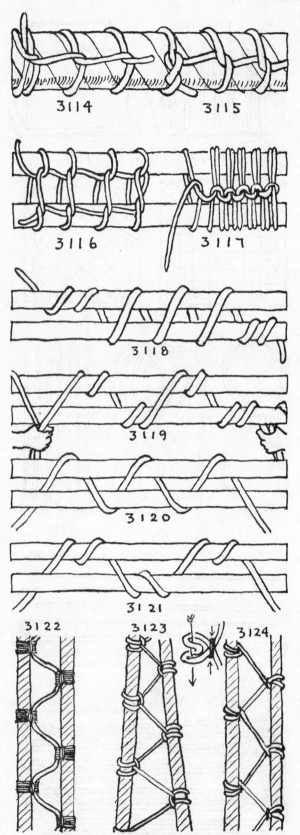

3114. Half hitching. Unless put around a rope, this is really single hitching but it is commonly called *half hitching*. It is a method of lashing in which a series of SINGLE HITCHES is employed to secure one or several objects, and it is universally used in tying up parcels, bundles and bales.

3115. MARLINE HITCHING is used to secure parceling on standing rigging. It is preferred to half hitching, as service lies over it more smoothly. It is also used in lacing the foot and heads of fore-and-aft sails to booms and gaffs and in lashing hammocks. It is firmer than half hitching. The difference in construction between the two may be illustrated by tying a series on a cylinder and then slipping them off the end. Half hitching spills instantly and completely, whereas MARLINE HITCHING resolves itself into a series of OVERHAND KNOTS.

3116. The DOUBLE MARLINE HITCH is given in several of the works of seamanship of about 1860 as the proper method of seizing the parts of a fish davit tackle.

3117. *Kackling* or *keckling* consists of alternate right and left hitches around two parts of a cable. It is a secure method of seizing.

3118. *Nippering.* A hemp cable is hove in by attaching it to a continuous rope belt termed a *messenger* which passes around two capstans, one forward and one aft. The cable is held to the messenger with a series of short selvagees or sinnets termed *nippers*. A "nipper man," forward, passes these around the cable and the messenger, as pictured, and a number of "nipper boys," also termed "nippers," hold them in place, while the cable is hove from the forward capstan to the after one. Each boy holds the after end of one nipper and the forward end of a second one. When near the after capstan, the nippers are removed and brought back to the nipper man by the nipper boys. The nippers are never made fast to the cable.

3119. Gower, in 1808, recommends this method of passing a nipper as one that "will not jamb."

3120. Racking turns. These were used in nippering, as well as in seizing the parts of a tackle.

3121. Alternating racking and round turns. When the pull was very heavy, this was the proper way to pass nippers. If this slipped when the anchor refused to break out, sand or ashes were thrown on to make the nippers bite.

3122. *Snaking down the rigging.* This was applied to backstays before going into action, and was sometimes placed permanently between the two parts of double topmast stays. For the latter purpose a rope about half the diameter of the stay was staggered down the stay and carefully seized at regular intervals.

3123. CLOVE HITCHING was resorted to when there was insufficient time for seizing. Snaking was an emergency expedient and seizing was a slow process. In this case the rope was in short lengths for easier handling, with an eye in one end to which the next length was bent with a BECKET HITCH.

3124. Some of the older seamanship works picture *snaking* passed with a round turn. In this case it would have to be stopped, otherwise it would not hold if the rope parted. This latter method was probably the quickest of all.

3125. There are, nowadays, many more or less mechanical arrangements for bending sail, consisting of various metal slides and snaps, but here we are particularly concerned with rope practice. At the end of Chapter 16, "Binding Knots," are given a number of ROBAND HITCHES, which were formerly used in bending square sails. The following practices are for gaffs and booms.

The most usual way of bending a sail to a gaff is with marline seizings, consisting of several turns around the spar and boltrope with crossing turns added. In large craft, small stuff is used in much the same way. The number of turns may be few or many, depending entirely on the relative sizes of the sail and the line. Square sails have been bent in this way with two turns only, before jackstays came into use.

3126. Bending with a single short piece of rope, passed through an eyelet in the foot of a sail, and reef knotted below the boom, is the oldest known method of bending a sail. Later the two parts were seized together between the spar and boltrope.

3127. A Gloucesterman's boom was usually bent in the fashion shown here, with a lace line wrapped around and around, passing through an eyelet hole at each circuit. Gaffs were also frequently bent to in this same way.

3128. Both gaff and boom are often marled to the sail, and wire boltrope is marled in a similar way to a square sail with small stuff.

3129. *Lace line* and screw eyes. This has been common practice both in "pleasure boats" and small commercial craft for many years. The screw eyes are in the boom and the sail is laced through eyelet holes in the tabling or else to thimbles seized to the footrope.

3130. This is called a FOOT STOPPER or a BOOM STOPPER KNOT. With this contrivance, when on the wind, the foot of a sail is bent to the boom. When off the wind, the REEF KNOTS are cast adrift and the sail is loose-footed. So far as I know, its use is limited to small British craft.

To tie the knot: A short strap, that is whipped at each end, is middled through an eyelet hole in the foot of the sail. Each end is thrust through the lay of the other end, close up to the hole. The ends are then reef knotted around the boom. This knot is also shown in Chapter 16.

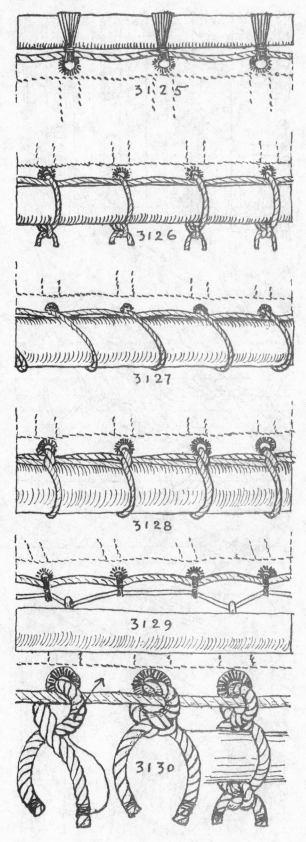

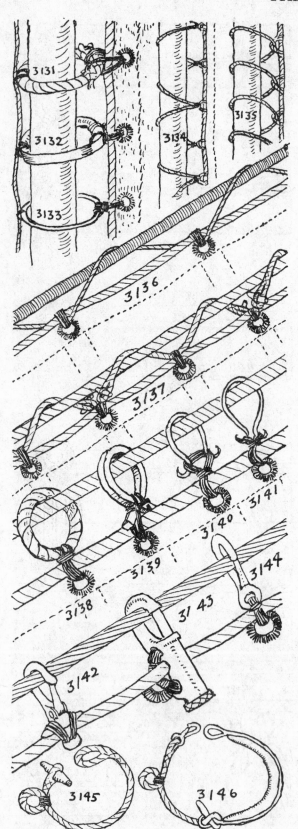

3131. The earliest *mast hoop* was a short spliced rope grommet, and these are still in use among the fishermen of the West Indies and elsewhere. The grommet is seized to the sail at the *center of the splice*. Nowadays a light line is sometimes seized to the front of each hoop, and at the top this is secured to the jaws of the gaff. The line lifts the front of the hoops and lessens the danger of jamming. There are two sets of crossing turns to the seizing, one at either side of the boltrope. These are shown as #3132.

3132. Wooden *mast hoops* are still the common practice. Hoops are also found on the head of a spanker, when the sail is run out on the gaff and brailed to the mast when furled.

3133. A galvanized *iron hoop* seized with crossing turns around all parts is common on fishing and other small commercial craft.

3134. This method of *lacing a sail* to the mast is pictured by Darcy Lever in 1808.

3135. In out-of-the-way places, both in Europe and America, sails are still laced to the mast of small craft. The best practice is to reeve the lace line through cringles on the boltrope, but frequently they lace through eyelet holes in the tabling. In either case the lace line is seized in.

3136. A lace line on a ship's staysail is seized as shown here.

3137. Luce and Ward's *Seamanship* (1884) shows a similar practice. But in this case *bridles* of short length are fitted at one end with a toggle and at the other end with an eye. Lace lines on staysails should always be rove opposite to the lay of the stay, as they are less apt to twist when the downhaul is pulled.

3138. Rope grommets were seized on staysail hoists before *wooden hanks* appeared, which was about the middle of the eighteenth century. These were rove on the stay while it was being rigged and were seized in when the sails were bent as #3133.

3139. The wooden hank was a great improvement over the grommet, as it would run freely without jamming. It was made of hickory or ash in America, of oak in England. Each end was notched and it was seized as pictured. If one broke, a new one could be sprung around the stay.

Wooden hanks are still used, but not often; galvanized iron ones have taken their place.

3140. The earlier form of *iron hank* had the ends well spaced so that a new one could be easily fitted. Seizing turns were taken on the horns of the hook itself.

3141. It was found that iron hanks did not have to be replaced often and, when they were, they could easily be sprung around the stay. The shape was modified so that the seizing was simpler.

3142, 3143, 3144. On small-boat staysails, particularly on racing craft, *snap hooks* of various patterns are used. Number 3142 is the common everyday model, #3143 is found on racing sails and #3144 is the earlier form with a spring steel tongue.

3145. Storm trysails are sometimes fitted with beckets which toggle to the mast. The beckets reeve through eyelet holes in the luff and a round turn is seized in. These contrivances are quickly buttoned into place without disturbing other gear on the mast.

3146. Fishermen have an iron-bound, *half mast hoop* which serves a similar purpose. A bridle or span is seized into each eyelet hole of the sail. When setting the sail, the bridles are either snapped to the hoops or else they are secured with BECKET HITCHES.

3147. Most blocks nowadays are iron-bound, but *rope-strapped blocks* are lighter and do less chafing against sails, spars, and rigging.

The *selvagee, salvagee* or *warped strap* is a skein or coil of marline or rope yarn that is laid up as smoothly as possible, generally around two belaying pins, and then is marled over. Made in this way, the strap is used to wrap around stays to hook a block to and, being much softer than rope, it has a better cling. Small *selvagees*, served or grafted over, are used for block straps. Large ones, similarly made but not served, are used for cargo slings. They are soft and pliant, and do not mar the cargo.

3148. A strap with a large eye is used for either toggling or lashing. A block that is to be bent to a spar is fitted in this fashion with a round seizing.

3149. A *selvagee* for a block strap is parceled and served over (two processes described later in the chapter). This illustration shows an old block, with selvagee strap, turned in with a throat seizing (#3377 and #3411).

3150. A tail block is employed when making a tackle fast to standing rigging. A *selvagee* is doubled and served over at the center with spun yarn and seized snugly around the block with a round seizing. The yarns are opened and scraped down, so that the length tapers very moderately to a point. It is then carefully marled (#3115). A single tail should always be dogged with the lay.

3151. A similar tail block is made of FLAT SINNET. An ordinary rope is first spliced snugly around the block as pictured. The ends are stuck only once. They are then scraped down and a round seizing put on (#3396). At six inches from the block, a snaked whipping is put on (#3453) and then the rope is made into seven foxes, tapered and platted.

3152. A *double tail block* may be made either selvagee-fashion or of FLAT SINNET. The two tails are made as described for the single tail (#3151).

3153. The oldest method of strapping a block, and one that is still used, was with a SHORT SPLICE (#2648). The splice was always placed at the breech of the block.

3154. A block with a thimble seized in the strap is termed an *eye block*. On shipboard a thimble was seized in by means of a Spanish windlass. The circumference of rope needed in making a strap is approximately one fourth to one third of the length of the block. A block strap that is over three and one half inches in circumference should be wormed and parceled before being served. The length of rope required for the strap is about one and one half times the round of the block. One half a turn should be removed from the lay of the rope before the ends are crotched. There should be four to seven lower turns in an eye seizing, and one less riding turn. Methods of seizing are given later in this chapter.

3155. Blocks are of two kinds: "*made*" blocks, of several pieces, and "*morticed*" blocks, which are chiseled out of a single piece of wood. The early name for the grooved wheel in a block was *shiver* which, after 1627, was contracted to shiv, the name that is used at present.

3156. The several parts of a made block are riveted together.

3157. A hook block. Nowadays all blocks are strapped with grommets (#2864), selvagee straps being obsolete. When a grommet is made for a hook block, it has to be made through the hole in the hook.

3158. *Jumpsurgee block* is the old name for the block that Luce calls a *grafted block*. Frequently they are grafted, only at the breech. (See SPLICE #2678.)

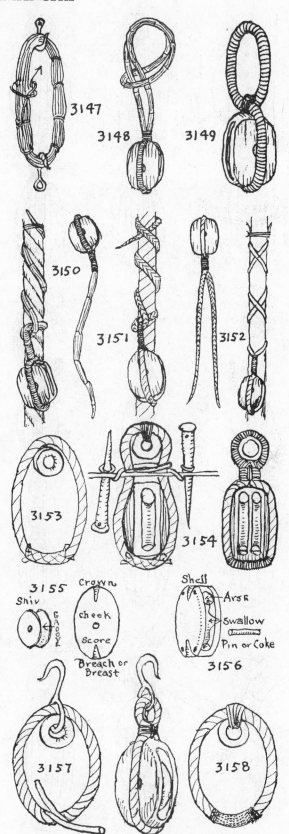

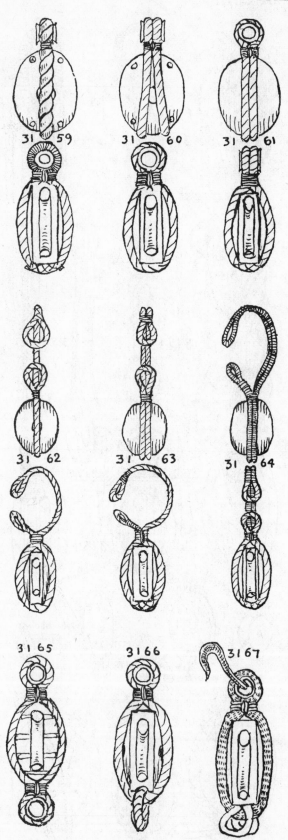

Blocks are spoken of as *eye blocks*, *hook blocks* or *tail blocks* according to their equipment; as *double*, *threefold* or *fourfold* according to their size; as *inner* and *outer*, *upper* and *lower*, or as *working* and *load*, according to their positions; and as *fall* or *loose*, according to the lead of the fall. Ashore the latter are sometimes termed the *stationary* and *movable* blocks.

3159. With a *single-strapped block*, the thimble and the shiv are ordinarily at right angles to each other.

3160. Two single straps are used where great strength is needed for heavy lifts.

3161. A *double strap* allows the thimble to lie in the same plane with the shiv.

3162. A *single strap with lashing eyes*. These are to be seized or lashed around a spar. An EYE SPLICE is made at either end of the strap and the strap seized or lashed in place.

3163. Heavy blocks for the same purpose have a double strap.

3164. If a different lead is required, it may be provided with two single straps.

3165. *Clump blocks* of the eighteenth century were turned on a lathe before morticing. The strap shown here has a thimble seized in at either end.

3166. For attaching the standing part of the fall to the block, a becket of some sort must be added. Notches are made on the breech of the block to admit the becket, which is at right angles to the strap. The one shown here is a small grommet, which should be half the diameter of the strap.

3167. An old way of fitting a block was with a double becket. The block pictured is one of a white whalebone pair that were made at sea about 1825. The shells are six inches long and the selvagee straps are grafted over. The becket in this case is a small grafted grommet.

Straps were commonly served over, but sometimes they were covered with leather or canvas and sometimes they were grafted over. This was to prevent chafe. But some authorities held that straps should never be covered, as they were apt to rot inside and fail without warning. In recent years, only hemp straps have been served over.

3168. The customary way of attaching the end of a fall to a block is to eye splice it around the strap at the breech of the block. The splice should be carefully tapered and served with spun yarn so that, when the tackle is chockablock, the splice will not suffer.

3169. To make the thimble of a single block lie in the plane of the shiv, a throat seizing (#3376 or #3410) is employed. The two ends of a block are not interchangeable. Only one end is sufficiently open for reeving the fall. In this case the fall is eye spliced to the thimble at the breech of the block.

3170. A *two-shiv block* leads better if the standing part of the fall is secured to the cheek. If it is not fitted with an offset becket, the fall may be spliced around the eye or hook and seized to the strap twice, at either end of the block.

3171. A *quarter-tackle block strap* is eye spliced around the block and has a long pendant bearing a hook in the end.

3172. *Swig blocks* have no shivs and are used to set up on the lashings of a whaleboat on the cranes. They resemble snatch blocks without shivs.

3173. A *topsail halyard block* is seized into a long grommet with a hook at the end.

3174. A *pendant block strap* is made with a LONG EYE that is seized around the block with a racking seizing (#3400).

3175. *Span blocks* for studding-sail halyards are lashed around masts in pairs. The blocks are seized in with a round seizing (#541).

3176. A *sheet block pendant* for jibs and staysails. The blocks are eye spliced to the two ends of a pendant. One block is rove through the clew and given a BECKET HITCH, the knot is drawn up and strongly seized, and the clew is seized close up to the knot. This was shown by Lever (1808) and it is still in use today.

3177. *Brace blocks* are secured to stays with a seized CLOVE HITCH. A small MOUSE is raised on the stay and the hitch is seized above it.

3178. A *block with a collar* is seized to a spar. The long leg is hauled through the eye, laid back on its own part and seized in several places according to its length.

3179. A *"strap-bound block"* is used on tacks, spritsail sheets, etc. The block was made and strapped in this manner to minimize chafing against the sails. The two ends of a strap were passed around the breech of the block and up through the two holes. After seizing in, the rope was opened and a SPRITSAIL SHEET KNOT tied in the six strand ends. The knot was buttoned to the clew of a sail, after which the clew was stopped.

3180. A *button and eye strap*, for quick adjustment to a spar. Either a MATTHEW WALKER KNOT or a MANROPE KNOT may be used.

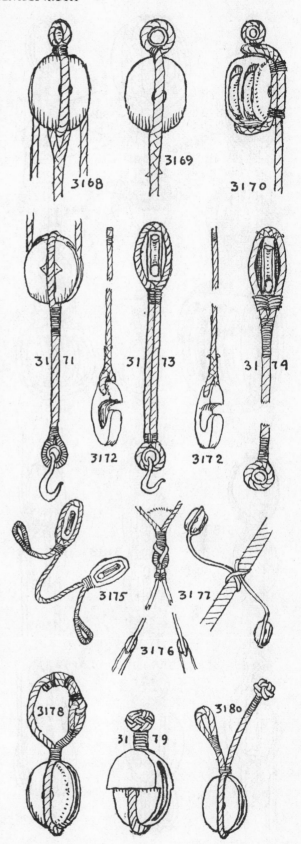

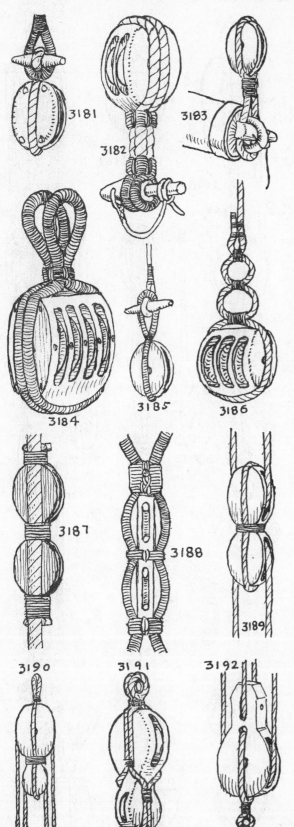

3181. A clew line block is fitted with a **toggle**. The toggle is buttoned to an eye, termed the clew, in the corner of the sail. It is a very practical method of fitting a block. A similar block is often toggled to pendants for various purposes. If to be left in place for any considerable time, the eye may be closed with a seizing.

3182. The lower block of a *whaler's cutting tackle* is fitted with long double straps which are rove through a hole cut in the blanket piece (blubber), and the toggle is passed through a double thimble.

3183. A *fid block* for a studding-sail tack is toggled to a metal eye in the end of a yard.

3184. A *"heaving-down" block*. The British equivalent would be a "careening" block. I saw what was probably the last merchant ship to be hove down in America. The 384-ton whaling bark *Josephine* was hove down at Merrill's Wharf, New Bedford, in 1893, there being no railway in the neighborhood that could take her, and no drydock available. Peter Black, an ancient master rigger, who in the 1840s had been the last to put the *Constitution* in active commission, resurrected his heaving-down tackle and, with no trouble at all, and much saving of expense, the ship was hove down. She was then breamed, scraped, caulked, payed, sheathed and coppered in record time. The gear he used is pictured on page 530.

3185. A *strap with a* Long Eye, made with throat seizing ✳3411, was often attached to a pendant bearing a toggle. The same shaped strap was employed in 1808 on lower square-sail sheets. It passed around the necks of the clews, and tacks were buttoned to the clews with Tack Knots (✳846).

3186. This method of strapping a *three-shiv block* is given by Vial du Clairbois, in his *Encyclopédie Méthodique Marine* (1787), and it is also given by Roding (1795). It consists of three throat seizings and an end seizing. Nowadays huge blocks such as this are generally strapped as ✳3184.

3187. *Sister blocks.* Two independent tackles, or on occasions one tackle and one bridle, are rove through the two ends of a sister block. This one is scored down one side and is to be seized to a shroud. Shown by Lever (1808).

3188. Sister blocks with scores down both cheeks are seized between two forward shrouds below the topmast crosstrees and are employed for the topsail lift and reef tackle.

3189. In the merchant service sister blocks may have but one shiv, the other end having only a hole which takes a bridle. The strap holds the shiv pin in place. It is hove taut around the shell by a seizing between the two halves.

3190. A *fiddle block* will lie flatter to a yard or mast than a double block will.

3191, 3192. *Shoe blocks* have their shivs at right angles to each other; ✳3191 is eighteenth-century and is double strapped; ✳3192 is seventeenth-century. It is strapped through a hole between the two shivs. Recently shoe blocks have been used for buntlines.

3193. A *lower lift purchase* with standing part strapped to the block.

3194. Two straps may be quickly adjusted to a block in this manner. If there is time they should be seized in.

3195. A CUT SPLICE with single block seized in.

3196. A *pendant block* of about 1600 is shown by R. C. Anderson in his *Treatise on Rigging* (circa 1625).

3197. A *double pendant block* is given by Roding (1795). I do not know its purpose. It may be a fair-leader.

3198. A block from Furttenbach (1629), representative of one of the earliest types known. The standing part is knotted into the breech. The shell is actually a block of wood which, of course, is the origin of the name.

3199. A strap fitted with STOPPER KNOTS from Roding (1795). A lanyard was eye spliced around the neck of one of these STOPPERS and the block was lashed in the rigging just as CABLE STOPPER ⌗1765 is clapped on.

3200. The earliest way of strapping a block was to reeve it through a hole in the upper end of the shell. The method is shown by Furttenbach in 1629. The STOPPER KNOT used at this period would probably be a wall upon a wall (⌗684).

3201. The early method of strapping, just described, is still employed on snatch blocks. I have one, incised "Bark *America*" on the back, that dates from the first half of the nineteenth century. This method of strapping is also used today on the blocks of tropical jalousies and awning gear.

3202. Quarter blocks are double and have a round seizing. The legs are of equal length, with eyes in each end which lash together over the topgallant yard. The forward shiv takes the topgallant clew line and the after one takes the royal sheet, according to Brady (1841).

3203. A euphroe block has "many holes but no shivers" and is used to extend the edge of an awning.

3204. To strap a reef tackle block: Make a grommet and seize in two thimbles the width of the block apart. Notch the block deeply at the breech and strap in the usual way. Reeve the fall through the two thimbles. The purpose is to prevent reef earings and reef points from fouling in the shivs.

3205, 3206. These are taken from Crescentio's *Nautica Mediterrania* of 1607. Multi-shiv blocks were used to disperse the strain of running rigging that was made fast to the stays. They served a purpose similar to euphroe blocks (see ⌗3276).

3207. This is a threefold block from Roding (1795).
A tackle (pronounced tai'cle at sea) is generally rove in the same

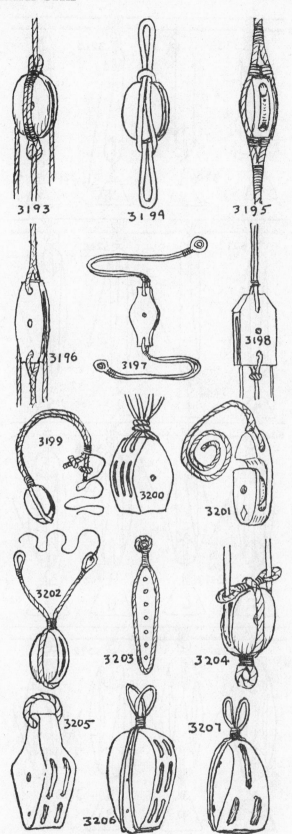

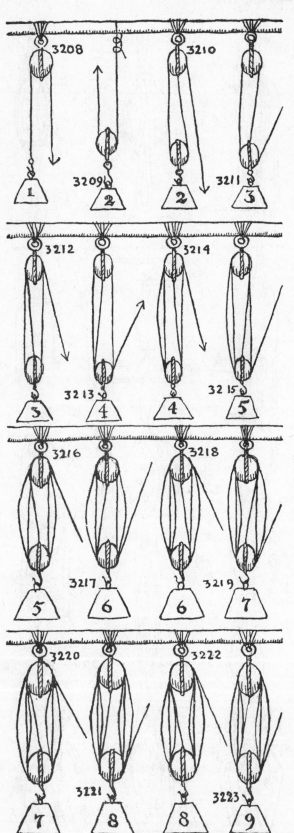

direction that a rope is coiled (clockwise). The blocks are placed together on a clean deck and the bottom shivs are rove first. Apparently the point is not considered important as, even on well-found ships, tackles are rove in both ways.

Running rigging may be rove off by marrying the end of the new rope to the old fall and hauling the new one through. Power is increased by adding to the number of shivs around which a rope (called the fall) passes.

3208. A single whip is called a tackle, although it does not increase the power.

On the accompanying diagrams, the figure placed on the weight represents the increase of power at that point, no allowance being made for loss by friction or otherwise. The figure 1 on the weight means that the pull and the lift are equal.

3209. A *runner* is the same as a single whip, reversed. The figure 2 means that the lift is double the effort spent.

3210. A *single purchase*. A purchase is a tackle that has the same number of shivs in both blocks. With the fall leading to the upper block of a purchase, the increase in power is always represented by an even number.

3211. A gun tackle.

3212. A luff tackle.

3213. Luff tackle inverted.

3214. Double purchase (mechanically the same as long tackle #3232).

3215. Double tackle.

3216. Winding tackle. This is about the largest tackle commonly found on sailing ships. It is used as a fish tackle (at the anchor) and also as a cargo tackle. Lever (1808) gives it for a jear tackle and Anderson (1625) gives the same thing for jears, except that the standing part is bent to the yard instead of to the fall block, the principle being the same. As each shiv added increases the time required to lift a load, blocks larger than are needed should be avoided. On blocks with over two shivs, the standing part should lead to the cheek of the block and not to the breech, as shown in #3170.

3217. Winding tackle reversed.

3218. Threefold or triple purchase.

3219. Threefold or triple tackle.

3220. Four-by-three tackle.

3221. Three-by-four tackle.

3222. Fourfold purchase.

3223. Fourfold or quadruple tackle.

Purchases of five and six shivs with steel wire rope are used for steamship cargo tackles. Ball or roller bearings are employed.

3224. *Whip upon whip.*

3225. A *double whip.*

3226. A *sail tackle* is used when bending sails. A fair-lead block is seized to the lower block. Fair-leads are used with many tackles; often they are snatch blocks (#3201), which are instantly removable. They are secured wherever convenient, provided they admit of a proper exertion of power.

3227. *Quarter tackle* or *yard tackle*. This is attached to a yard when needed to break out supplies. There is a long pendant to the lower block.

3228. *Topgallant halyard purchase.*

3229. *Watch tackle, handy-billy* or *tail tackle* is a small *luff tackle* with a tail on the fall block. This is always kept handy for any emergency and may be bent to either rigging or yard. The tail is tapered and platted or else made selvagee-fashion.

3230. *Jiggers* or *jig tackles* with double tails are used for the same purpose and are also called *handy-billies.* They are handy tackles kept for odd jobs alow and aloft.

3231. A *top burton* is mechanically the same as the luff tackle. The fiddle block allows the tackle to lie flat close to a spar.

3232. A *long tackle*. This also lies close to a spar and is for the same purpose as the former, but has more power.

3233. The *Spanish burton, single burton*, or *dory tackle* is the tackle with which Gloucestermen handle their dories. The upper block may be fitted with either an eye, a hook or a tail. The tackle is very economical of power but it is practical only for short lifts.

In running rigging the fall block is generally fitted with a thimble and eye or a shackle. Tackles for occasional use are more apt to have hooks.

Due to friction, the greatest strain is on the hauling part of the rope in hoisting, but in lowering, it is on the standing part.

A tackle with eyes on both blocks is called an *eye tackle*. A tackle with hooks on both blocks is called a *hook tackle*.

The power of a tackle may be computed by counting the number of parts in the rope between the two blocks. If the pull is away from the fall or lead block, the fall also is added to the total of parts. If two tackles are compounded by hooking one to the fall of the other, each tackle is counted separately and the two sums are multiplied together. If there is any doubt (as there may well be when tackles such as the burtons are elaborately compounded) it is an easy matter to decide empirically. Lay out the tackle on the deck or floor and secure the upper block. Overhaul (lengthen) the tackle several feet. Put a stop for a marker on the fall where it leads from the block, then measure the distance the marker moves in hauling the lower block one foot. This will be the figure wanted. If it is six feet, the power is one to six. At sea an allowance is made for loss of power of from five to eight per cent for each shiv in the tackle.

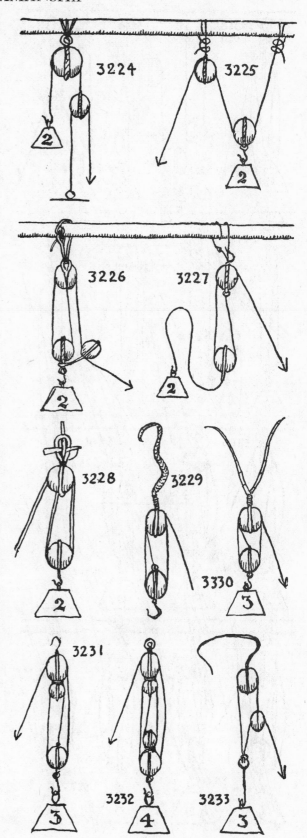

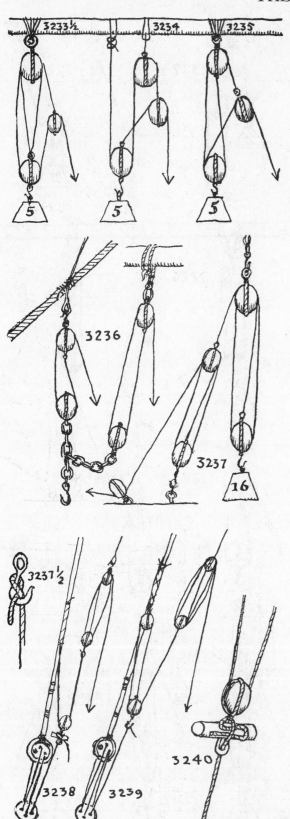

3233½. The double Spanish burton (1). The more common one.

3234. Double Spanish burton (2). The rarer one.

3235. Double Spanish burton (3). This is the same as the former, except that the standing end is bent to a becket in the upper block, instead of to a spar.

3236. The water whip is a light tackle, used when watering at sea. As a ship is not under way when watering, a large crew is available and a large tackle is unnecessary. The casks are hoisted with the yard tackle, then are eased aboard with the stay tackle and lowered away with both. The detail of the stay lashing or seizing is given as ⚓ 1998.

3237. Luff upon luff. The main tackle is much heavier cordage than the jigger.

3237½. The BLACKWALL HITCH is commonly tied in the end of a lanyard when setting up rigging.

3238. A tackle for setting up shrouds. This is the preferred method for attaching lanyards which, being seldom adjusted, are apt to be exceedingly stiff.

3239. An alternate method. Every boatswain is bound to employ something a little different.

3240. Detail of the LANYARD HITCH shown in ⚓ 3238.

3241. A method of setting up a mainstay or other large fore-and-aft stay, a much heavier task than setting up a single shroud. After the stay is brought home, a racking seizing (⚓3362) is put on at the bull's-eye and then a number of round seizings are added, the number depending on the length of the doubling. The upper end of a shroud or stay, where it passes over a top, is prepared in the rigging loft. The lower block is secured to the end of the shroud with a BALE SLING HITCH. The upper block is fitted with tails and the fairlead block is made fast to the mast.

3242. A fish tackle from Lever (1808). After the anchor has been catted, the shank and flukes are hoisted with the fish tackle.

3243. A *runner tackle* is a luff or jig tackle added to the end of a whip.

3244. *Runner and tackle* for setting up on a backstay. In heavy lifting, a lead block is always advisable. In a straight downward pull a man can haul no more than his own weight. In a short lifting pull, he can exert several times that amount of power. From the lead block the fall is usually led to a belaying pin and one man at the pin rail takes up slack so that at no time is the load liable to get adrift.

3245. Throat halyard and jig tackle. On small and medium-sized schooners, after a sail is hoisted and the halyard fall has been hauled hand taut and belayed, a jig tackle on the standing end of the main tackle is employed to send the halyard home.

3246. The peak halyards are treated in the same manner. On yachts nowadays small winches have taken the place of many of the heavier tackles, and also serve in place of jig tackles.

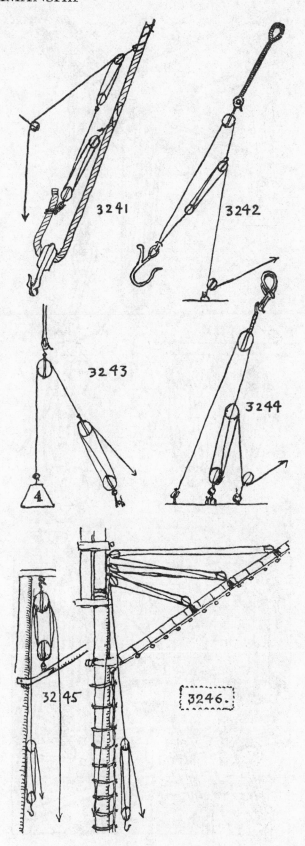

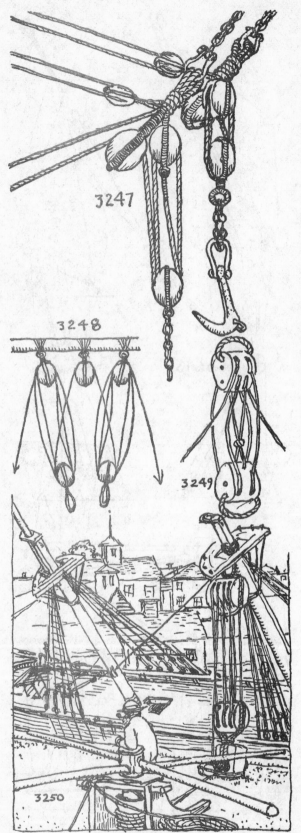

3247

3248

3249

3250

3247. This was the whaling bark *Sunbeam's* "cutting tackle." There were two tackles which worked independently and alternately, one blanket piece being hoisted while another was being lowered. The two single purchases shown at the top were guys to hold the tackle over the main hatch and the two falls, at the left, led forward to the windlass. Although the lift was exceedingly heavy and the blocks and falls enormous, the power was provided by a windlass, so a compounded tackle was unnecessary, the lift in this case being only four times the pull.

3248. A double threefold purchase, for getting a gun, boiler or other heavy weight aboard, was given in Knight's *Seamanship* of 1908.

3249. A tackle that was shown by Bartolomeo Crescentio in 1607. There are four shivs to each block, but the fall is divided into two hauling parts and two standing parts, so that the total power of the tackle is only three to one.

3250. This is the heaving-down tackle with which Peter Black, master rigger, *hove down* the bark *Josephine* in 1893. Although I was a small boy at the time, I was tremendously interested in the operation and the sketch given here is made from a photograph taken at the time.

The lower three-shiv block is attached to a heaving-down post, the details of which are given as ✳2017. The upper block is suspended from the main top. The shell of the fall block is in my own collection and measures 24″ × 19½″ × 19½″. It took from four to six hands to man each of the four arms of the heaving-down winch.

The fall runs from a lead block at the base of the heaving-down post to the winch, and the standing end is made fast at the foot of the mainmast. The increase of power is nine times the force exerted at the winch. The shrouds at the starboard side are reinforced with chains.

Peter Black was the last rigger to fit out the U.S.S. *Constitution* for sea duty. There was no better rigger than he, so it is interesting to see that his tackle is rigged so that there is friction between the two back leads at the left. It would seem that the methods of reeving large blocks used nowadays and (shown on the next two pages) were not widely known in 1893. The earliest record I have found of the method on page 531 is in Axel S. Blomgren's *Seamanship* (Stockholm, 1923). He gives the threefold purchase. Knight, in 1908, gives a threefold purchase by the method on page 532.

3251–57. With a three-shiv, or larger, block much is gained by having the fall lead to the center shiv. If led to an end shiv, the block will cant, so that the fall will chafe against the shell. The tackles described on this page are sometimes termed "right-angle tackles." Numbers 3251 and 3253 are the only ones I have ever seen described or in use, but in case someone should have occasion to employ something else I have rounded out the series up to five shivs. The proportions of the blocks are exaggerated and the details eliminated to make the lead of the fall clearer to the eye. The shivs are numbered without being drawn. So if the falls are rove in rotation as numbered, the working end will always lead to the center shiv (which is most desirable). The general rule is to reeve at the fall block from the center outward and at the lower block to reeve from the outside inward. The cycle in each case is from the innermost shiv to an outermost shiv to the innermost remaining shiv, to the outermost remaining shiv, etc.

3258. This fivefold purchase presents a variation from the rule just given. The working end is led each time to the innermost vacant shiv until all are full. This might prove the more practical way, but on paper an adherence to the rule given above promises better.

For very heavy lifts, hooks on blocks are seldom used. Double eye straps are preferable, and these may be either lashed or toggled.

3251. Luff tackle (equivalent).

3252. Double purchase.

3253. Winding tackle (equivalent).

3254. Threefold or triple purchase.

3255. Four-by-three shiv tackle.

3256. Fourfold purchase.

3257. Five-by-four shiv tackle.

3258. Fivefold purchase.

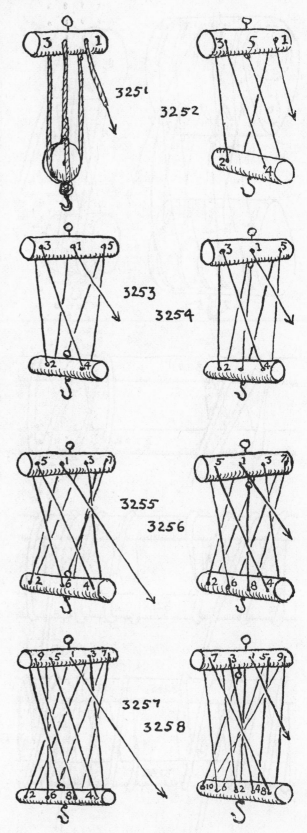

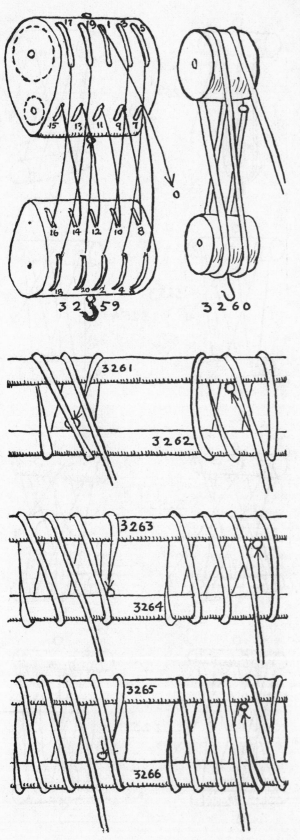

3259. Smeaton's blocks. A tenfold purchase. I once saw **a** drawing of this with the name attached and that is all I know about it. The larger the number of shivs, the less efficient is the block. If the nautical rule of subtraction, for loss by friction, is applied, by the time the becket is reached, at the higher figure of eight per cent per shiv, a hundred and sixty per cent of the power will have been expended, which is excessive, and if we apply the lower figure of five per cent per shiv, exactly one hundred per cent has gone. That is to say, there might not be enough power left when the standing part is reached to take up the slack. It would, moreover, take twenty minutes to move a load that, with a whip, could be moved in one minute. If, however, the shivs have ball bearings (which they probably have) and steel rope is used (which is undoubtedly what was planned), the figures would be quite different.

3260. By the method here shown, tackles may be rove with the two blocks in the same plane and with the fall invariably leading to a central shiv. Axel S. Blomgren, in his *Seamanship* (Stockholm, 1923), shows ⚓3262. I have not seen the method published elsewhere. I have tried out ⚓3261 with a farm tackle and found it satisfactory.

3260. Double purchase.

3261. Winding tackle (equivalent).

3262. Threefold purchase.

3263. Four-by-three shiv tackle.

3264. Fourfold purchase.

3265. Five-by-four shiv tackle.

3266. Fivefold purchase.

3267. *Mousing a hook.* If any considerable load is to be put on a block, the hook should be moused. A length of marline is doubled and a BALE SLING HITCH put over the bill which is slipped to the back of the hook. A number of turns are taken around the back and bill, the ends being led in opposite circuits. Cross the ends while there is still material and put on tight frapping turns in both directions from the center. Then add riding turns back to the center and finish off with a REEF KNOT. This serves the double purpose of strengthening the hook and preventing the hook from spilling.

3268. The names of the different parts of a hook are noted in the diagram opposite.

3269. A *mousing* of five or six turns of marline. Cross the ends at the middle and, using both ends, add frapping turns to the end of the mousing. Stick the ends through the middle of the mousing turns and tie an OVERHAND KNOT in each end.

3270. Nowadays hooks are often moused with wire. Frapping turns are added and riding turns may be put on if desired but are usually omitted. Without frapping turns there would be no tension on the wire and consequently no support to the hook until it starts to straighten.

To make: Double the wire and, without knotting, lead the ends around the neck of the hook, lay them up together and take a number of turns around the neck and the bill, pulling each turn as taut as possible. At the last turn lead the ends to the back of the hook around opposite sides and twist them up together. Cut off the ends and hammer them down and out of the way.

I have seen frapping turns of marline added to a wire mousing of the sort just described.

3271. *Sister hooks* are used for a variety of purposes. They are often found on lightweight jib sheets. Ordinarily they are stopped with a number of round turns and a REEF KNOT.

3272. If a shackle of the right size can be found it will prove stronger than a mousing but it should fit very snugly.

3273. A *crowfoot*, spread along the front rim of the fore and main tops and leading to a tackle on the stay, was common in the days of single topsails to prevent the foot of the sails fouling in the tops.

3274. The crowfoot nowadays is used to spread awnings and canvas swimming pools on shipboard. In circuses it is indispensable for spreading safety nets under trapeze performers. A euphroe block, also called a centipede block, is used to dissipate the lines of the crowfoot.

3275. The drawing shows a crowfoot at the head of a lateen yard. From Furttenbach (1629). In this period blocks with shivs, instead of euphroes, were used.

3276. Before staysails came into use in the eighteenth century, double mainstays were sometimes led to the forward shrouds and secured with a crowfoot at either side. This left the space above the main hatch clear.

3277. Catharpins stiffened the backstays by frapping them to the tops, and were a variety of crowfoot. The ends were eye spliced and seized similarly to ratlines (※3438). Sometimes they had a euphroe block, at other times they were merely lashed. Catharpins were still to be seen occasionally at the turn of the present century.

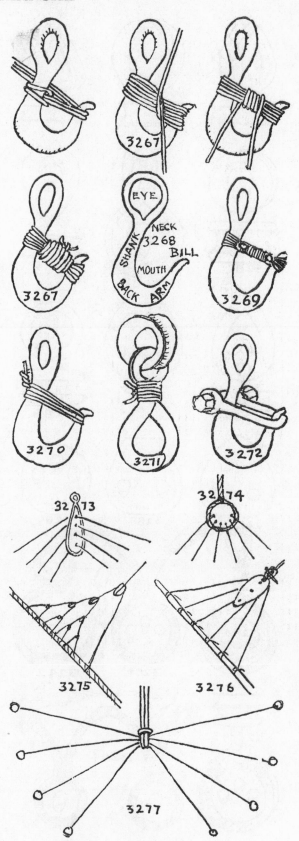

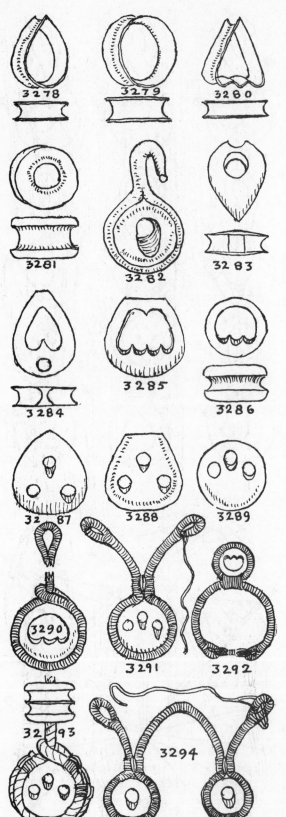

3278. An oval thimble. This is the ordinary thimble for wire rigging but it is not often used in hemp.

3279. A round thimble is made of galvanized iron or of other metal. It is the oldest type of thimble and still is commonly used with fiber rope.

3280. A lashing thimble for wire rigging.

3281. A lignum vitae truck, thimble or bull's-eye was lashed or seized wherever needed and was often employed as a fair-leader.

3282. The ordinary bull's-eye was the means of securing the ends of various stays.

3283. This is a white whalebone bull's-eye that was used on a whaleboat's backstay lashing (see ⚹3300).

3284. A whalebone heart (see ⚹3301). This specimen probably was made in the mid-nineteenth century.

3285. An eighteenth-century heart was shown by Admiral Paris, in his *Dictionary of the Marine* (Paris, 1877).

3286. The common nineteenth- and twentieth-century heart. It is circular and sometimes has four grooves through the hole instead of three, which is more common. In England and the United States hearts, deadeyes and bull's-eyes were made of elm wood before the nineteenth century; later ones are of lignum vitae.

3287. A *deadeye*. This is from a painting of 1640. The detail may be correct but the painting as a whole is not authoritative.

3288. From Crescentio's *Nautica Mediterrania* (1607).

3289. The common deadeye of the past century or two. The left hole is where the knot ordinarily is tied and it should be noted that the edge is left sharp while the other holes are gouged to soften the sharp turn of the lanyards.

3290. A forestay strap is made of the same material as the stay. A length about four times the circumference of the bowsprit is short spliced to form a grommet. Two eyes are seized in and one eye is rove through the other, to enclose a large heart through which the lanyards are rove.

3291. A deadeye collar has a span of Eye Splices which is lashed around the bowsprit. It was given by Lever (1808).

3292. A heart turned in with a throat seizing and lashing eyes, for securing a forestay.

3293. The cutter stay method of turning in deadeyes was employed in the mid-nineteenth century. Staysails could be set much more snugly to the mast than by the ordinary method. In Great Britain this method was also used on shrouds. The end of the shroud, having been doubled around the standing part, was seized as closely as possible with a racking seizing. Then two or three round seizings were put on and the turning was hammered into place with commanders.

3294. Bowsprit shroud collars were often made double in the manner here illustrated. The eyes were lashed around the bowsprit.

Deadeyes and lanyards form a sort of tackle that is found in the ends of standing rigging. They do not require shivs as they are seldom adjusted. When adjustment is necessary the holes and lanyards are both well tallowed, and the lanyards are set up with jig tackles.

3295. The illustration represents the *bronze deadeyes* of a Viking ship. They are borrowed from Konijnenburg's *Ship Building from Its Beginnings* (Brussels, N.D.).

3296. Anderson, in his *Treatise on Rigging* (circa 1625), pictures a *deadeye of four holes*. The French *Manuel de Manœuvrier* (Paris, 1891) gives exactly the same deadeye and a method of reeving and setting up. With more than three turns a lanyard is always hauled at both ends, so there is no LANYARD KNOT and the ends are seized to adjacent parts. In a modern French lanyard the center is secured with a RING HITCH below the lower deadeye.

3297. Bartolemeo Crescentio in his *Nautica Mediterrania* (Rome, 1607), in an illustration of the battle of Lepanto (1571) pictures deadeyes almost identical with those of the present day. They are differently turned in, however. The upper one has an eye strap which toggles to the shroud. Artiñano gives a reproduction of a picture of 1498 and another of 1504, both presumably contemporary, which show the usual three-hole deadeye. A painting by Pieter Breughel, dated 1564, appears to show ordinary three-hole deadeyes without the toggles.

3298. In early small craft, where masts and rigging were struck whenever sails were lowered, it was the custom to set up stays with shiv blocks instead of deadeyes. Dutch boats of the present day are rigged in this way. The illustration showing blocks is from a photograph of the stone monument to Saint Peter Martyr by Giovanni di Balduccio in the Basílica Sant' Eustorgio at Milan. The monument was completed in 1339.

3299. This was a common way of setting up the backstays of a whaleboat. Whaleboat stays have to be let go instantly, so lanyards are always secured with a SLIPPED HITCH.

3300. An earlier *whaleboat lanyard* having the white whalebone bull's-eye (#3283).

3301. A *white whalebone heart* (#3284). This appears too complicated for a whaleboat backstay lashing and it may have belonged to a whaleboat's gripe.

3302. A *rigging stopper* or a *fighting stopper* was employed to repair a shroud or other stay that was carried away in action. Each deadeye was strapped with two tails. A long lanyard was rove with a knotted EYE SPLICE at each end (see #2781, #2782, or #2783). After the tail was stopped at either end of the wounded rigging a tackle was hooked to the handiest eye; and the other knotted eye acted as a LANYARD KNOT.

3303. The eyes of the jib sheets and the clew of the sail were lashed in this manner so that the sheets would lead fair.

3304. A round-turn lashing. This generally starts with an EYE SPLICE in the lanyard to a thimble or eye in the stay; after a number of frapping turns have been added to the round turns, the end is secured under the last few turns.

3305. A *cross-turn lashing* (the name is from Steel, 1794; Biddlecomb calls it a *cross lashing*) is made with a series of racking turns. It is started either with an EYE SPLICE or else a RUNNING EYE and finished off with frapping turns. Rope jackstays were formerly lashed together at the center of the yard in this way.

3306. A common practice on small commercial boats is to finish off the backstay lashing with a series of HALF HITCHES instead of frapping turns.

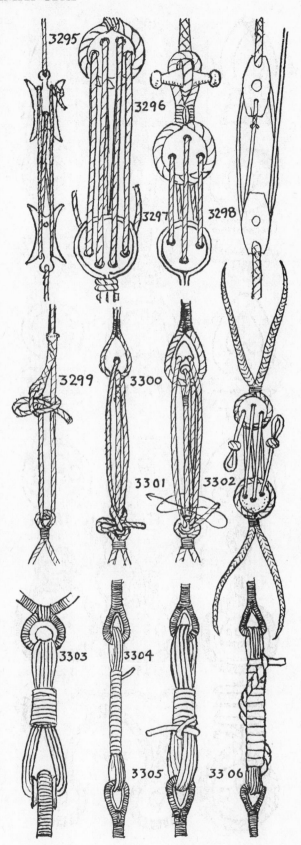

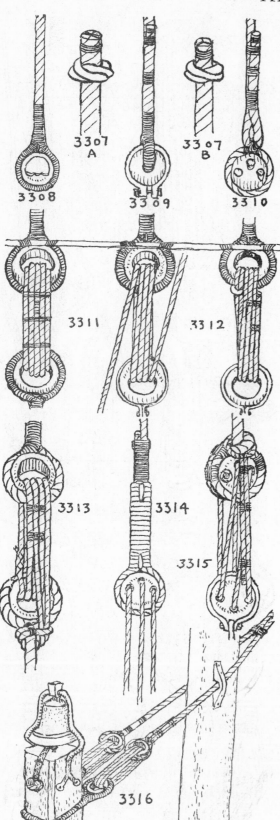

3307. The FOUR-STRAND LANYARD KNOT (A) is used at the dead-eyes in the lower rigging (❋688). The MATTHEW WALKER KNOT (B) is used aloft and elsewhere (❋682).

3308. In wire rigging, where no considerable stretch is to be allowed for, wire EYE SPLICES are not uncommonly used around *deadeyes* and *hearts*.

3309. Royal backstays and topgallant mast shrouds generally have no lanyards and many of the upper fore-and-aft stays are rove through *iron-strapped bull's-eyes* and doubled back with a racking seizing.

3310. A *throat seizing* has been the preferred method of turning in deadeyes on American ships since the middle of the eighteenth century. In the sixteenth and seventeenth centuries a round seizing appears to have been used. Seizings will be described later in this chapter. The turn around the deadeye should always be right-handed as illustrated, except when cable-laid rigging is used. The end should always be inboard.

3311. *Forestay lanyards* of 1891 (from the *Manual of the Sea* of that date) are rove through hearts. Any lanyard lashing with four turns or over should be set up at both ends.

Four turns having been taken, the lanyards are set up with two tackles and held with stops while seizings are added. Riding turns are put on the seizings. The two lanyard ends are cut off where they meet and are carefully whipped. Three or four seizings are put on each lashing.

3312. A *heart lashing in the bowsprit rigging* is sometimes started at the outer end with a LONG RUNNING EYE and the working end is seized directly to the turns without the addition of a Cow HITCH.

3313. To reeve the *lanyard of a jib-boom guy:* The end of a lanyard in a heart lashing is made fast with an EYE SPLICE to the inner heart and is brought up through the outer heart. After three turns a Cow HITCH (❋1673) is taken around the neck of the iron strap and the end is seized in as illustrated.

3314. Steel, in 1794, describes as contemporary practice the following. The end of the lanyard, after setting up for a full due, is seized or stopped with racking turns as ❋3362. The end is then rove outward over the upper deadeye and under the throat seizing and there hitched. It is then expended with round turns around the doubling of the shroud. The end is stopped with spun yarn to the shroud.

3315. The way in which the Cow HITCH was taken with a cutter-turned deadeye is shown here and also a way of attaching the standing end of the lanyard to an eyebolt fixed to the channel; a method that was highly thought of in the 1880s, but soon went out of practice. Boyd (1857) described a practice of securing the standing end of a lanyard with a RUNNING EYE round the neck of the *lower* deadeye. Nares, in 1874, shows the lanyard secured with a round turn, which is obviously bad as the lanyard would have a tendency to work down and fetch against the end seizings.

3316. A double main topmast stay that was secured to the Samson post or Samson knee, forward of the foremast. More often than not, no lanyards were used here, the ends of the stay being rove through a buil's-eye as pictured in ⚓3309 and ⚓3358. The Samson post provided a step for the bowsprit and held the pawls of the windlass in the earlier part of the nineteenth century. The more common *bowsprit bitts* served the same purpose but were double instead of single posts.

3317. Lanyards are rove in the same direction that rope is coiled (right-handed). The standing end is knotted at the inboard side of the left hole of the upper deadeye. On square-rigged vessels lanyard stuff for all lower rigging is four-strand tarred hemp, in diameter one half the diameter of the shroud or stay that it leads to. Topmast lanyards are three-strand stuff.

On some smart naval craft the knots were at the forward hole of the deadeye on both sides of the ship, left-laid rigging being used on the port side. If cable-laid rigging was used, all the knots were on the right side of the deadeye.

The common way of securing the end of a lanyard in hemp rigging. A Cow Hitch is taken around the doubled shroud above the shear pole and the end is carried down and seized three times between two standing parts.

3318. This is a common Lanyard Hitch since the advent of wire rigging. The hemp lanyard should be very little smaller than the size of the wire rigging itself. The greater bother of adjusting hemp lanyards is more than offset by their greater elasticity and in times of stress they can easily be chopped away. Today they are much preferred on power fishermen, particularly on swordfishermen, because the stiffness of wire rigging makes the lookout a most uncomfortable perch.

3319. To *scow a grapnel*. This method is used in small-boat fishing on rocky bottom. If the grapnel fouls and refuses to break out, the stop will part and free it. The roding or warp is led tightly around the crotch and is stopped to the ring with a single rope yarn. When the stop parts, the flukes are lifted and the grapnel breaks out.

3320. To *crown or scow an anchor*. This is similar in principle to the foregoing but the warp is made fast to the crown of the anchor with a Clove Hitch which may be seized in. Haul taut and stop to the ring with a single rope yarn if the anchor is not a heavy one. Ansted, *A Dictionary of Sea Terms* (Glasgow, 1917), calls this "becueing an anchor."

3321. A *rider for a cable*. If your cable is short and you are riding uncomfortably, make a grommet of some sort, of either wire, rope or an old mast hoop, and tie a bag of sand or any other available weight to it and allow it to slide down the cable for a length a little greater than your depth.

3322. To *secure a buoy rope*. The commonest way is as shown, a Clove Hitch at the crown, three seizings and a Buoy Rope Knot (⚓719) on the shank. This is from Lever (1808).

3323. A better Buoy Rope Hitch is described by Hutchinson (1744), who says, "It takes much less rope than the clumsy method of a clove hitch." In the days before power capstans and windlasses it was often necessary to break out an anchor with a buoy rope, a method which requires far less effort than tripping with the cable alone.

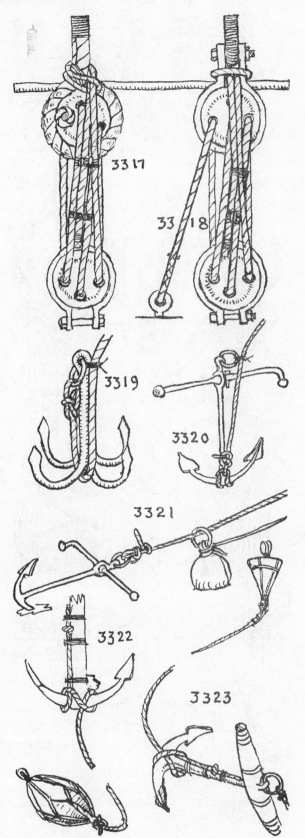

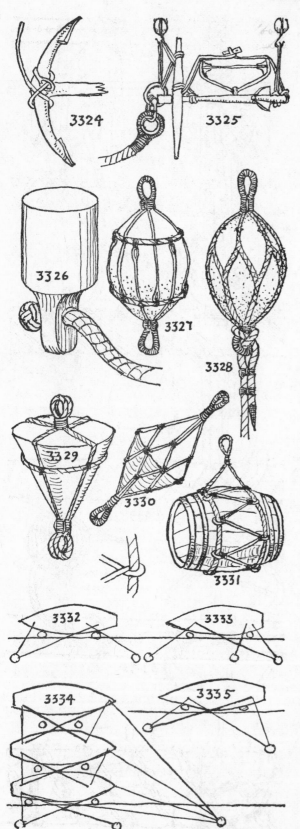

3324. A BUOY ROPE HITCH from Brady (New York, 1841). Brady gives a method of making fast to the crown of the anchor without leading the end up the shank. A RUNNING EYE SPLICE is put around one arm, a SINGLE HITCH is taken around the other arm, and the hitch is seized "in the cross."

3325. The following is a *method of boating anchors,* employed when kedging ship, before the days of steam. The anchor was lowered into the water by the tackles shown. The boat was drifted over the anchor, and the anchor was toggled to the boat by straps around her midship section. The tackles having been removed, the boat was pulled out ahead of the ship and the anchor dropped by driving out the toggle.

3326. A *mooring buoy of 1750* was made of a section of an old mast or spar. The buoy rope bore a SPRITSAIL SHEET KNOT.

3327. To *strap a buoy.* Buoys were formerly made caskwise by a cooper. It is only since the days of Galvin that iron buoys have proved universally practical. Two grommets were made to pass around the buoy, halfway from the center to the end. Four straps of equal length were made with EYE SPLICES in each end. The straps, two for each end, were seized to the grommets. The grommets were driven taut and double beckets were seized into the bights of the straps at each end of the buoy. All crossings were seized.

3328. Six straps of equal length were cut and two sets of three were stopped together at the middle. The ends of each set were side spliced to the opposite straps and triple beckets were seized in at each end of the buoy.

3329. A nun buoy strap was tightened by seizing in the eyes. A nun buoy had a head similar to a hogshead or cask. It was used for a channel marker as well as for an anchor buoy.

3330. This one is tightened by seizing different parts together. Two straps are employed, which makes a DOUBLE EYE at each end. The eyes are seized in and served.

3331. An ordinary keg serves as a swordfish or a seine buoy. Two grommets are used for hoops and a line is snaked to the grommets around the body of the keg, being either seized or clove hitched to them. A short bridle is eye spliced and seized to the grommets and also has a thimble seized in at the center, to which the buoy line is bent.

3332. Posts and bollards on wharfs are never placed twice alike, so there is considerable variety in the ways of tying up, though the principle is always the same. This shows a boat tied up with a bow line, stern line and a forward spring line. This triangulates the mooring.

3333. A boat with the same gear but with the addition of a *breast line.* The spring line in this case leads aft.

3334. Three fishermen are here tied up abreast, with breast lines at the quarters to hold them against wind and current. There is a tacit understanding that boats anchored alongside each other must each have at least one line to shore.

3335. A boat with crossed spring lines.

The greater the fall and rise of the tide, the farther apart the posts must be and the nearer parallel with the wharf the warps must lead. The warps or lines must form triangles, with either the wharf or the boat acting as one side of each triangle. Larger vessels require more lines of the same sort along the middle length. Otherwise the principle of tying up is the same.

3336. Manropes, yoke ropes, etc., are canvas-covered and then wormed *over* the canvas with fishline. This is hove in as described below, and NARROW TURK'S-HEADS of fishline are added at intervals of every two or three feet, wherever there is a joint in the canvas. Very small rope is parceled without being wormed.

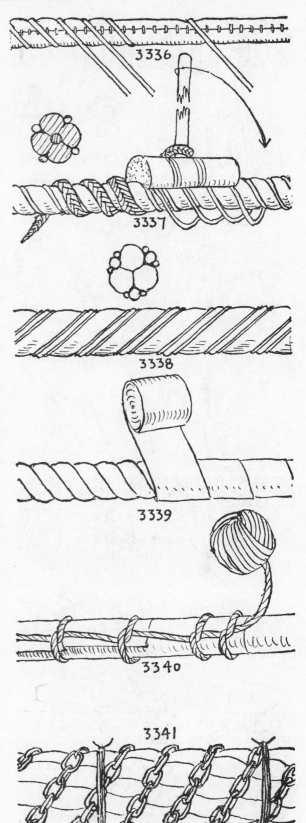

3337. *Worming.* Large standing rigging is always wormed before parceling, the purpose being to fill all cracks and keep out moisture. If worming is put in for a short distance only, it may be hove in sufficiently by hand, providing there is a helper to open the lay slightly. A large rope may be opened by means of a heaver (#2718). When any considerable length is to be wormed, however, the rope is first stretched with a tackle or winch and secured in the loft about waist-high. The worming is laid in by hand and pulled hand taut. Then a medium-sized serving mallet is taken and fitted with a tail or tails, called "trailors," which may be either of sinnet or the single strand of a large rope. The tails are secured to the handle with a RUNNING EYE or a BALE SLING HITCH. With this apparatus, heave in the worming; the pull of the trailor does the entire work of tightening. All ends are then stopped. Most rigging is four-strand and requires four pieces or parts of worming. The length of material needed is about once and a half the length of the stay that is to be wormed. Where a stay is to be turned in around a thimble or eye, the worming must be slack, otherwise it may part. Worming, parceling and service in standing rigging are always put on with materials well soaked in rigging tar.

3338. *Sister worming,* also called *backing* and *side worming.* Cable-laid rigging has large cuntlines and the worming requires *backing* with smaller stuff at either side. This can generally be put in by hand alone. Four-strand cable has sometimes been used for large fore-and-aft stays.

3339. Parceling at sea is made of old canvas, preferably cut up in long strips. It is soaked in rigger's tar and put on snugly in the manner of a bandage, *always with the lay* of the stay. It must also be put on from the bottom upward so that the parts will overlap as shingles do and tend to keep out moisture. But if parceling is *not to be served,* it should be put on against the lay.

3340. *Parceling* at sea is often made of old bits of canvas closely marled to hold it in place while being served.

3341. *Link worming.* In the days of hemp cables link worming was used on very rocky bottom. Three small chains, each about fifteen fathoms long, were shackled to the anchor ring and wormed in the manner described for rope. The cable was stopped at frequent intervals and was seized at the ends of the chains.

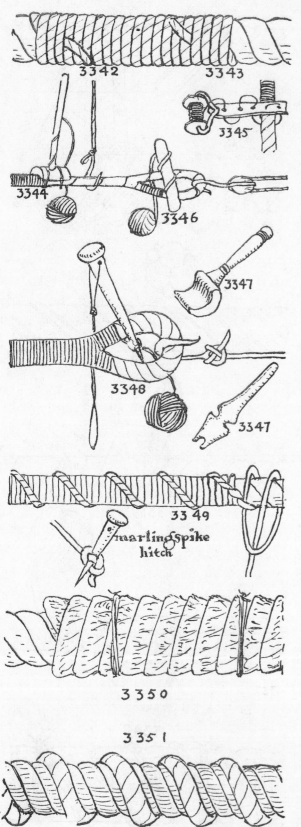

3342. Service is applied to standing rigging to protect it from wear and weather. After worming and parceling it is tightly bound with well-tarred spun yarn or marline. Service is started by taking two or three turns by hand over the rope and drawing them taut with a marlingspike. The rigger's mallet then takes over the work.

3343. When the job is completed the end is rove under the last three or four turns and all is hove taut with the marlingspike, when both ends are trimmed. Whenever necessary another piece of service is bent on with either SPLICE ⚹2680 or BENDS ⚹1480 and ⚹1485.

3344. For applying service a tool called a *serving mallet* is required. A large one with a reel is pictured in the heading of this chapter. Formerly a rigger's apprentice or helper with a large ball of marline walked backward, ahead of the rigger, and passed the ball around the stay at the same time the rigger revolved his mallet. The marline was passed several times around the head of the mallet and then a number of times around the handle. The friction on the head and handle was regulated by the number of the turns that were taken. And the number of the turns decided the tightness of the service. Serving turns were always passed contrary to the lay of the rope, so that as the rope stretched in use the service tended to tighten rather than slacken. A swifter (the foremost shroud) was served its full length, as it took most of the chafe of the sail. The remaining shrouds were served one third down to take the wear of the yard. In very early days the swifter was the aftermost shroud.

3345. Nowadays smaller mallets and reels are used that do away with the need of a helper. The one pictured consists of a brass plate with several holes drilled through it, and with spring-steel jaws to provide tension for the reel.

3346. For EYE SPLICES a "serving stick" is often used.

3347. Riggers and sailors commonly use a *serving board* for eyes.

3348. But *marlingspike service* is required for very small eyes and also when repairing broken service. A MARLINGSPIKE HITCH is taken over the point and the hitch is drawn taut by prying against the rope. This hitch is quickly made by the method shown as ⚹2030 ("Occasional Knots"). Photographs of old serving tools are shown among the frontispieces.

3349. *Grapevine service* consists of a series of hitches, all being in the same direction. Esparteiro shows it made with two lines hitched on opposite sides, which he terms "*d'Americana.*"

3350. *Rounding.* This is *service* of old rope, formerly put on ships' cables, to prevent chafe at the hawse holes. Nowadays the same thing is used by fishermen on flounder gear. It is patched as soon as worn through, so it is generally most untidy but very efficient. The ends of rounding are sometimes tucked through the strands of the rope that is being covered. It is tightened with a heaver (⚹2023).

When dragged constantly over rough bottom in one direction, rounding will wear with the saw-tooth effect that is pictured.

3351. *Cackling* or *kackling.* A three-inch rope was sometimes wormed along a single cuntline of the ship's cable to protect it at the anchor ring and at the hawse pipe.

Ropes that are bound together or to other objects, more or less permanently, are said to be seized. Ordinary *rigger's seizings* are made with *marline*, large seizings with *small stuff. Sailmaker's seizings* are of sail twine.

Seizings require less material than knots and splices; they have little give and little tendency to mark and injure the rope.

3352. The end of a shroud or stay is *capped* with metal or tarred canvas to protect it from the weather.

3353–57. An *end seizing* (#3353) is often a *rigger's stopping* (#3380), which has no crossing turns. The *upper seizing* (#3354) is sometimes made as a flat seizing (without riding turns), #3383. As many as five seizings may be used on a fore-and-aft stay; #3355 is a *middle seizing;* #3356 is a *quarter seizing;* and #3357 an *eye seizing.* All of these may be round seizings except the eye seizing, which is generally a throat (#3410) or a round seizing (#3388); less often it is a racking seizing (#3400).

3358. The drawing illustrates a bull's-eye seized in with a *double racking seizing* (#3401), which is best for wire. Although a *throat seizing* (#3410) has been favored since the middle of the eighteenth century for deadeyes, the *round seizing* is the earlier practice.

3359. Spun yarn or marline seizings are started with TUCKED EYE #2772, the end of which is gripped by the next few turns.

3360. Seizings of small stuff are started with an EYE SPLICE (#2725), with long ends that are tucked once only.

3361. *Round turns.* If a TUCKED EYE is used, the turns are carefully laid over the end to hold it. A SPLICED EYE is generally tucked but once, the ends being held by the turns. The turns of a seizing should always be taken contrary to the lay of the rope, and each turn is·hove taut with a marlingspike.

3362. *Racking turns* are often used on wire rope.

3363. *Double racking turns* are used when there is need of haste.

3364. *Riding turns,* or *riders,* form a second layer of service on top of the first layer or under turns. The riders are always one less in number than the under turns, and are not set up so hard, in order not to disturb the under turns.

3365. *Crossing turns* are added to take up slack.

3366, 3367. Patent deadeyes for wire rigging were invented in the early seventies; the stay was turned in around a thimble and held with five seizings. They were soon superseded by turnbuckles.

3368. *Cross* or *right-angle seizings* are employed for seizing battens which sometimes take the place of ratlines, and for securing mast hoops.

3369. An X seizing has the same number of turns in each diagonal. It is completed with crossing turns and finished off with SEIZING HITCH #3390.

3370. *Figure-eight turns* may be used either with or without crossing turns. Similar turns may be added on the opposite side of the seizing, one set being horizontal, the other vertical. These are often found on the battens of a swordfisherman's shrouds.

3371. *Frapping turns* are added with a needle to the face of a figure-eight seizing.

3372. A TRANSOM KNOT serves the same purpose.

3373. *Flat seizing* (#3383) is frequently used as an end seizing.

3374. *Round seizing* (#3388) is the usual middle seizing of a shroud end.

3375. A *quarter seizing* is commonly put in as a round seizing.

3376. The *throat seizing* is used when turning in a shroud (#3410).

3377. Shear poles are secured to the shroud doublings with flat seizings (#3383).

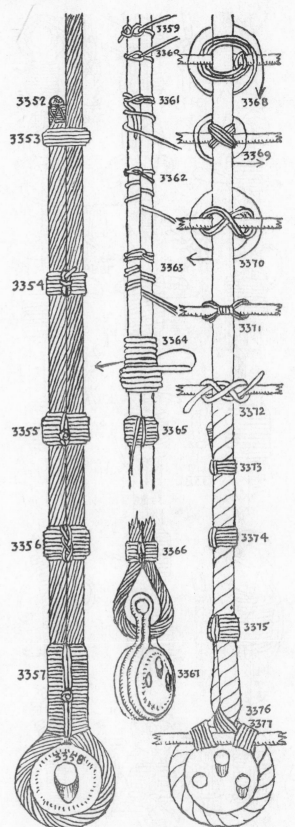

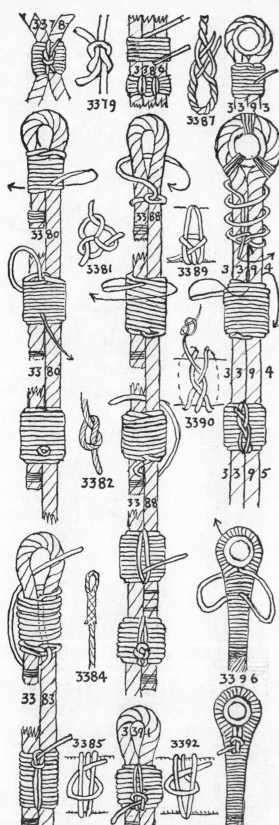

3378. *Ordinary stopping* consists of a number of round turns, with the two ends tied together.

3379. The SQUARE or REEF KNOT is used to finish off a stopping.

3380. A rigger's stopping differs from a seizing only in having no crossing turns. A layer of *riding turns* is added that is one less than the number of under turns. Riding turns are put on only hand taut; when the last one has been added the end is stuck down through the initial eye between the two layers of turns, and up to the surface under two turns. It is finished off either with a WALL KNOT or an OVERHAND KNOT, according to the size of the seizing stuff.

3381. The WALL KNOT is tied in the ends of small-stuff seizings.

3382. The OVERHAND KNOT is tied in spun yarn and marline seizings.

3383. The *flat seizing* has no *riding turns*. When sufficient lower turns are taken the end is tucked down and brought up through the eye. *Crossing turns* are taken and a FLAT KNOT (%3385) added.

3384. A *seizing of small stuff* is started with an EYE SPLICE, tucked once only, and with the ends "trimmed long."

3385. The FLAT KNOT is used in finishing off small seizings; it is sometimes wrongly called a SQUARE KNOT.

3386. A *lanyard seizing* passes around three parts of the rope. Two sets of crossing turns are made with the two ends of the seizing and are finished off between the parts of the lanyard with an OVERHAND KNOT.

3387. A TWO-STRAND EYE SPLICE (%2770) is used in starting a marline seizing. The ends are tucked but once and are then buried carefully under the turns of the seizing.

3388. The *round seizing* (1). This is the most common and practical seizing for general purposes. Make eight or ten lower turns toward the eye. When the riders, one less in number than the lower turns, have been added, the end is stuck down through the initial EYE SPLICE and two crossing turns are added. The back of the knot is shown in the fourth and fifth illustrations. Finally bring the end up *between* the two crossing turns and *under* two turns and finish off with a WALL KNOT, or if the seizing is of yarn or marline, make an OVERHAND or else a FLAT KNOT (%3385).

3389. This knot, closely related to %3385, has the loop underneath and the end differently disposed.

3390. The SEIZING HITCH is often, wrongly, called CLOVE HITCH.

3391. The round seizing, finished off with a FLAT KNOT.

3392. A SEIZING KNOT that is shown by Öhrvall in *Om Knutar* is closely related to the FLAT KNOT (%3385).

3393. A *stopping* is often finished off in a way similar to a whipping. This is not a very good stopping, although it does very well for starting service. The ends of the eye are secured as in %3361.

3394. The *round seizing* (2). Put on eight or ten turns, starting at the bottom. At the top, pass the end down underneath all turns to the bottom again and stick it up through the EYE SPLICE. Add seven or nine riders and stick the end down below the top *under turn*. Add crossing turns and finish off with SEIZING HITCH %3390.

3395. *Small seizings* either with or without riders are commonly finished off with the SEIZING HITCH (%3390). Generally an OVERHAND KNOT is tied in the end.

3396. A wire EYE SPLICE is always served and seized. The turns are started at the neck. When they have reached the thimble, the end is shoved through from front to back, several of the last turns are crossed, and the end is rove through again, this time from back to front. When there are three crossing parts on the back and two on the front, the turns are knotted with a FLAT KNOT (%3385).

3397. The *clews of square sails* originally were a part of the bolt-rope, and were seized in with a short round seizing. Fourteen turns were allowed for the eye.

3398. A *double strapped block* had a "double crossed" round seizing.

3399. To *seize in a thimble by hand*. Stop the cringle with marline or small stuff at the breast of the eye with several round turns, and hold it in a vise with the legs uppermost. With racking turns heave the eye around the thimble. Put on a round seizing. If the rope is large, a Spanish windlass (%2024) may be required.

3400. *Racking seizings* are always used with wire rigging or wherever excessive strain is expected. The under turns are racked and set up with a marlingspike. The riders are set up hand taut and crossing turns are added. Finish off as a round seizing.

3401. *Double racking seizing*. When sufficient turns have been taken, stick the parallel ends out to the surface at the center. Take riding turns with each end away from the center and lead ends underneath and back to center. Add crossing turns with the ends in opposite directions. Tie a WALL in each end, on opposite sides.

3402. A *lineman's seizing* is made of "electric tape."

3403. When a CUT SPLICE was not served over it was seized. Beginning with round turns at the neck, it was finished off at both ends with racking turns through the crotch.

3404. A *single* or *simple clinch* is also called single throat seizing, *pigtail* and *monkey's tail* when used as a stopper. It has neither riders nor crossing turns and the ends are secured as in %3393. Pigtails are put in running rigging about ten feet from the ends to prevent unreeving at the fair-leader racks.

3405. A "*half a crown*" is put in the middle of the back ropes and passes around the end of the dolphin striker. It has both riding turns and crossing turns.

3406. A CUCKOLD'S NECK is a SEIZED EYE without riding turns, but with crossing turns; it is to be found in jib and staysail pendants, bridles for various purposes, and in can-hook straps.

3407. An INSIDE CLINCH has two or three round seizings (%3395), which are termed "bends." Formerly the RUNNING CLINCH was the conventional method for bending a cable to the bower anchor. It was also used in making fast buntlines and in securing bowline bridles to the cringles.

3408. The OUTSIDE CLINCH was sometimes used on an anchor, or "on any rope you wish to let go smartly," but the INSIDE CLINCH was safer. Any clinch, to be safe, must be smaller than the ring or cringle to which it is bent.

3409. A nineteenth-century *forestay collar* was placed around the bowsprit and was lashed to the ends of a double forestay.

3410. A *throat seizing* is a seized round turn. It is used when turning in deadeyes, and has *riding turns* but no *crossing turns*. The end of the stay or shroud should first be stopped around the deadeye as shown. At sea a Spanish windlass (%2024) is generally used for the purpose. Ashore rigging screws and vises are employed.

3411. *Single crossing turns* are sometimes added to one side of the seizing of a CUCKOLD'S NECK (%3406). This was done with a marling needle, on the inner side of the seizing only.

3412. In the nineteenth century a throat seizing was sometimes used for strapping blocks. The crossing turns were taken only in

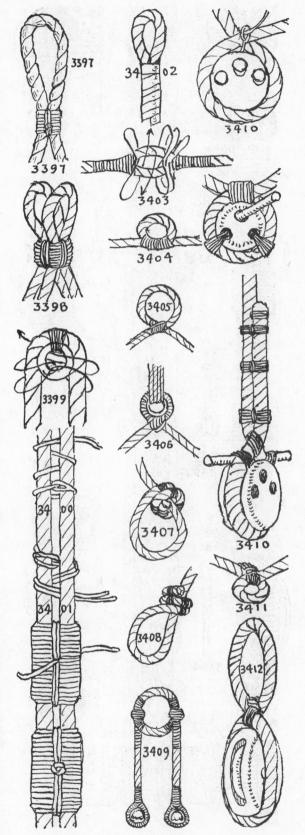

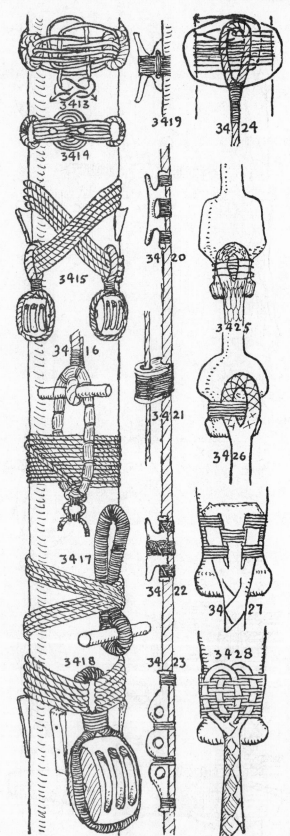

the upper half of the seizing. A sail needle or marling needle was used, and the seizing is similar to #3411.

3413. A *rose seizing*, or *rose lashing* (1), is used when blocks or stays are to be lashed to spars. The eyes are lashed with racking turns and, in finishing off, the end of the seizing is passed alternately over and under each part and when the rope has been expended the two ends are reef knotted together.

3414. *Rose seizing* or *rose lashing* (2). For securing a stay. This is similar to the last except that, in expending the two ends, they spiral in the same direction and pass between the layers of racking turns, one outside the other. They are finished off with two WALL KNOTS.

3415. To suspend jear blocks, for supporting a lower yard: Two stop cleats were nailed to the mast, screws not being used in the last century. The eye of each block was then lashed separately as depicted.

3416. A *garland* is a heavy selvagee strap that serves as a sling; it is lashed around a lower or top mast when it is to be hoisted. Shears are first put in place, then the garland is lashed with a series of turns, beginning at the bottom. The upper turn is led to the bottom and the two ends are throat seized together twice (#3410). The tackle block should be toggled, not hooked, to the garland, as a hook is not strong enough for so heavy a lift.

3417. A *French garland* is for the same purpose. The toggle prevents the garland from rendering. The tackle block is toggled to the eye shown above the lashing. Both garlands are pictured in Luce's *Seamanship.*

3418. A *block lashing* for a derrick arm is given by Knight. Cleats are nailed to the derrick arm and the eye of the block strap is lashed with racking turns.

3419. A *mast cleat* from Lever (1808). (See #1630.)

3420. A galvanized iron *shroud cleat* is lashed as pictured, *without* crossing turns.

3421. *Seizing trucks* or *fair-leaders* are lashed here and there in the rigging, generally to the shrouds. They are sometimes of elm, sometimes of lignum vitae.

3422. A *lashing cleat* of wood (oak or hickory) is seized as pictured; the central seizing is snaked to save wear on the turns. This is also from Lever (1808).

3423. A *comb* or "*bee*" cleat, or a fair-leader, is lashed wherever required. Anything, except a block, that alters or directs the lead of a rope, is called a fair-leader.

3424. A *rose seizing* is employed to secure the eye of a footrope to the yard. A series of turns are passed about the yard and alternately over and under the parts of the eye. It is finished off by reeving between the racking turns in circular fashion and tying an OVERHAND KNOT with the end.

3425. A *ship's bell rope* is sometimes seized to the flight of the bell clapper in a manner similar to the rose lashing.

3426. The common method is to put on a *stopping* through the eye.

3427. A *whiplash tongue* of three parts is secured as shown here.

3428. If the thongs have been middled, they are seized in much the same way. It is well to shellac the whipstock and to seize while it is still tacky.

3429. A whiplash with a single tongue should first be laid down the whipstock and seized, and then laid up and a series of riding turns added. The end of the seizing should be tucked under the last four or five turns.

3430. If the tongue of the whiplash is in two separate parts, the parts may be laid down the end of the whipstock opposite each other. First shellac the tip of the stock and, after the shellac has set, serve the end tightly. Then seize on the tongue. Preferably the stock should have a button at the end as pictured in #3429.

3431. This fly driver is not to be confused with a swatter. Its purpose is merely to direct flies into the open. I saw it in a Negro log cabin at the Kinloch Plantations on the Santee River. A helical groove was whittled around the end and a jute cord was tied at the tip and then laid tightly in the groove and held there. A piece of heavy Manila wrapping paper had been deeply fringed (about twenty inches) with streamers about one half inch wide, and an uncut border of about five inches was left. This border was swabbed with flour paste and snugly rolled around the end of the stock. The cord was tightly wound in wide turns up and down several times over the pasted border and finally the bound section was neatly hitched over.

3432. Gammoning is a method of holding down the bowsprit. It was universally in use before the days of the bobstay, and was still in service in 1869 according to Admiral Smyth. The gammoning started with a RUNNING EYE through the hole in the cutwater and consisted of eight to twelve round turns. A half dozen frapping turns were added, hove taut and the end seized to the standing part. On large ships chain gammoning was used.

3433. A series of racking turns taken through single holes in the cheeks of a pilot ladder are knotted at both ends of the seizing. The hole should be no bigger than is necessary.

3434. "*Preventers*" were used in the Navy for quick repairs in the lighter rigging. The same thing was called a *leech rope stopper* when employed to repair a parted boltrope. A man was lowered in a BOWLINE from a yardarm above the break to make the repair, which was done just as a deck stopper is applied. (See #1765).

3435. To pass a *head earing*, first splice it to the cringle with a LONG RUNNING EYE. Lead it through the strap on the end of the yard and back through the cringle. Follow with two turns around the jackstay and through the cringle, then three or four turns through the cringle and around the yard *and* the jackstay. Add a crossing turn under the jackstay and then one around all; finally secure the end with a CLOVE HITCH.

3436. A *reef earing* is secured to the *lower* eyelet hole of a REEF CRINGLE with a LONG RUNNING EYE. The sail is hauled well out by two turns around an outer cleat. One turn of the earing is taken around the yardarm only and then the end is expended with a number of turns through the cringle and around the yard; the end is clove hitched to the lift.

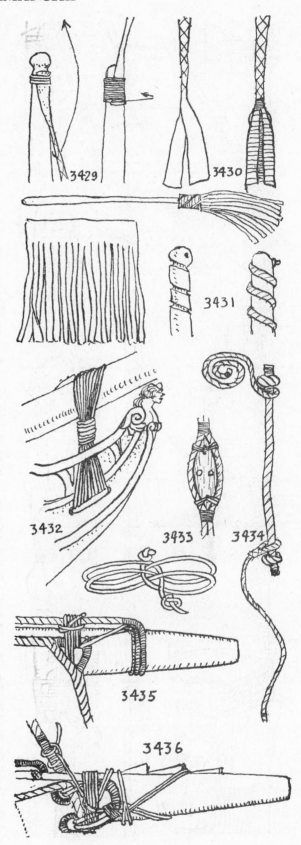

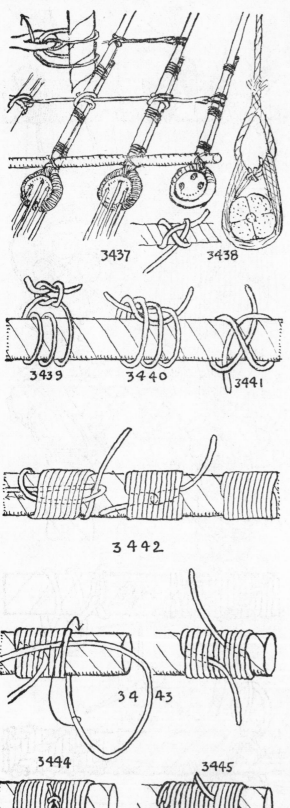

3437   3438

3439   3440   3441

3442

34 43

3444   3445

3437. Shrouds are always said to be "rattled down" although foi many years they have actually been rattled up. Ratlines are light tarred hemp lines, passing between the shrouds, that serve as the rungs of a ladder by which sailors climb aloft. The ratlines bear an Eye Splice at either end, and these eyes are seized to forward and after shrouds, and are clove hitched to the intervening ones. The two lower ratlines are heavier than the others, to support the crew before the men stretch aloft. The ratline is seized at its forward end. Every fifth ratline, termed a *catch ratline*, goes to the swifter or forward shroud; the remainder are seized to the second shroud.

Generally they are fifteen to sixteen inches apart. On boys' training ships they may be only thirteen or fourteen inches apart. Such ratlines on a merchant ship are termed in derision "ladies' ladders."

The Clove Hitches are always on the outer side of the shrouds, and they are tied so that the lower end of the hitch *always* leads aft.

Wire shrouds are served so that ratlines will not slip.

3438. The Eye Splice in a ratline is tucked once and a half times and is seized in a horizontal position, for the sake of neatness. The manner of passing the seizing is illustrated alongside. A lanyard of marline is eye spliced through the end of the ratline. There are no crossing turns and the end of the seizing is secured with a hitch at the center of the eye.

3439. *Stopping* may be either a temporary whipping or a seizing, the commonest variety consisting of a few round turns finished off with a Reef Knot. The purpose of a *whipping* is to prevent the end of a rope from fraying. A *seizing* holds several objects together.

3440. The Strangle Knot is a neater and more secure stopping than the last. It is first tied loosely and then worked snug.

3441. The Constrictor Knot is the firmest of the three *stoppings* shown, although the Strangle Knot is perhaps neater.

3442. *Common, plain* or *ordinary whipping* is tied by laying a loop along the rope and then making a series of turns over it. The working end is finally stuck through this loop and the end hauled back out of sight. Both ends are then trimmed short. A whipping should be, in width, about equal to the diameter of the rope on which it is put.

3443. The *sailor's whipping* is the one that is most commonly seen. An end is laid down and a number of turns taken about it, after which it is hauled taut and laid out. Then the second end is laid back along the rope and additional turns, not less than four, are made around the end, with the loop that is formed. It is finally tightened by pulling on the two ends.

This is the whipping with which the "all square" and "sharp up" marks are put in braces, which aid in trimming sail at night, when a sailor must "see with his hands."

3444. *American whipping* is the name given by the British to *sailor's whipping* (⚹3443) when the ends, after being hauled out at the center, are reef knotted together before being trimmed. It is said to be the "best whipping for hawsers." When putting this and ⚹3443 in the bight of a rope, the last four or five turns are taken around a needle or a loop, and are hauled back tightly.

3445. A *rigger's whipping* is made in the same way as Stopping ⚹3393. The ends of the Eye Splice are tucked once and are held by the turns.

3446. *Palm-and-needle whipping*, or *sailmaker's whipping*, is the most satisfactory of all. Two of them, a short distance apart, are put in the ends of every reef point, where the constant "whipping" against the sail makes the wear excessive; this is said to be the source of the name *whipping*. Where the whipping is a short one, the needle is thrust through one strand from one side of the whipping diagonally to the other as shown. To start: Wax a double thread and stitch twice through a strand to secure the end. After the correct number of turns is taken, the thread is wormed back to the left side, and then thrust as pictured and wormed again in the same way as before. The worming having been followed twice, the end is trimmed close, after a final diagonal stitch.

3447. A *second method* for *palm-and-needle whipping* is employed when the width of the whipping is too wide to be crossed with a single diagonal thrust of the needle. In this case the needle is thrust straight through a strand at one side of the turns and then is wormed to the other side of the whipping, where it is thrust through another strand. Then it is wormed back again to the first side. The needle is thrust either three or six times, to make the worming either single or double.

3448. The British Admiralty *Manual of Seamanship* gives a very ingenious way of whipping that superficially resembles palm-and-needle whipping. An ordinary three-strand rope is *opened* for one and one half to two inches, after first stopping the end of each strand. A waxed twine is middled and a loose loop laid around one strand, then both ends are brought out at the opposite cuntline. The rope end is carefully laid up again and stopped. The loop and the working end having been left long, with the working end make the required number of turns and put the loop that was left at the bottom over the top of the strand that it encircles. The standing end is now pulled taut, which draws up the loop and tightens the worming. The standing end is next wormed to the top and reef knotted to the working end, between the strands, where it does not show.

3449. In a similar way a whipping may be put on a four-strand rope. Open the rope for a couple of inches and with a waxed thread make a figure eight between the strands as pictured. The two loops are left well open. Turn both loops down and the *standing end up*. With the working end put on turns around the rope and the standing end, which has been led to the top. Worm the two loops to the top and put each over the end of the proper strand. With a pricker pull on the standing end and tighten both loops. Finally bring the two ends across the top between the proper strands and reef knot them together. The objection to these two whippings is that the lay is disturbed and the end of the rope tends to "blossom."

3450. *French whipping* is merely a series of HALF HITCHES. Start with a RUNNING EYE and finish up with the end tucked back under the last few hitches. The ridge of the hitches should follow the lay of the rope.

3451. *Crown whipping*. Knot or side splice a piece of marline or fishline to the center of another piece that is twice as long. Place it in the center of the rope and, with ends protruding at different cuntlines, crown them continuously to the right, pulling all tight at each operation. When the length is sufficient tuck each end back under the last two or three crowns, using a needle for the task.

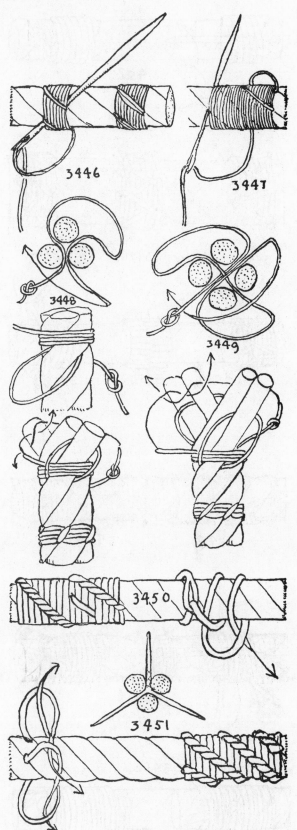

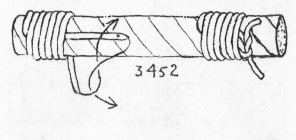

3452

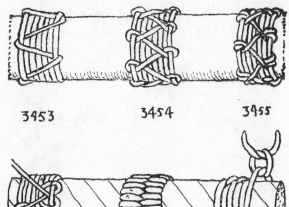

3453   3454   3455

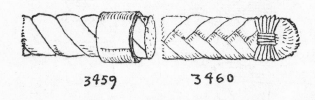

3556   3457   3458

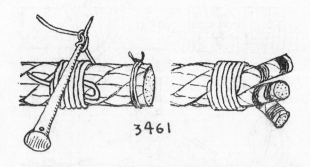

3459   3460

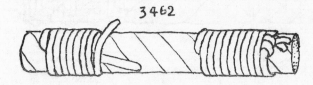

3461

3462

3452. *Portuguese whipping* is the quickest of all to apply; the ends are merely reef knotted together. It is given by Esparteiro in his *Dicionario de Marinharia* (Lisboa, 1936).

3453. *Snaking* is added to whippings on yoke ropes, manropes and pointings. On large ropes it is added for security. It is added to a sailor's whipping (＃3443). With a needle the end is thrust under and over the outer turns at either end.

3454. A regular *snaking* is made by taking a hitch at each outer turn.

3455. A *round turn* is sometimes taken about the outer edge, which is presumably a decorative feature.

3456. A Cow Hitch Snaking.

3457. A decorative snaking. Tie ＃3440 with *five* turns. Thrust the needle alternately left and right, each time under the two outside turns and at right angles to the rope at either end. The initial five turns should be slackly taken.

3458. *West Country whipping* was the name given by Biddlecombe in 1848 to this particular practice, but most subsequent seamanship books, including the British Admiralty *Manual of Seamanship*, have modified the name to *West County whipping*. The thread or yarn having been middled, the ends are passed around the rope and are half knotted together. Each end is next led one *half* a turn to the opposite side and again the two are half knotted. The ends are again led one half a turn around the rope and *half knotted*. This is continued on alternate sides until the required width is reached, when the ends are securely *reef knotted* and cut off. I have not seen this whipping used but it has this advantage: if any part breaks it will be a very long while before the whole whipping lets go. The break will be evident and the whipping can be replaced in time.

3459. A *lineman's whipping* is made of "electric tape." Although far from handsome, it is very practical. Start with the end laid under one strand of the rope.

3460. *Sinnet whipping* requires a palm and needle. It is used on the ends of gaskets, points, robands and anywhere where FLAT or FRENCH SINNET is practically used. A photograph among the frontispieces shows *sinnet whipping* tied on an old *cat-o'-nine-tails*. A number of turns having been taken, the needle is thrust through the flat of the sinnet and brought out again at the other side. Generally three crossing turns are added in this manner, then the end is buried with one or two invisible stitches.

3461. *Cable whipping* requires more care than hawser whipping, because the rope is harder laid. The end of the cable is first stopped temporarily and then a whipping of marline is clapped on a number of inches from the end. The turns are taken in a direction contrary to the lay of the cable and hove very taut with a marlingspike. The stopping is next removed and each of the three component ropes is whipped twice, preferably with a palm-and-needle whipping, but if the ropes are large ＃3442 will be found about the best.

3462. Wire whipping is made with a special, soft galvanized iron wire that is made for the purpose. But if this is not available, galvanized stovepipe wire will serve adequately. Pliers may be used to tighten but care must be exercised not to score the wire. The first end is laid under the turns as in whipping ＃3452, and instead of knotting, the ends are twisted and hammered flat.

CHAPTER 41: DECORATIVE MARLINGSPIKE SEAMANSHIP (APPLIED KNOTS)

Add to all this labor, the neat work upon the rigging; the knots,
Flemish-eyes, splices, seizings, coverings, pointings and graftings,
which show a ship in crack order.

RICHARD H. DANA, JR., *Two Years Before the Mast*, 1841

In the days of hand-made rope a great quantity of "*small stuff*" was wanted aboard ship, which could have been easily supplied by the ropewalks ashore, but was more cheaply produced aboard ship by the sailors themselves. Many ships carried small ropemaker's winches for the purpose. But most of the stuff used by the sailor for his "fancy" knot work was made wholly by hand. The material for this manufacture was called "junk." Old cable and rope were chopped into workable lengths, opened and reduced to their component yarns. These yarns were twisted together by rolling with the palm, against the thigh or belly, or else they were twisted up between thumb and fingers and then were laid up into foxes and nettles. These were called "twice-laid stuff." Yarns were larger around then than they are at the present time, and the hemp fiber then used was stronger than Manila. A single yarn of hemp was supposed to bear a weight of a hundred pounds.

Nowadays small stuff approximating foxes and nettles can be procured, ready-made, at slight cost. Italian marline will serve nicely instead of a Spanish fox, and a good quality of common marline is much like an ordinary fox. Four-thread stuff (two-strand) and six-thread stuff (three-strand) are made for crab- and lobster-pot buoy ropes, and these closely resemble nettle stuff.

[549]

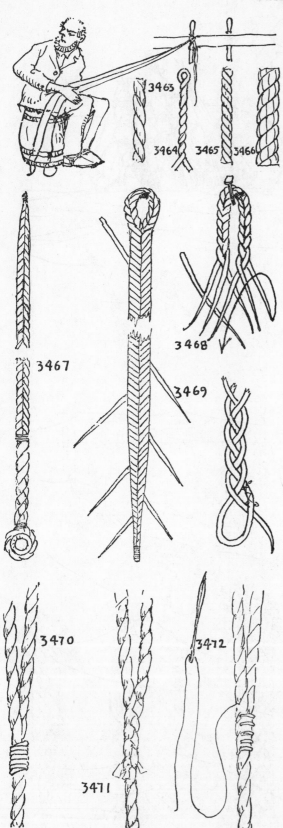

3463. *Spun yarn* consists of two or three (occasionally four) rope yarns, placed together and first rolled between palm and knee and finally twisted tightly with the fingers. The direction is contrary to the lay of yarns. It differs from rope and cord, inasmuch as no additional twist is imparted to the individual yarns. Before slacking up, the spun yarn is well rubbed with a patch of old tarry canvas. It is at once wound into a tight ball.

3464. A *Spanish fox* is made of a single rope yarn that is split into either two or three equal parts. The several parts of the yarn, originally right-handed, are given a left twist, which first untwists the original lay and then twists the individual parts reversely. The several parts are then laid up together right-handed.

The purpose of reversing the twist is to smooth out any inequalities which are bound to exist in the interior of an old hard-laid rope. *Spanish foxes* are more commonly made of the two halves of a single yarn. As the length grows, other half yarns are added by tying ROPE YARN KNOTS, the ends being first scraped to a taper to keep the knot small.

3465. An *ordinary fox* is formed by laying up two or three right-handed yarns, which makes the fox left-handed.

3466. *Nettle stuff* or *nettles* (also called *knittles*, *knettles* and *nittles*) are composed of two, three or (very seldom) four *foxes*. They are right-handed. Three or four rope yarns laid up together would also be termed nettle stuff. In fact, a good working definition of nettle stuff might be: "A hand-made rope of about the size of clothesline, or smaller."

The four products so far described are rubbed smooth with a patch of old tarred parceling.

3467. Stirrups support the *footropes* which hang below the yards. One end has a THIMBLE SPLICE through which the footrope is rove. Before *jackstays* came into use the other end was platted for a length sufficient to pass two or three times helically around the yard, to which it was nailed. Small leather washers were placed under the nailheads.

3468, 3469. *Robands* and *sea gaskets* are made alike but in varying sizes. A *roband* serves to bend a sail to either a yard or a jackstay, and a gasket is for lashing a furled sail. Three, four or five foxes are middled and platted together from mid-length into a FLAT SINNET for a distance sufficient to form an eye. All the strands are then brought together and laid up into a wider FLAT SINNET for a short distance, where another single strand is introduced. After another interval, equal to one round of the yard (for a gasket, but less for a roband) a single strand is laid out, and then at a shorter interval another from the opposite side of the sinnet. This continues until there are but *two* strands left, where one of these is tucked back parallel with the one last laid out, making three in all. The two opposing ends are spliced or seized together, and the three parts are then platted to the end and seized.

3470, 3471, 3472. Although in making reef points, gaskets, etc., it is commonly recommended to "lay out *nettles* and trim them off";

unless they are first secured in some manner the sinnet will fret. An end may be tapered and seized to a remaining nettle (#3470). It may be side spliced, in which case it requires only one tuck per strand (#3471), or else a few stitches with sail twine will be sufficient to hold it (#3472).

3473. *Double reef points* are made in the same manner as gaskets but the eye is much longer in proportion. Three foxes form the eye and the manner of platting is the same as already described. A *reef point* is rove through the eyelet hole in the sail from either side. Then a round turn is put in each of the two eyes and the opposite point is rove through the doubled eye, after which a man on either side of the sails hauls them home.

3474. *Robands* are made and rove in much the same manner, but the eye is shorter and is not doubled; moreover there is a short leg and a long leg and the short leg is rove from the back of the sail forward.

3475. A *single roband* may have two sinnet tails at opposite ends with a rope center, in which case it is bent to the headrope, as pictured, and is seized in.

3476. *Single reef points* are started at the center with SEVEN-STRAND FLAT SINNET and are platted and tapered toward both ends. In bending these a SINGLE OVERHAND KNOT is placed in each. After the *point* is hove taut and rove through the eyelet hole, another knot is added close to the other side and this is hove taut by placing the feet against a block shiv that is put over the *point*.

Points got their name because of their tapered or pointed form when they were made of sinnet. When *rope points* came into use, in the latter part of the eighteenth century, they were first called reef hanks; but it was the older name that survived.

3477. The *harbor gasket* is made of FRENCH SINNET #2976 and is reserved for dress-up occasions. In the Navy they were tarred black for appearance' sake and were lined with white duck so as not to mark the sails.

To make: Take six nettles, middle them and lay up a section of SIX-STRAND ROUND SINNET sufficient to take the thimble. Lay out one nettle and lay up a section of ELEVEN-STRAND FRENCH SINNET in length equal to one round of the yard. Then taper for an equal length.

The eye is served over and the thimble is seized in.

The earlier harbor gasket had a FRENCH SINNET EYE and no thimble.

3478. Another harbor gasket is started with an iron ring instead of a thimble, and the ring is covered with RINGBOLT HITCHING (#3605).

Several nettles are middled and rove through the ring, and a single nettle is eye spliced to the ring in order to give an odd number of strands. This is not necessary, but it is customary, as an odd number makes a symmetrical FRENCH SINNET. One and one half tucks to the strand are sufficient for the EYE SPLICE since the nettles are to be laid up into sinnet.

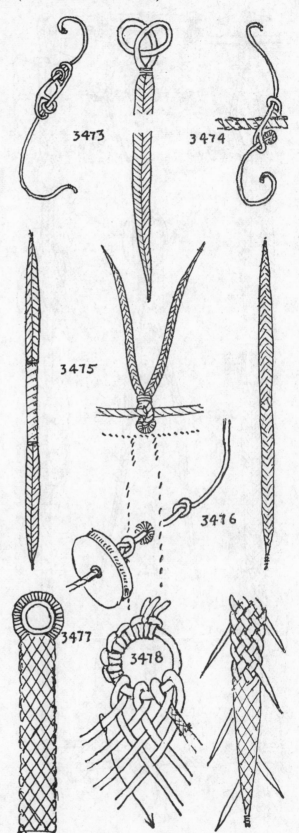

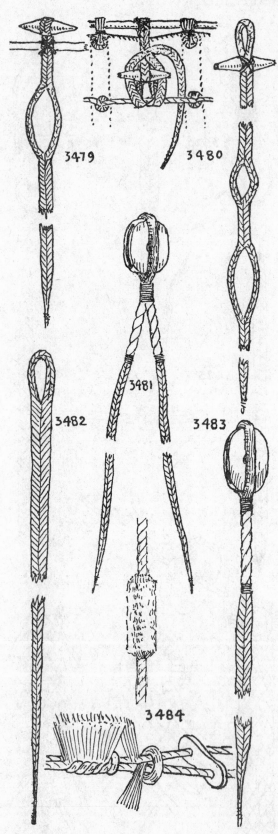

3479. *Reef beckets* appeared on naval ships and large merchant craft about 1860 and remained in use on training ships until the end of the century, but they were seldom seen on ordinary merchant ships.

To make: Double four nettles and make sufficient sinnet to form an eye around the toggle. Seize in the toggle and plat six inches of Eight-Strand Flat Sinnet. Then divide the strands and make an eye eight inches long. Next taper for nine inches more and seize, as described for ⚹3469.

3480. Another *reef becket* is designed to pass around a yard, after which the end is rove through the eye and the neck of the eye is seized to the jackstay. The eye is first formed, and then a section of Eight-Strand Flat Sinnet is made that is four inches longer than the round of the yard. The strands are next divided and an eye of four-inch length is made, followed by six inches of Eight-Strand Flat Sinnet; another eye eight inches long is made, and a final taper of nine inches is added.

3481. A *double tail block* is fitted with a long strap that is middled and seized. A short length of the rope is left, a snaked whipping (⚹3453) is put on, and the legs are opened up into yarns that are tapered and laid up into five nettles. These nettles are platted into Flat Sinnet and given a palm-and-needle whipping (⚹3446).

3482. *Sinnet earings* are made with a Long Eye that is bent to the eringles with a Bale Sling Hitch. They are made the same as gaskets and robands but are heavier and longer and are tapered gradually the full length. Eleven strands of four yarn nettles are used and, if great strength is required, the earing is made longer so that more turns may be passed. The method of passing is illustrated as ⚹3435 and ⚹3436.

3483. A *single tail block* is strapped with an Eye Splice. The single tail is made as one of the double tails already described (⚹3481).

3484. Railroad Sinnet (1). Aboard ship there is a constant rubbing and grinding of ropes, spars and sails one against another. Wherever there is danger of galling and fraying it is necessary to interpose something of a softer or smoother texture in order to save wear. Anything used for this purpose is termed *chafing gear*.

Railroad Sinnet is a kind of chafing gear, so named because it is made over two long parallel tracks of marline or other small stuff. These are usually stretched while being worked between the fife rail and the lee pin rail. Between these tracks, short thrums are knotted and packed tightly together.

Old rope or cable is chopped into short lengths of six inches to one foot, and the pieces separated into yarns. With back to the rail, and with tracks tucked under one arm, the boatswain middles a thrum and leads it over both tracks, one end down each side, then brings the left end up between the tracks and follows with the right one. He grasps the two ends and draws them strongly toward him. Each thrum is jammed against the preceding one. A stick, a few inches long, with either a notch or a hole at each end, is kept a few inches in advance of the work, to hold the tracks apart. Holes are preferable as the stick cannot then fall to deck. The completed sinnet is wound helically and snugly around ropes and spars. Around a rope the end is tucked and seized in; around a spar the end is tacked or nailed.

3485. RAILROAD SINNET (2). Baggy wrinkle is the name applied to the RAILROAD SINNET chafing gear of a fisherman's topping lift. There are a number of variants of the name, which may mean that it is not yet old enough to have become standardized. The title that heads this paragraph is from Waldo Howland. Gershom Bradford speaks of "*bagy wrinkles*," Rodman Swift of "*baggy winkles*," James B. Connolly of "*boogy winkles*." Captain Daniel Mullins calls them "bag wrinkles" and Charles G. Davis, "bag-a-wrinkle." Bag or baggy may be derived from the bag of the sail where the topping-lift chafe centers and where wrinkles are apt to form, unless the wind is strong enough to flatten them out. Winkles or wrinkles are spirally marked sea shells that wind in much the same manner that RAILROAD SINNET twists around the lift in forming a baggy wrinkle. It is an amusing name, of recent coinage, but its origin is already obscured.

3486. RAILROAD SINNET (3). Platted corn-husk mats as well as chafing gear are made of THREE-STRAND SINNET thrumming. Rope yarns six to eight inches long, or the crotched ends of corn husks, are introduced at the top left of the sinnet each time that a strand is led to the right. When the strands have crossed the sinnet one to three times they are laid out at the right side.

A *corn-husk rug* is either sewed flat as other braided rugs are or else it is made thicker by being sewed with the sinnet on edge. In the latter case all ends are laid out at the upper edge of the sinnet.

The fuses of Chinese firecrackers are platted in this same way to form the crackers into "bunches."

3487. *Sallie tucks*, *tucking* or "*sallies*" are used on the bell ropes of chimes to cushion the hands when pulling. They are usually made of bright-colored worsted yarns, the different colors serving to identify the bells. A number of short yarns are tucked between the strands and these are trimmed off evenly. If four-strand bell rope is used, the yarns are stuck through the center of the rope in alternating directions and crowded together compactly. The length of the "*sallie*" is governed by the size and swing of the bell.

3488. Marline or other two-strand material is thrummed with the fingers or else with a large blunted needle. A number of long yarns are threaded at one time and sewed either back and forth or over and over. They are packed down hard and trimmed.

3489. For heavy chafing gear a single strand may be removed from a three-strand rope and separated into yarns, which in turn are cut up into thrums. These are rove through the remaining two strands in the manner illustrated. Thrums are sometimes called "rovings," and they have also been called "rovens," "fillers," and "filling."

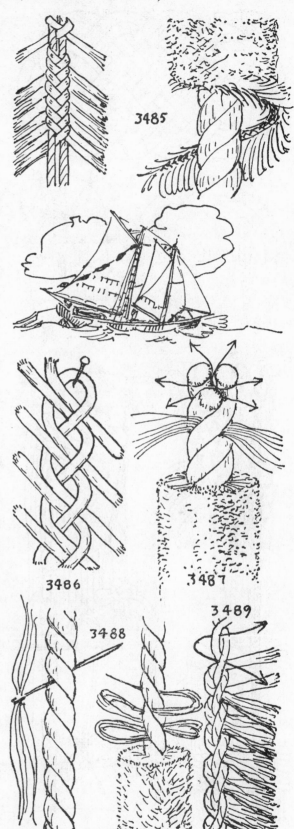

3485

3486

3487

3488

3489

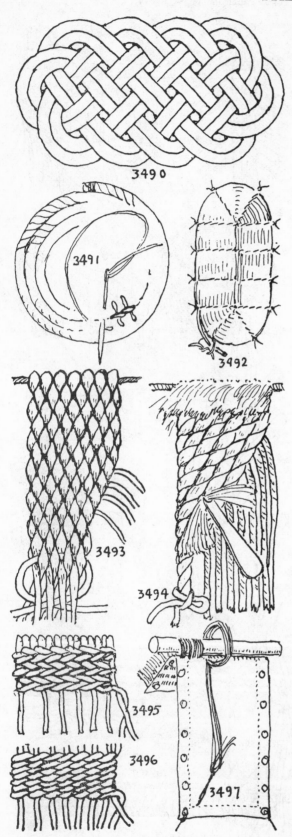

3490. The PROLONG KNOT is described at length on page 362. It is one of the BASKET WEAVE KNOTS.

Mats of one sort or another form the greater part of chafing gear.

3491. A *Flemish flake* with the turns sewed together on the back with a herringbone stitch is often tacked to the deck for the helmsman to stand on and is also used to take up the thump of sheet blocks.

3492. *Door mats* are frequently made by sailors ashore. Marline or lobster cord warps are sometimes used and these are half knotted around each turn of the rope. The flakes may be made either round or elliptical. It will take about three hundred feet of 2½-inch rope and twelve pieces of white marline to make the mat pictured. The HALF KNOTS are tied alike, GRANNY-fashion. When the rope is exhausted finish off the warps with REEF KNOTS. Both ends of the rope should be whipped.

3493. To "shoulder" a *woven* or *sword mat*. The sketch alongside shows how sword mat #2964 may be tapered if an odd shape is required to pass around a bolt or cleat on a yard. The method of doing this is given in detail with the hammock clews, page 588. Either one or both shoulders may be narrowed. OVERHAND KNOTS are tied in the strands that are laid out.

3494. *Punch mat* (also called wrought mat) is often spelled either *panch* or *paunch*, but I can find no record of its being pronounced at sea in any way except *punch*. Originally it was the name for any large, heavily padded and thrummed mat. Nowadays it always refers to one made in a certain way. The method of making this is shown as #2963. A wooden tool with a notched end, called a punch, has been employed in thrumming a mat but more often this is done with the fingers alone. Thrums six to eight inches long are middled and punched halfway through the fabric and the bights are afterward punched back again through a different part of the weave. When all thrums are in place the bights are trimmed.

To *selvage off the bottom of a punch mat*, stretch a rope for the foot. Pass the left strand around this, remove the second strand and back the left strand into its score two, three, four, or more tucks, withdrawing the second strand by the same amount. Half knot opposite ends and leave out, one on each side of the mat. Treat the remaining pairs the same way, but bringing all ends out at different lengths of the mat. Each end is opened and trimmed to the same length as the thrums.

3495. *Crown and wall mat.* This is made the same as the foregoing, but instead of always leading from the right side and working downward diagonally to the left, this one is started at the right side and each strand in turn is engaged with its next neighbor. At the left edge the process is reversed and the strands are worked back to the right.

3496. A *crowned mat* is much the same. In the illustration it is started on the left side, each strand in turn is engaged with its neighbor to the right, but when the right edge is reached the mat is turned over (to the left) and the back side is worked across exactly the same as the front, from left to right.

3497. To thrum a canvas mat that is to be laced about a spar: Take a sailmaker's "rubber" (seam rubber), turn the canvas edge down a short distance parallel with the edge and crease it well. Take a roping needle with several long yarns on it and sew over and over along the crease and around a spool. With a very sharp knife or razor blade cut the yarns in a straight line along the top of the spool. Make another crease a half or three quarters of an inch away and repeat.

3498. A MOUSE or mousing (plural "MOUSES") is a knob that is raised on the messenger to prevent nippers from slipping. Enough spun yarn is wound around the messenger to form a shallow knob. Then a small rope is worked through the strands of the rope and jammed against the MOUSE much in the same way that a snaking is added to a whipping. The two ends are reef knotted.

3499. A MOUSE on a stay was formerly of spun yarn, but Lever, in 1808, recommends that narrow parceling, marled down, be used instead. This method of "parsling" was first mentioned by Falconer in 1769. "MOUSES" are grafted over and the grafting is carried down the stay a short distance. Then, when the stay is served, the ends of the grafting are covered over.

3500. *Puddening an anchor ring* is serving it with several parallel lengths of small rope. Lever describes it as made with five. These are stopped onto the ring and, after being set up with a heaver and trailer, are seized and snaked. The method of employing the heaver is described under worming (#3337).

3501. A *pudding* was formerly a pad to protect a mast where it is crossed by a yard. Later it was any sort of a *soft* fender. The name comes from *bagpudding*. Brady (1841) says, "If intended for a yard generally it is covered with leather or rawhide, if for a mast it is pointed over for neatness."

Puddings are also used for fenders.

An EYE SPLICE is put in both ends of a short piece of rope and spun yarn is wound around it. When the shape is satisfactory the pudding is marled and covered either with grafting or hitching. Nowadays they are often canvas-covered.

One of the neatest ways to make a pudding is as follows: Take a piece of hawser and splice in two THIMBLE EYES for the ends, leaving all ends very long for crowning. Whip all strands and tuck them twice. (Tuck bights instead of ends, and draw the ends through afterward to prevent torsion.) Raise the pudding with old strands, first, and finish with spun yarn. Crown both sets of strands to the right until they meet. Side splice (#2828) extra strands as needed, an equal number at each end. When the pudding is completely covered, lay opposite ends "in and out" and scatter the joints before trimming.

3502. A *dolphin* is started the same as a *pudding* but is not padded. An eye is spliced in each end of a short rope and the rope is wormed and parceled, and then grafted over.

3503. The *bow fender* of a towboat is similar to a pudding, being large enough and soft enough to allow a tug to push directly against the side of the ship. Sometimes bow fenders are made of punch matting, thrummed, stuffed and sewed together on the back, and sometimes they are hitched over. They may be made around dolphins with several THIMBLE EYES spliced in; by means of these they are lashed into place.

3504. A *dolphin* is also the name for a series of fenders, made on one rope, which pass in a continuous line below the gunnel of a boat. The ends are lashed at the stern. These are made as described for #3501.

3505. A *fisherman's fender*. Fishermen's gear is essentially practical, although often far from shipshape. This fender consists of several turns of an old hawser served over with smaller rope. The ends of the latter are rove through the end turns of the former.

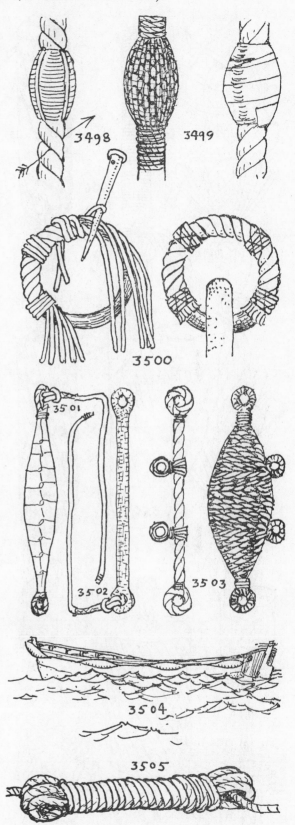

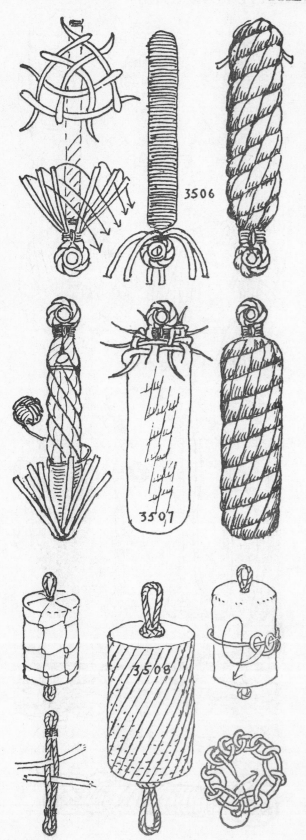

3506. CROWN SINNET-covered *boat fenders* are both common and practical. Take a piece of 2½-inch rope, middle it and seize in a THIMBLE EYE. Take a piece of hawser the length of the fender and whip both ends. If it is desired to add to the diameter, wind spun yarn evenly around it until sufficient in size. Open both ends of the rope as far as the eye, then crown the strands as in the lower illustration. Make several tiers of CROWNS (see SINNET №2913), then push the short piece of hawser down into the center, work the CROWNS taut around it and put a CONSTRICTOR (№1249) around all to hold the hawser core in place while working. Continue to crown until sufficient length is made, then add the knot pictured at the top, and, when partly drawn up, pull the ends well back with a wire loop under the sinnet. Then draw everything taut.

3507. CROWN SINNET *boat fender* of four-strand rope. This will be found more shipshape than the one just described. Middle a long rope and seize in an eye. Take a shorter piece of the same size rope and seize in or side splice below the thimble seizing. Lay these three up by hand into a cable the length of the desired fender and seize strongly. Cut off the shortest rope and open the two remaining ends. Make a CROWN SINNET of the eight strands around the cable core. When the neck is reached, crown as KNOT №956 and with a wire loop pull the ends well down under the sinnet and out to the surface, get everything taut and cut off the ends flush. If the strands are pulled very taut they will work back out of sight. Roll the fender under a plank or beat well with a mallet to even out any irregularities.

3508. A *hitched fender*. Splice the ends of a short piece of rope together, form a strap and seize in an eye at either end. Make of the desired shape and proportion by worming and winding oakum or other material around the doubled rope. If a large fender is planned, make a cylinder of corrugated board around the strap, and, after marling carefully, cover it over with sacking and stuff tightly with oakum or cotton.

Take a long single strand of 2½-inch rope and cover the cylinder with needle hitching (№3544). Use a marlingspike, heavy wire loop or pliers for tools. This is simple but heavy work. Finish off very tightly at the neck of the EYE SPLICES. Tuck each strand through the two parts of the strap below the eye and form a STANDING TURK'S-HEAD (№1283).

In covering a fender with CROWN SINNET, the strands may be untwisted slightly, which allows them to lie flatter as they pass over each other. But in general the tighter the lay, the greater the resistance to surface wear.

The making of fenders may be expedited if the helical crowning method described as №2931 is resorted to. But this method requires greater skill than crowning in successive tiers, so if possible have a mate to help.

3509. "UNDERHAND ROUND-TURN HITCHING." A bumper is used when landing heavy cargo, particularly kegs and casks. An X-shaped dolphin is formed of two pieces of heavy rope, seized together where they cross. These are inserted in a heavy sack or a carton and an EYE SPLICE is placed at each of the four corners. The cavity is then well stuffed.

A Noose is put around one end of this, with the end of a small rope, and a series of turns (not too close together) is taken to the bottom end, where a Half Hitch is made with the working end around the last turn. The lead is then deflected at right angles across the end of the sack or carton to the back, where a series of underhand round turns is taken around each rope that is crossed. This is shown in the upper left drawing. When the front and back are completely covered, the lead is again deflected at right angles, in the same way as before, and the remaining four sides are completely covered. The bumper is finished off with a Clove Hitch and the end is tucked out of the way.

3510. An Overhand Round-Turn Hitching is a bit simpler than the former, as the end is stuck under one strand only at a time, instead of two. The process of making the bumper and winding the first set of turns is the same. These two are made generally of small stuff instead of single strands. They are often a part of the equipment of brewery trucks, where they are used to drop kegs from the tailboard.

3511. Footrope Knot fender. Two sections of rope are required and these are wormed, parceled and canvas-covered. Middle the ropes. Seize an eye in the center of one, then reeve the other rope through this eye and seize them together snugly. Serve them for a length equal to the proposed knot, and tie a Wall at the bottom, which completes the first drawing. Lead the four ends upward in a right helix and stop them at the eye. Crown the ends to the right and tuck them downward, one tier at a time, over one and under one, to the bottom. (The final tuck will be under two, which includes the original Wall.) After drawing up, seize the four ends.

3512. An old *sinnet fender* of canvas-covered strands. An eye is seized into a doubled rope, with a round seizing having five riding turns. Then the rope is opened and the six canvas-covered strands are laid up into Six-Strand Round Sinnet (⚹3021) to the end, which is canvas-capped, whipped with seven turns and snaked as ⚹3454. Two Turk's-Heads are added, of small stuff, about eighteen-thread cotton rope. The upper one is a Five-Lead, Four-Bight, Three-Ply Knot, the lower one a Six-Lead, Five-Bight, Three-Ply One (see Chapter 17).

3513. A Turk's-Head *fender* of small hawser, made by Rodman Swift. It provides a fender that is practically round and very neat. If the Turk's-Head is to be three-ply only, it will not require a core. Tie a Three-Lead, Four-Bight Turk's-Head (⚹1305), form an eye with a bight near the center of the rope on the inside and put in a throat seizing (⚹3410) and a round seizing close to it. Follow the lead around once with each end, and work taut with a marlingspike. Serve or ringbolt hitch over the eye.

3514. A second way is *to worm a short rope* with which to form an eye, and then seize and cover the eye with Ringbolt Hitching (⚹3604). Tie a round Spritsail Sheet Knot (⚹887) with the ends, wind a little spun yarn over the knot to round it out and place a Monkey's Fist (⚹2206) over it.

3515. A Flattened Turk's-Head makes an excellent fender for a dinghy. The ends should be seized on the underside and the eye made with a throat seizing in the outer ply.

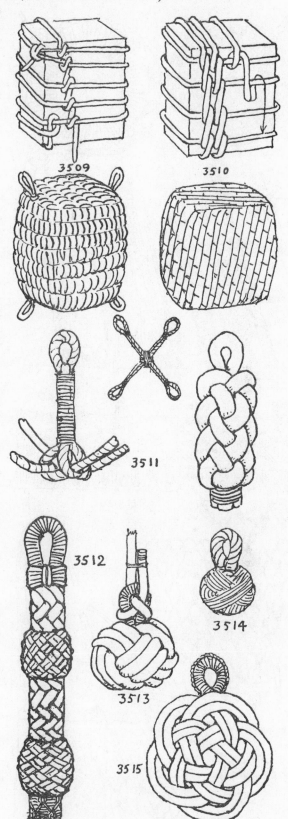

3509   3510

3511

3512   3514

3513

3515

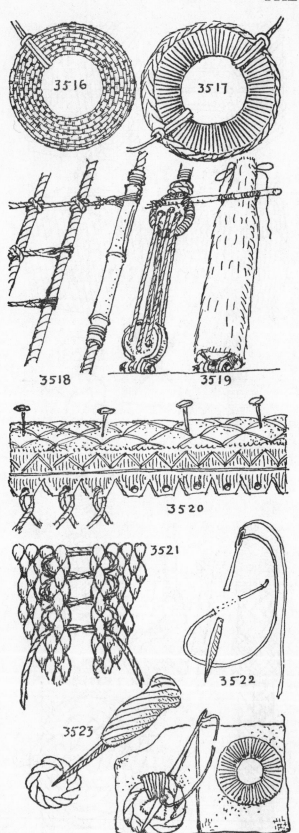

3516. A *grommet fender* "is merely a rope grommet grafted over" according to Alston. Grafting is described as ✳3557, this chapter. The grommet should be wormed and parceled before grafting, and may also be served with spun yarn.

3517. An old truck-tire fender, unfortunately, is about the most practical fender there is. Fishermen use them naked and they are far from handsome. But if they are ringbolt hitched with rope or large strands from a rope, they become as handsome as any (see ✳3605 or ✳3606).

3518. *Scotchmen* are fenders or chafing gear of stiff material that are seized or lashed to shrouds and stays. The simplest are made of bamboo, split down the middle, with the valves gouged out. They are also made of other woods, of iron and of hide. Iron ones are used to protect the rigging from the futtock shrouds. Ashore iron pipes are put over telephone-pole guys either to serve the same purpose or to protect pedestrians.

3519. *Hide Scotchmen* are of pickled hide with the hair still on. Holes are punched along the edges and they are laced into place with rawhide thongs. Applying them is spoken of as "hiding" a stay or a spar.

3520. *Automobile-tire Scotchmen* are either nailed or laced according to where they are placed. The edges are serrated with a chisel and mallet and the holes are punched. I have seen them on fishermen, neatly made and aluminum-painted, and they were not half bad in appearance.

3521. To sew two *punch* or *sword mats* together. Two marline needles and doubled marline are required and the two selvages are joined with a *cobbler's stitch*.

3522. This shows the sailor's way of securing his thread by making an OVERHAND KNOT in the canvas itself. A first short stitch is taken and then a second stitch of equal length crosses underneath the first one diagonally.

3523. In making *eyelet holes* in a sail, *small grommets* (✳2864) of the right size are first to be made, either a single strand or a full-size piece of marline being used, according to the size required. The ends of the grommet need be stuck but once. A hole is pricked through the canvas, either with a stabber, which has three edges, or with a pegging awl, which has four. The grommet is placed on top of the hole and the needle is stuck down at the far side of the grommet and up through the hole. One should always sew to the right along the far side, and put the stitches close together, covering the grommet completely and evenly. A number of threads are put in the needle at a time and these are well waxed and sewed "over and over."

Often small galvanized iron rings are used in sails instead of grommets, and sometimes grommets are made of wire.

The sailor is a very proficient needleman. Not only has he his own wardrobe to care for, but the ship's as well. The canvas is a constant care, requiring various roping, seaming, and mending stitches. For these purposes three-sided needles are used, which on occasion may be fully seven inches long, and these are thrust with a leather-mounted thimble called a palm (✳101B). For wardrobe and fancy work smaller needles of the same sort are used, and an ordinary uncapped thimble is worn. It is not at all uncommon to see a sailor wearing his thimble on his thumb.

DECORATIVE MARLINGSPIKE SEAMANSHIP (APPLIED KNOTS)

I was reared in a town that was steeped in nautical tradition and the youth of my town scorned almost any activity that was of inland origin, unless perhaps it had to do with the pioneer, the cowboy, or the Indian. So, although "store" *baseballs* were preferred in practice, every boy felt the urge at some time to make himself a ball, in a manner that was undoubtedly handed down from an older generation of seafaring ancestors.

Around a hard round core of ivory, stone, rubber or even a glass alley (agate) spun yarn or cord was wound meticulously, round and tight, to form a ball. And this was stitched over (※3544) with hard fishline and soaked in thinned shellac or rigger's tar. I remember many such balls being made, but very few ever being played with. In late years I have conducted a search for one, but have failed to find a single survivor. The puppies of the last two score years must have accounted for them all. For such needlework a somewhat blunted needle is used. If the object is of large diameter, the end of the needle may be heated in a candle flame and bent slightly to allow easy entering.

Most sailors' needlework with which I am familiar is in the nature of coverings. But there are colored worsted embroidered pictures of ships made by foreign sailors that would not greatly lower the average of many contemporary fine arts exhibitions, and I have seen elaborate doilies and cushion covers of knotted and sewed wicking that are said to have been made at sea.

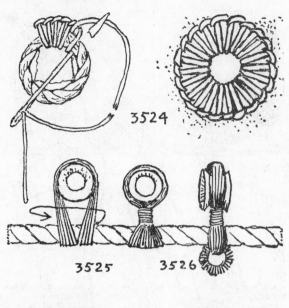

3524. *Hitched eyelet holes* were often made by the sailor on his clothes and ditty bags, and I have a ditty bag that has "buttonholing" (※3611).

3525. *Thimbles* are frequently added to the boltrope of small-boat sails without the employment of eyelet holes. After the groove of the thimble is well filled with sail twine, it may be served, before frapping turns are added. The drawing shows a thimble lying *parallel with the sail.*

3526. If the *thimble* is to be *at right angles with the sail*, round turns are taken and frapping turns added. The drawing shows a thimble seized to an eyelet hole.

3527. *Seizing in a square-sail reef point.* This is done with needle and thread and frapping turns are added. In reefing square sails the points are led either to the yard or around the jackstay so that the weight of the sail is below the spar. The reef point is sewed to the upper edge of the eyelet hole. Formerly reef points were knotted in, as ※1938.

3528. The reef point of a fore-and-aft sail is sewed with the same stitch, but to the bottom of the eyelet hole, as the pull is upward, away from the boom.

3529. Another way of sewing in reef points on fore-and-aft sails. After the point is rove the two halves are seized together *through* the sail, just below the eyelet hole, and frapping turns are added on both sides of the canvas.

3530. *Crowfooting a reef point* is a method used on large fore-and-aft sails. Grasp the point at the center with both hands, push the two parts together, at the same time twisting them strongly against the lay. The lay will open and as the twisting is continued a loop will erupt from each strand. Seize the point at either side of the loops and reeve it through the hole. Stitch the loops flat to the port side of the sail.

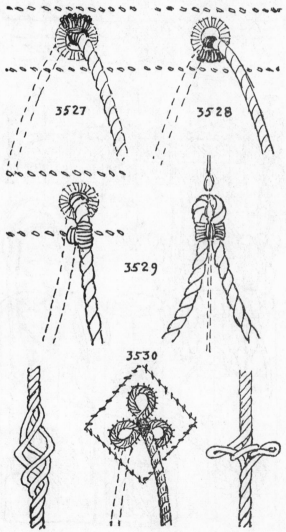

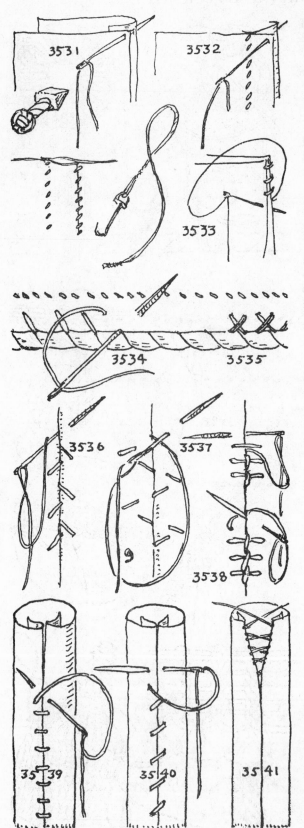

The blade of a sail needle is much larger than the shank and eye, so that it makes a large hole when it enters and the thread is easily drawn through. A number of threads, each from a different spool, are threaded at the same time, the number depending on the weight of the canvas to be used. Sometimes as many as six spools are employed. The needle is thrust with a palm, of which there are two sorts—one for seaming, and one for roping.

3531. Cloths are sewed together with what is termed a *flat seam*. The *Naval Expositor* of 1750 called it a *monk's seam*, but Admiral Smyth, in 1867, says that a monk's seam is a reinforcement between the two other lines of flat seaming.

To sew a flat seam in a new sail: With the cloths lying flat on the loft floor turn up the right selvage edges of the different cloths and crease them well with a "seam rubber." Nowadays a colored thread in the canvas marks the width of the seam; formerly it was marked with a pencil. Take two cloths, arrange as in the first drawing, the selvage of the top cloth above the crease of the lower. Sew from left to right and away from you (as shown by the arrows). When the seam is finished, open the cloths and rub the seam down flat, with the seam rubber.

3532. Fold back the second cloth and sew the selvage of the first cloth to the doubled part of the second cloth. Rub the seam smooth.

3533. "*Round seaming*" is the earliest practice; it is mentioned in the *Expositor* of 1750. The two selvages are laid together without overlapping and the edges are sewed over and over.

3534. *Roping stitches* are also taken to the right, and more threads are required than in seaming. These are well waxed and rubbed. The boltrope is held on a stretch and the canvas is sewed on slackly to make allowance for the stretch of the boltrope, which is always three-strand. The needle is thrust first through the boltrope, then up through the doubled canvas edge. In heavy sewing a heaver (#101J) is used to pull the canvas snugly down into the cuntlines. Several turns of the thread are taken around the heaver and then the heaver is twisted. Square sails are always roped on the after side, fore-and-aft sails always on the port side, to save wear of the stitches against the spar. Ropes are sewed to a doubled edge or hem termed the *tabling*. The end or point of the heaver is cupped and a reluctant needle may be shoved well into the rope by this means.

3535. *Cross stitches* are added at all clews, cringles, splices, etc.

3536. The sailor's stitch, also called "baseball stitch," is employed in mending garments and sometimes in mending sail.

3537. The double sailor's stitch is used in mending where the material is very weak.

3538. *Herringboning*, or herringbone stitch, is the preferred stitch in mending a ripped sail or where two selvages or hems are to be brought together.

3539. A round seam (1) is ordinarily made in covering manropes, yoke ropes and the like.

3540. The round seam (2) is preferable, the only difference being in the direction of the needle thrust. The covering will be firmer if the stitch passes through the rope. A worming will also contribute to the firmness of the covering.

3541. An "*invisible stitch*" is sewed with two needles and the two stitches are taken directly opposite each other and along the exact

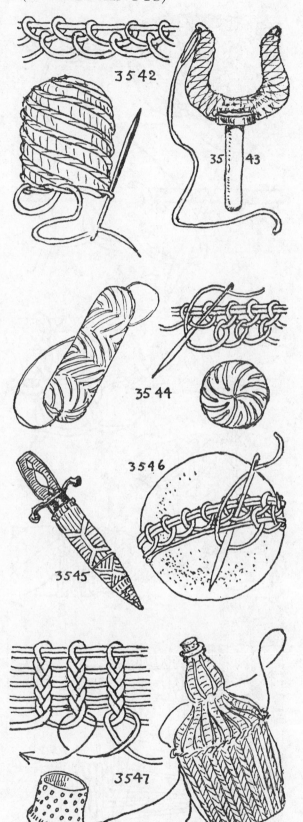

tage of the hems. The width of material required must be ascertained and the canvas marked precisely with a pencil. If well done, this makes the neatest manrope, as the seam will scarcely show.

3542. The *round-turn stitch* is the simplest of the *covering stitches* employed by the sailor. It is worked either to the left or to the right, and frequently sections of left and right are worked in alternation. The same stitch presents two different aspects, according to whether it is drawn taut in the direction of the needle's progress, or contrary to it.

3543. *Muffled oars* were generally muffled rowlocks. In the whaling service the covering was of marline hitched over with needle stitch ✳3344. Frequently leather bushings were added, or else the marline was thrummed with a needle and rope yarns.

3544. *Needle hitching* is the name for the commonest of the sailor's covering stitches. It is also called *half hitching* and *hitching over*. Admiral Luce speaks of it as "loop stitch." At sea it is often referred to merely as *hitching*. I should repeat here that at sea the verb *to hitch* does not apply to knots.

A single knot that is designated "a hitch" is always "made fast" or "put on." Needle hitchings are commonly started with two or three turns around the thickest part of the object to be covered. If the object tapers much it is worked in both directions away from the fattest part.

This particular object is a sailor's needle case, shaped from the solid wood. The center is bored out, the outside is turned on a lathe and a shoulder is left for the cover to fit against. The round turns already mentioned are taken at the edges of the cover and body, and are worked both ways toward the two round ends. As the ends are reached, hitches are omitted at regular intervals to allow the covering to close at the center. Gimlet holes are made at the two ends and a light lanyard is rove through and knotted on the inside of the box. The illustrations show that the hitches have been alternated at regular intervals from right-hand to left-hand hitches, which gives a "herringbone pattern." Needle boxes are from six to ten inches long, generally of soft wood but also of tin, albatross wing, bone, beef marrow bone and bamboo.

3545. The knife sheath that is pictured here is covered with needle hitching ✳3544. The pattern is made by working some sections horizontally, some vertically and others diagonally. To taper a section to a point, make each line with one less stitch than the preceding one.

3546. This stitch is similar to ✳3344 but an extra turn of the line is taken around the object after each row of hitches is added. This line is encompassed by the next row of hitches. The illustration shows the covering of a baseball.

3547. The rib stitch, when finished, closely resembles knitting, particularly if the stitches are kept well together. If they are widely separated the ribs generally helix in one direction or the other.

At sea many bottles were covered with hitching (generally ✳3344). Loops, through which a lanyard was rove, were added at the sides and on the bottom. As the bottle narrows toward the neck, hitches were omitted at regular intervals. These bottles were taken ashore by the sailor when watering, wooding and recruiting. Alongside is pictured a sailor's thimble.

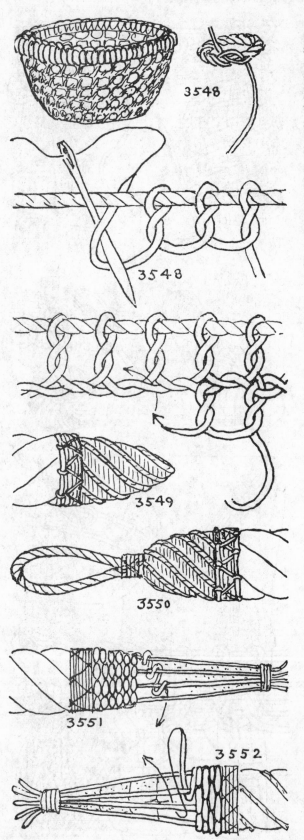

3548. A *fishline basket* was stretched over the bottom of a bowl or bottle and soaked and then allowed to dry. When dry it was shellacked and painted. Similar baskets of crocheting were made ashore, but whatever their origin, their destination was the same: they always stood on the whatnot in the corner of the parlor and held souvenirs. The one shown here is sailor's work; it was started with a small grommet in the end of the fishline at the bottom. Eight stitches (as illustrated) are taken around the grommet, then an in-and-out turn is taken about the structure, which passes through the bottom loops of each of the hitches. The short end of the grommet is left eight or ten inches long, and the two ends are brought together. The needle end takes a turn around the loose end, as illustrated at the right in the lower drawing. Then another series of hitches is added. It will be noted that the turn of the cord that is added after the first line of hitches doubles the number of the bights at the lower edge. The next tier of hitches is taken through all these bights, which gives sixteen hitches, the next tier omits every third bight, which gives twenty-four hitches, and the next tier also omits every third bight, which gives thirty-two hitches. Five uniform tiers are made with the thirty-two hitches and the final row is buttonholed over, making the top rim of the basket.

Pointing was named and described by Sir Henry Manwayring in 1644. Cables were pointed to make reeving through the hawse pipes easier, and to keep them from fraying. They were frequently finished off with an eye so that they could be hauled out with a smaller rope. On running rigging the avowed purpose of pointing was to make reeving off tackles easier, but another and equally important purpose was to prevent sailors from pilfering ropes' ends for their own use. This purpose was mentioned by Sir Henry Manwayring in 1644.

3549. Luce calls this a *hitched end*. It was made with a needle. With a knife or scissors, trim the end into the shape illustrated. Take a number of close turns at the base and then hitch to the end as ⌗3344. Snake the first four or five turns.

3550. A SHORT HAWSER POINTING, *with an eye*. The eye in this case is for bending a heaving line. To make: An EYE SPLICE is put into a short piece of small rope. The hawser is opened up and the small rope is short spliced to the heart, or the center yarns, which are laid up for the purpose. The ends of the splice are trimmed and the hawser is tapered and hitched over as ⌗3549. The neck of the point is whipped and snaked.

3551. UNDERHAND ROUND-TURN POINTING is put on with a needle. Whip and open the rope, and lay back and stop a number of the surface yarns. Scrape the inside yarns to an even taper point. Parcel and marl or else cover them with adhesive tape. Next lay down the surface yarns tightly and seize them at the tip of the point. Take the long end of the whipping that was first put on, "thread" it on a sail needle and with it progress around the *pointing*, first forward, *under* two strands, then back *over* one, and forward again *under* two, etc. Drop out yarns if the taper requires. When the point is covered, whip and snake the tip.

3552. OVERHAND ROUND-TURN POINTING is made in much the same way but the needle is thrust back under one, then forward over two, and back under one, forward over two, etc., until complete.

3553. OVERHAND ROUND-TURN GRAFTING is also called OVERHAND SPANISH HITCHING, and resembles the pointing just shown. But in this case the turns are in the fillers and not in the warp. An overhand round turn is taken with each filler in rotation around the warp, which is at all times held taut. The warp should be of stiffer material than the fillers. Tarred fishline is excellent for the purpose.

3554. UNDERHAND ROUND-TURN GRAFTING, also called UNDERHAND SPANISH HITCHING. Each filler in rotation takes a round turn about the warp, and the warp is kept straight. The texture of this suggests snakeskin and is very handsome.

3555, 3556. HALF KNOT GRAFTING can hardly be told from the ROUND-TURN GRAFTING just shown. Structurally the only difference is that the turns in the fillers are taken in a direction opposite to the lead of the warp. To make: Half knot and pull on the warp sufficiently to keep it straight.

3557. To *point a rope in the early way:* Put on a whipping at some distance from the end, open the rope, and lay back all the *surface yarns.* Make these up into tapered nettles as described at the beginning of this chapter. Scrape the underneath yarns that were left and make a smooth pencil-point taper; parcel and marl it over with sail twine. It is now ready to graft, which is done in one of two ways. The first, using an odd number of nettles, has already been described as ⚓2678. The commoner way, perhaps, is to employ an even number of nettles. Arrange the nettles in two sets, the odd ones up, the even ones down. The long end of the whipping, which was left for the purpose, is to be used for the warp. With this warp take a SINGLE HITCH around the whole structure and draw it snug close to the juncture of the two sets. Next turn the upper set of nettles down and the lower set up, and single hitch again. Repeat until the point is covered. With the same warp, whip and snake the tip. Put a snaking on the base as well.

3558. Pointing with the yarns of the rope itself has been obsolete for many years. The recent method has been to cover with fishline, or sometimes with marline, after the rope's end has been tapered. A number of short pieces of line are doubled and seized at the base of the pointing with several turns of the warp. With these ends and the fishline warp, proceed exactly as described in ⚓3557. The illustration shows two turns at a time taken in the warp.

3559. The most common pointing is needle hitching, described as ⚓3544. Pointings are seldom used nowadays except on manropes, yoke ropes and life lines, or on any other rope that has to be frequently rove. Points are often needle hitched to the end, as in ⚓3549.

3560. Grafting three turns of the warp is shown here, the last being hitched as illustrated in ⚓3557. When the warp is multiplied in this manner it should be of much smaller material than the nettles. The tip, having been reduced to a few nettles, may be crowned and the ends withdrawn under the covering, employing a loop buttoner for the purpose. The base of the point in the illustration bears a TURK'S-HEAD.

3561. The texture of grafting may be varied. This illustrates a *point* in which two sets of nettles are always turned down and one set up. The nettles should taper and, in this case, their number is not divisible by three.

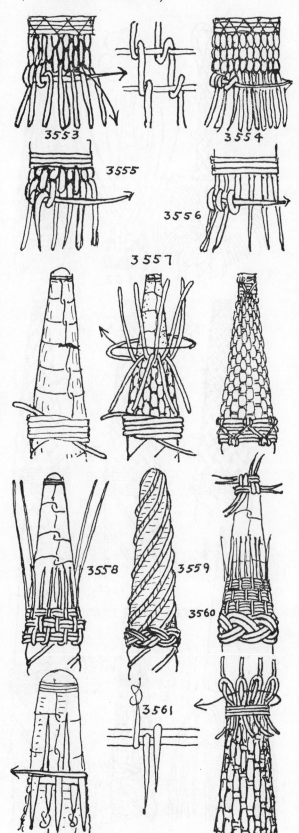

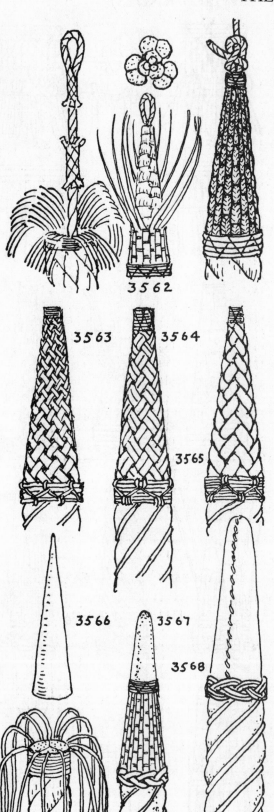

3562

3563   3564

3565

3566   3567

3568

3562. A *pointed cable* generally has an EYE SPLICE in the end so that by means of a smaller rope it may be hauled out the hawse hole.

A whipping is put on at about two feet from the end, for a twelve-inch cable. The end is opened, and the surface yarns laid back and stopped. The three center strands (one from each of the three ropes that constitute the cable) are laid up into a rope. A short piece of rope somewhat smaller than one of the component ropes of the cable has an EYE SPLICE put into it, and this in turn is spliced to the heart that was just made. The remaining yarns of the cable are trimmed and scraped to a symmetrical point, which is parceled and marled over. The surface yarns that were laid out are next scraped and tapered, waxed and laid up into an odd number of THREE- or FIVE-STRAND FLAT SINNETS. These sinnets are now grafted in the same way that the nettles were in ✻2678. The tip is whipped and snaked and also the base. This point is described by Sir Henry Manwayring in 1644.

ROUND SINNET, CROSS-POINTING and CROSS-GRAFTING are made alike, but ROUND SINNET has no core, CROSS-POINTING has a tapered core and CROSS-GRAFTING has a cylindrical core. All three require an even number of strands.

ROUND SINNET is made of four, six, and sometimes eight strands. Beyond that it requires a core and becomes automatically, according to the shape of the core, either pointing or grafting.

The strands for pointings should be tapered; if the strands have insufficient taper, superfluous ones must be cut out from time to time.

3563. CROSS-POINTING is made like ROUND SINNET. The surface yarns are laid up into an even number of nettles, which are divided, and alternate strands are turned down. Proceed as directed for ✻3024. Finish off in one of the ways already given—that is, with a seizing, a snaking or a TURK'S-HEAD. Steel (1796) gives "CROSS-POINTING" as the proper covering for a MOUSE or splice.

3564. A coachwhipped point is similar to the last but is either two-, three-, or four-ply. This is made directly as ✻3022 with double strands.

3565. A pointing may be covered with EIGHT- or TWELVE-STRAND SQUARE SINNET. The texture is distinctive, quite different from COACHWHIPPING (✻3564).

Still another texture may be obtained by helixing and seizing one set of strands at the tip of the pointing and then tucking the other set in the opposite direction, over two and under two, or over three and under three.

3566. Dana says, "If rope is too weak for pointing, put in a piece of stick." This cone is grafted over as ✻3557, with fishline seized to the rope's end.

3567. The tip of a point was often rounded and covered with white duck or turkey red cloth.

3568. Manrope points are often canvas-covered and painted. The canvas cover is a continuation or the beginning of the canvas covering of the rope proper. The ends of the worming are hidden at the base of the point by a NARROW TURK'S-HEAD.

3569. A *sailmaker's taper point* or *rattail* is put into the ends of the boltrope of small-boat sails, doing away with a leech rope. They are sewed to the leech just below the peak and just above the clew. Even large and heavy sails might be improved if leech rope were done away with and a wide and heavier tabling substituted.

Make the rattail as described in Long Short Splice #2643; continue the taper until only two or three yarns are left in each strand. Give the end a palm-and-needle whipping (#3446). Sailmakers, in derision, characterize a poorly made rattail, a "carrot."

3570. Rough Pointing. For use when a rope or strand is to be rove in an emergency. Open the end and, with a knife, shears or an ax, cut off the strands or yarns at different lengths with long diagonal cuts. Lay up and serve over, against the lay, with electrician's tape, starting at the base. Tallow well and reeve. Useful when splicing hawsers and cable.

3571. A cloth *cap* is sometimes seen on yoke ropes instead of knots. The macramé bag shown among the frontispieces has them of turkey red. The end is raveled and trimmed to acorn shape. A piece of red cloth is seized over the acorn and a Four-Bight, Three-Lead, Three-Ply Turk's-Head is put over the seizing.

3572. A *shroud cap*. The upturned ends of shrouds, after they have turned the deadeyes, are *capped* with brass, a piece of tarred canvas, rawhide or sheet lead to keep out the moisture. The end is served over and snaked.

3573. This illustrates a white cotton yoke rope with a thistle-shaped cap. The end is seized, raveled and encircled with a Four-Lead, Five-Bight, Three-Ply Turk's-Head over the whipping, the whipping having been first "built up," somewhat in the manner of a Mouse.

3574. The caps of yacht shrouds, before the days of turnbuckles, were sometimes finished off with a Wide Turk's-Head. A Five-Lead, Four-Bight, Two-Ply Turk's-Head is illustrated here (see #1322 for details of manufacture).

3575. *Pigtails* were put on the hooks of davit tackle falls on all whale ships. This allowed of instant and certain uncoupling. A Matthew Walker Knot was put in the end of the *pigtail*, the other end was opened and rove through the eye of the hook and then was strongly grafted (#3557) to the shank. The end of the grafting was seized around the hook and pigtail.

3576, 3577. Queues were worn in the Navy by enlisted men well into the nineteenth century. They were made in two ways—either laid up into a rattail similar to #3569, or else platted as ordinary Four-Strand Square Sinnet (#2999). A cask of eelskins, well pickled in brine, was kept handy. The queue was tightly worked to a point, and the eelskin, having been carefully rolled wrong side out into the form of a doughnut, was rolled back over the queue and seized. On dress occasions it was finished off with ribbon and bow. Every three or four months it had to be replenished, which was made necessary by the normal growth of the hair.

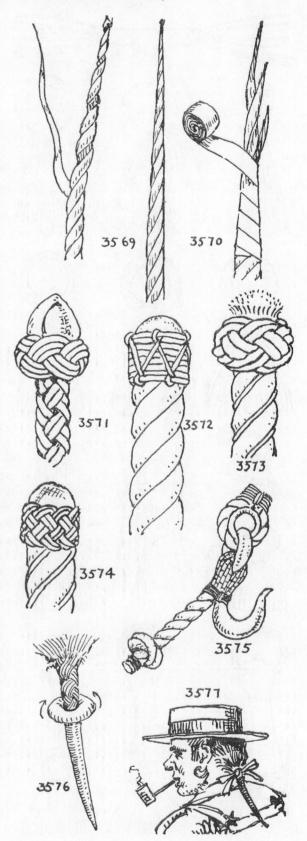

[565]

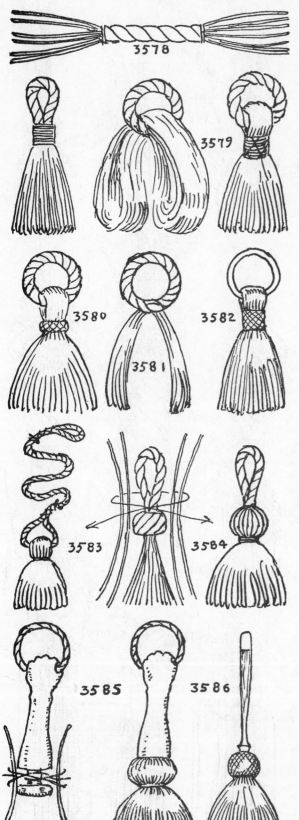

We are now come to the subject of swabs (deck, hand and dish). Ashore these are generally termed mops. Since they are structurally the same, tassels also will be discussed at the same time. Mops have wooden handles; deck swabs have a long rope lanyard and the head may be two or three feet long. Aboard oystermen very large swabs five to eight feet long are used for mopping up the starfish, which are the natural enemy of the oyster. A long line of mops is dragged over the beds and the starfish cling to them and are hauled aboard. Cabin, table and dish swabs are often fitted with beckets.

3578. The simplest swab is made of a middled and seized piece of rope with the strands raveled out. If for dishes or the table, the swab is used without a lanyard, but if for swabbing deck, a long lanyard, finished off with either a Dog's Point or an Eye Splice, is made fast to the becket with a Becket Hitch. As this knot is always used for the purpose, it is sometimes called the Swab Hitch.

3579. A more elaborate and fuller swab is made through a grommet. Rope yarns are wound into a skein, which is middled and put through the grommet and there seized and snaked.

3580. The swab just described is sometimes finished off with a Turk's-Head instead of a seizing.

3581. After the grommet is made, the ends need not be trimmed short; they can be utilized as the center of the swab, so that fewer turns need be added.

3582. A tassel is often made through a metal ring instead of a grommet, in the same manner as through a grommet (#3579).

3583. Deck swabs have long lanyards to give them greater scope. On small craft they are often dipped directly overside, but on larger craft they are dipped into tubs on deck that have been filled by draw buckets.

3584. Table and dish swabs are often ornamented. In this case a rope is formed into an eye which serves as a handle. A Matthew Walker Knot is tied in the six strands of the handle, and the ends are raveled out. Yarns are laid along the rope and are middled and seized to the handle just above the knot. They are faired, led downward, and a final seizing is put on, close below the knot.

3585. A groove is sometimes cut around a wooden handle and a seizing is tied over the groove; this allows the seizing to sink, making it firmer and less subject to wear. Elaborate dish mop handles were often made at sea to be taken home as gifts.

3586. Frequently the bulbous parts of mops and swabs are hitched over (#3544). As this is one of the points of greatest wear, the life of the mop is much lengthened thereby.

3587. A swab or tassel similar to #3584 may be made around a single rope by tying a FIGURE-EIGHT KNOT in the lanyard. After seizing the yarns above and below the knot, mouse over the knob with yarn and encircle it with a WIDE TURK'S-HEAD.

3588. Needlework covering #3544 or #3547 may be used on either swab #3584 or #3585. A small sail needle is required for this purpose.

3589. Tie two WALL KNOTS and a full MATTHEW WALKER KNOT near the end of a lanyard, put seizings over the swab between the knots and put NARROW TURK'S-HEADS over the seizings. Almost any of the swabs that have been shown may be employed for tassels, although some of the tassels that follow will hardly do for swabs.

3590. A tassel that is based on SHROUD KNOT #1590. Make this of three-strand rope. Manila is best, flax will do and cotton is apt to be a bit difficult. Tie the SHROUD KNOT as directed, then cut off the rope and ravel the inside rope as well as the outside one.

3591. A Chinese tassel. Whittle off the rims from a large linen thread spool. Countersink the bottom end to allow it to hold a knot. With an awl make six small holes from the outside into the center hole near the top end. With a needle reeve silk thread through all six holes and allow all ends to hang several inches below the spool. Seize temporarily with a CONSTRICTOR. Reeve a lanyard down through the center hole and knot with a FIGURE-EIGHT. Smooth out the silk threads and serve over the whole length of the spool with silk in two or more colors, and trim the tassel ends all square. Make with different-colored worsted if preferred, or with colored string. Secure the ends of the service as described for whipping #3443.

3592. This tassel is from a Chinese priest cord that is photographically reproduced among the frontispieces. The mold is turned on a lathe and the tassel is covered with netting, but ribbing #3547 will do nicely. A larger hole is countersunk at the bottom, the cord is rove through it and knotted. Silk, worsted, or cotton threads are middled and knotted into the groove with a CONSTRICTOR KNOT and then the ends are trimmed.

3593. A simple tassel for a fringe, window-shade or electric-light pull. Take a piece of cardboard of twice the length of the tassel and fold it lengthwise. Cut two crosswise slits near the top as shown in the illustration, and punch small holes at the ends of the slits. Lay a lanyard across the top. Wind yarn, thread or cord lengthwise on the cardboard. Tie two CONSTRICTOR KNOTS around the structure and through the slits. Secure the lanyard and draw the knots tight. Cut all strands at the bottom and remove the card.

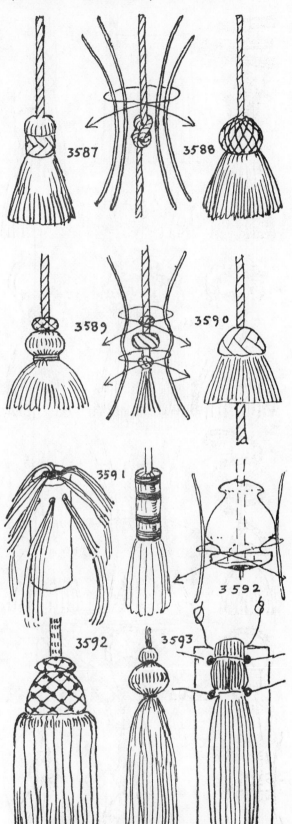

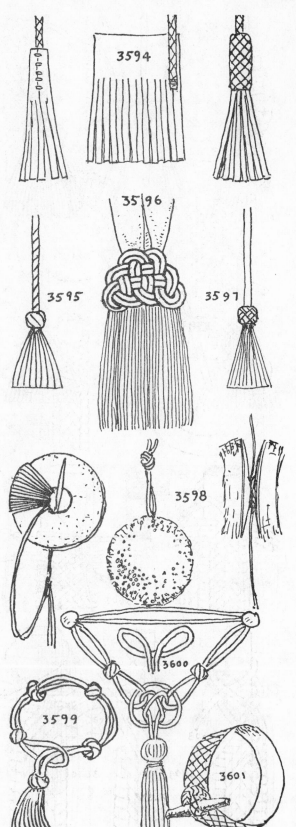

3594. A leather tassel for a horse's bridle. Slit only the bottom edge of a rectangular piece of leather into a series of narrow widths. Sew the end of a platted lanyard to the edge, on the rough side. Soak in warm water and roll the leather tightly around the lanyard. Roll underfoot to make smooth. Seize it temporarily to hold in position, sew it tightly in place. Cover the solid neck with a TURK's-HEAD of the same or other material.

3595. A tassel for cord shoestrings on bathing shoes and other summer footgear. The shoestring itself may first be made as described for foxes and nettles at the beginning of this chapter. If desired, different-colored strands may be laid up together. Having a string of the right length, tie a MATTHEW WALKER KNOT a little way from the ends and then ravel the end.

3596. This flat tassel of white silk was on the sash of a maroon bathrobe. Two FLAT KNOTS are required for each tassel and they are made three-ply and completed before being put in place. The tassel is made on a card as ⅜3593 and is sewed flat to the sash, which is pleated once to correspond to the width of the knots. Two knots are sewed to each end of the sash, one on each side covering the upper part of the tassel. Sew carefully around the edges and tack a few times through the center. To tie one of the knots: Enlarge the drawing and pin the knot out over the copy. Any other FLAT KNOT may be employed in this way if desired.

3597. Another shoestring tassel similar to ⅜3595 is an adaptation of DIAMOND KNOT ⅜735.

3598. A pompon is made by cutting out two flat doughnut-shaped pieces of cardboard, placing them together and sewing around and around with cord, string, or yarn, until the center hole is tightly filled. Then take a safety-razor blade and carefully cut along the edge. Insert a wire between the sheets of cardboard and wind it several times *very tightly* around the center core and twist the ends together. Finally remove the two cards and trim carefully with scissors until a uniformly round ball is made.

For a pendant ball for curtains, shades, fringes, etc., instead of wire take a stout cord and tie a CONSTRICTOR in the center bight, around the core between the two cards. Either leave the ends long for a lanyard or else bend them together so that the knot is hidden in the texture of the ball.

3599. A decorative curtain holdback may be made with a series of any of the TWO-CORD LANYARD KNOTS of Chapter 8. Make the loop first and finish off with a tassel.

3600. Another curtain holdback. Make tassel ⅜3584 with a light cord and a LONG EYE. Make a separate doubled cord with a loop at either end or else with two rings. Loop the tassel eye as in the upper drawing, bring one of these loops up through one eye of the holdback, do likewise with the other. Place one loop of the tassel over the other and reeve the tassel through them both.

3601. A more formal holdback may be made as sea gasket ⅜3477. A MULTI-STRAND BUTTON from Chapter 9 or 10 may be put in one end, or a neatly turned toggle may be seized in.

3602. Ringbolt Hitching. Whenever a ship laid to anchor, before the days of chain cables, her hemp cable was made fast by means of stoppers to two rows of ringbolts that were fastened along the deck. The chafing gear on these rings was termed "Ringbolt Hitching." Another old name for it was "platted rings." Nowadays it is sometimes called "hog backing," which is, I believe, a literal translation of the Swedish name. A picturesque needlework term, "cockscombing," has recently been applied. In the old days ringbolts were sometimes grafted over, but on slovenly craft they were merely served over.

Ringbolt Hitching is also put on the eyes of chest beckets and hammock clews, and occasionally it is seen on the clews of light sails, on the eyes of block straps and ditty bag lanyards. Single hitching is the simplest form. The circumference of the outside of the ring being greater than the inside, service did not fill up the spaces and was very apt to "work" and chafe. So hitches were added which filled up the interstices of the outer edge and held all firm.

3603. Double Hitching is used on a heavy ring—that is, one in which the wire is large in proportion to the diameter.

3604. *Kackling* or *keckling* is probably the commonest of the knotted forms. It consists of a series of alternate left and right hitches.

3605. Ringbolt Hitching, per se, is made with three strands which are led in regular rotation; each time a strand is worked, the lead is reversed and a Single Hitch taken around the ring. The ends should be seized when starting the hitching. When completed, a skillful workman will take a needle and, withdrawing a strand from one end, will lay in a strand from the opposite end, so that the ends are scattered as in a Long Splice.

3606. Five-Strand Ringbolt Hitching is worked in exactly the same manner and resembles Five-Strand Flat Sinnet. Keep all strands snug at all times. If the material is slippery the ring may be shellacked and covered while "tacky," or it may be parceled first with adhesive tape.

3607. The semblance of French Sinnet may be applied to Ringbolt Hitching. Having noted that the previous forms resemble Flat or English Sinnet, it was a simple matter to evolve this.

3608. Two-Ply Hitching is made with two strands which are both knotted to the right as pictured, and then they are reversed and both knotted to the left, and so on, alternately.

3609. Two-Strand Ringbolt Hitching superficially resembles ⌗3605, but the two strands have separate cycles: one is always hitched to the right and the other always to the left.

3610. Zigzag Hitching may be made with any number of strands, but three, four or five are ample. All are hitched in regular order, first to the left as pictured and then to the right, and so continued alternately.

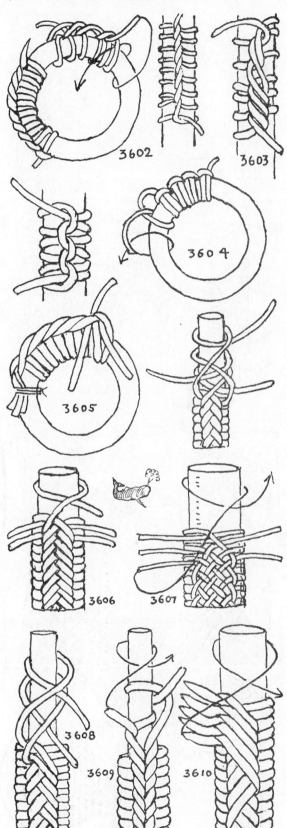

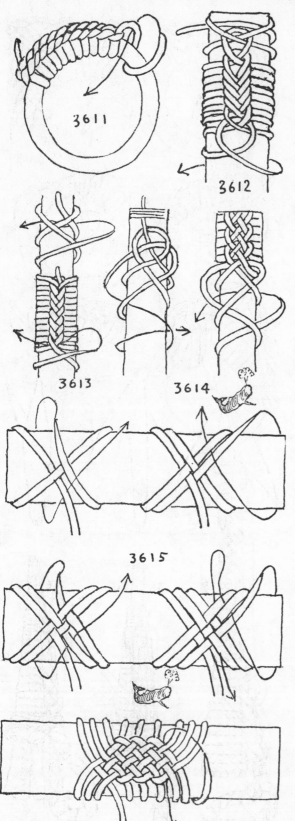

3611. *Buttonholing* is sometimes found around the eyes of chest beckets and on ditty bag eyelets. It is put in with a sail needle as are the remaining RINGBOLT HITCHES on this page. There are a number of different ways of making the buttonhole stitch. The technique given here was shown me by Mrs. H. R. Scudder.

3612. The stitch required in RIB STITCH HITCHING has already been shown as ⌗3547, but in ringbolt hitching only a single rib is made around the outer circumference of the ring.

3613. SINGLE-STRAND RINGBOLT HITCHING, per se. The needle passes under one more part than in ⌗3614, otherwise it is worked about the same, but the effect is a little fuller. It can scarcely be told, when completed, from THREE-STRAND HITCHING (⌗3605). Start as in the upper diagram, continue as below.

3614. SINGLE-STRAND FRENCH SINNET HITCHING. Start as in ⌗3613 but tuck *under one* part on the downward passage and follow with a hitch around the ring instead of a turn. When leading the strand from the left side, it is passed over the first strand and under the last strand to be crossed and then is single hitched around the ring to the right. It is then thrust to the left under three strands, which completes the full cycle.

Griswold, in *Handicraft*, gives a thong work edging on page 70 that is very closely related to this RINGBOLT HITCHING.

3615. A wider SINGLE-STRAND FRENCH SINNET HITCHING may be made which superficially resembles FIVE-STRAND HITCHING (⌗3607). It may appear a little complicated at the start, but is not difficult to work. Until the fourth diagram is reached it closely resembles a TURK'S-HEAD, each diagonal being crossed with alternate over-and-under sequence. But when diagram 4 is half completed the needle crosses the front of the ring downward under all five leads. The needle is then turned and takes a right upward diagonal, crossing three leads: over, under, over. It is then led around the ring to the right and finally makes a left upward diagonal, over, under, over, which completes the cycle. It is now ready to be led downward again under five leads. Exercise care in drawing up and keep the structure fair and taut at all times.

3616. *Commercial window-shade rings* may be covered in the manner illustrated, using for a tool a crochet or netting needle, but the same thing may be made with the fingers. Tie a SLIP KNOT around the ring, then bring a loop up at the back (the second diagram). A bight from the standing part is next brought across the front of the ring and through both loops, as shown with an arrow in the second diagram. Everything being firmly in place, another loop is brought up at the back and then the course indicated by the arrow is repeated.

3617. Another Loop Hitching. Bring a loop up first from one face of the ring and then the other. Each time it is thrust through the previous loop, which is then drawn snug.

3618. A hitching with a very pronounced ridge is made with a sail needle. Start as in the first diagram, proceed as in the second diagram and continue as in the third, and thereafter repeat two and three alternately. Draw up snugly, but not enough to distort.

3619. A *ringbolt hitched harpoon mounting*, on a two-flued Arctic iron, that was collected in Provincetown. The two-flued iron has been out of use in the whaling industry for almost exactly one hundred years, which approximately places the date of this mounting. The becket is wormed and all six strands are seized and *tapered*. One strand takes a round turn about the socket toward the rim and then is teased and laid down the socket to be covered by the remaining five strands. The five are hitched as in ✻3606 and when the shank is reached they are opened, teased and served over for several inches. A Three-Bight, Five-Lead, Three-Ply Turk's-Head is put on at the base of the socket.

3620. A one-flued iron with a grafted mounting. This iron was in use about 1840.

3621. Ringbolt Hitching applied to an early toggle iron, circa 1845. The eye is spliced directly around the socket, and a becket for bending the whale line is formed with the bight. The end of the hitching is seized and snaked. These three harpoons are now in the collection of the Mariners' Museum in Newport News.

The most familiar bit of sailor's knot work that remains to us is his sea chest beckets. They have survived because the chest itself was too practical a piece of furniture to be cast aside. When brought back from sea it has generally been put to some domestic task; to serve perhaps as woodbox or coal scuttle, as clothes chest or cellarette, as grain or vegetable bin, as attic catchall—I have even seen one in a barn serving as a nesting place for a setting hen.

Often a sea chest has a sloping front designed to keep it from being topheavy and also to save the sailor's shins in a seaway. Sometimes the back also slopes, and, very rarely, the ends as well. The best type of becket clears the lid of the chest just enough to spare the sailor's knuckles.

Richard H. Dana, Jr., in the *Seaman's Manual* (1841), defines the word *becket* as follows: "A handle made of rope in the form of a circle, as the handle of a chest, is called a becket." W. Clark Russell (*Sailors' Language*, London, 1883) and Olsen (*Fisherman's Seamanship*, Grimsby, 1885) give similar definitions. Several writers of fiction and verse have called them shackles, a name suggested no doubt by their shape, and the title, so sponsored, has even entered the Oxford Dictionary, while the real name is still knocking at the door.

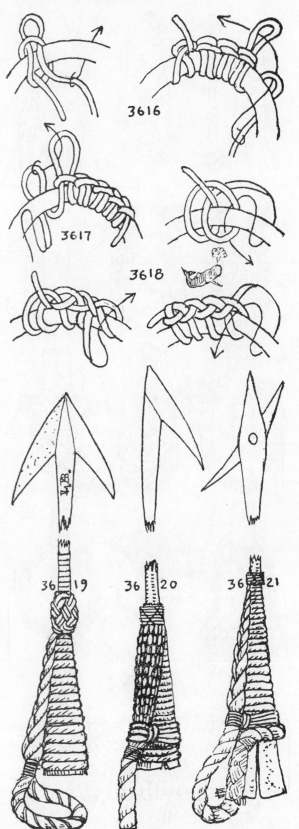

3616

3617

3618

36 19   36 20   36 21

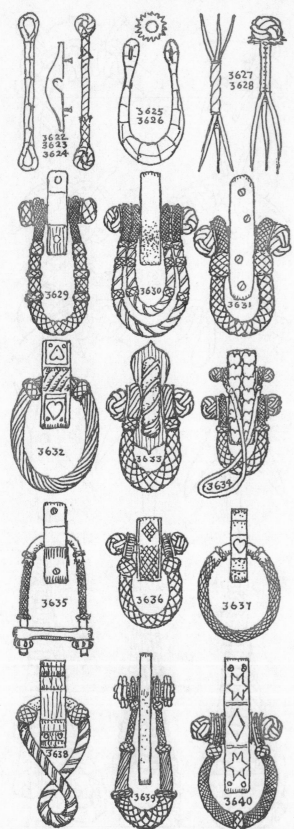

3622. A selvagee bail for a chest becket.

3623. A cleat of the usual type by means of which the becket is attached to the sea chest.

3624. A rope bail with EYE SPLICES.

3625. Pinked washers, four to each becket, generally are made of boot-top leather, red leather when it is obtainable.

3626. The handle or grip is shaped by mousing.

3627. The bolt is either three- or four-strand rope, leather-covered where it passes through the cleat. The strands, where they are knotted, are canvas-covered.

3628. After a knot is tied in one end, the becket is ready to be assembled. The second knot on the bolt is the last thing to be made.

3629. The beckets on this page are taken from the end papers of this book and are in the same order.

This one is from an officer's chest, which is much larger than a sailor's chest, the latter being limited to thirty-six inches over all, as two chests must stand end to end in front of each tier of berths. The material is hard-twisted fishline, painted red clay and dark blue. Knobs are FIVE-BIGHT × FOUR-LEAD × EIGHT-PLY TURK'S-HEADS, over MANROPE KNOTS, navy workmanship, probably. The eyes and necks are grafted, the remainder is TEN-STRAND ROUND SINNET. The TURK'S-HEADS on the bail are FOUR-PLY KNOTS. They are, top to bottom, FIVE-LEAD × FOUR-BIGHT, FOUR-LEAD × FIVE-BIGHT, and THREE-LEAD × FOUR-BIGHT.

3630. *Double beckets*, for two hands, are very rare. A large officer's chest of teakwood. Knobs, THREE-STRAND MANROPES. Eyes, needle hitching #3544. TURK'S-HEADS, THREE-LEAD × FOUR-BIGHT × FOUR-PLY. Bails, cloth-covered and wormed.

3631. A pine chest with slope front and back. Knobs, FOUR-STRAND MANROPES' EYES grafted. TURK'S-HEADS, SEVEN-LEAD × SIX-BIGHT × FOUR-PLY. Bail, THREE-PLY, EIGHT-STRAND COACHWHIPPING.

3632. A brassbound teakwood chest, carved cleats, hitched grommet, THREE-LEAD × FIVE-BIGHT × THREE-PLY TURK'S-HEADS.

3633. A Chinese brassbound camphor chest. Cleats of teak carved to represent wormed rope. Knobs, FOUR-STRAND, TWO-PLY MANROPES, HITCHED EYES. Bails, EIGHT-STRAND ROUND SINNET. TURK'S-HEAD, THREE-LEAD × FOUR-BIGHT × THREE-PLY.

3634. A pine chart chest, 14″ × 14″ × 42″, with double beckets. The long upper beckets allow one man to carry the chest, as charts weigh very little. MANROPE KNOBS, long beckets parceled with blue jeans and wormed. The short beckets are EIGHT-STRAND ROUND SINNET strands covered with blue jeans. Eyes grafted.

3635. A pine officer's chest owned by Mrs. Frank Wood. The center is UNDERHAND GRAFTING #3554. MATTHEW WALKER KNOTS covered with leather slashed and collared. White whalebone grips.

3636. A ship's papers chest, owned by Mrs. F. Gilbert Hinsdale. Carved cleats, SIX-STRAND ROUND SINNET bails. MANROPE KNOBS.

3637. A small chest, with drawnwork fringe, whale ivory hearts inlaid on the cleats. Becket made as #3632, red-cloth-covered and wormed with fishline.

3638. A slope-front teak chest, with wormed grommets.

3639. Mahogany chest. Knobs are THREE-STRAND STAR. The eyes are ringbolt hitched. Bail (top to bottom), TURK'S-HEAD, THREE-LEAD × FIVE-BIGHT × THREE-PLY, fine CROSS-POINTING. TURK'S-HEAD, THREE-LEAD × FOUR-BIGHT × FOUR-PLY ribbing, EIGHT-STRAND STAR KNOTS. Grip, FOUR-PLY COACHWHIPPING.

3640. A pine officer's chest. THREE-STRAND MANROPE KNOBS. Eyes ringbolt hitched. Bail grafted, TURK'S-HEADS, THREE-LEAD × FOUR-BIGHT × THREE-PLY.

3641. Knobs, Six-Strand Manrope Knots. Eyes and necks grafted. Turk's-Heads Five-Bight × Three-Lead × Four-Ply. Bail, coachwhipped.

3642. Knobs, Four-Strand Manrope Knots. Rope wormed. Lanyard Knot below and the whipping snaked. A similar becket in the Mystic Marine Museum has Eye Splice ⚓2783 instead of a Manrope Knot at the top.

3643. Knobs, Three-Strand Manrope Knots. Eyes and neck duck-covered. Bail, Ten-Strand Round Sinnet, strand duck-covered. Turk's-Heads all Five-Bight × Three-Lead × Three-Ply.

3644. Knobs, Five-Strand Manrope Knots. Eyes ringbolt hitched (⚓3608). Leather collars, pinked, Five-Bight × Three-Lead × Three-Ply Turk's-Heads. Legs, Overhand Spanish Hitchings. Grip, Eight-Strand Coachwhipping of black enamel cloth.

3645. This *becket* is of interest because it is on the miniature chest which held the papers of the ship *Acushnet*. The name decorates the front of the box. It was on this ship that Herman Melville made his whaling voyage to the South Seas in 1837. The beckets are only three and a half inches in their outside diameter.

3646. Manrope Knots. The eyes and neck are *grafted*.

When the point where the grip is started is reached forty-eight larger threads (fishline) are substituted for those that were being used and the joint is covered by a Three-Lead × Six-Bight × Five-Ply Turk's-Head. The forty-eight threads are divided into sets of four, and are grafted as follows: Four knots are taken as ⚓3555 and then four as ⚓3556. This is continued alternately until six complete tiers of the warp have been taken. Then six more rows are taken exactly in the same way *except* that ⚓3556 now comes below the first ⚓3555 and they continue to alternate. This is repeated until four rows of six have been completed, when one extra thread is added to each set of four so that there are sixty threads in all. Six rows of six knots are made this size, then the extra threads are dropped out and the becket finished as it was begun.

3647. Four-Strand Manrope Knots. Eyes and necks are *needle hitched*. Mid-sections of nettles made into Twelve-Strand Round Sinnet. Grip is *coachwhipped* of the same nettles. Turk's-Heads Five-Bight × Three-Lead × Three-Ply.

3648. Unusual pattern, perhaps unique. I have never seen another. They are very old but never were used. Pinked leather collar. Three-Strand Manrope Knobs. Duck-covered and wormed Four-Bight × Three-Lead × Three-Ply Turk's-Heads. The seizings of fishline have riding but no crossing turns.

3649. Four-Strand Manrope Knots. Eyes, bolt and grips are of grafting. Mid-sections are Ten-Strand Round Sinnet.

3650. Three-Strand Manrope Knobs, eyes *ringbolt hitched* (⚓3605), grips grafted, mid-section cloth-covered and wormed.

3651. A *toggle grip becket*, grafted.

3652. Five-Strand Manrope Knobs. Eyes and neck hitched over, grip canvas-covered and wormed.

3653. A bedroom knocker with a brass plate. A Flat Sinnet hinge (⚓2971) is knotted on the back of the plate. Small Turk's-Heads on a leather collar keep the knocker from shifting. Shroud Knot ⚓1583 is at the bottom.

3654. All the knots above the white whalebone grip are Four-Strand Star Knots and the becket is of Four-Strand Round Sinnet with a knot every two and a half inches. Below the grip are two Matthew Walker Knots with slashed leather covers (⚓724).

3655. A small *grafted becket* with a Turk's-Head at the bottom makes an attractive bedroom knocker.

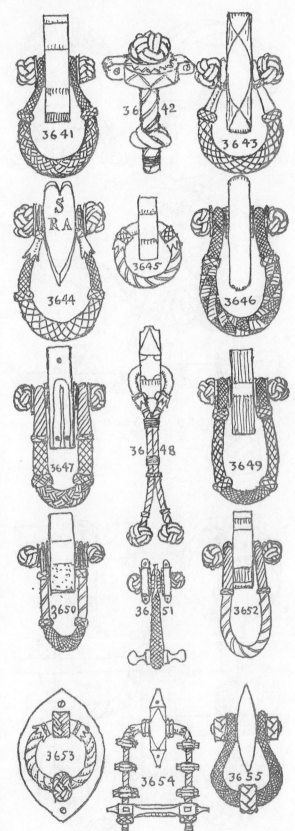

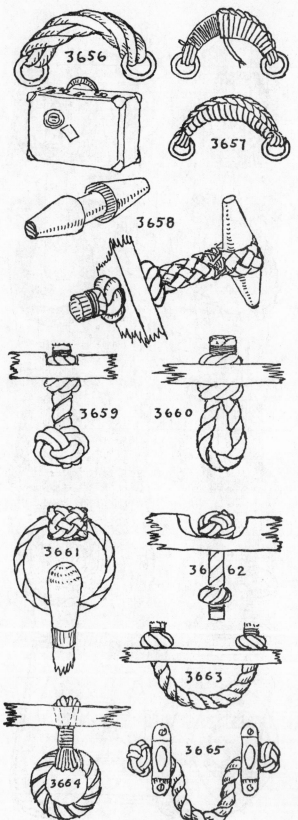

3656. If your *satchel or suitcase handle* fails you and there is no time to visit the luggage shop, make yourself a cringle (※2848).

3657. But if there is sufficient time at your disposal, form the handle *selvagee-fashion* (※3622), marl with waxed sail twine, shape it nicely (※3626) with spun yarn or other soft stuff and cover with a Ringbolt Hitching (※3604) of Italian marline, which has a nice brown color.

3658. *Drawer pulls* on a yacht should be shipshape. These were on Waldo Howland's sloop *Escape*. The eye around the toggle was made of Four-Strand French Sinnet. It was seized close and a short section of Eight-Strand Round Sinnet laid up. An Eight-Strand, Three-Tuck Matthew Walker Knot was formed close to the outside of the drawer and a Wall Knot on the inside. The end was whipped and snaked, and the Wall Knot countersunk.

3659. A neat *knob for a swing door* on a boat can be formed of a Four-Strand Manrope Knot. If the door opens two ways, have a Manrope Knot at both sides. Close to each side of the door make either a Wall Knot (※671) or a Single Diamond (※693).

3660. A *Knotted Eye*. Either ※2981 or ※2982 will serve nicely or the rope ends may be opened and seized flatly together and a Diamond Knot or Matthew Walker Knot (※682) tied. For the inside a Diamond or a Wall will serve. This makes a nice drawer pull.

3661. An *umbrella strap* was made of a silk cord with the ends bent together with a Shroud Knot (※1587). A grommet will also serve nicely as an umbrella cord.

3662. For lifting a scuttle, employ any Flat Multi-Strand Button Knot. Bore a hole through the scuttle large enough to take the rope. Leave a stem about three inches long and tie a Matthew Walker Knot on the underside, whipping the end. Have the countersunk hole just large enough so that the knot can be easily reached with the fingers.

3663. The simplest form of chest becket. If the wood is thick enough, knots may be countersunk.

3664. A *grommet drawer handle* may be seized in by boring two small holes about a quarter of an inch apart, one above the other, three eighths of an inch in diameter. Use Italian yacht marline and add a smooth layer of frapping turns.

3665. The *handles* pictured here are on the ends of the benches in "The Galley," a restaurant on a wharfhead in Fairhaven. Manrope Knots are used.

3666. *Deck bucket bails* commonly are of three-strand rope and are finished off with Matthew Walker Knots (※682). These are whipped but not snaked. Serrated leather washers are worn between the bucket ear and the knot. On a well-made bail a leather collar is added.

3667. A *kit* is a *deck bucket*, larger at the bottom than at the top. It is less apt to slop over in a seaway. This also is equipped with MATTHEW WALKER KNOTS.

3668. *Mess bucket* and *fire bucket bails* are four-strand ropes, wormed, and generally finished off with LANYARD KNOTS, and sometimes with MANROPE KNOTS.

3669. Many *mess buckets* have hickory bails and the hinge is often a bone or ivory button, with a small hickory fid on the inside.

3670. *Draw buckets* are heavily made, as they are subjected to very hard service. The heaviest canvas is used, and the best-made ones have chafing gear added wherever it will serve a purpose. This one has a grommet at the rim and bottom, and a rope yarn sinnet is appliquéd to the canvas surface. The bail is eye spliced to the grommet rim, an eye is seized into the bail to which the bucket rope is made fast, with a SINGLE BECKET HITCH. The end of the bucket rope is generally finished off either with an EYE SPLICE or a DOG'S POINT (※2813).

3671. This is an old, heavy-duty *draw bucket* from a high-sided ship, which I donated to the half-size model ship *Lagoda*. The canvas is of two pieces sewed flat together. An iron hoop at the top is hemmed over, SEVEN-STRAND FLAT SINNET is appliquéd in different designs to the two sides. The bail passes entirely around the bucket and a thimble is seized in at the top. The bucket rope is eye spliced to the thimble and the splice itself is hitched over. There is a LONG EYE SPLICE in the end of the bucket rope. It came from a junk shop in San Francisco. Small mast hoops have often been used at the tops and bottoms of draw buckets; not uncommonly they have wooden bottoms.

3672. This is a *ship's paper case;* it was always taken ashore by the captain when the ship made port. The case was often made of brass, but old ones were also of wood, canvas-covered. This one bears the name of the ship on its side. The canvas is sewed through awl holes in the wood around the upper edge. The top of the lid is hitched over decoratively with linen thread. The bottom is surrounded with about eight circuits of hitching and there is a linen thread seizing across the center.

3673. The most efficient means of crushing ice that I have found is a hand-sewn No. 1 canvas bag twenty-two inches long and ten inches wide. This is filled with ice and beaten with a heavy lignum-vitae mallet against a stone hearth. If the edges of the mallet are rounded slightly with a file, the bag will last a lifetime and give better service than any other hand-driven device for the same purpose. It is equally effective if the bag is held by the neck and swung against the stone, but this requires more energy than should be exerted in warm weather.

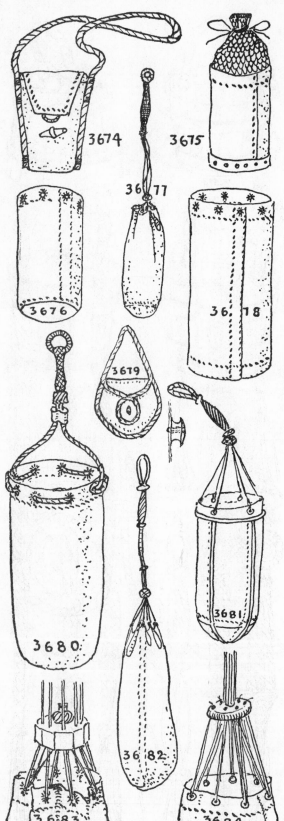

3674

3675

36 77

3676

36 18

3679

3680

3681

36 82

36 83

3684

3674. A *binoculars case* that was used at the "lookout" of a whaler. The flap is secured with a little wooden toggle.

3675. This *ditty bag* was from the Nantucket Shoals Lightship. It has a knitted "purse" of fishline (※2877) and a wooden bottom, leather-taped and studded with brass tacks.

3676. An *ordinary ditty bag* is made from two pieces of light duck, preferably linen, with from four to twelve eyelet holes around the hem for splicing in the lanyard legs. The bottom is round.

3677. The average size of a *ditty bag* is about seven inches by fourteen inches. The lanyard is about eighteen inches long and the handle or grip is about eight inches of the length. The length of the legs exceeds one half the circumference of the bag.

3678. A *clothesbag* is usually of heavier material, and is anywhere from one foot to two feet in diameter and from thirty inches to forty-two inches in length.

There are from six to twelve eyelet holes and the length of the bag plus the length of lanyard should not exceed six feet since it is designed to be hung in the forecastle. The legs of the lanyard should be equal in length to the diameter of the bag, so a wide bag should be short and a long bag should be narrow. The seams are made as the seams of a sail (※3531 and ※3532).

3679. A *roped canvas game bag* with a wooden thimble or button sewed flat against the surface.

3680. This *clothesbag lanyard* is a sport. It has but two legs with EYE SPLICES in the ends. The becket is an iron ring, hitched over with ※3605; the handle is SIX-STRAND ROUND SINNET finished off with SINNET KNOT (※757), and a TURK'S-HEAD closes the bag.

3681. Many old *ditty bags* have their seams piped, often in red and blue wool. Clothesbags are more seldom piped. The handle of this bag is EIGHT-STRAND SQUARE SINNET.

3682. A *clothesbag*. A RUNNING TURK'S-HEAD of stiff fishline slides up and down the legs and serves to close the bag. The ends of the legs are eye spliced to the eyelet holes.

3683. The strands on this bag lead through an ivory sleeve and finish off with a MATTHEW WALKER KNOT (see frontispiece). The weight of the bag automatically closes the top when it is hung up.

3684. Here the strands are knotted to a small brass sleeve, and the legs draw together when the weight of the bag is put on a hook.

3685. A commercial *handbag* with frogs and loops.

3686. A loop and button fastening (※699).

3687. A ten-legged *clothesbag lanyard*. Lay up a three-inch section of EIGHT-STRAND CROWN SINNET around a two-strand core and put MULTI-STRAND BUTTON ※964 on the short ends. Add SINNET KNOT ※757 to the long ends. Lay up one and a half inches of TEN-STRAND ROUND SINNET (※3021). Add a series of six STAR KNOTS (※727) one and a half inches apart with ROUND SINNET in between them. After the second STAR KNOT, lay out two heart strands, and after the fourth knot, two strands more; seize and cut the ends off. After the six STAR KNOTS, make another one and a half inches of ROUND SINNET and finish off with SINNET KNOT ※757. Seize two small grommets opposite each other below the top button and cover the seizing with a THREE-LEAD × FIVE-BIGHT × THREE-PLY TURK'S-HEAD.

3688. The typical *ditty bag lanyard* of six strands is as follows: Middle and lay up three pieces of small line to form an eye about one and a half inches long. Tie a MATTHEW WALKER KNOT (※731) and add a section of ROUND SINNET six inches long. Follow with a DIAMOND KNOT (※693) and another section of ROUND SINNET and finally add another knot the same as the first one.

3689. Make in the following order: A becket of FOUR-STRAND SQUARE SINNET/ EIGHT-STRAND MATTHEW WALKER/ EIGHT-STRAND CROWN SINNET/ SIX-STRAND STAR/ EIGHT-STRAND CROWN SINNET/ EIGHT-STRAND MATTHEW WALKER/ Two legs FOUR-STRAND SQUARE SINNET/ EIGHT-STRAND SIX-PART MATTHEW WALKER/ EIGHT-STRAND ROUND SINNET/ TWO-STRAND LANYARD KNOT #792/ SIX-STRAND ROUND SINNET/ SIX-STRAND SINNET KNOT #757.

3690. The strands of a lanyard laid out ready to be tied into knots. First an eye; then SIX-STRAND ROUND SINNET/ Lanyard, TWELVE-STRAND MATTHEW WALKER/ TWELVE-STRAND SQUARE SINNET/ TWO-STRAND STANDING TURK'S-HEAD #1293/ EIGHT-STRAND ROUND SINNET (leaving two heart strands)/ SINGLE-STRAND TURK'S-HEAD/ NINE-STRAND TRIANGULAR SINNET #3028/ SINGLE-STRAND TURK'S-HEAD/ EIGHT-STRAND SQUARE SINNET/ FOUR-STRAND STANDING TURK'S-HEAD/ FOUR-STRAND SQUARE SINNET/ ONE-STRAND TURK'S-HEAD/ THREE-STRAND FLAT SINNET/ ONE-STRAND TURK'S-HEAD/ TWO-STRAND SINNET #2907/ ONE-STRAND TURK'S-HEAD/ ONE-STRAND CHAIN #2869.

3691. Eye, SIX-STRAND ROUND SINNET/ SINGLE DIAMOND/ EIGHT-STRAND ROUND SINNET, four-strand core/ TWELVE-STRAND SINGLE DIAMOND/ EIGHT-STRAND CROWN SINNET with four-strand core/ DOUBLE DIAMOND/ TWELVE-STRAND CROWN SINNET/ DOUBLE DIAMOND KNOT/ CROWN AND REVERSE SINNET/ FOOTROPE KNOT.

3692. Eye, SIX-STRAND ROUND SINNET/ lanyard, TWELVE-STRAND SINNET KNOT/ ROUND SINNET over urn-shaped wooden core/ THREE-LEAD, FOUR-BIGHT, FOUR-PLY TURK'S-HEAD/ two legs of SIX-STRAND ROUND SINNET/ TWELVE-STRAND SINNET KNOT/ three legs FOUR-STRAND SQUARE SINNET/ FOUR-STRAND DIAMOND KNOT tied in four units of three strands each.

3693. A SIX-STRAND ROUND SINNET becket, with a six-strand core/ lanyard, TWELVE-STRAND FULL MATTHEW WALKER over twelve-strand core/ TWELVE-STRAND ROUND SINNET over twelve-strand core/ SIX-STRAND DIAMOND KNOT, of double strands over twelve-strand core/ CROWN SINNET, six units of two strands each/ seize the twelve-strand core and with surface strands tie a 12 × 12 MATTHEW WALKER KNOT. Lay up the ends into eight three-strand *nettles*.

3694. An eight-strand *ditty bag lanyard*. The eye is a series of FOUR-STRAND WALLS over a four-strand core/ lanyard, EIGHT-STRAND CROWN AND REVERSE, by pairs/ handle, EIGHT-STRAND CROWN SINNET over a wooden mold. FOUR-LEAD CROWN KNOT worked in units of two strands, similar CROWN over the end, seized.

3695. Eight-strand *clothesbag lanyard*, becket ringbolt hitched (#3604), MATTHEW WALKER/ lanyard, handle *needle hitched* over wooden mold/ EIGHT-STRAND MATTHEW WALKER/ EIGHT-STRAND SQUARE SINNET, finished off with SINNET KNOT #757.

3696. Four-strand *ditty bag lanyard*. Eye laid up with two strands/ FOUR-STRAND LANYARD KNOT/ lanyard, four-strand handle of CROWN SINNET over a wooden mold/ LANYARD KNOT.

3697. A four-strand *becket/* EIGHT-STRAND FULL MATTHEW WALKER KNOT/ lanyard handle, EIGHT-STRAND ROUND SINNET over a wooden mold/ DOUBLE EIGHT-STRAND STANDING TURK'S-HEAD/ EIGHT-STRAND CROWN SINNET/ FULL MATTHEW WALKER.

3698. Three-strand *rope becket/* SIX-STRAND SINNET KNOT #757/ lanyard of SIX-STRAND ROUND SINNET, SIX-STRAND DOUBLE WALL KNOT/ handle of CROWN SINNET over a wooden mold/ SIX-STRAND ROUND SINNET/ SIX-STRAND SINNET KNOT #757.

3699. A becket of three strands. SIX-STRAND MATTHEW WALKER/ lanyard of SIX-STRAND CROWN SINNET/ SIX-STRAND MATTHEW WALKER/ SIX-STRAND ROUND SINNET/ SIX-STRAND DIAMOND.

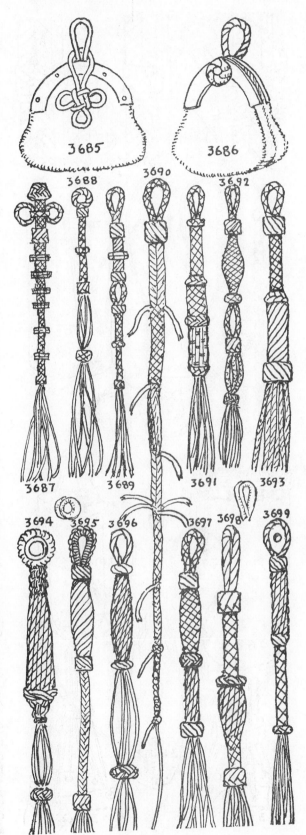

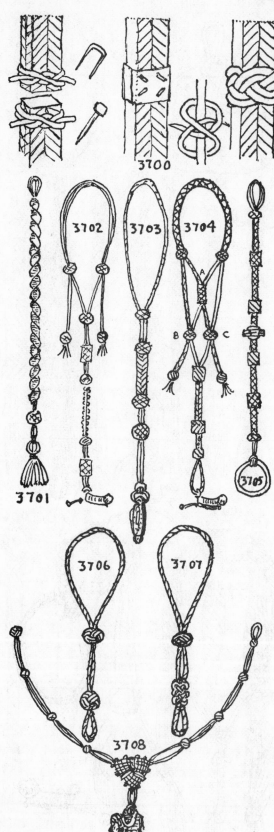

3700. To join two ends of a SQUARE SINNET.

Seize the ends with CONSTRICTOR KNOTS (#1249), and cut them off square with a razor blade. Saturate the ends with Duco cement, butt them, and cover the joint with a thin strip of leather and rivet with copper tacks. Cover joint with a TURK'S-HEAD.

3701. To make a *window-shade pull:*

Middle two cords each about four feet long and form an eye. Middle and knot another ten-foot cord (#2489) around the base of the eye. With the long cord make three inches of LEFT-HAND BANNISTER BARS #2494. Make an equal section of RIGHT BANNISTER BARS. Continue, reversing the HALF KNOTS every three inches. Add a tassel to the end.

3702. A *whistle* or *knife lanyard.*

Middle a long cord and leave a loop four inches long. Tie CHINESE KNOT #818 and at a distance of one and a half inches tie KNIFE LANYARD KNOT #787, then follow with five inches of IDIOT'S DELIGHT (#2896). Repeat LANYARD #787 and CHINESE KNOT #818 spaced as before. Leave three feet clear, and tie KNOT #546 in each end. Lay the ends parallel in contrary directions and add three RUNNING TURK'S-HEADS.

3703. *Whistle* or *knife lanyard.* Middle four cords and make three feet of FOUR-STRAND SQUARE SINNET (#2999) in the center.

Tie a DOUBLE DIAMOND KNOT and make four inches of EIGHT-STRAND SQUARE SINNET (#3001). Lay out alternate ends. Make twelve inches of IDIOT'S DELIGHT with two of the remaining ends and two inches only with the other pair. Crotch the eight strands and tie KNOT #1593. Add a RUNNING TURK'S-HEAD to the neck section.

3704. Take four small lines each five feet long. With the center of two, lay up six inches of two-strand rope for a becket. Place the two ropes together and tie a FOUR-STRAND MATTHEW WALKER.

Lay up two inches of FOUR-STRAND SQUARE SINNET, then middle the other two lines and lay the bights across the top of the sinnet just made and seize all eight lines together. All the ends being in the same direction, tie an EIGHT-STRAND SINNET KNOT (#757). Lay up six inches of EIGHT-STRAND SQUARE SINNET and tie a FULL MATTHEW WALKER. Divide the strands and lay up twelve inches of FOUR-STRAND SQUARE SINNET with each set. Bring the ends together and tie a FULL MATTHEW WALKER. Now work fourteen inches of EIGHT-STRAND ROUND SINNET and tie another MATTHEW WALKER. Divide the strands again and lay up two FOUR-STRAND SQUARE SINNETS fourteen inches long, seize the ends at equal length, tie a MATTHEW WALKER in the end of each of the sinnets, add tassels.

Open the first double section of FOUR-STRAND ROUND SINNET and spread the two legs slightly. Turn the EIGHT-STRAND SQUARE section around to the left and place one leg of the last FOUR-STRAND SQUARE section across a bight of the first section. Bring the second leg down to the left of the other. Arrange the lanyard symmetrically as pictured and seize strongly at B and C. Cover each seizing permanently with a THREE-LEAD × FOUR-BIGHT × THREE-PLY TURK'S-HEAD. At A, put a RUNNING TURK'S-HEAD, SEVEN-LEAD × THREE-BIGHT × THREE-PLY.

3705. A *window-shade lanyard.* Double two cords, leave a two-inch loop and tie DIAMOND KNOT #694. Make four inches of FOUR-STRAND SQUARE SINNET and tie #742, then make four inches more of FOUR-STRAND SQUARE SINNET and tie a MATTHEW WALKER. Add one and a half inches more of FOUR-STRAND SQUARE SINNET and tie a STAR KNOT (#727). Follow with one and a half inches of FOUR-STRAND SQUARE SINNET and tie a MATTHEW WALKER KNOT. Make four inches of FOUR-STRAND SQUARE SINNET and tie #742. Make four inches more of FOUR-STRAND SQUARE SINNET and seize, make a two-inch loop with two strands and crotch with the other two strands. Make SHROUD KNOT #1593 and double it.

3706, 3707. These are *common knife lanyards.* Both are started at the bottom loop. Either a ROUND KNIFE LANYARD KNOT (#787) or a CHINESE KNOT (#818) is made and the ends are spliced together at the side of the neckpiece with a LONG SPLICE. A RUNNING TURK'S-HEAD is added, for a puckering knot.

3708. A *locket lanyard* of two cords. The large PECTORAL KNOT is #842. All the rest are Two-Strand MATTHEW WALKER KNOTS, except the upper left BUTTON which is Two-Strand MANROPE KNOT #980. The necklace starts at the upper right with an eye and is completed with the MANROPE KNOT.

3709. The following three *knife* or *whistle lanyards* were made by Edward M. Stetson.

The neckpiece of the first lanyard is a separate section of EIGHT-STRAND SQUARE SINNET with the ends of FOUR-STRAND SINNET doubled back into two long loops. The joints are seized and covered with FOUR-LEAD × FIVE-BIGHT × THREE-PLY TURK'S-HEADS. A similar loop is made for each leg and is knotted into the first two with CARRICK LOOPS before the leg is made. Put similar TURK'S-HEADS over the seizings and on one leg make a RIGHT CROWN SINNET of three strands around a core of five to the next TURK'S-HEAD, which is FIVE-BIGHT × THREE-LEAD × TWO-PLY. From this point the sinnet is reversed to a LEFT CROWN. The crowning for the right leg is the reverse of the left leg. There is a RUNNING TURK'S-HEAD over this section, of larger cord. At the top of the PECTORAL KNOT a FIVE-BIGHT × FOUR-LEAD × THREE-PLY TURK'S-HEAD covers a seizing. The diamond-shaped PECTORAL KNOT consists of BANNISTER BARS over two-strand cores and all joints are seized and covered with FOUR-LEAD × FIVE-BIGHT × TWO-PLY TURK'S-HEADS. The bottom loop is of THREE-STRAND SINNET, the TURK'S-HEAD that is seized to it is FOUR-LEAD × FIVE-BIGHT × THREE-PLY and the pendant section above the loop is a BANNISTER BAR with four strands for a core. The RUNNING TURK'S-HEAD is a FOUR-LEAD × FIVE-BIGHT × THREE-PLY TURK'S-HEAD of larger material than the sinnet and the three vertically central TURK'S-HEAD of the PECTORAL KNOTS are TWO-PLY KNOTS of the same heavier material. All others are of the same material as the cord itself.

3710. The bottom loop of this lanyard is THREE-STRAND SINNET, the pendant is SIX-STRAND ROUND SINNET, the legs are FIVE-STRAND FRENCH SINNET and the neckband is SEVEN-STRAND FRENCH SINNET. The RUNNING TURK'S-HEAD is SEVEN-LEAD × FIVE-BIGHT × TWO-PLY. And the STANDING TURK'S-HEAD at the nape of the neck is the same. The others are all FOUR-LEAD × FIVE-BIGHT × THREE-PLY TURK'S-HEADS. The leg and neckband joint is shown in detail.

3711. The third lanyard is of *square knotting* in two-inch sections. Two strands form the core for each leg. Beginning at the bottom, the loop is THREE-STRAND SINNET/ TURK'S-HEAD, FOUR-LEAD × FIVE-BIGHT × TWO-PLY/ SOLOMON BARS/ four uncomplicated cords/ SOLOMON BARS/ BANNISTER BARS/ SOLOMON BARS/ four uncomplicated cords/ SOLOMON BARS/ two TURK'S-HEADS as before. The RUNNING TURK'S-HEAD is FOUR-LEAD × FIVE-BIGHT × THREE-PLY. Two uncomplicated cords pass around the neck.

3712. A *knife* or *whistle lanyard*. Middle two pieces of fishline. Leave an eight-inch loop in one piece and seize the two together. Tie a FOUR-STRAND DOUBLE DIAMOND KNOT (#695).

Lay out the two left ends and, at six inches, seize in another middled section to the right ends. Tie a DOUBLE DIAMOND KNOT (#695). Make four inches of SQUARE SINNET and add FOOTROPE KNOT #696. Shape a neckband for sixteen inches by winding spun yarn around one of the strands and CROWN SINNET around this core with the other three strands. Tie a DOUBLE DIAMOND and add four inches of SQUARE SINNET. Crotch and seize-in the two long ends from the first loop. Cut out two of the four strands from the neck band and tie SHROUD KNOT #1593. Add a RUNNING TURK'S-HEAD for a gathering knot.

3713. The common marlingspike lanyard is of tarred hemp with two LONG EYE SPLICES in it.

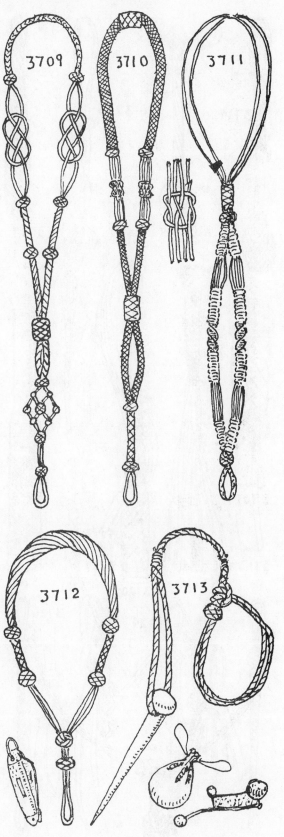

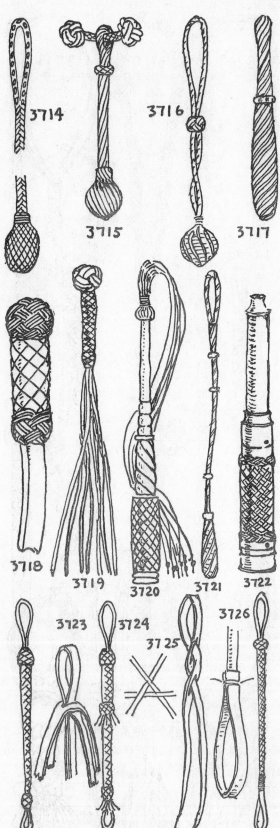

3714. A *"life preserver"* twenty-two inches long. Becket of FOUR-STRAND SQUARE SINNET, the lanyard EIGHT-STRAND SQUARE SINNET, DIAMOND KNOT in end. A leather bag containing shot is needle hitched and seized around the neck of a knot on the lanyard.

3715. A blackjack, ten and a half inches long, that started out to be a *chest becket*. Evidently the sailor's requirements changed as his ship neared port. The knobs are MANROPE KNOTS, the bolt, eye, and lanyard are *needle hitched*. The lead ball is *rib hitched*.

3716. A *blackjack* consisting of a *rib hitched* lead ball, a tarred codfish line lanyard, and a DOUBLE KNIFE LANYARD KNOT.

3717. A wooden *"night stick,"* ten and one half inches long, *single hitched*, with a narrow TURK'S-HEAD.

3718. A razor-blade knife. The handle is of wood *cross grafted* with ten leather thongs. The TURK'S-HEADS are small tarred fishline, the guard being FIVE-LEAD × FOUR-BIGHT × FIVE-PLY.

3719. A cat with seven tails of FIVE-STRAND FLAT SINNET tapered and *whipped* (#3460). The knob is a THREE-LEAD × FOUR-BIGHT × TWO-PLY TURK'S-HEAD of FLAT SINNET tied over a MANROPE KNOT (#847). The handle is TWELVE-LEAD, FOUR-PLY COACHWHIPPING, the guard, a FIVE-LEAD × FOUR-BIGHT × FIVE-PLY TURK'S-HEAD.

3720. *A whale ship's cat-o'-nine-tails* with a fourteen-inch handle of white whalebone. Five cords are middled and seized around a button on the end of the handle. One tail is cut out.

3721. A thirty-two-inch blackjack. The *becket* is an EYE SPLICE, the neck of which is hitched over. The loaded end is also hitched over. FOUR TURK'S-HEADS (THREE-LEAD × FOUR-BIGHT × THREE-PLY) are added and the rope is wormed.

3722. A *spyglass*, covered with COACHWHIPPING put on with a needle and finished off with a TURK'S-HEAD of larger cord.

3723. A *rawhide quirt* of three thongs.

Slit two of them in the center to admit a bight for a wrist strap from the center of the third thong. Taper an eighteen-inch piece of sash cord, parcel with "electric tape" and cross graft it with six strands (#2563). Seize in a loop of THREE-STRAND FLAT SINNET. Add two SEVEN-LEAD × FIVE-BIGHT × SINGLE-PLY TURK'S-HEADS.

3724. To make a loaded quirt, serve a piece of sash cord with a strip of quarter-inch wide sheet lead.

Separate the turns of the lead by winding a piece of soft cord between them. Seize both ends and serve over with butcher's cord. Add a wrist strap, and loop as #3723. Make an additional cover for the handle that is several inches long, first arranging strands as in the center sketch. Leave the ends long and seize them. Add three SEVEN-LEAD × FIVE-BIGHT TURK'S-HEADS and fringe all ends.

3725. A quirt lash is tapered both ways from the middle. Attach to the quirt with a RING HITCH (#1493).

3726. A riding crop with a tapered black whalebone core. If unobtainable, rawhide, rattan or elm root will do.

Form a loop of 7/16-inch leather strap and stop it tightly to the small end of the core. Take four long leather strips the size of shoestrings. Middle and form the wrist strap either of FOUR-STRAND SQUARE or FRENCH SINNET. Seize together and make an EIGHT-STRAND DIAMOND KNOT over the big end of the core. Then cover the core with EIGHT-STRAND SQUARE SINNET, seize and cut off where it meets the end loop. Whip the joint.

3727. A dog's leash of three thongs. Taper both ways from the middle and lay up a wrist strap of THREE-STRAND SINNET.

With six strands tie SINNET KNOT #757. Plat half the length into SIX-STRAND ROUND SINNET, then lay out two strands and complete with FOUR-STRAND SQUARE SINNET. Form a collar loop with one strand, seize all four and tie a DIAMOND KNOT (#693). Add TURK'S-HEADS where shown.

3728. A *flat belt*. Tie KNOT #825, then a series of LANYARD KNOTS (#818) and finish off with BUTTON #656.

3729. A *leash* for a large dog of rawhide belt lacing.

Taper and skive four thongs, form a loop with the small end of the longest strand, and seize all strands together. Lay up a FOUR-STRAND SQUARE SINNET. Surmount it with a large BUTTON KNOT. Cover the seizing with a leather shoestring TURK'S-HEAD.

3730. A CARRICK BEND *belt*. Make the eye first and finish with BUTTON #603. Reverse the knots alternately to avoid torsion.

3731. A *twelve-strand leash* of tarred fishline.

Sinnets and knots alternate. Loop is SIX-STRAND ROUND SINNET/ TWELVE-STRAND MATTHEW WALKER/ SIX-STRAND SPIRAL CROWN SINNET with a six-strand core/ NINE-LEAD × FOUR-BIGHT × TWO-PLY TURK'S-HEAD/ EIGHT-STRAND ROUND SINNET with a four-strand core/ FOUR-STRAND DOUBLE DIAMOND KNOT/ EIGHT-STRAND SQUARE SINNET/ TWO-STRAND STANDING TURK'S-HEAD/ SIX-STRAND ROUND SINNET/ TWO-STRAND STANDING TURK'S-HEAD/ FOUR-STRAND SQUARE SINNET/ a twisted loop of two strands/ seize and tie SHROUD KNOT #1593.

3732. A *lady's belt*. Loop is THREE-STRAND FLAT SINNET/ SIX-STRAND DIAMOND KNOT/ SIX-STRAND ROUND SINNET/ SIX-STRAND FOOT-ROPE KNOT/ two parallel THREE-STRAND FLAT SINNETS/ and any SIX-STRAND BUTTON.

3733. A *lady's belt*. A single length of FOUR-STRAND SINNET in two colors with ends seized together. Add three SEVEN-LEAD × FOUR-BIGHT × THREE-PLY TURK'S-HEADS.

3734. A *toggle and loop belt*. FOUR-STRAND FRENCH SINNET around the toggle/ seize and make two short sections of FOUR-STRAND SQUARE SINNET/ a section of EIGHT-STRAND SQUARE SINNET/ a loop of FOUR-STRAND SQUARE SINNET/ add three TURK'S-HEADS.

3735. A *belt* of SIX-STRAND ROUND SINNET, made as #3733. Loops are knotted together with a tasseled cord.

3736. A *sword mat* (#2964) or any FLAT SINNET may be made into a belt by using two rings. Divide strands for the top ring and sew the sinnet to the back at the bottom ring. Sew a thong to one ring and tie with a LATIGO KNOT (#1528).

3737. A loop *key guard* of three thongs. Middle and make a section of SIX-STRAND ROUND SINNET. Slit the ends to take the keys.

3738. With an even number of loops, double the cords and seize with a CONSTRICTOR KNOT.

3739. A knob *key guard*. Double two pieces of fishline, tie a FOOTROPE KNOT. SQUARE SINNET and tie any FOUR-STRAND BUTTON.

3740. When employing *an odd number of strands* or making a guard for a considerable number of keys, knot one end of any cord and seize the strands together below this knot.

3741. A knob *key guard* of TRIANGULAR SINNET. Middle five strands, tie a BUTTON KNOT. Cut one strand close to knot and make sinnet (#3028). Tie a SINNET KNOT and put EYE SPLICES in ends.

3742. For an extra key, side splice to one of the strands.

3743. A two-strand guard for an ignition key. Make the loop and tie a MATTHEW WALKER KNOT, finish off with #980.

3744. Instead of knotting strands as #3740, if a small knot is needed tuck the ends through the strands as shown here and seize tightly with a CONSTRICTOR, or else tie #560.

3745. A ring key guard. Middle three or more leather shoestrings through a ring. Make a short length of FRENCH SINNET and seize ends evenly *by pairs*. Lay up ends alternately front and back, making long loops of equal length for the keys. Tie a DIAMOND KNOT and draw all ends snug. Keep the knot flat.

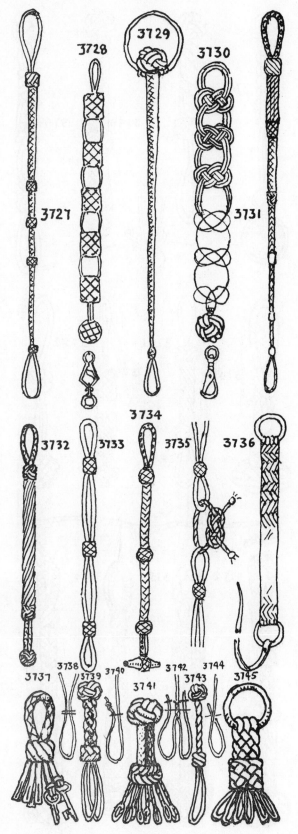

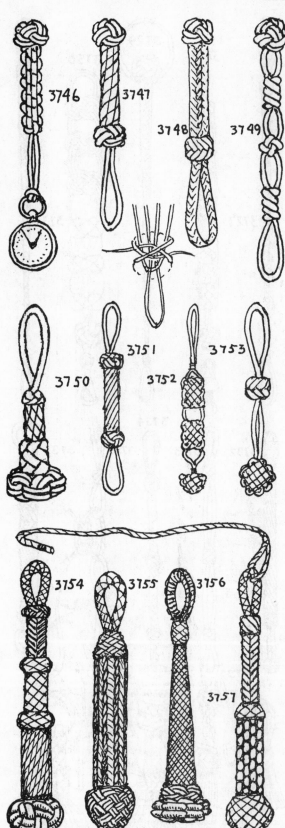

3746. The common shoestring watch guard of REVERSE CROWN SINNET (#2917). Middle two long *flat* leather shoestrings and form a three-inch loop with one bight. Then introduce the other bight, stopping all four legs loosely together. Tie a RIGHT WALL KNOT (#671) with all four strands, draw it up tightly and remove the seizing. Tie a LEFT CROWN and continue to alternate RIGHT and LEFT CROWNS. When sufficient is made, finish off with a MANROPE KNOT (#847) or any FOUR-STRAND BUTTON KNOT.

3747. A watch guard of HELICAL CROWN SINNET, CROWNS tied in one direction (see #2932). To be tied with round cords. Arrange the cords as before and tie a DOUBLE FOOTROPE KNOT (#694), remove the stopping and draw up snugly. Then crown successively to the right. Finish off with any FOUR-STRAND BUTTON.

3748. A TRIANGULAR SINNET watch guard of small linen cord. The loop is of FIVE-STRAND FLAT SINNET. Seize the legs together, tie LANYARD KNOT #737 (over four and under four). Cut off one strand and make NINE-STRAND SINNET #3028. Seize and finish off with any BUTTON of nine or less strands, cutting out any superfluous strands.

3749. A two-cord guard for an *automobile key*. It will neither rattle nor mar the instrument board. Middle the cord and form the loop, then tie KNOTS #777 and #808, in the order pictured, and finish off with a TWO-STRAND BUTTON (#601).

3750. A STAR KNOT watch guard of fairly heavy cord. Make a loop of THREE-STRAND SINNET and tie a FOOTROPE KNOT, follow with a SIX-STRAND ROUND SINNET, add a SIX-STRAND DIAMOND KNOT over the ROUND SINNET, and finish with a SIX-STRAND STAR KNOT.

3751. A DOUBLE LOOP key guard. Splice the ends of a short line together and seize in two loops. Secure four extra strands and cover the center part with CROWN SINNET and add two FOOTROPE KNOTS.

3752. A flat watch guard. Seize in a loop, tie two or three CHINESE KNOTS and terminate with KNOT #2459.

3753. A watch guard. Divide the cord a little off center and tie BUTTON #2460. Then tie KNOT #792. Tuck one end back into the knot parallel with the other, leaving enough material for a loop. Withdraw the other end several tucks, replacing it with the end that formed the loop. Draw all snug.

3754. Ship's bell ropes, being much exposed to the weather, are always painted. The becket is seized to the flight of the bell clapper. Form the becket of FOUR-STRAND SQUARE SINNET, add EIGHT-STRAND DIAMOND KNOT #693. Follow with EIGHT-STRAND SQUARE SINNET, then an EIGHT-STRAND DIAMOND KNOT. Next an EIGHT-STRAND ROUND SINNET, and KNOT #792, of two strands only. A SIX-STRAND CROWN SINNET and a SPRITSAIL SHEET KNOT (#887) completes the bell rope.

3755. A five-sided bell rope. Middle four strands, make a becket of FOUR-STRAND SQUARE SINNET. Seize in eight strands to make SINNET #3080, cover the joint with a TURK'S-HEAD, finish off with any EIGHT-STRAND BUTTON from Chapter 10.

3756. Middle four strands, make a becket of FOUR-STRAND ROUND SINNET, seize, and *ringbolt hitch* the becket (#3605); make an EIGHT-STRAND ROUND SINNET. At half length seize five *large* strands outside At full length seize and cut off original eight strands. Taper with spun yarn and either graft or coachwhip the full length. With the five large strands, tie STAR #885. Add a TURK'S-HEAD at the neck of the becket and tie a STANDING TURK'S-HEAD with five ends above the STAR KNOT.

3757. A *bell rope*. Make a loop of Four-Strand Square Sinnet, tie an Eight-Strand Matthew Walker Knot and follow with Eight-Strand Square Sinnet, after which Sinnet Knot #761 follows. Add Crown Sinnet #2920 and finish off with a Double Matthew Walker, covered with Knot #954.

"Outside" knot work is painted to save weathering. Before painting, it should be sized with casein, glue or shellac. Manropes, bell ropes, life lines, etc., are always treated in this way. Manropes reeve through stanchions let in the rail, and provide a handhold for anyone coming aboard. When ships were high-sided and visitors mounted through an "entering port" they were called "entering ropes." *The Naval Repository* of 1762 gives the following: "The Entering Rope is suspended from the Top of the Ladder by which you enter the ship; and for the most Part covered with Scarlet Cloth curiously fringed and tasseled, the genteeler to accommodate the Captain or any Visitor, it seldom being used at any other Time." For a short while before the term "manrope" was adopted, they were called "sideropes."

3758. *Manropes* are made of four-strand rope, canvas-covered. A Narrow Turk's-Head of small fishline covers each joint of the canvas. The joints are the width of a cloth apart. The knob is generally a Two- or Three-Ply Manrope Knot tied with *canvas-covered strands* and furnished with a pinked leather washer. Often the point is finished off with an eye, by which it is lashed.

Admiral Luce recommends that manropes be "pointed over with neat small line, the job is a tedious one, but worth the expense and trouble." Alston described them coachwhipped the full length.

3759. A *manrope stanchion* of white whalebone. The hole is eleven sixteenths of an inch in diameter, indicating that it was made for either linen or hemp rope.

3760. A coachwhipped yoke rope of fishline with a very attenuated grafted point bearing a tassel. The knob is a Manrope Knot, covered with Nine-Lead × Eight-Bight × Three-Ply Turk's-Head. The pointing in this case is pure swank, as it could not be used practically on account of the tassel. The points in this case were not rove; the knots were buttoned instead to two beckets in the yoke. A square knotted yoke rope is described on page 404.

3761. A *deck stopper* is made of hawser-laid rope one half the size of the cable and one fathom in length. The lanyard is twice as long as the stopper itself and one third the diameter. In one end is a Stopper Knot (#674), in the other end is a shackle or hook. The ends are laid up three or four inches after the knot has been tied and is strongly whipped and snaked.

3762. A *manrope* with a Matthew Walker Knot covered with a red slashed leather cap (see #724). There is a Turk's-Head around the leather collar and the point is canvas-covered.

3763. A bronze *manrope stanchion*. Similar but shorter stanchions are used at the knightheads to hold a net on which the headsails are doused.

3764. A *deck stopper* for a large ship was sometimes of cable. Often the three heart strands were cut out and a Spritsail Sheet Knot tied with the remaining strands.

3765, 3766. *Mess kid* and *mess table pendants* are shown in a drawing by Cruickshank (1815). The table is held with Multi-Strand Stopper Knots, presumably Matthew Walkers. The tassels were probably of brightly colored yarns.

3767. A *bell rope*. A small rope is middled to form the eye and is shaped with worming and spun yarn. The middle section is *needle hitched* once, and the bulbous parts are covered with Turk's-Heads.

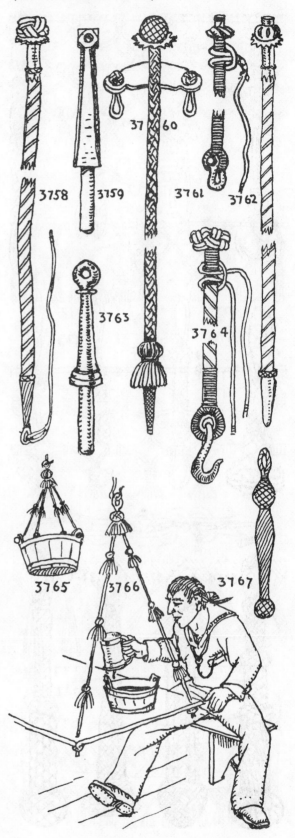

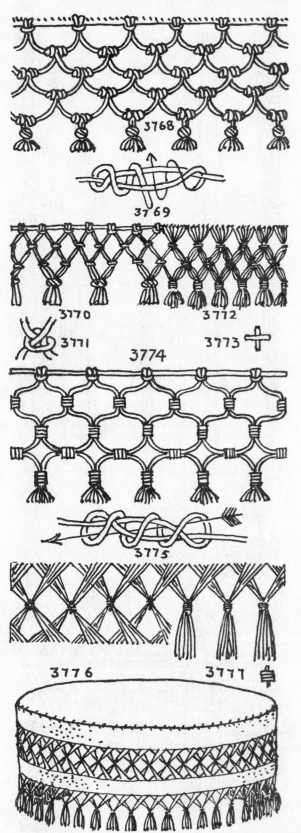

I have read frequent references to *knotted drawnwork fringes* made by sailors on canvas sea chest covers. But all the drawnwork covers that I have ever seen have had *seized* fringes. The only *knotted chest fringes* that I have encountered were made of fishline that was sewed through the hem of the cover. The "D.M.C. Library" has published a booklet entitled *Knotted Fringes* containing twenty pages of illustration. Drawnwork is exhaustively treated in various books on needlework (see the Bibliography).

3768. A fish scale fringe may be tied in cord, using the BARREL KNOT (#1413) in rather coarse fishline. At the edge it is raveled and then OVERHAND KNOTS added to form a short tassel. Tassels for this series are found on pages 566, 567, and 568.

3769. A BARREL KNOT fringe.

3770. A *diamond-pattern fringe* of half knotted cord with raveled ends.

3771. The MARLING KNOT is tied with one end around the other; always the same end is employed.

3772. A similar seized *drawnwork fringe* on a sea chest cover. This is shown in one of the end paper photographs.

3773. The X *seizing* is of very heavy linen thread with an equal number of horizontal and vertical turns. The ends are reef knotted at the back. A sailor always waxes his sewing thread, even when he mends his trousers.

3774. A FOURFOLD OVERHAND KNOT fringe with turnip-shaped meshes. Tie the vertical knots with the left diagonal cords and the horizontal knots with the right diagonal cords, the knots being identical.

3775. The arrow represents the cord around which the knot is tied with the other end.

3776. A *line tub* (whale line) *cover* of light linen canvas. The cross threads having been withdrawn from two sections of canvas, the threads are grouped in half-inch sections four inches wide with a two-inch section of undisturbed canvas left between them. This is in the New Bedford Whaling Museum.

3777. The seizing is an X but with twice the number of horizontal turns that there are vertical turns. To make: The first half-inch section of warps is seized at the center to the fourth section. The centers of the even-numbered sections are brought to the left over all while the centers of the odd-numbered sections are brought to the right under all.

Line tub covers and *chest covers* are always painted over. The former are subjected to the weather. The latter are subjected to much wear and are often wet from rain-soaked clothes. Sea chests are the only seats that sailors have in the forecastle. Netting is also to be found in Chapter 2 under "The Netmaker," and in Chapter 18, "Bends," where only the knots used are discussed.

3778. Very heavy rope is employed for *cargo nets,* flounder dredging, and boarding nets. Ropes are seized together in pairs, with round seizings, after which the pairs are assembled.

3779. Nowadays heavy nets are frequently made with metal clips, and the floors of deep-sea dredges are usually of mail.

Boarding nets were formerly made of ratline stuff and, after being well soaked in tar, were *sanded* and allowed to dry. A net so treated cannot be cut with a sharp knife.

It is possible that nets covered in this manner with beach sand would be of value in the fisheries. Beach sand, being round, will not cut the hands or abrade the deck, but would protect the rope.

3780. A CLOVE HITCH for bending to a headrope.

3781. A BALE SLING or STRAP HITCH is used for the same purpose.

3782. A *decorative net* may be made as follows: Stretch a headrope shoulder-high, middle a number of mesh ropes and make them fast to the headrope at regular intervals with either a CLOVE HITCH, which is the usual procedure, or with a BALE or STRAP HITCH, which is perhaps more decorative. Adjacent strands are knotted together. A spool may be employed to keep the meshes of equal length and the same pair are not tied together twice in succession.

3783. The CARRICK BEND lends itself effectively to decorative netting.

3784. A *decorative netting* that makes a handsome fringe. Any TWO-STRAND LANYARD KNOT having a proper lead may be used for such a purpose.

3785. *Cargo nets* are ordinarily made of four-strand rope. One set of ropes is rove through the center strands of the other ropes at regular intervals, and seized in. Sometimes they are rove as KNOT #2856 and not seized. Braiding nets may be made in the same way. All ends are spliced (#2855) into a much heavier headrope, or else are eye spliced around it. The net is fitted with clews for hoisting. More frequently cargo nets are square.

3786. The GRANNY MESH KNOT has several points in its favor. It is more compact and more regular, and has a better lead than the common MESH KNOT. Although it tends to slip, it cannot spill. The ordinary MESH KNOT (#402 and #403) tends to capsize but ordinarily does not slip.

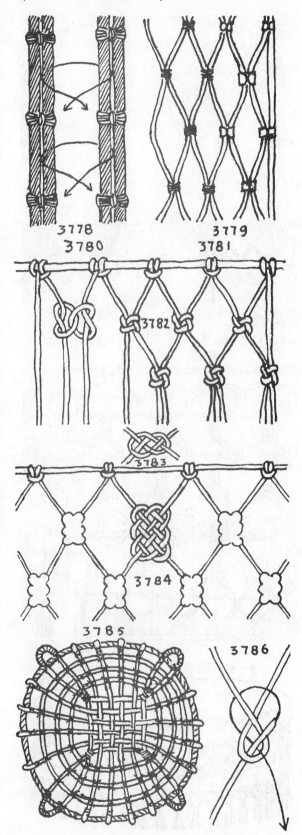

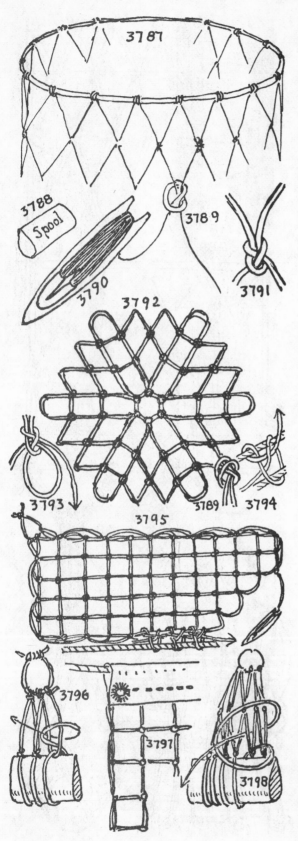

3787. A *crab or dip net* is cylindrical in form. With a netting needle (♯3790) make a series of evenly spaced CLOVE HITCHES (♯3793) around a hoop, leaving a long end and using a spool (♯3788). When the circuit is completed, tie the working and standing ends together as ♯3789. The methods of tying the MESH KNOT (♯3791) have already been described as ♯402 and ♯403. Holding the spool in the left hand, add a second row of meshes. When a sufficient number of rows is completed the bottom row of meshes may be clove hitched to a small ring or else a heavy cord is rove through the meshes and tied. This net may be more quickly made if the meshes helix continuously in one direction instead of being arranged in tiers.

3788. The net is tapered by tying every second, third or fourth knot through two adjoining meshes instead of merely one, as ♯3798.

3789. The OVERHAND BEND is the most practical knot for closing the final mesh in a cylindrical net.

3790. The *netting* or *seine needle*.

3791. The MESH KNOT.

3792. A round flat net is called a *shot*, *treasure* or *cabbage net*. Make a ring or grommet equal in size to twice the round of your spool plus an added length for "take-up." Leave a long end, and put a series of six equally spaced knots around the ring and tie the long end that was left and the working end together with an OVERHAND BEND (♯1410) to form the last mesh (♯3788). The second row of meshes is knotted twice to each of the first row of six meshes, making twelve meshes in all. The third row of meshes is knotted twice to every second mesh. At this point it will be apparent that there are six radiating rows of rectangular meshes. Each time one of these six is worked, two knots are tied, so that six are added in each circuit. The other meshes are knotted but once. When the net is complete the edge is roped by putting CLOVE HITCHES in the last row of meshes, or else the boltrope is marline hitched to the last row.

3793. DOUBLE MESH KNOT.

3794. The LACING KNOT attaches the foot of a tennis net to the boltrope.

3795. A *lawn tennis net* is made in such manner that the sides of the meshes are parallel with the sides of the net. Horizontal and vertical lines are much less distracting to the eyes of a tennis player than the diagonal meshes of the early nets. The spool used is three and one half inches in girth.

Make a ring that is three inches in diameter. Bend the end of your mesh line to this ring and make two meshes. Next turn the structure over and make two knots, the first a regular MESH KNOT, the second a DOUBLE MESH KNOT (♯3793), which makes three for that row. Continue to net rows in the ordinary manner, except that the final knot of *each row* is a DOUBLE MESH KNOT until twenty-two meshes are in one row. This being reached, on finishing the next row stick your needle up through the *two* final meshes and knot, as in the final diagram of ♯3798. At the end of the next row make a DOUBLE MESH KNOT and thereafter at the ends of rows alternate the two knots. When there are two hundred and ninety meshes along the head of the net, tie no more DOUBLE MESH KNOTS but knot to two meshes at the end of each row. The cord should be black (tarred or dyed) thirty-six-thread cotton. Sew a five-inch-wide white canvas tape, doubled along the head of the finished net and reeve through it a small galvanized wire rope with an EYE SPLICE in each end. A piece of tarred ratline stuff should be seized along the bottom of the net as illustrated. If a net is exposed to excessive wear it may be reinforced along the upper half of the center section. This is worked with a needle on which two parallel cords are wound. The lower section is worked with another needle, carrying a single cord only. The sections are worked separately and, whenever they meet each other, all three threads are joined with a compound OVERHAND BEND (#3789), and each needle is then reversed and a new row of meshes is started in each direction. After ninety-six single meshes are made along the head of the net, one hundred double meshes should follow and then a final ninety-six single meshes. There should be only eleven horizontal rows of double meshes at the top of the mid-section of the net.

3796. The ordinary way of tying the MESH KNOT.

3797. To add the tape: The tape is held taut by means of a cord attached to the eyelet.

3798. Narrowing the mesh.

3799–3812. This *tennis-ball bag* was designed and made for my cousin Hope Knowles. Use a spool two and three quarters inches in girth. A galvanized iron mast hoop or lobster pot ring about seven inches in diameter is called for and a 1⅜-inch galvanized iron eyelet hole ring.

Parcel the seven-inch ring with one-inch adhesive surgical tape and cover #3810 with RINGBOLT HITCHING #3613. Use small hard white fishline. Reef knot the ends of the RINGBOLT HITCHING together.

Take a fifty-foot piece of small soft cotton fishline and wind it at both ends onto two netting needles. Clove hitch (#3799) sixteen meshes around the small ring. If the ring is not completely covered substitute enough ROLLING HITCHES (#3800) to fill. Hang the ring by a toggled cord (#3802) and proceed to make cylindrical net #3787. Make nine rows of meshes (#3801), completing each tier with OVERHAND BEND #3803. When complete, bend the two ends together with HARNESS BEND #3804, well up on the side of the mesh.

Take eight feet of cotton cord about twice the diameter of the netting material, and arrange it on the large ring, as in #3806, reeving the cord through the meshes of the net as pictured in #3809, and tying the ends together with a REEF KNOT placed as #3805. Seize the strands below the ring with a CONSTRICTOR #3808. Have all the loops of even length. Take several feet of the netting material, leaving the ends long, and tie KNOT #3807, which holds the material in place. Draw very tight, making certain that the ends of the RINGBOLT HITCHING are covered. With the ends of the cord serve the knob over tightly and evenly. Then cover with TURK'S-HEAD #3811, which was designed for this bag and is given in detail as #1393. Make the knot three- or four-ply in order to completely cover all underneath material. Add a RUNNING TURK'S-HEAD (#3812) of very hard cord (log or fishline) around the lanyards for a puckering knot.

Columbus' diary states that he found the inhabitants of the Bahama Islands slept in "nets of cotton" suspended at either end, "which they called hamacs." The name has been adopted the world over. Although Columbus remarked upon this as something new and strange in furniture, Alcibiades is credited with the invention of the swinging canvas bed, which is still used in the Navy. It was not until the days of the Greenland whale fishery that bunks were first introduced for sailors, and only then because it was found impossible for a sailor to keep warm in a hammock in Northern latitudes. I do not know when "Cape Ann" hammocks were first made, but they are by no means a recent invention, for I have an old one made of linen homespun canvas.

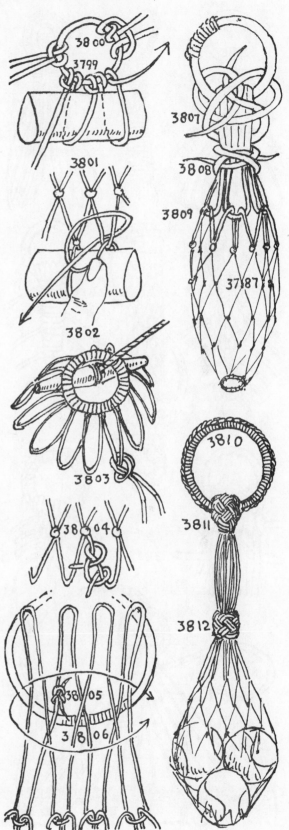

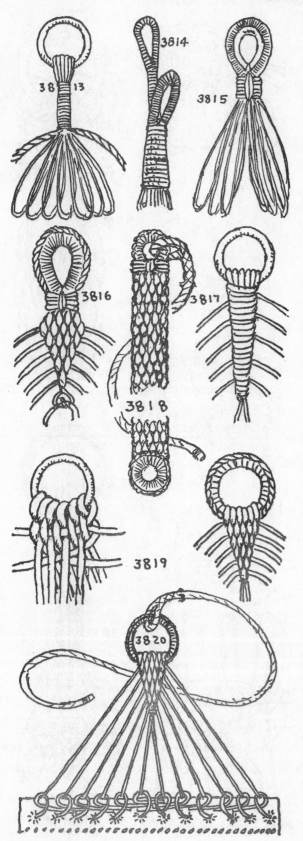

3813. The simplest *hammock clew* is made by holding an iron ring in a vise and driving a nail in the bench about two feet away. A number of turns are taken through the ring and around the nail. When sufficient in number, the upper part is served tightly over, close up to the ring. Netted hammocks are generally reinforced with ropes along the edges. A small rope twice the length of the hammock is middled through the ring and the turns in the light material are taken in such way as to cover it. The splice is taken at the other end, where it is served over in making the other clew. Sufficient netting is made between the two clews to suit the length of the boltrope.

3814. A *Pullman hammock clew* is made so that the length of the hammock has three adjustments. Each end has two loops, one being made of the side rope, the other of the mesh material. The overall length is about five feet ten inches. Every berth on a small boat should be provided with a hammock of this sort to hold clothes.

3815. A *seized clew* is made around two nails. The center section is grafted or served over, and a thimble is seized in with a round seizing.

3816. *Navy clews* are made of either six or twelve lengths of nettle stuff; twelve was the older practice. These are middled and the eye is either grafted, ringbolt hitched, or served over. They are then seized together either with or without a thimble. A sword mat is started and, after all twelve ends are worked once or twice, two ends, one at each side, are laid out each time the warps are passed, in the manner described for "shouldering" (※3493). Some old seamanship books say that the last pair should be half knotted. But the best practice is to seize them.

3817. An *old boat gripe* that I have examined was made as follows: Twelve strands were middled, and the center section *ringbolt hitched*. The strands were brought together, seized and then laid up into a six-foot length of sword matting. At the bottom end the strands were made into an ARTIFICIAL EYE, which was ringbolt hitched as far as possible and then buttonholed across the matted part.

3818. A *Spanish hammock clew* is made with six lengths of material middled. The twelve strands that are formed are served from the ring down and every four turns two opposite strands are laid out. The end of the service is finished off around the two last strands.

3819. A *sword mat ring clew* is made as pictured with six lengths of material in a way similar to ※3816. The ring is hitched over (see pages 569, 570).

3820. The *sailor's hammock* is of heavy canvas six feet long and three feet wide with a selvage at both edges. At the head and foot is a tabling with twelve eyelet holes to which the nettles are made fast as pictured. Every hammock clew has a lanyard for slinging spliced in.

In stowing such a hammock, seven MARLINE HITCHES were formerly recommended. Nowadays five SINGLE HITCHES are deemed sufficient.

3821. A *knitted hammock.* Using *hammock clew* ⚓3813 with fifteen loops as a base, and two broomstick handles for needles, Caleb Stabler used to knit a complete hammock of lobster cord in one evening. Two stitches were taken in each clew loop.

3822. A *netted hammock.* Make clew ⚓3813 or ⚓3815 with twelve loops two feet long and one doubled rope with two twelve-foot legs. Using a spool five inches in girth, the first row of meshes should be KNOT ⚓3793. This will give a row of twenty-four meshes. Now add a 6½-foot length of ordinary mesh. Reeve the side ropes through the outer meshes along each side. Splice the two ends of the side rope together at the proper length and make a second clew exactly like the first one. The splice should be hidden inside the clew.

Netted hammocks are sometimes made with several different lengths of stitches, and frequently the number of meshes in a row is diminished toward the ends. Frequently double threads are used to strengthen the mid-section (see ⚓3795).

3823. I haven't seen a *barrel-stave hammock* for years, but when I was a youngster I made one. Secure a clean flour or sugar barrel, take it apart and bore two ⅜-inch holes in the end of each stave just inside the chines and one half or three quarters of an inch from the sides. Take two lengths of sash cord each about twenty-two feet long.

Middle one of the ropes and reeve one of the ends, first down and then up, through the holes in one end of each stave to the other end of the hammock. Do the same with the other end of the same rope through the holes at the other ends of the staves in the same direction. From the other direction repeat the performance with the other rope, the order for each stave being up and then down, and the up tuck should be taken to the left of the first rope and the down tuck should be to the right of it. After the staves are all evenly spaced and about a half inch apart, the total stave length should be six to six and one half feet and the whole hammock, including clews, about twelve feet. Each clew is made up of one loop and two rope ends. The rope ends pass around the thimble in opposite directions and the clew is tightly seized in close up to the thimble as ⚓3815 and then is served over.

3824. There are at least two peculiar HAMMOCK HITCHES by which clews are secured to "Cape Ann" hammocks. These are given as ⚓1832 and ⚓1833.

3825. When timber on a strange shore failed to grow at the water's edge, hammocks were slung by "wooding and watering parties" from oars that were lashed together. With miasma, serpents and cannibals to contend with, a sailor couldn't be too careful.

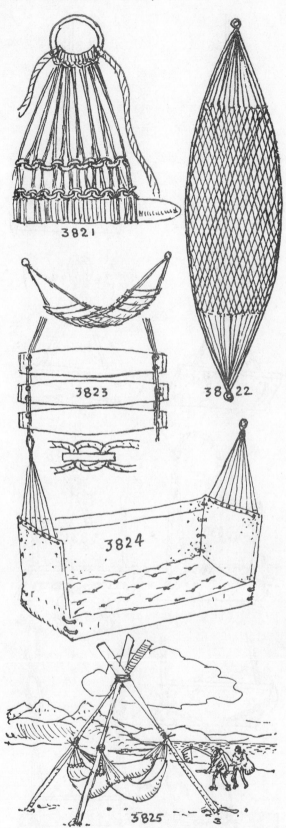

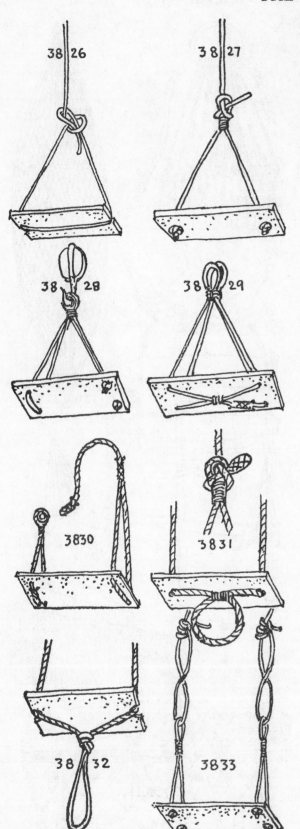

3826. The *boatswain's chair* is a very important article of ship's furniture, and ashore *house painters, flagpole climbers* and *steeplejacks* cannot get along without it. This is the simplest form made, with slotted ends in the seat and a *bowline knot* in the rope.

3827. A more finished and safer chair is made with holes in the seat. The seat strap is fastened in the holes with two MATTHEW WALKER KNOTS, and there is a becket seized in at the top, to which the pendant is bent.

3828. A more stable *boatswain's chair* is suspended at four corners and has a *double becket* seized in. The two knots are MATTHEW WALKERS.

3829. The most approved *strap for a boatswain's chair* is the one illustrated here. The ends are short spliced on the bottom, and the bights are seized together where they cross. The seized-in double-eyed becket has two sets of crossing turns, and altogether the chair is as safe as can be.

3830. An elaborate *boatswain's chair* that is so rigged in order to be bent to a becket on a tackle block. After it is bent to the tackle the end of the strap is adjusted to its own THIMBLE EYE and secured with a BECKET HITCH. An interesting feature of this is the DOG'S POINT on the end of the strap, which makes the BECKET HITCH doubly secure.

3831. A method of *shortening swing ropes* ashore by seizing in a round turn under the seat. The seizing should have *crossing turns*.

3832. The more common method is to tie an OVERHAND KNOT in the bight; this is very difficult to untie, and a DOUBLE FIGURE-EIGHT KNOT is better. These loops are much favored when the swinger has a ground crew to assist. It offers an excellent handhold.

3833. I have seen an *adjustable swing* made as illustrated. The rope ends, after passing through THIMBLE EYES on the seat straps, were first rove through the strands of the standing part of the ropes and then made fast with ROLLING HITCHES, presumably beyond the reach of the younger children. The ends of the ROLLING HITCHES were seized (not shown).

3834. A *knotted bathing ladder* for a small boat. The knot is given by Bocher. It is very comfortable for bare feet and it has the advantage that it may be stowed anywhere and will not mark or bruise other stowed articles. Take a piece of 2¼-inch (circumference) rope and middle it. Leave a loop at the center and seize in an eye. At a distance of one foot from the eye tie the series of knots that are pictured. Splice the ends together or else leave them long and put a MATTHEW WALKER KNOT in each end. A somewhat similar knot, that is perhaps more difficult to tie, is given as №800.

3835. This *chock ladder*, also for barefoot use, is given by Paul N. Hasluck. It would seem that there might be a tendency to spin, in which case, if used as a bathing ladder, toes might be pinched. But hanging free over the stern of a boat or from the branch of a tree, it would do nicely. The chocks are turned, about five inches in diameter with lengthwise holes about seven eighths of an inch in diameter. The ropes should be a little smaller than the holes; if of the same size, they may swell and split the chocks. Put a THIMBLE

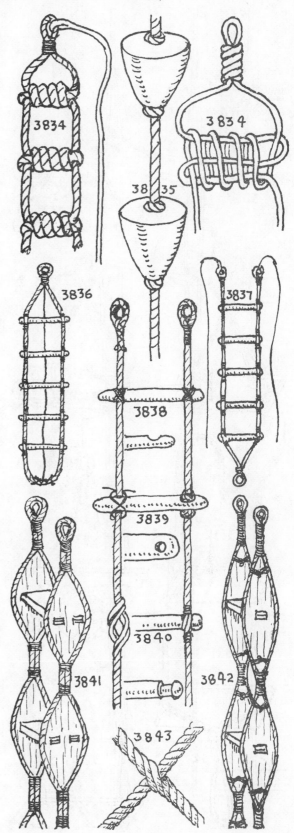

EYE in the end of a four-strand rope. Mark the rope with light stops at fifteen-inch intervals. Reeve all chocks and stop them near the bottom of the rope. Hang the rope upside down at a good working height and at the first stopping put in a STANDING TURK'S-HEAD (#1582) of heavy marline, FOUR-BIGHT × THREE-LEAD × THREE-PLY. Put the first chock in place and add a similar knot close to the other end of the chock. Continue until all chocks are in place, then leave a two-foot end and tie a MATTHEW WALKER KNOT (#682).

3836. A *Jacob's ladder* has round rungs that are generally of oak or ash but sometimes of iron. A pilot's ladder (#3841) has flat treads and generally side pieces as well. Except for this distinction, ladders are classified according to their material, position or use: as side, rope, accommodation, companion, stern, hatchway, etc.

The sides of *Jacob's ladders* are made preferably of four-strand rope, and, if of Manila, these are about two and one quarter inches in circumference. Middle a rope and seize in a THIMBLE EYE. The strands are opened enough to receive the rungs, which are seized in at approximately sixteen-inch intervals. Finally the lower ends of the rope are spliced together. According to Steel's text and illustrations, a light line called a "concluding line" is added as shown, presumably for gathering up the ladder. There is another interpretation of the "concluding line," given here as #3844.

3837. Sometimes *Jacob's ladders* are fitted with a pair of beckets instead of a single one; this is to prevent spinning.

3838. A rung notched on one side only and made fast with an X seizing.

3839. A large flattened rung with a hole bored in each end is occasionally seen and is very comfortable indeed for bare feet. Sailors of many nations go barefoot except when in cold waters. This rung is generally seized in, but it may have a STANDING TURK'S-HEAD above and below.

3840. The most usual way of fitting is the one given here. The rung is turned in a lathe with knobs in each end. The knob is entered between the strands of the rope and either sized in or else secured above and below with STANDING TURK'S-HEADS.

3841. A *pilot ladder* consists of a series of sections, each composed of two "punkin-seed cheeks" morticed to a flat tread. Sometimes two parallel rungs, close together, were used instead of a single flat tread. The edges of the cheeks are deeply grooved to receive the ropes. The side ropes are doubled and a THIMBLE EYE is seized in the center of each; a second seizing is put in a short distance below the first, and then a cheek is seized in. Between two cheeks on a side is a doubled section of rope several inches in length. Without these the ladder will not fold up into convenient form for stowing.

3842. Another type of *pilot ladder* is made with longer, narrower cheeks and narrower treads.

3843. Between two of these cheeks, one of each pair of ropes is rove between the strands of its companion rope and, after being pulled up snug around a cheekpiece, the two are given a long seizing. Seizing #3433 is then put into each end of the cheeks.

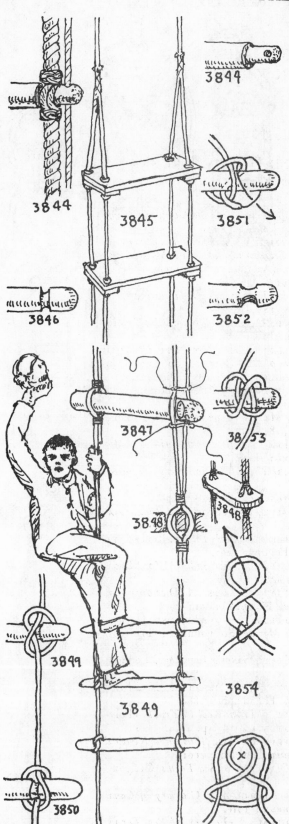

3844. *"Concluding lines,"* to hold rungs in place. According to Admiral Paris, these were rove through holes in the middle of the ends of rungs. The rungs were seized in or else STANDING TURK'S-HEADS were placed above and below them on the side ropes.

3845. A large State-of-Maine schooner carried this ladder, which was neither pilot nor Jacob's ladder. It had lanyards at the top which were long enough to lash either to eyebolts or to belaying pins inside the rail. The steps had cleats at either end which were supported by STANDING TURK'S-HEADS.

3846. The common grooved rung was turned in a lathe.

3847. "The most general way of making these ladders," according to Brady (1841), was with two small ropes at each side which were seized together above and below the slots in the rungs.

3848. Instead of a round rung, a flat one with two holes in each end was also used, which was easier for the feet.

3849. The remainder of the ladders shown are simple makeshift ones for shore use. The first and simplest is from Lowney Brothers' Circus and led to the flying trapeze. It consisted of two ropes tied in a series of MARLINE HITCHES around sections of broom handle which had been slightly scored with a rasp to receive them. The tendency of the rung to roll was frustrated by having the knots in one rope on the front of the rung, and the knots of the other rope on the reverse side.

3850. A HALF HITCH is as simple to make and, used for this purpose, is more secure than the MARLINE HITCH. The hitches in one rope should oppose those on the other end of the rung.

3851. If the last knot is given one additional tuck, as indicated by the single arrow in the diagram, CROSSING KNOT #1193 is formed and the pull on the knot will be at opposite sides of the rung.

3852. The common way of notching a rung, when two ropes are used at one end, is #3841. Shallow notches may be made with a rasp. Single ropes may be secured to this rung, as #3840 and #3844.

3853. A secure ladder can be very quickly made by tying the CONSTRICTOR KNOT. The knots at one end of the rung should be on the side opposite the knots of the other end.

3854. CROSSING KNOT #1192 makes an excellent temporary LADDER KNOT, as the pull is at the top and bottom of the rung. For this reason, the two sets of knots do not have to be tied reversely. Moreover, it is simpler to tie than #3850.

The subject of knots is still very much alive; for there is more rope in use today than ever before, more even than in the days of the clipper ship, and a rope cannot be put to work without the tying of a knot.

There are still old knots that are unrecorded, and so long as there are new purposes for rope, there will always be new knots to discover.

So it is possible that someday I may find something further to say on knots, although it seems to me at present that eleven years is long enough service to have given to one cause.

But now, in the words of Captain John Smith, "Sometimes Governour of Virginia, and Admirall of New England," we will "Make an End of this Discourse with a Knot."

A LIST OF BOOKS, BELONGING TO THE AUTHOR, WHICH CONTAIN MATERIAL ON KNOTS

PART I

MARINE DICTIONARIES, ENCYCLOPEDIAS, AND VOCABULARIES
(Arranged Chronologically)

MANWAYRING, SIR HENRY. *The Sea-mans Dictionary or, an Exposition and Demonstration of all the Parts and Things belonging to a Shippe.* Published posthumously. London: 1644. Privately circulated in MS. form for twenty years previous to publication.

SMITH, CAPTAINE JOHN, Sometimes Governour of Virginia and Admirall of New England. *An Accidence for Young Sea-men or the Pathway to Experience.* London: 1626 (Reprint, Edinburgh: 1910).

———. *A Sea Grammar.* London: 1627 (Reprint, Glasgow: 1907).

BUTLER, CAPTAINE NATHANIEL. *Boteler's Dialogues.* Written about 1634, published 1688. (Navy Records Society reprint, London: 1929.)

GUILLET, SAINT GEORGES. *The Gentleman's Dictionary* (Part III, "The Art of Navigation"). Paris: 1678. (First English translation, London: 1705.)

AUBIN. *Dictionnaire de Marine.* Amsterdam: 1702.

WARD, EDWARD ("NED"). *The Wooden World.* 1707. (The Society for Nautical Research reprint, London: 1929.)

ANONYMOUS: *A Military Dictionary and a Sea Dictionary by officers who serv'd several years at Sea and Land.* London: 1708.

BLANCKLEY, THOMAS RILEY. *A Naval Expositor.* London: 1750.

AN OFFICER OF THE NAVY. *The Naval Repository.* London: 1762.

FALCONER, WILLIAM. *An Universal Dictionary of the Marine.* London: 1769, 1771, 1780, and 1789.

MONTAINE, WILLIAM. *Seaman's Vade Mecum.* London: 1782.

LESCALLIER, M. *Vocabulaire des Termes de Marine.* London: 1783. (Eng.-Fr.)

DU CLAIRBOIS, VIAL, and BLONDEAU, M. *Encyclopédie Méthodique Marine.* Vols. I–IV. Paris: 1783.

LIDDEL, R. *Seaman's New Vede Mecum.* London: 1794.

ANONYMOUS. (J. Debrett, publisher.) *A Vocabulary of Sea Phrases by a Captain of the British Navy.* London: 1799.

MOORE, J. J. *British Mariner's Vocabulary or Universal Dictionary of Technical Terms and Sea Phrases.* London: 1801.

NORIE, J. W. *Mariner's New and Complete Naval Dictionary.* London: 1804.

DUANE, WILLIAM. *The Mariner's Dictionary or American Seaman's Vocabulary.* Washington City: 1805. (Appears to be a literal copy of Moore, 1801.)

ROMME, CHARLES. *Dictionnaire de la Marine Française.* Paris: 1813.

WILLAUMEZ, VICE-ADMIRAL. *Dictionnaire de Marine.* Paris: 1820.

BURNEY, WILLIAM, LL.D. *New and Universal Dictionary of the Marine.* London: 1830. (Revised edition of Falconer's Dictionary.)

DANA, R. H., JR. *Seaman's Friend.* Boston, New York: 1841.

———. *Seaman's Manual* (same as above). London: 1841, 1844, 1846, etc.

D'AMORINN, JOÃO PEDRO. *Diccionario de Marinha.* Lisboa: 1841.

YOUNG, ARTHUR. *Nautical Dictionary.* Dundee: 1847.

JAL, A. *Glossaire Nautique.* Paris: 1848.

GREENWOOD, JAMES, ESQ. *Sailor's Sea Book.* London: 1850.

LEES, JAMES. *Dana's Seaman's Friend.* Revised and enlarged. London: 1867.

SMYTH, ADMIRAL W. H. *The Sailor's Word Book.* London: 1867.

CHAPMAN, CAPTAIN CHARLES. *A Dictionary of Modern Sea Terms.* London: 1869.

PARIS, VICE-ADMIRAL FRANÇOIS EDMOND. *Dictionary of the Marine.* Six volumes folio. Paris: 1877.

RUSSELL, W. CLARK. *Sailor's Language.* London: 1883.

HAMERSLY, LEWIS R., and ASSOCIATES. *Naval Encyclopaedia.* Philadelphia: 1884.

PAASCH, CAPTAIN H. *From Keel to Truck.* (Polyglot Dictionary.) Antwerp: 1894.

PATTERSON, CAPTAIN HOWARD. *Illustrated Nautical Encyclopedia.* Cleveland: 1901.

ANSTED, A. *A Dictionary of Sea Terms.* Glasgow: 1917.

DE SALIS, HENRY RODOLPH. *A Glossary of Canal Terms.* London: 1918.

BRADFORD, GERSHOM. *A Glossary of Sea Terms.* New York: 1927.

ESPARTEIRO, ANTONIO MARQUES. *Dicionario de Marinharia.* Lisboa: 1936.

PART II

SEAMANSHIP, SAILMAKING, RIGGING, ETC.

(Arranged Alphabetically)

ADMIRALTY, THE. *Manual of Seamanship for Boys' Training Ships.* Vols. I–II. London: 1932.

ALSTON, LIEUTENANT A. H. (R.N.). *Seamanship and Naval Duties.* London: 1860; ALSTON, CAPTAIN A. H., *Seamanship and Naval Duties.* Portsmouth: 1871.

ANDERSON, R. C. *Rigging of Ships in the Days of the Spritsail Topsail.* Salem: 1927.

——, editor. *Treatise on Rigging.* Circa 1625. (Publication of the Society for Nautical Research.) London: 1921.

ANONYMOUS. *The Mate and his Duties.* Liverpool: 1875.

——. *Manual of Seamanship.* London: 1891.

BANDEIRO DE SOUSA, JOÃO. *Tratado de Apparelho do Navio.* Lisboa: 1896.

BATHURST, HON., and REV. CHARLES, LL.D. *Notes on Nets.* London: N. D.

BIDDLECOMBE, GEORGE. *Art of Rigging.* London: 1848.

BLOOMGREN, AXEL S. *Lärobok I. Sjömanskap.* Stockholm: 1923.

BLUNT, GEORGE W. *Sheet Anchor,* by Darcy Lever, with additions by G. W. Blunt. New York: 1858.

BOYD, JOHN McNEILL. *Manual for Naval Cadets.* London: 1857.

BRADY, WILLIAM N. (Boatswain, U.S.N.). *The Naval Apprentice's Kedge Anchor.* New York: 1841.

——. (Sailing Master, U.S.N.). *Kedge Anchor.* Eighth edition, New York: 1855; Eighteenth edition, 1893.

BURNEY, COMMANDER CHARLES. *Young Seaman's Manual and Rigger's Guide.* London: 1878.

BUSHELL. *The Rigger's Guide.* London: 1854; Portsmouth: 1893.

CHALLAMEL, AUGUSTIN, editor. *Manuel du Manœuvrier.* Vols. I–II. Paris: 1891.

CLARKE, FRANCIS G. *The Seaman's Manual.* Portland, Maine: 1830.

——. *American Ship Master's Guide.* Boston: 1845.

CLOWES, G. S. LAIRD, editor. *Length of Mast and Yards in 1640.* London: 1931.

DANA, R. H., JR. *Seaman's Friend.* Boston and New York: 1841; Boston: 1857.

——. *Seaman's Manual.* London: 1841, 1844, 1846, 1867. (Revised by James Lees.)

DE PARFOURU, R. *Manuel du Marin.* Paris: 1921.

DICK, ADMIRAL. *Leitfaden der Seemännschaft.* Berlin: 1927.

GOWER, RICHARD HALL. *Treatise on Seamanship.* London: 1808.

HARRIS, COMMANDER R. H. Alston's *Seamanship* revised. Portsmouth: 1871.

HEATHCOTE, CAPTAIN SIR HENRY (R.N.). *Treatise on Staysails.* London: 1824.

KENEALY, CAPTAIN A. J. *Boat Sailing.* New York: 1901.

KIPPING, ROBERT. *Elements of Sailmaking.* London: 1847.

——. *Masting, Mast-making and Rigging.* London: 1877.

——. *Sails and Sailmaking.* London: 1880.

KNIGHT, LIEUTENANT COMMANDER AUSTIN M. *Modern Seamanship.* New York: 1901.

LAVIEUVILLE, ODIN and DOUXAMI. *Manuel des Écoles de Pêche Maritime.* Paris: 1902.

LEVER, DARCY. *Sheet Anchor.* London: 1808.

——. *Sheet Anchor,* with additions by George W. Blunt. New York: 1858.

LUCE, S. B. *Seamanship for Use of U. S. Naval Academy.* Newport, R. I.: 1862.

——, LIEUTENANT COMMANDER. *Seamanship.* New York: 1873.

——, ADMIRAL. *Seamanship,* revised by Lieutenant Aaron Ward. New York: 1884.

MIDDENDORF, F. L. *Bemastung und Tackelung der Schiffe.* Berlin: 1903.

MOFFAT, JAMES B. *Seamanship and Rigging.* London: 1861.

MURPHY and JEFFERS. *Nautical Routine and Stowage.* New York: 1849.

NARES, LIEUTENANT GEORGE S. *Naval Cadet's Guide or Seaman's Companion.* London: 1860.

——, CAPTAIN SIR GEORGE S. *Seamanship.* Portsmouth: 1877, 1882.

——, VICE-ADMIRAL SIR GEORGE S. *Seamanship.* Portsmouth: 1897.

OLSEN, O. T. *Fisherman's Seamanship.* Grimsby: 1885.

QUALTROUGH, LIEUTENANT E. F. (U.S.N.). *The Boat Sailor's Manual.* New York: 1886.

RIESENBERG, FELIX. *Seamanship for the Merchant Service.* New York: 1922.

RÖDING, JOHANN. *Allgemeines Wörterbuch der Marine.* Vols. I–III. Hamburg: 1795.

STEEL, DAVID. *Elements and Practice of Rigging and Seamanship.* Vols. I, II. London: 1794.

——. *Art of Sailmaking.* London: 1796.

SUTHERLAND, WILLIAM. *Shipbuilder's Assistant and Marine Architecture.* (Chapter 5, "The Boatswain's Art.") London: 1755.

TAUNT, LIEUTENANT EMERY H. *Young Sailor's Assistant in Practical Seamanship.* Washington: 1883.

TODD and WHALL. *Practical Seamanship for the Merchant Marine.* London: 1896.

WALKER, T. P. Alston's *Seamanship*, revised. Portsmouth: 1902.

WARD, LIEUTENANT AARON. Luce's *Seamanship*, revised. New York: 1884.

WILCOCKS, J. C. *The Sea Fisherman*. London: 1868.

WILSON-BARKER, D. *Manual of Elementary Seamanship*. London: 1897.

PART III
KNOT MONOGRAPHS

ALDRIDGE, A. F. *Knots*. New York: 1918.

BELASH, CONSTANTINE A. *Braiding and Knotting for Amateurs*. Boston: 1936.

BERGER, A. A. *Rope and Its Uses*. Iowa State College: 1927.

BIDDLE, TYRREL. *How to Make Knots, Bends and Splices*. London: N. D.

BOCHER, EMMANUEL. *Cordes, tresses, nœuds*. (Vol. III, "Needlework".) Paris: 1914.

BOITARD, M. *Nouveau Manuel du Cordier*. Paris: 1839.

BOWLING, TOM (pseudonym), PAUL RAPSEY HODGE or FREDERICK CHAMIER. *The Book of Knots*. Edinburgh: 1866; London: 1870, 1876, 1882, 1890.

BRAINARD, F. R. *Knots, Splices, Hitches, Bends and Lashings*. New York: 1893.

BURGESS, J. TOM. *Knots, Ties and Splices*. London: N. D.; Glasgow: N. D.

BYERS, CHESTER. *Roping*. New York: 1928.

COE, CHARLES H. *Juggling a Rope*. Pendleton, Oregon: 1927.

COLUMBIAN ROPE CO. *Rope Knowledge for Scouts*. Auburn: N. D.

COMÉT, N. R. *Sjömansknopen*. Malmo: 1908.

DAY, CYRUS LAWRENCE. *Sailor's Knots*. New York: 1935.

DE DILLMONT, THÉRÈSE. *Knotted Fringes*. Mulhouse: N. D.

——. *Macramé*. Mulhouse: N. D.

DORN, J. C., publisher. *Useful Hitches and Splices* (pamphlet). Chicago: N. D.

DREW, JAMES M. *Ropework, Knots, Hitches, Splices, Halters*. St. Paul: 1936.

——. *Some Knots and Splices*, Farmer's Library. St. Paul: 1912.

ELIASON, ELDRIDGE. *Practical Bandaging*. Philadelphia: 1930.

FEHRE, HANS. *Seemännische Handarbeiten*. Hamburg: 1925.

FLATHER, J. J. *Rope Driving*. New York: 1895.

FREAR, J. B. *Rope and Its Use on the Farm*. University of Minnesota. St. Paul: 1915.

GIBSON, J. *Boy Scout Knot Book*. Glasgow: 1928.

——. *Girl Scout Knot Book* (same as above). Glasgow: 1928.

GILBERT, ALFRED C. *Knots and Splices with Rope-Tying Tricks*. New Haven: 1920.

"GILCRAFT" (pseudonym). *Knotting*. London: 1931.

GRAUMONT and HENSEL. *Encyclopedia of Knots*. New York: 1939.

HASLUCK, PAUL N. *Knotting and Splicing*. London: 1918–21.

HERWIG, PHILIP C. *Square Knot Book*. Brooklyn: 1926.

HOUDINI, HARRY. *Magical Rope Ties and Escapes*. London: N. D.

HUNT, C. W., Co. *Knots, Hitches and Bends* (pamphlet). Philadelphia: 1916.

HUNTER, W. A. *Fisherman's Knots and Wrinkles*. London: 1927.

IRVING, COMMANDER J. *Knots, Ties and Splices*. New York: 1934.

ANONYMOUS. *Jewellers' Book of Patterns in Hairwork*. London: circa 1865.

JUTSUM, CAPTAIN J. NETHERCLIFT. *Knots, Bends and Splices*. Glasgow: 1908, 1917.

KUNHARDT, C. P. *Ropes: Their Knots and Splices*. New York: 1893.

LATTER, LUCY R. *Knotting, Looping and Plaiting*. London: N. D.

LE BLANC, H. *The Art of Tying the Cravat*. Philadelphia and Paris: 1828; London and New York: 1829.

LOCKE, L. LELAND. *Ancient Quipu or Peruvian Knot Record*. New York: 1923.

MILBURN, GEORGE. *How to Tie All Kinds of Knots*. Gerard, Kansas: 1927.

NATIONAL SAFETY COUNCIL. *Knots, Bends, Hitches and Slings* (pamphlet). Chicago: N. D.

"NAUTICUS" (pseudonym). *The Splicing of Ropes (Cotton and Wire)*. London: N. D.

NEW BEDFORD CORDAGE CO. *The Knot Book*. New Bedford: 1935.

ÖHRVALL, HJALMAR. *De Viktigaste Knutarna*. Stockholm: 1912.

——. *Om Knutar*. Stockholm: 1908, 1916.

OSBORN, E. H. *Rope Work*. Sauk Center: 1915.

PASKINS, T. F. *Splicing and Socketing Wire Rope*. Musselburgh: N. D.

PLYMOUTH ROPE CO. *Useful Knots and How to Tie Them* (pamphlet). Plymouth: N. D.

POST, CHARLES JOHNSON. *Horse Packing*. New York: 1914.

POST OFFICE DEPARTMENT, GREAT BRITAIN. *Cordage and Tackle, Knotting and Splicing*. London: 1926.

RENNER, KAPITÄN C. *Knoten, Spleissen und andere Seemännische Handarbeiten*. Berlin: 1927.

RILEY, HOWARD W. *Knots, Hitches and Splices*. Ithaca: 1912.

RILEY, H. W., ROBB, B. B., and BEHRENDS, F. G. *Knots, Hitches and Splices*. Ithaca: 1922.

ROEHL, LOUIS M. *Rope Work*. Milwaukee: 1921.

SAITO, YEN. *Knots and Paper Folding*. Tokyo: 1918.

SCHÖMANN, A. *Das Tauwerk*. Hamburg: 1925.

SCOATES, DANIELS. *Rope Work*. Department of Agriculture, Washington, D. C.: 1915.

SHAW, GEORGE RUSSELL. *Knots, Useful and Ornamental*. Boston: 1924.

——. The same, enlarged. Boston: 1933.

SIMMONS, JOHN, Co. *Knots and How to Tie Them* (pamphlet). New York: N. D.

SKIRVING, R. SCOT. *Wire Splicing for Yachtsmen*. Sidney: 1931.

SMITH, JOHNSON, publisher. *Rope Splicing, Useful Knots, etc.* (pamphlet). Chicago: N. D.

SPENCER, CHARLES L. *Knots, Splices and Fancy Work*. Glasgow: 1934.

STOPFORD, CAPTAIN P. J. (R. N.). *Cordage and Cables*. Glasgow: 1925.

WALKER, LOUISA. *Varied Occupations in String-work*. London: 1896.

WHITLOCK CORDAGE Co. *Knots the Sailors Use* (pamphlet). New York: N. D.

WOODHOUSE and KILGOUR. *Cordage and Cordage Hemp and Fibres*. London: 1918.

PART IV

PRACTICES ALLIED TO KNOTTING

ANONYMOUS. *Rigging*. War Department, Washington: 1924.

BOCHER, EMMANUEL. *Needlework*. Four folio volumes. Paris: 1914.

CAULFIELD and SAWARD. *Dictionary of Needlework*. London: 1882.

CRAMPTON, CHARLES. *Canework*. Leicester: 1928.

DE DILLMONT, THÉRÈSE. *Encyclopedia of Needle Work*. Paris: N. D.

——. *Macramé*. (Abstracted in part from the above work with additional photographic illustrations) "D.M.C. Library." Mulhouse.

——. *Knotted Fringes*. "D.M.C. Library." Mulhouse: N. D.

ELIASON, ELDRIDGE. *Practical Bandaging*. Philadelphia: 1930.

GRISWOLD, LESTER. *Handicraft*. (Includes quill, thong, bead, rope and hair work. An excellent instruction book, well illustrated.) Denver: 1931.

HADDON, KATHLEEN. *Artists in String*. (Cat's Cradles.) New York: 1930.

——. *Cat's Cradles from Many Lands*. London: 1912.

HOLDEN, G. P. *Streamcraft and Angling Manual*. (Fly tying.) Cincinnati: 1920.

HERWIG, P. C. *The Square Knot Book*. (Macramé. Good elementary instruction.) 97 Sands St., Brooklyn: N. D.

JAYNE, C. F. *String Figures*. (Cat's Cradles.) New York: 1906.

LAMBERT, MISS. *Handbook of Needlework*. New York: 1842.

POST, CHARLES J. *Horse Packing*. New York: 1914.

ROLLO, W. KEITH. *Art of Fly Fishing*. London: 1931.

ROUSE-BALL, W. W. *String Figures*. (Cat's Cradles.) Cambridge: 1928.

Starlight Manual of Knitting and Crocheting. Boston: 1887.

WALKER, LOUISA. *Varied Occupations in Stringwork*. London: 1896.

WALLACE, DILLON. *Packing and Portaging*. New York: 1916.

WHITE, MARY. *How to Make Baskets*. (Good elementary instruction.) New York: 1907.

Various museum bulletins (American Museum of Natural History, Smithsonian, etc.) have excellent instruction on basketry, hat braiding, rugmaking, cat's cradles, trapping, etc., which are easily procurable.

A GLOSSARY OF TERMS, MAINLY NAUTICAL, PERTAINING TO KNOTS AND ROPE WORK

ADRIFT: A piece of rigging goes adrift when the end unreeves; a knot when it spills.

AGAINST THE SUN: Counterclockwise.

AMBULANCE KNOT: The REEF KNOT, a needle-work term.

ARSE: The hole in a block through which the fall is rove.

ARTIFICER'S KNOT: The CLOVE HITCH.

"AS THEY LIE": Ends tucked directly under instead of first *over* and then *under*.

(A) 'VAST!: Stop or halt. " 'Vast heaving" is the order to stop work at the capstan.

BACK A STRAND, TO: (1) In the LONG SPLICE, to fill the score vacated by one strand, with one of the opposite strands. (2) In the BACK-HANDED SPLICE, to tuck one strand in a helix around the opposing one.

BACKHANDED ROPE: The yarns and strands have a right twist and the rope itself a left twist.

BACK SPLICE: The strands are first crowned, then tucked back over and under as in a SHORT SPLICE.

BACKING: Small flanking wormings at either side of the main worming, in large hawsers and cables.

BARBER'S KNOT: The SHEET BEND when used for tying hair in wigmaking.

HAVE A BEARING, TO: To be properly couched.

BECKET: (1) The rope handle of a sea chest. (2) The eye or hook of a block strap. (3) A short rope with an eye at one end and a button at the other, used to confine and secure spars, oars, etc.

BELAY, TO: To secure a rope with S or figure-eight turns around a belaying pin, cleat or bitts.

BELAYING PIN: A wood, metal or bone pin inserted through a hole in a rail, to which running rigging is made fast.

BEND, A: A knot which ties two ropes' ends together.

BEND, TO: (1) To tie two ropes together. (2) To tie to an anchor. (3) To tie a rope to a spar. (4) To secure a sail to a spar.

BENDS: Small ropes used as seizings in clinching a cable.

BIGHT or BITE: Any slack part of a rope between the two ends, particularly when curved or looped.

BIND, TO: (1) To jam. (2) To seize or lash.

BITTS: Upright timbers, usually in pairs, for making fast hawsers and cables.

BITT, TO: To take a turn around a bitt.

BITTER END: The inactive inboard end of a cable abaft the Carrick bitts.

BLACK KNOT: A hard knot or tangle.

BLOCK: A machine with grooved wheels for diverting the lead of a rope or, when compounded, for increasing the power of a tackle.

BLOCK AND FALL: A tackle. At sea these generally bear specific names, so the expression is more common ashore.

BLOCK-A-BLOCK, "BLOCK AND BLOCK," "TWO BLOCKS" and "CHOCK-A-BLOCK": The blocks of a tackle hauled together. The term is commonly used to mean that the limit or capacity (of anything) has been reached.

BOLLARD or BOLLARDS: (1) Originally the knight-heads of a ship when extended above the rail and used for making fast. (2) A pair of posts at either side of a dock or lock. (3) Posts of iron or wood on a wharf or the deck of a ship, either single or double. Sometimes the distinction is made that bollards belong to the wharf and not the deck. Captain Francis Stone always called a single post or pile, suitable for mooring, a bollard. At the present time bollards are generally of cast iron, are either single or double, and commonly are round, while bitts are usually rectangular.

BOLT: A heaver, q.v.

BOLTROPE: Three-strand rope sewed around the edges of sails.

BOND: A knot that binds.

BOURCHIER KNOT: In heraldry, the REEF KNOT.

BOW GRACE: Old rope and cable nailed to the planking of a ship as a protection against ice.

BOWLINE: (1) A rope that trims the forward leech of a square sail. (2) Nowadays the *knot* formerly employed in making the bowline fast to the BOWLINE CRINGLES.

BOUSE or BOWSE: To move an object about deck by means of a small tackle.

BRACES: Ropes with which to trim the yards.

BRACE UP, TO: To take up slack and to sail "full and by."

BRAILS: Ropes leading through cringles in the leech of the spanker and spencers, to assist in furling, similar to buntlines.

BRIDLE: A span of rope used in attaching halyards, fore-and-aft sheets, bowlines, etc.

BRING UP, TO: To fetch, to come in contact.

BRING UP WITH A ROUND TURN, TO: To check, or be checked, suddenly.

BUILDER'S KNOT: The CLOVE HITCH, one of "Tom Bowling's" names.

BULL'S-EYE: A wooden thimble or block having no shiv, usually of lignum vitae; early ones of elm.

BUNT: The central section of the foot of a square sail or seine.

BUNTLINE: For hauling up the bunt when furling and reefing.

BUTTON: (1) A KNOB KNOT. (2) A leather washer used under nailheads when securing stirrups to the yards.

BY THE RUN: To let go by the run is to let go or cast off instantly, instead of slacking off gradually.

CABLE or CABLE-LAID ROPE: Three hawsers or ropes twisted and laid up, or closed, together.

CABLE'S LENGTH: As a unit of measurement, 100 fathoms. The actual length of a cable depends upon the length of the ropewalk, usually about 120 fathoms.

CABLETS: Cable-laid rope under nine inches in circumference.

CANT ROPE: An old name for four-strand rope without a core. Also called "four cant" (Admiral Smyth).

CAPSIZE, TO: To change its form under stress, to pervert. Said of a knot.

CAPSTAN KNOT: A name loosely applied to several knots, none of which appear to have any purpose connected with the capstan.

CARRY AWAY, TO: To break and go adrift. Applied to both sails and rigging.

CAST, TO: To tie a knot (generally a KNOB KNOT). "It has a Matthew Walker's knot cast in the end." (Lever, 1808.)

CAST LOOSE or CAST OFF: (1) To remove the turns from a belaying pin. (2) To untie a knot, to unbend. (3) To cut seizings or stops.

CASTING LINE: A heaving line. Also, in *angling*, the leader.

CHAFE, TO: To fray, fret, gall or rub.

CHAFING GEAR: Mats, baggy wrinkles, Scotchmen, rounding, etc., for protecting rigging and spars from wear of different sorts.

CHECK, TO: To slacken and hold alternately with a turn around a pin or bitt.

CHEERLY: Quickly, with a will, heartily. Often applied to hoisting.

CHINCKLE: A small bight (kink) in a line. (Admiral Smyth.)

CLAP ON, TO: An expression used in seizing, nippering, stopping and stoppering. The two hands are brought together and the ends exchanged, for passing the turns.

CLEAR, TO: To remove kinks and snarls from a rope.

CLEAT. An object with two horns, for belaying ropes.

CLEWS: Eyes in the lower corners of a square sail, and in the after lower corner of a fore-and-aft sail.

CLOSE, TO: To lay three plain-laid ropes together to form a cable.

CLUE: A thread which, if followed, leads to the solution of a problem.

COACHWHIPPING: A sinnet made around a core in which several strands are worked as a unit. Also any sinnet worked around a core.

COAX A STRAND, TO: To tighten a knot gradually by taking up a little slack at a time, and working each strand in turn until all is snug.

COCKSCOMB: A serrated stop cleat on the end of a yard, to which reef earings are hauled out and lashed. (Also spelled coxcomb.)

COCKSCOMBING: A needlework term that has recently been applied to RINGBOLT HITCHING.

COIL: A series of flakes in a rope, one turn upon another, so arranged for convenience in handling and storing.

COME AND GO, THE: The play or scope allowed any rope or gear.

COME UP, TO (A ROPE or TACKLE): To slacken it gently.

COMMON KNOT: A loose name for the REEF, OVERHAND and other knots. Also applied as an adjective to many others as COMMON WEAVER'S KNOT, COMMON BEND, etc.

CONTLINES: See CUNTLINES.

CONT SPLICE: See CUNT SPLICE.

CORD: Several yarns hard-twisted together.

CORDAGE: All twisted rope of whatever material or size.

CORDED: Hard-twisted. Sometimes it means lashed. A trunk is often corded, and so also is an old-fashioned rope bed.

CORE: The heart of a rope or sinnet; heart is the sailor's term.

COUCH, TO: To rest in the proper niche. "The strands Couch better." (Steel.)

CROSSING KNOT: Found in lashings and parcels where two parts are engaged where they cross each other at right angles.

CROSSING TURNS: Similar to frapping turns but found in seizings and mousings. They are at right angles to the underneath turns and serve to tighten them and keep them compact.

CROTCH or CRUTCH, TO: To marry the opened ends of two ropes preliminary to splicing or shroud knotting.

CROWFOOT: Radiating lines from a euphroe block with which to stretch awnings, nets, etc.

CUNTLINES: The surface seams between the strands of a rope.

CUNT SPLICE: Two ends side spliced together, with a gap between the two parts.

DIAMOND HITCH: A method of pack lashing.

DIP, TO: In knotting, to tuck. The term is employed by both Alston and Luce.

DOG'S COCK or PRICK: The common name for the crowned and back spliced end of a rope. Found on bucket lanyards, hand lead lines, etc.

DOGSHANK: A literal translation of the French name for SHEEPSHANK.

GLOSSARY

Dog, To: To back the tail of a block several turns around a stay, with the lay of the rope.

Doublings: The overlap where two ropes or two parts of the same rope parallel each other, as the shrouds above the deadeyes. The term is usually applied to the overlap of two spars at the tops.

Double, To: To follow the lay of a decorative knot an additional circuit, as in a Turk's-Head or Manrope. If there are three parallel parts (a Three-Ply Knot) the sailor describes it in his own way as having been "doubled three times."

Douse, To: To lower and stow a sail hastily.

Draw, To (A Knot): To untie it.

Drift or Play: Margin allowed for stretch or shrinkage. "Allow two feet six inches drift for setting up with a lanyard." (Bushell, 1854.)

Earings: Ropes with which to bend the corners of a square sail. There are also reef earings at the ends of reef bands.

Ease or Ease Off, To: To slacken.

Elbow: Cables crossed twice.

End: The termination of a rope or the free end leading from the top of a Stopper Knot.

End for End: To shift each end of a rope to the position that has been held by the other.

Enter, To: To tuck a strand.

Entering Rope: An old name for a manrope.

Eye: A spliced, seized or knotted loop.

Fag End: The unfinished end of a rope, left in manufacture.

Fag, To: To fray.

Fagged Out: Worn and raveled.

Fair, To: To smooth out, to even a knot, splice or sinnet. A shipbuilding term.

Fair-Leaders: Boards lashed in the rigging with holes to direct the lead of running rigging. Also various other fittings for similar purposes.

Fake: See Flake.

Fall: (1) The whole rope of a tackle. (2) The hauling end only of a tackle.

Fall Block: The block in a tackle where energy is first applied.

Fancy Knot: Any decorative or trick knot, even one that serves a practical purpose.

Fast: Secure.

Fay, To: A strand is said to be fayed down when it is teased, tapered and laid flat against a rope, spar or hook for seizing, serving or pointing over.

Fetch, To: To bring up, to reach the objective.

Fid: A long tapering cone, generally of hard wood, for rounding out eyes, cringles, etc.

Fid Out, To: To ream or round out an Eye Splice, cringle, clew, eyelet hole, grommet, etc., preliminary to inserting a thimble or otherwise finishing off.

Filling: Material used in worming a rope, weaving a sword mat, etc.

Finish Off, To: To add the final flourish, as to whip an end, knot a seizing, etc.

Fish, To: To mend broken spars by binding wooden splints along the injured parts.

Fist, To: To grasp a rope or sail and handle it quickly.

Flake: A single turn, or a tier of turns, in a coil. The dictionary form *fake* is unknown at sea, although so spelled by Captain John Smith (1627). Boteler uses the form *flake* in 1688.

Flaking: Coiling in various ways.

Flatten, To; Flatten Out, To; Haul Flat: A sheet is hauled flat when it is "sheeted home."

Fleet, To: To come up on a tackle and draw the blocks apart for another pull.

Fleet the Messenger, To: To rearrange the turns when they have crawled too high on the capstan.

Foul, To: To become entangled with some other object. A *foul* cable is caught on the fluke of an anchor, etc.

Follow the Lead, To: In Turk's-Heads and other knots, to parallel alongside the first-laid strand with identical over-and-under.

For a Full Due: To set up (rigging) to the desired tautness in one uninterrupted haul.

Fox: Yarns twisted together in several ways.

Frapping: A number of crossing turns in a lashing or the leads of a tackle, which serve to both tighten and secure them. When at anchor halyards are frapped to prevent slatting at night.

Fray, To: To fret, ravel, unravel. Generally applied to a rope's end.

Freshen, To: To shift a rope so that chafe will come at a new place in a hawse pipe, chock, fair-leader, etc. Usually the order is "Freshen the hawse."

Fret, To: To chafe or wear on the surface through rubbing.

Frog Knot: A flat appliquéd knot used decoratively on dresses and uniforms. Often called "military frogs."

Full: A term sometimes used instead of Double in describing a knot, as Full Matthew Walker and Full Carrick Bend.

Furl, To: To gather and secure sails with stops, gaskets, etc. Square sails are lifted for this purpose; most fore-and-aft sails are lowered; and a few are brailed to the mast.

Gall, To: To chafe or fret. Applies particularly to hawsers and cables.

Gang: A set of rigging for a mast or yard. Also a gang of knots in a footrope.

Ganging Line or a Ganging: A short line attached at one end to a hook and at the other end to the ground line of a trawl.

Gaskets: Of French or Flat Sinnet, for furling sail to yards.

Gear: The paraphernalia of commercial fishing. In amateur fishing "fishing tackle" is called for.

GIVE, To: To start, to ease, to render, to slacken, to slip.

GOKE: An old name for the heart or core of a shroud-laid rope.

GORDIAN KNOT: A legendary one that was difficult to untie. Some authors have contended that it was the first splice. Also a certain trick knot.

GOUTY END: A weathered and swelled end in running rigging.

GRAFT: Originally a kind of splice, now the method that was used in covering the splice.

GRINDS: Kinks or "half kinks" in a hempen cable.

GRIPE: A rope employed in lashing a boat.

GROUND TACKLE: General term for all hawsers, cables, buoy ropes and warps employed in anchoring, mooring and sometimes in towing a vessel.

GROW, To: A cable grows in the direction it leads from the hawse hole.
(Q) "How does she grow?" (A) "Dead ahead, sir!"

GUYS: Stays for cranes, shears, derricks, poles, booms, etc.

HAGSTEETH or HAKESTEETH: Irregularities in mats, points, sinnets, etc.

HALTER: The rope used in a hanging, or one with which a domestic animal is "hitched" or led.

HALYARDS or HALLIARDS: Ropes for hoisting sails and yards.

HAND, To: To furl. A hand is a sailor. To "hand, reef and steer" is termed the "sailor's A.B.C."

HAND OVER HAND: To haul rapidly on a rope, employing alternate hands.

HANDSOMELY: Slowly, carefully, gently, gradually; as to lower away handsomely.

HAND TAUT or TIGHT: Set up by hand alone without use of tackle.

HANDY: Ready at hand, as a tool. Also dexterous, skillful.

HANDY BILLY: A small tackle kept handy for small jobs.

HANG ON, To: To hold fast without belaying.

HANK: The spliced grommet first used on stays for bending staysails and jibs. Wooden and iron hanks were invented in the latter part of the eighteenth century. Also a skein of yarn; also a coil of cord consisting of a number of long turns covered with tight crossing turns.

HARD KNOT: (1) Any knot that jams. (2) A REEF KNOT as opposed to a GRANNY. (3) A REEF KNOT as opposed to a HALF BOW or DRAW-KNOT.

HARD-LAID or SHORT-LAID: Tightly twisted rope.

HAUL, To: To pull by hand on a rope or tackle. Formerly to pull on a single rope without blocks.

HAUL HOME, To: To sheet home. To pull until your rope fetches up, chockablock.

HAWSER: A plain-laid rope big enough for towing and mooring.

HEART: A slack-twisted rope or strand employed as a core in shroud-laid rope, wire rope and sinnet.

HEART: A sort of deadeye with a single hole, having either three or four grooves to hold the parts of a lanyard in place.

HEART YARNS: The center yarns of a strand, which do not appear on the surface.

HEAVE, To: To exert leverage on a windlass brake, capstan bar, marlingspike, etc.

HEAVE DOWN: To pull a vessel over on its side, to careen, so that the bottom is exposed.

HEAVER: A sailmaker's tool, also called "stitch mallet," illustrated in Chapter 1. Also a stick with rope tails used in ropemaking, splicing and worming.

HEAVING LINE: A light line secured to the eye of a mooring rope and bearing a heavy knot, often a weighted one, which is tossed to the wharf and by means of which the mooring line is hauled ashore.

HERALDIC KNOTS: Pictured knots on family devices. Only a few of these will form tangible knots.

HERCULES KNOT: The Roman name for the REEF KNOT.

HITCH, A: A knot that secures a rope to another object. This can be another rope if the latter is inert.

HOBBLE, To: To secure a domestic animal by one or more of its feet or to tie two feet together.

HOIST, To: To lift by means of a tackle.

HOIST, THE: The perpendicular edge of a sail or flag that is next to the mast.

HOME: In place, sharp up, to the limit, chockablock.

HONDA or HONDA KNOT: The eye in a lariat through which the rope is rove to form the required NOOSE.

HORNS: The arms of a cleat.

HORSES: An old name for footropes. Now applied only to the Flemish horses on the extremities of the topsail yards.

IRISH PENNANTS: Frayed rope yarns and loose ends in reef points, gaskets, service, seizings, etc.

IRISH SPLICE: A ratline, tightened or loosened by twisting the lay.

JACKSTAYS: Ropes, wooden battens or iron bars stretched along the yards, to which the sails are bent.

JAM, To: To refuse to render, to draw up into a tight knot that is difficult to untie.

JUNK: Old rope and cable cut up into short lengths, for working up into twice-laid stuff.

KACKLING or KECKLING: Old rope passed around hawsers and cable to prevent chafe at the hawse pipes, etc.

KEDGE, To: To move a vessel ahead by boating anchors and heaving at alternate cables.

KINK: "When a roape which should run smooth in the block, hath got a little turne." (Sir Henry Manwayring.)

KNOB KNOT: A bunch in a rope to prevent unreeving or slipping.

GLOSSARY

KNOT: (1) Specifically, a KNOB KNOT. (2) Broadly, any complication in rope except (a) accidental ones, as snarls and kinks, and (b) arrangements for storage, coils, balls, skeins, hanks, etc. (3) The same as (2) but further excluding sinnets, splices, hitches and bends.

KOP KNOT: An old name for the TACK or MANROPE KNOT, given by Norie (1804).

LACING or LACE LINE: A long line used in bending and reefing sail.

LAIR ROPE: A rope used in making up a pack for animal transportation.

LANYARD: (1) A small rope for making fast the end of a stay, etc. (2) Handles for marlingspikes, clothesbags, ditty bags, jackknives, whistles, etc., commonly ornamented with knots and sinnets.

LARIAT: Lasso, riata, rope, etc., for snaring running animals from horseback.

LARK: The French name for a RING or TAG KNOT (*Tête d'allouette*).

LASH, TO: (1) To bind two or more objects together. (2) To wrap a single object with a series of turns or hitches. (3) To secure any movable object on shipboard in order to prevent shifting.

LAY: The direction of the twist in a rope, the lead of the strands, also the nature of the twist, as hard, soft, left, right, long or short. To "open the lay" is to separate the strands with a fid or fingers.

LAY, TO: To form a rope in a ropewalk by twisting the strands together.

LAY UP, TO: To restore the lay of a rope's end after it has been opened, particularly after a STOPPER KNOT has been tied. A short length of rope is relaid and a whipping added.

LAY HOLD, TO: To seize a rope and stand by.

LAY OFF, TO: To quit, as to lay off a yard.

LAY OUT, TO: To take a position on a yardarm or a jib boom.

LEAD: The direction of a rope. The direction of a strand in a knot.

LEADS: The parts of a tackle between the two blocks, as opposed to the standing part and fall.

LEECH: The side edges of a square sail and the after edge of a fore-and-aft sail.

LEFT-HANDED KNOT: A mirrored or perverted knot, tied contrary to the prevailing practice.

LEFT-HANDED or LEFT-LAID ROPE: The reverse of right-handed or plain-laid rope. The yarns and rope have a left twist and the strands a right one.

LEGS: When a rope branches into two or more parts they are often termed legs, as the legs of a crowfoot or a bowline. Also the opened strands of a rope's end employed in splicing or knotting.

LEND A HAND, TO: To assist, to aid in hauling, etc.

LET GO, TO: To cast off. To let go "by the run" is to cast off all at once.

LIE FAIR, TO: To be ready, in position.

LIGATURE KNOT: A SURGEON'S KNOT for constricting.

LIGHT, TO: To move a heavy cable in short shifts, by hand.

LINE: A common name for various cordage, without specific meaning, as fishline, clew line, heaving line, whale line, spring line, towline, clothesline, mooring line.

LIZARD: A short pennant with a bull's-eye or thimble spliced in one end.

LONG-JAWED ROPE: Old rope that has stretched and lost much of its twist.

LOOP KNOT: A closed and knotted bight. An EYE SPLICE is a MULTI-STRAND LOOP KNOT.

LOOSE, TO (A SAIL): To unfurl it. To loose a knot is to untie or spill it.

MAGGED ROPE: Worn or fretted rope.

MAKE FAST, TO: (1) To secure a rope with a hitch. (2) To finish off belaying with a SINGLE HITCH.

MAKE SAIL: Being under way, to set additional sail.

MANHANDLE: To move heavy objects by manpower alone, without the aid of tackle or other machine.

MANROPES: Originally the jib-boom footropes. The name was afterwards applied to the entering ropes which provide a handhold to anyone coming overside.

MARL, TO: To secure parceling with a series of MARLINE HITCHES.

MARLINGSPIKE or MARLINESPIKE: A conical rigger's tool of metal, with a knobbed head for pounding, used to tighten seizings, service and whippings and to open strands when knotting and splicing.

MARLINGSPIKE SAILOR: One handy with knots and splices. A term used by Brady (*Kedge Anchor*, 1841).

MARRY, TO: (1) To butt two ropes' ends and worm over the joint, adding four stops. Used in reeving off. (2) To open and crotch two ropes' ends preparatory to splicing or shroud knotting.

MESH: One of the compartments of a net.

MESSENGER: A rope belt passing around two capstans, by means of which the cable is hove in.

MIDDLE, TO: To determine the center of a piece of rope by laying the two ends together.

MOOR, TO: To tie up to a wharf or buoy, or else to anchor both bow and stern.

NECK OF A KNOT: The stem.

NETTLES, KNITTLES, KNETTLES: Small, twice-laid stuff made of rope yarns, used in sinnets, seizings, etc.

NIP, THE: The spot within a knot where the end is gripped and is thereby made secure. To nip is to cease giving and to become secure.

NIPPERS: Small ropes which hold the messenger to the cable.

NOOSE: A loop which passes around its own standing part and draws tight when hauled upon.

GLOSSARY

Norman: The horizontal iron pin in a bitt.

Oakum: Old yarn picked apart. Used in calking, stuffing oil bags, etc.

Open, To: To separate the strands or yarns of a rope. To untie a knot.

Over and Under: Descriptive of the weave of certain knots, as Turk's-Heads.

Overhaul (a Tackle): To separate the blocks for another haul.

Palm: A narrow mitt with a thumb hole and a checkered piece of metal at the palm for pushing a sail needle.

Parcel, To: To bind strips of canvas around rope before marling; the direction is with the lay.

Part, To: To break.

Part, Standing: In a tackle the part spliced to a block. In a rope the inactive part as opposed to the bight and end.

Part, A: Each reappearance of a strand on the surface of a knot.

Pass, To: To shift regularly from one hand to another or from one person to another, as in passing gaskets, stoppers, nippers and seizings.

Pay Out, To (a Cable): To slack away slowly, to allow it to run out.

Pendant: A short rope with a thimble spliced in one end to which a tackle is hooked.

Picket, To: To stake out an animal, generally for the night.

Pigtail: A wisp of fiber middled, twisted and the two legs laid up together, particularly hemp and flax. A short tail attached to a hook, for loosing.

Pinion, To: To bind the arms or wings of any creature.

Plain-Laid: Hawser-laid. Three-strand, right-handed rope.

Plait: Pronounced plat, which see.

Plat: Sinnet. Flat and French Sinnet specifically.

Play: Drift, margin allowed for shrinkage and stretching.

Point: A decorative cone-shaped termination on cables and running rigging. Ostensibly to aid in reeving but really to prevent pilfering.

Pricker: A tool smaller than a marlingspike, generally with a wooden handle.

Purchase: An arrangement of blocks and fall in which the standing part and the fall both lead to the same block.

Quilting: Mats nailed to planking as protection against ice.

Quoyle: Coil. (Boteler, 1634.)

Rack a Fall, To: To stop the fall to one of the leads of a tackle with a series of racking turns.

Racking Turns: Seizing and lashing turns taken figure-eight-fashion.

Racks: Long fair-leaders with many holes, lashed in the rigging above the shear pole.

Raddle, To: To plat, according to Smyth.

Ravel and Unravel: To fray.

Range of Cable: Sufficient cable for the depth, laid out in flakes on deck, ready for anchoring.

Rattle Down, To: To secure ratlines to the shrouds, so forming a ladder aloft.

Reef Hanks: When reef points were first made of rope instead of sinnet they were called hanks; later the earlier name point was returned.

Reeve, To: To pass the end of a rope through any hole or opening.

Reeve Off, To: To reeve new running rigging through the blocks from unbroken coils, first marrying the old rope to the new.

Render, To: To slacken, give, ease off.

Ride, To: A rope is said to ride a capstan when one turn settles over another.

Riders or Riding Turns: In seizings and whippings a second tier of turns, always one less in number than the ground or under turns.

Rigging: In its narrowest meaning the lower shrouds alone. Broadly, all the rope in a ship except ground tackle is divided into standing and running rigging. Standing rigging is permanently secured at both ends, running rigging at one end only.

Right-Handed: Plain- or hawser-laid rope, which is right-handed like a corkscrew.

Robands, Rope Bands (pronounced robbins): The lines with which square sails are bent.

Roding: Originally the anchor warp or cable of a coasting schooner, nowadays of any small craft. Derived from roadstead and roadster.

Rope: Anything in cordage over one inch in circumference.

Rope Yarn: A single thread from the strand of a rope.

Ropes: There is an old saying that "there are seven ropes on a ship." Luce gives a list of about forty ropes and there are at least twenty more, but all these were never in use at the same time.

Roping: To strengthen the edges of a sail. Square sails are roped on the after side and fore-and-aft sails on the port side.

Roping: Lashing a trunk or parcel, a shore term.

Round of a Rope, The: The length of a single strand in one complete passage around the rope.

Rounding: Old three-inch rope served on a cable at the hawse pipe for chafing gear.

Round Up: To take up the slack on a tackle.

Rousing or Rowsing: To pull together by hand on the cable, to haul in slack.

Running Rigging: All rigging that is rove through blocks.

Run Out, To: To boat a warp, and make fast the end.

Sailor's Knot: Carrick Bend, Sheet Bend, Reef Knot, Bowline, etc. The name is loosely applied to any good or unfamiliar knot.

Seam Rubber: A tool for turning a seam and creasing it, also called merely "a rubber."

SEND DOWN, TO (or SEND ALOFT): Preferred to *lower* and *hoist* when speaking of spars, sails or other heavy gear.

SEINE NEEDLE: A netting needle. Illustrated in Chapter 1.

SEIZING: A lashing of spun yarn, marline or small stuff either with or without riding turns.

SERVICE: Marline or small stuff, bound around standing rigging for protection against wear and weather.

SERVING BOARD: A small tool for putting on and tightening service.

SERVING MALLET: A larger tool for the same purpose.

SET UP, TO: To tighten rigging at the lanyards with a tackle.

SHAKE OUT, TO (A REEF): To remove the gaskets or untie the reef points and to loosen the sail.

SHAKINGS: Odds and ends of old rope, saved for making oakum.

SHARP UP: Yards braced as far as they will go.

SHEARS: Two spars lashed together at the top and guyed; used for raising masts and hoisting heavy weights.

SHEET: A rope that trims the lower corner of a sail. To *sheet home* or *sheet flat* is to haul the sheet taut.

SHELL: The carcass of a block.

SHIFT, TO: To move a short distance or to substitute one thing for another, as to shift places.

SHIV: The grooved wheel of a block. The earliest form of the word was *shiver*.

SHORT-LAID: Hard-laid rope.

SHOT OF CABLE: Two cables spliced together make a "shot." A single cable is usually about 120 fathoms long, depending upon the length of the ropewalk.

SHOULDER KNOT: Tied in braid and worn on the shoulder of a uniform.

SHROUD-LAID: Four-strand, right-handed rope made around a heart.

SHROUD TRUCK: A single fair-leader, lashed to a shroud.

SHROUDS: The lower standing rigging which lead from the channels to the tops.

SIDE ROPES: A name for manropes, from Biddlecombe.

SICK SEAMS: A sailmaking term. Indicates that the stitches are worn and giving way.

SIMPLE HITCH: Another name for the SINGLE HITCH.

SIMPLE KNOT: A name for the OVERHAND KNOT.

SINKING A STRAND: In splicing a three-strand and a four-strand rope together, the extra strand of the latter is "sunk as it lies."
In a WIRE LONG SPLICE the heart is cut out for a length, and the end of a strand is "sunk" to take its place.

SINKING A YARN: In tapering a strand individual yarns are cut out and the ends tucked under the remaining yarns.

SINNET: "Sinnet is braided cordage." (Steel.) Also spelled *synnet, sennit, sinnit, sennet*, etc.

SINNET LINE: The original name for braided rope, used at sea for signal halyards as early as 1860

SISTER STRANDS: Where there are two opposed sets of strands, as in SHORT SPLICES and SHROUD KNOTS, the related members of each set are referred to as sister strands.

SLACK, THE: Loose and superfluous material that must be worked out to complete a knot.

SLACK OF A ROPE: Any loose or inactive part.

SLACK OFF or AWAY, TO: To ease off or to let out.

SLACK-LAID: See soft-laid.

SLATCH: The loose or slack part of a rope.

SLICK: Smooth and slippery as wet rope fiber.

SLING or SLINGS: A wreath or rope encompassing an object and by means of which it is to be hoisted.

SLIP KNOT: Any knot which may be spilled by pulling on the end, so withdrawing a loop.

SLIP A CABLE, TO: To buoy an anchor and put to sea without hoisting it.

SLIPPERING HITCH: A name used by Moore (1801) for the SLIPPERY HITCH.

SLUE, TO: To turn anything around without changing its base.

SMALL STUFF: Rope that is under one inch in circumference.

SMARTLY: Together, with precision and alacrity.

SNARE: A NOOSE for catching birds and animals.

SNARL: A confusion and entanglement of cordage.

SNUB, TO: To check a line, generally with a round turn, on a post or pin.

SNUG: Compact, neat, tight.

SO!: Order to cease hauling for the moment. Norie gives "Thus!" with the same meaning.

SOFT KNOT: Bow, HALF BOW or DRAWKNOT, in contradistinction to the HARD or SQUARE KNOT.

SOFT-LAID: Loose-twisted rope.

SPAN: A short rope fast at both ends, to be hauled on at the center; a bridle.

SPILL, TO: To untie accidentally, to let go completely.

SPLICE, TO: To secure two ropes or two parts of the same rope together by interweaving the strands.

SPOOL: (1) A small stick used as a gauge, around which meshes are formed in netting. (2) The apparatus used by children in making LOOP SINNET.

SPRING LINE: A long central diagonal employed in tying up to a wharf.

SPUN YARN: Yarn made from old rope.

STAFFORD KNOT: The OVERHAND KNOT when pictured in heraldry.

STAND BY, TO: To take hold of a rope and stand ready to haul, slacken or belay.

STANDING: When prefixed to the name of a knot it indicates that the knot is of a semipermanent nature, as STANDING TURK'S-HEAD, STANDING BOWLINE, as opposed to "RUNNING."

GLOSSARY

STANDING PART (OF A ROPE): The inactive part as opposed to the end and bight.

START, TO (A SHEET OR TACK): To slack off a bit, sufficiently to ease the strain on the gear.

STAYS: Standing rigging. Fore-and-aft stays lead forward from the tops. Backstays lead to the ship's sides abaft the shrouds.

STEM: The neck of a KNOB KNOT.

STICK, TO: To tuck a strand. Specifically to make the first tuck in an EYE SPLICE or the final tuck in a MULTI-STRAND BUTTON or STOPPER KNOT.

STIRRUP: The strap or pennant that suspends a footrope which was formerly nailed to the yard, but now is secured to the jackstays.

STITCH MALLET: A heaver. A sailmaker's tool that is pictured in Chapter 1.

STOP, TO: To seize or whip temporarily, often finished off with a REEF KNOT.

STOPPER: A short rope or cable with a knot at one end and a hook or shackle at the other for securing the cable to deck.

STOPPER KNOT: Any TERMINAL KNOT for preventing unreeving in which the end departs from the knot at the top.

STOPS: Canvas bands or short ropes for furling fore-and-aft sails.

STOUT ROPE: Of large circumference for its purpose.

STRAND (OF A ROPE): Two or more yarns twisted together.

STRANDED ROPE: A rope with one broken or badly galled strand.

STRAP: (Often spelled strop, but always pronounced strap.) The wreath around a block; some of them have a tail by which the block can be lashed in the rigging.

STRETCH ALONG, TO: To lay the end of a brace or sheet along the deck in readiness for a number of men to lay hold.

STRIKE, TO: To lower something from aloft as colors, mast or sail:

STROP: See STRAP.

SUN, WITH THE: In coiling rope, etc., the same direction as taken by a clock hand.

SURGE, TO: To slack up suddenly on a pin, windlass tackle, etc.

SWAG, TO: To sag, as the center of a horizontal rope.

SWALLOW: The mortice between the cheeks of a block.

SWAY, TO: To haul vertically on the fall of a tackle. Particularly to hoist upper yards.

SWIFT, TO: To set up on the rigging. To bring two shrouds or stays close together with a rope.

SWIFTER: The forward lower shroud (formerly the after one), also the rope which holds the ends of capstan bars in place.

SWIG, SWIGGING OFF: To pull on the center of a taut rope at right angles to the fall, and to give the slack so gained to the man at the pin.

TABLING: The wide hem at the edges of a sail, to which the boltrope is sewed.

TACK: A tapered rope, frequently cable-laid, that trims forward the weather clew of a course.

TACKLE: (Pronounced tāy'kle.) A mechanism of blocks and rope for increasing power.

TAIL ON! or TALLY ON!: An order to grasp and haul.

TAKE A TURN, TO: To put a turn on a belaying pin.

TAKE IN, TO: To furl a sail.

TAKE-UP: The amount of material expended in making a knot, splice or sinnet.

TAPER, TO: To diminish a rope gradually by scraping and teasing or by systematically cutting out yarns. The surface is usually covered with needlework.

TAUT: Tight.

TEASE, TO (OUT STRANDS): Derived from teasel. To open the end of a rope and comb out with the fingers.

TETHER, TO (AN ANIMAL): To tie it out for grazing.

THOROUGHFOOT: A tangle in a tackle due to a block's turning through the fall.

THREAD: A yarn. Small rope is frequently designated by the total number of its component threads, as nine-thread or twelve-thread stuff.

THROW, TO: Pack lashing ashore is always "thrown" from man to man or from hand to hand.

THRUMS: Short pieces of yarn for tufting chafing gear.

THUMB KNOT: The OVERHAND and WEAVER'S KNOTS, also applied to the OVERHAND BEND.

TIE, TO: About the only time a sailor "ties" is when he forsakes the sea. Then he "ties up to" a wharf.

TIER: One range of turns in a coil.

TOP: A ropemaking tool, with grooves for the strands, which "lays" the rope after the strands have been twisted.

TOW, TO: To draw (a boat or car) with a rope.

TRAILER: A sinnet tail on a heaver or woolder.

TRICE, TO: To haul up by a single rope or whip.

TRIM, TO: To adjust sheets and braces to a favorable length.

TRUSS, TO: To bind, to lash, to truss up.

TURK'S-HEAD: A platted wreath or ring, a section of which is similar to sinnet.

TURN: One round of rope on a pin or cleat, one round of a coil.

TURN IN, TO (A DEADEYE): To seize a shroud or stay securely around it.

TURN, TO TAKE A: To belay.

TWICE-LAID STUFF: Nettles, foxes, sinnets. Small stuff made by hand from old cables and rope.

UNBEND: To cast off.

UNLAY: To open a rope.

VANGS: Ropes with which to trim the peak of a spencer or spanker.

[604]

VEER, TO, or TO VEER AWAY: To slacken and pay out gradually.

VEER AND HAUL, TO: To slack on one rope and haul on another that leads to the same spar (Braces, etc.).

WAKE KNOT: A name for the CARRICK BEND in heraldry.

WARP, TO: To shift a vessel by means of hawsers. A warp is generally hawser-laid.

WATER-LAID ROPE: (1) Three-strand, left-laid rope. (2) Rope that is moistened in the making instead of being oiled, sometimes called "white rope." (3) Cable-laid rope, which is said to absorb less water than hawser-laid rope.

WEED, TO: To clear rigging, cable and clotheslines of stops, rope yarns, etc.

WHIP, TO: To bind the end of a rope to prevent fraying.

WITH THE LAY, or WITH THE SUN (TO COIL): A right-hand or clockwise coil.

WOOLDER: A ropemaker's tool consisting of a stick with one or two trailers, for twisting, holding and laying rope. Nowadays called a *heaver*.

WORK, TO: To draw up and mold a knot. To *work up yarn* is to make small stuff of it by hand.

WORM A ROPE, TO: To fill the seams with spun yarn, marline or fishline.

YARN: A number of fibers twisted together.

INDEX

The number of an index item refers to the page on which the illustration of a knot appears
The description is on the same or the facing page.

INDEX

INDEX

INDEX

INDEX

INDEX

INDEX

INDEX

INDEX

Wrap Hitch, 40
Wrought mat, 488, 554

"X" seizings, 541, 584

Yachtsman, the, 82
Yardarm Knot, 209

Yard tackle, 527
Yard Hitches, 13
Yarn, 23
Yarn Splice, 568
Yoke rope, of cotton, 565; square knotted, 604
Young, Louria, 73

Zigzag Bar, 400
Zigzag Knot, 217
Zigzag Lanyard Knot, 134
Zigzag Ring Hitching, 389

[620]

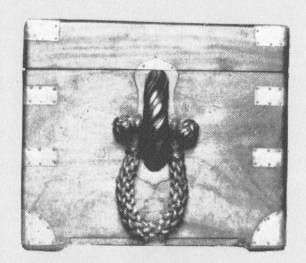